T0202783

Lecture Notes in Artificial Intelligence 11716

Subseries of Lecture Notes in Computer Science

Pascal Fontaine (Ed.)

Automated Deduction – CADE 27

27th International Conference on Automated Deduction
Natal, Brazil, August 27–30, 2019
Proceedings

 Springer

Editor
Pascal Fontaine
University of Lorraine
Villers-lès-Nancy, France

ISSN 0302-9743 ISSN 1611-3349 (electronic)
Lecture Notes in Artificial Intelligence
ISBN 978-3-030-29435-9 ISBN 978-3-030-29436-6 (eBook)
https://doi.org/10.1007/978-3-030-29436-6

LNCS Sublibrary: SL7 – Artificial Intelligence

This Springer imprint is published by the registered company Springer Nature Switzerland AG
The registered company address is: Gewerbestrasse 11, 6330 Cham, Switzerland

Preface

This volume contains the proceedings of the 27th International Conference on Automated Deduction (CADE 27). The conference was hosted by the Universidade Federal do Rio Grande do Norte, in Natal, Brazil, during August 27–30, 2019. CADE is the major forum for the presentation of research in all aspects of automated deduction, including foundations, applications, implementations, and practical experience.

The Program Committee accepted 34 papers (27 full papers and 7 system descriptions) out of 65 submissions (53 full papers and 12 system descriptions). Each submission was reviewed by at least three Program Committee (PC) members or external reviewers appointed by the PC members in charge. The main criteria for evaluation were originality and significance, technical quality and completeness, comparison with related work and completeness of references, quality of presentation, clarity, and readability. All papers containing experimental data were also evaluated with respect to reproducibility.

The technical program of the conference included three invited talks:

- Cas Cremers (CISPA Helmholtz Center for Information Security, Saarbrücken, Germany): "Automated Reasoning for Security Protocols"
- Assia Mahboubi (Inria, LS2N, Université de Nantes, France and Vrije Universiteit Amsterdam, the Netherlands): "Computer Deduction and (Formal) Proofs in Mathematics"
- Cesare Tinelli (Department of Computer Science, The University of Iowa, USA): "From Counter-Model-based Quantifier Instantiation to Quantifier Elimination in SMT"

During the conference, the Herbrand Award for Distinguished Contributions to Automated Reasoning was presented to Nikolaj Bjørner and Leonardo de Moura in recognition of their numerous and important contributions to SMT solving, including its theory, implementation, and application to a wide range of academic and industrial needs. The Selection Committee for the Herbrand Award consisted of Bruno Dutertre, Juergen Giesl, Dale Miller (chair), and Larry Paulson.

The Thoralf Skolem Awards were conferred this year to reward CADE papers that have passed the test of time by being most influential papers in the field for 1979, 1990, 1999, and 2009. The authors receiving an award were:

- Peter Andrews for the paper entitled "General Matings," published in the CADE 4 proceedings in 1979.

  The paper is recognized for its invention of the generalized mating method for constructing refutations of formulas in negative normal form. This development paved the way for the subsequent construction of many non-resolution methods in automated deduction, including the well-known connection method.

- Leo Bachmair and Harald Ganzinger for the paper entitled "On Restrictions of Ordered Paramodulation with Simplification," published in the CADE 10 proceedings in 1990.

  The paper is recognized for its development of the superposition calculus for equational first-order clauses alongside a new and powerful framework for proving completeness and accommodating redundancy. This framework forms the basis of many advanced modern theorem provers, and has been highly influential in accelerating progress in the area of automated deduction.
- Christoph Weidenbach for the paper "Towards an Automated Analysis of Security Protocols," published in the CADE 16 proceedings in 1999.

  The paper is recognized for two main contributions to automated deduction: first, its novel application of general theorem proving techniques to a key-exchange security protocol; and, second, its development of new decidability and undecidability results for fragments of monadic Horn theories.
- Rajeev Goré and Florian Widmann for the paper entitled "An Optimal On-the-Fly Tableau-Based Decision Procedure for PDL-Satisfiability," published in the CADE 22 proceedings in 2009.

  The paper is recognized for presenting the first decision procedure for propositional dynamic logic which is both theoretically optimal and effective in practice. Previous decision procedures are either suboptimal in the worst case, or worst-case optimal but with poor average-case performance. The solution in this paper thereby closed a problem that had been open for almost 30 years.

The conference issued a call for workshops out of which the following five proposals were approved:

- Automated Reasoning: Challenges, Applications, Directions, Exemplary Achievements (ARCADE)
- Deduction Mentoring Workshop (DeMent 2019)
- Logical and Semantic Frameworks, with Applications (LSFA)
- Proof eXchange for Theorem Proving (PxTP)
- Theorem Prover Components for Educational Software (ThEdu 2019).

In addition, the conference included a two-day program of introductory tutorials. The first day was dedicated to tutorials given by local organizers, with an aim to promote among local and foreign students the research on automated reasoning carried out locally:

- Cláudia Nalon: "Machine Oriented Reasoning"
- Carlos Olarte: "Building Theorem Provers Using Rewriting Logic"
- Giselle Reis: "Intuitionistic Logic"

A one-day tutorial, titled "Build Your Own First-Order Prover," was given by Jens Otten on the second day.

During the conference, the CADE 27 ATP System Competition (CASC 27) was held, organized by Geoff Sutcliffe. The description of the competition is available as an abstract in these proceedings.

I would like to thank the many people without whom the conference would not have been possible. First, I would like to thank all authors who submitted papers, all participants of the conference as well as the invited keynote speakers, the tutorial speakers, and the workshop organizers for their contributions. I am very grateful to the members of the PC and the external reviewers for carefully reviewing and selecting the papers. In particular, I would like to thank Philipp Rümmer and Roberto Sebastiani who acted as chairs for the papers I was conflicting with. Many thanks to Andrei Voronkov for providing the EasyChair system which greatly facilitated the reviewing process, the electronic PC meeting, and the preparation of the proceedings. I also thank the Trustees of CADE Inc. for their advice and support. Special thanks go to Elaine Pimentel, who as conference chair was involved in almost every aspect of the organization of the conference, and the members of the local organization team, Carlos Olarte, João Marcos, Cláudia Nalon, and Giselle Reis, for the tremendous effort they devoted to the organization of the conference. I am extremely grateful to Geoff Sutcliffe, for organizing CASC 27 and being the publicity chair, and to Giles Reger, the workshop chair.

CADE 27 received support from many organizations. On behalf of all organizers, I would like to thank the Universidade Federal do Rio Grande do Norte, DMAT, ProEx, PPG, PROPESQ, the Universidade de Brasilia, CAPES, CNPq, CMU Qatar, the Association for Symbolic Logic, IBM, Imandra, Microsoft, and Springer.

August 2019   Pascal Fontaine

Organization

Program Committee

Carlos Areces	FaMAF, Universidad Nacional de Córdoba, Argentina
Franz Baader	TU Dresden, Germany
Clark Barrett	Stanford University, USA
Jasmin Christian Blanchette	Vrije Universiteit Amsterdam, The Netherlands
Maria Paola Bonacina	Università degli Studi di Verona, Italy
Leonardo de Moura	Microsoft, USA
Hans de Nivelle	School of Science and Technology, Nazarbayev University, Kazakhstan
Clare Dixon	University of Liverpool, UK
Mnacho Echenim	University of Grenoble, France
Marcelo Finger	University of São Paulo, Brazil
Pascal Fontaine	University of Lorraine, CNRS, Inria, LORIA, France
Silvio Ghilardi	Dipartimento di Matematica, Università degli Studi di Milano, Italy
Jürgen Giesl	RWTH Aachen University, Germany
Rajeev Gore	The Australian National University, Australia
Stefan Hetzl	Vienna University of Technology, Austria
Marijn Heule	The University of Texas at Austin, USA
Nao Hirokawa	JAIST, Japan
Moa Johansson	Chalmers University of Technology, Sweden
Cezary Kaliszyk	University of Innsbruck, Austria
Deepak Kapur	University of New Mexico, USA
Benjamin Kiesl	CISPA Helmholtz Center for Information Security, Germany
Konstantin Korovin	The University of Manchester, UK
Laura Kovacs	Vienna University of Technology, Austria
Ramana Kumar	DeepMind, UK
Cláudia Nalon	University of Brasília, Brazil
Vivek Nigam	Federal University of Paraíba, Brazil and Fortiss, Germany
Carlos Olarte	Universidade Federal do Rio Grande do Norte, Brazil
Jens Otten	University of Oslo, Norway
André Platzer	Carnegie Mellon University, USA
Andrew Reynolds	University of Iowa, USA
Philipp Rümmer	Uppsala University, Sweden
Renate A. Schmidt	The University of Manchester, UK
Stephan Schulz	DHBW Stuttgart, Germany
Roberto Sebastiani	University of Trento, Italy

Natarajan Shankar	SRI International, USA
Viorica Sofronie-Stokkermans	University Koblenz-Landau, Germany
Martin Suda	Czech Technical University, Czech Republic
Geoff Sutcliffe	University of Miami, USA
René Thiemann	University of Innsbruck, Austria
Uwe Waldmann	Max Planck Institute for Informatics, Germany
Christoph Weidenbach	Max Planck Institute for Informatics, Germany
Sarah Winkler	University of Innsbruck, Austria

Conference Chair

| Elaine Pimentel | Universidade Federal do Rio Grande do Norte, Brazil |

Local Organization

Carlos Olarte	Universidade Federal do Rio Grande do Norte, Brazil
João Marcos	Universidade Federal do Rio Grande do Norte, Brazil
Cláudia Nalon	Universidade de Brasilia, Brazil
Giselle Reis	CMU, Qatar

Workshop Chair

| Giles Reger | The University of Manchester, UK |

Publicity Chair

| Geoff Sutcliffe | University of Miami, USA |

System Competition

| Geoff Sutcliffe | University of Miami, USA |

Additional Reviewers

Aoto, Takahito
Aravantinos, Vincent
Atig, Mohamed Faouzi
Avanzini, Martin
Backeman, Peter
Barbosa, Haniel
Benedikt, Michael
Bentkamp, Alexander
Berger, Gerald
Bottesch, Ralph
Brown, Chad

Cordwell, Katherine
Cruanes, Simon
Das, Anupam
Dawson, Jeremy
Ebner, Gabriel
El Ouraoui, Daniel
Fervari, Raul
Fiorentini, Camillo
Fiorino, Guido
Fleury, Mathias
Frohn, Florian

Board of Trustees of CADE Inc.

Board of the Association for Automated Reasoning

Abstracts

Automated Reasoning for Security Protocols

Cas Cremers

CISPA Helmholtz Center for Information Security, Saarbrücken, Germany

Abstract. Security protocols are a prime example of seemingly simple algorithms for which it would be highly desirable, and possibly feasible, to provide formal proofs of their security. Yet despite several decades of active research, this goal has remained elusive. In this talk we will revisit the security protocol problem, why it is so crucial, and how forms of automated reasoning have helped advance the state of the art, using the TLS 1.3 protocol as an example. We highlight some of the many open general questions and how future advancements in automated reasoning might help towards the ultimate goal of deploying provably secure protocols.

Computer Deduction and (Formal) Proofs in Mathematics

Assia Mahboubi

Inria, LS2N, Université de Nantes, Vrije Universiteit Amsterdam

Abstract. In 1976, K. Appel and W. Haken announced a computer-assisted proof of the Four Color theorem, solving a long standing open question in graph theory. Since, experimental mathematics have gained momentum and computers have even changed the very nature of peer-reviewed mathematical proofs. This phenomenon can be observed in a broad spectrum of fields, including number theory, dynamical systems, combinatorics, etc.

A vast variety of software is available today for doing computer-aided mathematics. Tools, and the algorithms they implement, are usually grouped in two partially overlapping categories: the symbolic ones, typically computer algebra systems, and the numerical ones. This talk is about a different flavor of software for doing mathematics with a computer: proof assistants. So far proof assistants have been mostly used for research projects in computer science, often related to program verification. But proof assistants, and in particular those based on dependent type theory, are receiving these days an increased attention from users with a background in mathematics. Designing formal libraries about contemporary mathematics raises specific issues and challenges for proof assistants, that we will discuss.

From Counter-Model-Based Quantifier Instantiation to Quantifier Elimination in SMT

Andrew Reynolds and Cesare Tinelli

The University of Iowa, Iowa City, USA

Abstract. Despite decades of research, reasoning efficiently about formulas containing both quantifiers and built-in symbols for a given background theory remains a challenge in automated deduction. Nevertheless, several exciting advances have been made in the last few years, mainly in two directions: (*i*) integrating theory reasoning in saturation-based calculi for first-order logic and (*ii*) integrating quantified reasoning into frameworks for ground Satisfiability Modulo Theories (SMT). Focusing on the latter, this talk provides an overview of a general, refutation-based approach for reasoning about quantified formulas in SMT. The approach maintains a set S of ground formulas that is incrementally expanded with selected instances of quantified input formulas, with the selection based on counter-models of S. In addition to being quite effective in practice, for several logical theories that admit quantifier elimination and have a decidable universal fragment this approach also leads to practically efficient decision procedures for the full theory. While the approach applies to traditional theories with quantifier elimination such as linear real and integer arithmetic, this talk will present new promising developments for the theory of fixed-sized bit vectors and the theory of floating point arithmetic whose full-fragments are notoriously difficult to reason about.

The CADE-27 ATP System Competition - CASC-27

Geoff Sutcliffe[ID]

University of Miami, Miami, USA
http://www.cs.miami.edu/~geoff

The CADE ATP System Competition (CASC) [4] is the annual evaluation of fully automatic, classical logic Automated Theorem Proving (ATP) systems – the world championship for such systems. One purpose of CASC is to provide a public evaluation of the relative capabilities of ATP systems. Additionally, CASC aims to stimulate ATP research, motivate development and implementation of robust ATP systems that are useful and easily deployed in applications, provide an inspiring environment for personal interaction between ATP researchers, and expose ATP systems within and beyond the ATP community. Fulfillment of these objectives provides insight and stimulus for the development of more powerful ATP systems, leading to increased and more effective use. CASC-27 was held on 29th August 2019 in Natal, Brazil, as part of the 27th International Conference on Automated Deduction (CADE-27). CASC-27 was the twenty-fourth competition in the CASC series; see [6] and citations therein for information about individual previous competitions. The CASC-27 web site provides access to all competition resources: http://www.tptp.org/CASC/27. (Information about previous competitions is available from http://www.tptp.org/CASC.)

CASC is divided into divisions according to problem and system characteristics. The divisions reflect active areas of research and application of ATP. Each division uses problems that have certain logical, language, and syntactic characteristics, so that the systems that compete in the division are, in principle, able to attempt all the problems in the division. Some divisions are further divided into problem categories that make it possible to analyze, at a more fine-grained level, which systems work well for what types of problems. Table 1 catalogs the divisions and problem categories of CASC-27.

Problems for the THF, TFA, FOF, FNT, UEQ, and EPR divisions are taken from the TPTP Problem Library [5]. The TPTP version used for CASC is not released until after the competition has started, so that new problems have not been seen by the entrants. In order to ensure that no system receives an advantage or disadvantage due to the specific presentation of the problems in the TPTP, the problems are obfuscated by stripping out all comment lines, randomly reordering the formulae/clauses, randomly swapping the arguments of associative connectives, randomly reversing implications, and randomly reversing equalities. The problems have to meet certain criteria to be eligible for selection: they may not be designed specifically to be suited or ill-suited to some ATP system, calculus, or control strategy; they must be syntactically non-propositional; generally they must have a TPTP difficulty rating in the range 0.21 to 0.99 (some exceptions are permitted). The problems used are randomly selected

Table 1. Divisions and problem categories

Div'n	Problems	Problem Categories
THF	Monomorphic Typed Higher-order Form theorems (axioms with a provable conjecture).	TNE – THF with No Equality TEQ – THF with EQuality
TFA	Monomorphic Typed First-order form theorems with Arithmetic (axioms with a provable conjecture).	TFI – TFA with only Integer arithmetic TFE – TFA with only rEal arithmetic
FOF	First-Order Form theorems (axioms with a provable conjecture).	FNE – FOF with No Equality FEQ – FOF with EQuality
FNT	FOF Non-Theorems (axioms with a countersatisfiable conjecture, and satisfiable axioms sets).	FNN – FNT with No equality FNQ – FNT with eQuality
EPR	Effectively PRopositional theorems and non-theorems in clause normal form (unsatisfiable and satisfiable clause sets). *Effectively propositional* means that the problems are known to be reducible to propositional form.	EPT – Effectively Propositional Theorems (unsatisfiable clause sets) EPS – Effectively Propositional non-theorems (Satisfiable clause sets)
UEQ	Clause normal form non-propositional Unit EQuality theorems (unsatisfiable clause sets).	
LTB	Theorems (axioms with a provable conjecture) from Large Theories, presented in Batches. A large theory typically has many functors and predicates, and many axioms of which only a few are required for the proof of a theorem. The problems in each batch all use a common core set of axioms, and the problems in each batch are given to the ATP systems all at once.	HL4 – Problems exported from the HOL4 library. A set of training problems and their solutions, taken from the same exports as the competition problems, is provided. The training data can be used for system tuning during (typically at the start of) the competition.

from the eligible problems based on a seed supplied by the competition panel. The selection is constrained so that no division or category contains an excessive number of very similar problems, and is biased to select problems that are new in the TPTP version used. The problems are given to the systems in TPTP format, with include directives, and are given to the systems in increasing order of TPTP difficulty rating. A CPU time limit is imposed for each problem.

The problems for the CASC-27 LTB division were taken from the HOL4 [2] library. For CASC-27 multiple exports [1] of the library were used, so that multiple versions of each problem were available – two FOF versions, two TF0 versions, one TF1 version, two TH0 versions, and one TH1 version. Systems could attempt as many of the versions as they want, in any order including in parallel, and a solution to any version counted as a solution to the problem. The LTB problems are not obfuscated, thus allowing the systems to take advantage of natural structure that occurs in the problems. The batch presentation of the LTB division allows the systems to load and process the common core set of axioms just once. The set of training problems and solutions facilitates system tuning by learning from previous proofs. The batch presentation allows proofs and other control information to be used between proof searches for further incremental tuning. The problems are given to the systems in TPTP format, with include directives, and the problems are given to the systems in the natural order of their creation (i.e., for CASC-27, in their natural HOL4 order). Systems are allowed to attempt the problems in any order, and to make multiple attempts on each problem. An overall wall clock time limit is imposed for all proof attempts and system tuning. No CPU time limits are imposed.

The THF, TFA, FOF, FNT, and UEQ, and LTB divisions are ranked according to the number of problems solved with an acceptable proof/model output (where "acceptable" includes criteria such as derivations starting from problem formulae and ending at the conjecture/refutation, derivations documenting the input, output, and inference rule of each inference step, derivation inference steps being reasonably fine-grained, and models documenting the domain, function maps, and predicate maps). The EPR division is ranked according to the number of problems solved, but not necessarily accompanied by a proof or model. Ties are broken according to the average time taken over problems solved (CPU time or wall clock time, depending on the type of limit in the division).

The competition was run on computers provided by the StarExec project [3].

References

1. Brown, C., Gauthier, T., Kaliszyk, C., Sutcliffe, G., Urban, J.: GRUNGE: a grand unified ATP challenge. In: Fontaine, P. (ed.) CADE 2019. LNCS, vol. 11716, pp. 123–141. Springer, Heidelberg (2019). https://doi.org/10.1007/978-3-030-29436-6_8
2. Slind, K., Norrish, M.: A brief overview of HOL4. In: Mohamed O.A., Muñoz C., Tahar S. (eds.) TPHOLs 2008. LNCS, vol. 5170, pp. 28–32. Springer, Heidelberg (2008). https://doi.org/10.1007/978-3-540-71067-7_6
3. Stump A., Sutcliffe G., Tinelli C.: StarExec: a cross-community infrastructure for logic solving. In: Demri S., Kapur D., Weidenbach C. (eds.) IJCAR 2014. LNCS (LNAI), vol. 8562, pp. 367–373. Springer, Cham (2014). https://doi.org/10.1007/978-3-319-08587-6_28
4. Sutcliffe, G.: The CADE ATP system competition - CASC. AI Mag. 37(2), 99–101 (2016)
5. Sutcliffe, G.: The TPTP problem library and associated infrastructure. From CNF to TH0, TPTP v6.4.0. J. Autom. Reason. 59(4), 483–502 (2017)
6. Sutcliffe, G.: The 9th IJCAR automated theorem proving system competition - CASC-29. AI Commun. 31(6), 495–507 (2018)

Contents

Unification Modulo Lists with Reverse Relation with Certain Word Equations

Siva Anantharaman[1(✉)], Peter Hibbs[2,4P], Paliath Narendran[2], and Michael Rusinowitch[3]

[1] LIFO - Université d'Orléans, Orléans, France
siva@univ-orleans.fr
[2] University at Albany–SUNY, Albany, USA
peter.s.hibbs@gmail.com, pnarendran@albany.edu
[3] Loria-Inria Université de Lorraine, Nancy, France
rusi@loria.fr
[4] Google Inc., Mountain View, USA

Abstract. Decision procedures for various list theories have been investigated in the literature with applications to automated verification. Here we show that the unifiability problem for some list theories with a *reverse* operator is NP-complete. We also give a unifiability algorithm for the case where the theories are extended with a *length* operator on lists.

1 Introduction

Reasoning about data types such as lists and arrays is an important research area with many applications, such as formal program verification [13, 19]. Early work on this [10] focused on proving inductive properties. Important outcomes of this work include *satisfiability modulo theories* (SMT), starting with the pioneering work of Nelson and Oppen [21] and of Shostak [25]. (See [3] for a more recent syntactic, inference-rule based approach to developing SMT algorithms for lists and arrays.)

In this paper, we investigate the *unification* problem modulo two simple equational theories for lists. The constructors we shall use are the usual 'nil' and 'cons'. We only consider nil-terminated lists, or equivalently, only finite lists that are *proper* in the sense of LISP. (All our lists can actually be visualized as *flat-lists* in the sense of LISP.) We first examine lists with *right cons* (*rcons*) as the only operator (observer), and propose an algorithm for the unification problem modulo this theory (Sect. 2). We then consider the theory extended with a second operator *reverse* (named *rev*) and develop an algorithm to solve the unification problem over *rev* (Sect. 3). In both cases, the algorithm is based on a suitable reduction of the unification problem to solving equations on finite words over a finite alphabet, where every equation of the problem has at most one word variable on either side. Further reductions will then lead us to the case where the equations will be 'independent,' and each equation will involve a single word variable; they can be solved by the techniques presented in [8]. All of this can be done in NP with respect to the lengths of the equations of the initial problem. In Sect. 4 we show how the considerations of length of words can be built into the unification algorithms for the

© Springer Nature Switzerland AG 2019
P. Fontaine (Ed.): CADE 2019, LNAI 11716, pp. 1–17, 2019.
https://doi.org/10.1007/978-3-030-29436-6_1

theories *rcons* and *reverse*. These could be of use in formal techniques based on word constraints (e.g., [2, 11, 16, 17]) or in constraint programming [7]. Several examples are given in Sect. 5, to illustrate how the method we have developed in this paper operates.

Related Work. Motivated by constraint logic programming [7], some existential theories of list concatenation have been investigated in [26]. But these works do not consider any list reverse operator. With a view to derive NP decision procedures we reduce our unification problems, on lists with a reverse operator but without concatenation, to systems of word equations that are special case of quadratic word equations. It is stated in [24] that solving systems of quadratic word equations is in NP *if* a simple exponential bound can be obtained on their shortest solution; however, to our knowledge this simple exponential bound has not yet been proved. In [11] it is shown that *if* word equations can be converted to a solved form, then satisfiability of word equations with length constraints is decidable. Satisfiability of quadratic regular-oriented word equations with length constraints is shown decidable in [11]. Again these results do not consider a reverse operator.

2   List Theory with *rcons*

The reader is assumed to be familiar with the concepts and notation used in [4]. For terminology and a more in-depth treatment of unification the reader is referred to [6].

The signature underlying our study below, will be 2-sorted with two disjoint types: *element* and *list*. We assume there are finitely many constants (at least 2) of type *element*, while nil will be the unique constant of type *list*. The unification problems we consider are instances of *unification with constants* in the terminology of [6].

For better comprehension, we shall use in general the lower-case letters $x, y, z, u, v, \ldots$ for the variables to which are assigned terms of type *element*, and the upper-case letters $X, Y, Z, U, V, \ldots$, for the variables to which are assigned terms of type *list*; possibly with suffixes or indices, in both cases.

We introduce now the equational axioms of List theory with *rcons*:

$$rcons(\text{nil}, x) \approx cons(x, \text{nil})$$
$$rcons(cons(x, Y), z) \approx cons(x, rcons(Y, z))$$

where nil and cons are constructors; and cons, *rcons* are typed respectively as:

$$cons : \text{element} \times \text{list} \longrightarrow \text{list}$$
$$rcons : \text{list} \times \text{element} \longrightarrow \text{list}$$

We refer to this equational theory as RCONS. Orienting these from left to right produces a convergent system:

$$(1) \qquad rcons(\text{nil}, x) \longrightarrow cons(x, \text{nil})$$
$$(2) \quad rcons(cons(x, y), z) \longrightarrow cons(x, rcons(y, z))$$

The following result helps simplifying equations in RCONS:

Lemma 1. *Let* s_1, s_2, t_1, t_2 *be terms such that* $rcons(s_1, t_1) \approx_{\text{RCONS}} rcons(s_2, t_2)$.

$$Then \quad s_1 \approx_{\text{RCONS}} s_2 \quad and \quad t_1 \approx_{\text{RCONS}} t_2.$$

2.1 Unifiability Complexity Analysis

Theorem 1. *Unifiability modulo* RCONS *is NP-hard.*

Proof. We will show this by reduction from 1-in-3-SAT. Given an instance of 1-in-3-SAT, we will construct a unification problem in our theory such that a unifier exists *if and only if* the instance of 1-in-3-SAT is satisfiable. The set of equations thus constructed will be referred to as S.

For each clause $C_i = (a_i \vee b_i \vee c_i)$ in the instance of 1-in-3-SAT, we add the following equation into S:

$$S_i : \; \mathrm{cons}(0, \mathrm{cons}(0, \mathrm{cons}(1, L_i))) \approx^? rcons(rcons(rcons(L_i, x_i), y_i), z_i)$$

where 0 and 1 are constants. Note that this equation has the following three solutions:

1. $L_i \mapsto \mathrm{nil}, x_i \mapsto 0, y_i \mapsto 0, z_i \mapsto 1$
2. $L_i \mapsto \mathrm{cons}(0, \mathrm{nil}), x_i \mapsto 0, y_i \mapsto 1, z_i \mapsto 0$
3. $L_i \mapsto \mathrm{cons}(0, \mathrm{cons}(0, \mathrm{nil})), x_i \mapsto 1, y_i \mapsto 0, z_i \mapsto 0.$

it also has the following solution:

$$L_i \mapsto \mathrm{cons}(0, \mathrm{cons}(0, \mathrm{cons}(1, rcons(rcons(rcons(M_i, x_i), y_i), z_i))))$$

but if we substitute this solution back into equation S_i and apply a series of decompositions, this gives us the following equation:

$$\mathrm{cons}(0, \mathrm{cons}(0, \mathrm{cons}(1, M_i))) \approx^? rcons(rcons(rcons(M_i, x_i), y_i), z_i)$$

Therefore, clearly $\{M_i, x_i, y_i, z_i\}$ has the same solution set as $\{L_i, x_i, y_i, z_i\}$ and must ultimately terminate in a solution of type 1, 2, or 3. If it does not terminate, then the unifier for L_i must be infinitely large and is thus not a valid unifying assignment. We associate the solutions of type 1, 2, and 3 with the truth assignments $\{a_i = false, b_i = false, c_i = true\}$, $\{a_i = false, b_i = true, c_i = false\}$, and $\{a_i = true, b_i = false, c_i = false\}$ respectively. Thus, if the constructed unification problem has a set of finite unifiers for these variables, then the original 1-in-3-SAT problem has a solution (which is given by the previous associations.) Similarly, if there is some satisfying assignment of the 1-in-3-SAT, then a set of finite unifiers for the unification problem can be constructed from that assignment by running the previous associations backward. □

To show that the problem is in NP, we first consider the set of variables of type *element* in the problem, and guess equivalence classes in this set. We then select one representative element from each equivalence class, and replace all instances of the other variables in that class with the chosen representative; whenever possible, choose a constant as representative. Clearly, no equivalence class may contain more than one constant. For every representative x of type *element* that is not a constant, introduce a fresh (symbolic) constant c_x to act as the representative of its class. This guessing step is clearly in NP. (If a unifier is found involving c_x, then all instances of c_x may be replaced by x once again.)

Once this guessing step is done, all equations of the given unification problem will be of the following form (after RCONS-normalization if necessary):

$$\mathsf{cons}(a_1,...(\mathsf{cons}(a_k, rcons(rcons(...rcons(X,b_l)...,b_1)))))$$
$$\approx^? \mathsf{cons}(c_1,...(\mathsf{cons}(c_m, rcons(rcons(...rcons(Y,d_n),...,d_1)))))$$

with X and Y not necessarily distinct. We will represent the sequences $\{a_i\}$, $\{b_i\}$, $\{c_i\}$, $\{d_i\}$ as finite words α, β, γ, δ respectively, over the constants. Such an equation can then be expressed as a word equation as follows:

$$\alpha X \beta \approx^? \gamma Y \delta$$

Clearly, this equation does not have a solution unless either α is a prefix of γ or vice-versus. Without loss of generality, let α be a prefix of γ and let $\alpha^{-1}\gamma$ denote the suffix of γ after α is removed. The equation may be simplified to the following: $X\beta \approx^? \alpha^{-1}\gamma Y\delta$. Similarly, either β or δ is a suffix of the other; there are two cases:

β is a suffix of δ. Let $\delta\beta^{-1}$ denote the remaining prefix of δ. The equation is then simplified to $X \approx^? \alpha^{-1}\gamma Y\delta\beta^{-1}$
δ is a suffix of β. Let $\beta\delta^{-1}$ denote the remaining prefix of β. The equation is thus simplified to $X\beta\delta^{-1} \approx^? \alpha^{-1}\gamma Y$

A word equation $\alpha X \beta \approx^? \gamma Y \delta$, is said to be *pruned*, if all common (non-empty) prefixes and suffixes from the two sides of the equation have been removed. If this cannot be done, the equation is unsolvable. Every pruned 1-variable equation is either of the form $\alpha X \approx^? X\beta$, or of the form $X \approx^? \gamma$, and every pruned 2-variable equation is either of the form $X \approx^? \alpha Y\beta$, or of the form $\alpha X \approx^? Y\beta$, for words α, β, γ. Equations of the form $X \approx^? \gamma$ or of the form $X \approx^? \alpha Y\beta$ are said to be in *solved form*. Those of the other types are said to be *unsolved*.

In the following subsection, we present a nondeterministic algorithm to solve any set of such equations, on finite words over a finite alphabet, each equation involving at most two variables, one on either side, appearing at most once. Such a set of equations will be said to be a *simple system*, or a *simple set*, of word equations. The following notions will be useful for presenting and analyzing our algorithm.

Definition 1. *Let U be a simple set of word equations.*

(i) *The relation graph G_U of U is the undirected graph $G = (\mathcal{V}, \mathcal{E})$ where the set of vertices $\mathcal{V}$ is the set of variables in U and the set of edges $\mathcal{E}$ contains (X, Y) iff there is an equation of the form $\alpha X \beta \approx^? \gamma Y \delta$ in U.*

(ii) *For any two variables X, Y in U, the variable Y is said to be dependent on X iff the graph G_U has an edge defined by an equation of the form $Y \approx^? \alpha X \beta$, with α or β (or both) non-empty; such a dependency is denoted as $Y \succ_U X$, or as $X \prec_U Y$.*

(iii) *The graph G_U is said to present a dependency cycle from a variable Y in U, iff for some variables $X_1, X_2, ...X_p$ in U, we have: $Y \succ_U X_1 \succ_U \cdots \succ_U X_p \succ_U Y$.*

Given a dependency relation $Y \approx^? \alpha X \beta$ on the variables X, Y in U, the variable Y is said to be the 'lhs' (left-hand-side) of this dependency; the edge on G_U between Y and X is called a *directed dependency edge* from Y to X. (By definition, at least one of α, β is supposed to be non-empty.) A *dependency path* from a node V to a node W is a sequence of dependency edges on G_U, from V to W.

2.2 NP-Solvability of Simple Sets: Algorithm A

Algorithm **A** presented below is nondeterministic. We will show that, for any run of Algorithm **A** (successful or not) on any given simple set U of word equations, the total number of steps is polynomial w.r.t. inputs. Moreover the equations generated in a run will be shown to have polynomial size w.r.t. inputs (Sect. 2.3). Consequently, Algorithm **A** will produce, when successful on U, a system containing only a polynomial number of dependencies and 1-variable equations, each of them of polynomial size. By applying to this resulting system of 1-variable equations, (Lemma 3 followed by) a polynomial solvability check from [8], we will deduce that solvability of simple systems of word equations is in NP.

Under the runs of Algorithm **A**, dependencies chosen in Step 2 get marked; we assume that, initially, none of the dependencies in the given set U is marked.

Step 1. (*Pruning*) For each equation in U of the form $\alpha X \beta \approx^? \gamma Y \delta$, remove all common prefixes and suffixes from the two sides of that equation.

(i) If the two sides of some equation have non-common prefixes or suffixes, then EXIT with failure.

(ii) If for some variable X in U, there is a dependency cycle at X in the graph G_U, then EXIT with failure.

Step 2. Choose an *unmarked* dependency $X \approx^? \alpha Y \beta$ in U; replace all instances of X in all the other equations by $\alpha Y \beta$; *mark the chosen dependency*. GOTO Step 1.

Step 3.a. Select an arbitrary equation such that the variables on the right and left hand sides of the equation are distinct. If no such equation is available, EXIT.

Step 3.b. Let the selected equation be of the form $\alpha X \approx^? Y \beta$.

Guess a word u in $Prefixes(\alpha)$,

(i) If $\alpha = uv$ and $\beta = vw$, with $v \neq \lambda$, then *replace* the selected equation on X, Y by the two equations $\{X \approx^? w, Y \approx^? u\}$ and propagate this substitution through G_U; GOTO Step 1.

(ii) (*Splitting*) Otherwise, let Z be a fresh variable; and *replace* the selected equation on X, Y by the two solved forms: $X \approx^? Z\beta$ and $Y \approx^? \alpha Z$; GOTO Step 1.

Proposition 1. *Let U be a simple set of word equations. The number of steps needed for Algorithm **A** to halt is bounded by $5n$ where n is the initial number of variables in the given problem U.*

Proof. Let d be the number of unsolved variables (i.e., that are not the lhs of an equation). Initially $d \leq n$ where n is the initial number of variables in U. Let $d(k)$ be the value of d when we enter for the kth time in Step 3. Since Step 3 generates one fresh variable and two solved variables (that were not solved at previous steps: otherwise they would have been replaced at Step 2) we have $d(k+1) < d(k)$. Therefore Step 3 is applied at most n times. Hence the number of fresh variables generated (under Splitting) is at most n, and the maximum number of variables at any stage is at most $2n$. Therefore Step 2 can be applied at most $2n$ times, and the same holds also for Step 1. □

When a fresh variable 'Z' is introduced in Step 3.b. (ii) the graph G_U will be *dynamically extended* by the addition of a fresh node labelled with the variable Z; we also introduce two dependency edges from the nodes X and Y to the node Z, corresponding respectively to the two solved forms $X \approx^? Z\beta$, and $Y \approx^? \alpha Z$. Similarly, each time an equation derived under this step turns out (after Pruning) to be a solved form, a dependency edge will be added on the extended graph, between the corresponding nodes.

We note that when Algorithm **A** halts (without failure) on a given problem, we will be left with a set of equations each being either in solved form, or a simple 1-variable equation. Note also that the variables that are lhs of solved forms have a unique occurrence. Hence the resulting system is solvable iff each subsystem of 1-variable equations, on a given variable, is solvable.

We prove in Lemma 3 below, that every subsystem of the resulting 1-variable equations, on a given variable, can be replaced by a single equation (that may not be necessarily simple) on that variable, at polynomial cost; each such 1-variable equation can be checked for solvability, by a known polynomial algorithm from [8]. Prior to that we need to show that, when **A** halts without failure on any problem U, the length of any resulting simple 1-variable equation is polynomially bounded, w.r.t. the size of U. In the following section we shall actually show more.

2.3 Lengths of Prefixes/Suffixes of Equations Are Polynomially Bounded

Note that in Steps 2 and 3.b of Algorithm **A**, when a dependency $X = \mu$ is selected, then every other equation e containing at least one occurrence of X is replaced by $e[X \leftarrow \mu]$ and immediately simplified by Pruning (Step 1). After these operations the resulting equation e' *replaces e*.

Suppose now, that a derived equation e' replaces an equation e under the propagation of a dependency (and after Pruning); let α, β denote respectively the prefix and suffix of the equation e, and α', β' those of e'. The replacing equation e' is said to be in '*excess-size*' w.r.t. the equation it replaces, iff $|\alpha'| > |\alpha|$, or $|\beta'| > |\beta|$, or both.

It is easy to see that the propagation of solved forms of the type $Y \approx^? X$, or of the type $Y \approx^? \gamma$, cannot lead to replacing equations in excess-size. We can also check that, in any run of **A**, a 1-*variable equation is never replaced by an equation in excess-size*; this follows from a simple case analysis (cf. [1], Appendix A). It can also be checked (cf. loc. cit), that the cases of Steps 2 and 3.b of **A** that can lead to replacing equations possibly in excess-size, are as follows:

- a 2-variable equation in *excess-size* can get derived, when a dependency is applied to the lhs (or the rhs) of a 2-variable equation.
- a 1-variable equation in *excess-size* can get derived, when a dependency is propagated onto a 2-variable equation on the same two variables.
- a solved form equation in *excess-size* can get derived when a dependency is propagated onto a solved form for the same variable, or on a 2-variable equation.

We already know that Algorithm **A** halts in polynomially many steps w.r.t. the number of variables n of the given problem, and that the number of equations in U when **A** halts, is also polynomially bounded w.r.t. n (each step generates at most one equation). We show now, that in the equations derived under **A**, even when they are in excess-size, the lengths of the prefixes/suffixes remain polynomially bounded w.r.t. U.

Let us consider a 2-variable equation that gets derived under **A**: for instance, the 2-variable equation $\alpha_1 Y \approx^? W\beta_1$, on which is propagated the dependency $Y \approx^? \alpha X \beta$. The 2-variable equation will be replaced (after Pruning) by a 2-variable equation of the form $\alpha_1' X \approx^? W\beta_1'$, where: $|\alpha_1'| = \alpha_1 \alpha| \leq |\alpha_1| + |\alpha|$, and $|\beta_1'| \leq |\beta_1|$. To the variable X, brought in by the substitution in the equation derived $\alpha_1' X \approx^? W\beta_1'$, we attach the singleton sequence $[Y \succ X]$, and refer to it as the 'prefix-tag' (or 'ptag') of X in this equation. (Remember: by definition, either the prefix or the suffix of a dependency must be non-empty.) This ptag is to be seen as a tag, to notify that the unique dependency with Y as lhs, has served in the derivation of this fresh equation.

The replacing equation (in the example) will be in excess-size, iff α is non-empty. In the prefix $\alpha_1 \alpha$ of X in the equation, α_1 is contributed by the 2-variable equation $\alpha_1 Y \approx^? W\beta_1$, and α is contributed by the dependency $Y \approx^? \alpha X \beta$ that is applied to that 2-variable equation. In other words, *if the equation derived is in excess-size*, the ptag *also carries the information* that the excess in the length of the prefix, is due to a portion contributed by the prefix of the dependency.

The ptag sequences grow incrementally, when a fresh equation derived gets replaced in turn, under a subsequent step of **A**, by a new fresh equation. For instance, suppose on the same example, that we have a second dependency of the form $X \approx^? \theta V \delta$. The fresh (replacing) 2-variable equation derived would then be of the form: $\alpha_1' \theta V \approx^? W\beta_1'$. The ptag of V (the variable brought in) in this equation (not necessarily in excess-size) would then be, by definition, the sequence $[Y \succ X, X \succ V]$.

Suffix-tags ('stags') are defined analogously: on the same example above, suppose for instance that we have a dependency $W \approx^? \tau Z \eta$. We would then derive an equation of the form $\alpha'' V \approx^? Z\beta''$; the ptag of V in this equation would still be $[Y \succ X, X \succ V]$, while the stag of Z (the variable brought in by the substitution) would be $[W \succ Z]$.

The ptags and stags can be defined, in formal terms, (recursively,) as follows:

Definition 2. *(i) For any variable in an equation of the given problem U, the ptag attached, w.r.t. that equation, is set to be the empty sequence* $[\,]$.

*(ii) Suppose that, under some step of the algorithm **A**:*

- *a dependency of the form $Y \approx^? \alpha X \beta$ is propagated onto an equation of the form $\gamma_1 Y \approx^? W\delta_1$ (resp. of the form $X \approx^? \gamma_1 Z \delta_1$);*
- *that the variable Y in $\gamma_1 Y \approx^? W\delta_1$ (resp. Z in $X \approx^? \gamma_1 Z \delta_1$) has an attached ptag of the form $[c]$, where c is a (possibly empty) finite sequence of dependency relations on the graph G_U;*
- *and that from the propagation of the dependency (after Pruning), we derive an equation of the form $\gamma_1' X \approx^? W \delta_1'$ (resp. of the form $Y \approx^? \gamma_1' Z \delta_1'$).*

Then, the ptag attached to the variable X (resp. the variable Z), brought in by the substitution in the replacing equation, is set to be $[c, Y \succ X]$

(iii) stags are defined analogously.

Note that the ptags/stags define a dependency chain of the form $Y \succ X \succ V \succ W \dots$, on the variables of equations that get derived, under the Steps 2 and 3.b of **A**.

Lemma 2. *Assume that algorithm* **A** *halts without failure on a given problem U. Then, no variable can appear more the once in the dependency chain defined by the ptag, or stag, of any equation derived under the runs of* **A** *on U.*

Proof. If we assume the contrary, then we get a dependency cycle on the (extended) relation graph of U; but then **A** would have exited with failure on U.   □

Corollary 1. *Assume that algorithm* **A** *halts without failure, on a given problem U. Then the length of the prefix of any resulting equation is polynomially bounded, w.r.t. Ns, where N is the total number of equations in U, and s is the maximum size of the prefixes or suffixes of the equations in U.*

Proof. By the above Lemma, the number of dependency relations in any ptag or stag is at most the number N_1 of dependencies, initial or derived under the runs of **A**; and we also know that N_1 is polynomial on N. On the other hand, the maximal (or 'worst') growth in the prefix size of any derived equation e, when **A** halts, would be when *each* dependency relation in its ptag sequence corresponds to a derived equation in excess-size. But, as observed above, this means, that the prefix α (or suffix β) of a dependency of the form $Y \approx^? \alpha X \beta$ whose propagation led to the derivation of the equation e, has contributed to the excess-size in the prefix (or suffix) of the variable X in e. On the other hand, we know that the length of the prefix (or suffix) of any dependency in the problem, initial or derived under Steps 2 and 3.b on a first run of **A**, is polynomial on Ns (cf. [1], Appendix A); an inductive argument, on the number of steps of **A** before it halts, proves that the same bound holds also for all derivations under the subsequent runs of **A**. That proves the corollary.   □

Note however, that when **A** halts without failure on a given problem, the resulting 1-variable equations may not be all independent. So, to be able to apply [8] and conclude, it remains now to replace every subsystem formed of the resulting simple 1-variable equations *on the same variable*, by an equivalent single equation (which may not be simple) on that variable, but of polynomial size w.r.t. the size of U. This is the objective of our next lemma:

Lemma 3. *Any system S of 1-variable equations, of size m, on a given variable X, is equivalent to a* single *1-variable equation of size $p(m)$ for some fixed polynomial p (where X can appear more than once on either side).*

Proof. We first recall the well-known 'trick' (see [15]) to build such a single equation from two equations:

$$\begin{cases} u = v \\ u' = v' \end{cases} \equiv \quad uau'ubu' = vav'vbv'$$

where a, b are two distinct constants. The resulting equation is of size $2|S| + 4$. Since the initial system S is of size $|S| \geq 4$, we deduce that the resulting single equation has size $\leq 3|S|$. To iterate the process on a system W of n equations (indexed from 1 to n) we consider an integer k such that $k - 1 \leq \log n < k$; by adding to the system $2^k - n$ trivial equations $X = X$, we get an extended system $V = (V_i)$ with equations indexed from 1 to 2^k. We shall show by induction, that V is equivalent to a single equation of size $\leq 3^k|V|$.

Assume (as inductive hypothesis) that we have derived, for the two systems $V' = (V_i)_1^{2^{k-1}}$ and $V'' = (V_i)_{2^{k-1}+1}^{2^k}$ two equivalent single equations e' and e'' respectively, of size $\leq 3^{k-1}|V'|$ and $\leq 3^{k-1}|V''|$ respectively. Now if we combine e' and e'' we obtain an equivalent single equation of size bounded by $\leq 3(3^{k-1}|V'|+3^{k-1}|V''|) = 3^k(|V'|+|V''|) = 3^k(|V|)$. Getting back to system W, this means that W is equivalent to a single equation of size $\leq 3^k(|W|+2^k-n)$. Since $k \leq \log n + 1$ we have $3^k(|W|+2^k-n) \leq 3^{\log n+1}(|W|+2^{\log n+1}-n) \leq 3n^{\log 3}(|W|+2n^{\log 2}-n)$. Since n is bounded by $|W|$, we deduce the assertion of the lemma. □

Theorem 2. *Solvability of a simple set U of word equations is in NP.*

Proof. Assume that Algorithm **A** halts without failure on the given problem U. We shall then be left with a final system of solved form equations, along with several (simple) 1-variable equations. Moreover (see Lemma 2, and Corollary 1) the size of these 1-variable equations is polynomially bounded w.r.t. the size of U. Thanks to Lemma 3, every subsystem of these 1-variable equations involving a given variable X is equivalent to a single 1-variable equation in X (that may not be simple). Each of these resulting 1-variable equations can then be solved, *independently*, in polynomial time (see [8]). □

We can now conclude:

Theorem 3. *Unifiability modulo* RCONS *is NP-complete.*

3   List Theory with *rev*

The axioms of this theory are

$$rcons(\text{nil},x) \approx cons(x,\text{nil})$$
$$rcons(cons(x,Y),z) \approx cons(x,rcons(Y,z))$$
$$rev(\text{nil}) \approx \text{nil}$$
$$rev(cons(x,Y)) \approx rcons(rev(Y),x)$$

where nil and cons are constructors. Orienting each of the above equations to the right yields a convergent rewrite system (with 4 rules). But the term rewriting system we shall consider here, for the theory *rev*, is the following system of six rewrite rules:

$$
\begin{aligned}
&(1) & rcons(\text{nil},x) &\rightarrow cons(x,\text{nil}) \\
&(2) & rcons(cons(x,Y),z) &\rightarrow cons(x,rcons(Y,z)) \\
&(3) & rev(\text{nil}) &\rightarrow \text{nil} \\
&(4) & rev(cons(x,Y)) &\rightarrow rcons(rev(Y),x) \\
&(5) & rev(rcons(X,y)) &\rightarrow cons(y,rev(X)) \\
&(6) & rev(rev(X)) &\rightarrow X
\end{aligned}
$$

which is again convergent. We shall refer to this equational theory as REV.

Actually, the two added rules (5) and (6) are derivable as inductive consequences of the first four rules. We shall prove this by induction on the length of the list-term X, where by 'length' of any ground list-term X, we shall mean the number of applications of cons in X at the outermost level.

We first prove the claim for the added rule (5): $rev(rcons(X,y)) \to cons(y, rev(X))$. Suppose we have some ground term X. If $X = $ nil, then

$$rev(rcons(X,y)) \approx rev(rcons(\text{nil}, y)) \to^+ cons(y, \text{nil}) \text{ and}$$
$$cons(y, rev(X)) \approx cons(y, rev(\text{nil})) \to^+ cons(y, \text{nil})$$

If $X = cons(a, Y)$ for some term a and some term Y of length n, then

$$rev(rcons(X,y)) \approx rev(rcons(cons(a,Y),y)) \to^+ rcons(rev(rcons(Y,y)), a) \text{ and}$$
$$cons(y, rev(X)) \approx cons(y, rev(cons(a,Y))) \to^+ rcons(cons(y, rev(Y)), a)$$

By the inductive assumption $rev(rcons(Y,y)) = cons(y, rev(Y))$ and we are done. We prove then the claim for the added rule (6): $rev(rev(X)) \to X$.

Clearly $rev(rev(\text{nil})) \to^+ \text{nil}$. Let $X = cons(a, Y)$ for some term a and some term Y of length n. Then $rev(rev(X)) \approx rev(rev(cons(a,Y))) \to rev(rcons(rev(Y), a))$ $\to cons(a, rev(rev(Y))) \to cons(a, Y) = X$.

From this point on, without loss of generality, we will consider all terms to be in normal form modulo this term rewrite system.

Lemma 4. *Let S_1, S_2, t_1, t_2 be terms such that: $rcons(S_1, t_1) =_{\text{REV}} rcons(S_2, t_2)$.*

$$\text{Then} \quad S_1 =_{\text{REV}} S_2 \quad \text{and} \quad t_1 =_{\text{REV}} t_2.$$

Lemma 5. *Let S_1, S_2 be terms such that: $rev(S_1) =_{\text{REV}} rev(S_2)$. Then $S_1 =_{\text{REV}} S_2$.*

Lemma 6. *Unifiability modulo REV is NP-hard.*

Proof. The NP-hardness proof for unifiability modulo RCONS (as given in Sect. 2) remains valid for unifiability modulo REV as well. □

Theorem 4. *Unifiability modulo REV is in NP and is therefore NP-Complete.*

Proof. After normalization with the rules of REV, we can assume that, for every equation in the given unification problem, its lhs as well as its rhs are of one of the following two types:

$$cons(x_1, cons(x_2, \ldots (rcons(rcons(\ldots (rcons(X, y_1) \ldots)))),$$
$$\text{or}$$
$$cons(x_1, cons(x_2, \ldots (rcons(rcons(\ldots (rcons(rev(Y), z_1) \ldots)))$$

If the lhs and the rhs of an equation are both of the first type, or both of the second type, then we can associate with it a word equation of the form $\alpha X \beta \approx^? \alpha' Y \beta'$, as in Sect. 2; we deal with all such equations first, exactly as we did in Sect. 2.

Once done with such equations, we consider equations (in the unification problem) whose lhs are of the first type, while their rhs are of the second type, or vice versa. To each such equation we can associate either a word equation of the form $\alpha X \beta \approx^? \alpha' Y^R \beta'$, or a word equation of the form $\alpha X \beta \approx^? \alpha' X^R \beta'$, where Y^R (resp.

X^R) is a variable that stands for $rev(Y)$ (resp. for $rev(X)$); naturally, all these will be duly pruned.

The (pruned) word equations of a 'mixed' type, of the form $\alpha X \approx^? Y^R \beta$ involving two different variables X, Y will be handled by the addition of an *extra splitting inference step* to the algorithm **A**, say between its Steps 2 and 3. In concrete terms, such an equation will first get split by writing: $X \approx^? Z\beta$, and $Y^R \approx^? \alpha Z$, where Z is a fresh variable, then 'solving it locally' as $X \approx^? Z\beta'$, $Y \approx^? Z^R \alpha^R$; this substitution will then be propagated to all the other equations of the problem involving X or Y; the resulting equations derived thereby, will be treated similarly, and by the procedure that we present below for the equations involving a single variable.

We present now the part of the algorithm that deals with all the (pruned) word equations of the form $\alpha X \beta \approx^? \alpha' X^R \beta'$, on a given variable X of the problem. This part will be referred to as the *palindrome discovery* step of the algorithm. We will use the word *palindrome* to refer to a variable X that has to satisfy $X = X^R$. We maintain a list of variables that are known to be palindromes in our algorithm, which is initially empty. Clearly, if X is known to be a palindrome, then $\alpha X \beta \approx^? \alpha' X^R \beta'$ is the same as $\alpha X \beta \approx^? \alpha' X \beta'$ and need not be considered at this step in the algorithm.

In this part, we have two cases to consider:

Case 1: $X \approx^? \alpha'' X^R \beta''$. In this case, if $|\alpha'' \beta''| = 0$, then we conclude that X is a palindrome. Else, if $|\alpha'' \beta''| \neq 0$, then there is clearly no solution and we terminate with failure.

Case 2: $\alpha'' X \approx^? X^R \beta''$. In this case, we check for the existence of words u, v such that $\alpha'' = u^R v$, $\beta'' = vu$. If such a pair exists, we may conclude that $X = u$, and this solution can be propagated through the dependency graph, as in the flat-list case. Again, there cannot be more than $min(|\alpha|, |\beta|)$ of these solutions. If all such pairs are checked without finding a solution, then we resort to splitting and write $X = Z\beta''$, $X^R = \alpha'' Z$, where Z is fresh. This second equation gives us $X = Z^R \alpha''^R$ and therefore $Z\beta'' = Z^R \alpha''^R$. If $\beta'' \neq \alpha''^R$, then there is no solution and we may terminate with failure. Otherwise we may conclude that $Z = Z^R$ (and is therefore a palindrome) and replace all occurrences of X with $Z\beta''$.

Once we have finished this, we have to check with the equations of the form $\alpha X \approx^? X\beta$ involving the same variable X studied above. If X is not a palindrome, then we may use (possibly after grouping several equations with Lemma 3) the algorithm given in [8] to find a solution. If X is known to be a palindrome, then we still run the algorithm given in [8] to check for a solution, but we first check that the prefixes and suffixes of each equation (i.e., α, β) meet certain criteria.

In the case where $|\alpha|$ or $|\beta| \geq |X|$, the equation $\alpha X \approx^? X\beta$ implies that X has to be a prefix of α and a suffix of β. Therefore we may exhaustively check all palindrome prefixes and suffixes of α and β respectively for validity.

Remains to consider the case where $|\alpha|$ and $|\beta| < |X|$; then, according to the following Lemma 7, X is a solution if and only if there exist palindromes u, v, and a positive integer k such that $\alpha = uv$, $\beta = vu$ and $X = (uv)^k u$.

Lemma 7. *Let α, β and A be non-empty words such that A is a palindrome and $|\alpha| = |\beta| < |A|$. Then $\alpha A = A\beta$ if and only if there exist palindromes u, v, and a positive integer k such that $\alpha = uv$, $\beta = vu$ and $A = (uv)^k u$.*

Proof. If $\alpha = uv$, $\beta = vu$ and $A = (uv)^k u$ for palindromes u, v then

$$\alpha A = uv(uv)^k u = (uv)^{k+1} u = (uv)^k uvu = A\beta$$

Also, $A^R = ((uv)^k u)^R = u^R (v^R u^R)^k = u(vu)^k = (uv)^k u = A$. So, A is indeed a palindrome and satisfies $\alpha A = A\beta$.

It is well-known that for any equation $\alpha A = A\beta$ where $0 < |\alpha| = |\beta| < |A|$, α and β must be *conjugates*. That is, there must exist some pair of words u, v, such that $\alpha = uv$ and $\beta = vu$. Furthermore, A must be $(uv)^k u$ for some k. If A is also a palindrome, then α must be a prefix of A and β must be a suffix of A. Because A is a palindrome, α^R is therefore also a suffix of A. So, because $|\alpha| = |\beta|$, we may conclude that $\alpha^R = \beta$. The proof proceeds as follows:

$$\alpha^R = \beta \text{ implies } (uv)^R = vu \text{ implies } v^R u^R = vu \text{ implies } (v^R = v \text{ and } u^R = u)$$

Thus u and v are palindromes, $\alpha = uv$, $\beta = vu$, and $A = (uv)^k u$ for some $k > 0$.   □

4   List Theories with *length*

In many cases of practical interest, list data types are 'enriched' with a length operator, under which, e.g., the list $cons(a, nil)$ will have length 1, the list $cons(a, cons(b, nil))$ will have length 2, etc. Solving equations on list terms in these cases will need to take into account length constraints. For instance $cons(a, X) = cons(a, Y)$ cannot be solved if $length(X) = s(length(Y))$ (where s stands for the successor function on natural integers). We shall be assuming in this section that a length operator is defined on the lists we consider, and that this operator is formally defined in terms of a (typed) convergent rewrite system, presented below in Sects. 4.1 and 4.2. Our objective will be to solve equations on list terms subject to certain given length constraints. We will again reduce the problem to solving some word equations. It seems appropriate here to quote [17]: "The problem of solving a word equation with a length constraint (i.e., a constraint relating the lengths of words in the word equation) has remained a long-standing open problem". However, thanks to the special form of the word equations we deal with, we will be able to provide a decision algorithm in our case.

4.1   *length* with *rcons*

The Term Rewrite System: The (typed) rewrite rules for *rcons* with *length* are given below, where the unary functions s and *length* are typed as $s : \text{nat} \to \text{nat}$, $length : \text{list} \to \text{nat}$; the constant 0 is typed $0 \to \text{nat}$;. This rewrite system is convergent:

$$length(\text{nil}) \to 0$$
$$length(cons(x, Y)) \to s(length(Y))$$
$$rcons(\text{nil}, x) \to cons(x, \text{nil})$$
$$rcons(cons(x, Y), z) \to cons(x, rcons(Y, z))$$
$$length(rcons(X, y)) \to s(length(X))$$

Variables of type nat will be denoted (in general) by the lower case letters $i, j, k, m, n, \ldots$ The last rule above, $length(rcons(x, y)) \to s(length(x))$, is derived easily from the preceding rules, by induction.

The Unification Algorithm. We shall assume that all instances of s and 0 in the equations of the given problem have been removed by successive applications of the inference rules below, where $\mathscr{E}\mathscr{Q}$ is a set of equations and $\uplus$ is the disjoint union:

$$\frac{\mathscr{E}\mathscr{Q} \uplus \{n \approx^? 0\}}{\mathscr{E}\mathscr{Q} \cup \{n \approx^? length(X'), X' \approx^? nil\}}$$

$$\frac{\mathscr{E}\mathscr{Q} \uplus \{n \approx^? s(m)\}}{\mathscr{E}\mathscr{Q} \cup \{n \approx^? length(X'), m \approx^? length(Y'), X' \approx^? cons(x',Y')\}}$$

Assume further that our given unification problem U has been transformed into word equations of the form $\alpha X \beta \approx^? \gamma Y \delta$ and that those equations have been reduced to a set of mutually independent systems S_i of equations on one variable X_i. Let us call this set $\mathbb{S} = \bigcup S_i$ where each S_i is a set of equations on one variable. These independent systems of equations S_i may be solved, each producing a solution-set which forms a regular language [8]. We shall use L_i to refer to the solution-set to the system of equations S_i. By Theorem 3 in [8] either $L_i = F_i$ or $L_i = F_i \cup (u_i v_i)^+ u_i$ for some words u_i, v_i and some finite set of words F_i.

In the version of this problem without *length*, the problem of *unifiability* is now solved by simply checking each element of $\{L_i\}$ for (non-)emptiness. However, here the solutions may still be related by *length* equations. We must find a set of words $\{w_i \mid w_i \in L_i\}$ which satisfy length constraints of the form $|w_i| = |w_j| + c_{ij}$ for a constant, non-negative integer c_{ij}. Note that not all pairs i, j need have a constraint of this form.

For w_i we either try elements of F_i or a word of type: $(u_i v_i)^{n_i} u_i$. For the latter case constraints of the type $|w_i| = |w_j| + c_{ij}$ are equivalent to $(|u_i| + |v_i|)n_i + |u_i| = (|u_j| + |v_j|)n_j + |u_j| + c_{ij}$, where n_i, n_j are non-negative integer variables; so we can always reduce our problem to solving a finite number of linear diophantine equations.

4.2 *length* with *rcons* and *rev*

The Term Rewrite System: We now add the rewrite rules of *rev* as defined in Sect. 3. The resulting rewrite system (where $0, s, length$ are typed as in Sect. 4.1) is convergent:

$$length(nil) \rightarrow 0$$
$$length(cons(x,y)) \rightarrow s(length(y))$$
$$rcons(nil,x) \rightarrow cons(x,nil)$$
$$rcons(cons(x,y),z) \rightarrow cons(x,rcons(y,z))$$
$$rev(nil) \rightarrow nil$$
$$rev(cons(x,y)) \rightarrow rcons(rev(y),x)$$
$$rev(rev(x)) \rightarrow x$$
$$length(rcons(x,y)) \rightarrow s(length(x))$$
$$length(rev(x)) \rightarrow length(x)$$

The last rule, $length(rev(x)) \rightarrow length(x)$, is not originally in the theories of RCONS, REV or LENGTH but can be easily derived by induction from the other rules.

The Unification Algorithm. We again assume that all instances of s and 0 have been removed from the equations of the given problem, by successive applications of the same two inference rules presented above in Sect. 4.1, for *rcons*.

We thus assume once more that our unification problem has been transformed into word equations of the form $\alpha X \beta \approx^? \gamma Y \delta$ and that those equations have been reduced to a set of mutually independent systems of equations on one variable (without reverse) which may be required to be a palindrome. As before, let $\mathbb{S} = \{S_i\}$ where each S_i is a set of equations on one variable which are respectively solved by the languages L_i.

Now suppose that S_i has variable X that is not required to be a palindrome, then its solution-set is either F_i or $F_i \cup (u_i v_i)^+ u_i$ for some words u_i, v_i and some finite set of words F_i according to Theorem 3 of [8]. If X is required to be a palindrome then its solution-set contains either a finite set of palindromes F_i or $F_i \cup (u_i v_i)^+ u_i$, where u_i, v_i, are such that $\alpha = u_i v_i$, $\beta = v_i u_i$ according to Lemma 7 and Theorem 3 of [8].

The algorithm now continues as in the previous *length* with *rcons* case: if two solution-sets are related by *length* equations, satisfiability may be checked by solving a finite set of linear diophantine equations.

5 Some Illustrative Examples

The following simple examples illustrate how our methods presented above will operate (either directly, or indirectly) in concrete situations.

Example 1. cof two 'list equations':

$$cons(x, X) \approx^? rev((cons(y, Y))), \ cons(a, X) \approx^? rev(cons(a, rev(X)))$$

As described in Sect. 3, this system will first get transformed to a system of two word equations: $xX \approx^? Y^R y$, $aX \approx^? X a$.

We can apply the Splitting step of algorithm **A** to the first word equation, and derive: $X \approx^? Zy$, $Y^R \approx^? xZ$, where Z is fresh; the latter of these two will get transformed to the solved form: $Y \approx^? Z^R x$. We have thus derived two solved forms: $X \approx^? Zy$, $Y \approx^? Z^R x$. Propagating for X from the first of these solved forms in the second word equation would a priori give: $aZy \approx^? Zya$, so Pruning would imply: $y = a$. And the variable Z has to satisfy: $aZ \approx^? Za$; which is true for any of the assignments: $Z = nil$, $Z = a$, $Z = aa$, $Z = aaa$, etc. If we choose $Z = nil$, and $x = a$, we get the following solution for the given list equations: $X = rcons(nil, a)$, $Y = rcons(nil, a)$.

Example 2. Consider the single 1-variable word equation $abX \approx^? Xba$.

For solving this 1-variable equation, (instead of appealing to the general result of [8]) we could choose to see the equation as an instance of a 2-variable equation, and use Splitting, as an ad hoc technique: i.e., replace the X on the lhs by Zba, and the X on the rhs by abZ.

The equation would then become: $abZba \approx^? abZba$, on the single variable Z, which admits any value of Z as a solution. Now, each of the assignments $Z = a$, $Z = aba$, $Z = ababa$ satisfies the equalities $X = abZ = Zba$. So each of the assignments $X = aba$, $X = ababa$, $X = abababa$, is a solution for the given problem.

Example 3. We consider now the set of word equations: $abX \approx^? Yba, Y \approx^? X^R$.

The equations are first replaced as: $abX \approx^? X^R ba$ and the equality $Y = X^R$. For solving the former we use Splitting, and write: $X \approx^? Zba$ and $X^R \approx^? abZ$. The fresh variable Z has then to satisfy the condition that $Zba = Z^R ba$. That is to say: Z must be a palindrome. Any palindrome (on the given alphabet) is actually a solution. We thus deduce that the assignments $X = Zba, Y = abZ$, where Z is *any* palindrome, is a solution for the given set of equations.

Note: This also shows that unification modulo the theory rev is infinitary. (It is not difficult to see that unification modulo the theory rcons is not finitary either.)

Example 4. We consider now the set of word equations, subject to a length constraint:

$$abX \approx^? Xba, \ X \approx^? ababY, \ length(Y) = 1$$

This set would be transformed into a set of word equations:

$$\{abX \approx^? Xba, \ X \approx^? ababY, \ Y \approx^? yZ, \ Z \approx^? nil\}.$$

Propagation of the first dependency would give us the 1-variable equation $abababY \approx^? ababYba$, which, once pruned, would become: $abY \approx^? Yba$. Propagation of the other dependencies would give us the equation $aby \approx^? yba$; which admits as solution $y = a$. Thus the given problem admits as solution: $X = ababa, Y = a, Z = nil$.

Suppose now, that the length constraint given is either $length(Y) = 0$, or $length(Y) = 3$, instead of the one given above. Then, by what we have seen in the previous two examples (we know the forms of the possible solutions for Y, after the propagation of the first dependency; therefore) the problem thus modified would be unsatisfiable.

6 Conclusion and Future Work

We have shown that unifiability modulo the two theories RCONS, REV are both NP-complete. For that we have identified a new class of word equations, *simple sets*, which can be solved in NP. One possible direction for our future work would be to investigate other problems for these list theories; for instance we can show that the uniform word problem for RCONS is undecidable (cf. [1], Appendix B). A second direction of future work would be to identify a class of *non-simple* sets of word equations, which can be solved by a suitable adaptation (and extension) of the algorithm **A**.

We also plan to investigate the interesting question of whether the results, such as membership in NP, hold with the addition of linear constant restrictions (as in [5,26]), to the theory of REV. This could lead to a method to solve the positive fragment of REV. Disunification modulo REV is another interesting problem to investigate, and that may be reducible to the previous one.

References

1. Anantharaman, S., Hibbs, P., Narendran, P., Rusinowitch, M.: Unification of lists with reverse as solving simple sets of word equations. Research-Report. https://hal.archives-ouvertes.fr/hal-02123648
2. Abdulla, P.A., et al.: String constraints for verification. In: Biere, A., Bloem, R. (eds.) CAV 2014. LNCS, vol. 8559, pp. 150–166. Springer, Cham (2014). https://doi.org/10.1007/978-3-319-08867-9_10
3. Armando, A., Bonacina, M.P., Ranise, S., Schulz, S.: New results on rewrite-based satisfiability procedures. ACM Trans. Comput. Log. **10**(1), 4:1–4:51 (2009)
4. Baader, F., Nipkow, T.: Term Rewriting and All That. Cambridge University Press, Cambridge (1999)
5. Baader, F., Schulz, K.U.: Unification in the union of disjoint equational theories: combining decision procedures. J. Symb. Comput. **21**(2), 211–243 (1996)
6. Baader, F., Snyder, W.: Unification theory. In: Robinson, J.A., Voronkov, A. (eds.) Handbook of Automated Reasoning, pp. 445–532. Elsevier and MIT Press (2001)
7. Colmerauer, A.: An introduction to Prolog III. Commun. ACM **33**(7), 69–90 (1990)
8. Dabrowski, R., Plandowski, W.: On word equations in one variable. Algorithmica **60**(4), 819–828 (2011)
9. Diekert, V., Jez, A., Plandowski, W.: Finding all solutions of equations in free groups and monoids with involution. Inf. Comput. **251**, 263–286 (2016)
10. Guttag, J.V., Horowitz, E., Musser, D.R.: Abstract data types and software validation. Commun. ACM **21**(12), 1048–1064 (1978)
11. Ganesh, V., Minnes, M., Solar-Lezama, A., Rinard, M.: Word equations with length constraints: what's decidable? In: Biere, A., Nahir, A., Vos, T. (eds.) HVC 2012. LNCS, vol. 7857, pp. 209–226. Springer, Heidelberg (2013). https://doi.org/10.1007/978-3-642-39611-3_21
12. Hibbs, P.: Unification modulo common list functions. Doctoral Dissertation. University at Albany–SUNY (2015)
13. Kapur, D.: Towards a theory for abstract data types. Doctoral Dissertation. Massachusetts Institute of Technology (1980)
14. Kapur, D., Musser, D.R.: Proof by consistency. Artif. Intell. **31**(2), 125–157 (1987)
15. Karhumäki, J.: Combinatorics on Words: A New Challenging Topic, p. 12. Turku Centre for Computer Science, Turku (2004)
16. Liang, T., Tsiskaridze, N., Reynolds, A., Tinelli, C., Barrett, C.: A decision procedure for regular membership and length constraints over unbounded strings. In: Lutz, C., Ranise, S. (eds.) FroCoS 2015. LNCS, vol. 9322, pp. 135–150. Springer, Cham (2015). https://doi.org/10.1007/978-3-319-24246-0_9
17. Lin, A.W., Majumdar, R.: Quadratic word equations with length constraints, counter systems, and Presburger arithmetic with divisibility. arXiv preprint arXiv:1805.06701 (2018)
18. Morita, K.: Universality of a reversible two-counter machine. Theoret. Comput. Sci. **168**(2), 303–320 (1996)
19. Musser, D.R.: Abstract data type specification in the AFFIRM system. IEEE Trans. Softw. Eng. **6**(1), 24–32 (1980)
20. Musser, D.R.: On proving inductive properties of abstract data types. In: Proceedings of the Seventh Annual ACM Symposium on Principles of Programming Languages (POPL), pp. 154–162 (1980)
21. Nelson, G., Oppen, D.C.: Simplification by cooperating decision procedures. ACM Trans. Program. Lang. Syst. **1**(2), 245–257 (1979)

22. Oppen, D.C.: Reasoning about recursively defined data structures. J. ACM **27**(3), 403–411 (1980)
23. Plandowski, W.: An efficient algorithm for solving word equations. In: Proceedings of the ACM Symposium on the Theory of Computing, pp. 467–476 (2006)
24. Robson, J.M., Diekert, V.: On quadratic word equations. In: Meinel, C., Tison, S. (eds.) STACS 1999. LNCS, vol. 1563, pp. 217–226. Springer, Heidelberg (1999). https://doi.org/10.1007/3-540-49116-3_20
25. Shostak, R.E.: Deciding combinations of theories. J. ACM **31**(1), 1–12 (1984)
26. Schulz, K.U.: On existential theories of list concatenation. In: Pacholski, L., Tiuryn, J. (eds.) CSL 1994. LNCS, vol. 933, pp. 294–308. Springer, Heidelberg (1995). https://doi.org/10.1007/BFb0022264

On the Width of Regular Classes
of Finite Structures

Alexsander Andrade de Melo[1] and Mateus de Oliveira Oliveira[2(⊠)]

[1] Federal University of Rio de Janeiro, Rio de Janeiro, Brazil
aamelo@cos.ufrj.br
[2] University of Bergen, Bergen, Norway
mateus.oliveira@uib.no

Abstract. In this work we introduce the notion of decisional width of a finite relational structure and the notion of regular-decisional width of a regular class of finite structures. Our main result states that the first-order theory of any regular-decisional class of finite structures is decidable. Building on the proof of this decidability result, we show that the problem of counting satisfying assignments for a first-order logic formula in a structure of constant width is fixed parameter tractable when parameterized by the width parameter and can be solved in quadratic time with respect to the length of the input representation of the structure.

Keywords: Automatic structures · Width measures ·
First order logic

1 Introduction

The notion of relational structure can be used to formalize a wide variety of mathematical constructions—such as graphs, hypergraphs, groups, rings, databases, etc. Not surprisingly, relational structures are a central object of study in several subfields of computer science, such as database theory, learning theory [15], constraint satisfaction theory [7,22], and automated theorem proving [9,10,25,28,30].

Let $\mathcal{C}$ be a class of finite structures and let $\mathcal{L}$ be a logic, such as first-order logic (FO) or monadic second-order logic (MSO). The $\mathcal{L}$ theory of $\mathcal{C}$ is the set $\mathcal{T}(\mathcal{L}, \mathcal{C})$ of all logical sentences from $\mathcal{L}$ that are satisfied by at least one structure in $\mathcal{C}$. We say that $\mathcal{T}(\mathcal{L}, \mathcal{C})$ is decidable if the problem of determining whether a given sentence φ belongs to $\mathcal{T}(\mathcal{L}, \mathcal{C})$ is decidable.

Showing that the $\mathcal{L}$ theory of a particular class of structures $\mathcal{C}$ is decidable is an endeavour of fundamental importance because many interesting mathematical statements can be formulated as the problem of determining whether some/every/no structure in a given class $\mathcal{C}$ of finite structures satisfies a given logical sentence φ. For instance, when considering the celebrated 4-color theorem, which states that every planar graph is 4-colorable, the class $\mathcal{C}$ is the set

© Springer Nature Switzerland AG 2019
P. Fontaine (Ed.): CADE 2019, LNAI 11716, pp. 18–34, 2019.
https://doi.org/10.1007/978-3-030-29436-6_2

of all planar graphs, while formula φ is a particular formula in the monadic second order logic of graphs expressing the 4-colorability property. While it can be shown that the monadic second-order theory of planar graphs is undecidable, one can show using automata-theoretic techniques that for each fixed k, the MSO_1 theory[1] of graphs of clique width at most k is decidable [10, 30], and that the MSO_2 theory of the class of graphs of treewidth at most k is decidable [9, 30].

The problem of deciding logical properties of relational structures has also been studied extensively in the field of automatic structure theory. Intuitively, a relational structure is automatic if its domain and each of its relations can be defined by finite automata. Although the idea of representing certain relational structures using automata dates back to seminal work of Büchi and Rabin, and it has been well studied in the realm of automatic group theory [14], Khoussainov and Nerode were the first to define and investigate a general notion of automatic structure [21]. Among other results that can be proved, automatic structures can be used to provide an elegant proof of a celebrated theorem of Presburger stating that the first order theory of $(\mathbb{N}, +)$ is decidable. In [24] Kruckman et al. introduced the notion of structure with advice and used it to show that the first-order theory of $(\mathbb{Q}, +)$ is decidable. The theory of automatic structures with advice was recently extended by Zaid, Grädel and Reinhardt and used to define classes of structures. They show that the notion of automatic classes of structures with advice has decidable first-order logic theory if and only if the set of used advices has a decidable monadic second-order logic theory [30].

In this work we introduce a notion of width for relational structures based on the notion of ordered decision diagrams (ODD's). ODD's may be regarded as a special case of acyclic finite automata where states are split into a sequence of levels, and transitions are split into layers which send states in level i to states in level $i + 1$. We note that ODD's over binary alphabets are widespread in the literature and usually called OBDDs. This formalism has been used extensively in the filed of symbolic computation due to its ability to represent in a concise way combinatorial structures with exponentially many elements in the domain [3, 4, 18, 26, 29]. An important complexity measure when dealing with ODD's is the notion of width. This is simply the maximum number of states in a level of the ODD. We say that a relational structure is (Σ, w)-decisional if its domain and each of its relations can be represented by an ODD of width w over an alphabet Σ. We then use finite automata over alphabets of tuples of layers to define infinite classes of finite structures. We call these classes regular-decisional. We show that, given a first order formula ψ and a constant w, the class of finite structures of decisional width at most w that satisfy ψ is regular-decisional. From this result, it follows that the first-order theory of regular-decisional classes of finite structures is decidable. Finally, we show that the problem of counting the number of satisfying assignments for a fixed first-order logic formula ψ with respect to a decisional finite τ-structure $\mathfrak{A}$ is fixed parameter tractable when

---

[1] MSO_1 denotes the MSO logic of graphs where edge-set quantifications are not allowed, while MSO_2 is the extension of MSO_1 where we can also quantify over sets of edges.

parameterized by the width of the input representation $\mathcal{D}$ of $\mathfrak{A}$, and that such a problem can be solved in time quadratic in the length of $\mathcal{D}$.

An interesting feature of our width measure for classes of structures is that it behaves very differently from usual complexity measures for graphs studied in structural complexity theory. As an example of this fact, we note that the family of hypercube graphs has regular-decisional width 2, while it has unbounded width in many of the studied measures, such as treewidth and cliquewidth. This class of graphs has also unbounded degeneracy, and therefore it is not no-where dense. As a consequence, we have that most algorithmic metatheorems proved so far dealing with the interplay between first-order logic and structural graph theory [16, 17, 23] fail on graphs of constant decisional-width.

2   Preliminaries

We denote by $\mathbb{N} \doteq \{0, 1, \ldots\}$ the set of natural numbers (including zero), and by $\mathbb{N}_+ \doteq \mathbb{N} \setminus \{0\}$ the set of positive natural numbers. For each $c \in \mathbb{N}_+$, we let $[c] \doteq \{1, 2, \ldots, c\}$ and $[\![c]\!] \doteq \{0, 1, \ldots, c-1\}$. Given a set S and a number $a \in \mathbb{N}_+$, we let $S^{\times a}$ be the set of all a-tuples of elements from S.

Relational Structures. A *relational vocabulary* is a tuple $\tau = (\mathsf{R}_1, \ldots, \mathsf{R}_l)$ of *relation symbols* where for each $i \in [l]$, the relation symbol R_i is associated with an arity $\mathsf{a}_i \in \mathbb{N}_+$. Let $\tau = (\mathsf{R}_1, \ldots, \mathsf{R}_l)$ be a relational vocabulary. A finite τ-*structure* is a tuple $\mathfrak{A} = (\mathsf{R}_0(\mathfrak{A}), R_1(\mathfrak{A}), \ldots, R_l(\mathfrak{A}))$ such that

1. $\mathsf{R}_0(\mathfrak{A})$ is a non-empty finite set, called the *domain* of $\mathfrak{A}$;
2. for each $i \in [l], R_i(\mathfrak{A}) \subseteq \mathsf{R}_0(\mathfrak{A})^{\times \mathsf{a}_i}$ is an a_i-ary relation.

Let $\mathfrak{A}$ and $\mathfrak{A}'$ be τ-structures. An *isomorphism from $\mathfrak{A}$ to $\mathfrak{A}'$* is a bijection $\pi \colon \mathsf{R}_0(\mathfrak{A}) \to \mathsf{R}_0(\mathfrak{A}')$ such that, for each $i \in [l]$, $(u_1, \ldots, u_{\mathsf{a}_i}) \in R_i(\mathfrak{A})$ if and only if $(\pi(u_1), \ldots, \pi(u_{\mathsf{a}_i})) \in R_i(\mathfrak{A}')$. If there exists an isomorphism from $\mathfrak{A}$ to $\mathfrak{A}'$, then we say that $\mathfrak{A}$ is *isomorphic* to $\mathfrak{A}'$, and we denote this fact by $\mathfrak{A} \simeq \mathfrak{A}'$.

First-Order Logic. Now, we briefly recall some basic concepts from first-order logic. Extensive treatments of this subject can be found in [11, 12].

Let $\tau = (\mathsf{R}_1, \ldots, \mathsf{R}_l)$ be a relational vocabulary. We denote by $\mathrm{FO}\{\tau\}$ the set of all *first-order logic formulas over τ*, i.e. the logic formulas comprising: variables to be used as placeholders for elements from the domain of a τ-structure; the Boolean connectives $\vee, \wedge, \neg, \to$ and $\leftrightarrow$; the quantifiers $\exists$ and $\forall$ that can be applied to the variables; and the two following atomic logic formulas $x = y$, where x and y are variables, and $R_i(x_1, \ldots, x_{\mathsf{a}_i})$ for some $i \in [l]$, where $x_1, \ldots, x_{\mathsf{a}_i}$ are variables.

A variable x is said to be *free* in a formula $\psi \in \mathrm{FO}\{\tau\}$, if x is not within the scope of any quantifier in ψ. The set of free variables of ψ is denoted by $\mathrm{freevar}(\psi)$. We write $\psi(x_1, \ldots, x_t)$ to indicate that $\mathrm{freevar}(\psi) \subseteq \{x_1, \ldots, x_t\}$. A *sentence* is a formula without free variables.

Let $\mathfrak{A} = (\mathsf{R}_0(\mathfrak{A}), \mathsf{R}_1(\mathfrak{A}), \ldots, \mathsf{R}_l(\mathfrak{A}))$ be a finite τ-structure, $\psi(x_1, \ldots, x_t) \in \mathrm{FO}\{\tau\}$ and $u_1, \ldots, u_t \in \mathsf{R}_0(\mathfrak{A})$. We write $\mathfrak{A} \models \psi[u_1, \ldots, u_t]$ to mean that $\mathfrak{A}$

satisfies ψ when all the free occurrences of the variables $x_1, \ldots, x_t$ are interpreted by the values $u_1, \ldots, u_t$, respectively. In particular, if ψ is a sentence, then we may write $\mathfrak{A} \models \psi$ to mean that $\mathfrak{A}$ satisfies ψ. In this case, we also say that $\mathfrak{A}$ is a *model* of ψ. If $\psi(x_1, \ldots, x_t) \equiv \mathsf{R}_i(x_{\beta(1)}, \ldots, x_{\beta(\mathfrak{a}_i)})$ for some mapping $\beta \colon [\mathfrak{a}_i] \to [t]$ and some $i \in [l]$, then $\mathfrak{A} \models \psi[u_1, \ldots, u_t]$ if and only if $(u_{\beta(1)}, \ldots, u_{\beta(\mathfrak{a}_i)}) \in \mathsf{R}_i(\mathfrak{A})$. The semantics of the equality symbol, of the quantifiers $\exists$ and $\forall$, and of the Boolean connectives $\vee, \wedge, \neg, \to$ and $\leftrightarrow$ are the usual ones.

Languages. An *alphabet* Σ is any finite, non-empty set of symbols. A *string* over Σ is any finite sequence of symbols from Σ. We denote by Σ^+ the set of all (non-empty) strings over Σ. A *language* over Σ is any subset L of Σ^+. In particular, for each $k \in \mathbb{N}_+$, we let Σ^k be the language of all strings of length k over Σ, and we let $\Sigma^{\leq k} \doteq \Sigma^1 \cup \cdots \cup \Sigma^k$ be the language of all (non-empty) strings of length at most k over Σ.

For each alphabet Σ, we let $\square$ be a special symbol, called the *padding symbol*, such that $\square \notin \Sigma$, and we write $\Sigma \uplus \{\square\}$ to denote the disjoint union between Σ and $\{\square\}$. For each $\sigma \in \Sigma \uplus \{\square\}$ and each $c \in \mathbb{N}_+$, we let $\sigma^{\times c}$ denote the tuple $(\sigma, \ldots, \sigma)$ composed by c copies of the symbol σ.

Tensor Product. Let $\Sigma_1, \ldots, \Sigma_c$ be c alphabets, where $c \in \mathbb{N}_+$. The *tensor product* of $\Sigma_1, \ldots, \Sigma_c$ is defined as the alphabet

$$\Sigma_1 \otimes \cdots \otimes \Sigma_c \doteq \{(\sigma_1, \ldots, \sigma_c) \colon \sigma_i \in \Sigma_i, \, i \in [c]\}.$$

In particular, for each $c \in \mathbb{N}_+$ and each alphabet Σ, we define the *c-th tensor power* of Σ as the alphabet $\Sigma^{\otimes c} \doteq \overbrace{\Sigma \otimes \cdots \otimes \Sigma}^{c \text{ times}}$. Note that, the tensor product of $\Sigma_1, \ldots, \Sigma_c$ (the c-th tensor power of Σ) may be simply regarded as the Cartesian product of $\Sigma_1, \ldots, \Sigma_c$ (the c-ary Cartesian power of Σ, respectively). Also, note that $\Sigma^{\otimes 1} = \Sigma$.

For each $i \in [c]$, let $s_i = \sigma_{i,1} \cdots \sigma_{i,k_i}$ be a string of length k_i, where $k_i \in \mathbb{N}_+$, over the alphabet Σ_i. The *tensor product* of $s_1, \ldots, s_c$ is defined as the string

$$s_1 \otimes \cdots \otimes s_c \doteq (\widetilde{\sigma}_{1,1}, \ldots, \widetilde{\sigma}_{c,1}) \cdots (\widetilde{\sigma}_{1,k}, \ldots, \widetilde{\sigma}_{c,k})$$

of length $k = \max\{k_1, \ldots, k_c\}$ over the alphabet $(\Sigma_1 \uplus \{\square\}) \otimes \cdots \otimes (\Sigma_c \uplus \{\square\})$ such that, for each $i \in [c]$ and each $j \in [k]$,

$$\widetilde{\sigma}_{i,j} \doteq \begin{cases} \sigma_{i,j} & \text{if } j \leq k_i \\ \square & \text{otherwise.} \end{cases}$$

For instance, the tensor product of the strings $aabab$ and abb over the alphabet $\{a, b\}$ is the string $(a, a)(a, b)(b, b)(a, \square)(b, \square)$ over the alphabet $(\{a, b\} \uplus \{\square\})^{\otimes 2}$.

For each $i \in [c]$, let $L_i \subseteq \Sigma_i^+$ be a language over the alphabet Σ_i. The *tensor product* of $L_1, \ldots, L_c$ is defined as the language

$$L_1 \otimes \cdots \otimes L_c \doteq \{s_1 \otimes \cdots \otimes s_c \colon s_i \in L_i, i \in [c]\}.$$

We remark that, in the literature [1,2,20,30], the tensor product of strings (as well as the tensor product of languages) is also commonly called of *convolution*.

Finite Automata. A *finite automaton* is a tuple $\mathcal{F} = (\Sigma, Q, T, I, F)$, where Σ is an alphabet, Q is a finite set of *states*, $T \subseteq Q \times \Sigma \times Q$ is a set of *transitions*, $I \subseteq Q$ is a set of *initial states* and $F \subseteq Q$ is a set of *final states*. The size of a finite automaton $\mathcal{F}$ is defined as $|\mathcal{F}| \doteq |Q| + |T|$.

Let $k \in \mathbb{N}_+$ and $s = \sigma_1 \cdots \sigma_k \in \Sigma^k$. We say that $\mathcal{F}$ *accepts* s if there exists a sequence of transitions $\langle (q_0, \sigma_1, q_1), (q_1, \sigma_2, q_2), \ldots, (q_{k-1}, \sigma_k, q_k) \rangle$, called *accepting sequence* for s in $\mathcal{F}$, such that $q_0 \in I$, $q_k \in F$ and, for each $i \in [k]$, $(q_{i-1}, \sigma_i, q_i) \in T$. The language of $\mathcal{F}$, denoted by $\mathcal{L}(\mathcal{F})$, is defined as the set of all strings accepted by $\mathcal{F}$, i.e. $\mathcal{L}(\mathcal{F}) \doteq \{s \in \Sigma^+ : s \text{ is accepted by } \mathcal{F}\}$.

Regular Relations. Let Σ be an alphabet. A language $L \subseteq \Sigma^+$ is called *regular* if there exists a finite automaton $\mathcal{F}$ over Σ such that $\mathcal{L}(\mathcal{F}) = L$.

For each $\mathfrak{a} \in \mathbb{N}_+$ and each language $L \subseteq (\Sigma^{\otimes \mathfrak{a}})^+$ over the alphabet $\Sigma^{\otimes \mathfrak{a}}$, we let $\mathsf{rel}(L) \doteq \{(s_1, \ldots, s_\mathfrak{a}): s_1 \otimes \cdots \otimes s_\mathfrak{a} \in L\}$ be the *relation associated with* L. On the other hand, for each $\mathfrak{a} \in \mathbb{N}_+$ and each $\mathfrak{a}$-ary relation $R \subseteq (\Sigma^+)^{\times \mathfrak{a}}$, we let $\mathsf{lang}(R) \doteq \{s_1 \otimes \cdots \otimes s_\mathfrak{a} : (s_1, \ldots, s_\mathfrak{a}) \in R\}$ be the *language associated with* R. We say that such a relation R is *regular* if its associated language $\mathsf{lang}(R)$ is a regular subset of $(\Sigma^{\otimes \mathfrak{a}})^+$.

3 Ordered Decision Diagrams

Let Σ be an alphabet and $w \in \mathbb{N}_+$. A (Σ, w)-*layer* is a tuple $B \doteq (\ell, r, T, I, F, \iota, \phi)$, where $\ell \subseteq [\![w]\!]$ is a set of *left states*, $r \subseteq [\![w]\!]$ is a set of *right states*, $T \subseteq \ell \times (\Sigma \uplus \{\square\}) \times r$ is a set of *transitions*, $I \subseteq \ell$ is a set of *initial states*, $F \subseteq r$ is a set of *final states* and $\iota, \phi \in \{0, 1\}$ are Boolean flags satisfying the following conditions: i) $I = \emptyset$ if $\iota = 0$, and ii)$F = \emptyset$ if $\phi = 0$. We remark that, possibly, $\iota = 1$ and $I = \emptyset$. Similarly, it might be the case in which $\phi = 1$ and $F = \emptyset$.

In what follows, we may write $\ell(B), r(B), T(B), I(B), F(B), \iota(B)$ and $\phi(B)$ to refer to the sets ℓ, r, T, I and F and to the Boolean flags ι and ϕ, respectively.

We let $\mathcal{B}(\Sigma, w)$ denote the set of all (Σ, w)-layers. Note that, $\mathcal{B}(\Sigma, w)$ is non-empty and has at most $2^{\mathcal{O}(|\Sigma| \cdot w^2)}$ elements. Therefore, $\mathcal{B}(\Sigma, w)$ may be regarded as an alphabet.

Let $k \in \mathbb{N}_+$. A (Σ, w)-*ordered decision diagram* (or simply, (Σ, w)-*ODD*) of *length* k is a string $D \doteq B_1 \cdots B_k \in \mathcal{B}(\Sigma, w)^k$ of length k over the alphabet $\mathcal{B}(\Sigma, w)$ satisfying the following conditions:

1. for each $i \in [k-1]$, $\ell(B_{i+1}) = r(B_i)$;
2. $\iota(B_1) = 1$ and, for each $i \in \{2, \ldots, k\}$, $\iota(B_i) = 0$;
3. $\phi(B_k) = 1$ and, for each $i \in [k-1]$, $\phi(B_i) = 0$.

The *width* of D is defined as $\omega(D) \doteq \max\{|\ell(B_1)|, \ldots, |\ell(B_k)|, |r(B_k)|\}$. We remark that $\omega(D) \leq w$.

For each $k \in \mathbb{N}_+$, we denote by $\mathcal{B}(\Sigma, w)^{\circ k}$ the set of all (Σ, w)-ODDs of length k. And, more generally, we let $\mathcal{B}(\Sigma, w)^{\circledast}$ be the set of all (Σ, w)-ODDs, i.e. $\mathcal{B}(\Sigma, w)^{\circledast} \doteq \bigcup_{k \in \mathbb{N}_+} \mathcal{B}(\Sigma, w)^{\circ k}$.

Let $D = B_1 \cdots B_k \in \mathcal{B}(\Sigma, w)^{\circ k}$ and $s = \sigma_1 \cdots \sigma_{k'} \in \Sigma^{\leq k}$. A *valid sequence* for s in D is a sequence of transitions $\langle (\mathfrak{p}_1, \widetilde{\sigma}_1, \mathfrak{q}_1), \ldots, (\mathfrak{p}_k, \widetilde{\sigma}_k, \mathfrak{q}_k) \rangle$ satisfying the following conditions:

1. for each $i \in [k]$, $\widetilde{\sigma}_i = \sigma_i$ if $i \leq k'$, and $\widetilde{\sigma}_i = \square$ otherwise;
2. for each $i \in [k]$, $(\mathfrak{p}_i, \widetilde{\sigma}_i, \mathfrak{q}_i) \in T(B_i)$;
3. for each $i \in [k-1]$, $\mathfrak{p}_{i+1} = \mathfrak{q}_i$.

Such a sequence is called *accepting* for s if, in addition to the above conditions, $\mathfrak{p}_1 \in I(B_1)$ and $\mathfrak{q}_k \in F(B_k)$. We say that D *accepts* s if there exists an accepting sequence for s in D. The language of D, denoted by $\mathcal{L}(D)$, is defined as the set of all strings accepted by D, i.e. $\mathcal{L}(D) \doteq \{ s \in \Sigma^{\leq k} : s \text{ is accepted by } D \}$.

Proposition 3.1. *Let Σ be an alphabet, $w, k \in \mathbb{N}_+$ and $D \in \mathcal{B}(\Sigma, w)^{\circ k}$. For each natural number $k' \geq k$, there exists an ODD $D' \in \mathcal{B}(\Sigma, w)^{\circ k'}$ such that $\mathcal{L}(D') = \mathcal{L}(D)$.*

4 Regular-Decisional Classes of Finite Relational Structures

In this section we combine ODDs with finite automata in order to define infinite classes of finite structures. We start by defining the notion of (Σ, w, τ)-structural tuples of ODDs as a way to encode single finite τ-structures. Subsequently, we use finite automata over a suitable alphabet in order to uniformly define infinite families of finite τ-structures.

4.1 Decisional Relations and Decisional Relational Structures

Let Σ be an alphabet and $\mathfrak{a}, w \in \mathbb{N}_+$. A *finite $\mathfrak{a}$-ary relation* $R \subseteq (\Sigma^+)^{\times \mathfrak{a}}$ is said to be *strongly (Σ, w)-decisional* if there exists an ODD D in $\mathcal{B}(\Sigma^{\otimes \mathfrak{a}}, w)^{\circledast}$ such that $\mathrm{rel}(\mathcal{L}(D)) = R$. Given a set S, we say that a relation $R \subseteq S^{\times \mathfrak{a}}$ is (Σ, w)-decisional if R is isomorphic to some strongly (Σ, w)-decisional structure.

Let $\tau = (\mathsf{R}_1, \ldots, \mathsf{R}_l)$ be a relational vocabulary, Σ be an alphabet and $w \in \mathbb{N}_+$. We say that a tuple $\mathcal{D} = (D_0, D_1, \ldots, D_l)$ of ODDs is (Σ, w, τ)-*structural* if there exists a positive natural number $k \in \mathbb{N}_+$, called the *length of* $\mathcal{D}$, such that the following conditions are satisfied:

1. D_0 is an ODD in $\mathcal{B}(\Sigma, w)^{\circ k}$;
2. for each $i \in [l]$, D_i is an ODD in $\mathcal{B}(\Sigma^{\otimes \mathfrak{a}_i}, w)^{\circ k}$;
3. for each $i \in [l]$, $\mathcal{L}(D_i) \subseteq \mathcal{L}(D_0)^{\otimes \mathfrak{a}_i}$.

Let $\mathcal{D} = (D_0, D_1, \ldots, D_l)$ be a (Σ, w, τ)-structural tuple. The τ-*structure derived from* $\mathcal{D}$ is defined as the finite τ-structure

$$\mathfrak{s}(\mathcal{D}) \doteq (\mathsf{R}_0(\mathfrak{s}(\mathcal{D})), \mathsf{R}_1(\mathfrak{s}(\mathcal{D})), \ldots, \mathsf{R}_l(\mathfrak{s}(\mathcal{D}))),$$

with domain $R_0(\mathfrak{s}(\mathcal{D})) = \mathcal{L}(D_0)$, such that $R_i(\mathfrak{s}(\mathcal{D})) = \mathrm{rel}(\mathcal{L}(D_i))$ for each $i \in [l]$.

We say that a finite τ-structure $\mathfrak{A}$ is *strongly (Σ, w)-decisional* if there exists some (Σ, w, τ)-structural tuple $\mathcal{D}$ such that $\mathfrak{A} = \mathfrak{s}(\mathcal{D})$. We say that a finite τ-structure $\mathfrak{A}$—whose domain is not necessarily a subset of Σ^+—is (Σ, w)-*decisional* if $\mathfrak{A}$ is isomorphic to some strongly (Σ, w)-decisional structure.

The Σ-*decisional width* of a finite τ-structure $\mathfrak{A}$, denoted by $\omega(\Sigma, \mathfrak{A})$, is defined as the minimum $w \in \mathbb{N}_+$ such that $\mathfrak{A}$ is (Σ, w)-decisional. The following proposition states that if a relation is (Σ, w)-decisional, then it is also $(\{0, 1\}, w')$-decisional for a suitable $w' \in \mathbb{N}_+$.

Proposition 4.1. *Let $\tau = (R_1, \ldots, R_l)$ be a relational vocabulary, Σ be an alphabet and $w \in \mathbb{N}_+$. If $\mathfrak{A}$ is a finite τ-structure with $\omega(\Sigma, \mathfrak{A}) \leq w$ for some $w \in \mathbb{N}_+$, then $\omega(\{0, 1\}, \mathfrak{A}) \leq w^2 \cdot |\Sigma|^{\max\{1, a_1, \ldots, a_l\}}$.*

The Hypercube Graph $\mathcal{H}_k$. Let $k \in \mathbb{N}_+$. The k-*dimensional hypercube graph* is the graph $\mathcal{H}_k = (R_0(\mathcal{H}_k), R_1(\mathcal{H}_k))$ whose vertex set $R_0(\mathcal{H}_k) = \{0, 1\}^k$ is the set of all k-bit binary strings, and whose edge set $R_1(\mathcal{H}_k)$ is the set of all pairs of k-bit strings that differ in exactly one position.

$$R_1(\mathcal{H}_k) = \{(b_1 b_2 \cdots b_k, b_1' b_2' \cdots b_k') : \text{There is a unique } i \in [k] \text{ such that } b_i \neq b_i'\}.$$

Therefore, the k-dimensional hypercube is equal to the structure derived from the structural pair $\mathcal{D}_k = (D_0, D_1)$, where the ODD $D_0 \in \mathcal{B}(\{0, 1\}, 2)^{\circ k}$ accepts all k-bit strings of length k, and $D_1 \in \mathcal{B}(\{0, 1\}^{\otimes 2}, 2)^{\circ k}$ is the ODD that accepts all strings of the form $b_1 \cdots b_k \otimes b_1' \cdots b_k'$ such that $b_1 \cdots b_k$ and $b_1' \cdots b_k'$ differ in exactly one entry. In other words, we have $\mathcal{H}_k = \mathfrak{s}(\mathcal{D}_k)$. This structural pair is depicted in Fig. 1.

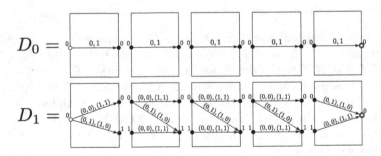

Fig. 1. An example of a $(\{0, 1\}, 2, \tau)$-structural pair $\mathcal{D}_5 = (D_0, D_1)$, where τ is the relational vocabulary of directed graphs. The ODD D_0 accepts all binary strings of length 5. The odd D_1 accepts all strings of the form $b_1 \cdots b_5 \otimes b_1' \cdots b_5' = (b_1, b_1') \cdots (b_5, b_5')$ such that $b_1 \cdots b_5$ and $b_1' \cdots b_5'$ differ in exactly one bit. The structure derived from $\mathcal{D}_5$ is the 5-dimensional directed hypercube $\mathcal{H}_5 = \mathfrak{s}(\mathcal{D}_5)$.

4.2   Regular-Decisional Classes

Let Σ be an alphabet, $w \in \mathbb{N}_+$ and $\tau = (R_1, \ldots, R_l)$ be a relational vocabulary. We let $\mathcal{R}(\Sigma, w, \tau)$ denote the relation constituted by all (Σ, w, τ)-structural tuples. Note that the relation $\mathcal{R}(\Sigma, w, \tau)$ is a subset of the following set of tuples of ODDs

$$\bigcup_{k \in \mathbb{N}_+} \mathcal{B}(\Sigma, w)^{\circ k} \times \mathcal{B}(\Sigma^{\otimes a_1}, w)^{\circ k} \times \cdots \times \mathcal{B}(\Sigma^{\otimes a_l}, w)^{\circ k}.$$

Since each (Σ, w, τ)-structural tuple $\mathcal{D} \in \mathcal{R}(\Sigma, w, \tau)$ corresponds to a (Σ, w)-decisional structure $\mathfrak{s}(\mathcal{D})$, we can associate with each sub-relation $R \subseteq \mathcal{R}(\Sigma, w, \tau)$ a class $\mathfrak{s}(R) = \{\mathfrak{A} : \mathcal{D} \in R, \mathfrak{s}(\mathcal{D}) \simeq \mathfrak{A}\}$ of (Σ, w)-decisional τ-structures.

Definition 4.2. Let Σ be an alphabet, $w \in \mathbb{N}_+$, and τ be a relational vocabulary. We say that a class $\mathcal{C}$ of *finite* τ-structures is (Σ, w)-*regular-decisional* if there exists a regular sub-relation $R \subseteq \mathcal{R}(\Sigma, w, \tau)$ such that $\mathcal{C} = \mathfrak{s}(R)$.

The Σ-*regular-decisional width* of a class $\mathcal{C}$ of finite τ-structures, denoted by $\omega(\Sigma, \mathcal{C})$, is defined as the minimum $w \in \mathbb{N}_+$ such that $\mathcal{C}$ is (Σ, w)-regular-decisional. We note that this minimum w may not exist. In this case, we set $\omega(\Sigma, \mathcal{C}) = \infty$.

Now, consider the alphabet

$$\mathcal{B}(\Sigma, w, \tau) \doteq \mathcal{B}(\Sigma, w) \otimes \mathcal{B}(\Sigma^{\otimes a_1}, w) \otimes \cdots \otimes \mathcal{B}(\Sigma^{\otimes a_l}, w). \tag{1}$$

Then a class $\mathcal{C}$ of finite τ-structures is (Σ, w)-decisional if and only if there exists a finite automaton $\mathcal{F}$ over $\mathcal{B}(\Sigma, w, \tau)$ such that $\mathsf{rel}(\mathcal{L}(\mathcal{F})) \subseteq \mathcal{R}(\Sigma, w, \tau)$, and $\mathcal{C} = \mathfrak{s}(\mathsf{rel}(\mathcal{L}(\mathcal{F})))$. This implies, in particular, that in order to show that a class $\mathcal{C}$ of finite τ-structures is (Σ, w)-decisional, it is enough to construct a finite automaton $\mathcal{F}$ over $\mathcal{B}(\Sigma, w, \tau)$ such that a string of the form $D_0 \otimes D_1 \otimes \ldots \otimes D_l$ belongs to $\mathcal{L}(\mathcal{F})$ if and only if $\mathcal{D} = (D_0, D_1, \ldots, D_l)$ is a (Σ, w, τ)-structural tuple and $\mathfrak{s}(\mathcal{D}) \in \mathcal{C}$. To illustrate this type of construction, we show in Proposition 4.3 that the class $\mathcal{H}$ of hypercubes is $(\{0, 1\}, 2)$-regular-decisional. Since it can be easily shown that this class is not $(\{0, 1\}, 1)$-regular-decisional, we have that the $\{0, 1\}$-regular-decisional width of $\mathcal{H}$ is 2.

Proposition 4.3. *Let $\mathcal{H} \doteq \{\mathcal{H}_k : k \in \mathbb{N}_+\}$ be the class of all hypercube graphs. The class $\mathcal{H}$ is $(\{0, 1\}, 2)$-regular-decisional.*

Proof. In Fig. 2 we depict an automaton $\mathcal{F}$ which accepts a string $D_0 \otimes D_1$ of length k if and only if the pair $\mathcal{D}_k = (D_0, D_1)$ is a structural pair whose derived structure $\mathfrak{s}(\mathcal{D}_k)$ is the hypercube graph $\mathcal{H}_k$.   □

An interesting aspect of Proposition 4.3 is that it states that the class $\mathcal{H}$ of hypercube graphs has regular-decisional width 2, while this class has unbounded width with respect to most traditional width measures studied in structural

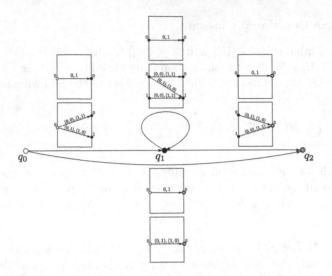

Fig. 2. An automaton $\mathcal{F}$ over the alphabet $\mathcal{B}(\{0,1\}, 2, \tau)$, where τ is the vocabulary of directed graphs. This automaton accepts exactly one string of length k for each $k \in \mathbb{N}_+$. For each such k, if $D_0 \otimes D_1$ is the unique string of length k accepted by $\mathcal{F}$, then the pair $\mathcal{D}_k = (D_0, D_1)$ is structural, and $\mathfrak{s}(\mathcal{D}_k)$ is the hypercube graph $\mathcal{H}_k$. In particular, the string $D_0 \otimes D_1$ represented in Fig. 1 is accepted by $\mathcal{F}$ upon following the sequence of states $q_0 q_1 q_1 q_1 q_2$.

graph theory. For instance, it can be shown that the hypercube graph $\mathcal{H}_k$ has treewidth $\Theta(2^k/\sqrt{k})$ [8] and cliquewidth $\Omega(2^k/\sqrt{k})$ [5]. Therefore, $\mathcal{H}_k$ has also exponential bandwidth, carving width, pathwidth, treedepth and rank-width. Additionally, since all vertices of $\mathcal{H}_k$ have degree k, the degeneracy of the family $\mathcal{H}$ is $\Theta(k)$. Therefore, $\mathcal{H}$ is *not* a nowhere dense class of graphs. This also implies that the graphs in $\mathcal{H}$ have unbounded genus, unbounded local treewidth, etc.

5   First-Order Definable Classes of Constant Width

For each FO$\{\tau\}$-sentence ψ, we let $\mathcal{R}(\Sigma, w, \tau, \psi)$ denote the sub-relation of $\mathcal{R}(\Sigma, w, \tau)$ consisting of all tuples $\mathcal{D} \in \mathcal{R}(\Sigma, w, \tau)$ whose associated structure $\mathfrak{s}(\mathcal{D})$ satisfies ψ, i.e. $\mathcal{R}(\Sigma, w, \tau, \psi) \doteq \{\mathcal{D} \in \mathcal{R}(\Sigma, w, \tau): \mathfrak{s}(\mathcal{D}) \models \psi\}$. The next theorem (Theorem 5.1), which is the main technical result of this section, states that the relation $\mathcal{R}(\Sigma, w, \tau, \psi)$ is regular.

Theorem 5.1. *Let Σ be an alphabet, $w \in \mathbb{N}_+$ and $\tau = (\mathsf{R}_1, \ldots, \mathsf{R}_l)$ be a relational vocabulary. For each FO$\{\tau\}$-sentence ψ, the relation $\mathcal{R}(\Sigma, w, \tau, \psi)$ is regular.*

A constructive proof of Theorem 5.1 will be given in Sect. 6. As a consequence of Theorem 5.1, we have that the first-order theory of any regular-decisional class of finite structures is decidable.

Theorem 5.2. *Let Σ be an alphabet, $w \in \mathbb{N}_+$, $\tau = (\mathsf{R}_1, \ldots, \mathsf{R}_l)$ be a relational vocabulary and $\mathcal{C}$ be a fixed (Σ, w, τ)-regular-decisional class of finite structures. The following problem is decidable: Given an $\mathrm{FO}\{\tau\}$-sentence ψ is there a τ-structure $\mathfrak{A} \in \mathcal{C}$ that satisfies ψ?*

Proof. Since $\mathcal{C}$ is (Σ, w)-regular-decisional, there exists a regular relation $R \subseteq \mathcal{R}(\Sigma, w, \tau)$ such that $\mathcal{C} = \mathfrak{s}(R) = \{\mathfrak{A} : \mathcal{D} \in R, \mathfrak{s}(\mathcal{D}) \simeq \mathfrak{A}\}$. Let $\mathcal{F}$ be a finite automaton over the alphabet $\mathcal{B}(\Sigma, w, \tau)$ such that $\mathcal{L}(\mathcal{F}) = \mathsf{lang}(R)$. From Theorem 5.1 it follows that there exists a finite automaton $\mathcal{F}'$ over the alphabet $\mathcal{B}(\Sigma, w, \tau)$ such that $\mathcal{L}(\mathcal{F}') = \mathsf{lang}(\mathcal{R}(\Sigma, w, \tau, \psi))$. Additionally, since the proof of Theorem 5.1 is constructive, the automaton $\mathcal{F}'$ can be effectively constructed from the input representation of the FO sentence ψ. Therefore, one can decide whether there exists a finite τ-structure $\mathfrak{A} \in \mathcal{C}$ that satisfies ψ by simply checking whether $\mathcal{L}(\mathcal{F}) \cap \mathcal{L}(\mathcal{F}') \neq \emptyset$. $\square$

Let $\tau = (\mathsf{R}_1, \ldots, \mathsf{R}_l)$ be a relational vocabulary. We denote by $\mathrm{MSO}\{\tau\}$ the set of all monadic second-order logic formulas over τ, i.e. the extension of $\mathrm{FO}\{\tau\}$ that, additionally, allows variables to be used as placeholders for sets of elements from the domain of a finite τ-structure and allows quantification over such variables. We note that neither Theorem 5.1 nor Theorem 5.2 can be generalized to the logic $\mathrm{MSO}\{\tau\}$ for an arbitrary relational vocabulary τ. Indeed, it is well known that the MSO theory of unlabeled grids is already undecidable [19,27][2].

For a given alphabet Γ, we let $\varrho(\Gamma)$ be the vocabulary of strings over Γ. A celebrated result of Büchi [6] and Elgot [13] states that a language $L \subseteq \Gamma^+$ can be represented by a finite automaton over Γ if and only if L can be defined by an $\mathrm{MSO}\{\varrho(\Gamma)\}$-sentence. In particular, let $\mathcal{B}(\Sigma, w, \tau)$ be the alphabet defined in Eq. 1, and let $\mathcal{B}(\Sigma, w, \tau)^{\circledast}$ be the set of strings $D_0 \otimes D_1 \otimes \ldots \otimes D_l$ over $\mathcal{B}(\Sigma, w, \tau)$ such that $(D_0, D_1, \ldots, D_l)$ is a (Σ, w, τ)-structural tuple. Then, we have that a language $L \subseteq \mathcal{B}(\Sigma, w, \tau)^{\circledast}$ is regular if and only if L can be defined by an $\mathrm{MSO}\{\varrho(\mathcal{B}(\Sigma, w, \tau))\}$-sentence.

Theorem 5.3. *Let Σ be an alphabet, $w \in \mathbb{N}_+$ and $\tau = (\mathsf{R}_1, \ldots, \mathsf{R}_l)$ be a relational vocabulary. Given an $\mathrm{MSO}\{\varrho(\mathcal{B}(\Sigma, w, \tau))\}$-sentence φ and an $\mathrm{FO}\{\tau\}$-sentence ψ, one can decide whether there exists some string $\mathbb{S} = D_0 \otimes D_1 \otimes \ldots \otimes D_l \in \mathcal{B}(\Sigma, w, \tau)^{\circledast}$ such that $\mathbb{S} \models \varphi$ and $\mathfrak{s}(\mathcal{D}) \models \psi$, where $\mathcal{D} = (D_0, D_1, \ldots, D_l)$.*

Proof. By using Büchi-Elgot's Theorem, one can construct a finite automaton $\mathcal{F}_1$ over $\mathcal{B}(\Sigma, w, \tau)$ that accepts a string $\mathbb{S} \in \mathcal{B}(\Sigma, w, \tau)^+$ if and only if $\mathbb{S} \models \varphi$. Now, from Theorem 5.1, we can construct a finite automaton $\mathcal{F}_2$ over $\mathcal{B}(\Sigma, w, \tau)$ which accepts a string $D_0 \otimes D_1 \otimes \ldots \otimes D_l \in \mathcal{B}(\Sigma, w, \tau)^+$ if and only if $\mathcal{D} = (D_0, D_1, \ldots, D_l)$ is a (Σ, w, τ)-structural tuple and $\mathfrak{s}(\mathcal{D}) \models \psi$. Let $\mathcal{F}_{\cap}$ be a finite automaton that accepts the language $\mathcal{L}(\mathcal{F}_1) \cap \mathcal{L}(\mathcal{F}_2)$. Then, we have that $\mathcal{L}(\mathcal{F}_{\cap})$ is non-empty if and only if there exists some string $\mathbb{S} = D_0 \otimes D_1 \otimes \ldots \otimes D_l \in$

---

[2] Note that Theorem 5.2 implies that the first-order theory of *unlabeled* grids is *decidable*, since unlabeled grids have constant decisional-width. Nevertheless, it is known that the first-order theory of *labeled* grids is undecidable. In this latter case, we may have labeled grids that require ODDs of arbitrarily high width to be represented.

$\mathcal{B}(\Sigma, w, \tau)^{\circledast}$ such that $\mathbb{S} \models \varphi$ and $\mathfrak{s}(\mathcal{D}) \models \psi$, where $\mathcal{D} = (D_0, D_1, \ldots, D_l)$. Since emptiness is decidable for finite automata, the theorem follows. □

6   Proof of Theorem 5.1

We dedicate this section to the proof of Theorem 5.1. The proof follows a traditional strategy combined with new machinery for the implicit manipulation of ODDs. More precisely, given an alphabet Σ, $w \in \mathbb{N}_+$, a relational vocabulary $\tau = (\mathsf{R}_1, \ldots, \mathsf{R}_l)$ and an FO$\{\tau\}$-formula $\psi(x_1, \ldots, x_t)$ with free variables freevar$(\psi) \subseteq X_t = \{x_1, \ldots, x_t\}$, we define $\mathcal{R}(\Sigma, w, \tau, \psi, X_t)$ as the relation containing precisely the tuples of the form $(D_0, D_1, \ldots, D_l, u_1, \ldots, u_t)$ such that $\mathcal{D} = (D_0, D_1, \ldots, D_l)$ is (Σ, w, τ)-structural and $\mathfrak{s}(\mathcal{D}) \models \psi[u_1, \ldots, u_t]$. The Boolean connectives $\wedge, \vee$ and $\neg$ and the existential quantification $\exists$ are handled using closure properties from regular languages.

The technically involved part of the proof however will be the construction of an "initial" automaton which accepts precisely those strings

$$D_0 \otimes D_1 \otimes \ldots \otimes D_l \otimes u_1 \ldots u_t$$

such that $(D_0, D_1, \ldots, D_l)$ is a (Σ, w, τ)-structural tuple, and $u_1, \ldots, u_t$ belong to the domain $\mathcal{L}(D_0)$. The difficulty lies in the fact that we need to guarantee that, for each $i \in [l]$, the language $\mathcal{L}(D_i)$ is contained in the tensored language $\mathcal{L}(D_0)^{\otimes a_i}$. This will require the introduction of new machinery for the implicit manipulation of ODDs that may be of independent interest.

6.1   Basic General Operations

In this section, we introduce some basic low-level operations that will be used repeatedly in the proof of Theorem 5.1. More precisely, we consider the following operations: *projection, identification, permutation of coordinates, fold, unfold, direct sum, union, intersection* and *complementation*.

Let Σ be an alphabet, $\mathfrak{a} \in \mathbb{N}_+$ and $R \subseteq (\Sigma^+)^{\times \mathfrak{a}}$ be an $\mathfrak{a}$-ary relation.

For each permutation $\pi \colon [\mathfrak{a}] \to [\mathfrak{a}]$, we let perm$(R, \pi)$ be the relation obtained from R by permuting the coordinates of each tuple in R according to π. In other words, perm$(R, \pi) \doteq \big\{ (s_{\pi(1)}, \ldots, s_{\pi(\mathfrak{a})}) \colon (s_1, \ldots, s_{\mathfrak{a}}) \in R \big\}$.

For each $i \in [\mathfrak{a}]$, the *projection of the i-th coordinate of R* is defined as the $(\mathfrak{a} - 1)$-ary relation proj$(R, i) \doteq \{(s_1, \ldots, s_{i-1}, s_{i+1}, \ldots, s_{\mathfrak{a}}) \colon (s_1, \ldots, s_{\mathfrak{a}}) \in R\}$ obtained from R by removing the i-th coordinate of each tuple in R. More generally, for each $J \subseteq [\mathfrak{a}]$, we let proj$(R, J)$ denote the relation obtained from R by removing all the i-th coordinates of each tuple in R, where $i \in J$.

For each $i, j \in [\mathfrak{a}]$, the *identification of the i-th and j-th coordinates of R* is defined as the relation ident$(R, i, j) \doteq \{(s_1, \ldots, s_{\mathfrak{a}}) \in R \colon s_i = s_j\}$ obtained from R by removing each tuple $(s_1, \ldots, s_{\mathfrak{a}}) \in R$ such that $s_i \neq s_j$. More generally, for each $J \subseteq [\mathfrak{a}] \times [\mathfrak{a}]$, we let ident$(R, J) \doteq \{(s_1, \ldots, s_{\mathfrak{a}}) \in R \colon s_i = s_j, (i, j) \in J\}$.

For each $i, j \in [\mathfrak{a}]$, with $i \leq j$, we let

$$\mathsf{fold}(R, i, j) \doteq \{(s_1, \ldots, s_{i-1}, s_i \otimes \cdots \otimes s_j, s_{j+1}, \ldots, s_{\mathfrak{a}}) \colon (s_1, \ldots, s_{\mathfrak{a}}) \in R\}.$$

On the other hand, if $R = \text{fold}(R', i, j)$ for some relation R' and some $i, j \in [\mathfrak{a}]$, with $i \leq j$, then we let $\text{unfold}(R, i) = R'$, i.e. the inverse operation of fold.

Let Σ_1 and Σ_2 be two alphabets, $\mathfrak{a}_1, \mathfrak{a}_2 \in \mathbb{N}_+$, $R_1 \subseteq (\Sigma_1^+)^{\times \mathfrak{a}_1}$ be an $\mathfrak{a}_1$-ary relation and $R_2 \subseteq (\Sigma_2^+)^{\times \mathfrak{a}_2}$ be an $\mathfrak{a}_2$-ary relation. If R_1 and R_2 are non-empty, then we define the *direct sum* of R_1 with R_2 as the $(\mathfrak{a}_1 + \mathfrak{a}_2)$-ary relation

$$R_1 \oplus R_2 \doteq \big\{ (s_1, \ldots, s_{\mathfrak{a}_1}, s'_1, \ldots, s'_{\mathfrak{a}_2}) : (s_1, \ldots, s_{\mathfrak{a}_1}) \in R_1, (s'_1, \ldots, s'_{\mathfrak{a}_2}) \in R_2 \big\}.$$

Otherwise, we let $R_1 \oplus \emptyset \doteq R_1$ and $\emptyset \oplus R_2 \doteq R_2$.

Proposition 6.1. *Let Σ_1 and Σ_2 be two alphabets, $\mathfrak{a}_1, \mathfrak{a}_2 \in \mathbb{N}_+$, $R_1 \subseteq (\Sigma_1^+)^{\times \mathfrak{a}_1}$ be a regular $\mathfrak{a}_1$-ary relation and $R_2 \subseteq (\Sigma_2^+)^{\times \mathfrak{a}_2}$ be a regular $\mathfrak{a}_2$-ary relation. The following closure properties are held:*

1. *for each permutation $\pi \colon [\mathfrak{a}_1] \to [\mathfrak{a}_1]$, $\text{perm}(R_1, \pi)$ is regular;*
2. *for each $J \subseteq [\mathfrak{a}_1]$, $\text{proj}(R_1, J)$ is regular;*
3. *for each $J \subseteq [\mathfrak{a}_1] \times [\mathfrak{a}_1]$, $\text{ident}(R_1, J)$ is regular;*
4. *for each $i, j \in [\mathfrak{a}_1]$, with $i \leq j$, $\text{fold}(R_1, i, j)$ is regular;*
5. *if $R_1 = \text{fold}(R'_1, i, j)$ for some relation R'_1 and some $i, j \in [\mathfrak{a}_1]$, with $i \leq j$, then $\text{unfold}(R_1, i) = R'_1$ is regular;*
6. *$R_1 \oplus R_2$ is regular.*

Besides the operations described above, it is worth noting that, if R_1 and R_2 have the same arity, i.e. $\mathfrak{a}_1 = \mathfrak{a}_2$, then the *union* $R_1 \cup R_2$ and the *intersection* $R_1 \cap R_2$ of R_1 and R_2 are regular relations. Moreover, if $R \subseteq (\Sigma^+)^{\times \mathfrak{a}}$ is a regular $\mathfrak{a}$-ary relation, then the *complement* $\neg R \doteq (\Sigma^+)^{\times \mathfrak{a}} \setminus R$ of R is also a regular $\mathfrak{a}$-ary relation.

6.2   Core Relations

In this subsection we introduce some non-standard relations and prove that these relations are regular. Intuitively, these relations will be used to implicitly manipulate tuples of ODDs, and in particular to construct a finite automaton accepting a string $D_0 \otimes D_1 \otimes \ldots \otimes D_l \otimes u_1 \ldots u_t$ if and only if the tuple $(D_0, D_1, \ldots, D_l)$ is (Σ, w, τ)-structural and $u_1, \ldots, u_t$ belong to the domain $\mathcal{L}(D_0)$.

Proposition 6.2. *For each alphabet Σ and each $w \in \mathbb{N}_+$, the language $\mathcal{B}(\Sigma, w)^{\circledast}$ is regular.*

Let Σ be an alphabet and $w \in \mathbb{N}_+$. We let $\mathcal{R}_\in(\Sigma, w)$ be the relation defined as follows: $\mathcal{R}_\in(\Sigma, w) \doteq \big\{ (D, s) : D \in \mathcal{B}(\Sigma, w)^{\circledast}, s \in \mathcal{L}(D) \big\}$.

Proposition 6.3. *For each alphabet Σ and each $w \in \mathbb{N}_+$, the relation $\mathcal{R}_\in(\Sigma, w)$ is regular.*

Proof. Consider the finite automaton $\mathcal{F}$ over the alphabet $\mathcal{B}(\Sigma, w) \otimes (\Sigma \uplus \{\Box\})$ defined in the following way:

- $Q(\mathcal{F}) = \{q_I\} \cup \{q_{B, [\mathfrak{p}, \tilde{\sigma}, \mathfrak{q}]} : B \in \mathcal{B}(\Sigma, w), (\mathfrak{p}, \tilde{\sigma}, \mathfrak{q}) \in T(B)\};$

$$- \ T(\mathcal{F}) = \big\{(q_I, (B, \widetilde{\sigma}), q_{B,[\mathfrak{p},\widetilde{\sigma},\mathfrak{q}]}) \colon q_{B,[\mathfrak{p},\widetilde{\sigma},\mathfrak{q}]} \in Q(\mathcal{F}) \setminus \{q_I\}, \mathfrak{p} \in I(B)\}$$

$$\cup \big\{(q_{B',[\mathfrak{p}',\widetilde{\nu},\mathfrak{q}']}, (B, \widetilde{\sigma}), q_{B,[\mathfrak{p},\widetilde{\sigma},\mathfrak{q}]}) \colon q_{B',[\mathfrak{p}',\widetilde{\nu},\mathfrak{q}']}, \ q_{B,[\mathfrak{p},\widetilde{\sigma},\mathfrak{q}]} \in Q(\mathcal{F}) \setminus \{q_I\},$$

$$\ell(B) = r(B'), \phi(B') = 0, \iota(B) = 0, \mathfrak{p} = \mathfrak{q}'\big\};$$

$$- \ I(\mathcal{F}) = \{q_I\}; \ F(\mathcal{F}) = \big\{q_{B,[\mathfrak{p},\widetilde{\sigma},\mathfrak{q}]} \in Q(\mathcal{F}) \setminus \{q_I\} \colon \mathfrak{q} \in F(B)\}.$$

One can verify that $\mathcal{L}(\mathcal{F}) = \{D \otimes s \colon D \in \mathcal{B}(\Sigma, w)^{\circledast}, s \in \mathcal{L}(D)\}$. In other words, $\mathrm{rel}(\mathcal{L}(\mathcal{F})) = \mathcal{R}_{\in}(\Sigma, w)$. Therefore, $\mathcal{R}_{\in}(\Sigma, w)$ is a regular relation. $\qquad\square$

Lemma 6.4. *For each alphabet Σ and each $w, c \in \mathbb{N}_+$, the following relations are regular:*

1. $\widetilde{\mathcal{R}}_{\in}(\Sigma, w, c) \doteq \big\{(D, s_1, \ldots, s_c) \colon D \in \mathcal{B}(\Sigma, w)^{\circledast}, \ s_1, \ldots, s_c \in \mathcal{L}(D)\big\};$
2. $\widetilde{\mathcal{R}}(\Sigma, w, c) \doteq \big\{(D, s_1, \ldots, s_c) \colon D \in \mathcal{B}(\Sigma, w)^{\circ k}, \ s_1, \ldots, s_c \in \Sigma^{\leq k}, k \in \mathbb{N}_+\big\};$
3. $\widetilde{\mathcal{R}}_{\notin}(\Sigma, w, c) \doteq \big\{(D, s_1, \ldots, s_c) \colon D \in \mathcal{B}(\Sigma, w)^{\circ k}, \ s_1, \ldots, s_c \in \Sigma^{\leq k},$

$$s_i \notin \mathcal{L}(D) \text{ for some } i \in [c], \ k \in \mathbb{N}_+\big\}.$$

Lemma 6.5. *For each two alphabets Σ_1 and Σ_2 and each $w \in \mathbb{N}_+$, the relation $\mathcal{R}(\Sigma_1, \Sigma_2, w) \doteq \{(D, D') \colon D \in \mathcal{B}(\Sigma_1, w)^{\circledast}, \ D' \in \mathcal{B}(\Sigma_2, w)^{\circledast}\}$ is regular.*

Proof. It follows from Proposition 6.2 that $\mathcal{B}(\Sigma_1, w)^{\circledast}$ and $\mathcal{B}(\Sigma_2, w)^{\circledast}$ are regular languages. In other words, $R_1 = \mathcal{B}(\Sigma_1, w)^{\circledast}$ and $R_2 = \mathcal{B}(\Sigma_2, w)^{\circledast}$ are regular unary relations. Therefore, $\mathcal{R}(\Sigma_1, \Sigma_2, w)$ is regular, since it may be simply regarded as the regular relation $R_1 \oplus R_2$. $\qquad\square$

Let Σ be an alphabet and $w, \mathfrak{a} \in \mathbb{N}_+$. We let $\mathcal{R}_{\subseteq}(\Sigma, w, \mathfrak{a})$ be the relation defined as follows:

$$\mathcal{R}_{\subseteq}(\Sigma, w, \mathfrak{a}) \doteq \big\{(D, D') \colon D \in \mathcal{B}(\Sigma, w)^{\circledast}, \ D' \in \mathcal{B}(\Sigma^{\otimes \mathfrak{a}}, w)^{\circledast}, \mathcal{L}(D') \subseteq \mathcal{L}(D)^{\otimes \mathfrak{a}}\big\}.$$

Proposition 6.6. *For each alphabet Σ and each $w, \mathfrak{a} \in \mathbb{N}_+$, the relation $\mathcal{R}_{\subseteq}(\Sigma, w, \mathfrak{a})$ is regular.*

Proof. Consider the relation $R = \mathrm{fold}(\widetilde{\mathcal{R}}_{\notin}(\Sigma, w, \mathfrak{a}), 2, \mathfrak{a}+1) \oplus \mathcal{R}_{\in}(\Sigma^{\otimes \mathfrak{a}}, w)$. Note that, R consists of all tuples of the form $(D, s_1 \otimes \cdots \otimes s_{\mathfrak{a}}, D', s'_1 \otimes \cdots \otimes s'_{\mathfrak{a}})$ satisfying the following conditions:

- $D \in \mathcal{B}(\Sigma, w)^{\circ k}, \ s_1, \ldots, s_{\mathfrak{a}} \in \Sigma^{\leq k}$ but, for some $i \in [\mathfrak{a}], \ s_i \notin \mathcal{L}(D)$;
- $D' \in \mathcal{B}(\Sigma, w)^{\circ k'}$, and $s'_1 \otimes \cdots \otimes s'_{\mathfrak{a}} \in \mathcal{L}(D')$,

where $k, k' \in \mathbb{N}_+$. Let $R' = \mathrm{ident}(R, 2, 4)$. By definition, R' is the sub-relation of R comprised of all tuples $(D, s_1 \otimes \cdots \otimes s_{\mathfrak{a}}, D', s'_1 \otimes \cdots \otimes s'_{\mathfrak{a}}) \in R$ such that $s_i = s'_i$ for each $i \in [\mathfrak{a}]$. Thus, $\mathrm{proj}(R', \{2, 4\})$ consists of all tuples $(D, D') \in \mathcal{B}(\Sigma, w)^{\circ k} \times \mathcal{B}(\Sigma^{\otimes \mathfrak{a}}, w)^{\circ k'}$ such that there exist $s_1, \ldots, s_{\mathfrak{a}} \in \Sigma^{\leq k}$ with $s_1 \otimes \cdots \otimes s_{\mathfrak{a}} \in \mathcal{L}(D')$ but, for some $i \in [\mathfrak{a}], \ s_i \notin \mathcal{L}(D)$, where $k, k' \in \mathbb{N}_+$. In other words, we have that

$$\mathrm{proj}(R', \{2, 4\}) = \big\{(D, D') \colon D \in \mathcal{B}(\Sigma, w)^{\circledast}, \ D' \in \mathcal{B}(\Sigma^{\otimes \mathfrak{a}}, w)^{\circledast}, \mathcal{L}(D') \nsubseteq \mathcal{L}(D)^{\otimes \mathfrak{a}}\big\},$$

Now, let $\mathcal{R}(\Sigma, \Sigma^{\otimes \mathfrak{a}}, w) = \{(D, D') \colon D \in \mathcal{B}(\Sigma, w)^{\circledast}, \ D' \in \mathcal{B}(\Sigma^{\otimes \mathfrak{a}}, w)^{\circledast}\}$. By Lemma 6.5, $\mathcal{R}(\Sigma, \Sigma^{\otimes \mathfrak{a}}, w)$ is regular. Therefore, $\mathcal{R}_{\subseteq}(\Sigma, w, \mathfrak{a})$ is regular, since it may be simply regarded as the relation $\mathcal{R}(\Sigma, \Sigma^{\otimes \mathfrak{a}}, w) \cap \neg \mathrm{proj}(R', \{2, 4\})$. $\qquad\square$

6.3   Regular-Structural Relations

Let Σ be an alphabet, $w \in \mathbb{N}_+$, $\tau = (\mathsf{R}_1, \ldots, \mathsf{R}_l)$ be a relational vocabulary and $t \in \mathbb{N}$. We let $\mathcal{R}(\Sigma, w, \tau, t)$ be the relation defined as follows:

$$\mathcal{R}(\Sigma, w, \tau, t) \doteq \big\{ (D_0, D_1, \ldots, D_l, u_1, \ldots, u_t) :$$
$$(D_0, D_1, \ldots, D_l) \in \mathcal{R}(\Sigma, w, \tau),\ u_1, \ldots, u_t \in \mathcal{L}(D_0) \big\}.$$

In particular, note that, if $t = 0$, then $\mathcal{R}(\Sigma, w, \tau, t) = \mathcal{R}(\Sigma, w, \tau)$.

Lemma 6.7. *Let Σ be an alphabet, $w \in \mathbb{N}_+$, $\tau = (\mathsf{R}_1, \ldots, \mathsf{R}_l)$ be a relational vocabulary and $t \in \mathbb{N}$. The relation $\mathcal{R}(\Sigma, w, \tau, t)$ is regular.*

Proof. Consider the relations $R = \mathcal{R}_{\subseteq}(\Sigma, w, \mathfrak{a}_1) \oplus \cdots \oplus \mathcal{R}_{\subseteq}(\Sigma, w, \mathfrak{a}_l) \oplus \widetilde{\mathcal{R}}_{\in}(\Sigma, w, t)$ and $R' = \mathrm{ident}(R, \{(2i + 1, 2i + 3) : i \in [\![l]\!]\})$. One can verify that R' consists of tuples of the form $(D_0, D_1, \ldots, D_0, D_l, D_0, u_1, \ldots, u_t)$ satisfying the conditions: $(D_0, D_1, \ldots, D_l) \in \mathcal{R}(\Sigma, w, \tau)$ and $u_1, \ldots, u_t \in \mathcal{L}(D_0)$. Therefore, $\mathcal{R}(\Sigma, w, \tau, t)$ is regular, since it may regarded as the relation $\mathrm{proj}(R', \{2i + 1 : i \in [\![l]\!]\})$. $\square$

Let $\psi(x_1, \ldots, x_t)$ be an $\mathrm{FO}\{\tau\}$-formula, with $t \in \mathbb{N}$. If $X_t = \{x_1, \ldots, x_t\}$, then we let $\mathcal{R}(\Sigma, w, \tau, \psi, X_t)$ denote the relation defined as follows:

$$\mathcal{R}(\Sigma, w, \tau, \psi, X_t) \doteq \big\{ (D_0, D_1, \ldots, D_t, u_1, \ldots, u_t) \in \mathcal{R}(\Sigma, w, \tau, t) :$$
$$\mathfrak{s}(D_0, D_1, \ldots, D_t) \models \psi[u_1, \ldots, u_t] \big\}.$$

We remark that, if $t = 0$, then $\mathcal{R}(\Sigma, w, \tau, \psi, X_t)$ coincides with the relation $\mathcal{R}(\Sigma, w, \tau, \psi)$, in which ψ is an $\mathrm{FO}\{\tau\}$-sentence.

Finally, we show in Theorem 6.8 that, for each $\mathrm{FO}\{\tau\}$-formula $\psi(x_1, \ldots, x_t)$, the relation $\mathcal{R}(\Sigma, w, \tau, \psi, X_t)$ is regular. As a result, we obtain that $\mathcal{R}(\Sigma, w, \tau, \psi)$ is also a regular relation, concluding the proof of Theorem 5.1. We note that Theorem 6.8 is proven by induction on the structure of the input formula $\psi(x_1, \ldots, x_t)$. The base case follows straightforwardly from the results proven in this section, the induction step follows from the fact that regular languages are closed under, negation, union, intersection and projection.

Theorem 6.8. *Let Σ be an alphabet, $w \in \mathbb{N}_+$, $\tau = (\mathsf{R}_1, \ldots, \mathsf{R}_l)$ be a relational vocabulary and $\psi(x_1, \ldots, x_t)$ be an $\mathrm{FO}\{\tau\}$-formula, with $t \in \mathbb{N}$. The relation $\mathcal{R}(\Sigma, w, \tau, \psi, X_t)$ is regular, where $X_t = \{x_1, \ldots, x_t\}$.*

7   Counting Satisfying Assignments

Let $\tau = (\mathsf{R}_1, \ldots, \mathsf{R}_l)$ be a relational vocabulary, $\psi(x_1, \ldots, x_t)$ be an $\mathrm{FO}\{\tau\}$-formula with $\mathrm{freevar}(\psi) \subseteq \{x_1, \ldots, x_t\}$, and let $\mathfrak{A}$ be a finite τ-structure. We say that an assignment $(u_1, \ldots, u_t)$ of elements from the domain $\mathsf{R}_0(\mathfrak{A})$ to the free occurrences of the variables $x_1, \ldots, x_t$ *satisfies* ψ *with respect to* $\mathfrak{A}$ if $\mathfrak{A} \models \psi[u_1, \ldots, u_t]$.

The next theorem states that, if we are given a (Σ, w, τ)-structural tuple $\mathcal{D}$ such that $\mathfrak{s}(\mathcal{D}) = \mathfrak{A}$, then the problem of counting the number of assignments to the free occurrences of the variables $x_1, \ldots, x_t$ that satisfy ψ with respect to $\mathfrak{A}$ is fixed parameter tractable when parameterized by Σ, w, τ, ψ and t. More specifically, such a problem can be solved in time quadratic in the length of the (Σ, w, τ)-structural tuple $\mathcal{D}$. We remark that, in most applications, the parameters Σ, τ, ψ, t are naturally already fixed, and therefore the only complexity parameter that is indeed relevant in these situations is the width w.

Theorem 7.1. *Let Σ be an alphabet, $w \in \mathbb{N}_+$, $\tau = (\mathsf{R}_1, \ldots, \mathsf{R}_l)$ be a relational vocabulary and $\psi(x_1, \ldots, x_t)$ be an FO$\{\tau\}$-formula. Given a (Σ, w, τ)-structural tuple $\mathcal{D} = (D_0, D_1 \ldots D_l)$ of length k, one can count in time $f(\Sigma, w, \tau, \psi, t) \cdot k^2$, for some computable function f, the number of assignments that satisfy ψ with respect to $\mathfrak{s}(\mathcal{D})$.*

8 Conclusion

In this work we have introduced the notion of decisional-width of a relational structure, as a measure that intuitively tries to provide a quantification of how difficult it is to define the relations of the structure. Subsequently we provided a suitable way of defining infinite classes of structures of small width. Interestingly, there exist classes of structures of constant width that have very high width with respect to most width measures defined so far in structural graph theory. As an example, we have shown that the class of hypercube graphs has regular-decisional width 2, while it is well known that they have unbounded treewidth and cliquewidth. Additionally, this family is not nowhere-dense. Therefore, first-order model-checking and validity-testing techniques developed for these well studied classes of graphs do not generalize to graphs of constant decisional width. Other examples of families of graphs of constant decisional width are paths, cliques (which have unbounded treewidth), unlabeled grids (which have unbounded treewidth and cliquewidth) and many others. It is interesting to note that these mentioned classes have all a regular structure and, therefore, are "easy" to describe.

Acknowledgments. Alexsander Andrade de Melo acknowledges support from the Brazilian agencies CNPq/GD 140399/2017-8 and CAPES/PDSE 88881.187636/2018-01; and Mateus de Oliveira Oliveira acknowledges support from the Bergen Research Foundation and from the Research Council of Norway.

References

1. Blumensath, A.: Automatic structures. Diploma thesis. Rheinisch-Westfälische Technische Hochschule Aachen (1999)
2. Blumensath, A., Gradel, E.: Automatic structures. In: Proceedings of the 15th Annual IEEE Symposium on Logic in Computer Science, pp. 51–62. IEEE (2000)

3. Bollig, B.: On symbolic OBDD-based algorithms for the minimum spanning tree problem. Theoret. Comput. Sci. **447**, 2–12 (2012)
4. Bollig, B.: On the width of ordered binary decision diagrams. In: Zhang, Z., Wu, L., Xu, W., Du, D.-Z. (eds.) COCOA 2014. LNCS, vol. 8881, pp. 444–458. Springer, Cham (2014). https://doi.org/10.1007/978-3-319-12691-3_33
5. Bonomo, F., Grippo, L.N., Milanič, M., Safe, M.D.: Graph classes with and without powers of bounded clique-width. Discrete Appl. Math. **199**, 3–15 (2016)
6. Büchi, J.R.: Weak second order arithmetic and finite automata. Z. Math. Logik Grundl. Math. **6**, 66–92 (1960)
7. Bulatov, A.A.: Graphs of relational structures: restricted types. In: Proceedings of the 31st Annual ACM/IEEE Symposium on Logic in Computer Science, pp. 642–651. ACM (2016)
8. Chandran, L.S., Kavitha, T.: The treewidth and pathwidth of hypercubes. Discrete Math. **306**(3), 359–365 (2006)
9. Courcelle, B.: The monadic second-order logic of graphs. I. Recognizable sets of finite graphs. Inf. Comput. **85**(1), 12–75 (1990)
10. Courcelle, B., Makowsky, J.A., Rotics, U.: Linear time solvable optimization problems on graphs of bounded clique-width. Theory Comput. Syst. **33**(2), 125–150 (2000)
11. Ebbinghaus, H.D., Flum, J., Thomas, W.: Mathematical Logic. Springer, New York (2013)
12. Ebbinghaus, H.D., Flum, J.: Finite Model Theory. Springer, Heidelberg (2005)
13. Elgot, C.C.: Decision problems of finite automata and related arithmetics. Trans. Am. Math. Soc. **98**, 21–52 (1961)
14. Farb, B.: Automatic groups: a guided tour. Enseign. Math. (2) **38**(3–4), 291–313 (1992)
15. Getoor, L., Friedman, N., Koller, D., Taskar, B.: Learning probabilistic models of relational structure. In: ICML, vol. 1, pp. 170–177 (2001)
16. Grohe, M.: Algorithmic meta theorems. In: Broersma, H., Erlebach, T., Friedetzky, T., Paulusma, D. (eds.) WG 2008. LNCS, vol. 5344, p. 30. Springer, Heidelberg (2008). https://doi.org/10.1007/978-3-540-92248-3_3
17. Grohe, M.: Algorithmic meta theorems for sparse graph classes. In: Hirsch, E.A., Kuznetsov, S.O., Pin, J.É., Vereshchagin, N.K. (eds.) CSR 2014. LNCS, vol. 8476, pp. 16–22. Springer, Cham (2014). https://doi.org/10.1007/978-3-319-06686-8_2
18. Hachtel, G.D., Somenzi, F.: A symbolic algorithm for maximum flow in 0-1 networks. In: Proceedings of the 1993 IEEE/ACM International Conference on Computer-Aided Design, pp. 403–406. IEEE Computer Society Press (1993)
19. Hliněný, P., Seese, D.: Trees, grids, and MSO decidability: from graphs to matroids. Theoret. Comput. Sci. **351**(3), 372–393 (2006)
20. Khoussainov, B., Minnes, M.: Three lectures on automatic structures. In: Proceedings of Logic Colloquium, pp. 132–176 (2007)
21. Khoussainov, B., Nerode, A.: Automatic presentations of structures. In: Leivant, D. (ed.) LCC 1994. LNCS, vol. 960, pp. 367–392. Springer, Heidelberg (1995). https://doi.org/10.1007/3-540-60178-3_93
22. Kolaitis, P.G., Vardi, M.Y.: A game-theoretic approach to constraint satisfaction. In: AAAI/IAAI, pp. 175–181 (2000)
23. Kreutzer, S.: Algorithmic meta-theorems. In: Grohe, M., Niedermeier, R. (eds.) IWPEC 2008. LNCS, vol. 5018, pp. 10–12. Springer, Heidelberg (2008). https://doi.org/10.1007/978-3-540-79723-4_3

24. Kruckman, A., Rubin, S., Sheridan, J., Zax, B.: A Myhill-Nerode theorem for automata with advice. In: Proceedings of GANDALF 2012. Electronic Proceedings in Theoretical Computer Science, vol. 96, pp. 238–246 (2012)
25. Poon, H., Domingos, P.M., Sumner, M.: A general method for reducing the complexity of relational inference and its application to MCMC. In: AAAI, vol. 8, pp. 1075–1080 (2008)
26. Sawitzki, D.: Implicit flow maximization by iterative squaring. In: Van Emde Boas, P., Pokorný, J., Bieliková, M., Štuller, J. (eds.) SOFSEM 2004. LNCS, vol. 2932, pp. 301–313. Springer, Heidelberg (2004). https://doi.org/10.1007/978-3-540-24618-3_26
27. Seese, D.: The structure of the models of decidable monadic theories of graphs. Ann. Pure Appl. Log. **53**(2), 169–195 (1991)
28. Sutskever, I., Tenenbaum, J.B., Salakhutdinov, R.R.: Modelling relational data using Bayesian clustered tensor factorization. In: Advances in Neural Information Processing Systems, pp. 1821–1828 (2009)
29. Woelfel, P.: Symbolic topological sorting with OBDDs. J. Discrete Algorithms **4**(1), 51–71 (2006)
30. Zaid, F.A., Grädel, E., Reinhardt, F.: Advice automatic structures and uniformly automatic classes. In: 26th EACSL Annual Conference on Computer Science Logic (CSL 2017). LIPIcs, vol. 82, pp. 35:1–35:20 (2017)

Extending SMT Solvers to Higher-Order Logic

Haniel Barbosa[1], Andrew Reynolds[1], Daniel El Ouraoui[2(✉)], Cesare Tinelli[1], and Clark Barrett[3]

[1] The University of Iowa, Iowa City, USA
[2] University of Lorraine, CNRS, Inria, and LORIA, Nancy, France
`daniel.elouraoui@gmail.com`
[3] Stanford University, Stanford, USA

Abstract. SMT solvers have throughout the years been able to cope with increasingly expressive formulas, from ground logics to full first-order logic (FOL). In contrast, the extension of SMT solvers to higher-order logic (HOL) is mostly unexplored. We propose a pragmatic extension for SMT solvers to support HOL reasoning natively without compromising performance on FOL reasoning, thus leveraging the extensive research and implementation efforts dedicated to efficient SMT solving. We show how to generalize data structures and the ground decision procedure to support partial applications and extensionality, as well as how to reconcile quantifier instantiation techniques with higher-order variables. We also discuss a separate approach for redesigning an HOL SMT solver from the ground up via new data structures and algorithms. We apply our pragmatic extension to the CVC4 SMT solver and discuss a redesign of the veriT SMT solver. Our evaluation shows they are competitive with state-of-the-art HOL provers and often outperform the traditional encoding into FOL.

1   Introduction

Higher-order (HO) logic is a pervasive setting for reasoning about numerous real-world applications. In particular, it is widely used in proof-assistants (also known as interactive theorem provers) to provide trustworthy, formal, and machine-checkable proofs of theorems. A major challenge in these applications is to automate as much as possible the production of these formal proofs, thereby reducing the burden of proof on the users. An effective approach to achieve stronger automation in proof assistants is to rely on less expressive but more automatic theorem provers to discharge some of the proof obligations. Systems such as HOLYHammer, MizAR, Sledgehammer, and Why3, which provide a one-click connection from proof-assistants to first-order (FO) provers, have led in recent

---

This work was partially supported by the National Science Foundation under award 1656926.

years to considerable improvements in proof-assistant automation [14]. A similar layered approach is also used by automatic HO provers such as Leo-III [43] and Satallax [17], which regularly invoke FO provers to discharge intermediate goals that depend solely on FO reasoning. However, as noted in previous work [12,30,48], in both cases the reduction to FOL has its own disadvantages: full encodings into FO, such as those performed by the *hammers*, may lead to issues with performance, soundness, or completeness. On the other hand, the combination of FO and HO reasoning in automatic HO provers may suffer from the HO prover itself having to perform substantial FO reasoning, since it is not optimized for FO proving. This would be the case in HO problems with a large FO component, which occur often in practice. We aim to overcome these shortcomings by extending Satisfiability Modulo Theories (SMT) [8] solvers, a class of highly successful automatic FO provers, to natively support HOL.

The two main challenges for extending SMT solvers to HOL lie in dealing with *partial function applications* and with *functional variables*, i.e., quantifier variables of higher-order type. The former mainly affects term representation and core algorithms, which in FOL are based on the fact that all function symbols are fully applied. The latter impacts quantifier instantiation techniques, which must now account for quantified variables occurring in function symbol positions. Moreover, often HO problems can only be proven if functional variables are instantiated with synthesized λ-terms, typically via HO unification [23], which is undecidable in general.

Contributions. We present two approaches for extending SMT solvers to natively support HO reasoning (HOSMT). The first one, the *pragmatic* approach (Sect. 3), targets existing state-of-the-art SMT solvers with large code bases and complex data structures optimized for the FO case. In this approach, we extend a solver with only minimal modifications to its core data structures and algorithms. In the second approach, the *redesign* approach (Sect. 4), we rethink a solver's data structures and develop new algorithms aimed specifically at HO reasoning. This approach may lead to better results but is better suited to *lightweight* solvers, i.e., less optimized solvers with a smaller code base. Moreover, this approach provides more flexibility to later develop new techniques especially suited for higher-order reasoning. A common theme of both approaches is that the instantiation algorithms are *not* extended with HO unification. This is a significant enough challenge that we plan to explore in a later phase of this work. We include proofs, more examples, and related work in a technical report [5].

We present an extensive experimental evaluation (Sect. 5) of our pragmatic and redesign approaches as implemented respectively in the state-of-the-art SMT solver CVC4 [6] and the lightweight solver veriT [16]. Besides comparisons against state-of-the-art HO provers, we also evaluate these solvers against themselves, comparing a native HO encoding using the extensions in this paper to the base versions of the solvers with the more traditional FO encoding (not using the extensions).

Related Work. The pioneering work of Robinson [41] on using a translation to reduce higher-order reasoning to first-order logic inspired the successful tools such as Sledgehammer [36] and CoqHammer [19] that build on this idea by automating HO reasoning via automatic FO provers. Earlier works on native HO proving are, e.g., Andrews's higher-order resolution [1] and Kohlhase's higher-order tableau [29], inspire the modern day HO provers such as LEO-II [11] and Leo-III [43], implementing variations of HO resolution, and Satallax [17], based on a HO tableau calculus guided by a SAT solver. Our approach however is conceptually closer to recent work by Blanchette et al. [9,48] on *gracefully* generalizing the superposition calculus [2,33] to support higher-order reasoning. As a first step, they have targeted the λ-free fragment of higher-order logic, presenting a refutationally complete calculus [9] and an initial implementation as a prototype extension of the Zipperposition prover [18]. More recently they integrated their approach into the state-of-the-art FO prover E [48], showing competitive results against state-of-the-art HO provers. Their next step, as is ours, is to extend their calculus to superposition with λ-terms while preserving their completeness guarantees.

2   Preliminaries

Our monomorphic higher-order language $\mathscr{L}$ is defined in terms of right-associative binary *sort constructors* $\rightarrow$, $\times$ and pairwise-disjoint countably infinite sets $\mathcal{S}$, $\mathcal{X}$ and $\mathcal{F}$, of *atomic sorts*, *variables*, and *function symbols*, respectively. We use the notations $\bar{a}_n$ and $\bar{a}$ to denote the tuple $(a_1, \ldots, a_n)$ or the cross product $a_1 \times \cdots \times a_n$, depending on context, with $n \geq 0$. We extend this notation to pairwise binary operations over tuples in the natural way. A *sort* τ is either an element of $\mathcal{S}$ or a *functional sort* $\bar{\tau}_n \rightarrow \tau$ from sorts $\bar{\tau}_n = \tau_1 \times \cdots \times \tau_n$ to sort τ. The elements of $\mathcal{X}$ and $\mathcal{F}$ are annotated with sorts, so that $x : \tau$ is a variable of sort τ and $\mathsf{f} : \bar{\tau}_n \rightarrow \tau$ is an *n-ary* function symbol of sort $\bar{\tau}_n \rightarrow \tau$. We identify function symbols of sort $\bar{\tau}_0 \rightarrow \tau$ with function symbols of sort τ, which we call *constants* when τ is not a functional sort. Whenever convenient, we drop the sort annotations when referring to symbols.

The set of terms is defined inductively: every variable $x : \tau$ is a term of sort τ. For variables $\bar{x}_n : \bar{\tau}_n$ and a term $t : \tau$ of sort τ, the expression $\lambda \bar{x}_n. t$ is a term of sort $\bar{\tau}_n \rightarrow \tau$, called a λ-*abstraction*, with *bound* variables $\bar{x}_n$ and *body* t. A variable occurrence is *free* in a term if it is not bound by a λ-abstraction. For a term $t : \bar{\tau}_n \rightarrow \tau$ and terms $t_1 : \tau_1, \ldots, t_m : \tau_m$ with $m \leq n$, the expression $\mathsf{f}(\bar{t}_n)$ is a term, called an *application of* f, the *head* of the application, to the *arguments* $\bar{t}_m$. The application is *total* and has sort τ if $m = n$; it is *partial* and has sort $\tau_{m+1} \times \cdots \times \tau_n \rightarrow \tau$ if $m < n$. A λ-*application* is an application whose head is a λ-abstraction. The subterm relation is defined recursively: a term is a subterm of itself; if a term is an application, all subterms of its arguments are also its subterms. Note this is not the standard definition of subterms in HOL, which also includes application heads and all partial applications. The *set of all subterms in a term* t is denoted by $\mathbf{T}(t)$. We assume $\mathcal{S}$ contains a sort o, the Boolean sort, and that $\mathcal{F}$ contains Boolean constants $\top$, $\bot$, a Boolean unary function $\neg$, Boolean binary functions $\wedge$, $\vee$, and, for every sort τ, a family of equality symbols $\simeq : \tau \times \tau \to o$ and a family of symbols ite $: o \times \tau \times \tau \to \tau$. These symbols are interpreted in the usual way as, respectively, logical constants, connectives, identity, and *if-then-else* (ITE). We refer to terms of sort o as *formulas* and to terms of sort $\bar{\tau} \to o$ as *predicates*. An *atom* is a total predicate application. A *literal* or *constraint* is an atom or its negation. We assume the language contains the $\forall$ and $\exists$ binders over formulas, defined as usual, in addition to the λ binder. A formula or a term is *ground* if it is binder-free. We use the symbol $=$ for syntactic equality on terms. We reserve the names $\mathsf{a}, \mathsf{b}, \mathsf{c}, \mathsf{f}, \mathsf{g}, \mathsf{h}, \mathsf{p}$ for function symbols; w, x, y, z for variables in general; F, G for variables of functional sort; r, s, t, u for terms; and φ, ψ for formulas. The notation $t[\bar{x}_n]$ stands for a term whose free variables are included in the tuple of distinct variables $\bar{x}_n$; $t[\bar{s}_n]$ is the term obtained from t by a simultaneous substitution of $\bar{s}_n$ for $\bar{x}_n$.

We assume $\mathcal{F}$ contains a family $@ : (\bar{\tau}_n \to \tau) \times \tau_1 \to (\tau_2 \times \cdots \times \tau_n \to \tau)$ of *application symbols* for all $n > 1$. We use it to model (curried) applications of terms of functional sort $\bar{\tau}_n \to \tau$. For example, given a function symbol $\mathsf{f} : \tau_1 \times \tau_2 \to \tau_3$ and application symbols $@ : (\tau_1 \times \tau_2 \to \tau_3) \times \tau_1 \to (\tau_2 \to \tau_3)$ and $@ : (\tau_2 \to \tau_3) \times \tau_2 \to \tau_3$, $@(\mathsf{f}, t_1)$ and $@(@(\mathsf{f}, t_1), t_2)$ have, respectively, the same denotation as $\lambda x_2 : \tau_2.\mathsf{f}(t_1, x_2)$ and $\mathsf{f}(t_1, t_2)$.

An *applicative encoding* is a well-known approach for performing HO reasoning using FO provers. This encoding converts every functional sort into an atomic sort, every n-ary symbol into a nullary symbol, and uses $@$ to encode applications. Thus, all applications, partial or not, become total, and quantification over functional variables becomes quantification over regular FO variables. We adopt Henkin semantics [10,27] with extensionality and choice, as is standard in automatic HO theorem proving.

2.1 SMT Solvers and Quantified Reasoning

SMT solvers that process quantified formulas can be seen as containing three main components: a preprocessing module, a ground solver, and an instantiation module. Given an input formula φ, the preprocessing module applies various transformations (for instance, Skolemization, clausification and so on) to it to obtain another, equisatisfiable, formula φ'. The ground solver operates on the formula φ'. It abstracts all of its atoms and quantified formulas and treats them as if they were propositional variables. The solver for ground formulas provides an *assignment* $E \cup Q$, where E is a set of ground literals and Q is a set of quantified formulas appearing in φ', such that $E \cup Q$ propositionally entails φ'. The ground solver then determines the satisfiability of E according to a decision procedure for a combination of background theories. If E is satisfiable, the instantiation module of the solver generates new *instances*, ground formulas of the form $\neg(\forall \bar{x}.\, \psi) \vee \psi\sigma$ where $\forall \bar{x}.\, \psi$ is a quantified formula in Q and σ is a substitution from the variables in $\bar{x}$ to ground terms. These instances will be, after preprocessing, added conjunctively to the input of the ground solver, which will proceed to derive a new assignment $E' \cup Q'$, if possible. This interplay may terminate either if φ' is proven unsatisfiable or if a model is found for an assignment $E \cup Q$ that is also a model of φ'.

Extending SMT solvers to HOL can be achieved by extending these three components so that: (1) the preprocessing module eliminates λ-abstractions; (2) the ground decision procedure supports a ground extensional logic with partial applications, which we denote QF_HOSMT; and (3) the instantiation module instantiates variables of functional type and takes into account partial applications and equations between functions. We can perform each of these tasks pragmatically without heavily modifying the solver, which is useful when extending highly optimized state-of-the-art SMT solvers (Sect. 3). Alternatively, we can perform these extensions in a more principled way by redesigning the solver, which better suits lightweight solvers (Sect. 4).

3   A Pragmatic Extension for HOSMT

We pragmatically extend the ground SMT solver to QF_HOSMT by removing λ-expressions (Sect. 3.1), checking ground satisfiability (Sect. 3.2), and generating models (Sect. 3.3). Extensions to the instantiation module are discussed in Sect. 3.4.

3.1   Eliminating λ-Abstractions and Partial Applications of Theory Symbols

To ensure that the formulas that reach the core solving algorithm are λ-free, a preprocessing pass is used to first eliminate λ-applications and then eliminate any remaining λ-abstractions. The former are eliminated via β-reduction, with each application $(\lambda \bar{x}. t[\bar{x}])\bar{u}$ replaced by the equivalent term $t[\bar{u}]$. The substitution renames bound variables in t as needed to avoid capture.

Two main approaches exist for eliminating (non-applied) λ-abstractions: reduction to combinators [35] and λ-lifting [28]. Combinators allow λ-terms to be synthesized during solving without the need for HO unification. This translation, however, introduces a large number of quantifiers and often leads to performance loss [13, Sect. 6.4.2]. We instead apply λ-lifting in our pragmatic extension.

In λ-lifting, each λ-abstraction is replaced by a fresh function symbol, and a quantified formula is introduced to define the symbol in terms of the original expression. Note this is similar to the typical approach used for eliminating ITE expressions in SMT solvers. The new function takes as arguments the variables bound by the respective λ-abstraction and the free variables occurring in its body. More precisely, λ-abstractions of the form $\lambda \bar{x}_n. t[\bar{x}_n, \bar{y}_m]$ of type $\bar{\tau}_n \to \tau$ with $\bar{y}_m : \bar{v}_m$ occurring in a formula φ are lifted to (possibly partial) applications $f(\bar{y}_m)$ where f is a fresh function symbol of type $\bar{v}_m \times \bar{\tau}_n \to \tau$. Moreover, the formula $\forall \bar{y}_m \bar{x}_n. f(\bar{y}_m, \bar{x}_n) \simeq t[\bar{x}_n, \bar{y}_m]$ is added conjunctively to φ. To minimize the number of new functions and quantified formulas introduced, eliminated expressions are cached so that the same definition can be reused.

In the presence of a background theory T, the norm in SMT, a previous preprocessing step is also needed to make all applications of theory, or *interpreted*, symbols total: each term of the form $h(\bar{t}_m)$, where $h : \bar{\tau}_n \to \tau$ is a symbol of T and $m < n$, is converted to $\lambda \bar{x}_{n-m}.h(\bar{t}_m, \bar{x}_{n-m})$, which is then λ-lifted as above to an uninterpreted symbol f, defined by the quantified formula $\forall \bar{y} \forall \bar{x}_{n-m}.f(\bar{x}_{n-m}) \simeq h(\bar{t}_m, \bar{x}_{n-m})$, with $\bar{y}$ collecting the free variables of $\bar{t}_m$.

We stress that careful engineering is required to perform λ-lifting correctly in an SMT solver not originally designed for it. For instance, using the existing machinery for ITE removal may be insufficient, since this may not properly handle instances occurring inside binders or as the head of applications.

3.2   Extending the Ground Solver to QF_HOSMT

Since we operate after preprocessing in a λ-free setting in which only uninterpreted functions may occur partially applied, lifting the ground solver to QF_HOSMT amounts to extending the solver for ground literals in the theory of Equality and Uninterpreted Functions (EUF) to handle partial applications and extensionality.

The decision procedure for ground EUF adopted by SMT solvers is based on classical congruence closure algorithms [24,31]. While the procedure is easily extensible to HOL (with partial applications but no λ-abstractions) via a uniform applicative encoding [32], many SMT solvers require that function symbols occurring in (FO) terms be fully applied. Instead of redesigning the solver to accommodate partial applications, we apply a *lazy applicative encoding* where only partial applications are converted.

Concretely, during term construction, all partial applications are converted to total applications by means of the binary symbol @, while fully applied terms are kept in their regular representation. Determining the satisfiability of a set of EUF constraints E containing terms in both representations is done in two phases: if E is determined to be satisfiable by the regular first-order procedure, we introduce equalities between regular terms (i.e., fully applied terms without the @ symbol) and their applicative counterpart and recheck the satisfiability of the resulting set of constraints. However, we only introduce these equalities for regular terms which interact with partially applied ones. This interaction is characterized by function symbols appearing as members of congruence classes in the *E-graph*, the congruence closure of E built by the EUF decision procedure. A function symbol occurs in an equivalence class if it is an argument of an @ symbol or if it appears in an equality between function symbols. The equalities between regular terms and their applicative encodings are kept internal to the E-graph, therefore not affecting other parts of the ground decision procedure.

Example 1. Given $f : \tau \times \tau \to \tau$, $g, h : \tau \to \tau$ and $a : \tau$, consider the set of constraints $E = \{@(f, a) \simeq g, f(a, a) \not\simeq g(a), g(a) \simeq h(a)\}$. We have that E is initially found to be satisfiable. However, since f and g occur partially applied, we augment the set of constraints with a correspondence between the HO and FO applications of f, g:

$$E' = E \cup \{@(@(f, a), a) \simeq f(a, a), @(g, a) \simeq g(a)\}$$

When determining the satisfiability of E', the equality $@(@(f, a), a) \simeq @(g, a)$ will be derived by congruence and hence, $f(a, a) \simeq g(a)$ will be derived by transitivity, leading to a conflict. Notice that we do not require equalities between fully applied terms whose functions *do not* appear in the E-graph and their equivalent in the applicative encoding. In particular, the equality $h(a) \simeq @(h, a)$ is not introduced in this example.   •

$$\frac{t \in \mathbf{T}(E)}{t \simeq t} \text{ REFL} \qquad \frac{t \simeq u}{u \simeq t} \text{ SYM} \qquad \frac{s \simeq t, \, t \simeq u}{s \simeq u} \text{ TRANS}$$

$$\frac{\bar{t}_n \simeq \bar{u}_n \quad f(\bar{t}_n), f(\bar{u}_n) \in \mathbf{T}(E)}{f(\bar{t}_n) \simeq f(\bar{u}_n)} \text{ CONG} \qquad \frac{t \simeq u, \, t \not\simeq u}{\bot} \text{ CONFLICT}$$

$$\frac{f(\bar{t}_n), f \in \mathbf{T}(E)}{f(\bar{t}_n) \simeq @(\dots (@(f, t_1), \dots), t_n)} \text{ APP-ENCODE}$$

$$\frac{f \not\simeq g \quad f, g : \bar{\tau}_n \to \tau \quad n > 0}{f(sk_1, \dots, sk_n) \not\simeq g(sk_1, \dots, sk_n)} \text{ EXTENSIONALITY}$$

where $sk_1, \dots, sk_n$ are fresh symbols of respective sorts $\tau_1, \dots, \tau_n$.

Fig. 1. Derivation rules for checking satisfiability of QF_HOSMT constraints in EUF.

We formalize the above procedure via the calculus in Fig. 1. The derivation rules operate on a current set E of constraints. A derivation rule can be applied if its premises are met. A rule's conclusion either adds an equality literal to E or replaces it by $\bot$ to indicate unsatisfiability. A rule application is *redundant* if its conclusion leaves E unchanged. A constraint set is *saturated* if it admits only redundant rule applications.

Rules REFL, SYM, TRANS, CONG and CONFLICT are standard for EUF decision procedures based on congruence closure, i.e., the smallest superset of a set of equations that is closed under entailment in the theory of equality. The rule APP-ENCODE equates a full application to its applicative encoding equivalent, and it is applied only to applications of functions which occur as subterms in E. As mentioned above, this can only be the case if the function itself appears as an argument of an application, which happens when it is partially applied (as argument of @ or $\simeq$).

Rule EXTENSIONALITY is similar to how extensionality is handled in decision procedures for extensional arrays [21,44]. If two non-nullary functions are disequal in E, then a witness of their disequality is introduced. The extensionality property is characterized by the axiom $\forall \bar{x}_n. \, f(\bar{x}_n) \simeq g(\bar{x}_n) \Leftrightarrow f \simeq g$, for all functions f and g of the same type. The rule ensures the left-to-right direction of the axiom (the opposite one is ensured by APP-ENCODE together with the congruence closure rules). To simplify the presentation we assume that, for every term $@(\ldots (@(\mathsf{f}, t_1), \ldots), t_m) : \bar{\tau}_n \to \tau \in \mathbf{T}(E)$, there is a fresh symbol $\mathsf{f}' : \bar{\tau}_n \to \tau$ such that $@(\ldots (@(\mathsf{f}, t_1), \ldots), t_m) \simeq \mathsf{f}' \in E$.

Example 2. Consider the function symbols $\mathsf{f}, \mathsf{g} : \tau \to \tau$, $\mathsf{a} : \tau$, and the set of constraints $E = \{\mathsf{f} \simeq \mathsf{g}, \mathsf{f}(\mathsf{a}) \not\simeq \mathsf{g}(\mathsf{a})\}$. The constraints are initially satisfiable with respect to the congruence closure rules, however, since $\mathsf{f}, \mathsf{g} \in \mathbf{T}(E)$, the rule APP-ENCODE will be applied twice to derive $\mathsf{f}(\mathsf{a}) \simeq @(\mathsf{f}, \mathsf{a})$ and $\mathsf{g}(\mathsf{a}) \simeq @(\mathsf{g}, \mathsf{a})$. Then, via CONG, from $\mathsf{f} \simeq \mathsf{g}$ we infer $@(\mathsf{f}, \mathsf{a}) \simeq @(\mathsf{g}, \mathsf{a})$, which leads to a conflict via transitivity.   •

Decision Procedure. Any derivation strategy for the calculus that does not stop until it saturates or generates $\perp$ yields a decision procedure for the satisfiability of QF_HOSMT constraints in the EUF theory, according to the following results for the calculus.

Proposition 1 (Termination). *Every sequence of non-redundant rule applications is finite.*

Proposition 2 (Refutation Soundness). *A constraint set is unsatisfiable if $\perp$ is derivable from it.*

Proposition 3 (Solution Soundness). *Every saturated constraint set is satisfiable.*

Even though we could apply the rules in any order, for better performance we only apply APP-ENCODE and EXTENSIONALITY once other rules have only redundant applications. Moreover, APP-ENCODE has precedence over EXTENSIONALITY.

3.3   Model Generation for Ground Formulas

When our decision procedure for QF_HOSMT saturates, it can produce a first-order model M as a witness for the satisfiability of its input. Typically, the models generated by SMT solvers for theories in first-order logic map uninterpreted functions $\mathsf{f} : \bar{\tau}_n \to \tau$ to functions, denoted $M(\mathsf{f})$, of the form

$$\lambda \bar{x}_n. \, \mathsf{ite}(x_1 \simeq t_1^1 \wedge \ldots x_n \simeq t_n^1, s_1, \ldots, \mathsf{ite}(x_1 \simeq t_1^{m-1} \wedge \ldots x_n \simeq t_n^{m-1}, s_{m-1}, s_m) \ldots)$$

in which every entry but the last corresponds to an application $\mathsf{f}(t_1^i, \ldots, t_n^i)$, modulo congruence, occurring in the problem. In other words, functions are interpreted in models M as almost constant functions.

In the presence of partial applications, this scheme can sometimes lead to functions with exponentially many entries. For example, consider the satisfiable formula

$$\mathsf{f}_1(\mathsf{a}) \simeq \mathsf{f}_1(\mathsf{b}) \wedge \mathsf{f}_1(\mathsf{b}) \simeq \mathsf{f}_2 \wedge \mathsf{f}_2(\mathsf{a}) \simeq \mathsf{f}_2(\mathsf{b}) \wedge \mathsf{f}_2(\mathsf{b}) \simeq \mathsf{f}_3 \wedge \mathsf{f}_3(\mathsf{a}) \simeq \mathsf{f}_3(\mathsf{b}) \wedge \mathsf{f}_3(\mathsf{b}) \simeq \mathsf{c}$$

in which $f_1 : \tau \times \tau \times \tau \to \tau$, $f_2 : \tau \times \tau \to \tau$, $f_3 : \tau \to \tau$, and $a, b, c : \tau$. To produce the model values of f_1 as a list of total applications with three arguments into an element of the interpretation of τ, we would need to account for 8 cases. In other words, we require 8 ite cases to indicate $f_1(x, y, z) \simeq c$ for all inputs where $x, y, z \in \{a, b\}$. The number of entries in the model is exponential on the "depth" of the chain of functions that each partial application is equal to, which can make model building unfeasible if just a few functions are chained as in the above example.

To avoid such an exponential behavior, model building assigns values for functions in terms of the other functions that their partial applications are equated to. In the above example f_1 would have only two model values, depending on its application's first argument being a or b, by using the model values of f_2 applied on its two other arguments. In other words, we construct $M(f_1)$ as the term:

$$\lambda xyz.\, \mathsf{ite}(x \simeq a,\, M(f_2)(y, z), \mathsf{ite}(x \simeq b,\, M(f_2)(y, z), \_))$$

where $M(f_2)$ is the model for f_2 and $\_$ is an arbitrary value. The model value of f_2 would be analogously built in terms of the model value of f_3. This guarantees a polynomial construction for models in terms of the number of constraints in the problem in the presence of partial applications.

Extensionality and Finite Sorts. Model construction assigns different values to terms not asserted equal. Therefore, if non-nullary functions $f, g : \bar{\tau}_n \to \tau$ occur as terms in different congruence classes but are not asserted disequal, we ensure they are assigned different model values by introducing disequalities of the form $f(\bar{sk}_n) \not\simeq g(\bar{sk}_n)$ for fresh $\bar{sk}_n$. This is necessary because model values for functions are built based on their applications occurring in the constraint set. However, such disequalities are only always guaranteed to be satisfied if $\bar{\tau}_n, \tau$ are infinite sorts.

Example 3. Let E be a saturated set of constraints s.t. $p_1, p_2, p_3 : \tau \to o \in \mathbf{T}(E)$ and $E \not\models p_1 \simeq p_2 \vee p_1 \simeq p_3 \vee p_2 \simeq p_3 \vee p_1 \not\simeq p_2 \vee p_1 \not\simeq p_3 \vee p_2 \not\simeq p_3$. In the congruence closure of E the functions p_1, p_2, p_3 each occur in a different congruence class but are not asserted disequal, so a naive model construction would, in order to build their model values, introduce disequalities $p_1(sk_1) \not\simeq p_2(sk_1)$, $p_1(sk_2) \not\simeq p_3(sk_2)$, and $p_2(sk_3) \not\simeq p_3(sk_3)$, for fresh $sk_1, sk_2, sk_3 : \tau$. However, if τ has cardinality one these disequalities make E unsatisfiable, since sk_1, sk_2, sk_3 must be equal and o has cardinality 2. $\qquad\bullet$

To prevent this issue, whenever the set of constraints E is saturated, we introduce, for every pair of functions $f, g : \bar{\tau}_n \to \tau \in \mathbf{T}(E)$ s.t. $n > 0$ and $E \not\models f \simeq g \vee f \not\simeq g$, the splitting lemma $f \simeq g \vee f \not\simeq g$. In the above example this would amount to add the lemmas $p_1 \simeq p_2 \vee p_1 \not\simeq p_2$, $p_1 \simeq p_3 \vee p_1 \not\simeq p_3$, and $p_2 \simeq p_3 \vee p_2 \not\simeq p_3$, thus ensuring that the decision procedure detects the inconsistency before saturation.

3.4   Extending the Quantifier Instantiation Module to HOMST

The main quantifier instantiation techniques in SMT solving are trigger-based [22], conflict-based [4,38], model-based [26,40], and enumerative [37]. Lifting any of them to HOSMT presents its own challenges. We focus here on extending the E-matching [20] algorithm, the keystone of trigger-based instantiation, the most commonly used technique in SMT solvers. In this technique, instantiations are chosen for quantified formulas φ based on *triggers*. A trigger is a term (or set of terms) containing the free variables occurring in φ. Matching a trigger term against ground terms in the current set of assertions E results in a substitution that is used to instantiate φ.

The presence of higher-order constraints poses several challenges for E-matching. First, notice that the @ symbol is an overloaded operator. Applications of this symbol can be selected as terms that appear in triggers. Special care must be taken so that applications of @ are not matched with ground applications of @ whose arguments have different types. Second, functions can be equated in higher-order logic. As a consequence, a match may involve a trigger term and a ground term with different head symbols. Third, since we use a lazy applicative encoding, our ground set of terms may contain a mixture of partially and fully applied function applications. Thus, our indexing techniques must be robust to handle combinations of the two. The following example demonstrates the last two challenges.

Example 4. Consider E with the equality @$(f, a) \simeq g$ and the term $f(a, b)$ where $f : \tau \times \tau \to \tau$ and $g : \tau \to \tau$. Notice that $g(x)$ is equivalent modulo E to the term $f(a, b)$ under the substitution $x \mapsto b$. Such a match is found by indexing all terms that are applications of *either* @(f, a) or g in a common term index. This ensures when matching $g(x)$, the term $f(a, b)$, whose applicative counterpart is @$(@(f, a), b)$, is considered.

We extended the regular first-order E-matching algorithm of CVC4 as described in this section. Extensions to the other instantiation techniques of CVC4, such as model-based quantifier instantiation, are left as future work.

Extending Expressivity via Axioms. Even though not synthesizing λ-abstractions prevents us from fully lifting the above instantiation techniques to HOL, we remark that, as we see in Sect. 5, this pragmatic extension very often can prove HO theorems, many times even at higher rates than full-fledged HO provers. Success rates can be further improved by using well-chosen axioms to prove problems that otherwise cannot be proved without synthesizing λ-abstractions.

Example 5. Consider the ground formula $\varphi = a \not\simeq b$ with a, b of sort τ and the quantified formula $\psi = \forall F, G : \tau \to \tau. F \simeq G$. Intuitively ψ states that all functions of sort $\tau \to \tau$ are equal. However, this is inconsistent with φ, which forces τ to contain at least two elements and therefore $\tau \to \tau$ to contain at least four functions. For a prover to detect this inconsistency it must apply an instantiation like $\{F \mapsto (\lambda w.\, \mathsf{a}),\, G \mapsto (\lambda w.\, \mathsf{b})\}$ to ψ, which would need HO unification. However, adding the axiom

$$\forall F : \tau \to \tau.\, \forall x, y : \tau.\, \exists G : \tau \to \tau.\, \forall z : \tau.\, G(z) \simeq \mathsf{ite}(z \simeq x,\, y,\, F(z)) \qquad \text{(SAX)}$$

makes the problem provable without the need to synthesize λ-abstractions.   •

We denote the above axiom as the *store axiom* (SAX) because it simulates how arrays are updated via the store operation. As we note in Sect. 5, introducing this axiom for all functional sorts occurring in the problem often allows our pragmatically extended solver to prove problems it would not be able to prove otherwise. Intuitively, the reason is that instances can be generated not only from terms in the original problem, but also from the larger set of functions representable in the formula signature.

4 Redesigning a Solver for HOSMT

In the previous section we discussed how to address the challenges of HO reasoning in SMT while minimally changing the SMT solver. Alternatively, we can redesign the solver to support HO features directly. However, this requires a redesign of the core data structures and algorithms. We propose one such redesign below. We again assume that the solver operates on formulas with no λ-abstraction and no partial applications of theory symbols, which can be achieved via preprocessing (Sect. 3.1).

4.1 Redesigning the Core Ground Solver for HOSMT

Efficient implementations of the congruence closure (CC) procedure for EUF reasoning operate on Union-Find data structures and have asymptotic time complexity $\mathcal{O}(n \log n)$. To accommodate partial applications, we propose a simpler algorithm which operates on an E-graph where nodes are terms, and edges are relations (equality, congruence, disequality) between them. An equivalence class is a connected component without disequality edges. All operations on the graph (incremental addition of new constraints, backtracking, conflict analysis, proof production) are implemented straightforwardly. This simpler implementation comes at the cost of higher worse-case time complexity (the CC algorithm becomes quadratic) but integrates better with various other features such as term addition, support of injective functions, rewriting or even computation, in particular for β- and η-conversion, which now can be done during solving rather than as preprocessing. In the redesigned approach, the solver keeps two term representations, a curried representation and a regular one. In the regular one, partial and total applications are distinguished by type information. The curried representation is used only by the congruence closure algorithm. It is integrated with the rest of the solver via an interface with translation functions **curry** and **uncurry** between the two different representations. For conciseness, instead of writing $@(\ldots (@(\mathsf{f}, t_1), \ldots), t_n)$ below, we use the curried notation $(\cdots ((\mathsf{f}\ t_1) \cdots)\ t_n)$, omitting parenthesis when unambiguous.

Example 6. Given $f : \tau \times \tau \to \tau$, $g, h : \tau \to \tau$ and $a : \tau$, consider the constraints $\{f(a) \simeq g,\ f(a, a) \not\simeq g(a),\ g(a) \simeq h(a)\}$. The congruence closure module will operate on $\{f\,a \simeq g,\ f\,a\,a \not\simeq g\,a,\ g\,a \simeq h\,a\}$, thanks to the curry translation. •

SMT solvers generally perform theory combination via equalities over terms shared between different theories. Given the different term representations kept between the CC procedure and the rest of the solver, to ensure that theory combination is done properly, the redesigned core ground solver keeps track of terms shared with other theory solvers. Whenever an equality is inferred on a term whose translation is shared with another theory, a shared equality is sent out in terms of the translation.

Example 7. Consider the function symbols $f : \text{Int} \to \text{Int}$, $p : \text{Int} \to o$, a, b, $c_1, c_2, c_3, c_4 : \text{Int}$, the set of arithmetic constraints $\{a \leq b,\ b \leq a,\ p(f(a) - f(b)),\ \neg p(0),\ c_1 \simeq c_3 - c_4,\ c_2 \simeq 0\}$, and the set of curried equality constraints $E = \{p\,c_1,\ \neg(p\,c_2),\ c_3 \simeq f\,a,\ c_4 \simeq f\,b\}$. The equalities $c_3 \simeq f\,a$ and $c_4 \simeq f\,b$ keep track of the fact that $f\,a$ and $f\,b$ are shared. The arithmetic module deduces $a \simeq b$, which is added to $E' = E \cup \{a \simeq b\}$. By congruence, $f\,a \simeq f\,b$ is derived, which propagates $c_3 \simeq c_4$ to the arithmetic solver. With this new equality, arithmetic reasoning derives $c_1 \simeq c_2$, whose addition to the equality constraints produces the unsatisfiable constraint set $E' \cup \{c_1 \simeq c_2\}$. •

Extensionality. The EXTENSIONALITY rule (Fig. 1) is sufficient for handling extensionality at the ground level. However, it has shortcomings when quantifiers, even just first-order ones, are considered, as shown in the example below. In the redesigned solver, extensionality is better handled via axioms.

Example 8. Consider the constraints $E = \{h\,f \simeq b,\ h\,g \not\simeq b,\ \forall x.\, f(x) \simeq a,\ \forall x.\, g(x) \simeq a\}$, with $h : \tau \to \tau \to \tau$, $f, g : \tau \to \tau$, $a, b : \tau$. The pragmatic solver could prove this problem unsatisfiable only with a ground decision procedure that derives consequences of disequalities, since deriving $f \not\simeq g$ is necessary to derive $f(\mathsf{sk}) \not\simeq g(\mathsf{sk})$, via extensionality, which then leads to a conflict. But SMT solvers are well known not to propagate all disequalities for efficiency considerations. In contrast, with the axiom $\forall F, G : \bar{\tau}_n \to \tau.\, F \not\simeq G \Rightarrow F(\mathsf{sk}_1, \ldots, \mathsf{sk}_n) \not\simeq G(\mathsf{sk}_1, \ldots, \mathsf{sk}_n)$, the instantiation $\{F \mapsto f,\ G \mapsto g\}$ (which may be derived, e.g., via enumerative instantiation, since $f, g \in \mathbf{T}(E)$), provides the splitting lemma $f \simeq g \vee f(\mathsf{sk}) \not\simeq g(\mathsf{sk})$. The case $E \cup \{f \simeq g\}$ leads to a conflict by pure ground reasoning, while the case $E \cup \{f\,\mathsf{sk} \not\simeq g\,\mathsf{sk}\}$ leads to a conflict from the instances $f(\mathsf{sk}) \simeq a$, $g(\mathsf{sk}) \simeq a$ of the quantified formulas in E. •

4.2 Quantifier Instantiation Module

In the pragmatic approach, the challenges for the E-matching procedure lied in properly accounting for the @ symbol, functional equality, and the mixture of partial and total applications, all of which lead to different term representations, in the term indexing data structure. In the redesign approach, the second challenge remains the same, and term indexing is extended in the same manner of Sect. 3.4 to cope with it. The first and third challenge present themselves in a different way, however, since the curried representation of terms is only used inside the E-graph of the new CC procedure. To apply E-matching properly, term indexing is extended to perform query by types, returning all the subterms of a given type that occur in the E-graph, but translated back to the uncurried representation.

Example 9. Consider $E = \{f(a, g(b, c)) \simeq a, \forall F. F(a) \simeq h, \forall y. h(y) \not\simeq a\}$ and the set of triggers $\{F(a), h(y)\}$ where $a, b, c : \tau$, $h : \tau \to \tau$ and $f, g : \tau \times \tau \to \tau$. The set of ground curried terms in E is $\{f\,a\,(g\,b\,c), f\,a, g\,b, g\,b\,c, f, g, a, b, c\}$. To do E-matching with $F(a)$ and $h(y)$ the index returns the sets of uncurried subterms $\{f(a, g(b, c)), a, g(b, c), b, c\}$ and $\{f(a), g(b)\}$ for the types τ and $\tau \to \tau$, respectively. •

Since we do not perform HO unification, to instantiate functional variables it suffices to extend the standard E-matching algorithm applied by SMT solvers by accounting for function applications with variable heads. When matching a term $F(\bar{s}_n)$ with a ground term t the procedure essentially matches F with the head of ground terms $f(\bar{t}_n)$ congruent to t, as long as each s_i in $\bar{s}_n$ can be matched with each t_i in $\bar{t}_n$. In the above example, matching the trigger $F(a)$ with the term $f(a)$ yields the substitution $\{F \mapsto f\}$.

5 Evaluation

We have implemented the above techniques in the state-of-the-art CVC4 solver and in the lightweight veriT solvers. We distinguish between two main versions of each solver: one that performs a full applicative encoding (Sect. 2) into FOL a priori, denoted @cvc and @vt, and another that implements the pragmatic (Sects. 3) or redesigned (Sect. 4) extensions to HOL within the solvers, denoted cvc and vt. Both CVC4 modes eliminate λ-abstractions via λ-lifting. Neither veriT configuration supports benchmarks with λ-abstractions. The CVC4 configurations that employ the "store axiom" (Sect. 3.4) are denoted by having the suffix -sax.

We use the state-of-the-art HO provers Leo-III [43], Satallax [17,25] and Ehoh [42,48] as baselines in our evaluation. The first two have refutationally complete calculi for extensional HOL with Henkin semantics, while the third only supports λ-free HOL without first-class Booleans. For Leo-III and Satallax we use their configurations from the CASC competition [47], while for Ehoh we report on their best non-portfolio configuration from Vukmirović et al., Ehoh hb, [48].

We split our account between the case of proving HO theorems and that of producing countermodels for HO conjectures since the two require different strengths from the system considered. We discus only two of them, CVC4 and Satallax, for the second evaluation. The reason is that Leo-III and veriT do not provide models and Ehoh is not model-sound with respect to Henkin semantics, only with respect to λ-free Henkin semantics. We ran our experiments on a cluster equipped with Intel E5-2637 v4 CPUs running Ubuntu 16.04, providing one core, 60 s, and 8 GB RAM for each job. The full experimental data is publicly available.[1]

We consider the following sets[2] of HO benchmarks: the 3,188 monomorphic HO benchmarks in TPTP [46], split into three subsets: the 530 problems that are both λ-free and without first-class Booleans (TH0); the 743 that are only λ-free (oTH0); and the 1,915 that are neither (λoTH0). The next sets are Sledgehammer (SH) benchmarks from the Judgment Day test harness [15], consisting of 1,253 provable goals *manually* chosen from different Isabelle theories [34] and encoded into λ-free monomorphic HOL problems without first-class Booleans. The encoded problems are such that they are provable only if the original goal is. These problems are split into four subsets, JD_{lift}^{32}, JD_{combs}^{32}, JD_{lift}^{512}, and JD_{combs}^{512} depending, respectively, on whether they have 32 or 512 Isabelle lemmas, or facts, and whether λ-abstractions are removed via λ-lifting or via SK-style combinators. The last set, $λoSH^{1024}$, has 832 SH benchmarks from 832 provable goals *randomly* selected from different Isabelle theories, encoded with 1,024 facts and preserving λs and first-class Booleans. Considering a varying number of facts in the SH benchmarks emulates the needs of increasingly larger problems in interactive verification, while different λ handling schemes allow us to measure from which alternative each particular solver benefits more.

We point out that our extensions of CVC4 and veriT do not significantly compromise their performance on FO benchmarks. The pragmatic extension of CVC4 has virtually the same performance as the original solver on SMT-LIB [7], the standard SMT test suite. The redesigned veriT does have a considerably lower performance. However, while it is, for example, three times slower on the QF_UF category of SMT-LIB due to its slower ground solver for EUF, it still performs better on this category than CVC4. This shows that despite the added cost of supporting higher-order reasoning, the FO performance of veriT is still on par with the state of the art.

5.1   Proving HO Theorems

The number of theorems proved by each solver configuration per benchmark set is given in Table 1. Grayed out cells represent unsupported benchmark sets. Figure 2 compares benchmarks solved per time. It only includes benchmark sets supported by all solvers (namely TH0 and the JD benchmarks).

As expected, the results vary significantly between benchmark sets. Leo-III and Satallax have a clear advantage on TPTP, which contains a significant number of small logical problems meant to exercise the HO features of a prover. Considering the TPTP benchmarks from less to more expressive, i.e., including first-class Booleans and then λs, we see the advantages of these systems only

---

[1] http://matryoshka.gforge.inria.fr/pubs/hosmt/.

[2] Since veriT does not parse TPTP, its reported results are on the equivalent benchmarks as translated by CVC4 into the HOSMT language [3].

Table 1. Proved theorems per benchmark set. Best results are in **bold**.

Solver	Total	TH0	oTH0	λoTH0	$\mathrm{JD}^{32}_{\mathrm{lift}}$	$\mathrm{JD}^{32}_{\mathrm{combs}}$	$\mathrm{JD}^{512}_{\mathrm{lift}}$	$\mathrm{JD}^{512}_{\mathrm{combs}}$	$\lambda o\mathrm{SH}^{1024}$
#	9032	530	743	1915	1253	1253	1253	1253	832
@cvc	4318	384	344	940	457	459	655	667	**412**
@cvc-sax	4348	390	373	937	456	457	655	**668**	**412**
cvc	4232	389	342	865	463	447	**667**	654	405
cvc-sax	4275	389	376	883	458	443	**667**	654	405
Leo-III	**4410**	**402**	452	1178	**491**	**482**	609	565	231
Satallax	3961	392	**457**	**1215**	394	390	407	404	302
@vt		370	332		404	396	525	529	
vt		369	346		426	424	550	556	
Ehoh		394			489	481	637	630	

increase. We also observe that both @cvc and cvc, but especially the latter, benefit from -sax as more complex benchmarks are considered in TPTP, showing that the disadvantage of not synthesizing λ-abstractions can sometimes be offset by well-chosen axioms. Nevertheless, the results on λoTH0 show that this axiom alone is far from enough to offset the gap between @cvc and cvc, with cvc giving up more often from lack of instantiations to perform.

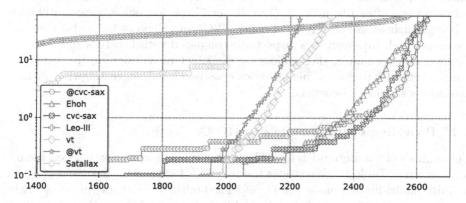

Fig. 2. Execution times in secs on 5,543 benchmarks, from TH0 and JD, supported by all solvers.

Sledgehammer-generated problems stem from formalization efforts across different applications. As others note [45, 48], the bottleneck in solving these problems is often scalability and efficient FO reasoning, rather than a refined handling of HO constructs, especially as more facts are considered. Thus, the ability to synthesize λ-abstractions is not sufficient for scalability as more facts are considered, and Ehoh and the CVC4 extensions eventually surpass the native HO provers. In particular, in the largest set we considered, $\lambda o\mathrm{SH}^{1024}$, both @cvc and cvc have significant advantages. As in λoTH0, @cvc also solves more problems than cvc in $\lambda o\text{SH}^{1024}$, which we attribute again to @cvc being able to perform more instantiations than cvc On commonly solved problems, however, cvc is often faster than @cvc, albeit by a small margin: 15% on average.

Both CVC4 configurations dominate JD^{512} with a significantly margin over Ehoh and Leo-III. Comparing the results between using λ-lifting or combinators, the former favors cvc and the latter, @cvc. These results, as well as the previously discussed ones, indicate that for unsatisfiable benchmarks the pragmatic extension of CVC4 should not, in its current state, substitute an encoding-based approach but complement it. In fact, a virtual best solver of all the CVC4 configurations, as well as others employing interleaved enumerative instantiation [37], in portfolio, would solve 703 problems in $\text{JD}^{512}_{\text{lift}}$, 702 in $\text{JD}^{512}_{\text{combs}}$, 453 in $\lambda o\text{SH}^{1024}$, and 408 in TH0, the most in these categories, even also considering a virtual best solver of all Ehoh configurations from [48]. The CVC4 portfolio would also solve 482 problems in $\text{JD}^{32}_{\text{lift}}$, and 482 in $\text{JD}^{32}_{\text{combs}}$, doing almost as well as Leo-III, and 1,001 problems in $\lambda o\text{TH0}$, The virtual best CVC4 has a success rate 3% points higher than @cvc on Sledgehammer benchmarks, as well as overall, which represents a significant improvement when considering the usage of these solvers as backends for interactive theorem provers.

Differently from the pragmatic extension in CVC4, which provides more of an alternative to the full applicative encoding, the redesigned veriT is an outright improvement, with vt consistently solving more problems and with better solving times than @vt, especially on harder problems, as seen by the wider separation between them after 10s in Fig. 2. Overall, veriT's performance, consistently with it being a lightweight solver, lags behind CVC4 and Ehoh as bigger benchmarks are considered. However, it is respectable compared with Leo-III's and ahead of Satallax's performance, thus validating the effort of redesigning the solver for a more refined handling of higher-order constructs and suggesting that further extensions should be beneficial.

5.2   Providing Countermodels to HO Conjectures

The number of countermodels found by each solver configuration per benchmark set is given in Table 2. We consider the two CVC4 extension, @cvc and cvc, run in finite-model-finding mode (-fmf) [39]. The builtin HO support in cvc is vastly superior to @cvc when it comes to model finding, as cvc-fmf greatly outperforms @cvc-fmf-sax. We note that @cvc-fmf is only model-sound if combined with -sax.

Table 2. Conjectures with found countermodels per benchmark set. Best results in **bold**.

Solver	Total	TH0	oTH0	λoTH0	$\text{JD}^{32}_{\text{lift}}$	$\text{JD}^{32}_{\text{combs}}$	$\text{JD}^{512}_{\text{lift}}$	$\text{JD}^{512}_{\text{combs}}$	$\lambda o\text{SH}^{1024}$
#	9032	530	743	1915	1253	1253	1253	1253	832
@cvc-fmf-sax	224	58	**43**	80	20	18	1	1	**3**
cvc-fmf	**482**	**90**	17	**205**	**93**	**73**	1	1	2
Satallax	186	72	15	98	0	0	0	0	1

Differently from cvc-fmf, which fails to provide a model as soon as it is faced with quantification over a functional sort, in @cvc-fmf functional sorts are encoded as atomic sorts. Thus it needs the extra axiom to ensure model soundness. For example, @cvc-fmf considers Example 5 satisfiable while @cvc-fmf-sax properly reports it unsatisfiable.

The high number of countermodels in JD^{32} indicates, not surprisingly, that providing few facts makes several SH goals unprovable. Nevertheless, it is still useful to know where exactly the Sledgehammer generation is being "incomplete" (i.e., making originally provable goals unprovable), something that is difficult to determine without effective model finding procedures.

6 Concluding Remarks

We have presented extensions for SMT solvers to handle HOSMT problems. The pragmatic extension of CVC4, which can be implemented in other state-of-the-art SMT solver with similar level of effort, performs similarly to the standard encoding-based approach despite its limited support for HO instantiation. Moreover, it allows numerous new problems to be solved by CVC4, with a portfolio approach performing very competitively and often ahead of state-of-the-art HO provers. The redesigned veriT on the other hand consistently outperforms its standard encoding-based counterpart, showing it can be the basis for future advancements towards stronger HO automation.

Acknowledgments. We are grateful to Jasmin Blanchette and Pascal Fontaine for numerous discussions throughout the development of this work, for providing funding for research visits and for suggesting many improvements. We also thank Jasmin for generating several of the benchmarks with which we evaluate our approach; Simon Cruanes and Martin Riener for many fruitful discussions on the intricacies of HOL; Andres Nötzli for help with the table and plot scripts; Mathias Fleury, Hans-Jörg Schurr and Sophie Tourret for suggesting many improvements. This work was partially supported by the National Science Foundation under Award 1656926 and the European Research Council (ERC) under starting grant Matryoshka (713999).

References

1. Andrews, P.B.: Resolution in type theory. J. Symb. Log. **36**(3), 414–432 (1971)
2. Bachmair, L., Ganzinger, H.: Rewrite-based equational theorem proving with selection and simplification. J. Log. Comput. **4**(3), 217–247 (1994)
3. Barbosa, H., Blanchette, J.C., Cruanes, S., El Ouraoui, D., Fontaine, P.: Language and proofs for higher-order SMT (work in progress). In: Dubois, C., Paleo, B.W. (eds.) PXTP 2017. EPTCS, vol. 262, pp. 15–22 (2017)
4. Barbosa, H., Fontaine, P., Reynolds, A.: Congruence closure with free variables. In: Legay, A., Margaria, T. (eds.) TACAS 2017. LNCS, vol. 10206, pp. 214–230. Springer, Heidelberg (2017). https://doi.org/10.1007/978-3-662-54580-5_13
5. Barbosa, H., Reynolds, A., El Ouraoui, D., Tinelli, C., Barrett, C.: Extending SMT solvers to higher-order logic. Technical report. The University of Iowa, May 2019

6. Barrett, C., et al.: CVC4. In: Gopalakrishnan, G., Qadeer, S. (eds.) CAV 2011. LNCS, vol. 6806, pp. 171–177. Springer, Heidelberg (2011). https://doi.org/10. 1007/978-3-642-22110-1_14

7. Barrett, C., Fontaine, P., Tinelli, C.: The SMT-LIB standard: version 2.6. Technical report. Department of Computer Science, The University of Iowa (2017)

8. Barrett, C., Sebastiani, R., Seshia, S., Tinelli, C.: Satisfiability modulo theories, Chap. 26. In: Biere, A., Heule, M.J.H., van Maaren, H., Walsh, T. (eds.) Handbook of Satisfiability. FAIA, vol. 185, pp. 825–885. IOS Press (2009)

9. Bentkamp, A., Blanchette, J.C., Cruanes, S., Waldmann, U.: Superposition for lambda-free higher-order logic. In: Galmiche, D., Schulz, S., Sebastiani, R. (eds.) IJCAR 2018. LNCS, vol. 10900, pp. 28–46. Springer, Cham (2018). https://doi. org/10.1007/978-3-319-94205-6_3

10. Benzmüller, C., Miller, D.: Automation of higher-order logic. In: Siekmann, J.H. (ed.) Computational Logic. Handbook of the History of Logic, vol. 9, pp. 215–254. Elsevier (2014)

11. Benzmüller, C., Sultana, N., Paulson, L.C., Theiss, F.: The higher-order prover LEO-II. J. Autom. Reason. **55**, 389–404 (2015)

12. Bhayat, A., Reger, G.: Set of support for higher-order reasoning. In: Konev, B., Urban, J., Rümmer, P. (eds.) PAAR-2018. CEUR Workshop Proceedings, vol. 2162, pp. 2–16. CEUR-WS.org (2018)

13. Blanchette, J.C.: Automatic proofs and refutations for higher-order logic. Ph.D. thesis. Technical University Munich (2012)

14. Blanchette, J.C., Kaliszyk, C., Paulson, L.C., Urban, J.: Hammering towards QED. J. Formaliz. Reason. **9**(1), 101–148 (2016)

15. Böhme, S., Nipkow, T.: Sledgehammer: judgement day. In: Giesl, J., Hähnle, R. (eds.) IJCAR 2010. LNCS, vol. 6173, pp. 107–121. Springer, Heidelberg (2010). https://doi.org/10.1007/978-3-642-14203-1_9

16. Bouton, T., Caminha B. de Oliveira, D., Déharbe, D., Fontaine, P.: veriT: an open, trustable and efficient SMT-solver. In: Schmidt, R.A. (ed.) CADE 2009. LNCS, vol. 5663, pp. 151–156. Springer, Heidelberg (2009). https://doi.org/10.1007/978-3-642-02959-2_12

17. Brown, C.E.: Satallax: an automatic higher-order prover. In: Gramlich, B., Miller, D., Sattler, U. (eds.) IJCAR 2012. LNCS, vol. 7364, pp. 111–117. Springer, Heidelberg (2012). https://doi.org/10.1007/978-3-642-31365-3_11

18. Cruanes, S.: Superposition with structural induction. In: Dixon, C., Finger, M. (eds.) FroCoS 2017. LNCS, vol. 10483, pp. 172–188. Springer, Cham (2017). https://doi.org/10.1007/978-3-319-66167-4_10

19. Czajka, Ł., Kaliszyk, C.: Hammer for Coq: automation for dependent type theory. J. Autom. Reason. **61**, 423–453 (2018)

20. de Moura, L., Bjørner, N.: Efficient E-matching for SMT solvers. In: Pfenning, F. (ed.) CADE 2007. LNCS, vol. 4603, pp. 183–198. Springer, Heidelberg (2007). https://doi.org/10.1007/978-3-540-73595-3_13

21. de Moura, L., Bjørner, N.: Generalized, efficient array decision procedures. In: FMCAD 2009, pp. 45–52. IEEE (2009)

22. Detlefs, D., Nelson, G., Saxe, J.B.: Simplify: a theorem prover for program checking. J. ACM **52**, 365–473 (2005)

23. Dowek, G.: Higher-order unification and matching. In: Robinson, J.A., Voronkov, A. (eds.) Handbook of Automated Reasoning, vol. II, pp. 1009–1062. Elsevier and MIT Press (2001)

24. Downey, P.J., Sethi, R., Tarjan, R.E.: Variations on the common subexpression problem. J. ACM **27**, 758–771 (1980)

25. Färber, M., Brown, C.: Internal guidance for Satallax. In: Olivetti, N., Tiwari, A. (eds.) IJCAR 2016. LNCS, vol. 9706, pp. 349–361. Springer, Cham (2016). https://doi.org/10.1007/978-3-319-40229-1_24

26. Ge, Y., de Moura, L.: Complete instantiation for quantified formulas in satisfiabiliby modulo theories. In: Bouajjani, A., Maler, O. (eds.) CAV 2009. LNCS, vol. 5643, pp. 306–320. Springer, Heidelberg (2009). https://doi.org/10.1007/978-3-642-02658-4_25

27. Henkin, L.: Completeness in the theory of types. J. Symb. Log. **15**(2), 81–91 (1950)

28. Hughes, R.J.M.: Super combinators: a new implementation method for applicative languages. In: Symposium on LISP and Functional Programming, pp. 1–10 (1982)

29. Kohlhase, M.: Higher-order tableaux. In: Baumgartner, P., Hähnle, R., Possega, J. (eds.) TABLEAUX 1995. LNCS, vol. 918, pp. 294–309. Springer, Heidelberg (1995). https://doi.org/10.1007/3-540-59338-1_43

30. Meng, J., Paulson, L.C.: Translating higher-order clauses to first-order clauses. J. Autom. Reason. **40**(1), 35–60 (2008)

31. Nelson, G., Oppen, D.C.: Fast decision procedures based on congruence closure. J. ACM **27**, 356–364 (1980)

32. Nieuwenhuis, R., Oliveras, A.: Fast congruence closure and extensions. Inf. Comput. IC **2005**(4), 557–580 (2007)

33. Nieuwenhuis, R., Rubio, A.: Paramodulation-based theorem proving. In: Robinson, A., Voronkov, A. (eds.) Handbook of Automated Reasoning, vol. 1, pp. 371–443. Elsevier Science (2001)

34. Nipkow, T., Wenzel, M., Paulson, L.C.: Isabelle/HOL: A Proof Assistant for Higher-Order Logic. LNCS, vol. 2283. Springer, Heidelberg (2002). https://doi.org/10.1007/3-540-45949-9

35. Noshita, K.: Translation of Turner combinators in O(n log n) space. IPL **20**, 71–74 (1985)

36. Paulson, L.C., Blanchette, J.C.: Three years of experience with Sledgehammer, a practical link between automatic and interactive theorem provers. In: Sutcliffe, G., Schulz, S., Ternovska, E. (eds.) IWIL-2010. EPiC, vol. 2, pages 1–11. EasyChair (2012)

37. Reynolds, A., Barbosa, H., Fontaine, P.: Revisiting enumerative instantiation. In: Beyer, D., Huisman, M. (eds.) TACAS 2018. LNCS, vol. 10806, pp. 112–131. Springer, Cham (2018). https://doi.org/10.1007/978-3-319-89963-3_7

38. Reynolds, A., Tinelli, C., de Moura, L.: Finding conflicting instances of quantified formulas in SMT. In: FMCAD 2014, pp. 195–202. IEEE (2014)

39. Reynolds, A., Tinelli, C., Goel, A., Krstić, S.: Finite model finding in SMT. In: Sharygina, N., Veith, H. (eds.) CAV 2013. LNCS, vol. 8044, pp. 640–655. Springer, Heidelberg (2013). https://doi.org/10.1007/978-3-642-39799-8_42

40. Reynolds, A., Tinelli, C., Goel, A., Krstić, S., Deters, M., Barrett, C.: Quantifier instantiation techniques for finite model finding in SMT. In: Bonacina, M.P. (ed.) CADE 2013. LNCS, vol. 7898, pp. 377–391. Springer, Heidelberg (2013). https://doi.org/10.1007/978-3-642-38574-2_26

41. Robinson, J.A.: Mechanizing higher order logic. Mach. Intell. **4**, 151–170 (1969)

42. Schulz, S.: E - a brainiac theorem prover. AI Commun. **15**, 111–126 (2002)

43. Steen, A., Benzmüller, C.: The higher-order prover Leo-III. In: Galmiche, D., Schulz, S., Sebastiani, R. (eds.) IJCAR 2018. LNCS, vol. 10900, pp. 108–116. Springer, Cham (2018). https://doi.org/10.1007/978-3-319-94205-6_8

44. Stump, A., Barrett, C.W., Dill, D.L., Levitt, J.R.: A decision procedure for an extensional theory of arrays. In: LICS 2001, pp. 29–37. IEEE Computer Society (2001)

45. Sultana, N., Blanchette, J.C., Paulson, L.C.: LEO-II and Satallax on the Sledge-hammer test bench. J. Appl. Log. **11**, 91–102 (2013)
46. Sutcliffe, G.: The TPTP problem library and associated infrastructure. J. Autom. Reason. **43**, 337–362 (2009)
47. Sutcliffe, G.: The CADE ATP system competition - CASC. AI Mag. **37**, 99–101 (2016)
48. Vukmirović, P., Blanchette, J.C., Cruanes, S., Schulz, S.: Extending a brainiac prover to lambda-free higher-order logic. In: Vojnar, T., Zhang, L. (eds.) TACAS 2019. LNCS, vol. 11427, pp. 192–210. Springer, Cham (2019). https://doi.org/10.1007/978-3-030-17462-0_11

Superposition with Lambdas

Alexander Bentkamp[1]([✉]), Jasmin Blanchette[1,2], Sophie Tourret[2],
Petar Vukmirović[1], and Uwe Waldmann[2]

[1] Vrije Universiteit Amsterdam, Amsterdam, The Netherlands
{a.bentkamp,j.c.blanchette,p.vukmirovic}@vu.nl
[2] Max-Planck-Institut für Informatik,
Saarland Informatics Campus, Saarbrücken, Germany
{jblanche,stourret,uwe}@mpi-inf.mpg.de

Abstract. We designed a superposition calculus for a clausal fragment of extensional polymorphic higher-order logic that includes anonymous functions but excludes Booleans. The inference rules work on $\beta\eta$-
equivalence classes of λ-terms and rely on higher-order unification to
achieve refutational completeness. We implemented the calculus in the
Zipperposition prover and evaluated it on TPTP and Isabelle benchmarks. The results suggest that superposition is a suitable basis for
higher-order reasoning.

1 Introduction

Superposition [5] is widely regarded as the calculus par excellence for reasoning
about first-order logic with equality. To increase automation in proof assistants
and other verification tools based on higher-order formalisms, we propose to
generalize superposition to an extensional, polymorphic, clausal version of higher-
order logic (also called simple type theory). Our ambition is to achieve a *graceful*
extension, which coincides with standard superposition on first-order problems
and smoothly scales up to arbitrary higher-order problems.

Bentkamp, Blanchette, Cruanes, and Waldmann [10] recently designed a family of superposition-like calculi for a λ-free fragment of higher-order logic, with
currying and applied variables. We adapt their "extensional nonpurifying" calculus to also support λ-expressions (Sect. 3). Our calculus does not support first-
class Booleans; it is conceived as the penultimate milestone towards a superposition calculus for full higher-order logic. If desired, Booleans can be encoded in our
logic fragment using an uninterpreted type and uninterpreted "proxy" symbols
corresponding to equality, the connectives, and the quantifiers.

Designing a higher-order superposition calculus poses three main challenges:

1. In first-order logic, superposition is parameterized by a ground-total simplification order $\succ$, but such orders do not exist for λ-terms considered equal
   up to β-conversion. The relations designed for proving termination of higher-
   order term rewriting systems, such as HORPO [39] and CPO [21], lack many
   of the desired properties (e.g., transitivity, stability under substitution).

© Springer Nature Switzerland AG 2019
P. Fontaine (Ed.): CADE 2019, LNAI 11716, pp. 55–73, 2019.
https://doi.org/10.1007/978-3-030-29436-6_4

2. Higher-order unification is undecidable and may give rise to an infinite set of incomparable unifiers. For example, the constraint $f(y\,a) \overset{?}{=} y(f\,a)$ admits infinitely many independent solutions of the form $\{y \mapsto \lambda x.\, f^n\, x\}$.

3. In first-order logic, to rewrite into a term s using an oriented equation $t \approx t'$, it suffices to find a subterm of s that is unifiable with t. In higher-order logic, this is insufficient. Consider superposition from $f\,c \approx a$ into $y\,c \not\approx y\,b$. The left-hand sides can obviously be unified by $\{y \mapsto f\}$, but the more general substitution $\{y \mapsto \lambda x.zx(f\,x)\}$ also gives rise to a subterm $f\,c$ after β-reduction. The corresponding inference generates the clause $z\,c\,a \not\approx z\,b\,(f\,b)$.

To address the first challenge, we adopt η-short β-normal form to represent $\beta\eta$-equivalence classes of λ-terms. In the spirit of Jouannaud and Rubio's early joint work [38], we state requirements on the term order only for ground terms (i.e., closed monomorphic $\beta\eta$-equivalence classes); the nonground case is connected to the ground case via stability under substitution. Even on ground terms, it is impossible to obtain all desirable properties. We sacrifice compatibility with arguments (the property that $s' \succ s$ implies $s'\,t \succ s\,t$) and compensate for it with an *argument congruence* rule (ARGCONG), as in Bentkamp et al. [10].

For the second challenge, we accept that there might be infinitely many incomparable unifiers and enumerate a complete set (including the notorious flex–flex pairs [36]), relying on heuristics to keep the combinatorial explosion under control. The saturation loop must also be adapted to interleave this enumeration with the theorem prover's other activities (Sect. 6). Despite its reputation for explosiveness, higher-order unification is a conceptual improvement over SK combinators, because it can often *compute* the right unifier. Consider the conjecture $\exists z.\, \forall x\,y.\, z\,x\,y \approx f\,y\,x$. After negation, clausification, and skolemization, it becomes $z\,(sk_x\,z)\,(sk_y\,z) \not\approx f\,(sk_y\,z)\,(sk_x\,z)$. Higher-order unification quickly computes the unique unifier: $\{z \mapsto \lambda x\,y.\, f\,y\,x\}$. In contrast, an encoding approach based on combinators, similar to the one implemented in Sledgehammer [48], would blindly enumerate all possible SK terms for z until the right one, $S\,(K\,(S\,f))\,K$, is found. Given the definitions $S\,z\,y\,x \approx z\,x\,(y\,x)$ and $K\,x\,y \approx x$, the E prover [55] in *auto* mode needs to perform 3756 inferences to derive the empty clause.

For the third challenge, when applying $t \approx t'$ to perform rewriting inside a higher-order term s, the idea is to encode an arbitrary context as a fresh higher-order variable z, unifying s with $z\,t$; the result is $(z\,t')\sigma$, for some unifier σ. This is performed by a dedicated *fluid subterm superposition* rule (FLUIDSUP).

Functional extensionality (the property that $\forall x.\, y\,x \approx z\,x$ implies $y \approx z$) is also considered a challenge for higher-order reasoning [13], although similar difficulties arise with the first-order theories of sets and arrays [33]. Our approach is to add extensionality as an axiom and provide optional rules as optimizations (Sect. 5). With this axiom, our calculus is refutationally complete with respect to extensional Henkin semantics (Sect. 4). Detailed proofs are included in a technical report [11], together with more explanations, examples, and discussions.

We implemented the calculus in the Zipperposition prover [27] (Sect. 6). Our empirical evaluation includes benchmarks from the TPTP [59] and interactive verification problems exported from Isabelle/HOL [22] (Sect. 7). The results appear promising and suggest that an optimized implementation inside a competitive prover such as E [55], SPASS [64], or Vampire [44] would outperform existing higher-order automatic provers.

2 Logic

Our extensional polymorphic clausal higher-order logic is a restriction of full TPTP THF [15] to rank-1 polymorphism, as in TH1 [40]. In keeping with standard superposition, we consider only formulas in conjunctive normal form. Booleans can easily be axiomatized [11, Sect. 2.3]. We use Henkin semantics [14,31,34].

We fix a set Σ_{ty} of type constructors with arities and a set $\mathcal{V}_{\mathsf{ty}}$ of type variables. We require a binary function type constructor $\to\;\in \Sigma_{\mathsf{ty}}$ to be present. A type τ, υ is either a type variable $\alpha \in \mathcal{V}_{\mathsf{ty}}$ or has the form $\kappa(\bar{\tau}_n)$ for an n-ary type constructor $\kappa \in \Sigma_{\mathsf{ty}}$ and types $\bar{\tau}_n$. We use the notation $\bar{a}_n$ or $\bar{a}$ to stand for the tuple $(a_1, \ldots, a_n)$ or product $a_1 \times \cdots \times a_n$, where $n \geq 0$. We write κ for $\kappa()$ and $\tau \to \upsilon$ for $\to(\tau, \upsilon)$. A type declaration is an expression of the form $\Pi\bar{\alpha}_m.\ \tau$ (or simply τ if $m = 0$), where all type variables occurring in τ belong to $\bar{\alpha}_m$.

We fix a nonempty set Σ of (function) symbols $\mathsf{a, b, c, f, g, h}, \ldots$, with type declarations, written as $\mathsf{f} : \Pi\bar{\alpha}_m.\ \tau$ or f, and a set $\mathcal{V}$ of term variables with associated types, written as $x : \tau$ or x. The sets $(\Sigma_{\mathsf{ty}}, \mathcal{V}_{\mathsf{ty}}, \Sigma, \mathcal{V})$ form the signature. The set of raw λ-terms is defined inductively as follows. Every $x : \tau \in \mathcal{V}$ is a raw λ-term of type τ. If $\mathsf{f} : \Pi\bar{\alpha}_m.\ \tau \in \Sigma$ and $\bar{\upsilon}_m$ is a tuple of types, called type arguments, then $\mathsf{f}\langle\bar{\upsilon}_m\rangle$ (or simply f if $m = 0$) is a raw λ-term of type $\tau\{\bar{\alpha}_m \mapsto \bar{\upsilon}_m\}$. If $x : \tau$ and $t : \upsilon$, then the λ-expression $\lambda x.\, t$ is a raw λ-term of type $\tau \to \upsilon$. If $s : \tau \to \upsilon$ and $t : \tau$, then the application $s\, t$ is a raw λ-term of type υ.

The α-renaming rule is defined as $(\lambda x.\, t) \to_\alpha (\lambda y.\, t\{x \mapsto y\})$, where y does not occur free in t and is not captured by a λ in t. Raw λ-terms form equivalence classes modulo α-renaming, called λ-terms. A variable occurrence is free in a λ-term if it is not bound by a λ-expression. A λ-term is ground if it is built without using type variables and contains no free term variables. Using the spine notation [25], λ-terms can be decomposed in a unique way as a non-application head t applied to zero or more arguments: $t\, s_1 \ldots s_n$ or $t\, \bar{s}_n$ (abusing notation).

The β- and η-reduction rules are defined on λ-terms as $(\lambda x.t)u \to_\beta t\{x \mapsto u\}$ and $(\lambda x.\, t\, x) \to_\eta t$. For β, bound variables in t are renamed to avoid capture; for η, the variable x must not occur free in t. The λ-terms form equivalence classes modulo $\beta\eta$-reduction, called $\beta\eta$-equivalence classes or simply terms. When defining operations that need to analyze the structure of terms, we use the η-short β-normal form $t{\downarrow}_{\beta\eta}$, obtained by applying $\to_\beta$ and $\to_\eta$ exhaustively, as a representative of the equivalence class t. Many authors prefer the η-long β-normal form [36,38,47], but in a polymorphic setting it has the drawback that instantiating a type variable by a function type can lead to η-expansion. We reserve the letters s, t, u, v for terms and w, x, y, z for variables, and write $: \tau$ to indicate their type.

An equation $s \approx t$ is formally an unordered pair of terms s and t. A literal is an equation or a negated equation, written $\neg\, s \approx t$ or $s \not\approx t$. A clause $L_1 \vee \cdots \vee L_n$ is a finite multiset of literals L_j. The empty clause is written as $\bot$.

In general, a substitution $\{\bar{\alpha}_m, \bar{x}_n \mapsto \bar{\upsilon}_m, \bar{s}_n\}$, where each x_j has type τ_j and each s_j has type $\tau_j\{\bar{\alpha}_m \mapsto \bar{\upsilon}_m\}$, maps m type variables to m types and n term variables to n terms. The letters θ, ρ, σ are reserved for substitutions. Substitutions are lifted to terms and clauses in a capture-avoiding way. The composition $\rho\sigma$ applies ρ first: $t\rho\sigma = (t\rho)\sigma$. A *complete set of unifiers* on a set X of variables for s and t is a set U of unifiers of s and t such that for every unifier ρ of s and t there exists a member $\sigma \in U$ and a substitution θ such that $x\sigma\theta = x\rho$ for all $x \in X$. We use $\mathrm{CSU}_X(s,t)$ to denote a fixed complete set of unifiers on X for s and t. The set X will consist of the free variables of the clauses in which s and t occur and will be left implicit.

3   The Calculus

Our superposition calculus for clausal higher-order logic is inspired by the λ-free *extensional nonpurifying* calculus described by Bentkamp et al. [10]. The text of this section is partly based on that paper (with Cruanes's permission). The central idea is that superposition inferences are restricted to unapplied subterms occurring in the "first-order outer skeleton" of the superterm—that is, outside λ-expressions and outside the arguments of applied variables. We call these "green subterms." Thus, an equation $\mathsf{g} \approx (\lambda x.\, \mathsf{f}\, x\, x)$ cannot be used directly to rewrite $\mathsf{g}\,\mathsf{a}$ to $\mathsf{f}\,\mathsf{a}\,\mathsf{a}$, because g is applied in $\mathsf{g}\,\mathsf{a}$. A separate inference rule, ARGCONG, takes care of deriving $\mathsf{g}\, x \approx \mathsf{f}\, x\, x$, which can be oriented independently of its parent clause and used to rewrite $\mathsf{g}\,\mathsf{a}$ or $\mathsf{f}\,\mathsf{a}\,\mathsf{a}$.

A term (i.e., a $\beta\eta$-equivalence class) t is defined to be a *green subterm* of a term s if either $s = t$ or $s = \mathsf{f}\langle\bar{\tau}\rangle\,\bar{s}$ for some function symbol f, types $\bar{\tau}$ and terms $\bar{s}$, where t is a green subterm of s_i for some i. In $\mathsf{f}\,(\mathsf{g}\,\mathsf{a})\,(y\,\mathsf{b})\,(\lambda x.\,\mathsf{h}\,\mathsf{c}\,(\mathsf{g}\,x))$, the green subterms are a, $\mathsf{g}\,\mathsf{a}$, $y\,\mathsf{b}$, $\lambda x.\,\mathsf{h}\,\mathsf{c}\,(\mathsf{g}\,x)$, and the entire term. We write $t = s\langle u\rangle$ to express that u is a green subterm of t and call $s\langle\ \rangle$ a *green context*.

Another key notion is that of a "fluid" term. A subterm t of $s[t]$ is called *fluid* if (1) $t{\downarrow}_{\beta\eta}$ is of the form $y\,\bar{u}_n$, where y is not bound in $s[t]$ and $n \geq 1$, or (2) $t{\downarrow}_{\beta\eta}$ is a λ-expression and there exists a substitution σ such that $t\sigma{\downarrow}_{\beta\eta}$ is not a λ-expression (due to η-reduction). A necessary condition for case (2) is that $t{\downarrow}_{\beta\eta}$ contains an applied variable that is not bound in $s[t]$. Intuitively, fluid subterms are terms whose η-short β-normal form can change radically as a result of instantiation. For example, applying the substitution $\{z \mapsto (\lambda x.\, x)\}$ to the fluid term $\lambda x.\, y\,\mathsf{a}\,(z\, x)$ makes the λ-expression vanish: $(\lambda x.\, y\,\mathsf{a}\,x) = y\,\mathsf{a}$.

Term Order. The calculus is parameterized by a well-founded strict total order $\succ$ on ground terms satisfying the following properties:

- *green subterm property*: $t\langle s\rangle \succeq s$ (i.e., $t\langle s\rangle \succ s$ or $t\langle s\rangle = s$);
- *compatibility with green contexts*: $s' \succ s$ implies $t\langle s'\rangle \succ t\langle s\rangle$.

The literal and clause orders are defined as multiset extensions in the standard way [5]. Two properties that are not required are *compatibility with λ-expressions* ($s' \succ s$ implies $(\lambda x.\, s') \succ (\lambda x.\, s)$) and *compatibility with arguments* ($s' \succ s$ implies $s'\, t \succ s\, t$). The latter would even be inconsistent with totality. To see why, consider the symbols $c \succ b \succ a$ and the terms $\lambda x.\, b$ and $\lambda x.\, x$. Owing to totality, one of the terms must be larger than the other, say, $(\lambda x.\, b) \succ (\lambda x.\, x)$. By compatibility with arguments, we get $(\lambda x.\, b)\, c \succ (\lambda x.\, x)\, c$, i.e., $b \succ c$, a contradiction. A similar line of reasoning applies if $(\lambda x.\, b) \prec (\lambda x.\, x)$, using a instead of c.

For nonground terms, $\succ$ is extended to a strict partial order so that $t \succ s$ if and only if $t\theta \succ s\theta$ for all grounding substitutions θ. We also introduce a quasiorder $\succsim$ such that $t \succsim s$ if and only if $t\theta \succeq s\theta$ for all grounding substitutions θ, and similarly for literals and clauses. The quasiorder $\succsim$ is more precise than $\succeq$; for example, given $a, b : \iota$ with $b \succ a$, we can have $x\, b \succsim x\, a$ even though $x\, b \not\succeq x\, a$.

Our approach to derive a suitable order is to encode η-short β-normal forms into untyped λ-free higher-order terms and apply an order $\succ_{\mathsf{base}}$ such as the λ-free Knuth–Bendix order (KBO) [8], the λ-free lexicographic path order (LPO) [20], or the embedding path order (EPO) [9]. The encoding, denoted by $[\,]$, translates $\lambda x : \tau.\, t$ to $\mathsf{lam}\, [\tau]\, [t]$ and uses De Bruijn symbols db_i to represent bound variables x [24]. It replaces fluid terms t by fresh variables z_t and maps type arguments to term arguments; thus, $[\lambda x{:}\iota.\lambda y{:}\iota.\, x] = \mathsf{lam}\,\iota\,(\mathsf{lam}\,\iota\,(\mathsf{db}_1\,\iota))$ and $[\mathsf{f}\langle\iota\rangle(y\,\mathsf{a})] = \mathsf{f}\,\iota\,z_{y\mathsf{a}}$. We then define the *metaorder* $\succ_{\mathsf{meta}}$ induced by $\succ_{\mathsf{base}}$ in such a way that $t \succ_{\mathsf{meta}} s$ if and only if $[t] \succ_{\mathsf{base}} [s]$. The use of De Bruijn indices and the monolithic encoding of fluid terms ensure stability under α-renaming and under substitution.

The Inference Rules. The calculus is parameterized by a selection function, which maps each clause to a subclause consisting of negative literals. A literal $L\langle y\rangle$ must not be selected if $y\,\bar{u}_n$, with $n > 0$, is a $\succsim$-maximal term of the clause.

A literal L is *(strictly) eligible* in C if it is selected in C or if there are no selected literals in C and L is (strictly) maximal in C. A variable is *deep* in a clause C if it occurs inside a λ-expression or inside an argument of an applied variable; these cover all occurrences that may correspond to positions inside λ-expressions after applying a substitution.

We regard positive and negative superposition as two cases of a single rule

$$\frac{\overbrace{D' \vee t \approx t'}^{D} \quad \overbrace{C' \vee [\lnot]\, s\langle u\rangle \approx s'}^{C}}{(D' \vee C' \vee [\lnot]\, s\langle t'\rangle \approx s')\sigma}\ \mathrm{SUP}$$

with the following side conditions:

1. u is not a fluid subterm;
2. u is not a deep variable in C;
3. if u is a variable y, there must exist a grounding θ such that $t\sigma\theta \succ t'\sigma\theta$ and $C\sigma\theta \prec C\{y \mapsto t'\}\sigma\theta$;
4. $\sigma \in \mathrm{CSU}(t, u)$;   5. $t\sigma \not\precsim t'\sigma$;   6. $s\langle u\rangle\sigma \not\precsim s'\sigma$;   7. $C\sigma \not\precsim D\sigma$;

8. $(t \approx t')\sigma$ is strictly eligible in $D\sigma$;
9. $([\neg] s\langle u \rangle \approx s')\sigma$ is eligible in $C\sigma$, and strictly eligible if it is positive.

There are four main differences with the statement of the standard superposition rule: Contexts $s[\ ]$ are replaced by green contexts $s\langle\ \rangle$. The standard condition $u \notin \mathcal{V}$ is generalized by conditions 2 and 3. Most general unifiers are replaced by complete sets of unifiers. And $\not\succeq$ is replaced by the more restrictive $\not\succ$.

The second rule is a variant of SUP that focuses on fluid subterms occurring in green contexts. Its statement is

$$\frac{\overbrace{D' \vee t \approx t'}^{D} \quad \overbrace{C' \vee [\neg] s\langle u \rangle \approx s'}^{C}}{(D' \vee C' \vee [\neg] s\langle z\, t' \rangle \approx s')\sigma} \text{ FluidSup}$$

with the following side conditions, in addition to SUP's conditions 5 to 9:

1. u is either a deep variable in C or a fluid subterm;
2. z is a fresh variable;   3. $\sigma \in \mathrm{CSU}(z\, t, u)$;   4. $z\, t' \neq z\, t$.

The next two rules are almost identical to their standard counterparts:

$$\frac{C' \vee u \not\approx u'}{C'\sigma} \text{ EqRes} \qquad \frac{C' \vee u' \approx v' \vee u \approx v}{(C' \vee v \not\approx v' \vee u \approx v')\sigma} \text{ EqFact}$$

For EqRes: $\sigma \in \mathrm{CSU}(u, u')$ and $(u \not\approx u')\sigma$ is eligible in the premise. For EqFact: $\sigma \in \mathrm{CSU}(u, u')$, $u'\sigma \not\succ v'\sigma$, $u\sigma \not\succ v\sigma$, and $(u \approx v)\sigma$ is eligible in the premise.

Argument congruence, a higher-order concern, is embodied by the rule

$$\frac{C' \vee s \approx s'}{C'\sigma \vee (s\sigma)\, \bar{x}_n \approx (s'\sigma)\, \bar{x}_n} \text{ ArgCong}$$

where σ is the most general type substitution that ensures well-typedness of the conclusion. In particular, if the result type of s is not a type variable, σ is the identity substitution; and if the result type is a type variable, it is instantiated with $\bar{\alpha}_n \to \beta$, where $\bar{\alpha}_n$ and β are fresh type variables, yielding infinitely many conclusions, one for each n. The literal $s\sigma \approx s'\sigma$ must be strictly eligible in $(C' \vee s \approx s')\sigma$, and $\bar{x}_n$ is a nonempty tuple of distinct fresh variables.

The rules are complemented by an axiom expressing functional extensionality:

$$y\, (\mathsf{diff}\langle \alpha, \beta \rangle\, y\, z) \not\approx z\, (\mathsf{diff}\langle \alpha, \beta \rangle\, y\, z) \vee y \approx z$$

The symbol $\mathsf{diff} : \Pi\alpha, \beta.\ (\alpha \to \beta) \to (\alpha \to \beta) \to \alpha$ is a Skolem symbol.

Rationale for the Rules. The calculus realizes the following division of labor: SUP and FLUIDSUP are responsible for green subterms, which are outside λs, ARGCONG indirectly gives access to the remaining positions outside λs, and the extensionality axiom takes care of subterms occurring inside λs.

Example 1. Applied variables give rise to subtle situations with no counterparts in first-order logic. Consider the clauses

$$\mathsf{f\, a} \approx \mathsf{c} \qquad\qquad \mathsf{h}\,(y\,\mathsf{b})\,(y\,\mathsf{a}) \not\approx \mathsf{h}\,(\mathsf{g}\,(\mathsf{f}\,\mathsf{b}))\,(\mathsf{g}\,\mathsf{c})$$

where $\mathsf{f\, a} \succ \mathsf{c}$. It is easy to see that the clause set is unsatisfiable, by grounding the second clause with $\theta = \{y \mapsto (\lambda x.\, \mathsf{g}\,(\mathsf{f}\,x))\}$. However, to mimic the superposition inference that can be performed at the ground level, it is necessary to superpose at an imaginary position *below* the applied variable y and yet *above* its argument a, namely, into the subterm $\mathsf{f\, a}$ of $\mathsf{g}\,(\mathsf{f}\,\mathsf{a}) = (\lambda x.\, \mathsf{g}\,(\mathsf{f}\,x))\,\mathsf{a} = (y\,\mathsf{a})\theta$. FLUIDSUP's z variable effectively transforms $\mathsf{f\, a} \approx \mathsf{c}$ into $z\,(\mathsf{f}\,\mathsf{a}) \approx z\,\mathsf{c}$, whose left-hand side can be unified with $y\,\mathsf{a}$ by taking $\{y \mapsto (\lambda x.\, z\,(\mathsf{f}\,x))\}$. The resulting clause is $\mathsf{h}\,(z\,(\mathsf{f}\,\mathsf{b}))\,(z\,\mathsf{c}) \not\approx \mathsf{h}\,(\mathsf{g}\,(\mathsf{f}\,\mathsf{b}))\,(\mathsf{g}\,\mathsf{c})$, which has the right form for EQRES.

Example 2. Third-order clauses in which variables are applied to λ-expressions can be even more stupefying. The clause set

$$\mathsf{f\, a} \approx \mathsf{c} \qquad\qquad \mathsf{h}\,(y\,(\lambda x.\, \mathsf{g}\,(\mathsf{f}\,x))\,\mathsf{a})\,y \not\approx \mathsf{h}\,(\mathsf{g}\,\mathsf{c})\,(\lambda w\,x.\, w\,x)$$

is unsatisfiable. To see this, apply $\theta = \{y \mapsto (\lambda w\,x.\, w\,x)\}$ to the second clause: $\mathsf{h}\,(\mathsf{g}\,(\mathsf{f}\,\mathsf{a}))\,(\lambda w\,x.\, w\,x) \not\approx \mathsf{h}\,(\mathsf{g}\,\mathsf{c})\,(\lambda w\,x.\, w\,x)$. Let $\mathsf{f\, a} \succ \mathsf{c}$. A SUP inference is possible between the two ground clauses. But at the nonground level, the subterm $\mathsf{f\, a}$ is not clearly localized: $\mathsf{g}(\mathsf{f}\mathsf{a}) = (\lambda x.\mathsf{g}(\mathsf{f}x))\mathsf{a} = (\lambda w x.w x)(\lambda x.\mathsf{g}(\mathsf{f}x))\mathsf{a} = (y(\lambda x.\mathsf{g}(\mathsf{f}x))\mathsf{a})\theta$. FLUIDSUP can cope with this. One of the unifiers of $z\,(\mathsf{f}\,\mathsf{a})$ and $y\,(\lambda x.\, \mathsf{g}\,(\mathsf{f}\,x))\,\mathsf{a}$ will be $\{y \mapsto (\lambda w\,x.\, w\,x),\, z \mapsto \mathsf{g}\}$, yielding $\mathsf{h}\,(\mathsf{g}\,\mathsf{c})\,(\lambda w\,x.\, w\,x) \not\approx \mathsf{h}\,(\mathsf{g}\,\mathsf{c})\,(\lambda w\,x.\, w\,x)$.

Because it gives rise to flex–flex pairs (unification constraints where both sides are applied variables), FLUIDSUP can be very prolific. The extensionality axiom is another prime source of flex–flex pairs.

Due to order restrictions and fairness, we cannot postpone solving flex–flex pairs indefinitely. Thus, we cannot use Huet's pre-unification procedure [36] and must instead choose a complete procedure such as Jensen and Pietrzykowski's [37] or Snyder and Gallier's [57]. On the positive side, optional inference rules can efficiently cover many cases where FLUIDSUP or the extensionality axiom would otherwise be needed, and heuristics can help keep the explosion under control. Moreover, flex–flex pairs are not always as bad as their reputation; for example, $y\,\mathsf{a}\,\mathsf{b} \overset{?}{=} z\,\mathsf{c}\,\mathsf{d}$ admits a most general unifier: $\{y \mapsto (\lambda w\,x.\, y'\,w\,x\,\mathsf{c}\,\mathsf{d}),\, z \mapsto y'\,\mathsf{a}\,\mathsf{b}\}$.

The calculus is a graceful generalization of standard superposition, except for the extensionality axiom. From $\mathsf{g}\,x \approx \mathsf{f}\,x\,x$, the axiom can be used to derive clauses such as $(\lambda x.\, y\,x\,(\mathsf{g}\,x)) \approx (\lambda x.\, y\,x\,(\mathsf{f}\,x\,x))$, which are useless if the problem is first-order.

Redundancy Criterion. A redundant (or composite) clause is usually defined as a clause whose ground instances are entailed by smaller ($\prec$) ground instances of existing clauses. This would be too strong for our calculus; for example, it would make ARGCONG inferences redundant. Our solution is to base the redundancy criterion on a weaker ground logic in which argument congruence and extensionality are not guaranteed to hold.

The weaker logic is defined via an encoding $\lfloor\ \rfloor$ of ground λ-terms into first-order terms. The $\lfloor\ \rfloor$ encoding indexes each symbol occurrence with its type arguments and argument count. Thus, $\lfloor f \rfloor = f_0$, $\lfloor f\ a \rfloor = f_1(a_0)$, and $\lfloor g\langle\iota\rangle \rfloor = g_0^\iota$. In addition, it conceals λs by replacing them with fresh symbols. These measures effectively disable argument congruence and extensionality. For example, the clause sets $\{g_0 \approx f_0,\ g_1(a_0) \not\approx f_1(a_0)\}$ and $\{b_0 \approx a_0,\ c_0 \not\approx d_0\}$ are satisfiable, even though $\{g \approx f,\ g\ a \not\approx f\ a\}$ and $\{b \approx a,\ (\lambda x.\ b) \not\approx (\lambda x.\ a)\}$ are unsatisfiable.

Given a ground higher-order signature $(\Sigma_{\mathsf{ty}}, \{\}, \Sigma, \{\})$, we define a first-order signature $(\Sigma_{\mathsf{ty}}, \{\}, \Sigma^\downarrow, \{\})$ as follows. The type constructors Σ_{ty} are the same in both signatures, but $\rightarrow$ is uninterpreted in first-order logic. For each ground instance $f\langle\bar{v}\rangle : \tau_1 \rightarrow \cdots \rightarrow \tau_n \rightarrow \tau$ of a symbol $f \in \Sigma$, we introduce a first-order symbol $f_j^{\bar{v}} \in \Sigma^\downarrow$ with argument types $\bar{\tau}_j$ and result type $\tau_{j+1} \rightarrow \cdots \rightarrow \tau_n \rightarrow \tau$, for each j. Moreover, for each ground term $\lambda x.t$, we introduce a symbol $\lfloor \lambda x.t \rfloor \in \Sigma^\downarrow$ of the same type.

The $\lfloor\ \rfloor$ encoding is defined on ground η-short β-normal forms so that $\lambda x.t$ is mapped to the symbol $\lfloor \lambda x.t \rfloor$ and $\lfloor f\langle\bar{v}\rangle\ \bar{s}_j \rfloor = f_j^{\bar{v}}(\lfloor \bar{s}_j \rfloor)$ recursively. The encoding is extended to literals and clauses elementwise. Using the inverse mapping $\lceil\ \rceil$, the order $\succ$ can be transferred to the first-order level by defining $t \succ s$ as $\lceil t \rceil \succ \lceil s \rceil$. A crucial property of $\lfloor\ \rfloor$ is that green subterms of a term t correspond to first-order subterms of $\lfloor t \rfloor$. Thus, the subterms considered by SUP and FLUIDSUP coincide with the subterms exposed to the redundancy criterion.

In standard superposition, redundancy employs the entailment relation $\models$ on ground clauses. We define redundancy of higher-order clauses in the same way, but using $\models$ on the $\lfloor\ \rfloor$-encoded clauses. This definition gracefully generalizes the standard first-order notion of redundancy. Formally, a clause C is *redundant with respect to a set of clauses* N if for each ground instance $C\theta$, $\lfloor C\theta \rfloor$ is entailed by ground instances of clauses in $\lfloor \mathcal{G}_\Sigma(N) \rfloor$ that are smaller than $\lfloor C\theta \rfloor$. Here, $\mathcal{G}_\Sigma(N)$ denotes the set of ground instances of clauses in N. We call N *saturated up to redundancy* if for each inference from clauses in N, its premise is redundant with respect to N or its conclusion is contained in N or redundant with respect to N.

The saturation procedures of superposition-based provers aggressively delete clauses that are strictly subsumed by other clauses. A clause C *subsumes* D if there exists a substitution σ such that $C\sigma \subseteq D$. A clause C *strictly subsumes* D if C subsumes D but D does not subsume C. For example, $x \approx c$ strictly subsumes both $a \approx c$ and $b \not\approx a \vee x \approx c$. The proof of refutational completeness of resolution and superposition provers relies on the well-foundedness of the strict subsumption relation [54, Section 7]. Unfortunately, this property does not hold for higher-order logic, where $f\ x\ x \approx c$ is strictly subsumed by $f\ (x\ a)\ (x\ b) \approx c$, which is strictly subsumed by $f\ (x\ a\ a)\ (x\ b\ b') \approx c$, and so on. Subsumption must be restricted to prevent such infinite chains—for example, by requiring that the subsumer is syntactically smaller than or of the same size as the subsumee.

4 Refutational Completeness

Besides soundness, the most important property of the higher-order superposition calculus introduced in Sect. 3 is refutational completeness:

Theorem 3. *Let $N \not\ni \bot$ be a clause set that is saturated up to redundancy and that contains the extensionality axiom. Then N has a Henkin model.*

The proof is adapted from Bentkamp et al. [10]. We present a brief outline in this section and point to our technical report [11] for the details. Let $N \not\ni \bot$ be a higher-order clause set saturated up to redundancy with respect to the inference rules and that contains the extensionality axiom. The proof proceeds in two steps:

1. Construct a model of the first-order grounded clause set $\lfloor \mathcal{G}_\Sigma(N) \rfloor$, where $\lfloor\ \rfloor$ is the encoding of ground terms used to define redundancy.
2. Lift this first-order model to a higher-order interpretation and show that it is a model of $\mathcal{G}_\Sigma(N)$ and hence of N.

The first step follows the same general idea as the completeness proof for standard superposition [5,50,63]. We construct a term rewriting system R_∞ and use it to define a candidate interpretation that equates all terms that share the same normal form with respect to R_∞. At this level, expressions $\lambda x.\, t$ are regarded as uninterpreted symbols $\lfloor \lambda x.\, t \rfloor$.

As in the standard proof, it is the set N, and not its grounding $\mathcal{G}_\Sigma(N)$, that is saturated. We must show that there exist nonground inferences corresponding to all necessary ground SUP, EQRES, and EQFACT inferences. We face two specifically higher-order difficulties. First, in standard superposition, we can avoid SUP inferences into variables x by exploiting the order's compatibility with contexts: If $t' \prec t$, we have $C\{x \mapsto t'\} \prec C\{x \mapsto t\}$, which allows us to invoke the induction hypothesis at a key point in the argument to establish the truth of $C\{x \mapsto t'\}$. This technique fails for higher-order variables x that occur applied in C, because the order lacks compatibility with arguments. Hence, our SUP rule must perform some inferences into variables. The other difficulty also concerns applied variables. We must show that any necessary ground SUP inference into a position corresponding to a fluid term or a deep variable on the nonground level can be lifted to a FLUIDSUP inference. This involves showing that the z variable in FLUIDSUP can represent arbitrary contexts around a term t.

For the first-order model construction, $\beta\eta$-normalization is the proverbial dog that did not bark. At the ground level, the rules SUP, EQRES, and EQFACT preserve η-short β-normal form, and so does first-order term rewriting. Thus, we can completely ignore $\to_\beta$ and $\to_\eta$. At the nonground level, β- and η-reduction can arise only through instantiation. This poses no difficulties thanks to the order's stability under substitution.

The second step of the completeness proof consists of constructing a higher-order interpretation and proving that it is a model of $\mathcal{G}_\Sigma(N)$, and hence of N. The difficulty is to show that the symbols representing λ-expressions behave like the λ-expressions they represent. This step relies on saturation with respect to the ARGCONG rule—which connects a λ-expression with its value when applied to an argument x—and on the presence of the extensionality axiom.

5   Extensions

The calculus can be extended to make it more practical. The familiar simplification machinery can be adapted to higher-order terms by considering green contexts instead of arbitrary contexts. Optional inference rules provide lightweight alternatives to the extensionality axiom.

Two of the rules below are based on "orange subterms." A λ-term t is an *orange subterm* of a λ-term s if $s = t$; or if $s = f\langle\bar{\tau}\rangle\,\bar{s}$ and t is an orange subterm of s_i for some i; or if $s = x\,\bar{s}$ and t is an orange subterm of s_i for some i; or if $s = (\lambda x.\,u)$ and t is an orange subterm of u. In $f\,(g\,a)\,(y\,b)\,(\lambda x.\,h\,c\,(g\,x))$, the orange subterms include b, c, x, $g\,x$, $h\,c\,(g\,x)$, and all the green subterms. This notion is lifted to $\beta\eta$-equivalence classes via representatives in η-short β-normal form. We write $t = s\langle\!\langle\bar{x}_n.\,u\rangle\!\rangle$ to indicate that u is an orange subterm of t, where $\bar{x}_n$ are the variables bound in the *orange context* around u.

Once a term $s\langle\!\langle\bar{x}_n.\,u\rangle\!\rangle$ has been introduced, we write $s\langle\!\langle\bar{x}_n.\,u'\rangle\!\rangle_\eta$ to denote the same context with a different subterm u' at that position. The η subscript is a reminder that u' is not necessarily an orange subterm of $s\langle\!\langle\bar{x}_n.\,u'\rangle\!\rangle_\eta$ due to potential applications of η-reduction. For example, if $s\langle\!\langle x.\,g\,x\,x\rangle\!\rangle = (\lambda x.\,g\,x\,x)$, then $s\langle\!\langle x.\,f\,x\rangle\!\rangle_\eta = (\lambda x.\,f\,x) = f$.

Demodulation, which destructively rewrites using an equality $t \approx t'$, is available at green positions. A variant rewrites inside λ-expressions:

$$\frac{t \approx t' \quad C\langle s\langle\!\langle\bar{x}.\,t\sigma\rangle\!\rangle\rangle}{t \approx t' \quad C\langle s\langle\!\langle\bar{x}.\,t'\sigma\rangle\!\rangle_\eta\rangle \quad s\langle\!\langle\bar{x}.\,t\sigma\rangle\!\rangle \approx s\langle\!\langle\bar{x}.\,t'\sigma\rangle\!\rangle_\eta} \text{\small λDemodExt}$$

where $s\langle\!\langle\bar{x}.\,t\sigma\rangle\!\rangle{\downarrow}_{\beta\eta}$ is a λ-expression or an applied variable. The term $t\sigma$ may refer to the bound variables $\bar{x}$. Side condition: The second premise is larger than $(\succ)$ the second and third conclusion. This ensures that this premise is redundant with respect to these conclusions and may be removed. The double bar indicates that the conclusions collectively make the premises redundant and can replace them. An instance of the rule, where $g\,z$ is rewritten to $f\,z\,z$ under a λ, follows:

$$\frac{g\,x \approx f\,x\,x \quad k\,(\lambda z.\,h\,(g\,z)) \approx c}{g\,x \approx f\,x\,x \quad k\,(\lambda z.\,h\,(f\,z\,z)) \approx c \quad (\lambda z.\,h\,(g\,z)) \approx (\lambda z.\,h\,(f\,z\,z))} \text{\small λDemodExt}$$

The next simplification rule can be used to prune arguments to variables that can be expressed as functions of the remaining arguments. For example, the clause $C[y\,a\,b\,(f\,b\,a),\,y\,b\,d\,(f\,d\,b)]$, in which y occurs twice, can be simplified to $C[y'\,a\,b,\,y'\,b\,d]$. The rule can also be used to remove the repeated arguments in $y\,b\,b \not\approx y\,a\,a$, the static argument a in $y\,a\,c \not\approx y\,a\,b$, and all four arguments in $y\,a\,b \not\approx z\,b\,d$. It is stated as

$$\frac{C}{C\{y \mapsto (\lambda\bar{x}_j.\,y'\,\bar{x}_{j-1})\}} \text{\small PruneArg}$$

where y' is a fresh variable, the minimum number k of arguments passed to any occurrence of y in the clause $C{\downarrow}_{\beta\eta}$ is at least j, and there exists a term t

containing no variables bound in the clause such that $s_j = t\, \bar{s}_{j-1}\, s_{j+1} \ldots s_k$ for all terms of the form $y\, \bar{s}_k$ occurring in the clause. For example, clauses with a static argument correspond to the case $t := (\lambda \bar{x}_{j-1}\, x_{j+1} \ldots x_k.\, u)$, where u is the static argument (containing no variables bound in t) and j is its index in y's argument list.

Following the literature [33,58], we provide a rule for negative extensionality:

$$\frac{C \vee s \not\approx s'}{C \vee s\, (\mathsf{sk}\langle \bar{\alpha}_m \rangle\, \bar{y}_n) \not\approx s'\, (\mathsf{sk}\langle \bar{\alpha}_m \rangle\, \bar{y}_n)}\ \text{NegExt}$$

where sk is a fresh Skolem symbol, $\bar{\alpha}_m, \bar{y}_n$ are the variables occurring free in the literal $s \not\approx s'$, and $s \not\approx s'$ is eligible in the premise. Negative extensionality can also be applied as a simplification rule to all literals in the initial problem.

Superposition can be generalized to orange subterms as follows:

$$\frac{D' \vee t \approx t' \quad C' \vee [\neg]\, s\langle\!\langle \bar{x}.\, u \rangle\!\rangle \approx s'}{(D' \vee C' \vee [\neg]\, s\langle\!\langle \bar{x}.\, t' \rangle\!\rangle_\eta \approx s')\sigma\rho}\ \lambda\text{Sup}$$

Sup's side conditions apply. We also require that $\bar{x}\sigma = \bar{x}$ and that the variables $\bar{x}$ do not occur in $y\sigma$ for all variables y in u. Moreover, let $P_y = \{y\}$ for all type and term variables $y \notin \bar{x}$. For each i, let P_{x_i} be recursively defined as the union of all P_y such that y occurs free in the λ-expression that binds x_i in $s\langle\!\langle \bar{x}.\, u \rangle\!\rangle\sigma$ or that occurs free in the corresponding subterm of $s\langle\!\langle \bar{x}.\, t' \rangle\!\rangle_\eta\sigma$. The substitution ρ is defined as $\{x_i \mapsto \mathsf{sk}_i\langle \bar{\alpha}_i \rangle\, \bar{y}_i$ for each $i\}$, where $\bar{y}_i$ are the term variables in P_{x_i} and $\bar{\alpha}_i$ are the type variables in P_{x_i} and the type variables occurring in the type of the λ-expression binding x_i. The rule can be justified in terms of paramodulation and extensionality, with the Skolem terms standing for diff terms. An instance of the rule follows:

$$\frac{n \approx \mathsf{zero} \vee \mathsf{div}\, n\, n \approx \mathsf{one} \quad \mathsf{prod}\, K\, (\lambda k.\, \mathsf{div}\, (\mathsf{succ}\, k)\, (\mathsf{succ}\, k)) \not\approx \mathsf{one}}{\mathsf{succ}\, \mathsf{sk} \approx \mathsf{zero} \vee \mathsf{prod}\, K\, (\lambda k.\, \mathsf{one}) \not\approx \mathsf{one}}\ \lambda\text{Sup}$$

Intuitively, the term $\mathsf{prod}\, K\, (\lambda k.\, u)$ is intended to denote the product $\prod_{k \in K} u$, where k ranges over a finite set K of natural numbers.

6 Implementation

Zipperposition [26,27] is an open source superposition prover written in OCaml.[1] Originally designed for polymorphic first-order logic (TF1 [19]), it was later extended with an incomplete higher-order mode based on pattern unification [49]. Bentkamp et al. [10] extended it further with a complete λ-free higher-order mode. As a prototype, we have now implemented a Boolean-free higher-order mode based on our calculus.

---

[1] https://github.com/c-cube/zipperposition.

We use a metaorder induced by a λ-free KBO [8]. We currently use $\succeq$ as the nonstrict term order but could improve precision by employing a more precise computable approximation of $\succsim$.

Except for FLUIDSUP, the core calculus rules already existed in Zipperposition in a similar form. To retrieve candidate right premises for FLUIDSUP, we created an index of all fluid green subterms in the active clause set. Among the proposed higher-order optional rules, we implemented NEGEXT, λSUP, a mildly incomplete variant of λDEMODEXT without the third conclusion, and a variant of the PRUNEARG rule that removes most functional dependencies that occur in practice.

For unification, we started with Jensen and Pietrzykowski's procedure [37]. The procedure is not ideal because it computes a nonminimal set of unifiers; for example, given the flex–flex constraint $y\,\mathsf{a} \stackrel{?}{=} z\,\mathsf{b}$, it generates not only the most general unifier $\{y \mapsto (\lambda w.\, y'\,w\,\mathsf{b}),\, z \mapsto y'\,\mathsf{a}\}$ but also infinitely many superfluous unifiers. It is not clear whether Snyder and Gallier's procedure [57] would behave better. To support polymorphism, we extended Jensen and Pietrzykowski's projection rule to check type unifiability instead of equality and their iteration rule to consider the possibility that a type variable is instantiated with a function type. On the other hand, polymorphism allows us to avoid the enumeration of types in the iteration rule.

To interleave the unification with other computation, our unification procedure returns a possibly infinite stream of subsingletons (sets of cardinality 0 or 1) computed on demand. It can even cope with nonterminating unification problems that do not yield any unifiers, by representing them as an infinite stream of empty sets. We use this procedure for inference rules, keeping simpler pattern-style unification for simplification rules. The inference rules turn the possibly infinite streams of unifiers into possibly infinite streams of clauses—the conclusions of inferences. To consume these streams fairly while giving flexibility to heuristics, we designed a priority queue that associates a weight with each stream. This queue is used in the main given clause loop to store new streams resulting from inferences and to extract clauses, which are then moved to the passive clause set.

Based on informal experiments, we developed or tuned a few general heuristics of Zipperposition. Definition unfolding, in conjunction with β-reduction, transforms many higher-order TPTP problems into first-order problems. We also modified KBO's weight generation scheme to take symbol frequencies into account and modified other heuristics to prioritize clauses containing symbols present in the conjecture.

7   Evaluation

We evaluated our prototype implementation of the calculus in Zipperposition with other higher-order provers and with Zipperposition's modes for less expressive logics. All of the experiments presented in this section were performed on StarExec nodes equipped with Intel Xeon E5-2609 0 CPUs clocked at 2.40 GHz.

	TFF	TH0λf	TH0λ	SH256-ll	SH16-ll	SH256-λ	SH16-λ
Leo-III	85	387	**42**	234	323	228	338
Satallax	–	400	**42**	495	371	516	384
Ehoh	–	396	–	**671**	397	–	–
FOZip	**238**	–	–	–	–	–	–
@+FOZip	194	398	–	495	389	–	–
λfreeZip	233	401	–	603	**401**	–	–
λZip-full	178	388	27	394	351	385	348
λZip-pragmatic	227	416	27	560	386	**567**	**387**
λZip-competitive	216	**418**	40	413	351	399	357
Leo-III-meta	252	438	44	706	412	688	416
Satallax-meta	–	427	42	491	372	513	385

Fig. 1. Number of proved problems

Provers were invoked with a CPU time limit of 300 s. The raw data are available online.[2]

We used both standard TPTP benchmarks [59] and Sledgehammer-generated benchmarks. From the TPTP, we selected all 709 TFF (monomorphic and polymorphic first-order) problems without arithmetic and all 597 TH0 (monomorphic higher-order) problems without first-class Booleans and arithmetic. We partitioned the TH0 problems into those containing no λs (TH0λf, 545 problems) and those containing λs (TH0λ, 52 problems). The Sledgehammer benchmarks, corresponding to Isabelle's Judgment Day suite [22], were regenerated to target Boolean-free higher-order logic. They comprise 5012 problems, divided in two groups based on the number of Isabelle facts (lemmas, definitions, etc.) selected for inclusion in each problem: either 256 (SH256) or 16 facts (SH16). Each group is further divided into two subgroups based on the processing of λ-expressions: SH256-λ and SH16-λ preserve λ-expressions, whereas SH256-ll and SH16-ll encode them as λ-lifted supercombinators [48] to make the problems accessible to λ-free higher-order provers.

We chose Leo-III 1.3 and Satallax 3.3 as representatives of the state of the art. These are cooperative higher-order provers that can be set up to regularly invoke first-order provers as terminal proof procedures. Leo-III can be used on its own or as a metaprover (Leo-III-meta) with CVC4, E, and iProver as backends. Satallax can be used on its own or as a metaprover (Satallax-meta) with E. We also included Ehoh [62], the λ-free higher-order mode of E 2.3. For Zipperposition, we included its first-order and λ-free modes (FOZip and λfreeZip) as well as a mode that performs an applicative encoding [62, Section 2] before invoking the first-order mode (@+FOZip). We experimented with three variants of our calculus implementation. λZip-full is designed to be refutationally complete. λZip-pragmatic disables FLUIDSUP and the extensionality axiom, and uses a lightweight higher-order unification algorithm instead of

---

[2] http://matryoshka.gforge.inria.fr/pubs/lamsup_results.tgz.

Jensen and Pietrzykowski's procedure. Finally, λZip-competitive is a variant of λZip-pragmatic that is further tuned for small problems requiring a substantial amount of higher-order reasoning.

A summary of our experiments is presented in Fig. 1. To enhance readability, we highlight in bold the winning system for each column *excluding the metaprovers*. We observe that Leo-III-meta emerges as winner on all benchmark sets, but λZip-pragmatic and λZip-competitive compare very well with Leo-III and Satallax. In contrast, λZip-full cannot seem to keep its FLUIDSUP rule and extensionality under control. More research into heuristics design appears necessary.

It is disappointing that on Sledgehammer problems (SH256 and SH16), we obtain better performance by using λfreeZip with λ-lifting than using λZip with native λs. On TH0λf problems, the situation is reversed. This seems to suggest that λ reasoning is rarely needed for Sledgehammer problems. Clearly, this is another area where research into heuristics design could be beneficial.

8   Discussion and Related Work

Bentkamp et al. [10] introduced four calculi for λ-free higher-order logic organized along two axes: *intensional* versus *extensional*, and *nonpurifying* versus *purifying*. The purifying calculi flatten the clauses containing applied variables, thereby eliminating the need for superposition into variables. As we extended their work to support λs, we found the purification approach problematic and quickly gave it up because it needs x to be smaller than $x\ t$, which is impossible to achieve with a term order on $\beta\eta$-equivalence classes. As for extensionality, it is the norm for higher-order unification [30] and is employed in the TPTP THF format [60] and in proof assistants such as HOL4, HOL Light, Isabelle/HOL, Lean, Nuprl, and PVS. Bentkamp et al. viewed their approach as "a stepping stone towards full higher-order logic." It already included a notion analogous to green subterms and an ARGCONG rule, which help cope with the complications occasioned by β-reduction.

Our superposition calculus joins the family of proof systems for higher-order logic. Closely related are Andrews's higher-order resolution [1], Huet's constrained resolution [35], Jensen and Pietrzykowski's ω-resolution [37], Snyder's higher-order E-resolution [56], Benzmüller and Kohlhase's extensional higher-order resolution [13], and Benzmüller's higher-order unordered paramodulation and RUE resolution [12]. A noteworthy variant is Steen and Benzmüller's higher-order ordered paramodulation [58], whose order restrictions undermine refutational completeness but yield good empirical results. Other approaches are based on analytic tableaux [6,42,43,52], connections [2], sequents [46], and satisfiability modulo theories [7]. Andrews [3] and Benzmüller and Miller [14] provide excellent surveys.

The main advantage of our calculus is that it gracefully generalizes the highly successful first-order superposition rules without sacrificing refutational completeness. It also includes a powerful simplification rule, PRUNEARG, that could be useful in other provers. Among the drawbacks of our approach are the need to solve flex–flex pairs eagerly and the explosion caused by the extensionality axiom. We believe that this is a reasonable trade-off, especially for large problems with a substantial first-order component, such as those originating from proof assistants.

Our prototype λZipperposition joins the league of higher-order automatic theorem provers. We briefly list some of its rivals. TPS [4] is based on the connection method and expansion proofs. LEO [13] and LEO-II [16] implement variants of RUE resolution. Leo-III [58] is based on higher-order paramodulation. Satallax [23] implements a higher-order tableau calculus guided by a SAT solver. LEO-II, Leo-III, and recent versions of Satallax integrate first-order provers as terminal procedures. AgsyHOL [46] is based on a focused sequent calculus guided by narrowing. Finally, there is ongoing work by the developers of CVC4, veriT, and Vampire to extend their provers to higher-order logic [7,17].

Half a century ago, Robinson [53] proposed to reduce higher-order logic to first-order logic via a translation. Tools such as Sledgehammer [51], MizAR [61], HOLyHammer [41], and CoqHammer [28] have since popularized this approach. Such translations must eliminate the λ-expressions, typically using SKBCI combinators or λ-lifting [48], and encode typing information [18]. Most translations are implemented outside provers, but hybrid approaches are also possible [17,29].

9 Conclusion

We presented a superposition calculus for a Boolean-free fragment of extensional polymorphic higher-order logic. With the notable exception of a functional extensionality axiom, it gracefully generalizes standard superposition. Our prototype prover Zipperposition shows promising results on TPTP and Isabelle benchmarks. In future work, we plan to pursue five main avenues of investigation.

We first plan to *extend the calculus to support Booleans and Hilbert choice.* Booleans are notoriously explosive. We want to experiment with both axiomatizations and native support in the calculus. Native support would likely take the form of a primitive substitution rule that enumerates predicate instantiations [2], delayed clausification rules [32], and rules for reasoning about Hilbert choice.

We want to investigate techniques to *curb the explosion caused by functional extensionality.* The extensionality axiom reintroduces the search space explosion that the calculus's order restrictions aim at avoiding.

We will also look into approaches to *curb the explosion caused by higher-order unification.* Our calculus suffers because it needs to solve flex–flex pairs. Existing procedures [37,57] enumerate redundant unifiers. This can probably be avoided to some extent. It could also be interesting to investigate unification algorithms that would delay imitation/projection choices via special schematic variables, inspired by Libal's concise representation of regular unifiers [45].

We clearly need to *fine-tune and develop heuristics.* We expect heuristics to be a fruitful area for future research in higher-order reasoning. Proof assistants are an inexhaustible source of easy-looking benchmarks that are beyond the power of today's provers. Whereas "hard higher-order" may remain forever out of reach, there is a substantial "easy higher-order" fragment that awaits automation.

Finally, we plan to *implement the calculus in a state-of-the-art prover*. A suitable basis for an optimized implementation of our calculus would be Ehoh, the λ-free higher-order version of the E prover developed by Vukmirović et al. [62].

Acknowledgment. Simon Cruanes patiently explained Zipperposition's internals and allowed us to continue the development of his prover. Christoph Benzmüller and Alexander Steen shared insights and examples with us, guiding us through the literature and clarifying how the Leos work. Maria Paola Bonacina and Nicolas Peltier gave us some ideas on how to treat the extensionality axiom as a theory axiom, ideas we have yet to explore. Mathias Fleury helped us set up regression tests for Zipperposition. Ahmed Bhayat, Tomer Libal, and Enrico Tassi shared their insights on higher-order unification. Andrei Popescu and Dmitriy Traytel explained the terminology surrounding the λ-calculus. Haniel Barbosa, Daniel El Ouraoui, Pascal Fontaine, and Hans-Jörg Schurr were involved in many stimulating discussions. Christoph Weidenbach made this collaboration possible. Ahmed Bhayat, Mark Summerfield, and the anonymous reviewers suggested several textual improvements. We thank them all.

Bentkamp, Blanchette, and Vukmirović's research has received funding from the European Research Council (ERC) under the European Union's Horizon 2020 research and innovation program (grant agreement No. 713999, Matryoshka). Bentkamp and Blanchette also benefited from the Netherlands Organization for Scientific Research (NWO) Incidental Financial Support scheme. Blanchette has received funding from the NWO under the Vidi program (project No. 016.Vidi.189.037, Lean Forward).

References

1. Andrews, P.B.: Resolution in type theory. J. Symb. Log. **36**(3), 414–432 (1971)
2. Andrews, P.B.: On connections and higher-order logic. J. Autom. Reason. **5**(3), 257–291 (1989)
3. Andrews, P.B.: Classical type theory. In: Robinson, J.A., Voronkov, A. (eds.) Handbook of Automated Reasoning, vol. II, pp. 965–1007. Elsevier and MIT Press (2001)
4. Andrews, P.B., Bishop, M., Issar, S., Nesmith, D., Pfenning, F., Xi, H.: TPS: a theorem-proving system for classical type theory. J. Autom. Reason. **16**(3), 321–353 (1996)
5. Bachmair, L., Ganzinger, H.: Rewrite-based equational theorem proving with selection and simplification. J. Log. Comput. **4**(3), 217–247 (1994)
6. Backes, J., Brown, C.E.: Analytic tableaux for higher-order logic with choice. J. Autom. Reason. **47**(4), 451–479 (2011)
7. Barbosa, H., Reynolds, A., Fontaine, P., El Ouraoui, D., Tinelli, C.: Higher-order SMT solving (work in progress). In: Dimitrova, R., D'Silva, V. (eds.) SMT 2018 (2018)
8. Becker, H., Blanchette, J.C., Waldmann, U., Wand, D.: A transfinite Knuth–Bendix order for lambda-free higher-order terms. In: de Moura, L. (ed.) CADE 2017. LNCS (LNAI), vol. 10395, pp. 432–453. Springer, Cham (2017). https://doi.org/10.1007/978-3-319-63046-5_27
9. Bentkamp, A.: Formalization of the embedding path order for lambda-free higher-order terms. Archive of Formal Proofs (2018). http://isa-afp.org/entries/Lambda_Free_EPO.html

10. Bentkamp, A., Blanchette, J.C., Cruanes, S., Waldmann, U.: Superposition for lambda-free higher-order logic. In: Galmiche, D., Schulz, S., Sebastiani, R. (eds.) IJCAR 2018. LNCS (LNAI), vol. 10900, pp. 28–46. Springer, Cham (2018). https:// doi.org/10.1007/978-3-319-94205-6_3

11. Bentkamp, A., Blanchette, J., Tourret, S., Vukmirović, P., Waldmann, U.: Superposition with lambdas (technical report). Technical report (2019). http://matryoshka. gforge.inria.fr/pubs/lamsup_report.pdf

12. Benzmüller, C.: Extensional higher-order paramodulation and RUE-resolution. In: Ganzinger, H. (ed.) CADE 1999. LNCS (LNAI), vol. 1632, pp. 399–413. Springer, Heidelberg (1999). https://doi.org/10.1007/3-540-48660-7_39

13. Benzmüller, C., Kohlhase, M.: Extensional higher-order resolution. In: Kirchner, C., Kirchner, H. (eds.) CADE 1998. LNCS (LNAI), vol. 1421, pp. 56–71. Springer, Heidelberg (1998). https://doi.org/10.1007/BFb0054248

14. Benzmüller, C., Miller, D.: Automation of higher-order logic. In: Siekmann, J.H. (ed.) Computational Logic, Handbook of the History of Logic, vol. 9, pp. 215–254. Elsevier (2014)

15. Benzmüller, C., Paulson, L.C.: Multimodal and intuitionistic logics in simple type theory. Log. J. IGPL 18(6), 881–892 (2010)

16. Benzmüller, C., Sultana, N., Paulson, L.C., Theiss, F.: The higher-order prover Leo-II. J. Autom. Reason. 55(4), 389–404 (2015)

17. Bhayat, A., Reger, G.: Set of support for higher-order reasoning. In: Konev, B., Urban, J., Rümmer, P. (eds.) PAAR-2018. CEUR Workshop Proceedings, vol. 2162, pp. 2–16. CEUR-WS.org (2018)

18. Blanchette, J.C., Böhme, S., Popescu, A., Smallbone, N.: Encoding monomorphic and polymorphic types. Log. Meth. Comput. Sci. 12(4) (2016)

19. Blanchette, J.C., Paskevich, A.: TFF1: the TPTP typed first-order form with rank-1 polymorphism. In: Bonacina, M.P. (ed.) CADE 2013. LNCS (LNAI), vol. 7898, pp. 414–420. Springer, Heidelberg (2013). https://doi.org/10.1007/978-3-642-38574-2_29

20. Blanchette, J.C., Waldmann, U., Wand, D.: A lambda-free higher-order recursive path order. In: Esparza, J., Murawski, A.S. (eds.) FoSSaCS 2017. LNCS, vol. 10203, pp. 461–479. Springer, Heidelberg (2017). https://doi.org/10.1007/978-3-662-54458-7_27

21. Blanqui, F., Jouannaud, J.P., Rubio, A.: The computability path ordering. Log. Meth. Comput. Sci. 11(4) (2015)

22. Böhme, S., Nipkow, T.: Sledgehammer: Judgement Day. In: Giesl, J., Hähnle, R. (eds.) IJCAR 2010. LNCS (LNAI), vol. 6173, pp. 107–121. Springer, Heidelberg (2010). https://doi.org/10.1007/978-3-642-14203-1_9

23. Brown, C.E.: Satallax: an automatic higher-order prover. In: Gramlich, B., Miller, D., Sattler, U. (eds.) IJCAR 2012. LNCS (LNAI), vol. 7364, pp. 111–117. Springer, Heidelberg (2012). https://doi.org/10.1007/978-3-642-31365-3_11

24. de Bruijn, N.G.: Lambda calculus notation with nameless dummies, a tool for automatic formula manipulation, with application to the Church-Rosser theorem. Indag. Math. 75(5), 381–392 (1972)

25. Cervesato, I., Pfenning, F.: A linear spine calculus. J. Log. Comput. 13(5), 639–688 (2003)

26. Cruanes, S.: Extending superposition with integer arithmetic, structural induction, and beyond. Ph.D. thesis, École polytechnique (2015)

27. Cruanes, S.: Superposition with structural induction. In: Dixon, C., Finger, M. (eds.) FroCoS 2017. LNCS (LNAI), vol. 10483, pp. 172–188. Springer, Cham (2017). https://doi.org/10.1007/978-3-319-66167-4_10

28. Czajka, Ł., Kaliszyk, C.: Hammer for Coq: automation for dependent type theory (2018)
29. Dougherty, D.J.: Higher-order unification via combinators. Theor. Comput. Sci. **114**(2), 273–298 (1993)
30. Dowek, G.: Higher-order unification and matching. In: Robinson, J.A., Voronkov, A. (eds.) Handbook of Automated Reasoning, vol. II, pp. 1009–1062. Elsevier and MIT Press (2001)
31. Fitting, M.: Types, Tableaus, and Gödel's God. Kluwer (2002)
32. Ganzinger, H., Stuber, J.: Superposition with equivalence reasoning and delayed clause normal form transformation. Inf. Comput. **199**(1–2), 3–23 (2005)
33. Gupta, A., Kovács, L., Kragl, B., Voronkov, A.: Extensional crisis and proving identity. In: Cassez, F., Raskin, J.-F. (eds.) ATVA 2014. LNCS, vol. 8837, pp. 185–200. Springer, Cham (2014). https://doi.org/10.1007/978-3-319-11936-6_14
34. Henkin, L.: Completeness in the theory of types. J. Symb. Log. **15**(2), 81–91 (1950)
35. Huet, G.P.: A mechanization of type theory. In: Nilsson, N.J. (ed.) IJCAI 1973, pp. 139–146. William Kaufmann (1973)
36. Huet, G.P.: A unification algorithm for typed lambda-calculus. Theor. Comput. Sci. **1**(1), 27–57 (1975)
37. Jensen, D.C., Pietrzykowski, T.: Mechanizing ω-order type theory through unification. Theor. Comput. Sci. **3**(2), 123–171 (1976)
38. Jouannaud, J.P., Rubio, A.: Rewrite orderings for higher-order terms in eta-long beta-normal form and recursive path ordering. Theor. Comput. Sci. **208**(1–2), 33–58 (1998)
39. Jouannaud, J.P., Rubio, A.: Polymorphic higher-order recursive path orderings. J. ACM **54**(1), 2:1–2:48 (2007)
40. Kaliszyk, C., Sutcliffe, G., Rabe, F.: TH1: the TPTP typed higher-order form with rank-1 polymorphism. In: Fontaine, P., Schulz, S., Urban, J. (eds.) PAAR 2016. CEUR Workshop Proceedings, vol. 1635, pp. 41–55. CEUR-WS.org (2016)
41. Kaliszyk, C., Urban, J.: HOL(y)Hammer: online ATP service for HOL Light. Math. Comput. Sci. **9**(1), 5–22 (2015)
42. Kohlhase, M.: Higher-order tableaux. In: Baumgartner, P., Hähnle, R., Possega, J. (eds.) TABLEAUX 1995. LNCS, vol. 918, pp. 294–309. Springer, Heidelberg (1995). https://doi.org/10.1007/3-540-59338-1_43
43. Konrad, K.: Hot: a concurrent automated theorem prover based on higher-order tableaux. In: Grundy, J., Newey, M. (eds.) TPHOLs 1998. LNCS, vol. 1479, pp. 245–261. Springer, Heidelberg (1998). https://doi.org/10.1007/BFb0055140
44. Kovács, L., Voronkov, A.: First-order theorem proving and VAMPIRE. In: Sharygina, N., Veith, H. (eds.) CAV 2013. LNCS, vol. 8044, pp. 1–35. Springer, Heidelberg (2013). https://doi.org/10.1007/978-3-642-39799-8_1
45. Libal, T.: Regular patterns in second-order unification. In: Felty, A.P., Middeldorp, A. (eds.) CADE 2015. LNCS (LNAI), vol. 9195, pp. 557–571. Springer, Cham (2015). https://doi.org/10.1007/978-3-319-21401-6_38
46. Lindblad, F.: A focused sequent calculus for higher-order logic. In: Demri, S., Kapur, D., Weidenbach, C. (eds.) IJCAR 2014. LNCS (LNAI), vol. 8562, pp. 61–75. Springer, Cham (2014). https://doi.org/10.1007/978-3-319-08587-6_5
47. Mayr, R., Nipkow, T.: Higher-order rewrite systems and their confluence. Theor. Comput. Sci. **192**(1), 3–29 (1998)
48. Meng, J., Paulson, L.C.: Translating higher-order clauses to first-order clauses. J. Autom. Reason. **40**(1), 35–60 (2008)
49. Miller, D.: A logic programming language with lambda-abstraction, function variables, and simple unification. J. Log. Comput. **1**(4), 497–536 (1991)

50. Nieuwenhuis, R., Rubio, A.: Paramodulation-based theorem proving. In: Robinson, J.A., Voronkov, A. (eds.) Handbook of Automated Reasoning, vol. I, pp. 371–443. Elsevier and MIT Press (2001)

51. Paulson, L.C., Blanchette, J.C.: Three years of experience with Sledgehammer, a practical link between automatic and interactive theorem provers. In: Sutcliffe, G., Schulz, S., Ternovska, E. (eds.) IWIL-2010. EPiC, vol. 2, pp. 1–11. EasyChair (2012)

52. Robinson, J.: Mechanizing higher order logic. In: Meltzer, B., Michie, D. (eds.) Machine Intelligence, vol. 4, pp. 151–170. Edinburgh University Press (1969)

53. Robinson, J.: A note on mechanizing higher order logic. In: Meltzer, B., Michie, D. (eds.) Machine Intelligence, vol. 5, pp. 121–135. Edinburgh University Press (1970)

54. Schlichtkrull, A., Blanchette, J.C., Traytel, D., Waldmann, U.: Formalizing Bachmair and Ganzinger's ordered resolution prover. In: Galmiche, D., Schulz, S., Sebastiani, R. (eds.) IJCAR 2018. LNCS (LNAI), vol. 10900, pp. 89–107. Springer, Cham (2018). https://doi.org/10.1007/978-3-319-94205-6_7

55. Schulz, S.: System description: E 1.8. In: McMillan, K., Middeldorp, A., Voronkov, A. (eds.) LPAR 2013. LNCS, vol. 8312, pp. 735–743. Springer, Heidelberg (2013). https://doi.org/10.1007/978-3-642-45221-5_49

56. Snyder, W.: Higher order E-unification. In: Stickel, M.E. (ed.) CADE 1990. LNCS (LNAI), vol. 449, pp. 573–587. Springer, Heidelberg (1990). https://doi.org/10.1007/3-540-52885-7_115

57. Snyder, W., Gallier, J.H.: Higher-order unification revisited: complete sets of transformations. J. Symb. Comput. **8**(1/2), 101–140 (1989)

58. Steen, A., Benzmüller, C.: The higher-order prover Leo-III. In: Galmiche, D., Schulz, S., Sebastiani, R. (eds.) IJCAR 2018. LNCS (LNAI), vol. 10900, pp. 108–116. Springer, Cham (2018). https://doi.org/10.1007/978-3-319-94205-6_8

59. Sutcliffe, G.: The TPTP problem library and associated infrastructure-from CNF to TH0, TPTP v6.4.0. J. Autom. Reason. **59**(4), 483–502 (2017)

60. Sutcliffe, G., Benzmüller, C., Brown, C.E., Theiss, F.: Progress in the development of automated theorem proving for higher-order logic. In: Schmidt, R.A. (ed.) CADE 2009. LNCS (LNAI), vol. 5663, pp. 116–130. Springer, Heidelberg (2009). https://doi.org/10.1007/978-3-642-02959-2_8

61. Urban, J., Rudnicki, P., Sutcliffe, G.: ATP and presentation service for Mizar formalizations. J. Autom. Reason. **50**(2), 229–241 (2013)

62. Vukmirović, P., Blanchette, J.C., Cruanes, S., Schulz, S.: Extending a brainiac prover to lambda-free higher-order logic. In: Vojnar, T., Zhang, L. (eds.) TACAS 2019. LNCS, vol. 11427, pp. 192–210. Springer, Cham (2019). https://doi.org/10.1007/978-3-030-17462-0_11

63. Waldmann, U.: Automated reasoning II. Lecture notes, Max-Planck-Institut für Informatik (2016). http://resources.mpi-inf.mpg.de/departments/rg1/teaching/autrea2-ss16/script-current.pdf

64. Weidenbach, C., Dimova, D., Fietzke, A., Kumar, R., Suda, M., Wischnewski, P.: SPASS version 3.5. In: Schmidt, R.A. (ed.) CADE 2009. LNCS (LNAI), vol. 5663, pp. 140–145. Springer, Heidelberg (2009). https://doi.org/10.1007/978-3-642-02959-2_10

Restricted Combinatory Unification

Ahmed Bhayat$^{(\boxtimes)}$ and Giles Reger

University of Manchester, Manchester, UK
ahmed.bhayat@manchester.ac.uk

Abstract. First-order theorem provers are commonly utilised as back-ends to proof assistants. In order to improve efficiency, it is desirable that such provers can carry out some higher-order reasoning. In his 1991 paper, Dougherty proposed a combinatory unification algorithm for higher-order logic. The algorithm removes the need to deal with λ-binders and α-renaming, making it attractive to implement in first-order provers. However, since publication it has garnered little interest due to a number of characteristics that make it unsuitable for a practical implementation. It fails to terminate on many trivial instances and requires polymorphism. We present a restricted version of Dougherty's algorithm that is incomplete, terminating and does not require polymorphism. Further, we describe its implementation in the Vampire theorem prover, including a novel use of a substitution tree as a filtering index for higher-order unification. Finally, we analyse the performance of the algorithm on two benchmark sets and show that it is competitive.

1 Introduction

Higher-order logic has many applications from the formalisation of mathematics through to uses in verifying the safety and security of computer systems. This has led to a growing interest in the *automation* of reasoning in higher-order logic. A successful step in this direction has been via translation to first-order logic and utilisation of first-order theorem provers, made possible by the high level of maturity and sophistication of such provers. Proof assistants such as Isabelle [23] and Coq [9] along with automated provers such as Leo-III [29], interact with first-order provers by translating their native logic into first-order logic [21]. These translations tend to be incomplete and suffer from a number of problems of which two of the most important are highlighted below. This paper addresses these problems with a higher-order unification algorithm for combinatory logic and its pragmatic realisation within the first-order Vampire theorem prover [17].

The translation of nameless or λ-functions is often carried out using combinators. However, when translating to monomorphic first-order logic, supported by most first-order provers, an infinite set of combinators is required to guarantee completeness. Thus, most translation schemes suffice with including the combinators necessary to translate the λ-functions present in the input. Consider the somewhat contrived conjecture $\exists X : X\,b\,a = a$. On negation, this becomes

© Springer Nature Switzerland AG 2019
P. Fontaine (Ed.): CADE 2019, LNAI 11716, pp. 74–93, 2019.
https://doi.org/10.1007/978-3-030-29436-6_5

$X\, b\, a \neq a$. As there are no 'λ's there would be no combinators present in the translation. Accordingly, the prover would be unable to synthesise the combinatory equivalent (which is **CK**) of the λ-term $\lambda xy.y$ and would be unable to find a proof. Now consider the same conjecture, but assume that some combinator axioms are present in the first-order translation (this could be via the heuristic addition of combinator axioms, an option in Vampire). In this case, the axioms can superpose amongst themselves. For example, the **C** combinator axiom $\mathbf{C}\, X\, Y\, Z = X\, Z\, Y$ could superpose onto the right hand side of the **S** combinator axiom $\mathbf{S}\, X'\, Y'\, Z' = X'\, Z'(Y'\, Z')$ with unifier $\{X \to \mathbf{C}\, X', Y \to Z', Z \to Y'\, Z'\}$ to produce the equation $\mathbf{S}\,(\mathbf{C}\, X)\, Y'\, Z' = X\,(Y'\, Z')Z'$. A consequence of the combinator axioms has been derived that is of no use in proving the goal.

Both of these problems stem from attempting to achieve what the goal-oriented procedure of higher-order unification (HOU) does using the non-goal-oriented superposition calculus. Thus, there is a strong argument that introducing some form of higher-order unification into first-order provers would significantly improve their performance on problems generated by proof-assistants. This is particularly so if this can be achieved without harming performance on the first-order portion of the problems. We are not attempting to solve problems which require complex higher-order unifiers. Rather, the aim is to introduce limited HOU into a first-order prover to allow it to deal with 'nearly first-order' problems.

Consider for example, the TPTP problem NUM020^1. The problems posits the existence of the Church numeral 2 and requires provers to synthesise the lambda function $\lambda XY.X(XY)$. Despite its simple nature, no current first-order prover would be able to solve the problem unless provided with the definition of the Church numeral 2.

An option is to convert combinatory terms used in the first-order prover into λ-terms at the point of unification and then run a HOU algorithm on these terms. However, the usage of λ-binders adds complications and subtleties to the implementation of higher-order unification. It is precisely to deal with such issues that explicit substitution calculi [10,12] have been investigated.

First-order provers are generally not able to handle binders, so rather than explicit substitution calculi, we focus on higher-order unification in the setting of combinatory logic. The only existing algorithm in this setting is Dougherty's algorithm. The algorithm is a complete unification procedure for *polymorphic* higher-order terms. It is unattractive for implementation because it produces many redundant unifiers and does not terminate in many cases.

Contribution. Our main contributions in this paper are:

- A modification of Dougherty's algorithm that works on *monomorphic* higher-order terms (Sect. 4). Our algorithm is incomplete, but terminating and has shown strong experimental results.
- A method of imperfect filtering that facilitates the implementation of higher-order unification without harming performance on first-order problems (Sect. 5).

These techniques are implemented in the Vampire theorem prover [17] (along with other extensions reported elsewhere for higher-order reasoning) and experimental results (Sect. 6) show that combinatory unification can help solve previously unsolved problems.

2 Preliminaries

In this paper some knowledge of first-order unification and substitution tree indexing is assumed. The reader is referred to [15] and [14] for further details. We present the logical terminology used throughout the rest of the paper. We work with the combinatory-logic (CL) first developed by Schönfinkel, but popularised by Curry. As Dougherty's original algorithm works with polymorphic terms and our modification works with monomorphic terms, both are presented here.

Terms are built over a set of types. Let S be a set of sort symbols that act as syntactic identifiers for the base types of the logic and V_{ty} be a set of sort variables. The set of types is defined as:

$$\textbf{Monomorphic Types} \quad \tau ::= \sigma \mid \tau \to \tau \quad \text{where } \sigma \in S$$

$$\textbf{Polymorphic Types} \quad \tau ::= \sigma \mid \alpha \mid \tau \to \tau \quad \text{where } \sigma \in S, \alpha \in V_{ty}$$

A *polymorphic* type declaration is of the form $\Pi \overline{\alpha_m}.\tau$ where each α_i is a type variable and τ is a potentially polymorphic type containing type variables from $\overline{\alpha_m}$ ($\overline{\alpha_m}$ is a list of type variables). A *monomorphic* type declaration is simply τ for some monomorphic type τ.

For each type τ let V_τ be a set of term variables of type τ and let $V = \bigcup_{\tau \in T} V_\tau$. Further, let Σ be a set of typed constant symbols. When working in monomorphic CL, for every type τ, there exists a constant $\mathsf{I} : \tau \to \tau \in \Sigma$. For every pair of types τ, ρ, there exists a constant $\mathsf{K} : \tau \to \rho \to \tau \in \Sigma$ and for every triple of types τ, ρ, σ, there exists a constant $\mathsf{S} : (\tau \to \rho \to \sigma) \to (\tau \to \rho) \to \tau \to \sigma \in \Sigma$. The constants I, K and S are known as *basic combinators*. When working in polymorphic CL, the existence of only three polymorphic basic combinators is required. From now on, unless required for clarity, type subscripts are omitted.

We define monomorphic and polymorphic terms together as follows. Let $f : \Pi \overline{\alpha_m}.\tau$ be a member of Σ. In the monomorphic case, $m = 0$. Then, f applied to m type arguments: $f\langle \overline{\sigma_m} \rangle$ is a term of type $\tau\{\overline{\alpha_m} \to \overline{\sigma_m}\}$ for some tuple of types $\overline{\sigma_m}$. For all $X \in V_\tau$, X is a term of type τ. If t is a term of type $\tau \to \sigma$ and t' is a term of type τ, then tt' is a term of type σ. Where type arguments are irrelevant, they are dropped from the presentation.

Terms of the form tt' are called *applications*. Non-applicative terms are called *heads*. A term can be decomposed uniquely into a head and n arguments, e.g., $\zeta t_1 \ldots t_n$ or in shorter form $\zeta \overline{t_n}$. By $head(t)$ the unique head of t is intended, e.g., $head(f\,a\,b) = f$ or $head(g\langle \alpha \rangle\, a) = g\langle \alpha \rangle$. A head is first-order if it is not a variable or combinator. A term is *passive* if it does not have a combinator head. The positions $pos(t)$ of term t are defined in the standard fashion; we write $t|_p$

for the subterm of t at position p. Recall the partial ordering $<$ on positions such that $p < p'$ if $t|_{p'}$ is a subterm of $t|_p$. The set of all positions over t is denoted $pos(t)$ and the size of t, denoted $|t|$, is the cardinality of $pos(t)$. A *higher-order subterm*[1] is a subterm with a variable or combinator head. A term that contains no higher-order subterms is called first-order. The set of *first-order positions* over a term t is defined as all $p \in pos(t)$ such that, for all $p' < p$, $head(t|_{p'})$ is not a variable or combinator. In a term $\zeta \overline{t_n}$, subterms of the form $\zeta \overline{t_i}$ for $i < n$ are known as *prefix* subterms.

In what follows, capital letters such as $X, Y, Z \ldots$ are used to denote variables, s, t, u denote arbitrary terms, $a, b, c \ldots$ denote constants.

Unification. Unification involves substituting terms for (free) variables in order to make two or more terms equal. This equality could be syntactic equality, as is generally the case in first-order theorem proving, or equality modulo a set of axioms. In classic HOU, the goal is to find substitution(s) $\theta_1 \ldots \theta_n$ for terms $t_1, t_2 \ldots t_n$ such that $t_1 \theta_i =_{\beta\eta} t_2 \theta_i =_{\beta\eta} \ldots =_{\beta\eta} t_n \theta_i$ for all i in $\{1 \ldots n\}$ where $=_{\beta\eta}$ is equality modulo the axioms of β and η reduction. In this paper, we are interested in the relationship $=_c$ (defined below) on terms of the combinatory logic. A substitution that unifies two or more terms is known as a *unifier*. When working with polymorphic terms, a substitution θ is a *pair*, a term substitution θ_0 and a type substitution θ_1. By an abuse of notation, the same symbols are used to refer to these dual substitutions and standard monomorphic substitutions.

For two unifiers σ and θ, σ is more general than θ ($\sigma \leq \theta$) iff there exists a substitution γ such that $\sigma\gamma = \theta$. In this case, θ is *redundant*. If neither $\sigma \leq \theta$, nor $\theta \leq \sigma$ then σ and θ are *independent*. In syntactic first-order unification, if two terms have a unifier then they have a unique (up to variable naming) *most general unifier* (mgu). This is not the case with HOU and the notion of mgu is generalised to that of *complete set of unifiers* (csu). Let Γ be a set of unifiers of terms $t_1 \ldots t_n$. Γ is a csu iff for all $\sigma \in unifiers(\overline{t_n})$ such that $\sigma \notin \Gamma$, we have $\exists \sigma' \in \Gamma$ such that $\sigma' \leq \sigma$. Γ is a minimal csu iff for all $\sigma_1, \sigma_2 \in \Gamma$, σ_1 and σ_2 are independent. With respect to HOU, all minimal csus may be infinite.

The HOU problem is undecidable and any complete algorithm must produce redundant unifiers [16]. Let $\overset{up}{=}$ be the least congruence relation on combinatory terms which contains $\{(t_1, t_2)|head(t_1), head(t_2) \in V\}$. The pre-unification problem is to find substitutions $\theta_1 \ldots \theta_n$ such that for terms $t_1 \ldots t_n$, $t_i \theta_k \overset{up}{=} t_j \theta_k$ for all i, j and k. Huet devised a famous complete algorithm for pre-unification [16] that is irredundant.

Definition 1. *For CL terms t_1 and t_2, $t_1 =_c t_2$ or equivalently t_1 is C-equal to t_2, iff $\Lambda(t_1) =_{\beta\eta} \Lambda(t_2)$ where Λ is the following translation between combinatory terms and terms of the λ-calculus.*

$\Lambda(a) = a$ *for a not a combinator* $\qquad\qquad \Lambda(\mathsf{S}) = \lambda XYZ.XZ(YZ)$
$\Lambda(\mathsf{I}) = \lambda X.X \qquad\qquad \Lambda(\mathsf{K}) = \lambda XY.X \qquad \Lambda(t_1 t_2) = \Lambda(t_1)\Lambda(t_2)$

---

[1] Note that the definition of higher-order subterm here is different to its usage in [3].

The translation Λ can be used to derive unifiers of λ-terms from unifiers of CL terms. The details can be found in Dougherty's paper [11]. If θ is a substitution such that θ unifies two or more terms with respect to $=_c$, θ is referred to as a C-unifier.

Following Dougherty, a *system* is defined as a multiset of pairs of CL terms. A pair is *trivial* if its components are identical and it is valid if its components are C-equal. The definition of flex-flex, flex-rigid and rigid-rigid pairs is as common in HOU literature [27]. The definitions of *trivial* and *valid* are extended to systems in the obvious way. The *extensional combinatory unification* problem is to find, for any given system $\mathcal{S}$, a set of unifiers U such that $\forall \langle t_1, t_2 \rangle \in \mathcal{S}$ and $\forall \theta \in U$ $t_1 \theta =_c t_2 \theta$. A system $\mathcal{S}$ is *simple* if for all pairs $\langle t, t' \rangle$ in $\mathcal{S}$, terms t and t' do not have identical rigid heads and both are passive.

Definition 2 (Solved System). *For some system $\mathcal{S}$, a pair $\langle X, t_2 \rangle \in \mathcal{S}$ is solved if X doesn't occur in t_2 or in any other pair in $\mathcal{S}$. A system $\mathcal{S}$ is solved if $\forall p \in \mathcal{S}$, either p is trivial or solved.*

The importance of the concept of solved systems can be seen from the fact that the solved pairs of a solved system $\mathcal{S}$ form a *most general unifier* of $\mathcal{S}$ (see [11]).

3   Dougherty's Combinatory Unification Algorithm

Dougherty's algorithm is a complete, finitely-branching, polymorphic HOU algorithm. It is presented here as a set of non-deterministic transformation rules that act on a system of unification pairs. Let $\Longrightarrow$ represent the application of a transformation rule to a system, $\Longrightarrow^+$ the transitive closure of $\Longrightarrow$ and $\Longrightarrow^*$ its reflexive transitive closure. We use $\uplus$ for the multiset sum of two multisets. It assumed that the order of the terms in the pairs is immaterial.

Polymorphism is an essential feature in Dougherty's algorithm even if the initial terms are monomorphic. In the SXX'-narrow transform (given below) an applied variable head is replaced with the term $\mathbf{S}\,X'\,X''$ and then reduced. Applying this transform to the system $\{\langle X_{\iota \to \iota}\, a_\iota, b_\iota \rangle\}$ results in $\{\langle X'a(X''a), b \rangle\}$. Because the type of a is ι the type of the fresh variable X'' must be $\iota \to ?$, but there is no way to determine what type ? should be. Similarly the type of X' must be $\iota \to ? \to \iota$, but again ? cannot be determined. Thus, in both cases ? is set to a type variable which may be instantiated during subsequent unification. In only this transformation are the types of the introduced variables not deducible.

Our presentation differs from that of Dougherty's by having WEAKREDUCE as a separate transformation, rather than a special case of HEADNARROW.

1. ADDARG

$$\{\langle t_1, t_2 \rangle\} \uplus \mathcal{S} \;\Longrightarrow\; \{\langle t_1 \theta\, d, t_2 \theta\, d \rangle\} \uplus \mathcal{S}\theta$$

Where either t_1 or t_2 has an under applied combinator as its head, d is a fresh constant and θ is the type-unifier of the types of t_1, t_2 and $\alpha \to \tau$ for fresh type variables α and τ (in case t_1 and t_2 are both of atomic type).

2. SPLIT:

$$\{\langle X \overline{t_n}, h \overline{s'_m} \overline{s''_n}\rangle\} \uplus \mathcal{S} \implies \{\langle h \overline{X'_m} \overline{t_n}, h \overline{s'_m} \overline{s''_n}\rangle\}\theta \uplus \mathcal{S}\theta$$

Where $\theta = (\theta_0, \theta_1)$, $\theta_0 = \{X \to h \overline{X'_m}\}$ and θ_1 is the mgu of $type(X)$ and $type(h \overline{s'_m})$. Each X'_i is a fresh variable.

3. WEAKREDUCE:

$$\{\langle \mathsf{I} t \overline{t_n}, s'\rangle\} \uplus \mathcal{S} \implies \{\langle t \overline{t_n}, s'\rangle\} \uplus \mathcal{S} \qquad \text{(I-reduce)}$$

$$\{\langle \mathsf{K} t t' \overline{t_n}, s'\rangle\} \uplus \mathcal{S} \implies \{\langle t \overline{t_n}, s'\rangle\} \uplus \mathcal{S} \qquad \text{(K-reduce)}$$

$$\{\langle \mathsf{S} t t' t'' \overline{t_n}, s'\rangle\} \uplus \mathcal{S} \implies \{\langle t t'' (t't'') \overline{t_n}, s'\rangle\} \uplus \mathcal{S} \qquad \text{(S-reduce)}$$

4. HEADNARROW: The variables introduced by the rules are assumed to be fresh for the system in all cases. In all rules, $\theta = (\theta_0, \theta_1)$ where θ_0 is the syntactic unifier of a non-variable prefix subterm and the left-hand side of a suitably renamed combinator axiom and θ_1 is the relevant type unifier. For example, in the first rule $\theta_0 = \{X \to \mathsf{I}\}$ and $\theta_1 = mgu(type(X), type(\mathsf{I}))$.

$$\{\langle X t \overline{t_n}, s'\rangle\} \uplus \mathcal{S} \implies \{\langle t \overline{t_n}, s'\rangle\}\theta \uplus \mathcal{S}\theta \qquad \text{(I-narrow)}$$

$$\{\langle X t \overline{t_n}, s'\rangle\} \uplus \mathcal{S} \implies \{\langle X' \overline{t_n}, s'\rangle\}\theta \uplus \mathcal{S}\theta \qquad \text{(KX-narrow)}$$

$$\{\langle X t t' \overline{t_n}, s'\rangle\} \uplus \mathcal{S} \implies \{\langle t \overline{t_n}, s'\rangle\}\theta \uplus \mathcal{S}\theta \qquad \text{(K-narrow)}$$

$$\{\langle X t \overline{t_n}, s'\rangle\} \uplus \mathcal{S} \implies \{\langle X' t (X'' t) \overline{t_n}, s'\rangle\}\theta \uplus \mathcal{S}\theta \qquad \text{(SXX'-narrow)}$$

$$\{\langle X t t' \overline{t_n}, s'\rangle\} \uplus \mathcal{S} \implies \{\langle X' t' (t t') \overline{t_n}, s'\rangle\}\theta \uplus \mathcal{S}\theta \qquad \text{(SX-narrow)}$$

$$\{\langle X t t' t'' \overline{t_n}, s'\rangle\} \uplus \mathcal{S} \implies \{\langle t t'' (t' t'') \overline{t_n}, s'\rangle\}\theta \uplus \mathcal{S}\theta \qquad \text{(S-narrow)}$$

These four transformation rules are collectively known as the HUT-transformations. They are used alongside syntactic transformations DECOMP, ELIMINATE and TYPEUNIFY. For a system $\mathcal{S}$, its *derived* system is the system of type pairs formed by replacing each term in $\mathcal{S}$ with its type.

5. DECOMP:

$$\{\langle f \overline{t_n}, f \overline{s_n}\rangle\} \uplus \mathcal{S} \implies \{\langle t_1, s_1\rangle \ldots \langle t_n, s_n\rangle\} \uplus \mathcal{S}$$

6. ELIMINATE:

$$\{\langle X, t\rangle\} \uplus \mathcal{S} \implies \{\langle X, t\rangle\} \uplus \mathcal{S}\theta$$

where $\theta = \{X \to t\}$ and X does not occur in t.

7. TypeUnify

$$S \implies S\theta$$

Where θ is the most general type unifier of the derived system of S.

For any system S, an exhaustive application of WeakReduce, Decomp and AddArg results in a simple system S' with the same unifiers as S as proved by Dougherty. Dougherty [11] proves the following non-deterministic algorithm, called U, for enumerating C-unifiers to be sound and complete.

1. Reduce the system to a simple system then apply some HUT-transformation out of an unsolved pair.
2. If at any point the system is syntactically unifiable by a pure substitution then optionally return a most general unifier of the system.

A substitution σ is *pure* if $\forall x \in dom(\sigma)$, $\sigma(x)$ does not contain any constants introduced by AddArg. Unfortunately U contains infinite computation paths in many cases where Huet's classical algorithm does terminate. Worse, even when restricted to pre-unification, the algorithm produces redundant unifiers.

Lemma 1. *If, for a system of unification pairs Σ, there exists a computation path of U that includes a HeadNarrow step, then there exists an infinite computation path of U on S.*

Proof. Let ty_1 and ty_2 be meta-type variables, standing for arbitrary types. We show that if a pair of the form $\langle X_{ty_1 \to ty_2} \, t_{ty_1} \, \overline{t_n}, t' \rangle$ (*) is part of a simple system, then an SXX'-narrow step can be applied and the resulting system transformed to a simple system containing a pair of the same form.

For the application of a HeadNarrow step, there must exist a simple system S_1 such that $S \implies^* S_1$ by a series of U-steps and S_1 includes a pair $p = \langle X_{\alpha \to \tau} \, t_\alpha \, \overline{t_n}, t' \rangle$. Assume that t' has a rigid head or a flexible head different to X (if the head of t' is X, the proof still holds, but is slightly more complex). The pair p is of the form (*). The following HeadNarrow step can then be applied:

$$S_1 = p \uplus S_2 \implies_{SXX'-narrow} \{\langle X'_{\alpha \to \gamma \to \tau} \, t_\alpha (X''_{\alpha \to \gamma} \, t_\alpha) \, \overline{t_n}, t' \rangle\} \theta \uplus S_2 \theta = S_3$$

The algorithm proceeds by reducing S_3 to a simple system S_4. As $head(t') \neq X$, we have that $head(t') = head(t'\theta)$. Since neither X' nor $head(t')$ is a combinator, no WeakReduce or AddArg rules can be applied to the pair during the reduction phase. As X' is not rigid, Decomp is not applicable either. Therefore, the pair $\langle (X'_{\alpha \to \gamma \to \tau} \, t_\alpha \, (X'' \, t) \, \overline{t_n}) \theta \sigma, t \theta \sigma \rangle$ is a part of S_4 where σ is a possibly empty type substitution introduced by AddArg steps. By taking $ty_1 = \alpha \theta \sigma$ and $ty_2 = (\gamma \to \tau) \theta \sigma$, we have that S_4 is a simple system that contains a pair of form (*).

Lemma 2. *Even if U is restricted, such that no transformation steps are carried out on flex-flex pairs, U can still produce redundant unifiers.*

Proof. Consider the simple system $\{\langle Xa, a \rangle\}$. Then by a single application of I-narrow the unifier $\{X \to I\}$ can be produced. Alternatively the derivation path $\{\langle Xa, a \rangle\} \Longrightarrow_{SXX'-narrow} \{\langle X'a(X''a), a \rangle\} \Longrightarrow_{K-narrow} \Longrightarrow \{\langle a, a \rangle\}$ can be followed leading to the unifier $\{X \to SKX''\}$. $SKX'' =_c I$ and is thus a redundant unifier.

Lemmas 1 and 2 show that Dougherty's algorithm, whilst interesting from a theoretical aspect, is not suitable for a practical implementation. In as yet unpublished work [4], Bentkamp et al. present a modification of the given-clause algorithm that deals with possibly infinite streams of unifiers. But even such a method would be unable to handle Dougherty's algorithm as almost all unification problems are likely to be non-terminating quickly leading to memory issues on difficult problems. Instead, we propose a modification to the algorithm that eliminates these unpleasant properties at the cost of completeness.

4   Restricted Combinatory Unification

The pair of problems with Dougherty's algorithm identified in the previous section are both linked to the SXX'-narrow transform. As this step introduces type variables, typing cannot be used to restrict its application. In our modification of Dougherty's algorithm, we remove this head-narrow step. As this step was the only one to introduce type variables, polymorphism can now be eliminated. The three polymorphic combinator axioms used in the HEADNARROW step now become an infinite set of monomorphic axioms. To this set the **C** and **B** combinator axioms schemas are added. These schemas are $\mathbf{B}XYZ = X(YZ)$ and $\mathbf{C}XYZ = XZY$. The **C** and **B** combinators are redundant, in the sense that they can be defined in terms of **S, K** and **I**, yet their usage often makes combinatory terms smaller.

Below, the modifications to Dougherty's algorithm are presented. The resulting algorithm is referred to as Restricted Combinatory Unification or RCU. In the calculation of the unifier θ in the steps below, no type unification is required. Further Dougherty's syntactic transformation step TYPEUNIFY is no longer required resulting in DECOMP and ELIMINATE being the only syntactic transforms needed.

Definition 3. *The set of all variables contained in a system $\mathcal{S}$, denoted $vars(\mathcal{S})$, is divided into two disjoint subsets R and B. Members of R are referred to as red variables and members of B as blue variables. We define $R = \{X \in vars(\mathcal{S}) \mid X$ introduced by CX-narrow transform$\}$ and $B = vars(\mathcal{S}) - R$.*

1. The following WEAKREDUCE rules are added in addition to the three in Dougherty's algorithm.

$$\{\langle \mathbf{B}\, t\, t'\, t''\, \overline{t_n}, s' \rangle\} \uplus \mathcal{S} \qquad \Longrightarrow \{\langle t\, (t't'')\, \overline{t_n}, s' \rangle\} \uplus \mathcal{S} \qquad \text{(B-reduce)}$$

$$\{\langle \mathbf{C}\, t\, t'\, t''\, \overline{t_n}, s' \rangle\} \uplus \mathcal{S} \qquad \Longrightarrow \{\langle t\, t''\, t'\, \overline{t_n}, s' \rangle\} \uplus \mathcal{S} \qquad \text{(C-reduce)}$$

2. The SXX'-narrow step is removed from Dougherty's rules and the following HEADNARROW steps are added. In all cases, θ is the syntactic (first-order) unifier of a non-variable prefix subterm and the left-hand side of a suitably renamed combinator axiom.

$$\{\langle X\ t\ t'\ \overline{t_n}, s'\rangle\} \uplus \mathcal{S} \qquad \Longrightarrow \{\langle X'\ (t\ t')\ \overline{t_n}, s'\rangle\}\theta \uplus \mathcal{S}\theta \qquad \text{(BX-narrow)}$$

$$\{\langle X\ t\ t'\ t''\ \overline{t_n}, s'\rangle\} \uplus \mathcal{S} \qquad \Longrightarrow \{\langle t\ (t'\ t'')\ \overline{t_n}, s'\rangle\}\theta \uplus \mathcal{S}\theta \qquad \text{(B-narrow)}$$

$$\{\langle X\ t\ t'\ \overline{t_n}, s'\rangle\} \uplus \mathcal{S} \qquad \Longrightarrow \{\langle X'\ t'\ t\ \overline{t_n}, s'\rangle\}\theta \uplus \mathcal{S}\theta \qquad \text{(CX-narrow)}$$

Where X is not a red variable

$$\{\langle X\ t\ t'\ t''\ \overline{t_n}, s'\rangle\} \uplus \mathcal{S} \qquad \Longrightarrow \{\langle t\ t''\ t'\ \overline{t_n}, s'\rangle\}\theta \uplus \mathcal{S}\theta \qquad \text{(C-narrow)}$$

The reason for the restriction on the CX-narrow step is to prevent infinite computation paths such as $\langle Xab, s\rangle \Longrightarrow \langle X'ba, s\rangle \Longrightarrow \langle X''ab, s\rangle \Longrightarrow \ldots$. The convention that no transformations are carried out on solved or trivial pairs is adopted.

Restricting Dougherty's algorithm would be of little interest if the restricted version suffered the same problems as the original. This is not the case with RCU.

Theorem 1. *Every sequence of RCU transformations terminates.*

Proof. A proof sketch is provided here (see Appendix A for full proof). Dougherty proves that the set of transforms WEAKREDUCE, DECOMP and ADDARG are terminating. We reduce the proof of termination of RCU to this proof by showing that the remaining transformation can only appear finitely many times on a computation path. Intuitively, for any type σ, $size(\sigma)$ is the number of '$\rightarrow$'s in σ.

- Each of transforms ELIMINATE and SPLIT, reduce the number of unsolved variables in a system by 1, whilst all other transforms maintain or reduce this measure.
- For HEADNARROW, consider the measure $(\sum_{v \in vars(\mathcal{S})} size(type(v)), \#\mathcal{S})$ where $\#\mathcal{S}$ is the number of blue variables in a system $\mathcal{S}$. HEADNARROW reduces this measure whilst WEAKREDUCE, DECOMP and ADDARG maintain or reduce it.

An obvious corollary of Theorem 1 is that RCU is not a complete HOU algorithm. It does not, in general, find a csu. It would be of interest to compare RCU with other restricted forms of higher-order unification such as pattern unification [22]. However, it is not readily comparable with pattern unification and similar restrictions, as these tend to be restrictions on the *input terms* whilst RCU is a restriction on the *transformations*. As such, it most closely resembles a depth-bound version of Huet's algorithm. We have not studied the complexity of RCU, but in Sect. 6, empirical evidence is presented that suggests its performance is reasonable.

5   Imperfect Filtering

In first-order provers, unification is generally carried out via term-indexes. Let R be a relationship on terms. A term-indexing data-structure stores terms in a manner that facilitates the rapid retrieval of all terms l such that $R(l, t)$ for some *query term* t. In the context of theorem-proving, the relationship R could be "is unifiable with", "is a generalisation of" etc. Indexing structures for first-order theorem proving have been intensively studied and efficient indexing structures such as substitution trees, fingerprint indexes and perfect discrimination trees have been developed.

These structures are either *perfect* or *imperfect* depending on whether they return all and only those terms that match the query, or they return some sub/superset of the same. Substitution trees store substitutions in their nodes. Variables of the form $*_i$ are used to denote substitutions in the tree. The equation $*_i = t$ represents the substitution of the variable $*_i$ by the term t. A path from the root to a leaf represents a term formed by the composition of substitutions on the path (view Fig. 1). Substitution trees act as perfect filters for first-order unification. This is achieved by traversing the tree left-right depth-first. In the root, the query term is unified with $*_0$. Each time we move down to a node $*_i = t$ the current unifier is extended with the unifier of $(*_i, t)$ in what is known as *incremental unification*. On backtracking, the unifier is reset to its previous value.

With respect to higher-order unification, some work has been carried out on developing indexing data structures [20, 24], but has gained little acceptance. Steen [28] suggests that the reason for this is the complexity or undecidability of many of the operations required to build and maintain higher-order indexing structures. For example, higher-order unification, anti-unification and matching are all either undecidable or have large complexities. This is a daunting obstacle to developing perfect higher-order indexing structures. However, it does not preclude the development of imperfect filters.

We have modified substitution trees to act as imperfect filters for higher-order unification. The insights behind this modification are two-fold:

1. If two terms disagree on a function symbol that is not below an applied variable or combinator, then the terms have no higher-order unifier
2. Two terms that are first-order can only have a first-order unifier

Description of Filtering Algorithm. Prior to any term being inserted into the tree all higher-order subterms are replaced with special sort-correct constants $\#_\tau$ not appearing in the input. We call this process *hashing* and its inverse *dehashing*. When performing incremental unification, '#'s unify with all terms. Let t be a query term and T a hashed substitution tree. The filtering algorithm works as follows:

1. Calculate $t' = hash(t)$.

2. Run the standard first-order algorithm to find all unification partners of t' in T. Let $U = \{\langle \sigma_i, t_i \rangle | t_i$ unifies with t' with unifier $\sigma_i\}$ be the output of this algorithm.
3. For all $\langle \sigma_i, t_i \rangle$ in U, if both t and $dehash(t_i)$ are first-order then return σ_i as the only unifier of t and $dehash(t_i)$.
4. Otherwise the pair $\langle t, t_i \rangle$ has passed filtering and is handed over to RCU.

Correctness of Algorithm. To show that the algorithm is correct, we need to show that (1) if incremental unification at a node $*_i = t$ fails due to CLASH or OCCURSCHECK (terminology from [1]), then for all terms sharing this substitution, none of them can have a higher-order unifier with the query term. We also need to show that (2) if two terms are first-order then higher-order unification can only produce the first-order unifier. The following two lemmas are used to show (1).

Lemma 3. *If $t|_p = s$ for first-order position p, then $(t\theta|_p) = s\theta$ for all substitutions θ.*

Proof. Proof is by induction on the length of p. If $p = \epsilon$ then $t\theta|_\epsilon = t\theta = s\theta$. In the inductive case, $t\theta|_p = t\theta|_{p'.i} \overset{IH}{=} (\zeta \ s'_1 \ldots s'_{i-1}, s, s'_{i+1} \ldots s'_n)\theta|_i = (\zeta \ s'_1\theta \ldots s'_{i-1}\theta, s\theta, s'_{i+1}\theta \ldots s'_n\theta)|_i = s\theta$.

Lemma 4. *Let p be a first-order position in terms t_1 and t_2. Then t_1 and t_2 have no higher-order unifiers if:*

1. *Both $head(t_1|_p)$ and $head(t_2|_p)$ are first order and $head(t_1|_p) \neq head(t_2|_p)$, or*
2. *$t_1|_p = X$, X occurs in $t_2|_p$ at a first-order position and $X \neq t_2|_p$ or vice versa.*

Proof. Assume that θ is a unifier of t_1 and t_2. Let $t_1|_p$ be s_1 and $t_2|_p$ be s_2. By Lemma 3, $(t_1|_p)\theta = s_1\theta$ and $(t_2|_p)\theta = s_2\theta$. Therefore, we must have that $s_1\theta = s_2\theta$. In case (1), $s_1 = f \ \overline{s'_n}$, $s_2 = g \ \overline{t'_m}$ and $f \neq g$. However, $s_1\theta = (f \ \overline{s'_n})\theta = f \ (\overline{s'_n}\theta) \neq g \ (\overline{t'_m}\theta) = (g \ \overline{t'_m})\theta$ and thus θ cannot be a unifier. In case (2), $s_1 = X$ and $s_2 = \zeta \ \overline{t_n}$ such that for some t_i and position p', $t_i|_{p'} = X$. By Lemma 3 and the fact $i.p'$ is a first-order position in s_2, we have that $s_2\theta|_{i.p'} = X\theta$. But then we cannot have that $s_1\theta = s_2\theta$ since $|s_1\theta| = |X\theta| \leq |t_i\theta| < |\zeta \ (\overline{t_n})\theta| = |s_2\theta|$.

Now consider incremental unification at a node $*_i = t$. Assume that $*_i$ is bound to a subterm t' of the hashed query term. If a CLASH occurs in unifying t with t', then the query term and all terms sharing the substitution $*_i = t$ must disagree on a head symbol occurring at a first-order position. By Lemma 4, the query term and all terms sharing the substitution $*_i = t$ can have no higher-order unifiers. The case where unification of t and t' fails due to OCCURSCHECK is similar.

To show (2) we prove the following lemma.

Terms in tree:

1. $g(X\,a)b$

2. $g(\boldsymbol{I}\,a)c$

3. $g(f\,a)b$

4. $g(f(Z\,d))b$

Query term:
g (f X) b

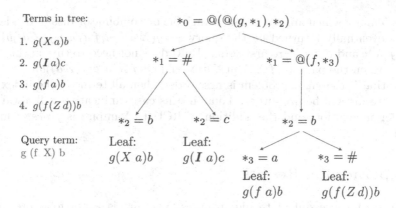

Fig. 1. Example of substitution tree being used as a filter for higher-order unification. The query will return terms (1), (3) and (4). Higher-order unification only needs to be run on the pairs $\langle g(f\,X)b,\ g(X\,a)b\rangle$ and $\langle g(f\,X)b,\ g(f(Z\,d))b\rangle$

Lemma 5. *Let t_1 and t_2 be first-order terms. Then, for any computation path $\{\langle t_1, t_2\rangle\} \Longrightarrow^* S'$, we have:*

1. *All terms in S' are first-order.*
2. *In the computation path, only DECOMP and ELIMINATE are used.*

Proof. Proof by induction on the length of the $\Longrightarrow^*$ path. The base case is trivial. In the inductive case, after p steps the original system is transformed into $\{\langle s_1, s_2\rangle \ldots \langle s_{n-1}, s_n\rangle\}$ where each s_i is first-order by the induction hypothesis. In the $p+1$ step, an arbitrary pair $\langle s_i, s_{i+1}\rangle$ is transformed. If either s_i or s_{i+1} is a variable than the transformation is ELIMINATE and the resulting system again contains only first-order terms. Otherwise s_i and s_{i+1} are of the form $\zeta\,\overline{t_m}$ and $\zeta\,\overline{r_m}$ and the only applicable step is DECOMP. After performing DECOMP, the resulting system is $\{\langle s_1, s_2\rangle \ldots \langle t_m, r_m\rangle \ldots \langle s_{n-1}, s_n\rangle\}$ and again all terms are first-order.

Since the usage of DECOMP and ELIMINATE is deterministic, and these two transforms form a sound and complete unification algorithm for syntactic first-order unification [1], we have that if two terms are first-order and unifiable then running RCU on the terms will result in the single mgu produced by first-order unification. The result is presented in terms of RCU, but is in reality general.

Example. Consider searching the tree in Fig. 1 for unifiers of $g(f\,X)b$. The original substitution is $\sigma_0 = \{*_0 \to g(f\,X)b\}$. In the root, the substitution is extended to unify $*_0$ with $g\,*_1\,*_2$ resulting in $\sigma_1 = \sigma_0 \cup \{*_1 \to f\,X, *_2 \to b\}$. In the left child, $*_1$ is unified with $\#$. This succeeds without adding anything to the unifier, so $\sigma_3 = \sigma_2$. Finally, in the left-most leaf, $*_2$ is unified with b, again succeeding with the empty substitution. The search then backtracks and attempts to enter the second-to-left leaf. This requires unifying $*_2$ which is bound to b, with c and fails due to CLASH. The terms $g(f\,X)b$ and $g(\boldsymbol{I}\,a)c$ can have no unifiers as symbols b and c which are not below a variable or combinator disagree. The set of terms eventually returned by the query is $\{g(X\,a)b, g(f\,a)b, g(f(Z\,d))b\}$. As both $g(f\,X)b$ and $g(f\,a)b$ are first-order, RCU does not need to run on this pair. RCU is run on the pairs $\langle g(f\,X)b, g(X\,a)b\rangle$ and $\langle g(f\,X)b, g(f(Z\,d))b\rangle$

Note that if the input problem is first-order, then all terms in the index and all query terms will be first-order. Thus, in this case, unification will always be first-order unification, and the addition of RCU to Vampire is *graceful* in the sense of [3].

6   Experimental Results

As with most successful first-order provers, Vampire is a portfolio prover. In finding a proof, it runs a set of *strategies* known as a *schedule*. Each strategy is a predefined set of proof search parameters. Normally, if a problem is solvable, it is solvable within a short space of time using a particular strategy. In this section we examine whether the new RCU option can be used to complement the existing set of options available for higher-order reasoning in Vampire. To test this we first heuristically created a custom higher-order schedule that includes various options (including RCU) linked to higher-order proof search. Some details regarding these options can be found in [5]. Two options in particular are relevant to the experiments below:

comb_unif: this option can be set to on or off toggling combinatory unification as described in this paper

combinator_elimination: this option can be set to axioms in which case combinators are axiomatised. It can be set to inference_rules to enable a set of inferences that rewrite fully applied combinators. Axioms and rewriting can be used together by setting the option to both or the option can be set to off

The higher-order schedule represents our current best-effort prior to these experiments. It is Vampire trying its hardest rather than a default baseline.

Experiments were run across two benchmark sets. The first set consists of TPTP library benchmarks [31]. From the TPTP library we selected higher-order monomorphic problems that are designated as theorems, unsatisfiable or unknown giving a total of 2727 problems. Satisfiable problems were excluded as both Vampire and Leo-III are incomplete. The second benchmark set was produced by the Isabelle theorem prover's Sledgehammer system. It contains 1253 benchmarks kindly made available to us by the Matryoshka team and is called SH-λ following their naming convention.

We ran Vampire's higher-order schedule across both benchmark sets multiple times with comb_unif and combinator_elimination forced to various values across the whole schedule. A (wall-clock) time limit of 520s was used for experiments over the TPTP problem set and 300s for experiments over the SH-λ problem set. Experiments were performed on StarExec [30] nodes equipped with four 2.40 GHz Intel Xeon CPUs.

Table 1. Number of problems proved theorem or unsat

	TPTP problems			SH-λ		
	Number	Uniques		Number	Uniques	
	Solved	All	A vs B	Solved	All	A vs B
Vampire-HOL-RCUon	1907	7		713	0	
Vampire-HOL-RCUon-CEaxs	1538	2		708	0	
Vampire-HOL-RCUon-CEinf (A)	1728	0	276	714	0	16
Vampire-HOL-RCUon-CEoff	1500	0		700	0	
Vampire-HOL-RCUoff	1920	30		725	1	
Vampire-HOL-RCUoff-CEaxs (B)	1637	15	175	715	0	17
Vampire-HOL-RCUoff-CEinf	1672	0		720	0	
Vampire-HOL-RCUoff-CEoff	1186	0		692	0	
Union	*2018*			*734*		
Vampire-HOL	1958	31		719	55	
Leo-III	2097	58		668	31	
Satallax	2095	92		513	8	

The results of two sets of experiments can be found in Table 1. In the first set, **Vampire-HOL-RCUxx-CEyyy** refers to Vampire running its higher-order schedule, with `comb_unif` forced to value **xx** and `combinator_elimination` forced to value **yyy**. The second set compares **Vampire-HOL** (higher-order schedule with nothing forced) to the CASC-2018 versions of leading higher-order theorem provers, Leo-III version 1.3 and Satallax version 3.3 [6]. The number of problems solved uniquely are given separately for the two sets of experiments. As explained below, we make an additional comparison in the first set. Our experimental data is publicly available.[2]

Firstly, we consider the choice between reasoning solely with axioms or solely with RCU. To do this we compare **Vampire-HOL-RCUon-CEinf** (A) and **Vampire-HOL-RCUoff-CEaxs** (B). In (B) the only method of synthesising higher-order functions is via combinators and in (A) it is via RCU, making these suitable versions for comparing the two methods. RCU is run in conjunction with inference rules in our comparison due to the implementation of RCU which does not weak reduce terms on the application of a combinatory unifier. Across the TPTP benchmark set, RCU significantly outperforms axioms. Across the SH-λ problem set, the performance of the two is similar.

Next we consider the other combinations of options more broadly. The strategies that solve the most problems do not force RCU on. Indeed, between them, strategies forcing RCU off solve 93 problems unsolved by forcing RCU on, conversely 68 are solved by forcing it on as opposed to off. This is expected as RCU is expensive and many problems do not require it. It is the 68 problems gained with the new option that are of interest. We also draw attention to the fact that

---

[2] https://github.com/vprover/vampire_publications/tree/master/experimental_data/ CADE-2019-RCU.

Table 2. Efficiency of RCU

Problem category	Average time spent on combinatory unification (as % of total time)	Average number of unifiers produced per problem
SYO	11.71%	63764
SEU	9.5%	42968
SET	9.89%	57339
NUM	9.55%	22779
ALG	11.08%	54723

for both problem sets, the union of all problems solved by the various Vampire versions exceeds the number of problems solved by our current schedule. This suggests that the schedule could easily be improved by incorporating some of these strategies.

It is interesting to note that on the SH-λ problems **Vampire-HOL-RCUoff-CEoff** which treats combinators as uninterpreted symbols and cannot synthesise higher-order functions outperforms Leo-III suggesting that this problem set is highly first-order in nature. This may well explain why RCU performs poorly across the problem set in general (adding it as an option to the schedule actually reduces the number of proofs). We suspect that RCU is becoming trapped in the high-order portions of the problems which do not need to be explored to find a proof. The 16 problems solved by RCU that cannot be solved with combinators show that RCU is still a valuable option to include in the schedule. However, for these mostly first-order problems, the schedule requires tweaking to reduce the prominence of RCU.

Amongst the TPTP benchmarks, Vampire solves 31 problems not solved by Leo-III and Satallax.[3] Out of these, 2 (SEV016^5[4] and SEV032^5) are difficulty rating 1.00 problems, meaning that they are unsolvable by any current theorem prover. Amongst the 31 problems 17 are solved by strategies that utilise combinatory unification, showing its value. On the SH-λ benchmarks, Vampire solves 55 problems that Leo-III and Satallax cannot. Out of these, 33 are solved by strategies that use combinatory unification.

Finally, we investigated the efficiency of combinatory unification. It would have been interesting to compare it against first-order unification, but this is not possible in Vampire as first order unification is carried out incrementally whilst RCU is carried out term-to-term. Instead, the amount of time spent on RCU in each run was recorded as well as the number of unifiers produced. The results can be found in Table 2. It can be seen that combinatory unification is not dominating the running time. Further the number of combinatory unifiers

---

[3] Some of these problems are marked as being solvable by Satallax on the TPTP website. However, the CASC-2018 version of Satallax that we used in our tests was unable to find a proof.

[4] This problem can be solved by the new version of E, Ehoh developed by Vukmirović et al. [32].

produced suggests that whatever the worst case complexity is, in practice the procedure is efficient.

7   Conclusion and Related Work

Pragmatic approaches to higher-order theorem proving include Otter-λ, a prover for lambda logic [2] developed by Michael Beeson. Lambda logic is a relatively weak extension of first-order logic. Also included is Cruanes' prover Zipperposition [8] which he extended to HOL. The prover rewrites using the combinator definitions which resembles our approach, but is less goal directed.

Dowek et al. developed the deduction modulo framework [7,13] which can be used to turn higher-order logic into a first-order theory. It involves replacing unification with unification modulo and adding rewrite rules for literals. Their proof methods don't extend to superposition and in the absence of an efficient, complete unification algorithm modulo the combinator axioms, their work remains of academic interest.

The approach we present here resembles that taken by the Leo-III higher-order prover [29]. Leo-III implements Huet's complete algorithm for higher-order unification, but then imposes a depth bound, thereby losing completeness. We feel that RCU is more amenable to implementation within a first-order prover than depth-bound Huet's algorithm and therefore our approach is complementary. By retaining the ordering restrictions of the superposition calculus, our approach further resembles that of Leo-III which makes use of the computational path order (CPO) further losing completeness.

Related to our work is the Matryoshka team's extension of superposition to lambda-free higher-order logic [3] and, in as yet unpublished work, to full higher-order logic [4]. Their approach aims for completeness and thus has to deal with possible infinite sets of unifiers. Due to the incompleteness of our method, there will certainly be problems provable by a complete calculus that are inaccessible to us. On the other hand, it appears likely that, at least on some problems, the overhead of dealing with infinite streams of possibly redundant unifiers will allow lightweight but incomplete solutions such as RCU to outperform complete methods. However, what promises to be an interesting empirical comparison of the two approaches is future work.

As far as restrictions to higher-order unification are concerned, our approach adds to a long list of attempts to devise useful restrictions. Foremost amongst these are *pattern unification* [22] and its generalisation by Libal and Miller [19]. Pattern unification has gained popularity because it is decidable and mgus exist. Bounding the number of 'λ's that can appear in a unifier has been shown to make higher-order unification decidable [26]. Various other restrictions have been shown to either be decidable or undecidable in [18] and [25]. As far as we are aware, we are the first to address restrictions to combinatory higher-order unification algorithms.

On the mildly higher-order Sledgehammer benchmarks, Vampire with RCU outperformed full higher-order solvers. It remains to be seen whether this results holds across larger proof assistant generated benchmark sets. Other lines of investigation, include implementing Dougherty's algorithm, but utilising it in a limited form. Consider the following inference which we call HYPEREQRES:

$$\frac{t_1 \neq t_2 \vee t_3 \neq t_4 \ldots \vee t_{n-1} \neq t_n}{\square} \text{ HYPEREQRES}$$

where Dougherty's algorithm is used to find a unifier θ that simultaneously unifies each pair of terms. As this leads directly to a refutation, the problem of redundant unifiers is circumvented. Likewise, polymorphism can be restricted to the unification algorithm. Finally, it would be interesting to evaluate the usage of substitution trees as imperfect filters. On average what percentage of terms in the index are discarded? In practice, how often does first-order unification suffice?

Acknowledgements. Thanks to Jasmin Blanchette, Alexander Bentkamp, Simon Cruanes and Petar Vukmirović for many discussions on aspects of this research. A big thanks to the Matryoshka team as a whole for sharing their benchmarks. We would also like to thank Andrei Voronkov, Michael Rawson, Alexander Steen, the maintainers of StarExec and the anonymous paper reviewers. Special thanks to Martin Riener for proof-reading the paper. The first author thanks the family of James Elson for funding his research.

A   Restricted Combinatory Unification Is Terminating

We prove the termination of an algorithm identical to RCU, except that reductions can be performed at all positions. That RCU is terminating follows immediately. A straight-forward corollary of this is that RCU is incomplete.

Lemma 6. *For any (finite) system S, if there exists an infinite RCU computation path on S, then there exists a system S' such that $S \Longrightarrow^* S'$ and there exists an infinite computation path on S' that does not include the ELIMINATE or SPLIT transforms.*

Proof. Both ELIMINATE and SPLIT reduce the number of unsolved variables in S. As S is finite, it can only contain a finite number of unsolved variables. A case analysis of the other rules shows that either they reduce the number of unsolved variables or leave it unchanged. Thus SPLIT and ELIMINATE can only be carried out a finite number of times. $\square$

Based on Lemma 6, to prove that RCU is terminating, it suffices to prove that RCU without the eliminate and split transforms is terminating. Call the resulting set of transformation rules RCU−. Next a result analogous to Lemma 6 is proved with respect to the HEADNARROW transformation.

Definition 4 (Size). *The size of a type σ is defined inductively as follows:*

- σ *is atomic, the* $size(\sigma) = 0$

- $\sigma = \alpha \to \beta$, then $size(\sigma) = size(\alpha) + size(\beta) + 1$

For a term t, its type is denoted by $\tau(t)$

Intuitively, $size(\sigma)$ is the number of '$\to$'s in σ.

Lemma 7. *For any (finite) system S, if there exists an infinite RCU– computation path on S, then there exists a system S' such that $S \Longrightarrow^* S'$ and there exists an infinite computation path on S' that does not include the head narrow transform.*

Proof. Consider the following measure on systems:

$$\left(\sum_{v \in vars(S)} size(\tau(v)), \#S \right)$$

Where the pairs are compared lexicographically and $\#S$ denotes the number of blue variables in S or equivalently, the cardinality of B. The transformation rules of RCU–, other than head narrow, keep this measure constant or reduce it. HEADNARROW reduces the measure, so there can only be a finite number of applications of head narrow. The former claim is demonstrated for a number of HEADNARROW steps:

1. KX-narrow. For a variable X to be eligible for a KX-narrow step, it must have type $\alpha \to \beta$. It is replaced by a term $\mathbf{K}_{\beta \to \alpha \to \beta} X'_\beta$. Clearly $size(\tau(X')) < size(\tau(X))$ and so the first item of the measure is reduced.
2. BX-narrow. For a variable X to be eligible for a BX-narrow step, it must have type $(\alpha \to \beta) \to \alpha \to \gamma$. It is replaced by a term $\mathbf{B}_{(\beta \to \gamma) \to (\alpha \to \beta) \to \alpha \to \gamma} X'_{\beta \to \gamma}$. Again $size(\tau(X')) < size(\tau(X))$ and so the first item of the measure is reduced.
3. CX-narrow. In this case, the size of the type of the variable being narrowed is not reduced. For a variable X to be eligible for a CX-narrow step, it must have type $\alpha \to \beta \to \gamma$. It is replaced by a term $\mathbf{C}_{(\beta \to \alpha \to \gamma) \to \alpha \to \beta \to \gamma} X'_{\beta \to \alpha \to \gamma}$. Here $size(\tau(X')) = size(\tau(X))$. However, each CX-narrow step replaces a blue variable with a red variable and therefore the second item of the measure is reduced. $\square$

Based on Lemma 7 to prove that RCU– is terminating, it suffices to prove that RCU– without the HEADNARROW transformation is terminating. This is precisely Dougherty's VT transformations which he has proven to be terminating in [11]. Therefore we have:

Theorem 2. *Every sequence of RCU transformations terminates.*

References

1. Baader, F., Nipkow, T.: Term Rewriting and All That. Cambridge University Press, Cambridge (1999)

2. Beeson, M.: Lambda logic. In: Basin, D., Rusinowitch, M. (eds.) IJCAR 2004. LNCS (LNAI), vol. 3097, pp. 460–474. Springer, Heidelberg (2004). https://doi.org/10.1007/978-3-540-25984-8_34

3. Bentkamp, A., Blanchette, J.C., Cruanes, S., Waldmann, U.: Superposition for lambda-free higher-order logic. In: Galmiche, D., Schulz, S., Sebastiani, R. (eds.) IJCAR 2018. LNCS (LNAI), vol. 10900, pp. 28–46. Springer, Cham (2018). https://doi.org/10.1007/978-3-319-94205-6_3

4. Bentkamp, A., Blanchette, J.C., Tourret, S., Vukmirović, P., Waldmann, U.: Superposition with lambdas (2019, submitted for publication)

5. Bhayat, A., Reger, G.: Set of support for higher-order reasoning. In: PAAR 2018. CEUR Workshop Proceedings, vol. 2162, pp. 2–16 (2018)

6. Brown, C.E.: Satallax: an automatic higher-order prover. In: Gramlich, B., Miller, D., Sattler, U. (eds.) IJCAR 2012. LNCS (LNAI), vol. 7364, pp. 111–117. Springer, Heidelberg (2012). https://doi.org/10.1007/978-3-642-31365-3_11

7. Burel, G.: Embedding deduction modulo into a prover. In: Dawar, A., Veith, H. (eds.) CSL 2010. LNCS, vol. 6247, pp. 155–169. Springer, Heidelberg (2010). https://doi.org/10.1007/978-3-642-15205-4_15

8. Cruanes, S.: Superposition with structural induction. In: Dixon, C., Finger, M. (eds.) FroCoS 2017. LNCS (LNAI), vol. 10483, pp. 172–188. Springer, Cham (2017). https://doi.org/10.1007/978-3-319-66167-4_10

9. Czajka, Ł., Kaliszyk, C.: Hammer for coq: automation for dependent type theory. J. Autom. Reason. **61**(1), 423–453 (2018)

10. de Moura, F.L.C., Ayala-Rincón, M., Kamareddine, F.: Higher-order unification: a structural relation between Huet's method and the one based on explicit substitutions. J. Appl. Logic **6**(1), 72–108 (2008)

11. Dougherty, D.J.: Higher-order unification via combinators. Theor. Comput. Sci. **114**(2), 273–298 (1993)

12. Dowek, G.: Higher order unification via explicit substitutions. Inf. Comput. **157**(1–2), 183–235 (2000)

13. Dowek, G., Hardin, T., Kirchner, C.: Theorem proving modulo. J. Autom. Reason. **31**(1), 33–72 (2003)

14. Graf, P.: Substitution tree indexing. In: Hsiang, J. (ed.) RTA 1995. LNCS, vol. 914, pp. 117–131. Springer, Heidelberg (1995). https://doi.org/10.1007/3-540-59200-8_52

15. Hoder, K., Voronkov, A.: Comparing unification algorithms in first-order theorem proving. In: Mertsching, B., Hund, M., Aziz, Z. (eds.) KI 2009. LNCS (LNAI), vol. 5803, pp. 435–443. Springer, Heidelberg (2009). https://doi.org/10.1007/978-3-642-04617-9_55

16. Huet, G.: A unification algorithm for typed λ-calculus. Theor. Comput. Sci. TCS **1**(1), 27–57 (1975)

17. Kovács, L., Voronkov, A.: First-order theorem proving and VAMPIRE. In: Sharygina, N., Veith, H. (eds.) CAV 2013. LNCS, vol. 8044, pp. 1–35. Springer, Heidelberg (2013). https://doi.org/10.1007/978-3-642-39799-8_1

18. Levy, J.: Decidable and undecidable second-order unification problems. In: Nipkow, T. (ed.) RTA 1998. LNCS, vol. 1379, pp. 47–60. Springer, Heidelberg (1998). https://doi.org/10.1007/BFb0052360

19. Libal, T., Miller, D.: Functions-as-constructors higher-order unification. In: 1st International Conference on Formal Structures for Computation and Deduction (FSCD 2016). Schloss Dagstuhl-Leibniz-Zentrum fuer Informatik (2016)

20. Libal, T., Steen, A.: Towards a substitution tree based index for higher-order resolution theorem provers. In: PAAR 2016. CEUR Workshop Proceedings, vol. 1635 (2016)
21. Meng, J., Paulson, L.C.: Translating higher-order clauses to first-order clauses. J. Autom. Reason. **40**(1), 35–60 (2008)
22. Miller, D.: Unification of simply typed lambda-terms as logic programming. In: Logic Programming Conference, pp. 255–269. MIT Press (1991)
23. Paulson, L.C., Blanchette, J.C.: Three years of experience with sledgehammer, a practical link between automatic and interactive theorem provers. In: IWIL 2010, vol. 2, pp. 1–11 (2010)
24. Pientka, B.: Higher-order term indexing using substitution trees. ACM Trans. Comput. Logic **11**(1), 6:1–6:40 (2009)
25. Prehofer, C.: Decidable higher-order unification problems. In: Bundy, A. (ed.) CADE 1994. LNCS, vol. 814, pp. 635–649. Springer, Heidelberg (1994). https://doi.org/10.1007/3-540-58156-1_46
26. Schmidt-Schauß, M., Schulz, K.U.: Decidability of bounded higher-order unification. J. Symb. Comput. **40**(2), 905–954 (2005)
27. Snyder, W., Gallier, J.: Higher-order unification revisited: complete sets of transformations. J. Symb. Comput. **8**(1–2), 101–140 (1989)
28. Steen, A.: Extensional Paramodulation for Higher-Order Logic and its Effective Implementation Leo-III. Ph.D. thesis, Freie Universität Berlin (2018)
29. Steen, A., Benzmüller, C.: The higher-order prover Leo-III. In: Galmiche, D., Schulz, S., Sebastiani, R. (eds.) IJCAR 2018. LNCS (LNAI), vol. 10900, pp. 108–116. Springer, Cham (2018). https://doi.org/10.1007/978-3-319-94205-6_8
30. Stump, A., Sutcliffe, G., Tinelli, C.: StarExec: a cross-community infrastructure for logic solving. In: Demri, S., Kapur, D., Weidenbach, C. (eds.) IJCAR 2014. LNCS (LNAI), vol. 8562, pp. 367–373. Springer, Cham (2014). https://doi.org/10.1007/978-3-319-08587-6_28
31. Sutcliffe, G.: The TPTP problem library and associated infrastructure, from CNF to TH0, TPTP v6.4.0. J. Autom. Reason. **59**(4), 483–502 (2017)
32. Vukmirović, P., Blanchette, J.C., Cruanes, S., Schulz, S.: Extending a brainiac prover to lambda-free higher-order logic. In: Vojnar, T., Zhang, L. (eds.) TACAS 2019. LNCS, vol. 11427, pp. 192–210. Springer, Cham (2019). https://doi.org/10.1007/978-3-030-17462-0_11

dL$_\iota$: Definite Descriptions in Differential Dynamic Logic

Rose Bohrer[1]([mail]) [iD], Manuel Fernández[1] [iD], and André Platzer[1,2] [iD]

[1] Computer Science Department, Carnegie Mellon University,
Pittsburgh, USA
rose.bohrer.cs@gmail.com, {manuelf,aplatzer}@andrew.cmu.edu
[2] Fakultät für Informatik, Technische Universität München,
Munich, Germany

Abstract. We introduce dL$_\iota$, which extends differential dynamic logic (dL) for hybrid systems with definite descriptions and tuples, thus enabling its theoretical foundations to catch up with its implementation in the theorem prover KeYmaera X. Definite descriptions enable partial, nondifferentiable, and discontinuous terms, which have many examples in applications, such as divisions, nth roots, and absolute values. Tuples enable systems of multiple differential equations, arising in almost every application. Together, definite description and tuples combine to support long-desired features such as vector arithmetic.

We overcome the unique challenges posed by extending dL with these features. Unlike in dL, definite descriptions enable non-locally-Lipschitz terms, so our differential equation (ODE) axioms now make their continuity requirements explicit. Tuples are simple when considered in isolation, but in the context of hybrid systems they demand that differentials are treated in full generality. The addition of definite descriptions also makes dL$_\iota$ a free logic; we investigate the interaction of free logic and the ODEs of dL, showing that this combination is sound, and characterize its expressivity. We give an example system that can be defined and verified using these extensions.

Keywords: Dynamic logic · Definite description · Hybrid systems · Theorem proving · Uniform substitution · Partial functions

1 Introduction

Cyber-physical systems (CPSs) such as self-driving cars, trains, and airplanes combine discrete control and continuous physical dynamics and are often safety-critical because they operate around humans. Thus, it is essential to achieve the highest possible confidence in their correctness, e.g., using formal methods with strong theoretical foundations. Differential dynamic logic (dL) [18,22,23] is a

This research was sponsored by NDSEG, the AFOSR under grant number FA9550-16-1-0288, and the Alexander von Humboldt Foundation.

P. Fontaine (Ed.): CADE 2019, LNAI 11716, pp. 94–110, 2019.
https://doi.org/10.1007/978-3-030-29436-6_6

logic for formal verification of *hybrid systems* [10], widely-used models of CPSs that incorporate both their discrete and continuous behaviors. Among formal methods for CPSs, dL is notable both for its case studies [12,15,16] using the KeYmaera X [9] theorem prover, and for its strong foundations, as evidenced by its completeness results [18,22,23,25] and a formal proof of soundness in both Isabelle/HOL and Coq [4].

However, there is a tension between the goals of practical applicability and rigorous foundations. In practice, theorem prover implementations often demand new features which were not anticipated in theory. Formalizations of KeYmaera X [5], Coq [2], and NuPRL [1] all omit or simplify whichever practical features are most theoretically challenging for their specific logic: discontinuous and partial terms in KeYmaera X, termination-checking in Coq, or context management in NuPRL. When formalizations of theorem provers *do* succeed in reflecting the implementation [13], they owe a credit to the generality of the underlying theory: it is much more feasible to formalize a general base theory than to formalize multiple ad-hoc extensions as they arise.

This paper introduces dL$_\iota$, a new, generalized foundation for dL where *definite description* $\iota x\, \phi$ denotes the unique x for which ϕ holds, enabling practical extensions like divisions θ_1/θ_2, roots $\sqrt[n]{\theta}$, and the functions $\min(\theta_1, \theta_2)$, $\max(\theta_1, \theta_2)$, and $|\theta|$, while pairs (θ_1, θ_2) enable differential equation (ODE) *systems*. Useful new features like trigonometric functions and vectors are also definable, and existing features like differentials $(\theta)'$ have elegant new axiomatizations in dL$_\iota$.

The term $\iota x\, \phi$ is the definite (i.e., requiring unique existence) counterpart of Hilbert's choice $\varepsilon x\, \phi$; both have seen success in HOL-style theorem provers [17,26]. We chose definite $\iota x\, \phi$ over $\varepsilon x\, \phi$ because uniqueness significantly simplifies continuity and differential reasoning. In adopting definite descriptions and tuples in dL, we solve the novel challenges of integrating them with differential equations, dL's distinguishing feature. Definite descriptions allow partiality, discontinuity, and nondifferentiability, all of which interact subtly with sound ODE reasoning. Multidimensional systems, enabled by tuples, demand a general treatment of differentials and expose subtle variable dependencies in some advanced ODE reasoning principles.

An example demonstrates the power of definite description: definite descriptions allow non-polynomial terms and thus non-polynomial ODEs, which need not have unique solutions. While non-polynomial ODEs (and all of dL$_\iota$) are reducible to dL in theory, the reduction of $\iota x\, \phi$ is completely impractical [3]. Expressivity comes with deep semantic changes: supporting partiality makes dL$_\iota$ a free logic, for which we adopt a 3-valued Łukasiewicz semantics. We show this profound change in foundations needs only small changes to the proof calculus with additional definedness conditions. We develop the theory of dL$_\iota$, show that the proof calculus is sound and show the nontrivial reduction from dL$_\iota$ to dL.

2   Syntax

We present the core syntax of dL$_\iota$, which extends dL with definite descriptions and tuples. We describe the constructs informally here, deferring formal semantics to Sect. 3. As a free logic [8], dL_ι contains terms that do not denote and formulas whose truth values are unknown (truth is indicated $\oplus$, falsehood by $\ominus$, and unknown by $\oslash$), a major point of difference between our semantics and proof calculus vs. those of dL. Our calculus uses uniform substitution [6, §35,§40], where symbols ranging over predicates, programs, etc. are explicitly represented in the syntax, because it has simplified the construction of dL calculi [23], implementations [9], and machine-checked correctness proofs [4]. This will ease implementing dL_ι and mechanizing the soundness proof in future work. The syntax of dL_ι is divided into terms, programs, and formulas, whose definitions, unlike in dL, are all mutually recursive. The terms θ of dL_ι extend the terms of dL with definite descriptions, pairs, and reductions:

$$\theta ::= q \mid x \mid f(\theta) \mid \theta + \theta \mid \theta \cdot \theta \mid (\theta)' \mid \iota x\, \phi \mid (\theta, \theta) \mid \mathsf{red}(\theta, \mathsf{s}\,\theta, \mathbf{lr}\,\theta)$$

for literal $q \in \mathbb{Q}$ and variable $x \in \mathcal{V}$, where $\mathcal{V}$ is the set of all variable names, f is a function symbol, and ϕ is a formula. The first six cases, polynomials, differentials, and function symbols, are as in dL. Variables are *flexible*: they are modified by quantifiers and programs. Variables x always denote some value and so assignments succeed only when the RHS denotes a value. In contrast, $f(\theta)$ is an *uninterpreted function* f applied to term θ, but both θ and $f(\theta)$ are allowed to be non-denoting. While function symbols f rarely appear in theorem statements, they are essential for the axioms of Sect. 5. The definite description $\iota x\, \phi$ denotes the *unique* value of x that makes formula ϕ true, if exactly one such value exists, else it does not denote (since description is definite). Pairs (θ_1, θ_2) can be nested to arbitrary finite depth, so their eliminator is primitive recursion on binary trees with values at the leaves. Reduction $\mathsf{red}(\theta_1, s\, \theta_2, lr\, \theta_3)$ reduces every leaf $t \in \mathbb{R}$ to $\theta_2{}_s^t$ and reduces every pair a, b of recursive results to $\theta_3{}_l^a{}_r^b$, where e_x^y is the capture-avoiding substitution of y for every x in e. For example, if $\theta_1 = ((-1, 2), -3)$, then the reduction $\mathsf{red}(\theta_1, s\, s^2, lr\, (r, l))$ is the elementwise square of the reverse tree, $(9, (4, 1))$.

The programs α, β of dL_ι are *hybrid programs*, a program syntax for *hybrid systems* combining discrete and continuous dynamics. Hybrid programs of dL_ι are identical to those of dL with the exception that any formula or term contained therein is again any formula or term of dL_ι, not necessarily just dL. For any starting state, a program α might transition to zero, one, or many final states. Whenever a program transitions to zero states, we say it *aborts*.

$$\alpha, \beta ::= x := \theta \mid x' = \theta \,\&\, \psi \mid ?\phi \mid \alpha \cup \beta \mid \alpha; \beta \mid \alpha^* \mid a$$

Assignments $x := \theta$ assign the value of term θ to variable x, if θ denotes a value, else they abort. Tests $?\phi$ abort execution if formula ϕ is not true, else they are no-ops. Nondeterministic choices $\alpha \cup \beta$ behave as either α or β, nondeterministically. Sequential composition $\alpha; \beta$ performs β in any state resulting from α. Loops α^* repeat α sequentially any number of times, nondeterministically. The defining construct of hybrid programs are the differential equations $x' = \theta \,\&\, \psi$, which continuously evolve x according to the differential equation $x' = \theta$ for any duration such that term θ denotes and formula ψ is true throughout. Note the core syntax of dL$_\iota$ need only contain systems of a single variable x: in Sect. 4 we will derive systems with multiple variables from systems of one variable. Uninterpreted program constants a range over programs. We parenthesize programs α as $\{\alpha\}$ with braces for disambiguation and readability. The formulas ϕ, ψ of dL$_\iota$ are defined inductively:

$$\phi, \psi :: = \phi \wedge \psi \mid \neg\phi \mid \forall x\, \phi \mid \theta_1 \geq \theta_2 \mid [\alpha]\phi \mid p(\theta)$$

Conjunctions $\phi \wedge \psi$, negations $\neg\phi$, and quantifiers $\forall x\, \phi$ are as is standard in first-order Łukasiewicz [14] logic. The quantifier $\exists x\, \phi$ is also as in first-order Łukasiewicz logic and can be derived $\exists x\, \phi \equiv \neg\forall x\, \neg\phi$. In comparing $\theta_1 \geq \theta_2$, if terms θ_1 and θ_2 both denote reals, those reals are compared, if they both denote tuples they are compared elementwise, in all other cases the result is unknown ($\oslash$). The defining construct of dynamic logics is $[\alpha]\phi$, which says ϕ holds in all states reachable by running α. Its dual, $\langle\alpha\rangle\phi$, says there exists a state reachable by running α where ϕ holds, and can be derived by the equivalence $\langle\alpha\rangle\phi \equiv \neg[\alpha]\neg\phi$. Uninterpreted predicate symbols p expect terms θ, which are also allowed not to denote, as arguments, and are allowed truth value unknown ($\oslash$). We write P, Q for predicates which take *all* variables as arguments. We sometimes write the implication $\phi \to \psi$ as $\psi \leftarrow \phi$ for emphasis on ψ.

Example 1 (Robot Water Cooler). The textbook examples of non-Lipschitz ODEs are those of form $h' = k \cdot \sqrt{h}$ for constant k. In dL$_\iota$, in contrast to dL, non-Lipschitz terms simplify describing a hybrid system with such ODEs, which we base on Hubbard's leaky bucket [11, §4.2]. Consider a water cooler of height h and an opening of surface area a in its bottom of surface area A, where g is acceleration due to gravity. Suppose an enterprising student has equipped the cooler's valve with robotic control. We could then model the cooler as:

$$\alpha_B \equiv \left\{\left\{\{?h > 0;\ a := 1\} \cup a := 0\right\}; h' = -\sqrt{2gh}\frac{a}{A} \,\&\, h \geq 0\right\}^*$$

This says that so long as there is water in the cooler ($?h > 0$) we can choose to open the valve ($a := 1$), but we can always close the valve ($a := 0$). Then the water drains out the cooler at a rate proportional to the square root of the current volume by Torricelli's Law [7], or rate 0 if the valve is closed. This control process repeats arbitrarily often. The constructs $\sqrt{2gh}$ (root) and $\frac{a}{A}$ (division) are not core dL, but we can rewrite α_B using definite descriptions:

$$\left\{\left\{\{?h > 0;\ a := 1\} \cup a := 0\right\}; h' = -(\iota y\, y^2 = 2gh \wedge y \geq 0)(\iota z\, zA = a) \,\&\, h \geq 0\right\}^*$$

This example is representative because the ODE is non-Lipschitz: the solution is unique at $h = 0$ *only* within the constraint $h \geq 0$. The terms $\sqrt{2gh}$ and $\frac{a}{A}$ are also both *partial*: defined only assuming $gh \geq 0$ and $A \neq 0$, respectively. The interactions between partiality, uniqueness, and the constraint combine to make the proof subtle, even if short.

Common dL (and likewise, dL_ι) theorems include *safety assertions* of the form $\phi \to [\alpha]\psi$ which say that if ϕ holds initially, then ψ will necessarily hold after α. For example, we might wish to prove the final water height of α_B never exceeds the initial height, so it is actually *leaky* (or at least is not filling up):

Proposition 1 (Leakiness). *This is valid (definitely true $\oplus$ in all states):*

$$g > 0 \land h = h_0 \land h_0 > 0 \land A > 0 \to [\alpha_B](h \le h_0)$$

We will prove Proposition 1 after we have introduced a proof calculus for dL_ι in Sect. 5.

3   Denotational Semantics

We now formally define the semantics of dL_ι terms, formulas, and programs. Due to the presence of definite descriptions $\iota x\, \phi(x)$, not every dL_ι term denotes in every state, i.e., dL_ι is a *free logic* [8]. We write $\bot$ for the interpretation of a term that does not denote any value. When a term denotes, it denotes a *finite, binary* tree with real values at the leaves: a scalar denotes a singleton tree, while (arbitrarily nested) pairs denote non-singleton trees. We refer to the set of all real trees as **Tree**$(\mathbb{R})$, where for any S, **Tree**(S) is the smallest set such that: (i) $S \subseteq$ **Tree**(S), and (ii) for any l and $r \in$ **Tree**(S), $(l, r) \in$ **Tree**(S). Typing is extrinsic, i.e., we do not make typing distinctions between $\mathbb{R}$ and **Tree**$(\mathbb{R})$ in the semantics; typing constraints will be expressed explicitly as predicates. To account for non-denoting terms, formulas can take on three truth values: $\oplus$ (definitely true), $\oslash$ (unknown), and $\ominus$ (definitely false). Thus dL_ι is a *3-valued* logic, and first-order connectives use the Łukasiewicz [14] interpretation.

The interpretation functions are parameterized by state $\omega : \mathcal{V} \to$ **Tree**$(\mathbb{R})$ mapping variables to values, and by an interpretation I mapping function symbols, predicate symbols, and program constants to their interpretation, including the possibility of not denoting a value. Writing $\mathcal{S}$ for the set of all states, we have $I(f) : ($**Tree**$(\mathbb{R}) \cup \bot) \to ($**Tree**$(\mathbb{R}) \cup \bot)$, $I(p) : ($**Tree**$(\mathbb{R}) \cup \bot) \to \{\oplus, \oslash, \ominus\}$, and $I(a) : \wp(\mathcal{S} \times \mathcal{S})$, where $\wp(U)$ is the power set of a set U. Below, ω_x^t is the state that is equal to ω except at x, where $\omega_x^t(x) = t$.

Definition 1 (Term semantics). *The denotation of a term is either a tree or undefined, i.e.* $I\omega[\![\theta]\!] :$ **Tree**$(\mathbb{R}) \cup \{\bot\}$*, and is inductively defined as:*

$$I\omega[\![q]\!] = q \quad I\omega[\![x]\!] = \omega(x) \quad I\omega[\![f(\theta)]\!] = I(f)(I\omega[\![\theta]\!])$$
$$I\omega[\![\theta_1 + \theta_2]\!] = I\omega[\![\theta_1]\!] + I\omega[\![\theta_2]\!] \; \text{if} \; I\omega[\![\theta_1]\!], I\omega[\![\theta_2]\!] \in \mathbb{R}$$
$$I\omega[\![\theta_1 \cdot \theta_2]\!] = I\omega[\![\theta_1]\!] \cdot I\omega[\![\theta_2]\!] \; \text{if} \; I\omega[\![\theta_1]\!], I\omega[\![\theta_2]\!] \in \mathbb{R}$$

$$I\omega[\![\iota x\,\phi]\!] = \begin{cases} t & \text{if a unique } t \in \mathbf{Tree}(\mathbb{R}) \text{ has } I\omega_x^t[\![\phi]\!] = \oplus \\ \bot & \text{otherwise} \end{cases}$$

$$I\omega[\![(\theta_1, \theta_2)]\!] = (I\omega[\![\theta_1]\!], I\omega[\![\theta_2]\!]) \text{ if } I\omega[\![\theta_1]\!], I\omega[\![\theta_2]\!] \neq \bot$$

$$I\omega[\![\mathsf{red}(\theta_1, s\ \theta_2, lr\ \theta_3)]\!] = \mathsf{Fold}(I\omega[\![\theta_1]\!], s\ \theta_2, lr\ \theta_3, I\omega) \text{ if } I\omega[\![\theta_1]\!] \neq \bot$$

$$I\omega[\![(\theta)']\!] = \sum_{x \in \mathcal{V}} \omega(x') \frac{\partial I\omega[\![\theta]\!]}{\partial x} \text{ if } I[\![\theta]\!] \text{ totally differentiable at } \omega$$

$$I\omega[\![\theta]\!] = \bot \text{ in all other cases}$$

where $\omega(x')\frac{\partial I\omega[\![\theta]\!]}{\partial x}$ abuses notation: when $\omega(x)$ is a tuple, the partial is taken w.r.t. each leaf in x, scaled by the corresponding component of x'; the subtleties of semantics for differentials are discussed at greater length in the companion report [3]. In previous formalisms for dL [23] the semantics of $(\theta)'$ do not explicitly require that θ is totally differentiable because all pure dL terms are already smooth, thus totally differentiable. In contrast, not all dL$_\iota$ terms are smooth, thus we require total differentiability explicitly, as it is required for soundness (specifically of DI$_\geq$, Sect. 5). If differentiability conditions are not met, then $I\omega[\![(\theta)']\!] = \bot$. Reductions $\mathsf{Fold}(t, s\ \theta_R, lr\ \theta_T, I\omega)$ recurse on t:

$$\mathsf{Fold}(t, s\ \theta_R, lr\ \theta_T, I\omega) = I\omega_s^t[\![\theta_R]\!] \text{ when } t \in \mathbb{R}$$

$$\mathsf{Fold}((L, R), s\ \theta_R, lr\ \theta_T, I\omega) = I\omega_l^{K\ S}[\![\theta_T]\!] \text{ where}$$

$$K = \mathsf{Fold}(L, s\ \theta_R, lr\ \theta_T, I\omega), S = \mathsf{Fold}(R, s\ \theta_R, lr\ \theta_T, I\omega)$$

That is, they reduce singletons t by binding s to t in θ_R, and reduce node (L, R) by binding l, r to the reductions of the respective branches in θ_T.

Definition 2 (Formula semantics). *The formula semantics are 3-valued:*

$$I\omega[\![\phi \wedge \psi]\!] = I\omega[\![\phi]\!] \sqcap I\omega[\![\psi]\!] \qquad\qquad I\omega[\![\neg\phi]\!] = \overline{I\omega[\![\phi]\!]}$$

$$I\omega[\![\forall x\,\phi]\!] = \bigsqcap_{t \in \mathbf{Tree}(\mathbb{R})} I\omega_x^t[\![\phi]\!] \qquad I\omega[\![[\alpha]\phi]\!] = \bigsqcap_{(\omega,\nu) \in I[\![\alpha]\!]} I\nu[\![\phi]\!]$$

$$I\omega[\![\theta_1 \geq \theta_2]\!] = \mathsf{Geq}(I\omega[\![\theta_1]\!], I\omega[\![\theta_2]\!]) \qquad I\omega[\![p(\theta)]\!] = I(p)(I\omega[\![\theta]\!])$$

$$\mathsf{Geq}(r_1, r_2) = r_1 \geq r_2 \text{ if } r_1, r_2 \in \mathbb{R}$$

$$\mathsf{Geq}((l_1, r_1), (l_2, r_2)) = \mathsf{Geq}(l_1, l_2) \sqcap \mathsf{Geq}(r_1, r_2)$$

$$\mathsf{Geq}(v_1, v_2) = \oslash \text{ otherwise}$$

$p \sqcap q$	$q = \oplus$	$\oslash$	$\ominus$	$\bar{p}$	$p = \oplus$	$\oslash$	$\ominus$
$p = \oplus$	$\oplus$	$\oslash$	$\ominus$		$\ominus$	$\oslash$	$\oplus$
$p = \oslash$	$\oslash$	$\oslash$	$\ominus$				
$p = \ominus$	$\ominus$	$\ominus$	$\ominus$				

$p \to q$	$q = \oplus$	$\oslash$	$\ominus$	$p \leftrightarrow q$	$q = \oplus$	$\oslash$	$\ominus$
$p = \oplus$	$\oplus$	$\oslash$	$\ominus$	$p = \oplus$	$\oplus$	$\oslash$	$\ominus$
$p = \oslash$	$\oplus$	$\oplus$	$\oslash$	$p = \oslash$	$\oslash$	$\oplus$	$\oslash$
$p = \ominus$	$\oplus$	$\oplus$	$\oplus$	$p = \ominus$	$\ominus$	$\oslash$	$\oplus$

Implication $p \to q$ can be intuited as $p \leq q$, (where $\ominus < \oslash < \oplus$) so $(p \to q)$ is $\oplus$ even when $p = q = \oslash$. Conjunction $p \sqcap q$ takes the minimum value of the arguments, and is unknown $\oslash$ when the least conjunct is $\oslash$. Equivalence $p \leftrightarrow q$ is reflexive (even $(\oslash \leftrightarrow \oslash)$ is $\oplus$), but is $\oslash$ in all other cases where some argument is $\oslash$. We say a formula ϕ is *valid* if $I\omega[\![\phi]\!] = \oplus$ for all ω and I. Comparisons $\theta_1 \geq \theta_2$ are taken elementwise and are unknown $(\oslash)$ for differing shapes. Predicates p are interpreted by the interpretation I. The meaning of quantifiers $\forall x\, \phi$ and $[\alpha]\phi$ are taken as conjunctions $\sqcap_S$ over potentially-uncountable index sets S. The value of $\sqcap_S$ is the least value of any conjunct, one of $\{\ominus, \oslash, \oplus\}$.

Definition 3 (Program semantics). *Program semantics generalize those of dL as conservatively as possible so that verification finds as many bugs as possible: e.g. assignments of non-denoting terms and tests of unknown formulas abort. The denotation of a program α is a relation $I[\![\alpha]\!]$ where $(\omega, \nu) \in I[\![\alpha]\!]$ whenever final state ν is reachable from initial state ω by running α.*

$$I[\![x := \theta]\!] = \{(\omega, \omega_x^{I\omega[\![\theta]\!]}) \mid I\omega[\![\theta]\!] \neq \bot\} \qquad I[\![?\phi]\!] = \{(\omega, \omega) \mid I\omega[\![\phi]\!] = \oplus\}$$

$$I[\![\alpha \cup \beta]\!] = I[\![\alpha]\!] \cup I[\![\beta]\!] \qquad I[\![\alpha; \beta]\!] = I[\![\alpha]\!] \circ I[\![\beta]\!]$$

$$I[\![\alpha^*]\!] = I[\![\alpha]\!]^* = \bigcup_{n \in \mathbb{N}} I[\![\underbrace{\alpha; \cdots; \alpha}_{n \text{ times}}]\!]$$

$$I[\![x' = \theta \,\&\, \psi]\!] = \{(\omega, \nu) \mid \omega = \varphi(0) \text{ on } \{x'\}^{\complement} \text{ and } \nu = \varphi(r) \text{ for some } \varphi : [0, r] \to S$$

$$\text{which solves } x' = \theta \,\&\, \psi, \text{ i.e., for } s \in [0, r], \frac{\partial \varphi(t)(x)}{\partial t}(s) = \varphi(s)(x')$$

$$\text{and } I\varphi(s)[\![x' = \theta \wedge \psi]\!] = \oplus \text{ and } \varphi(s) = \varphi(0) \text{ on } \{x, x'\}^{\complement}\}$$

where $X^{\complement}$ is the complement of set X. ODEs $x' = \theta \,\&\, \psi$ are initial value problems: $(\omega, \nu) \in I[\![x' = \theta \,\&\, \psi]\!]$ if some solution φ of some duration $r \in \mathbb{R}_{\geq 0}$ takes ω to ν while satisfying ψ throughout. A solution φ must satisfy $x' = \theta$ as an equation, satisfy constraint ψ, and assign the time-derivative of each x to each x'. The initial value of x' is overwritten and variables except x, x' are not changed. Assignments $x := \theta$ are strict: they store the value of θ in variable x, or abort if θ does not denote a value. Tests $?\phi$ succeed if ϕ is definitely true $(\oplus)$; both the unknown $(\oslash)$ and definitely false $(\ominus)$ cases abort execution. Likewise, the domain constraint ψ of a differential equation $x' = \theta \,\&\, \psi$ must be definitely-true $(\oplus)$ throughout the entire evolution and the term θ implicitly must denote values throughout the evolution, since $I\varphi(s)[\![x' = \theta \wedge \psi]\!] = \oplus$.

4   Derived Constructs

A key benefit of dL$_\iota$ is extensibility: Many term constructs can be defined with definite descriptions $\iota x\,\phi$ and tuples which otherwise require unwieldy encodings as formulas. In this section we reap the benefits of extensibility by defining such new term constructs.

Arithmetic Operations. In practice, we often wish to use arithmetic operations beyond the core dL operations. Figure 1 demonstrates basic arithmetic operations which have simple definitions in dL$_\iota$ but not as terms in dL: Of these, max, min, and $|\cdot|$ preserve Lipschitz-continuity but not differentiability. Roots $\sqrt{\theta}$ can violate even Lipschitz-continuity and both roots and divisions are non-total. In practice (as in Example 1), these operators are used in ODE models, making their continuity properties essential. Since pure dL requires smooth terms [23], even *functions* max and min would be encoded as formulas in pure dL.

$$
\begin{aligned}
(\mathsf{if}(\phi)(\theta_1)\mathsf{else}(\theta_2)) &= \iota x\,(\phi \wedge x{=}\theta_1) \vee (\neg\phi \wedge x{=}\theta_2)\\
\max(\theta_1,\theta_2) &= \iota x\,(\theta_1 \geq \theta_2 \wedge x = \theta_1) \vee (\theta_2 \geq \theta_1 \wedge x = \theta_2)\\
\min(\theta_1,\theta_2) &= \iota x\,(\theta_1 \geq \theta_2 \wedge x = \theta_2) \vee (\theta_2 \geq \theta_1 \wedge x = \theta_1)\\
|\theta| &= \max(\theta,-\theta) \quad \sqrt{\theta} = \iota x\,(x^2{=}\theta \wedge x \geq 0) \quad \theta_1/\theta_2 = \iota x\,(x \cdot \theta_2{=}\theta_1)\\
(\sin\theta,\cos\theta) &= \iota z\,[t := 0; s := 0; c := 1; s'{=}c, c'{=}{-}s, t'{=}1; ?t{=}\theta]z{=}(s,c)
\end{aligned}
$$

Fig. 1. Derived arithmetic operations (for fresh x, t, c, s, z)

Tuples. We make tuples first-class in dL$_\iota$ to simultaneously simplify the treatment of ODEs compared to prior work [18] and provide support for data structures such as vectors, widely used in physical computations. In contrast to the flexible function symbols (think: unbounded arrays) of Qd$\mathcal{L}$ [20], they are equipped with a primitive recursion operator, making it easier to write sophisticated functional computations. These structures can be used in systems with non-scalar inputs, for example a robot which avoids a list of obstacles [16].

While pairs (θ_1,θ_2) are core dL$_\iota$ constructs, the left and right projections $\pi_1\theta$ and $\pi_2\theta$ are derivable, as are convenience predicates $\mathsf{inR}(\theta)$ and $\mathsf{isT}(\theta)$ which hold exactly for scalars and tuples, respectively:

$$
\begin{aligned}
\pi_1\theta &\equiv \iota l\,\exists r\,(\theta = (l,r)) & \pi_2\theta &\equiv \iota r\,\exists l\,(\theta = (l,r))\\
\mathsf{inR}(\theta) &\equiv (\mathsf{red}(\theta, s\,1, lr\,0) = 1) & \mathsf{isT}(\theta) &\equiv (\mathsf{red}(\theta, s\,1, lr\,0) = 0)
\end{aligned}
$$

When combined with the reduce operation on trees, these operations can be used to implement a variety of data structures. Figure 2 shows an example library of operations on lists. Lists are represented as nested pairs, with no special terminator. We name an argument L to indicate its intended use as a list rather than an arbitrary tree. Lists are trees whose left-projections are never pairs. Additional data structures are shown in the report [3].

Systems of ODEs. Tuples reduce ODE systems to individual ODEs, e.g.:

$$\{x_1'{=}\theta_1,\, x_2'{=}\theta_2\} \;\equiv\; (z := (x_1, x_2);\, \{z' = (\theta_1{}_{x_j}^{\pi_j z}, \theta_2{}_{x_j}^{\pi_j z})\});\; x_1 := \pi_1 z;\; x_2 := \pi_2 z)$$

While this encoding is simple, it will enable us in Sect. 5 to support systems of any finite dimension in axiom DG, which implementation experience [9] has shown challenging due to the variable dependencies involved.

$$\mathsf{map2}(T, f(x, y)) = \mathsf{red}(T, s\ s, lr\ \mathsf{if}(\mathsf{in}\mathbb{R}(r))(f(l, r))\mathsf{else}\{(f(\pi_1 l, \pi_2 l), r)\})$$
$$\mathsf{snoc}(L, x) = \mathsf{red}(L, s\ (s, x), lr\ (\pi_1 l, r)) \quad \mathsf{rev}(L) = \mathsf{red}(L, s\ s, lr\ \mathsf{snoc}(r, l))$$
$$\mathsf{zip}(L_1, L_2) = \pi_1 \mathsf{red}(\mathsf{rev}(L_1), s\ ((s, \pi_1 L_2), \pi_2 L_2), lr\ (((\pi_1\pi_1 l, \pi_1\pi_2 r), \pi_1 r), \pi_2\pi_2 r))$$
$$(L_1{+}L_2) = \mathsf{map2}(\mathsf{zip}(L_1, L_2), x + y)$$
$$L_1{\cdot}L_2 = \mathsf{red}(\mathsf{map2}(\mathsf{zip}(L_1, L_2), x \cdot y), s\ s, lr\ l + r)$$

Fig. 2. Example vector functions

Types and Definedness. Many of the operations in dL_ι expect, for example, reals or terms that denote values. For simplicity, we make these type distinctions extrinsically: core dL terms are untyped, and proposition $\mathsf{in}\mathbb{R}(\theta)$ says θ belongs to type $\mathbb{R}$. Typed quantifiers are definable, e.g., $\forall x{:}\mathbb{R}\ \phi \equiv \forall x\,(\mathsf{in}\mathbb{R}(x) \to \phi)$. Whether a term denotes is also treated extrinsically. Formula $\mathsf{E}(\theta) \equiv \mathsf{D}(\theta = \theta)$ only holds for terms that denote, where $\mathsf{D}(\phi)$ says ϕ *is definitely true*, which has truth value $\oplus$ when ϕ has truth value $\oplus$ and has value $\ominus$ otherwise. We give its truth table and a definition:

p	$\oplus$	$\oslash$	$\ominus$
$\mathsf{D}(p)$	$\oplus$	$\ominus$	$\ominus$

$$\mathsf{D}(\phi) \equiv \neg(\phi \to \neg\phi)$$

That is, $\mathsf{D}(\phi)$ collapses $\oslash$ into $\ominus$. These constructs are used in the axioms of Sect. 5. In the same spirit, we sometimes need to know that a function $f(x)$ (of any dimension) is continuous, but derive this notion. We write $\mathsf{Con}(f(x))$ to say that $f(x)$ is continuous as x varies around its current value:

$$\mathsf{Con}(f(x)) \equiv \mathsf{D}(\forall \xi\, \exists \delta\, \forall y\, (0 < \|y - x\| < \delta \to \|f(y) - f(x)\| < \xi))$$

Note that when $\mathsf{Con}(f(x))$ holds, the shape of $f(x)$ is constant in a neighborhood of x, since the Euclidean norm $\|f(y) - f(x)\|$ does not exist when $f(y)$ and $f(x)$ differ in shape. Likewise, $\mathsf{Con}(f(x))$ requires only continuity on y whose shape agrees with that of x, since the Euclidean norm $\|y - x\|$ does not otherwise exist.

5   dL$_\iota$ Axioms

Our proof system is given in the Hilbert style, with a minimum number of proof rules and larger number of axioms, each of which is an individual concrete formula. The core proof rule is uniform substitution [23][6, §35,§40]: from the validity of ϕ we can conclude validity of $\sigma(\phi)$ where the uniform substitution σ specifies concrete replacements for some or all predicates, functions, and program constants in a formula ϕ:

$$\text{(US)} \ \frac{\phi}{\sigma(\phi)}$$

The soundness side-conditions to US about σ are non-trivial, and make up much of its soundness proof in Sect. 6. The payoff is that uniform substitution enables a modular design where such subtle arguments need only be done once in the soundness proof of the US rule, and every axiom, which is now an individual concrete dL$_\iota$ formula, is significantly simpler to prove valid and to implement.

$[\cdot] \ \langle a \rangle P \leftrightarrow \neg [a] \neg P$
$\qquad$
K $[a] \, (P \rightarrow Q) \rightarrow ([a]P \rightarrow [a]Q)$

$[:=] \ ([x := f]p(x) \leftrightarrow p(f)) \leftarrow \mathsf{E}(f)$
$\qquad$
I $[a^*]\mathsf{D}(P \rightarrow [a]P) \rightarrow \mathsf{D}(P \rightarrow [a^*]P)$

$[?] \ [?Q]P \leftrightarrow (\mathsf{D}(Q) \rightarrow P)$
$\qquad$
V $p \rightarrow [a]p$

$[\cup] \ [a \cup b]P \leftrightarrow [a]P \wedge [b]P$
$\qquad$
G $\dfrac{P}{[a]P}$

$[;] \ [a;b]P \leftrightarrow [a][b]P$

$[*] \ [a^*]P \leftrightarrow P \wedge [a][a^*]P$
$\qquad$
$\forall \ \dfrac{p(x)}{\forall x \, p(x)}$

$\forall i \ (\forall x \, p(x)) \rightarrow (\mathsf{E}(f) \rightarrow p(f))$
$\qquad$
MP $\dfrac{P \rightarrow Q \quad P}{Q}$

$\forall \rightarrow \ \forall x \, (p(x) \rightarrow q(x)) \rightarrow \forall x \, p(x) \rightarrow \forall x \, q(x)$
$\qquad$
$V_\forall \ p \rightarrow \forall x \, p$

Fig. 3. Discrete dL axioms

Figure 3 gives axioms and rules for the discrete programming constructs, which are generalizations of corresponding axioms [23] for dl to account for non-denoting terms and unknown formulas. Axioms are augmented with definedness conditions whenever multiple occurrences of terms or formulas differ in their tolerance for partiality. The conclusion (in canonical usage) of each axiom is highlighted in blue, while any difference from the dL axioms is highlighted in red. Recall the operator $\mathsf{D}(\phi)$ says ϕ is *definitely* true. For example, axiom $[?]$ says that a test $?Q$ succeeds when Q is definitely true. The induction axiom I requires the inductive step proved definitely true, but concludes definite truth. The other axioms for program constructs ($[\cdot], [\cup], [;], [*]$) carry over from dL without modification, since partiality primarily demands changes when mediating between formulas and programs or between terms and program variables. As is standard in free logics, axiom $\forall i$ says that since quantifiers range over values, they must be instantiated only to terms that denote values. Assignments $[:=]$ require the assigned term to denote a value, since program variables x range over values.

Figure 4 gives the dL$_\iota$ generalizations of dL's axioms for reasoning about differential equations: DC is generalized by analogy to $[?]$ to require definite truth

DW $[x' = f(x)\&q(x)]q(x)$

DC $\big([x' = f(x)\&q(x)]p(x) \leftrightarrow [x' = f(x)\&q(x) \wedge r(x)]p(x)\big) \leftarrow \mathsf{D}([x' = f(x)\&q(x)]r(x))$

DE $[x' = f(x)\&q(x)][x' := f(x)]p(x, x') \leftrightarrow [x' = f(x)\&q(x)]p(x, x')$

DI$_\geq$ $\quad\dfrac{([x' = h(x)\&q(x)]f(x) \geq g(x) \leftrightarrow [?q(x)]f(x) \geq g(x))}{\leftarrow [x' = h(x)\&q(x)](f(x))' \geq (g(x))'}$

DG $\quad\dfrac{\forall x\,(q(x) \rightarrow \mathsf{Con}(a(x)) \wedge \mathsf{Con}(b(x)))}{\rightarrow \big([x' = f(x)\&q(x)]p(x) \leftrightarrow \exists y : \mathbb{R}\ [x'{=}f(x),\ y' = a(x)y + b(x)\&q(x)]p(x)\big)}$

DS $\big(\forall t : \mathbb{R}\ ((\forall 0 \leq s \leq t\, q(x + fs)) \rightarrow [x := x + ft]p(x))\big) \rightarrow [x' = f\,\&\,q(x)]p(x)$

$(\theta)'$ $\quad\dfrac{(f(x))' = x' \cdot \iota M\,\forall \xi {>} 0\,\exists \delta\,\forall y\,\mathsf{D}(0 {<} \|y{-}x\| {<} \delta \rightarrow f(y) {-} f(x) {-} M(y{-}x) {<} \xi \|y{-}x\|)}{\leftarrow \mathsf{E}((f(x))')}$

E($'$) $\mathsf{E}((f(x))') \leftarrow \mathsf{E}(\iota M\,\forall \xi {>} 0\,\exists \delta\,\forall y\,\mathsf{D}(0 {<} \|y{-}x\| {<} \delta \rightarrow f(y) {-} f(x) {-} M(y{-}x) {<} \xi \|y{-}x\|))$

Fig. 4. Differential equation axioms and differential axioms

and DG is generalized to require continuity, otherwise the axioms carry over unchanged. DW says the constraint of an ODE always holds as a postcondition. DC says any postcondition which is proven (definitely) true may be added to the constraint. DE says the ODE holds as an equation in the postcondition. DI$_\geq$ is the *differential induction* [19] axiom for proving nonstrict inequalities $f(x) \geq g(x)$ follow from their *differential formula* $(f(x))' \geq (g(x))'$. The strict case $f(x) > g(x)$ is analogous; axioms for equality, inequality, conjunction, and disjunction can be derived from these. Note the assumptions in DI$_\geq$ hold only when $f(x)$ and $g(x)$ are *totally* differentiable within the constraint, as required for soundness. DG allows extending a system with an additional ghost dimension, and is used for everything from solving systems to reasoning about exponentially-decaying systems [25]. The new dimension is required to be Lipschitz so that solutions exist and is required to be linear in the new variables so that the solutions of the extended system exist as long as those of the initial system. DS says the solution of a constant ODE system is linear. To solve multidimensional systems with DS, interpret $x + fs$ and $x + ft$ as pairwise vector sums per Fig. 2. Axiom $(\theta)'$ expands a differential $(f(x))'$ according to the definition of total differential. It assumes $\mathsf{E}((f(x))')$ because equalities are not allowed to hold between non-denoting terms; proving these assumptions is enabled by axiom E($'$). In practice, axioms are derived from E($'$) for each case and applied recursively to automatically prove existence, for example:

$$\mathsf{E}((f(x))') \wedge \mathsf{E}((g(x))') \rightarrow \mathsf{E}(((f + g)(x))')$$

is used to show differentials of sums exist. Likewise, axiom $(\theta)'$ is long-winded for practical proving, so we will use it to implement simpler special-case axioms in Example 2. The definition of $(\theta)'$ above only supports real-valued x and $f(x)$, because scalar differences $f(y) - f(x)$ and $y - x$ only denote a value when $x, y, f(x)$, and $f(y)$ are reals. The report [3] discusses its generalization to tree-valued functions of tree-valued arguments.

$$\iota\ p(\iota z\,p(z)) \leftrightarrow \exists x\left(p(x) \wedge \forall y\,(p(y) \rightarrow y = x)\right) \qquad =\!T\ l_1{=}l_2 \wedge r_1{=}r_2 \leftrightarrow (l_1, r_1){=}(l_2, r_2)$$

$$\text{QE}\ \dfrac{*}{\left(\bigwedge_{x \in V(\phi)} \text{in}\mathbb{R}(x)\right) \rightarrow \phi} \qquad\qquad (\text{where } \phi \text{ is valid in first-order real arithmetic})$$

redT $\text{red}((L, R), s\ f(s), lr\ g(l, r)) = g\big(\text{red}(L, s\ f(s), lr\ g(l, r)), \text{red}(R, s\ f(s), lr\ g(l, r))\big)$

redR $\text{in}\mathbb{R}(r) \rightarrow \text{red}(r, s\ f(s), lr\ g(l, r)) = f(r)$

TreeI $\text{D}\Big(p(\iota x\,0 = 1) \wedge \forall s\,\big(\text{in}\mathbb{R}(s) \rightarrow p(s)\big) \wedge \forall lr\,\big(p(l) \wedge p(r) \rightarrow p((l, r))\big)\Big) \rightarrow \text{D}(p(t))$

Fig. 5. Axioms for datatypes

Figure 5 gives axioms for definite descriptions and tuples. Axiom ι fully characterizes definite descriptions, and it is used to derive axioms for defined term constructs like those in Example 2. Axiom $=\!T$ enables comparisons on tuples. Quantifier elimination rule QE uses that first-order real arithmetic, a fragment, is decidable [27]. Since variables of dL$_\iota$ may range over tuples, which are not part of first-order arithmetic, it must first check that all variables of the formula (written $V(\phi)$) are indeed real-valued. Axioms redT and redR evaluate reductions when their shape is known, and axiom TreeI allows proving a property of an arbitrary value by induction on its shape, including a second base case $p(\iota x\,0 = 1)$ where the argument to p does not denote.

Example 2 (Derived axioms). The following are examples of derived axiom schemata that have been proved from those above. Proofs are in the report [3].

$$\pi_1(l, r) = l \qquad \pi_2(l, r) = r \qquad \text{in}\mathbb{R}(f) \vee \text{isT}(f) \leftarrow \text{E}(f) \qquad (x)' = x'$$

$$(f(x) + g(x))' = (f(x))' + (g(x))' \leftarrow \text{E}((f(x))') \wedge \text{E}((g(x))') \qquad (f)' = 0 \leftarrow \text{E}(f)$$

$$(f(x) \cdot g(x))' = (f(x))' \cdot g(x) + (g(x))' \cdot f(x) \leftarrow \text{E}((f(x))') \wedge \text{E}((g(x))')$$

It is significant that the differential axioms of Example 2 are *derived*: when new term constructs are added in the future, we expect to derive their differential axioms as well, so that these extensions lie entirely *outside* the core dL$_\iota$ calculus. Note that these axioms also conclude (by applying axiom E($'$)) that the differential of the larger term exists, because it equals something. Thus, these axioms are suitable both for showing differentials exist and what form differentials take.

Example 3 (Proof of leakiness). Proposition 1 of Sect. 2 is provable in dL.

Proof (Sketch). By axiom I with loop invariant $P \equiv (g > 0 \land A > 0 \land 0 \le h \le h_0)$. The first two conditions are trivially invariant by axiom V because g and A are constant throughout α_B. Proceed by cases with axiom [U]. In each case, show $h \le h_0$ to be an invariant of the ODE by $DI_\ge$. Because $h \le h_0$ holds initially and the ODE is locally Lipschitz-continuous given constraint $h \ge 0$, it suffices to show $(h)' \le (h_0)' = 0$ throughout. Then $(h)' \le 0 \iff -\sqrt{2gh}\frac{a}{A} \le 0 \iff \sqrt{h} \ge 0$ by algebra and DE, which is true by DW, showing $h \le h_0$.   □

6   Theory

Proofchecking is decidable, and provable formulas are valid.

Theorem 1 (Proofchecking decidability). *There exists an algorithm which decides whether a derivation $\mathcal{D}$ is a proof of a given dL_ι formula ϕ.*

Theorem 2 (Soundness of dL_ι). *If ϕ is provable in dL_ι, then ϕ is valid.*

The proof of soundness proceeds by induction on the structure of derivations. That is, we prove each axiom (which is an individual formula) to be *valid* and prove every proof rule to be *sound* (producing valid conclusions from valid premises). Because dL_ι supports the formula and program connectives of dL, many of the axioms are extensions of corresponding dL axioms. The axiom validity proofs also have a similar flavor to those of dL: each axiom is proven valid by direct proof, showing truth of the axiom according to the denotational semantics in an arbitrary state. The full proofs for each axiom and rule are given in the report [3]; Lemma 1 gives an example.

Lemma 1 (Assignment axiom is valid). *The following formula is valid:*
$([x := f]p(x) \leftrightarrow p(f)) \leftarrow E(f)$

Proof. Assume (1) $I\omega[\![E(f)]\!] = \oplus$ for some state ω and interpretation I, then observe $I\omega[\![[x := f]p(x)]\!] = I\omega[\![p(f)]\!]$ by the chain of equalities $I\omega[\![[x := f]p(x)]\!] = \bigsqcap_{\nu \mid (\omega,\nu) \in \{(\omega,\omega_x^{I\omega[\![f]\!]})\}, I\omega[\![f]\!] \neq \bot} I\nu[\![p(x)]\!] = I\omega_x^{I\omega[\![f]\!]}[\![p(x)]\!] = I(p)(I(f)) = I\omega[\![p(f)]\!]$ □

6.1   Uniform Substitution

The uniform substitution proof rule in dL_ι is analogous to that in dL:

$$(US) \; \frac{\phi}{\sigma(\phi)}$$

In dL, the US rule is sound when the substitution σ does not introduce free references to bound variables, in a sense made precise elsewhere [23]. Such substitutions are called *admissible*, a condition which can be checked syntactically.

We show that the same holds of dL_ι when adding terms $\iota x \phi, (\theta_1, \theta_2)$ and $red(\theta_1, s \; \theta_2, lr \; \theta_3)$ and generalizing dL to a three-valued semantics. As in dL, we formulate admissibility in terms of U-admissibility (Definition 4) checks.

Definition 4 (Admissible uniform substitution). *A substitution σ is U-admissible for ϕ (or θ or α) with respect to a set $U \subseteq \mathcal{V} \cup \mathcal{V}'$ iff $FV(\sigma|_{\Sigma(\phi)}) \cap U = \emptyset$ where $\sigma|_{\Sigma(\phi)}$ is the restriction of σ that only replaces symbols that occur in ϕ and $FV(\sigma) = \bigcup_{f \in \sigma} FV(\sigma f(\cdot)) \cup \bigcup_{p \in \sigma} FV(\sigma p(\cdot))$ are the free variables that σ introduces, and where $\mathcal{V}' = \{x' \mid x \in \mathcal{V}\}$. The substitution σ is admissible for ϕ (or θ or α) if all such checks during its applications hold, per Fig. 6.*

Case	Replacement	Admissible when
$\sigma((\theta_1, \theta_2)) = (\sigma(\theta_1), \sigma(\theta_2))$		
$\sigma(\mathsf{red}(\theta_1, s\,\theta_2, lr\,\theta_3)) = \mathsf{red}(\sigma(\theta_1), s\,\sigma(\theta_2), lr\,\sigma(\theta_3))$		σ is $\{s\}$-admissible for θ_2
		σ is $\{l, r\}$-admissible for θ_3
$\sigma(\iota x\,\phi) = \iota x\,\sigma(\phi)$		σ is $\{x\}$-admissible for ϕ
$\sigma(\forall x\,\phi) = \forall x\,\sigma(\phi)$		σ is $\{x\}$-admissible for ϕ
$\sigma([\alpha]\phi) = [\sigma(\alpha)]\sigma(\phi)$		σ is $BV(\sigma(\alpha))$-admissible for ϕ
$\sigma(f(\theta)) = f(\sigma(\theta))$, if $f \notin \sigma$, else $\sigma f(\sigma(\theta))$		

Fig. 6. Uniform substitution algorithm (selected cases)

In Fig. 6, σf denotes the replacement for symbol f provided by σ. We give the new cases of $FV(\cdot)$ here and the full static semantics in the report [3]:

$$FV((\theta_1, \theta_2)) = FV(\theta_1) \cup FV(\theta_2) \qquad FV(\iota x\,\phi) = FV(\phi) \setminus \{x\}$$
$$FV(\mathsf{red}(\theta_1, s\,\theta_2, lr\,\theta_1)) = FV(\theta_1) \cup (FV(\theta_2) \setminus \{s\}) \cup (FV(\theta_3) \setminus \{l, r\})$$

Admissibility checks employ static semantics consisting of free-variable ($FV(\cdot)$), may-bound-variable ($BV(\cdot)$), and must-bound-variable ($MBV(\cdot)$) computations. Generally speaking, the free variables of a compound expression θ are the free variables of its immediate subexpressions, minus any variables that it binds. Formally, $FV(\theta)$ (or ϕ, α) contains all variables that influence meaning:

Lemma 2 (Coincidence). *The interpretation of an expression depends only on the values of its free variables and constants, e.g. for any term θ, any interpretations I and J that agree on the signature (mentioned predicate symbols, function symbols, and program constants) $\Sigma(\theta)$ of θ, and any states ω and $\tilde{\omega}$ that agree on $FV(\theta)$, we have $I\omega[\![\theta]\!] = J\tilde{\omega}[\![\theta]\!]$.*

The substitution result for a compound expression is found by substituting in each immediate subexpression, and is defined so long as all admissibility checks hold recursively. In general, the admissibility check for each constructor says that the substitution result must not contain any new occurrences of the variables bound at that constructor.

Theorem 3 (Uniform substitution). *Rule US is sound.*

Soundness of the proof system then follows from validity of the axioms and soundness of US and of the other proof rules.

6.2   Expressive Power

After showing soundness of dL_ι, we explore its expressive power: can dL_ι express formulas that are inexpressible in dL, or is its advantage the ease with which certain formulas are expressed? Conversely, are all dL formulas expressible in dL_ι? Because dL_ι is an extension of dL, it is unsurprising that it can express all dL formulas. However, a valid dL formula ϕ is not always valid in dL_ι.

Remark 1 (Conservativity counterexample). There exist valid formulas of dL that are not valid formulas of dL_ι.

Proof. The formula $\phi \equiv (x \cdot x \geq 0)$ is not conserved, because it is true for all real values of x, but fails when x is a tuple such as $(0, 0)$, outside the domain of multiplication. This is why rule QE requires $\mathsf{in}\mathbb{R}(x)$ for each mentioned x.   □

We transform dL quantifiers to real-valued dL_ι quantifiers to close the gap:

Theorem 4 (Converse reducibility). *There exists a linear-time transformation T such that for all ϕ in dL, $T(\phi)$ is valid in dL_ι iff ϕ is valid in dL.*

The greater challenge is to show that dL also suffices to express all dL_ι formulas and thus dL and dL_ι are equiexpressive:

Theorem 5 (Reducibility). *There is a computable T s.t. for all formulas ϕ, interpretations I, and states ω in dL_ι, $I\omega[\![\phi]\!] = \oplus$ in dL_ι iff $I\omega[\![T(\phi)]\!] = \oplus$ in dL.*

While this result might be misread to suggest that dL_ι is not truly necessary, definite descriptions enable us to define constructs that have no description as terms in dL, even if they can be expressed through a sufficiently complex formula translation. The key is that the reduction from dL_ι to dL is indeed complex, exploiting for example Gödel encodings for tuples and continuous functions [21, 24]. On the contrary, the complexity of the reduction shows that native support for definite descriptions is essential for practical proving. The equiexpressiveness result is of theoretical interest because it allows us to inherit results from dL [18]:

Theorem 6 (Completeness and decidability). dL_ι *is reducible to* dL, *and therefore semidecidable relative to properties of differential equations.*

While the reduction gives a semi-decision procedure for dL_ι in principle, it is infeasible for implementation, especially since deciding even core dL is hard in practice. Moreover, this would defeat our purpose: easing implementation of practical term language extensions in dL, where interactive proof is common.

7   Conclusion and Future Work

In this paper we developed dL_ι, an extension to differential dynamic logic (dL) for formal verification of hybrid systems models of safety-critical cyber-physical systems. The key feature of dL_ι is definite description $\iota x\, \phi$, which provides a foundation for defining new term language constructs from their characteristic formulas. We develop the theory of dL$_\iota$, including semantics, a proof calculus, and soundness and expressiveness proofs. We apply dL$_\iota$ to verify a classic example of a non-Lipschitz ODE, which could not be directly verified in dL.

In particular, we give a novel axiomatization that accounts for the interactions between non-differentiable and partially defined operators with systems of differential equations, an interaction which does not occur for dL's simpler language where all terms are smooth. More generally, example applications abound: almost every serious case study of dL employs these constructs in practice; we give a fully rigorous foundation to these case studies. In future work, implementing dL$_\iota$ in KeYmaera X would enable case studies to soundly employ the constructs given herein and to define their own. We expect few core changes would be needed, thanks to our use of uniform substitution, rather the challenge is to efficiently prove and track the new assumptions on existence and continuity.

Acknowledgments. We thank Martin Giese for discussions on the use of definite descriptions in theorem provers and the referees for their thoughtful feedback.

References

1. Anand, A., Rahli, V.: Towards a formally verified proof assistant. In: Klein, G., Gamboa, R. (eds.) ITP 2014. LNCS, vol. 8558, pp. 27–44. Springer, Cham (2014). https://doi.org/10.1007/978-3-319-08970-6_3
2. Barras, B.: Sets in Coq, Coq in sets. J. Formaliz. Reason. **3**(1), 29–48 (2010). https://doi.org/10.6092/issn.1972-5787/1695
3. Bohrer, R., Fernández, M., Platzer, A.: dL$_\iota$: definite descriptions in differential dynamic logic. Technical report. CMU-CS-19-111, School of Computer Science, Carnegie Mellon University, Pittsburgh, PA (2019)
4. Bohrer, R., Rahli, V., Vukotic, I., Völp, M., Platzer, A.: Formally verified differential dynamic logic. In: Bertot, Y., Vafeiadis, V. (eds.) CPP, pp. 208–221. ACM (2017). https://doi.org/10.1145/3018610.3018616
5. Bohrer, R., Tan, Y.K., Mitsch, S., Myreen, M.O., Platzer, A.: VeriPhy: verified controller executables from verified cyber-physical system models. In: Grossman, D. (ed.) PLDI, pp. 617–630. ACM (2018). https://doi.org/10.1145/3192366.3192406
6. Church, A.: Introduction to Mathematical Logic. Princeton University Press, Princeton (1956)
7. Driver, R.: Torricelli's law: an ideal example of an elementary ODE. Am. Math. Mon. **105**(5), 453–455 (1998)
8. Fitting, M., Mendelsohn, R.L.: First-Order Modal Logic. Kluwer, Norwell (1999)
9. Fulton, N., Mitsch, S., Quesel, J.-D., Völp, M., Platzer, A.: KeYmaera X: an axiomatic tactical theorem prover for hybrid systems. In: Felty, A.P., Middeldorp, A. (eds.) CADE 2015. LNCS (LNAI), vol. 9195, pp. 527–538. Springer, Cham (2015). https://doi.org/10.1007/978-3-319-21401-6_36
10. Henzinger, T.A.: The theory of hybrid automata. In: LICS. IEEE (1996). https://doi.org/10.1109/LICS.1996.561342
11. Hubbard, J.H., West, B.H.: Differential Equations: A Dynamical Systems Approach. Springer, Heidelberg (1991). https://doi.org/10.1007/978-1-4612-4192-8
12. Jeannin, J., et al.: A formally verified hybrid system for safe advisories in the next-generation airborne collision avoidance system. STTT **19**(6), 717–741 (2017). https://doi.org/10.1007/s10009-016-0434-1

13. Kumar, R., Arthan, R., Myreen, M.O., Owens, S.: Self-formalisation of higher-order logic: semantics, soundness, and a verified implementation. J. Autom. Reason. **56**(3), 221–259 (2016). https://doi.org/10.1007/s10817-015-9357-x
14. Łukasiewicz, J.: O logice tr ojwartościowej (on 3-valued logic). Ruch Filozoficzny **5**, 169–171 (1920)
15. Mitsch, S., Gario, M., Budnik, C.J., Golm, M., Platzer, A.: Formal verification of train control with air pressure brakes. In: Fantechi, A., Lecomte, T., Romanovsky, A. (eds.) RSSRail. LNCS, vol. 10598, pp. 173–191. Springer, Cham (2017). https://doi.org/10.1007/978-3-319-68499-4_12
16. Mitsch, S., Ghorbal, K., Vogelbacher, D., Platzer, A.: Formal verification of obstacle avoidance and navigation of ground robots. Int. J. Robot. Res. **36**(12), 1312–1340 (2017). https://doi.org/10.1177/0278364917733549
17. Nipkow, T., Paulson, L.C., Wenzel, M.: Isabelle/HOL - A Proof Assistant for Higher-Order Logic. LNCS, vol. 2283. Springer, Heidelberg (2002). https://doi.org/10.1007/3-540-45949-9
18. Platzer, A.: Differential dynamic logic for hybrid systems. J. Autom. Reason. **41**(2), 143–189 (2008). https://doi.org/10.1007/s10817-008-9103-8
19. Platzer, A.: Differential-algebraic dynamic logic for differential-algebraic programs. J. Log. Comput. **20**(1), 309–352 (2010). https://doi.org/10.1093/logcom/exn070
20. Platzer, A.: A complete axiomatization of quantified differential dynamic logic for distributed hybrid systems. Log. Method Comput. Sci. **8**(4), 1–44 (2012). https://doi.org/10.2168/LMCS-8(4:17)2012. Special issue for selected papers from CSL2010
21. Platzer, A.: The complete proof theory of hybrid systems. In: LICS, pp. 541–550. IEEE (2012). https://doi.org/10.1109/LICS.2012.64
22. Platzer, A.: Logics of dynamical systems. In: LICS, pp. 13–24. IEEE (2012). https://doi.org/10.1109/LICS.2012.13
23. Platzer, A.: A complete uniform substitution calculus for differential dynamic logic. J. Autom. Reason. **59**(2), 219–265 (2017). https://doi.org/10.1007/s10817-016-9385-1
24. Platzer, A.: Differential hybrid games. ACM Trans. Comput. Log. **18**(3), 19:1-19:44 (2017). https://doi.org/10.1145/3091123
25. Platzer, A., Tan, Y.K.: Differential equation axiomatization: the impressive power of differential ghosts. In: Dawar, A., Grädel, E. (eds.) LICS, pp. 819–828. ACM, New York (2018). https://doi.org/10.1145/3209108.3209147
26. Slind, K., Norrish, M.: A brief overview of HOL4. In: Mohamed, O.A., Muñoz, C., Tahar, S. (eds.) TPHOLs 2008. LNCS, vol. 5170, pp. 28–32. Springer, Heidelberg (2008). https://doi.org/10.1007/978-3-540-71067-7_6
27. Tarski, A.: A decision method for elementary algebra and geometry. In: Caviness, B.F., Johnson, J.R. (eds.) Quantifier Elimination and Cylindrical Algebraic Decomposition. Texts and Monographs in Symbolic Computation (A Series of the Research Institute for Symbolic Computation, Johannes-Kepler-University, Linz, Austria), pp. 24–84. Springer, Vienna (1998). https://doi.org/10.1007/978-3-7091-9459-1_3

SPASS-SATT
A CDCL(LA) Solver

Martin Bromberger[1,2,3(✉)], Mathias Fleury[1,2,3], Simon Schwarz[1,2],
and Christoph Weidenbach[1,2]

[1] Max Planck Institute for Informatics, Saarland Informatics Campus,
Saarbrücken, Germany
{mbromber,mfleury,sschwarz,weidenb}@mpi-inf.mpg.de
[2] Saarland University, Saarland Informatics Campus, Saarbrücken, Germany
[3] Graduate School of Computer Science, Saarland Informatics Campus,
Saarbrücken, Germany

Abstract. SPASS-SATT is a CDCL(LA) solver for linear rational and
linear mixed/integer arithmetic. This system description explains its specific features: fast cube tests for integer solvability, bounding transformations for unbounded problems, close interaction between the SAT solver
and the theory solver, efficient data structures, and small-clause-normal-
form generation. SPASS-SATT is currently one of the strongest systems
on the respective SMT-LIB benchmarks.

Keywords: Linear arithmetic · Integer arithmetic · SMT ·
Preprocessing

1 Introduction

SPASS-SATT (v1.1) is a sound and complete CDCL(LA) solver for quantifier-
free linear rational and linear mixed/integer arithmetic. It is a from-scratch
implementation except for some basic data structures taken from the SPASS [32]
superposition theorem prover. It is available through the SPASS-Workbench [3].
We participated with SPASS-SATT in the main track of the 13th International
Satisfiability Modulo Theories Competition (SMT-COMP 2018) and ranked first
in the category QF_LIA (quantifier-free linear integer arithmetic) [1] and second
in the category QF_LRA (quantifier-free linear rational arithmetic) [2]. This
system description explains the main features that led to the success of SPASS-
SATT. We do not only describe the relevant techniques, but also show their
specific impact on dedicated groups of examples from the SMT-LIB by experiments.

By far not all techniques presented in this system description are unique
features of SPASS-SATT. The techniques that appeared first in SPASS-SATT
are the unit cube test and bounding transformations explained in Sect. 2. Concerning preprocessing, SPASS-SATT is the first SMT solver implementing the

© Springer Nature Switzerland AG 2019
P. Fontaine (Ed.): CADE 2019, LNAI 11716, pp. 111–122, 2019.
https://doi.org/10.1007/978-3-030-29436-6_7

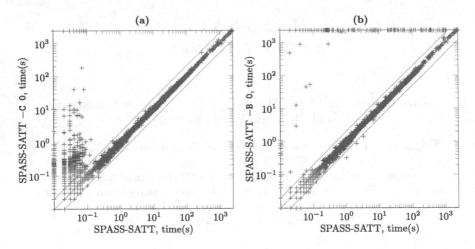

Fig. 1. Impact of our BnB extensions on the QF LIA benchmarks (a) QF_LIA with(out) unit cube tests (b) QF_LIA with(out) bounding transf.

small-clause-normal-form algorithm, see Sect. 4. Further important techniques implemented in SPASS-SATT have already been available in other SMT solvers such as CVC4 [4], MathSAT [12], Yices [16], and Z3 [14], but not all in one tool: (i) the implementation of branch and bound as a separate theory solver and a number of improvements to the simplex implementation such as a priority queue for pivot selection, integer coefficients instead of rational coefficients, dynamically switching between native and arbitrary precision integers, and backing-up versus recalculating simplex states, all in Sect. 2, (ii) decision recommendations, unate propagations, and bound refinements for the interaction between the SAT and theory solver, in Sect. 3, and (iii) preprocessing techniques for if-then-else operators and pseudo-boolean inequalities, in Sect. 4. Although these techniques are contained in existing SMT solvers, not all have been described in the respective literature. The paper ends with a discussion of future extensions to SPASS-SATT in Sect. 5.

The benchmark experiments with SPASS-SATT consider the 6947 SMT-LIB benchmarks for quantifier-free linear integer arithmetic (QF_LIA) [5]. For the experiments, we used a Debian Linux cluster and gave SPASS-SATT for each problem one core of an Intel Xeon E5620 (2.4 GHz) processor, 8 GB RAM, and 40 min. The results are depicted as scatter plots and in each of them we compare the default configuration (i.e., without any command line options) of SPASS-SATT (horizontal axis) with an alternative configuration of SPASS-SATT (vertical axis). (The SMT-COMP results were obtained with the default configuration; by default all presented techniques are turned on.)

2   SPASS-IQ: An LA Theory Solver

SPASS-SATT's theory solver, called SPASS-IQ, decides conjunctions of linear arithmetic inequations. It is divided into two main components: a simplex implementation for handling linear rational arithmetic and a branch-and-bound implementation for handling linear mixed/integer arithmetic.

However, the division between the two components is in all truth not that strict. The branch-and-bound implementation is more of a supervisor for the simplex implementation. To be more precise, the branch-and-bound implementation coordinates the search for a mixed or integer solution, but the majority of the actual search/calculation is still done by the simplex implementation. For most QF_LIA benchmark instances (4894 out of 6947 instances), this supervision is not even necessary; i.e., SPASS-SATT solves these instances with just the simplex implementation as its theory solver. This means that SPASS-SATT's efficiency on the QF_LIA benchmarks also highly depends on the efficiency of our simplex implementation and not just on the extensions and optimizations to our branch-and-bound implementation.

The *simplex implementation* inside SPASS-IQ is based on a specific version [17] of the dual simplex algorithm [29]. The overall efficiency of our simplex implementation is heavily influenced by the efficiency of the data structures that we use. Our most important data structure features are:

(1) *Priority Queue for Pivot Selection:* Instead of iterating over all basic variables when searching for violated basic variables, we collect the basic variables in a priority queue as soon as they become violated.

(2) *Integer Coefficients Instead of Rational Coefficients:* We avoid rational coefficients in our simplex tableau by multiplying each equation in the tableau with the common denominator of the equations coefficients. As a result, each basic variable also has a coefficient, but all coefficients are integers. This transformation roughly halves the cost of most tableau operations because we do not need to consider rationals which are typically represented by two integers (the numerator and the denominator).

(3) *Dynamically Switching between Native and Arbitrary-Precision Integers:* We use the *arbitrary-precision arithmetic library* FLINT to represent our integers [21]. It dynamically switches between native C integer and arbitrary-precision types.

(4) *Backup vs. Recalculation:* In contrast to Dutertre and de Moura's version of the simplex algorithm, our simplex backtrack function recalculates a satisfiable assignment instead of loading a backup of the last satisfiable assignment.

SPASS-IQ's second set of decision procedures revolves around an *implementation of the branch-and-bound (BnB) algorithm* [29]. Most SMT solvers implement branch and bound through a technique called *splitting-on-demand* [6], which delegates some of the branch-and-bound reasoning to the SAT solver. In order to keep more control over the branch-and-bound reasoning, we decided against splitting-on-demand and implemented branch and bound as a theory solver separate from the SAT solver. This also made it easier to complement branch and bound with other decision procedures:

The first two extensions that we discuss here are *simple rounding* (turn off with −LASR 0) and *bound propagation* (turn off with −LABP 0) [29], which are both classical additions to most branch-and-bound implementations. For simple rounding, we round any rational solution computed during the branch-and-bound search to the closest integer assignment and check whether this is already an integer solution. For bound propagation, we propagate new bounds from existing bounds at every node in our branching tree. Although both techniques are very popular, we could only measure a minor impact on SPASS-SATT's performance on the QF_LIA benchmarks. With simple rounding we solve only one instance faster and with bound propagations we solve only 10 additional instances. In part, this is due to our next two extensions that make simple rounding and bound propagation in many cases unnecessary.

The next extension we discuss is the *unit cube test* (turn off with −C 0). It determines in polynomial time whether a polyhedron, i.e., the geometric representation of a system of inequalities, contains a hypercube parallel to the coordinate axes with edge length one [9,10]. The existence of such a hypercube guarantees a mixed/integer solution for the system of inequalities.

The unit cube test is only a sufficient and not a necessary test for the existence of a solution. There is at least one class of inequality systems, viz., absolutely unbounded inequality systems [9,10], where the unit cube test is also a necessary test and which are much harder for many complete decision procedures.

The plot in Fig. 1(a) shows that SPASS-SATT employing the unit cube test solves 56 additional benchmark instances from the QF_LIA benchmarks and solves 705 instances more than twice as fast.[1] Moreover, the unit cube test causes only a minor overhead on problems where it is not successfully applicable.

The final extension that we discuss are *bounding transformations* (turn off with −B 0). Branch and bound alone is an incomplete decision procedure and only guarantees termination on bounded problems, i.e., problems where all variables have an upper and a lower bound. For this reason, we developed two transformations that reduce any unbounded problem into an equisatisfiable problem that is bounded [7]. The transformed problem can then be solved with our branch-and-bound implementation because it is complete for bounded problems.

The plot in Fig. 1(b) shows that SPASS-SATT employing the bounding transformation solves 169 additional benchmark instances from the QF_LIA benchmarks and solves 167 instances more than twice as fast.[2] Moreover, the bounding transformation causes only a minor, almost immeasurable overhead on problem instances where it is not successfully applicable.

3   CDCL(LA): SAT and Theory Solver Interaction

SPASS-SATT uses at its core a CDCL(LA) implementation that combines our CDCL (conflict-driven-clause-learning)-based SAT solver SPASS-SAT with our

---

[1] These instances belong to the `dillig` [15], `CAV-2009` [15], `slacks` [22], `20180326-Bromberger` [7], and `prime-cone` benchmark families [22], which together contain more than 1483 instances of absolutely unbounded problems.

[2] These instances belong to the `20180326-Bromberger` [7], `arctic-matrix` [13], `cut_lemmas` [19], `slacks` [22], and `tropical-matrix` [13] benchmark families.

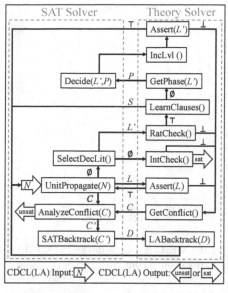

Decide(L,P): if P is $\top$, then L is added to the model; otherwise, $\neg L$ is added.

SelectDecLit(): returns $\emptyset$ if the model satisfies all clauses; otherwise, returns a literal L that is undefined in the model.

UnitPropagate(N): returns $\emptyset$ if no literal can be unit propagated; otherwise, selects a literal L that can be unit propagated and adds it to the model; if a clause $C \in N$ evaluates to $\bot$ under the new model, then returns C; otherwise, returns L.

AnalyzeConflict(C): derives a clause C' which is the negation of the literals that led to the conflict in C; ends CDCL(LA) and returns *unsat* if C' is empty; otherwise, returns C'.

SATBacktrack(C'): adds C' to the clause set N and backtracks to the maximum decision level D where C' is still satisfiable; retuns D.

Assert(L): returns $\bot$ if the literal L contradicts another asserted literal.

IncLvl(): notifies the theory solver that a new decision level was reached.

GetPhase(L): selects the phase P for the decision literal L.

LearnClauses(): Adds a set S of clauses to N that correspond to unate propagations and bound refinements; returns $\emptyset$ if there are no clauses to learn.

RatCheck(): determines a rational solution for the asserted literals; returns $\top$ if a rational solution exists; otherwise, returns $\bot$.

IntCheck(): determines an integer solution for the asserted literals; ends CDCL(LA) and returns *sat* if an integer solution exists; otherwise, returns $\bot$.

GetConflict(): returns a clause C that explains the theory conflict.

LABacktrack(D): removes all asserted literals that were added after decision level D; recalculates a rational solution for the remaining asserted literals.

Fig. 2. CDCL(LA) as implemented in SPASS-SATT

LA theory solver SPASS-IQ. The result is a decision procedure for ground linear-arithmetic formulae in clause normal form. In this section, we quickly explain how our theory solver and SAT solver interact. To this end, we list in Fig. 2 the main interface functions of our SAT solver and theory solver and show through a flow graph how they interact. The main focus of this section, however, is to explain in which way our implementation of CDCL(LA) differs from more general frameworks for CDCL(T), also called DPLL(T) [6,18,26,27].

There are three key points that we have changed compared to the more general frameworks for CDCL(T). First of all, we rely on "weakened early pruning" [30], i.e., we only use a weaker but faster check to determine theory satisfiability for partial (propositionally abstracted) models. We do so because IntCheck(), i.e., checking for an integer solution, is too expensive and not incrementally efficient enough to be checked more than once per complete

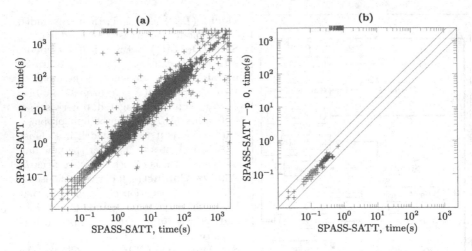

Fig. 3. Impact of decision recommendations on the QF_LIA benchmarks (a) QF_LIA with(out) decision recom. (b) `convert` with(out) decision recom.

(propositionally abstracted) model. As a compromise, we at least check the partial model with RatCheck(), i.e., we check for a rational solution, before we add a(nother) decision literal to the model with Decide(L,P).

As our second key change, we let the theory solver select via GetPhase(L) the phase of the next decision literal L, i.e., whether Decide(L,P) will add the positive or the negated version of L to the model. We call this technique a *decision recommendation* (turn off with −p 0).[3] Finally, we use theory reasoning via the function LearnClauses() to find and learn new clauses implied by the input formula. The reasoning techniques we use for this purpose are *unate propagations* and *bound refinements* as proposed in [17].

In Fig. 3(a), we examine the impact that decision recommendations have on SPASS-SATT's performance on the QF_LIA benchmarks. With decision recommendations it can solve 129 additional problems. Moreover, it becomes more than twice as fast on 389 problems, but only twice as slow on 58 problems. The benchmark family that is impacted the most by decision recommendations is `convert` with 116 additionally solved problems (see Fig. 3(b)). Although SPASS-SATT frequently and regularly performs unate propagations on the QF_LIA benchmarks, we are unable to observe any consistent benefit or drawback from this interaction technique. The impact of bound refinements is also relatively minor and SPASS-SATT solves only 24 additional problem instances if they are activated.

---

[3] In our own theory solver, GetPhase(L) = ⊤ if the current theory assignment satisfies L or if Assert($\neg L$) would return ⊥. Otherwise, GetPhase(L) = ⊥. (If unate propagations are enabled, then the case that Assert($\neg L$) would return ⊥ is impossible because L would have been unate propagated.).

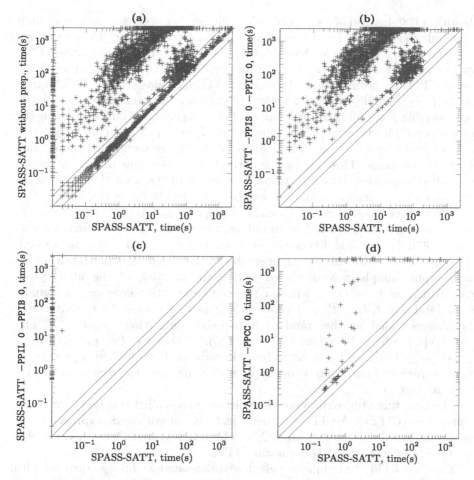

Fig. 4. Impact of our preprocessing techniques on (a) the QF_LIA benchmarks and more specifically (b) `nec_smt`, (c) `rings`, and (d) `pb2010`

4 Preprocessing

Many real world applications can be encoded as linear integer arithmetic formulas, and some of those applications are too specialized to be efficiently handled by our rather general CDCL(LA) implementation. To resolve this, we have complemented SPASS-SATT with several specialized preprocessing techniques.[4]

Complex input formulas are typically transformed into CNF by a Tseitin-style renaming [31] using a static criterion which subformula to replace by a fresh propositional variable. SPASS-SATT includes the small clause normal form

---

[4] All preprocessing techniques are also contained in CVC4 [4] with the exception of the small CNF. The implementation is so efficient because we employ a shared term representation and cache all intermediate results.

algorithm [28]. Instead of a static criterion, the number of clauses with or without a renaming is compared and a fresh propositional variable is introduced only if a renaming eventually yields fewer clauses. This results in a more compact CNF with strictly fewer additional propositional variables. To this end we extended the small clause normal form algorithm to ITE formulas. For an ITE formula (ite t_1 t_2 t_3), simplified by the below techniques and potentially contained in some formula f, we compare the number of clauses generated out of replacing the formula with a fresh variable P in f and adding $P \leftrightarrow [(t_1 \rightarrow t_2) \wedge (\neg t_1 \rightarrow t_3)]$ with a direct replacement of the ITE formula by the before mentioned conjunction of two implications. This test can be carried out in constant time after having once filled respective data structures. The set up of the data structures needs one run on the overall formula, i.e., can be computed in linear time [28].

SPASS-SATT also has five specialized preprocessing techniques for *if-then-else expressions* (ITE). Our first technique, *if-then-else reconstruction* (turn off with −PPIR 0), rebuilds if-then-else operations that were already preprocessed-away by the creators of the input problem. The reconstruction then allows us to apply simplifications missed during the creation of the input problem. To this end, we check whether the first conjunctive layer of our formula $f := (\text{and} \dots t_i \dots t_i' \dots)$ contains any pair of clauses t_i, t_i' that match the clauses added by the standard if-then-else elimination, i.e., $t_i \in T_i$ and $t_i' \in T_i \backslash \{t_i\}$, where $T_i = \{(\text{or } t_{i1} (= y_i \ t_{i3})), (\text{or } (\text{not } t_{i1}) (= y_i \ t_{i2})), (\text{or } (= y_i \ t_{i2}) (= y_i \ t_{i3}))\}$ and y_i is an arithmetic variable. If we find such pairs t_i, t_i', then we remove them from f and replace all remaining occurrences of y_i in f with (ite t_{i1} t_{i2} t_{i3}).

The next three techniques are all dedicated to so-called *constant if-then-else expressions* (CITEs). A CITE is either a leaf, i.e., an arithmetic expression that can be simplified to a number $a_{ij} \in \mathbb{Q}$, or a branch, i.e., an if-then-else expression (ite t_1 t_2 t_3) where t_2 and t_3 are again CITEs.

The first CITE technique is called *shared monomial lifting* (turn off with −PPIL 0) and we use it to increase the number of CITEs in our formula. It traverses the subterms in our formula in bottom-up order and transforms all subterms $t := (\text{ite } t_1 (+ q \ q') (+ q \ \hat{q}))$ into $(+ q (* 1 (\text{ite } t_1 (+ q') (+ \hat{q}))))$. (We assume here for simplicity that the shared part q appears after the unshared parts q' and $\hat{q}$. In reality SPASS-SATT has to find and extract the shared parts.)

The second technique is called *CITE simplification* (turn off with −PPIS 0) and it simplifies atoms $(o \ t_1 \ t_2)$, where t_1 and t_2 are CITEs and o is one of the operators $<=, =, >=$. To be more precise, the technique essentially pushes the comparison operator o recursively down the CITE branches and greedily simplifies any branch to *true* or *false* if possible. For more details, see Sect. 4 in the paper by Kim et al. on efficient term-ITE conversion [24].

The third technique is called *CITE bounding* (turn off with −PPIB 0) and eliminates the remaining CITEs. Thanks to it, we only introduce one new variable for each topmost CITE instead of one variable for each CITE branch. Moreover, this new variable describes only a small set of values (often equivalent to just the CITE leaves) because it is bounded as tightly as possible.

As its first step, CITE bounding creates one new integer variable x_j for each topmost CITE expression t_j and replaces the occurrences of t_j in our formula f with x_j. As its second step, CITE bounding extends f to the formula $f' := ($and f f_1 f_1' $\ldots$ f_m $f_m')$, where (i) f_j is equivalent to t_j except that all leaves a_{ij} of t_j are replaced by the equations ($=$ x_j a_{ij}), (ii) $f_j' := ($and ($>=$ x_j a_{minj}) ($<=$ x_j a_{maxj})), and (iii) a_{minj} is the smallest leaf in t_j and a_{maxj} is the largest leaf in t_j. As its last step, CITE bounding replaces all occurrences of x_j in f' with ($*$ a_{gj} x_j), where a_{gj} is the greatest common divisor of the leaves a_{ij} in t_j.

The final ITE technique handles *nested conjunctive if-then-else expressions* (AND-ITEs). An AND-ITE is a series of nested if-then-else expressions that can be simplified to a conjunction. For instance, if $t_i := ($ite t_i' t_{i+1} *false*$)$ for $i = 1, \ldots, n$, then t_1 is an AND-ITE equivalent to (and t_1' $\ldots$ t_n' t_{n+1}). Naturally, we transform these AND-ITEs into actual conjunctions and we call this process compression. However, we compress an AND-ITE t_1 only if all of its actual AND-ITE subterms t_i appear only inside t_1 and only once. If this is the case, then we first replace all occurrences of t_1 in f by a new propositional variable p_j and extend our formula f to the formula (and f ($=$ p_j t_1')), where t_1' is the compressed form of t_1. (If this is not the case, then we simply replace and compress the AND-ITE subterms in t_i first.) We do the compression in this way to strengthen the connection of the AND-ITEs that have multiple occurrences in f. The above described technique is called *if-then-else compression* (turn off with $-$PPIC 0) and it was first presented by Burch in [11]. However, Burch used it to simplify control circuits and not SMT input problems.

Last but not least, SPASS-SATT also provides a preprocessing technique for *pseudo-boolean problems* [20], i.e., linear arithmetic problems where all integer variables x_j have bounds $0 \le x_j \le 1$, which we call *pseudo-boolean variables*. To be more precise, SPASS-SATT recognizes clauses that are encoded as linear pseudo-boolean inequalities (i.e., inequalities containing just pseudo-boolean variables) and turns them into actual clauses (turn off with $-$PPCC 0). (This technique goes back to the NP-hardness proof of 0-1 programming [23].) However, SPASS-SATT only transforms inequalities containing at most three variables because it would otherwise fail to solve some of the problems from the **pidgeons** benchmark family.

The **convert** benchmark family contains problems that are relatively hard unless SPASS-SATT uses the right combination of techniques. To be more precise, SPASS-SATT solves only two-thirds of the 319 instances if one of the following three techniques is missing: (i) recalculating simplex states during backtracking (Sect. 2), (ii) decision recommendations (Sect. 3), or (iii) the small CNF transformation. SPASS-SATT with all three techniques solves all instances in less than 2 s (see Fig. 3(b)).

The **nec_smt** benchmark family contains problems with many nested if-then-else and let expressions. SPASS-SATT can handle most of them if we first apply our constant if-then-else simplifications and our conjunctive if-then-else compression. In Fig. 4(b), we see that SPASS-SATT without our preprocessing techniques solves only 1422 out of the 2800 benchmark instances and is by far slower on the instances it can solve. SPASS-SATT with our preprocessing techniques solves 2782 out of the 2800 benchmark instances.

The `rings` benchmark family encodes associative properties on modular arithmetic with the help of if-then-else expressions. With a combination of shared monomial lifting and constant if-then-else bounding, these problems become almost trivial to solve. In fact, SPASS-SATT needs less than one second for each problem instance and needs only techniques for linear rational arithmetic to solve each of them (Fig. 4(c)).

The `rings_preprocessed` benchmark family is equivalent to the `rings` benchmark family except that all if-then-else-operations were eliminated by standard if-then-else elimination [19]. We can use the same trick as for the `rings` benchmark family if we first use our if-then-else reconstruction technique that reverses the standard if-then-else elimination.

The `pb2010` benchmark family is a set of industrial problems taken from the pseudo-boolean competition 2010. With its pseudo-boolean preprocessing, SPASS-SATT solves 22 additional benchmark instances from the 81 instances in the `pb2010` benchmark family (see Fig. 4(e)). Moreover, SPASS-SATT solves all of these instances without its branch-and-bound implementation.

5   Conclusion and Future Work

We have presented SPASS-SATT our complete solver for ground linear arithmetic and have explained which techniques make it so efficient in practice. To summarize, SPASS-SATT is so efficient because (i) we have optimized the data structures in our simplex implementation, (ii) we have combined branch and bound with the unit cube test and the bounding transformation, (iii) we have added decision recommendations to our CDCL(LA) framework, (iv) we have added a small CNF transformation, and (v) we have added specialized preprocessing techniques for if-then-else expressions and pseudo-boolean inequalities.

Almost all of the presented techniques can be applied incrementally, however this is not always useful. For the partial models computed by the SAT solver, we only apply the simplex method, unate propagation, and bound refinements incrementally. If we ever extend SPASS-SATT to handle theory combinations or incremental SMT-LIB problems, then we would also apply branch-and-bound, unit cubes, and bounding transformations incrementally; but only on the models generated during Nelson-Oppen combination or between two (check-sat) calls.

For future research, we plan to extend SPASS-SATT to quantified linear arithmetic. Moreover, we plan to complement SPASS-SATT with several specialized decision procedures. For instance, SPASS-SATT could handle (almost) pseudo-boolean problems (e.g., benchmark families `pb2010`, `miplib2003`) much more efficiently if we extended branch and bound with a SAT based arithmetic decision procedure [8, 22, 25].

References

1. SMT-COMP 2018 results for QF_LIA (main track). http://smtcomp.sourceforge.net/2018/results-QF_LIA.shtml
2. SMT-COMP 2018 results for QF_LRA (main track). http://smtcomp.sourceforge.net/2018/results-QF_LRA.shtml
3. The SPASS workbench. https://www.spass-prover.org/
4. Barrett, C., Conway, C.L., Deters, M., Hadarean, L., Jovanović, D., King, T., Reynolds, A., Tinelli, C.: CVC4. In: Gopalakrishnan, G., Qadeer, S. (eds.) CAV 2011. LNCS, vol. 6806, pp. 171–177. Springer, Heidelberg (2011). https://doi.org/10.1007/978-3-642-22110-1_14
5. Barrett, C., Fontaine, P., Tinelli, C.: The satisfiability modulo theories library (SMT-LIB) (2016). www.SMT-LIB.org
6. Barrett, C., Nieuwenhuis, R., Oliveras, A., Tinelli, C.: Splitting on demand in SAT modulo theories. In: Hermann, M., Voronkov, A. (eds.) LPAR 2006. LNCS (LNAI), vol. 4246, pp. 512–526. Springer, Heidelberg (2006). https://doi.org/10.1007/11916277_35
7. Bromberger, M.: A reduction from unbounded linear mixed arithmetic problems into bounded problems. In: Galmiche, D., Schulz, S., Sebastiani, R. (eds.) IJCAR 2018. LNCS (LNAI), vol. 10900, pp. 329–345. Springer, Cham (2018). https://doi.org/10.1007/978-3-319-94205-6_22
8. Bromberger, M., Sturm, T., Weidenbach, C.: Linear integer arithmetic revisited. In: Felty, A.P., Middeldorp, A. (eds.) CADE 2015. LNCS (LNAI), vol. 9195, pp. 623–637. Springer, Cham (2015). https://doi.org/10.1007/978-3-319-21401-6_42
9. Bromberger, M., Weidenbach, C.: Fast cube tests for LIA constraint solving. In: Olivetti, N., Tiwari, A. (eds.) IJCAR 2016. LNCS (LNAI), vol. 9706, pp. 116–132. Springer, Cham (2016). https://doi.org/10.1007/978-3-319-40229-1_9
10. Bromberger, M., Weidenbach, C.: New techniques for linear arithmetic: cubes and equalities. Formal Methods Syst. Des. **51**(3), 433–461 (2017). https://doi.org/10.1007/s10703-017-0278-7
11. Burch, J.R.: Techniques for verifying superscalar microprocessors. In: DAC, pp. 552–557. ACM Press (1996). https://doi.org/10.1145/240518.240623
12. Cimatti, A., Griggio, A., Schaafsma, B.J., Sebastiani, R.: The MathSAT5 SMT solver. In: Piterman, N., Smolka, S.A. (eds.) TACAS 2013. LNCS, vol. 7795, pp. 93–107. Springer, Heidelberg (2013). https://doi.org/10.1007/978-3-642-36742-7_7
13. Codish, M., Fekete, Y., Fuhs, C., Giesl, J., Waldmann, J.: Exotic semi-ring constraints. In: SMT@IJCAR. EPiC Series in Computing, vol. 20, pp. 88–97. EasyChair (2012). https://doi.org/10.29007/qqvt
14. de Moura, L., Bjørner, N.: Z3: an efficient SMT solver. In: Ramakrishnan, C.R., Rehof, J. (eds.) TACAS 2008. LNCS, vol. 4963, pp. 337–340. Springer, Heidelberg (2008). https://doi.org/10.1007/978-3-540-78800-3_24
15. Dillig, I., Dillig, T., Aiken, A.: Cuts from proofs: a complete and practical technique for solving linear inequalities over integers. In: Bouajjani, A., Maler, O. (eds.) CAV 2009. LNCS, vol. 5643, pp. 233–247. Springer, Heidelberg (2009). https://doi.org/10.1007/978-3-642-02658-4_20
16. Dutertre, B.: Yices 2.2. In: Biere, A., Bloem, R. (eds.) CAV 2014. LNCS, vol. 8559, pp. 737–744. Springer, Cham (2014). https://doi.org/10.1007/978-3-319-08867-9_49
17. Dutertre, B., de Moura, L.: A fast linear-arithmetic solver for DPLL(T). In: Ball, T., Jones, R.B. (eds.) CAV 2006. LNCS, vol. 4144, pp. 81–94. Springer, Heidelberg (2006). https://doi.org/10.1007/11817963_11

18. Ganzinger, H., Hagen, G., Nieuwenhuis, R., Oliveras, A., Tinelli, C.: DPLL(T): fast decision procedures. In: Alur, R., Peled, D.A. (eds.) CAV 2004. LNCS, vol. 3114, pp. 175–188. Springer, Heidelberg (2004). https://doi.org/10.1007/978-3-540-27813-9_14

19. Griggio, A.: A practical approach to satisfiability modulo linear integer arithmetic. JSAT **8**(1/2), 1–27 (2012)

20. Hammer, P.L., Rudeanu, S.: Boolean Methods in Operations Research and Related Areas. Econometrics and Operations Research, vol. 7. Springer, Heidelberg (2012). https://doi.org/10.1007/978-3-642-85823-9

21. Hart, W., Johansson, F., Pancratz, S.: FLINT: fast library for number theory, version 2.4.0 (2013). http://flintlib.org

22. Jovanović, D., de Moura, L.: Cutting to the chase solving linear integer arithmetic. In: Bjørner, N., Sofronie-Stokkermans, V. (eds.) CADE 2011. LNCS (LNAI), vol. 6803, pp. 338–353. Springer, Heidelberg (2011). https://doi.org/10.1007/978-3-642-22438-6_26

23. Karp, R.M.: Reducibility among combinatorial problems. In: Complexity of Computer Computations. The IBM Research Symposia Series, pp. 85–103. Plenum Press, New York (1972). https://doi.org/10.1007/978-1-4684-2001-2_9

24. Kim, H., Somenzi, F., Jin, H.S.: Efficient term-ITE conversion for satisfiability modulo theories. In: Kullmann, O. (ed.) SAT 2009. LNCS, vol. 5584, pp. 195–208. Springer, Heidelberg (2009). https://doi.org/10.1007/978-3-642-02777-2_20

25. Nieuwenhuis, R.: The IntSat method for integer linear programming. In: O'Sullivan, B. (ed.) CP 2014. LNCS, vol. 8656, pp. 574–589. Springer, Cham (2014). https://doi.org/10.1007/978-3-319-10428-7_42

26. Nieuwenhuis, R., Oliveras, A.: DPLL(T) with exhaustive theory propagation and its application to difference logic. In: Etessami, K., Rajamani, S.K. (eds.) CAV 2005. LNCS, vol. 3576, pp. 321–334. Springer, Heidelberg (2005). https://doi.org/10.1007/11513988_33

27. Nieuwenhuis, R., Oliveras, A., Tinelli, C.: Solving SAT and SAT modulo theories: from an abstract Davis-Putnam-Logemann-Loveland procedure to DPLL(T). J. ACM **53**(6), 937–977 (2006). https://doi.org/10.1145/1217856.1217859

28. Nonnengart, A., Weidenbach, C.: Computing small clause normal forms. In: Handbook of Automated Reasoning, vol. 1. Elsevier (2001). https://doi.org/10.1016/b978-044450813-3/50008-4

29. Schrijver, A.: Theory of Linear and Integer Programming. Wiley, New York (1986)

30. Sebastiani, R.: Lazy satisability modulo theories. JSAT **3**(3–4), 141–224 (2007)

31. Tseitin, G.S.: On the complexity of derivation in propositional calculus. In: Siekmann, J.H., Wrightson, G. (eds.) Automation of Reasoning: Classical Papers on Computational Logic, vol. 2, pp. 466–483. Springer, Heidelberg (1983). https://doi.org/10.1007/978-3-642-81955-1_28. First Published. In: Slisenko, A.O. (ed.) Studies in Constructive Mathematics and Mathematical Logic (1968)

32. Weidenbach, C., Dimova, D., Fietzke, A., Kumar, R., Suda, M., Wischnewski, P.: SPASS version 3.5. In: Schmidt, R.A. (ed.) CADE 2009. LNCS (LNAI), vol. 5663, pp. 140–145. Springer, Heidelberg (2009). https://doi.org/10.1007/978-3-642-02959-2_10

GRUNGE: A Grand Unified ATP Challenge

Chad E. Brown[1], Thibault Gauthier[1], Cezary Kaliszyk[2,3], Geoff Sutcliffe[4],
and Josef Urban[1(✉)]

[1] Czech Technical University in Prague, Prague, Czech Republic
josef.urban@gmail.com
[2] University of Innsbruck, Innsbruck, Austria
[3] University of Warsaw, Warsaw, Poland
[4] University of Miami, Coral Gables, USA

Abstract. This paper describes a large set of related theorem proving problems obtained by translating theorems from the HOL4 standard library into multiple logical formalisms. The formalisms are in higher-order logic (with and without type variables) and first-order logic (possibly with types, and possibly with type variables). The resultant problem sets allow us to run automated theorem provers that support different logical formalisms on corresponding problems, and compare their performances. This also results in a new "grand unified" large theory benchmark that emulates the ITP/ATP hammer setting, where systems and metasystems can use multiple formalisms in complementary ways, and jointly learn from the accumulated knowledge.

Keywords: Theorem proving · Higher-order logic ·
First-order logic · Many-sorted logic

1 Introduction

A hammer [7] for an interactive theorem prover (ITP) [22] typically translates an ITP goal into a formalism used by an automated theorem prover (ATP). Since the most successful ATPs have so far been for untyped first-order logic, the focus has been on first-order translations. There is also interest in ATPs working in richer formalisms, such as monomorphic and polymorphic, typed first-order, and higher-order logics. The TPTP formats for various formalisms have been adopted for this work, viz. FOF [46] TF0 [47], TF1 [8], TH0 [5], and TH1 [26]. An interesting related task is the creation of a (grand) unified large-theory benchmark that allows fair comparison of such ATP systems, their combination and integration with premise selectors and machine learners [1], across different formalisms. As

Supported by the ERC grant no. 649043 AI4REASON and no. 714034 SMART, by the Czech project AI&Reasoning CZ.02.1.01/0.0/0.0/15_003/0000466, the European Regional Development Fund, and the National Science Foundation Grant 1730419 - "CI-SUSTAIN: StarExec: Cross-Community Infrastructure for Logic Solving".

P. Fontaine (Ed.): CADE 2019, LNAI 11716, pp. 123–141, 2019.
https://doi.org/10.1007/978-3-030-29436-6_8

a step towards creating such benchmarks we present two families of translations from the language of HOL4 [42] to the various TPTP formats. We have implemented these translations and plan to use them as the first "GRand UNified ATP challenGE" (GRUNGE) benchmarks, generalizing existing benchmarks such as the CakeML export [31] that was used in the large-theory benchmark (LTB) division of the CASC-J9 ATP competition [48].

The rest of the paper is structured as follows. Section 2 introduces notation and the HOL syntax. Section 3 introduces the problems – the HOL4 standard library. Section 4 introduces the first family of translations, and Sect. 5 introduces the second family of translations. Section 6 discusses and compares the translations on an example, and Sect. 7 evaluates the translations using existing ATPs. Section 8 describes the CASC-27 LTB division, which is based on these translations. Related work is discussed in Sect. 9.

2   Preliminaries

Since this work is based on the HOL4 standard library, it is necessary to start with brief comments about the syntax and notion of proof in HOL4. More detailed information is in [19,42]. HOL4, like several other ITPs (e.g., Isabelle/HOL [36], HOL Light [20] or ProofPower [28]), is based on an extension of Church's simple type theory [12] that includes prefix polymorphism and type definitions [19]. HOL4 includes a type o of propositions, a type ι of individuals and a type $(\sigma \to \tau)$ of functions from a type σ to a type τ. Parentheses are omitted, with $\to$ associating to the right. In addition, there are type variables α and defined types. At each point in the development of the HOL4 library there is a finite set of (previously defined) constants c, and a finite set of (previously defined) type constructors κ giving a type $\kappa(\sigma_1, \ldots, \sigma_n)$ for types $\sigma_1, \ldots, \sigma_n$. For simplicity we consider the signature to be fixed, to avoid the need to specify the types and terms relative to an evolving signature.

Terms are generated from constants c and variables x using application $(s\ t)$ and λ-abstractions $(\lambda x : \sigma.t)$ in the expected way, for terms s and t. Parentheses are omitted, with application associating the left. Binders have scope as far to the right as possible, consistent with parentheses. Multiple binders over the same type can be written in a combined form, e.g., $\lambda xy : \sigma.t$ means $\lambda x : \sigma.\lambda y : \sigma.t$.

Constants may be polymorphic. There are two primitive polymorphic logical constants: $=^\alpha$ is polymorphic with type $\alpha \to \alpha \to o$ and ε^α is polymorphic with type $(\alpha \to o) \to \alpha$, where α is a type variable. When terms are defined, such constants are used with a fixed type for α written as a superscript. New polymorphic constants can be defined within a HOL4 theory.

Aside from $=^\alpha$ and ε^α, implication $\Rightarrow$ of type $o \to o \to o$ is primitive. From these primitive logical constants it is possible to define $\wedge$, $\vee$ and $\neg$, as well as polymorphic operators $\forall^\alpha$ and $\exists^\alpha$. The usual notation is used for these logical connectives, so that the binder notation $\forall^\sigma(\lambda x : \sigma.t)$ is written as $\forall x : \sigma.t$, using the same binding conventions as for λ-abstractions. Similarly, $\exists^\sigma(\lambda x : \sigma.t)$ is written as $\exists x : \sigma.t$.

Terms of type o are called propositions, and we use φ and ψ to range over propositions. A sequent is a pair $\Gamma \vdash \varphi$ where Γ is a finite set of propositions and φ is a proposition. There is a notion of HOL4 provability for sequents. While our translations map HOL4 sequents to TPTP formulae, it is not our intention to mirror HOL4 provability in the target format. The intention, roughly speaking, is to gain information about when a HOL4 theorem is a consequence of previous HOL4 theorems, in some logic weaker than HOL4.

From the simplest perspective, each translation translates HOL4 types and HOL4 terms (including propositions) to terms in the target format. A type, term or sequent with no type variables is called *monomorphic*. As an optimization, some of the translations translate some monomorphic HOL4 types to types in the target language. As a common notation throughout this paper, a HOL4 type σ translated as a term is written as $\hat{\sigma}$, and σ translated as a type is written as $\tilde{\sigma}$. Another optimization is to translate HOL4 propositions (and sequents) to the level of formulae in the target language.

3   Problem Set: The HOL4 Standard Library

Version Kananaskis-12 of the HOL4 standard library contains 15733 formulae: 8 axioms, 2294 definitions, and 13431 theorems. If most of the formulae were monomorphic and fell into a natural first-order fragment of HOL4, then there would be a natural translation into the FOF format. However, many formulae are either polymorphic or higher-order (or both), as Table 1 shows (note that the numbers are not cumulative, e.g., the 2232 monomorphic first-order formulae do not include the 1632 uni-sorted first-order formulae, which could also be processed by an ATP that can handle the monomorphic types). The problem set consists of 12140 theorems proven in the HOL4 standard library[1], in the context of a finite set of dependencies used in the HOL4 proof [16].

Table 1. Number of HOL4 formulae in each category.

	First-order	Higher-order	Combined
Uni-sorted	1632 (FOF)	0	1632
Monomorphic	2232 (TF0)	3683 (TH0)	5915
Polymorphic	1536 (TF1)	6650 (TH1)	8186
Combined	5400	10333	15733

---

[1] 1291 theorems were not included due to dependencies being erased during the build of the HOL4 library.

4   Syntactic Translations via First-Order Encodings

There already exist many families of translations for HOL to the TPTP format, usually developed for hammers [27,35]. We have adopted and adapted them: (i) We have made the translations more local, by making them independent for each theorem, i.e., unaffected by other theorems. In particular, this means that when the same lambda function appears in two theorems, lambda-lifting will produce two new functions. (ii) We have made more problems provable (in principle) by introducing additional axioms and relying on an embedding of polymorphic types instead of relying on heuristic monomorphization. (iii) For the TF0 and TH0 formats, we have made use of their polysortedness by expressing the type of monomorphic constants directly using TF0 and TH0 types.

The translations are described in the order TH1 → TF1 → FOF → TF0 → TH0, as translations to the later formats take advantage of translation techniques used for earlier formats.

4.1   Translating to TH1

TH1 is a language that is strictly more expressive than HOL4. Therefore HOL4 formulae can be represented in TH1 with minimal effort. This produces the TH1-I collection of ATP problems.

Alignment of Logical Constructions. The TPTP format contains a set of defined constructs that have implicit definitions, and HOL4 objects are mapped to their TPTP counterparts in a natural way. The boolean type o of HOL4 is mapped to the defined TPTP type $o. The arrow type operator is mapped to the TPTP arrow >. All other type operators are declared to take n types and give a type, using the TPTP "type of types" $tType. For example, the type operator *list* has type $tType > $tType.

The TPTP logical connectives $\wedge, \vee, \Rightarrow, \neg, =, \forall, \exists$ are used at the top-level of the translated formula whenever possible, but the corresponding HOL4 constants are used when necessary. Equivalences relating HOL4 logical constants to TPTP connectives are included.

Explicit Type Arguments. A HOL4 constant c carries a type ν'. This type is an instance of type ν that was given to c when c was created. By matching ν with ν', a type substitution s can be inferred. Ordering the type variables in the domain of s, the implicit type arguments of c are deduced. Making the quantification of type variables and the type arguments explicit is required in the TH1 format. The effect that this requirement has on a constant declaration and a formula is shown in Example 1.

Example 1. Explicit type arguments and type quantifications

	HOL4	TH1
Type of I	$\alpha \to \alpha$	$\forall \alpha : \$tType.\ \alpha \to \alpha$
Formula	$\forall x : \alpha.\ (I\ x) = x$	$\forall \alpha : \$tType.\ \forall x : \alpha.\ ((I\ \alpha)\ x) = x$

4.2 Translating to TF1

To produce the TF1-I collection of ATP problems, all the higher-order features of the HOL4 problems have to be eliminated. This is done in a sequence of steps.

Lambda-Lifting and Boolean-Lifting. One of the higher-order features is the presence of lambda-abstraction. The translation first uses the extensionality property to add extra arguments to lambdas appearing on either side of an equality, and then beta-reduce the formula. Next lambda-lifting [14, 35] is used. Lambda-lifting creates a constant **f** for the leftmost outermost lambda-abstractions appearing at the term-level. This constant **f** replaces the lambda-abstraction in the formula. A definition is given for **f**, which may involve some variable capture - see Example 2. This procedure is repeated until all the atoms are free of lambda-abstractions. The definitions are part of the background theory, and are considered to be axioms in the TF1 problem even if they were created from the conjecture.

Example 2. Lambda-lifting with variable capture

$$\text{Original formula: } \forall k.\ \text{linear}\ (\lambda x.\ k \times x)$$
$$\text{Additional definition: } \forall k\ x.\ \mathbf{f}\ k\ x = k \times x$$
$$\text{New formula: } \forall k.\ \text{linear}\ (\mathbf{f}\ k)$$

A similar method can be applied to move some logical constants from the term-level to the formula-level - see Example 3 (this optimization is not applied in our second family of translations).

Example 3. Boolean-lifting

$$\text{Original formula: } \forall x.\ x = \text{COND}\ (x = 0)\ 0\ x$$
$$\text{Additional definition: } \forall x.\ \mathbf{f}\ x \Leftrightarrow (x = 0)$$
$$\text{New formula: } \forall x.\ x = \text{COND}\ (\mathbf{f}\ x)\ 0\ x$$

To allow the ATPs to create their own encoded lambda-abstractions, axioms for the combinators S, K and I are added to every problem. These axioms are omitted in the second family of translations. In the TH0-II versions of the problem, combinators are not needed since all simply typed λ-calculus terms are already representable. In the TF0-II and FOF-II versions only an axiom for I and a partially applied axiom for K are included. Combinator axioms enlarge the search space, which hinders the ATPs unnecessarily because they are not needed for proving most of the theorem.

Apply Operator and Arity Equations. As functions cannot be passed as arguments in first-order logic, an explicit apply operator ap is used to apply a function to an argument. This way all objects (constants and variables) have arity zero except for the apply operator which has arity two. The HOL4 functional extensionality axiom is added to all problems, as it expresses the main property of the apply operator:

$$\forall f\ g\ (\forall x.\ \mathsf{ap}\ f\ x = \mathsf{ap}\ g\ x) \Rightarrow f = g$$

This axiom also demonstrates how the higher-order variables f and g become first-order variables after the introduction of ap.

To limit the number of apply operators in a formula, versions of each constant are defined for all its possible arities, in terms of the zero-arity version. These constants are used in the translated formula - see Example 4.

Example 4. Using constants with their arity

$$\text{Original formula: } \mathsf{SUC}\ 0 = 1 \wedge \exists y.\ \mathsf{MAP}\ \mathsf{SUC}\ y \neq y$$
$$\text{Arity equations: } \mathsf{SUC}_1\ x = \mathsf{ap}\ \mathsf{SUC}_0\ x,\ \ldots$$
$$\text{New formula: } \mathsf{SUC}_1\ 0_0 = 1_0 \wedge \exists y.\ \mathsf{MAP}_2\ \mathsf{SUC}_0\ y \neq y$$

If the return type of a constant is a type variable then some of its instances can expect an arbitrarily large numbers of arguments. In the case where the number of arguments n' of an instance exceeds the number of arguments n of the primitive constant, variants of this constant are not created for this arity. Instead, the apply operator is used to reduce the number of arguments to n. For example, the term $\mathsf{I}\ \mathsf{I}\ x$ is not translated to $\mathsf{I}_2\ \mathsf{I}_0\ x$ but instead to $\mathsf{ap}\ (\mathsf{I}_1\ \mathsf{I}_0)\ x$.

TF1 types. As a final step, type arguments and type quantifications are added as in Sect. 4.1. Moreover, the boolean type of HOL4 is replaced by \$o at the formula-level, and by o at the term-level (because \$o is not allowed at the term-level in a first-order formula). This causes a mismatch between the type of the atom o and the type of the logical connective \$o. Therefore an additional operator $\mathsf{p}:o \rightarrow \$o$ is applied on top of every atom. The following properties of p and o are added to every translated problem (written here in the first-order style for function application):

$$\forall xy:o.\ (\mathsf{p}(x) \Leftrightarrow \mathsf{p}(y)) \Rightarrow (x = y)$$
$$\mathsf{p}(\mathsf{true}),\ \neg\mathsf{p}(\mathsf{false}),\ \forall x:o.\ x = \mathsf{true} \vee x = \mathsf{false}$$

In a similar manner, the TPTP arrow type cannot be used whenever a function appears as an argument. Instead the type constructor fun is used, as illustrated by the following constant declaration:

$$\mathsf{ap} : \forall \alpha : \$tType\ \beta : \$tType.\ ((\mathsf{fun}(\alpha, \beta) \times \alpha) \rightarrow \beta)).$$

4.3   Translating to FOF

The translation to FOF, which produces the FOF-I collection of ATP problems, follows exactly the same path as the translation to TF1 except that the types are encoded as first-order terms. To represent the fact that a first-order term t has type ν, the tagging function s, introduced by Hurd [23], is used: every term t of type ν is replaced by $\mathsf{s}(\hat{\nu}, t)$. Going from the type ν to the term $\hat{\nu}$ effectively transforms type variables into term variables, and type operators into first-order functions and constants. Type arguments are unnecessary as the tags contain enough information. In practice, the s tagging function prevents terms of different types from unifying, and allows instantiation of type variables - see Example 5.

Example 5. Type instantiation

TF1	FOF
$\forall x\!:\!\alpha.\ \mathsf{I}(\alpha, x) = x$	$\forall \hat{\alpha}\ \hat{x}.\ \mathsf{s}(\hat{\alpha}, \hat{\mathsf{I}}(\mathsf{s}(\hat{\alpha}, \hat{x}))) = \mathsf{s}(\hat{\alpha}, \hat{x})$
$\forall x\!:\!\mathsf{num}.\ \mathsf{I}(\mathsf{num}, x) = x$	$\forall \hat{x}.\ \mathsf{s}(\widehat{\mathsf{num}}, \hat{\mathsf{I}}(\mathsf{s}(\widehat{\mathsf{num}}, \hat{x}))) = \mathsf{s}(\widehat{\mathsf{num}}, \hat{x})$

4.4   Translating to TF0

An easy way to translate HOL4 formulae to TF0, which produces the TF0-I collection of ATP problems, is to take the translation to FOF and inject it into TF0.

Trivial Injection from FOF to TF0. The first step is to give types to all the constants and variables appearing in the FOF formula. A naive implementation would be to give the type $\iota^n \to \iota$ to symbols with arity n. However, since it is known that the first argument comes from the universe of non-empty types, and the second argument comes from the universe of untyped terms, an explicit distinction can be made. The type of s is defined to be $\delta \times \mu \to \iota$, with δ being the universe of non-empty types, μ being the universe of untyped terms, and ι being the universe of typed terms. After this translation a type operator (or type variable) with m arguments has type $\delta^m \to \delta$, and a function (or term variable) with n arguments has type $\iota^n \to \mu$. The type of p is $\mathsf{p} : \iota \to \$\mathsf{o}$. Declaring the type of all these objects achieves a trivial translation from FOF with tags to TF0.

Using Special Types. To take full advantage of the polysortedness of TF0, a constant $\tilde{c}_n{}^\nu$ is declared for every constant c_n, with arity n and monomorphic type ν. The type of $\tilde{c}_n{}^\nu$ is declared to be $(\tilde{\nu}_1 \times \ldots \times \tilde{\nu}_n) \to \tilde{\nu}_0$, where $\tilde{\nu}_1, \ldots, \tilde{\nu}_n$, and $\tilde{\nu}_0$ are basic types. A basic type constructs a single type from a monomorphic type, e.g., *list_real* for *list*[*real*], *fun_o_o* for *fun*(*o*, *o*). The basic types are special types, and are declared using $\mathtt{\$tType}$. Thanks to these new constants monomorphic formulae can be expressed in a natural way, without type encodings in the formula. Nevertheless, an ATP should still be able to perform a type instantiation if necessary. That is why we relate the monomorphic representation with its tagged counterpart.

If a term has a basic type then it lives in the monomorphic world where as a term of type ι it belongs to the tagged world. All monomorphic terms (constructed from monomorphic variables and constants) can be expressed in the monomorphic world. To relate the two representations of the same HOL4 term an "injection" i_ν and a "surjection" j_ν are defined for each basic type $\tilde{\nu}$. The constants $i_\nu : \tilde{\nu} \to \mu$ and $j_\nu : \iota \to \tilde{\nu}$ must respect the following properties, which are included as axioms in the translated problems:

$$\forall x : \mu.\ \mathsf{s}(\hat{\nu}, i_\nu(j_\nu(\mathsf{s}(\hat{\nu}, x)))) = \mathsf{s}(\hat{\nu}, x)$$
$$\forall x : \tilde{\nu}.\ j_\nu(\mathsf{s}(\hat{\nu}, i_\nu(x))) = x$$

Whenever $\tilde{c}_n{}^\nu$ is an instance of a polymorphic function $\hat{c}_n$, the following equation is included in the TF0 problem, which relates the two representatives:

$$\forall x_1 : \tilde{\nu}_1.. x_n : \tilde{\nu}_n.\ \mathsf{s}(\nu_0, i_{\nu_0}(\tilde{c}_n{}^\nu(x_1,.., x_n))) = \mathsf{s}(\nu_0, \hat{c}_n(\mathsf{s}(\nu_1, i_{\nu_1}(x_1)),.., \mathsf{s}(\nu_n, i_{\nu_n}(x_n)))$$

Example 6 shows how "injections", "surjections", and special types can be used to translate a theorem mixing polymorphic and monomorphic elements.

Example 6. Special types
The polymorphic function I is applied to the monomorphic variable x. Using special types, type tags can be dropped for x.

$$\text{FOF}: \quad \forall \hat{x}.\ \mathsf{s}(\widehat{\mathsf{num}}, \hat{I}(\ \mathsf{s}(\widehat{\mathsf{num}}, \hat{x})\ )) = \mathsf{s}(\widehat{\mathsf{num}}, \hat{x})$$
$$\text{TF0}: \quad \forall \tilde{x} : \widetilde{\mathsf{num}}.\ j_{\mathsf{num}}(\hat{I}(\ \mathsf{s}(\widehat{\mathsf{num}}, i_{\mathsf{num}}(\tilde{x}))\ )) = \tilde{x}$$

Effect on Defined Operators. The ap operator is treated in the same way as every other constant. In particular, a different version of ap is created for each monomorphic type. The type of p becomes $\tilde{o} \to \$o$, and the projection j_o is used to transfer atoms from the tagged world to the monomorphic world.

If the presence of the p predicate and the inclusion of additional equations are ignored, our translation of a HOL4 first-order monomorphic formula using special types to TF0 is simply the identity transformation.

4.5   Translating to TH0

Translating from HOL4 to TH0, which produces the TH0-I collection of ATP problems, is achieved in a way similar to the translation to TF0. The HOL4 formulae are first translated to FOF and then trivially injected into TH0. Special types are used for basic types extracted from monomorphic types. The set of higher-order basic types is slightly different from the first-order one, where we recursively remove arrow types until a non-arrow constructor is found. In the higher-order setting a single monomorphic constant $\tilde{c}^\nu$ is used to replace all arity versions of c: $\forall f\ x.\ \tilde{\mathsf{ap}}^\nu\ f\ x = f\ x$. Another benefit of the expressivity of TH0 is that the basic type $\tilde{o}$ can be replaced by $\$o$, and the predicate p can be omitted. The effect of the previous steps is illustrated in Example 7.

Example 7. Translations of $\exists f.\ f\ 0 = 0$

In this example $\tilde{\mathsf{ap}}^\nu$ has type $(\mathsf{fun\_num\_num} \times \widetilde{\mathsf{num}}) \to \widetilde{\mathsf{num}}$ where $\mathsf{fun\_num\_num}$ is the special type corresponding to $\mathsf{num} \to \mathsf{num}$.

$$\mathsf{TF0}:\ \exists \tilde{f}:\mathsf{fun\_num\_num}.\ \tilde{\mathsf{ap}}^\nu\ (\tilde{f}, \tilde{0}^{\mathsf{num}}) = \tilde{0}^{\mathsf{num}}$$

$$\mathsf{TH0}:\ \exists \tilde{f}:\widetilde{\mathsf{num}} \to \widetilde{\mathsf{num}}.\ \tilde{f}\ \tilde{0}^{\mathsf{num}} = \tilde{0}^{\mathsf{num}}$$

In order to have the same shallowness result for TH0 as for TF0, it would be necessary to replace monomorphic constants created by the lifting procedure by their lambda-abstractions. We chose to keep the definitions for the lifted constants, as they allow some term-level logical operators to be pushed to the formula level.

5   Semantic Translations via Set Theory Encodings

The second family of translations into TH0, TF0, and FOF is semantically motivated [38]: we make use of constructors known to be definable in set theory. Types and terms are translated to sets, where types must translate to non-empty sets. The translation may optionally use other special types for monomorphic types in the HOL4 source. In the TH0 case the builtin type $\$o$ can be used for the HOL4 type o. In the first-order cases HOL4 terms of type o are sometimes translated to terms, and sometimes to formulae, depending on how the HOL4 term is used. In the TF0 case a separate type $\tilde{o}$ of booleans is declared, which is used as the type of terms translated from HOL4 terms of type o. In the FOF case this approach is not possible, as all terms have the same type (intuitively representing sets). The other main difference between the translation to TH0 and the translations to the first-order languages is that the first-order translations make use of lambda lifting [14,35]. As a result of the translations we obtain three new collections of ATP problems are produced: TH0-II, TF0-II and FOF-II.

5.1   Translating to TH0

The base type o for propositions is written as $\$o$ in TH0, and ι for individuals is written as $\$i$. In addition a base type δ is declared. The translation treats elements of type ι as sets, and elements of type δ as non-empty sets. The basic constants used in the ATP problems are as follows:

- bool : δ is used for a fixed two element set.
- ind : δ is used for a fixed non-empty set corresponding to HOL4's type of individuals.
- arr : $\delta \to \delta \to \delta$ is used to construct the function space of two sets.
- mem : $\iota \to \delta \to o$ corresponds to the membership relation on sets, where the second set is known to be non-empty. The term mem $s\ t$ is written as $s \in t$, and the term $\forall x.x \in s \to t$ is written as $\forall x \in s.t$.

- ap : $\iota \to \iota \to \iota$ corresponds to set theory level application (represented as a set).
- lam : $\delta \to (\iota \to \iota) \to \iota$ is used to build set bounded λ-abstractions as sets.
- p : $\iota \to o$ is a predicate that indicates whether or not an element of bool is true or not.
- i_o : $o \to \iota$ is an injection of o into ι, essentially translating false to a set and true to a different set.

The basic axioms included in each ATP problem are:

Inj$_o$: $\forall X : o.i_o X \in$ bool.
Iso$_o^1$: $\forall X : o.\mathsf{p}(i_o X) = X.$
Iso$_o^2$: $\forall X \in$ bool.$i_o(\mathsf{p}X) = X.$
ap$_{\mathbf{tp}}$: $\forall AB : \delta.\forall f \in (\mathsf{arr}\ A\ B).\forall x \in A.(\mathsf{ap}\ f\ x) \in B.$
lam$_{\mathbf{tp}}$: $\forall AB : \delta.\forall F : \iota \to \iota.(\forall x \in A.F\ x \in B) \to (\mathsf{lam}\ A\ F) \in (\mathsf{arr}\ A\ B).$
FunExt: $\forall AB : \delta.\forall f \in (\mathsf{arr}\ A\ B).\forall g \in (\mathsf{arr}\ A\ B).$
   $(\forall x \in A.\mathsf{ap}\ f\ x = \mathsf{ap}\ g\ x) \to f = g.$
beta: $\forall A : \delta.\forall F : \iota \to \iota.\forall x \in A.(\mathsf{ap}\ (\mathsf{lam}\ A\ F)\ x) = F\ x.$

If ι is interpreted using a model of ZFC and δ using a copy of the non-empty sets in this model, then the constants above can be interpreted in an obvious way so as to make the basic axioms true.

Given this theory, a basic translation from HOL4 to TH0 is as follows. Each HOL4 type α (including type variables) is mapped to a term $\hat{\alpha}$ of type δ. HOL4 type variables (constants) are mapped to TH0 variables (constants) of type δ. For the remaining cases bool, ind, and arr are used. Each HOL4 term $s : \alpha$ is mapped to a TH0 term $\hat{s}$ of type ι, for which the context $\hat{s} \in \hat{\alpha}$ is always known. The invariant can be maintained by including the hypothesis $\hat{x} \in \hat{\alpha}$ whenever x is a variable or a constant. The ap and lam constants are used to handle HOL4 applications and λ-abstractions. The axioms **ap$_{\mathbf{tp}}$** and **lam$_{\mathbf{tp}}$** ensure the invariant is maintained. Finally HOL4 propositions (which may quantify over type variables) are translated to TH0 propositions in an obvious way, using p to go from ι to o, and i_o to go from o to ι, when necessary. As an added heuristic, the translation makes use of TH0 connectives and quantifiers as deeply as possible, delaying the use of p whenever possible.

Using Special Types. As with the first family of translations, the second family optimizes by using special types for HOL4 types with no type variables, e.g., num and list num. Unlike the first family, special types are not used for monomorphic function types. As a result it is not necessary to consider alternative ap operators. A *basic monomorphic type* is a monomorphic type that is not of the form $\alpha \to \beta$. If special types are used, then for each basic monomorphic type occurring in a proposition a corresponding TH0 type γ is declared, mappings and axioms relating γ to the type ι of sets are declared, and the type γ is used to translate terms of the type and quantifiers over the type when possible. For example, if a basic monomorphic type ν (e.g., num) occurs in a HOL4 proposition, then in addition to translating ν as a term $\hat{\nu} : \iota$ we also declare a TH0 type $\tilde{\nu}$, $i_\nu : \tilde{\nu} \to \iota$

and $j_\nu : \iota \rightarrow \tilde{\nu}$ along with axioms $\forall x : \tilde{\nu}.j_\nu(i_\nu x) = x$ and $\forall x : \iota.x \in \hat{\nu} \rightarrow i_\nu(j_\nu x) = x$.

One obvious basic monomorphic type is o. In the case of o a new type is not declared, but instead the TH0 type $o is used. That is, $\tilde{o}$ denotes $o. Note that $i_o : \tilde{o} \rightarrow \iota$ is already declared. Additionally, j_o is used as shorthand for p, which has the desired type $\iota \rightarrow \tilde{o}$.

Suppose a HOL4 constant c has type $\alpha_1 \rightarrow \ldots \rightarrow \alpha_n \rightarrow \beta$, where $\alpha_1, \ldots, \alpha_n, \beta$ are basic monomorphic types with corresponding TH0 types $\tilde{\alpha}_1, \ldots, \tilde{\alpha}_n, \tilde{\beta}$. Instead of translating a term $ct_1 \cdots t_n$ as a term of type ι, each t_i is translated to a term $\hat{t}_i$ of type $\tilde{\alpha}_i$, and a first order constant $\tilde{c} : \tilde{\alpha}_1 \rightarrow \cdots \rightarrow \tilde{\alpha}_n \rightarrow \tilde{\beta}$ is used to translate to the term $\tilde{c}\hat{t}_1 \cdots \hat{t}_n$ of type $\tilde{\beta}$. In such a case an equation relating $\hat{c}$ to $\tilde{c}$ is also included. Since the translation may return a term of type ι or $\tilde{\alpha}$, where α is a basic monomorphic type, i_α and j_α are used to obtain a term of type $\tilde{\alpha}$ or ι when one is required. If a quantifier ranges over a monomorphic type α, a quantifier over type $\tilde{\alpha}$ is used instead of using a quantifier over type ι and using $\in$ to guard the quantifier.

5.2   Translating to TF0

There are two main modifications to the translation to TH0 when targeting TF0. Firstly, propositions cannot be treated as special kinds of terms in TF0. In order to deal with this o is treated like other special types by declaring a new type $\tilde{o}$ and functions $i_o : \tilde{o} \rightarrow \iota$ and $j_o : \iota \rightarrow \tilde{o}$ along with corresponding axioms as above. Note that unlike the TH0 case, j_o differs from p. In TF0 p is a unary predicate on ι, and j_o is a function from ι to $\tilde{o}$. In the TF0 versions of the axioms $\mathbf{Iso}_o^1$ and $\mathbf{Iso}_o^2$, p is replaced with j_o. Secondly, the background theory cannot include the higher-order lam operator. Therefore the lam operator is omitted, and lambda lifting is used to translate (most) HOL4 λ-abstractions. The two higher-order axioms $\mathbf{lam_{tp}}$ and **beta** are also omitted.

In the TH0 case, the background axioms are enough to infer the following (internal) propositional extensionality principle

$$\forall Q \in \mathsf{bool}.\forall R \in \mathsf{bool}.(\mathsf{p}\ Q \leftrightarrow \mathsf{p}\ R) \rightarrow Q = R$$

from the corresponding extensionality principle $\forall QR : o.(Q \leftrightarrow R) \rightarrow Q = R$ valid in TH0. This is no longer the case in TF0, so propositional extensionality is added as an axiom.

There are two special cases where lambda lifting can be avoided: identity and constant functions. For this purpose a new unary function I on sets and a new binary function K on sets are added. Two new basic axioms are added to the ATP problem for these functions:

Id: $\forall A : \delta.\forall X \in A.(\mathsf{ap}\ (\mathsf{I}\ A)\ X) = X$.
Const: $\forall A : \delta.\forall Y : \iota.\forall X \in A.(\mathsf{ap}\ (\mathsf{K}\ A\ Y)\ X) = Y$.

A HOL4 term $\lambda x : \alpha.x$ is translated as $\mathsf{I}\ \hat{\alpha}$. For a HOL4 term $\lambda x : \alpha.t$, where x is not free in t, t is translated to a first-order term $\hat{t}$ of type ι, and the λ-term is translated to $\mathsf{K}\,\hat{\alpha}\,\hat{t}$. If there is already a function defined for $\lambda x : \alpha.t$ (with the same variable names), then that function is reused. Otherwise, lambda lifting of $\lambda x : \alpha.t$ proceeds as follows. Let $\alpha_1,\ldots,\alpha_m$ be type variables occurring in $\lambda x : \alpha.t$ and $y_1 : \beta_1,\ldots,y_n : \beta_n$ be the free variables occurring in $\lambda x : \alpha.t$. Assume $\hat{t}$ is a first-order term translation of t, with $\hat{x}$ of type ι corresponding to the variable x. (Note that this may have involved some lambda lifting.) Let $\mathbf{f}$ be a new $m + n$-ary function returning sets. If special types are not being used, then each argument of $\mathbf{f}$ is a set. If special types are used, then each argument is a set unless it corresponds to $y_i : \beta_i$, where β_i is a monomorphic type in which case the argument has type $\tilde{\beta}_i$. The following axioms about $\mathbf{f}$ are added to the ATP problem:

$\mathbf{f_{tp}}$: $\forall A_1 \cdots A_n : \delta.\forall Y_1 \cdots Y_m : \iota.\cdots (\mathbf{f}\ A_1 \cdots A_n\ Y_1 \cdots Y_m) \in \hat{\alpha}.$
$\mathbf{f_{beta}}$: $\forall A_1 \cdots A_n : \delta.\forall Y_1 \cdots Y_m : \iota.\cdots \forall X \in \hat{\alpha}.\mathsf{ap}\ (\mathbf{f}\ A_1 \cdots A_n\ Y_1 \cdots Y_m)\ X = \hat{t}.$

In these axioms the preconditions that each Y_i must be in $\hat{\beta}_i$ if Y_i has type ι have been elided (otherwise special types are being used, β_i is monomorphic, Y_i has type $\tilde{\beta}_i$, and no guard is required).

5.3 Translating to FOF

In order to translate to FOF, all terms must be translated to the same type, effectively the type ι. This requires omission of any special treatment of monomorphic types, and instead all HOL4 terms are translated to terms of type ι. The type δ of non-empty sets is also omitted. Instead, ι is used wherever δ was used in the TF0 setting, and quantifiers that were over δ are guarded by a new non-emptiness predicate ne : $\iota \to o$. Aside from these changes, the translation proceeds using lambda lifting as in the TF0 case.

6 Case Study

A very simple HOL4 theorem is $\forall f : \alpha \to \beta.\forall x : \alpha.\mathsf{LET}^{\alpha,\beta}\ f\ x = f\ x$, where $\mathsf{LET}^{\alpha,\beta}$ is defined to be $\lambda f : \alpha \to \beta.\lambda x : \alpha.fx$. Informally the proof is clear: expand the definition of LET and perform two β-reductions. However, proving various translated versions of the problem range from trivial to challenging.

The first family of translations make use of a preprocessing step (Sect. 4.2) that changes the definition of LET from $\mathsf{LET}^{\alpha,\beta} = \lambda f : \alpha \to \beta.\lambda x : \alpha.fx$ to

$$\forall x : \alpha \to \beta.\forall x' : \alpha.\mathsf{LET}^{\alpha,\beta}\ x\ x' = x\ x'.$$

This step makes the definition of LET the same (up to α-conversion) as the theorem. Even if further encodings are applied to obtain a first-order problem, the axiom will still be the same as the conjecture. Consequently all versions resulting from the first family of translations are trivially provable.

The TH0-II version has conjecture

$$\forall AB : \delta.\forall f \in (\mathsf{arr}\ A\ B).\forall x \in A.\mathsf{ap}\ (\mathsf{ap}\ (\mathsf{LET}\ A\ B)\ f)\ x = \mathsf{ap}\ f\ x$$

and the axiom (corresponding to the definition of LET)

$$\forall AB : \delta.\mathsf{LET}\ A\ B = \mathsf{lam}\ (\mathsf{arr}\ A\ B)\ (\lambda f : \iota.\mathsf{lam}\ A\ (\lambda x : \iota.\mathsf{ap}\ f\ x)).$$

The axiom defining LET combined with the basic axiom **beta** is enough to prove the theorem. However, the TH0-II version also includes all the other basic axioms along with internal versions of the logical constants for universal quantification and equality. The extra axioms make the problem hard for ATP systems, but if only the necessary axioms are provided the problem is easy. In TF0-II and FOF-II the conjecture is the same as in the TH0-II version, but the definition of LET is split into two functions declared when lambda lifting:

$$\forall A \cdots \forall B \cdots \mathsf{LET}\ A\ B = \mathbf{f_{14}}\ A\ B,$$

$$\forall A \cdots \forall B \cdots \forall f \in (\mathsf{arr}\ A\ B).\mathsf{ap}\ (\mathbf{f_{14}}\ A\ B)\ f = \mathbf{f_{13}}\ A\ B\ f$$

and

$$\forall A \cdots \forall B \cdots \forall f \in (\mathsf{arr}\ A\ B).\forall x \in A.\mathsf{ap}\ (\mathbf{f_{13}}\ A\ B\ f)\ x = \mathsf{ap}\ f\ x.$$

All the first-order versions of this problem are easy for current ATP systems.

7 Results

Since the HOL4 library has a natural order of the problems, each translation can generate two versions of each problem. The *bushy* (small) version contains only the (translated) library facts that were needed for the HOL4 proof of the theorem. The *chainy* (large) version contains all the facts that precede the theorem in the library order, i.e., the real task faced by hammer systems. Chainy problems typically include thousands of axioms, requiring the use of *premise selection* algorithms [1] as a front-end in the ATP systems. Thus, in order to maintain the focus on ATP system performance, the results of running the ATP systems on the bushy problems are presented here.

Nineteen ATPs were run on the 12140 problems in each of the bushy problem sets, according to the ATPs' support for the various TPTP formats. In each case we ran the ATP with a CPU time limit of 60s per problem. Table 2 summarizes the results. In union, more proofs were found in the first family of translations than in the second family, in all formats. However, some provers like Vampire 4.3 and SPASS 3.9 do better on FOF-II than on FOF-I. This indicates that these provers are probably better at reasoning with type guards than with type tags. Of the 12140 problems 7412 (61.1%) were solved by some ATP in one of the representations.

The TacticToe [17, 18] prover built into HOL4 has been tested as a baseline comparison, and it (re)proves 5327 of 8855 chainy versions of the problems (60.2%). TacticToe is a machine-learning guided prover that searches for a tactical proof by selecting suitable tactics and theorems learned from human-written tactical proofs. By design, this system works in the chainy setting. In total 8840 (72.8%) of the 12140 problems can be proved by either TacticToe or one of the ATPs using one of the translations.

Table 2. Number of theorems proved, out of 12140. Each ATP is evaluated on all its supported TPTP formats.

System	TH1-I	TH0-I	TH0-II	TF1-I	TF0-I	TF0-II	FOF-I	FOF-II	Union
agsyHOL 1.0 [32]		1374	1187						1605
Beagle 0.9.47 [3]					2008	2047	2449	2498	3183
cocATP 0.2.0		899	599						1000
CSE_E 1.0 [51]							4251	3102	4480
CVC4 1.6 [2]					4851	3991	5030	3746	5709
E 2.2 [41]					4277	3622	4618	3844	5118
HOLyHammer 0.21 [27]	5059								5059
iProver 2.8 [29]							2778	2894	3355
iProverModulo 2.5-0.1 [11]					2435	1639	1433	1263	2852
LEO-II 1.7.0 [4]		2579	1923				2119	1968	3702
Leo-III 1.3 [43,44]	6668	5018	3485	3458	4032	3421	3986	3185	7090
Metis 2.4 [24]							2353	474	2356
Princess 170717 [39,40]					3646	2138	3162	2086	4096
Prover9 1109a [33]							2894	1742	3128
Satallax 3.3 [10]		2207	1292						2494
SPASS 3.9 [50]							2850	3349	3821
Vampire 4.3 [30]					4837	4693	4008	4928	5929
ZenonModulo [15]				1071	1038	1041	1026	1198	1751
Zipperposition 1.4 [13]		2252	2161	3771	3099	2576	2531	1795	4251
Union	6824	5209	3771	4663	5732	5074	5909	5249	**7412**

8   GRUNGE as CASC LTB Division

The CADE ATP System Competition (CASC) [45] is the annual evaluation of fully automatic, classical logic Automated Theorem Proving (ATP) systems – the world championship for such systems. CASC is divided into divisions according to problem and system characteristics. Each competition division uses problems that have certain logical, language, and syntactic characteristics, so that the systems that compete in the division are, in principle, able to attempt all the problems in the division. For example, the First-Order Form (FOF) division uses problems in full first-order logic, with each problem having axioms and a conjecture to be proved.

While most of the CASC divisions present the problems to the ATP systems one at a time, with an individual CPU or wall clock time limit per problem, the Large Theory Batch (LTB) division presents the problems in batches, with an overall wall clock time limit on the batch. As the name also suggests, the problems in each batch come from a "large theory", which typically has many functors and predicates, and many axioms of which only a few are required for the proof of a theorem. The problems in a batch typically have a common core set of axioms used by all problems, and each problem typically has additional axioms that are specific to the problem. The batch presentation allows the ATP systems to load and preprocess the common core set of axioms just once, and to share logical and control results between proof searches. Each batch is accompanied by a set of training problems and their solutions, taken from the same source as the competition problems. The training data can be used for ATP system tuning and learning during (typically at the start of) the competition.

In CASC-J9 [48] – the most recent edition of the competition – the LTB division used FOF problems exported from CakeML [31]. At the time there was growing interest in an LTB division for typed higher-order problems, and it became evident that a multi-format LTB division would add a valuable dimension to CASC. For the CASC-27 LTB division each problem was presented in multiple formats: TH1, TH0, TF1, TF0, and FOF. The work described in this paper provides the problems. Systems were able to attempt whichever versions they support, and a solution to any version constitutes a solution to the problem. For example, Leo-III is able to handle all the formats, while E can attempt only the tffzero and FOF formats.

The batch presentation of problems in the LTB division provides interesting opportunities for ATP systems, including making multiple attempts on problems and learning search heuristics from proofs found. The multi-format LTB division extends these possibilities by allowing multiple attempts on problems by virtue of the multiple formats available, and learning from proofs found in one format to improve performance on problems in another format. The latter is especially interesting, with little known research in this direction.

9 Related Work

The HOL4 library already has translations for SMT solvers such as Yices [49], Z3 [9] and Beagle. A link to first-order ATPs is also available thanks to exports [16] of HOL4 theories to the HOL(y)Hammer framework [27]. Another notable project that facilitates the export of HOL4 theories is Open Theory [25]. The general approach for higher-order to first-order translations is laid out in Hurd [23]. An evaluation of the effect of different translations on ATP-provability was performed in [35]. A further study shows the potential improvements provided by the use of supercombinators [14]. In our work, the use of lambda-lifting (or combinators) is not necessary in TH0-II thanks to the use of the higher-order operator lam. This is similar to using higher-order abstract syntax to model syntax with binders [37].

A method for encoding of polymorphic types as terms through type tags (as in our first translation) or type guards (as in our second translation) is described in [6]. Translations [21,44] from a polymorphic logic to a monomorphic poly-sorted logic without encoding typically rely on heuristic instantiations of type variables. However, heuristics may miss useful instantiations, and make the translation less modular (i.e., context dependent). Our translations to TH0 and TF0 try to get the best of both worlds by using a type encoding for polymorphic types and special types for basic monomorphic types.

10   Conclusion

This work has defined, compared, and evaluated ATP performance on two families of translations of the HOL4 logic to a number of ATP formalisms, and described a new unified large-theory ATP benchmark (GRUNGE) based on them. The first family is designed to play to the strengths of the calculi of most ATP systems, while the second family is based on more straightforward semantics rooted in set theory. The case study shows how different the translated problems may be, even in a simple example. A number of methods and optimizations have been used, however it is clear that the translations can be further optimized and that different encodings favour different provers. Out of 12140 HOL4 theorems, the ATP systems can solve 7412 problems in one or more of the formats. The TacticToe system that works directly in the HOL4 formalism and uses HOL4 tactics could solve 5327 problems. Together the total number of problems solved is 8840. Leo-III was the strongest system in the higher-order representations. In the first-order representations the strongest systems were Zipperposition, CVC4, E and Vampire. A pre-release of the bushy versions of the problems was provided before CASC-27[2], to allow system developers to adapt and tune their systems before the competition.

References

1. Alama, J., Heskes, T., Kühlwein, D., Tsivtsivadze, E., Urban, J.: Premise selection for mathematics by corpus analysis and kernel methods. J. Autom. Reason. **52**(2), 191–213 (2014). https://doi.org/10.1007/s10817-013-9286-5
2. Barrett, C., et al.: CVC4. In: Gopalakrishnan, G., Qadeer, S. (eds.) CAV 2011. LNCS, vol. 6806, pp. 171–177. Springer, Heidelberg (2011). https://doi.org/10.1007/978-3-642-22110-1_14
3. Baumgartner, P., Waldmann, U.: Hierarchic superposition with weak abstraction. In: Bonacina, M.P. (ed.) CADE 2013. LNCS (LNAI), vol. 7898, pp. 39–57. Springer, Heidelberg (2013). https://doi.org/10.1007/978-3-642-38574-2_3
4. Benzmüller, C., Paulson, L.C., Theiss, F., Fietzke, A.: LEO-II - a cooperative automatic theorem prover for classical higher-order logic (system description). In: Armando, A., Baumgartner, P., Dowek, G. (eds.) IJCAR 2008. LNCS (LNAI), vol. 5195, pp. 162–170. Springer, Heidelberg (2008). https://doi.org/10.1007/978-3-540-71070-7_14
5. Benzmüller, C., Rabe, F., Sutcliffe, G.: THF0 – the core of the TPTP language for higher-order logic. In: Armando, A., Baumgartner, P., Dowek, G. (eds.) IJCAR 2008. LNCS (LNAI), vol. 5195, pp. 491–506. Springer, Heidelberg (2008). https://doi.org/10.1007/978-3-540-71070-7_41. http://christoph-benzmueller.de/papers/C25.pdf
6. Blanchette, J.C., Böhme, S., Popescu, A., Smallbone, N.: Encoding monomorphic and polymorphic types. In: Piterman, N., Smolka, S.A. (eds.) TACAS 2013. LNCS, vol. 7795, pp. 493–507. Springer, Heidelberg (2013). https://doi.org/10.1007/978-3-642-36742-7_34

---

[2] http://www.tptp.org/CASC/27/TrainingData.HL4.tgz.

7. Blanchette, J.C., Kaliszyk, C., Paulson, L.C., Urban, J.: Hammering towards QED. J. Formalized Reason. **9**(1), 101–148 (2016). https://doi.org/10.6092/issn.1972-5787/4593
8. Blanchette, J.C., Paskevich, A.: TFF1: the TPTP typed first-order form with rank-1 polymorphism. In: Bonacina, M.P. (ed.) CADE 2013. LNCS (LNAI), vol. 7898, pp. 414–420. Springer, Heidelberg (2013). https://doi.org/10.1007/978-3-642-38574-2_29
9. Böhme, S., Weber, T.: Fast LCF-style proof reconstruction for Z3. In: Kaufmann, M., Paulson, L.C. (eds.) ITP 2010. LNCS, vol. 6172, pp. 179–194. Springer, Heidelberg (2010). https://doi.org/10.1007/978-3-642-14052-5_14
10. Brown, C.E.: Satallax: an automatic higher-order prover. In: Gramlich, B., Miller, D., Sattler, U. (eds.) IJCAR 2012. LNCS (LNAI), vol. 7364, pp. 111–117. Springer, Heidelberg (2012). https://doi.org/10.1007/978-3-642-31365-3_11
11. Burel, G.: Experimenting with deduction modulo. In: Bjørner, N., Sofronie-Stokkermans, V. (eds.) CADE 2011. LNCS (LNAI), vol. 6803, pp. 162–176. Springer, Heidelberg (2011). https://doi.org/10.1007/978-3-642-22438-6_14
12. Church, A.: A formulation of the simple theory of types. J. Symb. Logic **5**, 56–68 (1940)
13. Cruanes, S.: Extending superposition with integer arithmetic, structural induction, and beyond. (Extensions de la Superposition pour l'Arithmétique Linéaire Entière, l'Induction Structurelle, et bien plus encore). Ph.D. thesis, École Polytechnique, Palaiseau, France (2015). https://tel.archives-ouvertes.fr/tel-01223502
14. Czajka, L.: Improving automation in interactive theorem provers by efficient encoding of lambda-abstractions. In: Avigad, J., Chlipala, A. (eds.) Proceedings of the 5th ACM SIGPLAN Conference on Certified Programs and Proofs, Saint Petersburg, FL, USA, 20–22 January 2016, pp. 49–57. ACM (2016). https://doi.org/10.1145/2854065.2854069
15. Delahaye, D., Doligez, D., Gilbert, F., Halmagrand, P., Hermant, O.: Zenon modulo: when achilles outruns the tortoise using deduction modulo. In: McMillan et al. [34], pp. 274–290. https://doi.org/10.1007/978-3-642-45221-5_20
16. Gauthier, T., Kaliszyk, C.: Premise selection and external provers for HOL4. In: Certified Programs and Proofs (CPP 2015). ACM (2015). https://doi.org/10.1145/2676724.2693173
17. Gauthier, T., Kaliszyk, C., Urban, J.: TacticToe: learning to reason with HOL4 tactics. In: Eiter, T., Sands, D. (eds.) 21st International Conference on Logic for Programming, Artificial Intelligence and Reasoning, LPAR-21, Maun, Botswana, 7–12 May 2017. EPiC Series in Computing, vol. 46, pp. 125–143. EasyChair (2017). http://www.easychair.org/publications/paper/340355
18. Gauthier, T., Kaliszyk, C., Urban, J., Kumar, R., Norrish, M.: Learning to prove with tactics. CoRR (2018). http://arxiv.org/abs/1804.00596
19. Gordon, M.J.C., Melham, T.F. (eds.): Introduction to HOL: A Theorem Proving Environment for Higher Order Logic. Cambridge University Press (1993). http://www.cs.ox.ac.uk/tom.melham/pub/Gordon-1993-ITH.html
20. Harrison, J.: HOL light: a tutorial introduction. In: Srivas, M., Camilleri, A. (eds.) FMCAD 1996. LNCS, vol. 1166, pp. 265–269. Springer, Heidelberg (1996). https://doi.org/10.1007/BFb0031814
21. Harrison, J.: Optimizing proof search in model elimination. In: McRobbie, M.A., Slaney, J.K. (eds.) CADE 1996. LNCS, vol. 1104, pp. 313–327. Springer, Heidelberg (1996). https://doi.org/10.1007/3-540-61511-3_97

22. Harrison, J., Urban, J., Wiedijk, F.: History of interactive theorem proving. In: Siekmann, J.H. (ed.) Computational Logic, Handbook of the History of Logic, vol. 9, pp. 135–214. Elsevier (2014). https://doi.org/10.1016/B978-0-444-51624-4. 50004-6

23. Hurd, J.: First-order proof tactics in higher-order logic theorem provers. Design and Application of Strategies/Tactics in Higher Order Logics, number NASA/CP-2003-212448 in NASA Technical reports, pp. 56–68 (2003)

24. Hurd, J.: System description: the metis proof tactic. In: Benzmueller, C., Harrison, J., Schurmann, C. (ed.) Workshop on Empirically Successful Automated Reasoning in Higher-Order Logic (ESHOL), pp. 103–104 (2005). https://arxiv.org/pdf/cs/0601042

25. Hurd, J.: The opentheory standard theory library. In: Bobaru, M., Havelund, K., Holzmann, G.J., Joshi, R. (eds.) NFM 2011. LNCS, vol. 6617, pp. 177–191. Springer, Heidelberg (2011). https://doi.org/10.1007/978-3-642-20398-5_14

26. Kaliszyk, C., Sutcliffe, G., Rabe, F.: TH1: the TPTP typed higher-order form with rank-1 polymorphism. In: Fontaine, P., Schulz, S., Urban, J. (eds.) Proceedings of the 5th Workshop on Practical Aspects of Automated Reasoning. CEUR Workshop Proceedings, vol. 1635, pp. 41–55 (2016)

27. Kaliszyk, C., Urban, J.: Learning-assisted automated reasoning with Flyspeck. J. Autom. Reason. 53(2), 173–213 (2014). https://doi.org/10.1007/s10817-014-9303-3

28. King, D., Arthan, R., Winnersh, I.: Development of practical verification tools. ICL Syst. J. 11, 106–122 (1996)

29. Korovin, K.: iProver – an instantiation-based theorem prover for first-order logic (system description). In: Armando, A., Baumgartner, P., Dowek, G. (eds.) IJCAR 2008. LNCS (LNAI), vol. 5195, pp. 292–298. Springer, Heidelberg (2008). https://doi.org/10.1007/978-3-540-71070-7_24

30. Kovács, L., Voronkov, A.: First-order theorem proving and VAMPIRE. In: Sharygina, N., Veith, H. (eds.) CAV 2013. LNCS, vol. 8044, pp. 1–35. Springer, Heidelberg (2013). https://doi.org/10.1007/978-3-642-39799-8_1

31. Kumar, R., Myreen, M.O., Norrish, M., Owens, S.: CakeML: a verified implementation of ML. In: Jagannathan, S., Sewell, P. (eds.) The 41st Annual ACM SIGPLAN-SIGACT Symposium on Principles of Programming Languages, POPL 2014, San Diego, CA, USA, 20–21 January 2014, pp. 179–192. ACM (2014). https://doi.org/10.1145/2535838.2535841

32. Lindblad, F.: A focused sequent calculus for higher-order logic. In: Demri, S., Kapur, D., Weidenbach, C. (eds.) IJCAR 2014. LNCS (LNAI), vol. 8562, pp. 61–75. Springer, Cham (2014). https://doi.org/10.1007/978-3-319-08587-6_5

33. McCune, W.: Prover9 and Mace4 (2005–2010). http://www.cs.unm.edu/~mccune/prover9/

34. McMillan, K.L., Middeldorp, A., Voronkov, A. (eds.): LPAR 2013. LNCS, vol. 8312. Springer, Heidelberg (2013). https://doi.org/10.1007/978-3-642-45221-5

35. Meng, J., Paulson, L.C.: Translating higher-order clauses to first-order clauses. J. Autom. Reason. 40(1), 35–60 (2008)

36. Nipkow, T., Wenzel, M., Paulson, L.C. (eds.): Isabelle/HOL. LNCS, vol. 2283. Springer, Heidelberg (2002). https://doi.org/10.1007/3-540-45949-9

37. Pfenning, F., Elliot, C.: Higher-order abstract syntax. In: Proceedings of the ACM SIGPLAN 1988 Conference on Programming Language Design and Implementation, PLDI 1988, pp. 199–208. ACM, New York (1988). https://doi.org/10.1145/53990.54010

38. Pitts, A.: The HOL logic. In: Gordon and Melham [19]. http://www.cs.ox.ac.uk/tom.melham/pub/Gordon-1993-ITH.html

39. Rümmer, P.: A constraint sequent calculus for first-order logic with linear integer arithmetic. In: Cervesato, I., Veith, H., Voronkov, A. (eds.) LPAR 2008. LNCS (LNAI), vol. 5330, pp. 274–289. Springer, Heidelberg (2008). https://doi.org/10.1007/978-3-540-89439-1_20

40. Rümmer, P.: E-matching with free variables. In: Bjørner, N., Voronkov, A. (eds.) LPAR 2012. LNCS, vol. 7180, pp. 359–374. Springer, Heidelberg (2012). https://doi.org/10.1007/978-3-642-28717-6_28

41. Schulz, S.: System description: E 1.8. In: McMillan et al. [34], pp. 735–743. https://doi.org/10.1007/978-3-642-45221-5_49

42. Slind, K., Norrish, M.: A brief overview of HOL4. In: Mohamed, O.A., Muñoz, C., Tahar, S. (eds.) TPHOLs 2008. LNCS, vol. 5170, pp. 28–32. Springer, Heidelberg (2008). https://doi.org/10.1007/978-3-540-71067-7_6

43. Steen, A., Benzmüller, C.: The higher-order prover Leo-III. In: Galmiche, D., Schulz, S., Sebastiani, R. (eds.) IJCAR 2018. LNCS (LNAI), vol. 10900, pp. 108–116. Springer, Cham (2018). https://doi.org/10.1007/978-3-319-94205-6_8. http://christoph-benzmueller.de/papers/C70.pdf

44. Steen, A., Wisniewski, M., Benzmüller, C.: Going polymorphic - TH1 reasoning for Leo-III. In: Eiter, T., Sands, D., Sutcliffe, G., Voronkov, A. (eds.) IWIL@LPAR 2017 Workshop and LPAR-21 Short Presentations, Maun, Botswana, 7–12 May 2017, vol. 1. Kalpa Publications in Computing, EasyChair (2017). http://www.easychair.org/publications/paper/346851

45. Sutcliffe, G.: The CADE ATP system competition - CASC. AI Mag. 37(2), 99–101 (2016)

46. Sutcliffe, G.: The TPTP problem library and associated infrastructure. From CNF to TH0, TPTP v6.4.0. J. Autom. Reason. 59(4), 483–502 (2017)

47. Sutcliffe, G., Schulz, S., Claessen, K., Baumgartner, P.: The TPTP typed first-order form with arithmetic. In: Bjørner, N., Voronkov, A. (eds.) LPAR 2012. LNCS, vol. 7180, pp. 406–419. Springer, Heidelberg (2012). https://doi.org/10.1007/978-3-642-28717-6_32

48. Sutcliffe, G.: The 9th IJCAR automated theorem proving system competition - CASC-J9. AI Commun. 31(6), 495–507 (2018). https://doi.org/10.3233/AIC-180773

49. Weber, T.: SMT solvers: new oracles for the HOL theorem prover. Int. J. Softw. Tools Technol. Transfer 13(5), 419–429 (2011). https://doi.org/10.1007/s10009-011-0188-8

50. Weidenbach, C., Dimova, D., Fietzke, A., Kumar, R., Suda, M., Wischnewski, P.: SPASS version 3.5. In: Schmidt, R.A. (ed.) CADE 2009. LNCS (LNAI), vol. 5663, pp. 140–145. Springer, Heidelberg (2009). https://doi.org/10.1007/978-3-642-02959-2_10

51. Xu, Y., Liu, J., Chen, S., Zhong, X., He, X.: Contradiction separation based dynamic multi-clause synergized automated deduction. Inf. Sci. 462, 93–113 (2018)

Model Completeness, Covers
and Superposition

Diego Calvanese[1], Silvio Ghilardi[2], Alessandro Gianola[1(✉)], Marco Montali[1],
and Andrey Rivkin[1]

[1] Faculty of Computer Science, Free University of Bozen-Bolzano, Bolzano, Italy
{calvanese,gianola,montali,rivkin}@inf.unibz.it
[2] Dipartimento di Matematica, Università degli Studi di Milano, Milan, Italy
silvio.ghilardi@unimi.it

Abstract. In ESOP 2008, Gulwani and Musuvathi introduced a notion
of cover and exploited it to handle infinite-state model checking problems. Motivated by applications to the verification of data-aware processes, we show how covers are strictly related to model completions, a
well-known topic in model theory. We also investigate the computation
of covers within the Superposition Calculus, by adopting a constrained
version of the calculus, equipped with appropriate settings and reduction
strategies.

1 Introduction

Declarative approaches to infinite state model checking [40] need to manipulate logical formulae in order to represent sets of reachable states. To prevent divergence, various abstraction strategies have been adopted, ranging from
interpolation-based [33] to sophisticated search via counterexample elimination [26]. Precise computations of the set of reachable states require some form
of quantifier elimination and hence are subject to two problems, namely that
quantifier elimination might not be available at all and that, when available, it
is computationally very expensive.

To cope with the first problem, [25] introduced the notion of a *cover* and
proved that covers exist for equality with uninterpreted symbols (EUF) and its
combination with linear arithmetic; also, it was shown that covers can be used
instead of quantifier elimination and yield a precise computation of reachable
states. Concerning the second problem, in [25] it was observed (as a side remark)
that computing the cover of a conjunction of literals becomes tractable when only
free unary function symbols occur in the signature. It can be shown (see [10])
that the same observation applies when also free relational symbols occur.

In [11,12] we propose a new formalism for representing *read-only database
schemata* towards the verification of integrated models of processes and data
[9], in particular so-called *artifact systems* [7,15,31,43]; this formalism (briefly
recalled in Sect. 4.1 below) uses precisely signatures comprising unary function

© Springer Nature Switzerland AG 2019
P. Fontaine (Ed.): CADE 2019, LNAI 11716, pp. 142–160, 2019.
https://doi.org/10.1007/978-3-030-29436-6_9

symbols and free n-ary relations. In [11,12] we apply model completeness techniques for verifying transition systems based on read-only databases, in a framework where such systems employ both individual and higher order variables.

In this paper we show (see Sect. 3 below) that covers are strictly related to *model completions* and to *uniform interpolation* [39], thus building a bridge between different research areas. In particular, we prove that computing covers for a theory is *equivalent* to eliminating quantifiers in its model completion. Model completeness has other well-known applications in computer science. It has been applied: *(i)* to reveal interesting connections between temporal logic and monadic second order logic [22,23]; *(ii)* in automated reasoning to design complete algorithms for constraint satisfiability in combined theories over non disjoint signatures [1,17,20,34–36] and theory extensions [41,42]; *(iii)* to obtain combined interpolation for modal logics and software verification theories [18,19].

In the last part of the paper (Sect. 5 below), we prove that covers for EUF can be computed through a constrained version of the *Superposition Calculus* [38] equipped with appropriate settings and reduction strategies; the related completeness proof requires a careful analysis of the constrained literals generated during the saturation process. Not all proofs could be included here: for the missing ones, we refer to the online available extended version [10] (the proofs of our results from Sect. 5 are however reported in full detail).

2   Preliminaries

We adopt the usual first-order syntactic notions of signature, term, atom, (ground) formula, and so on; our signatures are multi-sorted and include equality for every sort. Hence variables are sorted as well. For simplicity, some basic definitions will be supplied for single-sorted languages only (the adaptation to multi-sorted languages is straightforward). We compactly represent a tuple $\langle x_1, \ldots, x_n \rangle$ of variables as $\underline{x}$. The notation $t(\underline{x}), \phi(\underline{x})$ means that the term t, the formula ϕ has free variables included in the tuple $\underline{x}$. We assume that a function arity can be deduced from the context. Whenever we build terms and formulae, we always assume that they are well-typed, i.e., that the sorts of variables, constants, and function sources/targets match. A formula is said to be *universal* (resp., *existential*) if it has the form $\forall \underline{x}(\phi(\underline{x}))$ (resp., $\exists \underline{x}(\phi(\underline{x}))$), where ϕ is a quantifier-free formula. Formulae with no free variables are called *sentences*. From the semantic side, we use the standard notion of Σ-structure $\mathcal{M}$ and of truth of a formula in a Σ-structure under a free variables assignment. The *support* $|\mathcal{M}|$ of $\mathcal{M}$ is the disjoint union of the interpretations of the sorts in Σ. The interpretation of a (sort, function, predicate) symbol σ in $\mathcal{M}$ is denoted $\sigma^{\mathcal{M}}$.

A Σ-*theory* T is a set of Σ-sentences; a *model* of T is a Σ-structure $\mathcal{M}$ where all sentences in T are true. We use the standard notation $T \models \phi$ to say that ϕ is true in all models of T for every assignment to the variables occurring free in ϕ. We say that ϕ is T-*satisfiable* iff there is a model $\mathcal{M}$ of T and an assignment to the variables occurring free in ϕ making ϕ true in $\mathcal{M}$.

We now focus on the constraint satisfiability problem and quantifier elimination for a theory T. A Σ-formula ϕ is a Σ-*constraint* (or just a constraint) iff it is a conjunction of literals. The *constraint satisfiability problem* for T is the following: we are given a constraint (equivalently, a quantifier-free formula) $\phi(\underline{x})$ and we are asked whether there exist a model $\mathcal{M}$ of T and an assignment $\mathcal{I}$ to the free variables $\underline{x}$ such that $\mathcal{M}, \mathcal{I} \models \phi(\underline{x})$. A theory T has *quantifier elimination* iff for every formula $\phi(\underline{x})$ in the signature of T there is a quantifier-free formula $\phi'(\underline{x})$ such that $T \models \phi(\underline{x}) \leftrightarrow \phi'(\underline{x})$. Since we are in a computational logic context, when we speak of quantifier elimination, we assume that it is effective, namely that it comes with an algorithm for computing ϕ' out of ϕ. It is well-known that quantifier elimination holds in case we can eliminate quantifiers from *primitive* formulae, i.e., formulae of the kind $\exists y\, \phi(\underline{x}, y)$, with ϕ a constraint.

We recall also some basic notions from logic and model theory. Let Σ be a first-order signature. The signature obtained from Σ by adding to it a set $\underline{a}$ of new constants (i.e., 0-ary function symbols) is denoted by $\Sigma^{\underline{a}}$. Analogously, given a Σ-structure $\mathcal{M}$, the signature Σ can be expanded to a new signature $\Sigma^{|\mathcal{M}|} := \Sigma \cup \{\bar{a} \mid a \in |\mathcal{M}|\}$ by adding a set of new constants $\bar{a}$ (the *name* for a), one for each element a in $\mathcal{M}$, with the convention that two distinct elements are denoted by different "name" constants. $\mathcal{M}$ can be expanded to a $\Sigma^{|\mathcal{M}|}$-structure $\overline{\mathcal{M}} := (\mathcal{M}, a)_{a \in |\mathcal{M}|}$ just interpreting the additional constants over the corresponding elements. From now on, when the meaning is clear from the context, we will freely use the notation $\mathcal{M}$ and $\overline{\mathcal{M}}$ interchangeably: in particular, given a Σ-structure $\mathcal{M}$ and a Σ-formula $\phi(\underline{x})$ with free variables that are all in $\underline{x}$, we will write, by abuse of notation, $\mathcal{M} \models \phi(\underline{a})$ instead of $\overline{\mathcal{M}} \models \phi(\bar{\underline{a}})$.

A Σ-*homomorphism* (or, simply, a homomorphism) between two Σ-structures $\mathcal{M}$ and $\mathcal{N}$ is a map $\mu : |\mathcal{M}| \longrightarrow |\mathcal{N}|$ among the support sets $|\mathcal{M}|$ of $\mathcal{M}$ and $|\mathcal{N}|$ of $\mathcal{N}$ satisfying the condition $(\mathcal{M} \models \varphi \;\Rightarrow\; \mathcal{N} \models \varphi)$ for all $\Sigma^{|\mathcal{M}|}$-atoms φ ($\mathcal{M}$ is regarded as a $\Sigma^{|\mathcal{M}|}$-structure, by interpreting each additional constant $a \in |\mathcal{M}|$ into itself and $\mathcal{N}$ is regarded as a $\Sigma^{|\mathcal{M}|}$-structure by interpreting each additional constant $a \in |\mathcal{M}|$ into $\mu(a)$). In case the last condition holds for all $\Sigma^{|\mathcal{M}|}$-literals, the homomorphism μ is said to be an *embedding* and if it holds for all first order formulae, the embedding μ is said to be *elementary*. If $\mu : \mathcal{M} \longrightarrow \mathcal{N}$ is an embedding which is just the identity inclusion $|\mathcal{M}| \subseteq |\mathcal{N}|$, we say that $\mathcal{M}$ is a *substructure* of $\mathcal{N}$ or that $\mathcal{N}$ is an *extension* of $\mathcal{M}$.

Let $\mathcal{M}$ be a Σ-structure. The *diagram* of $\mathcal{M}$, written $\Delta_\Sigma(\mathcal{M})$ (or just $\Delta(\mathcal{M})$), is the set of ground $\Sigma^{|\mathcal{M}|}$-literals that are true in $\mathcal{M}$. An easy but important result, called *Robinson Diagram Lemma* [13], says that, given any Σ-structure $\mathcal{N}$, the embeddings $\mu : \mathcal{M} \longrightarrow \mathcal{N}$ are in bijective correspondence with expansions of $\mathcal{N}$ to $\Sigma^{|\mathcal{M}|}$-structures which are models of $\Delta_\Sigma(\mathcal{M})$. The expansions and the embeddings are related in the obvious way: $\bar{a}$ is interpreted as $\mu(a)$.

3   Covers, Uniform Interpolation and Model Completions

We report the notion of *cover* taken from [25]. Fix a theory T and an existential formula $\exists \underline{e}\, \phi(\underline{e}, y)$; call a *residue* of $\exists \underline{e}\, \phi(\underline{e}, y)$ any quantifier-free formula belonging to the set of quantifier-free formulae $Res(\exists \underline{e}\, \phi) = \{\theta(y, \underline{z}) \mid T \models \phi(\underline{e}, y) \to \theta(y, \underline{z})\}$. A quantifier-free formula $\psi(y)$ is said to be a T-*cover* (or, simply, a cover) of $\exists \underline{e} \, \phi(\underline{e}, \underline{y})$ iff $\psi(\underline{y}) \in Res(\exists \underline{e} \, \phi)$ and $\psi(\underline{y})$ implies (modulo T) all the other formulae in $Res(\exists \underline{e} \, \phi)$. The following Lemma (to be widely used throughout the paper) supplies a semantic counterpart to the notion of a cover:

Lemma 1. *A formula $\psi(\underline{y})$ is a T-cover of $\exists \underline{e} \, \phi(\underline{e}, \underline{y})$ iff it satisfies the following two conditions: (i) $T \models \forall \underline{y} \, (\exists \underline{e} \, \phi(\underline{e}, \underline{y}) \rightarrow \psi(\underline{y}))$; (ii) for every model $\mathcal{M}$ of T, for every tuple of elements $\underline{a}$ from the support of $\mathcal{M}$ such that $\mathcal{M} \models \psi(\underline{a})$ it is possible to find another model $\mathcal{N}$ of T such that $\mathcal{M}$ embeds into $\mathcal{N}$ and $\mathcal{N} \models \exists \underline{e} \, \phi(\underline{e}, \underline{a})$.* ◁

Proof. Suppose that $\psi(\underline{y})$ satisfies conditions (i) and (ii) above. Condition (i) says that $\psi(\underline{y}) \in Res(\exists \underline{e} \, \phi)$, so ψ is a residue. In order to show that ψ is also a cover, we have to prove that $T \models \forall \underline{y}, \underline{z}(\psi(\underline{y}) \rightarrow \theta(\underline{y}, \underline{z}))$, for every $\theta(\underline{y}, \underline{z})$ that is a residue for $\exists \underline{e} \, \phi(\underline{e}, \underline{y})$. Given a model $\mathcal{M}$ of T, take a pair of tuples $\underline{a}, \underline{b}$ of elements from $|\mathcal{M}|$ and suppose that $\mathcal{M} \models \psi(\underline{a})$. By condition (ii), there is a model $\mathcal{N}$ of T such that $\mathcal{M}$ embeds into $\mathcal{N}$ and $\mathcal{N} \models \exists \underline{e} \phi(\underline{e}, \underline{a})$. Using the definition of $Res(\exists \underline{e} \, \phi)$, we have $\mathcal{N} \models \theta(\underline{a}, \underline{b})$, since $\theta(\underline{y}, \underline{z}) \in Res(\exists \underline{x} \, \phi)$. Since $\mathcal{M}$ is a substructure of $\mathcal{N}$ and θ is quantifier-free, $\mathcal{M} \models \theta(\underline{a}, \underline{b})$ as well, as required.

Suppose that $\psi(\underline{y})$ is a cover. The definition of residue implies condition (i). To show condition (ii) we have to prove that, given a model $\mathcal{M}$ of T, for every tuple $\underline{a}$ of elements from $|\mathcal{M}|$, if $\mathcal{M} \models \psi(\underline{a})$, then there exists a model $\mathcal{N}$ of T such that $\mathcal{M}$ embeds into $\mathcal{N}$ and $\mathcal{N} \models \exists \underline{x} \phi(\underline{x}, \underline{a})$. By reduction to absurdity, suppose that this is not the case: this is equivalent (by using Robinson Diagram Lemma) to the fact that $\Delta(\mathcal{M}) \cup \{\phi(\underline{e}, \underline{a})\}$ is a T-inconsistent $\Sigma^{|\mathcal{M}| \cup \{\underline{e}\}}$-theory. By compactness, there is a finite number of literals $\ell_1(\underline{a}, \underline{b}), ..., \ell_m(\underline{a}, \underline{b})$ (for some tuple $\underline{b}$ of elements from $|\mathcal{M}|$) such that $\mathcal{M} \models \ell_i$ (for all $i = 1, \ldots, m$) and $T \models \phi(\underline{e}, \underline{a}) \rightarrow \neg(\ell_1(\underline{a}, \underline{b}) \wedge \cdots \wedge \ell_m(\underline{a}, \underline{b}))$, which means that $T \models \phi(\underline{e}, \underline{y}) \rightarrow (\neg \ell_1(\underline{y}, \underline{z}) \vee \cdots \vee \neg \ell_m(\underline{y}, \underline{z}))$, i.e. that $T \models \exists \underline{e} \phi(\underline{e}, \underline{y}) \rightarrow (\neg \ell_1(\underline{y}, \underline{z}) \vee \cdots \vee \neg \ell_m(\underline{y}, \underline{z}))$. By definition of residue, clearly $(\neg \ell_1(\underline{y}, \underline{z}) \vee \cdots \vee \neg \ell_m(\underline{y}, \underline{z})) \in Res(\exists \underline{x} \, \phi)$; then, since $\psi(\underline{y})$ is a cover, $T \models \psi(\underline{y}) \rightarrow (\neg \ell_1(\underline{y}, \underline{z}) \vee \cdots \vee \neg \ell_m(\underline{y}, \underline{z}))$, which implies that $\mathcal{M} \models \neg \ell_j(\underline{a}, \underline{b})$ for some $j = 1, \ldots, m$, which is a contradiction. Thus, $\psi(\underline{y})$ satisfies conditions (ii) too. ⊣

We say that a theory T has *uniform quantifier-free interpolation* iff every existential formula $\exists \underline{e} \, \phi(\underline{e}, \underline{y})$ (equivalently, every primitive formula $\exists \underline{e} \, \phi(\underline{e}, \underline{y})$) has a T-cover.

It is clear that if T has uniform quantifier-free interpolation, then it has ordinary quantifier-free interpolation [8], in the sense that if we have $T \models \phi(\underline{e}, \underline{y}) \rightarrow \phi'(\underline{y}, \underline{z})$ (for quantifier-free formulae ϕ, ϕ'), then there is a quantifier-free formula $\theta(\underline{y})$ such that $T \models \phi(\underline{e}, \underline{y}) \rightarrow \theta(\underline{y})$ and $T \models \theta(\underline{y}) \rightarrow \phi'(\underline{y}, \underline{z})$. In fact, if T has uniform quantifier-free interpolation, then the interpolant θ is independent on ϕ' (the same $\theta(\underline{y})$ can be used as interpolant for all entailments $T \models \phi(\underline{e}, \underline{y}) \rightarrow \phi'(\underline{y}, \underline{z})$, varying ϕ').

We say that a *universal* theory T has a *model completion* iff there is a stronger theory $T^* \supseteq T$ (still within the same signature Σ of T) such that (i) every Σ-constraint that is satisfiable in a model of T is satisfiable in a model of T^*; (ii) T^* eliminates quantifiers. Other equivalent definitions are possible [13]: for instance, (i) is equivalent to the fact that T and T^* prove the same quantifier-free formulae or again to the fact that every model of T can be embedded into a model of T^*. We recall that the model completion, if it exists, is unique and that its existence implies the amalgamation property for T [13]. The relationship between uniform interpolation in a propositional logic and model completion of the equational theory of the variety algebraizing it was extensively studied in [24]. In the context of first order theories, we prove an even more direct connection:

Theorem 1. *Suppose that T is a universal theory. Then T has a model completion T^* iff T has uniform quantifier-free interpolation. If this happens, T^* is axiomatized by the infinitely many sentences $\forall \underline{y} \, (\psi(\underline{y}) \rightarrow \exists \underline{e} \, \phi(\underline{e}, \underline{y}))$, where $\exists \underline{e} \, \phi(\underline{e}, \underline{y})$ is a primitive formula and ψ is a cover of it.*   ◁

The proof (via Lemma 1, by iterating a chain construction) is in [10].

4   Model-Checking Applications

In this section we supply old and new motivations for investigating covers and model completions in view of model-checking applications. We first report the considerations from [11,12,25] on symbolic model-checking via model completions (or, equivalently, via covers) in the basic case where system variables are represented as individual variables (for more advanced applications where system variables are both individual and higher order variables, see [11,12]). Similar ideas ('use quantifier elimination in the model completion even if T does not allow quantifier elimination') were used in [41] for interpolation and symbol elimination.

Definition 1. *A (quantifier-free) transition system is a tuple*

$$\mathcal{S} = \langle \Sigma, T, \underline{x}, \iota(\underline{x}), \tau(\underline{x}, \underline{x}') \rangle$$

where: (i) Σ is a signature and T is a Σ-theory; (ii) $\underline{x} = x_1, \ldots, x_n$ are individual variables; (iii) $\iota(\underline{x})$ is a quantifier-free formula; (iv) $\tau(\underline{x}, \underline{x}')$ is a quantifier-free formula (here the $\underline{x}'$ are renamed copies of the $\underline{x}$).   ◁

A *safety* formula for a transition system $\mathcal{S}$ is a further quantifier-free formula $\upsilon(\underline{x})$ describing undesired states of $\mathcal{S}$. We say that $\mathcal{S}$ is *safe with respect to* υ if the system has no finite run leading from ι to υ, i.e. (formally) if there are no model $\mathcal{M}$ of T and no $k \geq 0$ such that the formula

$$\iota(\underline{x}^0) \wedge \tau(\underline{x}^0, \underline{x}^1) \wedge \cdots \wedge \tau(\underline{x}^{k-1}, \underline{x}^k) \wedge \upsilon(\underline{x}^k) \tag{1}$$

is satisfiable in $\mathcal{M}$ (here $\underline{x}^i$'s are renamed copies of $\underline{x}$). The *safety problem* for $\mathcal{S}$ is the following: *given υ, decide whether $\mathcal{S}$ is safe with respect to υ.*

Suppose now that the theory T mentioned in Definition 1(i) is universal, has decidable constraint satisfiability problem and admits a model completion T^*. Algorithm 1 describes the *backward reachability algorithm* for handling the safety problem for S (the dual algorithm working via forward search is described in equivalent terms in [25]). An integral part of the algorithm is to compute preimages. For that purpose, for any $\phi_1(\underline{x}, \underline{x}')$ and $\phi_2(\underline{x})$, we define $Pre(\phi_1, \phi_2)$ to be the formula $\exists \underline{x}'(\phi_1(\underline{x}, \underline{x}') \wedge \phi_2(\underline{x}'))$. The *preimage* of the set of states described by a state for-

---
Algorithm 1: Backward reachability algorithm

Function BReach(v)

1    $\phi \longleftarrow v; B \longleftarrow \perp;$

2   **while** $\phi \wedge \neg B$ *is T-satisfiable* **do**

3   **if** $\iota \wedge \phi$ *is T-satisfiable.* **then**
         $\lfloor$ **return** unsafe

4       $B \longleftarrow \phi \vee B;$

5       $\phi \longleftarrow Pre(\tau, \phi);$

6       $\phi \longleftarrow QE(T^*, \phi);$

   return (safe, B);

---

mula $\phi(\underline{x})$ is the set of states described by $Pre(\tau, \phi)$. The subprocedure $QE(T^*, \phi)$ in Line 6 applies the quantifier elimination algorithm of T^* to the existential formula ϕ. Algorithm 1 computes iterated preimages of v and applies to them quantifier elimination, until a fixpoint is reached or until a set intersecting the initial states (i.e., satisfying ι) is found. *Inclusion* (Line 2) and *disjointness* (Line 3) tests produce proof obligations that can be discharged thanks to the fact that T has decidable constraint satisfiability problem.

The proof of Proposition 1 consists just in the observation that, thanks to quantifier elimination in T^*, (1) is a quantifier-free formula and that a quantifier-free formula is satisfiable in a model of T iff so is it in a model of T^*:

Proposition 1. *Suppose that the universal Σ-theory T has decidable constraint satisfiability problem and admits a model completion T^*. For every transition system $S = \langle \Sigma, T, \underline{x}, \iota, \tau \rangle$, the backward search algorithm is effective and partially correct for solving safety problems for S.*[1] $\triangleleft$

Despite its simplicity, Proposition 1 is a crucial fact. Notice that it implies decidability of the safety problems in some interesting cases: this happens, for instance, when in T there are only finitely many quantifier-free formulae in which $\underline{x}$ occur, as in case T has a purely relational signature or, more generally, T is *locally finite*[2]. Since a theory is universal iff it is closed under substructures [13] and since a universal locally finite theory has a model completion iff it has the amalgamation property [44], it follows that Proposition 1 can be used to cover the decidability result stated in Theorem 5 of [7] (once restricted to transition systems over a first-order definable class of Σ-structures).

---

[1] *Partial correctness* means that, when the algorithm terminates, it gives a correct answer. *Effectiveness* means that all subprocedures in the algorithm can be effectively executed.

[2] We say that T is locally finite iff for every finite tuple of variables $\underline{x}$ there are only finitely many non T-equivalent atoms $A(\underline{x})$ involving only the variables $\underline{x}$.

4.1   Database Schemata

In this subsection, we provide a new application for the above explained model-checking techniques [11,12]. The application relates to the verification of integrated models of business processes and data [9], referred to as artifact systems [43], where the behavior of the process is influenced by data stored in a relational database (DB) with constraints. The data contained therein are read-only: they can be queried by the process and stored in a working memory, which in the context of this paper is constituted by a set of system variables. In this context, safety amounts to checking whether the system never reaches an undesired property, irrespectively of what is contained in the read-only DB.

We define next the two key notions of (read-only) DB schema and instance, by relying on an algebraic, functional characterization.

Definition 2. *A* DB schema *is a pair* $\langle \Sigma, T \rangle$*, where: (i)* Σ *is a* DB signature*, that is, a finite multi-sorted signature whose function symbols are all unary; (ii)* T *is a* DB theory*, that is, a set of universal* Σ*-sentences.*   ◁

We now focus on extensional data conforming to a given DB schema.

Definition 3. *A* DB instance *of DB schema* $\langle \Sigma, T \rangle$ *is a* Σ*-structure* $\mathcal{M}$ *such that* $\mathcal{M}$ *is a model of* T*.*[3]   ◁

One might be surprised by the fact that signatures in our DB schemata contain unary function symbols, beside relational symbols. As shown in [11,12], the algebraic, functional characterization of DB schema and instance can be actually reinterpreted in the classical, relational model so as to reconstruct the requirements posed in [31]. Definition 2 naturally corresponds to the definition of relational database schema equipped with single-attribute *primary keys* and *foreign keys*. To see this connection, we adopt the *named perspective*, where each relation schema is defined by a signature containing a *relation name* and a set of *typed attribute names*. Let $\langle \Sigma, T \rangle$ be a DB schema. Each sort S from Σ corresponds to a dedicated relation R_S with the following attributes: (i) one identifier attribute id_S with type S; (ii) one dedicated attribute a_f with type S' for every function symbol f from Σ of the form $f : S \longrightarrow S'$.

The fact that R_S is constructed starting from functions in Σ naturally induces corresponding functional dependencies within R_S, and inclusion dependencies from R_S to other relation schemas. In particular, for each non-id attribute a_f of R_S, we get a functional dependency from id_S to a_f. Altogether, such dependencies witness that id_S is the *primary key* of R_S. In addition, for each non-id attribute a_f of R_S whose corresponding function symbol f has id sort S' as image, we get an inclusion dependency from a_f to the id attribute $id_{S'}$ of $R_{S'}$. This captures that a_f is a *foreign key* referencing $R_{S'}$.

---

[3] One may restrict to models interpreting sorts as *finite* sets, as customary in database theory. Since the theories we are dealing with usually have finite model property for constraint satisfiability, assuming such restriction turns out to be irrelevant, as far as safety problems are concerned (see [11,12] for an accurate discussion).

Given a DB instance $\mathcal{M}$ of $\langle \Sigma, T \rangle$, its corresponding relational instance $\mathcal{R}[\mathcal{M}]$ is the minimal set satisfying the following property: for every id sort S from Σ, let $f_1, \dots, f_n$ be all functions in Σ with domain S; then, for every identifier $\mathrm{o} \in S^{\mathcal{M}}$, $\mathcal{R}[\mathcal{M}]$ contains a *labeled fact* of the form $R_S(id_S : \mathrm{o}^{\mathcal{M}}, a_{f_1} : f_1^{\mathcal{M}}(\mathrm{o}), \dots, a_{f_n} : f_n^{\mathcal{M}}(\mathrm{o}))$. In addition, $\mathcal{R}[\mathcal{M}]$ contains the tuples from $r^{\mathcal{M}}$, for every relational symbol r from Σ (these relational symbols represent plain relations, i.e. those not possessing a key).

We close our discussion by focusing on DB theories. Notice that EUF suffices to handle the sophisticated setting of database-driven systems from [12] (e.g., key dependencies). The role of a non-empty DB theory is to encode background axioms to express additional constraints. We illustrate a typical background axiom, required to handle the possible presence of *undefined identifiers/values* in the different sorts. This, in turn, is essential to capture artifact systems whose working memory is initially undefined, in the style of [16,31]. To accommodate this, we add to every sort S of Σ a constant $\mathbf{undef}_S$ (written by abuse of notation just $\mathbf{undef}$ from now on), used to specify an undefined value. Then, for each function symbol f of Σ, we can impose additional constraints involving $\mathbf{undef}$, for example by adding the following axioms to the DB theory:

$$\forall x \ (x = \mathbf{undef} \leftrightarrow f(x) = \mathbf{undef}) \tag{2}$$

This axiom states that the application of f to the undefined value produces an undefined value, and it is the only situation for which f is undefined. A slightly different approach may handle *many* undefined values for each sort; the reader is referred to [11,12] for examples of concrete database instances formalized in our framework. We just point out that in most cases the kind of axioms that we need for our DB theories T are just *one-variable universal axioms* (like Axioms 2), so that they fit the hypotheses of Proposition 2 below.

We are interested in applying the algorithm of Proposition 1 to what we call *simple artifact systems*, i.e. transition systems $\mathcal{S} = \langle \Sigma, T, \underline{x}, \iota(\underline{x}), \tau(\underline{x}, \underline{x}') \rangle$, where $\langle \Sigma, T \rangle$ is a DB schema in the sense of Definition 2. To this aim, it is sufficient to identify a suitable class of DB theories having a model completion and whose constraint satisfiability problem is decidable. A first result in this sense is given below. We associate to a DB signature Σ the edge-labeled graph $G(\Sigma)$ whose nodes are the sorts in Σ, and such that $G(\Sigma)$ contains a labeled edge $S \xrightarrow{f} S'$ if and only if Σ contains a function symbol whose source sort is S and whose target sort is S'. We say that Σ is *acyclic* if $G(\Sigma)$ is so.

Proposition 2. *A DB theory T has decidable constraint satisfiability problem and admits a model completion in case it is axiomatized by finitely many universal one-variable formulae and Σ is acyclic.* $\triangleleft$

The proof is given in [10]. Since acyclicity of Σ yields local finiteness, we immediately get as a Corollary the decidability of safety problems for transitions systems based on DB schema satisfying the hypotheses of the above theorem.

5   Covers via Constrained Superposition

Of course, a model completion may not exist at all; Proposition 2 shows that it exists in case T is a DB theory axiomatized by universal one-variable formulae and Σ is acyclic. The second hypothesis is unnecessarily restrictive and the algorithm for quantifier elimination suggested by the proof of Proposition 2 is highly impractical: for this reason we are trying a different approach. In this section, we drop the acyclicity hypothesis and examine the case where the theory T is empty and the signature Σ may contain function symbols of any arity. Covers in this context were shown to exist already in [25], using an algorithm that, very roughly speaking, determines all the conditional equations that can be derived concerning the nodes of the congruence closure graph. An algorithm for the generation of interpolants, still relying on congruence closure [28] and similar to the one presented in [25], is supplied in [29].

We follow a different plan and we want to produce covers (and show that they exist) using *saturation-based theorem proving*. The natural idea to proceed in this sense is to take the matrix $\phi(\underline{e}, \underline{y})$ of the primitive formula $\exists \underline{e}\, \phi(\underline{e}, \underline{y})$ we want to compute the cover of: this is a conjunction of literals, so we consider each variable as a free constant, we saturate the corresponding set of ground literals and finally we output the literals involving only the $\underline{y}$. For saturation, one can use any version of the superposition calculus [38]. This procedure however for our problem is not sufficient. As a trivial counterexample consider the primitive formula $\exists e\, (R(e, y_1) \wedge \neg R(e, y_2))$: the set of literals $\{R(e, y_1), \neg R(e, y_2)\}$ is saturated (recall that we view e, y_1, y_2 as constants), however the formula has a non-trivial cover $y_1 \neq y_2$ which is *not* produced by saturation. If we move to signatures with function symbols, the situation is even worse: the set of literals $\{f(e, y_1) = y_1', f(e, y_2) = y_2'\}$ is saturated but the formula $\exists e\, (f(e, y_1) = y_1' \wedge f(e, y_2) = y_2')$ has the *conditional equality* $y_1 = y_2 \rightarrow y_1' = y_2'$ as cover. *Disjunctions of disequations* might also arise: the cover of $\exists e\, h(e, y_1, y_2) \neq h(e, y_1', y_2')$ (as well as the cover of $\exists e\, f(f(e, y_1), y_2) \neq f(f(e, y_1'), y_2')$, see Example 1 below) is $y_1 \neq y_1' \vee y_2 \neq y_2'$. [4]

Notice that our problem is different from the problem of producing ordinary quantifier-free interpolants via saturation based theorem proving [30]: for ordinary Craig interpolants, we have as input *two* quantifier-free formulae $\phi(\underline{e}, \underline{y}), \phi'(\underline{y}, \underline{z})$ such that $\phi(\underline{e}, \underline{y}) \rightarrow \phi'(\underline{y}, \underline{z})$ is valid; here we have a *single* formula $\phi(\underline{e}, \underline{y})$ in input and we are asked to find an interpolant which is good *for all possible* $\phi'(\underline{y}, \underline{z})$ such that $\phi(\underline{e}, \underline{y}) \rightarrow \phi'(\underline{y}, \underline{z})$ is valid. Ordinary interpolants can be extracted from a refutation of $\phi(\underline{e}, \underline{y}) \wedge \neg\phi'(\underline{y}, \underline{z})$, here we are not given any refutation at all (and we are not even supposed to find one).

What we are going to show is that, nevertheless, saturation via superposition can be used to produce covers, if suitably adjusted. In this section we consider signatures with n-ary function symbols (for all $n \geq 1$). For simplicity, we omit

---

[4]   This example points out a problem that needs to be fixed in the algorithm presented in [25]: that algorithm in fact outputs only equalities, conditional equalities and single disequalities, so it cannot correctly handle this example.

n-ary relation symbols (you can easily handle them by rewriting $R(t_1, \ldots, t_n)$ as $R(t_1, \ldots, t_n) = true$, as customary in the paramodulation literature [38]).

We are going to compute the cover of a primitive formula $\exists \underline{e}\, \phi(\underline{e}, \underline{y})$ to be fixed for the remainder of this section. We call variables $\underline{e}$ *existential* and variables $\underline{y}$ *parameters*. By applying abstraction steps, we can assume that ϕ is *primitive flat*. i.e. that it is a conjunction of $\underline{e}$-*flat literals*, defined below. [By an abstraction step we mean replacing $\exists \underline{e}\, \phi$ with $\exists \underline{e}\, \exists e'(e' = u \wedge \phi')$, where e' is a fresh variable and ϕ' is obtained from ϕ by replacing some occurrences of a term $u(\underline{e}, \underline{y})$ by e'].

A term or a formula are said to be $\underline{e}$-*free* iff the existential variables do not occur in it. An $\underline{e}$-flat term is an $\underline{e}$-free term $t(\underline{y})$ or a variable from $\underline{e}$ or again it is of the kind $f(u_1, \ldots, u_n)$, where f is a function symbol and $u_1, \ldots, u_n$ are $\underline{e}$-free terms or variables from $\underline{e}$. An $\underline{e}$-flat literal is a literal of the form

$$t = a, \quad a \neq b$$

where t is an $\underline{e}$-flat term and a, b are either $\underline{e}$-free terms or variables from $\underline{e}$.

We assume the reader is familiar with standard conventions used in rewriting and paramodulation literature: in particular $s_{|p}$ denotes the subterm of s in position p and $s[u]_p$ denotes the term obtained from s by replacing $s_{|p}$ with u. We use $\equiv$ to indicate coincidence of syntactic expressions (as strings) to avoid confusion with equality symbol; when we write equalities like $s = t$ below, we may mean both $s = t$ or $t = s$ (an equality is seen as a multiset of two terms). For information on reduction ordering, see for instance [2].

We first replace variables $\underline{e} = e_1, \ldots, e_n$ and $\underline{y} = y_1, \ldots, y_m$ by free constants - we keep the names $e_1, \ldots, e_n, y_1, \ldots, y_m$ for these constants. Choose a reduction ordering $>$ total for ground terms such that $\underline{e}$-flat literals $t = a$ are always oriented from left to right in the following two cases: (i) t is not $\underline{e}$-free and a is $\underline{e}$-free; (ii) t is not $\underline{e}$-free, it is not equal to any of the $\underline{e}$ and a is a variable from $\underline{e}$. To obtain such properties, one may for instance choose a suitable Knuth-Bendix ordering taking weights in some transfinite ordinal, see [32].

Given two $\underline{e}$-flat terms t, u, we indicate with $E(t, u)$ the following procedure:

- $E(t, u)$ fails if t is $\underline{e}$-free and u is not $\underline{e}$-free (or vice versa);
- $E(t, u)$ fails if $t \equiv e_i$ and (either $t \equiv f(t_1, \ldots, t_k)$ or $u \equiv e_j$ for $i \neq j$);
- $E(t, u) = \emptyset$ if $t \equiv u$;
- $E(t, u) = \{t = u\}$ if t and u are different but both $\underline{e}$-free;
- $E(t, u)$ fails if none of t, u is $\underline{e}$-free, $t \equiv f(t_1, \ldots, t_k)$ and $u \equiv g(u_1, \ldots, u_l)$ for $f \not\equiv g$;
- $E(t, u) = E(t_1, u_1) \cup \cdots \cup E(t_k, u_k)$ if none of t, u is $\underline{e}$-free, $t \equiv f(t_1, \ldots, t_k)$, $u \equiv f(u_1, \ldots, u_k)$ and none of the $E(t_i, u_i)$ fails.

Notice that, whenever $E(t, u)$ succeeds, the formula $\bigwedge E(t, u) \to t = u$ is universally valid. The definition of $E(t, u)$ is motivated by the next lemma.

Lemma 2. *Let R be a convergent (i.e. terminating and confluent) ground rewriting system, whose rules consist of $\underline{e}$-free terms. Suppose that t and u are $\underline{e}$-flat terms with the same R-normal form. Then $E(t, u)$ does not fail and all pairs from $E(t, u)$ have the same R-normal form as well.*   ◁

Proof. This is due to the fact that if t is not $\underline{e}$-free, no R-rewriting is possible at root position because rules from R are $\underline{e}$-free.   ⊣

In the following, we handle *constrained* ground flat literals of the form $L \parallel C$ where L is a ground flat literal and C is a conjunction of ground equalities among $\underline{e}$-free terms. The logical meaning of $L \parallel C$ is the Horn clause $\bigwedge C \to L$.

In the literature, various calculi with constrained clauses were considered, starting e.g. from the non-ground constrained versions of the Superposition Calculus of [4,37]. The calculus we propose here is inspired by such versions and it has close similarities with a subcase of hierarchic superposition calculus [5], or rather to its "weak abstraction" variant from [6] (we thank an anonymous referee for pointing out this connection).

The rules of our *Constrained Superposition Calculus* follow; each rule applies provided the E subprocedure called by it does not fail. The symbol $\bot$ indicates the empty clause. Further explanations and restrictions to the calculus are given in the Remarks below.

Superposition Right (**Constrained**)	$\dfrac{l = r \parallel C \qquad s = t \parallel D}{s[r]_p = t \parallel C \cup D \cup E(s_{\mid p}, l)}$	if $l > r$ and $s > t$
Superposition Left (**Constrained**)	$\dfrac{l = r \parallel C \qquad s \neq t \parallel D}{s[r]_p \neq t \parallel C \cup D \cup E(s_{\mid p}, l)}$	if $l > r$ and $s > t$
Reflexion (**Constrained**)	$\dfrac{t \neq u \parallel C}{\bot \parallel C \cup E(t, u)}$	
Demodulation (**Constrained**)	$\dfrac{L \parallel C, \qquad l = r \parallel D}{L[r]_p \parallel C}$	if $l > r$, $L_{\mid p} \equiv l$ and $C \supseteq D$

Remark 1. The first three rules are inference rules: they are non-deterministically selected for application, until no rule applies anymore. The selection strategy for the rule to be applied is not relevant for the correctness and completeness of the algorithm (some variant of a 'given clause algorithm' can be applied). An inference rule *is not applied in case one premise is $\underline{e}$-free* (we have no reason to apply inferences to $\underline{e}$-free premises, since we are not looking for a refutation).   ◁

Remark 2. The Demodulation rule is a simplification rule: its application not only adds the conclusion to the current set of constrained literals, but it also removes the first premise. It is easy to see (e.g., representing literals as multisets of terms and extending the total reduction ordering to multisets), that one cannot have an infinite sequence of consecutive applications of Demodulation rules.   ◁

Remark 3. The calculus takes $\{L \parallel \emptyset \mid L$ is a flat literal from the matrix of $\phi\}$ as the initial set of constrained literals. It terminates when a *saturated* set of constrained literals is reached. We say that S is saturated iff every constrained literal that can be produced by an inference rule, after being exhaustively simplified via Demodulation, is already in S (there are more sophisticated notions of 'saturation up to redundancy' in the literature, but we do not need them). When it reaches a saturated set S, the algorithm outputs the conjunction of the clauses $\bigwedge C \to L$, varying $L \parallel C$ among the $\underline{e}$-free constrained literals from S.   ◁

We need some rule application policy to ensure termination: without any such policy, a set like $\{e = y \,\|\, \emptyset, f(e) = e\|\, \emptyset\}$ may produce by Right Superposition the infinitely many literals (all oriented from right to left) $f(y) = e \,\|\, \emptyset$, $f(f(y)) = e \,\|\, \emptyset$, $f(f(f(y))) = e \,\|\, \emptyset$, etc. The next Remark explains the policy we follow.

Remark 4. First, we apply Demodulation *only in case the second premise is of the kind* $e_j = t(\underline{y}) \,\|\, D$, *where t is $\underline{e}$-free*. Demodulation rule is applied with higher priority with respect to the inference rules. Inside all possible applications of Demodulation rule, we give priority to the applications where *both premises have the form* $e_j = t(\underline{y}) \,\|\, D$ (for the same e_j but with possibly different D's - the D from the second premise being included in the D of the first). In case we have two constrained literals of the kind $e_j = t_1(\underline{y}) \,\|\, D$, $e_j = t_2(\underline{y}) \,\|\, D$ inside our current set of constrained literals (notice that the e_j's and the D's here are the same), among the two possible applications of the Demodulation rule, we apply the rule that keeps the smallest t_i. Notice that in this way two different constrained literals cannot simplify each other.   ◁

We say that a constrained literal $L \,\|\, C$ belonging to a set of constrained literals S is *simplifiable in S* iff it is possible to apply (according to the above policy) a Demodulation rule removing it. A first effect of our policy is:

Lemma 3. *If a constrained literal $L \,\|\, C$ is simplifiable in S, then after applying to S any sequence of rules, it remains simplifiable until it gets removed. After being removed, if it is regenerated, it is still simplifiable and so it is eventually removed again.*   ◁

Proof. Suppose that $L \,\|\, C$ can be simplified by $e = t \,\|\, D$ and suppose that a rule is applied to the current set of constrained literals. Since there are simplifiable constrained literals, that rule cannot be an inference rule by the priority stated in Remark 4. For simplification rules, keep in mind again Remark 4. If $L \,\|\, C$ is simplified, it is removed; if none of $L \,\|\, C$ and $e = t \,\|\, D$ get simplified, the situation does not change; if $e = t \,\|\, D$ gets simplified, this can be done by some $e = t' \,\|\, D'$, but then $L \,\|\, C$ is still simplifiable - although in a different way - using $e = t' \,\|\, D'$ (we have that D' is included in D, which is in turn included in C). Similar observations apply if $L \,\|\, C$ is removed and re-generated.   ⊣

Due to the above Lemma, if we show that a derivation (i.e. a sequence of rule applications) can produce terms only from a finite set, it is clear that when no new constrained literal is produced, saturation is reached. First notice that

Lemma 4. *Every constrained literal $L \,\|\, C$ produced during the run of the algorithm is $\underline{e}$-flat.*   ◁

Proof. The constrained literals from initialization are $\underline{e}$-flat. The Demodulation rule, applied according to Remark 4, produces an $\underline{e}$-flat literal out of an $\underline{e}$-flat literal. The same happens for the Superposition rules: in fact, since both the terms s and l from these rules are $\underline{e}$-flat, a Superposition may take place at root position or may rewrite some $l \equiv e_j$ with $r \equiv e_i$ or with $r \equiv t(\underline{y})$.   ⊣

There are in principle infinitely many $\underline{e}$-flat terms that can be generated out of the $\underline{e}$-flat terms occurring in ϕ (see the above counterexample). We show however that only finitely many $\underline{e}$-flat terms can in fact occur during saturation and that one can determine in advance the finite set they are taken from.

To formalize this idea, let us introduce a hierarchy of $\underline{e}$-flat terms. Let D_0 be the $\underline{e}$-flat terms occurring in ϕ and let D_{k+1} be the set of $\underline{e}$-flat terms obtained by simultaneous rewriting of an $\underline{e}$-flat term from $\bigcup_{i \leq k} D_i$ via rewriting rules of the kind $e_j \to t_j(\underline{y})$ where the t_j are $\underline{e}$-flat $\underline{e}$-free terms from $\bigcup_{i \leq k} D_i$. The *degree* of an $\underline{e}$-flat term is the minimum k such that it belongs to set D_k (it is necessary to take the minimum because the same term can be obtained in different stages and via different rewritings).[5]

Lemma 5. *Let the $\underline{e}$-flat term t' be obtained by a rewriting $e_j \to u(\underline{y})$ from the $\underline{e}$-flat term t; then, if t has degree $k > 1$ and u has degree at most $k - 1$, we have that t' has degree at most k.*   ◁

Proof. This is clear, because at the k-stage one can directly produce t' instead of just t: in fact, all rewriting producing directly t' replace an occurrence of some e_i by an $\underline{e}$-free term, so they are all done in parallel positions.   ⊣

Proposition 3. *The saturation of the initial set of $\underline{e}$-flat constrained literals always terminates after finitely many steps.*   ◁

Proof. We show that all $\underline{e}$-flat terms that may occur during saturation have at most degree n (where n is the cardinality of $\underline{e}$). This shows that the saturation must terminate, because only finitely many terms may occur in a derivation (see the above observations). Let the algorithm during saturation reach the status S; we say that *a constraint C allows the explicit definition of e_j in S* iff S contains a constrained literal of the kind $e_j = t(\underline{y}) \,\|\, D$ with $D \subseteq C$. Now we show by mutual induction two facts concerning a constrained literal $L \,\|\, C \in S$:

(1) if an $\underline{e}$-flat term u of degree k occurs in L, then C allows the explicit definition of k different e_j in S;
(2) if L is of the kind $e_i = t(\underline{y})$, for an $\underline{e}$-flat $\underline{e}$-free term t of degree k, then either $e_i = t \,\|\, C$ can be simplified in S or C allows the explicit definition of $k + 1$ different e_j in S (e_i itself is of course included among these e_j).

Notice that (1) is sufficient to exclude that any $\underline{e}$-flat term of degree bigger than n can occur in a constrained literal arising during the saturation process.

We prove (1) and (2) by induction on the length of the derivation leading to $L \,\|\, C \in S$. Notice that it is sufficient to check that (1) and (2) hold for the first time where $L \,\|\, C \in S$ because if C allows the explicit definition of a certain variable in S, it will continue to do so in any S' obtained from S by continuing the derivation (the definition may be changed by the Demodulation rule, but the fact that e_i is explicitly defined is forever). Also, by Lemma 3, a literal cannot become non simplifiable if it is simplifiable.

---

[5] Notice that, in the above definition of degree, constraints (attached to the rewriting rules occurring in our calculus) are ignored.

(1) and (2) are evident if S is the initial status. To show (1), suppose that u occurs for the first time in $L \parallel C$ as the effect of the application of a certain rule: we can freely assume that u does not occur in the literals from the premisses of the rule (otherwise induction trivially applies) and that u of degree k is obtained by rewriting *in a non-root position* some u' occurring in a constrained literal $L' \parallel D'$ via some $e_j \to t \parallel D$. This might be the effect of a Demodulation or Superposition in a non-root position (Superpositions in root position do not produce new terms). If u' has degree k, then by induction D' contains the required k explicit definitions, and we are done because D' is included in C. If u' has lower degree, then t must have degree at least $k - 1$ (otherwise u does not reach degree k by Lemma 5). Then by induction on (2), the constraint D (also included in C) has $(k-1) + 1 = k$ explicit definitions (when a constraint $e_j \to t \parallel D$ is selected for Superposition or for making Demodulations in a non-root position, it is itself not simplifiable according to the procedure explained in Remark 4).

To show (2), we analyze the reasons why the non simplifiable constrained literal $e_i = t(\underline{y}) \parallel C$ is produced (let k be the degree of t). Suppose it is produced from $e_i = u' \parallel C$ via Demodulation with $e_j = u(\underline{y}) \parallel D$ (with $D \subseteq C$) in a non-root position; if u' has degree at least k, we apply induction for (1) to $e_i = u' \parallel C$: by such induction hypotheses, we get k explicit definitions in C and we can add to them the further explicit definition $e_i = t(\underline{y})$ (the explicit definitions from C cannot concern e_i because $e_i = t(\underline{y}) \parallel C$ is not simplifiable). Otherwise, u' has degree less than k and u has degree at least $k - 1$ by Lemma 5 (recall that t has degree k): by induction, $e_j = u \parallel D$ is not simplifiable (it is used as the active part of a Demodulation in a non-root position, see Remark 4) and supplies k explicit definitions, inherited by $C \supseteq D$. Note that e_i cannot have a definition in D, otherwise $e_i = t(\underline{y}) \parallel C$ would be simplifiable, so with $e_i = t(\underline{y}) \parallel C$ we get the required $k + 1$ definitions.

The remaining case is when $e_i = t(\underline{y}) \parallel C$ is produced via Superposition Right. Such a Superposition might be at root or at a non-root position. We first analyse the case of a root position. This might be via $e_j = e_i \parallel C_1$ and $e_j = t(\underline{y}) \parallel C_2$ (with $e_j > e_i$ and $C = C_1 \cup C_2$ because $E(e_j, e_i) = \emptyset$), but in such a case one can easily apply induction. Otherwise, we have a different kind of Superposition at root position: $e_i = t(\underline{y}) \parallel C$ is obtained from $s = e_i \parallel C_1$ and $s' = t(\underline{y}) \parallel C_2$, with $C = C_1 \cup C_2 \cup E(s, s')$. In this case, by induction for (1), C_2 supplies k explicit definitions, to be inherited by C. Among such definitions, there cannot be an explicit definition of e_i otherwise $e_i = t(\underline{y}) \parallel C$ would be simplifiable, so again we get the required $k + 1$ definitions.

In case of a Superposition at a non root-position, we have that $e_i = t(\underline{y}) \parallel C$ is obtained from $u' = e_i \parallel C_1$ and $e_j = u(\underline{y}) \parallel C_2$, with $C = C_1 \cup C_2$; here t is obtained from u' by rewriting e_j to u. This case is handled similarly to the case where $e_i = t(\underline{y}) \parallel C$ is obtained via Demodulation rule.   ⊣

Having established termination, we now prove that our calculus computes covers; to this aim, we rely on refutational completeness of unconstrained Superposition Calculus (thus, our technique resembles the technique used [5,6] in order to prove refutational completeness of hierarchic superposition, although it is not clear whether Theorem 2 below can be derived from the results concerning hierarchic superposition - we are not just proving refutational completeness and we need to build proper superstructures):

Theorem 2. *Suppose that the above algorithm, taking as input the primitive $\underline{e}$-flat formula $\exists\underline{e}\,\phi(\underline{e}, y)$, gives as output the quantifier-free formula $\psi(y)$. Then the latter is a cover of $\exists\underline{e}\,\phi(\underline{e}, y)$.*   ◁

Proof. Let S be the saturated set of constrained literals produced upon termination of the algorithm; let $S = S_1 \cup S_2$, where S_1 contains the constrained literals in which the $\underline{e}$ do not occur and S_2 is its complement. Clearly $\exists\underline{e}\,\phi(\underline{e}, y)$ turns out to be logically equivalent to

$$\bigwedge_{L \,\|\, C \in S_1} (\bigwedge C \to L) \wedge \exists\underline{e} \bigwedge_{L \,\|\, C \in S_2} (\bigwedge C \to L)$$

so, as a consequence, in view of Lemma 1 it is sufficient to show that every model $\mathcal{M}$ satisfying $\bigwedge_{L \,\|\, C \in S_1}(\bigwedge C \to L)$ via an assignment $\mathcal{I}$ to the variables y can be embedded into a model $\mathcal{M}'$ such that for a suitable extension $\mathcal{I}'$ of $\mathcal{I}$ to the variables $\underline{e}$ we have that $(\mathcal{M}', \mathcal{I}')$ satisfies also $\bigwedge_{L \,\|\, C \in S_2}(\bigwedge C \to L)$.

Fix $\mathcal{M}, \mathcal{I}$ as above. The diagram $\Delta(\mathcal{M})$ of $\mathcal{M}$ is obtained as follows. We take one free constant for each element of the support of $\mathcal{M}$ (by Löwenheim-Skolem theorem you can keep $\mathcal{M}$ at most countable, if you like) and we put in $\Delta(\mathcal{M})$ all the literals of the kind $f(c_1, \ldots, c_k) = c_{k+1}$ and $c_1 \neq c_2$ which are true in $\mathcal{M}$ (here the c_i are names for the elements of the support of $\mathcal{M}$). Let R be the set of ground equalities of the form $y_i = c_i$, where c_i is the name of $\mathcal{I}(y_i)$. Extend our reduction ordering in the natural way (so that $y_i = c_i$ and $f(c_1, \ldots, c_k) = c_{k+1}$ are oriented from left to right). Consider now the set of clauses

$$\Delta(\mathcal{M}) \,\cup\, R \,\cup\, \{\bigwedge C \to L \mid (L \,\|\, C) \in S\} \tag{3}$$

(below, we distinguish the positive and the negative literals of $\Delta(\mathcal{M})$ so that $\Delta(\mathcal{M}) = \Delta^+(\mathcal{M}) \cup \Delta^-(\mathcal{M})$). We want to saturate the above set in the standard Superposition Calculus. Clearly the rewriting rules in R, used as reduction rules, replace everywhere y_i by c_i inside the clauses of the kind $\bigwedge C \to L$. At this point, the negative literals from the equality constraints all disappear: if they are true in $\mathcal{M}$, they $\Delta^+(\mathcal{M})$-normalize to trivial equalities $c_i = c_i$ (to be eliminated by standard reduction rules) and if they are false in $\mathcal{M}$ they become part of clauses subsumed by true inequalities from $\Delta^-(\mathcal{M})$. Similarly all the $\underline{e}$-free literals not coming from $\Delta(\mathcal{M}) \cup R$ get removed. Let $\tilde{S}$ be the set of survived literals involving the $\underline{e}$ (they are not constrained anymore and they are $\Delta^+(\mathcal{M}) \cup R$-normalized): we show that they cannot produce new clauses. Let in fact (π) be an inference from the Superposition Calculus [38] applying to them. Since no superposition with $\Delta(\mathcal{M}) \cup R$ is possible, this inference must involve only literals from $\tilde{S}$; suppose it produces a literal $\tilde{L}$ from the literals $\tilde{L}_1, \tilde{L}_2$ (coming via $\Delta^+(\mathcal{M}) \cup R$-normalization from $L_1 \,\|\, C_1 \in S$ and $L_2 \,\|\, C_2 \in S$) as parent clauses. Then, by Lemma 2, our constrained inferences produce a constrained literal $L \,\|\, C$ such that the clause $\bigwedge C \rightarrow L$ normalizes to $\tilde{L}$ via $\Delta^+(\mathcal{M}) \cup R$. Since S is saturated, the constrained literal $L \,\|\, C$, after simplification, belongs to S. Now simplifications via our Constrained Demodulation and $\Delta(\mathcal{M})^+ \cup R$-normalization commute (they work at parallel positions, see Remark 4), so the inference (π) is redundant because $\tilde{L}$ simplifies to a literal already in $\tilde{S} \cup \Delta(\mathcal{M})$.

Thus the set of clauses (3) saturates without producing the empty clause. By the completeness theorem of the Superposition Calculus [3,27,38] it has a model $\mathcal{M}'$. This $\mathcal{M}'$ by construction fits our requests by Robinson Diagram Lemma. ⊣

Theorem 2 also proves the existence of the model completion of EUF.

Example 1. We compute the cover of the primitive formula $\exists e\, f(f(e, y_1), y_2) \neq f(f(e, y_1'), y_2')$ (one more example, taken from [25], is analyzed in [10]). Flattening gives the set of literals $\{\, f(e, y_1) = e_1,\ f(e_1, y_2) = e_1',\ f(e, y_1') = e_2,\ f(e_2, y_2') = e_2',\ e_1' \neq e_2' \,\}$. Superposition Right produces the constrained literal $e_1 = e_2 \,\|\, \{y_1 = y_1'\}$; supposing that we have $e_1 > e_2$, Superposition Right gives first $f(e_2, y_2) = e_1' \,\|\, \{y_1 = y_1'\}$ and then also $e_1' = e_2' \,\|\, \{y_1 = y_1', y_2 = y_2'\}$. Superposition Left and Reflexion now produce $\bot \,\|\, \{y_1 = y_1', y_2 = y_2'\}$. Thus the clause $y_1 = y_1' \wedge y_2 = y_2' \rightarrow \bot$ will be part of the output (actually, this will be the only clause in the output). ◁

In the special case where the signature Σ contains only unary function symbols, only empty constraints can be generated; in case Σ contains also relation symbols of arity $n > 1$, the only constrained clauses that can be generated have the form $\bot \,\|\, \{t_1 = t_1', \ldots, t_{n-1} = t_{n-1}'\}$. Also, it is not difficult to see that in a derivation at most one explicit definition $e_i = t(\underline{y}) \,\|\, \emptyset$ can occur for every e_i: as soon as this definition is produced, all occurrences of e_i are rewritten to t. This shows that Constrained Superposition computes covers in polynomial time for the empty theory, whenever the signature Σ matches the restrictions of Definition 2 for DB schemata. More details on complexity are given in [10] (where a quadratic bound is obtained).

6 Conclusions and Future Work

As evident from Subsect. 4.1, our main motivation for investigating covers originated from the verification of data-aware processes. Such applications require database (DB) signatures to contain only unary function symbols (besides relations of every arity). We observed that computing covers of primitive formulae in such signatures requires only polynomial time. In addition, if relation symbols are at most binary, *the cover of a primitive formula is a conjunction of literals*: this is crucial in applications, because model checkers like MCMT [21] and CUBICLE [14] represent sets of reachable states as primitive formulae. This makes cover computations a quite attractive technique in database-driven model checking.

Our cover algorithm for DB signatures has been implemented in the model checker MCMT. A first experimental evaluation (based on the existing benchmark provided in [31], which samples 32 real-world BPMN workflows taken from the BPMN official website http://www.bpmn.org/) is described in [11]. The benchmark set is available as part of the last distribution 2.8 of MCMT http://users. mat.unimi.it/users/ghilardi/mcmt/ (see the subdirectory /examples/dbdriven of the distribution). The user manual, also included in the distribution, contains a dedicated section giving essential information on how to encode relational artifact systems (comprising both first order and second order variables) in MCMT specifications and how to produce user-defined examples in the database driven framework. Although an extensive experimentation is outside the focus of this paper, we mention that the first experiments were very encouraging: the tool was able to solve in few seconds all the proposed benchmarks and the cover computations generated automatically during model-checking search were discharged instantaneously.

This experimental setup motivates new research to extend Proposition 2 to further theories axiomatizing integrity constraints used in DB applications. Combined cover algorithms (along the perspectives in [25]) could be crucial also in this setting. Practical algorithms for the computation of covers in the theories falling under the hypotheses of Proposition 2 need to be designed: as a little first example, in [10] we show how to handle Axiom (2) by light modifications to our techniques. Symbol elimination of function and predicate variables should also be combined with cover computations.

Acknowledgements. This research has been partially supported by the UNIBZ CRC projects *REKAP: Reasoning and Enactment for Knowledge-Aware Processes* and *PWORM: Planning for Workflow Management*.

References

1. Baader, F., Ghilardi, S., Tinelli, C.: A new combination procedure for the word problem that generalizes fusion decidability results in modal logics. Inf. Comput. **204**(10), 1413–1452 (2006)
2. Baader, F., Nipkow, T.: Term Rewriting and All That. Cambridge University Press, Cambridge (1998)
3. Bachmair, L., Ganzinger, H.: Rewrite-based equational theorem proving with selection and simplification. J. Log. Comput. **4**(3), 217–247 (1994)
4. Bachmair, L., Ganzinger, H., Lynch, C., Snyder, W.: Basic paramodulation. Inf. Comput. **121**(2), 172–192 (1995)
5. Bachmair, L., Ganzinger, H., Waldmann, U.: Refutational theorem proving for hierarchic first-order theories. Appl. Algebra Eng. Commun. Comput. **5**, 193–212 (1994)
6. Baumgartner, P., Waldmann, U.: Hierarchic superposition with weak abstraction. In: Bonacina, M.P. (ed.) CADE 2013. LNCS (LNAI), vol. 7898, pp. 39–57. Springer, Heidelberg (2013). https://doi.org/10.1007/978-3-642-38574-2_3
7. Bojańczyk, M., Segoufin, L., Toruńczyk, S.: Verification of database-driven systems via amalgamation. In: Proceedings of PODS, pp. 63–74 (2013)
8. Bruttomesso, R., Ghilardi, S., Ranise, S.: Quantifier-free interpolation in combinations of equality interpolating theories. ACM Trans. Comput. Log. **15**(1), 5:1–5:34 (2014)

9. Calvanese, D., De Giacomo, G., Montali, M.: Foundations of data aware process analysis: a database theory perspective. In: Proceedings of PODS (2013)
10. Calvanese, D., Ghilardi, S., Gianola, A., Montali, M., Rivkin, A.: Quantifier elimination for database driven verification. CoRR, abs/1806.09686 (2018)
11. Calvanese, D., Ghilardi, S., Gianola, A., Montali, M., Rivkin, A.: Verification of data-aware processes via array-based systems (extended version). Technical report arXiv:1806.11459, arXiv.org (2018)
12. Calvanese, D., Ghilardi, S., Gianola, A., Montali, M., Rivkin, A.: From model completeness to verification of data aware processes. In: Lutz, C., Sattler, U., Tinelli, C., Turhan, A.Y., Wolter, F. (eds.) Description Logic, Theory Combination, and All That. LNCS, vol. 11560, pp. 212–239. Springer, Cham (2019). https://doi.org/10.1007/978-3-030-22102-7_10
13. Chang, C.-C., Keisler, J.H.: Model Theory, 3rd edn. North-Holland Publishing Co., Amsterdam (1990)
14. Conchon, S., Goel, A., Krstić, S., Mebsout, A., Zaïdi, F.: Cubicle: a parallel SMT-based model checker for parameterized systems. In: Madhusudan, P., Seshia, S.A. (eds.) CAV 2012. LNCS, vol. 7358, pp. 718–724. Springer, Heidelberg (2012). https://doi.org/10.1007/978-3-642-31424-7_55
15. Deutsch, A., Hull, R., Patrizi, F., Vianu, V.: Automatic verification of data-centric business processes. In: Proceedings of ICDT, pp. 252–267 (2009)
16. Deutsch, A., Li, Y., Vianu, V.: Verification of hierarchical artifact systems. In: Proceedings of PODS, pp. 179–194. ACM Press (2016)
17. Ghilardi, S.: Model theoretic methods in combined constraint satisfiability. J. Autom. Reason. 33(3–4), 221–249 (2004)
18. Ghilardi, S., Gianola, A.: Interpolation, amalgamation and combination (the non-disjoint signatures case). In: Dixon, C., Finger, M. (eds.) FroCoS 2017. LNCS (LNAI), vol. 10483, pp. 316–332. Springer, Cham (2017). https://doi.org/10.1007/978-3-319-66167-4_18
19. Ghilardi, S., Gianola, A.: Modularity results for interpolation, amalgamation and superamalgamation. Ann. Pure Appl. Log. 169(8), 731–754 (2018)
20. Ghilardi, S., Nicolini, E., Zucchelli, D.: A comprehensive combination framework. ACM Trans. Comput. Log. 9(2), 54 p. (2008). Article no. 8
21. Ghilardi, S., Ranise, S.: MCMT: a model checker modulo theories. In: Giesl, J., Hähnle, R. (eds.) IJCAR 2010. LNCS (LNAI), vol. 6173, pp. 22–29. Springer, Heidelberg (2010). https://doi.org/10.1007/978-3-642-14203-1_3
22. Ghilardi, S., van Gool, S.J.: Monadic second order logic as the model companion of temporal logic. In: Proceedings of LICS, pp. 417–426 (2016)
23. Ghilardi, S., van Gool, S.J.: A model-theoretic characterization of monadic second order logic on infinite words. J. Symb. Log. 82(1), 62–76 (2017)
24. Ghilardi, S., Zawadowski, M.: Sheaves, Games, and Model Completions: A Categorical Approach to Nonclassical Propositional Logics. Trends in Logic-Studia Logica Library, vol. 14. Kluwer Academic Publishers, Dordrecht (2002)
25. Gulwani, S., Musuvathi, M.: Cover algorithms and their combination. In: Drossopoulou, S. (ed.) ESOP 2008. LNCS, vol. 4960, pp. 193–207. Springer, Heidelberg (2008). https://doi.org/10.1007/978-3-540-78739-6_16
26. Hoder, K., Bjørner, N.: Generalized property directed reachability. In: Cimatti, A., Sebastiani, R. (eds.) SAT 2012. LNCS, vol. 7317, pp. 157–171. Springer, Heidelberg (2012). https://doi.org/10.1007/978-3-642-31612-8_13
27. Hsiang, J., Rusinowitch, M.: Proving refutational completeness of theorem-proving strategies: the transfinite semantic tree method. J. ACM 38(3), 559–587 (1991)

28. Kapur, D.: Shostak's congruence closure as completion. In: Comon, H. (ed.) RTA 1997. LNCS, vol. 1232, pp. 23–37. Springer, Heidelberg (1997). https://doi.org/10.1007/3-540-62950-5_59

29. Kapur, D.: Nonlinear polynomials, interpolants and invariant generation for system analysis. In: Proceedings of the 2nd International Workshop on Satisfiability Checking and Symbolic Computation Co-Located with ISSAC (2017)

30. Kovács, L., Voronkov, A.: Interpolation and symbol elimination. In: Schmidt, R.A. (ed.) CADE 2009. LNCS (LNAI), vol. 5663, pp. 199–213. Springer, Heidelberg (2009). https://doi.org/10.1007/978-3-642-02959-2_17

31. Li, Y., Deutsch, A., Vianu, V.: VERIFAS: a practical verifier for artifact systems. PVLDB **11**(3), 283–296 (2017)

32. Ludwig, M., Waldmann, U.: An extension of the knuth-bendix ordering with LPO-like properties. In: Dershowitz, N., Voronkov, A. (eds.) LPAR 2007. LNCS (LNAI), vol. 4790, pp. 348–362. Springer, Heidelberg (2007). https://doi.org/10.1007/978-3-540-75560-9_26

33. McMillan, K.L.: Lazy abstraction with interpolants. In: Ball, T., Jones, R.B. (eds.) CAV 2006. LNCS, vol. 4144, pp. 123–136. Springer, Heidelberg (2006). https://doi.org/10.1007/11817963_14

34. Nicolini, E., Ringeissen, C., Rusinowitch, M.: Data structures with arithmetic constraints: a non-disjoint combination. In: Ghilardi, S., Sebastiani, R. (eds.) FroCoS 2009. LNCS (LNAI), vol. 5749, pp. 319–334. Springer, Heidelberg (2009). https://doi.org/10.1007/978-3-642-04222-5_20

35. Nicolini, E., Ringeissen, C., Rusinowitch, M.: Satisfiability procedures for combination of theories sharing integer offsets. In: Kowalewski, S., Philippou, A. (eds.) TACAS 2009. LNCS, vol. 5505, pp. 428–442. Springer, Heidelberg (2009). https://doi.org/10.1007/978-3-642-00768-2_35

36. Nicolini, E., Ringeissen, C., Rusinowitch, M.: Combining satisfiability procedures for unions of theories with a shared counting operator. Fundam. Inform. **105**(1–2), 163–187 (2010)

37. Nieuwenhuis, R., Rubio, A.: Theorem proving with ordering and equality constrained clauses. J. Symb. Comput. **19**(4), 321–351 (1995)

38. Nieuwenhuis, R., Rubio, A.: Paramodulation-based theorem proving. In: Handbook of Automated Reasoning, vol. 2, pp. 371–443. MIT Press (2001)

39. Pitts, A.M.: On an interpretation of second order quantification in first order intuitionistic propositional logic. J. Symb. Log. **57**(1), 33–52 (1992)

40. Rybina, T., Voronkov, A.: A logical reconstruction of reachability. In: Broy, M., Zamulin, A.V. (eds.) PSI 2003. LNCS, vol. 2890, pp. 222–237. Springer, Heidelberg (2004). https://doi.org/10.1007/978-3-540-39866-0_24

41. Sofronie-Stokkermans, V.: On interpolation and symbol elimination in theory extensions. In: Olivetti, N., Tiwari, A. (eds.) IJCAR 2016. LNCS (LNAI), vol. 9706, pp. 273–289. Springer, Cham (2016). https://doi.org/10.1007/978-3-319-40229-1_19

42. Sofronie-Stokkermans, V.: On interpolation and symbol elimination in theory extensions. Log. Methods Comput. Sci. **14**(3), 1–41 (2018)

43. Vianu, V.: Automatic verification of database-driven systems: a new frontier. In: Proceedings of ICDT, pp. 1–13 (2009)

44. Wheeler, W.H.: Model-companions and definability in existentially complete structures. Isr. J. Math. **25**(3–4), 305–330 (1976)

A Tableaux Calculus for Default Intuitionistic Logic

Valentin Cassano[1], Raul Fervari[1], Guillaume Hoffmann[1], Carlos Areces[1(✉)], and Pablo F. Castro[2]

[1] CONICET and Universidad Nacional de Córdoba, Córdoba, Argentina
carlos.areces@gmail.com
[2] CONICET and Universidad Nacional de Río Cuarto, Río Cuarto, Argentina

Abstract. We build a Default Logic variant on Intuitionistic Propositional Logic and develop a sound, complete, and terminating, tableaux calculus for it. We also present an implementation of the calculus. We motivate and illustrate the technical elements of our work with examples.

1 Introduction

Non-monotonic formalisms have traditionally been defined with a classical semantics [20]. More recently –following the seminal work of Gabbay [19]– there is an interest in the interplay between non-monotonic formalisms and Intuitionistic Logic (IL). E.g., in [38] a formalization of a notion of non-monotonic implication capturing non-monotonic consequence based on IL is proposed; in [39] the work of Gabbay in [19] is revised; in [30] a characterization of answer sets for logic programs with nested expressions is offered in terms of provability in IL (generalizing earlier proposals of Pearce in [32,33]). The articles just mentioned have in common a study of the interplay between non-monotonic formalisms and IL from a theoretical perspective. Another interesting take on this interplay can be found in the area of Normative Systems or Legal Artificial Intelligence. E.g., in [22] a Description Logic built on IL is presented as a way to deal with conflicts present in laws and normative systems. These conflicts usually lead to logical inconsistencies when they are formally analyzed, bringing to the fore the need for an adequate semantics for negation in such a context. Another example is [31], where a construction of an I/O Logic –a general framework to study and reason about conditional norms [28]– is carried out on IL.

The interplay between non-monotonic formalisms and IL in normative systems is succinctly illustrated by the following motivating example (adapted from [26]). Let the possible outcomes of a trial be the verdicts of *guilty* or *not guilty*. A verdict of *guilty* is obtained when the evidence presented by the prosecution meets the so-called "beyond reasonable doubt" standard of proof. A verdict of *not guilty* is obtained when the evidence fails to meet said standard of proof; say because the defense manages to pinpoint contradictions in what the prosecution has presented. In such a context, the proposition *guilty or not*

© Springer Nature Switzerland AG 2019
P. Fontaine (Ed.): CADE 2019, LNAI 11716, pp. 161–177, 2019.
https://doi.org/10.1007/978-3-030-29436-6_10

guilty is not understood as plainly true. Associated to it there is a proof of guiltiness; or a proof that this leads to contradictions. This intuitive understanding of *guilty or not guilty* departs from its classical interpretation and better fits in an intuitionistic setting.

Furthermore, as stated in [26], a proposition such as: *a verdict of guilty implies not innocent* is intuitively correct. The reason for this is that a verdict of *guilty*, as mentioned, is backed up by evidence meeting a standard of proof "beyond reasonable doubt", and such a proof can be used to convert any proof of *innocent* into a contradiction. But we might be more reluctant to accept the contraposition: *innocent implies not guilty* as intuitively correct. Being *innocent*, as a concept, is not backed up by any notion of evidence, neither it has to meet any standard of proof. A common starting point of a trial is the so-called principle of *presumption of innocence*, whereby someone *accused* of committing a crime is *a priori innocent*. In other words, some care needs to be taken in an intuitionistic setting for the law of contraposition does not necessarily hold.

The principle of *presumption of innocence* is clearly *defeasible*. If we only know that a person has been *accused of committing a crime*, we must conclude that this person is *innocent*. However, if additional information is brought up, e.g., a *credible witness*, the *murder weapon*, etc., the principle ceases to apply and the conclusion that the person is *innocent* is withdrawn. In other words, the principle of *presumption of innocence* behaves non-monotonically.

Here, we build a default logic over Intuitionistic Propositional Logic (IPL). Our aim is to formally reason about scenarios such as the one presented above. The choice of a default logic is not arbitrary. Since their introduction in [37], it has become clear that default logics have a special status in the literature on non-monotonic logic due to a relatively simple syntax and semantics, natural representation capabilities, and direct connections to other non-monotonic logics [2,5]. From a logic engineering point of view default logics are also interesting since they can be modularly built on an underlying logic having some minimal properties [8]. Moreover, we develop a tableaux calculus for our default logic taking some ideas from [7,9]. The resulting calculus is sound, complete, and terminating. Not many proof calculi for default logics built over IL exist. Important works are [1,14]. In [1], a tableaux method is presented for a default logic built on IPL which allows for the computation of extensions, but not for checking default consequence. The latter is covered in [14], where a sequent calculus is presented. The calculi introduced in [1,14] are related to ours but differ in some important aspects, in particular, in their construction. In addition, we present a prototype implementation which enables automated reasoning, a feature missing in [1,14].

Structure. In Sect. 2 we introduce preliminary definitions and results. More precisely, we present Intuitionistic Propositional Logic (IPL), and a default logic built over IPL ($\mathscr{D}$IPL). In Sect. 3 we recall tableaux for IPL and develop a tableaux calculus for default consequence in $\mathscr{D}$IPL. In Sect. 4 we present an implementation of our calculus. In Sect. 5 we report on a preliminary empirical evaluation of our implementation. In Sect. 6 we conclude the paper and discuss future research.

2 Basic Definitions

This section introduces basic definitions to make the paper self-contained.

Intuitionistic Logic. The syntax and semantics of Intuitionistic Propositional Logic (IPL) is defined below.

Definition 1 (Syntax). *The set $\mathscr{F}$ of wffs of* IPL *is defined on an enumerable set $\mathscr{P} = \{\, p_i \mid 0 \le i \,\}$ of proposition symbols, and is determined by the grammar*

$$\varphi ::= p_i \mid \varphi \wedge \varphi \mid \varphi \vee \varphi \mid \neg\varphi \mid \varphi \supset \varphi.$$

We write $\perp$ as an abbreviation for $p \wedge \neg p$, and $\top$ for $\neg\perp$.

As in [35], we define the semantics for IPL via intuitionistic Kripke models.

Definition 2 (Models). *A Kripke model $\mathfrak{M}$ is a tuple $\langle W, \preccurlyeq, V \rangle$ where: W is a non-empty set of elements (a.k.a. worlds); $\preccurlyeq \subseteq W \times W$ is the accessibility relation; and $V : W \to 2^{\mathscr{P}}$ is the valuation function. An intuitionistic Kripke model is a Kripke model $\mathfrak{M}$ in which $\preccurlyeq$ is reflexive and transitive, and in which V satisfies the so-called heredity condition: for all $w \preccurlyeq w'$, if $w \in V(p)$, $w' \in V(p)$.*

Definition 3 (Semantics). *Let $\mathfrak{M} = \langle W, \preccurlyeq, V \rangle$ be an intuitionistic Kripke model, $w \in W$, and $\varphi \in \mathscr{F}$, we define the satisfiability relation $\mathfrak{M}, w \models \varphi$ s.t.:*

$$\begin{aligned}
\mathfrak{M}, w &\models p && \textit{iff } p \in V(w) \\
\mathfrak{M}, w &\models \varphi \wedge \psi && \textit{iff } \mathfrak{M}, w \models \varphi \textit{ and } \mathfrak{M}, w \models \psi \\
\mathfrak{M}, w &\models \varphi \vee \psi && \textit{iff } \mathfrak{M}, w \models \varphi \textit{ or } \mathfrak{M}, w \models \psi \\
\mathfrak{M}, w &\models \neg\varphi && \textit{iff } \textit{for all } w \preccurlyeq w', \ \mathfrak{M}, w' \nvDash \varphi \\
\mathfrak{M}, w &\models \varphi \supset \psi && \textit{iff } \textit{for all } w \preccurlyeq w', \textit{ if } \mathfrak{M}, w' \models \varphi \textit{ then } \mathfrak{M}, w' \models \psi.
\end{aligned}$$

Notice that, unlike Classical Propositional Logic, $\mathfrak{M}, w \nvDash \varphi$ is not equivalent to $\mathfrak{M}, w \models \neg\varphi$. For any $\Phi \subseteq \mathscr{F}$, we say that $\mathfrak{M}, w \models \Phi$ iff $\mathfrak{M}, w \models \varphi$, for all $\varphi \in \Phi$.

Next, we introduce the definition of *consequence* for IPL.

Definition 4 (Consequence). *Let $\Phi \subseteq \mathscr{F}$ and $\varphi \in \mathscr{F}$; we say that φ is a logical consequence of Φ, notation $\Phi \models \varphi$, iff for every $\mathfrak{M}$ and w in $\mathfrak{M}$, if $\mathfrak{M}, w \models \Phi$, then $\mathfrak{M}, w \models \varphi$[1]. We use $\models \varphi$ as an abbreviation for $\emptyset \models \varphi$. We say that Φ is consistent if $\Phi \nvDash \perp$, otherwise it is inconsistent.*

It is well known that $\models$ satisfies *reflexivity, monotonicity, cut, structurality* and *compactness* (see e.g. [18] for details). In Definition 4 consequence in IPL is characterized semantically in terms of Kripke models. In Sect. 3 we present a syntactic characterization based on a proof system.

---

[1] This notion is referred to as *local consequence* in the literature on Modal Logic.

Default Logic. First introduced in [37], *Default Logic* comprises a sub-class of non-monotonic logics, characterized by so-called *defaults* and *extensions*. A default is a 3-tuple of formulas, notation $\pi \overset{\rho}{\Rightarrow} \chi$. Intuitively, we can think of a default as a *defeasible conditional* which given some conditions on π and ρ enables us to obtain χ. Extensions formalize what are these conditions. Defaults and extensions are introduced below.

Definition 5 (Defaults and Default Theories). *We call $\mathscr{D} = \mathscr{F}^3$ the set of all defaults. Let $\Delta \subseteq \mathscr{D}$, $\Delta^{\Pi} = \{\pi \mid \pi \overset{\rho}{\Rightarrow} \chi \in \Delta\}$, $\Delta^{P} = \{\rho \mid \pi \overset{\rho}{\Rightarrow} \chi \in \Delta\}$ and $\Delta^{X} = \{\chi \mid \pi \overset{\rho}{\Rightarrow} \chi \in \Delta\}$. A default theory Θ is a pair (Φ, Δ) where $\Phi \subseteq \mathscr{F}$ and $\Delta \subseteq \mathscr{D}$. For any default theory $\Theta = (\Phi, \Delta)$, we define $\Phi_{\Theta} = \Phi$ and $\Delta_{\Theta} = \Delta$.*

In what follows we restrict our attention to finite default theories, i.e., default theories Θ in which both Φ_{Θ} and Δ_{Θ} are finite sets. Though our definitions extend directly to infinite default theories, there are some subtleties involved in dealing with infinite sets of defaults which we wish to avoid here (see [8] for details).

Definition 6 (Triggered). *Let Θ be a default theory, and $\Delta \cup \{\delta\} \subseteq \Delta_{\Theta}$; we say that δ is* triggered *by Δ iff $(\Phi_{\Theta} \cup \Delta^{X}) \vDash \delta^{\Pi}$.*

Definition 7 (Blocked). *Let Θ be a default theory, and $\Delta \cup \{\delta\} \subseteq \Delta_{\Theta}$; we say that δ is* blocked *by Δ iff there is $\rho \in (\Delta \cup \delta)^{P}$ s.t. $\Phi_{\Theta} \cup (\Delta \cup \delta)^{X} \cup \rho$ is inconsistent.*

Definition 8 (Detached). *Let Θ be a default theory and $\Delta \cup \{\delta\} \subseteq \Delta_{\Theta}$; we say that δ is* detached *by Δ if δ is triggered and not blocked by Δ.*

Intuitively, for a default $\pi \overset{\rho}{\Rightarrow} \chi$ in the context of a default theory Θ, the notion of detachment in Definition 8 tells us under which conditions on π and ρ we can obtain χ. The definition of detachment is an intermediate step towards the definition of an extension.

Definition 9 (Generating Set). *Let Θ be a default theory and $\Delta \subseteq \Delta_{\Theta}$; we call Δ a* generating set *iff there is a total ordering $\prec$ on Δ_{Θ} s.t. $\Delta = \mathsf{D}_{\Theta}^{\prec}(n)$ for $n = |\Delta_{\Theta}|$, and $\mathsf{D}_{\Theta}^{\prec}$ is defined as:*

$$\mathsf{D}_{\Theta}^{\prec}(0) = \emptyset$$

$$\mathsf{D}_{\Theta}^{\prec}(i{+}1) = \begin{cases} \mathsf{D}_{\Theta}^{\prec}(i) \cup \delta & \text{if } \delta \in \Delta_{\Theta} \backslash \mathsf{D}_{\Theta}^{\prec}(i) \text{ is detached by } \mathsf{D}_{\Theta}^{\prec}(i), \text{ and} \\ & \quad \text{for all } \eta \neq \delta \in \Delta_{\Theta} \backslash \mathsf{D}_{\Theta}^{\prec}(i), \text{ if } \eta \text{ is detached by } \mathsf{D}_{\Theta}^{\prec}(i), \delta \prec \eta \\ \mathsf{D}_{\Theta}^{\prec}(i) & \text{otherwise.} \end{cases}$$

Definition 10 (Extension). *Let Θ be a default theory, we say that $E \subseteq \mathscr{F}$ is an extension of Θ iff $E = \Phi_{\Theta} \cup \Delta^{X}$ where $\Delta \subseteq \Delta_{\Theta}$ is a generating set.*

Intuitively, we can think of an extension of a default theory Θ as a set of formulas which contains Φ_{Θ} and which is closed under detachment. We are now in a position to define our default logic.

Definition 11 ($\mathscr{D}$IPL). *The default logic $\mathscr{D}$IPL is the 3-tuple $\langle \mathscr{F}, \vDash, \mathscr{E} \rangle$ where:* (i) $\mathscr{F}$ *is the set of all formulas of* IPL; *(ii)* $\vDash$ *is the consequence relation of* IPL; *and (iii)* $\mathscr{E} : (2^{\mathscr{F}} \times 2^{\mathscr{D}}) \to 2^{(2^{\mathscr{F}})}$ *is a function which maps every default theory Θ to its set of extensions, i.e., $E \in \mathscr{E}(\Theta)$ iff E is an extension of Θ (see Definition 10).*

The notion of consequence for $\mathscr{D}$IPL is introduced below.

Definition 12 (Default Consequence). *We say that a formula φ is a default consequence of a default theory Θ, notation $\Theta \approx \varphi$, iff for all $E \in \mathscr{E}(\Theta)$, $E \vDash \varphi^2$.*

Some Comments and Easily Established Properties of $\mathscr{D}$IPL. Definition 10 corresponds to extensions as defined by Łukaszewicz in [27]. This definition of extensions is better behaved than Reiter's original proposal [37]. In particular, it guarantees existence, i.e., for any default theory Θ, $\mathscr{E}(\Theta) \neq \emptyset$. Definition 10 also guarantees *semi-monotonicity*. For default theories Θ_1 and Θ_2, define $\Theta_1 \sqsubseteq \Theta_2$ iff $\Phi_{\Theta_1} \subseteq \Phi_{\Theta_2}$ and $\Delta_{\Theta_1} \subseteq \Delta_{\Theta_2}$. Semi-monotonicity implies that for any two default theories $\Theta_1 \sqsubseteq \Theta_2$, if $\Phi_{\Theta_1} = \Phi_{\Theta_2}$, then for all $E_1 \in \mathscr{E}(\Theta_1)$, there is $E_2 \in \mathscr{E}(\Theta_2)$ s.t. $E_1 \subseteq E_2$. As we will see in Sect. 3, semi-monotonicity is important because it allows us to define a tableaux calculus for default consequence that can take advantage of a partial use of default theories. $\mathscr{D}$IPL is non-monotonic; in the sense that there are default theories Θ_1 and Θ_2 s.t. $\Theta_1 \sqsubseteq \Theta_2$, $\Theta_1 \approx \varphi$, and $\Theta_2 \not\approx \varphi$.

We conclude this section with an example illustrating some of the features and technical elements of $\mathscr{D}$IPL. The following terminology and notation is useful. A default $\pi \overset{\rho}{\Rightarrow} \chi$ is *normal* iff $\rho = \chi$. Normal defaults are written $\pi \Rightarrow \chi$. Let $\Theta_1 = (\Phi_1, \Delta_1)$ and $\Theta_2 = (\Phi_2, \Delta_2)$, define $\Theta_1 \sqcup \Theta_2 = (\Phi_1 \cup \Phi_2, \Delta_1 \cup \Delta_2)$. If Θ_1 is a default theory, Φ a set of formulas, and Δ a set of defaults, we use $\Theta_1 \sqcup \Phi$ to mean $\Theta \sqcup (\Phi, \emptyset)$, and $\Theta \sqcup \Delta$ to mean $\Theta \sqcup (\emptyset, \Delta)$.

Example 1 (Presumption of Innocence). Consider the following propositions:

(1) 'accused'. (2) 'guilty or not guilty'. (3) 'guilty implies not innocent'. (4) 'the affidavit of a credible witness, the murder weapon, and the results of forensic tests, imply sufficient evidence'. (5) 'sufficient evidence implies a verdict of guilty'.

In IPL, we would typically formalize (1) to (5) as:

(1') a.　　(2') $g \vee \neg g$.　　(3') $g \supset \neg i$.　　(4') $(c \wedge w \wedge f) \supset e$.　　(5') $e \supset g$.

In turn, consider the principle of presumption of innocence, i.e., 'an accused of committing a crime is *a priori* innocent'; because of its defeasible status, we choose to formalize it as the (normal) default (6') $a \Rightarrow i$.

Let $\Theta = (\{g \vee \neg g, g \supset \neg i, (c \wedge w \wedge f) \supset e, e \supset g\}, \{a \Rightarrow i\})$; then:

---

[2] This notion is referred to as *sceptical consequence* in the literature on Default Logics.

(a) $\Theta \approx g \vee \neg g$ (e) $\Theta \sqcup \{a\} \approx a$ (h) $\Theta \sqcup \{a, c, w, f\} \approx a$

(b) $\Theta \approx g \supset \neg i$ (f) $\Theta \sqcup \{a\} \approx i$ (i) $\Theta \sqcup \{a, c, w, f\} \not\approx i$

(c) $\Theta \approx (c \wedge w \wedge f) \supset e$ (g) $\Theta \sqcup \{a\} \not\approx g$ (j) $\Theta \sqcup \{a, c, w, f\} \approx g$

(d) $\Theta \approx e \supset g$

Intuitively, the default theory Θ captures the basic set of assumptions discussed in the example in Sect. 1. These assumptions include the possible outcomes of the trial, i.e., the verdict of guilty or not guilty, i.e., $g \vee \neg g$; the consideration that guilty implies not innocent, i.e., $g \supset \neg i$; what constitutes sufficient evidence, i.e., $(c \wedge w \wedge f) \supset e$; and the claim that sufficient evidence leads to a verdict of guilty, i.e., $e \supset g$. Each of these assumptions is a default consequence of Θ. $\Theta \sqcup \{a\}$ considers the particular situation at the beginning of a trial, i.e., someone is accused of committing a crime. It follows that a and i are default consequences of $\Theta \sqcup \{a\}$; i.e., if the only thing we know is that someone is accused of committing a crime, we must conclude that said person is innocent, as per the principle of presumption of innocence. In turn, $\Theta \sqcup \{a, c, w, f\}$ captures the idea that if we acquire sufficient evidence, in the form of a credible witness affidavit, the murder weapon, and the results of forensic tests, we obtain a verdict of guilt, and in such a situation the principle of presumption of innocence no longer holds (i.e., no longer can be used as a basis for establishing the innocence of the accused).

3   Tableaux Proof Calculus

We develop a tableaux proof calculus for $\mathscr{D}$IPL based on one for IPL. The calculus captures default consequence in $\mathscr{D}$IPL and it is sound, complete, and terminating (using loop-checks).

Intuitionistic Tableaux. We begin by recalling the basics of a tableaux calculus for IPL. We follow closely the style of presentation of [35].

A *tableau* is a tree whose nodes are of two different kinds. The first kind corresponds to a pair of a formula φ and a natural number i, called a *label*, appearing in positive form, notation $@_i^+ \varphi$, or negative form, notation $@_i^- \varphi^3$. The second kind corresponds to a pair of labels i and j, notation (i, j). Intuitively, $@_i^+ \varphi$ means "φ holds at world i"; and $@_i^- \varphi$ means "φ does not hold at world i"[4]. Intuitively, (i, j) means that world j is accessible from world i.

A tableau for φ is a tableau having $@_0^- \varphi$ as its root. A tableau for φ is *well-formed* if it is constructed according to the expansion rules in Fig. 1. In this figure, $(\wedge^+)$, $(\wedge^-)$, $(\vee^+)$ and $(\vee^-)$, are rules for the logical connectives of conjunction and disjunction. The "positive rules" $(\supset^+)$ and $(\neg^+)$ for the logical connectives of implication and negation are applied for every j in the branch, whereas the "negative rules" $(\supset^-)$ and $(\neg^-)$ for these logical connectives create

---

[3] The '@' notation is borrowed from Hybrid Logic [3].

[4] The signs $+$ and $-$ are necessary since in IPL we cannot use the symbol $\neg$ of negation for expressing that a formula does not hold in a world.

a "new" label j. The latter implies that the positive rules might need to be re-applied, e.g., if a new (i, j) is introduced in the branch. The rules (ref) and (trans) correspond to the reflexivity and transitivity constraints for the accessibility relation. The rule (her) corresponds to the heredity condition in Kripke models, propagating the valuation of a positive proposition symbol from a world to all its successors. The rule (A) occupies a special place in the construction of a tableau and will be discussed immediately below. Rules are applied as usual: premisses must belong to the branch; side conditions must be met (if any); the branch is extended at the level of leaves according to the consequents.

$$\frac{@_i^+(\varphi \wedge \psi)}{\begin{array}{c}@_i^+\psi\\@_i^+\varphi\end{array}} \; (\wedge^+) \qquad \frac{@_i^-(\varphi \wedge \psi)}{@_i^-\varphi \quad @_i^-\psi} \; (\wedge^-) \qquad \frac{@_i^+(\varphi \vee \psi)}{@_i^+\varphi \quad @_i^+\psi} \; (\vee^+) \qquad \frac{@_i^-(\varphi \vee \psi)}{\begin{array}{c}@_i^-\psi\\@_i^-\varphi\end{array}} \; (\vee^-)$$

$$\frac{\begin{array}{c}@_i^+(\varphi \supset \psi)\\(i,j)\end{array}}{@_j^-\varphi \quad @_j^+\psi} \; (\supset^+) \qquad \frac{@_i^-(\varphi \supset \psi)}{\begin{array}{c}(i,j)\\@_j^+\varphi\\@_j^-\psi\end{array}} \; (\supset^-)^\dagger \qquad \frac{@_i^+\neg\varphi}{\begin{array}{c}(i,j)\\@_j^-\varphi\end{array}} \; (\neg^+) \qquad \frac{@_i^-\neg\varphi}{\begin{array}{c}(i,j)\\@_j^+\varphi\end{array}} \; (\neg^-)^\dagger$$

$$\frac{\begin{array}{c}@_i^+p\\(i,j)\end{array}}{@_j^+p} \; (\text{her})^\ddagger \qquad \frac{}{(i,i)} \; (\text{ref})^* \qquad \frac{\begin{array}{c}(i,j)\\(j,k)\end{array}}{(i,k)} \; (\text{trans})^\P \qquad \frac{}{@_0^+\varphi} \; (\text{A}) \; \text{ for } \varphi \in \Phi$$

$\dagger$ for j new (i.e., not used before in the branch).
$\ddagger$ for $j \neq i$ in the branch.
$*$ for i in the branch.
$\P$ for i, j, k in the branch.

Fig. 1. Tableau rules for IPL

Definition 13 (Closedness and Saturation). *A branch is* closed, *tagged* ($\blacktriangle$), *if* $@_i^+\varphi$ *and* $@_i^-\varphi$ *occur in the branch; otherwise it is* open, *tagged* ($\blacktriangledown$). *A branch is* saturated, *tagged* ($\blacklozenge$), *if the application of any expansion rule is redundant.*

Definition 14 (Provability). *A tableau τ for φ is an attempt at proving φ. We call τ a* proof *of φ if all branches in τ are closed. We write $\vdash \varphi$ if there is a proof of φ.*

Definition 13 introduces standard conditions of *closedness* and *saturation* for a tableau. Given these conditions, we define a tableau proof in Definition 14. The resulting proof calculus is sound and complete, i.e., $\vdash \varphi$ iff $\vDash \varphi$ (see [35]). Termination is ensured using loop-checks. Loop-checks are a standard termination technique in tableaux systems that require the re-application of expansion rules [17,23].

Tableaux constructed without the rule (A) formulate a *proof calculus* for *provability*, i.e., proofs without assumptions. Including the rule (A) in the construction of a tableau gives us a proof calculus for *deducibility* (proofs from a set

Φ of assumptions). Intuitively, (A) can be understood as stating that assumptions are always true in the "current" world. This rule is not strictly necessary: $\Phi \vDash \varphi$ iff $\vDash \wedge \Phi \supset \varphi$, for Φ finite. Nonetheless, incorporating a primitive rule for assumptions simplifies the definitions and understanding of tableaux for $\mathscr{D}$IPL. When (A) is involved, we talk about a tableau for φ from Φ. Such a tableau is *well-formed* if: its root is $@_0^- \varphi$; the rules in Fig. 1 are applied as usual; and (A) is applied w.r.t. the formulas in Φ. The precise definition of the proof calculus for deducibility is given in Definition 15. By adapting the argument presented in [35], it is possible to prove that the calculus for deducibility is also *sound* and *complete*, i.e., $\Phi \vdash \varphi$ iff $\Phi \vDash \varphi$. Termination is also guaranteed with loop-checks.

Definition 15 (Deducibility). *A tableau τ for φ from Φ is an attempt at proving that φ follows from Φ. We call τ a proof of φ from Φ if all branches in τ are closed. We write $\Phi \vdash \varphi$ if there is a proof of φ from Φ.*

An interesting feature of the tableaux calculus of Definition 15 is that not only it allows us to find proofs, but also lack of proofs. The latter is done by inspecting particular proof attempts, i.e., tableaux having a branch that is both open and saturated. These tableaux serve as counter-examples (i.e., they result in a description of a model which satisfies the assumptions but invalidates the formula we are trying to prove). This claim is made precise in Prop. 1. We resort to this feature as a way of *checking consistency of a set of formulas*. This check will be used in the definition of an expansion rule for tableaux for $\mathscr{D}$IPL.

Proposition 1. *If a tableau for φ from Φ has an open and saturated branch, then, $\Phi \nvdash \varphi$.*

Corollary 1. $\Phi \nvdash \perp$ *iff* $\Phi \nvDash \perp$.

Summing up, Definition 15 characterizes *proof theoretically*, via tableaux, the semantically defined notion of logical consequence in Definition 4. We repeat that termination of the proof calculus is not ensured by a simple exhaustive application of rules, and *loop-checks* are required. Intuitively, a loop-check restricts the application of an expansion rule ensuring that only "genuinely new worlds" are created. This technique, traced back to [17, 23], is nowadays standard in tableaux systems.

Default Tableaux. *Default tableaux* extend tableaux for IPL with the addition of a new kind of node corresponding to the use of defaults. More precisely, a default tableau is a tree whose nodes are as in tableaux for IPL, together with a third kind that corresponds to the use of a default $\pi \overset{\rho}{\Rightarrow} \chi$. By a default tableau for φ from Θ, where φ is a formula and Θ is a default theory, we mean a default tableau having $@_0^- \varphi$ at its root. Such a default tableau is *well-formed* if it is constructed according to the expansion rules in Figs. 1 and 2. Rules in Fig. 1 are applied as before, with rule (A) being applied w.r.t. formulas in Φ_Θ. Rule (D) in Fig. 2 is applied w.r.t. the defaults in Δ_Θ. Note that rule (D) is applicable only if its side condition is met. This side condition can be syntactically decided using auxiliary tableaux in IPL to verify detachment, i.e., to prove that a default is triggered and not blocked.

$$\frac{\begin{array}{ccccc} \delta_1 & & \delta_i & & \delta_n \\ @_0^+ \delta_1^\times & \cdots & @_0^+ \delta_i^\times & \cdots & @_0^+ \delta_n^\times \end{array}}{} \quad (D)^\dagger$$

for $\{\, \delta_i \mid i \in [1,n] \,\} = \{\, \delta \in \Delta_\Theta \backslash \Delta_B \mid \delta$ is detached by $\Delta_B \,\}$
where Δ_B is the set of defaults in the branch.

Fig. 2. Tableau rule for defaults

Definition 16 (Default Deducibility). *Any well-formed default tableau τ for φ from Θ is an attempt at proving that φ follows from Θ by default. We call τ a default proof of φ from Θ if all branches of τ are closed. We write $\Theta \vdash \varphi$ if there is a default proof of φ from Θ.*

The proof calculus just introduced is *sound* and *complete*. Termination is guaranteed by the termination of tableaux for IPL. Figure 3 shows a default proof.

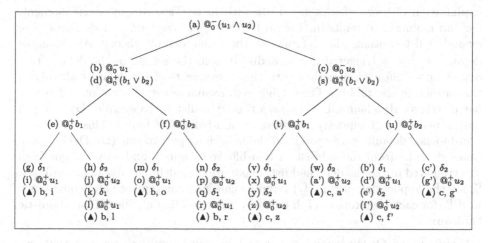

Fig. 3. Default tableau for $u_1 \wedge u_2$ from $\langle \{b_1 \vee b_2\}, \{\top \xRightarrow{u_i \wedge \neg b_i} u_i \mid i \in \{1,2\} \} \rangle$.

Theorem 1. $\Theta \vdash \varphi$ iff $\Theta \approx \varphi$. *Since $\vdash$ terminates, $\vdash$ also terminates.*

Proof (Sketch). We make use of the already known soundness and completeness of deducibility of the tableaux calculus for IPL. The proof of soundness and completeness of default deducibility depends on the following two observations: (i) a branch of a default tableau contains a branch of a tableau for deducibility in IPL (just remove default nodes); and (ii) defaults appearing in an open and saturated branch of a default tableau define a generating set (as per Definition 9) by construction. (i) and (ii) implies that if there is an open and saturated branch of a default tableau, then, there is an extension which serves as a counter-example. This proves that if $\Theta \approx \varphi$, then $\Theta \vdash \varphi$. For the converse, suppose that $\Theta \not\approx \varphi$; hence there is an extension $E \in \mathscr{E}(\Theta)$ s.t. $E \not\vdash \varphi$. Let τ be any saturated default tableau for φ from Θ; by construction, there is an open branch of τ which contains a set of defaults which is a generating set for E. The result follows from the completeness of deducibility for IPL.

4   Implementation

Overview. DefTab is an implementation of the default tableau calculus presented in Sect. 3. It is available at http://tinyurl.com/deftab0.

Given Θ and φ as input, DefTab builds proof attempts of $\Theta \vdash \varphi$ by searching for Kripke models for φ, and subsequently restricting these models with the use of sentences from Φ_Θ and defaults from Δ_Θ. DefTab reports whether or not a default proof has been found. In the latter case, DefTab exhibits an extension of Θ from which φ does not follow.

Defaults Detachment Rule and Sub-tableaux. The following is a brief explanation of how defaults are dealt with in DefTab. At any given moment, DefTab maintains defaults in three lists: *available*, *triggered*, and *detached*. The available list contains the defaults of the input default theory. An available default $\pi \overset{\beta}{\Rightarrow} \chi$ is triggered if π is deduced from the set Φ_Θ of the default theory Θ under question, together with the consequents of the defaults already in the branch of the tableau. Once triggered, available defaults are moved to the list of triggered defaults. DefTab uses the latter list to apply rule (D) in Fig. 2 and generates a (temporary) sub-list of non-blocked defaults. This sub-list of non-blocked defaults corresponds to the branching part of rule (D). DefTab then takes defaults from the sub-list of non-blocked defaults and moves them from the triggered list to the detached list, expanding the default tableau accordingly. Since the application of rule (D) requires checking consequence and consistency in IPL, for each (D)-step, DefTab builds a corresponding number of intuitionistic tableaux.

Blocking and Optimizations. For loop-checking intuitionistic rules that create new labels, DefTab uses a blocking technique called *pattern-based blocking* [25], initially designed for modal logics. In the present tableau system, when rule $(\neg^-)$ can be applied to some formula $@_i^- \neg\varphi$, it is first checked that no label k exists such that the set of formulas $\{@_k^- \varphi\} \cup @_k C(i)$ hold, where $C(i)$ are the constraints that formulas at label i forces on all its successors. If such a label exists, then the rule is not applied. The same occurs for rule $(\supset^-)$.

DefTab does not include semantic branching, or any other optimization based on Boolean negation and the excluded middle (which are usually unsound in an intuitionistic setup). Backjumping [24], on the other hand, is intuitionistically sound, and preliminary testing shows that it greatly improves performance.

We take special care of tracking dependencies of the consequent formulas introduced by the application of rule (D). That is, once a default $\pi \overset{\beta}{\Rightarrow} \chi$ is triggered, we bookkeep it along with the set of formulas that triggered it. Concretely, this bookkeeping is the union of the dependencies of all defaults Δ s.t. $\Phi_\Theta \cup \Delta^X \models \pi$. Note that this set can overestimate the set of dependencies of the triggered rule. This is a trade-off between being precise and limiting the number of sub-tableaux runs.

Usage. DefTab takes as input a file indicating the underlying logic to be used, a default theory partitioned into its set of formulas and set of defaults, and the formula to be checked. The structure of this input file is illustrated in the following example file `presumption.dt`. This file corresponds to Example 1 where: $g \mapsto$ P1, $i \mapsto$ P2, $a \mapsto$ P3, $c \mapsto$ P4, $w \mapsto$ P5, $f \mapsto$ P6, $e \mapsto$ P7.

```
intuitionistic
facts:
P1 v !P1; P1 -> !P2;
(P4 ^ P5 ^ P6) -> P7;
P7 -> P1; P3;
defaults:
P3 --> P2;
consequence:
P2
```

- The keyword `intuitionistic` indicates that the prover will work over IPL as the underlying logic.
- The keyword `facts` indicates the beginning of the set of formulas of the default theory.
- The keyword `defaults` indicates the beginning of the set of defaults. The syntax for a default $\pi \overset{\rho}{\Rightarrow} \chi$ is π `---` ρ `-->` χ. Normal default rules can be written as π `-->` χ.
- The keyword `consequence` indicates the formula to be proven.

DefTab is executed from the command line as

```
$ ./deftab -f presumption.dt
```

```
------------------------------------
Indeed a sceptical consequence.
Total time: 8.01513e-4
```

The output indicates that P2 is a sceptical consequence of the default theory. If we add the facts P4; P5; P6;, we obtain that P2 is not a sceptical consequence, indicated by the output: `Not a sceptical consequence, found bad extension: []`. The list `[]` indicates the defaults in the extension, in this case none. DefTab includes in the output a counter-example for disproving the candidate default consequence. Such counter-example consists of the generator set of the corresponding extension. In this case, the empty list indicates that the set of facts itself (without any default) is enough to generate the extension.

5   Preliminary Testing

To our knowledge, there is no standard test set for automated reasoning for default logic, and less so (if possible) for default reasoning based on IL. Moreover, our tool is a first prototype which still needs the implementation of many natural optimizations (e.g., catching for sub-tableaux results). Hence, any empirical testing is, by force, very preliminary, and should be taken only as a first evaluation of the initial performance of the tool, and of its current usability. Still, the results are encouraging and the prover seems to be able to handle examples which are well beyond what can be computed by hand, making it already a useful tool. We discuss below the tests sets we evaluated. All tests were performed on a machine running Ubuntu 16.04 LTS, with 8 GB of memory and an Intel Core i7-5500U CPU @ 2.40 Ghz.

Purely Intuitionistic Problems. When no defaults are specified in the input file, DefTab behaves as a prover for consequence in IPL (but it has not particular optimization for the case where the input is just an intuitionistic formula). Even though DefTab is still a prototype, we carried out a comparison of its performance w.r.t. existing provers for IPL.

We extend the comparison of provers for IPL carried out in [11] which compares their own prover (intuit) that implements satisfiability checking in IPL by an SMT (Satisfiability Modulo Theories) reasoner implemented over MiniSAT [13], with IntHistGC [21] and fCube [16]. These two last provers perform a backtracking search directly on a proof calculus, and are rather different from the approach taken by intuit, and closer to DefTab. IntHistGC implements clever backtracking optimizations that avoid recomputations in many cases. fCube implements several pruning techniques on a tableau-based calculus. Tests are drawn from three different benchmark suites.

1. ILTP [36] includes 12 problems parameterized by size. The original benchmark is limited, and hence it was extended as follows: two problems were generated up to size 38 and all other problems up to size 100, leading up to a total of 555 problem instances.
2. Benchmarks crafted by IntHistGC developers. These are 6 parameterized problems. They are carefully constructed sequences of formulas that separate classical and intuitionistic logic. The total number of instances is 610.
3. API solving; these are 10 problems where a rather large API (set of functions with types) is given, and the problem is to construct a new function of a given type. Each problem has variants with API sizes that vary in size from a dozen to a few thousand functions. These problems were constructed by the developers of intuit in an attempt to create practically useful problems. The total number of instances is 35.

Figure 4 shows a scatterplot (logscale) of the performance of DefTab with the other three provers, discriminating between valid and not valid formulas. Times shown are in seconds, and the timeout was set to 300 seconds. Point below the diagonal show cases where DefTab performance is worse that the other provers. The empirical tests show that specialized provers for IPL (and in particular intuit) outperforms DefTab, specially on valid, complex formulas. On simple, not valid formulas, the performance of DefTab in this test is better than fCube and comparable to IntHistGC.

Broken Arms [34]. Consider an assembly line with two mechanical arms. We assume that an arm is usable (u_i), but sometimes it can be broken (b_i), although a broken arm is an exception. In the literature on Default Logic such default assumptions have been formalized either as:

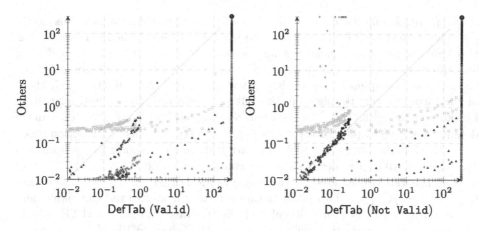

Fig. 4. Comparison on IPL: □ fCube, ◇ intuit, △ IntHistGC.

$$\Delta_1 = \left\{ \top \xrightarrow{u_i \wedge \neg b_i} u_i \;\middle|\; i \in \{1,2\} \right\} \text{ or } \Delta_2 = \left\{ (b_i \vee \neg b_i) \xrightarrow{u_i \wedge \neg b_i} u_i \;\middle|\; i \in \{1,2\} \right\}.$$

Δ_1 can be found in Poole's original discussion of the example (see [34]), whereas Δ_2 is found in, e.g., [1,14]. Suppose that we know as a fact that one of the arms is broken, but we do not know which one, i.e., $b_1 \vee b_2$. Let $\Theta_1 = (\{b_1 \vee b_2\}, \Delta_1)$ and $\Theta_2 = (\{b_1 \vee b_2\}, \Delta_2)$; it is possible to prove that $\Theta_1 \hspace{1pt}\vdash\hspace{-6pt}\sim u_1 \wedge u_2$ and that $\Theta_2 \not\hspace{1pt}\vdash\hspace{-6pt}\sim u_1 \wedge u_2$. Poole introduces this example to argue that having $u_1 \wedge u_2$ as a default consequence of Θ_1 is counter-intuitive; as we have as a fact that one of the arms is broken. This counter-intuitive result has inspired some important work on Default Logic [6,12,29]. Here, we choose this example, and Θ_1 in particular, merely as a test case. First, observe that Θ_1 can easily be made parametric on the number of arms (the number of defaults grows linearly with the number of arms). Second, observe that since defaults do not block each other, they can all be detached at any given time in a default proof attempt. The latter means that the prover needs, a priori, to consider a large number of combinations, leading to a potentially large search space. On the other hand, the intuitionistic reasoning needed is controlled, and as a result, the test case should mostly highlight how default are handled by the prover. These observations make this example a good candidate for testing the implementation of our proof calculus in order to evaluate its performance in a small, but non-trivial case. The results of running DefTab with n defaults are reported below.

No. of defaults	10	20	40	60	80
run time	0.038 s	0.499 s	8.667 s	49.748 s	177.204 s

Abstract. The following example, actually, an example template, is a variation of Broken Arms, where defaults do not block one another, but in which the detachment of defaults involves "non-trivial" intuitionistic formulas. This example is built on the ILTP library. To provide a bit of context, the ILTP library has two kinds of problems: those testing consequence in IPL, i.e., problems $\Phi \vdash \varphi$; and those testing not-consequence in IPL, i.e., problems $\Phi \not\vdash \varphi$. Of the problems testing not-consequence, we are interested in a particular sub-class, i.e., those of the form $\Phi \not\vdash \neg\varphi$. Problems in this sub-class can directly be used for testing blocking of defaults. Now, for each pair $\Phi_1 \vdash \varphi_1$ and $\Phi_2 \not\vdash \neg\varphi_2$, we construct a default theory $\Theta = (\Phi_1 \cup \Phi_2, \{\varphi_1 \overset{\varphi_2}{\Longrightarrow} p\})$. We carry out this construction guaranteeing that the languages of $\Phi_i \cup \varphi_i$ are disjoint via renaming of proposition symbols and that p is new. Then, we consider a family $\{\Theta_i \mid i \in [1, n]\}$ of default theories constructed in the way just described. It can be proven that $(\bigsqcup_{i=1}^{n} \Theta_i) \vdash (\bigwedge_{i=1}^{n} p_i)$. This construction serves as a way to test our implementation on increasingly more difficult default theories built on the ILTP library. The next table reports the results of running DefTab on $\Theta_n^m \vdash (\bigwedge_{i=1}^{n} r_i)$ where:

$$\Theta_b^a = \bigsqcup_{i=1}^{a}(\Phi_i^b \cup \Gamma_i^b, \{p_{i_0} \overset{q_{i_0}}{\Longrightarrow} r_i\})$$
$$\Phi_b^a = \{\quad p_{b_a}, \textstyle\bigwedge_{i=1}^{a}(p_{b_i} \supset (p_{b_i} \supset p_{b_{(i-1)}}))\}$$
$$\Gamma_b^a = \{\neg\neg q_{b_a}, \textstyle\bigwedge_{i=1}^{a}(q_{b_i} \supset (q_{b_i} \supset q_{b_{(i-1)}}))\}.$$

$n \backslash m$	1	2	3	4	5
1	2.20e−3 s	1.50e−2 s	0.15 s	1.15 s	11.29 s
2	1.99e−3 s	2.23e−2 s	0.25 s	2.17 s	17.17 s
3	2.8e−3 s	3.7e−2 s	0.39 s	3.29 s	26.08 s

Intuitively, Θ_n^m contains m instances of sub-problems $\Phi_m^n \vdash p_{m_0}$ and $\Gamma_m^n \not\vdash \neg q_{m_0}$ of size n taken from the ILTP. The sub-indices in Φ_m^n and Γ_m^n ensure languages are disjoint. It follows that every default $p_{i_0} \overset{q_{i_0}}{\Longrightarrow} r_i$ is detached by $\Phi_i^n \cup \Gamma_i^n$; and also that no default blocks any other. Thus, $\Theta_n^m \vdash (\bigwedge_{i=1}^{m} r_i)$. The times show the progression of running DefTab on increasingly larger default theories Θ_n^m. Note the increase on complexity is both on m and n.

6 Final Remarks

We introduced $\mathscr{D}$IPL, a Default Logic to reason non-monotonically over Propositional Intuitionistic Logic. This logic is motivated by Normative Systems and Legal Artificial Intelligence in order to deal, e.g., with legal conflicts due to logical inconsistencies. Our contribution is twofold. First, we present a sound, complete and terminating tableaux calculus for $\mathscr{D}$IPL, which decides if a formula φ is a logical consequence of a default theory Θ. The calculus is based on tableaux for IPL as presented in [35], combined with the treatment for defaults of [7]. Second, we provide a prototype implementation for our calculus in the DefTab prover.

To the best of our knowledge, this is the first prover combining Intuitionistic Logic with Non-monotonic Reasoning. For instance, DeReS [10] is a default logic reasoner with an underlying propositional tableaux calculus. It is designed to check logical consequence by combining defaults reasoning and the underlying logic reasoning as 'black boxes'. This contrasts with DefTab which integrates these two reasonings in a same tableaux calculus. On the other hand DefTab only supports sceptical consequence checking, while DeReS also supports credulous consequence checking. In [15], a tableaux calculus for Intuitionistic Propositional Logic is presented, with a special treatment for nested implications. The implementation is no longer available, but it would be interesting to implement their specialized rules in DefTab. More directly related to our work are [1], where the authors present a sequent calculus for a Non-monotonic Intuitionistic Logic; and [14], where a tableaux method is presented but only for the computation of extensions, and with no implementation.

We ran an empirical evaluation of our prover and obtained preliminary results concerning the implementation. To test purely intuitionistic reasoning we used the ILTP problem library [36]. We tested non-monotonic features in two, very small, case examples (*broken arms* and *abstract*). Clearly further testing is necessary. In particular, we are interested in crafting examples that combine the complexities of non-monotonic and intuitionistic reasoning.

For future work there are several interesting lines of research. As we mentioned, the treatment of defaults in the calculus is almost independent from the underlying logic. As a consequence, it would be interesting to define a calculus which is parametric on the rules for the underlying logic (see, e.g., [8] for such a proposal). We believe that (modulo some refactoring in the current source code) the implementation of DefTab can be generalized to handle defaults over different underlying logics obtaining a prover for a wide family of Default Logics.

Ackowledgements. This work was partially supported by ANPCyT-PICTs-2017-1130 and 2016-0215, MinCyT Córdoba, SeCyT-UNC, the Laboratoire International Associé INFINIS and the European Union's Horizon 2020 research and innovation programme under the Marie Skodowska-Curie grant agreement No. 690974 for the project MIREL: MIning and REasoning with Legal texts.

References

1. Amati, G., Aiello, L., Gabbay, D., Pirri, F.: A proof theoretical approach to default reasoning I: tableaux for default logic. J. Log. Comput. **6**(2), 205–231 (1996)
2. Antoniou, G.: Nonmonotonic Reasoning. The MIT Press, Cambridge (1997)
3. Areces, C., ten Cate, B.: Hybrid logics. In: Blackburn, et al. [4], pp. 821–868
4. Blackburn, P., van Benthem, J., Wolter, F. (eds.): Handbook of Modal Logic. Elsevier, Amsterdam (2007)
5. Bochman, A.: Non-monotonic reasoning. In: Gabbay and Woods [20], pp. 555–632
6. Brewka, G.: Cumulative default logic: in defense of nonmonotonic inference rules. Artif. Intell. **50**(2), 183–205 (1991)

7. Cassano, V., Areces, C., Castro, P.: Reasoning about prescription and description using prioritized default rules. In: Barthe, G., Sutcliffe, G., Veanes, M. (eds.) 22nd International Conference on Logic for Programming, Artificial Intelligence and Reasoning (LPAR-22), EPiC Series in Computing, vol. 57, pp. 196–213. EasyChair (2018)

8. Cassano, V., Fervari, R., Areces, C., Castro, P.F.: Interpolation and beth definability in default logics. In: Calimeri, F., Leone, N., Manna, M. (eds.) JELIA 2019. LNCS (LNAI), vol. 11468, pp. 675–691. Springer, Cham (2019). https://doi.org/10.1007/978-3-030-19570-0_44

9. Cassano, V., Pombo, C.G.L., Maibaum, T.S.E.: A propositional tableaux based proof calculus for reasoning with default rules. In: De Nivelle, H. (ed.) TABLEAUX 2015. LNCS (LNAI), vol. 9323, pp. 6–21. Springer, Cham (2015). https://doi.org/10.1007/978-3-319-24312-2_2

10. Cholewinski, P., Marek, V., Truszczynski, M.: Default reasoning system DeReS. In: 5th International Conference on Principles of Knowledge Representation and Reasoning (KR 1996), pp. 518–528. Morgan Kaufmann (1996)

11. Claessen, K., Rosén, D.: SAT modulo intuitionistic implications. In: Davis, M., Fehnker, A., McIver, A., Voronkov, A. (eds.) LPAR 2015. LNCS, vol. 9450, pp. 622–637. Springer, Heidelberg (2015). https://doi.org/10.1007/978-3-662-48899-7_43

12. Delgrande, J., Schaub, T., Jackson, W.: Alternative approaches to default logic. Artif. Intell. **70**(1–2), 167–237 (1994)

13. Eén, N., Sörensson, N.: An extensible SAT-solver. In: Giunchiglia, E., Tacchella, A. (eds.) SAT 2003. LNCS, vol. 2919, pp. 502–518. Springer, Heidelberg (2004). https://doi.org/10.1007/978-3-540-24605-3_37

14. Egly, U., Tompits, H.: A sequent calculus for intuitionistic default logic. In: 12th Workshop Logic Programming (WLP 1997), pp. 69–79 (1997)

15. Ferrari, M., Fiorentini, C., Fiorino, G.: A tableau calculus for propositional intuitionistic logic with a refined treatment of nested implications. J. Appl. Non-Class. Log. **19**, 149–166 (2009)

16. Ferrari, M., Fiorentini, C., Fiorino, G.: FCUBE: an efficient prover for intuitionistic propositional logic. In: Fermüller, C.G., Voronkov, A. (eds.) LPAR 2010. LNCS, vol. 6397, pp. 294–301. Springer, Heidelberg (2010). https://doi.org/10.1007/978-3-642-16242-8_21

17. Fitting, M.: Proof Methods for Modal and Intuitionistic Logics. Springer, Dordrecht (1983). https://doi.org/10.1007/978-94-017-2794-5

18. Font, J.: Abstract Algebraic Logic: An Introductory Textbook, 1st edn. College Publications (2016)

19. Gabbay, D.M.: Intuitionistic basis for non-monotonic logic. In: Loveland, D.W. (ed.) CADE 1982. LNCS, vol. 138, pp. 260–273. Springer, Heidelberg (1982). https://doi.org/10.1007/BFb0000064

20. Gabbay, D., Woods, J. (eds.): Handbook of the History of Logic: The Many Valued and Nonmonotonic Turn in Logic, vol. 8. North-Holland, Amsterdam (2007)

21. Goré, R., Thomson, J., Wu, J.: A history-based theorem prover for intuitionistic propositional logic using global caching: IntHistGC system description. In: Demri, S., Kapur, D., Weidenbach, C. (eds.) IJCAR 2014. LNCS (LNAI), vol. 8562, pp. 262–268. Springer, Cham (2014). https://doi.org/10.1007/978-3-319-08587-6_19

22. Haeusler, E., de Paiva, V., Rademaker, A.: Intuitionistic logic and legal ontologies. In: 23rd International Conference on Legal Knowledge and Information Systems (JURIX 2010), Frontiers in Artificial Intelligence and Applications, vol. 223, pages 155–158. IOS Press (2010)

23. Hughes, G., Cresswell, M.: An Introduction to Modal Logic. Methuen, London (1968)
24. Hustadt, U., Schmidt, R.A.: Simplification and backjumping in modal tableau. In: de Swart, H. (ed.) TABLEAUX 1998. LNCS (LNAI), vol. 1397, pp. 187–201. Springer, Heidelberg (1998). https://doi.org/10.1007/3-540-69778-0_22
25. Kaminski, M., Smolka, G.: Terminating tableau systems for hybrid logic with difference and converse. J. Log. Lang. Inf. 18(4), 437–464 (2009)
26. Kapsner, A.: The logic of guilt, innocence and legal discourse. In: Urbaniak, R., Payette, G. (eds.) Applications of Formal Philosophy. LARI, vol. 14, pp. 7–24. Springer, Cham (2017)
27. Łukaszewicz, W.: Considerations on default logic: an alternative approach. Comput. Intell. 4, 1–16 (1988)
28. Makinson, D., van der Torre, L.: What is input/output logic? Input/output logic, constraints, permissions. In: Boella, G., van der Torre, L., Verhagen, H. (eds.) Normative Multi-agent Systems, Dagstuhl Seminar Proceedings, vol. 07122. Internationales Begegnungsund Forschungszentrum für Informatik (2007)
29. Mikitiuk, A., Truszczynski, M.: Constrained and rational default logics. In: 14th International Joint Conference on Artificial Intelligence (IJCAI 1995), pp. 1509–1517 (1995)
30. Osorio, M., Navarro Pérez, J., Arrazola, J.: Applications of intuitionistic logic in answer set programming. TPLP 4(3), 325–354 (2004)
31. Parent, X., Gabbay, D., Torre, L.: Intuitionistic basis for input/output logic. In: Hansson, S.O. (ed.) David Makinson on Classical Methods for Non-Classical Problems. OCL, vol. 3, pp. 263–286. Springer, Dordrecht (2014). https://doi.org/10.1007/978-94-007-7759-0_13
32. Pearce, D.: Stable inference as intuitionistic validity. J. Log. Program. 38(1), 79–91 (1999)
33. Pearce, D., Sarsakov, V., Schaub, T., Tompits, H., Woltran, S.: A polynomial translation of logic programs with nested expressions into disjunctive logic programs: preliminary report. In: Stuckey, P.J. (ed.) ICLP 2002. LNCS, vol. 2401, pp. 405–420. Springer, Heidelberg (2002). https://doi.org/10.1007/3-540-45619-8_28
34. Poole, D.: What the lottery paradox tells us about default reasoning. In: 1st International Conference on Principles of Knowledge Representation and Reasoning (KR 1989), pp. 333–340 (1989)
35. Priest, G.: An Introduction to Non-Classical Logic: From If to Is. Cambridge University Press, Cambridge (2000)
36. Raths, T., Otten, J., Kreitz, C.: The ILTP problem library for intuitionistic logic. J. Autom. Reason. 38(1–3), 261–271 (2007)
37. Reiter, R.: A logic for default reasoning. Artif. Intell. 13(1–2), 81–132 (1980)
38. Servi, G.: Nonmonotonic consequence based on intuitionistic logic. J. Symb. Log. 57(4), 1176–1197 (1992)
39. Wansing, H.: Semantics-based nonmonotonic inference. Notre Dame J. Formal Log. 36(1), 44–54 (1995)

NIL: Learning Nonlinear Interpolants

Mingshuai Chen[1,2]([✉]) [iD], Jian Wang[1,2] [iD], Jie An[3] [iD], Bohua Zhan[1,2]([✉]) [iD], Deepak Kapur[4] [iD], and Naijun Zhan[1,2]([✉]) [iD]

[1] State Key Laboratory of Computer Science,
Institute of Software, CAS, Beijing, China
{chenms,bzhan,znj}@ios.ac.cn
[2] University of Chinese Academy of Sciences, Beijing, China
[3] School of Software Engineering, Tongji University, Shanghai, China
[4] Department of Computer Science, University of New Mexico, Albuquerque, USA

Abstract. Nonlinear interpolants have been shown useful for the verification of programs and hybrid systems in contexts of theorem proving, model checking, abstract interpretation, etc. The underlying synthesis problem, however, is challenging and existing methods have limitations on the form of formulae to be interpolated. We leverage classification techniques with space transformations and kernel tricks as established in the realm of machine learning, and present a counterexample-guided method named NIL for synthesizing polynomial interpolants, thereby yielding a unified framework tackling the interpolation problem for the general quantifier-free theory of nonlinear arithmetic, possibly involving transcendental functions. We prove the soundness of NIL and propose sufficient conditions under which NIL is guaranteed to converge, i.e., the derived sequence of candidate interpolants converges to an actual interpolant, and is complete, namely the algorithm terminates by producing an interpolant if there exists one. The applicability and effectiveness of our technique are demonstrated experimentally on a collection of representative benchmarks from the literature, where in particular, our method suffices to address more interpolation tasks, including those with perturbations in parameters, and in many cases synthesizes simpler interpolants compared with existing approaches.

Keywords: Nonlinear Craig interpolant ·
Counterexample-guided learning · Program verification ·
Support vector machines (SVMs)

1 Introduction

Interpolation-based technique provides a powerful mechanism for local and modular reasoning, thereby improving scalability of various verification techniques,

This work has been supported through grants by NSFC under grant No. 61625206 and 61732001, by the CAS Pioneer Hundred Talents Program under grant No. Y9RC585036, and by the National Science Foundation Award DMS-1217054.

P. Fontaine (Ed.): CADE 2019, LNAI 11716, pp. 178–196, 2019.
https://doi.org/10.1007/978-3-030-29436-6_11

e.g., theorem proving, model checking and abstract interpretation, to name just a few. The study of interpolation was pioneered by Krajíček [27] and Pudlák [35] in connection with theorem proving, by McMillan [30] in the context of model checking, by Graf and Saïdi [17], McMillan [31] and Henzinger et al. [20] pertaining to abstraction like CEGAR [8], and by Wang et al. [24] in the context of learning-based invariant generation. Developing efficient algorithms for generating interpolants for various theories and their combination has become an active research area, see e.g., [7,25,26,31,32,36,46].

Though established methods addressing interpolant generation for Presburger arithmetic, decidable fragments of first-order logic, theory of equality over uninterpreted functions (EUFs) as well as their combination have been extensively studied in the literature, there appears to be little work on synthesizing nonlinear interpolants. Dai et al. proposed an algorithm in [11] for generating interpolants for nonlinear polynomial inequalities based on the existence of a witness guaranteed by Stengle's Positivstellensatz [16] that can be computed using semi-definite programming (SDP). A major limitation of this method is that the two mutually contradictory formulas to be interpolated must share the same set of variables. Okudono et al. extended [11] in [33] to cater for the so-called sharper and simpler interpolants by developing a continuous fraction-based algorithm that rounds off numerical solutions. In [14], Gan et al. considered the interpolation for inequalities combined with EUFs by employing the hierarchical calculus framework proposed in [38] (and its extension [39]), while the inequalities are limited to be of the concave quadratic form. In [15], Gao and Zufferey transformed proof traces from δ-complete decision procedures into interpolants, composed of Boolean combinations of linear constraints, which can deal with certain transcendental functions beyond polynomials. The techniques of encoding interpolants as logical combinations of linear constraints, including [15,28,37], however, yield potentially large interpolants (requiring even an infinite length in the worst case) and their usage thus becomes difficult in practical applications (cf. Example 1).

Interpolants can be viewed as classifiers that distinguish, in the context of program verification for instance, positive program states from negative ones (unreachable/error states) and consequently the state-of-the-art classification algorithms can be leveraged for synthesizing interpolants. The universal applicability of classification techniques substantially extends the scope of theories admitting interpolant generation. This idea was first employed by Sharma et al. in [37], which infers linear interpolants through hyperplane-classifiers generated by support vector machines (SVMs) [3,45] whilst handles superficial nonlinearities by assembling interpolants in the form purely of conjunctions (or dually, disjunctions) of linear half-spaces, which addresses only a limited category of formulae featuring nonlinearities. The learning-based paradigm has also been exploited in the context of nonlinear constraint solving, see e.g., [12].

In this paper, we present a classification-based learning method for the synthesis of polynomial interpolants for the quantifier-free theory of nonlinear arithmetic. Our approach is based on techniques of space transformations and kernel tricks pertinent to SVMs that have been well-developed in the realm of machine learning. Our method is described by an algorithm called NIL (and its several variants) that adopts the counterexample-guided inductive synthesis framework [22,40]. We prove the soundness of NIL and propose sufficient conditions under which NIL is guaranteed to converge, that is, the derived sequence of classifiers (candidate interpolants) converges to an actual interpolant, and is complete, i.e., if an interpolant exists, the method terminates with an actual interpolant. In contrast to related work on generation of nonlinear interpolants, which restrict the input formulae, our technique provides a uniform framework, tackling the interpolation problem for the general quantifier-free theory of nonlinear arithmetic, possibly involving transcendental functions. The applicability and effectiveness of NIL are demonstrated experimentally on a collection of representative benchmarks from the literature; as is evident from experimental results, our method is able to address more demands on the nature of interpolants, including those with perturbations in parameters (due to the robustness inherited from SVMs); in many cases, it synthesizes simpler interpolants compared with other approaches, as shown by the following example.

Example 1 ([15]). Consider two mutually contradictory inequalities $\phi \,\widehat{=}\, y \geq x^2$ and $\psi \,\widehat{=}\, y \leq -\cos(x) + 0.8$. Our NIL algorithm constructs a single polynomial inequality $I \,\widehat{=}\, 15x^2 < 4 + 20y$ as the interpolant, namely, $\phi \models I$ and $I \wedge \psi$ is unsatisfiable; while the interpolant generated by the approach in [15], only when provided with sufficiently large finite domains, e.g., $x \in [-\pi, \pi]$ and $y \in [-0.2, \pi^2]$, is $y > 1.8 \vee (0.59 \leq y \leq 1.8 \wedge -1.35 \leq x \leq 1.35) \vee (0.09 \leq y < 0.59 \wedge -0.77 \leq x \leq 0.77) \vee (y \geq 0 \wedge -0.3 \leq x \leq 0.3)$. As will be discussed later, we do not need to provide a priori information to our algorithm such as bounds on variables.

The rest of the paper is organized as follows. Section 2 introduces some preliminaries on Craig interpolants and SVMs. In Sect. 3, we present the NIL algorithm dedicated to synthesizing nonlinear interpolants, followed by the analysis of its soundness, conditional completeness and convergence in Sect. 4. Section 5 reports several implementation issues and experimental results on a collection of benchmarks (with the robustness discussed in Sect. 6). The paper is then concluded in Sect. 7.

2 Preliminaries

Let $\mathbb{N}$, $\mathbb{Q}$ and $\mathbb{R}$ be the set of natural, rational and real numbers, respectively. We denote by $\mathbb{R}[\mathbf{x}]$ the polynomial ring over $\mathbb{R}$ with variables $\mathbf{x} = (\mathbf{x}_1, \ldots, \mathbf{x}_n)$, and $\|\mathbf{x}\|$ denotes the ℓ^2-norm [4]. For a set $X \subseteq \mathbb{R}^n$, its convex hull is denoted by $\text{conv}(X)$. For $\boldsymbol{x}, \boldsymbol{x}' \in X$, $\text{dist}(\boldsymbol{x}, \boldsymbol{x}') = \|\boldsymbol{x} - \boldsymbol{x}'\|$ denotes the Euclidean distance between two points, which generalizes to $\text{dist}(\boldsymbol{x}, X') = \min_{\boldsymbol{x}' \in X'} \text{dist}(\boldsymbol{x}, \boldsymbol{x}')$. Given $\delta \geq 0$, define $\mathcal{B}(\boldsymbol{x}, \delta) = \{\boldsymbol{x}' \in \mathbb{R}^n \,|\, \|\boldsymbol{x}' - \boldsymbol{x}\| \leq \delta\}$ as the closed ball of radius δ centered at $\boldsymbol{x}$. Consider the quantifier-free fragment of a first-order theory of polynomials over the reals, denoted by $\mathcal{T}_P$, in which a formula φ is of the form

$$\varphi \,\widehat{=}\, p(\mathbf{x}) \diamond 0 \mid \varphi \wedge \varphi \mid \varphi \vee \varphi \mid \neg\varphi$$

where $p(\mathbf{x}) \in \mathbb{R}[\mathbf{x}]$ and $\diamond \in \{<, >, \leq, \geq, =\}$. A natural extension of our method to cater for more general nonlinearities involving transcendental functions will be demonstrated in subsequent sections. In the sequel, we use $\bot$ to stand for *false* and $\top$ for *true*. Let $\mathbb{R}[\mathbf{x}]_m$ consist of all polynomials $p(\mathbf{x})$ of degree $\leq m \in \mathbb{N}$. We abuse the notation $\varphi \in \mathbb{R}[\mathbf{x}]_m$ to abbreviate $\varphi \stackrel{\frown}{=} p(\mathbf{x}) \diamond 0$ and $p(\mathbf{x}) \in \mathbb{R}[\mathbf{x}]_m$ if no ambiguity arises.

Given formulas ϕ and ψ in a theory $\mathcal{T}$, ϕ is *valid* w.r.t. $\mathcal{T}$, written as $\models_{\mathcal{T}} \phi$, iff ϕ is true in all models of $\mathcal{T}$; ϕ *entails* ψ w.r.t. $\mathcal{T}$, written as $\phi \models_{\mathcal{T}} \psi$, iff every model of $\mathcal{T}$ that makes ϕ true makes ψ also true; ϕ is *satisfiable* w.r.t. $\mathcal{T}$, iff there is a model of $\mathcal{T}$ in which ϕ is true; otherwise *unsatisfiable*. It follows that ϕ is unsatisfiable iff $\phi \models_{\mathcal{T}} \bot$. The set of all the models that make ϕ true is denoted by $[\![\phi]\!]_{\mathcal{T}}$.

2.1   Craig Interpolant

Craig showed in [10] that given two formulas ϕ and ψ in a first-order logic $\mathcal{T}$ s.t. $\phi \models_{\mathcal{T}} \psi$, there always exists an *interpolant* I over the common symbols of ϕ and ψ s.t. $\phi \models_{\mathcal{T}} I$ and $I \models_{\mathcal{T}} \psi$. In the verification literature, this terminology has been abused by [31], which defined an interpolant over the common symbols of ϕ and ψ as

Definition 1 (Interpolant). *Given ϕ and ψ in a theory $\mathcal{T}$ s.t. $\phi \wedge \psi \models_{\mathcal{T}} \bot$, a formula I is a* (reverse) interpolant *of ϕ and ψ if (i) $\phi \models_{\mathcal{T}} I$; (ii) $I \wedge \psi \models_{\mathcal{T}} \bot$; and (iii) I contains only common symbols shared by ϕ and ψ.*

It is immediately obvious that $\phi \models_{\mathcal{T}} \psi$ iff $\phi \wedge \neg \psi \models_{\mathcal{T}} \bot$, namely, I is an interpolant of ϕ and ψ iff I is a reverse interpolant in McMillan's sense of ϕ and $\neg \psi$. We follow McMillan in continuing to abuse the terminology.

2.2   Support Vector Machines

In machine learning, support vector machines [3,45] are supervised learning models for effective classification based on convex optimization. In a binary setting, we are given a training dataset $X = X^+ \uplus X^-$ of n sample points $\{(\boldsymbol{x}_1, y_1), (\boldsymbol{x}_2, y_2), \ldots, (\boldsymbol{x}_n, y_n)\}$, where $\boldsymbol{x}_i \in \mathbb{R}^d$, and y_i is either 1, indicating a positive sample $\boldsymbol{x}_i \in X^+$, or -1, indicating a negative one in X^-. The goal of classification here is to find a potential hyperplane (a.k.a. *linear classifier*) to separate the positive samples from the negative ones. There however might be various or even infinite number of separating hyperplanes, and an SVM aims to construct a separating hyperplane that yields the largest distance (so-called *functional margin*) to the nearest positive and negative samples. Such a classification hyperplane is called the *optimal-margin classifier* while the samples closest to it are called the *support vectors*.

Linear SVMs. Assume that X^+ and X^- are *linearly separable*, meaning that there exists a *linear separating hyperplane* $\boldsymbol{w}^{\mathrm{T}} \mathbf{x} + b = 0$ such that $y_i(\boldsymbol{w}^{\mathrm{T}} \boldsymbol{x}_i + b) > 0$, for all $(\boldsymbol{x}_i, y_i) \in X$. Then the functional margin can be formulated as

$$\gamma \widehat{=} 2 \min_{1 \leq i \leq n} 1/\|\boldsymbol{w}\| |\boldsymbol{w}^{\mathrm{T}} \boldsymbol{x}_i + b|.$$

Linear SVMs are committed to finding appropriate parameters $(\boldsymbol{w}, b)$ that maximize the functional margin while adhering to the constraints of separability, which reduces equivalently to the following convex quadratic optimization problem [2] that can be efficiently solved by off-the-shelf packages for quadratic programming:

$$\underset{\boldsymbol{w}, b}{\text{minimize}} \quad \frac{1}{2} \boldsymbol{w}^{\mathrm{T}} \boldsymbol{w} \quad \text{subject to} \quad y_i(\boldsymbol{w}^{\mathrm{T}} \boldsymbol{x}_i + b) \geq 1, \quad i = 1, 2, \ldots, n. \qquad (1)$$

Lemma 1 (Correctness of SVMs [37]). *Given positive samples X^+ which are linearly separable from negative samples X^-, SVMs produce, under computations of infinite precision, a half-space h s.t. $\forall \boldsymbol{x} \in X^+.\ h(\boldsymbol{x}) > 0$ and $\forall \boldsymbol{x} \in X^-.\ h(\boldsymbol{x}) < 0$.*

Corollary 1 (Separation of Convex Hulls [1]). *The half-space h in Lemma 1 satisfies that $\forall \boldsymbol{x} \in \text{conv}(X^+).\ h(\boldsymbol{x}) > 0$ and $\forall \boldsymbol{x} \in \text{conv}(X^-).\ h(\boldsymbol{x}) < 0$.*

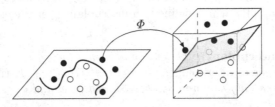

Fig. 1. Mapping from a two-dimensional input space into a three-dimensional feature space with linear separation thereof.

Nonlinear SVMs. When ϕ and ψ are formulas over nonlinear arithmetic, often after sampling X, it is not possible to find a linearly separable hyperplane in the common variables. However, a nonlinear surface that can be described as a linear hyperplane in the space of monomials of bounded degree may separate X^+ and X^-. The above construction is generalized by introducing a transformation from $\mathbb{R}^d$ to $\mathbb{R}^{\tilde{d}}$, the vector space of monomials in the common variables up to some bounded degree, with $y_i(\boldsymbol{w}^{\mathrm{T}} \boldsymbol{x}_i + b) \geq 1$ in (1) replaced by $y_i(\boldsymbol{w}^{\mathrm{T}} \Phi(\boldsymbol{x}_i) + b) \geq 1$, where Φ is a linear expression in monomials in the common variables up to a bounded degree. Here, the vectors $\Phi(\mathbf{x})$ span the *feature space*.

Consider the Lagrangian dual [3] of the modified optimization problem:

$$\underset{\alpha}{\text{minimize}} \quad \frac{1}{2} \sum_{i=1}^n \sum_{j=1}^n \alpha_i \alpha_j y_i y_j \Phi(\boldsymbol{x}_i)^{\mathrm{T}} \Phi(\boldsymbol{x}_j) - \sum_{i=1}^n \alpha_i$$

$$\text{subject to} \quad \sum_{i=1}^n \alpha_i y_i = 0, \text{ and } \alpha_i \geq 0 \text{ for } i = 1, 2, \ldots, n.$$

A *kernel function* $\kappa \colon \mathbb{R}^d \times \mathbb{R}^d \mapsto \mathbb{R}$ is defined as $\kappa(\mathbf{x}, \mathbf{x}') \widehat{=} \Phi(\mathbf{x})^{\mathrm{T}} \Phi(\mathbf{x}')$. The introduction of the dual problem and the kernel function [3] reduces the computational complexity essentially from $\mathcal{O}(\tilde{d})$ down to $\mathcal{O}(d)$. For the sake of post-verifying a candidate interpolant given by SVMs, we adopt an inhomogeneous polynomial kernel function of the form

$$\kappa(\mathbf{x}, \mathbf{x}') \cong (\beta \mathbf{x}^T \mathbf{x}' + \theta)^m,$$

where m is the polynomial degree describing complexity of the feature space, $\theta \geq 0$ is a parameter trading off the influence of higher-order versus lower-order terms in the polynomial, and β is a scalar parameter. Henceforth, the optimal-margin classifier (if there exists one) can be derived as $\mathbf{w}^T \Phi(\mathbf{x}) = \sum_{i=1}^{n} \alpha_i \kappa(\mathbf{x}_i, \mathbf{x}) = 0$, with $\mathbf{x}_i$ being a support vector iff $\alpha_i > 0$. In practice, usually a large amount of α_is turn out to be zero and this leads to a simple representation of a classifier. Figure 1 illustrates the intuitive idea of the transformation from the original input space to the feature space. We will show in the sequel that the resulting classifier can be viewed as a candidate interpolant, while its optimal-margin feature contributes to a certain "medium" logical strength of the interpolant, which is thus robust to perturbations (in the feature space) in the formulae to be interpolated.

3   Learning Interpolants

In this section, we present the NIL algorithm for synthesizing nontrivial (reverse) Craig interpolants for the quantifier-free theory of nonlinear arithmetic. It takes as input a pair $\langle \phi, \psi \rangle$ of formulas in $\mathcal{T}_P$ as well as a positive integer m, and aims to generate an interpolant I of maximum degree m, i.e., $I \in \mathbb{R}[\mathbf{x}]_m$, if it exists, such that $\phi \models_{\mathcal{T}_P} I$ and $I \wedge \psi \models_{\mathcal{T}_P} \bot$. Here, $\langle \phi, \psi \rangle$ can be decorated as $\langle \phi(\mathbf{x}, \mathbf{y}), \psi(\mathbf{x}, \mathbf{z}) \rangle$ with variables involved in the predicates, and thus $\mathbf{x}$ denotes variables that are common to ϕ and ψ. In the sequel, we drop the subscript $\mathcal{T}_P$ in $\models_{\mathcal{T}_P}$ and $\llbracket \cdot \rrbracket_{\mathcal{T}_P}$ wherever the context is unambiguous.

Due to the decidability of the first-order theory of real-closed fields established by Tarski [44], $\mathcal{T}_P$ admits *quantifier elimination* (QE). This means that the satisfiability of any formula in $\mathcal{T}_P$ can be decided (in doubly exponential time in the number of variables for the worst case). If the formula is satisfiable, models satisfying the formula can also be constructed algorithmically (following the same time complexity). Though the introduction of general forms of transcendental functions renders the underlying theory undecidable, there does exist certain extension of $\mathcal{T}_P$ with transcendental functions (involving exponential functions, logarithms and trigonometric functions), e.g. that identified by Strzeboński in [43] and references therein, which still admits QE. This allows a straightforward extension of NIL to such a decidable fragment involving transcendental functions. Specifically, the decidability remains when the transcendental functions involved are real univariate exp-log functions [41] or tame elementary functions [42] which admit a real root isolation algorithm.

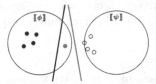

Algorithm NIL: Learning nonlinear interpolant

input : ϕ and ψ in $\mathcal{T}_P$ over common variables $\mathbf{x}$;
         m, degree of the polynomial kernel, and hence
         maximum degree of the interpolant.
/* checking unsatisfiability */
1 if $\phi \wedge \psi \not\models \perp$ then
         /* no interpolant exists */
2   abort;

   /* generating initial sample points */
3 $\langle X^+, X^- \rangle \leftarrow$ **Sampling**(ϕ, ψ);
   /* counterexample-guided learning */
4 while $\top$ do
         /* generating a classifier by SVMs */
5         $C \leftarrow$ **SVM**(X^+, X^-, m);
         /* checking classification result */
6   if $C =$ Failed then
              /* no interpolant exists in $\mathbb{R}[\mathbf{x}]_m$ */
7   abort;
         /* classifier as candidate interpolant */
8   else
9              $I \leftarrow C$;
         /* valid interpolant found */
10   if $\phi \models I$ and $I \wedge \psi \models \perp$ then
11   return I;
         /* adding counterexamples */
12   else
13             $X^+ \leftarrow X^+ \uplus$ **FindInstance**$(\phi \wedge \neg I)$;
14             $X^- \leftarrow X^- \uplus$ **FindInstance**$(I \wedge \psi)$;

Fig. 2. In NIL, a candidate interpolant (black line as its boundary) is refined to an actual one (red line as its boundary) by adding a counterexample (red dot). (Color figure online)

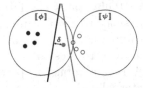

Fig. 3. In NIL$_\delta$, a counterexample (red dot) stays at least a distance of δ away from the candidate interpolant (black line as its boundary) to be refined, leading to an interpolant (red line as its boundary) with tolerance δ. (Color figure online)

3.1   The Core Algorithm

The basic idea of NIL is to view interpolants as classifiers and use SVMs with the kernel trick to perform effective classification. The algorithm is based on the sampling-guessing-refining technique: in each iteration, it is fed with a classifier (candidate interpolant) for a finite set of sample points from $[\![\phi]\!]$ and $[\![\psi]\!]$ (line 5), and verify the candidate (line 10) by checking the entailment problem that defines an interpolant (as in Definition 1). If the verification succeeds, the interpolant is returned as the final result. Otherwise, a set of counterexamples is obtained (line 13 and 14) as new sample points to further refine the classifier. In what follows, we explain the steps of the interpolation procedure in more detail.

Initial Sampling. The algorithm begins by checking the satisfiability of $\phi \wedge \psi$. If the formula is satisfiable, it is then impossible to find an interpolant, and the algorithm stops declaring no interpolant exists.

Next, the algorithm attempts to sample points from both $[\![\phi]\!]$ and $[\![\psi]\!]$. This initial sampling stage can usually be done efficiently using the Monte Carlo method, e.g. by (uniformly) scattering a number of random points over certain bounded range and then selecting those fall in $[\![\phi]\!]$ and $[\![\psi]\!]$ respectively. However, this method fails when one or both of the predicates is very unlikely to be satisfied. One common example is when the predicate involves equalities. For such situations, solving the satisfiability problem using QE is guaranteed to succeed in producing the sample points.

To meet the condition that the generated interpolant can only involve symbols that are common to ϕ and ψ, we can project the points sampled from $[\![\phi]\!]$ (resp. $[\![\psi]\!]$) to the space of $\mathbf{x}$ by simply dropping the components that pertain to $\mathbf{y}$ (resp. $\mathbf{z}$) and thereby obtain sample points in X^+ (resp. X^-).

Entailment Checking. The correctness of SVM given in Lemma 1 only guarantees that the candidate interpolant separates the finite set of points sampled from $[\![\phi]\!]$ and $[\![\psi]\!]$, not necessarily the entirety of the two sets. Hence, post-verification by checking the entailment problem (line 10) is needed for the candidate to be claimed as an interpolant of ϕ and ψ. This can be achieved by solving the equivalent QE problems $\forall \mathbf{x}.\ \phi(\mathbf{x}, \mathbf{y})|_{\mathbf{x}} \implies I(\mathbf{x})$ and $\forall \mathbf{x}.\ I(\mathbf{x}) \wedge \psi(\mathbf{x}, \mathbf{z})|_{\mathbf{x}} \implies \perp$, where $\cdot|_{\mathbf{x}}$ is the *projection* to the common space over $\mathbf{x}$. The candidate will be returned as an actual interpolant if both formulae reduce to $\top$ after eliminating the universal quantifiers. The satisfiability checking at line 1 can be solved analogously. Granted, the entailment checking can also be encoded in SMT techniques by asking the satisfiability of the negation of the universally quantified predicates, however, limitations of current SMT solvers in nonlinear arithmetic hinders them from being practically used in our framework, as demonstrated later in Sect. 5.

Counterexample Generation. If a candidate interpolant cannot be verified as an actual one, then at least one witness can be found as a counterexample to that candidate, which can be added to the set of sample points in the next iteration to refine further candidates (cf. Fig. 2). Multiple counterexamples can be obtained at a time thereby effectively reducing the number of future iterations.

In general, we have little control over which counterexample will be returned by QE. In the worst case, the counterexample can lie almost exactly on the hyperplane found by SVM. This poses issues for the termination of the algorithm. We will address this theoretical issue by slightly modifying the algorithm, as explained in Sects. 3.3 and 4.

3.2   Comparison with the Naïve QE-Based Method

Simply performing QE on $\exists \mathbf{y}.\ \phi(\mathbf{x}, \mathbf{y})$ yields already an interpolant for mutually contradictory ϕ and ψ. Such an interpolant is actually the *strongest* in the sense of [13], which presents an ordered family of interpolation systems due to the logical strength of the synthesized interpolants. Dually, the negation of the result when performing QE over $\exists \mathbf{z}.\ \psi(\mathbf{x}, \mathbf{z})$ is the *weakest* interpolant. However, as argued by D'Silva et al. in [13], a good interpolant (approximation of ϕ or ψ) –when computing invariants of transition systems using interpolation-based model checking– should be coarse enough to enable rapid convergence but strong enough to be contained within the weakest inductive invariant. In contrast, the advantages of NIL are two-fold: first, it produces better interpolants (in the above sense) featuring "medium" strength (due to the way optimal-margin classifier is defined) which are thus more effective in practical use and furthermore resilient to perturbations in ϕ and ψ (i.e., the robustness shown later in Sect. 6); second, NIL always returns a single polynomial inequality as the interpolant which is often simpler than that derived from the naïve QE-based method, where the direct projection of $\phi(\mathbf{x}, \mathbf{y})$ onto the common space over $\mathbf{x}$ can be as complex as the original ϕ.

These issues can be avoided by combining this method with a template-based approach, which in turn introduces fresh quantifiers over unknown parameters to be eliminated. Note that in NIL the candidate interpolants $I \in \mathbb{R}[\mathbf{x}]_m$ under verification are polynomials without unknown parameters, and therefore, in contrast to performing QE over an assumed template, the learning-based technique can practically generate polynomial interpolants of higher degrees (with acceptable rounds of iterations). For example, NIL is able to synthesize an interpolant of degree 7 over 2 variables (depicted later in Fig. 4(b)), which would require a polynomial template with $\binom{7+2}{2} = 36$ unknown parameters that goes far beyond the capability of QE procedures.

On the other hand, performing QE within every iteration of the learning process, for entailment checking and generating counterexamples, limits the efficiency of the proposed method, thereby confining NIL currently to applications only of small scales. Potential solutions to the efficiency bottleneck will be discussed in Sect. 5.

3.3   Variants of NIL

While the above basic algorithm is already effective in practice (as demonstrated in Sect. 5), it is guaranteed to terminate only when there is an interpolant with positive functional margin between $[\![\phi]\!]$ and $[\![\psi]\!]$. In this section, we present two variants of the algorithm that have nicer theoretical properties in cases where the two sets are only separated by an interpolant with zero functional margin, e.g., cases where $[\![\phi]\!]$ and $[\![\psi]\!]$ share adjacent or even coincident boundaries.

Entailment Checking with Tolerance δ. When performing entailment checking for a candidate interpolant I, instead of using, e.g., the formula $p(\mathbf{x}) \geq 0$ for I, we can introduce a tolerance of δ. That is, we check the satisfiability of $\phi \wedge (p(\mathbf{x}) < -\delta)$ and $(p(\mathbf{x}) \geq \delta) \wedge \psi$ instead of the original $\phi \wedge (p(\mathbf{x}) < 0)$ and $(p(\mathbf{x}) \geq 0) \wedge \psi$. This means that a candidate that is an interpolant "up to a tolerance of δ" will be returned as a true interpolant, which may be acceptable in some applications. If the candidate interpolant is still not verified, the counterexample is guaranteed to be at least a distance of δ away from the separating hyperplane. Note the distance δ is taken in the feature space $\mathbb{R}^{\tilde{d}}$, not in the original space. We let $\mathrm{NIL}_\delta(\phi, \psi, m)$ denote the version of NIL with this modification (cf. Fig. 3). In the next section, we show $\mathrm{NIL}_\delta(\phi, \psi, m)$ terminates as long as $[\![\phi]\!]$ and $[\![\psi]\!]$ are bounded, including the case where they are separated only by interpolants of functional margin zero.

Varying Tolerance During the Execution. A further refinement of the algorithm can be made by varying the tolerance δ during the execution. We also introduce a bounding box B of the varying size to handle unbounded cases. Define algorithm $\mathrm{NIL}^*_{\delta,B}(\phi, \psi, m)$ as follows. Let $\delta_1 = \delta$ and $B_1 = B$. For each iteration i, execute the core algorithm, except that the counterexample must be a distance of at least δ_i away from the separating boundary, and have absolute value in each dimension at most B (both in $\mathbb{R}^{\tilde{d}}$). After the termination of iteration i, begin iteration $i + 1$ with $\delta_{i+1} = \delta_i/2$ and $B_{i+1} = 2B_i$. This continues until an interpolant is found or until a pre-specified cutoff. For any $[\![\phi]\!]$ and $[\![\psi]\!]$ (without the boundedness condition), this variant of the algorithm *converges* to an interpolant in the limit, which will be made precise in the next section.

4 Soundness, Completeness and Convergence

In this section, we present theoretical results obtained for the basic NIL algorithm and its variants. Proofs are available in the appendix of [6].

First, the basic algorithm is sound, as captured by Theorem 1.

Theorem 1 (Soundness of NIL). *$NIL(\phi, \psi, m)$ terminates and returns I if and only if I is an interpolant in $\mathbb{R}[\mathbf{x}]_m$ of ϕ and ψ.*

Under certain conditions, the algorithm is also terminating (and hence complete). We prove two such situations below. In both cases, we require boundedness of the two sets that we want to separate. In the first case, there exists an interpolant with positive functional margin between the two sets.

Theorem 2 (Conditional Completeness of NIL). *If $[\![\phi]\!]$ and $[\![\psi]\!]$ are bounded and there exists an interpolant in $\mathbb{R}[\mathbf{x}]_m$ of ϕ and ψ with positive functional margin γ when mapped to $\mathbb{R}^{\tilde{d}}$, then $NIL(\phi, \psi, m)$ terminates and returns an interpolant I of ϕ and ψ.*

The standard algorithm is not guaranteed to terminate when $[\![\phi]\!]$ and $[\![\psi]\!]$ are only separated by interpolants of functional margin zero. However, the modified algorithm $NIL_\delta(\phi, \psi, m)$ does terminate (with the cost that the resulting answer is an interpolant with tolerance δ).

Theorem 3 (Completeness of NIL_δ with zero margin). *If $[\![\phi]\!]$ and $[\![\psi]\!]$ are bounded, and $\delta > 0$, then $NIL_\delta(\phi, \psi, m)$ terminates. It returns an interpolant I of ϕ and ψ with tolerance δ whenever such an interpolant exists.*

By iteratively decreasing δ during the execution of the algorithm, as well as introducing an iteratively increasing bounding box, as in $NIL^*_{\delta,B}(\phi, \psi, m)$, we can obtain more and more accurate candidate interpolants. We now show that this algorithm *converges* to an interpolant without restrictions on ϕ and ψ. We first make this convergence property precise in the following definition.

Definition 2 (Convergence of a sequence of equations to an interpolant). *Given two sets $[\![\phi]\!]$ and $[\![\psi]\!]$ that we want to separate, and an infinite sequence of equations $I_1, I_2, \ldots$, we say the sequence I_n converges to an interpolant of ϕ and ψ if, for each point p in the interior of $[\![\phi]\!]$ or $[\![\psi]\!]$, there exists some integer K_p such that I_k classifies p correctly for all $k \geq K_p$.*

Theorem 4 (Convergence of $NIL^*_{\delta,B}$). *Given two regions $[\![\phi]\!]$ and $[\![\psi]\!]$. Suppose there exists an interpolant of ϕ and ψ, then the infinite sequence of candidates produced by $NIL^*_{\delta,B}(\phi, \psi, m)$ converges to an interpolant in the sense of Definition 2.*

5 Implementation and Experiments

5.1 Implementation Issues

We have implemented the core algorithm NIL as a prototype[1] in Wolfram Mathematica with LIBSVM [5] being integrated as an engine to perform SVM classifications. Despite featuring no completeness for adjacent $[\![\phi]\!]$ and $[\![\psi]\!]$ nor convergence for unbounded $[\![\phi]\!]$ or $[\![\psi]\!]$, the standard NIL algorithm yields already promising results as shown later in the experiments. Key Mathematica functions that are utilized include REDUCE, for entailment checking, e.g., the unsatisfiability checking of $\phi \wedge \psi$ and the post-verification of a candidate interpolant, and FINDINSTANCE, for generating counterexamples and sampling initial points (when the random sampling strategy fails). The REDUCE command implements a decision procedure for $\mathcal{T}_P$ and its appropriate extension to catering for transcendental functions (cf. [43]) based on *cylindrical algebraic decomposition* (CAD), due to Collins [9]. The underlying quantifier-elimination procedure, albeit inducing rather high computation complexity, cannot in practice be replaced by SMT-solving techniques (by checking the negation of a universally quantified predicate) as in the linear arithmetic. For instance, the off-the-shelf SMT solver Z3 fails to accomplish our tasks particularly when the coefficients occurring in the entailment problem to be checked get larger[2].

Numerical Errors and Rounding. LIBSVM conducts floating-point computations for solving the optimization problems induced by SVMs and consequently yields numerical errors occurring in the candidate interpolants. Such numerical errors may block an otherwise valid interpolant from being verified as an actual one and additionally bring down the simplicity and thereby the effectiveness of the synthesized interpolant, thus not very often proving humans with clear-cut understanding. This is a common issue for approaches that reduce the interpolation problem to numerical solving techniques, e.g. SDP solvers exploited in [11,14,33], while an established method to tackle it is known as *rational recovery* [29,47], which retrieves the nearest rational number from the continued fraction representation of its floating-point approximation at any given accuracy (see e.g. [47] for theoretical guarantees and [33] for applications in interpolation). The algorithm implementing rational recovery has been integrated in our implementation and the consequent benefits are two-fold: (i) NIL can now cope with interpolation tasks where only exact coefficients suffice to constitute an actual interpolant while any numerical error therein will render the interpolant invalid, e.g., cases where $[\![\phi]\!]$ and $[\![\psi]\!]$ share parallel, adjacent, or even coincident boundaries, as demonstrated later by examples with ID 10–17 in Table 1; (ii) rationalizing coefficients moreover facilitates simplifications over all of the candidate interpolants and therefore practically accelerating the entailment checking and counterexample generation processes, which in return yields simpler interpolants, as shown in Table 2 in the following section.

---

[1] Available at http://lcs.ios.ac.cn/~chenms/tools/NIL.tar.bz2.

[2] As can be also observed at https://github.com/Z3Prover/z3/issues/1765.

5.2   Benchmark and Experimental Results

Table 1 collects a group of benchmark examples from the literature on synthesizing nonlinear interpolants as well as some geometrically contrived ones. All of the experiments have been evaluated on a 3.6 GHz Intel Core-i7 processor with 8 GB RAM running 64-bit Ubuntu 16.04.

In Table 1, we group the set of examples into four categories comprising 20 cases in total. For each example, **ID** numbers the case, ϕ, ψ and I represent the two formulas to be interpolated and the synthesized interpolant by our method respectively, while **Time/s** indicates the total time in seconds for interpolation. The categories are described as follows, and the visualization of a selected set of typical examples thereof is further depicted in Fig. 4.

Cat. I: with/without rounding. This category includes 9 cases, for which our method generates the polynomial interpolants correctly with or without the rounding operation.

Cat. II: with rounding. For cases 10 to 17 in this category, where $[\![\phi]\!]$ and $[\![\psi]\!]$ share parallel, adjacent, or even coincident boundaries, our method produces interpolants successfully with the rouding process based on rational recovery.

Cat. III: beyond polynomials. This category encloses two cases beyond the theory $\mathcal{T}_P$ of polynomials: for case 18, a verified polynomial interpolant is obtained in spite of the transcendental term in ψ; while for case 19, the SVM classification fails since $[\![\phi]\!]$ and $[\![\psi]\!]$ are not linearly separable in any finite-dimensional feature space and hence no polynomial interpolant exists for this example. Note that our counterexample-guided learning framework admits a straightforward extension to a decidable fragment of more general nonlinear theories involving transcendental functions, as investigated in [43].

Cat. IV: unbalanced. The case 20, called Unbalanced, instantiates a particular scenario where ϕ and ψ have extraordinary "unbalanced" number of models that make them true respectively. For this example, there are an infinite number of models satisfying ϕ yet one single model (i.e., $x = 0$) satisfying ψ. The training process in SVMs may fail when encountering extremely unbalanced number of positive/negative samples. This is solved by specifying a *weight* factor for the positive set of samples as the number of negative ones, and dually for the other way around, to balance biased number of training samples before triggering the classification. Such a balancing trick is supported in LIBSVM.

Remark that examples named CAV13-1/3/4 are taken from [11] (and the latter two originally from [28] and [18] respectively), where interpolation is applied to discovering *inductive invariants* in the verification of programs and hybrid systems. For instance, CAV13-3 is a program fragment describing an accelerating car and the synthesized interpolant by NIL suffices to prove the safety property of the car concerning its velocity.

Applicability and Comparison with Existing Approaches. As shown in Table 1, our learning-based technique succeeds in all of the benchmark examples

Table 1. Benchmark examples for synthesizing nonlinear interpolants.

Category	ID	Name	ϕ	ψ	I	Time/s
	1	Dummy	$x \le -1$	$x \ge 1$	$x < 0$	0.11
	2	Necklace	$y - x^2 - 1 = 0$	$y + x^2 + 1 = 0$	$-y < 0$	0.21
	3	Face	$(x+4)^2 + y^2 - 1 \le 0 \vee$ $(x-4)^2 + y^2 - 1 \le 0$	$x^2 + y^2 - 64 \le 0 \wedge$ $(x+4)^2 + y^2 - 9 \ge 0 \wedge$ $(x-4)^2 + y^2 - 9 \ge 0$	$\frac{x^4}{223} - \frac{356}{} + x^2\left(\frac{y^2}{45} - \frac{170}{} - \frac{y}{9}\right) +$ $\frac{y^3}{89} + \frac{y^2}{68} - \frac{1}{74} + \frac{y}{55}\left(\frac{}{}\right) + \frac{y^4}{146}$ $\frac{y^3}{95} + \frac{y^2}{37} + \frac{y}{366} + 1 < 0$	0.33
	4	Twisted	$x^2 - 2xy^2 + 3zx - y^2$ $-y + x^2 - 1 \ge 0 \wedge$ $-\frac{1}{120}(-x^6 - y^6) + x^2z^2 -$ $x^2 + \frac{1}{6}(x^4 + 2x^2y^2 + y^4) +$ $y^2z^2 - y^2 - 4 \le 0$	$w^2 + 4(x-y)^4 + (x+y)^2 - 80 \le 0 \wedge$ $-w^2(x-y)^4 + 100(x+y)^2 - 3000 \ge 0$	$-\frac{x^4}{160} + x^3\left(\frac{y}{170} - \frac{1}{113}\right) + x^2\left(\frac{y^2}{225} + \frac{y}{76} + \frac{2}{27}\right) +$ $x\left(\frac{y^3}{259} + \frac{y^2}{63} + \frac{5y}{51} - \frac{1}{316}\right) - \frac{y^4}{183} + \frac{y^3}{94} + \frac{y^2}{14} + \frac{y}{255} - 1 < 0$	140.62
with/without rounding	5	Ultimate	$(x^2 + y^2 - 3.8025 \le 0 \wedge y \ge 0) \vee$ $(x-1)^2 + y^2 - 0.9025 \le 0) \wedge$ $(x+1)^2 + y^2 - 0.09 > 0 \wedge$ $(x+1)^2 + y^2 - 1.1025 \ge 0 \vee$ $-\frac{1}{25} \le 0$	$(-3.8025 + x^2 + y^2 \le 0 \wedge -w \ge 0 \vee$ $-0.9025 + (-1-x)^2 + y^2 \le 0) \wedge$ $-0.09 + (-1-x)^2 + y^2 > 0 \wedge$ $-1.1025 + (1-x)^2 + y^2 \ge 0$ $-\frac{1}{25} + (1-x)^2 + y^2 \le 0$	$\frac{x^7}{27} + x^6\left(-\frac{y}{5} - \frac{1}{96}\right) + x^5\left(\frac{2y^2}{3} - \frac{32}{} - \frac{1}{}\right) +$ $x^4\left(-\frac{2y^3}{9} + \frac{y}{3} + \frac{1}{31}\right) + x^3\left(\frac{y^4}{11} - \frac{y^2}{10} - \frac{13}{}\right) +$ $x^2\left(\frac{y^5}{18} - \frac{y^4}{3} + \frac{y}{10} - \frac{1}{32}\right) +$ $\frac{y^6}{71} - \frac{2y^4}{11} - \frac{y^3}{25} - \frac{y^2}{45} - \frac{3}{8}\left(\frac{}{}\right) +$ $\frac{y^6}{48} - \frac{y^5}{7} + \frac{y^4}{6} - \frac{y^3}{2} + \frac{y^2}{59} + \frac{y}{85} - 1 < 0$	48.82
	6	DCAR16-4 [14]	$-x_1^2 + 4x_1 + x_2 - 4 \ge 0 \wedge$ $-x_1 - x_2 + 3 - y^2 > 0$ $1 - a^2 - b^2 > 0 \wedge a^2 + b - 1 - x = 0 \wedge$ $b + bx + 1 - y = 0$	$-3x_1^2 - x_2^2 + 1 \ge 0 \wedge x_2 - x^2 \ge 0$	$1 - \frac{3x_1}{4} - x_2^2 < 0$	0.16
	7	CAV13-1 [11]		$x^2 - 2y^2 - 4 > 0$	$-1 + \frac{x^2}{2} - \frac{y}{3} + \frac{xy}{3} - \frac{y^2}{4} < 0$	3.25
	8	CAV13-2 [11]	$x^2 + y^2 - 2 \ge 0 \wedge$ $1.2x^2 + y^2 + xz = 0$	$20 - 3x^2 - 4y^2 - 10z^2 \ge 0 \wedge$ $x^2 + y^2 - z - 1 = 0$	$105x^4 + x^2(140y^2 + 24y(5x+7) + 35x(3x+8)) +$ $2(70y^3 + 5y^2(12z^2 + 21z + 28) - 14y(6z^3 + 5z^2 +$ $10) - 35(3z^4 + 8z^2 + 4z - 9)) < 14x(20z^2(x+1) +$ $10y^2(x+2) + 3) - 3y(4z^2 - 5z + 4) - 20z(x^2 + 2)$	3857.89
	9	CAV13-3 [11]	$wc < 49.61 \wedge fa = 0.5418wc^2 \wedge$ $fr = 1000 - fa \wedge ac = 0.0005fr \wedge$ $wc_1 = wc + ac$	$wc_1 \ge 49.61$	$-1 + \frac{2wc_1}{99} < 0$	40.63
	10	Parallel parabola	$y - x^2 - 1 \ge 0$	$y - x^2 < 0$	$\frac{1}{2} + x^2 < y$	4.50
	11	Parallel halfplane	$y - x - 1 \ge 0$	$y - x + 1 < 0$	$x < y$	2.46
	12	Sharper-1 [33]	$y + 1 < 0$	$x^2 + 1 \le 0$	$2 + y < y^2$	2.19
	13	Sharper-2 [33]	$y - x > 0 \wedge x + y > 0$	$x^2 + y \le 0$	$y > 0$	2.38
	14	Coincident	$x + y > 0 \vee x + y < 0$	$x + y = 0$	$(x+y)^2 > 0$	0.18
	15	Adjacent	$y - 2 > 0$	$-x^2 + y \le 0$	$x^2 < y$	0.25
with rounding	16	DCAR16-2 [14]	$-y_1 + x_1 - 2 \ge 0 \wedge 2x_1 - x_1 - 1 > 0 \wedge$ $-x_1^2 - x_2^2 + 2x_1y_1 - 2y_1 + 2x_1 \ge 0 \wedge$ $-y_1^2 - y_1^2 - 2 - 4y_1 + x_2y_1 - x_2 \ge 0 \wedge$ $xx_1^2 + 2yx_1 \ge 0 \wedge x_1 - x_1 = 0 \wedge 2x_1 + y \ge 0$	$-y_1 + x_1 - 2 \ge 0 \wedge 2x_1 - x_1 - 1 > 0 \wedge$ $-x_1^2 - 4x_2^2 + 4x_2y_1 + 3x_1 - 6x_2 - 2 \ge 0 \wedge$ $-x_2^2 - x_1^2 - x_2^2 + x_1 + x_1 - 2x_2 - 1 \ge 0$	$2xa + 4ya > 5$	12.33
	17	CAV13-4 [11]	$y = y_1 + yx_1 - y_1 = 0 \wedge -x_1 - 1 = 0 \wedge xa + yx < 0$	$-x_1^2 - 4x_2^2 + 4x_2y_1 + 3x_1 - 6x_2 - 2 \ge 0$	$2xa + 4ya > 5$	3.10
beyond polynomials	18	TACAS16 [15]	$y - x^2 \ge 0$	$y + \cos x - 0.8 \le 0$	$15x^2 < 4 + 20y$	12.71
	19	Transcendental	$\sin x \ge 0.6$	$\sin x \le 0.4$	SVM failed	–
unbalanced	20	Unbalanced	$x > 0 \vee x < 0$	$x = 0$	$x^2 > 0$	0.11

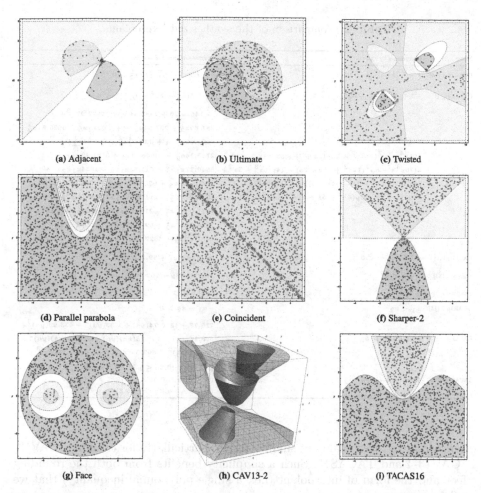

(a) Adjacent   (b) Ultimate   (c) Twisted

(d) Parallel parabola   (e) Coincident   (f) Sharper-2

(g) Face   (h) CAV13-2   (i) TACAS16

Fig. 4. Visualization in NIL on a selected set of examples. Legends: gray region: $[\![\phi]\!]$, blue region: $[\![\psi]\!]$, pink region: $[\![I]\!]$ with a valid interpolant I, red dots: X^+, blue dots: X^-, circled dots: support vectors. Sample points are hidden in 3D-graphics for a clear presentation.

that admit polynomial interpolants. Due to theoretical limitations of existing approaches as elaborated in Sect. 1, none of the aforementioned methods can cope with as many cases in Table 1 as NIL can. For instances, the Twisted example as depicted in Fig. 4(c) falls beyond the scope of concave quadratic formulas and thus cannot be addressed by the approach in [14], while the Parallel parabola example as shown in Fig. 4(d) needs an infinite combination of linear constraints as an interpolant when performing the technique in [15] and hence not of practical use, to name just a few. Moreover, we list in Table 2 a comparison of the synthesized interpolants against works where the benchmark examples are collected from. As being immediately obvious from Table 2, our technique

Table 2. Comparison of the synthesized interpolants.

Name	Interpolants by NIL	Interpolants from the sources
UCAR16-1 [14]	$1 - \frac{3x_1}{4} - \frac{x_2}{2} < 0$	$-3 + 2x_1 + x_1^2 + \frac{1}{2}x_2^2 > 0$
CAV13-1 [11]	$-1 + \frac{x^2}{2} - \frac{y}{3} + \frac{xy}{3} - \frac{y^2}{4} < 0$	$436.45(x^2 - 2y^2 - 4) + \frac{1}{2} \le 0$
CAV13-2 [11]	$105x^4 + x^2(140y^2 + 24y(5z+7) + 35z(3z+8)) + 2(70y^3 z + 5y^2(12z^2 + 21z + 28) - 14y(6z^3 + 5z^2 + 10) - 35(3z^4 + 8z^2 + 4z - 9)) < 14x(20x^2(z+1) + 10y^2(z+2) - 3y(4z^2 - 5z + 4) - 20z(z^2 + 2))$	$-14629.26 + 2983.44x_3 + 10972.97x_3^2 + 297.62x_2 + 297.64x_2x_3 + 0.02x_2x_3^2 + 9625.61x_2^2 - 1161.80x_2^2x_3 + 0.01x_2^2x_3^2 + 811.93x_2^3 + 2745.14x_2^4 - 10648.11x_1 + 3101.42x_1x_3 + 8646.17x_1x_3^2 + 511.84x_1x_2 - 1034x_1x_2x_3 + 0.02x_1x_2x_3^2 + 9233.66x_1x_2^2 + 1342.55x_1x_2^2x_3 - 138.70x_1x_2^3 + 11476.61x_1^2 - 3737.70x_1^2x_3 + 4071.65x_1^2x_3^2 - 2153.00x_1 2x_2 + 373.14x_1^2x_2x_3 + 7616.18x_1^2x_2^2 + 8950.77x_1^3 + 1937.92x_1^3x_3 - 64.07x_1^3x_2 + 4827.25x_1^4 > 0$
CAV13-3 [11]	$-1 + \frac{2vc_1}{99} < 0$	$-1.3983vc_1 + 69.358 > 0$
Sharper-1 [33]	$2 + y < y^2$	$34y^2 - 68y - 102 \ge 0$
Sharper-2 [33]	$y > 0$	$8y + 4x^2 > 0$
UCAR16-2 [14]	$x_1 < x_2$	$-x_1 + x_2 > 0$
CAV13-4 [11]	$2xa + 4ya > 5$	$716.77 + 1326.74(ya) + 1.33(ya)^2 + 433.90(ya)^3 + 668.16(xa) - 155.86(xa)(ya) + 317.29(xa)(ya)^2 + 222.00(xa)^2 + 592.39(xa)^2(ya) + 271.11(xa)^3$
TACAS16 [15]	$15x^2 < 4 + 20y$	$y > 1.8 \lor (0.59 \le y \le 1.8 \land -1.35 \le x \le 1.35) \lor (0.09 \le y < 0.59 \land -0.77 \le x \le 0.77) \lor (y \ge 0 \land -0.3 \le x \le 0.3)$

often produces interpolants of simpler forms, particularly for examples CAV13-2, CAV13-4 and TACAS16. Such a simplicity benefits from both the rounding effect and the form of interpolant (i.e., a single polynomial inequality) that we tend to construct.

Bottleneck of Efficiency and Potential Solutions. The current implementation of NIL works promisingly for small examples; it does not scale to interpolation problems with large numbers of common variables, as reported in Table 1. The bottleneck stems from quantifier eliminations performed within every iteration of the learning process, for entailment checking and generating counterexamples. We pose here several potential solutions that are expected to significantly reduce computational efforts: (i) substitute general purpose QE procedure that perform CAD by the so-called variant quantifier-elimination (VQE) algorithm [21], which features singly-exponential complexity in the number of variables. This however requires a careful inspection of whether our problem meets the geometric conditions imposed by VQE; (ii) incorporate relaxation schemes, e.g., Lagrangian relaxation and sum-of-squares decompositions [34], and complement with QE only when the relaxation fails to produce desired results.

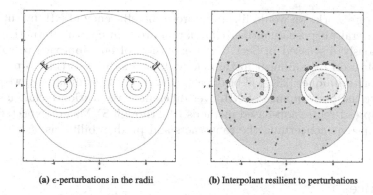

(a) ϵ-perturbations in the radii   (b) Interpolant resilient to perturbations

Fig. 5. ϵ-Face: introducing perturbations (with ϵ up to 0.5) in the Face example. The synthesized interpolant is resilient to any ϵ-perturbation in the radii satisfying $-0.5 \leq \epsilon \leq 0.5$.

6 Taming Perturbations in Parameters

An interpolant synthesized by the SVM-based technique features inherent robustness due to the way optimal-margin classifier is defined (Sect. 2). That is, the validity of such an interpolant is not easily perturbed by changes (in the feature space) in the formulae to be interpolated. It is straightforward in NIL to deal with interpolation problems under explicitly specified perturbations, which are treated as constraints over fresh variables. An example named ϵ-Face is depicted in Fig. 5, which perturbs $\langle \phi, \psi \rangle$ in the Face example as $\phi \,\widehat{=}\, -0.5 \leq \epsilon_1 \leq 0.5 \wedge ((x+4)^2 + y^2 - (1+\epsilon_1)^2 \leq 0 \vee (x-4)^2 + y^2 - (1+\epsilon_1)^2 \leq 0)$ and $\psi \,\widehat{=}\, -0.5 \leq \epsilon_2 \leq 0.5 \wedge x^2 + y^2 - 64 \leq 0 \wedge (x+4)^2 + y^2 - (3+\epsilon_2)^2 \geq 0 \wedge (x-4)^2 + y^2 - (3+\epsilon_2)^2 \geq 0$. The synthesized interpolant over common variables of ϕ and ψ is $\frac{x^4}{139} + \frac{x^3 y}{268} + x^2 \left(\frac{y^2}{39} - \frac{11}{36} \right) + x \left(-\frac{y^3}{52} - \frac{y^2}{157} - \frac{y}{52} - \frac{1}{116} \right) + \frac{y^4}{25} - \frac{y^3}{182} + \frac{2y^2}{19} - \frac{y}{218} + 1 < 0$ which is hence resilient to any ϵ-perturbation in the radii satisfying $-0.5 \leq \epsilon \leq 0.5$, as illustrated in Fig. 5(b).

7 Conclusions

We have presented a unified, counterexample-guided method named NIL for generating polynomial interpolants over the general quantifier-free theory of nonlinear arithmetic. Our method is based on classification techniques with space transformations and kernel tricks as established in the community of machine-learning. We proved the soundness of NIL and proposed sufficient conditions for its completeness and convergence. The applicability and effectiveness of our technique are demonstrated experimentally on a collection of representative benchmarks from the literature, including those extracted from program verification. Experimental results indicated that our method suffices to address more interpolation tasks, including those with perturbations in parameters, and in many cases synthesizes simpler interpolants compared with existing approaches.

For future work, we would like to improve the efficiency of NIL by substituting the general purpose quantifier-elimination procedure with alternative methods previously discussed in Sect. 5. An extension of our approach to cater for the combination of nonlinear arithmetic with EUFs, by resorting to predicate-abstraction techniques [23], will be of particular interest. Additionally, we plan to investigate the performance of NIL over different classification techniques, e.g., the widespread regression-based methods [19], though SVMs are expected to be more competent concerning the robustness and predictability, as also observed in [37].

References

1. Bennett, K.P., Bredensteiner, E.J.: Duality and geometry in SVM classifiers. In: ICML 2000, pp. 57–64 (2000)
2. Bishop, C.M.: Pattern Recognition and Machine Learning, pp. 326–328. Springer, New York (2006)
3. Boser, B.E., Guyon, I., Vapnik, V.: A training algorithm for optimal margin classifiers. In: COLT 1992, pp. 144–152 (1992)
4. Bourbaki, N.: Topological Vector Spaces. Elements of Mathematics. Springer, Heidelberg (1987). https://doi.org/10.1007/978-3-642-61715-7
5. Chang, C., Lin, C.: LIBSVM: a library for support vector machines. ACM TIST **2**(3), 27:1–27:27 (2011)
6. Chen, M., Wang, J., An, J., Zhan, B., Kapur, D., Zhan, N.: NIL: learning nonlinear interpolants (full version). http://lcs.ios.ac.cn/~chenms/papers/CADE-27_FULL.pdf
7. Cimatti, A., Griggio, A., Sebastiani, R.: Efficient interpolant generation in satisfiability modulo theories. In: Ramakrishnan, C.R., Rehof, J. (eds.) TACAS 2008. LNCS, vol. 4963, pp. 397–412. Springer, Heidelberg (2008). https://doi.org/10.1007/978-3-540-78800-3_30
8. Clarke, E., Grumberg, O., Jha, S., Lu, Y., Veith, H.: Counterexample-guided abstraction refinement. In: Emerson, E.A., Sistla, A.P. (eds.) CAV 2000. LNCS, vol. 1855, pp. 154–169. Springer, Heidelberg (2000). https://doi.org/10.1007/10722167_15
9. Collins, G.E.: Quantifier elimination for real closed fields by cylindrical algebraic decompostion. In: Brakhage, H. (ed.) GI-Fachtagung 1975. LNCS, vol. 33, pp. 134–183. Springer, Heidelberg (1975). https://doi.org/10.1007/3-540-07407-4_17
10. Craig, W.: Linear reasoning. A new form of the Herbrand-Gentzen theorem. J. Symb. Log. **22**(3), 250–268 (1957)
11. Dai, L., Xia, B., Zhan, N.: Generating non-linear interpolants by semidefinite programming. In: Sharygina, N., Veith, H. (eds.) CAV 2013. LNCS, vol. 8044, pp. 364–380. Springer, Heidelberg (2013). https://doi.org/10.1007/978-3-642-39799-8_25
12. Dathathri, S., Arechiga, N., Gao, S., Murray, R.M.: Learning-based abstractions for nonlinear constraint solving. In: IJCAI 2017, pp. 592–599 (2017)
13. D'Silva, V., Kroening, D., Purandare, M., Weissenbacher, G.: Interpolant strength. In: Barthe, G., Hermenegildo, M. (eds.) VMCAI 2010. LNCS, vol. 5944, pp. 129–145. Springer, Heidelberg (2010). https://doi.org/10.1007/978-3-642-11319-2_12

14. Gan, T., Dai, L., Xia, B., Zhan, N., Kapur, D., Chen, M.: Interpolant synthesis for quadratic polynomial inequalities and combination with *EUF*. In: Olivetti, N., Tiwari, A. (eds.) IJCAR 2016. LNCS (LNAI), vol. 9706, pp. 195–212. Springer, Cham (2016). https://doi.org/10.1007/978-3-319-40229-1_14

15. Gao, S., Zufferey, D.: Interpolants in nonlinear theories over the reals. In: Chechik, M., Raskin, J.-F. (eds.) TACAS 2016. LNCS, vol. 9636, pp. 625–641. Springer, Heidelberg (2016). https://doi.org/10.1007/978-3-662-49674-9_41

16. Gilbert, S.: A nullstellensatz and a positivstellensatz in semialgebraic geometry. Math. Ann. **207**(2), 87–97 (1974)

17. Graf, S., Saidi, H.: Construction of abstract state graphs with PVS. In: Grumberg, O. (ed.) CAV 1997. LNCS, vol. 1254, pp. 72–83. Springer, Heidelberg (1997). https://doi.org/10.1007/3-540-63166-6_10

18. Gulavani, B.S., Chakraborty, S., Nori, A.V., Rajamani, S.K.: Automatically refining abstract interpretations. In: Ramakrishnan, C.R., Rehof, J. (eds.) TACAS 2008. LNCS, vol. 4963, pp. 443–458. Springer, Heidelberg (2008). https://doi.org/10.1007/978-3-540-78800-3_33

19. Hastie, T., Tibshirani, R., Friedman, J.: The Elements of Statistical Learning: Data Mining, Inference, and Prediction. SSS, 2nd edn. Springer, New York (2009). https://doi.org/10.1007/978-0-387-84858-7

20. Henzinger, T.A., Jhala, R., Majumdar, R., McMillan, K.L.: Abstractions from proofs. In: POPL 2004, pp. 232–244 (2004)

21. Hong, H., Din, M.S.E.: Variant quantifier elimination. J. Symb. Comput. **47**(7), 883–901 (2012)

22. Jha, S., Gulwani, S., Seshia, S.A., Tiwari, A.: Oracle-guided component-based program synthesis. In: ICSE 2010, pp. 215–224 (2010)

23. Jhala, R., Podelski, A., Rybalchenko, Λ.: Predicate abstraction for program verification. In: Clarke, E., Henzinger, T., Veith, H., Bloem, R. (eds.) Handbook of Model Checking, pp. 447–491. Springer, Cham (2018). https://doi.org/10.1007/978-3-319-10575-8_15

24. Jung, Y., Lee, W., Wang, B.-Y., Yi, K.: Predicate generation for learning-based quantifier-free loop invariant inference. In: Abdulla, P.A., Leino, K.R.M. (eds.) TACAS 2011. LNCS, vol. 6605, pp. 205–219. Springer, Heidelberg (2011). https://doi.org/10.1007/978-3-642-19835-9_17

25. Kapur, D., Majumdar, R., Zarba, C.G.: Interpolation for data structures. In: FSE 2006, pp. 105–116 (2006)

26. Kovács, L., Voronkov, A.: Interpolation and symbol elimination. In: Schmidt, R.A. (ed.) CADE 2009. LNCS (LNAI), vol. 5663, pp. 199–213. Springer, Heidelberg (2009). https://doi.org/10.1007/978-3-642-02959-2_17

27. Krajíček, J.: Interpolation theorems, lower bounds for proof systems, and independence results for bounded arithmetic. J. Symb. Log. **62**(2), 457–486 (1997)

28. Kupferschmid, S., Becker, B.: Craig interpolation in the presence of non-linear constraints. In: Fahrenberg, U., Tripakis, S. (eds.) FORMATS 2011. LNCS, vol. 6919, pp. 240–255. Springer, Heidelberg (2011). https://doi.org/10.1007/978-3-642-24310-3_17

29. Lang, S.: Introduction to Diophantine Approximations: New Expanded Edition. Springer, New York (2012)

30. McMillan, K.L.: Interpolation and SAT-based model checking. In: Hunt, W.A., Somenzi, F. (eds.) CAV 2003. LNCS, vol. 2725, pp. 1–13. Springer, Heidelberg (2003). https://doi.org/10.1007/978-3-540-45069-6_1

31. McMillan, K.L.: An interpolating theorem prover. In: Jensen, K., Podelski, A. (eds.) TACAS 2004. LNCS, vol. 2988, pp. 16–30. Springer, Heidelberg (2004). https://doi.org/10.1007/978-3-540-24730-2_2

32. McMillan, K.L.: Quantified invariant generation using an interpolating saturation prover. In: Ramakrishnan, C.R., Rehof, J. (eds.) TACAS 2008. LNCS, vol. 4963, pp. 413–427. Springer, Heidelberg (2008). https://doi.org/10.1007/978-3-540-78800-3_31

33. Okudono, T., Nishida, Y., Kojima, K., Suenaga, K., Kido, K., Hasuo, I.: Sharper and simpler nonlinear interpolants for program verification. In: Chang, B.-Y.E. (ed.) APLAS 2017. LNCS, vol. 10695, pp. 491–513. Springer, Cham (2017). https://doi.org/10.1007/978-3-319-71237-6_24

34. Parrilo, P.A.: Semidefinite programming relaxations for semialgebraic problems. Math. Program. **96**(2), 293–320 (2003)

35. Pudlák, P.: Lower bounds for resolution and cutting plane proofs and monotone computations. J. Symb. Log. **62**(3), 981–998 (1997)

36. Rybalchenko, A., Sofronie-Stokkermans, V.: Constraint solving for interpolation. In: Cook, B., Podelski, A. (eds.) VMCAI 2007. LNCS, vol. 4349, pp. 346–362. Springer, Heidelberg (2007). https://doi.org/10.1007/978-3-540-69738-1_25

37. Sharma, R., Nori, A.V., Aiken, A.: Interpolants as classifiers. In: Madhusudan, P., Seshia, S.A. (eds.) CAV 2012. LNCS, vol. 7358, pp. 71–87. Springer, Heidelberg (2012). https://doi.org/10.1007/978-3-642-31424-7_11

38. Sofronie-Stokkermans, V.: Interpolation in local theory extensions. In: Furbach, U., Shankar, N. (eds.) IJCAR 2006. LNCS (LNAI), vol. 4130, pp. 235–250. Springer, Heidelberg (2006). https://doi.org/10.1007/11814771_21

39. Sofronie-Stokkermans, V.: On interpolation and symbol elimination in theory extensions. In: Olivetti, N., Tiwari, A. (eds.) IJCAR 2016. LNCS (LNAI), vol. 9706, pp. 273–289. Springer, Cham (2016). https://doi.org/10.1007/978-3-319-40229-1_19

40. Solar-Lezama, A., Rabbah, R.M., Bodík, R., Ebcioglu, K.: Programming by sketching for bit-streaming programs. In: PLDI 2005, pp. 281–294 (2005)

41. Strzeboński, A.W.: Real root isolation for exp-log functions. In: ISSAC 2008, pp. 303–314 (2008)

42. Strzeboński, A.W.: Real root isolation for tame elementary functions. In: ISSAC 2009, pp. 341–350 (2009)

43. Strzeboński, A.W.: Cylindrical decomposition for systems transcendental in the first variable. J. Symb. Comput. **46**(11), 1284–1290 (2011)

44. Tarski, A.: A Decision Method for Elementary Algebra and Geometry. University of California Press, Berkeley (1951)

45. Vladimir, V.: Pattern recognition using generalized portrait method. Autom. Remote Control **24**, 774–780 (1963)

46. Yorsh, G., Musuvathi, M.: A combination method for generating interpolants. In: Nieuwenhuis, R. (ed.) CADE 2005. LNCS (LNAI), vol. 3632, pp. 353–368. Springer, Heidelberg (2005). https://doi.org/10.1007/11532231_26

47. Zhang, J., Feng, Y.: Obtaining exact value by approximate computations. Sci. China Ser. A Math. **50**(9), 1361 (2007)

ENIGMA-NG: Efficient Neural and Gradient-Boosted Inference Guidance for E

Karel Chvalovský[(⊠)], Jan Jakubův, Martin Suda, and Josef Urban

Czech Technical University in Prague, Prague, Czech Republic
karel@chvalovsky.cz

Abstract. We describe an efficient implementation of given clause selection in saturation-based automated theorem provers, extending the previous ENIGMA approach. Unlike in the first ENIGMA implementation where a fast linear classifier is trained and used together with manually engineered features, we have started to experiment with more sophisticated state-of-the-art machine learning methods such as gradient boosted trees and recursive neural networks. In particular, the latter approach poses challenges in terms of efficiency of clause evaluation, however, we show that deep integration of the neural evaluation with the ATP datastructures can largely amortize this cost and lead to competitive real-time results. Both methods are evaluated on a large dataset of theorem proving problems and compared with the previous approaches. The resulting methods improve on the manually designed clause guidance, providing the first practically convincing application of gradient-boosted and neural clause guidance in saturation-style automated theorem provers.

1 Introduction

Automated theorem provers (ATPs) have been developed for decades by manually designing proof calculi and search heuristics. Their power has been growing and they are already very useful, e.g., as parts of large interactive theorem proving (ITP) verification toolchains (hammers) [5]. On the other hand, with small exceptions, ATPs are still significantly weaker than trained mathematicians in finding proofs in most research domains.

Recently, machine learning over large formal corpora created from ITP libraries [24,32,42] has started to be used to develop guidance of ATP systems [2,30,44]. This has already produced strong systems for selecting relevant facts for proving new conjectures over large formal libraries [1,4,13]. More recently, machine learning has also started to be used to guide the internal search of the ATP systems. In sophisticated saturation-style provers this has been done

---

Supported by the ERC Consolidator grant no. 649043 AI4REASON, and by the Czech project AI&Reasoning CZ.02.1.01/0.0/0.0/15_003/0000466 and the European Regional Development Fund.

© Springer Nature Switzerland AG 2019
P. Fontaine (Ed.): CADE 2019, LNAI 11716, pp. 197–215, 2019.
https://doi.org/10.1007/978-3-030-29436-6_12

by feedback loops for strategy invention [21,38,43] and by using supervised learning [19,31] to select the next given clause [35]. In the simpler connection tableau systems such as LeanCoP [34], supervised learning has been used to choose the next tableau extension step [25,45] and first experiments with Monte-Carlo guided proof search [12] and reinforcement learning [26] have been done.[1]

In this work, we add two state-of-the-art machine learning methods to the ENIGMA [19,20] algorithm that efficiently guides saturation-style proof search. The first one trains gradient boosted trees on efficiently extracted manually designed (handcrafted) clause features. The second method removes the need for manually designed features, and instead uses end-to-end training of recursive neural networks. Such architectures, when implemented naively, are typically expensive and may be impractical for saturation-style ATP. We show that deep integration of the neural evaluation with the ATP data-structures can largely amortize this cost, allowing competitive performance.

The rest of the paper is structured as follows. Section 2 introduces saturation-based automated theorem proving with the emphasis on machine learning. Section 3 briefly summarizes our previous work with handcrafted features in ENIGMA and then extends the previously published ENIGMA with additional classifiers based on decision trees (Sect. 3.3) and simple feature hashing (Sect. 3.4). Section 4 presents our new approach of applying neural networks for ATP guidance. Section 5 provides experimental evaluation of our work. We conclude in Sect. 6.

2   Automated Theorem Proving with Machine Learning

State-of-the-art saturation-based automated theorem provers (ATPs) for first-order logic (FOL), such as E [40] and Vampire [28] are today's most advanced tools for general reasoning across a variety of mathematical and scientific domains. Many ATPs employ the *given clause algorithm*, translating the input FOL problem $T \cup \{\neg C\}$ into a refutationally equivalent set of clauses. The search for a contradiction is performed maintaining sets of *processed* (P) and *unprocessed* (U) clauses. The algorithm repeatedly selects a *given clause* g from U, moves g to P, and extends U with all clauses inferred with g and P. This process continues until a contradiction is found, U becomes empty, or a resource limit is reached. The size of the unprocessed set U grows quickly and it is a well-known fact that the selection of the right given clause is crucial for success. Machine learning from a large number of proofs and proof searches may help guide the selection of the given clauses.

E allows the user to select a *proof search strategy* $\mathcal{S}$ to guide the proof search. An E strategy $\mathcal{S}$ specifies parameters such as term ordering, literal selection function, clause splitting, paramodulation setting, premise selection, and, most importantly for us, the *given clause selection* mechanism. The given clause selection in E is implemented using a list of priority queues. Each priority queue stores

---

[1] Other, less immediately relevant, previous work on combining machine learning with automated theorem proving includes, e.g., [6,8,9,11,39].

all the generated clauses in a specific order determined by a clause *weight function*. The clause weight function assigns a numeric (real) value to each clause, and the clauses with smaller weights ("lighter clauses") are prioritized. To select a given clause, one of the queues is chosen in a round robin manner, and the clause at the front of the chosen queue gets processed. Each queue is additionally assigned a *frequency* which amounts to the relative number of clause selections from that particular queue. Frequencies can be used to prefer one queue over another. We use the following notation to denote the list of priority queues with frequencies f_i and weight functions $\mathcal{W}_i$:

$$(f_1 * \mathcal{W}_1, \ldots, f_k * \mathcal{W}_k).$$

To facilitate machine learning research, E implements an option under which each successful proof search gets analyzed and outputs a list of clauses annotated as either *positive* or *negative* training examples. Each processed clause that is present in the final proof is classified as positive. On the other hand, processing of clauses not present in the final proof was redundant, hence they are classified as negative. Our goal is to learn such classification (possibly conditioned on the problem and its features) in a way that generalizes and leads to solving previously unsolved related problems.

Given a set of problems $\mathcal{P}$, we can run E with a strategy $\mathcal{S}$ and obtain positive and negative training data $\mathcal{T}$ from each of the successful proof searches. In this work, we use three different machine learning methods to learn the clause classification given by $\mathcal{T}$, each method yielding a *classifier* or *model* $\mathcal{M}$. The concrete structure of $\mathcal{M}$ depends on the machine learning method used, as explained in detailed below. With any method, $\mathcal{M}$ provides a function to compute the weight of an arbitrary clause. This weight function is then used in E to guide further proof runs.

A model $\mathcal{M}$ can be used in E in different ways. We use two methods to combine $\mathcal{M}$ with a strategy $\mathcal{S}$. Either (1) we use $\mathcal{M}$ to select *all* the given clauses, or (2) we combine $\mathcal{M}$ with the given clause guidance from $\mathcal{S}$ so that roughly half of the clauses are selected by $\mathcal{M}$. We denote the resulting E strategies as (1) $\mathcal{S} \odot \mathcal{M}$, and (2) $\mathcal{S} \oplus \mathcal{M}$. The two strategies are equal up to the priority queues for given clause selection which are changed ($\rightsquigarrow$) as follows.

in $\mathcal{S} \odot \mathcal{M}$: $(f_1 * \mathcal{W}_1, \ldots, f_k * \mathcal{W}_k) \rightsquigarrow (1 * \mathcal{M})$,
in $\mathcal{S} \oplus \mathcal{M}$: $(f_1 * \mathcal{W}_1, \ldots, f_k * \mathcal{W}_k) \rightsquigarrow ((\sum f_i) * \mathcal{M}, f_1 * \mathcal{W}_1, \ldots, f_k * \mathcal{W}_k)$.

The strategy $\mathcal{S} \oplus \mathcal{M}$ usually performs better in practice as it helps to counter overfitting by combining powers with the original strategy $\mathcal{S}$. The strategy $\mathcal{S} \odot \mathcal{M}$ usually provides additional proved problems, gaining additional training data, and it is useful for the evaluation of the training phase. When $\mathcal{S} \odot \mathcal{M}$ performs better than $\mathcal{S}$, it indicates that $\mathcal{M}$ has learned the training data well. When it performs much worse, it indicates that $\mathcal{M}$ is not very well-trained. The strategy $\mathcal{S} \oplus \mathcal{M}$ should always perform better than $\mathcal{S}$, otherwise the guidance of $\mathcal{M}$ is not useful. Additional indication of successful training can be obtained from the number of clauses processed during a successful proof search. The strategy $\mathcal{S} \odot \mathcal{M}$

should run with much fewer processed clauses, in some cases even better than $S \oplus M$, as the original S might divert the proof search. In the best case, when M would learn to guide for certain problem perfectly, the number of processed clauses would not need to exceed the length of the proof.

It is important to combine a model M only with a "compatible" strategy S. For example, let us consider a model M trained on samples obtained with another strategy S_0 which has a different term ordering than S. As the term ordering can change term normal forms, the clauses encountered in the proof search with S might look quite different from the training clauses. This may be an issue unless the trained models are independent of symbol names, which is not (yet) our case. Additional complications might arise as term orderings and literal selection might change the proof space and the original proofs might not be reachable. Hence we only combine M with the strategy S which provided the examples on which M was trained.

3   ATP Guidance with Handcrafted Clause Features

In order to employ a machine learning method for ATP guidance, first-order clauses need to be represented in a format recognized by the selected learning method. A common approach is to manually extract a finite set of various properties of clauses called *features*, and to encode these clause features by a fixed-length numeric vector. Various machine learning methods can handle numeric vectors and their success heavily depends on the selection of correct clause features. In this section, we work with handcrafted clause features which, we believe, capture information important for ATP guidance.

ENIGMA [19,20] is our *efficient* learning-based method for guiding given clause selection in saturation-based ATPs. Sections 3.1 and 3.2 briefly summarizes our previous work. Sections 3.3 and 3.4 describe extensions, first presented in this work.

3.1   ENIGMA Clause Features

So far the development of ENIGMA has focused on fast and practically usable methods, allowing E users to directly benefit from our work. Various possible choices of efficient clause features for theorem prover guidance have been experimented with [19,20,26,27]. The original ENIGMA [19] uses term-tree walks of length 3 as features, while the second version [20] reaches better results by employing various additional features. In particular, the following types of features are used (see [19, Sec. 3.2] and [20, Sec. 2] for details):

Vertical Features are (top-down-)oriented term-tree walks of length 3. For example, the unit clause $P(f(a,b))$ contains only features (P,f,a) and (P,f,b).

Horizontal Features are horizontal cuts of a term tree. For every term $f(t_1,\ldots,t_n)$ in the clause, we introduce the feature $f(s_1,\ldots,s_n)$ where s_i is the top-level symbol of t_i.

Symbol Features are various statistics about clause symbols, namely, the number of occurrences and the maximal depth for each symbol.

Length Features count the clause length and the numbers of positive and negative literals.

Conjecture Features embed information about the conjecture being proved into the feature vector. In this way, ENIGMA can provide conjecture-dependent predictions.

Since there are only finitely many features in any training data, the features can be serially numbered. This numbering is fixed for each experiment. Let n be the number of different features appearing in the training data. A clause C is translated to a feature vector φ_C whose i-th member counts the number of occurrences of the i-th feature in C. Hence every clause is represented by a sparse numeric vector of length n.

With conjecture features, instead of using the vector φ_C of length n, we use a vector (φ_C, φ_G) of length $2n$ where φ_G contains the features of the conjecture G. For a training clause C, G corresponds to the conjecture of the proof search where C was selected as a given clause. When classifying a clause C during proof search, G corresponds to the conjecture currently being proved. When the conjecture consists of several clauses, their vectors are computed separately and then summed (except for features corresponding to maxima, such as the maximal symbol depth, where maximum is taken instead).

3.2 ATP Guidance with Fast Linear Classifiers

ENIGMA has so far used simple but fast linear classifiers such as *linear SVM* and *logistic regression* efficiently implemented by the LIBLINEAR open source library [10]. In order to employ them, clause representation by numeric feature vectors described above in Sect. 3.1 is used. Clausal training data T are translated to a set of fixed-size labeled vectors. Each (typically sparse) vector of length n is labeled either as positive or negative.

The labeled numeric vectors serve as an input to LIBLINEAR which, after the training, outputs a model M consisting mainly of a weight vector w of length n. The main cost in classifying a clause C consists in computing its feature vector φ_C and its dot product with the weight vector $p = \varphi_C \cdot w$. ENIGMA the assigns to the positively classified clauses (i.e., $p \geq 0$) a chosen small weight (1.0) and a higher weight (10.0) to the negatively classified ones (i.e., $p < 0$). This weight is then used inside E to guide given clause selection as described in Sect. 2.

The training data obtained from the proof runs are typically not balanced with respect to the number of positive and negative examples. Usually, there are many more negative examples and the method of *Accuracy-Balancing Boosting* [20] was found useful in practice to improve precision on the positive training data. This is done as follows. Given training data T we create a LIBLINEAR classifier M, test M on the training data, and collect the positives mis-classified by M. We then repeat (*boost*) the mis-classified positives in the training data, yielding updated T_1 and an updated classifier M_1. We iterate this process, and with every iteration, the accuracy on the positive samples increases, while the accuracy on the negatives typically decreases. We finish the boosting when the positive accuracy exceeds the negative one. See [20, Sec. 2] for details.

3.3   ATP Guidance with Gradient Boosted Trees

Fast linear classifiers together with well-designed features have been used with good results for a number of tasks in areas such as NLP [23]. However, more advanced learning models have been recently developed, showing improved performance on a number of tasks, while maintaining efficiency. One such method is *gradient boosted trees* and, in particular, their implementation in the XGBoost library [7]. Gradient boosted trees are ensembles of decision trees trained by tree boosting.

The format of the training and evaluation data used by XGBoost is the same as the input used by LIBLINEAR (sparse feature vectors). Hence, we use practically the same approach for obtaining the positive and negative training examples, extracting their features, and clause evaluation during proof runs as described in Sects. 3.1 and 3.2. XGBoost, however, does not require the accuracy-balancing boosting. This is because XGBoost can deal with unbalanced training data by setting the ratio of positive and negative examples.[2]

The model $\mathcal{M}$ produced by XGBoost consists of a set (*ensemble* [37]) of decision trees. The inner nodes of the decision trees consist of conditions on feature values, while the leafs contain numeric scores. Given a vector φ_C representing a clause C, each tree in $\mathcal{M}$ is navigated to a unique leaf using the values from φ_C, and the corresponding leaf scores are aggregated across all trees. The final score is translated to yield the probability that φ_C represents a positive clause. When using $\mathcal{M}$ as a weight function in E, the probabilities are turned into binary classification, assigning weight 1.0 for probabilities ≥ 0.5 and weight 10.0 otherwise. Our experiments with scaling of the weight by the probability did not yet yield improved functionality.

3.4   Feature Hashing

In the previous version of ENIGMA, the vectors representing clauses had always length n where n is the total number of features in the training data $\mathcal{T}$ (or $2n$ with conjecture features). Experiments revealed that both LIBLINEAR and XGBoost are capable of dealing with vectors up to the length of 10^5 with a reasonable performance. This might be enough for smaller benchmarks, but with the need to train on bigger training data, we might need to handle much larger feature sets. In experiments with the whole translated Mizar Mathematical Library [42], the feature vector length can easily grow over 10^6. This significantly increases both the training and the clause evaluation times. To handle such larger data sets, we have implemented a simple *hashing* method to decrease the dimension of the vectors.

---

[2] We use the XGBoost parameter `scale_pos_weight`.

Instead of serially numbering all features, we represent each feature f by a unique string and apply a general-purpose string hashing function to obtain a number n_f within a required range (between 0 and an adjustable *hash base*). The value of f is then stored in the feature vector at the position n_f. If different features get mapped to the same vector index, the corresponding values are summed up.

We use the following hashing function *sdbm* coming from the open source SDBM project. Given a string s, the value h_i is computed for every character as follows:

$$h_i = s_i + (h_{i-1} \ll 6) + (h_{i-1} \ll 16) - h_{i-1}$$

where $h_0 = 0$, s_i is the ASCII code of the character at the i-th position, and the operation $\ll$ stands for a bit shift. The value for the last character is computed with a fixed-size data type (we use 64-bit unsigned integers) and this value modulo the selected hash base is returned. We evaluate the effect of the selected hashing function later in Sect. 5.

4   Neural Architecture for ATP Guidance

Although the handcrafted clause features described in Sect. 3.1 lead to very good results, they naturally have several limitations. It is never clear whether the selected set of features is the best available given the training data. Moreover, a rich set of features can easily lead to long sparse vectors and thus using them for large corpora requires the use of dimensionality reduction techniques (c.f. Sect. 3.4). Hence selecting the features automatically is a natural further step.

Among various techniques used to extract features fully automatically, neural networks (NN) have recently become the most popular thanks to many successful applications in, e.g., computer vision and natural language processing. There have been several attempts to use NNs for guiding ATPs. However, such attempts have so far typically suffered from a large overhead needed to evaluate the used NN [31], making them impractical for actual proving.

A popular approach for representing tree-structured data, like logical formulae, is based on recursive NNs [16]. The basic idea is that all objects (tree nodes, subterms, subformulas) are represented in a high dimensional vector space and these representations are subject to learning. Moreover, the representation of more complex objects is a function of representations of their arguments. Hence constants, variables, and atomic predicates are represented as directly learned vectors, called *vector embeddings*. Assume that all such objects are represented by n-dimensional vectors. For example, constants a and b are represented by learned vectors v_a and v_b, respectively. The representation of $f(a, b)$ is then produced by a learned function (NN), say v_f, that has as an input two vectors and returns a vector; hence $v_f(v_a, v_b) \in \mathbf{R}^n$. Moreover, the representation of $P(f(a, b), a)$ is obtained similarly, because from our point of view a representation is just a function of arguments. Therefore we have

$$v_f \colon \underbrace{\mathbf{R}^n \times \cdots \times \mathbf{R}^n}_{k\text{-times}} \to \mathbf{R}^n \qquad \text{for every } k\text{-ary, } k \geq 0, \text{ function symbol } f,$$

$$v_P \colon \underbrace{\mathbf{R}^n \times \cdots \times \mathbf{R}^n}_{k\text{-times}} \to \mathbf{R}^n \qquad \text{for every } k\text{-ary, } k \geq 0, \text{ predicate symbol } P,$$

in our language. We treat all variables as a single symbol, i.e., we always represent a variable by a fixed learned vector, and similarly for Skolem names. This is in line with how the ENIGMA features are constructed and thus allows for a more straightforward comparison. We also replace symbols that appear rarely (fewer than 10 times) in our training set by a representative, e.g., all rare binary functions become the same binary function. Loosely speaking, we learn a general binary function this way. Because we treat equality and negation as learned functions, we have described how a representation of a literal is produced.

We could now produce the representation of clauses by assuming that disjunction is a binary connective, however, we instead use a more direct approach and we treat clauses directly as sequences of literals. Recurrent neural networks (RNN) are commonly used to process arbitrary sequences of vectors. Hence we train an RNN, called Cl, that consumes the representations of literals in a clause and produces the representation of the clause, $Cl \colon \mathbf{R}^n \times \cdots \times \mathbf{R}^n \to \mathbf{R}^n$.

Given a representation of a clause we could learn a function that says whether the clause is a good given clause. However, without any context this may be hard to decide. As in ENIGMA and [31], we introduce more context into our setting by using the problem's conjecture. The negated conjecture is translated by E into a set of clauses. We combine the vector representations of these clauses by another RNN, called $Conj$ and defined by $Conj \colon \mathbf{R}^n \times \cdots \times \mathbf{R}^n \to \mathbf{R}^n$.

Now that we know how to represent a conjecture and a given clause by a vector, we can define a function that combines them into a decision, called Fin and defined by $Fin \colon \mathbf{R}^n \times \mathbf{R}^n \to \mathbf{R}^2$. The two real values can later be turned into probabilities of whether the clause will (will not) be useful, see Sect. 4.2.

Although all the representations have been vectors in $\mathbf{R}^n$, this is an unnecessary restriction. It suffices if the objects of the same type are represented by vectors of the same length. For example, we have experimented with $Conj$ where outputs are shorter (and inputs to Fin are changed accordingly) with the aim to decrease overfitting to a particular problem.

4.1 Neural Model Parameters

The above mentioned neural model can be implemented in many ways. Although we have not performed an extensive grid search over various variants, we can discuss some of them shortly. The basic parameter is the dimension n of the vectors. We have tried various models with $n \in \{8, 16, 32, 64, 128\}$. The functions used for v_f and v_P can be simple linear transformations (tensors), or more complex combinations of linear and nonlinear layers. An example of a frequently used nonlinearity is the rectified linear unit (ReLU), defined by $\max(0, x)$.[3]

---

[3] Due to various numerical problems with deep recursive networks we have obtained better results with ReLU6, defined by $\min(\max(0, x), 6)$, or tanh.

For *Cl* and *Conj* we use (multi-layer) long short-term memory (LSTM) RNNs [18]. We have tried to restrict the output vector of *Conj* to $m = \frac{n}{2}$ or $m = \frac{n}{4}$ to prevent overfitting with inconclusive results. The *Fin* component is a sequence of alternating linear and nonlinear layers (ReLU), where the last two linear layers are $\mathbf{R}^{n+m} \rightarrow \mathbf{R}^{\frac{n}{2}}$ and $\mathbf{R}^{\frac{n}{2}} \rightarrow \mathbf{R}^2$.

4.2   ATP Guidance with Pytorch

We have created our neural model using the Pytorch library and integrated it with E using the library's C++ API.[4] This API allows to load a previously trained model saved to a file in a special TorchScript format. We use a separate file for each of the neural parts described above. This includes computing of the vector embeddings of terms, literals, and clauses, as well as the conjecture embedding *Conj* summarizing the conjecture clauses into one vector, and finally the part *Fin*, which classifies clauses into those deemed useful for proving the given conjecture and the rest.

We have created a new clause weight function in E called TorchEval which interfaces these parts and can be used for evaluating clauses based on the neural model. One of the key features of the interface, which is important for ensuring reasonable evaluation speed, is *caching* of the embeddings of terms and literals. Whenever the evaluation encounters a term or a literal which was evaluated before, its embedding is simply retrieved from the memory in constant time instead of being computed from the embeddings of its subterms recursively. We use the fact that terms in E are perfectly shared and thus a pointer to a particular term can be used as a key for retrieving the corresponding embedding. Note that this pervasive caching is possible thanks to our choice of recursive neural networks (that match our symbolic data) and it would not work with naive use of other neural models such as convolutional or recurrent networks without further modifications.

The clause evaluation part of the model returns two real outputs x_0 and x_1, which can be turned into a probability that the given clause will be useful using the sigmoid (logistic) function:

$$p = \frac{1}{1 + e^{(x_0 - x_1)}}. \tag{1}$$

However, for classification, i.e. for a yes-no answer, we can just compare the two numbers and "say yes" whenever

$$x_0 < x_1. \tag{2}$$

After experimenting with other schemes that did not perform so well,[5] we made TorchEval return 1.0 whenever condition (2) is satisfied and 10.0 otherwise.

---

[4] https://pytorch.org/cppdocs/.

[5] For instance, using the probability (1) for a more fine-grained order on clauses dictated by the neural model.

This is in accord with the standard convention employed by E that clauses with smaller weight should be preferred and also corresponds to the ENIGMA approach. Moreover, E implicitly uses an ever-increasing clause id as a tie breaker, so among the clauses within the same class, both TorchEval and ENIGMA behave as FIFO.

Another performance improvement was obtained by forcing Pytorch to use just a single core when evaluating the model in E. The default Pytorch setting was causing degradation of performance on machines with many cores, probably by assuming by default that multi-threading will speed up frequent numeric operations such as matrix multiplication. It seems that in our case, the overhead for multi-threading at this point might be higher than the gain.

5 Experimental Evaluation

We experimentally evaluated the three learning-based ATP guidance methods on the MPTP2078 benchmark [1].[6] MPTP2078 contains 2078 problems coming from the MPTP translation [42] of the Mizar Mathematical Library (MML) [3] to FOL. The consistent use of symbol names across the MPTP corpus is crucial for our symbol-based learning methods. We evaluated ATP performance with a good-performing baseline E strategy, denoted S, which was previously optimized [22] on Mizar problems (see Appendix A for details).

Section 5.1 provides details on model training and the hyperparameters used, and analyzes the most important features used by the tree model. The model based on linear regression (Sect. 3.2) is denoted $\mathcal{M}_{\text{lin}}$, the model based on decision trees (Sect. 3.3) is denoted $\mathcal{M}_{\text{tree}}$, and the neural model (Sect. 4) is denoted $\mathcal{M}_{\text{nn}}$. Sections 5.2 and 5.3 evaluate the performance of the models both by standard machine learning metrics and by plugging them into the ATPs. Section 5.4 evaluates the effect of the feature hashing described in Sect. 3.4.

All experiments were run on a server with 36 hyperthreading Intel(R) Xeon(R) Gold 6140 CPU @ 2.30 GHz cores, with 755 GB of memory available in total. Each problem is always assigned one core. For training of the neural models we used NVIDIA GeForce GTX 1080 Ti GPUs. As described above, neither GPU nor multi-threading was, however, employed when using the trained models for clause evaluation inside the ATP.

5.1 Model Training, Hyperparameters and Feature Analysis

We evaluated the baseline strategy S on all the 2078 benchmark problems with a fixed CPU time limit of 10 s per problem.[7] This yielded 1086 solved problems and provided the training data for the learning methods as described in Sect. 2. For $\mathcal{M}_{\text{lin}}$ and $\mathcal{M}_{\text{tree}}$, the training data was translated to feature vectors (see

---

[6] The benchmark can be found at https://github.com/JUrban/MPTP2078. For all the remaining materials for reproducing the experiments please check out the repository https://github.com/ai4reason/eprover-data/tree/master/CADE-19.

[7] This appears to be a reasonable waiting time for, e.g., the users of ITP hammers [5].

Sect. 3) which were then fed to the learner. For $\mathcal{M}_{nn}$ we used the training data directly without any feature extraction.

Training Data and Training of Linear and Tree Models: The training data consisted of around 222 000 training samples (21 000 positives and 201 000 negatives) with almost 32 000 different ENIGMA features. This means that the training vectors for $\mathcal{M}_{lin}$ and $\mathcal{M}_{tree}$ had dimension close to 64 000,[8] and so had the output weight vector of $\mathcal{M}_{lin}$. For $\mathcal{M}_{tree}$, we reused the parameters that performed well in the ATPBoost [36] and rlCoP [26] systems and produced models with 200 decision trees, each with maximal depth 9. The resulting models—both linear and boosted trees—were about 1MB large in their native representation. The training time for $\mathcal{M}_{lin}$ was around 8 min (five iterations of accuracy-balancing boosting), and approximately 5 min for $\mathcal{M}_{tree}$. Both of them were measured on a single CPU core. During the boosting of $\mathcal{M}_{lin}$, the positive samples were extended from 21k to 110k by repeating the mis-classified vectors.

Learned Tree Features: The boosted tree model $\mathcal{M}_{tree}$ allows computing statistics of the most frequently used features. This is an interesting aspect that goes in the direction of *explainable* AI. The most important features can be analyzed by ATP developers and compared with the ideas used in standard clause evaluation heuristics. There were 200 trees in $\mathcal{M}_{tree}$ with 20215 decision nodes in total. These decision nodes refer to only 3198 features out of the total 32000. The most frequently used feature was the clause length, used 3051 times, followed by the conjecture length, used 893 times, and by the numbers of the positive and negative literals in the clauses and conjectures. In a crude way, the machine learning here seems to confirm the importance assigned to these basic metrics by ATP researchers. The set of top ten features additionally contains three symbol counts (including "$\in$" and "$\subseteq$") and a vertical feature corresponding to a variable occurring under negated set membership $\in$ (like in "$x \notin \cdot$" or "$\cdot \notin x$"). This seems plausible, since the Mizar library and thus MPTP2078 are based on set theory where membership and inclusion are key concepts.

Neural Training and Final Neural Parameters: We tried to improve the training of $\mathcal{M}_{nn}$ by randomly changing the order of clauses in conjectures, literals in clauses, and terms in equalities. If after these transformations a negative example pair (C, G) was equivalent to a positive one, we removed the negative one from the training set. This way we reduced the number of negative examples to 198k. We trained our model in batches[9] of size 128 and used the negative log-likelihood as a loss function (the learning rate is 10^{-3}), where we applied log-softmax on the output of *Fin*. We weighted positive examples more to simulate a balanced training set. All symbols of the same type and arity that have less than 10 occurrences in the training set were represented by one symbol. We set the vector dimension to be $n = 64$ for the neural model $\mathcal{M}_{nn}$ and we set the output of *Conj* to be $m = 16$. All the functions representing function symbols

---

[8] Combining the dimensions for the clause and the conjecture.

[9] Moreover, we always try to put examples with the same conjecture G into the same batch to share the time for recomputing the representation of G.

Table 1. True Positive Rate (TPR) and True Negative Rate (TNR) on training data.

	$\mathcal{M}_{lin}$	$\mathcal{M}_{tree}$	$\mathcal{M}_{nn}$
TPR	90.54%	99.36%	97.82%
TNR	83.52%	93.32%	94.69%

and predicates were composed of a linear layer and ReLU6. *Fin* was set to be a sequence of linear, ReLU, linear, ReLU, and linear layers. The training time for $\mathcal{M}_{nn}$ was around 8 min per epoch and the model was trained for 50 epochs. Note that we save a model after each epoch and randomly test few of these generated models and select the best performing one (in our case the model generated after 35 epochs).

5.2 Evaluation of the Model Performance

Training Performance of the Models: We first evaluate how well the individual models managed to learn the training data. Due to possible overfitting, this is obviously used only as a heuristic and the main metric is provided by the ultimate ATP evaluation. Table 1 shows for each model the *true positive* and *true negative* rates (TPR, TNR) on the training data, that is, the percentage of the positive and negative examples, classified correctly by each model.[10] The highest TPR, also called sensitivity, is achieved by $\mathcal{M}_{tree}$ while the highest TNR, also called specificity, by $\mathcal{M}_{nn}$. As expected, the accuracy of the linear model is lower. Its main strength seems to come from the relatively high speed of evaluation (see below).

ATP Performance of the Models: Table 2 shows the total number of problems solved by the four methods. For each learning-based model $\mathcal{M}$, we always consider the model alone ($\mathcal{S} \odot \mathcal{M}$) and the model combined equally with $\mathcal{S}$ ($\mathcal{S} \oplus \mathcal{M}$). All methods are using the same time limit, i.e., 10 s. This is our ultimate "real-life" evaluation, confirming that the boosted trees indeed outperform the guidance by the linear classifier and that the recursive neural network and its caching implementation is already competitive with these methods in real time. The best method $\mathcal{S} \oplus \mathcal{M}_{tree}$ solves 15.7% more problems than the original strategy $\mathcal{S}$, and 3.8% problems more than the previously best linear strategy $\mathcal{S} \oplus \mathcal{M}_{lin}$.[11] Table 2 provides also further explanation of these aggregated numbers. We show the number of unique solutions provided by each of the methods and the difference to the original strategy. Table 3 shows how useful are the particular methods when used together. Both the linear and the neural

---

[10] For $\mathcal{M}_{lin}$, we show the numbers after five iterations of the boosting loop (see Sect. 3.2). The values in the first round were 40.81% for the positive and 98.62% for the negative rate.

[11] We have also measured how much $\mathcal{S}$ benefits from increased time limits. It solves 1099 problems in 20 s and 1137 problems in 300 s.

Table 2. Number of problems solved (and uniquely solved) by the individual models. $\mathcal{S}+$ and $\mathcal{S}-$ indicate the number of problems gained and lost w.r.t. the baseline $\mathcal{S}$.

	$\mathcal{S}$	$\mathcal{S} \odot \mathcal{M}_{\text{lin}}$	$\mathcal{S} \oplus \mathcal{M}_{\text{lin}}$	$\mathcal{S} \odot \mathcal{M}_{\text{tree}}$	$\mathcal{S} \oplus \mathcal{M}_{\text{tree}}$	$\mathcal{S} \odot \mathcal{M}_{\text{nn}}$	$\mathcal{S} \oplus \mathcal{M}_{\text{nn}}$
Solved	1086	1115	1210	1231	**1256**	1167	1197
Unique	0	3	7	10	**15**	3	2
$\mathcal{S}+$	0	+119	+138	+155	**+173**	+114	+119
$\mathcal{S}-$	0	−90	−14	−10	**−3**	−33	−8

Table 3. The greedy sequence—methods sorted by their greedily computed contribution to all the problems solved.

	$\mathcal{S} \oplus \mathcal{M}_{\text{tree}}$	$\mathcal{S} \oplus \mathcal{M}_{\text{lin}}$	$\mathcal{S} \odot \mathcal{M}_{\text{nn}}$	$\mathcal{S} \odot \mathcal{M}_{\text{tree}}$	$\mathcal{S} \odot \mathcal{M}_{\text{lin}}$	$\mathcal{S} \oplus \mathcal{M}_{\text{nn}}$	$\mathcal{S}$
Addition	1256	33	13	11	3	2	0
Total	1256	1289	1302	1313	1316	1318	1318

models complement the boosted trees well, while the original strategy is made completely redundant.

Testing Performance of the Models on Newly Solved Problems: There are 232 problems solved by some of the six learning-based methods but not by the baseline strategy $\mathcal{S}$. To see how the trained models behave on new data, we again extract positive and negative examples from all successful proof runs on these problems. This results in around 31 000 positive testing examples and around 300 000 negative testing examples.

Table 4 shows again for each of the previously trained models the *true positive* and *true negative* rates (TPR, TNR) on these testing data. The highest TPR is again achieved by $\mathcal{M}_{\text{tree}}$ and the highest TNR by $\mathcal{M}_{\text{nn}}$. The accuracy of the linear model is again lower. Both the TPR and TNR testing scores are significantly lower for all methods compared to their training counterparts. TPR decreases by about 15% and TNR by about 20%. This likely shows the limits of our current learning and proof-state characterization methods. It also points to the very interesting issue of obtaining many *alternative proofs* [29] and learning from them. It seems that just using learning or reasoning is not sufficient in our AI domain, and that feedback loops combining the two multiple times [36,44] are really necessary for building strong ATP systems.

5.3   Speed of Clause Evaluation by the Learned Models

The number of generated clauses reported by E can be used as a rough estimate of the amount of work done by the prover. If we look at this statistic for those runs that timed out—i.e., did not find a proof within the given time limit—we can use it to estimate the slowdown of the clause processing rate incurred by employing a machine learner inside E. (Note that each generated clause needs to be evaluated before it is inserted on the respective queue.)

Table 4. True Positive Rate (TPR) and True Negative Rate (TNR) on testing data from the newly solved 232 problems.

	$\mathcal{M}_{lin}$	$\mathcal{M}_{tree}$	$\mathcal{M}_{nn}$
TPR	80.54%	83.35%	82.00%
TNR	62.28%	72.60%	76.88%

Table 5. The ASRPA and NSRGA ratios. ASRPA are the average ratios (and standard deviations) of the relative number of *processed* clauses with respect to $\mathcal{S}$ on problems on which all runs succeeded. NSRGA are the average ratios (and standard deviations) of the relative number of *generated* clauses with respect to $\mathcal{S}$ on problems on which all runs timed out. The numbers of problems were 898 and 681, respectively.

	$\mathcal{S}$	$\mathcal{S} \odot \mathcal{M}_{lin}$	$\mathcal{S} \oplus \mathcal{M}_{lin}$	$\mathcal{S} \odot \mathcal{M}_{tree}$	$\mathcal{S} \oplus \mathcal{M}_{tree}$	$\mathcal{S} \odot \mathcal{M}_{nn}$	$\mathcal{S} \oplus \mathcal{M}_{nn}$
ASRPA	1 ± 0	2.18 ± 20.35	0.91 ± 0.58	0.60 ± 0.98	0.59 ± 0.36	0.59 ± 0.75	0.69 ± 0.94
NSRGA	1 ± 0	0.61 ± 0.52	0.56 ± 0.35	0.42 ± 0.38	0.43 ± 0.35	0.06 ± 0.08	0.07 ± 0.09

Complementarily, the number of processed clauses when compared across those problems on which all runs succeeded may be seen as an indicator of how well the respective clause selection guides the search towards a proof (with a perfect guidance, we only ever process those clauses which constitute a proof).[12]

Table 5 compares the individual configurations of E based on the seven evaluated models with respect to these two metrics. To obtain the shown values, we first normalized the numbers on per problem basis with respect to the result of the baseline strategy $\mathcal{S}$ and computed an average across all relevant problems. The comparison of thus obtained All Solved Relative Processed Average (ASRPA) values shows that, except for $\mathcal{S} \odot \mathcal{M}_{lin}$ (which has a very high standard deviation), all other configurations on average manage to improve over $\mathcal{S}$ and find the corresponding proofs with fewer iterations of the given clause loop. This indicates better guidance towards the proof on the selected benchmarks.

The None Solved Relative Generated Average (NSRGA) values represent the speed of the clause evaluation. It can be seen that while the linear model is relatively fast (approximately 60% of the speed of $\mathcal{S}$), followed closely by the tree-based model (around 40%), the neural model is more expensive to evaluate (achieving between 6% and 7% of $\mathcal{S}$).

We note that without caching, NSRGA of $\mathcal{S} \oplus \mathcal{M}_{nn}$ drops from 7.1% to 3.6% of the speed of $\mathcal{S}$. Thus caching currently helps to approximately double the speed of the evaluation of clauses with $\mathcal{M}_{nn}$.[13] It is interesting and encouraging that despite the neural method being currently about ten times slower than the linear method—and thus generating about ten times fewer inferences within the

---

[12] This metric is similar in spirit to *given clause utilization* introduced by Schulz and Möhrmann [41].

[13] Note that more global caching (of, e.g., whole clauses and frequent combinations of literals) across multiple problems may further amortize the cost of the neural evaluation. This is left as future work here.

10 s time limit used for the ATP evaluation—the neural model already manages to outperform the linear model in the unassisted setting. I.e., $\mathcal{S} \odot \mathcal{M}_{nn}$ is already better than $\mathcal{S} \odot \mathcal{M}_{lin}$ (recall Table 2), despite the latter being much faster.

5.4   Evaluation of Feature Hashing

Finally, we evaluate the feature hashing described in Sect. 3.4. We try different hash bases in order to reduce dimensionality of the vectors and to estimate the influence on the ATP performance. We evaluate on 6 hash bases from 32k (2^{15}), 16k (2^{14}), down to 1k (2^{10}). For each hash base, we construct models $\mathcal{M}_{lin}$ and $\mathcal{M}_{tree}$, we compute their prediction rates, and evaluate their ATP performance.

With the hash base n, each feature must fall into one of n *buckets*. When the number of features is greater than the base—which is our case as we intend to use hashing for dimensionality reduction—collisions are inevitable. When using hash base of 32000 (ca 2^{15}) there are almost as many hashing buckets as there are features in the training data (31675). Out of these features, ca 12000 features are hashed without a collision and 12000 buckets are unoccupied. This yields a 40% probability of a collision. With lower bases, the collisions are evenly distributed.

Lower hash bases lead to larger loss of information, hence decreased performance can be expected. On the other hand, dimensionality reduction sometimes leads to better generalization (less overfitting of the learners). Also, the evaluation in the ATP can be done more efficiently in a lower dimension, thus giving the ATP the chance to process more clauses. The prediction rates and ATP performance for models with and without hashing are presented in Table 6. We compute the true positive (TPR) and negative (TNR) rates as in Sect. 5.1, and we again evaluate E's performance based on the strategy $\mathcal{S}$ in the two ways ($\odot$ and $\oplus$) as in Sect. 5.2. The best value in each row is highlighted. Both models perform comparably to the version without hashing even when the vector dimension is reduced to just 25%, i.e. 8k. With reduction to 1000 (32x), the models still provide a decent improvement over the baseline strategy $\mathcal{S}$, which solved 1086 problems. The $\mathcal{M}_{tree}$ model deals with the reduction slightly better.

Table 6. Effect of feature hashing on prediction rates and ATP performance.

Model\hash size		*Without*	32k	16k	8k	4k	2k	1k
$\mathcal{M}_{lin}$	TPR [%]	90.54	89.32	88.27	89.92	82.08	**91.08**	83.68
	TNR [%]	83.52	82.40	**86.01**	83.02	81.50	76.04	77.53
	$\mathcal{S} \odot \mathcal{M}$	**1115**	1106	1072	1078	1076	1028	938
	$\mathcal{S} \oplus \mathcal{M}$	1210	**1218**	1189	1202	1189	1183	1119
$\mathcal{M}_{tree}$	TPR [%]	99.36	99.38	99.38	99.51	99.62	99.65	**99.69**
	TNR [%]	93.32	93.54	93.29	93.69	93.90	94.53	**94.88**
	$\mathcal{S} \odot \mathcal{M}$	1231	1231	**1233**	1232	1223	1227	1215
	$\mathcal{S} \oplus \mathcal{M}$	**1256**	1244	1244	**1256**	1245	1236	1232

Interestingly, the classification accuracy of the models (again, measured only on the training data) seems to increase with the decrease of hash base (especially for $\mathcal{M}_{\text{tree}}$). However, with this increased accuracy, the ATP performance mildly decreases. This could be caused by the more frequent collisions and thus learning on data that has been made less precise.

6   Conclusions and Future Work

We have described an efficient implementation of gradient-boosted and recursive neural guidance in E, extending the ENIGMA framework. The tree-based models improve on the previously used linear classifier, while the neural methods have, for the first time, been shown practically competitive and useful, by using extensive caching corresponding to the term sharing implemented in E. While this is clearly not the last word in this area, we believe that this is the first practically convincing application of gradient-boosted and neural clause guidance in saturation-style automated theorem provers.

There are a number of future directions. For example, research in better proof state characterization of saturation-style systems has been started recently [14, 15] and it is likely that evolving vectorial representations of the proof state will further contribute to the quality of the learning-based guidance. Our recursive neural model is just one of many, and a number of related and combined models can be experimented with.

A   Strategy $\mathcal{S}$ from Experiments in Sect. 5

The following E strategy has been used to undertake the experimental evaluation in Sect. 5. The given clause selection strategy (heuristic) is defined using parameter "-H".

```
--definitional-cnf=24 --split-aggressive --simul-paramod -tKBO6 -c1 -F1
-Ginvfreq -winvfreqrank --forward-context-sr --destructive-er-aggressive
--destructive-er --prefer-initial-clauses -WSelectMaxLComplexAvoidPosPred
-H'(1*ConjectureTermPrefixWeight(DeferSOS,1,3,0.1,5,0,0.1,1,4),
   1*ConjectureTermPrefixWeight(DeferSOS,1,3,0.5,100,0,0.2,0.2,4),
   1*Refinedweight(ConstPrio,4,300,4,4,0.7),
   1*RelevanceLevelWeight2(PreferProcessed,0,1,2,1,1,1,200,200,2.5,
                                                9999.9,9999.9),
   1*StaggeredWeight(DeferSOS,1),
   1*SymbolTypeweight(DeferSOS,18,7,-2,5,9999.9,2,1.5),
   2*Clauseweight(ConstPrio,20,9999,4),
   2*ConjectureSymbolWeight(DeferSOS,9999,20,50,-1,50,3,3,0.5),
   2*StaggeredWeight(DeferSOS,2))'
```

References

1. Alama, J., Heskes, T., Kühlwein, D., Tsivtsivadze, E., Urban, J.: Premise selection for mathematics by corpus analysis and kernel methods. J. Autom. Reason. **52**(2), 191–213 (2014)
2. Alemi, A.A., Chollet, F., Eén, N., Irving, G., Szegedy, C., Urban, J.: DeepMath - deep sequence models for premise selection. In: Lee, D.D., Sugiyama, M., Luxburg, U.V., Guyon, I., Garnett, R. (eds.) Advances in Neural Information Processing Systems 29: Annual Conference on Neural Information Processing Systems 2016, Barcelona, Spain, 5–10 December 2016, pp. 2235–2243 (2016)
3. Bancerek, G., et al.: Mizar: state-of-the-art and beyond. In: Kerber, M., Carette, J., Kaliszyk, C., Rabe, F., Sorge, V. (eds.) CICM 2015. LNCS (LNAI), vol. 9150, pp. 261–279. Springer, Cham (2015). https://doi.org/10.1007/978-3-319-20615-8_17
4. Blanchette, J.C., Greenaway, D., Kaliszyk, C., Kühlwein, D., Urban, J.: A learning-based fact selector for Isabelle/HOL. J. Autom. Reason. **57**(3), 219–244 (2016)
5. Blanchette, J.C., Kaliszyk, C., Paulson, L.C., Urban, J.: Hammering towards QED. J. Formalized Reason. **9**(1), 101–148 (2016)
6. Bridge, J.P., Holden, S.B., Paulson, L.C.: Machine learning for first-order theorem proving - learning to select a good heuristic. J. Autom. Reason. **53**(2), 141–172 (2014)
7. Chen, T., Guestrin, C.: XGBoost: a scalable tree boosting system. In: KDD, pp. 785–794. ACM (2016)
8. Denzinger, J., Fuchs, M., Goller, C., Schulz, S.: Learning from previous proof experience. Technical report AR99-4, Institut für Informatik, Technische Universität München (1999)
9. Ertel, W., Schumann, J.M.P., Suttner, C.B.: Learning heuristics for a theorem prover using back propagation. In: Retti, J., Leidlmair, K. (eds.) 5. Österreichische Artificial Intelligence-Tagung. INFORMATIK, vol. 208, pp. 87–95. Springer, Heidelberg (1989). https://doi.org/10.1007/978-3-642-74688-8_10
10. Fan, R.-E., Chang, K.-W., Hsieh, C.-J., Wang, X.-R., Lin, C.-J.: LIBLINEAR: a library for large linear classification. J. Mach. Learn. Res. **9**, 1871–1874 (2008)
11. Färber, M., Brown, C.: Internal guidance for satallax. In: Olivetti and Tiwari [33], pp. 349–361
12. Färber, M., Kaliszyk, C., Urban, J.: Monte Carlo tableau proof search. In: de Moura, L. (ed.) CADE 2017. LNCS (LNAI), vol. 10395, pp. 563–579. Springer, Cham (2017). https://doi.org/10.1007/978-3-319-63046-5_34
13. Gauthier, T., Kaliszyk, C.: Premise selection and external provers for HOL4. In: Certified Programs and Proofs (CPP 2015) (2015). https://doi.org/10.1145/2676724.2693173
14. Goertzel, Z., Jakubův, J., Schulz, S., Urban, J.: ProofWatch: watchlist guidance for large theories in E. In: Avigad, J., Mahboubi, A. (eds.) ITP 2018. LNCS, vol. 10895, pp. 270–288. Springer, Cham (2018). https://doi.org/10.1007/978-3-319-94821-8_16
15. Goertzel, Z., Jakubuv, J., Urban, J.: ProofWatch meets ENIGMA: first experiments. In: Barthe, G., Korovin, K., Schulz, S., Suda, M., Sutcliffe, G., Veanes, M. (eds.) LPAR-22 Workshop and Short Paper Proceedings. Kalpa Publications in Computing, vol. 9, pp. 15–22. EasyChair (2018)
16. Goller, C., Küchler, A.: Learning task-dependent distributed representations by backpropagation through structure. In: Proceedings of International Conference on Neural Networks (ICNN 1996), vol. 1, pp. 347–352, June 1996

17. Gottlob, G., Sutcliffe, G., Voronkov, A. (eds.): Global Conference on Artificial Intelligence, GCAI 2015, Tbilisi, Georgia, 16–19 October 2015. EPiC Series in Computing, vol. 36. EasyChair (2015)

18. Hochreiter, S., Schmidhuber, J.: Long short-term memory. Neural Comput. **9**, 1735–1780 (1997)

19. Jakubův, J., Urban, J.: ENIGMA: efficient learning-based inference guiding machine. In: Geuvers, H., England, M., Hasan, O., Rabe, F., Teschke, O. (eds.) CICM 2017. LNCS (LNAI), vol. 10383, pp. 292–302. Springer, Cham (2017). https://doi.org/10.1007/978-3-319-62075-6_20

20. Jakubův, J., Urban, J.: Enhancing ENIGMA given clause guidance. In: Rabe, F., Farmer, W.M., Passmore, G.O., Youssef, A. (eds.) CICM 2018. LNCS (LNAI), vol. 11006, pp. 118–124. Springer, Cham (2018). https://doi.org/10.1007/978-3-319-96812-4_11

21. Jakubův, J., Urban, J.: Hierarchical invention of theorem proving strategies. AI Commun. **31**(3), 237–250 (2018)

22. Jakubuv, J., Urban, J.: BliStrTune: hierarchical invention of theorem proving strategies. In: Bertot, Y., Vafeiadis, V. (eds.) Proceedings of the 6th ACM SIGPLAN Conference on Certified Programs and Proofs, CPP 2017, Paris, France, 16–17 January 2017, pp. 43–52. ACM (2017)

23. Joulin, A., Grave, E., Bojanowski, P., Mikolov, T.: Bag of tricks for efficient text classification. In: Proceedings of the 15th Conference of the European Chapter of the Association for Computational Linguistics, Short Papers, vol. 2, pp. 427–431. Association for Computational Linguistics, April 2017

24. Kaliszyk, C., Urban, J.: Learning-assisted automated reasoning with Flyspeck. J. Autom. Reason. **53**(2), 173–213 (2014)

25. Kaliszyk, C., Urban, J.: FEMaLeCoP: fairly efficient machine learning connection prover. In: Davis, M., Fehnker, A., McIver, A., Voronkov, A. (eds.) LPAR 2015. LNCS, vol. 9450, pp. 88–96. Springer, Heidelberg (2015). https://doi.org/10.1007/978-3-662-48899-7_7

26. Kaliszyk, C., Urban, J., Michalewski, H., Olšák, M.: Reinforcement learning of theorem proving. In: Bengio, S., Wallach, H.M., Larochelle, H., Grauman, K., Cesa-Bianchi, N., Garnett, R. (eds.) Advances in Neural Information Processing Systems 31: Annual Conference on Neural Information Processing Systems 2018, NeurIPS 2018, Canada, Montréal, 3–8 December 2018, pp. 8836–8847 (2018)

27. Kaliszyk, C., Urban, J., Vyskocil, J.: Efficient semantic features for automated reasoning over large theories. In: IJCAI, pp. 3084–3090. AAAI Press (2015)

28. Kovács, L., Voronkov, A.: First-order theorem proving and VAMPIRE. In: Sharygina, N., Veith, H. (eds.) CAV 2013. LNCS, vol. 8044, pp. 1–35. Springer, Heidelberg (2013). https://doi.org/10.1007/978-3-642-39799-8_1

29. Kuehlwein, D., Urban, J.: Learning from multiple proofs: first experiments. In: Fontaine, P., Schmidt, R.A., Schulz, S. (eds.) PAAR-2012. EPiC Series, vol. 21, pp. 82–94. EasyChair (2013)

30. Kühlwein, D., van Laarhoven, T., Tsivtsivadze, E., Urban, J., Heskes, T.: Overview and evaluation of premise selection techniques for large theory mathematics. In: Gramlich, B., Miller, D., Sattler, U. (eds.) IJCAR 2012. LNCS (LNAI), vol. 7364, pp. 378–392. Springer, Heidelberg (2012). https://doi.org/10.1007/978-3-642-31365-3_30

31. Loos, S.M., Irving, G., Szegedy, C., Kaliszyk, C.: Deep network guided proof search. In: Eiter, T., Sands, D. (eds.) LPAR-21, 21st International Conference on Logic for Programming, Artificial Intelligence and Reasoning, Maun, Botswana, 7–12 May 2017. EPiC Series in Computing, vol. 46, pp. 85–105. EasyChair (2017)

32. Meng, J., Paulson, L.C.: Translating higher-order clauses to first-order clauses. J. Autom. Reason. **40**(1), 35–60 (2008)
33. Olivetti, N., Tiwari, A. (eds.): IJCAR 2016. LNCS (LNAI), vol. 9706. Springer, Cham (2016). https://doi.org/10.1007/978-3-319-40229-1
34. Otten, J., Bibel, W.: leanCoP: lean connection-based theorem proving. J. Symb. Comput. **36**(1–2), 139–161 (2003)
35. Overbeek, R.A.: A new class of automated theorem-proving algorithms. J. ACM **21**(2), 191–200 (1974)
36. Piotrowski, B., Urban, J.: ATPBOOST: learning premise selection in binary setting with ATP feedback. In: Galmiche, D., Schulz, S., Sebastiani, R. (eds.) IJCAR 2018. LNCS (LNAI), vol. 10900, pp. 566–574. Springer, Cham (2018). https://doi.org/10.1007/978-3-319-94205-6_37
37. Polikar, R.: Ensemble based systems in decision making. IEEE Circuits Syst. Mag. **6**(3), 21–45 (2006)
38. Schäfer, S., Schulz, S.: Breeding theorem proving heuristics with genetic algorithms. In: Gottlob et al. [17], pp. 263–274
39. Schulz, S.: Learning search control knowledge for equational deduction. DISKI, vol. 230. Infix Akademische Verlagsgesellschaft (2000)
40. Schulz, S.: E - a brainiac theorem prover. AI Commun. **15**(2–3), 111–126 (2002)
41. Schulz, S., Möhrmann, M.: Performance of clause selection heuristics for saturation-based theorem proving. In: Olivetti and Tiwari [33], pp. 330–345
42. Urban, J.: MPTP 0.2: design, implementation, and initial experiments. J. Autom. Reason. **37**(1–2), 21–43 (2006)
43. Urban, J.: BliStr: the blind strategymaker. In: Gottlob et al. [17], pp. 312–319
44. Urban, J., Sutcliffe, G., Pudlák, P., Vyskočil, J.: MaLARea SG1 - machine learner for automated reasoning with semantic guidance. In: Armando, A., Baumgartner, P., Dowek, G. (eds.) IJCAR 2008. LNCS (LNAI), vol. 5195, pp. 441–456. Springer, Heidelberg (2008). https://doi.org/10.1007/978-3-540-71070-7_37
45. Urban, J., Vyskočil, J., Štěpánek, P.: MaLeCoP machine learning connection prover. In: Brünnler, K., Metcalfe, G. (eds.) TABLEAUX 2011. LNCS (LNAI), vol. 6793, pp. 263–277. Springer, Heidelberg (2011). https://doi.org/10.1007/978-3-642-22119-4_21

Towards Physical Hybrid Systems

Katherine Cordwell[1]($\boxtimes$) (iD) and André Platzer[1,2] (iD)

[1] Computer Science Department, Carnegie Mellon University, Pittsburgh, USA
{kcordwel,aplatzer}@cs.cmu.edu
[2] Fakultät für Informatik, Technische Universität München, Munich, Germany

Abstract. Some hybrid systems models are unsafe for mathematically correct but physically unrealistic reasons. For example, mathematical models can classify a system as being unsafe on a set that is too small to have physical importance. In particular, differences in measure zero sets in models of cyber-physical systems (CPS) have significant mathematical impact on the mathematical safety of these models even though differences on measure zero sets have no tangible physical effect in a real system. We develop the concept of "physical hybrid systems" (PHS) to help reunite mathematical models with physical reality. We modify a hybrid systems logic (differential temporal dynamic logic) by adding a first-class operator to elide distinctions on measure zero sets of time within CPS models. This approach facilitates modeling since it admits the verification of a wider class of models, including some physically realistic models that would otherwise be classified as mathematically unsafe. We also develop a proof calculus to help with the verification of PHS.

Keywords: Hybrid systems · Almost everywhere ·
Differential temporal dynamic logic · Proof calculus

1 Introduction

Hybrid systems [1,24], which have interacting discrete and continuous dynamics, provide all the necessary mathematical precision to describe and verify the behavior of safety-critical *cyber-physical systems* (CPS), such as self-driving cars, surgical robots, and drones. Ironically, however, hybrid systems provide so much mathematical precision that they can distinguish models that exhibit no physically measurable difference. More specifically, since mathematical models are

This material is based upon work supported by the National Science Foundation Graduate Research Fellowship under Grant No. DGE-1252522. Any opinions, findings, and conclusions or recommendations expressed in this material are those of the authors and do not necessarily reflect the views of the National Science Foundation. This research was also sponsored by the AFOSR under grant number FA9550-16-1-0288 and by the Alexander von Humboldt Foundation. The views and conclusions contained in this document are those of the authors and should not be interpreted as representing the official policies, either expressed or implied, of any sponsoring institution, the U.S. government or any other entity.

P. Fontaine (Ed.): CADE 2019, LNAI 11716, pp. 216–232, 2019.
https://doi.org/10.1007/978-3-030-29436-6_13

minutely precise, models can classify systems as being unsafe on minutely small sets—even when these sets have no physical significance. For example, a mathematical model could classify a system as being mathematically unsafe at a single instant in time—but why should the safety of a model give more weight to such glitches than even the very notion of solutions of differential equations, which is unaffected [30] by changes on sets of measure zero in time? Practically speaking, a physical system is only unsafe at a single instant of time if it is also already unsafe at a significantly larger set of times. In the worst case, such degenerate counterexamples could detract attention from real unsafeties in a model.

That is why this paper calls for a shift in perspective toward *physical hybrid systems* (PHS) that are more attuned to the limitations and necessities of physics than pure mathematical models. PHS are hybrid systems that behave safely "almost everywhere" (in a measure theoretic sense) and thus, physically speaking, are safe systems. While different flavors of attaining PHS are possible and should be pursued, we propose arguably the tamest one, which merely disregards differences in safety on sets of time of measure zero. As our ultimate hope is that models of PHS can be (correctly) formally verified without introducing any burden on the user, we introduce the ability to rigorously ignore sets of time of measure zero into logic. A major difficulty is that there is a delicate trade-off between the physical practicality of a definition (what real-world behavior it captures) and the logical practicality of a definition (what logical reasoning principles it supports). Our notion of safety almost everywhere in time not only enjoys a direct link with well-established mathematical principles of differential equations, but also satisfies key logical properties, such as compositionality.

We modify *differential temporal dynamic logic* (dTL) [15,25] to capture the notion of safety *time almost everywhere* (tae) along the execution trace of a hybrid system. dTL extends the hybrid systems logic *differential dynamic logic* (dL) with the ability to analyze system behavior over time. We call our new logic *physical differential temporal dynamic logic* (PdTL) to reflect its purpose. While PdTL is closely related to dTL in style and development, the formalization of safety tae is entirely new, and thus requires new reasoning. Guiding the development of PdTL is the following motivating example: Consider a train and a safety condition $v<100$ on the velocity of the train. Physically speaking, it is fine to allow $v = 100$ for a split-second, because this has no measurable impact. PdTL is designed to classify the situation where the train continuously accelerates until $v = 100$ and immediately brakes whenever it reaches $v = 100$ as tae safe.

2   Related Work

Since all systems inherently suffer from imprecision, several approaches develop *robust hybrid systems*, which are stable up to small perturbations—for example, in the contexts of decidability [2,10,11], runtime monitoring [8,9], and controls [18,19,22]. If systems are robust, they provide a fair amount of automation [11,17]. Both our approach and robustness hinge on building in an awareness of physics to hybrid systems verification. However, robustness is fundamentally different from our deductive verification approach. The analysis of robust systems often relies on a reachability analysis (see, e.g., [21]) which loses much of the logical precision present in deductive verification, e.g., decidability of differential equation invariants [27]. Further, by building on dL, which is a general purpose hybrid systems logic, we are able to handle a wide class of models, whereas tools like dReach [17] tend to be slightly more limited in scope. In particular, our deductive approach for PHS admits an induction principle—making it possible to verify safety properties of controllers that run in loops for any amount of time— whereas robustness approaches are presently limited to bounded model checking. We advocate for robustness in that models can, and should be, written with an awareness of imprecision. However, we recognize that modeling is difficult, and even well-intentioned models can suffer from nonphysical glitches—hence PHS.

Non-classical solutions of ODEs [4,6], especially Filippov and Carathéodory solutions, align well with the PHS intuition as they often inherently ignore sets of measure zero. *Filippov solutions* consider vector fields equivalent up to differences on sets of measure zero. *Carathéodory solutions* satisfy a differential equation everywhere except on a set of measure zero. Hybrid systems models do not usually make use of non-classical solutions, since admitting them would require a relaxed notion of safety. Non-classical solutions are sometimes used in the context of controls: Goebel et al. [13] generalized the notion of a solution to a hybrid system by using non-classical solutions of ODEs by Filippov and Krasovskii, with a view towards obtaining robustness properties, and a later work [12] allows solutions that fit a system of ODEs almost everywhere in a time interval. The temporal approach of PdTL naturally admits Carathéodory solutions.

Eliding sets of measure zero can be computationally significant—notably, in quantifier elimination, which arises in the last step of hybrid systems proofs. Despite having no physical meaning, measure zero sets have a significant impact on the efficiency of real arithmetic, and thus on the overall hybrid systems proofs. The enabling factor behind efficient arithmetic [20] is to ignore sets of measure zero and thus remove the need to compute with irrational algebraic numbers. A potential computational benefit is an encouraging motivation for PHS.

3   Syntax of PdTL

In pursuit of enabling the statement of physical safety properties of hybrid systems, we develop PdTL, which builds on concepts from dTL [15,25] to introduce an "almost everywhere in time" operator, $\Box_{\text{tae}}$, which makes it possible to disregard minor glitches violating safety conditions on sets of time of measure zero. When possible, we keep our notation consistent with that of dTL [25], so that the syntax of PdTL is very similar to the syntax of dTL—the key difference being that we eschew dTL trace formulas $\Box\phi$ and $\Diamond\phi$ in favor of $\Box_{\text{tae}}\phi$.

The new PdTL formula $[\alpha]\Box_{\text{tae}}\phi$ expresses that along each run of the hybrid system α, the formula ϕ is true at almost every time ("tae" stands for "time almost everywhere"). This formula remains true even in cases where ϕ is false at only a measure zero set of points in time along α. Because a hybrid system may exhibit different behaviors, the particular measure zero set of points in time at which ϕ is false is allowed to depend on the particular run of α.

Fix a set Σ containing real-valued variables, function symbols, and predicate symbols. In particular, Σ contains the symbols needed for first-order logic of real arithmetic (FOL). We use Σ_{var} to denote the set of real-valued variables in Σ, and let $\mathrm{Trm}(\Sigma)$ denote the set of (polynomial) terms over Σ (as in FOL).

We now define the syntax of *hybrid programs* (which model hybrid systems) and formulas capable of expressing physical properties of hybrid programs. Hybrid programs [25,26] are allowed to assign values to variables (with the := operator), test the truth of formulas (with the ? operator), evolve along systems of differential equations, and branch nondeterministically (with the $\cup$ operator). Hybrid programs are also sequentially composable with the ; operator, and can be run in loops with the * operator.

Definition 1. *Hybrid programs are given by a grammar, where α and β are hybrid programs, $e \in \mathrm{Trm}(\Sigma)$, x is a variable, and P and R are FOL formulas:*

$$\alpha, \beta \ ::= \ x := e \mid ?P \mid x' = f(x) \,\&\, R \mid \alpha \cup \beta \mid \alpha; \beta \mid \alpha^*$$

As in CTL* [7] and dTL, we split *PdTL formulas* into state formulas that are true or false in a *state* (i.e., at a snapshot in time) and trace formulas that are true or false along a fixed *trace* that keeps track of the behavior of a system over time.

Definition 2. *The state formulas are given by the following grammar, where $p \in \Sigma$ is a predicate symbol of arity $n \geq 0$, $e_1, \ldots, e_n \in \mathrm{Trm}(\Sigma)$, ϕ and ψ are state formulas, α is a hybrid program, κ is a trace formula, and x is a variable:*

$$\phi, \psi \ ::= \ p(e_1, \ldots, e_n) \mid \neg\phi \mid \phi \wedge \psi \mid \forall x\, \phi \mid [\alpha]\kappa \mid \langle \alpha \rangle \kappa$$

Trace formulas are given by the following grammar, where ϕ is a state formula:

$$\kappa \ ::= \ \phi \mid \square_{\mathrm{tae}}\phi$$

We will also allow the use of the standard logical operators $\vee$, $\rightarrow$, and $\leftrightarrow$, which are defined in terms of $\neg$ and $\wedge$ as usual in classical logic.

Our motivating example can be modeled in PdTL as follows:

$$a{=}0 \wedge v{=}0 \rightarrow [(((?(v{<}100); a := 1) \cup (?(v{=}100); a := -1));$$
$$\{x' = v, v' = a \,\&\, 0{\leq}v{\leq}100\})^*]\square_{\mathrm{tae}}v{<}100$$

This claims that if the initial velocity and acceleration are both 0, then along any run of the system, $v{<}100$ holds at almost all times. The train accelerates if $v{<}100$ and brakes if $v{=}100$; it moves according to the system of ODEs $x' = v, v' = a$. The evolution domain constraint $v{\leq}100$ indicates an event-triggered controller [26].

A natural question is why we choose to build in reasoning about $\Box_{tae}$ by developing PdTL instead of having the user edit the model by, for example, making the postcondition $v{\leq}100$ instead of $v{<}100$. Indeed, in this particular case that would make the program safe at every moment in time. However, in other examples, editing the postcondition in a similar way may be unwise. For example, although $[x := 0; y := 0; \{x' = 0, y' = 1\}]\Box_{tae}(y{>}0 \rightarrow x{>}1 \vee x{<}1)$ is valid, if we relax the inequalities, $[x := 0; y := 0; \{x' = 0, y' = 1\}]$ $\Box_{tae}(y \geq 0 \rightarrow x \geq 1 \vee x \leq 1)$ is not. As reasoning about hybrid systems is so subtle, the most user-friendly approach to eliding sets of measure zero is to specifically introduce the rigorous ability to ignore sets of measure zero into the logic.

4   Semantics of PdTL

We now report a trace semantics for hybrid programs, based on which we give meaning to the informal concept of formulas being true almost everywhere in time, first along an individual trace and then along all traces of a hybrid program.

4.1   Semantics of State Formulas

State formulas are evaluated at states, which capture the behavior of the hybrid program at an instant in time. Each state contains the values of all relevant variables at a given instant. We formalize this in the following definition.

Definition 3. *A state is a map $\omega : \Sigma_{var} \rightarrow \mathbb{R}$. We distinguish a separate state Λ to indicate the failure of a system run. The set of all states is $Sta(\Sigma_{var})$.*

We now give the semantics of state formulas. The $val(\omega, \phi)$ operator determines whether state formula ϕ is true or false in state ω. The valuations of the state formulas $[\alpha]\kappa$ and $\langle\alpha\rangle\kappa$ depend on the semantics of traces σ (especially the notion of first σ), which is explained in Definition 5, and on the semantics of the trace formula κ (i.e., $val(\omega, \kappa)$) which is given later, in Definition 12, and may be undefined.

Definition 4 ([25]). *The valuation of state formulas with respect to state ω is defined inductively:*

1. *$val(\omega, p(\theta_1, \ldots, \theta_n))$ is $p^\ell(val(\omega, \theta_1), \ldots, val(\omega, \theta_n))$ where p^ℓ is the relation associated with p under the semantics of real arithmetic*
2. *$val(\omega, \neg\phi)$ is true iff $val(\omega, \phi)$ is false*
3. *$val(\omega, \phi \wedge \psi)$ is true iff $val(\omega, \phi)$ is true and $val(\omega, \psi)$ is true*
4. *$val(\omega, \forall x\, \phi)$ is true iff $val(\omega_x^d, \phi)$ is true for all $d \in \mathbb{R}$, where ω_x^d is the state that is identical to ω, except x has the value d.*
5. *$val(\omega, [\alpha]\kappa)$ is true iff for every trace σ of α that starts in first $\sigma = \omega$, if $val(\sigma, \kappa)$ is defined, then $val(\sigma, \kappa)$ is true*
6. *$val(\omega, \langle\alpha\rangle\kappa)$ is true iff there is some trace σ of α where first $\sigma = \omega$ and $val(\sigma, \kappa)$ is true*

We write $\omega \models \phi$ when $val(\omega, \phi)$ is true. We write $\omega \not\models \phi$ when $val(\omega, \phi)$ is false.

4.2 Traces of Hybrid Programs

Trace formulas are evaluated with respect to an execution trace of a hybrid program. Intuitively, a trace of a hybrid program views its behavior over time as a sequence of functions, where each function corresponds to a particular discrete or continuous portion of the dynamics. Most hybrid systems are associated with multiple traces (to reflect the variety of behaviors that a given program can exhibit). Each function within a trace maps from a time interval to states of the hybrid program. Continuous portions of traces are functions from an uncountable time interval, and thus are associated to uncountably many states, whereas discrete portions involve just a single state. Significantly, traces are allowed to end in an abort state Λ, which indicates an unsuccessful run of a program. Aborts are incurred when tests fail and when evolution domain constraints are not initially satisfied. No program can run past Λ. We review the formal definition below.

Definition 5 ([25]). *A trace σ of a hybrid program α is a sequence of functions $\sigma = (\sigma_0, \sigma_1, \ldots, \sigma_n)$ where $\sigma_i : [0, r_i] \to Sta(\Sigma_{var})$. We will denote the length of the interval associated to σ_i by $|\sigma_i|$ (so that if σ_i maps from $[0, r_i]$ to states of α, $|\sigma_i| = r_i$). A position of σ is a tuple (i, ζ) where $i \in \mathbb{N}$, $\zeta \in [0, r_i]$. Each position (i, ζ) is associated with the corresponding state $\sigma_i(\zeta)$. A trace $(\sigma_0, \sigma_1, \ldots, \sigma_n)$ is said to terminate if it does not end in the abort state, i.e. if $\sigma_n(|\sigma_n|) \neq \Lambda$, and we write last $\sigma \equiv \sigma_n(|\sigma_n|)$ in that case. We write first $\sigma \equiv \sigma_0(0)$ for the first state.*

We now modify the trace semantics [25] using Carathéodory solutions for ODEs [30] using notation as in [26, Definition 2.6].

Definition 6. *The state ν is* reachable in the extended sense *from initial state ω by $x'_1 = \theta_1, \ldots, x'_n = \theta_n$ & R iff there is a function $\varphi : [0, r] \to Sta(\Sigma_{var})$ s.t.:*

1. *Initial and final states match: $\varphi(0) = \omega, \varphi(r) = \nu$.*
2. *φ is absolutely continuous.*
3. *φ respects the differential equations almost everywhere: For each variable x_i, $\varphi(z)(x_i)$ is continuous in z on $[0, r]$ and if $r > 0$, $\varphi(z)(x_i)$ has a time-derivative of value $\varphi(z)(\theta_i)$ at all $z \in [0, r] \setminus \mathcal{U}$, for some set $\mathcal{U} \subset [0, r]$ that has Lebesgue measure zero.*
4. *The value of other variables $y \notin \{x_1, \ldots, x_n\}$ remains constant throughout the continuous evolution, that is $\varphi(z)(y) = \omega(y)$ for all times $z \in [0, r]$;*
5. *φ respects the evolution domain at all times: $\varphi(z) \models R$ for all $z \in [0, r]$.*

If such a φ exists, we say that $\varphi \models x'_1 = \theta_1 \wedge \cdots \wedge x'_n = \theta_n$ & R almost everywhere.

This change highlights how the PHS intuition aligns with the intuition behind Carathéodory solutions. However, we have left the syntax of hybrid programs unchanged, and any system of differential equations in this syntax has a unique classical solution by Picard-Lindelöf [26]. We believe that in order to determine a suitable generalization of the syntax of hybrid programs to allow systems of ODEs with Carathéodory solutions, one should first develop strategies for reasoning about ODEs in PdTL that are beyond the scope of this work (for example, a notion of differential invariants—see [26,27]).

Note that in condition 5 of Definition 6, the solution is required to stay within the evolution domain constraint at *all* times. This is because evolution domain constraints, when used correctly, are nonnegotiable—for example, a correct use of evolution domain constraints is to reflect some underlying property of physics, like that the speed of a decelerating system is always nonnegative.

We define the trace semantics [25], with the above change for ODEs. Like evolution domain constraints, we treat tests as nonnegotiable, so as not to interfere with a user's ability to write precise models. We do not intend to secretly change the meaning of models, but rather to identify physically correct models.

Definition 7. *The trace semantics, $\tau(\alpha)$, of a hybrid program α is the set of all its possible hybrid traces and is defined inductively as follows (where $e \in Trm(\Sigma)$, $x'=f(x)$ is a vectorial ODE, R and P are FOL formulas, β is a hybrid program, and where for a state ω, $\hat{\omega}$ is the function from $[0,0] \to Sta(\Sigma_{var})$ with $\hat{\omega}(0) = \omega$):*

1. $\tau(x := e) = \{(\hat{\omega}, \hat{\nu}) : \nu = \omega_x^{val(\omega,e)} \ for \ \omega \in Sta(\Sigma_{var})\}$
2. $\tau(x'=f(x) \ \& \ R) = \{(\varphi) : \varphi \models x'=f(x) \ \& \ R \ almost \ everywhere\} \cup \{(\hat{\omega}, \hat{\Lambda}) : \omega \not\models R\}$
3. $\tau(\alpha \cup \beta) = \tau(\alpha) \cup \tau(\beta)$
4. $\tau(?P) = \{(\hat{\omega}) : val(\omega, P) = true\} \cup \{(\hat{\omega}, \hat{\Lambda}) : val(\omega, P) = false\}$
5. $\tau(\alpha; \beta) = \{\sigma \circ \zeta : \sigma \in \tau(\alpha), \zeta \in \tau(\beta) \ when \ \sigma \circ \zeta \ is \ defined\}$; *the composition of $\sigma = (\sigma_0, \sigma_1, \sigma_2, \dots)$ and $\zeta = (\zeta_0, \zeta_1, \zeta_2, \dots)$ is*

$$\sigma \circ \zeta := \begin{cases} (\sigma_0, \dots, \sigma_n, \zeta_0, \zeta_1, \dots) & \textit{if } \sigma \textit{ terminates at } \sigma_n \textit{ and last } \sigma = \textit{first } \zeta \\ \sigma & \textit{if } \sigma \textit{ does not terminate} \\ \textit{not defined} & \textit{otherwise} \end{cases}$$

6. $\tau(\alpha^*) = \bigcup_{n \in \mathbb{N}} \tau(\alpha^n)$, *where $\alpha^{n+1} := (\alpha^n; \alpha)$ for $n \geq 1$, and $\alpha^0 := ?(true)$*

As an important remark, notice that if we have a trace $\sigma = (\sigma_0, \dots, \sigma_n)$ and $|\sigma_i| > 0$, then $\sigma_i \in \tau(x' = f(x) \ \& \ R)$ for some (vectorial) ODE $x' = f(x)$ and some evolution domain constraint R. In other words, only continuous portions of a trace have nonzero duration, and continuous portions are only introduced when our system is evolving subject to a system of differential equations.

We are almost ready to give the semantics of trace formulas, but first we need to take a slight detour to discuss what formulas make "physical sense".

4.3 Physical Formulas

One feature of our motivating example is that $v<100$ is not a physically meaningful postcondition: If v is allowed to get arbitrarily close to 100, $v=100$ should also be allowed, since there is no physically measurable difference between $v<100$ and $v\leq100$. The postcondition $v\leq100$ is, mathematically speaking, less restrictive than $v<100$, but also practically speaking, the same as $v<100$. Motivated by this intuition, we define "physical formulas".

Physical Formulas and $\overline{\phi}$. Geometrically, the set of states in which a state formula ϕ in n variables is true is a subset, $[\![\phi]\!] = \{(x_1,\ldots,x_n) \in \mathbb{R}^n \mid \phi(x_1,\ldots,x_n)\}$, of $\mathbb{R}^n$. We use this correspondence to define the physical version of ϕ.

Definition 8. *A state formula ϕ is called* physical *iff $[\![\phi]\!]$ is topologically closed. If ϕ is a formula in n variables $x_1,\ldots,x_n$, then the physical version of ϕ is the closure, denoted by $\overline{\phi}$, and is, indeed, definable* [3] *by:*

$$\forall\epsilon{>}0\,\exists y_1,\ldots,y_n\ \left(\phi(y_1,\ldots,y_n)\wedge(x_1-y_1)^2+\cdots+(x_n-y_n)^2<\epsilon^2\right)$$

This satisfies $[\![\overline{\phi}]\!] = \overline{[\![\phi]\!]}$, where $\overline{[\![\phi]\!]}$ is the topological closure of $[\![\phi]\!]$. Quantifier elimination can compute a quantifier-free equivalent of $\overline{\phi}$ that is often preferable.

Associating a state formula to a subset of $\mathbb{R}^n$ is useful for identifying which points are "almost included", which will be crucial knowledge for our temporal approach. In the train example, $v{=}100$ is "almost included" in the postcondition $v{<}100$. These points that are "almost included" in formula ϕ are exactly the limit points of the set associated to ϕ, so $\overline{[\![\phi]\!]}$ adds in all of these limit points. We will make use of the following properties of the physical version of ϕ. Both are proved in a companion report [5].

Proposition 9. *For any state formula ϕ, $\phi \rightarrow \overline{\phi}$ is valid (i.e., true in all states).*

Proposition 10. *The following proof rule is sound for state formulas ϕ, ψ (i.e., the validity of all premises implies the validity of the conclusion):*

$$\frac{\phi \rightarrow \psi}{\overline{\phi} \rightarrow \psi}\ TopCl$$

4.4   Semantics of Trace Formulas

Intuitively, we want to say that, for a trace σ, $\sigma \models \Box_{\text{t.a.e}}\phi$ when there is only a "small" set of positions (i,ζ) where $\sigma_i(\zeta) \not\models \phi$ and where the discrete portions of σ satisfy a reasonable constraint. To formalize the notion of a "small" set of positions, we map positions of σ to $\mathbb{R}$, since $\mathbb{R}$ admits the Lebesgue measure.

Definition 11. *Given a trace $\sigma = (\sigma_0,\ldots,\sigma_n)$ of a hybrid program α with $|\sigma_i| = r_i$, map each position (i,ζ) of σ to $\zeta + i + \sum_{k=0}^{i-1}|\sigma_k|$, so that the positions $(0,0),\ldots,(0,r_0)$ cover the interval $[0,r_0]$, the positions $(1,0),\ldots,(1,r_1)$ cover the interval $[r_0 + 1, r_0 + r_1 + 1]$, and so on. In this way we have an injection, which we call f, from positions of a trace σ to (a subset of) $\mathbb{R}$.*

Figure 1 illustrates the mapping f, which is obtained by first concatenating the positions between each discrete step (i.e. the positions for each continuous function σ_i) and then projecting these concatenations onto a single time axis

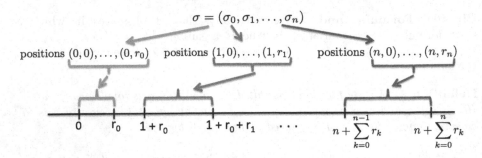

Fig. 1. Injectively mapping positions of a trace to times in $\mathbb{R}$

so that the images of the states for σ_i and the states for σ_j are disjoint when $i \neq j$. To ensure disjointness, our mapping places an open interval of unit length between the images of the states of σ_i and the states of σ_{i+1} (for all i). The unit length was chosen arbitrarily—any nonzero length would work—but it is important that the positions (i, r_i) and $(i+1, 0)$ have different projections, since discrete changes can cause their states $\sigma_i(r_i)$ and $\sigma_{i+1}(0)$ to be different.

Definition 12. *The valuation of a trace formula κ with respect to trace σ is defined as:*

1. $val(\sigma, \phi) = val(last\ \sigma, \phi)$ *if σ terminates. If σ does not terminate, then $val(\sigma, \phi)$ is undefined. We write $\sigma \models \phi$ when $val(\sigma, \phi)$ is true. We write $\sigma \not\models \phi$ when $val(\sigma, \phi)$ is false.*
2. *Let $\mathcal{U}$ be the set of positions (i, ζ) where corresponding states $\sigma_i(\zeta)$ satisfy $\sigma_i(\zeta) \not\models \phi$ and $\sigma_i(\zeta) \neq \Lambda$. We say that $val(\sigma, \Box_{tae}\phi)$ is true iff the following two conditions are satisfied:*
   (a) *(Discrete condition) For all i, if $|\sigma_i| = 0$ and $\sigma_i(0) \neq \Lambda$, then $\sigma_i(0) \models \overline{\phi}$.*
   (b) *(Continuous condition) $f(\mathcal{U}) \subseteq \mathbb{R}$ has measure zero with respect to the Lebesgue measure, where f is the mapping defined in Definition 11 for σ; i.e., for all $\epsilon > 0$ there exist intervals $I_p = [a_p, b_p]$ so that $f(\mathcal{U}) \subseteq \bigcup_{p=0}^{\infty} I_p$ and $\sum_{p=0}^{\infty} |b_p - a_p| < \epsilon$ (see [16, Section 1-1013], or [28]).*
   We write $\sigma \models \Box_{tae}\phi$ when $val(\sigma, \Box_{tae}\phi)$ is true. We write $\sigma \not\models \Box_{tae}\phi$ when $val(\sigma, \Box_{tae}\phi)$ is false.

A short primer on the measure theory we need is in a companion report [5].

With this mapping, the condition that $f(\mathcal{U})$ has measure zero with respect to the Lebesgue measure enforces the t.a.e. constraint for the continuous portions of our program. The image of the states for σ_i is an interval of length r_i. In order for the t.a.e constraint to be satisfied, σ_i cannot go wrong except at a "small set" of states, where we use our mapping to formalize the notion of a "small set" in terms of measure zero.

Next, the condition that $\sigma_i(0) \models \overline{\phi}$ whenever $|\sigma_i| = 0$ constrains the discrete portions of a program. This constraint will be important for induction; it also ensures that discrete programs behave reasonably within our logic. For example, let α be the fully discrete program $x := 5; (x := x + 1)^*$, and take a trace σ of α. The states of σ map to the points $5, 6, 7, \ldots, n$, and *without the discrete condition*, we would be able to show that $[x := 5; (x := x+1)^*]\Box_{\text{tae}}x{<}5$ is valid, even though x is never less than 5 along the trace.

To understand why the discrete condition specifies $\sigma_i(0) \models \overline{\phi}$ when $|\sigma_i| = 0$ instead of $\sigma_i(0) \models \phi$ when $|\sigma_i| = 0$, recall the motivating train control example. We want to allow the velocity of the train to evolve from a safe state where $v{<}100$ to an unsafe state where $v{=}100$, as long as the train then immediately brakes (sets its acceleration to a negative value). If we specified that $\sigma_i(0) \models \phi$, the train would *not* be allowed to accelerate from $v{<}100$ to $v{=}100$ and then brake, because at the discrete braking point, the train would be in a state that is unsafe mathematically (though still safe physically).

Given a hybrid program α, postcondition ϕ, and a state ω, we are interested in determining whether $\omega \models [\alpha]\Box_{\text{tae}}\phi$ holds, because when such a formula is true for a given hybrid program, that indicates that no matter how that particular hybrid program runs, it will be "safe almost everywhere". Following Definition 4, this is true iff for each trace $\sigma \in \tau(\alpha)$ with first $\sigma = \omega$, $\sigma \models \Box_{\text{tae}}\phi$.

5 Discussion

Now that we have developed the semantics, we step back to consider how PdTL makes progress towards PHS, and why PdTL is a good way to introduce PHS.

Impact on Modeling. PdTL allows the verification of several classes of physically realistic models that are mathematically not quite safe. For example, in Sect. 7 we will explain how PdTL allows the verification of the train control model. This simple train example is representative of a greater class of examples— tiny glitches are common in event-triggered controllers, since the event that is being detected is often an almost unsafe event that requires the controller to immediately change behavior.

Other examples do not involve time-triggered controllers, but rather suffer from tiny glitches at handover points between the discrete and continuous dynamics within a hybrid program. Consider the safety postcondition $x^2+y^2 < 1$ and the hybrid program $x := 0; y := 1; \{x' = -x, y' = -y\}$. The only glitch is that the program starts ever so slightly outside the safe set. Since it immediately moves into the safe set, all runs of this hybrid program are safe tae. PdTL is designed to classify $[x := 0; y := 1; \{x' = -x, y' = -y\}]\Box_{\text{tae}}x^2 + y^2{<}1$ as valid.

In another class of examples, our approach handles tiny glitches within the continuous portion of the program. This can easily happen if the postcondition is missing some small regions. For example, consider two robots that are moving, one in front of the other. Since we do not want the robots to collide, it is unsafe for the second robot to accelerate while the first robot is braking. Say we model this with safety postcondition $\neg(a_1 \le 0 \land a_2 \ge 0)$. This is a small modeling mistake, because we should allow the point where $a_1 = 0$ and $a_2 = 0$. Now, if our controller is $a_1 := -1; a_2 := -1; \{a_1' = 1, a_2' = 1\}$, any run of this hybrid program is tae safe, but not safe at all points in time (as some runs will contain the origin). Notably, the very similar controller $a_1 := -1; a_2 := -1; \{a'_1 = 1, a'_2 = 2\}$ is *not* tae safe. PdTL is designed to distinguish between these two controllers.

Why tae? The tae safety notion along the trace of a hybrid system is a natural approach with strong mathematical underpinnings (e.g., from the invariance of Lebesgue integrals up to sets of measure zero, and from Carathéodory solutions), and with physical motivation from examples like those just discussed. Introducing tae is a good way to begin PHS, because it may be the closest possible PHS construct to the canonical notion of "safety everywhere". However, this closeness to safety everywhere does make tae more restrictive than some other possible PHS notions—for example, a notion of safety "space almost everywhere", or sae.

Consider a self-driving car moving in $\mathbb{R}^3$. The final states of a hybrid program α modeling the car correspond to positions in $\mathbb{R}^3$, so here we may wish to consider safety almost everywhere with respect to the Lebesgue measure *on the set of all possible final states of* α as follows: Given a hybrid program α and precondition ψ, let $\mathcal{F} = \{\text{last } \sigma \text{ s.t. } \sigma \in \tau(\alpha), \text{first } \sigma \models \psi\}$. Say that $\psi \vdash [\alpha]\square_{\mu\text{sae}}\phi$ if $\mu(\{\omega \in \mathcal{F} \mid \omega \not\models \phi\}) = 0$, where μ is the Lebesgue measure on $\mathbb{R}^3$. This modality has an intuitive geometric interpretation and is more permissive than tae.

However, $\square_{\mu\text{sae}}$ applies only when there is a natural measure μ on the set of all possible final states of α. Furthermore, $\square_{\mu\text{sae}}$ is not compositional. Given $P \vdash [\alpha]\square_{\mu\text{sae}}P$ and $P \vdash [\beta]\square_{\mu\text{sae}}P$, in order to conclude that $P \vdash [\alpha; \beta]\square_{\mu\text{sae}}P$, one needs to know that β is sae safe when starting in $[\![P]\!] \cup Q$, for any measure zero set Q reachable from α. This is not always true—for example, let P be $x^2 + y^2 < 1$, α be $\{x' = 1, y' = 1 \ \& \ x^2 + y^2 \le 1\}$ and β be $?(x^2 + y^2 = 1); \{x' = 1, y' = 1\}$. Further, given α, it is unclear how to syntactically classify such sets Q—as sae is more relaxed than tae, it also seems to be less well-behaved. Thus, although $\square_{\mu\text{sae}}$ has some advantages, it is not clear how to constrain it to achieve desirable logical properties like compositionality. Although we hope that future work will develop a notion of safety sae, the challenges therein are no small matter. In contrast, tae satisfies many nice logical properties, which we now turn our attention to.

6   Proof Calculus and Properties of PdTL

Before developing the proof calculus for PdTL, we discuss some key properties. First, PdTL is a *conservative* extension of dL, i.e. all valid formulas of dL are still valid in PdTL. The proof of this, discussed in a companion report [5], is essentially the same as the proof that dTL is a conservative extension of dL [25, Proposition 4.1]. This conservativity property is useful, since if we are able to reduce temporal PdTL formulas to dL formulas, we can use the extensive machinery built for dL to close proofs. Indeed, our proof calculus is designed to reduce temporal PdTL formulas into nontemporal formulas to rely on dL's capabilities for the latter.

Key dL axioms are proved sound for PdTL in a companion report [5], which is useful as sometimes a dL axiom is needed to reduce the goal in a proof, as we will see when we analyze the train example in Sect. 7.

Next, we state three properties of temporal PdTL formulas which underlie some of the soundness proofs for rules in the proof calculus. These properties hold by construction. All proofs are in the companion report [5].

Lemma 13. *If* $\sigma \models \Box_{tae}\phi$ *for a terminating* σ*, then last* $\sigma \models \overline{\phi}$*.*

Corollary 14. *The formula* $[\alpha]\Box_{tae}\phi \to [\alpha]\overline{\phi}$ *is valid.*

Lemma 15. *If* ξ *and* η *are traces of hybrid programs where* ξ *terminates and* last $\xi =$ *first* η*, then* $\xi \circ \eta \models \Box_{tae}\phi$ *iff both* $\xi \models \Box_{tae}\phi$ *and* $\eta \models \Box_{tae}\phi$*.*

6.1 Proof Calculus

The proof calculus for PdTL is shown in Fig. 2. Intuitively, all of the axioms are designed to successively decompose complicated formulas into structurally simpler formulas while successively reducing trace formulas into state formulas. The test axiom, assignment axiom, solution axiom, and solution with evolution domain constraint axiom ($[?]_{tae}$, $[:=]_{tae}$, $[']_{tae}$, and $['\&]_{tae}$) remove instances of $\Box_{tae}$. The nondeterministic choice axiom $[\cup]_{tae}$ reduces a choice between two hybrid programs to two separate programs. The induction axiom I_{tae} reduces a loop property involving a trace formula to a loop property involving a state formula; I_{tae} also allows us to derive two very useful proof rules.

$$[?]_{tae} \quad [?P]\Box_{tae}\phi \leftrightarrow \overline{\phi}$$

$$[\cup]_{tae} \quad [\alpha \cup \beta]\Box_{tae}\phi \leftrightarrow [\alpha]\Box_{tae}\phi \wedge [\beta]\Box_{tae}\phi$$

$$[:=]_{tae} \quad [x := e]\Box_{tae}\psi \leftrightarrow \overline{\phi} \wedge [x := e]\overline{\phi}$$

$$[;]_{tae} \quad [\alpha; \beta]\Box_{tae}\phi \leftrightarrow ([\alpha]\Box_{tae}\phi \wedge [\alpha][\beta]\Box_{tae}\phi)$$

$$I_{tae} \quad [\alpha^*]\Box_{tae}\phi \leftrightarrow (\overline{\phi} \wedge [\alpha^*](\overline{\phi} \to [\alpha]\Box_{tae}\phi))$$

$$[']_{tae} \quad [x' = f(x)]\Box_{tae}P \leftrightarrow \overline{P} \wedge \forall t{\geq}0 Q$$

$$['\&]_{tae} \quad [x' = f(x)\&R]\Box_{tae}P \leftrightarrow \overline{P} \wedge$$
$$\forall t{>}0\,((\forall 0{\leq}s{\leq}t\,[x := y(s)]R) \to Q)$$

$$\frac{\phi}{[\alpha]\Box_{tae}\phi}\ G_{tae}$$

$$\frac{\overline{\phi} \to \overline{\psi} \quad [\alpha]\Box_{tae}(\phi \to \psi)}{[\alpha]\Box_{tae}\phi \to [\alpha]\Box_{tae}\psi}\ K_{tae}$$

$$\frac{\phi \to \psi}{\overline{\phi} \to \overline{\psi}}\ \text{TopCl}$$

$$\text{CGG} \quad [\alpha]\Box_{tae}\phi \to [\alpha]\overline{\phi}$$

Fig. 2. Proof calculus for PdTL (Here, α and β are hybrid programs, ϕ and ψ are state formulas, P is a FOL formula, $y(t)$ is the unique global polynomial solution to the differential equation $x' = f(x)$, and the formula Q in $[']_{tae}$ and $['\&]_{tae}$ is the FOL formula constructed by Proposition 16 for $P(y(t))$. Although the "for almost all" quantifier is in general *not* definable in FOL [23], Proposition 16 justifies that "for almost all $t{\geq}0[x := y(t)]P$" is logically equivalent to "$\forall t{\geq}0\,Q$".)

The Gödel generalization rule (G_{tae}) proves that if formula ϕ is valid, then it is also true, tae, along the trace of any hybrid program. The modal modus ponens rule (K_{tae}) allows us to derive a monotonicity property. Our approach occasionally introduces extra premises; for example, the modal modus ponens rule (K_{tae}) has an extra goal $\overline{\phi} \to \overline{\psi}$ due to the discrete condition of Definition 12. Many of these extra premises will be easy to prove—if our models make use of physical formulas, which are closed, then these extra cases will prove immediately.

Soundness proofs are in the report [5]. We discuss a few key high-level ideas.

Soundness of $[;]_{tae}$ *and* I_{tae}. Sequential composition and induction are subtly challenging for PHS—since we are allowed to leave the safe set, handover points between hybrid programs are no longer guaranteed to be safe points. However, sequential composition and induction are crucial for the practicality of verification, which is predicated on having a good way of breaking down complicated formulas into simpler components. The soundness proof of $[;]_{tae}$ exploits Lemma 15. The soundness proof of I_{tae} is based on Lemma 13, which in turn relies on the discrete condition of Definition 12.

Differential Equations. Reasoning about differential equations is one of the most challenging aspects of hybrid systems. In this work, we focus on relatively simple reasoning principles for differential equations, as justifying even simple principles is made much more challenging by introducing the notion of "safety almost everywhere". We leave the development of more complicated reasoning (for example, a notion of differential invariants for $\square_{tae}$) to future work.

For "sufficiently tame" systems of ODEs $x' = f(x)$, we might hope to replace $[x' = f(x)]\square_{tae}P$ with an equivalent expression without the $\square_{tae}$ modality. The cleanest case is when $x' = f(x)$ has a unique global polynomial solution, $y(t)$. Although we think of y as being a polynomial in t, y can involve any of the other parameters, call them $x_1, \ldots, x_n$, in f, from its dependency on initial values. We require that y is also polynomial in $x_1, \ldots, x_n$. This is the case handled by axiom $[']_{tae}$: $[x' = f(x)]\square_{tae}P \leftrightarrow \overline{P} \land \forall t \geq 0\, Q$, where Q is a FOL formula constructed so that "$\forall t \geq 0\, Q$" expresses "for almost all $t \geq 0\, [x := y(t)]P$". Axiom $['\&]_{tae}$ generalizes $[']_{tae}$ to ODEs with evolution domain constraints.

In particular, we get Q by applying Proposition 16 to $P(y(t))$, which is the formula obtained using the assignment axiom $[:=]$ of dL on $[x := y(t)]P$ (it is a FOL formula because $y(t)$ is polynomial and polynomials are closed under composition). Given any FOL formula P, Proposition 16 constructs a FOL formula Q so that "for almost all $t \geq 0\, P$" is semantically equivalent to $\forall t \geq 0\, Q$ (i.e., "for almost all $t \geq 0\, P$" is true in a state ω iff $\forall t \geq 0\, Q$ is true in ω).

Proposition 16. *Let P be a FOL formula. Using quantifier elimination [29], put it into one of the following normal forms: $e = 0$, $e \geq 0$, $e < 0$, $P_1 \land P_2$, and $P_1 \lor P_2$, where e is a polynomial and P_1, P_2 are FOL formulas. Construct the FOL formula $Q = g(P)$ by structural induction on P as follows: $g(e = 0)$ is $e = 0$, $g(e \geq 0)$ is $e \geq 0$, $g(e < 0)$ is $e \leq 0 \land ((a_n = 0 \land \cdots \land a_1 = 0) \to e < 0)$, $g(P_1 \land P_2)$ is $g(P_1) \land g(P_2)$, and $g(P_1 \lor P_2)$ is $g(P_1) \lor g(P_2)$.*

Then, for any state ω, the following hold:

1. *Locally false: If $\omega_t^k \not\models Q$ for some $k \geq 0$, then there is a nonempty interval $[k, \ell)$ so that for all $q \in [k, \ell)$, $\omega_t^q \not\models P$. Further, if $k > 0$, then there is an interval (ℓ_1, ℓ_2) with $\ell_1 < k < \ell_2$ so that for all $q \in (\ell_1, \ell_2)$, $\omega_t^q \not\models P$.*
2. *Finite difference: There are only finitely many values $k \geq 0$ where $\omega_t^k \models Q \wedge \neg P$.*

The proof is by induction on the structure of P; details are in the report [5].

6.2 Derived Rules

We highlight some of the most useful derived rules for PdTL formulas in Fig. 3. Monotonicity properties are fundamental in logic. Our rule M_{tae} intuitively says that if $\psi \to \phi$ is valid, then if ψ is true almost everywhere along every trace of a hybrid program, then ϕ is also true almost everywhere along every trace of that hybrid program. The rule Ind_{tae} reduces proving a safety property of hybrid program α^* to proving a safety property of program α. When its premise proves, it effectively removes the need to reason about loops. The rule loop_{tae} provides us with a loop invariant rule. The rule Comp_{tae} reduces a property of $\alpha; \beta$ to individual properties of α and β. The derivations are given in the report [5].

$$\frac{\psi \to \phi}{[\alpha]\square_{\text{tae}}\psi \to [\alpha]\square_{\text{tae}}\phi} \; M_{\text{tae}} \qquad\qquad \frac{\overline{\phi} \vdash [\alpha]\square_{\text{tae}}\phi}{\overline{\phi} \vdash [\alpha^*]\square_{\text{tae}}\phi} \; \text{Ind}_{\text{tae}}$$

$$\frac{\Gamma \vdash \overline{\psi}, \Delta \quad \overline{\psi} \vdash [\alpha]\square_{\text{tae}}\psi \quad \psi \vdash \phi}{\Gamma \vdash [\alpha^*]\square_{\text{tae}}\phi, \Delta} \; \text{loop}_{\text{tae}} \qquad \frac{\psi \to [\alpha]\square_{\text{tae}}\phi \quad \overline{\phi} \to [\beta]\square_{\text{tae}}\phi}{\psi \to [\alpha; \beta]\square_{\text{tae}}\phi} \; \text{Comp}_{\text{tae}}$$

Fig. 3. Derived rules for PdTL

7 Proof of Motivating Example

We now apply our proof calculus to the model of the train example (Sect. 3). Full details are in the report [5]. Using structural rule $\to R$ and our induction proof rule loop_{tae} with invariant $v < 100$, the proof reduces to showing $a=0 \wedge v=0 \vdash v \leq 100$ (which holds by real arithmetic), $v < 100 \vdash v < 100$ (identically true), and

$$v \leq 100 \vdash [((?(v < 100); a := 1) \cup (?(v = 100); a := -1));$$
$$\{x' = v, v' = a \; \& \; 0 \leq v \leq 100\}]\square_{\text{tae}} v < 100.$$

Axiom $[;]_{\text{tae}}$ splits this into goals (1) and (2):

$$v \leq 100 \vdash [(?(v < 100); a := 1) \cup (?(v = 100); a := -1)]\square_{\text{tae}} v < 100 \qquad (1)$$

$$v\leq100 \vdash [(?(v<100); a := 1) \cup (?(v=100); a := -1)]$$
$$[\{x' = v, v' = a \ \& \ 0\leq v\leq100\}]\Box_{\text{tae}}v<100. \tag{2}$$

(1) is straighforward. (2) is more complicated because it involves ODEs reasoning. The dL axioms $[\cup]$ and $\wedge R$ split the proof of (2) into (3) and (4):

$$v\leq100 \vdash [?(v<100); a := 1][\{x' = v, v' = a \ \& \ 0\leq v\leq100\}]\Box_{\text{tae}}v<100 \tag{3}$$
$$v\leq100 \vdash [?(v=100); a := -1][\{x' = v, v' = a \ \& \ 0\leq v\leq100\}]\Box_{\text{tae}}v<100 \tag{4}$$

(3) and (4) require similar reasoning, so we focus on (3). The dL axioms $[;], [:=]$, and $[?]$ reduce (3) to

$$v\leq100, v<100 \vdash [\{x' = v, v' = 1 \ \& \ 0\leq v\leq100\}]\Box_{\text{tae}}v<100 \tag{5}$$

To prove (5), we need to use axiom $['\&]_{\text{tae}}$, which says:

$$[x' = f(x)\&R]\Box_{\text{tae}}P \leftrightarrow \overline{P} \wedge \forall t>0 \, ((\forall 0\leq s\leq t \ [x := y(s)]R) \rightarrow Q)$$

For clarity, we use v_0 for the value of v in the initial state before it starts evolving along the ODEs, and similarly we use x_0 for the value of x in the initial state. Following Proposition 16, Q is $(1 = 0 \rightarrow t + v_0<100) \wedge t + v_0\leq100$. Since applying $['\&]_{tae}$ reduces our goal to a dL formula, and since PdTL is a conservative extension of dL, we can use the contextual equivalence rules of dL to replace Q with the logically equivalent formula $t + v_0\leq100$, obtaining:

$$v_0\leq100, v_0<100 \vdash v_0\leq100 \wedge \forall t>0$$
$$((\forall 0\leq s\leq t \ [x := .5s^2 + v_0 s + x_0][v := s + v_0]0\leq v\leq100) \rightarrow t + v_0\leq100) \tag{6}$$

After using the dL axiom $[:=]$, the proof closes by real arithmetic.

8   Conclusions and Future Work

We introduce PHS to help narrow the gap between mathematical models and physical reality. To enable logic to begin to distinguish between true unsafeties of systems and physically unrealistic unsafeties, we develop the notion of safety tae along the execution trace of a system. Our new logic, PdTL, contains the logical operator $\Box_{\text{tae}}$, which elides sets of time that have measure zero.

A cornerstone of our approach is its logical practicality—in order to support verification, we develop a proof calculus for PdTL. We demonstrate the capability of the proof calculus by applying it to a motivating example. We think it is an interesting and challenging problem for future work to develop new ways of thinking about PHS, such as the notion of space almost everywhere discussed in Sect. 5, while maintaining this logical practicality.

Future work could continue to develop PdTL. It would be especially interesting to develop further differential equations reasoning, including an appropriate generalization of the syntax of hybrid programs to admit Carathéodory solutions.

Acknowledgements. We very much appreciate Yong Kiam Tan and Rose Bohrer for many useful discussions and for feedback on the paper. Thank you also to the anonymous CADE'19 reviewers for their thorough feedback.

References

1. Alur, R., Courcoubetis, C., Henzinger, T.A., Ho, P.H.: Hybrid automata: an algorithmic approach to the specification and verification of hybrid systems. In: Grossman et al. [14], pp. 209–229
2. Asarin, E., Bouajjani, A.: Perturbed turing machines and hybrid systems. In: Proceedings of the 16th Annual IEEE Symposium on Logic in Computer Science, Boston, Massachusetts, USA, 16–19 June 2001, pp. 269–278. IEEE Computer Society (2001). https://doi.org/10.1109/LICS.2001.932503
3. Bochnak, J., Coste, M., Roy, M.F.: Real Algebraic Geometry. Springer, Heidelberg (1998). https://doi.org/10.1007/978-3-662-03718-8
4. Ceragioli, F.: Some remarks on stabilization by means of discontinuous feedbacks. Syst. Control Lett. **45**(4), 271–281 (2002). https://doi.org/10.1016/S0167-6911(01)00185-2
5. Cordwell, K., Platzer, A.: Towards physical hybrid systems. CoRR abs/1905.09520 (2019). http://arxiv.org/abs/1905.09520
6. Cortes, J.: Discontinuous dynamical systems. IEEE Control Syst. **28**(3), 36–73 (2008). https://doi.org/10.1109/MCS.2008.919306
7. Dam, M.: CTL* and ECTL* as fragments of the modal μ-calculus. Theor. Comput. Sci. **126**(1), 77–96 (1994). https://doi.org/10.1016/0304-3975(94)90269-0
8. Donzé, A., Ferrère, T., Maler, O.: Efficient robust monitoring for STL. In: Sharygina, N., Veith, H. (eds.) CAV 2013. LNCS, vol. 8044, pp. 264–279. Springer, Heidelberg (2013). https://doi.org/10.1007/978-3-642-39799-8_19
9. Fainekos, G.E., Pappas, G.J.: Robustness of temporal logic specifications for continuous-time signals. Theor. Comput. Sci. **410**(42), 4262–4291 (2009). https://doi.org/10.1016/j.tcs.2009.06.021
10. Fränzle, M.: Analysis of hybrid systems: an ounce of realism can save an infinity of states. In: Flum, J., Rodriguez-Artalejo, M. (eds.) CSL 1999. LNCS, vol. 1683, pp. 126–139. Springer, Heidelberg (1999). https://doi.org/10.1007/3-540-48168-0_10
11. Gao, S., Avigad, J., Clarke, E.M.: Delta-decidability over the reals. In: Proceedings of the 27th Annual IEEE Symposium on Logic in Computer Science, LICS 2012, Dubrovnik, Croatia, 25–28 June 2012, pp. 305–314. IEEE Computer Society (2012). https://doi.org/10.1109/LICS.2012.41
12. Goebel, R., Sanfelice, R.G., Teel, A.R.: Hybrid dynamical systems. IEEE Control Syst. Mag. **29**(2), 28–93 (2009). https://doi.org/10.1109/MCS.2008.931718
13. Goebel, R., Hespanha, J., Teel, A.R., Cai, C., Sanfelice, R.: Hybrid systems: generalized solutions and robust stability. IIFAC Proc. Vol. **37**(13), 1–12 (2004). https://doi.org/10.1016/S1474-6670(17)31194-1. 6th IFAC Symposium on Nonlinear Control Systems 2004 (NOLCOS 2004), Stuttgart, Germany, 1–3 September 2004
14. Grossman, R.L., Nerode, A., Ravn, A.P., Rischel, H. (eds.): HS 1991–1992. LNCS, vol. 736. Springer, Heidelberg (1993). https://doi.org/10.1007/3-540-57318-6
15. Jeannin, J.-B., Platzer, A.: dTL^2: differential temporal dynamic logic with nested temporalities for hybrid systems. In: Demri, S., Kapur, D., Weidenbach, C. (eds.) IJCAR 2014. LNCS (LNAI), vol. 8562, pp. 292–306. Springer, Cham (2014). https://doi.org/10.1007/978-3-319-08587-6_22
16. Jeffreys, H., Swirles, B.: Methods of Mathematical Physics, 3rd edn. Cambridge University Press, Cambridge (1999). https://doi.org/10.1017/CBO9781139168489
17. Kong, S., Gao, S., Chen, W., Clarke, E.: dReach: δ-reachability analysis for hybrid systems. In: Baier, C., Tinelli, C. (eds.) TACAS 2015. LNCS, vol. 9035, pp. 200–205. Springer, Heidelberg (2015). https://doi.org/10.1007/978-3-662-46681-0_15

18. Manthanwar, A., Sakizlis, V., Dua, V., Pistikopoulos, E.: Robust model-based predictive controller for hybrid system via parametric programming. In: Puigjaner, L., Espuña, A. (eds.) European Symposium on Computer-Aided Process Engineering-15, 38th European Symposium of the Working Party on Computer Aided Process Engineering, Computer Aided Chemical Engineering, vol. 20, pp. 1249–1254. Elsevier (2005). https://doi.org/10.1016/S1570-7946(05)80050-1

19. Mayhew, C.G., Sanfelice, R.G., Teel, A.R.: Robust source-seeking hybrid controllers for autonomous vehicles. In: 2007 American Control Conference, pp. 1185–1190, July 2007. https://doi.org/10.1109/ACC.2007.4283016

20. McCallum, S.: Solving polynomial strict inequalities using cylindrical algebraic decomposition. Comput. J. **36**(5), 432–438 (1993). https://doi.org/10.1093/comjnl/36.5.432

21. Moggi, E., Farjudian, A., Duracz, A., Taha, W.: Safe & robust reachability analysis of hybrid systems. Theor. Comput. Sci. **747**, 75–99 (2018). https://doi.org/10.1016/j.tcs.2018.06.020

22. Moor, T., Davoren, J.M.: Robust controller synthesis for hybrid systems using modal logic. In: Di Benedetto, M.D., Sangiovanni-Vincentelli, A. (eds.) HSCC 2001. LNCS, vol. 2034, pp. 433–446. Springer, Heidelberg (2001). https://doi.org/10.1007/3-540-45351-2_35

23. Morgenstern, C.F.: The measure quantifier. J. Symb. Log. **44**(1), 103–108 (1979). https://doi.org/10.2307/2273708

24. Nerode, A., Kohn, W.: Models for hybrid systems: automata, topologies, controllability, observability. In: Grossman et al. [14], pp. 317–356

25. Platzer, A.: Logical Analysis of Hybrid Systems - Proving Theorems for Complex Dynamics. Springer, Heidelberg (2010). https://doi.org/10.1007/978-3-642-14509-4

26. Platzer, A.: Logical Foundations of Cyber-Physical Systems. Springer, Cham (2018). https://doi.org/10.1007/978-3-319-63588-0

27. Platzer, A., Tan, Y.K.: Differential equation axiomatization: the impressive power of differential ghosts. In: Dawar, A., Grädel, E. (eds.) LICS, pp. 819–828. ACM, New York (2018). https://doi.org/10.1145/3209108.3209147

28. Royden, H.L., Fitzpatrick, P.M.: Real Analysis (Classic Version), 4th edn. Pearson, London (2018)

29. Tarski, A.: A decision method for elementary algebra and geometry. In: Caviness, B.F., Johnson, J.R. (eds.) Quantifier Elimination and Cylindrical Algebraic Decomposition. TEXTSMONOGR, pp. 24–84. Springer, Vienna (1998). https://doi.org/10.1007/978-3-7091-9459-1_3

30. Walter, W.: Ordinary Differential Equations. Graduate Texts in Mathematics, vol. 182. Springer, New York (1998). https://doi.org/10.1007/978-1-4612-0601-9

SCL
Clause Learning from Simple Models

Alberto Fiori[1,2] and Christoph Weidenbach[1(✉)]

[1] Max Planck Institute for Informatics, Saarland Informatics Campus,
Saarbrücken, Germany
weidenbach@mpi-inf.mpg.de
[2] Graduate School of Computer Science, Saarbrücken, Germany

Abstract. Several decision procedures for the Bernays-Schoenfinkel (BS) fragment of first-order logic rely on explicit model assumptions. In particular, the procedures differ in their respective model representation formalisms. We introduce a new decision procedure SCL deciding the BS fragment. SCL stands for clause learning from simple models. Simple models are solely built on ground literals. Nevertheless, we show that SCL can learn exactly the clauses other procedures learn with respect to more complex model representation formalisms. Therefore, the overhead of complex model representation formalisms is not always needed. SCL is sound and complete for full first-order logic without equality.

1 Introduction

There has been intensive research into the development of decision procedures for the Bernays-Schoenfinkel (BS) first-order clause fragment without equality [1,3,4,7,9,14,17]. Even classical tableau can be turned into a decision procedure for BS [2]. The procedures follow three different paradigms. They either employ an explicit CDCL-style [12] partial model assumption [1,3,4,14], or they implement an abstraction-refinement approach [9,17], or merely rely on syntactic restrictions on inferences [7] yielding finite saturations.

The BS fragment is a natural generalization of propositional logic but still enjoys the finite-model property. Furthermore, any finite BS clause set can be transformed into a satisfiability equivalent SAT problem by finite instantiation at the price of a, worst case, exponentially larger clause set. For example, this relationship is used as a reasoning principle in Answer Set Programming (ASP) [8]. The exponential "overhead" is, in the worst case, unavoidable for any decision procedure, because BS satisfiability is NEXPTIME-complete [11,15]. This means, worst case, that an explicit model representation gets exponentially large, or satisfiability testing with respect to the model representation cannot be done in polynomial time. This justifies and motivates the research for procedures with different model representation formalisms as well as alternative approaches through abstraction or saturation. Actually, the leading systems at recent CASCs [16] have implemented a portfolio containing procedures from all of the aforementioned paradigms.

© Springer Nature Switzerland AG 2019
P. Fontaine (Ed.): CADE 2019, LNAI 11716, pp. 233–249, 2019.
https://doi.org/10.1007/978-3-030-29436-6_14

One contribution of this paper is a CDCL-style calculus deciding the BS fragment and being sound and complete for full first-order logic without equality. The model representation is simple: it consists of a sequence of ground literals. It is therefore properly contained in known model representation formalisms [1, 3,4,14]. However, we show that this model representation formalism together with the respective inference rules is sufficient to learn the very same clauses as in NRCL [1]. NRCL has one of the most expressive model representation formalisms. We call the procedure *SCL* for *clause learning from simple models*. The most important computations with respect to a model representation are the consistent extension of the current trail and the detection of a propagating literal or a false clause. The currently available procedures can be further divided into procedures where these computations can be done in polynomial time [3,6] and procedures where such computations are worst case NP-complete [1,14].[1] The advantages of the latter two formalisms are exponentially more compact model representations where the model representation language of the NRCL calculus [1] is more general than [3,6,14]. One contribution of this paper is that for model-driven clause learning, sophisticated model representations are not needed (Theorem 24). More precisely, we prove that any clause learned by the NRCL calculus can also be learned by our new SCL calculus, where the model representation consists of ground literals only. One of the simplest but also most efficient model representations known with respect to computations. This result holds for full first-order logic without equality. Model representations for BS clause sets with respect to ground literals can become exponentially larger compared to the above-mentioned more sophisticated model representations. The model size is exponential in the maximal arity of a predicate, which we will discuss in detail in Sect. 5. The implication of our result is that SCL can be efficiently used on problems where the ground literal model representation does not become "too large", further discussed in Sect. 6.

Another contribution in addition to SCL being sound, complete, and a decision procedure for the BS fragment is the fact that it only learns non-redundant clauses with respect to so-called *reasonable* strategies, see Sect. 3. A clause is *redundant* with respect to a clause set, if it is implied by smaller clauses, see Sect. 2. Non-redundancy is a powerful property: in the BS context, we prove it NEXPTIME-complete, Theorem 14. Practically, this implies that a clause generated by SCL with a reasonable strategy does not need to be tested for forward redundancy, e.g., forward Subsumption. Saturation-based theorem provers spent a substantial share of their run time on testing forward redundancy.

A third contribution concerning SCL is its ability to simulate resolution, Sect. 4, Theorem 20. Arbitrary resolution steps may generate redundant clauses, hence giving up a reasonable strategy is a prerequisite for the simulation. In this context we also discuss the performance of SCL with respect to proof length, Sect. 4, following [13].

Finally, we investigate a so called *weakly-reasonable* strategy, where propagations need not to be exhaustive, specifically unit clauses need not to be

---

[1] For [4] no complexity result has been published so far.

propagated. Although propagating unit clauses is typically a good strategy for SAT, for the BS fragment this depends already on the actual problem, because one unit clause may cause exponentially many subsequent propagation steps. In summary, the weakly-reasonable strategy generates non-redundant clauses with the exception of unit instances, Theorem 12, and allows for exponentially shorter proofs compared to a reasonable strategy, which exhausts propagation, Example 9. We end the paper with a short summary and discussion of the obtained results, Sect. 6.

2   Preliminaries

We assume a first-order language without equality where N denotes a clause set; C, D denote clauses; L, K, H denote literals; A, B denote atoms; P, Q, R denote predicates; t, s terms; f, g, h function symbols; a, b, c constants; and x, y, z variables. Atoms, literals, clauses and clause sets are considered as usual. The complement of a literal is denoted by the function comp. Semantic entailment $\models$ is defined as usual where variables in clauses are assumed to be universally quantified. Substitutions σ, τ are total mappings from variables to terms, where $\mathrm{dom}(\sigma) := \{x \mid x\sigma \neq x\}$ is finite and $\mathrm{codom}(\sigma) := \{t \mid x\sigma = t, x \in \mathrm{dom}(\sigma)\}$. Their application is extended to literals, clauses, and sets of such objects in the usual way. A term, atom, clause, or a set of these objects is *ground* if it does not contain any variable. A substitution σ is *ground* if $\mathrm{codom}(\sigma)$ is ground. A substitution σ is *grounding* for a term t, literal L, clause C if $t\sigma$, $L\sigma$, $C\sigma$ is ground, respectively. A *closure* is denoted as $C \cdot \sigma$ and is a pair of a clause C and a ground substitution σ. The function gnd computes the set of all ground instances of a literal, clause, or clause set. Note that for BS this set is always finite, whereas for first-order logic it is infinite, in general. The function mgu denotes the *most general unifier* of two terms, atoms, literals. We assume that any mgu of two terms or literals does not introduce any fresh variables and is idempotent.

In addition, we assume a well-founded, total, strict ordering $\prec$ on ground literals. This ordering is then lifted to clauses and clause sets by its respective multiset extension. We overload $\prec$ for literals, clauses, clause sets if the meaning is clear from the context. The ordering is lifted to the non-ground case via instantiation: we define $C \prec D$ if for all grounding substitutions σ it holds $C\sigma \prec D\sigma$. We define $\preceq$ as the reflexive closure of $\prec$ and $N^{\preceq C} := \{D \mid D \in N \text{ and } D \preceq C\}$.

Definition 1 (Clause Redundancy). *A ground clause C is redundant with respect to a ground clause set N and an order $\prec$ if $N^{\preceq C} \models C$. A clause C is redundant with respect to a clause set N and an order $\prec$ if for all $C' \in \mathrm{gnd}(C)$ C' is redundant with respect to $\cup_{D \in N} \mathrm{gnd}(D)$.*

3   SCL Rules and Properties

The inference rules of SCL are represented by an abstract rewrite system. They operate on a problem state, a five-tuple $(\Gamma; N; U; k; u)$ where Γ is a sequence of annotated ground literals, the *trail*; N and U are the sets of *initial* and *learned* clauses; k counts the number of decisions; and u is a status that is either true $\top$, false $\bot$, or a closure $C \cdot \sigma$. Literals in Γ are either annotated with a number, a level; i.e., they have the form L^k meaning that L is the k-th guessed decision literal, or they are annotated with a closure that propagated the literal to become true. A ground literal L is of *level* i with respect to a problem state $(\Gamma; N; U; k; u)$ if L or $\text{comp}(L)$ occurs in Γ and the first decision literal left from L ($\text{comp}(L)$) in Γ, including L, is annotated with i. If there is no such decision literal then its level is zero. A ground clause D is of *level* i with respect to a problem state $(\Gamma; N; U; k; u)$ if i is the maximal level of a literal in D; the level of the empty clause $\bot$ is 0. Recall u is a non-empty closure or $\top$ or $\bot$.

A literal L is *undefined* in Γ if neither L nor $\text{comp}(L)$ occur in Γ. The initial state for a first-order clause set N is $(\epsilon, N, \emptyset, 0, \top)$. The rules for conflict search are

Propagate $(\Gamma; N; U; k; \top) \Rightarrow_{\text{SCL}} (\Gamma, L\sigma^{(C \vee L) \cdot \sigma}; N; U; k; \top)$

provided $C \vee L \in (N \cup U)$, $C\sigma$ is ground and false under Γ, $L\sigma$ is undefined in Γ

Decide $(\Gamma; N; U; k; \top) \Rightarrow_{\text{SCL}} (\Gamma, L^{k+1}; N; U; k+1; \top)$

provided L is a ground literal undefined in Γ

Conflict $(\Gamma; N; U; k; \top) \Rightarrow_{\text{SCL}} (\Gamma; N; U; k; D \cdot \sigma)$

provided $D \in (N \cup U)$, $D\sigma$ false in Γ for a grounding substitution σ

These rules construct a (partial) model via the trail Γ for $N \cup U$ until a conflict, i.e., a false clause with respect to Γ is found. The above rules always terminate with respect to the BS fragment, but not for first-order logic, in general. In the special case of a unit clause L, the rule Propagate actually annotates the literal L with a closure of itself. So the propagated literals on the trail are annotated with the respective propagating clause and the decision literals with the respective level. If a conflict is found, it is resolved by the rules below. Before any Resolve step, we assume that the respective clauses are renamed such that they do not share any variables and that the grounding substitutions of closures are adjusted accordingly.

Skip $(\Gamma, L\delta^{(C \vee L) \cdot \delta}; N; U; k; D \cdot \sigma) \Rightarrow_{\text{SCL}} (\Gamma; N; U; k; D \cdot \sigma)$

provided $\text{comp}(L\delta)$ does not occur in $D\sigma$

Factorize $(\Gamma; N; U; k; (D \vee L \vee L') \cdot \sigma) \Rightarrow_{\text{SCL}} (\Gamma; N; U; k; (D \vee L)\eta \cdot \sigma)$

provided $L\sigma = L'\sigma$, $\eta = \text{mgu}(L, L')$

Resolve $(\Gamma, L\delta^{(C \vee L) \cdot \delta}; N; U; k; (D \vee L') \cdot \sigma) \Rightarrow_{\text{SCL}} (\Gamma, L\delta^{(C \vee L) \cdot \delta}; N; U; k; (D \vee C)\eta \cdot \sigma\delta)$

provided $D\sigma$ is of level k, $L\delta = \text{comp}(L'\sigma)$, $\eta = \text{mgu}(L, \text{comp}(L'))$

Backtrack $(\Gamma, K^{i+1}, \Gamma'; N; U; k; (D \vee L) \cdot \sigma) \Rightarrow_{\text{SCL}} (\Gamma; N; U \cup \{D \vee L\}; i; \top)$
provided $L\sigma$ is of level k and $D\sigma$ is of level i.

The clause $D \vee L$ added by the rule Backtrack to U is called a *learned clause*. The empty clause $\bot$ can only be generated by rule Resolve or be already present in N, hence, as usual for CDCL style calculi, the generation of $\bot$ together with the clauses in $N \cup U$ represent a resolution refutation. The rules for SCL are applied in a don't-care style, hence, the calculus offers freedom with respect to factorization. Literals in the conflict clause can, but do not have to be factorized. In particular, the Factorize rule may remove duplicate literals. The rule Resolve does not remove the literal resolved upon from the trail. Actually, Resolve is applied as long as the rightmost propagated trail literal occurs in the conflict clause. This literal is eventually removed by rule Skip from the trail.

For example, consider the clause set $N = \{D = Q \vee R(a, y) \vee R(x, b), C = Q \vee S(x, y) \vee P(x) \vee P(y) \vee \neg R(x, y)\}$ and a problem state:

$$(\neg P(a)^1, \neg P(b)^2, \neg S(a, b)^3, \neg Q^4, \neg R(a, b)^{C \cdot \{x \mapsto a, y \mapsto b\}}, N, \emptyset, 4, \top)$$

derived by SCL. The rule Conflict is applicable and yields the conflict state

$$(\neg P(a)^1, \neg P(b)^2, \neg S(a, b)^3, \neg Q^4, R(a, b)^{C \cdot \{x \mapsto a, y \mapsto b\}}; N; \emptyset; 4; D \cdot \{x \mapsto a, y \mapsto b\})$$

from which we can either learn the clause

$$C_1 = Q \vee S(x, b) \vee P(x) \vee P(b) \vee S(a, y) \vee P(a) \vee P(y)$$

or the clause

$$C_2 = Q \vee S(a, b) \vee P(a) \vee P(b)$$

depending on whether we first resolve or factorize. Note that C_2 does not subsume C_1. Both clauses are non-redundant. In order to learn C_1 we need to resolve twice with $R(a, b)^{C \cdot \{x \mapsto a, y \mapsto b\}}$.

The first property we prove about SCL is soundness. We prove it via the notion of a sound state.

Definition 2 (Sound States). *A state $(\Gamma; N; U; k; u)$ is sound if the following conditions hold*

1. *Γ is a consistent sequence of annotated ground literals,*
2. *for each decomposition $\Gamma = \Gamma_1, L\sigma^{C \vee L \cdot \sigma}, \Gamma_2$ we have that $C\sigma$ is false under Γ_1 and $L\sigma$ is undefined under Γ_1, $C \vee L \in (N \cup U)$,*
3. *for each decomposition $\Gamma = \Gamma_1, L^k, \Gamma_2$ we have that L is undefined in Γ_1,*
4. *$N \not\models U$,*
5. *if $u = C \cdot \sigma$ then $C\sigma$ is false under Γ and $N \models C$.*

Note that an initial state $(\epsilon, N, \emptyset, 0, \top)$ is sound. A rule is *sound* if it maps sound states to sound states.

Theorem 3 (Soundness of SCL). *The rules of SCL are sound, hence SCL starting with an initial state is sound.*

Proof. (Idea) By induction on the length of an SCL derivation and a case analysis for the different rules preserving soundness of states.   □

Next we introduce regular and weakly-regular runs. Regular runs always generate non-redundant clauses, but require exhaustive propagation. Weakly-regular runs do not require exhaustive propagation and almost always generate non-redundant clauses except for instances of unit clauses. However, although exhaustive propagation is typically done in CDCL style SAT, already for the BS fragment it should not always be preferred, because unit clauses can have already exponentially many ground instances.

Definition 4 (Regular States). *A state $(\Gamma; N; U; k; u)$ is regular if and only if the following hold:*

1. *for every decomposition $\Gamma = \Gamma_1, L^k, \Gamma_2$ there is no clause in $N \cup U$ that could propagate from Γ_1,*
2. *for each decomposition $\Gamma = \Gamma_1, L, \Gamma_2$ where L may be either propagated or decided, there is no clause from $\mathrm{gnd}(N \cup U)$ false under Γ_1.*

Definition 5 (Weakly-Regular States). *A state $(\Gamma; N; U; k; u)$ is weakly-regular if and only if the following hold:*

1. *for every decomposition $\Gamma = \Gamma_1, L^k, \Gamma_2$ there is no non-unit clause in $N \cup U$ that could propagate from Γ_1,*
2. *for each decomposition $\Gamma = \Gamma_1, L, \Gamma_2$ where L may be either propagated or decided, there is no clause from $\mathrm{gnd}(N \cup U)$ false under Γ_1.*

Some of the below results hold both for regular and weakly-regular states or runs. In this case we write "(weakly-) regular" meaning both cases.

Theorem 6 (Correct Termination). *If no rules are applicable to a (weakly-) regular state $(\Gamma; N; U; k; u)$ then either $u = \bot$ and N is unsatisfiable or N is satisfiable and $\Gamma \models N$.*

Proof. For a state $(\Gamma; N; U; k; u)$ where $u \notin \{\top, \bot\}$, one of the rules Resolve, Skip, Factorize or Backtrack is applicable. If the top level literal is a propagated literal then either Resolve or Skip are applicable. If the top level literal is a decision then one of the rules Backtrack or Factorize is applicable. If $u = \top$ and Propagate, Decide, and Conflict are not applicable it means that there are no undefined ground literals in Γ, so $\Gamma \models N$.   □

Definition 7 (Regular Runs). *A derivation of regular states is regular or a regular run if the rules Conflict and Propagate are always applied before all other rules in decreasing order of priority.*

Definition 8 (Weakly-Regular Runs). *A derivation of regular states is weakly-regular or a weakly-regular run if the following conditions hold:*

1. *Conflict has higher priority than all other rules,*
2. *if Conflict is not applicable and we can apply Propagate to a non-unit clause then Propagate has higher priority than any other rule,*
3. *Decide never adds a literal L to the trail if* comp(L) *is a unit clause in* gnd$(N \cup U)$,
4. *Resolve has higher priority than Backtrack if the current conflict clause is subsumed in N by a unit clause.*

Example 9 (Comparing Proof Length of Regular and Weakly-Regular Runs).
Proofs generated by weakly-regular runs can be exponentially shorter than proofs generated by regular runs. Consider the simple BS clause set

$$N = \{R(x_1, \ldots, x_n, a, b), P \vee Q, P \vee \neg Q, \neg P \vee Q, \neg P \vee \neg Q\}.$$

A weakly-regular run can ignore generating the 2^n different ground instances of $R(x_1, \ldots, x_n, a, b)$ and directly proceed in refuting the propositional part of N in the usual CDCL style by starting with a decision on P or Q. For the example it is obvious that the instances of $R(x_1, \ldots, x_n, a, b)$ can be ignored, but in general it is not. This phenomenon already occurs for NP-complete problems: when deciding linear integer arithmetic in a CDCL style, exhaustive propagation is not required by respective calculi for the very same reason [5].

Definition 10 (State Induced Ordering). *Let $(L_1, L_2, \ldots, L_n; N; U; k; u)$ be a sound state of SCL where the annotations of the L_i are ignored. The trail induces a total well-founded strict order on the defined literals by*

$$L_1 \prec_\Gamma \text{comp}(L_1) \prec_\Gamma L_2 \prec_\Gamma \text{comp}(L_2) \prec_\Gamma \cdots \prec_\Gamma L_n \prec_\Gamma \text{comp}(L_n).$$

We extend $\prec_\Gamma$ to a strict total order on all literals where all undefined literals are larger than comp(L_n). *We also extend $\prec_\Gamma$ to a strict total order on ground clauses by multiset extension and also on multisets of ground clauses and overload $\prec_\Gamma$ for all these cases. With $\preceq_\Gamma$ we denote the reflexive closure of $\prec_\Gamma$.*

Theorem 11 (Learned Clauses in Regular Runs). *Let $(\Gamma; N; U; k; C_0 \cdot \sigma_0)$ be the state resulting from the application of Conflict in a regular run and let C be the clause learned at the end of the conflict resolution, then C is not redundant with respect to $N \cup U$ and $\prec_\Gamma$.*

Proof. Consider the following fragment of a derivation learning a clause:

$$\Rightarrow_{\text{SCL}}^{\text{Conflict}} (\Gamma; N; U; k; C_0 \cdot \sigma_0) \Rightarrow_{\text{SCL}}^{\{\text{Skip, Fact., Res.}\}^*} (\Gamma'; N; U; k; C \cdot \sigma) \Rightarrow_{\text{SCL}}^{\text{Backtrack}}.$$

By soundness $N \cup \models C$ and $C\sigma$ is false under both Γ and Γ'. We prove that $C\sigma$ is non-redundant.

Assume there is an $S \subseteq \text{gnd}(N \cup U)^{\preceq_\Gamma C\sigma}$ s.t. $S \models C\sigma$. There is a clause $D \in S$ false under Γ, $S \preceq_\Gamma \{C\sigma\}$ and $C\sigma \notin S$. All clauses in S have a defined truth value (as all undefined literals are greater than all defined literals) and if $\Gamma \models S$ then $\Gamma \models C\sigma$, a contradiction.

We distinguish whether the two trails Γ and Γ' are equal or Γ' is a strict prefix of Γ.

If $\Gamma \neq \Gamma'$ then at least one Skip application was performed during conflict resolution, so $C\sigma$ does not contain the rightmost literal of Γ and since $D \prec_\Gamma C\sigma$ neither does D. So at a previous point in the derivation there must be a conflict search state such that D was false under the current trail but was not chosen as conflict instance, a contradiction to the exhaustive application of Conflict.

If $\Gamma = \Gamma'$ we distinguish two sub-cases according to whether the rightmost literal in Γ is the result of a Decision or a Propagation.

If the rightmost literal of $\Gamma = \Gamma'', L^k$ is a decision literal, then D is either true in Γ'' or has at least two literals undefined or of level k. Since D must be false under Γ, D must have two or more occurrences of literals undefined under Γ or of comp(L). Since $C\sigma$ has no undefined literal and exactly one occurrence of comp(L) we have a contradiction with $D \prec_\Gamma C\sigma$.

If $\Gamma = \Gamma'', L^{C' \cdot \delta}$ then at most one literal in $C\sigma$ is of level k and all other literals, if any, are of level at most $k - 1$. Moreover, D is also either true in Γ'' or has at least two literals undefined under Γ'' or of level k or $k = 0$. Backtrack requires the presence of at least one decision literal on the trail and so $k > 0$ so D must have at least two literals of level k. If both of those literal are different from comp(L) then by regularity, we would have applied Conflict instead of Propagate on the trail Γ''. So at least one of the literals of level k in D must be comp(L). Simple case analysis shows that under these conditions $C\sigma \prec_\Gamma D$, a contradiction. □

Theorem 12 (Learned Clauses in Weakly-Regular Runs). *Let the state* $(\Gamma; N; U; k; C_0 \cdot \sigma_0)$ *the result of a Conflict application in a weakly-regular run and let C be the clause learned at the end of the conflict resolution, then C is not redundant w.r.t. $N \cup U$ and $\prec_\Gamma$ or C is an instantiation of a unit clause in $N \cup U$.*

Proof. Consider the following fragment of a derivation learning a clause:

$$\Rightarrow_{\text{SCL}}^{\text{Conflict}} (\Gamma; N; U; k; C_0 \cdot \sigma_0) \Rightarrow_{\text{SCL}}^{\{\text{Skip, Fact., Res.}\}^*} (\Gamma'; N; U; k; C \cdot \sigma) \Rightarrow_{\text{SCL}}^{\text{Backtrack}}.$$

By soundness $N \cup U \models C$ and $C\sigma$ is false under both Γ and Γ'. We need to prove that there exists a ground instantiation of C that is non-redundant or that C is unit; we assume that C is not a unit and prove by contradiction that $C\sigma$ is non-redundant.

Assume there is an $S \subseteq \text{gnd}(N \cup U)^{\preceq_\Gamma C\sigma}$ s.t. $S \models C$. There is a clause $D \in S$ false under Γ; indeed since $S \prec_\Gamma \{C\sigma\}$ all clauses in S have a defined truth value and if all clauses in S were to be true under Γ we would also have that $C\sigma$ would be true under Γ by transitivity of entailment.

We distinguish whether the two trails Γ and Γ' are equal or Γ' is a strict prefix of Γ.

If $\Gamma \neq \Gamma'$ then rule Skip was applied at least once during conflict resolution, so $C\sigma$ does not contain the rightmost literal of Γ and since $D \prec_\Gamma C\sigma$ neither does D. So at a previous point in the derivation there must be a conflict search state such that D was false under the current trail but was not chosen as conflict instance, a contradiction to the exhaustive application of Conflict.

If $\Gamma = \Gamma'$ we distinguish two sub-cases according to whether the rightmost literal in Γ is the result of a Decision or a Propagation.

If the rightmost literal of $\Gamma = \Gamma'', L^k$ is a decision literal then D is either true in Γ'', a unit clause, or has at least two literals undefined or of level k. If D is a unit clause then it must be true or undefined in Γ'', and since decisions are restricted to never falsify unit clauses D cannot be false in Γ''. Otherwise, D must have two or more occurrences of literals undefined under Γ'' or of comp(L). Since $C\sigma$ has no undefined literal and exactly one occurrence of comp(L), we have a contradiction with $D \prec_\Gamma C\sigma$.

If $\Gamma = \Gamma'', L^{C' \cdot \delta}$ then at most one literal in $C\sigma$ is of level k and all other literals, if any, are of level at most $k - 1$, moreover D is either true in Γ'', a unit clause, or has at least two literals undefined or of level k. Under these conditions $D \prec_\Gamma C\sigma$ and $\Gamma \models \neg D$ imply $D = \neg L$ and $C\sigma = C'' \vee \neg L$, but then the next rule cannot be a Backtrack as by weak regularity Resolve would have higher priority. □

Proposition 13. *All regular runs are weakly-regular runs.*

Proof. There are four conditions that a weakly-regular run needs to satisfy. A regular run clearly respects the first two conditions, so we prove that regular runs respect the last two. In a regular run Propagate has always higher priority than Decide, so whenever we could decide a literal L s.t. comp$(L) \in$ gnd$(N \cup U)$ the literal comp(L) must have already been propagated and so L is not undefined. By Theorem 11 whenever we can apply Backtrack the conflict clause is not redundant in N and so not subsumed in N. □

Theorem 14 (BS Non-redundancy is NEXPTIME-Complete). *Deciding non-redundancy of a BS clause C with respect to a finite BS clause set $N^{\preceq C}$ is NEXPTIME-Complete.*

Proof. We only show hardness, because containment of the problem in NEXPTIME is obvious. To this end, let $N = \{C_1, \ldots, C_n\}$ be an arbitrary, finite BS clause set. We consider an LPO ordering $\prec_{\text{LPO}}$. Next we add two fresh predicates of arity zero, P, Q with $P \prec_{\text{LPO}} Q$, where P, Q are larger in the LPO precedence than any other symbol from N. Then obviously N is satisfiable iff the finite BS clause set $N' = \{P, Q, C_1 \vee \neg Q, C_2 \vee \neg P, C_3, \ldots, C_n\}$ is satisfiable. Furthermore, the clause $\neg P \vee \neg Q$ is $\prec_{\text{LPO}}$ larger than any clause in $N' \setminus \{P, Q\}$. The clause $\neg P \vee \neg Q$ is non-redundant with respect to $N' \setminus \{P, Q\}$ iff N' is satisfiable. □

Theorem 15 (Termination). *If N is a clause set and gnd(N) is finite then any (weakly-) regular run of SCL terminates.*

Proof. Any infinite run learns infinitely many clauses. Firstly, for a regular run, by Theorem 11, all learned clauses are non-redundant. The number of different ground clauses and literals is finite. So there is no infinite regular run. Secondly, for weakly-regular runs, the learned clause is either non-redundant, or an instance of a unit clause from N or from the set of learned clauses. However, there are also only finitely many instances of unit clauses from N. So there is no infinite weakly-regular run.   □

Theorem 16 (SCL Refutational Completeness). *If N is unsatisfiable, then there is a (weakly-) regular run of SCL deriving $\bot$.*

Proof. If N is unsatisfiable, then as a consequence of Herbrand's Theorem there is a finite set of ground instances N' from N that is unsatisfiable. Now restrict the rules Decide and Propagate to ground literals from N'. By Theorems 15 and 6 any (weakly-) regular run on this restriction derives $\bot$.   □

Theorem 17 (SCL decides the BS fragment). *SCL restricted to weakly-regular runs decides satisfiability of a BS clause set.*

Proof. There are only finitely many ground instances of a BS clause set. Following the proof of Theorem 15, any SCL (weakly-) regular run will terminate on a BS clause set.   □

4   Simulating Resolution by SCL

It is well-known that resolution inferences may generate redundant clauses. Therefore, by Theorems 11 and 12 (weakly-) regular runs cannot simulate resolution. However, the SCL calculus is still flexible enough to simulate arbitrary resolution inferences that do not result in tautologies by a non-regular strategy.

Lemma 18 (SCL Simulates Resolution). *Let N be a clause set, $C = C' \vee H$ and $D = D' \vee H'$ be clauses in N such that C' and D' are non-empty, $\eta = \mathrm{mgu}(H, \mathrm{comp}(H'))$ exists, the literals H and H' are not duplicated in either C or D and the three clauses $C\eta$, $D\eta$ and $(C' \vee D')\eta$ are not tautologies. Then, there is an SCL run starting from the state $(\epsilon; N; \emptyset; 0; \top)$ where the first learned clause is $(C' \vee D')\eta$.*

Proof. Let θ be a grounding substitution on the variables of $C\eta$ and $D\eta$ such that distinct literals are mapped to distinct ground literals, also let $\{L_1, \ldots, L_n\} = (C' \vee D')\eta\theta$.

We can start our derivation with n Decisions where at the i-th step we decide the literal $\mathrm{comp}(L_i)$ to obtain the state $(K_1^1, \ldots, K_n^n; N; U; n; \top)$, $K_i = \mathrm{comp}(L_i)$. This is possible as $(C' \vee D')$ is not a tautology.

$H\eta\theta$ is still undefined but every other literal in $C'\eta\theta$ is falsified under the current trail; so in the next step we can propagate $H\eta\theta$ on the trail.

$$(K_1^1, \ldots, K_n^n; N; \emptyset; n; \top) \Rightarrow_{\mathrm{SCL}}^{\mathrm{Propagate}} (K_1^1, \ldots, K_n^n, H\eta\theta^{C' \vee H \cdot \eta\theta}; N; \emptyset; n; \top)$$

Now the rule Conflict is applicable to $(D' \vee H')\eta\theta$ resulting in

$$(K_1^1, \ldots, K_n^n, H\eta\theta^{C' \vee H \cdot \eta\theta}; N; \emptyset; n; D' \vee H' \cdot \eta\theta).$$

We apply Resolve once and we reach the state

$$(K_1^1, \ldots, K_n^n; N; \emptyset; n; (C' \vee D')\eta \cdot \theta).$$

From this state we can backtrack to

$$(K_1^1, \ldots, K_k^k; N; \{(C' \vee D')\eta\}; k; \top).$$

□

Lemma 19 (SCL Simulates Factoring). *Let N be a clause set, $C = C' \vee H \vee H'$ a non-tautological clause with unifiable literals H and H'. There is a run starting from the state $(\epsilon; N; \emptyset; 0; \top)$ where the first learned clause is $(C' \vee H)\eta$ where $\eta = \mathrm{mgu}(H, K)$.*

Proof. Let $\{L_1, \ldots, L_k\} = C\eta$ and let ρ be a grounding of C injective on the literals of $C\eta$. By applying Decide k times we can reach a state $(K_1^1\rho, \ldots, K_k^k\rho; N; \emptyset; k; \top)$, $K_i = \mathrm{comp}(L_i)$, from which we can apply rule Conflict to $C\eta\rho$ resulting in $(K_1^1\rho, \ldots, K_k^k\rho; N; \emptyset; k; C \cdot \eta\rho)$. Now we can factorize H and H', deriving $\Rightarrow_{\mathrm{SCL}}^{\mathrm{Factorize}} (K_1^1\rho, \ldots, K_k^k\rho; N; \emptyset; k; (C' \vee H)\eta \cdot \rho)$ and, finally, backtrack and learn $(C' \vee H)\eta$. □

In order to simulate an overall refutation of the resolution calculus, an additional Restart rule is needed. Note that tautologies can be ignored in refutations by the resolution calculus.

Restart $(\Gamma; N; U; k; \top) \Rightarrow_{\mathrm{SCL}} (\epsilon; N; U; 0; \top)$
provided $\Gamma \not\models N$

Theorem 20 (SCL Simulates the Resolution Calculus). *SCL together with the Restart rule can simulate a resolution refutation by a non-regular strategy.*

Proof. By Lemmas 18 and 19. □

Consider another example, taken from [13], where exhaustive propagation leads to exponentially longer proofs compared to the shortest resolution proof. Let i be a positive integer and consider the clause set N^i with one predicate P of arity i consisting of the following clauses, where we write $\bar{x}, \bar{0}$ and $\bar{1}$ to denote sequences of the appropriate length of variables and constants to meet the arity of P:

$$P(\bar{0}) \qquad \neg P(\bar{1})$$

and i clauses of the form

$$\neg P(\bar{x}, 0, \bar{1}) \vee P(\bar{x}, 1, \bar{0})$$

where the length of $\bar{1}$ varies between 0 and $i - 1$. The example encodes an i-bit counter. A regular run of SCL (NRCL) on this clause set would find a conflict after $O(2^i)$ propagations without any application of Decide. For example, for $i = 4$ we get the clauses of N^4:

$$1 : P(0,0,0,0)$$
$$2 : \neg P(x_1, x_2, x_3, 0) \lor P(x_1, x_2, x_3, 1)$$
$$3 : \neg P(x_1, x_2, 0, 1) \lor P(x_1, x_2, 1, 0)$$
$$4 : \neg P(x_1, 0, 1, 1) \lor P(x_1, 1, 0, 0)$$
$$5 : \neg P(0, 1, 1, 1) \lor P(1, 0, 0, 0)$$
$$6 : \neg P(1, 1, 1, 1)$$

For this clause set a regular SCL (NRCL) generates all unit clauses from $P(0,0,0,0)$ to $P(1,1,1,1)$ via 2^4 applications of Propagate, then finds a conflict with clause 6 and then uses 2^4 times Resolve to end up in $\bot$.

Instead a short resolution refutation can be obtained by

$$2.2 \text{ Res } 3.1 \quad 7 : \neg P(x_1, x_2, 0, 0) \lor P(x_1, x_2, 1, 0)$$
$$7.2 \text{ Res } 2.1 \quad 8 : \neg P(x_1, x_2, 0, 0) \lor P(x_1, x_2, 1, 1)$$
$$8.2 \text{ Res } 4.1 \quad 9 : \neg P(x_1, 0, 0, 0) \lor P(x_1, 1, 0, 0)$$
$$9.2 \text{ Res } 8.1 \quad 10 : \neg P(x_1, 0, 0, 0) \lor P(x_1, 1, 1, 1)$$
$$10.2 \text{ Res } 5.1 \quad 11 : \neg P(0, 0, 0, 0) \lor P(1, 0, 0, 0)$$
$$11.2 \text{ Res } 10.1 \; 12 : \neg P(0, 0, 0, 0) \lor P(1, 1, 1, 1)$$
$$12.1 \text{ Res } 6.1 \quad 13 : \bot$$

In general, $O(2i)$ many resolution steps are sufficient to refute N^i. The above resolution proof cannot be simulated by an SCL weakly-regular run. As soon as we decide a ground literal $[\neg]P(\ldots)$ propagation using the two literal clauses yields a conflict with either $\neg P(1,1,1,1)$ or $P(0,0,0,0)$. The above resolution proof can only be simulated by a non-regular SCL run, Theorem 20. It is an open problem to find a notion of regularity that both guarantees non-redundant clause learning and can simulate resolution proofs of the above type.

5   Simulating NRCL by SCL

In this section we show that even under the restriction of a ground trail, SCL can generate any clause learned by NRCL. In the worst case, the trail generated by SCL may be exponentially longer than the NRCL trail, see Example 25. We use $\Gamma, \Gamma_1, \Gamma_2$ to denote SCL trails and $\Gamma', \Gamma_1', \Gamma_2'$ to denote NRCL trails.

The ordering $\prec_{\Gamma'}$ is defined as in [1] and concerning NRCL we exactly stick to the notions from [1]. Nevertheless, the most important notions from NRCL are recalled below.

Definition 21 (Constrained Clauses [1]). *A constrained clause $(C \cdot \sigma; \pi)$ is a pair of a closure $C \cdot \sigma$ and a constraint π of the form $\bigwedge_{i=0}^{n} \vec{s}_i \neq \vec{t}_i$ where $\vec{s}_i$ and $\vec{t}_i$ are tuples of terms of equal length. The set of ground instances of $(C \cdot \sigma; \pi)$ denoted as $\mathrm{gnd}(C \cdot \sigma; \pi)$ is $\{C\sigma\delta \mid C\sigma\delta \in \mathrm{gnd}(C\sigma) \text{ and } \pi\delta \text{ is true}\}$. A constraint $\pi = \bigwedge_{i=0}^{n} \vec{s}_i \neq \vec{t}_i$ is true if for all $0 \leq i \leq n$ $\vec{s}_i$ and $\vec{t}_i$ are not unifiable. A ground* *clause C' is covered by a constrained clause $(C \cdot \sigma; \pi)$ if $C' \in \mathrm{gnd}(C \cdot \sigma; \pi)$. We similarly define constrained literals $(L \cdot \sigma; \pi)$ and say that a ground literal L' is defined true by $(L \cdot \sigma; \pi)$ if it is covered by $(L \cdot \sigma; \pi)$ and defined false if it covered by $(\mathrm{comp}(L) \cdot \sigma; \pi)$.*

Definition 22 (State induced ordering in NRCL [1]). *A ground literal L is defined under a trail Γ' if L or $\mathrm{comp}(L)$ is covered by some constrained literals L' in Γ'. Such a literal is necessarily unique and is denoted by $\mathrm{def}(L)$. Given two defined ground literals L_1, L_2 we say $L_1 \prec_{\Gamma'} L_2$ if $\Gamma' = \Gamma_0', \mathrm{def}(L_1), \Gamma_1', \mathrm{def}(L_2), \Gamma_2'$.*

The proof of the simulation is done in two steps. Firstly, we show that we can generate via SCL a suitable ground instance of any NRCL trail, Lemma 23. Then we show that on this basis, we can actually learn exactly the clause NRCL learns, Theorem 24.

Lemma 23 (Simulating the NRCL Trail). *Let $(\Gamma'; N; U; k; \top)$ be a regular state in an NRCL run and let $\prec_0$ be a total order on ground literals compatible with $\prec_{\Gamma'}$. Then there is an SCL derivation starting from $(\epsilon; N; U; 0; \top)$ which produces a trail Γ such that for any ground literal L, L is true, false, undefined under Γ if and only if it is so under Γ', and for all ground literals $L_1, L_2 \in \mathrm{gnd}(\Gamma')$: $L_1 \prec_\Gamma L_2$ if and only if $L_1 \prec_0 L_2$. We call Γ a grounding of Γ'.*

Proof. By induction on the length of Γ'. If $\Gamma' = \epsilon$ then we choose $\Gamma = \epsilon$ satisfying the conjecture. If $\Gamma' = \Gamma_1', (L; \sigma; \pi)^k$ then all ground literals $\mathrm{gnd}(L; \sigma; \pi)$ are undefined in Γ_1 so we can simply decide every literal in $\mathrm{gnd}(L; \sigma; \pi)$ in increasing order according to $\prec_{\Gamma'}$ to obtain a trail Γ_2 that clearly satisfies the conjecture. If the rightmost literal of Γ' is a propagation then we apply Propagate instead of Decide on the SCL trail.   □

A consequence of Lemma 23 is that SCL can simulate the derivation of $\bot$ from a state without decisions. So this needs not to be considered anymore. The most sophisticated rule of NRCL to be considered for the simulation is Backjump, because its side conditions are substantially different from the side conditions of the SCL Backtrack rule.

Backjump $(\Gamma, K^{k'}, \Gamma'; N; U; k; (C \cdot \sigma; \pi)) \Rightarrow_{\mathrm{NRCL}} (\Gamma, K^{k'}; N; U \cup \{C\}; k'; \top)$
provided one of the following conditions hold (i) $k = 0$ and $C = \bot$, (ii) $k > 0$, all ground clauses covered by $(C\sigma; \pi)$ have exactly one literal of level k and $(C\sigma; \pi)$ has no false instances under Γ (iii) $k > 0$, the right-most element of Γ' is a decision, some ground clauses covered by $(C\sigma; \pi)$ have two or more literals of level k, $(C\sigma; \pi)$ has no false instances under Γ and Factorize cannot be applied.

Theorem 24 (SCL Simulates NRCL). *If from an NRCL conflict state we can learn a clause $C \neq \bot$, then we can learn the same clause C from a grounding of that state by SCL.*

Proof. Let $w_1' = (\Gamma_1'; N; U; k; (C_1; \sigma_1; \pi_1))$ be an NRCL conflict state from which we learn the clause C. We prove by induction on the length of conflict resolution that there exists an SCL state $w_1 = (\Gamma_1; N; U; k; C_1 \cdot \delta_1)$ obtained by grounding w_1' from which we can learn C.

As a base case, we prove that if we can apply Backjump to an NRCL state $(\Gamma_2'; N; U; k'; (C_2; \sigma_2; \pi_2))$ then we can also apply Backtrack to a grounding $(\Gamma_2; N; U; k; C_2 \cdot \delta_2)$. In particular, we choose $\delta_2 = \sigma_2 \rho$ where ρ is an injective mapping from the variables of C_2 to a set of fresh constants. If we can apply Backjump in NRCL then one of the three cases of the rule applies. We consider them separately. The first case cannot apply as we have assumed a clause different from $\bot$. The second case implies that we can backtrack to the very same level via SCL. For the third case, we note that in SCL there is no equivalent of the concept of blocking decisions or blocking clauses as they can only arise when a decision defines multiple ground literals. In SCL all literals defined by decisions in a conflict clause have different levels and thus we can always apply Backtrack from any grounding of the conflict clause if the third case of Backjump applies.

For the inductive step, consider a rule application $(\Gamma_1'; N; U; k'; (C_1; \sigma_1; \pi_1))$ $\Rightarrow_{\mathrm{NRCL}} (\Gamma_2'; N; U; k'; (C_2; \sigma_2; \pi_2))$ in a conflict resolution. For any grounding $(\Gamma_2; N; U; k; C_2 \cdot \delta_2)$ of $(\Gamma_2'; N; U; k'; (C_2; \sigma_2; \pi_2))$ we build a grounding $(\Gamma_1; N; U; k; C_1 \cdot \delta_1)$ of $(\Gamma_1'; N; U; k'; (C_1; \sigma_1; \pi_1))$ from which we can still learn the clause C. In particular we will need to define Γ_1 and δ_1 in terms of $(\Gamma_2; N; U; k; C_2 \cdot \delta_2)$

Case Resolve: we consider the NRCL rule application

$$(\Gamma_1', (L_0; \sigma_0; \pi_0)^{C_0 \vee L_0}; N; U; k'; (C_1 \vee L_1; \sigma_1; \pi_1))$$
$$\Rightarrow_{\mathrm{NRCL}}^{\mathrm{Resolve}} (\Gamma_2', (L_0; \sigma_0; \pi_0)^{C_0 \vee L_0}; N; U; k'; (C_2; \sigma_2; \pi_2))$$

by the conditions of Resolve in NRCL we have

1. there exists $\eta_0 = \mathrm{mgu}(\mathrm{comp}(L_0), L_1)$
2. there exists $\eta = \mathrm{mgu}(\mathrm{comp}(L_0)\sigma_0, L_1\sigma_1)$
3. $\eta_0 \sigma_2 = \sigma_1 \sigma_0 \eta$
4. $C_2 = (C_1 \vee C_0)\eta_0$

and from the grounding we have $\delta_i = \sigma_i \delta_i'$ for some δ_i', $i = 0, 1, 2$. It is clear that any grounding substitution δ_2 on the variables of $(C_1 \vee C_0)\eta_0$ can be induced by choosing opportune grounding substitutions δ_0 and δ_1. In particular, we can define δ_i for $i = 0, 1$ as the restriction of $\eta_0 \delta_2 \rho$ to the variables of $C_i \vee L_i$ where ρ is a grounding on $\mathrm{var}(L_0\eta_0, L_1\eta_0) \setminus \mathrm{var}(C_0\eta_0, C_1\eta_0)$. If there is a grounding ρ such that $L_0\eta_0\delta_2\rho$ is undefined in Γ_2 then we define Γ_1 as $\Gamma_2, L_0\eta_0\delta_2\rho^{C_0 \vee L_0 \cdot \eta_0\delta_2\rho}$. If such a substitution ρ does not exist then the literal $L_0\rho'^{C_0 \vee L_0 \cdot \rho'}$ is already defined in Γ_2 obtained from grounding the same literal $(L_0; \sigma_0; \pi_0)^{C_0 \vee L_0}$; we can then define Γ_1 equal to Γ_2 and resolve once more with the literal $L_0\rho'^{C_0 \vee L_0 \cdot \rho'}$.

Case Factorize: we consider the NRCL rule application

$$(\Gamma_1', (L_0; \sigma_0; \pi_0)^{C_0 \vee L_0}; N; U; k'; (C_1 \vee L_1 \vee L_1'; \sigma_1; \pi_1))$$
$$\Rightarrow_{\mathrm{NRCL}}^{\mathrm{Factorize}} (\Gamma_2', (L_0; \sigma_0; \pi_0)^{C_0 \vee L_0}; N; U; k'; (C_2 \vee L_2; \sigma_2; \pi_2))$$

by the conditions on Factorize in NRCL we have

1. there exists $\eta_0 = \text{mgu}(L_1, L_1')$
2. $C_2 = C_1\eta_0$ and $L_2 = L_1\eta_0$
3. there exists $\eta = \text{mgu}(\text{comp}(L_0)\sigma_0, L_1\sigma_1, L_1'\sigma_1)$
4. $\eta_0\sigma_2 = \sigma_1\eta$

and from the grounding we have $\delta_i = \sigma_i\delta_i'$. We can define $\delta_1 = \eta_0\delta_2$ which produces an acceptable grounding of $(C_1 \vee L_1 \vee L_1'; \sigma_1; \pi_1)$ as $\eta_0\delta_2 = \eta_2\sigma_2$ and so $\delta_1 = \sigma_1\delta_1'$ for $\delta_1' = \eta\delta_2'$. We can, moreover, define $\Gamma_1 = \Gamma_2$ as in SCL Factorize is not restricted to the rightmost literal.

Case Skip: we consider the NRCL rule application

$$(\Gamma_1', (L_0; \sigma_0; \pi_0)^{C_0 \vee L_0}; N; U; k'; (C_1; \sigma_1; \pi_1))$$

$$\Rightarrow^{\text{Skip}}_{\text{NRCL}} (\Gamma_2'; N; U; k'; (C_2 \vee L_2; \sigma_2; \pi_2)).$$

We can simply define $(\Gamma_1; N; U; k; C_1 \cdot \delta_1) = (\Gamma_2; N; U; k; C_2 \cdot \delta_2)$ where Factorize is independent from the trail in SCL and the induction step for Resolve can add any needed literal.   □

Example 25 (SCL Trails may be Exponentially Longer). Consider an unsatisfiable clause set

$$N^n = \begin{cases} Q_n(x_1, \ldots, x_n) \\ \neg Q_{i+1}(x_1, \ldots, x_i, 0) \vee \neg Q_{i+1}(x_1, \ldots, x_i, 1) \vee Q_i(x_1, \ldots, x_i) & \text{if } 0 \leq i < n \\ \neg Q_0 \end{cases}$$

NRCL can refute the clause set N^n at level $k = 0$ in linear time by building through rule Propagate the trail $\neg Q_0, Q_n(x_1, \ldots, x_n), Q_{n-1}(x_1, \ldots, x_{n-1}), \ldots, Q_1(x_1)$, where we do not show the clauses annotated to the literals, resulting in a conflict with $\neg Q_1(1) \vee \neg Q_1(0) \vee Q_0$. For SCL all ground instances of the $Q_i(x_1, \ldots, x_i)$ have to be enumerated and there are 2^i many such ground instances for each Q_i.

Another relevant aspect is whether the SCL run constructed in Theorem 24 is (weakly-) regular. The example below shows it is not, in general, however at least for the example below, it is the case that SCL can actually learn a more general clause by a regular run.

Example 26 (Simulating SCL Runs are not (Weakly-) Regular). Consider the clauses

$$Q(x) \vee \neg P(x) \qquad P(x) \vee P(a) \vee P(b) \vee P(c) \qquad P(a) \vee \neg P(b)$$
$$P(b) \vee \neg P(c) \qquad P(c) \vee \neg P(a)$$

In NRCL we can decide the literal $\neg Q(x)$, propagate $\neg P(x)$ and result in a conflict with $P(x) \vee P(a) \vee P(b) \vee P(c)$. After factorization and resolution with $Q(x) \vee \neg P(x)$, NRCL learns the clause $Q(a) \vee Q(b) \vee Q(c)$. This clause cannot be learned with a (weakly-) regular run in SCL. After deciding any ground instance of $\neg Q(x)$, immediately all ground literals $\neg P(a), \neg P(b), \neg P(c)$ are propagated through the two literal clauses. Now the conflict does not only rely on the first two clauses but also involves the two literal clauses. After resolution and factoring steps, if SCL started with $\neg Q(a)$ it eventually learns the clause $Q(a)$ which makes the NRCL learned clause $Q(a) \vee Q(b) \vee Q(c)$ redundant.

6   Conclusion

The contributions of this paper are: (i) a sound, complete, SCL calculus for full first-order logic learning non-redundant clauses with respect to regular runs, (ii) weakly-regular runs do not exhaustively propagate unit clauses but still learn non-redundant clauses except for unit instances, (iii) the used notion of non-redundancy is NEXPTIME-complete for the BS fragment, (iv) SCL simulates resolution by non-regular runs, (v) SCL simulates NRCL by non-regular runs, (vi) exhaustive propagation is not always a good strategy for the BS fragment and beyond, and (vii) SCL is a decision procedure for the BS fragment.

The price for the simple SCL models is that trails can be exponentially longer compared to trails of calculi with more expressive model representation languages. For a BS clause set N the overall trail size is bound by mr^k where k is the maximal arity of a predicate in N, m the number of predicates, and r the number of constant symbols in N. Exploiting the actual recursive structure of N this bound can be further refined for a specific problem [10]. So in a simple preprocessing step, it can be checked whether an SCL trail potentially becomes "too large". Then a procedure can either start with a more expressive trail language [1,3,4,7,9,14,17] or dynamically decide to switch the trail model representation formalism. In practice, there are many interesting problems where the maximal predicate arity is not larger than three and there are not "too many" constants. Recall that all our examples inducing an exponentially growing trail or an exponentially growing proof length include the encoding of some type of binary counter.

Although SCL with a regular strategy and also all other calculi with exhaustive propagation cannot simulate resolution, the resolution calculus has also drawbacks. Worst case, the resolution calculus may generate more clauses, even in a terminating setting [7], than there are potential ground model assumptions as they are explored by SCL. Still one open question is whether the advantages of resolution and SCL can be combined: learning only non redundant clauses via partial model assumptions and being able to simulate non-redundant resolution inferences, in general. Such a result would unify both paradigms.

Acknowledgments. This work was funded by DFG grant 389792660 as part of TRR 248.

References

1. Alagi, G., Weidenbach, C.: NRCL - a model building approach to the Bernays-Schönfinkel fragment. In: Lutz, C., Ranise, S. (eds.) FroCoS 2015. LNCS (LNAI), vol. 9322, pp. 69–84. Springer, Cham (2015). https://doi.org/10.1007/978-3-319-24246-0_5
2. Baumgartner, P.: Hyper tableau—the next generation. In: de Swart, H. (ed.) TABLEAUX 1998. LNCS (LNAI), vol. 1397, pp. 60–76. Springer, Heidelberg (1998). https://doi.org/10.1007/3-540-69778-0_14

3. Baumgartner, P., Fuchs, A., Tinelli, C.: Lemma learning in the model evolution calculus. In: Hermann, M., Voronkov, A. (eds.) LPAR 2006. LNCS (LNAI), vol. 4246, pp. 572–586. Springer, Heidelberg (2006). https://doi.org/10.1007/11916277_39
4. Bonacina, M.P., Plaisted, D.A.: Semantically-guided goal-sensitive reasoning: model representation. J. Autom. Reason. **56**(2), 113–141 (2016)
5. Bromberger, M., Sturm, T., Weidenbach, C.: Linear integer arithmetic revisited. In: Felty, A.P., Middeldorp, A. (eds.) CADE 2015. LNCS (LNAI), vol. 9195, pp. 623–637. Springer, Cham (2015). https://doi.org/10.1007/978-3-319-21401-6_42
6. Fermüller, C.G., Pichler, R.: Model representation over finite and infinite signatures. J. Log. Comput. **17**(3), 453–477 (2007)
7. Hillenbrand, T., Weidenbach, C.: Superposition for bounded domains. In: Bonacina, M.P., Stickel, M.E. (eds.) Automated Reasoning and Mathematics. LNCS (LNAI), vol. 7788, pp. 68–100. Springer, Heidelberg (2013). https://doi.org/10.1007/978-3-642-36675-8_4
8. Kaufmann, B., Leone, N., Perri, S., Schaub, T.: Grounding and solving in answer set programming. AI Mag. **37**(3), 25–32 (2016)
9. Korovin, K.: Inst-Gen – a modular approach to instantiation-based automated reasoning. In: Voronkov, A., Weidenbach, C. (eds.) Programming Logics. LNCS, vol. 7797, pp. 239–270. Springer, Heidelberg (2013). https://doi.org/10.1007/978-3-642-37651-1_10
10. Korovin, K.: Non-cyclic sorts for first-order satisfiability. In: Fontaine, P., Ringeissen, C., Schmidt, R.A. (eds.) FroCoS 2013. LNCS (LNAI), vol. 8152, pp. 214–228. Springer, Heidelberg (2013). https://doi.org/10.1007/978-3-642-40885-4_15
11. Lewis, H.R.: Complexity results for classes of quantificational formulas. J. Comput. Syst. Sci. **21**(3), 317–353 (1980)
12. Nieuwenhuis, R., Oliveras, A., Tinelli, C.: Solving sat and sat modulo theories: from an abstract Davis-Putnam-Logemann-Loveland procedure to DPLL (T). J. ACM **53**, 937–977 (2006)
13. Navarro, J.A., Voronkov, A.: Proof systems for effectively propositional logic. In: Armando, A., Baumgartner, P., Dowek, G. (eds.) IJCAR 2008. LNCS (LNAI), vol. 5195, pp. 426–440. Springer, Heidelberg (2008). https://doi.org/10.1007/978-3-540-71070-7_36
14. Piskac, R., de Moura, L.M., Bjørner, N.: Deciding effectively propositional logic using DPLL and substitution sets. J. Autom. Reason. **44**(4), 401–424 (2010)
15. Plaisted, D.A.: Complete problems in the first-order predicate calculus. J. Comput. Syst. Sci. **29**, 8–35 (1984)
16. Sutcliffe, G.: The CADE ATP system competition - CASC. AI Mag. **37**(2), 99–101 (2016)
17. Teucke, A., Weidenbach, C.: First-order logic theorem proving and model building via approximation and instantiation. In: Lutz, C., Ranise, S. (eds.) FroCoS 2015. LNCS (LNAI), vol. 9322, pp. 85–100. Springer, Cham (2015). https://doi.org/10.1007/978-3-319-24246-0_6

Names Are Not Just Sound and Smoke: Word Embeddings for Axiom Selection

Ulrich Furbach[1], Teresa Krämer[1], and Claudia Schon[2(✉)]

[1] Institute for Computer Science, University of Koblenz-Landau, Koblenz, Germany
{uli,tbergk}@uni-koblenz.de
[2] Institute for Web Science and Technologies, University of Koblenz-Landau,
Koblenz, Germany
schon@uni-koblenz.de

Abstract. First-order theorem proving with large knowledge bases makes it necessary to select those parts of the knowledge base, that are necessary to prove the theorem at hand. We extend syntactic axiom selection procedures like SInE to use semantics of symbol names. For this, not only occurrences of symbol names but also semantically similar names are taken into account. We use a similarity measure based on word embeddings. An evaluation of this similarity based SInE is given using problems from TPTP's CSR problem class and Adimen-SUMO. This evaluation is done with two very different systems, namely the Hyper tableau prover and the saturation based system E.

1 Introduction

Automated theorem proving attempts to find a proof (for the unsatisfiability) of a set of formulae. Most problems, even those from benchmark suites like TPTP [28], consist of hand-coded sets of logical formulae and hence used to be relatively small. This situation changed dramatically since automated theorem provers have been used in contexts with large background knowledge. This can be large ontologies like SUMO [19], CYC [11], Yago [27] or mathematical libraries, where the theorem prover has to face millions of formulae that are potentially necessary to find a proof of the problem under consideration. Once a proof is found, it typically turns out that only a very small part of the vast background knowledge was necessary to find the proof. This leads to the following challenge: Given a large background knowledge base and a problem, find a (preferably small) subset of the knowledge base with which a proof for the problem can be found.

One of the most used approaches for this task is the SInE selection method [9]. It's basic idea is to determine symbols relevant for a problem at hand and to select formulae to be included into the proof search based on this relevancy. This method is very well suited for many problem areas and it is used by many

---

Work supported by DFG grant CoRg – Cognitive Reasoning. Author names are given in alphabetical order.

P. Fontaine (Ed.): CADE 2019, LNAI 11716, pp. 250–268, 2019.
https://doi.org/10.1007/978-3-030-29436-6_15

theorem provers nowadays. However, in order to apply this method it is mandatory that the symbols are used in a consistent manner throughout all formulae in the knowledge base and in the axiomatisation of the problem. And, of course, this is fully consistent with the way the logical formulae are usually processed by theorem provers. To prove the unsatisfiability of a set of formulae it does not matter which symbols are used, it is only important that symbols, e.g., a predicate symbol p, is used consistently in the entire formulae set. If every occurrence of p is substituted by q the problem to prove the unsatisfiability of the formulae remains the same. This is why the SInE selection strategy only counts occurrences of symbol names and does not consider the meaning of symbol names.

In certain areas such as commonsense reasoning, however, symbol names in knowledge bases are anything but random. This is very obvious as soon as we have to apply reasoning within the context of natural language. Examples are the commonsense reasoning benchmarks from [13] where the task is to determine which one of the given alternatives is the most plausible one:

My body cast a shadow over the grass. What was the CAUSE of this?
1. The sun was rising.
2. The grass was cut.

In the approach followed in the project CoRg [24] these sentences are transfered into first-order logic as a starting point for reasoning. This is done automatically by KNEWS [3], which is based on Boxer, a system for translating natural language input into various logical output formats [5]. For the premise together with the first alternative from our example we get:

$$\exists A, B(\exists C, D, E, F(rover(D, B) \land \exists G(rtopic(G, A) \land arisingC(G))$$
$$\land rthat(B, C) \land rpatient(D, E) \land ragent(D, F)$$
$$\land vcast(D) \land nshadow(E) \land nbody(F) \land rof(F, E)$$
$$\land nperson(E)) \land nsun(A) \land ngrassC(B)).$$

So far, this approach follows very much the traditional paradigm in computational linguistics, namely to translate a natural language sentence into a metalanguage that represents the meaning of the sentence. In our case, first-order logic is used as a metalanguage, which has the advantage that powerful automatic reasoning systems can be used for further processing of the meaning of the sentence. The predicates in the resulting first-order logic formula are derived either directly from the words appearing in the English sentence or by portraying the connections. Examples for the former are $nbody$ or $vcast$ with a prefix indicating the word type (n for noun, v for verb), while the latter can be exemplified by $ragent(D, F)$ (r for role), which states that F (the noun body) has the role of the agent of D (the verb cast).

It is easy to see that the COPA task shown above can not be solved by simply applying a reasoning system to the formula generated from it. To reason that a shadow can be cast by an object and the sun needs more background knowledge. We use the ontology SUMO [19] as a knowledge base representing this background knowledge. The task of axiom selection is to consider those parts of SUMO for the reasoning process that contain the symbols of the formula or related ones. There are two problems: Firstly, a symbol might not be used in the ontology, but a synonym or a semantically similar one. E.g., *vcast* does not occur in the ontology (and neither does *cast*), but the symbol *project*, which has a similar meaning occurs in the ontology and can be used instead of *vcast*. This can be easily solved by the use of WordNet [17], which immediately gives us *project* as a synonym of *cast*. This is even supported by KNEWS, which determines WordNet synsets for the symbol names in the generated formulae. The use of WordNet is further discussed in Sect. 4.3.

The second problem is much more subtle. There is no guarantee that the symbols of the background knowledge in SUMO fit semantically to the symbols in the generated predicate logic formulae—even if synonyms are taken into account.

This is why we also want to consider symbols in the background knowledge that are semantically similar to the symbols in the formulae. This offers the possibility to select more relevant axioms for the reasoning process from the background knowledge. For such a similarity measure there is an obvious choice, namely the distributional semantics of natural language, which is applied in many statistical natural language processing systems. Firth, one of the founders of this approach, put it like this:

You shall know a word by the company it keeps [8].

For such a semantics, a large corpus of natural language text is evaluated to find co-occurences of words. Words that occur more frequently together are more similar compared to words with less frequent co-occurences. Similar to this co-occurrence information are word embeddings, which we use in our approach. More specifically, we use the word embedding ConceptNet Numberbatch [26] to give us a real-valued vector for a symbol, which can be used to compare symbols with respect to similarity. In our example Numberbatch gives us a similarity value for *cast* and *project* of 0.19337063, which appears to be pretty low— the reason certainly is that *project* is not only a verb but also a noun with a semantics very different from *cast*, and this is mirrored by the low value. On the other hand, if we compare *sun* and *shadow* the value is 0.25696868 and for *grass* and *shadow* we get 0.09716037, which clearly indicates that the first alternative from the example above is more plausible. There are numerous systems which use this kind of distributional semantics together with machine learning methods for solving commonsense reasoning tasks very successfully [12,32,33].

We use both kinds of semantics—translation into logic as a metalanguage and distributional semantics—together. This offers the possibility of getting insights into the reasoning process and applying statistical methods at the same time. For this, we introduce a selection technique that considers the meaning of symbol names. The main contributions are:

- A selection technique that takes the meaning of symbol names into account by using word embeddings.

- A discussion of the need of mapping symbol names from the problem description and the background knowledge base to the vocabulary of the word embedding.
- An evaluation of the methods presented, which demonstrates that these methods can be helpful for reasoning.

This paper is organized as follows: after discussing related work in Sect. 2, in Sect. 3 we review the SInE selection method from [9]. Sect. 4 introduces our approach for combining word embeddings with the SInE method and in Sect. 5 this method is evaluated. Finally we discuss future work.

2   Related Work

There are a number of papers on axiom selection in large theories. Most of them are of purely syntactic nature, like [14, 23] or [9]. In [30] there is a semantic approach for axiom selection. It is based on the computation of models for subsets of the available axioms and by consecutively extending these sets. This approach is model based and the meaning of symbol names is not taken into account. A very similar approach is described in [34], where it is used to search for conjectures which might be interesting.

In [10] the authors extend SInE by a method which is well known from market basket analysis, namely frequent item set mining. Instead of co-occurences given by word embeddings in our case, frequent item set mining is working directly on axiom sets in order to find symbols which frequently occur together. This information is then used for extending SInE. Frequent item mining is evaluated with prover E and with SPASS with the MPTP2078 benchmarks and with both provers there was no increase of performance with the extended SInE. Moreover, the authors state that in many cases the selection itself was too costly and often resulted in a timeout.

In [22] similarities of symbol names are used to define an extended unification method. The similarity is learned by neural networks which allow calculation of proof success with respect to a vector representation of symbol names. This method is used to improve the similarity measure and it is shown in this paper that it is well suited for inductive logic programming.

The observation that names are meaningful is explicitly formulated and evaluated in [7]. This approach is based on knowledge graphs as they are used in the semantic web area. The authors test and evaluate their hypothesis, namely that the names of IRIs (Internationalized Resource Identifiers) carry a kind of social semantics, and come to the conclusion that semantics encoded in the names of IRIs significantly coincides with the formal meaning of the denoted resources. Hence the authors prove, that names in RDF graphs encode semantics. The authors use this insight to motivate the development of semantic web tools that make use of the meaning of names.

3   Selection Techniques for Large Knowledge Bases

The reasoning task we are considering in this paper consists of a very large set of axioms called the knowledge base (KB), a small set of further axioms $F_1, \ldots, F_n$ called assumptions and a query Q. The task is to show that KB together with $F_1, \ldots, F_n$ implies Q. In classical logic, this can be reduced to showing that $F_1 \wedge \ldots \wedge F_n \rightarrow Q$ is entailed by KB. As suggested in [9], we will denote $F_1 \wedge \ldots \wedge F_n \rightarrow Q$ as *goal*.

Given a query and a real-world KB, automated theorem provers (ATP) nowadays are able to compute proofs quite efficiently. However, once the underlying KB has reached a certain size, it is not feasible to consider the entire KB when trying to find a proof. Analysis of proofs on large KBs has shown that in the vast majority of cases only a very small part of the KB has been used for the proof. This observation is the basis of a strategy for reasoning in large KB: starting from the goal an attempt is made to determine a subset of the KB that contains sufficient knowledge to construct a proof.

In [9] the relevance-based selection strategy SInE is introduced. This selection is based on a trigger relation that determines which symbols trigger an axiom. Assume for a given axiom A and a symbol s occurring in A, a relation $triggers(s, A)$.

Definition 1 (Trigger-based selection [9]). *Let KB be a knowledge base, A be an axiom in KB and s be a predicate or function symbol occurring in KB. Let furthermore g be a goal to be proven from KB.*

1. *If s is a symbol occurring in the goal g, then s is 0-step triggered.*
2. *If s is k-step triggered and s triggers A ($triggers(s, A)$), then A is $k + 1$-step triggered.*
3. *If A is k-step triggered and s occurs in A, then s is k-step triggered, too.*

An axiom or a symbol is called triggered if it is k-step triggered for some $k \geq 0$.

In order to obtain a selection strategy, it is necessary to define which symbols trigger an axiom. A naive choice for this relation would be to determine that an axiom is triggered by all symbols occurring in it. Usually there are symbols like *subClass* or *hasPart* in KBs that are very common. Therefore, this naive trigger relation would result in the selection of almost all axioms. The SInE selection defines the triggers relation such that only the least common symbol in an axiom is allowed to trigger this axiom. This ensures that common symbols do not lead to the selection of all axioms.

Definition 2 (Trigger relation for the SInE selection [9]). *Let KB be a knowledge base and s be a symbol. Let furthermore $occ(s)$ denote the number of axioms in which s occurs in KB. Then the triggers relation is defined as follows:*

$$triggers(s, A) \text{ iff for all symbols } s' \text{ occurring in } A \text{ we have } occ(s) \leq occ(s') \tag{1}$$

Definition 1 together with Definition 2 define a trigger-based selection strategy. If a trigger-based selection selects all k-step relevant axioms, we call this selection SInE with *recursion depth* k in the following.

The SInE selection is an incomplete selection technique. This means that it can happen that given a goal, SInE selects a set of axioms with which no proof for the goal can be found (see Example 1 in Sect. 4.3 for an example). One reason for the incompleteness is SInE's fragility w.r.t. the number of occurrences of a symbol: even if two symbols occurring in an axiom occur almost equally often in the KB, only the one with the least number of occurrences is allowed to trigger the axiom. In order to soften this effect, the tolerance parameter, a real number $t \geq 1$, was introduced. To take this parameter into account, Eq. (1) can be changed such that

$$triggers(s, A) \text{ iff for all symbols } s' \text{ occurring in } A \text{ we have } occ(s) \leq t \cdot occ(s')$$
$$(2)$$

This allows not only the symbol with the least number of occurrences to trigger an axiom but also symbols with t times more occurrences.

The SInE selection strategy is successfully used by many provers. One property of SInE is that it completely ignores the names of the symbols in the KB. The behaviour of the selection does not change if a symbol called *beer* would be renamed to p. In many areas where the names of symbols are not very meaningful, this is a legitimate approach. In commonsense KBs, the symbols usually have meaningful names and we suspect that this meaning can be very helpful for the selection process. In the following, we introduce a selection technique taking into account the symbol name's meaning which is implemented as a SInE extension.

4 Integration of Distributional Semantics into Axiom Selection

An example of a KB where symbols carry meanings, is SUMO [19,20]. To simplify its use, there is even a mapping offered that relates symbols occurring in SUMO to WordNet [17] synsets. SUMO is no exception; many other KBs in the commonsense reasoning area, like Cyc [11], also offer such mappings to WordNet or include the WordNet class hierarchy like Yago [27]. This illustrates the importance of symbol names in this area.

In current selection techniques, however, the meaning of the symbol names used in a KB is completely ignored. Intuitively, a symbol like *beer* in the goal should not only lead to the selection of axioms triggered by the symbol *beer*, but also to the selection of axioms triggered by symbols with a similar meaning, like *pilsner* for example. This is why we aim at including the meaning of the symbol names in the selection process. We semantically guide the selection process by integrating word-embeddings into the selection process by replacing the above trigger relation with one that takes a word embedding into account. Using this selection technique together with a theorem prover leads to a hybrid approach using both reasoning and statistical methods.

4.1   Distributional Semantics

The area of distributional semantics researches theories for quantifying semantic similarities between words based on their distributional properties in large text corpora. More specifically, distributional semantics is based on the distributional hypothesis [18], which states that linguistic elements with a similar distribution have a similar meaning. A currently very popular technique in the field of distributional semantics is word embeddings [16], which map words or phrases from a given vocabulary to vectors of real numbers. The rough idea behind the construction of word embeddings, as performed by methods like Word2vec [15], is to first determine word co-occurrences on a large text corpus and store them in a matrix. If the vocabulary V of the text corpus consists of $|V|$ words, this step leads to a $|V|$ times $|V|$ matrix. In the next step, Word2vec performs a dimensionality reduction that leads to a smaller matrix. Each column of the resulting matrix corresponds to the vector representation of a word. A nice property of these word embeddings is that relative similarities of the vectors correlate with semantic similarity. This means that the vector representations of *beer* and *pilsner* are closer together than the representations of *beer* and *stone*. More precisely, the similarity of two words w_1 and w_2 from the vocabulary can be calculated by as the cosine similarity of their vector representations x_{w_1} and x_{w_2}:

$$\frac{x_{w_1} \cdot x_{w_2}}{||x_{w_1}|| \, ||x_{w_2}||} \tag{3}$$

where $x_{w_1} \cdot x_{w_2}$ denotes the dot product and $||x_{w_1}||$ the magnitude of vector x_{w_1}. The value of this cosine similarity lies between -1 for completely opposite vectors to 1 for the same vectors.

Surprisingly, simple algebraic operations on the vector representations can be used to answer questions about analogies. For example the question: Which word w has the same relationship to *king* as *woman* to *man*? can be answered by calculating $x_y = x_{woman} - x_{man} + x_{king}$ where x_w denotes the vector representation of word w normalized to unit form. The vector x_y' with the greatest cosine similarity to x_y yields the expected answer $y = queen$.

The word embedding toolkits Word2vec [15] and GloVe [21] are able to learn vector representations for given text corpora. We exploit the possibility of using word embeddings to provide the k most similar words for a given word, and integrate this information into the selection of axioms. In the following, we assume a given word embedding. The word embedding we use in our experiments is ConceptNet Numberbatch [26], which was derived using ConceptNet, Word2vec, GloVe, and OpenSubtitles 2016 [31].

Definition 3 (Set of k vectors most similar to x_v). *Let V be a vocabulary and f a word embedding, i.e. $f : V \to \mathbb{R}^n$, $k \in \mathbb{N}$, $|V| > k$ and $x_v \in \mathbb{R}^n$ a vector. Then $simvecs_f(x_v, k)$, the set of k vectors in $f(V)$ most similar to vector x_v, is defined as*

$$simvecs_f(x_v, k) = \begin{cases} \{x_1, \ldots, x_k\} & \text{if } x_v \in f(V) \\ \emptyset & \text{else} \end{cases}$$

such that

- $\{x_1, \ldots x_k\} \subseteq f(V)$,
- $|\{x_1, \ldots, x_k\}| = k$ *and*
- *there is no* $x_j \in f(V)$ *with* $x_j \notin \{x_1, \ldots, x_k\}$ *and* $\frac{x_j \cdot x_v}{||x_j|| \, ||x_v||} > \frac{x_i \cdot x_v}{||x_i|| \, ||x_v||}$ *for some* $x_i \in \{x_1, \ldots, x_k\}$.

  Furthermore, $simwords_f(w, k)$, *the set of words similar to word* w, *is defined as*

$$simwords_f(w, k) = \begin{cases} \{w' \in V \mid f(w') \in simvecs_f(f(w), k)\} & if \ w \in V \\ \emptyset & else \end{cases}$$

Next, we show how to integrate a word embedding into the selection process.

4.2 Using Similarities for Axiom Selection

Using the example of the frequently used selection SInE, we now show how word embeddings can be integrated into the selection process. For this the trigger relation must be exchanged. The trigger-based selection presented in Definition 1 can be used unchanged. In the following definition we assume the set of predicate and function symbols coincide with the set of words in the vocabulary of the used word embedding. We do this only to increase the readability of the definition. Since this assumption does not apply in practice, the next section presents details on how to map the symbols from the KB to the vocabulary of the embedding and vice versa.

Definition 4 (Word embedding enhanced trigger relation). *Let KB be a knowledge base with* Σ *the set of function and predicate symbols occurring in KB, A an axiom in KB,* $s \in \Sigma$ *be a symbol and* $k \in \mathbb{N}$. *Let furthermore* $f : V \to \mathbb{R}^n$ *be a word embedding with vocabulary* $V = \Sigma$. *Then the word embedding enhanced set of symbols triggering axiom A is defined as follows:*

$$simtriggers_f(A, k) = \bigcup_{s \in \{s' | triggers(s', A)\}} (\{s\} \cup (simwords_f(s, k)))$$

Intuitively, not only the rarest symbol s is allowed to trigger an axiom but also all symbols which are among the k most similar symbols of s according to word embedding f. This can result in an axiom like $subClass(beer, beverage)$ to be triggered by *pilsner* which does not occur in the axiom but is clearly related to content of the axiom.

Setting $triggers(s, A)$ iff $s \in simtriggers_f(A, k)$ in Definition 1 for some embedding f and some $k \in \mathbb{N}$, results in a selection technique that takes word embedding f into account.

Definition 4 assumes that the symbols occurring in the KB coincide with the vocabulary of the word embedding. Next we describe problems occurring if this assumption is not true and we show how to solve these problems.

4.3   Relating Symbol Names to the Vocabulary of a Word Embedding

Usually, a KB does not come in combination with a suitable word embedding. There are a variety of word embeddings that can be downloaded and used directly. For the integration of a word embedding into axiom selection it is important that the word embedding used matches the KB from which the selection is to be made. In other words, the embedding should be calculated on a text that matches the KB thematically. Ideally, for example, a word embedding learned on the text of Wikipedia would be used for selection on Yago, since Yago contains the knowledge of Wikipedia. Even if there is a word embedding which is close to the content of the KB, we cannot assume all predicate and function symbols of the KB to have vector representations in the embedding. A disadvantage of word embeddings is that they usually do not distinguish between the different meanings of a word. This means, for example, that the meaning of the verb *project* together with the meaning of the noun *project* is represented by the same vector. Therefore, WordNet mappings for word embeddings are usually not offered. However, when relating symbol names with elements in the embedding's vocabulary, an existing WordNet mapping for the KB can be used. Such a WordNet mapping of a KB is a mapping of the symbol names occurring in the KB to WordNet synsets.[1] A WordNet synset represents a *set of synonyms*, meaning a set of words with a similar meaning. Figure 1 shows some of the noun senses in WordNet for the word *grass*.

- S: (n) grass (narrow-leaved green herbage: grown as lawns; used as pasture for grazing animals; cut and dried as hay)
- S: (n) supergrass, grass (a police informer who implicates many people)
- S: (n) pot, grass, green goddess, dope, weed, gage, sess, sens, smoke, skunk, locoweed, Mary Jane (street names for marijuana)

Fig. 1. Some of the noun senses of the word *grass* in WordNet. Each line represents one synset of the word *grass*. The text given in parentheses represents the sense. The synset shown in the third line contains the synonyms *supergrass* and *grass* and has the sense *a police informer who implicates many people*.

One way to relate a symbol name s of the KB to elements in the word embedding's vocabulary is to check for each symbol name, if the symbol name occurs as a word in the vocabulary. We create a relation rel from this information such that $rel(s, s)$ for all symbols names s that are contained in the embedding's vocabulary. If the symbols have meaningful names, this can produce a relation covering many symbol names.

To achieve a higher coverage of the relation between symbol names and elements in the word embedding's vocabulary, the WordNet mapping of the KB

---

[1] WordNet mappings usually also contain information about *subclass* or *instance of* relations. Since these relations are not relevant for this paper, they are omitted.

can be used as follows: the symbol name s is first mapped to a WordNet synset using the WordNet mapping and then for all synonyms l belonging to this synset it is checked if l is in the word embedding's vocabulary. Meaning that for all synonyms l occurring in the vocabulary of the embedding $rel(s, l)$ is added to the relation.

In the following definition, we omit all further information in WordNet and consider a synset to be a set of synonyms. Therefore, a WordNet mapping is assumed to be a mapping $w : \Sigma \rightarrow 2^{Synsets}$ with $Synsets$ the set of WordNet synsets and each synset $S = \{l_1, \ldots l_n\}$ a set of synonyms.

Definition 5 (Bridging relation between symbol names and a word embedding's vocabulary). *Let KB be a knowledge base with Σ the set of function and predicate symbols occurring in KB and $s \in \Sigma$ be a symbol. Let furthermore $f : V \rightarrow \mathbb{R}^n$ be a word embedding with vocabulary V. Let Synsets be the set of synsets in WordNet and $w : \Sigma \rightarrow 2^{Synsets}$ be a WordNet mapping of KB. Then the bridging relation $rel \subseteq \Sigma \times V$ is defined as $\{(s,s) \mid s \in \Sigma \cap V\} \cup \{(s,l) \mid S \in w(s) \text{ and } l \in S \text{ and } l \in V\}$.*

Note that the bridging relation rel is not total. So there may be symbol names not taking part in the relation and there may be words in the vocabulary not taking part in the relation. Furthermore, rel is not a function. So there may be distinct words w_1, w_2 in the vocabulary with $rel(s, w_1)$ and $rel(s, w_2)$ for some symbol s.

Definition 6 (Word embedding enhanced trigger relation using a bridging relation). *Let KB be a knowledge base with Σ the set of function and predicate symbols occurring in KB, A an axiom in KB, $s \in \Sigma$ be a symbol and $k \in \mathbb{N}$. Let furthermore $f : V \rightarrow \mathbb{R}^n$ be a word embedding with vocabulary V and rel a bridging relation between symbols in Σ and words in V. Then the word embedding enhanced set of symbols triggering axiom A using rel is defined as follows:*

$$simtriggers_f(A, k) = \bigcup_{s \in \{s' \mid triggers(s', A)\}} (\{s\} \cup \{s'' \mid rel(s, w) \text{ and } w' \in simwords_f(w, k)$$

$$and \; rel(s'', w')\})$$

We call the resulting selection *Similarity SInE*. Note that for an empty bridging relation rel Definition 6 is identical to Definition 4. In general, $simtriggers_f(A, k)$ does not necessarily contain $k + 1$ symbols. In general, it contains many less than $k + 1$ symbols, since not all words contained in $simwords_f(w, k)$ can be mapped by rel to a symbol in Σ. In extreme cases, if no additional similar symbols can be added to the triggers relation due to an empty bridging relation, the resulting selection behaves exactly like SInE. Conversely, it could also happen that more than $k + 1$ symbols end up in $simtriggers_f(A, k)$, since a symbol s can be associated with more than one word from V via rel, and for all these words the k most similar words are looked up in the word embedding. In Sect. 5, we present the experiences we have made in this respect in our experiments.

Example 1. We consider the following set of axioms, which is an extended version of the example given in [9]:

$$\forall X, Y, Z((subClass(X, Y) \land subClass(Y, Z)) \rightarrow subClass(X, Z)) \qquad (4)$$

$subClass(stone, liquid) \rightarrow \bot$	(5)	$subClass(pilsner, beer)$	(10)
$subClass(petrol, liquid)$	(6)	$subClass(coolant, liquid)$	(11)
$subClass(beverage, liquid)$	(7)	$subClass(lager, beer)$	(12)
$subClass(beer, beverage)$	(8)	$subClass(ale, beer)$	(13)
$subClass(guiness, beer)$	(9)		

The second column in Fig. 2 shows for each symbol the number of axioms it occurs in. This information is used to determine the set of axioms triggered by each symbol which is shown in the third column. The fourth column presents for each given symbol the set of similar symbols found by using *rel* to map the symbol name to the word embedding ConceptNet Numberbatch's vocabulary V, determining the $k = 100$ most similar words and using *rel* to map these words back (if possible) to symbols in the axiom set. For the example, we assume *rel* to be defined as $rel = \{(s, s) \mid s \in V \cap \Sigma\}$. Of course ConceptNet Numberbatch contains many other similar words that do not occur in the axioms. For example the 100 words most similar to *beverage* in ConceptNet Numberbatch's vocabulary contain *tea_like_drink*, *beverages*, *red_bull*, *beer_run* and *in_drink* all of which can not be mapped back to the symbols in our example. The last column of Fig. 2 presents for each symbol the axioms that are similarity triggered by this symbol.

We now consider the following conjecture:

$$?\,subClass(beer, liquid) \qquad (14)$$

With regular SInE symbols *subClass*, *beer* and *liquid* are 0-step triggered. *subClass* triggers axiom (4) whereas symbol *beer* and *liquid* do not trigger further axioms (see third column Fig. 2). With the one selected axiom a proof cannot be found.

With Similarity SInE symbols *subClass*, *beer* and *liquid* are 0-step triggered. Symbol *subClass* triggers axiom (4), *beer* triggers axioms (7), (8), (10), (12) and (13) causing the symbols *beverage*, *liquid*, *pilsner*, *lager* and *ale* to be 1-step triggered. The symbols *liquid*, *beverage*, *pilsner*, *lager* and *ale* do not trigger any further axioms. Using the selected axioms, a proof can be found.

Using a tolerance of 2 for regular SInE causes SInE to select axioms (4), (7) and (8), which are sufficient to find a proof. The extent to which tolerance must be increased, however, depends strongly on the axioms present in the KB. For example, if we add the information about two more beers and two more liquids to the KB, the tolerance must be set to 3 for SInE to select all necessary axioms. If we then add three more beers and three more liquids, SInE selects all axioms necessary for the proof only at tolerance 4.5. In our example, the

Symbol	Occurrences	triggers(s, A)	Similar symbols	simtriggers$_f$(s, A)
subClass	10	(4)		(4)
liquid	4			
beer	5		*ale, lager, pilsner, beverage*	(7), (8),(10), (12), (13)
beverage	2	(7), (8)	*beer*	(7), (8)
petrol	1	(6)		(6)
stone	1	(5)		(5)
guiness	1	(9)		(9)
pilsner	1	(10)	*lager, ale, beer*	(10), (12),(13)
coolant	1	(11)		(11)
lager	1	(12)	*pilsner, ale, beer*	(10), (12),(13)
ale	1	(13)	*lager, beer, pilsner*	(10), (12),(13)

Fig. 2. SInE's and Similarity SInE's trigger relation.

tolerance to be used depends on the relationship between the number of the occurrence of the *beverage* and *liquid* symbols as well as the relationship between the number of occurrences of the *beverage* and *beer* symbols. If the symbols *beer* and *liquid* occur much more frequently than the symbol *beverage*, a high tolerance is required to be able to select all necessary axioms with SInE. In contrast, Similarity SInE selection is less dependent on relationships between frequencies. Regardless of how many more beers and liquids are added, Similarity SInE always selects axioms (4), (7), (8), (10), (12) and (13).

5 Experiments

In order to evaluate Similarity SInE, we need KBs in which the symbols have meaningful names. In addition, the KBs used must be large, otherwise the use of selection techniques does not make sense. The LTB division of CASC [29] contains very large problems. Unfortunately, most of the problems in this division do not have meaningful symbol names. The CSR SUMO problems (CSR075 - CSR109 and CSR118) are a positive exception here, and therefore considered for the experiments. In addition to the CSR SUMO problems, we consider Adimen-SUMO for the experiments. It was obtained by translating a large part of SUMO into first-order logic [2]. The reason for choosing Adimen-SUMO over SUMO is the fact that the current version of Adimen-SUMO (v2.6), comes with a set of 8010 automatically generated white-box truth-tests [1]. These problems are supposed to be entailed by Adimen-SUMO and are therefore fit for the evaluation of Similarity SInE. Just like SUMO, Adimen-SUMO uses meaningful symbol names and provides a mapping to WordNet (which corresponds to SUMO's WordNet mapping). Since there is no word embedding that fits exactly to CSR SUMO or Adimen-SUMO, the word embedding ConceptNet Numberbatch was used for the experiments, which contains a broad general knowledge.

In the experiments, we use SInE and Similarity SInE with different parameters as selection techniques. We adapted E's SInE implementation, which can be used as a stand-alone program, such that it takes similar symbols into account. The resulting program is used to perform the Similarity SInE selection[2]. E's implementation of SInE is used in the experiments to perform the SInE selection. Since the selection of the formulae is completely independent of the ATP used afterwards, we were able to use two different ATPs, Hyper [4] and E [25], after the selection step. Hyper is a tableau prover that is very well suited for tasks within cognitive reasoning because of its compact proof structure, efficient equality handling and confluence property. E is one of the best high performance saturation-based first-order systems.

5.1   Relating Symbol Names to a Word Embedding's Vocabulary

For the experiments, we use the ConceptNet Numberbatch word embedding. Adimen-SUMO contains 3,917 symbols. Starting with an empty bridging relation 58% namely 2,279 of these symbols can be mapped to words in the vocabulary by throwing away prefixes and reformatting compound symbol names. E.g., symbol *c__FamilyBusiness* was mapped to word *family_business*, which occurs in ConceptNet Numberbatch's vocabulary, and led to adding *(c__FamilyBusiness, family_business)* to the bridging relation *rel*. For those 2,279 symbols for which this brute-force relating of symbols to words in ConceptNet Numberbatch's vocabulary worked, the $k = 100$ most similar words were determined. Of these words, on average, 2.4 (standard deviation 2.6) could be mapped back to symbol names of Adimen-SUMO. In total, 5,521 similar symbols were found and used in the triggers relation. The value of k has been determined by small normative experiments. Further values of k will be considered in future work.

The coverage with this brute-force relating of symbol names to the word embedding's vocabulary can be improved to 63% using a bridging relation derived from the SUMO WordNet mapping.

Not all the CSR SUMO problems include the same axiom sets. This is why it is not possible to present one single number for the coverage of the bridging relation *rel*. Depending on the included axiom sets, the CSR SUMO problems use 3,452 to 34,239 different symbols. Using the brute-force method to create the bridging relation *rel*, the coverage was between 14% and 21%. Using SUMO's WordNet mapping increases coverage to 20% to 31%. Note that even using SUMO's WordNet mapping, the coverage of the bridging relation for CSR SUMO is far below the coverage of the bridging relation for Adimen-SUMO. In order to evaluate if the coverage of the bridging relation plays an important role for the selection and the subsequent ATP run, we performed experiments with both the bridging relation created by brute-force and the improved bridging relation (using the WordNet mapping).

In our implementation, we take advantage of the fact that WordNet gives a list of synonyms ordered by relevance. Therefore, for a given symbol name s we only add (s, l) to *rel* for the most relevant word l occurring in the list of synonyms.

---

[2] Implementation (git hash 'eeee0fc0b46c688ec25e08806d39ec8cea93cbc0') available at https://gitlab.uni-koblenz.de/corg/similaritysine.

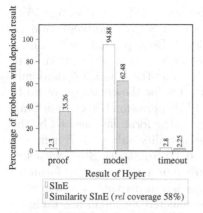

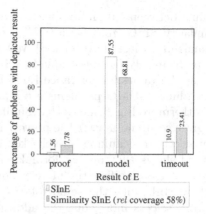

(a) Result of Hyper on the 6,701 problems, it was not able to solve without selection.

(b) Result of E on 3,405 problems, it was not able to solve without selection.

Fig. 3. Percentage of the considered Adimen-SUMO problems where Hyper or E found a proof, a model or ran into a timeout broken down by the selection technique used. For all selections, tolerance one and recursion depth 1–6 was used.

5.2 Experimental Results

All tests were carried out on a computer featuring an Intel(R) Xeon(R) CPU E5-2699 v3 @ 2.30GHz (only two cores were used) with 8GB RAM. For the provers used in the experiments, we used a timeout of 15 s (cpu time). The timeout is based on the experimental results from [1], where for the majority of the Adimen-SUMO problem's proofs were found in up to 10 s.

Hyper and E on Adimen-SUMO. For the Adimen-SUMO problems we first determined the set of problems for which selection makes sense for the used provers. For this, Hyper and E were run for all 8,010 Adimen-SUMO problems without using a selection technique. This resulted in 1,309 problems solved by Hyper and 4,605 problems solved by E without selection. For the sets of problems unsolved without selection (6,701 for Hyper and 3,405 for E) SInE and Similarity SInE (with 58% coverage of *rel*) were used to select formulae that were then fed into the respective prover. Figure 3a shows the results for Hyper, Fig. 3b for E. Hyper was able to find a proof for 2.3% of the problems using the formulae selected by SInE and for 35.26% of the problems using the Similarity SInE selected formulae. E was able to find a proof for 10.9% of the problems using the SInE selected formulae and for 23.41% using the formulae selected with Similarity SInE. This 12.51% increase shows that both tableau-based and saturation-based provers benefit from the Similarity SInE selection technique.

Experiments with Different Tolerance Values. To investigate the effect of the tolerance parameter on selection, we performed experiments with tolerance values between 1.0 and 6.0 with SInE, Similarity SInE (*rel* coverage 58%) and Similarity SInE (*rel* coverage 63%) on the CSR SUMO problems and on 1,000 randomly selected Adimen-SUMO problems. Both problem sets consist only of problems Hyper is not able to solve without selection. A comparison of Fig. 3a and the values for tolerance 1.0 in Fig. 4b shows that the 1,000 randomly selected Adimen-SUMO problems are representative for the entire set of problems. Furthermore Fig. 3 shows that Similarity SInE performs better than SInE for the given setup no matter the prover. Therefore the formulae selected by the different selection techniques are checked for satisfiability only with Hyper.

Figure 4 shows that on the formulae selected by Similarity SInE with low tolerance values, significantly more proofs were found than on the formulae selected by SInE with the same tolerance. This is due to the fact that Similarity SInE selects more, but the additionally selected formulae are targeted towards the goal due to the use of the similar symbols. SInE can catch up by using higher tolerance values. Starting from a tolerance value of 3.0 for CSR problems and 6.0 for Adimen-SUMO problems, more proofs can be found on the formulae selected with SInE than on the formulae selected with Similarity SInE. For these high tolerance values, too many additional formulae are selected with Similarity SInE. Figure 4b shows that a higher coverage of the bridging relation *rel* further improves the results for low tolerance values. On the CSR SUMO problems this effect is less clear, which we attribute to the fact that the CSR SUMO problems are generally more difficult to solve than the Adimen-SUMO problems. The fact that the improved coverage of the bridging relation for high tolerance values worsens the proportion of solved problems can be explained by the additionally selected formulae. For high tolerance values Similarity SInE with bridging relation with 58% coverage already selects too much. Similarity SInE with bridging relation with a coverage of 63% selects even more formulae for these high tolerance values, which exacerbates this problem.

Since the trigger relation of Similarity SInE extends SInE's trigger relation, Similarity SInE always selects a superset of the axioms selected by SInE. Figure 4 presents the number of selected axioms for both SInE and Similarity SInE. Even with a low tolerance, Similarity SInE already selects significantly more axioms than SInE. Nevertheless, there are not many more timeouts with the Similarity SInE selected axioms than with the SInE selected axioms (see Fig. 3).

5.3 Discussion

The experiments on the Adimen-SUMO problems reveal that the coverage of the bridging relation of symbol names to the used word embedding's vocabulary is crucial. Thus it is worthwhile to put work into a good coverage. Furthermore, the experiments have shown that Similarity SInE is superior to SInE selection at low tolerance values. Although SInE provides similar or better results with higher tolerance values, it must be taken into account that suitable tolerance values are not known in advance and are heavily dependent on the fact distributions in the KB.

To the best of our knowledge, the TPTP [28] does not include problems where background knowledge, like word embeddings or WordNet mappings, can be used to find a proof. Since background knowledge plays an important role in practice, we propose an extension of the TPTP by a problem class (domain BGK), where it is necessary to consult background knowledge to solve the tasks. This background knowledge could be specified WordNet mappings, word embeddings or even text corpora which may be used by provers, when solving problems. The SUMO problems of the CSR domain together with the SUMO WordNet mapping as well as problems from Yago [27], Yago-SUMO [6] and Cyc [11] would be a good starting point for this new domain.

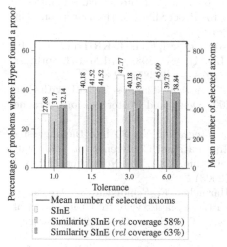 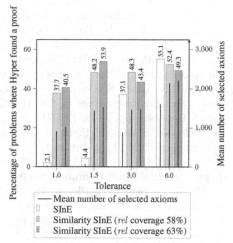

(a) Hyper on 224 CSR SUMO problems, it was not able to solve without selection.

(b) Hyper on 1,000 randomly selected Adimen-SUMO problems

Fig. 4. Percentage of the considered problems where Hyper found a proof using the selected formulae broken down by the selection technique and tolerance values used. For all selections recursion depth 1–6 was used.

6 Conclusion and Future Work

In many areas the symbol names in KBs are not chosen arbitrarily, but have a meaning. Although this meaning of symbol names is an interesting source of information, it has been ignored by previous axiom selection techniques. In this paper, we introduced a selection technique that uses word embeddings to consider the similarities of symbol names and thus includes their meaning in the selection process. Since the presented method is based on the SInE selection technique, it is called Similarity SInE. In future work, we will investigate different values for the number k of similar symbol names considered by Similarity SInE. Furthermore, we want to determine to what extent Similarity SInE is suitable as a selection technique for commonsense reasoning benchmarks such as the Choice of Plausible Alternatives Challenge [13]. More specifically, we want to analyze whether for a given problem, Similarity SInE is able to extract thematically appropriate modules from a background KB.

References

1. Álvez, J., Hermo, M., Lucio, P., Rigau, G.: Automatic white-box testing of first-order logic ontologies. CoRR, abs/1705.10219 (2017)
2. Álvez, J., Lucio, P., Rigau, G.: Adimen-SUMO: reengineering an ontology for first-order reasoning. Int. J. Seman. Web Inf. Syst. **8**, 80–116 (2012)
3. Basile, V., Cabrio, E., Schon, C.: KNEWS: using logical and lexical semantics to extract knowledge from natural language. In: Proceedings of the European Conference on Artificial Intelligence (ECAI) (2016)
4. Bender, M., Pelzer, B., Schon, C.: System description: E-KRHyper 1.4. In: Bonacina, M.P. (ed.) CADE 2013. LNCS (LNAI), vol. 7898, pp. 126–134. Springer, Heidelberg (2013). https://doi.org/10.1007/978-3-642-38574-2_8
5. Curran, J.R., Clark, S., Bos, J.: Linguistically motivated large-scale NLP with C&C and boxer. In: Proceedings of the ACL 2007 Demo and Poster Sessions, Prague, Czech Republic, pp. 33–36 (2007)
6. de Melo, G., Suchanek, F. M., Pease, A.: Integrating YAGO into the suggested upper merged ontology. In: 20th IEEE International Conference on Tools with Artificial Intelligence, ICTAI 2008, Dayton, Ohio, USA, 3–5 November 2008, vol. 1, pp. 190–193. IEEE Computer Society (2008)
7. de Rooij, S., Beek, W., Bloem, P., van Harmelen, F., Schlobach, S.: Are names meaningful? Quantifying social meaning on the semantic web. In: Groth, P., et al. (eds.) ISWC 2016. LNCS, vol. 9981, pp. 184–199. Springer, Cham (2016). https://doi.org/10.1007/978-3-319-46523-4_12
8. Firth, J.R.: Papers in Linguistics 1934–1951: Rep. Oxford University Press, Oxford (1991)
9. Hoder, K., Voronkov, A.: Sine qua non for large theory reasoning. In: Bjørner, N., Sofronie-Stokkermans, V. (eds.) CADE 2011. LNCS (LNAI), vol. 6803, pp. 299–314. Springer, Heidelberg (2011). https://doi.org/10.1007/978-3-642-22438-6_23
10. Kuksa, E., Mossakowski, T.: Prover-independent axiom selection for automated theorem proving in Ontohub. In: Fontaine, P., Schulz, S., Urban, J. (eds.) Proceedings of the 5th Workshop on Practical Aspects of Automated Reasoning Co-Located with International Joint Conference on Automated Reasoning, IJCAR 2016, Coimbra, Portugal, 2nd July 2016, volume 1635 of CEUR Workshop Proceedings, pp. 56–68. CEUR-WS.org (2016)
11. Lenat, D.B.: CYC: a large-scale investment in knowledge infrastructure. Commun. ACM **38**(11), 33–38 (1995)
12. Luo, Z., Sha, Y., Zhu, K.Q., Hwang, S., Wang, Z.: Commonsense causal reasoning between short texts. In: Baral, C., Delgrande, J.P., Wolter, J. (eds.) Principles of Knowledge Representation and Reasoning: Proceedings of the Fifteenth International Conference, KR 2016, Cape Town, South Africa, 25–29 April 2016, pp. 421–431. AAAI Press (2016)
13. Maslan, N., Roemmele, M., Gordon, A.S.: One hundred challenge problems for logical formalizations of commonsense psychology. In: Twelfth International Symposium on Logical Formalizations of Commonsense Reasoning, Stanford, CA (2015)

14. Meng, J., Paulson, L.C.: Lightweight relevance filtering for machine-generated resolution problems. J. Appl. Logic **7**(1), 41–57 (2009)
15. Mikolov, T., Chen, K., Corrado, G., Dean, J.: Efficient estimation of word representations in vector space. CoRR, abs/1301.3781 (2013)
16. Mikolov, T., Sutskever, I., Chen, K., Corrado, G.S., Dean, J.: Distributed representations of words and phrases and their compositionality. In: Burges, C.J.C., Bottou, L., Ghahramani, Z., Weinberger, K.Q. (eds.) Advances in Neural Information Processing Systems 26: 27th Annual Conference on Neural Information Processing Systems 2013. Proceedings of a Meeting Held, Lake Tahoe, Nevada, United States, 5–8 December 2013, pp. 3111–3119 (2013)
17. Miller, G.A.: WordNet: a lexical database for English. Commun. ACM **38**(11), 39–41 (1995)
18. Miller, G.A., Charles, W.G.: Contextual correlates of semantic similarity. Lang. Cogn. Process. **6**(1), 1–28 (1991)
19. Niles, I., Pease, A.: Towards a standard upper ontology. In: Proceedings of the international conference on Formal Ontology in Information Systems-Volume 2001, pp. 2–9. ACM (2001)
20. Pease, A.: Ontology: A Practical Guide. Articulate Software Press, Angwin (2011)
21. Pennington, J., Socher, R., Manning, C.D.: Glove: global vectors for word representation. In: Moschitti, A., Pang, B., Daelemans, W. (eds.) Proceedings of the 2014 Conference on Empirical Methods in Natural Language Processing, EMNLP 2014, Doha, Qatar, 25–29 October 2014, A Meeting of SIGDAT, A Special Interest Group of the ACL, pp. 1532–1543. ACL (2014)
22. Rocktäschel, T., Riedel, S.: End-to-end differentiable proving. In: NIPS, pp. 3791–3803 (2017)
23. Roederer, A., Puzis, Y., Sutcliffe, G.: Divvy: an ATP meta-system based on axiom relevance ordering. In: Schmidt, R.A. (ed.) CADE 2009. LNCS (LNAI), vol. 5663, pp. 157–162. Springer, Heidelberg (2009). https://doi.org/10.1007/978-3-642-02959-2_13
24. Schon, C., Siebert, S., Stolzenburg, F.: The CoRg project - cognitive reasoning. KI **33**(3) (2019, to appear)
25. Schulz, S.: System description: E 1.8. In: McMillan, K., Middeldorp, A., Voronkov, A. (eds.) LPAR 2013. LNCS, vol. 8312, pp. 735–743. Springer, Heidelberg (2013). https://doi.org/10.1007/978-3-642-45221-5_49
26. Speer, R., Chin, J., Havasi, C.: ConceptNet 5.5: an open multilingual graph of general knowledge. In: Singh, S.P., Markovitch, S. (eds.) Proceedings of the Thirty-First AAAI Conference on Artificial Intelligence, San Francisco, California, USA, 4–9 February 2017, pp. 4444–4451. AAAI Press (2017)
27. Suchanek, F.M., Kasneci, G., Weikum, G.: YAGO: a large ontology from Wikipedia and WordNet. Web Semant. **6**(3), 203–217 (2008)
28. Sutcliffe, G.: The TPTP problem library and associated infrastructure: from CNF to TH0, TPTP v6.4.0. J. Autom. Reason. 1–20 (2017)
29. Sutcliffe, G.: The 9th IJCAR automated theorem proving system competition CASC-J9. AI Commun. **31**(6), 495–507 (2018)
30. Sutcliffe, G., Puzis, Y.: SRASS - a semantic relevance axiom selection system. In: Pfenning, F. (ed.) CADE 2007. LNCS (LNAI), vol. 4603, pp. 295–310. Springer, Heidelberg (2007). https://doi.org/10.1007/978-3-540-73595-3_20
31. Tiedemann, J.: Parallel data, tools and interfaces in OPUS. In: Calzolari, N., (Conference Chair) et al. (eds.) Proceedings of the Eight International Conference on Language Resources and Evaluation, LREC 2012, Istanbul, Turkey. European Language Resources Association (ELRA), May 2012

32. Wang, L., Sun, M., Zhao, W., Shen, K., Liu, J.: Yuanfudao at SemEval-2018 task 11: three-way attention and relational knowledge for commonsense machine comprehension. In: Apidianaki, M., Mohammad, S.M., May, J., Shutova, E., Bethard, S., Carpuat, M. (eds.) Proceedings of The 12th International Workshop on Semantic Evaluation, SemEval@NAACL-HLT, New Orleans, Louisiana, 5–6 June 2018, pp. 758–762. Association for Computational Linguistics (2018)
33. Williams, B., Lieberman, H., Winston, P.H.: Understanding stories with large-scale common sense. In: Gordon, A.S., Miller, R., Turán, G. (eds.) Proceedings of the Thirteenth International Symposium on Commonsense Reasoning, COMMON-SENSE 2017, London, UK, 6–8 November 2017, volume 2052 of CEUR Workshop Proceedings. CEUR-WS.org (2017)
34. Zhang, J.: System description: MCS: model-based conjecture searching. CADE 1999. LNCS (LNAI), vol. 1632, pp. 393–397. Springer, Heidelberg (1999). https://doi.org/10.1007/3-540-48660-7_37

Computing Expected Runtimes
for Constant Probability Programs

Jürgen Giesl[1] , Peter Giesl[2] , and Marcel Hark[1(✉)]

[1] LuFG Informatik 2, RWTH Aachen University, Aachen, Germany
{giesl,marcel.hark}@cs.rwth-aachen.de
[2] Department of Mathematics, University of Sussex, Brighton, UK
p.a.giesl@sussex.ac.uk

Abstract. We introduce the class of *constant probability (CP) programs*
and show that classical results from probability theory directly yield
a simple decision procedure for (positive) almost sure termination of
programs in this class. Moreover, asymptotically tight bounds on their
expected runtime can always be computed easily. Based on this, we
present an algorithm to infer the *exact* expected runtime of any CP
program.

Keywords: Probabilistic programs · Expected runtimes ·
(Positive) almost sure termination · Complexity · Decidability

1 Introduction

Probabilistic programs are used to describe randomized algorithms and probability distributions, with applications in many areas. As an example, consider
the well-known program which models the race between a tortoise and a hare
(see, e.g., [10,24,30]). As long as the tortoise (variable t) is not behind the hare
(variable h), it does one step in each iteration. With probability $\frac{1}{2}$, the hare
stays at its position and with probabil-
ity $\frac{1}{2}$ it does a random number of steps
uniformly chosen between 0 and 10. The
race ends when the hare is in front of the
tortoise. Here, the hare wins with proba-

```
while (h ≤ t) {
  t = t + 1;
  {h = h + Unif(0, 10)} ⊕½ {h = h};
}
```

bility one and the technique of [30] infers the upper bound $\frac{2}{3} \cdot \max(t - h + 9, 0)$ on
the expected number of loop iterations. Thus, the program is positively almost
surely terminating.

Section 2 recapitulates preliminaries on probabilistic programs and on the
connection between their expected runtime and their corresponding recurrence
equation. Then we show in Sects. 3 and 4 that classical results on random walk
theory directly yield a very simple decision procedure for (positive) almost sure

Supported by the DFG Research Training Group 2236 UnRAVeL and the London
Mathematical Society (Grant 41662, Research in Pairs).

P. Fontaine (Ed.): CADE 2019, LNAI 11716, pp. 269–286, 2019.
https://doi.org/10.1007/978-3-030-29436-6_16

termination of *CP programs* like the tortoise and hare example. In this way, we also obtain asymptotically tight bounds on the expected runtime of any CP program. Based on these bounds, in Sect. 5 we develop the first algorithm to compute closed forms for the *exact* expected runtime of such programs. In Sect. 6, we present its implementation in our tool KoAT [9] and discuss related and future work. We refer to [20] for a collection of examples to illustrate the application of our algorithm and for all proofs.

2 Expected Runtimes of Probabilistic Programs

Example 1 (Tortoise and Hare). The program
$\mathcal{P}_{race}$ *on the right formulates the race of the tortoise and the hare as a CP program. In the loop guard, we use the scalar product*
$(1, -1) \bullet (t, h)$ *which stands for* $t - h$. *Exactly one of the instructions with numbers in brackets* [...] *is executed in each loop iteration and the number indicates the probability that the corresponding instruction is chosen.*

```
while ((1, −1) • (t, h) > −1) {
    (t, h) = (t, h) + (1, 0)    [6/11];
    (t, h) = (t, h) + (1, 1)    [1/22];
    (t, h) = (t, h) + (1, 2)    [1/22];
    (t, h) = (t, h) + (1, 3)    [1/22];
              ⋮
    (t, h) = (t, h) + (1, 10)   [1/22];
}
```

We now define the kind of probabilistic programs considered in this paper.

Definition 2 (Probabilistic Program). *A program has the form on the right, where* $\boldsymbol{x} = (x_1, \ldots, x_r)$ *for some* $r \geq 1$ *is a tuple of pairwise different program variables,* $\boldsymbol{a}, \boldsymbol{c}_1, \ldots, \boldsymbol{c}_n \in \mathbb{Z}^r$ *are tuples of integers, the* $\boldsymbol{c}_j$ *are pairwise distinct,* $b \in \mathbb{Z}$, $\bullet$ *is the scalar product (i.e.,* $(a_1, \ldots, a_r) \bullet (x_1, \ldots, x_r) = a_1 \cdot x_1 + \ldots + a_r \cdot x_r$), *and* $\boldsymbol{d} \in \mathbb{Z}^r$ *with* $\boldsymbol{a} \bullet \boldsymbol{d} \leq b$.

```
while (a • x > b) {
    x = x + c₁    [p_{c_1}(x)];
          ⋮
    x = x + cₙ    [p_{c_n}(x)];
    x = d         [p'(x)];
}
```

We require $p_{\boldsymbol{c}_1}(\boldsymbol{x}), \ldots, p_{\boldsymbol{c}_n}(\boldsymbol{x}), p'(\boldsymbol{x}) \in \mathbb{R}_{\geq 0} = \{r \in \mathbb{R} \mid r \geq 0\}$ *and* $\sum_{1 \leq j \leq n} p_{\boldsymbol{c}_j}(\boldsymbol{x}) + p'(\boldsymbol{x}) = 1$ *for all* $\boldsymbol{x} \in \mathbb{Z}^r$. *It is a program with direct termination if there is an* $\boldsymbol{x} \in \mathbb{Z}^r$ *with* $\boldsymbol{a} \bullet \boldsymbol{x} > b$ *and* $p'(\boldsymbol{x}) > 0$. *If all probabilities are constant, i.e., if there are* $p_{\boldsymbol{c}_1}, \ldots, p_{\boldsymbol{c}_n}, p' \in \mathbb{R}_{\geq 0}$ *such that* $p_{\boldsymbol{c}_j}(\boldsymbol{x}) = p_{\boldsymbol{c}_j}$ *and* $p'(\boldsymbol{x}) = p'$ *for all* $1 \leq j \leq n$ *and all* $\boldsymbol{x} \in \mathbb{Z}^r$, *we call it a constant probability (CP) program.*

Such a program means that the integer variables $\boldsymbol{x}$ are changed to $\boldsymbol{x} + \boldsymbol{c}_j$ with probability $p_{\boldsymbol{c}_j}(\boldsymbol{x})$. For inputs $\boldsymbol{x}$ with $\boldsymbol{a} \bullet \boldsymbol{x} \leq b$ the program terminates immediately. Note that the program in Example 1 has *no* direct termination (i.e., $p'(\boldsymbol{x}) = 0$ for all $\boldsymbol{x} \in \mathbb{Z}^r$). Since the values of the program variables only depend on their values in the previous loop iteration, our programs correspond to *Markov Chains* [32] and they are related to *random walks* [16,21,33], cf. [20] for details.

Clearly, in general termination is undecidable and closed forms for the runtimes of programs are not computable. Thus, decidability results can only be obtained for suitably restricted forms of programs. Our class nevertheless includes many examples that are often regarded in the literature on probabilistic programs. So while other approaches are concerned with *incomplete* techniques to analyze termination and complexity, we investigate classes of probabilistic programs where one can *decide* the termination behavior, *always* find complexity bounds, and even compute the expected runtime *exactly*. Our decision procedure could be integrated into general tools for termination and complexity analysis of probabilistic programs: As soon as one has to investigate a sub-program that falls into our class, one can use the decision procedure to compute its exact runtime. Our contributions provide a starting point for such results and the considered class of programs can be extended further in future work.

In probability theory (see, e.g., [2]), given a set Ω of possible events, the goal is to measure the probability that events are in certain subsets of Ω. To this end, one regards a set $\mathfrak{F}$ of subsets of Ω, such that $\mathfrak{F}$ contains the full set Ω and is closed under complement and countable unions. Such a set $\mathfrak{F}$ is called a σ-*field*, and a pair of Ω and a corresponding σ-field $\mathfrak{F}$ is called a *measurable space*.

A *probability space* $(\Omega, \mathfrak{F}, \mathbb{P})$ extends a measurable space $(\Omega, \mathfrak{F})$ by a *probability measure* $\mathbb{P}$ which maps every set from $\mathfrak{F}$ to a number between 0 and 1, where $\mathbb{P}(\Omega) = 1$, $\mathbb{P}(\varnothing) = 0$, and $\mathbb{P}(\biguplus_{j \geq 0} A_j) = \sum_{j \geq 0} \mathbb{P}(A_j)$ for any pairwise disjoint sets $A_0, A_1, \ldots \in \mathfrak{F}$. So $\mathbb{P}(A)$ is the probability that an event from Ω is in the subset A. In our setting, we use the probability space $((\mathbb{Z}^r)^\omega, \mathfrak{F}^{\mathbb{Z}^r}, \mathbb{P}^{\mathcal{P}}_{x_0})$ arising from the standard cylinder-set construction of MDP theory, cf. [20]. Here, $(\mathbb{Z}^r)^\omega$ corresponds to all infinite sequences of program states and $\mathbb{P}^{\mathcal{P}}_{x_0}$ is the probability measure induced by the program $\mathcal{P}$ when starting in the state $x_0 \in \mathbb{Z}^r$. For example, if $A \subseteq (\mathbb{Z}^2)^\omega$ consists of all infinite sequences starting with $(5,1)$, $(6,1)$, $(7,6)$, then $\mathbb{P}^{\mathcal{P}_{race}}_{(5,1)}(A) = \frac{6}{11} \cdot \frac{1}{22} = \frac{3}{121}$. So, if one starts with $(5,1)$, then $\frac{3}{121}$ is the probability that the next two states are $(6,1)$ and $(7,6)$. Once a state is reached that violates the loop guard, then the probability to remain in this state is 1. Hence, if B contains all infinite sequences starting with $(7,8)$, $(7,8)$, then $\mathbb{P}^{\mathcal{P}_{race}}_{(7,8)}(B) = 1$. In the following, for any set of numbers M let $\overline{M} = M \cup \{\infty\}$.

Definition 3 (Termination Time). *For a program $\mathcal{P}$ as in Definition 2, its termination time is the random variable $T^{\mathcal{P}} : (\mathbb{Z}^r)^\omega \to \overline{\mathbb{N}}$ that maps every infinite sequence $\langle z_0, z_1, \ldots \rangle$ to the first index j where z_j violates $\mathcal{P}$'s loop guard.*

Thus, $T^{\mathcal{P}_{race}}(\langle (5,1), (6,1), (7,8), (7,8), \ldots \rangle) = 2$ and $T^{\mathcal{P}_{race}}(\langle (5,1), (6,1), (5,6), (8,6), (9,6), \ldots \rangle) = \infty$ (i.e., this sequence always satisfies $\mathcal{P}_{race}$'s loop guard as the jth entry is $(5+j, 6)$ for $j \geq 3$). Now we can define the different notions of termination and the expected runtime of a probabilistic program. As usual, for any random variable X on a probability space $(\Omega, \mathfrak{F}, \mathbb{P})$, $\mathbb{P}(X = j)$ stands for $\mathbb{P}(X^{-1}(\{j\}))$. So $\mathbb{P}^{\mathcal{P}}_{x_0}(T^{\mathcal{P}} = j)$ is the probability that a sequence has termination time j. Similarly, $\mathbb{P}^{\mathcal{P}}_{x_0}(T^{\mathcal{P}} < \infty) = \sum_{j \in \mathbb{N}} \mathbb{P}^{\mathcal{P}}_{x_0}(T^{\mathcal{P}} = j)$. The *expected value* $\mathbb{E}(X)$ of a random variable $X : \Omega \to \overline{\mathbb{N}}$ for a probability space $(\Omega, \mathfrak{F}, \mathbb{P})$ is the weighted average under the probability measure $\mathbb{P}$, i.e., $\mathbb{E}(X) = \sum_{j \in \overline{\mathbb{N}}} j \cdot \mathbb{P}(X = j)$, where $\infty \cdot 0 = 0$ and $\infty \cdot u = \infty$ for all $u \in \mathbb{N}_{>0}$.

Definition 4 (Termination and Expected Runtime). *A program $\mathcal{P}$ as in Definition 2 is* almost surely terminating (AST) *if $\mathbb{P}^{\mathcal{P}}_{x_0}(T^{\mathcal{P}} < \infty) = 1$ for any* *initial value* $\boldsymbol{x}_0 \in \mathbb{Z}^r$. *For any* $\boldsymbol{x}_0 \in \mathbb{Z}^r$, *its* expected runtime $rt^{\mathcal{P}}_{\boldsymbol{x}_0}$ *(i.e., the expected number of loop iterations) is defined as the expected value of the random variable* $T^{\mathcal{P}}$ *under the probability measure* $\mathbb{P}^{\mathcal{P}}_{\boldsymbol{x}_0}$, *i.e.,* $rt^{\mathcal{P}}_{\boldsymbol{x}_0} = \mathbb{E}^{\mathcal{P}}_{\boldsymbol{x}_0}(T^{\mathcal{P}}) = \sum_{j \in \mathbb{N}} j \cdot \mathbb{P}^{\mathcal{P}}_{\boldsymbol{x}_0}(T^{\mathcal{P}}{=}j)$ *if* $\mathbb{P}^{\mathcal{P}}_{\boldsymbol{x}_0}(T^{\mathcal{P}}{<}\infty) = 1$, *and* $rt^{\mathcal{P}}_{\boldsymbol{x}_0} = \mathbb{E}^{\mathcal{P}}_{\boldsymbol{x}_0}(T^{\mathcal{P}}) = \infty$ *otherwise.*

The program $\mathcal{P}$ *is* positively almost surely terminating (PAST) *if for any initial value* $\boldsymbol{x}_0 \in \mathbb{Z}^r$, *the expected runtime of* $\mathcal{P}$ *is finite, i.e., if* $rt^{\mathcal{P}}_{\boldsymbol{x}_0} = \mathbb{E}^{\mathcal{P}}_{\boldsymbol{x}_0}(T^{\mathcal{P}}) < \infty$.

Example 5 (Expected Runtime for $\mathcal{P}_{race}$*). By the observations in Sect. 4 we will infer that* $\frac{2}{3} \cdot (t - h + 1) \leq rt^{\mathcal{P}_{race}}_{(t,h)} \leq \frac{2}{3} \cdot (t - h + 1) + \frac{16}{3}$ *holds whenever* $t - h > -1$, *cf. Example 22. So the expected number of steps until termination is finite (and linear in the input variables) and thus,* $\mathcal{P}_{race}$ *is PAST. The algorithm in Sect. 5 will even be able to compute* $rt^{\mathcal{P}_{race}}_{(t,h)}$ *exactly, cf. Example 34.*

If the initial values $\boldsymbol{x}_0$ violate the loop guard, then the runtime is trivially 0.

Corollary 6 (Expected Runtime for Violating Initial Values). *For any program* $\mathcal{P}$ *as in Definition 2 and any* $\boldsymbol{x}_0 \in \mathbb{Z}^r$ *with* $\boldsymbol{a} \bullet \boldsymbol{x}_0 \leq b$, *we have* $rt^{\mathcal{P}}_{\boldsymbol{x}_0} = 0$.

To obtain our results, we use an alternative, well-known characterization of the expected runtime, cf. e.g., [3,8,15,24–27,32,34]. To this end, we search for the *smallest* (or "*least*") solution of the recurrence equation that describes the runtime of the program as 1 plus the sum of the runtimes in the next loop iteration, multiplied with the corresponding probabilities. Here, functions are compared pointwise, i.e., for $f, g : \mathbb{Z}^r \to \overline{\mathbb{R}_{\geq 0}}$ we have $f \leq g$ if $f(\boldsymbol{x}) \leq g(\boldsymbol{x})$ holds for all $\boldsymbol{x} \in \mathbb{Z}^r$. So we search for the smallest function $f : \mathbb{Z}^r \to \overline{\mathbb{R}_{\geq 0}}$ that satisfies

$$f(\boldsymbol{x}) = \sum_{1 \leq j \leq n} p_{\boldsymbol{c}_j}(\boldsymbol{x}) \cdot f(\boldsymbol{x} + \boldsymbol{c}_j) + p'(\boldsymbol{x}) \cdot f(\boldsymbol{d}) + 1 \quad \text{for all } \boldsymbol{x} \text{ with } \boldsymbol{a} \bullet \boldsymbol{x} > b. \quad (1)$$

Equivalently, we can search for the least fixpoint of the "expected runtime transformer" $\mathcal{L}^{\mathcal{P}}$ which transforms the left-hand side of (1) into its right-hand side.

Definition 7 ($\mathcal{L}^{\mathcal{P}}$, cf. [32]). *For* $\mathcal{P}$ *as in Definition 2, we define the* expected runtime transformer $\mathcal{L}^{\mathcal{P}} : (\mathbb{Z}^r \to \overline{\mathbb{R}_{\geq 0}}) \to (\mathbb{Z}^r \to \overline{\mathbb{R}_{\geq 0}})$, *where for any* $f : \mathbb{Z}^r \to \overline{\mathbb{R}_{\geq 0}}$:

$$\mathcal{L}^{\mathcal{P}}(f)(\boldsymbol{x}) = \begin{cases} \sum_{1 \leq j \leq n} p_{\boldsymbol{c}_j}(\boldsymbol{x}) \cdot f(\boldsymbol{x} + \boldsymbol{c}_j) + p'(\boldsymbol{x}) \cdot f(\boldsymbol{d}) + 1, & \text{if } \boldsymbol{a} \bullet \boldsymbol{x} > b \\ f(\boldsymbol{x}), & \text{if } \boldsymbol{a} \bullet \boldsymbol{x} \leq b \end{cases}$$

Example 8 (Expected Runtime Transformer for $\mathcal{P}_{race}$*). For* $\mathcal{P}_{race}$ *from Example 1,* $\mathcal{L}^{\mathcal{P}_{race}}$ *maps any function* $f : \mathbb{Z}^2 \to \overline{\mathbb{R}_{\geq 0}}$ *to* $\mathcal{L}^{\mathcal{P}_{race}}(f)$, *where* $\mathcal{L}^{\mathcal{P}_{race}}(f)(t,h) =$

$$\begin{cases} \frac{6}{11} \cdot f(t+1,h) + \frac{1}{22} \cdot \sum_{1 \leq j \leq 10} f(t+1,h+j) + 1, & \text{if } t - h > -1 \\ f(t,h), & \text{if } t - h \leq -1 \end{cases} \quad (2)$$

Theorem 9 recapitulates that the least fixpoint of $\mathcal{L}^{\mathcal{P}}$ indeed yields an equivalent characterization of the expected runtime. In the following, let $\mathbf{o} : \mathbb{Z}^r \to \overline{\mathbb{R}_{\geq 0}}$ be the function with $\mathbf{o}(\boldsymbol{x}) = 0$ for all $\boldsymbol{x} \in \mathbb{Z}^r$.

Theorem 9 (Connection Between Expected Runtime and Least Fixpoint of $\mathcal{L}^{\mathcal{P}}$, cf. [32]). *For any $\mathcal{P}$ as in Definition 2, the expected runtime transformer $\mathcal{L}^{\mathcal{P}}$ is continuous. Thus, it has a least fixpoint $\mathrm{lfp}(\mathcal{L}^{\mathcal{P}}) : \mathbb{Z}^r \to \overline{\mathbb{R}_{\geq 0}}$ with $\mathrm{lfp}(\mathcal{L}^{\mathcal{P}}) = \sup\{0, \mathcal{L}^{\mathcal{P}}(0), (\mathcal{L}^{\mathcal{P}})^2(0), \ldots\}$. Moreover, the least fixpoint of $\mathcal{L}^{\mathcal{P}}$ is the expected runtime of $\mathcal{P}$, i.e., for any $x_0 \in \mathbb{Z}^r$, we have $\mathrm{lfp}(\mathcal{L}^{\mathcal{P}})(x_0) = rt_{x_0}^{\mathcal{P}}$.*

So the expected runtime $rt_{(t,h)}^{\mathcal{P}_{race}}$ can also be characterized as the smallest function $f : \mathbb{Z}^2 \to \overline{\mathbb{R}_{\geq 0}}$ satisfying $f(t,h) = (2)$, i.e., as the least fixpoint of $\mathcal{L}^{\mathcal{P}_{race}}$.

3 Expected Runtime of Programs with Direct Termination

We start with stating a decidability result for the case where for all x with $a \bullet x > b$, the probability $p'(x)$ for direct termination is at least p' for some $p' > 0$. Intuitively, these programs have a termination time whose distribution is closely related to the geometric distribution with parameter p' (which has expected value $\frac{1}{p'}$). By using the alternative characterization of $rt_{x_0}^{\mathcal{P}}$ from Theorem 9, one obtains that such programs are *always PAST* and their expected runtime is indeed *bounded by the constant* $\frac{1}{p'}$. This result will be used in Sect. 5 when computing the *exact* expected runtime of such programs. The more involved case where $p'(x) = 0$ is considered in Sect. 4.

Theorem 10 (PAST and Expected Runtime for Programs With Direct Termination). *Let $\mathcal{P}$ be a program as in Definition 2 where there is a $p' > 0$ such that $p'(x) \geq p'$ for all $x \in \mathbb{Z}^r$ with $a \bullet x > b$. Then $\mathcal{P}$ is PAST and its expected runtime is at most $\frac{1}{p'}$, i.e., $rt_{x_0}^{\mathcal{P}} \leq \frac{1}{p'}$ if $a \bullet x_0 > b$, and $rt_{x_0}^{\mathcal{P}} = 0$ if $a \bullet x_0 \leq b$.*

Example 11 (Example 1 with Direct Termination). Consider the variant $\mathcal{P}_{direct}$ of $\mathcal{P}_{race}$ on the right, where in each iteration, the hare either does nothing with probability $\frac{9}{10}$ or one directly reaches a configuration where the hare is ahead of the tortoise.

```
while ((1, -1) • (t, h) > -1) {
    (t, h) = (t, h) + (1, 0)    [9/10];
    (t, h) = (7, 8)              [1/10];
}
```

By Theorem 10 the program is PAST and its expected runtime is at most $\frac{1}{\frac{1}{10}} = 10$, i.e., independent of the initial state it takes at most 10 loop iterations on average. In Sect. 5 it will turn out that 10 is indeed the exact expected runtime, cf. Example 32.

4 Expected Runtimes of Constant Probability Programs

Now we present a very simple decision procedure for termination of CP programs (Sect. 4.2) and show how to infer their asymptotic expected runtimes (Sect. 4.3). This will be needed for the computation of exact expected runtimes in Sect. 5.

4.1   Reduction to Random Walk Programs

```
while (x > 0) {
    x = x + m    [p_m];
    ⋮
    x = x + 1    [p_1];
    x = x        [p_0];
    x = x - 1    [p_{-1}];
    ⋮
    x = x - k    [p_{-k}];
    x = d        [p'];
}
```

As a first step, we show that we can restrict ourselves to *random walk programs*, i.e., programs with a single program variable x and the loop condition $x > 0$.

Definition 12 (Random Walk Program). *A CP program $\mathcal{P}$ is called a* random walk program *if there exist $m, k \in \mathbb{N}$ and $d \in \mathbb{Z}$ with $d \leq 0$ such that $\mathcal{P}$ has the form on the right. Here, we require that $m > 0$ implies $p_m > 0$ and that $k > 0$ implies $p_{-k} > 0$.*

Definition 13 shows how to transform any CP program as in Definition 2 into a random walk program. The idea is to replace the tuple $\boldsymbol{x}$ by a single variable x that stands for $\boldsymbol{a} \bullet \boldsymbol{x} - b$. Thus, the loop condition $\boldsymbol{a} \bullet \boldsymbol{x} > b$ now becomes $x > 0$. Moreover, a change from $\boldsymbol{x}$ to $\boldsymbol{x} + \boldsymbol{c}_j$ now becomes a change from x to $x + \boldsymbol{a} \bullet \boldsymbol{c}_j$.

```
while (a • x > b) {
    x = x + c_1    [p_{c_1}];
    ⋮
    x = x + c_n    [p_{c_n}];
    x = d          [p'];
}
```

Definition 13 (Transforming CP Programs to Random Walk Programs). *Let $\mathcal{P}$ be the CP program on the left with $\boldsymbol{x} = (x_1, \ldots, x_r)$ and $\boldsymbol{a} \bullet \boldsymbol{d} \leq b$. Let $rdw_{\mathcal{P}}$ denote the affine map $rdw_{\mathcal{P}} : \mathbb{Z}^r \to \mathbb{Z}$ with $rdw_{\mathcal{P}}(\boldsymbol{z}) = \boldsymbol{a} \bullet \boldsymbol{z} - b$ for all $\boldsymbol{z} \in \mathbb{Z}^r$. Thus, $rdw_{\mathcal{P}}(\boldsymbol{d}) \leq 0$. Let $k_{\mathcal{P}}, m_{\mathcal{P}} \in \mathbb{N}$ be minimal such that $-k_{\mathcal{P}} \leq \boldsymbol{a} \bullet \boldsymbol{c}_j \leq m_{\mathcal{P}}$ holds for all $1 \leq j \leq n$. For $-k_{\mathcal{P}} \leq j \leq m_{\mathcal{P}}$, we define $p_j^{rdw} = \sum_{1 \leq u \leq n,\ \boldsymbol{a} \bullet \boldsymbol{c}_u = j} p_{c_u}$. This results in the random walk program $\mathcal{P}^{rdw}$ on the right.*

```
while (x > 0) {
    x = x + m_P    [p_{m_P}^{rdw}];
    ⋮
    x = x - k_P    [p_{-k_P}^{rdw}];
    x = rdw_P(d)   [p'];
}
```

Example 14 (Transforming $\mathcal{P}_{race}$). For the program $\mathcal{P}_{race}$ of Example 1, the mapping $rdw_{\mathcal{P}_{race}} : \mathbb{Z}^2 \to \mathbb{Z}$ is $rdw_{\mathcal{P}_{race}}(t, h) = (1, -1) \bullet (t, h) + 1 = t - h + 1$. Hence we obtain the random walk program $\mathcal{P}_{race}^{rdw}$ on the right, where $x = rdw_{\mathcal{P}_{race}}(t, h)$ represents the distance between the tortoise and the hare.

```
while (x > 0) {
    x = x + 1    [6/11];
    x = x        [1/22];
    x = x - 1    [1/22];
    x = x - 2    [1/22];
    ⋮
    x = x - 9    [1/22];
}
```

Approaches based on supermartingales (e.g., [1,4,10,12,13,17]) use mappings similar to $rdw_{\mathcal{P}}$ in order to infer a real-valued term which over-approximates the expected runtime. However, in the following (non-trivial) theorem we show that our transformation is not only an over- or under-approximation, but the termination behavior and the expected runtime of $\mathcal{P}$ and $\mathcal{P}^{rdw}$ are *identical*.

Theorem 15 (Transformation Preserves Termination & Expected Runtime). *Let $\mathcal{P}$ be a CP program as in Definition 2. Then the termination times $T^{\mathcal{P}}$ and $T^{\mathcal{P}^{rdw}}$ are identically distributed w.r.t. $rdw_{\mathcal{P}}$, i.e., for all $\boldsymbol{x}_0 \in \mathbb{Z}^r$*

with $x_0 = rdw_{\mathcal{P}}(x_0)$ and all $j \in \overline{\mathbb{N}}$ we have $\mathbb{P}_{x_0}^{\mathcal{P}}(T^{\mathcal{P}} = j) = \mathbb{P}_{x_0}^{\mathcal{P}^{rdw}}(T^{\mathcal{P}^{rdw}} = j)$. So in particular, $\mathbb{P}_{x_0}^{\mathcal{P}}(T^{\mathcal{P}} < \infty) = \mathbb{P}_{x_0}^{\mathcal{P}^{rdw}}(T^{\mathcal{P}^{rdw}} < \infty)$ and $rt_{x_0}^{\mathcal{P}} = \mathbb{E}_{x_0}^{\mathcal{P}}(T^{\mathcal{P}}) = \mathbb{E}_{x_0}^{\mathcal{P}^{rdw}}(T^{\mathcal{P}^{rdw}}) = rt_{x_0}^{\mathcal{P}^{rdw}}$. Thus, the expected runtimes of $\mathcal{P}$ on the input x_0 and of $\mathcal{P}^{rdw}$ on x_0 coincide.

The following definition identifies pathological programs that can be disregarded.

Definition 16 (Trivial Program). *Let $\mathcal{P}$ be a CP program as in Definition 2. We call $\mathcal{P}$ trivial if $a = 0 = (0,0, \ldots, 0)$ or if $\mathcal{P}^{rdw}$ is the program on the right.*

```
while (x > 0) {
    x = x      [1];
}
```

Note that a random walk program $\mathcal{P}$ is trivial iff it has the form $\texttt{while}(x > 0)\{x = x \ [1]; \}$, since $\mathcal{P} = \mathcal{P}^{rdw}$ holds for random walk programs $\mathcal{P}$. From now on, we will exclude trivial programs $\mathcal{P}$ as their termination behavior is obvious: for inputs x_0 that satisfy the loop condition $a \bullet x_0 > b$, the program never terminates (i.e., $rt_{x_0}^{\mathcal{P}} = \infty$) and for inputs x_0 with $a \bullet x_0 \leq b$ we have $rt_{x_0}^{\mathcal{P}} = 0$. Note that if $a = 0$, then the termination behavior just depends on b: if $b < 0$, then $rt_{x_0}^{\mathcal{P}} = \infty$ for all x_0 and if $b \geq 0$, then $rt_{x_0}^{\mathcal{P}} = 0$ for all x_0.

4.2 Deciding Termination

We now present a simple decision procedure for (P)AST of random walk programs $\mathcal{P}$. By the results of Sect. 4.1, this also yields a decision procedure for arbitrary CP programs. If $p' > 0$, then Theorem 10 already shows that $\mathcal{P}$ is PAST and its expected runtime is bounded by the constant $\frac{1}{p'}$. Thus, in the rest of Sect. 4 we regard *random walk programs without direct termination*, i.e., $p' = 0$.

Definition 17 introduces the *drift* of a random walk program, i.e., the expected value of the change of the program variable in one loop iteration, cf. [4].

Definition 17 (Drift). *Let $\mathcal{P}$ be a random walk program $\mathcal{P}$ as in Definition 12. Then its drift is $\mu_{\mathcal{P}} = \sum_{-k \leq j \leq m} j \cdot p_j$.*

Theorem 18 shows that to decide (P)AST, one just has to compute the drift.

Theorem 18 (Decision Procedure for (P)AST of Random Walk Programs). *Let $\mathcal{P}$ be a non-trivial random walk program without direct termination.*

- *If $\mu_{\mathcal{P}} > 0$, then the program is not AST.*
- *If $\mu_{\mathcal{P}} = 0$, then the program is AST but not PAST.*
- *If $\mu_{\mathcal{P}} < 0$, then the program is PAST.*

Example 19 ($\mathcal{P}_{race}$ is PAST). The drift of $\mathcal{P}_{race}^{rdw}$ in Example 14 is $\mu_{\mathcal{P}_{race}^{rdw}} = 1 \cdot \frac{6}{11} + \frac{1}{22} \cdot \sum_{-9 \leq j \leq 0} j = -\frac{3}{2} < 0$. So on average the distance x between the tortoise and the hare decreases in each loop iteration. Hence by Theorem 18, $\mathcal{P}_{race}^{rdw}$ is PAST and the following Corollary 20 implies that $\mathcal{P}_{race}$ is PAST as well.

Corollary 20 (Decision Procedure for (P)AST of CP programs). *For a non-trivial CP program $\mathcal{P}$, $\mathcal{P}$ is (P)AST iff $\mathcal{P}^{rdw}$ is (P)AST. Hence, Theorems 15 and 18 yield a decision procedure for AST and PAST of CP programs.*

In [20], we show that Theorem 18 follows from classical results on random walks [33]. Alternatively, Theorem 18 could also be proved by combining several recent results on probabilistic programs: The approach of [28] could be used to show that $\mu_{\mathcal{P}} = 0$ implies AST. Moreover, one could prove that $\mu_{\mathcal{P}} < 0$ implies PAST by showing that x is a *ranking supermartingale* of the program [4,10,13,17]. That the program is not PAST if $\mu_{\mathcal{P}} \geq 0$ and not AST if $\mu_{\mathcal{P}} > 0$ could be proved by showing that $-x$ is a $\mu_{\mathcal{P}}$-*repulsing supermartingale* [12].

While the proof of Theorem 18 is based on known results, the formulation of Theorem 18 shows that there is an extremely *simple* decision procedure for (P)AST of CP programs, i.e., checking the sign of the drift is much simpler than applying existing (general) techniques for termination analysis of probabilistic programs.

4.3   Computing Asymptotic Expected Runtimes

It turns out that for random walk programs (and thus by Theorem 15, also for CP programs), one can not only decide termination, but one can also infer tight bounds on the expected runtime. Theorem 21 shows that the computation of the bounds is again very *simple*.

Theorem 21 (Bounds on the Expected Runtime of CP Programs). *Let $\mathcal{P}$ be a non-trivial CP program as in Definition 2 without direct termination which is PAST (i.e., $\mu_{\mathcal{P}^{rdw}} < 0$). Moreover, let $k_{\mathcal{P}}$ be obtained according to the transformation from Definition 13. If $rdw_{\mathcal{P}}(\boldsymbol{x}_0) \leq 0$, then $rt^{\mathcal{P}}_{\boldsymbol{x}_0} = 0$. If $rdw_{\mathcal{P}}(\boldsymbol{x}_0) > 0$, then $\mathcal{P}$'s expected runtime is asymptotically linear and we have*

$$-\frac{1}{\mu_{\mathcal{P}^{rdw}}} \cdot rdw_{\mathcal{P}}(\boldsymbol{x}_0) \quad \leq \quad rt^{\mathcal{P}}_{\boldsymbol{x}_0} \quad \leq \quad -\frac{1}{\mu_{\mathcal{P}^{rdw}}} \cdot rdw_{\mathcal{P}}(\boldsymbol{x}_0) + \frac{1-k_{\mathcal{P}}}{\mu_{\mathcal{P}^{rdw}}}.$$

Example 22 (Bounds on the Runtime of $\mathcal{P}_{race}$). In Example 19 we saw that the program $\mathcal{P}^{rdw}_{race}$ from Example 14 is PAST as it has the drift $\mu_{\mathcal{P}^{rdw}_{race}} = -\frac{3}{2} < 0$. Note that here $k = 9$. Hence by Theorem 21 we get that whenever $rdw_{\mathcal{P}_{race}}(t, h) = t - h + 1$ is positive, the expected runtime $rt^{\mathcal{P}_{race}}_{(t,h)}$ is between $-\frac{1}{\mu_{\mathcal{P}^{rdw}_{race}}} \cdot rdw_{\mathcal{P}_{race}}(t, h) = \frac{2}{3} \cdot (t - h + 1)$ and $-\frac{1}{\mu_{\mathcal{P}^{rdw}_{race}}} \cdot rdw_{\mathcal{P}_{race}}(t, h) + \frac{1-k}{\mu_{\mathcal{P}^{rdw}_{race}}} = \frac{2}{3} \cdot (t - h + 1) + \frac{16}{3}$. The same upper bound $\frac{2}{3} \cdot (t - h + 1) + \frac{16}{3}$ was inferred in [30] by an incomplete technique based on several inference rules and linear programming solvers. In contrast, Theorem 21 allows us to read off such bounds directly from the program.

Our proof of Theorem 21 in [20] again uses the connection to random walks and shows that the classical Lemma of Wald [21, Lemma 10.2(9)] directly yields both the upper and the lower bound for the expected runtime. Alternatively, the upper bound in Theorem 21 could also be proved by considering that $rdw_{\mathcal{P}}(\boldsymbol{x}_0) +$

$(1 - k_\mathcal{P})$ is a *ranking supermartingale* [1,4,10,13,17] whose expected decrease in each loop iteration is $\mu_\mathcal{P}$. The lower bound could also be inferred by considering the *difference-bounded submartingale* $-rdw_\mathcal{P}(x_0)$ [7,19].

5   Computing Exact Expected Runtimes

While Theorems 10 and 21 state how to deduce the *asymptotic* expected runtime, we now show that based on these results one can compute the runtime of CP programs *exactly*. In general, whenever it is possible, then inferring the exact runtimes of programs is preferable to asymptotic runtimes which ignore the "coefficients" of the runtime.

Again, we first consider *random walk* programs and generalize our technique to CP programs using Theorem 15 afterwards. Throughout Sect. 5, for any random walk program $\mathcal{P}$ as in Definition 12, we require that $\mathcal{P}$ is PAST, i.e., that $p' > 0$ (cf. Theorem 10) or that the drift $\mu_\mathcal{P}$ is negative if $p' = 0$ (cf. Theorem 18). Note that whenever $k = 0$ and $\mathcal{P}$ is PAST, then $p' > 0$.[1]

To compute $\mathcal{P}$'s expected runtime exactly, we use its characterization as the least fixpoint of the expected runtime transformer $\mathcal{L}^\mathcal{P}$ (cf. Theorem 9), i.e., $rt_x^\mathcal{P}$ is the smallest function $f : \mathbb{Z} \to \overline{\mathbb{R}_{\geq 0}}$ satisfying the constraint

$$f(x) = \sum\nolimits_{-k \leq j \leq m} p_j \cdot f(x+j) + p' \cdot f(d) + 1 \quad \text{for all } x > 0, \qquad (3)$$

cf. (1). Since $\mathcal{P}$ is PAST, f never returns ∞, i.e., $f : \mathbb{Z} \to \mathbb{R}_{\geq 0}$. Note that the smallest function $f : \mathbb{Z} \to \mathbb{R}_{\geq 0}$ that satisfies (3) also satisfies

$$f(x) = 0 \quad \text{for all } x \leq 0. \qquad (4)$$

Therefore, as $d \leq 0$, the constraint (3) can be simplified to

$$f(x) = \sum\nolimits_{-k \leq j \leq m} p_j \cdot f(x+j) + 1 \quad \text{for all } x > 0. \qquad (5)$$

In Sect. 5.1 we recapitulate how to compute all solutions of such inhomogeneous recurrence equations (cf., e.g., [14, Ch. 2]). However, to compute $rt_x^\mathcal{P}$, the challenge is to find the *smallest* solution $f : \mathbb{Z} \to \mathbb{R}_{\geq 0}$ of the recurrence equation (5). Therefore, in Sect. 5.2 we will exploit the knowledge gained in Theorems 10 and 21 to show that there is only a *single* function f that satisfies both (4) and (5) *and* is bounded by a constant (if $p' > 0$, cf. Theorem 10) resp. by a linear function (if $p' = 0$, cf. Theorem 21). This observation then allows us to compute $rt_x^\mathcal{P}$ exactly. So the crucial prerequisites for this result are Theorem 9 (which characterizes the expected runtime as the smallest solution of the recurrence equation (5)), Theorem 18 (which allows the restriction to negative drift if $p' = 0$), and in particular Theorems 10 and 21 (since Sect. 5.2 will show that the results of Theorems 10 and 21 on the asymptotic runtime can be translated into suitable conditions on the solutions of (5)).

---

[1] If $p' = 0$ and $k = 0$ then $\mu_\mathcal{P} \geq 0$.

5.1   Finding All Solutions of the Recurrence Equation

Example 23 (Modification of $\mathcal{P}_{race}^{rdw}$). To illustrate our approach, we use a modified version of $\mathcal{P}_{race}^{rdw}$ from Example 14 to ease readability. In Sect. 6, we will consider the original program $\mathcal{P}_{race}^{rdw}$ resp. $\mathcal{P}_{race}$ from Example 14 resp. Example 1 again and show its exact expected runtime inferred by the implementation of our approach. In the modified program $\mathcal{P}_{race}^{mod}$ on the right, the distance between the tortoise and the hare still increases with proba-

```
while (x > 0) {
    x = x + 1    [6/11];
    x = x        [1/11];
    x = x - 1    [1/22];
    x = x - 2    [7/22];
}
```

bility $\frac{6}{11}$, but the probability of decreasing by more than two is distributed to the cases where it stays the same and where it decreases by two. We have $p' = 0$ and the drift is $\mu_{\mathcal{P}_{race}^{mod}} = 1 \cdot \frac{6}{11} + 0 \cdot \frac{1}{11} - 1 \cdot \frac{1}{22} - 2 \cdot \frac{7}{22} = -\frac{3}{22} < 0$. So by Theorem 18, $\mathcal{P}_{race}^{mod}$ is PAST. By Theorem 9, $rt_x^{\mathcal{P}_{race}^{mod}}$ is the smallest function $f : \mathbb{Z} \to \mathbb{R}_{\geq 0}$ satisfying

$$f(x) = \tfrac{6}{11} \cdot f(x+1) + \tfrac{1}{11} \cdot f(x) + \tfrac{1}{22} \cdot f(x-1) + \tfrac{7}{22} \cdot f(x-2) + 1 \text{ for all } x > 0. \quad (6)$$

Instead of searching for the *smallest* $f : \mathbb{Z} \to \mathbb{R}_{\geq 0}$ satisfying (5), we first calculate the set of *all* functions $f : \mathbb{Z} \to \mathbb{C}$ that satisfy (5), i.e., we also consider functions returning negative or complex numbers. Clearly, (5) is equivalent to

$$\begin{aligned} 0 = {} & p_m \cdot f(x+m) + \ldots + p_1 \cdot f(x+1) + (p_0 - 1) \cdot f(x) + \\ & p_{-1} \cdot f(x-1) + \ldots + p_{-k} \cdot f(x-k) + 1 \qquad \text{for all } x > 0. \end{aligned} \quad (7)$$

The set of solutions on $\mathbb{Z} \to \mathbb{C}$ of this linear, inhomogeneous recurrence equation is an affine space which can be written as an arbitrary particular solution of the inhomogeneous equation plus any linear combination of $k + m$ linearly independent solutions of the corresponding homogeneous recurrence equation.

We start with computing a solution to the inhomogeneous equation (7). To this end, we use the bounds for $rt_x^{\mathcal{P}}$ from Theorems 10 and 21 (where we take the upper bound $\frac{1}{p'}$ if $p' > 0$ and the lower bound $-\frac{1}{\mu_{\mathcal{P}}} \cdot x$ if $p' = 0$). So we define

$$C_{const} = \tfrac{1}{p'}, \text{ if } p' > 0 \qquad \text{and} \qquad C_{lin} = -\tfrac{1}{\mu_{\mathcal{P}}}, \text{ if } p' = 0.$$

One easily shows that if $p' > 0$, then $f(x) = C_{const}$ is a solution of the inhomogeneous recurrence equation (7) and if $p' = 0$, then $f(x) = C_{lin} \cdot x$ solves (7).

Example 24 (Example 23 cont.). In the program $\mathcal{P}_{race}^{mod}$ of Example 23, we have $p' = 0$ and $\mu_{\mathcal{P}_{race}^{mod}} = -\frac{3}{22}$. Hence $C_{lin} = \frac{22}{3}$ and $C_{lin} \cdot x$ is a solution of (6).

After having determined one particular solution of the inhomogeneous recurrence equation (7), now we compute the solutions of the *homogeneous* recurrence equation which results from (7) by replacing the add-on "+ 1" with 0. To this end, we consider the corresponding *characteristic polynomial $\chi_{\mathcal{P}}$*:[2]

$$\chi_{\mathcal{P}}(\lambda) = p_m \cdot \lambda^{k+m} + \ldots + p_1 \cdot \lambda^{k+1} + (p_0 - 1) \cdot \lambda^k + p_{-1} \cdot \lambda^{k-1} + \ldots + p_{-k} \quad (8)$$

---

[2] If $m = 0$ then $\chi_{\mathcal{P}}(\lambda) = (p_0 - 1) \cdot \lambda^k + p_{-1} \cdot \lambda^{k-1} + \ldots + p_{-k}$, and if $k = 0$ then $\chi_{\mathcal{P}}(\lambda) = p_m \cdot \lambda^m + \ldots + p_1 \cdot \lambda + (p_0 - 1)$. Note that $p_0 \neq 1$ since $\mathcal{P}$ is PAST and in Definition 12 we required that $m > 0$ implies $p_m > 0$ and $k > 0$ implies $p_{-k} > 0$. Hence, the characteristic polynomial has exactly the degree $k + m$, even if $m = 0$ or $k = 0$.

Let $\lambda_1, \ldots, \lambda_c$ denote the pairwise different (possibly complex) roots of the characteristic polynomial $\chi_{\mathcal{P}}$. For all $1 \leq j \leq c$, let $v_j \in \mathbb{N} \setminus \{0\}$ be the multiplicity of the root λ_j. Thus, we have $v_1 + \ldots + v_c = k + m$.

Then we obtain the following $k + m$ linearly independent solutions of the homogeneous recurrence equation resulting from (7):

$$\lambda_j^x \cdot x^u \quad \text{for all } 1 \leq j \leq c \text{ and all } 0 \leq u \leq v_j - 1$$

So $f : \mathbb{Z} \to \mathbb{C}$ is a solution of (5) (resp. (7)) iff there exist coefficients $a_{j,u} \in \mathbb{C}$ with

$$f(x) = C(x) + \sum_{1 \leq j \leq c} \sum_{0 \leq u \leq v_j - 1} a_{j,u} \cdot \lambda_j^x \cdot x^u \quad \text{for all } x > -k, \quad (9)$$

where $C(x) = C_{const} = \frac{1}{p'}$ if $p' > 0$ and $C(x) = C_{lin} \cdot x = -\frac{1}{\mu_{\mathcal{P}}} \cdot x$ if $p' = 0$. The reason for requiring (9) for all $x > -k$ is that $-k + 1$ is the smallest argument where f's value is taken into account in (5).

Example 25 (Example 24 cont.). The characteristic polynomial for the program $\mathcal{P}_{race}^{mod}$ of Example 23 has the degree $k + m = 2 + 1 = 3$ and is given by

$$\chi_{\mathcal{P}_{race}^{mod}}(\lambda) = \tfrac{6}{11} \cdot \lambda^3 - \tfrac{10}{11} \cdot \lambda^2 + \tfrac{1}{22} \cdot \lambda + \tfrac{7}{22}.$$

Its roots are $\lambda_1 = 1$, $\lambda_2 = -\frac{1}{2}$, and $\lambda_3 = \frac{7}{6}$. So here, all roots are real numbers and they all have the multiplicity 1. Hence, three linearly independent solutions of the homogeneous part of (6) are the functions $1^x = 1$, $(-\frac{1}{2})^x$, and $(\frac{7}{6})^x$. Therefore, a function $f : \mathbb{Z} \to \mathbb{C}$ satisfies (6) iff there are $a_1, a_2, a_3 \in \mathbb{C}$ such that

$$\begin{aligned} f(x) &= C_{lin} \cdot x + a_1 \cdot 1^x + a_2 \cdot (-\tfrac{1}{2})^x + a_3 \cdot (\tfrac{7}{6})^x \\ &= \tfrac{22}{3} \cdot x + a_1 + a_2 \cdot (-\tfrac{1}{2})^x + a_3 \cdot (\tfrac{7}{6})^x \quad \text{for } x > -2. \end{aligned} \quad (10)$$

5.2 Finding the Smallest Solution of the Recurrence Equation

In Sect. 5.1, we recapitulated the standard approach for solving inhomogeneous recurrence equations which shows that any function $f : \mathbb{Z} \to \mathbb{C}$ that satisfies the constraint (5) is of the form (9). Now we will present a novel technique to compute $rt_x^{\mathcal{P}}$, i.e., the *smallest non-negative* solution $f : \mathbb{Z} \to \mathbb{R}_{\geq 0}$ of (5). By Theorems 10 and 21, this function f is bounded by a constant (if $p' > 0$) resp. linear (if $p' = 0$). So, when representing f in the form (9), we must have $a_{j,u} = 0$ whenever $|\lambda_j| > 1$. The following lemma shows how many roots with absolute value less or equal to 1 there are (i.e., these are the only roots that we have to consider). It is proved using Rouché's Theorem which allows us to infer the number of roots whose absolute value is below a certain bound. Note that 1 is a root of the characteristic polynomial iff $p' = 0$, since $\sum_{-k \leq j \leq m} p_j = 1 - p'$.

Lemma 26 (Number of Roots With Absolute Value ≤ 1). *Let $\mathcal{P}$ be a random walk program as in Definition 12 that is PAST. Then the characteristic polynomial $\chi_{\mathcal{P}}$ has k roots $\lambda \in \mathbb{C}$ (counted with multiplicity) with $|\lambda| \leq 1$.*

Example 27 (Example 25 cont.). In $\mathcal{P}_{race}^{mod}$ of Example 23 we have $k = 2$. So by Lemma 26, $\chi_\mathcal{P}$ has exactly two roots with absolute value ≤ 1. Indeed, the roots of $\chi_\mathcal{P}$ are $\lambda_1 = 1$, $\lambda_2 = -\frac{1}{2}$, and $\lambda_3 = \frac{7}{6}$, cf. Example 25. So $|\lambda_3| > 1$, but $|\lambda_1| \leq 1$ and $|\lambda_2| \leq 1$.

Based on Lemma 26, the following lemma shows that when imposing the restriction that $a_{j,u} = 0$ whenever $|\lambda_j| > 1$, then there is only a *single* function of the form (9) that also satisfies the constraint (4). Hence, this must be the function that we are searching for, because the desired smallest solution $f : \mathbb{Z} \to \mathbb{R}_{\geq 0}$ of (5) also satisfies (4).

Lemma 28 (Unique Solution of (4) **and** (5) **when Disregarding Roots With Absolute Value** > 1**).** *Let $\mathcal{P}$ be a random walk program as in Definition 12 that is PAST. Then there is exactly one function $f : \mathbb{Z} \to \mathbb{C}$ which satisfies both (4) and (5) (thus, it has the form (9)) and has $a_{j,u} = 0$ whenever $|\lambda_j| > 1$.*

The main theorem of Sect. 5 now shows how to compute the expected runtime exactly. By Theorems 10 and 21 on the bounds for the expected runtime and by Lemma 28, we no longer have to search for the *smallest* function that satisfies (4) and (5), but we just search for *any* solution of (4) and (5) which has $a_{j,u} = 0$ whenever $|\lambda_j| > 1$ (because there is just a single such solution). So one only has to determine the values of the remaining k coefficients $a_{j,u}$ for $|\lambda_j| \leq 1$, which can be done by exploiting that $f(x)$ has to satisfy both (4) for all $x \leq 0$ and it has to be of the form (9) for all $x > -k$. In other words, the function in (9) must be 0 for $-k + 1 \leq x \leq 0$.

Theorem 29 (Exact Expected Runtime for Random Walk Programs). *Let $\mathcal{P}$ be a random walk program as in Definition 12 that is PAST and let $\lambda_1, \ldots, \lambda_c$ be the roots of its characteristic polynomial with multiplicities $v_1, \ldots, v_c$. Moreover, let $C(x) = C_{const} = \frac{1}{p'}$ if $p' > 0$ and $C(x) = C_{lin} \cdot x = -\frac{1}{\mu_\mathcal{P}} \cdot x$ if $p' = 0$. Then the expected runtime of $\mathcal{P}$ is $rt_x^\mathcal{P} = 0$ for $x \leq 0$ and*

$$rt_x^\mathcal{P} = C(x) + \sum_{1 \leq j \leq c, \, |\lambda_j| \leq 1} \sum_{0 \leq u \leq v_j - 1} a_{j,u} \cdot \lambda_j^x \cdot x^u \quad \text{for } x > 0,$$

where the coefficients $a_{j,u}$ are the unique solution of the k linear equations:

$$0 = C(x) + \sum_{1 \leq j \leq c, \, |\lambda_j| \leq 1} \sum_{0 \leq u \leq v_j - 1} a_{j,u} \cdot \lambda_j^x \cdot x^u \quad \text{for } -k+1 \leq x \leq 0 \quad (11)$$

So in the special case where $k = 0$, we have $rt_x^\mathcal{P} = C(x) = C_{const} = \frac{1}{p'}$ for $x > 0$.

Thus for $x > 0$, the expected runtime $rt_x^\mathcal{P}$ can be computed by summing up the bound $C(x)$ and an add-on $\sum_{1 \leq j \leq c, \, |\lambda_j| \leq 1} \sum_{0 \leq u \leq v_j - 1} \cdots$. Since $C(x)$ is an upper bound for $rt_x^\mathcal{P}$ if $p' > 0$ and a lower bound for $rt_x^\mathcal{P}$ if $p' = 0$, this add-on is non-positive if $p' > 0$ and non-negative if $p' = 0$.

Example 30 (Example 27 cont.). By Theorem 29, the expected runtime of the program $\mathcal{P}_{race}^{mod}$ from Example 23 is $rt_x^{\mathcal{P}_{race}^{mod}} = 0$ for $x \leq 0$ and

$$rt_x^{\mathcal{P}_{race}^{mod}} = \tfrac{22}{3} \cdot x + a_1 + a_2 \cdot (-\tfrac{1}{2})^x \quad \text{for} \quad x > 0, \text{ cf. } (10).$$

The coefficients a_1 and a_2 are the unique solution of the $k = 2$ linear equations

$$0 = \tfrac{22}{3} \cdot 0 + a_1 + a_2 \cdot (-\tfrac{1}{2})^0 = a_1 + a_2$$
$$0 = \tfrac{22}{3} \cdot (-1) + a_1 + a_2 \cdot (-\tfrac{1}{2})^{-1} = -\tfrac{22}{3} + a_1 - 2 \cdot a_2$$

So $a_1 = \tfrac{22}{9}$, $a_2 = -\tfrac{22}{9}$, and hence $rt_x^{\mathcal{P}_{race}^{mod}} = \tfrac{22}{3} \cdot x + \tfrac{22}{9} - \tfrac{22}{9} \cdot (-\tfrac{1}{2})^x$ for $x > 0$.

By Theorem 15, we can lift Theorem 29 to arbitrary CP programs $\mathcal{P}$ immediately.

Corollary 31 (Exact Expected Runtime for CP Programs). *For any CP program, its expected runtime can be computed exactly.*

Note that irrespective of the degree of the characteristic polynomial, its roots can always be approximated numerically with any chosen precision. Thus, "exact computation" of the expected runtime in the corollary above means that a closed form for $rt_x^{\mathcal{P}}$ can also be computed with any desired precision.

Example 32 (Exact Expected Runtime of $\mathcal{P}_{direct}$). Reconsider the program $\mathcal{P}_{direct}$ of Example 11 with the probability $p' = \tfrac{1}{10}$ for direct termination. $\mathcal{P}_{direct}$ is PAST and its expected runtime is at most $\tfrac{1}{p'} = 10$, cf. Example 11. The random walk program $\mathcal{P}_{direct}^{rdw}$ on the right is obtained

```
while (x > 0) {
    x = x + 1   [9/10];
    x = 0       [1/10];
}
```

by the transformation of Definition 13. As $k = 0$, by Theorem 29 we obtain $rt_x^{\mathcal{P}_{direct}^{rdw}} = \tfrac{1}{p'} = 10$ for $x > 0$. By Theorem 15, this implies $rt_{(t,h)}^{\mathcal{P}_{direct}} = rt_{rdw_{\mathcal{P}_{direct}}(t,h)}^{\mathcal{P}_{direct}^{rdw}} = 10$ if $rdw_{\mathcal{P}_{direct}}(t,h) = t - h + 1 > 0$, i.e., 10 is indeed the exact expected runtime of $\mathcal{P}_{direct}$.

Note that Theorem 29 and Corollary 31 imply that for any $x_0 \in \mathbb{Z}^r$, the expected runtime $rt_{x_0}^{\mathcal{P}}$ of a CP program $\mathcal{P}$ that is PAST and has only *rational* probabilities $p_{c_1}, \ldots, p_{c_n}, p' \in \mathbb{Q}$ is always an algebraic number. Thus, one could also compute a closed form for the exact expected runtime $rt_x^{\mathcal{P}}$ using a representation with algebraic numbers instead of numerical approximations.

Nevertheless, Theorem 29 may yield a representation of $rt_x^{\mathcal{P}}$ which contains complex numbers $a_{j,u}$ and λ_j, although $rt_x^{\mathcal{P}}$ is always real. However, one can easily obtain a more intuitive representation of $rt_x^{\mathcal{P}}$ without complex numbers:

Since the characteristic polynomial $\chi_\mathcal{P}$ only has real coefficients, whenever $\chi_\mathcal{P}$ has a complex root λ of multiplicity v, its conjugate $\overline{\lambda}$ is also a root of $\chi_\mathcal{P}$ with the same multiplicity v. So the pairwise different roots $\lambda_1, \ldots, \lambda_c$ can be distinguished into pairwise different real roots $\lambda_1, \ldots, \lambda_s$, and into pairwise different non-real complex roots $\lambda_{s+1}, \overline{\lambda_{s+1}}, \ldots, \lambda_{s+t}, \overline{\lambda_{s+t}}$, where $c = s + 2 \cdot t$.

For any coefficients $a_{j,u}, a'_{j,u} \in \mathbb{C}$ with $j \in \{s + 1, \ldots, s + t\}$ and $u \in \{0, \ldots, v_j - 1\}$ let $b_{j,u} = 2 \cdot \mathrm{Re}(a_{j,u}) \in \mathbb{R}$ and $b'_{j,u} = -2 \cdot \mathrm{Im}(a_{j,u}) \in \mathbb{R}$. Then $a_{j,u} \cdot \lambda_j^x + a'_{j,u} \cdot \overline{\lambda_j}^x = b_{j,u} \cdot \mathrm{Re}(\lambda_j^x) + b'_{j,u} \cdot \mathrm{Im}(\lambda_j^x)$. Hence, by Theorem 29 we get the following representation of the expected runtime which only uses *real* numbers:

$$
rt_x^{\mathcal{P}} = \begin{cases} C(x) + \displaystyle\sum_{1 \leq j \leq s, \, |\lambda_j| \leq 1} \; \sum_{0 \leq u \leq v_j - 1} a_{j,u} \cdot \lambda_j^x \cdot x^u \\[2mm] \quad + \displaystyle\sum_{s+1 \leq j \leq s+t, \, |\lambda_j| \leq 1} \; \sum_{0 \leq u \leq v_j - 1} \left(b_{j,u} \cdot \mathrm{Re}(\lambda_j^x) + b'_{j,u} \cdot \mathrm{Im}(\lambda_j^x) \right) \cdot x^u, \text{ for } x > 0 \\[4mm] 0, \hfill \text{for } x \leq 0 \end{cases}
$$
(12)

To compute $\mathrm{Re}(\lambda_j^x)$ and $\mathrm{Im}(\lambda_j^x)$, take the polar representation of the non-real roots $\lambda_j = w_j \cdot e^{\theta_j \cdot i}$. Then $\mathrm{Re}(\lambda_j^x) = w_j^x \cdot \cos(\theta_j \cdot x)$ and $\mathrm{Im}(\lambda_j^x) = w_j^x \cdot \sin(\theta_j \cdot x)$.

Therefore, we obtain the following algorithm to deduce the exact expected runtime automatically.

Algorithm 33 (Computing the Exact Expected Runtime). *To infer the runtime of a CP program $\mathcal{P}$ as in Definition 12 that is PAST, we proceed as follows:*

1. *Transform $\mathcal{P}$ into $\mathcal{P}^{rdw}$ by the transformation of Definition 13. Thus, $\mathcal{P}^{rdw}$ is a random walk program as in Definition 12.*
2. *Compute the solution $C(x) = C_{const} = \frac{1}{p'}$ resp. $C(x) = C_{lin} \cdot x = -\frac{1}{\mu_{\mathcal{P}^{rdw}}} \cdot x$ of the inhomogeneous recurrence equation (7).*
3. *Compute the $k + m$ (possibly complex) roots of the characteristic polynomial $\chi_{\mathcal{P}^{rdw}}$ (cf. (8)) and keep the k roots λ with $|\lambda| \leq 1$.*
4. *Determine the coefficients $a_{j,u}$ by solving the k linear equations in (11).*
5. *Return the solution (12) where $b_{j,u} = 2 \cdot \mathrm{Re}(a_{j,u})$, $b'_{j,u} = -2 \cdot \mathrm{Im}(a_{j,u})$, and for $\lambda_j = w_j \cdot e^{\theta_j \cdot i}$ we have $\mathrm{Re}(\lambda_j^x) = w_j^x \cdot \cos(\theta_j \cdot x)$ and $\mathrm{Im}(\lambda_j^x) = w_j^x \cdot \sin(\theta_j \cdot x)$. Moreover, x must be replaced by $rdw_{\mathcal{P}}(x)$.*

6   Conclusion, Implementation, and Related Work

We presented decision procedures for termination and complexity of classes of probabilistic programs. They are based on the connection between the expected runtime of a program and the smallest solution of its corresponding recurrence equation, cf. Sect. 2. For our notion of probabilistic programs, if the probability for leaving the loop directly is at least p' for some $p' > 0$, then the program is always PAST and its expected runtime is asymptotically constant, cf. Sect. 3. In Sect. 4 we showed that a very simple decision procedure for AST and PAST of CP programs can be obtained by classical results from random walk theory and that the expected runtime is asymptotically linear if the program is PAST. Based on these results, in Sect. 5 we presented our algorithm to automatically infer a closed form for the *exact* expected runtime of CP programs (i.e., with arbitrarily high precision). All proofs and a collection of examples to demonstrate our algorithm can be found in [20].

Implementation. We implemented Algorithm 33 in our tool KoAT [9], which was already one of the leading tools for complexity analysis of (non-probabilistic) integer programs. The implementation is written in OCaml and uses the Python libraries MpMath [22] and SymPy [29] for solving linear equations and for finding the roots of the characteristic polynomial. In addition to the closed form for the exact expected runtime, our implementation can also compute the concrete number of expected loop iterations if the user specifies the initial values of the variables. For further details, a set of benchmarks, and to download our implementation, we refer to https://aprove-developers.github.io/recurrence/.

Example 34 (Computing the Exact Expected Runtime of $\mathcal{P}_{race}$ Automatically).
For the tortoise and hare program $\mathcal{P}_{race}$ from Example 1, our implementation in
KoAT computes the following expected runtime within 0.49 s on an Intel Core
i7-6500 with 8 GB memory (when selecting a precision of 2 decimal places):

$$
\begin{aligned}
rt^{\mathcal{P}_{race}}_{(t,h)} = {} & 0.049 \cdot 0.65^{(t-h+1)} \cdot \sin\left(2.8 \cdot (t-h+1)\right) - 0.35 \cdot 0.65^{(t-h+1)} \cdot \cos\left(2.8 \cdot (t-h+1)\right) \\
& + 0.15 \cdot 0.66^{(t-h+1)} \cdot \sin\left(2.2 \cdot (t-h+1)\right) - 0.35 \cdot 0.66^{(t-h+1)} \cdot \cos\left(2.2 \cdot (t-h+1)\right) \\
& + 0.3 \cdot 0.7^{(t-h+1)} \cdot \sin\left(1.5 \cdot (t-h+1)\right) - 0.39 \cdot 0.7^{(t-h+1)} \cdot \cos\left(1.5 \,(t-h+1)\right) \\
& + 0.62 \cdot 0.75^{(t-h+1)} \cdot \sin\left(0.83 \cdot (t-h+1)\right) - 0.49 \cdot 0.75^{(t-h+1)} \cdot \cos\left(0.83 \cdot (t-h+1)\right) \\
& + \tfrac{2}{3} \cdot (t-h) \; + \; 2.3
\end{aligned}
$$

So when starting in a state with $t = 1000$ and $h = 0$, according to our implementation the number of expected loop iterations is $rt^{\mathcal{P}_{race}}_{(1000,0)} = 670$.

Related Work. Many techniques to analyze (P)AST have been developed, which mostly rely on ranking supermartingales, e.g., [1,4,10,12,13,17,19,28,30]. Indeed, several of these works (e.g., [1,4,17,19]) present complete criteria for (P)AST, although (P)AST is undecidable. However, the corresponding automation of these techniques is of course incomplete. In [13] it is shown that for affine probabilistic programs, a superclass of our CP programs, the existence of a linear ranking supermartingale is decidable. However, the existence of a linear ranking supermartingale is sufficient but not necessary for PAST or an at most linear expected runtime.

Classes of programs where termination is decidable have already been studied for deterministic programs. In [35] it was shown that for a class of linear loop programs over the reals, the halting problem is decidable. This result was transferred to the rationals [5] and under certain conditions to integer programs [5,18,31]. Termination analysis for probabilistic programs is substantially harder than for non-probabilistic ones [23]. Nevertheless, there is some previous work on classes of probabilistic programs where termination is decidable and asymptotic bounds on the expected runtime are computable. For instance, in [6] it was shown that AST is decidable for certain stochastic games and [11] presents an automatic approach for inferring asymptotic upper bounds on the expected runtime by considering uni- and bivariate recurrence equations.

However, our algorithm is the first which computes a general formula (i.e., a closed form) for the *exact* expected runtime of arbitrary CP programs. To our knowledge, up to now such a formula was only known for the very restricted special case of *bounded* simple random walks (cf. [16]), i.e., programs of the

form on the right for some $1 \geq p \geq 0$ and some $b \in \mathbb{Z}$.
Note that due to the *two* boundary conditions $x > 0$
and $b > x$, the resulting recurrence equation for the
expected runtime of the program only has a *single*
solution $f : \mathbb{Z} \to \mathbb{R}_{\geq 0}$ that also satisfies $f(0) = 0$
and $f(b) = 0$. Hence, standard techniques for solving

```
while (b > x > 0) {
    x = x + 1    [p];
    x = x - 1    [1 - p];
}
```

recurrence equations suffice to compute this solution. In contrast, we developed
an algorithm to compute the exact expected runtime of *unbounded arbitrary* CP
programs where the loop condition only has *one* boundary condition $x > 0$, i.e.,
x can grow infinitely large. For that reason, here the challenge is to find an
algorithm which computes the *smallest* solution $f : \mathbb{Z} \to \mathbb{R}_{\geq 0}$ of the resulting
recurrence equation. We showed that this can be done using the information on
the asymptotic bounds of the expected runtime from Sects. 3 and 4.

Future Work. There are several directions for future work. In Sect. 4.1 we
reduced CP programs to random walk programs. In future work, we will consider more advanced reductions in order to extend the class of probabilistic
programs where termination and complexity are decidable. Moreover, we want
to develop techniques to automatically *over- or under-approximate* the runtime
of a program $\mathcal{P}$ by the runtimes of corresponding CP programs $\mathcal{P}_1$ and $\mathcal{P}_2$ such
that $rt_x^{\mathcal{P}_1} \leq rt_x^{\mathcal{P}} \leq rt_x^{\mathcal{P}_2}$ holds for all $x \in \mathbb{Z}^r$. Furthermore, we will integrate the
easy inference of runtime bounds for CP programs into existing techniques for
analyzing more general probabilistic programs.

Acknowledgments. We would like to thank Nicos Georgiou and Vladislav Vysotskiy
for drawing our attention to Wald's Lemma and to the work of Frank Spitzer on
random walks, and Benjamin Lucien Kaminski and Christoph Matheja for many helpful
discussions. Furthermore, we thank Tom Küspert who helped with the implementation
of our technique in our tool KoAT.

References

1. Agrawal, S., Chatterjee, K., Novotný, P.: Lexicographic ranking supermartingales:
   an efficient approach to termination of probabilistic programs. Proc. ACM Program. Lang. (POPL) **2**, 34:1–34:32 (2018). https://doi.org/10.1145/3158122
2. Ash, R.B., Doleans-Dade, C.A.: Probability and Measure Theory. Else-
   vier/Academic Press (2000)
3. Bazzi, L., Mitter, S.: The solution of linear probabilistic recurrence relations. Algorithmica **36**(1), 41–57 (2003). https://doi.org/10.1007/s00453-002-1003-4
4. Bournez, O., Garnier, F.: Proving positive almost-sure termination. In: Giesl, J.
   (ed.) RTA 2005. LNCS, vol. 3467, pp. 323–337. Springer, Heidelberg (2005). https://
   doi.org/10.1007/978-3-540-32033-3_24
5. Braverman, M.: Termination of integer linear programs. In: Ball, T., Jones, R.B.
   (eds.) CAV 2006. LNCS, vol. 4144, pp. 372–385. Springer, Heidelberg (2006).
   https://doi.org/10.1007/11817963_34
6. Brázdil, T., Brozek, V., Etessami, K.: One-counter stochastic games. In: Lodaya,
   K., Mahajan, M. (eds.) FSTTCS 2010, LIPIcs, vol. 8, pp. 108–119 (2010). https://
   doi.org/10.4230/LIPIcs.FSTTCS.2010.108

7. Brázdil, T., Kučera, A., Novotný, P., Wojtczak, D.: Minimizing expected termination time in one-counter Markov decision processes. In: Czumaj, A., Mehlhorn, K., Pitts, A., Wattenhofer, R. (eds.) ICALP 2012. LNCS, vol. 7392, pp. 141–152. Springer, Heidelberg (2012). https://doi.org/10.1007/978-3-642-31585-5_16

8. Brázdil, T., Esparza, J., Kiefer, S., Kucera, A.: Analyzing probabilistic pushdown automata. Formal Methods Syst. Des. **43**(2), 124–163 (2013). https://doi.org/10.1007/s10703-012-0166-0

9. Brockschmidt, M., Emmes, F., Falke, S., Fuhs, C., Giesl, J.: Analyzing runtime and size complexity of integer programs. ACM Trans. Program. Lang. Syst. **38**(4), 13:1–13:50 (2016). https://doi.org/10.1145/2866575

10. Chakarov, A., Sankaranarayanan, S.: Probabilistic program analysis with martingales. In: Sharygina, N., Veith, H. (eds.) CAV 2013. LNCS, vol. 8044, pp. 511–526. Springer, Heidelberg (2013). https://doi.org/10.1007/978-3-642-39799-8_34

11. Chatterjee, K., Fu, H., Murhekar, A.: Automated recurrence analysis for almost-linear expected-runtime bounds. In: Majumdar, R., Kunčak, V. (eds.) CAV 2017. LNCS, vol. 10426, pp. 118–139. Springer, Cham (2017). https://doi.org/10.1007/978-3-319-63387-9_6

12. Chatterjee, K., Novotný, P., Zikelic, D.: Stochastic invariants for probabilistic termination. In: Castagna, G., Gordon, A.D. (eds.) POPL 2017, pp. 145–160 (2017). https://doi.org/10.1145/3093333.3009873

13. Chatterjee, K., Fu, H., Novotný, P., Hasheminezhad, R.: Algorithmic analysis of qualitative and quantitative termination problems for affine probabilistic programs. ACM Trans. Program. Lang. Syst. **40**(2), 7:1–7:45 (2018). https://doi.org/10.1145/3174800

14. Elaydi, S.: An Introduction to Difference Equations. Springer, New York (2005). https://doi.org/10.1007/0-387-27602-5

15. Esparza, J., Kucera, A., Mayr, R.: Quantitative analysis of probabilistic pushdown automata: expectations and variances. In: Panangaden, P. (ed.) LICS 2005, pp. 117–126 (2005). https://doi.org/10.1109/LICS.2005.39

16. Feller, W.: An Introduction to Probability Theory and Its Applications, Probability and Mathematical Statistics, vol. 1. Wiley, Hoboken (1950)

17. Fioriti, L.M.F., Hermanns, H.: Probabilistic termination: soundness, completeness, and compositionality. In: Rajamani, S.K., Walker, D. (eds.) POPL 2015, pp. 489–501 (2015). https://doi.org/10.1145/2676726.2677001

18. Frohn, F., Giesl, J.: Termination of triangular integer loops is decidable. In: Dillig, I., Tasiran, S. (eds.) CAV 2019. LNCS, vol. 11562, pp. 426–444. Springer, Cham (2019). https://doi.org/10.1007/978-3-030-25543-5_24

19. Fu, H., Chatterjee, K.: Termination of nondeterministic probabilistic programs. In: Enea, C., Piskac, R. (eds.) VMCAI 2019. LNCS, vol. 11388, pp. 468–490. Springer, Cham (2019). https://doi.org/10.1007/978-3-030-11245-5_22

20. Giesl, J., Giesl, P., Hark, M.: Computing expected runtimes for constant probability programs. CoRR abs/1905.09544 (2019). https://arxiv.org/abs/1905.09544

21. Grimmett, G., Stirzaker, D.: Probability and Random Processes. Oxford University Press, Oxford (2001)

22. Johansson, F., et al.: MpMath: a Python library for arbitrary-precision floating-point arithmetic. http://mpmath.org/

23. Kaminski, B.L., Katoen, J.: On the hardness of almost-sure termination. In: Italiano, G.F., Pighizzini, G., Sannella, D. (eds.) MFCS 2015. LNCS, vol. 9234, pp. 307–318. Springer, Heidelberg (2015). https://doi.org/10.1007/978-3-662-48057-1_24

24. Kaminski, B.L., Katoen, J.-P., Matheja, C., Olmedo, F.: Weakest precondition reasoning for expected run–times of probabilistic programs. In: Thiemann, P. (ed.) ESOP 2016. LNCS, vol. 9632, pp. 364–389. Springer, Heidelberg (2016). https://doi.org/10.1007/978-3-662-49498-1_15

25. Karp, R.M.: Probabilistic recurrence relations. J. ACM **41**(6), 1136–1150 (1994). https://doi.org/10.1145/195613.195632

26. Kozen, D.: Semantics of probabilistic programs. In: Kosaraju, S.R. (ed.) FOCS 1979, pp. 101–114 (1979). https://doi.org/10.1109/SFCS.1979.38

27. McIver, A., Morgan, C.: Abstraction, Refinement and Proof for Probabilistic Systems. Springer, New York (2005). https://doi.org/10.1007/b138392

28. McIver, A., Morgan, C., Kaminski, B.L., Katoen, J.: A new proof rule for almost-sure termination. Proc. ACM Program. Lang. (POPL) **2**, 33:1–33:28 (2018). https://doi.org/10.1145/3158121

29. Meurer, A., et al.: SymPy: symbolic computing in Python. Peer J Comput. Sci. **3**, e103 (2017). https://doi.org/10.7717/peerj-cs.103

30. Ngo, V.C., Carbonneaux, Q., Hoffmann, J.: Bounded expectations: resource analysis for probabilistic programs. In: Foster, J.S., Grossman, D. (eds.) PLDI 2018, pp. 496–512 (2018). https://doi.org/10.1145/3192366.3192394. Extended Version available at https://arxiv.org/abs/1711.08847

31. Ouaknine, J., Pinto, J.S., Worrell, J.: On termination of integer linear loops. In: Indyk, P. (ed.) SODA 2015, pp. 957–969 (2015). https://doi.org/10.1137/1.9781611973730.65

32. Puterman, M.L.: Markov Decision Processes: Discrete Stochastic Dynamic Programming. Wiley, New York (1994)

33. Spitzer, F.: Principles of Random Walk. Springer, New York (1964). https://doi.org/10.1007/978-1-4757-4229-9

34. Tassarotti, J., Harper, R.: Verified tail bounds for randomized programs. In: Avigad, J., Mahboubi, A. (eds.) ITP 2018. LNCS, vol. 10895, pp. 560–578. Springer, Cham (2018). https://doi.org/10.1007/978-3-319-94821-8_33

35. Tiwari, A.: Termination of linear programs. In: Alur, R., Peled, D.A. (eds.) CAV 2004. LNCS, vol. 3114, pp. 70–82. Springer, Heidelberg (2004). https://doi.org/10.1007/978-3-540-27813-9_6

Automatic Generation of Logical Models
with AGES

Raúl Gutiérrez[✉][iD] and Salvador Lucas[iD]

Valencian Research Institute for Artificial Intelligence (VRAIN),
Universitat Politècnica de València, Valencia, Spain
{rgutierrez,slucas}@dsic.upv.es

Abstract. We describe a new tool, AGES, which can be used to automatically generate models for order-sorted first-order theories. The tool uses linear algebra techniques to associate finite or infinite domains to the different sorts. Function and predicate symbols are then interpreted by means of piecewise interpretations with matrix-based expressions and inequalities. Relations interpreting binary predicates can be specified to be well-founded as an additional requirement for the generation of the model. The system is available as a web application.

Keywords: Abstraction · Logical models · First-order logic ·
Program analysis · Sorts

1 Introduction

Consider an interpretation $\mathscr{A}$ of the function and predicate symbols occurring in a first-order formula φ. A *valuation* α of the free variables occurring in φ as values of the domain of $\mathscr{A}$ *satisfies* φ *in* $\mathscr{A}$ if it makes φ true. We say that $\mathscr{A}$ is a *model* of φ if *all* valuations α satisfy φ in $\mathscr{A}$. If $\mathscr{A}$ is a *model* of φ for all formulas φ in a set $\mathscr{S}$ (often called a *theory*), we say that $\mathscr{A}$ is a *model* of $\mathscr{S}$. In program analysis and verification, the *synthesis of models* for theories representing program semantics and properties is useful for several purposes (see [11] and the references therein for a more detailed motivation). Our tool AGES (*Automatic GEneration of logical modelS*)

http://zenon.dsic.upv.es/ages/

gives support to this kind of analysis and verification purposes. AGES implements the methodology developed in [11] to generate a model $\mathscr{A}$ for a *theory* T of the *order-sorted, first-order logic* [8,18]. The meaning or use of such a model is up to the user. As a running example, consider the following Maude specification

Partially supported by the EU (FEDER), and projects RTI2018-094403-B-C32, PROMETEO/2019/098, and SP20180225. Raúl Gutiérrez was also supported by INCIBE program "Ayudas para la excelencia de los equipos de investigación avanzada en ciberseguridad".

P. Fontaine (Ed.): CADE 2019, LNAI 11716, pp. 287–299, 2019.
https://doi.org/10.1007/978-3-030-29436-6_17

(hopefully self-explained, but see [4]) of a many-sorted term rewriting system (MS-TRS) for the usual arithmetic operations over the naturals (sort N) together with function head, which returns the head of a list of natural numbers (sort LN) [10, Section 5.1]:

```
mod ExAddMulHead is
  sorts N LN .
  op Z : -> N .          op suc : N -> N . ops add mul : N N -> N .
  op head : LN -> N . op nil : -> LN .   op cons : N LN -> LN .
  vars x y : N .         var xs : LN .
  rl add(Z,x) => x . rl add(suc(x),y) => suc(add(x,y)) .
  rl mul(Z,x) => Z . rl mul(suc(x),y) => add(y,mul(x,y)) .
  rl head(cons(x,xs)) => x .
endm
```

We may express the claim of add being *commutative* as follows:

$$(\forall x : N)(\forall y : N)(\exists z : N) \; \text{add}(x, y) \rightarrow^* z \wedge \text{add}(y, x) \rightarrow^* z \qquad (1)$$

where $\rightarrow^*$ is the *many-step* rewrite relation associated to the system. By [10, Corollary 1], we can *disprove* (1) if we find a structure $\mathscr{A}$ which is a model of

$$\overline{\text{ExAddMulHead}} \cup H_N \cup \{\neg(1)\} \qquad (2)$$

with $\overline{\text{ExAddMulHead}}$ the corresponding (many-sorted) first-order theory in Fig. 1 and

$$H_N = \{(\forall x : N) \; x = Z \vee x = \text{suc}(Z) \vee x = \text{head}(\text{nil})\} \qquad (3)$$

a first-order theory which guarantees that the interpretation homomorphism $h_N : \mathscr{T}_{\Sigma N} \rightarrow \mathscr{A}_N$ is surjective (see [10, Sections 3 and 4] for further details). We obtain a model $\mathscr{A}$ of (2) with AGES, which we describe in Sect. 3. This formally proves that property (1) does not hold in ExAddMulHead. The main features of AGES can be summarized as follows: (a) supports order-sorted first-order logic, (b) generates finite and infinite, multidimensional domains, (c) supports overloaded function and predicate symbols, including equality, (d) supports the use of N and Z with most of the usual operations and predicates by means of predefined sorts Nat and Int, (e) generates piecewise function and predicate symbols, and (f) supports the definition of well-founded relations (over finite or infinite domains).

Section 2 explains the input format. Section 3 briefly introduces the kind of interpretations computed by AGES. Section 4 describes the structure of the tool. Section 5 provides experimental results showing the performance of the tool. Section 6 concludes.

$$(\forall x : \mathrm{N})\, x \to^* x$$
$$(\forall x : \mathrm{LN})\, x \to^* x$$
$$(\forall x, y, z : \mathrm{N})\, x \to y \wedge y \to^* z \Rightarrow x \to^* z$$
$$(\forall x, y, z : \mathrm{LN})\, x \to y \wedge y \to^* z \Rightarrow x \to^* z$$
$$(\forall x, y : \mathrm{N})\, x \to y \Rightarrow \mathsf{suc}(x) \to \mathsf{suc}(y)$$
$$(\forall x, y : \mathrm{N}, xs : \mathrm{LN})\, x \to y \Rightarrow \mathsf{cons}(x, xs) \to \mathsf{cons}(y, xs)$$
$$(\forall x : \mathrm{N}, xs, ys : \mathrm{LN})\, xs \to ys \Rightarrow \mathsf{cons}(x, xs) \to \mathsf{cons}(x, ys)$$
$$(\forall x, y, z : \mathrm{N})\, x \to y \Rightarrow \mathsf{add}(x, z) \to \mathsf{add}(y, z)$$
$$(\forall x, y, z : \mathrm{N})\, x \to y \Rightarrow \mathsf{add}(z, x) \to \mathsf{add}(z, y)$$
$$(\forall x, y, z : \mathrm{N})\, x \to y \Rightarrow \mathsf{mul}(x, z) \to \mathsf{mul}(y, z)$$
$$(\forall x, y, z : \mathrm{N})\, x \to y \Rightarrow \mathsf{mul}(z, x) \to \mathsf{mul}(z, y)$$
$$(\forall x, y : \mathrm{LN})\, x \to y \Rightarrow \mathsf{head}(x) \to \mathsf{head}(y)$$
$$(\forall x : \mathrm{N})\, \mathsf{add}(\mathrm{Z}, x) \to x$$
$$(\forall x, y : \mathrm{N})\, \mathsf{add}(\mathsf{suc}(x), y) \to \mathsf{suc}(\mathsf{add}(x, y))$$
$$(\forall x : \mathrm{N})\, \mathsf{mul}(\mathrm{Z}, x) \to \mathrm{Z}$$
$$(\forall x, y : \mathrm{N})\, \mathsf{mul}(\mathsf{suc}(x), y) \to \mathsf{add}(y, \mathsf{mul}(x, y))$$
$$(\forall x : \mathrm{N}, xs : \mathrm{LN})\, \mathsf{head}(\mathsf{cons}(x, xs)) \to x$$

Fig. 1. Horn theory for `ExAddMulHead` ($\to$ and $\to^*$ are overloaded)

2 Input Format

The main idea of order-sorted first-order logic (OS-FOL [8]) is distinguishing different kinds of objects by giving them a *sort s* from a set of sorts S which is ordered by a *subsort relation* $\le$. Variables have sorts and can be bound to objects of this sort only. The arguments of function and predicate symbols have sorts and only objects of these sorts are allowed in the arguments. The outcome of a function also has a sort.

We use Maude [4] as an appropriate basis to specify our order-sorted first-order theories, although we extend Maude syntax in different ways to fit our needs (and dismiss other Maude features which are not necessary). Our tool, though, is *not* meant to deal with Maude programs. We benefit from the order-sorted features of Maude to describe the *syntax* of the language we use as part of a *system module* $\mathscr{S}$ [4, Chapter 6]. The specification module may just define the signature (sorts, subsorts, and function and predicate symbols) with sorts `Bool`, `Nat` and `Int`, integer and natural numbers, relations =, > and >=, boolean constants `true` and `false`, and + and - operators with the standard meaning. The specification may also include *conditional rewrite rules* to define an *order-sorted conditional term rewriting system* (OS-CTRS). Rules are introduced as follows: `rl l => r` (or `crl l => r if c` for conditional rules), where l and r are terms (the conditional part c is of the form `s1 => t1 /\ ... /\ sn => tn` for terms `s1,t1,...,sn,tn`). Then, AGES obtains the *order-sorted first-order theory* $\overline{\mathscr{S}}$ from the OS-TRS $\mathscr{S}$ by specializing the inference rules in Fig. 2[1] and then treating inference rules $\frac{B_1 \cdots B_n}{A}$ as sentences $(\forall x : s)\, B_1 \wedge \cdots \wedge B_n \Rightarrow A$ where x are the variables $x_1, \ldots, x_m$ of sorts $s_1, \ldots, s_m$ occurring in $A, B_1, \ldots, B_n$.

$$(Rf)\ \frac{}{x \to^* x} \qquad\qquad (T)\ \frac{x \to y \quad y \to^* z}{x \to^* z}$$

$$(C)\ \frac{x_i \to y_i}{f(x_1, \ldots, x_i, \ldots, x_k) \to f(x_1, \ldots, y_i, \ldots, x_k)} \qquad (Rl)\ \frac{s_1 \to^* t_1 \quad \cdots \quad s_n \to^* t_n}{\ell \to r}$$

$$\text{where } f \in \Sigma_{w,s},\ w = s_1, \ldots, s_k, \text{ and } 1 \le i \le k \qquad \text{where } \ell \to r \Leftarrow s_1 \to t_1, \ldots, s_n \to t_n \in \mathscr{R}$$

Fig. 2. Schematic inference rules for Order-Sorted CTRSs $\mathscr{R}$

Example 1. Program `ExAddMulHead` is a valid AGES specification as it is. The theory which is obtained by AGES corresponds to the one displayed in Fig. 1.

The target theory $T = \overline{\mathscr{S}} \cup G$ for AGES consists of the theory $\overline{\mathscr{S}}$ obtained from the specification $\mathscr{S}$ together with a second component G.

Remark 1. The generation of $\overline{\mathscr{S}}$ from $\mathscr{S}$ using the inference rules in Fig. 2 can be *disabled* if this is not convenient for the analysis at hand. In this way, we can use the *goal* part G of the target theory T to provide a full, explicit description of the sentences to be considered in the generation process.

The set G of *goals* is given as a set of *quantifier-free formulas* $F_1, \ldots, F_k$ so that G is implicitly defined as follows:

$$\bigwedge_{1 \le i \le k} (\forall x_1 : s_1, \ldots, x_{q_i} : s_{q_i}) F_i \tag{4}$$

where $x_1, \ldots, x_{q_i}$ are the variables occurring in F_i (with sorts $s_1, \ldots, s_{q_i}$ respectively). Formulas F_i are built up using the symbols in the specification part. Predicates $\to$ and $\to^*$ can be used as `->` and `->*`, respectively. We can also use `true`, `false`, and `=` (the equality predicate), conjunction `/\`, disjunction `\/`, negation `~`, implication `=>`, and equivalence `<=>`, with the standard meaning.

Remark 2 (Predicate symbols in Maude specifications). Since Maude does not provide any specific means to specify predicate symbols, we assume that every function p returning values in the predefined sort `Bool` is a *predicate* symbol (see also Sect. 3).

The *sort* of each variable occurrence in the formula must be explicit. Note, however, that (4) contains universal quantifiers only. If existential quantifiers are necessary to specify a sentence (like in (1)) we need to first give it the appropriate format.

---

[1] Note that, following the semantics of *oriented* CTRSs [17, Section 7.1], (Rl) implements the treatment of the conditional part of rewrite rules as *reachability* tests (with $\to^*$ rather than $\to$).

Example 2. In order to find a model for (2), we need to write ¬(1) as a valid AGES goal (H_N has the required format). By applying well-known transformations, we obtain

$$(\exists x : N)(\exists y : N)(\forall z : N) \; \neg(\mathsf{add}(x, y) \rightarrow^* z \wedge \mathsf{add}(y, x) \rightarrow^* z)$$

Now we use *skolemization* to remove the existential quantifiers by introducing new constants declared by ops skX skY : -> N. (in the signature part) to obtain

$$(\forall z : N) \; \neg(\mathsf{add}(\mathsf{skX}, \mathsf{skY}) \rightarrow^* z \wedge \mathsf{add}(\mathsf{skY}, \mathsf{skX}) \rightarrow^* z)$$

which is in the appropriate format.[2] Thus, the model obtained by AGES (discussed in Sect. 3) is actually obtained for

$$\overline{\texttt{ExAddMulHead}} \cup H_N \cup \{(\forall z : N) \; \neg(\mathsf{add}(\mathsf{skX}, \mathsf{skY}) \rightarrow^* z \wedge \mathsf{add}(\mathsf{skY}, \mathsf{skX}) \rightarrow^* z)\} \, (5)$$

In AGES, we would enter module ExAddMulHead (including the declarations for skX and skY) in the *specification* part and, in the *goal* part:

```
x:N = Z \/ x:N = suc(Z) \/ x:N = head(nil)
~(add(skX,skY) ->* z:N /\ add(skY,skX) ->* z:N)
```

3 Interpretations Generated by AGES

In AGES, the *automatic generation* of models for a theory $T = \mathscr{S} \cup G$ proceeds *bottom-up* by (i) associating *parametric* expressions to sorts, function, and predicate *symbols* in the sentences of T, (ii) *combining* them according to their syntactic structure to obtain a set of conditional sentences of *linear arithmetic*, (iii) transforming the (parametric) sentences into equivalent *quantifier-free* formulas which actually are *constraints* over the parameters, and (iv) *solving* the constraints, to finally (v) give value to the initial parameters and then *synthesize* a structure which is (by construction) a model of T. For this purpose, sorts $s \in S$ are given *parametric* matrices C^s (of m_s rows and n_s columns) and vectors b^s so that each sort $s \in S$ is interpreted as the set $\mathscr{A}_s$ of vectors x of n_s integer components satisfying the linear inequality $C^s x \geq b^s$ (for some appropriate instantiation of the parameters in C^s and b^s). Sorts can be given values for m_s and n_s in the AGES specification $\mathscr{S}$. With

```
sort S [m=2 n=1].
```

we make explicit the *default* values $m_s = 2$ and $n_s = 1$ we use in the tool for all sorts s without explicit values for m_s and n_s as above (see [11, Remark 12]).

---

[2] These skolemization transformations are not implemented in AGES yet.

Example 3. In the model of (5) computed by AGES, sorts are interpreted by $\mathscr{A}_{\mathtt{N}} = \{-1, 0\}$ and $\mathscr{A}_{\mathtt{LN}} = \{0, 1\}$. The domains for sorts N and LN are defined by the inequalities $\begin{bmatrix} C_1^{\mathtt{N}} \\ C_2^{\mathtt{N}} \end{bmatrix} x \geq \begin{bmatrix} b_1^{\mathtt{N}} \\ b_2^{\mathtt{N}} \end{bmatrix}$ and $\begin{bmatrix} C_1^{\mathtt{LN}} \\ C_2^{\mathtt{LN}} \end{bmatrix} x \geq \begin{bmatrix} b_1^{\mathtt{LN}} \\ b_2^{\mathtt{LN}} \end{bmatrix}$, where, for $\mathscr{A}_{\mathtt{N}}$, we have $C_1^{\mathtt{N}} = 1$, $C_2^{\mathtt{N}} = -1$, $b_1^{\mathtt{N}} = -1$, and $b_2^{\mathtt{N}} = 0$, and x ranges over $\mathbb{Z}$. For $\mathscr{A}_{\mathtt{LN}}$, $C_1^{\mathtt{LN}} = 1$, $C_2^{\mathtt{LN}} = -1$, $b_1^{\mathtt{LN}} = 0$, and $b_2^{\mathtt{LN}} = -1$, and x ranges on $\mathbb{Z}$. The interpretation of, e.g., Nat is predefined, but obtained similarly as the solution of $C^{Nat}x \geq b^{Nat}$ (we do not need to use two parameters in the matrices because N is known to be infinite) by just providing predefined values $C^{Nat} = 1$ and $b^{Nat} = 0$ to the parameters.

Each *predicate symbol* $P \in \Pi_w$ with $w = s_1 \cdots s_n$ is interpreted by *piecewise* inequalities

$$R(x_1, \ldots, x_n) \Leftrightarrow \begin{cases} R_1^1 x_1 + \cdots + R_n^1 x_n \geq R_0^1 & \text{if } \widehat{R}_1^1 x_1 + \cdots + \widehat{R}_n^1 x_n \geq \widehat{R}_0^1 \\ \quad \vdots \\ R_1^{N_P} x_1 + \cdots + R_n^{N_P} x_n \geq R_0^{N_P} & \text{if } \widehat{R}_1^{N_P} x_1 + \cdots + \widehat{R}_n^{N_P} x_n \geq \widehat{R}_0^{N_P} \end{cases}$$

for some $N_P > 0$, where, for all $1 \leq i \leq n$ and $1 \leq j \leq N_P$, $R_i^j, R_i^j, \widehat{R}_i^j$, and $\widehat{R}_1^j$ are $m_P \times n_{s_i}$-matrices, R_0^j and $\widehat{R}_0^j$ are vectors of m_P rows for some $m_P \in \mathbb{N}$. In AGES, predicates $P \in \Pi_{s_1 \cdots s_n}$ can be given values for m_P and N_P as follows:

```
op P : S1 ... Sn -> Bool [m=1 N=1].
```

which actually shows the *default* values $m_P = 1$ and $N_P = 1$ we use for all predicates (but see [11, Example 13]). In this case, the generic expression above boils down into:

$$R(x_1, \ldots, x_n) \Leftrightarrow R_1 x_1 + \cdots + R_n x_n \geq R_0 \tag{6}$$

where R_i is a $2m_P \times n_{s_i}$-matrix, for $1 \leq i \leq n$, and R_0 is a vector [11, Remark14]. We can also use (6) directly, with matrices R_i of m rows for some $m > 0$.

Example 4. In the model of (5) computed by AGES, predicates are interpreted as follows: $x \to_{\mathtt{N}}^{\mathscr{A}} y \Leftrightarrow x(\to_{\mathtt{N}}^*)^{\mathscr{A}} y \Leftrightarrow x = y$, $x \to_{\mathtt{LN}}^{\mathscr{A}} y \Leftrightarrow x = y$, and $x(\to_{\mathtt{LN}}^*)^{\mathscr{A}} y$ is *true*. These are more readable formulations of the AGES output (after some variable renaming):

```
x:N -> y:N <=> ((y:N >= x:N) /\ (x:N >= y:N))
x:N ->* y:N <=> ((y:N >= x:N) /\ (x:N >= y:N))
x:LN -> y:LN <=> ((x:LN >= y:LN) /\ (y:LN >= x:LN))
x:LN ->* y:LN <=> (3 + x:LN + y:LN >= 0)
```

For instance, the interpretation of $\to_{\mathtt{N}}$ (first line), in matrix format (6), corresponds to

$$x \to_{\mathtt{N}}^{\mathscr{A}} y \Leftrightarrow \begin{bmatrix} -1 \\ 1 \end{bmatrix} x + \begin{bmatrix} 1 \\ -1 \end{bmatrix} y \geq \begin{bmatrix} 0 \\ 0 \end{bmatrix}$$

which is better understood as $x = y$. Note that since $3 + \text{x:LN} + \text{y:LN} >= 0$ holds for every value x and y in $\mathscr{A}_{\text{LN}} = \{0, 1\}$, $x(\to^*_{\text{LN}})^{\mathscr{A}} y$ is equivalent to *true*. Unfortunately, these kind of 'simplifications' are not implemented in AGES yet. However, we do not display *repeated* members in a conjunction of inequalities. This explains that the last line shows a single inequality instead of two.

A binary relation R on a set A is *well-founded* if there is no infinite sequence $a_1, a_2, \ldots$ such that for all $i \geq 1$, $a_i \in A$ and $a_i R a_{i+1}$. We can *require* that relation $P_{ss}^{\mathscr{A}}$ interpreting a binary predicate P_{ss} be *well-founded* [11, Section 8.3.1]:

```
op P : S S -> Bool [wellfounded].
```

Each *function symbol* $f : s_1 \cdots s_k \to s$ is interpreted as follows (for some $N_f > 0$):

$$F(x_1, \ldots, x_k) = \begin{cases} F_1^1 x_1 + \cdots + F_k^1 x_k + F_0^1 & \text{if } \widehat{F}_1^1 x_1 + \cdots + \widehat{F}_k^1 x_k \geq \widehat{F}_0^1 \\ \quad \vdots \\ F_1^{N_f-1} x_1 + \cdots + F_k^{N_f-1} x_k + F_0^{N_f-1} & \text{if } \widehat{F}_1^{N_f-1} x_1 + \cdots + \widehat{F}_k^{N_f-1} x_k \geq \widehat{F}_0^{N_f-1} \\ F_1^{N_f} x_1 + \cdots + F_k^{N_f} x_k + F_0^{N_f} & \text{otherwise} \end{cases}$$

where the *otherwise* in the last option guarantees that F is *total* [11, Remark 9]. The default option is $N_f = 1$ (signature declaration `op f : S1 ... Sk -> S [N=1].`), i.e., no pieces. Then, the generic expression above boils down into a linear expression:

$$F(x_1, \ldots, x_k) = F_1 x_1 + \cdots + F_k x_k + F_0 \tag{7}$$

where F_i is an $n_s \times n_{s_i}$-matrix, $1 \leq i \leq k$, and F_0 a vector of n_s rows.

Example 5. In our model of (5), function symbols are interpreted as follows:

$$\text{Z}^{\mathscr{A}} = -1 \qquad \text{nil}^{\mathscr{A}} = 0 \qquad \text{suc}^{\mathscr{A}}(x) = x \qquad \text{add}^{\mathscr{A}}(x, y) = y$$
$$\text{mul}^{\mathscr{A}}(x, y) = x \quad \text{cons}^{\mathscr{A}}(x, xs) = -x \quad \text{head}^{\mathscr{A}}(xs) = -xs$$

where x and y range on $\mathscr{A}_{\text{N}}$ and xs on $\mathscr{A}_{\text{LN}}$. The AGES output is as follows:

```
|[add(x_1_1:N,x_2_1:N)]| = x_2_1:N
|[head(x_1_1:LN)]| =  - x_1_1:LN
|[mul(x_1_1:N,x_2_1:N)]| = x_1_1:N
|[Z]| =  - 1
|[cons(x_1_1:N,x_2_1:LN)]| =  - x_1_1:N
|[nil]| = 0
|[suc(x_1_1:N)]| = x_1_1:N
```

Skolem symbols are interpreted as follows: $\text{skX}^{\mathscr{A}} = 0$ and $\text{skY}^{\mathscr{A}} = -1$. By [10, Section 6], we could use this information to conclude that terms add(head(nil), Z) and add(Z, head(nil)) explain why property (1) fails to hold (but AGES provides no support for such kind of issues yet).

4   User Interface

AGES is a web based application written in Haskell in 13705 lines of code. In order to use this application, the end user only needs an *HTML5* compatible browser. The main web page is divided in three areas: the input area, the configuration area and the information area. In the input area, two fields must be filled before generating a model:

- *Specification:* This field accepts the extended Maude specification as described in Sect. 2. It can be pasted from a text file, uploaded using the *Browse* button, or written in the text box.
- *Goal:* This field allows to add a goal to the model according to the format in Sect. 2. The goal can be a single formula or a list of formulas separated by newlines. If we do not want to add a goal, we can just write true in the field.

The configuration area permits to parameterize the search of the solution:

- *Predicates:* The user can select the interpretation of the relation $\rightarrow$ and $\rightarrow^*$ to well-known relations (i.e. $>$, $\geq$ or $=$) or allow the solver to search for it automatically.
- *Inference Rules:* The user can deactivate some of the inference rules of the OS-TRS logic (Fig. 2) in order to redefine them and obtain a new logic.
- *Convex Polytopic Domain:* permits the definition of common values m_s and n_s of C^s and b^s for all sorts s. The values are overridden by any specific value given in the specification (see Sect. 3).
- *Timeout:* for the SMT-based constraint solving. Maximum timeout is 300 s.
- *SMT Solver:* AGES uses external SMT solvers to find the model that satisfies the generated constraints in SMT-LIB format[3] in the QF_NIA domain. Currently, we can choose between SMT solvers Barcelogic [3], Yices [5] and Z3 [16].

All configuration fields have default values. The information area explains how to use the extended Maude configuration parameters described in Sect. 2. Pressing the *Generate* button starts the model generation process depicted in Fig. 3.

---

[3] http://smtlib.cs.uiowa.edu/.

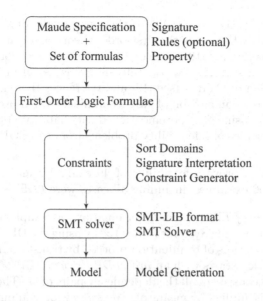

Fig. 3. AGES Workflow

5   Experimental Results

In order to evaluate the performance of AGES with respect to related tools (a nonexhaustive list includes FALCON [19], Mace4 [15], SEM [20], and the model generation subsystems of the theorem provers Alt-Ergo, PDL-tableau, Princess, or Vampire) we have compared AGES and Mace4, which is a good representative of what other similar model generation tools do. Mace4 generates (one-sorted) finite models only. Actually, this is not rare: to the best of our knowledge, all aforementioned systems generate models with finite domains only. Thus, as far as we known, AGES is the only tool which is able to generate infinite models for first-order theories. Mace4 is a very fast and easy to use tool. It is available as a desktop application in several platforms.

AGES and Mace4 are based on rather different ideas. Zhang [19] provides a comprehensive description of how Mace4-like tools work and [11] describes the approach implemented by AGES. Rather than directly comparing them as model generators, we compare them as *auxiliary tools* for other purposes. We have prepared three benchmarks suites which can be useful to compare both tools and evaluate their capabilities. The details of our benchmarks are available here:

http://zenon.dsic.upv.es/ages/benchmarks/cade27/

In the following, we explain each of them and comment on their results.

Proving Infeasibility. Given a (C)TRS $\mathcal{R}$ we say that a sequence $s_1 \to^* t_1, \ldots, s_n \to^* t_n$ is $\mathcal{R}$-infeasible if there is no substitution σ such that $\sigma(s_i) \to^*_{\mathcal{R}} \sigma(t_i)$ holds for all $1 \leq i \leq n$. In [12] it is proved that a sequence

$s_1 \to^* t_1, \ldots, s_n \to^* t_n$ is $\mathscr{R}$-infeasible if there is a model of $\overline{\mathscr{R}} \cup \{\neg(\exists x)\, s_1 \to^* t_1 \wedge \cdots \wedge s_n \to^* t_n\}$, where $\overline{\mathscr{R}}$ is the first-order theory associated to $\mathscr{R}$ (like the theory in Fig. 1 for ExAddMulHead, see [12, Section 3], for more details) and x refers all variables in $s_1, t_1, \ldots, s_n, t_n$. Infeasibility is useful in proofs of confluence and termination of CTRSs (see [12] and references therein).

We implemented a comparison of AGES and Mace4 when used to solve *infeasibility* problems by using the aforementioned satisfiability approach. We have considered 129 examples of infeasibility problems from the COPS database.[4] On this test suite,

> AGES was able to prove infeasibility of 49 examples and Mace4 proved infeasibility of 52 examples, including all cases were AGES succeeded.

Proving Termination of TRSs. Modern termination tools implement proofs of termination of Term Rewriting Systems (TRSs) $\mathscr{R}$ by using the DP Framework [7]. In the DP Framework, proofs of termination proceed by transforming DP problems. A proof of termination starts with an *initial DP Problem* $(\mathsf{DP}(\mathscr{R}), \mathscr{R})$ whose first component $\mathsf{DP}(\mathscr{R})$ consists of all the dependency pairs of $\mathscr{R}$. Then, a divide-and-conquer approach is applied by means of *processors* Proc mapping a DP problem τ into a (possibly empty) set $\mathsf{Proc}(\tau)$ of DP problems $\{\tau_1, \ldots, \tau_n\}$ (alternatively, they can return "no"). DP problems τ_i returned by Proc can now be treated independently by using other processors. In this way, a *DP proof tree* is built. One of the most important processors is the reduction pair processor Proc_{RP}. With Proc_{RP} we can remove a dependency pair $u \to v$ if we find a well-founded relation $\sqsupset$ such that $u \sqsupset v$ holds (among some additional conditions). Such well-founded relations can be generated by means of a model $\mathscr{A}$ of $\overline{\mathscr{R}}$ which also satisfies $(\forall x)\, u\pi_\sqsupset v$ for a new predicate symbol $\pi_\sqsupset$ representing the relation $\sqsupset$. If $\pi_\sqsupset^{\mathscr{A}}$ is guaranteed to be well-founded, then we can remove $u \to v$ from the current DP problem. In this way we introduce a simplification in the termination proof.

We have implemented (as part of our termination tool MU-TERM 6.0 [1][5]) the use of Proc_{RP} by using AGES and Mace4 to generate the required models and well-founded relations. As mentioned in Sect. 3, AGES provides explicit support for well-foundedness through the modifier `wellfounded` that can be specified in the predicate declaration. Mace4 does not provide any support for well-foundedness. However, we can use the fact that a finite relation R on a set A is well-founded iff R is not cyclic, i.e., there is no $a \in A$ such that $a\, R^+\, a$. As in [9], we instruct Mace4 to obtain a well-founded interpretation for $\pi_\sqsupset$ by adding the following sentences:

$$(\forall x)(\forall y) \quad x\, \pi_\sqsupset y \Rightarrow x\, \pi_\sqsupset^+ y \tag{8}$$

$$(\forall x)(\forall y)(\forall z) \quad x\, \pi_\sqsupset y \wedge y\, \pi_\sqsupset^+ z \Rightarrow x\, \pi_\sqsupset^+ z \tag{9}$$

$$\neg(\exists x) \quad x\, \pi_\sqsupset^+ x \tag{10}$$

where $\pi_\sqsupset^+$ is a new binary predicate symbol. We have used the Termination Problems Data Base (TPDB version 10.6) containing examples of TRS termination problems. On the 1498 examples of this test suite,

---

[4] http://project-coco.uibk.ac.at/2019/categories/infeasibility.php.

[5] Available at http://zenon.dsic.upv.es/muterm/.

MU-TERM 6.0+AGES was able to prove termination of 336 examples and MU-TERM 6.0+Mace4 proved termination of 109 examples.

The ability of AGES to generate models with infinite domains and different interpretations for sorts[6] could be essential for these good results. It is also interesting that Mace4 was able to prove termination of a few examples where AGES could not be used and that all the examples proved by AGES using Z3 and Yices are also proved by AGES using Barcelogic.

Proving Operational Termination of CTRSs. When *conditional* rewrite rules $\ell \to r \Leftarrow s_1 \approx t_1, \ldots, s_n \approx t_n$ are considered, besides the usual notion of termination as the absence of infinite sequences of reductions, a new source of nontermination arises: the possibility of 'getting lost' when trying to prove whether a single reduction step is possible [13, 14]. In this setting, describing rewriting computations as *proofs* of goals $s \to t$ and $s \to^* t$ with respect to an appropriate inference system is useful to approach the termination behavior of such systems as *the absence of infinite proof trees* [13]. In [14] appropriate notions of dependency pairs were introduced to capture operational termination (OT) of oriented[7] CTRSs. Given a CTRS $\mathscr{R}$, two new CTRSs $DP_H(\mathscr{R})$ and $DP_V(\mathscr{R})$ are introduced to capture the two *horizontal* and *vertical* dimensions of operational termination of CTRSs [14, Section 3]: the usual absence of infinite rewrite sequences (termination), and the absence of infinite 'climbings' on a proof tree when trying to prove a goal $s \to t$ or $s \to^* t$ (called V-termination [14, Definition 13]). Proofs of operational termination in the 2D DP Framework essentially proceed like in the DP Framework for TRSs. Thus, we have prepared MU-TERM 6.0 to work with AGES and Mace4 when trying to prove operational termination of CTRSs (again on the TPDB). On this test suite, over 121 examples,

MU-TERM 6.0+AGES proved OT of 85 examples and disproved OT of 17.
MU-TERM 6.0+Mace4 proved OT of 79 examples and disproved OT of 5.

Summary. In the first benchmark suite Mace4 slightly outperforms AGES. A possible explanation is that models with finite domains are usually well-suited to solve infeasibility problems. Mace4 computes fully general, extensional representations of functions and predicates, as sets of equations and atoms, respectively. AGES can simulate them using piecewise interpretations, but less efficiently, often running out of the timeout. The second and third benchmark suites show that MU-TERM+Mace4 proved termination of 23% of the TRSs handled by using AGES; in contrast, MU-TERM+Mace4 was able to (dis)prove operational termination of 80% of the CTRSs solved by using AGES. The first benchmark suite suggests a possible explanation. As remarked in [12], infeasibility (of conditional dependency pairs, of links between nodes in the dependency graph, etc.)

---

[6] Sorts can be used to treat dependency pairs [6, Sect. 5]; this is implemented in MU-TERM 6.0.

[7] Oriented CTRSs treat conditions $s_i \approx t_i$ in rules $\ell \to r \Leftarrow s_1 \approx t_1, \ldots, s_n \approx t_n$ as *rewriting* goals $\sigma(s_i) \to^* \sigma(t_i)$ for appropriate substitutions σ.

is important in proofs of operational termination of CTRSs. Infeasibility is tested in MU-TERM 6.0 as part of the proofs. Many proofs of operational termination finish with no use of well-founded relations. Thus, it is not so strange that Mace4 obtains better results when used in proofs of operational termination of CTRSs. Overall, the conclusion is that AGES is similar to Mace4 in proofs of infeasibility, whereas it is much better in the generation of well-founded models.

6   Conclusions

The main motivation to develop AGES was providing an appropriate framework to explore the applicability of the results in [11]: the generation of *convex domains* to interpret sorts of order-sorted signatures and the interpretation of function and predicate symbols by means of *piecewise matrix interpretations* which, for binary relations interpreting binary predicates, can be required to be well-founded. We have shown that this approach is applicable in practice, and can be competitive, as shown by our experiments (Sect. 5) and also in the 2017, 2018, and 2019 termination competitions,[8] where AGES was integrated as a backend of MU-TERM in the *conditional TRS* category, being the most successful tool for proving operational termination of CTRSs. Regarding future work, we plan to improve on efficiency, applications and extensions. With regard to *efficiency*, the generation of matrix-based models could benefit from the ideas in [2]. We will also improve our treatment of piecewise interpretations regarding the generation of the CNF formulae submitted to the backend solvers. With regard to *applications*, a deeper integration of AGES into MU-TERM would be necessary to test its impact in other TRS categories. We will also consider its integration/cooperation with other confluence and verification tools. Finally, with respect to *extensions*, we plan to include equational components in our input signature and give support to other input formats for rewriting-based systems.

Acknowledgments. We thank the anonymous referees for their comments and suggestions. We thank Patricio Reinoso for his work in the initial development of the tool.

References

1. Alarcón, B., Gutiérrez, R., Lucas, S., Navarro-Marset, R.: Proving termination properties with MU-TERM. In: Johnson, M., Pavlovic, D. (eds.) AMAST 2010. LNCS, vol. 6486, pp. 201–208. Springer, Heidelberg (2011). https://doi.org/10.1007/978-3-642-17796-5_12
2. Bau, A., Lohrey, M., Nöth, E., Waldmann, J.: Compression of rewriting systems for termination analysis. In: van Raamsdonk, F. (ed.) Proceedings of the 24th International Conference on Rewriting Techniques and Applications, RTA 2013, LIPICS, vol. 21, pp. 97–112 (2013). https://doi.org/10.4230/LIPIcs.RTA.2013.97

---

[8] http://termination-portal.org/wiki/Termination_Competition.

3. Bofill, M., Nieuwenhuis, R., Oliveras, A., Rodríguez-Carbonell, E., Rubio, A.: The barcelogic SMT solver. In: Gupta, A., Malik, S. (eds.) CAV 2008. LNCS, vol. 5123, pp. 294–298. Springer, Heidelberg (2008). https://doi.org/10.1007/978-3-540-70545-1_27

4. Clavel, M., et al.: All About Maude - A High-Performance Logical Framework. LNCS, vol. 4350. Springer, Heidelberg (2007). https://doi.org/10.1007/978-3-540-71999-1

5. Dutertre, B.: Yices 2.2. In: Biere, A., Bloem, R. (eds.) CAV 2014. LNCS, vol. 8559, pp. 737–744. Springer, Cham (2014). https://doi.org/10.1007/978-3-319-08867-9_49

6. Endrullis, J., Waldmann, J., Zantema, H.: Matrix interpretations for proving termination of term rewriting. J. Autom. Reasoning **40**(2–3), 195–220 (2008). https://doi.org/10.1007/s10817-007-9087-9

7. Giesl, J., Thiemann, R., Schneider-Kamp, P., Falke, S.: Mechanizing and improving dependency pairs. J. Autom. Reasoning **37**(3), 155–203 (2006). https://doi.org/10.1007/s10817-006-9057-7

8. Goguen, J.A., Meseguer, J.: Models and equality for logical programming. In: Ehrig, H., Kowalski, R., Levi, G., Montanari, U. (eds.) TAPSOFT 1987. LNCS, vol. 250, pp. 1–22. Springer, Heidelberg (1987). https://doi.org/10.1007/BFb0014969

9. Lucas, S.: Using Well-Founded Relations for Proving Operational Termination. J. Autom. Reasoning (2019). https://doi.org/10.1007/s10817-019-09514-2

10. Lucas, S.: Proving program properties as first-order satisfiability. In: Mesnard, F., Stuckey, P.J. (eds.) LOPSTR 2018. LNCS, vol. 11408, pp. 3–21. Springer, Cham (2019). https://doi.org/10.1007/978-3-030-13838-7_1

11. Lucas, S., Gutiérrez, R.: Automatic synthesis of logical models for order-sorted first-order theories. J. Autom. Reasoning **60**(4), 465–501 (2018). https://doi.org/10.1007/s10817-017-9419-3

12. Lucas, S., Gutiérrez, R.: Use of logical models for proving infeasibility in term rewriting. Inf. Process. Lett. **136**, 90–95 (2018). https://doi.org/10.1016/j.ipl.2018.04.002

13. Lucas, S., Marché, C., Meseguer, J.: Operational termination of conditional term rewriting systems. Inf. Process. Lett. **95**, 446–453 (2005). https://doi.org/10.1016/j.ipl.2005.05.002

14. Lucas, S., Meseguer, J.: Dependency pairs for proving termination properties of conditional term rewriting systems. J. Logical Algebraic Methods Program. **86**, 236–268 (2017). https://doi.org/10.1016/j.jlamp.2016.03.003

15. McCune, W.: Prover9 and Mace4 (2005–2010). http://www.cs.unm.edu/~mccune/prover9/

16. de Moura, L., Bjørner, N.: Z3: an efficient SMT solver. In: Ramakrishnan, C.R., Rehof, J. (eds.) TACAS 2008. LNCS, vol. 4963, pp. 337–340. Springer, Heidelberg (2008). https://doi.org/10.1007/978-3-540-78800-3_24

17. Ohlebusch, E.: Advanced Topics in Term Rewriting. Springer, New York (2002). https://doi.org/10.1007/978-1-4757-3661-8

18. Wang, H.: Logic of many-sorted theories. J. Symbolic Logic **17**(2), 105–116 (1952). https://doi.org/10.2307/2266241

19. Zhang, J.: Constructing finite algebras with FALCON. J. Autom. Reasoning **17**, 1–22 (1996). https://doi.org/10.1007/BF00247667

20. Zhang, J., Zhang, H.: System description generating models by SEM. In: McRobbie, M.A., Slaney, J.K. (eds.) CADE 1996. LNCS, vol. 1104, pp. 308–312. Springer, Heidelberg (1996). https://doi.org/10.1007/3-540-61511-3_96

Automata Terms in a Lazy WS*k*S
Decision Procedure

Vojtěch Havlena, Lukáš Holík, Ondřej Lengál$^{(\boxtimes)}$, and Tomáš Vojnar

FIT, IT4I Centre of Excellence,
Brno University of Technology, Brno, Czech Republic
lengal@fit.vutbr.cz

Abstract. We propose a lazy decision procedure for the logic WS*k*S.
It builds a term-based symbolic representation of the state space of the
tree automaton (TA) constructed by the classical WS*k*S decision procedure. The classical decision procedure transforms the symbolic representation into a TA via a bottom-up traversal and then tests its language
non-emptiness, which corresponds to satisfiability of the formula. On
the other hand, we start evaluating the representation from the top,
construct the state space on the fly, and utilize opportunities to prune
away parts of the state space irrelevant to the language emptiness test.
In order to do so, we needed to extend the notion of *language terms*
(denoting language derivatives) used in our previous procedure for the
linear fragment of the logic (the so-called WS1S) into *automata terms*.
We implemented our decision procedure and identified classes of formulae on which our prototype implementation is significantly faster than
the classical procedure implemented in the MONA tool.

1 Introduction

Weak monadic second-order logic of k successors (WS*k*S) is a logic for describing
regular properties of finite *k*-ary trees. In addition to talking about trees, WS*k*S
can also encode complex properties of a rich class of general graphs by referring
to their tree backbones [1]. WS*k*S offers extreme succinctness for the price of non-
elementary worst-case complexity. As noticed first by the authors of [2] in the
context of WS1S (a restriction that speaks about finite words only), the trade-
off between complexity and succinctness may, however, be turned significantly
favourable in many practical cases through a use of clever implementation techniques and heuristics. Such techniques were then elaborated in the tool MONA
[3,4], the best-known implementation of decision procedures for WS1S and WS2S.
MONA has found numerous applications in verification of programs with complex dynamic linked data structures [1,5–8], string programs [9], array programs
[10], parametric systems [11–13], distributed systems [14,15], hardware verification [16], automated synthesis [17–19], and even computational linguistics [20].

Despite the extensive research and engineering effort invested into MONA,
due to which it still offers the best all-around performance among existing
WS1S/WS2S decision procedures, it is, however, easy to reach its scalability

© Springer Nature Switzerland AG 2019
P. Fontaine (Ed.): CADE 2019, LNAI 11716, pp. 300–318, 2019.
https://doi.org/10.1007/978-3-030-29436-6_18

limits. Particularly, MONA implements the classical WS1S/WS2S decision procedures that build a word/tree automaton representing models of the given formula and then check emptiness of the automaton's language. The non-elementary complexity manifests in that the size of the automaton is prone to explode, which is caused mainly by the repeated determinisation (needed to handle negation and alternation of quantifiers) and synchronous product construction (used to handle conjunctions and disjunctions). Users of WSkS are then forced to either find workarounds, such as in [6], or, often restricting the input of their approach, give up using WSkS altogether [21].

As in MONA, we further consider WS2S only (this does not change the expressive power of the logic since k-ary trees can be easily encoded into binary ones). We revisit the use of tree automata (TAs) in the WS2S decision procedure and obtain a new decision procedure that is much more efficient in certain cases. It is inspired by works on *antichain algorithms* for efficient testing of universality and language inclusion of finite automata [22–25], which implement the operations of testing emptiness of a complement (universality) or emptiness of a product of one automaton with the complement of the other one (language inclusion) via an *on-the-fly* determinisation and product construction. The on-the-fly approach allows one to achieve significant savings by pruning the state space that is irrelevant for the language emptiness test. The pruning is achieved by early termination when detecting non-emptiness (which represents a simple form of *lazy evaluation*), and *subsumption* (which basically allows one to disregard proof obligations that are implied by other ones). Antichain algorithms and their generalizations have shown great efficiency improvements in applications such as abstract regular model checking [24], shape analysis [26], LTL model checking [27], or game solving [28].

Our work generalizes the above mentioned approaches of on-the-fly automata construction, subsumption, and lazy evaluation for the needs of deciding WS2S. In our procedure, the TAs that are constructed explicitly by the classical procedure are represented symbolically by the so-called *automata terms*. More precisely, we build automata terms for subformulae that start with a quantifier (and for the top-level formula) only—unlike the classical procedure, which builds a TA for every subformula. Intuitively, automata terms specify the set of leaf states of the TAs of the appropriate (sub)formulae. The leaf states themselves are then represented by *state terms*, whose structure records the automata constructions (corresponding to Boolean operations and quantification on the formula level) used to create the given TAs from base TAs corresponding to atomic formulae. The leaves of the terms correspond to states of the base automata. Automata terms may be used as state terms over which further automata terms of an even higher level are built. Non-leaf states, the transition relation, and root states are then given implicitly by the transition relations of the base automata and the structure of the state terms.

Our approach is a generalization of our earlier work [29] on WS1S. Although the term structure and the generalized algorithm may seem close to [29], the reasoning behind it is significantly more involved. Particularly, [29] is based on defining the semantics (language) of terms as a function of the semantics of their sub-terms. For instance, the semantics of the term $\{q_1, \ldots, q_n\}$ is defined as the union of languages of the state terms $q_1, \ldots, q_n$, where the language of a state of the base automaton consists of the words *accepted at that state*. With TAs, it is, however, not meaningful to talk about trees accepted from a leaf state, instead, we need to talk about a given state and its *context*, i.e., other states that could be obtained via a bottom-up traversal over the given set of symbols. Indeed, trees have multiple leafs, which may be accepted by a number of different states, and so a tree is *accepted from a set of states*, not from any single one of them alone. We therefore cannot define the semantics of a state term as a tree language, and so we cannot define the semantics of an automata term as the union of the languages of its state sub-terms. This problem seems critical at first because without a sensible notion of the meaning of terms, a straightforward generalization of the algorithm of [29] to trees does not seem possible. The solution we present here is based on defining the semantics of terms via the automata constructions they represent rather then as functions of languages of their sub-terms.

Unlike the classical decision procedure, which builds a TA corresponding to a formula *bottom-up*, i.e. from the atomic formulae, we build automata terms *top-down*, i.e., from the top-level formula. This approach offers a lot of space for various optimisations. Most importantly, we test non-emptiness of the terms *on the fly* during their construction and construct the terms *lazily*. In particular, we use *short-circuiting* for dealing with the $\wedge$ and $\vee$ connectives and *early termination* with possible *continuation* when implementing the fixpoint computations needed when dealing with quantifiers. That is, we terminate the fixpoint computation whenever the emptiness can be decided in the given computation context and continue with the computation when such a need appears once the context is changed on some higher-term level. Further, we define a notion of *subsumption* of terms, which, intuitively, compares the terms w.r.t the sets of trees they represent, and allows us to discard terms that are subsumed by others.

We have implemented our approach in a prototype tool. When experimenting with it, we have identified multiple parametric families of WS2S formulae where our implementation can—despite its prototypical form—significantly outperform MONA. We find this encouraging since there is a lot of space for further optimisations and, moreover, our implementation can be easily combined with MONA by treating automata constructed by MONA in the same way as if they were obtained from atomic predicates.

An extended version of this paper including proofs is available as [30].

2 Preliminaries

In this section, we introduce basic notation, trees, and tree automata, and give a quick introduction to the *weak monadic second-order logic of two successors* (WS2S) and its classical decision procedure. We give the minimal syntax of WS2S only; see, e.g., Comon *et al.* [31] for more details.

Basics, Trees, and Tree Automata. Let Σ be a finite set of symbols, called an *alphabet*. The set Σ^* of *words* over Σ consists of finite sequences of symbols from Σ. The *empty word* is denoted by ϵ, with $\epsilon \notin \Sigma$. The *concatenation* of two words u and v is denoted by $u.v$ or simply uv. The *domain* of a partial function $f : X \rightarrow Y$ is the set $\mathrm{dom}(f) = \{x \in X \mid \exists y : x \mapsto y \in f\}$, its *image* is the set $\mathrm{img}(f) = \{y \in Y \mid \exists x : x \mapsto y \in f\}$, and its *restriction* to a set Z is the function $f_{|Z} = f \cap (Z \times Y)$. For a binary operator $\bullet$, we write $A [\bullet] B$ to denote the augmented product $\{a \bullet b \mid (a,b) \in A \times B\}$ of A and B.

We will consider ordered binary trees. We call a word $p \in \{\mathrm{L},\mathrm{R}\}^*$ a *tree position* and $p.\mathrm{L}$ and $p.\mathrm{R}$ its *left* and *right child*, respectively. Given an alphabet Σ s.t. $\perp \notin \Sigma$, a *tree* over Σ is a finite partial function $\tau : \{\mathrm{L},\mathrm{R}\}^* \rightarrow (\Sigma \cup \{\perp\})$ such that (i) $\mathrm{dom}(\tau)$ is non-empty and prefix-closed, and (ii) for all positions $p \in \mathrm{dom}(t)$, either $\tau(p) \in \Sigma$ and p has both children, or $\tau(p) = \perp$ and p has no children, in which case it is called a *leaf*. We let $leaf(\tau)$ be the set of all leaves of τ. The position ϵ is called the *root*, and we write $\Sigma^{\maltese}$ to denote the set of all trees over Σ^1. We abbreviate $\{a\}^{\maltese}$ as $a^{\maltese}$ for $a \in \Sigma$.

The *sub-tree* of τ rooted at a position $p \in \mathrm{dom}(\tau)$ is the tree $\tau' = \{p' \mapsto \tau(p.p') \mid p.p' \in \mathrm{dom}(\tau)\}$. A *prefix* of τ is a tree τ' such that $\tau'_{|\mathrm{dom}(\tau')\setminus leaf(\tau')} \subseteq \tau_{|\mathrm{dom}(\tau)\setminus leaf(\tau)}$. The *derivative* of a tree τ wrt a set of trees $S \subseteq \Sigma^{\maltese}$ is the set $\tau - S$ of all prefixes τ' of τ such that, for each position $p \in leaf(\tau')$, the sub-tree of τ at p either belongs to S or it is a leaf of τ. Intuitively, $\tau - S$ are all prefixes of τ obtained from τ by removing some of the sub-trees in S. The derivative of a set of trees $T \subseteq \Sigma^{\maltese}$ wrt S is the set $\bigcup_{\tau \in T}(\tau - S)$.

A (binary) *tree automaton* (TA) over an alphabet Σ is a quadruple $\mathcal{A} = (Q, \delta, I, R)$ where Q is a finite set of *states*, $\delta : Q^2 \times \Sigma \rightarrow 2^Q$ is a *transition function*, $I \subseteq Q$ is a set of *leaf states*, and $R \subseteq Q$ is a set of *root* states. We use $(q,r)\text{-}\{a\}\mapsto s$ to denote that $s \in \delta((q,r),a)$. A *run* of $\mathcal{A}$ on a tree τ is a total map $\rho : \mathrm{dom}(\tau) \rightarrow Q$ such that if $\tau(p) = \perp$, then $\rho(p) \in I$, else $(\rho(p.\mathrm{L}), \rho(p.\mathrm{R}))\text{-}\{a\}\mapsto\rho(p)$ with $a = \tau(p)$. The run ρ is *accepting* if $\rho(\epsilon) \in R$, and the *language* $\mathcal{L}(\mathcal{A})$ of $\mathcal{A}$ is the set of all trees on which $\mathcal{A}$ has an accepting run. $\mathcal{A}$ is *deterministic* if $|I| = 1$ and $\forall q,r \in Q, a \in \Sigma : |\delta((q,r),a)| \leq 1$, and *complete* if $I > 1$ and $\forall q, r \in Q, a \in \Sigma : |\delta((q,r),a)| \geq 1$. Last, for $a \in \Sigma$, we shorten $\delta((q,r),a)$ as $\delta_a(q,r)$, and we use $\delta_\Gamma(q,r)$ to denote $\bigcup\{\delta_a(q,r) \mid a \in \Gamma\}$ for a set $\Gamma \subseteq \Sigma$.

Syntax and Semantics of WS2S. WS2S is a logic that allows quantification over second-order *variables*, which are denoted by upper-case letters $X, Y, \ldots$ and range over *finite sets* of tree positions in $\{\mathrm{L},\mathrm{R}\}^*$ (the finiteness of variable assignments is reflected in the name *weak*). See Fig. 1a for an example of a set of positions assigned to a variable. Atomic formulae (atoms) of WS2S are of the form: (i) $X \subseteq Y$, (ii) $X = S_{\mathrm{L}}(Y)$, and (iii) $X = S_{\mathrm{R}}(Y)$. Formulae are constructed from atoms using the logical connectives $\wedge, \neg$, and the quantifier $\exists \mathbb{X}$ where $\mathbb{X}$

---

^{1} Intuitively, the $[\cdot]^{\maltese}$ operator can be seen as a generalization of the Kleene star to tree languages. The symbol $\maltese$ is the Chinese character for a tree, pronounced *mù*, as in English *moo-n*, but shorter and with a falling tone, staccato-like.

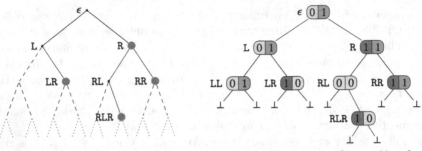

(a) Positions assigned to the variable X.

(b) Encoding of ν into a tree τ_ν; a node at a position p has the value $\boxed{x \mid y}$ where $x = 1$ iff $\tau_\nu(p)$ maps X to 1 and $y = 1$ iff $\tau_\nu(p)$ maps Y to 1.

Fig. 1. An example of an assignment ν to a pair of variables $\{X, Y\}$ s.t. $\nu(X) = \{LR, R, RLR, RR\}$ and $\nu(Y) = \{\epsilon, L, LL, R, RR\}$ and its encoding into a tree.

is a finite set of variables (we write $\exists X$ when $\mathbb{X}$ is a singleton set $\{X\}$). Other connectives (such as $\vee$ or $\forall$) and predicates (such as the predicate $Sing(X)$ for a singleton set X) can be obtained as syntactic sugar.

A *model* of a WS2S formula $\varphi(\mathbb{X})$ with the set of free variables $\mathbb{X}$ is an assignment $\nu : \mathbb{X} \to 2^{\{L, R\}^*}$ of the free variables of φ to finite subsets of $\{L, R\}^*$ for which the formula is *satisfied*, written $\nu \models \varphi$. Satisfaction of atomic formulae is defined as follows: (i) $\nu \models X \subseteq Y$ iff $\nu(X) \subseteq \nu(Y)$, (ii) $\nu \models X = S_L(Y)$ iff $\nu(X) = \{p.L \mid p \in \nu(Y)\}$, and (iii) $\nu \models X = S_R(Y)$ iff $\nu(X) = \{p.R \mid p \in \nu(Y)\}$. Informally, the $S_L(Y)$ function returns all positions from Y shifted to their left child and the $S_R(Y)$ function returns all positions from Y shifted to their right child. Satisfaction of formulae built using Boolean connectives and the quantifier is defined as usual. A formula φ is *valid*, written $\models \varphi$, iff all assignments of its free variables are its models, and *satisfiable* if it has a model. Wlog, we assume that each variable in a formula either has only free occurrences or is quantified exactly once; we denote the set of (free and quantified) variables occurring in a formula φ as $Vars(\varphi)$.

Representing Models as Trees. We fix a formula φ with variables $Vars(\varphi) = \mathbb{X}$. A *symbol* ξ over $\mathbb{X}$ is a (total) function $\xi : \mathbb{X} \to \{0, 1\}$, e.g., $\xi = \{X \mapsto 0, Y \mapsto 1\}$ is a symbol over $\mathbb{X} = \{X, Y\}$. We use $\Sigma_\mathbb{X}$ to denote the set of all symbols over $\mathbb{X}$ and $\vec{0}$ to denote the symbol mapping all variables in $\mathbb{X}$ to 0, i.e., $\vec{0} = \{X \mapsto 0 \mid X \in \mathbb{X}\}$.

A finite assignment $\nu : \mathbb{X} \to 2^{\{L, R\}^*}$ of φ's variables can be encoded as a finite tree τ_ν of symbols over $\mathbb{X}$ where every position $p \in \{L, R\}^*$ satisfies the following conditions: (a) if $p \in \nu(X)$, then $\tau_\nu(p)$ contains $\{X \mapsto 1\}$, and (b) if $p \notin \nu(X)$, then either $\tau_\nu(p)$ contains $\{X \mapsto 0\}$ or $\tau_\nu(p) = \bot$ (note that the occurrences of $\bot$ in τ are limited since τ still needs to be a tree). Observe that ν can have multiple encodings: the unique minimum one τ_ν^{min} and (infinitely many) extensions of τ_ν^{min} with $\vec{0}$-only trees. The *language* of φ is defined as the set of all encodings of its models $\mathcal{L}(\varphi) = \{\tau_\nu \in \Sigma_{\mathbb{X}}^* \mid \nu \models \varphi$ and τ_ν is an encoding of $\nu\}$.

Let ξ be a symbol over $\mathbb{X}$. For a set of variables $\mathbb{Y} \subseteq \mathbb{X}$, we define the *projection* of ξ wrt $\mathbb{Y}$ as the set of symbols $\pi_\mathbb{Y}(\xi) = \{\xi' \in \Sigma_\mathbb{X} \mid \xi_{|\mathbb{X}\setminus\mathbb{Y}} \subseteq \xi'\}$. Intuitively, the projection removes the original assignments of variables from $\mathbb{Y}$ and allows them to be substituted by any possible value. We define $\pi_\mathbb{Y}(\bot) = \bot$ and write π_Y if $\mathbb{Y}$ is a singleton set $\{Y\}$. As an example, for $\mathbb{X} = \{X, Y\}$ the projection of $\vec{0}$ wrt $\{X\}$ is given as $\pi_X(\vec{0}) = \{\{X \mapsto 0, Y \mapsto 0\}, \{X \mapsto 1, Y \mapsto 0\}\}$.[2] The definition of projection can be extended to trees τ over $\Sigma_\mathbb{X}$ so that $\pi_\mathbb{Y}(\tau)$ is the set of trees $\{\tau' \in \Sigma_\mathbb{X}^* \mid \forall p \in \mathrm{pos}(\tau) : \text{if } \tau(p) = \bot, \text{ then } \tau'(p) = \bot, \text{ else } \tau'(p) \in \pi_\mathbb{Y}(\tau(p))\}$ and subsequently to languages L so that $\pi_\mathbb{Y}(L) = \bigcup\{\pi_\mathbb{Y}(\tau) \mid \tau \in L\}$.

The Classical Decision Procedure for WS2S. The classical decision procedure for the WS2S logic goes through a direct construction of a TA $\mathcal{A}_\varphi$ having the same language as a given formula φ. Let us briefly recall the automata constructions used (cf. [31]). Given a complete TA $\mathcal{A} = (Q, \delta, I, R)$, the *complement* assumes that $\mathcal{A}$ is deterministic and returns $\mathcal{A}^\complement = (Q, \delta, I, Q \setminus R)$, the projection returns $\pi_X(\mathcal{A}) = (Q, \delta^{\pi_X}, I, R)$ with $\delta_a^{\pi_X}(q, r) = \delta_{\pi_X(a)}(q, r)$, and the *subset construction* returns the deterministic and complete automaton $\mathcal{A}^\mathcal{D} = (2^Q, \delta^\mathcal{D}, \{I\}, R^\mathcal{D})$ where $\delta_a^\mathcal{D}(S, S') = \bigcup_{q \in S, q' \in S'} \delta_a(q, q')$ and $R^\mathcal{D} = \{S \subseteq Q \mid S \cap R \neq \emptyset\}$. The binary operators $\circ \in \{\cup, \cap\}$ are implemented through a *product construction*, which—given the TA $\mathcal{A}$ and another complete TA $\mathcal{A}' = (Q', \delta', I', R')$—returns the automaton $\mathcal{A} \circ \mathcal{A}' = (Q \times Q', \Delta^\times, I^\times, R^\circ)$ where $\Delta_a^\times((q, r), (q', r')) = \Delta_a(q, q') \times \Delta_a'(r, r')$, $I^\times = I \times I'$, and for $(q, r) \in Q \times Q'$, $(q, r) \in R^\cap \Leftrightarrow q \in R \wedge r \in R'$ and $(q, r) \in R^\cup \Leftrightarrow q \in R \vee r \in R'$. The language non-emptiness test can be implemented through the equivalence $\mathcal{L}(\mathcal{A}) \neq \emptyset$ iff $\mathrm{reach}_\delta(I) \cap R \neq \emptyset$ where the set $\mathrm{reach}_\delta(S)$ of states *reachable* from a set $S \subseteq Q$ through δ-transitions is computed as the least fixpoint

$$\mathrm{reach}_\delta(S) = \mu Z.\, S \cup \bigcup_{q,r \in Z} \delta(q, r). \tag{1}$$

The same fixpoint computation is used to compute the derivative wrt a^* for some $a \in \Sigma$ as $\mathcal{A} - a^* = (Q, \delta, \mathrm{reach}_{\delta_a}(I), R)$: the new leaf states are all those reachable from I through a-transitions.

The classical WSkS decision procedure uses the above operations to constructs the automaton $\mathcal{A}_\varphi$ inductively to the structure of φ as follows: (i) If φ is an atomic formula, then $\mathcal{A}_\varphi$ is a pre-defined *base* TA over $\Sigma_\mathbb{X}$ (the particular base automata for our atomic predicates can be found, e.g., in [31], and we list them also in [30]). (ii) If $\varphi = \varphi_1 \wedge \varphi_2$, then $\mathcal{A}_\varphi = \mathcal{A}_{\varphi_1} \cap \mathcal{A}_{\varphi_2}$. (iii) If $\varphi = \varphi_1 \vee \varphi_2$, then $\mathcal{A}_\varphi = \mathcal{A}_{\varphi_1} \cup \mathcal{A}_{\varphi_2}$. (iv) If $\varphi = \neg\psi$, then $\mathcal{A}_\varphi = \mathcal{A}_\psi^\complement$. (v) Finally, if $\varphi = \exists X.\, \psi$, then $\mathcal{A}_\varphi = (\pi_X(\mathcal{A}_\psi))^\mathcal{D} - \vec{0}^*$.

---

[2] Note that our definition of projection differs from the usual one, which would in the example produce a single symbol $\{Y \mapsto 0\}$ over a different alphabet (the alphabet of symbols over $\{Y\}$).

Points (i) to (iv) are self-explanatory. In point (v), the projection implements the quantification by forgetting the values of the X component of all symbols. Since this yields non-determinism, projection is followed by determinisation by the subset construction. Further, the projection can produce some new trees that contain $\vec{0}$-only labelled sub-trees, which need not be present in some smaller encodings of the same model. Consider, for example, a formula ψ having the language $\mathcal{L}(\psi)$ given by the tree τ_ν in Fig. 1b and all its $\vec{0}$-extensions. To obtain $\mathcal{L}(\exists X.\psi)$, it is not sufficient to make the projection $\pi_X(\mathcal{L}(\psi))$ because the projected language does not contain the minimum encoding τ_ν^{min} of $\nu : Y \mapsto \{\epsilon, \mathrm{L}, \mathrm{LL}, \mathrm{R}, \mathrm{RR}\}$, but only those encodings ν' such that $\nu'(\mathrm{RLR}) = \{Y \mapsto 0\}$. Therefore, the $\vec{0}$-derivative is needed to saturate the language with *all* encodings of the encoded models (if some of these encodings were missing, the inductive construction could produce a wrong result, for instance, if the language were subsequently complemented). Note that the same effect can be achieved by replacing the set of leaf states I of $\mathcal{A}_\varphi$ by $reach_{\Delta_{\vec{0}}}(I)$ where Δ is the transition function of $\mathcal{A}_\varphi$. See [31] for more details.

3   Automata Terms

Our algorithm for deciding WS2S may be seen as an alternative implementation of the classical procedure from Sect. 2. The main innovation is the data structure of *automata terms*, which implicitly represent the automata constructed by the automata operations. Unlike the classical procedure—which proceeds by a bottom-up traversal on the formula structure, building an automaton for each sub-formula before proceeding upwards—automata terms allow for constructing parts of automata at higher levels from parts of automata on the lower levels even though the construction of the lower level automata has not yet finished. This allows one to test the language emptiness on the fly and use techniques of state space pruning, which will be discussed later in Sect. 4.

Syntax of Automata Terms. Terms are created according to the grammar in Fig. 2 starting from states $q \in Q_i$, denoted as *atomic states*, of a given finite set of *base automata* $\mathcal{B}_i = (Q_i, \delta_i, I_i, R_i)$ with pairwise disjoint sets of states. For simplicity, we assume that the base automata are complete, and we denote by $\mathcal{B} = (Q^\mathcal{B}, \delta^\mathcal{B}, I^\mathcal{B}, R^\mathcal{B})$ their component-wise union. *Automata terms A* specify the set of leaf states of an automaton. *Set terms S* list a finite number of the leaf

$$
\begin{aligned}
A &::= S \mid D & \textit{(automata term)} \\
S &::= \{t, \ldots, t\} & \textit{(set term)} \\
D &::= S - \vec{0}^* & \textit{(derivative term)} \\
t &::= q \mid t + t \mid t \,\&\, t \mid & \textit{(state term)} \\
  & \quad \bar{t} \mid \pi_X(t) \mid S \mid D &
\end{aligned}
$$

Fig. 2. Syntax of terms.

states explicitly, while *derivative terms* D specify them symbolically as states reachable from a set of states S via $\vec{0}$s. The states themselves are represented by *state terms* t (notice that set terms S and derivate terms D can both be automata and state terms). Intuitively, the structure of state terms records the automata constructions used to create the top-level automaton from states of the base automata. Non-leaf state terms, the state terms' transition function, and root state terms are then defined inductively from base automata as described below in detail. We will normally use t, u to denote terms of all types (unless the type of the term needs to be emphasized).

Example 1. Consider a formula $\varphi \equiv \neg \exists X.\ \mathrm{Sing}(X) \wedge X = \{\epsilon\}$ and its corresponding automata term $t_\varphi = \left\{ \overline{\{\pi_X(\{q_0\} \& \{p_0\})\} - \vec{0}^*} \right\}$ (we will show how t_φ was obtained from φ later). For the sake of presentation, we will consider the following base automata for the predicates $\mathrm{Sing}(X)$ and $X = \{\epsilon\}$: $\mathcal{A}_{\mathrm{Sing}(X)} = (\{q_0, q_1, q_s\}, \delta, \{q_0\}, \{q_1\})$ and $\mathcal{A}_{X=\{\epsilon\}} = (\{p_0, p_1, p_s\}, \delta', \{p_0\}, \{p_1\})$ where δ and δ' have the following sets of transitions (transitions not defined below go to the sink states q_s and p_s, respectively):

$$\delta : (q_0, q_0) \text{-}\{\{X \mapsto 0\}\}\text{-}q_0,\ (q_0, q_1) \text{-}\{\{X \mapsto 0\}\}\text{-}q_1, \qquad \delta' : (p_0, p_0) \text{-}\{\{X \mapsto 0\}\}\text{-}p_0,$$
$$(q_0, q_0) \text{-}\{\{X \mapsto 1\}\}\text{-}q_1,\ (q_1, q_0) \text{-}\{\{X \mapsto 0\}\}\text{-}q_1 \qquad\qquad (p_0, p_0) \text{-}\{\{X \mapsto 1\}\}\text{-}p_1.$$

The term t_φ denotes the TA $\left((\pi_X(\mathcal{A}_{\mathrm{Sing}(X)} \cap \mathcal{A}_{X=\{\epsilon\}}) - \vec{0}^*)^D \right)^C$ constructed by intersection, projection, derivative, subset construction, and complement. $\square$

Semantics of Terms. We will define the denotation of an automata term t as the automaton $\mathcal{A}_t = (Q, \Delta, I, R)$. For a set automata term $t = S$, we define $I = S$, $Q = reach_\Delta(S)$ (i.e., Q is the set of state terms reachable from the leaf state terms), and Δ and R are defined inductively to the structure of t. Particularly, R contains the terms of Q that satisfy the predicate $\mathcal{R}$ defined in Fig. 3, and Δ is defined in Fig. 4, with the addition that whenever the rules in Fig. 4 do not apply, then we let $\Delta_a(t, t') = \{\emptyset\}$. The $\emptyset$ here is used as a universal sink state in order to maintain Δ complete, which is needed for automata terms representing complements to yield the expected language.

$$\mathcal{R}(t + u) \Leftrightarrow \mathcal{R}(t) \vee \mathcal{R}(u) \quad (2)$$
$$\mathcal{R}(t \& u) \Leftrightarrow \mathcal{R}(t) \wedge \mathcal{R}(u) \quad (3)$$
$$\mathcal{R}(\pi_X(t)) \Leftrightarrow \mathcal{R}(t) \qquad\qquad (4)$$
$$\mathcal{R}(\bar{t}) \Leftrightarrow \neg \mathcal{R}(t) \qquad\qquad (5)$$
$$\mathcal{R}(S) \Leftrightarrow \exists t \in S.\, \mathcal{R}(t) \quad (6)$$
$$\mathcal{R}(q) \Leftrightarrow q \in R^\mathcal{B} \qquad\qquad (7)$$

Fig. 3. Root term states.

The transitions of Δ for terms of the type $+$, $\&$, π_X, $\overline{\cdot}$, and S are built from the transition function of their subterms analogously to how the automata operations of the product union, product intersection, projection, complement, and subset construction, respectively, build the transition function from the

$$\Delta_a(t + u, t' + u') = \Delta_a(t, t')\,[+]\,\Delta_a(u, u') \qquad (8)$$

$$\Delta_a(t \,\&\, u, t' \,\&\, u') = \Delta_a(t, t')\,[\&]\,\Delta_a(u, u') \qquad (9)$$

$$\Delta_a(\pi_X(t), \pi_X(t')) = \{\pi_X(u) \mid u \in \Delta_{\pi_X(a)}(t, t')\} \quad (10)$$

$$\Delta_a(\overline{t}, \overline{t'}) = \{\overline{u} \mid u \in \Delta_a(t, t')\} \qquad (11)$$

$$\Delta_a(S, S') = \left\{ \bigcup_{t \in S, t' \in S'} \Delta_a(t, t') \right\} \qquad (12)$$

$$\Delta_a(q, r) = \delta_a^{\mathcal{B}}(q, r) \qquad (13)$$

Fig. 4. Transitions among compatible state terms.

transition functions of their arguments (cf. Sect. 2). The only difference is that the state terms stay *annotated* with the particular operation by which they were made (the annotation of the set state terms are the set brackets). The root states are also defined analogously as in the classical constructions. In Figs. 3 and 4, the terms t, t', u, u' are arbitrary terms, S, S' are set terms, and $q, r \in Q^{\mathcal{B}}$.

Finally, we complete the definition of the term semantics by adding the definition of semantics for the derivative term $S - \vec{0}^*$. This term is a symbolic representation of the set term that contains all state terms upward-reachable from S in $\mathcal{A}_S$ over $\vec{0}$. Formally, we first define the so-called *saturation* of $\mathcal{A}_S$ as

$$(S - \vec{0}^*)^{\mathsf{s}} = reach_{\Delta_{\vec{0}}}(S) \qquad (14)$$

(with $reach_{\Delta_{\vec{0}}}(S)$ defined as the fixpoint (1)), and we complete the definition of Δ and $\mathcal{R}$ in Figs. 3 and 4 with three new rules to be used with a derivative term D:

$$\Delta_a(D, u) = \Delta_a(D^{\mathsf{s}}, u) \;\; (15) \quad \Delta_a(u, D) = \Delta_a(u, D^{\mathsf{s}}) \;\; (16) \qquad \mathcal{R}(D) \Leftrightarrow \mathcal{R}(D^{\mathsf{s}}) \quad (17)$$

The automaton $\mathcal{A}_D$ then equals $\mathcal{A}_{D^{\mathsf{s}}}$, i.e., the semantics of a derivative term is defined by its saturation.

Example 2. Let us consider a derivative term $t = \{\pi_X(\{q_0\}\,\&\,\{p_0\})\} - \vec{0}^*$, which occurs within the nested automata term t_φ of Example 1. The set term representing all terms reachable upward from t is then the term

$$t^{\mathsf{s}} = \{\pi_X(\{q_0\}\,\&\,\{p_0\}), \pi_X(\{q_1\}\,\&\,\{p_1\}), \pi_X(\{q_s\}\,\&\,\{p_s\}),$$
$$\pi_X(\{q_1\}\,\&\,\{p_s\}), \pi_X(\{q_0\}\,\&\,\{p_s\})\}.$$

The semantics of t is therefore the TA $\mathcal{A}_t$ with the set of states given by t^{s}. $\square$

Properties of Terms. An implication of the definitions above, essential for termination of our algorithm in Sect. 4, is that the automata represented by the terms indeed have finitely many states. This is the direct consequence of Lemma 1.

Lemma 1. *The size of $reach_\Delta(t)$ is finite for any automata term t.*

Intuitively, the terms are built over a finite set of states Q^B, they are finitely branching, and the transition function on terms does not increase their depth.

Let us further denote by $\mathcal{L}(t)$ the language $\mathcal{L}(\mathcal{A}_t)$ of the automaton induced by a term t. Lemma 2 below shows that languages of terms can be defined from the languages of their sub-terms if the sub-terms are set terms of derivative terms. The terms on the left-hand sides are implicit representations of the automata operations of the respective language operators on the right-hand sides. The main reason why the lemma cannot be extended to all types of sub-terms and yield an inductive definition of term languages is that it is not meaningful to talk about the bottom-up language of an isolated state term that is neither a set term nor a derivative term (which both are also automata terms). This is also one of the main differences from [29] where every term has its own language, which makes the reasoning and the correctness proofs in the current paper significantly more involved.

Lemma 2. *For automata terms A_1, A_2 and a set term S, the following holds:*

$$\mathcal{L}(\{A_1\}) = \mathcal{L}(A_1) \quad (a) \qquad\qquad \mathcal{L}(\{\overline{A_1}\}) = \overline{\mathcal{L}(A_1)} \quad (d)$$
$$\mathcal{L}(\{A_1 + A_2\}) = \mathcal{L}(A_1) \cup \mathcal{L}(A_2) \ (b) \qquad \mathcal{L}(\{\pi_X(A_1)\}) = \pi_X(\mathcal{L}(A_1)) \ (e)$$
$$\mathcal{L}(\{A_1 \& A_2\}) = \mathcal{L}(A_1) \cap \mathcal{L}(A_2) \ (c) \qquad\qquad \mathcal{L}(S - \vec{0}^{\,*}) = \mathcal{L}(S) - \vec{0}^{\,*} \ (f)$$

Terms of Formulae. Our algorithm in Sect. 4 will translate a WS2S formula φ into the automata term $t_\varphi = \{\langle\varphi\rangle\}$ representing a deterministic automaton with its only leaf state represented by the state term $\langle\varphi\rangle$. The base automata of t_φ include the automaton $\mathcal{A}_{\varphi_{atom}}$ for each atomic predicate φ_{atom} used in φ. The state term $\langle\varphi\rangle$ is then defined inductively to the structure of φ as shown in Fig. 5. In the definition, φ_0 is an atomic predicate, I_{φ_0} is the set of leaf states of $\mathcal{A}_{\varphi_{atom}}$, and φ and ψ denote arbitrary WS2S formulae. We note that the translation rules may create sub-terms of the form $\{\{t\}\}$, i.e., with nested set brackets. Since $\{\cdot\}$ semantically means determinisation by subset construction, such double determinisation terms can be always simplified to $\{t\}$ (cf. Lemma 2a). See Example 1 for a formula φ and its corresponding term t_φ. Theorem 1 establishes the correctness of the formula to term translation.

$$\langle\varphi_0\rangle = I_{\varphi_0} \tag{18}$$
$$\langle\varphi \wedge \psi\rangle = \langle\varphi\rangle \& \langle\psi\rangle \tag{19}$$
$$\langle\varphi \vee \psi\rangle = \langle\varphi\rangle + \langle\psi\rangle \tag{20}$$
$$\langle\neg\varphi\rangle = \overline{\langle\varphi\rangle} \tag{21}$$
$$\langle\exists X.\ \varphi\rangle = \{\pi_X(\langle\varphi\rangle)\} - \vec{0}^{\,*} \tag{22}$$

Fig. 5. From formulae to state-terms.

Theorem 1. *Let φ be a WS2S formula. Then $\mathcal{L}(\varphi) = \mathcal{L}(t_\varphi)$.*

The proof of Theorem 1 uses structural induction, which is greatly simplified by Lemma 2, but since Lemma 2 does not (and cannot, as discussed above) cover all used types of terms, the induction step must in some cases still rely on reasoning about the definition of the transition relation on terms.

4   An Efficient Decision Procedure

The development in Sect. 3 already implies a naïve automata term-based satisfiability check. Namely, by Theorem 1, we know that a formula φ is satisfiable iff $\mathcal{L}(\mathcal{A}_{t_\varphi}) \neq \emptyset$. After translating φ into t_φ using rules (18)–(22), we may use the definitions of the transition function and root states of $\mathcal{A}_{t_\varphi} = (Q, \Delta, I, F)$ in Sect. 3 to decide the language emptiness through evaluating the root state test $\mathcal{R}(reach_\Delta(I))$. It is enough to implement the equalities and equivalences (8)–(17) as recursive functions. We will further refer to this algorithm as the *simple recursion*. The evaluation of $reach_\Delta(I)$ induces nested evaluations of the fixpoint (14): the one on the top level of the language emptiness test and another one for every expansion of a derivative sub-term. The termination of these fixpoint computations is guaranteed due to Lemma 1.

Such a naïve implementation is, however, inefficient and has only disadvantages in comparison to the classical decision procedure. In this section, we will discuss how it can be optimized. Besides an essential *memoization* needed to implement the recursion efficiently, we will show that the automata term representation is amenable to optimizations that cannot be used in the classical construction. These are techniques of state space pruning: the fact that the emptiness can be tested on the fly during the automata construction allows one to avoid exploration of state space irrelevant to the test. The pruning is done through the techniques of *lazy evaluation* and *subsumption*. We will also discuss an optimization of the transition function of Sect. 3 through *product flattening*, which is an analogy to standard implementations of automata intersection.

4.1   Memoization

The simple recursion repeats the fixpoint computations that saturate derivative terms from scratch at every call of the transition function or root test. This is easily countered through *memoization*, known, e.g., from compilers of functional languages, which caches results of function calls in order to avoid their re-evaluation. Namely, after saturating a derivative sub-term $t = S - \vec{0}^{*}$ of t_φ for the first time, we simply *replace* t in t_φ by the saturation $t^{s} = reach_{\Delta_{\vec{0}}}(S)$. Since a derivative is a symbolic representation of its saturated version, the replacement does not change the language of t_φ. Using memoization, every fixpoint computation is then carried out once only.

4.2   Lazy Evaluation

The *lazy* variant of the procedure uses *short-circuiting* to optimize connectives $\wedge$ and $\vee$, and *early termination* to optimize fixpoint computation in derivative saturations. Namely, assume that we have a term $t_1 + t_2$ and that we test whether $\mathcal{R}(t_1 + t_2)$. Suppose that we establish that $\mathcal{R}(t_1)$; we can *short circuit* the evaluation and immediately return *true*, completely avoiding touching the potentially complex term t_2 (and analogously for a term of the form $t_1 \,\&\, t_2$ when one branch is *false*).

Furthermore, *early termination* is used to optimize fixpoint computations used to saturate derivatives within tests $\mathcal{R}(S - \vec{0}^{*})$ (obtained from sub-formulae such as $\exists X.\, \psi$). Namely, instead of first unfolding the whole fixpoint into a set $\{t_1, \ldots t_n\}$ and only then testing whether $\mathcal{R}(t_i)$ is true for some t_i, the terms t_i can be tested as soon as they are computed, and the fixpoint computation can be stopped early, immediately when the test succeeds on one of them. Then, instead of replacing the derivative sub-term by its full saturation, we replace it by the partial result $\{t_1, \ldots, t_i\} - \vec{0}^{*}$ for $i \leq n$.

Finishing the evaluation of the fixpoint computation might later be required in order to compute a transition from the derivative. We note that this corresponds to the concept of *continuations* from functional programming, used to represent a paused computation that may be required to continue later.

Example 3. Let us now illustrate the lazy decision procedure on our running example formula $\varphi \equiv \neg\exists X.\ \text{Sing}(X) \wedge X = \{\epsilon\}$ and the corresponding automata term $t_\varphi = \left\{ \overline{\{\pi_X(\{q_0\}\,\&\,\{p_0\})\} - \vec{0}^{\,*}} \right\}$ from Example 1. The task of the procedure is to compute the value of $\mathcal{R}(reach_\Delta(t_\varphi))$, i.e., whether there is a root state reachable from the leaf state $\langle\varphi\rangle$ of $\mathcal{A}_{t_\varphi}$. The fact that φ is ground allows us to slightly simplify the problem because any ground formula ψ is satisfiable iff $\bot \in \mathcal{L}(\psi)$, i.e., iff the leaf state $\langle\psi\rangle$ of $\mathcal{A}_{t_\psi}$ is also a root. It is thus enough to test $\mathcal{R}(\langle\varphi\rangle)$ where $\langle\varphi\rangle = \overline{\{\pi_X(\{q_0\}\,\&\,\{p_0\})\} - \vec{0}^{\,*}}$.

The computation proceeds as follows. First, we use (5) from Fig. 3 to propagate the root test towards the derivative, i.e., to obtain that $\mathcal{R}(\langle\varphi\rangle)$ iff $\neg\mathcal{R}(\{\pi_X(\{q_0\}\,\&\,\{p_0\})\} - \vec{0}^{\,*})$. Since the $\mathcal{R}$-test cannot be directly evaluated on a derivative term, we need to start saturating it into a set term, evaluating $\mathcal{R}$ on the fly, hoping for early termination. We begin with evaluating the $\mathcal{R}$-test on the initial element $t_0 = \pi_X(\{q_0\}\{p_0\})$ of the set. The test propagates through the projection π_X due to (4) and evaluates as *false* on the left conjunct (through, in order, (3), (6), and (7) since the state q_0 is not a root state. As a trivial example of short circuiting, we can skip evaluating $\mathcal{R}$ on the right conjunct $\{p_0\}$ and conclude that $\mathcal{R}(t_0)$ is *false*.

The fixpoint computation then continues with the first iteration, computing the $\vec{0}$-successors of the set $\{t_0\}$. We will obtain $\Delta_{\vec{0}}(t_0, t_0) = \{t_0, t_1\}$ with $t_1 = \pi_X(\{q_1\}\,\&\,\{p_1\})$. The test $\mathcal{R}(t_1)$ now returns *true* because both q_1 and p_1 are root states. With that, the fixpoint computation may terminate early, with the $\mathcal{R}$-test on the derivative subterm returning *true*. Memoization then replaces the derivative sub-term in $\langle\varphi\rangle$ by the partially evaluated version $\{t_0, t_1\} - \vec{0}^{\,*}$, and $\mathcal{R}(\langle\varphi\rangle)$ is evaluated as *false* due to (5). We therefore conclude that φ is unsatisfiable (and invalid since it is ground). $\square$

4.3 Subsumption

The next technique we use is based on pruning out parts of a search space that are *subsumed* by other parts. In particular, we generalize (in a similar way as we did for WS1S in our previous work [29]) the concept used in *antichain* algorithms for efficiently deciding language inclusion and universality of finite word and tree automata [22–25]. Although the problems are in general computationally infeasible (they are PSPACE-complete for finite word automata and EXPTIME-complete for finite tree automata), antichain algorithms can solve them efficiently in many practical cases.

We apply the technique by keeping set terms in the form of antichains of *simulation-maximal* elements and prune out any other simulation-smaller elements. Intuitively, the notion of a term t being simulation-smaller than t' implies that trees that might be generated from the leaf states $T \cup \{t\}$ can be generated from $T \cup \{t'\}$ too, hence discarding t does not hurt. Formally, we introduce the following rewriting rule:

$$\{t_1, t_2, \ldots, t_n\} \rightsquigarrow \{t_2, \ldots, t_n\} \qquad \text{for } t_1 \sqsubseteq t_2, \tag{23}$$

which may be used to simplify set sub-terms of automata terms. The rule (23) is applied after every iteration of the fixpoint computation on the current partial result.

Hence the sequence of partial results is monotone, which, together with the finiteness of $reach_\Delta(t)$, guarantees termination. The *subsumption* relation $\sqsubseteq$ used in the rule is defined in Fig. 6 where $S \sqsubseteq^{\forall\exists} S'$ denotes $\forall t \in S \; \exists t' \in S'. t \sqsubseteq t'$. Intuitively, on base TAs, subsumption corresponds to inclusion of the set terms (the left disjunct of (24). This clearly has the intended outcome: a larger set of states can always simulate a smaller set in accepting a tree. The rest of the definition is an inductive extension of the base case. It can be shown that $\sqsubseteq$ for any automata term t is an upward simulation on $\mathcal{A}_t$ in the sense of [25]. Consequently, rewriting sub-terms in an automata term according to the new rule (23) does not change its language. Moreover, the fixpoint computation interleaved with application of rule (23) terminates.

$$S \sqsubseteq S' \quad \Leftrightarrow S \subseteq S' \vee S \sqsubseteq^{\forall\exists} S' \quad (24)$$

$$t \,\&\, u \sqsubseteq t' \,\&\, u' \Leftrightarrow t \sqsubseteq t' \wedge u \sqsubseteq u' \quad (25)$$

$$t + u \sqsubseteq t' + u' \Leftrightarrow t \sqsubseteq t' \wedge u \sqsubseteq u' \quad (26)$$

$$\overline{t} \sqsubseteq \overline{t'} \quad \Leftrightarrow t' \sqsubseteq t \quad (27)$$

$$\pi_X(t) \sqsubseteq \pi_X(t') \Leftrightarrow t \sqsubseteq t' \quad (28)$$

Fig. 6. The subsumption relation $\sqsubseteq$

4.4 Product Flattening

Product flattening is a technique that we use to reduce the size of fixpoint saturations that generate conjunctions and disjunctions of sets as their elements.Consider a term of the form $D = \{\pi_X(S_0 \,\&\, S_0')\} - \vec{0}^*$ for a pair of sets of terms S_0 and S_0' where the TAs $\mathcal{A}_{S_0}$ and $\mathcal{A}_{S_0'}$ have sets of states Q and Q', respectively.The saturation generates the set $\{\pi_X(S_0 \,\&\, S_0'), \ldots, \pi_X(S_n \,\&\, S_n')\}$ with $S_i \subseteq Q, S_i' \subseteq Q'$ for all $0 \leq i \leq n$. The size of this set is $2^{|Q| \cdot |Q'|}$ in the worst case. In terms of the automata operations, this fixpoint expansion corresponds to first determinizing both $\mathcal{A}_{S_0}$ and $\mathcal{A}_{S_0'}$ and only then using the product construction (cf. Sect. 2). The automata intersection, however, works for nondeterministic automata too—the determinization is not needed. Implementing this standard product construction on terms would mean transforming the original fixpoint above into the following fixpoint with a *flattened product*: $D = \{\pi_X(S [\&] S')\} - \vec{0}^*$ where $[\&]$ is the augmented product for conjunction. This way, we can decrease the worst-case size of the fixpoint to $|Q| \cdot |Q'|$. A similar reasoning holds for terms of the form $\{\pi_X(S_0 + S_0')\} - \vec{0}^*$. Formally, the technique can be implemented by the following pair of sub-term rewriting rules where S and S' are non-empty sets of terms:

$$S + S' \rightsquigarrow S [+] S', \quad (29) \qquad\qquad S \,\&\, S' \rightsquigarrow S [\&] S'. \quad (30)$$

Observe that for terms obtained from WS2S formulae using the translation from Sect. 3, the rules are not really helpful as is. Consider, for instance, the term $\{\pi_X(\{r\} \,\&\, \{q\})\} - \vec{0}^*$ obtained from a formula $\exists X. \varphi \wedge \psi$ with φ and ψ being atoms. The term would be, using rule (30), rewritten into the term $\{\pi_X(\{r \,\&\, q\})\} - \vec{0}^*$. Then, during a subsequent fixpoint computation, we might obtain a fixpoint of the following form: $\{\pi_X(\{r \,\&\, q\}), \pi_X(\{r \,\&\, q, r_1 \,\&\, q_1\}), \pi_X(\{r_1 \,\&\, q_1, r_2 \,\&\, q_2\})\}$, where the occurrences of the projection π_X disallow one to perform the desired union of the inner sets, and so the application of rule (30) did not help. We therefore need to equip our procedure with a rewriting rule that can be used to push the projection inside a set term S:

$$\pi_X(S) \rightsquigarrow \{\pi_X(t) \mid t \in S\}. \tag{31}$$

In the example above, we would now obtain the term $\{\pi_X(r \,\&\, q)\}$ − $\vec{0}^*$ (we rewrote $\{\{\cdot\}\}$ to $\{\cdot\}$ as mentioned in Sect. 3) and the fixpoint $\{\pi_X(r \,\&\, q), \pi_X(r_1 \,\&\, q_1), \pi_X(r_2 \,\&\, q_2)\}$. The correctness of the rules is guaranteed by the following lemma:

Lemma 3. *For sets of terms S, S' s.t. $S \neq \emptyset$, $S' \neq \emptyset$ we have:*

$$\mathcal{L}\left(\{S + S'\}\right) = \mathcal{L}\left(\{S \,[+]\, S'\}\right), \quad (a) \qquad \mathcal{L}(\{\pi_X(S)\}) = \mathcal{L}(\{\pi_X(t) \mid t \in S\}). \quad (c)$$
$$\mathcal{L}\left(\{S \,\&\, S'\}\right) = \mathcal{L}\left(\{S \,[\&]\, S'\}\right), \quad (b)$$

However, we still have to note that there is a danger related with the rules (29)–(31). Namely, if they are applied to some terms in a partially evaluated fixpoint but not to all, the form of these terms might get different (cf. $\pi_X(\{r \,\&\, q\})$ and $\pi_X(r \,\&\, q)$), and it will not be possible to combine them as source states of TA transitions when computing Δ_a, leading thus to an incorrect result. We resolve the situation such that we apply the rules as a pre-processing step only before we start evaluating the top-level fixpoint, which ensures that all terms will subsequently be generated in a compatible form.

5   Experimental Evaluation

We have implemented the above introduced technique in a prototype tool written in Haskell.[3] The base automata, hard-coded into the tool, were the TAs for the basic predicates from Sect. 2, together with automata for predicates $\mathrm{Sing}(X)$ and $X = \{p\}$ for a variable X and a fixed tree position p. As an optimisation, our tool uses the so-called *antiprenexing* (proposed already in [29]), pushing quantifiers down the formula tree using the standard logical equivalences. Intuitively, antiprenexing reduces the complexity of elements within fixpoints by removing irrelevant parts outside the fixpoint.

We have performed experiments with our tool on various formulae and compared its performance with that of MONA. We applied MONA both on the original form of the considered formulae as well as on their versions obtained by antiprenexing (which is built into our tool and which—as we realised—can significantly help MONA too). Our preliminary implementation of product flattening (cf. Sect. 4.4) is restricted to parts below the lowest fixpoint, and our experiments showed that it does not work well when applied on this level, where the complexity is not too high, so we turned it off for the experiments. We ran all experiments on a 64-bit Linux Debian workstation with the Intel(R) Core(TM) i7-2600 CPU running at 3.40 GHz with 16 GiB of RAM. We used a timeout of 100 s.

We first considered various WS2S formulae on which MONA was successfully applied previously in the literature. On them, our tool is quite slower than MONA, which is not much surprising given the amount of optimisations built into MONA (for instance,

---

[3] The implementation is available at https://github.com/vhavlena/lazy-wsks.

Table 1. Experimental results over the family of formulae $\varphi_n^{pt} \equiv \forall Z_1, Z_2.\ \exists X_1,\ldots,X_n.\ edge(Z_1,X_1) \wedge \bigwedge_{i=1}^{n} edge(X_i,X_{i+1}) \wedge edge(X_n,Z_2)$ where $edge(X,Y) \equiv edge_L(X,Y) \vee edge_R(X,Y)$ and $edge_{L/R}(X,Y) \equiv \exists Z.\ Z = S_{L/R}(X) \wedge Z \subseteq Y$.

	Running time (sec)			# of subterms/states		
n	Lazy	Mona	Mona+AP	Lazy	Mona	Mona+AP
1	0.02	0.16	0.15	149	216	216
2	0.50	-	-	937	-	-
3	0.83	-	-	2487	-	-
4	34.95	-	-	8391	-	-
5	60.94	-	-	23827	-	-

for the benchmarks from [5], MONA on average took 0.1 s, while we timeouted).[4] Next, we identified several parametric families of formulae (adapted from [29]), such as, e.g., $\varphi_n^{horn} \equiv \exists X.\ \forall X_1.\ \exists X_2,\ldots X_n.\ ((X_1 \subseteq X \wedge X_1 \neq X_2) \Rightarrow X_2 \subseteq X) \wedge \ldots \wedge ((X_{n-1} \subseteq X \wedge X_{n-1} \neq X_n) \Rightarrow X_n \subseteq X)$, where our approach finished within 10 ms, while the time of MONA was increasing when increasing the parameter n, going up to 32 s for $n = 14$ and timeouting for $k \geq 15$. It turned out that MONA could, however, easily handle these formulae after antiprenexing, again (slightly) outperforming our tool. Finally, we also identified several parametric families of formulae that MONA could handle only very badly or not at all, even with antiprenexing, while our tool can handle them much better. These formulae are mentioned in the captions of Tables 1, 2 and 3, which give detailed results of the experiments.

Table 2. Experimental results over the family of formulae $\varphi_n^{cnst} \equiv \exists X.\ X = \{(LR)^4\} \wedge X = \{(LR)^n\}$.

	Running time (sec)			# of subterms/states		
n	Lazy	Mona	Mona+AP	Lazy	Mona	Mona+AP
80	14.60	40.07	40.05	1146	27913	27913
90	21.03	64.26	64.20	1286	32308	32308
100	28.57	98.42	98.91	1426	36258	36258
110	38.10	-	-	1566	-	-
120	49.82	-	-	1706	-	-

Particularly, Columns 2–4 give the running times (in seconds) of our tool (denoted Lazy), MONA, and MONA with antiprenexing. Columns 5–7 characterize the size of the generated terms and automata. Namely, for our approach, we give the

Table 3. Experiments over the family $\varphi_n^{sub} = \forall X_1,\ldots,X_n\ \exists X.\ \bigwedge_{i=1}^{n-1} X_i \subseteq X \Rightarrow (X_{i+1} = S_L(X) \vee X_{i+1} = S_R(X))$.

	Running time (sec)			# of subterms/states		
n	Lazy	Mona	Mona+AP	Lazy	Mona	Mona+AP
3	0.01	0.00	0.00	140	92	92
4	0.04	34.39	34.47	386	170	170
5	0.24	–	–	981	–	–
6	2.01	–	–	2376	–	–

---

[4] Building an optimised and overall competitive implementation is a subject of our further work. Our results with an implementation of a lazy decision procedure for WS1S from [29] suggest that this is possible.

number of nodes in the final term tree (with the leaves being states of the base TAs). For MONA, we give the sum of the numbers of states of all the minimal deterministic TAs constructed by MONA when evaluating the formula. The "–" sign means a timeout or memory shortage.

The formulae considered in Tables 1, 2 and 3 speak about various paths in trees. We were originally inspired by formulae kindly provided by Josh Berdine, which arose from attempts to translate separation logic formulae to WS2S (and use MONA to discharge them), which are beyond the capabilities of MONA (even with antiprenexing). We were also unable to handle them with our tool, but our experimental results on the tree path formulae indicate (despite the prototypical implementation) that our techniques can help one to handle some complex graph formulae that are out of the capabilities of MONA. Thus, they provide a new line of attack on deciding hard WS2S formulae, complementary to the heuristics used in MONA. Improving the techniques and combining them with the classical approach of MONA is a challenging subject for our future work.

6   Related Work

The seminal works [32,33] on the automata-logic connection were the milestones leading to what we call here the classical tree automata-based decision procedure for WSkS [34]. Its non-elementary worst-case complexity was proved in [35], and the work [2] presents the first implementation, restricted to WS1S, with the ambition to use heuristics to counter the high complexity. The authors of [31] provide an excellent survey of the classical results and literature related to WSkS and tree automata.

The tool MONA [3] implements the classical decision procedures for both WS1S and WS2S. It is still the standard tool of choice for deciding WS1S/WSkS formulae due to its all-around most robust performance. The efficiency of MONA stems from many optimizations, both higher-level (such as automata minimization, the encoding of first-order variables used in models, or the use of multi-terminal BDDs to encode the transition function of the automaton) as well as lower-level (e.g. optimizations of hash tables, etc.) [36,37]. The M2L(Str) logic, a dialect of WS1S, can also be decided by a similar automata-based decision procedure, implemented within, e.g., JMOSEL [38] or the symbolic finite automata framework of [39]. In particular, JMOSEL implements several optimizations (such as second-order value numbering [40]) that allow it to outperform MONA on some benchmarks (MONA also provides an M2L(Str) interface on top of the WS1S decision procedure).

The original inspiration for our work are the antichain techniques for checking universality and inclusion of finite automata [22–25] and language emptiness of alternating automata [22], which use symbolic computation together with subsumption to prune large state spaces arising from subset construction. This paper is a continuation of our work on WS1S, which started by [41], where we discussed a basic idea of generalizing the antichain techniques to a WS1S decision procedure. In [29], we then presented a complete WS1S decision procedure based on these ideas that is capable to rival MONA on already interesting benchmarks. The work in [42] presents a decision procedure that, although phrased differently, is in essence fairly similar to that of [29]. This paper generalizes [29] to WS2S. It is not merely a straightforward generalization of the word concepts to trees. A nontrivial transition was needed from language terms of [29], with their semantics being defined straightforwardly from the semantics of sub-terms, to tree automata terms, with the semantics defined as a language of an automaton with transitions defined inductively to the structure of the term. This change makes the reasoning and correctness proof considerably more complex, though the algorithm itself stays technically quite simple.

Finally, Ganzow and Kaiser [43] developed a new decision procedure for the weak monadic second-order logic on inductive structures within their tool TOSS. Their approach completely avoids automata; instead, it is based on the Shelah's composition method. The paper reports that the TOSS tool could outperform MONA on two families of WS1S formulae, one derived from Presburger arithmetics and one formula of the form that we mention in our experiments as problematic for MONA but solvable easily by MONA with antiprenexing.

Acknowledgement. We thank the anonymous reviewers for their helpful comments on how to improve the exposition in this paper. This work was supported by the Czech Science Foundation project 17-12465S, the FIT BUT internal project FIT-S-17-4014, and The Ministry of Education, Youth and Sports from the National Programme of Sustainability (NPU II) project IT4Innovations excellence in science—LQ1602.

References

1. Møller, A., Schwartzbach, M.: The pointer assertion logic engine. In: PLDI 2001. ACM Press (2001). Also in SIGPLAN Notices **36**(5) (2001)
2. Glenn, J., Gasarch, W.: Implementing WS1S via finite automata. In: Raymond, D., Wood, D., Yu, S. (eds.) WIA 1996. LNCS, vol. 1260, pp. 50–63. Springer, Heidelberg (1997). https://doi.org/10.1007/3-540-63174-7_5
3. Elgaard, J., Klarlund, N., Møller, A.: MONA 1.x: new techniques for WS1S and WS2S. In: Hu, A.J., Vardi, M.Y. (eds.) CAV 1998. LNCS, vol. 1427, pp. 516–520. Springer, Heidelberg (1998). https://doi.org/10.1007/BFb0028773
4. Klarlund, N., Møller, A.: MONA Version 1.4 User Manual. BRICS, Department of Computer Science, Aarhus University, January 2001. Notes Series NS-01-1. http://www.brics.dk/mona/. Revision of BRICS NS-98-3
5. Madhusudan, P., Parlato, G., Qiu, X.: Decidable logics combining heap structures and data. In: POPL 2011, pp. 611–622. ACM (2011)
6. Madhusudan, P., Qiu, X.: Efficient decision procedures for heaps using STRAND. In: Yahav, E. (ed.) SAS 2011. LNCS, vol. 6887, pp. 43–59. Springer, Heidelberg (2011). https://doi.org/10.1007/978-3-642-23702-7_8
7. Chin, W., David, C., Nguyen, H.H., Qin, S.: Automated verification of shape, size and bag properties via user-defined predicates in separation logic. Sci. Comput. Program. **77**(9), 1006–1036 (2012)
8. Zee, K., Kuncak, V., Rinard, M.C.: Full functional verification of linked data structures. In: POPL 2008, 349–361. ACM (2008)
9. Tateishi, T., Pistoia, M., Tripp, O.: Path- and index-sensitive string analysis based on monadic second-order logic. ACM Trans. Comput. Log. **22**(4), 33 (2013)
10. Zhou, M., He, F., Wang, B., Gu, M., Sun, J.: Array theory of bounded elements and its applications. J. Autom. Reasoning **52**(4), 379–405 (2014)
11. Baukus, K., Bensalem, S., Lakhnech, Y., Stahl, K.: Abstracting WS1S systems to verify parameterized networks. In: Graf, S., Schwartzbach, M. (eds.) TACAS 2000. LNCS, vol. 1785, pp. 188–203. Springer, Heidelberg (2000). https://doi.org/10.1007/3-540-46419-0_14

12. Bodeveix, J.-P., Filali, M.: FMona: a tool for expressing validation techniques over infinite state systems. In: Graf, S., Schwartzbach, M. (eds.) TACAS 2000. LNCS, vol. 1785, pp. 204–219. Springer, Heidelberg (2000). https://doi.org/10.1007/3-540-46419-0_15

13. Bozga, M., Iosif, R., Sifakis, J.: Structural invariants for parametric verification of systems with almost linear architectures. Technical report arXiv:1902.02696 (2019)

14. Klarlund, N., Nielsen, M., Sunesen, K.: A case study in verification based on trace abstractions. In: Broy, M., Merz, S., Spies, K. (eds.) Formal Systems Specification. LNCS, vol. 1169, pp. 341–373. Springer, Heidelberg (1996). https://doi.org/10.1007/BFb0024435

15. Smith, M.A., Klarlund, N.: Verification of a sliding window protocol using IOA and MONA. In: Bolognesi, T., Latella, D. (eds.) Formal Methods for Distributed System Development. ITIFIP, vol. 55, pp. 19–34. Springer, Boston, MA (2000). https://doi.org/10.1007/978-0-387-35533-7_2

16. Basin, D., Klarlund, N.: Automata based symbolic reasoning in hardware verification. In: CAV 1998. LNCS, pp. 349–361. Springer (1998)

17. Sandholm, A., Schwartzbach, M.I.: Distributed safety controllers for web services. In: Astesiano, E. (ed.) FASE 1998. LNCS, vol. 1382, pp. 270–284. Springer, Heidelberg (1998). https://doi.org/10.1007/BFb0053596

18. Hune, T., Sandholm, A.: A case study on using automata in control synthesis. In: Maibaum, T. (ed.) FASE 2000. LNCS, vol. 1783, pp. 349–362. Springer, Heidelberg (2000). https://doi.org/10.1007/3-540-46428-X_24

19. Hamza, J., Jobstmann, B., Kuncak, V.: Synthesis for regular specifications over unbounded domains. In: FMCAD 2010, pp. 101–109. IEEE Computer Science (2010)

20. Morawietz, F., Cornell, T.: The MSO logic-automaton connection in linguistics. In: Lecomte, A., Lamarche, F., Perrier, G. (eds.) LACL 1997. LNCS (LNAI), vol. 1582, pp. 112–131. Springer, Heidelberg (1999). https://doi.org/10.1007/3-540-48975-4_6

21. Wies, T., Muñiz, M., Kuncak, V.: An efficient decision procedure for imperative tree data structures. In: Bjørner, N., Sofronie-Stokkermans, V. (eds.) CADE 2011. LNCS (LNAI), vol. 6803, pp. 476–491. Springer, Heidelberg (2011). https://doi.org/10.1007/978-3-642-22438-6_36

22. Doyen, L., Raskin, J.-F.: Antichain algorithms for finite automata. In: Esparza, J., Majumdar, R. (eds.) TACAS 2010. LNCS, vol. 6015, pp. 2–22. Springer, Heidelberg (2010). https://doi.org/10.1007/978-3-642-12002-2_2

23. De Wulf, M., Doyen, L., Henzinger, T.A., Raskin, J.-F.: Antichains: a new algorithm for checking universality of finite automata. In: Ball, T., Jones, R.B. (eds.) CAV 2006. LNCS, vol. 4144, pp. 17–30. Springer, Heidelberg (2006). https://doi.org/10.1007/11817963_5

24. Bouajjani, A., Habermehl, P., Holík, L., Touili, T., Vojnar, T.: Antichain-based universality and inclusion testing over nondeterministic finite tree automata. In: Ibarra, O.H., Ravikumar, B. (eds.) CIAA 2008. LNCS, vol. 5148, pp. 57–67. Springer, Heidelberg (2008). https://doi.org/10.1007/978-3-540-70844-5_7

25. Abdulla, P.A., Chen, Y.-F., Holík, L., Mayr, R., Vojnar, T.: When simulation meets antichains (on checking language inclusion of NFAs). In: Esparza, J., Majumdar, R. (eds.) TACAS 2010. LNCS, vol. 6015, pp. 158–174. Springer, Heidelberg (2010). https://doi.org/10.1007/978-3-642-12002-2_14

26. Habermehl, P., Holík, L., Rogalewicz, A., Šimáček, J., Vojnar, T.: Forest automata for verification of heap manipulation. Formal Methods Syst. Des. 41(1), 83–106 (2012)

27. De Wulf, M., Doyen, L., Maquet, N., Raskin, J.-F.: Antichains: alternative algorithms for LTL satisfiability and model-checking. In: Ramakrishnan, C.R., Rehof, J. (eds.) TACAS 2008. LNCS, vol. 4963, pp. 63–77. Springer, Heidelberg (2008). https://doi.org/10.1007/978-3-540-78800-3_6

28. De Wulf, M., Doyen, L., Raskin, J.-F.: A lattice theory for solving games of imperfect information. In: Hespanha, J.P., Tiwari, A. (eds.) HSCC 2006. LNCS, vol. 3927, pp. 153–168. Springer, Heidelberg (2006). https://doi.org/10.1007/11730637_14

29. Fiedor, T., Holík, L., Janků, P., Lengál, O., Vojnar, T.: Lazy automata techniques for WS1S. In: Legay, A., Margaria, T. (eds.) TACAS 2017. LNCS, vol. 10205, pp. 407–425. Springer, Heidelberg (2017). https://doi.org/10.1007/978-3-662-54577-5_24

30. Havlena, V., Holík, L., Lengál, O., Vojnar, T.: Automata terms in a lazy WSkS decision procedure (technical report). Technical report arXiv:1905.08697 (2019)

31. Comon, H., et al.: Tree automata techniques and applications (2008)

32. Büchi, J.R.: On a decision method in restricted second-order arithmetic. In: International Congress on Logic, Methodology, and Philosophy of Science, pp. 1–11. Stanford University Press (1962)

33. Rabin, M.O.: Decidability of second order theories and automata on infinite trees. Trans. Am. Math. Soc. **141**, 1–35 (1969)

34. Thatcher, J.W., Wright, J.B.: Generalized finite automata theory with an application to a decision problem of second-order logic. Math. Syst. Theory **2**(1), 57–81 (1968)

35. Stockmeyer, L.J., Meyer, A.R.: Word problems requiring exponential time (preliminary report). In: Fifth Annual ACM Symposium on Theory of Computing, STOC 1973, pp. 1–9. ACM, New York (1973)

36. Klarlund, N., Møller, A., Schwartzbach, M.I.: MONA implementation secrets. Int. J. Found. Comput. Sci. **13**(4), 571–586 (2002)

37. Klarlund, N.: A theory of restrictions for logics and automata. In: Halbwachs, N., Peled, D. (eds.) CAV 1999. LNCS, vol. 1633, pp. 406–417. Springer, Heidelberg (1999). https://doi.org/10.1007/3-540-48683-6_35

38. Topnik, C., Wilhelm, E., Margaria, T., Steffen, B.: jMosel: a stand-alone tool and jABC plugin for M2L(Str). In: Valmari, A. (ed.) SPIN 2006. LNCS, vol. 3925, pp. 293–298. Springer, Heidelberg (2006). https://doi.org/10.1007/11691617_18

39. D'Antoni, L., Veanes, M.: Minimization of symbolic automata. In: POPL 2014, pp. 541–554 (2014)

40. Margaria, T., Steffen, B., Topnik, C.: Second-order value numbering. In: GraMoT 2010. Volume 30 of ECEASST, pp. 1–15. EASST (2010)

41. Fiedor, T., Holík, L., Lengál, O., Vojnar, T.: Nested antichains for WS1S. In: Baier, C., Tinelli, C. (eds.) TACAS 2015. LNCS, vol. 9035, pp. 658–674. Springer, Heidelberg (2015). https://doi.org/10.1007/978-3-662-46681-0_59

42. Traytel, D.: A coalgebraic decision procedure for WS1S. In: 24th EACSL Annual Conference on Computer Science Logic (CSL 2015). Volume 41 of Leibniz International Proceedings in Informatics (LIPIcs), pp. 487–503. Schloss Dagstuhl-Leibniz-Zentrum fuer Informatik, Dagstuhl, Germany (2015)

43. Ganzow, T., Kaiser, L.: New algorithm for weak monadic second-order logic on inductive structures. In: Dawar, A., Veith, H. (eds.) CSL 2010. LNCS, vol. 6247, pp. 366–380. Springer, Heidelberg (2010). https://doi.org/10.1007/978-3-642-15205-4_29

Confluence by Critical Pair Analysis Revisited

Nao Hirokawa[1]($\boxtimes$)(iD), Julian Nagele[2](iD), Vincent van Oostrom[3](iD),
and Michio Oyamaguchi[4]

[1] JAIST, Nomi, Japan
hirokawa@jaist.ac.jp
[2] Queen Mary University of London, London, UK
j.nagele@qmul.ac.uk
[3] University of Innsbruck, Innsbruck, Austria
Vincent.van-Oostrom@uibk.ac.at
[4] Nagoya University, Nagoya, Japan
oyamaguchi@za.ztv.ne.jp

Abstract. We present two methods for proving confluence of left-linear term rewrite systems. One is *hot-decreasingness*, combining the parallel/development closedness theorems with rule labelling based on a terminating subsystem. The other is *critical-pair-closing system*, allowing to boil down the confluence problem to confluence of a special subsystem whose duplicating rules are relatively terminating.

Keywords: Term rewriting · Confluence · Decreasing diagrams

1 Introduction

We present two results for proving confluence of first-order left-linear term rewrite systems, which extend and generalise three classical results: Knuth and Bendix' criterion [19] and strong and parallel closedness due to Huet [17]. Our idea is to reduce confluence of a term rewrite system $\mathcal{R}$ to that of a subsystem $\mathcal{C}$ comprising rewrite rules needed for *closing* the critical pairs of $\mathcal{R}$. In Sect. 3 we introduce *hot-decreasingness*, requiring that critical pairs can be closed using rules that are either below those in the peak or in a terminating subsystem $\mathcal{C}$. In Sect. 4 we introduce the notion of a *critical-pair-closing system* and present a confluence-preservation result based on relative termination $\mathcal{C}_d/\mathcal{R}$ of the duplicating part $\mathcal{C}_d$ of $\mathcal{C}$. For the left-linear systems we consider, our first criterion generalises both Huet's parallel closedness and Knuth and Bendix' criterion, and the second Huet's strong closedness. In Sect. 5, we assess viability of the new techniques, reporting on their implementation and empirical results.

Huet's parallel closedness result relies on the notion of overlap whose geometric intuition is subtle [1, 24], and reasoning becomes intricate for development

Supported by JSPS KAKENHI Grant Number 17K00011 and Core to Core Program.

P. Fontaine (Ed.): CADE 2019, LNAI 11716, pp. 319–336, 2019.
https://doi.org/10.1007/978-3-030-29436-6_19

closedness as covered by Theorem 2. We factor the classical theory of overlaps and critical pairs through the *encompassment* lattice in which overlapping redex-patterns *is* taking their join and the amount of overlap between redex-patterns is computed *via* their meet, thus allowing to reason algebraically about overlaps. Methodologically, our contribution here is the introduction of the lattice-theoretic language itself, relevant as it allows one to reason about occurrences of patterns[1] and their amount of (non-)overlap, omnipresent in deduction. Technically, whereas Huet's critical pair lemma [17] is well-suited for proving confluence of *terminating* TRSs, it is ill-suited to do so for *orthogonal* TRSs. Our lattice-theoretic results remedy this, allowing to decompose a reduction R both *horizontally* (as $R_1 \cdot R_2$) and *vertically* (as $R_1^{[x:=R_2]}$), enabling both termination and orthogonality reasoning in confluence proofs (Theorem 2).

In the last decade various classical confluence results for *term* rewrite systems have been factored through the decreasing diagrams method [28,30] for proving confluence of *abstract* rewrite systems, often leading to generalisations along the way: e.g. Felgenhauer's multistep labelling [13] generalises Okui's simultaneous closedness [27], the layer framework [12] generalises Toyama's modularity [33], critical pair systems [16] generalise both orthogonality [31] and Knuth and Bendix' criterion [19], and Jouannaud and Liu generalise, among others [20], parallel closedness, but in a way we do not know how to generalise to development closedness [29]. This paper fits into this line of research.[2]

We assume the reader is familiar with term rewriting [1,9,32] in general and confluence methods [17,19,30] in particular. Notions not explicitly defined in this paper can all be found in those works.

2   Preliminaries on Decreasingness and Encompassment

We recall the key ingredients of the decreasing diagrams method for proving confluence, see [20,26,30,32], and revisit the classical notion of critical pair, recasting its traditional account [1,17,19] based on redexes (substitution instances of left-hand sides) into one based on redex-patterns (left-hand sides).

Decreasingness. Consider an ARS comprising an I-indexed relation $\rightarrow = \bigcup_{\ell \in I} \rightarrow_\ell$ equipped with a well-founded strict order $\succ$. We refer to $\{\kappa \in I \mid \ell \succ \kappa\}$ by $\curlyvee\ell$, and to $\curlyvee\ell \cup \curlyvee\kappa$ by $\curlyvee\ell, \kappa$. For a subset J of I we define $\rightarrow_J$ as $\bigcup_{\ell \in J} \rightarrow_\ell$.

Definition 1. *A diagram for a peak $b \,_\ell\!\leftarrow a \rightarrow_\kappa c$ is decreasing if its closing conversion has shape $b \leftrightarrow^*_{\curlyvee\ell} \cdot \rightarrow^=_\kappa \cdot \leftrightarrow^*_{\curlyvee\ell,\kappa} \cdot \,^=_\ell\!\leftarrow \cdot \leftrightarrow^*_{\curlyvee\kappa} c$. An ARS in this setting is called decreasing if every peak can be completed into a decreasing diagram.*

One may think of decreasing diagrams as combining the diamond property [25, Theorem 1] (via the steps in the closing conversion with labels ℓ, κ) at the basis

---

[1] Modelled in various ways, via e.g.: tree homomorphisms (tree automata [7]), term-operations (algebra), context-variables, labelling (rippling [5]), to name a few.

[2] For space reasons we have omitted the proof by decreasing diagrams of Theorem 3.

of confluence of *orthogonal* systems [6,31], with local confluence diagrams [25, Theorem 3] (via the conversions with labels $\curlyvee \ell, \kappa$) at the basis of confluence of *terminating* systems [19,21].

Theorem 1 ([28,30]). *An ARS is confluent if it is decreasing. Conversely, every countable ARS that is confluent, is decreasing for some set of indices I.*

For the converse part it suffices that the set of *labels* I is a doubleton, a result that can be reformulated without referring to decreasing diagrams, as follows.

Lemma 1 ([11]). *A countable confluent rewrite relation has a spanning forest.*

Here a spanning forest for $\to$ is a relation $\rightarrowtail \subseteq \to$ that is *spanning* ($\leftarrowtail\rightarrowtail^* = \leftrightarrow^*$) and a *forest*, i.e. deterministic ($b \leftarrowtail a \rightarrowtail c$ implies $b = c$) and acyclic.

Critical Peaks Revisited. We introduce *clusters* as the structures obtained *after* the matching of the left-hand side of a rule in a rewrite step, but *before* its replacement by the right-hand side. When proving the aforementioned results in Sects. 3 and 4, we use them as a tool to analyse overlaps and critical peaks. To illustrate our notions we use the following running example. We refer to [16,32] for the notion of multistep.

Example 1. In the TRS $\mathcal{R}$ with $\varrho(x): f(f(x)) \to g(x)$ the term $t = f(f(f(f(a))))$ allows the step $f(\varrho(f(a))): t \to f(g(f(a)))$ and multistep $\varrho(\varrho(a)): t \multimap g(g(a))$.

Here $f(\varrho(f(a)))$ and $\varrho(\varrho(a))$ are so-called proofterms, *terms* representing *proofs* of rewritability in rewriting logic [22,32]. The source of a proofterm can be computed by the 2nd-order substitution src of the left-hand side of the rule for the rule symbol[3] $f(\varrho(f(a)))^{\text{src}} = f(\varrho(f(a)))^{[\![\varrho:=\lambda x.f(f(x))]\!]} = f(f(f(f(a))))$, and, *mutatis mutandis*, the same for the target via tgt. Proofclusters, introduced here, abstract from such proofterms by allowing to represent the matching and substitution phases of multisteps as well, by means of let-expressions.

Example 2. The multistep in Example 1 comprises three phases [28, Chapter 4]:

1. let $X, Y = \lambda x.f(f(x)), \lambda y.f(f(y))$ in $X(Y(a))$ denotes *matching* $f(f(x))$ twice;
2. let $X, Y = \lambda x.\varrho(x), \lambda x.\varrho(x)$ in $X(Y(a))$ denotes *replacing* by ϱ twice;
3. let $X, Y = \lambda x.g(x), \lambda x.g(x)$ in $X(Y(a))$ denotes *substituting* $g(x)$ twice.

To represent these we assume to have *proofterms* $t, s, u, \ldots$ over a signature comprising *function* symbols $f, g, h, \ldots$, *rule* symbols $\varrho, \theta, \eta, \ldots$, 2nd-order variables $X, Y, Z, \ldots$, all having natural number arities, and 1st-order variables $x, y, z, \ldots$ (with arity 0).We call proofterms without 2nd-order variables or rule symbols, 1*st-order* proofterms respectively *terms*, ranged over by $M, N, L, \ldots$.

---

[3] src can be viewed as tree homomorphism [7], or as a term algebra $\varrho^{\mathcal{L}\hbar\delta}(t) = \ell^{[x:=t]}$.

Definition 2. *A* proofcluster *is a let-expression* $\text{let } \boldsymbol{X} = \boldsymbol{Q} \text{ in } t$, *where*

- $\boldsymbol{X}$ *is a vector* $X_1, \ldots, X_n$ *of (pairwise distinct) second-order variables;*
- $\boldsymbol{Q}$ *is a vector of length* n *of closed* λ*-terms* $Q_i = \lambda \boldsymbol{x}_i.s_i$, *where* s_i *is a proofterm and the length of the vector* $\boldsymbol{x}_i$ *of variables is the arity of* X_i; *and*
- t *is a proofterm, the* body*, with its 2nd-order variables among* $\boldsymbol{X}$.

Its denotation $[\![\text{let } \boldsymbol{X} = \boldsymbol{Q} \text{ in } t]\!]$ *is* $t^{[\![\boldsymbol{X} := \boldsymbol{Q}]\!]}$. *It is a* cluster *if* $s_1, \ldots, s_n, t$ *are terms.*

We let $\varsigma, \zeta, \xi, \ldots$ range over (proof)clusters. They denote (proof)terms.

Example 3. Using ς, ζ, ξ for the three let-expressions in Example 2, each is a proofcluster and ς, ξ are clusters. Their denotations are the term $[\![\varsigma]\!] = f(f(f(f(a)))) = t$, proofterm $[\![\zeta]\!] = \varrho(\varrho(a))$, and term $[\![\xi]\!] = g(g(a))$.

We assume the usual variable renaming conventions, both for the 2nd-order ones in let-binders and the 1st-order ones in λ-abstractions. We say a proofcluster ς is *linear* if every (let or λ) binding binds exactly once, and *canonical* [23] if, when a binding variable occurs to the left of another such (of the same type), then the first bound occurrence of the former occurs before that of the latter in the pre-order walk of the relevant proofterm.

Example 4. Let ζ' and ξ' be the clusters $\text{let } X = \lambda x.f(f(x)) \text{ in } X(X(a))$ and $\text{let } X, Y = \lambda yz.f(f(y)), \lambda x.f(f(x)) \text{ in } Y(X(a, f(a)))$. Each of ς, ζ', ξ' denotes t in Example 1. The cluster ς is linear and canonical, ζ' is canonical but not linear (X occurs twice in the body), and ξ' is neither linear (z does not occur in $f(y)$) nor canonical (Y occurs outside of X in the body).

We adopt the convention that absent λ-binders are inserted linearly, canonically; $\text{let } X = f(f(x)) \text{ in } X(X(a))$ is ζ'. Clusters witness encompassment $\trianglerighteq$ [9].

Proposition 1. $t \trianglerighteq s$ *iff* $\exists u, X$ *s.t.* $[\![\text{let } X = s \text{ in } u]\!] = t$ *and* X *occurs once in* u.

We define the *size* $\|t\|$ of a proofterm t in a way that is compatible with encompassment. Formally, $\|t\|$ is the pair comprising the number of non-1st-order-variable symbols in t, and the sum over the 1st-order variables x, of the *square* of the number of occurrences of x in t. Then $\|t\| > \|s\|$ if $t \triangleright s$, where we (ab)use $>$ to denote the lexicographic product of the greater-than relation with itself, e.g. $\|g(a,a)\| = (3,0) > \|g(x,x)\| = (1,4) > \|g(x,y)\| = (1,2)$. For a proofcluster ς given by $\text{let } \boldsymbol{x} = \boldsymbol{s} \text{ in } t$ its *pattern*-size $[\![\varsigma]\!]$ is $\sum_i \|s_i\|$ (adding component-wise, with empty sum $(0,0)$) and its *body*-size $\|\varsigma\|$ is $\|t\|$. Encompassment $\trianglerighteq$ is at the basis of the theory of reducibility [7, Section 3.4.2]: t is reducible by a rule $\ell \to r$ iff $t \trianglerighteq \ell$. For instance, $\text{let } X = f(f(x)) \text{ in } f(X(f(a)))$ is a witness to reducibility of t in Example 1. We call it, or simply $f(f(x))$, a *pattern* in t.

Definition 3. *Let* ς *be a canonical linear proofcluster* $\text{let } \boldsymbol{X} = \boldsymbol{s} \text{ in } t$ *with term* t. *We say* ς *is a* multipattern *if each* s_i *is a non-variable 1st-order term, and* ς *is a* multistep *if each* s_i *has shape* $\varrho(\boldsymbol{x})$, *i.e. a rule symbol applied to a sequence of pairwise distinct variables. If* $\boldsymbol{X}$ *has length* 1 *we drop the prefix 'multi'.*

We use $\Phi, \Psi, \Omega, \ldots$ to range over multisteps, and $\phi, \psi, \omega, \ldots$ to range over steps. Taking their denotation yields the usual multistep [16,32] and step ARSs $\multimap\!\!\rightarrow$ and $\rightarrow$ underlying a TRS $\mathcal{R}$. These can be alternatively obtained by first applying src and tgt (of which only the former is guaranteed to yield a multipattern, by left-linearity) and then taking denotations: $[\![\Phi^{\mathsf{src}}]\!] = [\![\Phi]\!]^{\mathsf{src}}$ and $[\![\Phi^{\mathsf{tgt}}]\!] = [\![\Phi]\!]^{\mathsf{tgt}}$. Pattern- and body-sizes of multipatterns are compositional.

Proposition 2. *For multipatterns ς, ς if $\varsigma = \varsigma_0^{[x := \varsigma]}$ with each variable among x occurring once in the body of ς_0, then $[\![\varsigma]\!] = \sum_i \varsigma_i$, and $\|\varsigma\| \geqslant \|\varsigma_i\|$ for all i, with strict inequality holding in case the substitution is not a bijective renaming. Here multipattern-substitution substitutes in the body and combines let-bindings.*

Multipatterns are ordered by refinement $\sqsubseteq$.

Definition 4. *Let ς and ζ be multipatterns let $X = s$ in t and let $Y = u$ in w. We say ς refines ζ and write $\varsigma \sqsubseteq \zeta$, if there is a 2nd-order substitution σ on Y with $w^\sigma = t$ and $[\![$let $X = s$ in $Y_i(y_i)^\sigma]\!] = u_i$ for all i, with y_i the variables of u_i.*

Example 5. We have $\varsigma \sqsubseteq \varsigma'$ with ς' being let $Z = f(f(f(f(z))))$ in $Z(a)$, and ς as in Example 3, as witnessed by the 2nd-order substitution mapping Z to $\lambda x. X(Y(x))$.

Lemma 2. *$\sqsubseteq$ is a finite distributive lattice [8] on multipatterns denoting a 1st-order term t, with least element $\bot$ the empty let-expression let $=$ in t, and greatest element $\top$ of shape let $X = t'$ in $X(x)$ with x the vector of variables in t.*

Proof (Idea). Although showing that $\sqsubseteq$ is reflexive and transitive is easy, showing anti-symmetry or existence of/constructions for meets $\sqcap$ and joins $\sqcup$, directly is not. Instead, it *is* easy to see that each multipattern let $X = s$ in t is determined by the set of the (non-empty, convex,[4] pairwise disjoint) sets of node positions of its patterns s_i in t, and vice versa. For instance, the multipatterns ς and ς' in Example 5 are determined by $\{\{\varepsilon, 1\}, \{1 \cdot 1, 1 \cdot 1 \cdot 1\}\}$ and $\{\{\varepsilon, 1, 1 \cdot 1, 1 \cdot 1 \cdot 1\}\}$. Viewing multipatterns as sets in that way $\varsigma \sqsubseteq \zeta$ iff $\forall P \subset \varsigma, \exists Q \subset \zeta$ with $P \subseteq Q$. Saying $P, Q \in \varsigma \cup \zeta$ have *overlap* if $P \cap Q \neq \emptyset$, denoted by $P \between Q$, characterising meets and joins now also is easy: $\varsigma \sqcap \zeta = \{P \cap Q \mid P \in \varsigma, Q \in \zeta, \text{and } P \between Q\}$, and $\varsigma \sqcup \zeta = \{\bigcup P_\between \mid P \in \varsigma \cup \zeta\}$, where $P_\between = \{Q \in \varsigma \cup \zeta \mid P \between^* Q\}$, i.e. the sets connected to P by successive overlaps. On this set-representation $\sqsubseteq$ can be shown to be a finite distributive lattice by set-theoretic reasoning, using that the intersection of two overlapping patterns is a pattern again[5]. For instance, $\bot$ *is* the empty set and $\top$ *is* the singleton containing the set of all non-variable positions in t. $\square$

The (proof of the) lemma allows to freely switch between viewing multisteps and multipatterns as let-expressions and as sets of sets of positions, and to reason about (non-)overlap of multipatterns and multisteps in lattice-theoretic terms.

---

[4]   Here convex means that for each pair of positions p, q in the set, all positions on the shortest path from p to q in the term tree are also in the set, cf. [32, Definition 8.6.21].

[5]   This fails for, e.g., connected graphs; these may fall apart into non-connected ones.

We show any multistep Φ can be decomposed *horizontally* as ϕ followed by Φ/ϕ for any step $\phi \in \Phi$ [16,29], and *vertically* as some vector $\boldsymbol{\Phi}$ substituted in a prefix Φ_0 of Φ, and that peaks can be decomposed correspondingly.

Definition 5. *For a pair of multipatterns ς, ζ denoting the same term its amount of overlap[6] and non-overlap is $\varsigma \sqcap \zeta = [\![\varsigma \sqcap \zeta]\!]$ respectively $\varsigma \sqcup \zeta = [\![\varsigma \sqcup \zeta]\!]$, we say ς, ζ is overlapping if $\varsigma \sqcap \zeta \neq \bot$, and critically overlapping if moreover $\varsigma \sqcup \zeta = \top$ and $[\![\varsigma]\!] = [\![\zeta]\!]$ is linear. This extends to peaks $s \xleftarrow{\phi}\!\!\circ\!\!- t -\!\!\circ\!\!\rightarrow_\psi u$ via Φ^{src} and Ψ^{src}.*

Note ς, ζ is overlapping iff $\varsigma \sqcap \zeta \neq (0,0)$. Critical peaks $s \xleftarrow{\phi} t \rightarrow_\psi u$ are classified by comparing the root-positions p_ϕ, p_ψ of their patterns with respect to the prefix order $\prec_o$, into being *outer–inner* ($p_\phi \prec_o p_\psi$), *inner–outer* ($p_\psi \prec_o p_\phi$), or *overlay* ($p_\psi = p_\phi$), and induce the usual [1,9,17,19,26,32] notion of critical *pair* (s,u).[7]

Definition 6. *A pair (ς', ζ') of overlapping patterns such that ς', ζ' are in the multipatterns ς, ζ with $\top = \varsigma \sqcup \zeta$, is called* inner, *if it is minimal among all such pairs, comparing them in the lexicographic product of $\prec_o$ with itself, via the root-positions of their patterns, ordering these themselves first by $\preceq_o$. This extends to pairs of steps in peaks of multisteps via* src.

Proposition 3. *If (ϕ, ψ) is an inner pair for a critical peak $\circ\!\!-\!\!\circ \cdot -\!\!\circ\!\!\rightarrow_\psi$, and $\phi \in \Phi$, $\psi \in \Psi$ contract redexes at the same position, then $\phi = \Phi$ and $\psi = \Psi$.*

For patterns and peaks of ordinary steps, their join being top, entails they are overlapping, and the patterns in a join are joins of their constituent patterns.

Proposition 4. *Linear patterns ς, ζ are critically overlapping iff $\varsigma \sqcup \zeta = \top$.*

Lemma 3. *If $\xi = \varsigma \sqcup \zeta$ and $\varsigma, \zeta \sqsubseteq \xi$ are witnessed by the 2nd-order substitutions σ, τ, for multipatterns ς and ζ given by* let $X = t$ in M *and* let $Y = s$ in N, *then for all let-bindings $Z = u$ of ξ, $\top_u = ($let $X = t$ in $Z(z)^\sigma) \sqcup ($let $Y = s$ in $Z(z)^\tau)$.*

Lemma 4 (Vertical). *A peak $s \xleftarrow{\Phi}\!\!\circ\!\!- t -\!\!\circ\!\!\rightarrow_\Psi u$ of overlapping multisteps either is critical or it can be vertically decomposed as:*

$$s_0^{[x:=s]} \xleftarrow{\Phi_0^{[x:=\Phi]}}\!\!\circ\!\!- t_0^{[x:=t]} -\!\!\circ\!\!\rightarrow_{\Psi_0^{[x:=\Psi]}} u_0^{[x:=u]}$$

for peaks $s_i \xleftarrow{\Phi_i}\!\!\circ\!\!- t_i -\!\!\circ\!\!\rightarrow_{\Psi_i} u_i$ with $\Phi \sqcap \Psi \geqslant \Phi_i \sqcap \Psi_i$ and $\Phi \sqcup \Psi > \Phi_i \sqcup \Psi_i$, for all i.

Let Φ, Ψ in $s \xleftarrow{\Phi}\!\!\circ\!\!- t -\!\!\circ\!\!\rightarrow_\Psi u$ be given by let $X = \varrho(x)$ in M and let $Y = \theta(y)$ in N, for rules $\varrho_i(x_i) : \ell_i \to r_i$ and $\theta_j(y_j) : g_j \to d_j$. Lemma 2 entails that if Φ, Ψ are non-overlapping their patterns are (pairwise) disjoint, so that the join $\Phi^{\mathsf{src}} \sqcup \Psi^{\mathsf{src}}$ is given by taking the (disjoint) union of the let-bindings: let $XY = \ell g$ in L for some L such that $L^{[Y:=g]} = M$ and $L^{[X:=\ell]} = N$. We define the *join*[8] $\Phi \sqcup \Psi$ and

---

[6] For the amount of overlap for *redexes* in parallel reduction $-\!\!\twoheadrightarrow$, see e.g. [1,17,24].

[7] We exclude neither overlays of a rule with itself nor pairs obtained by symmetry.

[8] This does not create ambiguity with joins of multipatterns since if $\Phi \neq \Psi$, then $[\![\Phi]\!] \neq [\![\Psi]\!]$ unless the let-bindings of both are empty, so both are bottom.

residual Φ/Ψ by let $XY = \varrho(x)\theta(y)$ in L respectively let $X = \varrho(x)$ in $L^{[\![Y:=d]\!]}$, where, as substituting the right-hand sides d may lose being linear and canonical, we implicitly canonise and linearise the latter by reordering and replicating let-bindings. Then $t \ \text{-}\!\circ\!\!\to_{\Phi\sqcup\Psi} \cdot \ _{\Phi/\Psi}\!\!\leftarrow\!\circ\text{-}\ u$, giving rise to the classical residual theory [2, 4,6,18], see [32, Section 8.7]. We let $\phi \in \Phi$ abbreviate $\exists\Psi.\Phi = \phi \sqcup \Psi$.

Example 6. The steps ϕ and ψ given by let $X = \lambda x.\varrho(x)$ in $X(f(f(a)))$ respectively let $X = \lambda x.\varrho(x)$ in $f(f(Y(a)))$, are non-overlapping, $\phi, \psi \in \zeta$, $\phi \sqcup \psi = \zeta$, and $f(f(g(a))) \ \text{-}\!\circ\!\!\to_{\phi/\psi}\ g(g(a))$, for ζ and ϱ as in Example 3.

Lemma 5 (Horizontal). *A peak $t \ _{\Phi}\!\!\leftarrow\!\circ\text{-} \cdot \ \text{-}\!\circ\!\!\to_{\Psi}\ s$ of multisteps either*

1. *is non-overlapping and then $t \ \text{-}\!\circ\!\!\to_{\Psi/\Phi} \cdot \ _{\Phi/\Psi}\!\!\leftarrow\!\circ\text{-}\ s$, with the rule symbols occurring in Ψ/Φ contained in Ψ (and those in Φ/Ψ contained in Φ); or*
2. *it can be horizontally decomposed: $t \ _{\Phi/\phi}\!\!\leftarrow\!\circ\text{-} \cdot \ _{\phi}\!\!\leftarrow \cdot \rightarrow_{\psi} \cdot \ \text{-}\!\circ\!\!\to_{\Psi/\psi}\ s$ for some peak $_{\phi}\!\!\leftarrow \cdot \rightarrow_{\psi}$ of overlapping steps $\phi \in \Phi$ and $\psi \in \Psi$.*

The above allows to refactor the proof of the critical pair lemma [17, Lemma 3.1] for left-linear TRSs, as an induction on the amount of *non-overlap* between the steps in the peak, such that the critical peaks form the *base* case:

Lemma 6. *A left-linear TRS is locally confluent if all critical pairs are joinable.*

Proof. We show every peak $_{\phi}^{=}\!\!\leftarrow \cdot \rightarrow_{\psi}^{=}$ of empty or single steps is joinable, by induction on the amount of non-overlap ($\phi \uplus \psi$) ordered by $>$. We distinguish cases on whether ϕ, ψ are overlapping ($\phi \sqcap \psi \neq (0,0)$) or not. If ϕ, ψ do not have overlap, in particular when either ϕ or ψ is empty, then we conclude by Lemma 5(1). If ϕ, ψ do have overlap, then by Lemma 4 the peak either

- is critical and we conclude by assumption; or
- can be (vertically) *decomposed* into smaller such peaks $_{\phi_i}^{=}\!\!\leftarrow \cdot \rightarrow_{\psi_i}^{=}$. Since these are $>$-smaller, the induction hypothesis yields them joinable, from which we conclude by reductions and joins being closed under *composition*.   □

Remark 1. Apart from enabling our proof of Theorem 2 below, we think this refactoring is methodologically interesting, as it extends to (parallel and) simultaneous critical pairs, then yielding, we claim, simple statements and proofs of confluence results [13,27] based on these and their higher-order generalisations.

3   Confluence by Hot-Decreasingness

Linear TRSs have a critical-pair criterion for so-called rule-labelling [16,30,35]: If all critical peaks are decreasing with respect to some rule-labelling, then the TRS is decreasing, hence confluent. We introduce the hot-labelling extending that result to left-linear TRSs. To deal with non-right-linear rules we make use of a rule-labelling for multisteps that is invariant under duplication, cf. [13,35].

Remark 2. Naïve extensions fail. Non-left-linear TRSs need not be confluent even without critical pairs [32, Exercise 2.7.20]. That non-right-linear TRSs need not be confluent even if all critical peaks are decreasing for rule-labelling, is witnessed by [16, Example 8].

Definition 7. *For a TRS $\mathcal{R}$, terminating subsystem $\mathcal{C} \subseteq \mathcal{R}$, and labelling of $\mathcal{R} - \mathcal{C}$-rules into a well-founded order $\succ$, hot-labelling $\overset{\circ}{\mathcal{L}}$ maps a multistep Φ:*
$$t \overset{\circ}{\longrightarrow}_{\mathcal{R}} s$$

– to the term *t if Φ contains $\mathcal{C}$-rules only; and*
– to the set of $\succ$-maximal $\mathcal{R} - \mathcal{C}$-rules in Φ otherwise.

The hot-order *$\overset{\circ}{\succ}$ relates terms by $\to_{\mathcal{C}}^{+}$, sets by $\succ_{\mathsf{mul}}$, and all sets to all terms.*

Note $\overset{\circ}{\succ}$ is a well-founded order as series composition [3] of $\to_{\mathcal{C}}^{+}$ and $\succ_{\mathsf{mul}}$, which are well-founded orders by the assumptions on $\mathcal{C}$ and $\succ$. Taking the *set* of maximal rules in a multistep makes hot-labelling invariant under duplication. As with the notation $\curlyvee \ell$, we denote $\{\kappa \mid \ell \overset{\circ}{\succ} \kappa\}$ by $\overset{\circ}{\curlyvee}\ell$, and $\{\kappa \mid \ell \overset{\circ}{\succeq} \kappa\}$ by $\overset{\circ}{\curlyvee}\ell$.

Definition 8. *A TRS $\mathcal{R}$ is hot-decreasing if its critical peaks are decreasing for the hot-labelling, for some $\mathcal{C}$ and $\succ$, such that each outer–inner critical peak $\ell \leftarrow \cdot \to$ for label ℓ, is decreasing by a conversion of shape (oi): $\leftrightarrow_{\overset{\circ}{\curlyvee}\ell}^{*} \cdot \overset{\circ}{\curlyvee}\ell \leftarrow\!\circ\!\!-$.*

Theorem 2. *A left-linear TRS is confluent, if it is hot-decreasing.*

Before proving Theorem 2, we give (non-)examples and special cases.

Example 7. Consider the left-linear TRS $\mathcal{R}$:

$\varrho_1: nats \to 0 : inc(nats)$ $\varrho_3:$ $inc(x : y) \to s(x) : inc(y)$ $\varrho_5: hd(x : y) \to x$
$\varrho_2: d(x) \to x : (x : d(x))$ $\varrho_4: inc(tl(nats)) \to tl(inc(nats))$ $\varrho_6:$ $tl(x : y) \to y$

By taking $\mathcal{C} = \emptyset$, labelling rules by themselves, and ordering $\varrho_4 \succ \varrho_1, \varrho_3, \varrho_6$ the only critical peak $_{\{\varrho_4\}}\leftarrow \cdot \to_{\{\varrho_1\}}$ can be completed into the decreasing diagram:

$$
\begin{array}{ccccc}
tl(inc(nats)) & \xleftarrow{\quad\{\varrho_4\}\quad} & inc(tl(nats)) & \xrightarrow{\quad\{\varrho_1\}\quad} & inc(tl(0 : inc(nats))) \\
{\scriptstyle\{\varrho_1\}}\downarrow & & & & \downarrow{\scriptstyle\{\varrho_6\}} \\
tl(inc(0 : inc(nats))) & \xrightarrow[\{\varrho_3\}]{} & tl(s(0) : inc(inc(nats))) & \xrightarrow[\{\varrho_6\}]{} & inc(inc(nats))
\end{array}
$$

Since the peak is outer–inner, the closing conversion must be of (oi)-shape $\leftrightarrow_{\overset{\circ}{\curlyvee}\{\varrho_4\}}^{*} \cdot \overset{\circ}{\curlyvee}\{\varrho_4\}\leftarrow\!\circ\!\!-$. It is, so the system is confluent by Theorem 2.

Example 8. Consider the left-linear confluent TRS $\mathcal{R}$:

$\varrho_1: f(a, a) \to b$ $\varrho_3: f(c, x) \to f(x, x)$ $\varrho_5: f(c, c) \to f(a, c)$
$\varrho_2:$ $a \to c$ $\varrho_4: f(x, c) \to f(x, x)$

Since b is an $\mathcal{R}$-normal form, the only way to join the outer–inner critical peak $b \;_{\varrho_1}\!\leftarrow f(a, a) \to_{\varrho_2} f(c, a)$ is by a conversion starting with a step $b \;_{\varrho_1}\!\leftarrow f(a, a)$. As its label must be identical to the same step in the peak, not smaller, whether we choose ϱ_1 to be in $\mathcal{C}$ or not, the peak is not hot-decreasing, so Theorem 2 does not apply.

That hot-decreasingness in Theorem 2 cannot be weakened to (ordinary) decreasingness, can be seen by considering $\mathcal{R}'$ obtained by omitting ϱ_5 from $\mathcal{R}$. Although $\mathcal{R}'$ is not confluent [16, Example 8], by taking $\mathcal{C} = \varnothing$ and $\varrho_1 \succ \varrho_3, \varrho_4$, we can show that all critical peaks of $\mathcal{R}'$ are decreasing for the hot-labelling.

A special case of Theorem 2, is that a left-linear terminating TRS is confluent [19], if each critical pair is joinable, as can be seen by setting $\mathcal{C} = \mathcal{R}$.

Corollary 1. *A left-linear development closed TRS is confluent* [29, Corollary 24].

Proof. A TRS is development closed if for every critical pair (t,s) such that t is obtained by an outer step, $t \leftarrow\!\circ\!- s$ holds. Taking $\mathcal{C} = \emptyset$ and labelling all rules the same, say by 0, yields that each outer–inner or overlay critical peak is labelled as $t_{\{0\}} \leftarrow \cdot \rightarrow_{\{0\}} s$, and can be completed as $t_{\{0\}} \leftarrow\!\circ\!- s$, yielding a hot-decreasing diagram of (oi)-shape. We conclude by Theorem 2. □

The proof of Theorem 2 uses the following structural properties of decreasing diagrams specific to the hot-labelling. The labelling was designed so they hold.

Lemma 7. *1. If the peak $s \,_\ell\!\leftarrow\!\circ\!- t \, -\!\circ\!\rightarrow_\kappa u$ is hot-decreasing, then it can be completed into a hot-decreasing diagram of shape $s \leftrightarrow^*_{\overset{\ast}{\gamma}\ell} s' \, -\!\circ\!\rightarrow_\kappa s'' \leftrightarrow^*_{\overset{\ast}{\gamma}\ell\kappa} u'' \,_\ell\!\leftarrow\!\circ\!- u' \leftrightarrow^*_{\overset{\ast}{\gamma}\kappa} u$ such that the 1st-order variables in all terms in the diagram are contained in those of t.*
2. If the multisteps Φ, Ψ in the peak $s \,_\Phi\!\leftarrow\!\circ\!- t \, -\!\circ\!\rightarrow_\Psi u$ are non-overlapping, then the valley $s \, -\!\circ\!\rightarrow_{\Psi/\Phi} \cdot \,_{\Phi/\Psi}\!\leftarrow\!\circ\!- u$ completes it into a hot-decreasing diagram.
3. If the peak $s \leftarrow\!\circ\!- t \, -\!\circ\!\rightarrow u$ and vector of peaks $s \leftarrow\!\circ\!- t \, -\!\circ\!\rightarrow u$ have hot-decreasing diagrams, so does the composition $s^{[x:=s]} \leftarrow\!\circ\!- t^{[x:=t]} \, -\!\circ\!\rightarrow u^{[x:=u]}$.

The proof of Theorem 2 refines our refactored proof (see Lemma 6) of Huet's critical pair lemma, by wrapping the induction on the amount of non-overlap (⊎) between multisteps, into an outer induction on their amount of overlap (⋒).

Proof (of Theorem 2). We show that every peak $s \,_\Phi\!\leftarrow\!\circ\!- t \, -\!\circ\!\rightarrow_\Psi u$ of multisteps Φ and Ψ can be closed into a hot-decreasing diagram, by induction on the pair $(\Phi \!\Cap\! \Psi, \Phi \!\Cup\! \Psi)$ ordered by the lexicographic product of $>$ with itself. We distinguish cases on whether or not Φ and Ψ have overlap.

If Φ and Ψ do not have overlap, Lemma 5(1) yields $s \, -\!\circ\!\rightarrow_{\Psi/\Phi} \cdot \,_{\Phi/\Psi}\!\leftarrow\!\circ\!- u$. This valley completes the peak into a hot-decreasing diagram by Lemma 7(2).

If Φ and Ψ do have overlap, then we further distinguish cases on whether or not the overlap is critical.

If the overlap is not critical, then by Lemma 4 the peak can be vertically decomposed into a number of peaks between multisteps Φ_i, Ψ_i that have an amount of overlap that is not greater, $\Phi \Cap \Psi \geqslant \Phi_i \Cap \Psi_i$, and a strictly smaller amount of non-overlap $\Phi \Cup \Psi > \Phi_i \Cup \Psi_i$. Hence the I.H. applies and yields that each such peak can be completed into a hot-decreasing diagram. We conclude by vertically recomposing them yielding a hot-decreasing diagram by Lemma 7(3).

If the overlap is critical, then by Lemma 5 the peak can be horizontally decomposed as $s\ _{\Phi/\phi}\!\leftarrow\!\circ\!-\ s'\ _\phi\!\leftarrow\ t\ \rightarrow_\psi\ u'\ -\!\circ\!\rightarrow_{\Psi/\psi}\ u$ for some peak $s'\ _\phi\!\leftarrow\ t\ \rightarrow_\psi\ u'$ of overlapping steps $\phi \in \Phi$ and $\psi \in \Psi$, i.e. such that $\Phi = \phi \sqcup \Phi'$ $\Psi = \psi \sqcup \Psi'$ for some Φ', Ψ'. We choose (ϕ,ψ) to be *inner* among such overlapping pairs (see Definition 6), assuming w.l.o.g. that $p_\phi \preceq_o p_\psi$ for the root-positions p_ϕ, p_ψ of their patterns. We distinguish cases on whether or not p_ϕ is a strict prefix of p_ψ.

If $p_\phi = p_\psi$, then $\phi = \Phi$ and $\psi = \Psi$ by Proposition 3, so the peak *is* overlay, from which we conclude since such peaks are hot-decreasing by assumption.

Suppose $p_\phi \prec_o p_\psi$. We will construct a hot-decreasing diagram D for the peak $s\ _\Phi\!\leftarrow\!\circ\!-\ t\ -\!\circ\!\rightarrow_\Psi\ u$ out of several smaller such diagrams as illustrated in Fig. 1, using the multipattern $\varsigma = \Phi^{\mathsf{src}} \sqcup \psi^{\mathsf{src}}$ as a basic building block; it has as patterns those of Φ' and the join of the patterns of ϕ, ψ. To make ς explicit, unfold Φ and Ψ to let-expressions let $X = \varrho(x)$ in M respectively let $Y = \theta(y)$ in N, for rules of shapes $\varrho_i(x_i) : \ell_i \to r_i$ and $\theta_j(y_j) : g_j \to d_j$. We let $X = X'X$ and $Y = Y'Y$ be such that X and Y are the 2nd-order variables corresponding to $\phi \in \Phi$ and $\psi \in \Psi$ for rules $\varrho(x) : \ell \to r$ and $\theta(y) : g \to d$. By the choice of (ϕ,ψ) as inner, ϕ^{src} is the *unique* pattern in Φ^{src} overlapping ψ^{src}. As a consequence we can write ς as let $X'Z = \ell'\hat{t}$ in L, for some pattern $\hat{t}$, the join of the patterns of ϕ, ψ, such that σ maps Z to a term of shape $X(g_\psi)$ as ϕ is the outer step, and τ maps it to a term of shape $C[Y(\ell_\phi)]$,[9] where σ, τ witness $\Phi^{\mathsf{src}}, \psi^{\mathsf{src}} \sqsubseteq \varsigma$. That the other 2nd-order variables are X' follows by σ being the identity on them (their patterns do not overlap ψ), and that these are bound to the patterns ℓ' by τ mapping them to 1st-order terms (only Z can be mapped to a non-1st-order term).

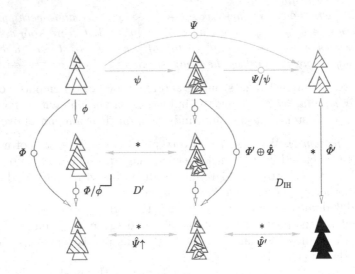

Fig. 1. Outer–inner critical peak construction

---

[9] C is a prefix of the left-hand side ℓ of ϱ. For instance, for a peak from $f(g(a))$ between $\varrho : f(g(a)) \to \ldots$ and $\theta : g(x) \to \ldots$, Z is mapped by σ to $X()$ and by τ to $f(Y(a))$.

We start with constructing a hot-decreasing diagram $\mathring{D}$ for the *critical* peak $\hat{s}\ _{\hat{\phi}}\!\leftarrow \hat{t} \rightarrow_{\hat{\psi}} \hat{u}$ encompassed by the peak between ϕ and ψ, as follows. We set $\hat{\phi}$ and $\hat{\psi}$ to let $X = \varrho(\boldsymbol{x})$ in $Z(\boldsymbol{z})^{\sigma}$ respectively let $Y = \theta(\boldsymbol{y})$ in $Z(\boldsymbol{z})^{\tau}$. This yields a peak as desired, which is outer–inner as $p_{\hat{\phi}} \prec_o p_{\hat{\psi}}$ by $p_{\phi} \prec_o p_{\psi}$, and critical by Lemma 3, hence by the hot-decreasingness assumption, it can be completed into a hot-decreasing diagram $\mathring{D}$ by a conversion of (oi)-shape: $\hat{s} \leftrightarrow^{*}_{\dot{\gamma}\mathring{\mathcal{L}}(\hat{\phi})} \hat{w} \ _{\dot{\gamma}\mathring{\mathcal{L}}(\hat{\phi})}\!\leftarrow\!\circ\!-\hat{u}$.

Below we refer to its conversion and multistep as $\hat{\Psi}$ and $\hat{\Phi}$. Based on $\mathring{D}$ we construct a hot-decreasing diagram D' (Fig. 1, left) for the peak $s\ _{\Phi}\!\leftarrow\!\circ\!- t \rightarrow_{\psi} u'$ by constructing a conversion $\hat{\Psi}{\uparrow}: s \leftrightarrow^{*} w''$ and a multistep $\Phi' \oplus \hat{\Phi}: u' \ \text{--}\!\circ\!\rightarrow w''$, with their composition (reversing the latter) of (oi)-shape.

The conversion $\hat{\Psi}{\uparrow}: s \leftrightarrow^{*} w''$ is constructed by lifting the closing conversion $\hat{\Psi}$ of the diagram $\mathring{D}$ back into ς. Formally, for any multistep $\hat{\Omega}$ given by let $\hat{Z} = \boldsymbol{\eta}(\boldsymbol{w})$ in $\hat{L}$ for rules $\eta_k(\boldsymbol{w_k})$, occurring anywhere in $\hat{\Psi}$, we define its *lifting* $\hat{\Omega}{\uparrow}$ to be let $\hat{Z} = \boldsymbol{\eta}(\boldsymbol{w})$ in $L^{[X',Z:=r',\hat{L}]}$. That is, we update ς by substituting[10] both $\hat{\Omega}$ (for Z, instead of binding that to $\hat{t}$) and the *right*-hand sides $\boldsymbol{r'}$ in its body. Because right-hand sides $\boldsymbol{r}$ need not be linear, the resulting proofclusters may have to be linearised (by replicating let-bindings) first to obtain multisteps. This extends to terms p by $p{\uparrow} = [\![(\text{let} = \text{in } p){\uparrow}]\!]$. That this yields multisteps and terms that connect into a conversion $s = \hat{s}{\uparrow} \leftrightarrow^{*}_{\hat{\Psi}{\uparrow}} \hat{w}{\uparrow} = w''$ as desired follows by *computation*. E.g., $s = M^{[X',X:=r',r]} = L^{[X',Z:=r',\hat{s}]} = \hat{s}{\uparrow}$ using that σ witnesses $\Phi^{\text{src}} \sqsubseteq \varsigma$ so that $M = L^{\sigma}$ and $\hat{s} = [\![\text{let } X = r \text{ in } Z(\boldsymbol{z})^{\sigma}]\!]$. That the labels in $\hat{\Psi}{\uparrow}$ are strictly below $\mathring{\mathcal{L}}(\Phi)$ follows for *set*-labels from that lifting clearly does not introduce rule symbols and from that labels of rule symbols in $\hat{\Psi}$ are, by assumption, strictly below the label of the rule ϱ of ϕ. In case Φ is *term*-labelled, by t, it follows from closure of $\rightarrow_c$-reduction under lifting (which also contracts Φ').

The multistep $\Phi' \oplus \hat{\Phi}: u' \ \text{--}\!\circ\!\rightarrow w''$ is the *combination* of the multisteps Φ' (the redex-patterns in Φ other than ϕ) and $\hat{\Phi}$, lifting the latter into ς. For $\hat{\Phi}: \hat{u} \ \text{--}\!\circ\!\rightarrow \hat{w}$ given by let $\hat{X} = \hat{\varrho}(\hat{\boldsymbol{x}})$ in $\hat{M}$, it is defined as let $X'\hat{X} = \varrho(\boldsymbol{x})'\hat{\varrho}(\hat{\boldsymbol{x}})$ in $L^{[Z:=\hat{M}]}$. Per construction it only contracts rules in $\Phi', \hat{\Phi}$, so has a label in $\dot{\gamma}\mathring{\mathcal{L}}(\Phi)$ by $\Phi = \phi \sqcup \Phi'$ and the label of $\hat{\Phi}$ is in $\dot{\gamma}\mathring{\mathcal{L}}(\hat{\phi})$ by the (oi)-assumption. That $\Phi' \oplus \hat{\Phi}: u' \ \text{--}\!\circ\!\rightarrow w''$ follows again by *computation*, e.g. $[\![\text{let } X'\hat{X} = r'\hat{r} \text{ in } L^{[Z:=\hat{M}]}]\!] = L^{[X',Z:=r',\hat{M}^{[\hat{X}:=\hat{r}]}]} = L^{[X',Z:=r',\hat{w}]} = \hat{w}{\uparrow} = w''$.

Finally, applying the I.H. to the peak $w''\ _{\Phi'\oplus\hat{\Phi}}\!\leftarrow\!\circ\!- u' \ \text{--}\!\circ\!\rightarrow_{\Psi/\psi} u$ yields some hot-decreasing diagram D_{IH} (Fig. 1, right). Prefixing $\hat{\Psi}{\uparrow}$ to its closing conversion between w'' and u, then closes the original peak $s\ _{\Phi}\!\leftarrow\!\circ\!- t \ \text{--}\!\circ\!\rightarrow_{\Psi} u$ into a hot-decreasing diagram D, because labels of steps in $\hat{\Psi}{\uparrow}$ are in $\dot{\gamma}\mathring{\mathcal{L}}(\Phi)$, $\mathring{\mathcal{L}}(\Phi) \succeq \mathring{\mathcal{L}}(\Phi' \oplus \hat{\Phi})$ as seen above, and $\mathring{\mathcal{L}}(\Psi) \succeq \mathring{\mathcal{L}}(\Psi/\psi)$. The I.H. applies since $\Phi \Cap \Psi > (\Phi' \oplus \hat{\Phi}) \Cap (\Psi/\psi)$: To see this, we define $L' = L^{[Z':=\ell']}$ and $F' = \text{let } \hat{X} = \hat{\ell} \text{ in } L'^{[Z:=\hat{M}]}$ and collect needed ingredients (the joins are disjoint):

---

[10] For this to be a valid 2nd-order substitution, the 1st-order variables of $\hat{\Omega}$ ($\hat{L}$) must be contained in those of $\hat{t}$, which we may assume by Lemma 7(1).

$$\begin{aligned}
D &= \Phi^{\text{src}} &&= (\text{let } \boldsymbol{X'} = \boldsymbol{\ell'} \text{ in } L^{[Z:=\hat{t}]}) \sqcup \phi^{\text{src}} &&= \Phi'^{\text{src}} \sqcup \phi^{\text{src}} \\
E &= \Psi^{\text{src}} &&= (\text{let } \boldsymbol{Y'} = \boldsymbol{g'} \text{ in } N^{[Y:=g]}) \sqcup \psi^{\text{src}} &&= \Psi'^{\text{src}} \sqcup \psi^{\text{src}} \\
D' &= (\Phi' \oplus \hat{\Phi})^{\text{src}} &&= (\text{let } \boldsymbol{X'} = \boldsymbol{\ell'} \text{ in } L^{[Z:=\hat{u}]}) \sqcup F' \\
E' &= (\Psi/\psi)^{\text{src}} &&= \text{let } \boldsymbol{Y'} = \boldsymbol{g'} \text{ in } N^{[Y:=d]}
\end{aligned}$$

Using these one may reason with sets of patterns (not let-expressions as $t \neq s'$; the sets are positions in both t,s') as follows, relying on distributivity:

$$(D \sqcap E) \sqsupseteq (D_- \sqcap E) = (D_- \sqcap E') = (D'_+ \sqcap E') \sqsupseteq (D' \sqcap E') \tag{1}$$

where F is the singleton $\{\{p \in \phi^{\text{src}} \mid p_\psi \not\preceq p\}\}$ having all positions in ϕ not below ψ's root, $D_- = \Phi'^{\text{src}} \sqcup F$, and $D'_+ = (D' - F') \sqcup F$. □

4 Confluence by Critical-Pair Closing Systems

We introduce a confluence criterion based on identifying for a term rewrite system $\mathcal{R}$ a subsystem $\mathcal{C}$ such that every $\mathcal{R}$-*critical peak* can be *closed* by means of $\mathcal{C}$-conversions, rendering the rules used in the peak redundant.

Definition 9. *A TRS $\mathcal{C}$ is* critical-pair closing *for a TRS $\mathcal{R}$, if $\mathcal{C}$ is a subsystem of $\mathcal{R}$ (namely $\mathcal{C} \subseteq \mathcal{R}$) and $s \leftrightarrow^*_{\mathcal{C}} t$ holds for all critical pairs (s,t) of $\mathcal{R}$.*

We phrase the main result of this section as a preservation-of-confluence result. We write $\to_{\mathcal{S}/\mathcal{R}}$ for $\twoheadrightarrow_{\mathcal{R}} \cdot \to_{\mathcal{S}} \cdot \twoheadrightarrow_{\mathcal{R}}$, and if it is terminating, $\mathcal{S}/\mathcal{R}$ is said to be *(relatively) terminating*. By $\mathcal{C}_d$ we denote the set of all duplicating rules in $\mathcal{C}$.

Theorem 3. *If $\mathcal{C}$ is a critical-pair-closing system for a left-linear TRS $\mathcal{R}$ such that $\mathcal{C}_d/\mathcal{R}$ is terminating, then $\mathcal{R}$ is confluent if $\mathcal{C}$ is confluent.*

Any left-linear TRS is critical-pair-closing for itself. However, the power of the method relies on choosing *small* $\mathcal{C}$. Before proving Theorem 3, we illustrate it by some (non-)examples and give a special case.

Example 9. Consider again the TRS $\mathcal{R}$ in Example 7. As we observed, the only critical pair originating from ϱ_4 and ϱ_1 is closed by $\to_{\varrho_1} \cdot \to_{\varrho_3} \cdot \to_{\varrho_6} \cdot {}_{\varrho_6}\!\leftarrow$. So the subsystem $\mathcal{C} = \{\varrho_1, \varrho_3, \varrho_6\}$ is a critical-pair-closing system for $\mathcal{R}$. As all $\mathcal{C}$-rules are linear, $\mathcal{C}_d/\mathcal{R}$ is vacuously terminating. Thus, by Theorem 3 it is sufficient to show confluence of $\mathcal{C}$. Because $\mathcal{C}$ has no critical pairs, the empty TRS $\emptyset$ is a critical-pair-closing TRS for $\mathcal{C}$. As $\emptyset/\mathcal{C}$ is terminating, confluence of $\mathcal{C}$ follows from that of $\emptyset$, which is trivial.

Observe how confluence was shown by successive applications of the theorem.

Remark 3. In our experiments (see Sect. 5), $\frac{3}{4}$ of the TRSs proven confluent by means of Theorem 3 used more than 1 iteration, with the maximum number of iterations being 6. For countable ARSs (see Corollary 2 below) 1 iteration suffices, which can be seen by setting $\mathcal{C}$ to the spanning forest obtained by Lemma 1. This provides the intuition underlying rule specialisation in Example 15 below.

Example 10. Although confluent, the TRS $\mathcal{R}$ in Example 8 does not have any confluent critical-pair-closing subsystem $\mathcal{C}$ such that $\mathcal{C}_d/\mathcal{R}$ is terminating, not even $\mathcal{R}$ itself: Because of b being in normal form in the critical pair induced by $b \;_{\varrho_1}\!\leftarrow f(a,a) \rightarrow_{\varrho_2} f(a,c)$, any such subsystem must contain ϱ_4, as one easily verifies, but ϱ_4 is both duplicating and non-terminating (looping).

Note that the termination condition of $\mathcal{C}_d/\mathcal{R}$ cannot be omitted from Theorem 3. Although the TRS $\mathcal{R}'$ in Example 8 is not confluent, it admits the confluent critical-pair-closing system $\{\varrho_1, \varrho_3, \varrho_4\}$.

Remark 4. The example is taken from [16] where it was used to show that decreasingness of *critical* peaks need not imply that of *all* peaks, for rule labelling. That example, in turn was adapted from Lévy's TRS in [17] showing that strong confluence need not imply confluence for left-linear TRSs.

Example 11. For *self-joinable* rules, i.e. rules that are self-overlapping and whose critical pairs need further applications of the rule itself to join, Theorem 3 is not helpful since the critical-pair-closing system $\mathcal{C}$ then contains the rule itself. Examples of self-joinable rules are associativity $(x \cdot y) \cdot z \rightarrow x \cdot (y \cdot z)$ and self-distributivity $(x \cdot y) \cdot z \rightarrow (x \cdot z) \cdot (y \cdot z)$, with confluence of the latter being known to be hard (currently no tool can handle it automatically).[11]

The special case we consider is that of TRSs that *are* ARSs, i.e. where all function symbols are nullary. The identification is justified by that any ARS in the standard sense [26,32] can be presented as $\rightarrow_{\mathcal{R}}$ for the TRS $\mathcal{R}$ having a nullary symbol for each object, and a rule for each step of the ARS. Since ARSs have no duplicating rules, Theorem 3 specialises to the following result.

Corollary 2. *If $\mathcal{C}$ is critical-pair-closing for ARS $\mathcal{R}$, $\mathcal{R}$ is confluent if $\mathcal{C}$ is.*

Example 12. Consider the TRS $\mathcal{R}$ given by $c \rightarrow a' \rightarrow a \rightarrow b$ and $a \rightarrow a' \rightarrow c$. It is an ARS having the critical-pair-closing system $\mathcal{C}$ given by the first part $c \rightarrow a' \rightarrow a \rightarrow b$. Since $\mathcal{C}$ is orthogonal it is confluent by Corollary 2, so $\mathcal{R}$ is confluent by the same corollary. In general, a confluent ARS may have many non-confluent critical-pair-closing systems. Requiring local confluence is no impediment to that: The subsystem $\mathcal{C}'$ of $\mathcal{R}$ obtained by removing $c \rightarrow a'$ allows to join all $\mathcal{R}$-critical peaks, but is not confluent; it simply is Kleene's example [32, Figure 1.2] showing that local confluence need not imply confluence.

For $\mathcal{C}_d/\mathcal{R}$ to be vacuously terminating it is sufficient that all rules are linear.

Example 13. Consider the linear TRS $\mathcal{R}$ consisting of $\rho_1 \colon f(x) \rightarrow f(f(x))$, $\rho_2 \colon f(x) \rightarrow g(x)$, and $\rho_3 \colon g(x) \rightarrow f(x)$. The subsystem $\mathcal{C} = \{\rho_1, \rho_3\}$ is critical-pair-closing and has no critical pairs, so $\mathcal{R}$ is confluent.

From the above it is apparent that, whereas usual redundancy-criteria are based on *rules* being redundant, the theorem gives a sufficient criterion for *peaks* of steps being redundant. This allows one to leverage the power of extant confluence methods. Here we give a generalisation of Huet's strong closedness theorem [17] as a corollary of Theorem 3.

---

[11] See problem 127 of http://cops.uibk.ac.at/results/?y=2019-full-run&c=TRS.

Definition 10. *A TRS $\mathcal{R}$ is strongly closed [17] if $s \twoheadrightarrow_{\mathcal{R}} \cdot \overset{=}{_{\mathcal{R}}}{\leftarrow} t$ and $s \to_{\overset{=}{\mathcal{R}}}$ $\cdot _{\mathcal{R}}{\leftarrow} t$ hold for all critical pairs (s,t).*

Corollary 3. *A left-linear TRS $\mathcal{R}$ is confluent if there exists a critical-pair-closing system $\mathcal{C}$ for $\mathcal{R}$ such that $\mathcal{C}$ is linear and strongly closed.*

Example 14. Consider the linear TRS $\mathcal{R}$:

$$\varrho_1: h(f(x,y)) \to f(h(r(x)),y) \qquad \varrho_2: f(x,k(y,z)) \to g(p(y),q(z,x))$$
$$\varrho_3: h(q(x,y)) \to q(x,h(r(y))) \qquad \varrho_4: q(x,h(r(y))) \to h(q(x,y))$$
$$\varrho_5: h(g(x,y)) \to g(x,h(y))$$
$$\varrho_6: a(x,y,z) \to h(f(x,k(y,z))) \qquad \varrho_7: \quad a(x,y,z) \to g(p(y),q(z,h(r(x))))$$

$\mathcal{C} = \{\varrho_1, \dots, \varrho_5\}$ is critical-pair-closing for $\mathcal{R}$, since the $\mathcal{R}$-critical peak between ϱ_6 and ϱ_7 can be $\mathcal{C}$-closed: $h(f(x,k(y,z))) \to_{\varrho_1} f(h(r(x)),k(y,z)) \to_{\varrho_2} g(p(y),q(z,h(r(x))))$. Because $\mathcal{C}$ is strongly closed and also linear, confluence of $\mathcal{R}$ follows by Corollary 3.

Remark 5. Neither of the TRSs in Examples 13 and 14 is strongly closed. The former not, because $f(f(x)) \twoheadrightarrow_{\mathcal{R}} \cdot \overset{=}{_{\mathcal{R}}}{\leftarrow} g(x)$ does not hold, and the latter not because $g(p(y),q(z,h(r(x)))) \twoheadrightarrow_{\mathcal{R}} \cdot \overset{=}{_{\mathcal{R}}}{\leftarrow} h(f(x,k(y,z)))$ does not hold.

Having illustrated the usefulness of Theorem 3, we now present its proof. In TRSs there are *two* types of peaks: overlapping and non-overlapping ones. As Example 10 shows, confluence criteria only addressing the former need not generalise from ARSs to TRSs. Note that one of the peaks showing non-confluence of $\mathcal{R}'$, the one between ϱ_2 and ϱ_3 (ϱ_4), is non-overlapping. Therefore, restricting to a subsystem without ϱ_2 can only provide a partial analysis of confluence of $\mathcal{R}'$; the (non-overlapping) interaction between $\mathcal{C}$ and $\mathcal{R} - \mathcal{C}$ is not accounted for, and indeed that is fatal here. The intuition for our proof is that the problem is that the number of such interactions is unbounded due to the presence of the duplicating and non-terminating rule ϱ_3 (and ϱ_4) in $\mathcal{C}$, and that requiring termination of $\mathcal{C}_d/\mathcal{R}$ bounds that number and suffices to regain confluence. This is verified by showing that $\twoheadrightarrow_{\mathcal{C}} \cdot \multimap\negmedspace\to_{\mathcal{R}}$ has the diamond property.

Lemma 8. *Let $\to_{\mathcal{A}} = \bigcup_{a \in I} \to_a$ be a relation equipped with a well-founded order $\succ$ on a label set I, and let $\to_{\mathcal{B}}$ be a confluent relation with $\to_{\mathcal{B}} \subseteq \twoheadrightarrow_{\mathcal{A}}$. The relation $\to_{\mathcal{A}}$ is confluent if*

1. $_a{\leftarrow} \cdot \to_b \subseteq (\to_{\mathcal{A}} \cdot _{\mathcal{A}}{\leftarrow}) \cup \bigcup_{\{a,b\} \succ_{\mathrm{mul}} \{a',b'\}} (_{a'}{\leftarrow} \cdot \overset{*}{\leftrightarrow}_{\mathcal{B}} \cdot \to_{b'})$ *for all $a,b \in I$; and*
2. $_a{\leftarrow} \cdot \to_{\mathcal{B}} \subseteq (\twoheadrightarrow_{\mathcal{B}} \cdot _a{\leftarrow}) \cup \bigcup_{a \succ a'} (\twoheadrightarrow_{\mathcal{B}} \cdot _{a'}{\leftarrow} \cdot \overset{*}{\leftrightarrow}_{\mathcal{B}})$ *for all $a \in I$.*

Here $\succ_{\mathrm{mul}}$ stands for the multiset extension of $\succ$.

Proof (Sketch). Let $\rightarrowtail = \twoheadrightarrow_{\mathcal{B}} \cdot \to_{\mathcal{A}}$. We claim that $_a{\leftarrow} \cdot \to^m_{\mathcal{B}} \cdot {}^n_{\mathcal{B}}{\leftarrow} \cdot \to_b \subseteq \rightarrowtail \cdot \leftarrowtail$ holds for all labels a,b and numbers $m,n \geqslant 0$. The claim is shown by well-founded induction on $(\{a,b\}, m+n)$ with respect to the lexicographic product of $\succ_{\mathrm{mul}}$ and the greater-than order $>$ on $\mathbb{N}$. Thus, the diamond property of $\rightarrowtail$ follows from the claim and confluence of $\mathcal{B}$. As $\to_{\mathcal{A}} \subseteq \rightarrowtail \subseteq \twoheadrightarrow_{\mathcal{A}}$, we conclude confluence of $\mathcal{A}$ by e.g. [32, Proposition 1.1.11].

Proof (of Theorem 3 by Lemma 8). Let I comprise pairs of a term and a natural number, and define $t \to_{(\hat{t},n)} s$ if $\hat{t} \twoheadrightarrow_{\mathcal{R}} t \multimap\!\!\!\to_{\mathcal{R}} s$ with n the maximal length of a development of the multistep,[12] and $\to_{\mathcal{B}} = \to_{\mathcal{C}}$, in Lemma 8. As well-founded order $\succ$ on indices we take the lexicographic product of $\mathcal{C}_d/\mathcal{R}$ and greater-than $>$. We only present the interesting case, leaving the others to the reader:

- Suppose $s \,_{(\hat{t},n)}\!\!\leftarrow t \to_{\mathcal{C}} u$ where the steps do not have overlap. Then by Lemma 5(1), $s \multimap\!\!\!\to_{\mathcal{C}} \cdot _{\mathcal{R}}\!\!\leftarrow\!\!\multimap u$, so $s \to_{\mathcal{C}} \cdot _{\mathcal{R}}\!\!\leftarrow\!\!\multimap u$. Distinguish cases on the type of the $\mathcal{C}$-rule employed in $t \to_{\mathcal{C}} u$.
  If the rule is duplicating, then $s \to_{\mathcal{C}} \cdot _{(u,m)}\!\!\leftarrow u$ for m the maximal length of a development of the $\multimap\!\!\!\to_{\mathcal{R}}$-step from u, and condition 2 is satisfied as $t \to_{\mathcal{C}_d} u$ implies $(\hat{t},n) \succeq (u,m)$.
  If the rule is non-duplicating, then $s \to_{\mathcal{C}} \cdot _{(\hat{t},n)}\!\!\leftarrow u$ as $\hat{t} \twoheadrightarrow_{\mathcal{R}} t \to_{\mathcal{R}} u$ by assumption and the length of the maximal development of the residual multistep does not increase when projecting over a linear rule. Again, condition 2 is satisfied. $\qquad\qquad\square$

5 Implementation and Experiments

The presented confluence techniques have been implemented in the confluence tool Saigawa version 1.12 [14]. We used the tool to test the criteria on 432 left-linear TRSs in COPS [15] Nos. 1–1036, where we ruled out duplicated problems. Out of 432 systems, 224 are known to be confluent and 173 are non-confluent.

We briefly explain how we automated the presented techniques. As illustrated in Example 9, Theorem 3 can be used as a stand-alone criterion. The condition $s \to_{\mathcal{R}}^{*} \cdot {}_{\mathcal{R}}^{=}\!\!\leftarrow t$ of strong closedness is tested by $s \to_{\mathcal{R}}^{\leqslant 5} \cdot {}_{\mathcal{R}}^{=}\!\!\leftarrow t$. For a critical peak $s \leftarrow \cdot \to t$ of $\mathcal{C}$, hot-decreasingness is tested by $s \to_{\mathcal{C}} \cdot {}_{\mathcal{C}}\!\!\leftarrow t$. For any other critical peak $s \,_{\ell}\!\!\leftarrow \cdot \to t$, we test the disjunction of $s \to_{\hat{\gamma}\ell}^{\leqslant 5} \cdot {}_{\hat{\gamma}\ell}\!\!\leftarrow\!\!\multimap t$ and $s \to_{\mathcal{C}} \cdot {}_{\hat{\gamma}\ell}\!\!\leftarrow\!\!\multimap t$ if it is outer–inner one, and if it is overlay, the disjunction of $s \to_{\hat{\gamma}\ell}^{\leqslant 5} \cdot {}_{\hat{\gamma}\ell}\!\!\leftarrow\!\!\multimap t$ and $s \to_{\mathcal{C}} \cdot {}_{\mathcal{C}}\!\!\leftarrow t$ is used. Order constraints for hot-labeling are solved by SMT solver Yices [10]. For proving (relative) termination we employ the termination tool NaTT version 1.8 [34]. Finally, suitable subsystems $\mathcal{C}$ used in our criteria are searched by enumeration.

Table 1 gives a summary of the results.[13] The tests were run on a PC equipped with Intel Core i7-8500Y CPU (1.5 GHz) and 16 GB memory using a timeout of 60 seconds. For the sake of comparison we also tested Knuth and Bendix' theorem (kb), the strong closedness theorem (sc), and development closedness theorem (dc). As theoretically expected, they are subsumed by their generalizations.

6 Conclusion and Future Work

We presented two methods for proving confluence of TRSs, dubbed critical-pair-closing systems and hot-decreasingness. We gave a lattice-theoretic characterisation of overlap. Since many results in term rewriting, and beyond, are based on

---

[12] By the Finite Developments Theorem lengths of such developments are finite [32].

[13] Detailed data are available from: http://www.jaist.ac.jp/project/saigawa/19cade/.

Table 1. Experimental results

	Theorem 2	Theorem 3	Corollary 3	kb	dc	sc
# proved (# timeouts)	101 (46)	81 (24)	94 (15)	45 (18)	34 (1)	62 (1)

reasoning about overlap, which is notoriously hard [24], we expect that formalising our characterisation could simplify or even enable formalising them. We expect that both methods generalise to commutation, extend to HRSs [21], and can be strengthened by considering rule *specialisations*.

Example 15. Analysing the TRS $\mathcal{R}$ of Example 10 one observes that for closing the critical pairs only (non-duplicating) *instances* of the duplicating rules ϱ_3 and ϱ_4 are used. Adjoining these specialisations allows the method to proceed: Adjoining $\varrho_3(a) : f(c, a) \to f(a, a)$ and $\varrho_4(a) : f(a, c) \to f(a, a)$ to $\mathcal{R}$ yields a (reduction-equivalent) TRS having critical-pair-closing system $\{\varrho_1, \varrho_3(a), \varrho_4(a), \varrho_5\}$. Since this is a linear system without critical pairs, it is confluent, so $\mathcal{R}$ is as well.

References

1. Baader, F., Nipkow, T.: Term Rewriting and All That. Cambridge University Press, Cambridge (1998)
2. Barendregt, H.: The Lambda Calculus: Its Syntax and Semantics, Studies in Logic and the Foundations of Mathematics, vol. 103. North-Holland (1985)
3. Bechet, D., de Groote, P., Retoré, C.: A complete axiomatisation for the inclusion of series-parallel partial orders. In: Comon, H. (ed.) RTA 1997. LNCS, vol. 1232, pp. 230–240. Springer, Heidelberg (1997). https://doi.org/10.1007/3-540-62950-5_74
4. Boudol, G.: Computational semantics of term rewriting systems. In: Nivat, M., Reynolds, J. (eds.) Algebraic Methods in Semantics, pp. 169–236. Cambridge University Press (1985)
5. Bundy, A., Basin, D., Hutter, D., Ireland, A.: Rippling: meta-level guidance for mathematical reasoning. In: Cambridge Tracts in Theoretical Computer Science, Cambridge University Press (2005). https://doi.org/10.1017/CBO9780511543326
6. Church, A., Rosser, J.: Some properties of conversion. Transact. Am. Math. Soc. **39**, 472–482 (1936)
7. Comon, H., et al.: Tree Automata Techniques and Applications (2007). http://www.grappa.univ-lille3.fr/tata
8. Davey, B., Priestley, H.: Introduction to Lattices and Order. Cambridge University Press, Cambridge (1990)
9. Dershowitz, N., Jouannaud, J.P.: Rewrite systems. In: van Leeuwen, J. (ed.) Handbook of Theoretical Computer Science, vol. B, Formal Models and Semantics, pp. 243–320. Elsevier (1990)
10. Dutertre, B.: Yices 2.2. In: Biere, A., Bloem, R. (eds.) CAV 2014. LNCS, vol. 8559, pp. 737–744. Springer, Cham (2014). https://doi.org/10.1007/978-3-319-08867-9_49

11. Endrullis, J., Klop, J., Overbeek, R.: Decreasing diagrams with two labels are complete for confluence of countable systems. In: Proceedings of 3rd FSCD. LIPIcs, vol. 108, pp. 14:1–14:15 (2018). https://doi.org/10.4230/LIPIcs.FSCD.2018.14
12. Felgenhauer, B., Middeldorp, A., Zankl, H., van Oostrom, V.: Layer systems for proving confluence. ACM Transact. Computat. Logic 16, 1–32 (2015)
13. Felgenhauer, B.: Labeling multi-steps for confluence of left-linear term rewrite systems. In: Tiwari, A., Aoto, T. (eds.) Proceedings of 4th IWC, pp. 33–37 (2015)
14. Hirokawa, H., Klein, D.: Saigawa: A confluence tool. In: Proceedings of 1st IWC, p. 49 (2012). http://www.jaist.ac.jp/project/saigawa/
15. Hirokawa, N., Nagele, J., Middeldorp, A.: Cops and CoCoWeb: infrastructure for confluence tools. In: Galmiche, D., Schulz, S., Sebastiani, R. (eds.) IJCAR 2018. LNCS (LNAI), vol. 10900, pp. 346–353. Springer, Cham (2018). https://doi.org/10.1007/978-3-319-94205-6_23
16. Hirokawa, N., Middeldorp, A.: Decreasing diagrams and relative termination. J. Autom. Reasoning 47(4), 481–501 (2011)
17. Huet, G.: Confluent reductions: abstract properties and applications to term rewriting systems. J. ACM 27(4), 797–821 (1980)
18. Huet, G., Lévy, J.J.: Computations in orthogonal rewriting systems, I. In: Lassez, J.L., Plotkin, G. (eds.) Computational Logic: Essays in Honor of Alan Robinson, chap. 11. The MIT Press (1991)
19. Knuth, D.E., Bendix, P.B.: Simple word problems in universal algebras. In: Leech, J. (ed.) Computational Problems in Abstract Algebra, Proceedings of a Conference held at Oxford under the Auspices of the Science Research Council Atlas Computer Laboratory, 29 August–2 September 1967. pp. 263–297 (1970)
20. Liu, J.L.: Propriétés de Confluence des Règles de Réécriture par des Diagrammes Décroissants. Ph.D. thesis, Tsinghua University and l'Université Paris-Saclay préparée à l'École Polytechnique (2016)
21. Mayr, R., Nipkow, T.: Higher-order rewrite systems and their confluence. Theoret. Comput. Sci. 192(1), 3–29 (1998). https://doi.org/10.1016/S0304-3975(97)00143-6
22. Meseguer, J.: Conditional rewriting logic as a unified model of concurrency. Theoret. Comput. Sci. 96, 73–155 (1992)
23. Métivier, Y.: About the rewriting systems produced by the Knuth–Bendix completion algorithm. Inf. Process. Lett. 16(1), 31–34 (1983)
24. Nagele, J., Middeldorp, A.: Certification of classical confluence results for left-linear term rewrite systems. In: Blanchette, J.C., Merz, S. (eds.) ITP 2016. LNCS, vol. 9807, pp. 290–306. Springer, Cham (2016). https://doi.org/10.1007/978-3-319-43144-4_18
25. Newman, M.: On theories with a combinatorial definition of equivalence. Ann. Math. 43(2), 223–243 (1942)
26. Ohlebusch, E.: Advanced Topics in Term Rewriting. Springer, Heidelberg (2002). https://doi.org/10.1007/978-1-4757-3661-8
27. Okui, S.: Simultaneous critical pairs and Church-Rosser property. In: Nipkow, T. (ed.) RTA 1998. LNCS, vol. 1379, pp. 2–16. Springer, Heidelberg (1998). https://doi.org/10.1007/BFb0052357
28. van Oostrom, V.: Confluence for Abstract and Higher-Order Rewriting. Ph.D. thesis, Vrije Universiteit, Amsterdam, March 1994
29. van Oostrom, V.: Developing developments. Theoret. Comput. Sci. 175(1), 159–181 (1997)

30. van Oostrom, V.: Confluence by decreasing diagrams. In: Voronkov, A. (ed.) RTA 2008. LNCS, vol. 5117, pp. 306–320. Springer, Heidelberg (2008). https://doi.org/10.1007/978-3-540-70590-1_21
31. Rosen, B.: Tree-manipulating systems and Church-Rosser theorems. J. ACM **20**, 160–187 (1973)
32. Terese: Term Rewriting Systems. Cambridge University Press (2003)
33. Toyama, Y.: On the Church-Rosser property for the direct sum of term rewriting systems. J. ACM **34**(1), 128–143 (1987)
34. Yamada, A., Kusakari, K., Sakabe, T.: Nagoya termination tool. In: Dowek, G. (ed.) RTA 2014. LNCS, vol. 8560, pp. 466–475. Springer, Cham (2014). https://doi.org/10.1007/978-3-319-08918-8_32
35. Zankl, H., Felgenhauer, B., Middeldorp, A.: Labelings for decreasing diagrams. J. Autom. Reasoning **54**(2), 101–133 (2015)

Composing Proof Terms

Christina Kohl[(✉)] and Aart Middeldorp

Department of Computer Science, University of Innsbruck, Innsbruck, Austria
{christina.kohl,aart.middeldorp}@uibk.ac.at

Abstract. Proof terms are a useful concept for comparing computations in term rewriting. We analyze proof terms with composition, with an eye towards automation. We revisit permutation equivalence and projection equivalence, two key notions presented in the literature. We report on the integration of proof terms with composition into ProTeM, a tool for manipulating proof terms.

Keywords: Proof terms · Term rewriting · Automation

1 Introduction

Proof terms represent proofs in rewriting logic [4,5]. Because proof terms are terms, they are subject to techniques common in automated reasoning, like termination orders and critical pair analysis. In term rewriting proof terms are used to study equivalence of reductions [6,7] and for confluence analysis [2]. In [7, Chapter 8] ([6] is a condensed version) van Oostrom and de Vrijer present a thorough study of five different notions of equivalence and argue that these are equivalent. Proof terms play a key role in three of these notions: *permutation equivalence, parallel standardization equivalence* and *projection equivalence*. In this paper we take a fresh look at permutation equivalence and projection equivalence, from the viewpoint of automation. This leads to a new understanding of the rewrite properties of the important residual operation. In particular, we show the analysis in [6,7] of the residual operation to be incorrect.

We implemented decision procedures for permutation equivalence and projection equivalence in ProTeM, a recent tool [3] for manipulating proof terms. Automating permutation equivalence is non-trivial since the rewrite system for parallel standardization is only complete modulo *structural equivalence*. The latter is a weaker notion of equivalence that is easily decidable by means of a confluent and terminating rewrite system, but no rewrite system is known that avoids rewriting modulo.

In the next section we recall proof terms and define structural equivalence. Permutation equivalence is the topic of Sect. 3. In Sect. 4 we study the residual operation on proof terms and the related notions of projection order and projection equivalence. We present a variant of the residual system defined in [7,

---

This research is supported by FWF (Austrian Science Fund) project P27528.

P. Fontaine (Ed.): CADE 2019, LNAI 11716, pp. 337–353, 2019.
https://doi.org/10.1007/978-3-030-29436-6_20

Definition 8.7.54 and proof of Theorem 8.7.57] and [6, Definition 6.9 and proof of Theorem 6.12]. By imposing an innermost evaluation strategy, we ensure that our rewrite system has a well-defined rewrite semantics. We establish (innermost) confluence and termination, and use these properties to define projection order and projection equivalence. The extensions to ProTeM are described in Sect. 5 before we conclude in Sect. 6.

We assume familiarity with first-order term rewriting [1,7] but knowledge of proof terms is not required. All definitions needed for this paper are given. Much more information on proof terms and notions of equivalence can be found in [7, Chapter 8]. Throughout the paper we deal with *left-linear* rewrite systems.

2   Proof Terms

Before formally defining proof terms, we give a motivating example that demonstrates their use. This example will reappear many times throughout the paper to illustrate the concepts we discuss.

Example 1. Consider the following TRS representing the necessary steps of computing the disjunctive normal form of a propositional formula:

$$\alpha \quad \neg(x \wedge y) \rightarrow \neg x \vee \neg y \qquad \gamma \quad x \wedge (y \vee z) \rightarrow (x \wedge y) \vee (x \wedge z)$$
$$\beta \quad \neg(x \vee y) \rightarrow \neg x \wedge \neg y \qquad \delta \quad (x \vee y) \wedge z \rightarrow (x \wedge z) \vee (y \wedge z)$$
$$\varepsilon \qquad \neg\neg x \rightarrow x$$

As illustrated by the diagram below there are 13 different rewrite sequences from $s = \neg(x \vee \neg(y \vee z))$ to $t = (\neg x \wedge y) \vee (\neg x \wedge z)$. If we want to compare them, for example to determine if some of them are equivalent, we can translate them into proof terms and do our analysis in the well-known realm of terms.

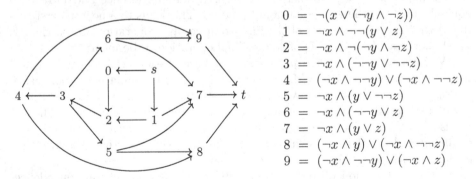

$$0 = \neg(x \vee (\neg y \wedge \neg z))$$
$$1 = \neg x \wedge \neg\neg(y \vee z)$$
$$2 = \neg x \wedge \neg(\neg y \wedge \neg z)$$
$$3 = \neg x \wedge (\neg\neg y \vee \neg\neg z)$$
$$4 = (\neg x \wedge \neg\neg y) \vee (\neg x \wedge \neg\neg z)$$
$$5 = \neg x \wedge (y \vee \neg\neg z)$$
$$6 = \neg x \wedge (\neg\neg y \vee z)$$
$$7 = \neg x \wedge (y \vee z)$$
$$8 = (\neg x \wedge y) \vee (\neg x \wedge \neg\neg z)$$
$$9 = (\neg x \wedge \neg\neg y) \vee (\neg x \wedge z)$$

We refer to a specific sequence from s to t by listing the numbers of the intermediate terms. For instance, the sequence $s \rightarrow \neg x \wedge \neg\neg(y \vee z) \rightarrow \neg x \wedge (y \vee z) \rightarrow t$ is named 17.

Proof terms are built from function symbols, variables, rule symbols as well as the binary *composition* operator ; which is used in infix notation. Rule symbols represent rewrite rules and have a fixed arity which is the number of different variables in the represented rule. We use Greek letters $(\alpha, \beta, \gamma, \dots)$ as rule symbols, and uppercase letters $(A, B, C, \dots)$ for proof terms. We can represent any rewrite sequence $\longrightarrow^*$ by a suitable proof term. A proof term without composition represents a multi-step ($\multimap\!\!\rightarrow$), a proof term without composition and nested rule symbols represents a parallel step ($\twoheadrightarrow$), and a proof term without composition and only one rule symbol represents a single step ($\longrightarrow$). If a proof term contains neither compositions nor rule symbols, it denotes an empty step ($=$).

If α is a rule symbol then lhs_α (rhs_α) denotes the left-hand (right-hand) side of the rewrite rule represented by α. Furthermore var_α denotes the list $(x_1, \dots, x_n)$ of variables appearing in α in some fixed order. The length of this list is the arity of α. Given a rule symbol α with $\mathsf{var}_\alpha = (x_1, \dots, x_n)$ and proof terms $A_1, \dots, A_n$, we write $\langle A_1, \dots, A_n \rangle_\alpha$ for the substitution $\{x_i \mapsto A_i \mid 1 \leqslant i \leqslant n\}$. A proof term A witnesses a rewrite sequence from its source $\mathsf{src}(A)$ to its target $\mathsf{tgt}(A)$, which are computed as follows:

$$\mathsf{src}(x) = \mathsf{tgt}(x) = x \quad \mathsf{src}(A \,;\, B) = \mathsf{src}(A) \quad \mathsf{tgt}(A \,;\, B) = \mathsf{tgt}(B)$$
$$\mathsf{src}(f(A_1, \dots, A_n)) = f(\mathsf{src}(A_1), \dots, \mathsf{src}(A_n))$$
$$\mathsf{src}(\alpha(A_1, \dots, A_n)) = \mathsf{lhs}_\alpha \langle \mathsf{src}(A_1), \dots, \mathsf{src}(A_n) \rangle_\alpha$$
$$\mathsf{tgt}(f(A_1, \dots, A_n)) = f(\mathsf{tgt}(A_1), \dots, \mathsf{tgt}(A_n))$$
$$\mathsf{tgt}(\alpha(A_1, \dots, A_n)) = \mathsf{rhs}_\alpha \langle \mathsf{tgt}(A_1), \dots, \mathsf{tgt}(A_n) \rangle_\alpha$$

Here f is an n-ary function symbol. The expression $\mathsf{lhs}_\alpha \langle \mathsf{src}(A_1), \dots, \mathsf{src}(A_n) \rangle_\alpha$ denotes the result of replacing every variable x_i in the left-hand side of α with the source of the corresponding argument A_i of α. We assume $\mathsf{tgt}(A) = \mathsf{src}(B)$ whenever the composition $A \,;\, B$ is used in a proof term. Proof terms A and B are *co-initial* if they have the same source. We omit parentheses in nested compositions in examples for better readability, assuming association to the right of the composition operator.

Example 2. The sequence 17 in Example 1 is represented by the proof term $\beta(x, \neg(y \vee z)) \,;\, \neg x \wedge \epsilon(y \vee z) \,;\, \gamma(\neg x, y, z)$. For the proof term $A = \alpha(\epsilon(x), \neg\epsilon(x))$ we have $\mathsf{src}(A) = \neg(\neg\neg x \wedge \neg\neg\neg x)$ and $\mathsf{tgt}(A) = \neg(x \vee \neg x)$. The proof term

$$\beta(x, \beta(y, z)) \,;\, \neg x \wedge \alpha(\neg y, \neg z) \,;\, \gamma(\neg x, \varepsilon(y), \varepsilon(z))$$

represents the sequence $s \multimap\!\!\rightarrow 2 \rightarrow 3 \multimap\!\!\rightarrow t$, which can be viewed as a compact version of 12348 and several other rewrite sequences from s to t. The expression $A \,;\, \beta(x, x)$ is not a proof term since $\mathsf{src}(\beta(x, x)) = \neg(x \vee x) \neq \mathsf{tgt}(A)$.

Structural equivalence [7, Definition 8.3.1] equates proof terms that only differ in the left-to-right order in which steps are executed.

Definition 1. *The* structural identities *consist of the following four equation schemas:*

$$A \,; t \approx A \tag{1}$$

$$t \,; A \approx A \tag{2}$$

$$(A \,; B) \,; C \approx A \,; (B \,; C) \tag{3}$$

$$f(A_1, \ldots, A_n) \,; f(B_1, \ldots, B_n) \approx f(A_1 \,; B_1, \ldots, A_n \,; B_n) \tag{4}$$

Here t denotes a term without rule symbols and composition whereas f denotes an arbitrary function symbol in the underlying TRS. The induced congruence relation $\equiv$ on proof terms is called structural equivalence. *The instances of scheme (4) are known as* functorial identities.

Structural equivalence is easily decidable by rewriting proof terms.

Definition 2. *The* canonicalization TRS *consists of the following rule schemas:*

$$A \,; t \rightarrow A \tag{5}$$

$$t \,; A \rightarrow A \tag{6}$$

$$(A \,; B) \,; C \rightarrow A \,; (B \,; C) \tag{7}$$

$$f(A_1, \ldots, A_n) \,; f(B_1, \ldots, B_n) \rightarrow f(A_1 \,; B_1, \ldots, A_n \,; B_n) \tag{8}$$

$$f(A_1, \ldots, A_n) \,; (f(B_1, \ldots, B_n) \,; C) \rightarrow f(A_1 \,; B_1, \ldots, A_n \,; B_n) \,; C \tag{9}$$

Normal forms of the canonicalization TRS are called canonical.

Example 3. Returning to Example 1, the proof terms

$$(\neg x \wedge \epsilon(y)) \vee (\neg x \wedge \neg\neg z) \,; (\neg x \wedge y) \vee (\neg x \wedge \epsilon(z)) \,; (\neg x \wedge y) \vee (\neg x \wedge z)$$
$$(\neg x \wedge \neg\neg y) \vee (\neg x \wedge \epsilon(z)) \,; (\neg x \wedge \epsilon(y)) \vee (\neg x \wedge z) \,; (\neg x \wedge y) \vee (\neg x \wedge z)$$

are structurally equivalent because both rewrite to the canonical proof term

$$(\neg x \wedge \epsilon(y)) \vee (\neg x \wedge \epsilon(z))$$

Theorem 1. *Canonical proof terms are unique representatives of structural equivalence classes.* □

A proof sketch is given in [7, Exercise 8.3.6]. We remark that automatic tools for proving confluence and termination are not applicable here since the rules in Definition 2 are rule schemas; for every function symbol f in the signature and every term t of the underlying TRS, the rule schemas are suitably instantiated to obtain a concrete (and infinite) rewrite system that operates on proof terms of the underlying TRS. Nevertheless, standard confluence and termination techniques are readily applicable. In particular, schema (9) is added to make the critical pair between (7) and (8) convergent.

3   Permutation Equivalence

Adjacent steps in which the contracted redexes are at parallel positions can be swapped, which is captured by structural equivalence. Permutation equivalence [7, Definition 8.3.1] extends this by also allowing swapping adjacent steps in which the contracted redexes are above each other. This is similar to the variable overlap case in the well-known critical pair lemma.

Definition 3. *The permutation* identities *consist of the structural identities of Definition 1 together with the following two equation schemas:*

$$\alpha(A_1, \ldots, A_n) \approx \mathsf{lhs}_\alpha\langle A_1, \ldots, A_n\rangle_\alpha \; ; \alpha(t_1, \ldots, t_n) \tag{10}$$

$$\alpha(A_1, \ldots, A_n) \approx \alpha(s_1, \ldots, s_n) \; ; \mathsf{rhs}_\alpha\langle A_1, \ldots, A_n\rangle_\alpha \tag{11}$$

Here $\mathsf{src}(A_i) = s_i$ *and* $\mathsf{tgt}(A_i) = t_i$ *and thus* s_i *and* t_i *are terms without rule symbols and compositions, for* $i = 1, \ldots, n$. *Furthermore,* α *ranges over the rule symbols of the underlying TRS. The induced congruence relation on proof terms is denoted by* $\cong$ *and called* permutation equivalence. *The permutation order* $\sqsubseteq$ *is defined as follows:* $A \sqsubseteq B$ *if there exists a proof term* C *such that* $A \; ; C \cong B$.

Example 4. We have $\neg x \wedge (\varepsilon(y) \vee \varepsilon(z)) \; ; \gamma(\neg x, y, z) \cong \gamma(\neg x, \varepsilon(y), \varepsilon(z))$ by an application of (10) from right to left (with $\alpha = \gamma$, $A_1 = \neg x$, $A_2 = \varepsilon(y)$, and $A_3 = \varepsilon(z)$). Hence $\neg x \wedge (\varepsilon(y) \vee \varepsilon(z)) \sqsubseteq \gamma(\neg x, \varepsilon(y), \varepsilon(z))$. Furthermore, $\gamma(\neg x, \varepsilon(y), \varepsilon(z)) \cong \gamma(\neg x, \neg\neg y, \neg\neg z) \; ; (\neg x \wedge \varepsilon(y)) \vee (\neg x \wedge \varepsilon(z))$ by using (11).

The following lemma generalizes the defining Eqs. (10) and (11). In Pro-TeM we use the second equation to move compositions inside arguments of rule symbols outside, which is necessary for translating proof terms into rewrite sequences.

Lemma 1. *For arbitrary proof terms* $A_1, \ldots, A_n$ *and* $B_1, \ldots, B_n$:

$$\alpha(A_1 \; ; B_1, \ldots, A_n \; ; B_n) \cong \mathsf{lhs}_\alpha\langle A_1, \ldots, A_n\rangle_\alpha \; ; \alpha(B_1, \ldots, B_n)$$

$$\alpha(A_1 \; ; B_1, \ldots, A_n \; ; B_n) \cong \alpha(A_1, \ldots, A_n) \; ; \mathsf{rhs}_\alpha\langle B_1, \ldots, B_n\rangle_\alpha$$

Proof. To simplify the notation, we assume the arity n of α equals 1:

$$\alpha(A_1 \; ; B_1) \cong \mathsf{lhs}_\alpha\langle A_1 \; ; B_1\rangle_\alpha \; ; \alpha(\mathsf{tgt}(B_1)) \tag{10}$$

$$\cong (\mathsf{lhs}_\alpha\langle A_1\rangle_\alpha \; ; \mathsf{lhs}_\alpha\langle B_1\rangle_\alpha) \; ; \alpha(\mathsf{tgt}(B_1)) \tag{$\star$}$$

$$\cong \mathsf{lhs}_\alpha\langle A_1\rangle_\alpha \; ; (\mathsf{lhs}_\alpha\langle B_1\rangle_\alpha \; ; \alpha(\mathsf{tgt}(B_1))) \tag{3}$$

$$\cong \mathsf{lhs}_\alpha\langle A_1\rangle_\alpha \; ; \alpha(B_1) \tag{10}$$

$$\alpha(A_1 \; ; B_1) \cong \alpha(\mathsf{src}(A_1)) \; ; \mathsf{rhs}_\alpha\langle A_1 \; ; B_1\rangle_\alpha \tag{11}$$

$$\cong \alpha(\mathsf{src}(A_1)) \; ; (\mathsf{rhs}_\alpha\langle A_1\rangle_\alpha \; ; \mathsf{rhs}_\alpha\langle B_1\rangle_\alpha) \tag{$\star$}$$

$$\cong (\alpha(\mathsf{src}(A_1)) \; ; \mathsf{rhs}_\alpha\langle A_1\rangle_\alpha) \; ; \mathsf{rhs}_\alpha\langle B_1\rangle_\alpha \tag{3}$$

$$\cong \alpha(A_1) \; ; \mathsf{rhs}_\alpha\langle B_1\rangle_\alpha \tag{11}$$

In the steps labeled $(\star)$ we use equation (4) repeatedly, depending on the structure of lhs_α and rhs_α. $\square$

The following lemma captures the connection between permutation equivalence and permutation order, a result that is mentioned in passing after the permutation order is introduced in [7, Definition 8.3.1].

Lemma 2. *For proof terms A and B, $A \cong B$ if and only if both $A \sqsubseteq B$ and $B \sqsubseteq A$.* $\square$

Standard Reductions are unique representatives of permutation equivalence classes, that are obtained by sorting rewrite steps in an outside-in and left-to-right order. For transforming reductions to outside-in order, called *parallel standard* form, the authors in [7, Section 8.5] propose two different approaches based on selection sort and insertion sort respectively. Since the latter, discussed in [7, Section 8.5.3], relies on proof terms it is of particular interest to us. Standard reductions are then obtained from parallel standard ones by imposing a left-to-right order when evaluating parallel steps.

Definition 4. *The* parallel standardization TRS *consists of the following rewrite schemas:*

$$\mathsf{lhs}_\alpha\langle A_1, \ldots, A_n \rangle_\alpha \, ; \alpha(t_1, \ldots, t_n) \;\to\; \alpha(A_1, \ldots, A_n) \tag{12}$$

$$\alpha(A_1, \ldots, A_n) \;\to\; \alpha(s_1, \ldots, s_n) \, ; \mathsf{rhs}_\alpha\langle A_1, \ldots, A_n \rangle_\alpha \tag{13}$$

These rules are applied modulo structural equivalence. The conditions on the symbols are the same as in Definition 3, but additionally we demand that in (13) at least one of $A_1, \ldots, A_n$ is not structurally equivalent to a proof term without rules symbols. A proof term is parallel standard *if it is in normal form with respect to parallel standardization.*

Parallel standardness is invariant with respect to structural equivalence by definition. As shown in the example below, structural equivalence is needed to move intermediate parallel reductions out of the way such that steps in the wrong order become adjacent. In particular, using canonical forms as representatives of structural equivalence classes, is not sufficient to compute parallel standard forms. This considerably complicates the automation of permutation equivalence.

Example 5. Consider $A = \varepsilon(x) \wedge \neg(y \wedge z) \, ; x \wedge \alpha(y, z) \, ; \gamma(x, \neg y, \neg z)$. The inner step $\varepsilon(x) \wedge \neg(y \wedge z)$ does not contribute to the outer step $\gamma(x, \neg y, \neg z)$ and hence these two steps need to be swapped to obtain a parallel standard normal form. To be able to apply the rules of the parallel standardization TRS, we first make the steps adjacent by moving the second step $x \wedge \alpha(y, z)$ out of the way with an appeal to structural equivalence:

$$A \equiv \varepsilon(x) \wedge \alpha(y, z) \; ; \gamma(x, \neg y, \neg z)$$
$$\equiv \neg\neg x \wedge \alpha(y, z) \; ; \varepsilon(x) \wedge (\neg y \vee \neg z) \; ; \gamma(x, \neg y, \neg z)$$
$$\rightarrow \neg\neg x \wedge \alpha(y, z) \; ; \gamma(\varepsilon(x), \neg y, \neg z)$$
$$\rightarrow \neg\neg x \wedge \alpha(y, z) \; ; \gamma(\neg\neg x, \neg y, \neg z) \; ; (\varepsilon(x) \wedge \neg y) \vee (\varepsilon(x) \wedge \neg z)$$

The resulting proof term is parallel standard. Note that the canonical form of A is $\varepsilon(x) \wedge \alpha(y, z) \; ; \gamma(x, \neg y, \neg z)$, which is a normal form with respect to (12).

The conditions on $A_1, \ldots, A_n$ in rule (13) are there to avoid trivial cases of non-termination; e.g. $\gamma(y) \rightarrow \gamma(y) \; ; y \equiv \gamma(y)$ is excluded. In [7, Section 8.5] a proof sketch of the following result is given.

Theorem 2. *The parallel standardization TRS is complete modulo structural equivalence.* $\qquad\qquad\square$

Instead of rule (12), in our implementation we use the more liberal rewrite rule

$$\mathsf{lhs}_\alpha\langle A_1, \ldots, A_n\rangle_\alpha \; ; \alpha(B_1, \ldots, B_n) \rightarrow \alpha(A_1 \; ; B_1, \ldots, A_n \; ; B_n) \qquad (14)$$

which is based on Lemma 1. Since we rewrite modulo structural equivalence, (14) simulates (12); simply substitute $\mathsf{tgt}(A_i)$ for B_i. So for the case that the B_i do not contain rule symbols, the two rules behave exactly the same. If there is some rule symbol contained in one of the B_i, the term $\mathsf{lhs}_\alpha\langle A_1, \ldots, A_n\rangle_\alpha \; ; \alpha(B_1, \ldots, B_n)$ with $\mathsf{tgt}(A_i) = \mathsf{src}(B_i) = t_i$ for $1 \leqslant i \leqslant n$ always rewrites to a proof term that is structurally equivalent to $\alpha(\mathsf{src}(A_1), \ldots, \mathsf{src}(A_n)) \; ; \mathsf{rhs}_\alpha\langle A_1 \; ; B_1, \ldots, A_n \; ; B_n\rangle_\alpha$ independent of which of the two rules we use:

$$\mathsf{lhs}_\alpha\langle A_1, \ldots, A_n\rangle_\alpha \; ; \alpha(B_1, \ldots, B_n)$$
$$\rightarrow \mathsf{lhs}_\alpha\langle A_1, \ldots, A_n\rangle_\alpha \; ; \alpha(t_1, \ldots, t_n) \; ; \mathsf{rhs}_\alpha\langle B_1, \ldots, B_n\rangle_\alpha \qquad (13)$$
$$\rightarrow \alpha(A_1, \ldots, A_n) \; ; \mathsf{rhs}_\alpha\langle B_1, \ldots, B_n\rangle_\alpha \qquad (12)$$
$$\rightarrow \alpha(\mathsf{src}(A_1), \ldots, \mathsf{src}(A_n)) \; ; \mathsf{rhs}_\alpha\langle A_1, \ldots, A_n\rangle_\alpha \; ; \mathsf{rhs}_\alpha\langle B_1, \ldots, B_n\rangle_\alpha \qquad (13)$$

and

$$\mathsf{lhs}_\alpha\langle A_1, \ldots, A_n\rangle_\alpha \; ; \alpha(B_1, \ldots, B_n)$$
$$\rightarrow \alpha(A_1 \; ; B_1, \ldots, A_n \; ; B_n) \qquad (14)$$
$$\rightarrow \alpha(\mathsf{src}(A_1), \ldots, \mathsf{src}(A_n)) \; ; \mathsf{rhs}_\alpha\langle A_1 \; ; B_1, \ldots, A_n \; ; B_n\rangle_\alpha \qquad (13)$$

Since it is not necessary to check whether the arguments of α are the targets of the A_i, rule (14) is easier to implement than rule (13). More details about the implementation can be found in Sect. 5.

4   Projection Equivalence

In the preceding section proof terms were declared to be equivalent if they can be obtained from each other by reordering (permuting) steps. In this section we give an account of *projection equivalence*, which is a completely different way of equating proof terms. It is based on the residual operation which computes which steps of A remain after performing B, for co-initial proof terms A and B. The steps in B need not be contained in A in order to compute their residual $A \mathbin{/} B$. The diagram on the left shows a desirable result of residuals and the diagram on the right provides the intuition behind Eqs. (17) and (18) below:

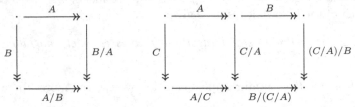

In [7, Definition 8.7.54] the residual $A \mathbin{/} B$ is defined by means of the following equations:

$$x \mathbin{/} x = x \tag{15}$$

$$f(A_1, \ldots, A_n) \mathbin{/} f(B_1, \ldots, B_n) = f(A_1 \mathbin{/} B_1, \ldots, A_n \mathbin{/} B_n)$$

$$\alpha(A_1, \ldots, A_n) \mathbin{/} \alpha(B_1, \ldots, B_n) = \mathsf{rhs}_\alpha\langle A_1 \mathbin{/} B_1, \ldots, A_n \mathbin{/} B_n\rangle_\alpha$$

$$\alpha(A_1, \ldots, A_n) \mathbin{/} \mathsf{lhs}_\alpha\langle B_1, \ldots, B_n\rangle_\alpha = \alpha(A_1 \mathbin{/} B_1, \ldots, A_n \mathbin{/} B_n) \tag{16}$$

$$\mathsf{lhs}_\alpha\langle A_1, \ldots, A_n\rangle_\alpha \mathbin{/} \alpha(B_1, \ldots, B_n) = \mathsf{rhs}_\alpha\langle A_1 \mathbin{/} B_1, \ldots, A_n \mathbin{/} B_n\rangle_\alpha$$

$$C \mathbin{/} (A \mathbin{;} B) = (C \mathbin{/} A) \mathbin{/} B \tag{17}$$

$$(A \mathbin{;} B) \mathbin{/} C = (A \mathbin{/} C) \mathbin{;} (B \mathbin{/} (C \mathbin{/} A)) \tag{18}$$

$$A \mathbin{/} B = \#(\mathsf{tgt}(B)) \qquad \text{(otherwise)}$$

Here A, B, C, $A_1, \ldots, A_n$, $B_1, \ldots, B_n$ are proof term *variables* that can be instantiated with arbitrary proof terms (so without $/$). The x in (15) denotes an *arbitrary* variable (in the underlying TRS), which cannot be instantiated.[1] In the final defining equation, $\#$ is the rule symbol of the special *error rule* $x \to \bot$. This rule is adopted to ensure that $A \mathbin{/} B$ is defined for arbitrary left-linear TRSs.[2] These defining equations are taken modulo (4) and

$$t \mathbin{;} t \approx t \tag{19}$$

The need for the functorial identities (4) is explained in the following example (Vincent van Oostrom, personal communication).

---

[1] In [7, Remark 8.2.21] variables are treated as constants and (15) is absent.
[2] In both [6, Definition 6.9] and [7, Definition 8.7.54] the wrong definition $A \mathbin{/} B = \#(\mathsf{tgt}(A))$ is given.

Example 6. Consider $A = f(g(\beta)\,;g(\gamma))$ and $B = \alpha(a)$ in the TRS

$$\alpha:\ f(g(x)) \to x \qquad\qquad \beta:\ a \to b \qquad\qquad \gamma:\ b \to c$$

When computing A/B without (4), the α-instance $f(g(A_1))/\alpha(B_1) = A_1/B_1$ of schema (16) does not apply to A/B since the g in $f(g(A_1))$ needs to be extracted from $g(\alpha)\,;g(\gamma)$ when computing $A\ /\ B$. As a consequence, the (otherwise) equation kicks in, producing the proof term $\#(b)$ that indicates an error. With (4) in place, the result of evaluating $A\ /\ B$ is the proof term $\beta\,;\gamma$, representing the desired sequence $a \to b \to c$.

It is not immediately clear that the defining equations on the preceding page constitute a well-defined definition of the residual operation. In [7, proof of Theorem 8.7.57] the defining equations together with (4) and (19) are oriented from left to right, resulting in a rewrite system $\mathcal{R}es$ that is claimed to be terminating and confluent. The residual of A over B is then defined as the unique normal form of $A\ /\ B$ in $\mathcal{R}es$.

There are two problems with this approach. First of all, when is the (otherwise) rule applied? In [7] this is not specified, resulting in an imprecise rewrite semantics of $\mathcal{R}es$. Keeping in mind that A/B is supposed to be a total operation on *proof terms* (so no $/$ in A and B), a natural solution is to adopt an innermost evaluation strategy. This ensures that $C\ /\ A$ is evaluated before $(C\ /\ A)\ /\ B$ in the right-hand side of (17) and before $B\ /\ (C\ /\ A)$ in the right-hand side of (18). The (otherwise) condition is taken into account by imposing the additional restriction that the (otherwise) rule is applied to A/B (with A and B in normal form) only if the other rules are not applicable. The second, and more serious, problem is that $\mathcal{R}es$ is *not* confluent.

Example 7. Consider the TRS consisting of the rules

$$\alpha:\ f(x,y) \to f(y,x) \qquad\qquad \beta:\ a \to b \qquad\qquad \gamma:\ f(a,x) \to x$$

and the proof terms $A = f(\beta, a)$, $B = \alpha(b, \beta)$, $C = \alpha(a, a)$, and $D = \gamma(a)$. There are two ways to compute $(A\,;B)\ /\ (C\,;D)$, starting with (17) or (18):

$$
\begin{aligned}
((A\,;B)\ /\ C)\ /\ D\ &\to\ ((A\ /\ C)\,;(B\ /\ (C\ /\ A)))\ /\ D \\
&\to^*\ (f(a\ /\ a, \beta\ /\ a)\,;(B\ /\ \alpha(a\ /\ \beta, a\ /\ a)))\ /\ D \\
&\to^*\ (f(a, \beta)\,;(B\ /\ \alpha(b, a)))\ /\ D \\
&\to\ (f(a, \beta)\,;f(\beta\ /\ a, b\ /\ b))\ /\ D \\
&\to^*\ (f(a, \beta)\,;f(\beta, b))\ /\ D \to f(a\,;\beta, \beta\,;b)\ /\ D \to \#(a) \\
(A\ /\ (C\,;D))\,;(B\ /\ ((C\,;D)\ /\ A)) & \\
&\to^*\ ((A\ /\ C)\ /\ D)\,;(B\ /\ ((C\ /\ A)\,;(D\ /\ (A\ /\ C)))) \\
&\to^*\ (f(a, \beta)\ /\ D)\,;(B\ /\ (\alpha(b, a)\,;(D\ /\ f(a, \beta)))) \\
&\to^*\ \beta\,;(B\ /\ (\alpha(b, a)\,;\gamma(b))) \to^*\ \beta\,;(f(\beta, b)\ /\ \gamma(b)) \\
&\to^*\ \beta\,;\#(b)
\end{aligned}
$$

The normal forms $\#(a)$ and $\beta\, ;\#(b)$ represent different failing computations: $a \to \bot$ and $a \to b \to \bot$.

To solve this problem we propose a drastic solution. When facing a term $A \,/\, B$ with A and B in normal form, the defining equations are evaluated from top to bottom and the first equation that matches is applied. This essentially means that the ambiguity between (17) and (18) is resolved by giving preference to the former. Due to innermost evaluation, no other critical situations arise. So we arrive at the following definition, where we turned Eq. (19) into rule (28), which is possible due to the presence of (29).

Definition 5. *The* residual TRS *for proof terms consists of the following rules:*

$$x \,/\, x \to x \tag{20}$$
$$f(A_1,\ldots,A_n) \,/\, f(B_1,\ldots,B_n) \to f(A_1 \,/\, B_1,\ldots,A_n \,/\, B_n) \tag{21}$$
$$\alpha(A_1,\ldots,A_n) \,/\, \alpha(B_1,\ldots,B_n) \to \mathsf{rhs}_\alpha\langle A_1 \,/\, B_1,\ldots,A_n \,/\, B_n\rangle_\alpha \tag{22}$$
$$\alpha(A_1,\ldots,A_n) \,/\, \mathsf{lhs}_\alpha\langle B_1,\ldots,B_n\rangle_\alpha \to \alpha(A_1 \,/\, B_1,\ldots,A_n \,/\, B_n) \tag{23}$$
$$\mathsf{lhs}_\alpha\langle A_1,\ldots,A_n\rangle_\alpha \,/\, \alpha(B_1,\ldots,B_n) \to \mathsf{rhs}_\alpha\langle A_1 \,/\, B_1,\ldots,A_n \,/\, B_n\rangle_\alpha \tag{24}$$
$$C \,/\, (A\,;B) \to (C \,/\, A) \,/\, B \tag{25}$$
$$(A\,;B) \,/\, C \to (A \,/\, C)\,;(B \,/\, (C \,/\, A)) \tag{26}$$
$$A \,/\, B \to \#(\mathsf{tgt}(B)) \tag{27}$$
$$x\,;x \to x \tag{28}$$
$$f(A_1,\ldots,A_n)\,;f(B_1,\ldots,B_n) \to f(A_1\,;B_1,\ldots,A_n\,;B_n) \tag{29}$$

We adopt innermost evaluation with the condition that the rules (20)–(27) *are evaluated from top to bottom.*

The residual TRS operates on *closed* proof terms, which are proof terms without proof term variables, to ensure that $\mathsf{tgt}(B)$ in the right-hand side of (27) can be evaluated. (Variables of the underlying TRS are allowed in proof terms.)

Lemma 3. *The residual TRS is terminating and confluent on closed proof terms.*

Proof. Confluence of the residual TRS is obvious because of the innermost evaluation strategy and the fact that there is no root overlap between its rules (due to the imposed evaluation order). Showing termination is non-trivial because of the nested occurrences of $/$ in the right-hand sides of (25) and (26). As suggested in [7, Exercise 8.7.58] one can use semantic labeling [8]. We take the well-founded algebra $\mathcal{A}$ with carrier $\mathbb{N}$ equipped with the standard order $>$ and the following weakly monotone interpretation and labeling functions:

$$\alpha_{\mathcal{A}}(x_1,\ldots,x_n) = f_{\mathcal{A}}(x_1,\ldots,x_n) = \max\{x_1,\ldots,x_n\}$$
$$;_{\mathcal{A}}(x,y) = x + y + 1 \qquad /_{\mathcal{A}}(x,y) = x \qquad \#_{\mathcal{A}}(x) = \perp_{\mathcal{A}} = 0$$
$$L_; = L_f = L_\alpha = L_\# = L_\perp = \varnothing \qquad L_/ = \mathbb{N} \qquad \mathsf{lab}_/(x,y) = x + y$$

The algebra $\mathcal{A}$ is a quasi-model of the residual TRS. Hence termination is a consequence of termination of its labeled version. The latter follows from LPO with well-founded precedence $/_i > /_j$ for all $i > j$ and $/_0 > \; ; \; > f > \alpha > \# > \perp$ for all function symbols f and rule symbols α. For instance, (26) gives rise to the labeled versions $(A\,;\,B)\,/_{a+b+c+1}\,C \;\to\; (A\,/_{a+c}\,C)\,;\,(B\,/_{b+c}\,(C\,/_{c+a}\,A))$ for all natural numbers a, b, and c, and each of them is compatible with the given LPO. □

The termination argument in the above proof does not depend on the imposed evaluation strategy. In the following we write $A\,!\,B$ for the unique normal form of $A\,/\,B$.

Definition 6. *The* projection order $\lesssim$ *and* projection equivalence $\simeq$ *are defined on co-initial proof terms as follows: $A \lesssim B$ if $A\,!\,B = \mathsf{tgt}(B)$ and $A \simeq B$ if both $A \lesssim B$ and $B \lesssim A$.*

Lemma 3 provides us with an easy decision procedure for projection equivalence: $A \simeq B$ if and only $A\,!\,B$ and $B\,!\,A$ coincide and contain neither rule symbols nor compositions.

Example 8. We can use this decision procedure to check which of the 13 sequences of Example 1 are projection equivalent. The (proof terms representing the) sequences 02357 and 12349 in Example 1 are projection equivalent since $02357/12349$ and $12349/02357$ rewrite to the same normal form $(\neg x \wedge y) \vee (\neg x \wedge z)$ in the residual TRS. As a matter of fact, all sequences from s to t are projection equivalent, except for 17. For instance, both $02357\,/\,17$ and $17\,/\,02357$ rewrite to $\#((\neg x \wedge y) \vee (\neg x \wedge z))\,;\,\#(\perp)$, but this normal form of the residual TRS contains the rule symbol $\#$ associated to the error rule.

Even though the residual TRS is designed to compute A/B for co-initial *proof terms*, there is no restriction on term formation. So in principle it is conceivable that $A\,!\,B$ is not a well-formed proof term, which can only happen if $A\,!\,B$ contains a subterm $A_1\,;\,A_2$ with $\mathsf{tgt}(A_1) \neq \mathsf{src}(A_2)$. The key properties that exclude this are $\mathsf{src}(A\,!\,B) = \mathsf{tgt}(B)$ and $\mathsf{tgt}(A\,!\,B) = \mathsf{tgt}(B\,!\,A)$, because then the right-hand sides of rules (25) and (26) are well-defined, meaning that one obtains proof terms as normal forms if A, B, C are instantiated by proof terms. The first property ($\mathsf{src}(A\,!\,B) = \mathsf{tgt}(B)$) can be proved by induction on the length of a normalizing sequence in the residual TRS starting from $A\,/\,B$. The second property ($\mathsf{tgt}(A\,!\,B) = \mathsf{tgt}(B\,!\,A)$, see also the diagrams at the beginning of this section) we have not yet been able to establish; the case where both A and B are headed by composition causes complications due to the imposed evaluation strategy.

5   Automation

In this section we describe the extensions to ProTeM[3] that we implemented as part of this work. ProTeM is a tool for manipulating proof terms and has been previously described in [3], with the focus on proof terms that represent multisteps, so without composition, and methods for measuring overlap between multisteps.

Apart from the decision procedure for projection equivalence based on the residual TRS described in the previous section, we implemented procedures dealing with parallel standardization as well as algorithms to translate between rewrite sequences and proof terms.

5.1   Rewrite Sequences and Proof Terms

We implemented an algorithm that takes as input two terms t and u, and computes a proof term A without compositions such that $\mathsf{src}(A) = t$ and $\mathsf{tgt}(A) = u$. If there is no multi-step $t \multimap u$, A does not exist. Otherwise, there may be different proof terms A that satisfy the requirements. ProTeM returns the first solution it encounters by trying to match the rules of the current TRS in top-down order and recursively in the arguments. This algorithm is extended to generate a proof term for a sequence of multisteps. We do this by applying it to each consecutive pair of terms, resulting in proof terms $A_1, \ldots, A_k$ for a sequence consisting of $k + 1$ terms, which are then combined into $A = A_1 ; \cdots ; A_k$.

Input: • proof term A
Output: • proof terms $B_1, \ldots, B_k$ without composition such that $A \cong B_1 ; \cdots ; B_k$

if $A = x$ **then return** A
else if $A = f(A_1, \ldots, A_n)$ or $A = \alpha(A_1, \ldots, A_n)$ **then**
    $B_1 := \mathsf{expand}(A_1); \ldots; B_n := \mathsf{expand}(A_n);$
    $m := $ maximum length of the sequences $B_1, \ldots, B_n;$
    for $i = 1, \ldots, n$ **do**
        extend B_i with $m - \mathsf{length}(B_i)$ copies of the term $\mathsf{tgt}(B_i)$
    if $A = f(A_1, \ldots, A_n)$ **then return**
        $f(B_1[1], \ldots, B_n[1]), \ldots, f(B_1[m], \ldots, B_n[m])$
    else return
        $\alpha(B_1[1], \ldots, B_n[1]), \mathsf{rhs}_\alpha\langle B_1[2], \ldots, B_n[2]\rangle_\alpha, \ldots, \mathsf{rhs}_\alpha\langle B_1[m], \ldots, B_n[m]\rangle_\alpha$
else if $A = A_1 ; A_2$ **then return** $\mathsf{expand}(A_1), \mathsf{expand}(A_2)$

Fig. 1. Expansion algorithm (expand).

Conversely, for a given proof term A, ProTeM computes terms $t_1, \ldots, t_n$ such that A represents the sequence $t_1 \multimap \ldots \multimap t_n$. To achieve this, first A is

---

[3] http://informatik-protem.uibk.ac.at/.

transformed into a permutation equivalent proof term $A_1 ; \ldots ; A_n$ such that the A_i themselves do not contain compositions. To move inner compositions outside we repeatedly apply the functorial identities (4) and a generalized form of (11) (similar to the extension of (12) to (14)). We call this procedure *expansion*. Detailed steps are displayed in Fig. 1. The terms $t_1, \ldots, t_n$ are then obtained by computing the sources and targets of $A_1, \ldots, A_n$. Expansion is also needed for the marking algorithm, presented in the next subsection. Here we give a simple example.

Example 9. Consider the TRS of Example 1. Expanding the proof term $A = \alpha(\beta(\neg x, \neg z) ; (\varepsilon(x) \wedge \varepsilon(y)), \varepsilon(z))$ yields the proof terms $A_1 = \alpha(\beta(\neg x, \neg z), \varepsilon(z))$ and $A_2 = \neg((\varepsilon(x) \wedge \varepsilon(y))) \vee \neg z$.

5.2 Standardization

In this subsection we report on ProTeM's implementations in connection with Sect. 3. When automating parallel standardization it is very useful to have some way of determining whether a given proof term is already parallel standard, other than going through all proof terms in its (theoretically infinite) structural equivalence class and trying to apply the parallel standardization rules. For this we use a modified version of the marking procedure [7, p. 366] that operates on proof terms instead of steps of a reduction. Our implementation is described in Fig. 2. We first transform the input A into its canonical form to get rid of trivial steps, then we use expansion to remove nested compositions and check if every proof term of the sequence $A_1, \ldots, A_n$ represents a parallel step (i.e., there are no nested rule symbols). Only then do we start with the actual marking. The basic idea is to go through the sequence $A_1, \ldots, A_n$ from left to right and mark the positions of the redexes. While moving right we check whether the next step contains markings below its redex pattern (i.e., in the arguments of its rule symbols). If it does we know that the next step takes place above the one that produced the marking and hence the given sequence of proof terms is not parallel standard.

Automating parallel standardization is a non-trivial task, since the rules of parallel standardization are applied modulo structural equivalence. Figure 3 displays our full algorithm to transform any proof term into a permutation equivalent parallel standard one. We start by computing the canonical form of our input A. Then we check if it is already parallel standard using the marking procedure. If not, we first apply the parallel standardization rules (13) and (14) as much as possible. If that does not result in a parallel standard proof term, a structurally equivalent proof term has to be computed to which we can again apply the parallel standardization rules. Structural equivalence classes are infinite, but only due to harmless compositions with trivial terms. Nevertheless, we do not search blindly through them. First we simplify our problem by determining which part of the proof term is not parallel standard and recursively call the parallel standardization algorithm on that subterm. When a composition $A_1 ; A_2$ is encountered where A_1 and A_2 are parallel standard but $A_1 ; A_2$ is not, neither A_1 nor A_2

Input: • proof term A
Output: • *yes* if A is parallel standard and *no* otherwise

$A_1, \ldots, A_n :=$ expand(canonical(A));
if one of $A_1, \ldots, A_n$ contains nested rule symbols then return *no*;
$M := \varnothing$;
for $i = 1, \ldots, n$ do
     $P := \{ p \in \mathcal{P}os(A_i) \mid A_i(p) \text{ is a rule symbol} \}$;
     for $p \in P$ do
         $\alpha(t_1, \ldots, t_m) := A_i|_p$;
         $t := \mathsf{lhs}_\alpha \langle t_1, \ldots, t_m \rangle \alpha$;
         mark the symbols in $A_i[t]_p$ at positions in M that are below p;
         if a symbol in $t_1, \ldots, t_m$ is marked then return *no*
     $M := \{ q \in M \mid q \text{ is parallel to all positions in } P \} \cup P$
return *yes*

Fig. 2. Marking algorithm (mark).

can contain nested rules symbols since these would have been expanded by (13). Because we always compute canonical forms of proof terms before trying the parallel standardization rules, A_1 and A_2 cannot have the same function symbol as root. The fact that $A_1 ; A_2$ is not parallel standard further implies that A_1 is of the form $A_1 = f(T_1, \ldots, T_n)$ and A_2 contains an outer step that must be performed before one of the inner steps in A_1. We try to find a structurally equivalent proof term $A = C_1 ; (C_2 ; A_2)$ with $C_1 = f(T_1, \ldots, \mathsf{src}(T_i), \ldots, T_n)$ and $C_2 = f(\mathsf{tgt}(T_1), \ldots, T_i, \ldots, \mathsf{tgt}(T_n))$ such that rule (13) is applicable to $C_2 ; A_2$. For each argument position i we first check if $C_2 ; A_2$ is already parallel standard to make sure not to perform useless steps which may cause non-termination of the procedure. If $C_2 ; A_2$ is parallel standard, we split A_1 at the next argument position. After we have identified C_1 and C_2 such that $C_2 ; A_2$ is not parallel standard, there is still the possibility that (13) is blocked, because C_2 contains composition. In that case C_2 is serialized into C_3 and C_4 such that $C_2 = C_3 ; C_4$ and C_4 contains exactly one rule symbol and no composition.

Since the parallel standardization TRS is terminating modulo structural equivalence (Theorem 2), its rules cannot be applied infinitely often to a proof term A and since we always perform at least one application of its rules in each iteration, our algorithm is bound to terminate after a finite number of steps.

Example 10. We apply the parallel standardization algorithm to the proof term A of Example 5. The canonical form of A is $A' = \varepsilon(x) \wedge \alpha(y, z) ; \gamma(x, \neg y, \neg z)$ and A' is not parallel standard according to the marking algorithm. Neither (12) nor (13) is applicable, though. Since both $\varepsilon(x) \wedge \alpha(y, z)$ and $\gamma(x, \neg y, \neg z)$ are parallel standard, we start splitting up $\varepsilon(x) \wedge \alpha(y, z)$ into $C_1 ; C_2$. For $i = 1$ we obtain $C_1 = \neg \neg x \wedge \alpha(y, z)$ and $C_2 = \varepsilon(x) \wedge (\neg y \vee \neg z)$, and so we try to apply (12) and (13) to the proof term $C_1 ; (C_2 ; A_2)$:

Input: • proof term A
Output: • canonical parallel standard proof term B such that $A \cong B$

$A := \mathsf{canonical}(A)$;
while $\mathsf{mark}(A) = \textit{false}$ **do**
    B is result of applying rules (12) and (13) to A;
    if $A \neq B$ **then** $A := \mathsf{canonical}(B)$
    else if $A = A_1 \,;\, A_2$ and $\mathsf{mark}(A_1) = \textit{false}$ **then**
        $A := \mathsf{canonical}(\mathsf{ps}(A_1) \,;\, A_2)$
    else if $A = A_1 \,;\, A_2$ and $\mathsf{mark}(A_2) = \textit{false}$ **then**
        $A := \mathsf{canonical}(A_1 \,;\, \mathsf{ps}(A_2))$
    else if $A = f(A_1, \ldots, A_n)$ **then**
        $A := \mathsf{canonical}(f(\mathsf{ps}(A_1), \ldots, \mathsf{ps}(A_n)))$
    else if $A = A_1 \,;\, A_2$ **then** $-\!\!-\ A_1 = f(T_1, \ldots, T_n)$
        $i := 0$;
        repeat
            $i\!+\!+$;
            $C_1 := f(T_1, \ldots, \mathsf{src}(T_i), \ldots, T_n)$;
            $C_2 := f(\mathsf{tgt}(T_1), \ldots, T_i, \ldots, \mathsf{tgt}(T_n))$
        until $\mathsf{mark}(C_2 \,;\, A_2) = \textit{false}$;
        B is result of applying rules (14) and (13) to $C_1 \,;\, (C_2 \,;\, A_2)$;
        if $A \neq B$ **then** $A := \mathsf{canonical}(B)$
        else
            C_2 is serialized into $C_3 \,;\, C_4$ such that C_4 contains one rule symbol;
            B is result of applying rules (12) and (13) to $C_1 \,;\, (C_3 \,;\, (C_4 \,;\, A_2))$;
            $A := \mathsf{canonical}(B)$;
return A

Fig. 3. Parallel standardization algorithm (ps).

$C_1 \,;\, (C_2 \,;\, A_2)$

$$\to\ \neg\neg x \wedge \alpha(y, z) \,;\, \gamma(\varepsilon(x), \neg y, \neg z) \tag{12}$$

$$\to\ \neg\neg x \wedge \alpha(y, z) \,;\, (\gamma(\neg\neg x, \neg y, \neg z) \,;\, (\varepsilon(x) \wedge \neg y) \vee (\varepsilon(x) \wedge \neg z)) \tag{13}$$

At this point we are done since the final term is parallel standard.

We also implemented full standardization of proof terms by serializing the parallel steps of parallel standard proof terms such that steps are performed in a left-to-right order.

6 Conclusion

In this paper we described the extensions to ProTeM that deal with the permutation and projection equivalences as well as the projection order, important notions to compare rewrite sequences. Along the way, we corrected a mistake in [6,7] concerning the well-definedness of the residual operation, which is used to decide projection equivalence.

This does not complete our investigations. We already remarked the difficulty of establishing $\mathsf{tgt}(A \mathbin{!} B) = \mathsf{tgt}(B \mathbin{!} A)$ which is needed to guarantee that $A \mathbin{/} B$ is a proper proof term. It is conceivable that the evaluation order we impose on the residual TRS needs to be relaxed to obtain this result. Then the error propagating rules $A \mathbin{;} \#(B) \to \#(A)$ and $\#(A) \mathbin{;} B \to \#(A)$ would be added to the residual TRS to resolve the non-confluence in Example 7. In addition the error rule $\# \colon x \to \bot$ would be promoted to the underlying TRS, in order to make $A \mathbin{;} \#(B)$, $\#(A) \mathbin{;} B$ and $\#(A)$ also permutation equivalent.

Another desirable result is a proof of equivalence of permutation and projection equivalence which is based on properties of the residual TRS. The question whether there exists a characterisation of permutation equivalence that avoids rewriting modulo structural equivalence is also worth investigating. Further, the complexity of computing (parallel) standard reductions and residuals needs to be investigated.

Acknowledgments. We thank Vincent van Oostrom and members of the master seminar of the Computational Logic research group for insightful discussions. Comments by the reviewers helped to improve the presentation.

References

1. Baader, F., Nipkow, T.: Term Rewriting and All That. Cambridge University Press (1998). https://doi.org/10.1017/CBO9781139172752
2. Hirokawa, N., Middeldorp, A.: Decreasing diagrams and relative termination. J. Autom. Reasoning **47**(4), 481–501 (2011). https://doi.org/10.1007/s10817-011-9238-x
3. Kohl, C., Middeldorp, A.: ProTeM: a proof term manipulator (system description). In: Kirchner, H. (ed.) Proceedings of 3rd International Conference on Formal Structures for Computation and Deduction. Leibniz International Proceedings in Informatics, vol. 108, pp. 31:1–31:8 (2018). https://doi.org/10.4230/LIPIcs.FSCD.2018.31
4. Martí-Oliet, N., Meseguer, J.: Rewriting logic: roadmap and bibliography. Theoret. Comput. Sci. **285**(2), 121–154 (2002). https://doi.org/10.1016/S0304-3975(01)00357-7
5. Meseguer, J.: Conditioned rewriting logic as a united model of concurrency. Theoret. Comput. Sci. **96**(1), 73–155 (1992). https://doi.org/10.1016/0304-3975(92)90182-F
6. van Oostrom, V., de Vrijer, R.: Four equivalent equivalences of reductions. In: Proceedings of 2nd International Workshop on Reduction Strategies in Rewriting and Programming. Electronic Notes in Theoretical Computer Science, vol. 70(6), pp. 21–61 (2002). https://doi.org/10.1016/S1571-0661(04)80599-1
7. Terese (ed.): Term Rewriting Systems, Cambridge Tracts in Theoretical Computer Science, vol. 55. Cambridge University Press (2003)
8. Zantema, H.: Termination of term rewriting by semantic labelling. Fundamenta Informaticae **24**, 89–105 (1995). https://doi.org/10.3233/FI-1995-24124

Combining ProVerif and Automated Theorem Provers for Security Protocol Verification

Di Long Li[✉] and Alwen Tiu

The Australian National University, Canberra, ACT 2600, Australia
dilong.li@anu.edu.au

Abstract. Symbolic verification of security protocols typically relies on an attacker model called the Dolev-Yao model, which does not model adequately various algebraic properties of cryptographic operators used in many real-world protocols. In this work we describe an integration of a state-of-the-art protocol verifier ProVerif, with automated first order theorem provers (ATP). The integration allows one to model directly algebraic properties of cryptographic operators as a first-order equational theory and the specified protocol can be exported to a first-order logic specification in the standard TPTP format for ATP. An attack on a protocol corresponds to a refutation using the encoded first order clauses. We implement a tool that analyses this refutation and extracts an attack trace from it, and visualises the deduction steps performed by the attacker. We show that the combination of ProVerif and ATP can find attacks that cannot be found by ProVerif when algebraic properties are taken into account in the protocol verification.

1 Introduction

Security protocols are used pervasively in communication networks, such as the SSL/TLS protocol [11] used in secure communication on the web. Designing a security protocol is an error-prone process due to the subtle security requirements and their dependency on the attacker model. Early work on symbolic analysis of protocols has uncovered many flaws in protocol designs, e.g., the classic example of Needham-Schröder's Public Key authentication protocol [20], whose flaw was found through a formal analysis in a model checker [18].

An important part of formal protocol analysis is the definition of the attacker model. A commonly used attacker model is the Dolev-Yao model [12], which assumes, among others, that encryption is perfect, i.e., an attacker will not be able to decrypt a cipher text unless he or she knows the decryption key. While this model has been shown effective in uncovering security flaws in many protocols (see, e.g., [18,25]), it also misses many attacks on protocols that rely on algebraic properties of the operators used in the protocols [9]. One example is the exclusive-or (XOR) operator commonly used in protocols for RFID. As shown in [10], some attacks on these protocols can only be found once the properties of XOR are taken into account, e.g., the associativity, commutativity, and inverse properties.

© Springer Nature Switzerland AG 2019
P. Fontaine (Ed.): CADE 2019, LNAI 11716, pp. 354–365, 2019.
https://doi.org/10.1007/978-3-030-29436-6_21

There are existing protocol verifiers that allow some algebraic properties in the attacker model, such as Maude-NPA [14,15] and Tamarin [13,19]. Maude-NPA, which is based on a rewriting framework, allows a rich set of algebraic properties, specified as equational theories and rewrite systems. These include associativity, commutativity and identity properties, and the finite variant class of equational theories [8]. However, there are some restrictions on how algebraic properties can be specified, and in certain cases [15], specific unification algorithms may need to be added to the prover. Tamarin has recently added support for XOR [13], which allows it to find flaws in the 5G network protocol [3], but just as Maude-NPA, it is not guaranteed to handle theories outside the finite variance class, e.g., XOR with a homomorphic function.

In this system description, we present a new tool, Proverif-ATP, which is a combination of a widely used protocol verifier ProVerif [4] and first-order automated theorem provers (ATP). Our tool allows a user to specify any algebraic properties in the attacker model as an equational theory, without having to modify the prover, or having to prove any particular meta-theory about the equational theory (e.g., whether the equational theory can be represented as a convergent rewrite system, or whether unification modulo the theory is decidable, etc), as this will be handled by the ATPs backend in our tool. Specifically, we made the following contributions:

- We implement an interface from ProVerif to arbitrary ATPs that allows the latter to verify the protocols specified in ProVerif. This is done via a translation from protocol specifications in ProVerif to first-order logic specifications in the TPTP format [24], a common input format accepted by a large number of ATPs. The TPTP output from ProVerif can then be fed into any ATP that accepts the TPTP input format.
- We implement a tool, called Narrator, that interprets the refutation proofs produced by the backend ATP and presents them in a form that is easier for the user to 'debug' a protocol specification. In particular it allows extraction of attack traces from the proofs. An issue with the default encoding from ProVerif to first-order specifications is that it obscures the structures of the original protocol, that makes it difficult to relate the resolution proofs produced by ATP (which can range in the thousands of steps) to attacks on the protocol. To this end, we introduce a tagging mechanism to annotate the encoding of a protocol with information about the protocol steps. This allows us to separate the attacker knowledge that is intercepted from protocol steps from the knowledge deduced by the attacker using (algebraic) properties of cryptographic operators. Narrator visualises the refutation proof as a directed acyclic graph, with different types of nodes color-coded to help the user to spot important steps in the protocol that contribute to the attack.

In Sect. 2 we give a brief overview of the architecture of ProVerif-ATP. Section 3 illustrates the use of ProVerif-ATP v0.1.0 through a running example of verifying a protocol featuring XOR [7]. Section 4 shows some results in using our tool to verify protocols that are currently out of the scope of ProVerif, and in some instances involving XOR with a homomorphic operator, also out of the scope of Tamarin.[1] Sect. 5 concludes the paper and discusses future work. The source code of the ProVerif-ATP tool and the example protocols tested are available online.[2]

2 Overview of the Proverif-ATP Tool

The Proverif-ATP tool consists of a version of ProVerif, modified to output protocol specifications in TPTP syntax, and a tool to interpret the resolution proof (in TPTP format [24]) in terms of attack traces and the visualisation of derivations of attacks. Figure 1 shows the architecture of Proverif-ATP. The backend solver can be any ATP, although in this work, we have used mainly Vampire [16]. We explain briefly each component in the following. More details of the implementation are available in the ProVerif-ATP repository.

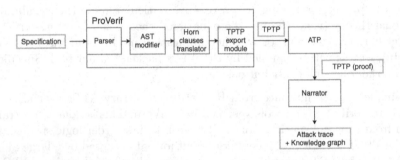

Fig. 1. Overall architecture of ProVerif-ATP

The components of Proverif-ATP are chained together using a script `pvatp`, which invokes the modified version of ProVerif, translates the ProVerif specification into a TPTP file, invokes the ATP, and generates the HTML files of the Narrator with both the ProVerif specification and Vampire output embedded.

ProVerif. A detailed explanation ProVerif is out of the scope of this system description, and the reader is referred to the ProVerif manual [6] for details. In our tool, we use the specification language based on the typed version of the applied-pi calculus [2]. The specification of algebraic properties of the attacker model can be accommodated within the syntax of ProVerif by simply writing down the equations corresponding to the algebraic properties of the model. So syntactically there is no change required to the specification language for protocols in ProVerif. However, the proof engine of ProVerif does not accept arbitrary equations, even if they are syntactically valid, and it also refuses to translate

---

[1] Some examples which Proverif-ATP can handle but which Tamarin fails are available via https://github.com/darrenldl/ProVerif-ATP/tree/master/related-work/.

[2] https://github.com/darrenldl/ProVerif-ATP.

these equations to first-order clauses. Since we will not be using ProVerif proof engine, the former is not a concern. We explain next how we address the latter.

Translation to First-Order Logic. The applied-pi calculus specification in ProVerif is translated to Horn clauses before it is given to its proof engine. This translation was proven correct by Abadi and Blanchet [1,5]. ProVerif has a built-in translator from the internal Horn clause representation of a protocol to a first-order specification in a format accepted by SPASS [27]. However, this translator cannot handle arbitrary equations – which is crucial to our aim. It attempts to perform reduction and syntactic unification to simplify certain terms in a protocol. In the case where the attacker model contains equational theories that cannot be represented as a convergent rewrite system, the simplification performed by ProVerif may fail and some parts of the protocol are not translated. To solve this, we modify the built-in translation of ProVerif to handle specific cases involving equations.

Proverif built-in translation also obscures the relative ordering of protocol steps and it is not obvious how to differentiate among clauses that encode only the attacker model and clauses from different steps of the protocol. To solve this, our tool tags all input (in the latest version) and output actions in the protocol. These tags do not change the meaning of the protocol (they preserve attacks), but it allows our tool (Narrator) to make sense of the refutation proof output by ATP. The tagging is done automatically at the abstract syntax of the applied-pi specification of the protocol, prior to the translation to TPTP.

Currently we only support secrecy queries, i.e., those queries that assert that the attacker knows a certain secret. Queries other than secrecy, such as authentication, need to be translated to an equivalent secrecy query. ProVerif provides a general authentication query, in the form of correspondence assertions [6,28], but their translation to first-order clauses is not yet supported. Since our goal here is to see how well ATP can handle algebraic properties in attacker models, we do not yet attempt to encode correspondence assertions in our translation, as this is orthogonal to the issue of algebraic models.

Note that if an attack is found, an attack trace is produced to serve as a proof certificate, which is to be manually verified in Narrator as described below, so in principle the correctness of the translation is not critical to the workflow.

ATP. The output (in TPTP format) of the translator of ProVerif is input to the ATP. The encoding of protocols as Horn clauses in ProVerif equates an attack on the protocol with provability of an attack goal. So if there is an attack on the protocol, we expect a proof of the attack goal as the output of the ATP (in the TPTP format for proofs). Since the expected input and output of an ATP are in TPTP format, we can in principle use any ATP as the backend prover in our tool, e.g., provers that compete in CASC competitions.[3] In this system description, we use Vampire [16] as the backend prover.

Narrator. The purpose of the Narrator is to make sense of the TPTP output, which can consist of thousands of inference steps. A lot of these steps are

---

[3] http://tptp.cs.miami.edu/~tptp/CASC/.

derivations of particular messages by the attacker, using the axioms for the attacker model. Some crucial information such as steps in the protocol responsible for the attacks, is not easy to spot from such a proof. The backend ATP may employ sophisticated inferences and rewriting of clauses that make it difficult to distinguish even basic information such as which properties of the operator are responsible for the attacks, which steps are involved, and whether a particular information provided by a protocol participant is useful in deriving the attack. Narrator aims to categorise various inference steps to make it easier for a user to spot relevant information from the resolution proof.

Narrator can also produce an attack trace, in the form of sequences of messages exchanged between roles of a protocol with the attacker. This feature is still at an experimental stage, as some crucial information, such as the actual messages that trigger the attack, may not be apparent from the trace. This is due to the fact that some provers (such as Vampire) do not provide the unifiers used in producing the proof, when the option for TPTP output is enforced. Vampire does provide this information in its native proof format (via the option --proof_extra) [21]. Narrator currently supports only the TPTP output format for the reason that it is a standard format supported by many theorem provers.

3   Protocol Verification with Proverif-ATP: An Example

We use the CH07 protocol [7], for mutually authenticating a RFID reader and a RFID tag, as an example. As shown in [10], the protocol fails to guarantee the aliveness property [17] of the tag to the reader - the reader completed a run of the protocol believing to have been communicating with a tag, while no tag was present. Figure 2a shows the CH07 protocol specification in a message sequence chart. In the figure, R denotes an instance of an RFID reader, and T denotes an instance of an RFID tag. The constant **k** denotes the secret key shared by R and T, and **ID** denotes an identifier of T (e.g., serial number). There are various bitwise manipulation functions used in the protocol: for simplicity, we shall treat these as uninterpreted function symbols except for $\oplus$, which denotes XOR.

R initiates the protocol by sending a query message containing a *nonce* (a fresh random number) $r1$ to **T**. **T** generates a nonce $r2$, and computes $\tilde{g}$, which is used to rotate ID to obtain $ID2$. **T** then sends out $r2$ along with the left half of $ID2$. **R** looks up the ID of **T**, and computes the same $\tilde{g}$ and $ID2$, then sends out the right half of $ID2$ as response to **T**. It is implicit that **R** and **T** check all received messages against the self-computed copies, namely $Left(ID2 \oplus \tilde{g})$ sent from **T** to **R**, and $Right(ID2, \tilde{g})$ sent from **R** to **T**. At the end of a successful run of the protocol, **R** is convinced of the identity of **T** and vice versa.

The attack shown in [10] consists of two sessions. In the first session, the attacker observes a completed run between R and a tag T, and records all messages exchanged. Then using these messages, the attacker impersonates T in the second session. This attack relies on the properties of XOR to craft a special value of r_2 in the second session (see [10] for details).

Figure 2b shows a fragment of the ProVerif specification of the protocol. Note that the properties of XOR are encoded as equations (line starting with equation

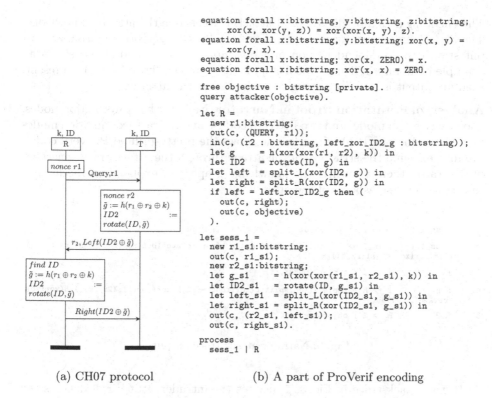

```
equation forall x:bitstring, y:bitstring, z:bitstring;
    xor(x, xor(y, z)) = xor(xor(x, y), z).
equation forall x:bitstring, y:bitstring; xor(x, y) =
    xor(y, x).
equation forall x:bitstring; xor(x, ZERO) = x.
equation forall x:bitstring; xor(x, x) = ZERO.

free objective : bitstring [private].
query attacker(objective).

let R =
    new r1:bitstring;
    out(c, (QUERY, r1));
    in(c, (r2 : bitstring, left_xor_ID2_g : bitstring));
    let g       = h(xor(xor(r1, r2), k)) in
    let ID2     = rotate(ID, g) in
    let left    = split_L(xor(ID2, g)) in
    let right   = split_R(xor(ID2, g)) in
    if left = left_xor_ID2_g then (
        out(c, right);
        out(c, objective)
    ).

let sess_1 =
    new r1_s1:bitstring;
    out(c, r1_s1);
    new r2_s1:bitstring;
    let g_s1      = h(xor(xor(r1_s1, r2_s1), k)) in
    let ID2_s1    = rotate(ID, g_s1) in
    let left_s1   = split_L(xor(ID2_s1, g_s1)) in
    let right_s1  = split_R(xor(ID2_s1, g_s1)) in
    out(c, (r2_s1, left_s1));
    out(c, right_s1).

process
    sess_1 | R
```

(a) CH07 protocol   (b) A part of ProVerif encoding

Fig. 2. CH07 specifications

in the figure). Since we cannot model authentication directly in Proverif-ATP, we reformulate the problem as a secrecy problem. For this, we assume that the attacker has obtained messages from the first session (process sess_1 in Fig. 2b). For the second session onwards, we modify the protocol so that the reader will output a secret (objective in Fig. 2b) after a successful authentication. To ensure that we capture the authentication property properly, we need to make sure that this secret is not accidentally output as a result of a legitmate interaction with **T**; this is modelled by simply removing the tag T from the protocol runs in the second session.

Before the protocol specification is translated to TPTP, the input/output actions in the protocol are tagged with constants denoting certain information, such as the principal performing those actions, and the steps within the protocol. The tagged protocol is then passed on to the translator unit to produce the TPTP specification of the protocol. The following is an example of a fragment of the TPTP file produced by the translation.

```
fof(ax226, axiom, pred_attacker(tuple_2(tuple_2(constr_QUERY, name_r1), constr_R_STEP_1))).

! [VAR_R2_293] : (pred_attacker(tuple_2(VAR_R2_293, constr_split_L(constr_xor(constr_rotate(
    name_ID, constr_h(constr_xor(constr_xor(name_r1, VAR_R2_293), name_k)))), constr_h(
    constr_xor(constr_xor(name_r1, VAR_R2_293), name_k)))))) => pred_attacker(tuple_2(
    name_objective, constr_R_STEP_3)))).
```

The encoding uses a predicate 'pred_attacker' to encode the attacker knowledge. The first clause above, for example, shows the knowledge obtained from an output step with no dependency on previous inputs. The second clause shows an example of an interactive protocol step: if the right condition (input) is present, then an output is sent (hence would be known to the attacker).

Analysis of Refutation Proof in Narrator. Narrator has three major modes, knowledge graph mode, and two ProVerif code + attack trace examination modes (one shows the raw ProVerif code, one shows the pretty-printed ProVerif code). We first examine the structure of the attack through the attack trace generated by Narrator, then we utilise the knowledge graph and explanation mechanism to further analyse aspects of the attack.

```
1.   sess_1.1    sess_1 -> I : r1_s1

2.   sess_1.2    sess_1 -> I : tuple_2(r2_s1,split_L(xor(rotate(ID,h(xor(xor(r1_s1,r2_s1),k)
     )),h(xor(xor(r1_s1,r2_s1),k)))))

3.   R.1         R -> I : tuple_2(QUERY,r1)

4.   R.3         I -> R : tuple_2(X28,split_L(xor(rotate(ID,h(xor(xor(r1,X28),k))),h(xor(xor
     (r1,X28),k)))))

5.   R.3         R -> I : objective
```

Fig. 3. Narrator attack trace output

In the attack trace in Fig. 3, I denotes the intruder/attacker, R denotes the reader, and sess_1 denotes the knowledge of a previous session as we have specified. Observe that the attacker is able to construct the appropriate message to send to R at step 4 (R.3 I -> R) for R to complete its execution and output objective at step 3. This matches the typical challenge and response structure - the reader R challenges the tag (attacker in this case) to give the appropriate message to solicit a response (message objective). The crucial step is step 4, which indicates that the reader somehow accepts the response from the attacker as legitimate. However, in this case, the backend ATP (Vampire) does not produce a ground instance of the message being sent; instead, there is a variable X28 whose value is supposed to be the nonce r_2 crafted by the attacker. Vampire can produce the substitutions produced at each step of inferences, but this feature is currently supported only in its native proof format, and not for the TPTP output. When we examine Vampire native proof output, we do see the exact term for X28 produced, which matches the attack mentioned in [10]. We have attempted running Vampire in the 'question-answering' mode, which would produce answer substitutions in TPTP format; but in that mode AVATAR must be disabled, which makes Vampire unable to find the attack for this protocol.

However, using Narrator we can still trace how the message at step 4 is constructed by the attacker, by observing the relationships between different nodes in the refutation proof. We represent the refutation proof as a directed acyclic graph, which we call *knowledge graph*. The nodes in the graph are color-coded to distinguish different categories of formulas as follows:

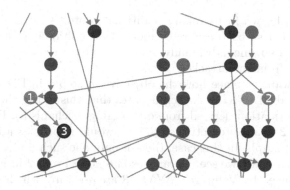

Fig. 4. Partial view of knowledge graph with manual numbering

```
From
  step R.1
  axiom ! [X17,X18] : attacker(tuple_2(X17,X18)) => attacker(X17)
  axiom ! [X19,X20] : attacker(tuple_2(X19,X20)) => attacker(X20)
attacker knows
  r1
...

From
  axiom ! [X2,X3] : xor(X2,X3) = xor(X3,X2)
  axiom ! [X4,X5,X6] : xor(X4,xor(X5,X6)) = xor(xor(X4,X5),X6)
  axiom ! [X8,X9] : (attacker(X9) & attacker(X8)) => attacker(xor(X8,X9))
  r1_s1
  xor(r1,r2_s1)
attacker knows
  xor(r1,xor(r1_s1,r2_s1))

From
  step sess_1.2
  axiom ! [X17,X18] : attacker(tuple_2(X17,X18)) => attacker(X17)
  axiom ! [X19,X20] : attacker(tuple_2(X19,X20)) => attacker(X20)
  axiom ! [X2,X3] : xor(X2,X3) = xor(X3,X2)
attacker learns
  split_L(xor(h(xor(k,xor(r1_s1,r2_s1))),rotate(ID,h(xor(k,xor(r1_s1,r2_s1))))))

Attacker rewrites
  split_L(xor(h(xor(k,X2)),rotate(ID,h(xor(k,X2)))))
to
  split_L(xor(h(xor(k,xor(r1,X0))),rotate(ID,h(xor(k,xor(r1,X0))))))

  xor(r1,X2)
to
  X0

From
  axiom ! [X15,X16] : (attacker(X16) & attacker(X15)) => attacker(tuple_2(X15,X16))
  split_L(xor(h(xor(k,xor(r1,X0))),rotate(ID,h(xor(k,xor(r1,X0))))))
  X0
attacker knows
  tuple_2(X0,split_L(xor(h(xor(k,xor(r1,X0))),rotate(ID,h(xor(k,xor(r1,X0)))))))
```

Fig. 5. Sample explanation given by Narrator (... indicates skip)

Unsure	Orange	NegatedGoal	Dark gray
Axiom	Light blue	Contradiction	Dark gray
InitialKnowledge	Light green	ProtocolStep	Light red
Rewriting	Dark blue	InteractiveProtocolStep	Dark red
Knowledge	Dark green	Alias	Light gray
Goal	Dark gray		

In this example, we focus on unconditional protocol steps (light red) and interactive protocol steps (dark red) nodes. Unconditional protocol steps are outputs that happen unconditionally, and interactive steps are outputs which depend on input from the attacker.

Suppose we want to trace how the objective in step 5 in Fig. 3 is triggered. That step is ascribed to R.3 – which denotes that this is the third step of the reader R (an information derived from our tagging mechanism). From the trace we know that R.3 is an interactive step, so it would appear as a dark-red node in the knowledge graph. In this case, there is only one such node. Tracing down the path from this node, we see it branches into node 1 and 2 in Fig. 4. The two nodes are introduced by Vampire's AVATAR architecture, which utilises a SAT or an SMT solver for improved capability [26]. By clicking on the two gray nodes individually, we can see the following two formulas

```
spl0_2 <=> ! [X0] : ~attacker(tuple_2(X0,split_L(xor(h(xor(k,xor(r1,X0))),rotate(ID,h(xor
(k,xor(r1,X0)))))))))
```

```
spl0_0 <=> attacker(tuple_2(objective,R_STEP_3))
```

The first formula corresponds to the message sent from I to R at step R.3. To see how this formula is constructed, we visit the next node from this grey node (node 3 in Fig. 4) and choose the "Explain construction of chain" option in the menu. Figure 5 contains the partial copy of the explanation shown, where X0 is equivalent to X28 in Fig. 3. See the full version of this paper in the project GitHub repository for the full explanation.

4   Evaluation

We evaluate the effectiveness of ProVerif-ATP on a number of protocol specifications under various attacker models featuring algebraic operators, such as, XOR, Abelian group operators, homomorphic encryption and associative pairing; see [9] for details of these properties. In most cases ProVerif simply fails because the equations modelling these properties are outside the scope of what it can handle. Table 1 shows the list of protocols verified and the results of the verification. We encode different attack queries as separate entries, thus there may be multiple entries for one protocol. See the full version of this paper on GitHub repository for more details of these protocols. Most of the protocols shown can be verified using Vampire version 4.2.2 as the ATP backend. In four protocols, involving XOR, Vampire fails due to out-of-memory error (indicated by 'MEM' in the table), and in one case, Vampire found a model (indicated by 'SAT' in the table) – meaning there is no attack under the corresponding attacker model, which is confirmed in ProVerif as well. The experiments were done in a dedicated virtual server, featuring a 8 core 3.6 GHz processor and 32GB RAM. Vampire was set to run in default mode, with a 24 h timeout and 30.9GB memory limit. In the default mode Vampire only uses one core.

Table 1. List of protocols tested with ProVerif-ATP

Protocol	ProVerif	Vampire	Vampire time (seconds)
LAK06 [10]	✗	✓	0.102
SM08 [10]	✗	✓	84.684
LD07 [10]	✗	✓	0.015
OTYT06 [10]	✗	✓	0.008
CH07 [10]	✗	✓	84.244
KCLL06 [10]	✗	✗ (MEM)	-
Bull Authentication Protocol [22]	✗	✗ (MEM)	-
Shamir-Rivest-Adleman Three Pass [9]	✓	✓	0.013
DH [9]	✓	✓	0.015
WEP [9]	✗	✓	0.182
Salary Sum [9]	✗	✓	0.571
NSPK (attack 1) [18]	✓	✓	3.151
NSPK (attack 2) [18]	✓	✓	2.629
NSLPK modified (attack 1) [9]	✗	✓	0.032
NSLPK modified (attack 2) [9]	✗	✓	0.034
NSLPK with ECB (attack 1) [9]	✗	✓	2.060
NSLPK with ECB (attack 2) [9]	✗	✓	2.300
NSLPK with XOR (attack 1) [23]	✗	✗ (MEM)	–
NSLPK with XOR (attack 2) [23]	✗	✗ (MEM)	–
NS with CBC (attack 1) [9]	✓	✓	0.070
NS with CBC (attack 2) [9]	No attack	SAT	–
NS with CBC (attack 3) [9]	✓	✓	0.087
Denning-Sacco Symmetric Key with CBC [9]	✓	✓	0.027

5   Conclusion and Future Work

Our preliminary tests suggest that the integration of ProVerif and ATP is useful as it improves the class of protocols one can verify. While we have not done a thorough comparison with other protocol verifiers, we do note that Tamarin can handle more security properties than Proverif-ATP (which is restricted to secrecy), but ProVerif-ATP can handle some cases where Tamarin cannot. Our aim is to show how an existing protocol verifier can benefit from ATPs to extend the coverage of its analysis with minimal efforts, ie., without coming up with dedicated procedures to solve equational reasoning needed in protocol analysis, as such we see our work as complementary to other dedicated protocol verifiers rather than their competitors or replacements.

A crucial part of our work is making the output of ATP intelligible for users, for which the unifiers used in the derivation of an attack would be very helpful. The current specification of the TPTP proof output format does not require unifiers to be included in the output proofs, something we hope will change in the future. As future work, we intend to compile a set of benchmark problems derived from protocol analysis (with algebraic operators) and propose its inclusion in the future CASC competition, to encourage developers of ATPs to improve their provers to solve this class of problems. Another direction is to also investigate the encoding of hyperproperties, such as non-inteference and equivalence.

References

1. Abadi, M., Blanchet, B.: Analyzing security protocols with secrecy types and logic programs. J. ACM **52**(1), 102–146 (2005). https://doi.org/10.1145/1044731. 1044735
2. Abadi, M., Fournet, C.: Mobile values, new names, and secure communication. In: Proceedings of the 28th ACM SIGPLAN-SIGACT Symposium on Principles of Programming Languages, POPL 2001, pp. 104–115. ACM, New York (2001). https://doi.org/10.1145/360204.360213
3. Basin, D., Dreier, J., Hirschi, L., Radomirovic, S., Sasse, R., Stettler, V.: A formal analysis of 5G authentication. In: Proceedings of the 2018 ACM SIGSAC Conference on Computer and Communications Security, CCS 2018, pp. 1383–1396. ACM, New York (2018). https://doi.org/10.1145/3243734.3243846
4. Blanchet, B.: An efficient cryptographic protocol verifier based on prolog rules. In: Proceedings of 14th IEEE Computer Security Foundations Workshop, 2001. pp. 82–96, June 2001. https://doi.org/10.1109/CSFW.2001.930138
5. Blanchet, B.: Modeling and verifying security protocols with the applied pi calculus and proVerif. Found. Trends® Priv. Secur. **1**(1–2), 1–135 (2016). https://doi.org/10.1561/3300000004
6. Blanchet, B., Smyth, B., Cheval, V., Sylvestre, M.: ProVerif 2.00: automatic cryptographic protocol verifier, user manual and tutorial. Technical report (2018)
7. Chien, H.-Y., Huang, C.-W.: A lightweight RFID protocol using substring. In: Kuo, T.-W., Sha, E., Guo, M., Yang, L.T., Shao, Z. (eds.) EUC 2007. LNCS, vol. 4808, pp. 422–431. Springer, Heidelberg (2007). https://doi.org/10.1007/978-3-540-77092-3_37
8. Comon-Lundh, H., Delaune, S.: The finite variant property: how to get rid of some algebraic properties. In: Giesl, J. (ed.) RTA 2005. LNCS, vol. 3467, pp. 294–307. Springer, Heidelberg (2005). https://doi.org/10.1007/978-3-540-32033-3_22
9. Cortier, V., Delaune, S., Lafourcade, P.: A survey of algebraic properties used in cryptographic protocols. J. Comput. Secur. **14**(1), 1–43 (2006). https://doi.org/10.3233/jcs-2006-14101
10. van Deursen, T., Radomirovic, S.: Attacks on RFID protocols. IACR Cryptology ePrint Archive 2008, 310 (2008). http://eprint.iacr.org/2008/310
11. Dierks, T., Rescorla, E.: The transport layer security (TLS) protocol version 1.2. Technical report, August 2008. https://doi.org/10.17487/rfc5246
12. Dolev, D., Yao, A.: On the security of public key protocols. IEEE Transact. Inf. Theory **29**(2), 198–208 (1983). https://doi.org/10.1109/TIT.1983.1056650
13. Dreier, J., Hirschi, L., Radomirovic, S., Sasse, R.: Automated unbounded verification of stateful cryptographic protocols with exclusive or. In: 2018 IEEE 31st Computer Security Foundations Symposium (CSF), pp. 359–373, July 2018. https://doi.org/10.1109/CSF.2018.00033
14. Escobar, S., Meadows, C., Meseguer, J.: Maude-NPA: cryptographic protocol analysis modulo equational properties. In: Aldini, A., Barthe, G., Gorrieri, R. (eds.) FOSAD 2007-2009. LNCS, vol. 5705, pp. 1–50. Springer, Heidelberg (2009). https://doi.org/10.1007/978-3-642-03829-7_1
15. Escobar, S., Meadows, C.A., Meseguer, J.: Maude-NPA, Version 3.1. Technical report (2017)
16. Kovács, L., Voronkov, A.: First-order theorem proving and VAMPIRE. In: Sharygina, N., Veith, H. (eds.) CAV 2013. LNCS, vol. 8044, pp. 1–35. Springer, Heidelberg (2013). https://doi.org/10.1007/978-3-642-39799-8_1

17. Lowe, G.: A hierarchy of authentication specifications. In: Proceedings 10th Computer Security Foundations Workshop, pp. 31–43, June 1997. https://doi.org/10.1109/CSFW.1997.596782
18. Lowe, G.: Breaking and fixing the Needham-Schroeder Public-Key protocol using FDR. In: Margaria, T., Steffen, B. (eds.) TACAS 1996. LNCS, vol. 1055, pp. 147–166. Springer, Heidelberg (1996). https://doi.org/10.1007/3-540-61042-1_43
19. Meier, S., Schmidt, B., Cremers, C., Basin, D.: The TAMARIN prover for the symbolic analysis of security protocols. In: Sharygina, N., Veith, H. (eds.) CAV 2013. LNCS, vol. 8044, pp. 696–701. Springer, Heidelberg (2013). https://doi.org/10.1007/978-3-642-39799-8_48
20. Needham, R.M., Schroeder, M.D.: Using encryption for authentication in large networks of computers. Commun. ACM **21**(12), 993–999 (1978). https://doi.org/10.1145/359657.359659
21. Reger, G.: Better proof output for vampire. In: Kovacs, L., Voronkov, A. (eds.) Proceedings of the 3rd Vampire Workshop, Vampire 2016. EPiC Series in Computing, vol. 44, pp. 46–60. EasyChair (2017). https://doi.org/10.29007/5dmz, https://easychair.org/publications/paper/1DlL
22. Ryan, P., Schneider, S.: An attack on a recursive authentication protocol a cautionary tale. Inf. Process. Lett. **65**(1), 7–10 (1998). https://doi.org/10.1016/S0020-0190(97)00180-4,. http://www.sciencedirect.com/science/article/pii/S0020019097001804
23. Steel, G.: Deduction with XOR constraints in security API modelling. In: Nieuwenhuis, R. (ed.) CADE 2005. LNCS (LNAI), vol. 3632, pp. 322–336. Springer, Heidelberg (2005). https://doi.org/10.1007/11532231_24
24. Sutcliffe, G.: The TPTP problem library and associated infrastructure. J. Autom. Reasoning **59**(4), 483–502 (2017). https://doi.org/10.1007/s10817-017-9407-7
25. Viganò, L.: Automated security protocol analysis with the AVISPA tool. Electron. Notes Theor. Comput. Sci. **155**, 61–86 (2006). https://doi.org/10.1016/j.entcs.2005.11.052. http://www.sciencedirect.com/science/article/pii/S1571066106001897 proceedings of the 21st Annual Conference on Mathematical Foundations of Programming Semantics (MFPS XXI)
26. Voronkov, A.: AVATAR: the architecture for first-order theorem provers. In: Biere, A., Bloem, R. (eds.) CAV 2014. LNCS, vol. 8559, pp. 696–710. Springer, Cham (2014). https://doi.org/10.1007/978-3-319-08867-9_46
27. Weidenbach, C., Dimova, D., Fietzke, A., Kumar, R., Suda, M., Wischnewski, P.: SPASS Version 3.5. In: Schmidt, R.A. (ed.) CADE 2009. LNCS (LNAI), vol. 5663, pp. 140–145. Springer, Heidelberg (2009). https://doi.org/10.1007/978-3-642-02959-2_10
28. Woo, T.Y.C., Lam, S.S.: Authentication for distributed systems. Computer **25**(1), 39–52 (1992). https://doi.org/10.1109/2.108052

Towards Bit-Width-Independent Proofs in SMT Solvers

Aina Niemetz[1], Mathias Preiner[1], Andrew Reynolds[2], Yoni Zohar[1(✉)],
Clark Barrett[1], and Cesare Tinelli[2]

[1] Stanford University, Stanford, USA
yoniz@cs.stanford.edu
[2] The University of Iowa, Iowa City, USA

Abstract. Many SMT solvers implement efficient SAT-based procedures for solving fixed-size bit-vector formulas. These approaches, however, cannot be used directly to reason about bit-vectors of symbolic
bit-width. To address this shortcoming, we propose a translation from
bit-vector formulas with parametric bit-width to formulas in a logic supported by SMT solvers that includes non-linear integer arithmetic, uninterpreted functions, and universal quantification. While this logic is undecidable, this approach can still solve many formulas by capitalizing on
advances in SMT solving for non-linear arithmetic and universally quantified formulas. We provide several case studies in which we have applied
this approach with promising results, including the bit-width independent verification of invertibility conditions, compiler optimizations, and
bit-vector rewrites.

1 Introduction

Satisfiability Modulo Theories (SMT) solving for the theory of fixed-size bit-
vectors has received a lot of interest in recent years. Many applications rely on
bit-precise reasoning as provided by SMT solvers, and the number of solvers that
participate in the corresponding divisions of the annual SMT competition is high
and increasing. Although theoretically difficult (e.g., [14]), bit-vector solvers are
in practice highly efficient and typically implement SAT-based procedures. Reasoning about fixed-size bit-vectors suffices for many applications. In hardware
verification, the size of a circuit is usually known in advance, and in software verification, machine integers are treated as fixed-size bit-vectors, where the width
depends on the underlying architecture. Current solving approaches, however, do
not generalize beyond this limitation, i.e., they cannot reason about parametric
circuits or machine integers of arbitrary size. This is a serious limitation when
one wants to prove properties that are bit-width independent. Further, when reasoning about machine integers of a fixed but large size, as employed, for example,

This work was supported in part by DARPA (awards N66001-18-C-4012 and FA8650-
18-2-7861), ONR (award N68335-17-C-0558), NSF (award 1656926), and the Stanford
Center for Blockchain Research.

P. Fontaine (Ed.): CADE 2019, LNAI 11716, pp. 366–384, 2019.
https://doi.org/10.1007/978-3-030-29436-6_22

in smart contract languages such as Solidity [28], current approaches do not perform as well in the presence of expensive operations such as multiplication [15].

To address this limitation we propose a general method for reasoning about bit-vector formulas with parametric bit-width. The essence of the method is to replace the translation from fixed-size bit-vectors to propositional logic (which is at the core of state-of-the-art bit-vector solvers) with a translation to the quantified theories of integer arithmetic and uninterpreted functions. We obtain a fully automated verification process by capitalizing on recent advances in SMT solving for these theories.

The reliability of our approach depends on the correctness of the SMT solvers in use. Interactive theorem provers, or proof assistants, such as Isabelle and Coq [20,29], on the other hand, target applications where trust is of higher importance than automation, although substantial progress towards increasing the latter has been made in recent years [5]. Our long-term goal is an efficient automated framework for proving bit-width independent properties within a trusted proof assistant, which requires both a formalization of such properties in the language of the proof assistant and the development of efficient automated techniques to reason about these properties. This work shows that state-of-the-art SMT solving combined with our encoding techniques make the latter feasible. The next steps towards this goal are described in the final section of this paper.

Translating a formula from the theory of fixed-size bit-vectors to the theory of integer arithmetic is not straightforward. This is due to the fact that the semantics of bit-vector operators are defined modulo the bit-width n, which must be expressed using exponentiation terms 2^n. Most SMT solvers, however, do not support unrestricted exponentiation. Furthermore, operators such as bitwise *and* and *or* do not have a natural representation in integer arithmetic. While they are definable in the theory of integer arithmetic using β-function encodings (e.g., [10]), such a translation is expensive as it requires an encoding of sequences into natural numbers. Instead, we introduce an uninterpreted function (UF) for each of the problematic operators and axiomatize them with quantified formulas, which shifts some of the burden from arithmetic to UF reasoning. We consider two alternative axiomatizations: a complete one relaying on induction, and a partial (hand-crafted) one that can be understood as an under-approximation.

To evaluate the potential of our approach, we examine three case studies that arise from real applications where reasoning about bit-width independent properties is essential. Niemetz et al. [19] defined invertibility conditions for bit-vector operators, which they then used to solve quantified bit-vector formulas. However, correctness of the conditions was only checked for specific bit-widths: from 1 to 65. As a first case study, we consider the bit-width independent verification of these invertibility conditions, which [19] left to future work. As a second case study, we examine the bit-width independent verification of compiler optimizations in LLVM. For that, we use the Alive tool [17], which generates verification conditions for such optimizations in the theory of fixed-size bit-vectors. Proving the correctness of these optimizations for arbitrary bit-widths would ensure their correctness for any language and underlying architecture rather than specific ones. As a third case study, we consider the bit-width independent verification of rewrite rules for the theory of fixed-size bit-vectors. SMT solvers for this theory heavily rely on such rules to simplify the input. Verifying their correctness is essential and is typically done by hand, which is both tedious and error-prone.

To summarize, this paper makes the following contributions.

- In Sect. 3, we study complete and incomplete encodings of bit-vector formulas with parametric bit-width into integer arithmetic.
- In Sect. 4, we evaluate the effectiveness of both encodings in three case studies.
- As part of the invertibility conditions case study, we introduce *conditional inverses* for bit-vector constraints, thus augmenting [19] with concrete parametric solutions.

Table 1. Considered bit-vector operators with SMT-LIB 2 syntax.

Symbol	SMT-LIB Syntax	Sort
$\approx, \not\approx$	=, distinct	$\sigma_{[n]} \times \sigma_{[n]} \to$ Bool
$<_u^{BV}, >_u^{BV}, <_s^{BV}, >_s^{BV}$	bvult, bvugt, bvslt, bvsgt	$\sigma_{[n]} \times \sigma_{[n]} \to$ Bool
$\leq_u^{BV}, \geq_u^{BV}, \leq_s^{BV}, \geq_s^{BV}$	bvule, bvuge, bvsle, bvsge	$\sigma_{[n]} \times \sigma_{[n]} \to$ Bool
$\sim^{BV}, -^{BV}$	bvnot, bvneg	$\sigma_{[n]} \to \sigma_{[n]}$
$\&^{BV}, |^{BV}, \oplus^{BV}$	bvand, bvor, bvxor	$\sigma_{[n]} \times \sigma_{[n]} \to \sigma_{[n]}$
$\ll^{BV}, \gg^{BV}, \gg_a^{BV}$	bvshl, bvlshr, bvashr	$\sigma_{[n]} \times \sigma_{[n]} \to \sigma_{[n]}$
$+^{BV}, \cdot^{BV}, \mathrm{mod}^{BV}, \mathrm{div}^{BV}$	bvadd, bvmul, bvurem, bvudiv	$\sigma_{[n]} \times \sigma_{[n]} \to \sigma_{[n]}$
$[u:l]^{BV}$	extract ($0 \leq l \leq u < n$)	$\sigma_{[n]} \to \sigma_{[u-l+1]}$
$\circ^{BV}$	concatenation	$\sigma_{[n]} \times \sigma_{[m]} \to \sigma_{[n+m]}$

Related Work. Bit-width independent bit-vector formulas were studied by Picora [22], who introduced a formal language for bit-vectors of parametric width, along with a semantics and a decision procedure. The language we use here is a simplified variant of that language. A unification-based algorithm for bit-vectors of symbolic lengths is discussed by Bjørner and Picora [4]. Bit-width independent formulas are related to parametric Boolean functions and circuits. An inductive approach for reasoning about such formalisms was developed by Gupta and Fisher [11,12] by considering a Boolean function for the base case of a circuit and another one for its inductive step. Reasoning about equivalence of such circuits can be embedded in the framework of [22].

2   Preliminaries

We briefly review the usual notions and terminology of many-sorted first-order logic with equality (denoted by $\approx$). See [10,30] for more detailed information. Let S be a set of *sort symbols*, and for every sort $\sigma \in S$, let X_σ be an infinite set of *variables of sort*σ. We assume that sets X_σ are pairwise disjoint and define X as the union of sets X_σ. A *signature* Σ consists of a set $\Sigma^s \subseteq S$ of sort symbols and a set Σ^f of function symbols. Arities of function symbols are defined in the usual way. Constants are treated as 0-ary functions. We assume that Σ includes a Boolean sort Bool and the Boolean constants $\top$ (true) and $\bot$ (false). Functions returning Bool are also called *predicates*.

We assume the usual definitions of well-sorted terms, literals, and formulas, and refer to them as Σ-terms, Σ-literals, and Σ-formulas, respectively. We define $\boldsymbol{x} = (x_1, ..., x_n)$ as a tuple of variables and write $Q\boldsymbol{x}\varphi$ with $Q \in \{\forall, \exists\}$ for a *quantified* formula $Qx_1 \cdots Qx_n\varphi$. For a Σ-term or Σ-formula e, we denote the *free variables* of e (defined as usual) as FV(e) and use $e[\boldsymbol{x}]$ to denote that the variables in $\boldsymbol{x}$ occur free in e. For a tuple of Σ-terms $\boldsymbol{t} = (t_1, ..., t_n)$ and a tuple of Σ-variables $\boldsymbol{x} = (x_1, ..., x_n)$, we write $e\{\boldsymbol{x} \mapsto \boldsymbol{t}\}$ for the term or formula obtained from e by simultaneously replacing each occurrence of x_i in e by t_i.

A Σ-*interpretation* $\mathcal{I}$ maps: each $\sigma \in \Sigma^s$ to a distinct non-empty set of values $\sigma^\mathcal{I}$ (the *domain* of σ in $\mathcal{I}$); each $x \in X_\sigma$ to an element $x^\mathcal{I} \in \sigma^\mathcal{I}$; and each $f^{\sigma_1 \cdots \sigma_n \sigma} \in \Sigma^f$ to a total function $f^\mathcal{I} : \sigma_1^\mathcal{I} \times ... \times \sigma_n^\mathcal{I} \to \sigma^\mathcal{I}$ if $n > 0$, and to an element in $\sigma^\mathcal{I}$ if $n = 0$. We use the usual inductive definition of a satisfiability relation $\models$ between Σ-interpretations and Σ-formulas.

A *theory* T is a pair (Σ, I), where Σ is a signature and I is a non-empty class of Σ-interpretations that is closed under variable reassignment, i.e., if interpretation $\mathcal{I}'$ only differs from an $\mathcal{I} \in I$ in how it interprets variables, then also $\mathcal{I}' \in I$. A Σ-formula φ is T-*satisfiable* (resp. T-*unsatisfiable*) if it is satisfied by some (resp. no) interpretation in I; it is T-*valid* if it is satisfied by all interpretations in I. We will sometimes omit T when the theory is understood from context.

The theory $T_{\mathrm{BV}} = (\Sigma_{\mathrm{BV}}, I_{\mathrm{BV}})$ of fixed-size bit-vectors as defined in the SMT-LIB 2 standard [3] consists of the class of interpretations I_{BV} and signature Σ_{BV}, which includes a unique sort for each positive integer n (representing the bit-vector width), denoted here as $\sigma_{[n]}$. For a given positive integer n, the domain $\sigma_{[n]}^\mathcal{I}$ of sort $\sigma_{[n]}$ in $\mathcal{I}$ is the set of all bit-vectors of size n. We assume that Σ_{BV} includes all *bit-vector constants* of sort $\sigma_{[n]}$ for each n, represented as bit-strings. However, to simplify the notation we will sometimes denote them by the corresponding natural number in $\{0, ..., 2^{n-1}\}$. All interpretations $\mathcal{I} \in I_{\mathrm{BV}}$ are identical except for the value they assign to variables. They interpret sort and function symbols as specified in SMT-LIB 2. All function symbols (of non-zero arity) in Σ_{BV}^f are overloaded for every $\sigma_{[n]} \in \Sigma_{\mathrm{BV}}^s$. We denote a Σ_{BV}-term (or *bit-vector term*) t of width n as $t_{[n]}$ when we want to specify its bit-width explicitly. We refer to the i-th bit of $t_{[n]}$ as $t[i]$ with $0 \leq i < n$. We interpret $t[0]$ as the least significant bit (LSB), and $t[n-1]$ as the most significant bit (MSB), and denote bit ranges over k from index j down to i as $t[j : i]$. The unsigned interpretation of a bit-vector $t_{[n]}$ as a natural number is given by $[t]_\mathbb{N} = \Sigma_{i=0}^{n-1} t[i] \cdot 2^i$, and its signed interpretation as an integer is given by $[t]_\mathbb{Z} = -t[n-1] \cdot 2^{n-1} + [t[n-2 : 0]^{\mathrm{BV}}]_\mathbb{N}$.

Without loss of generality, we consider a restricted set of bit-vector function and predicate symbols (or *bit-vector operators*) as listed in Table 1. The selection of operators in this set is arbitrary but complete in the sense that it suffices to express all bit-vector operators defined in SMT-LIB 2. We use $\max_{s[k]}^{BV}$ ($\min_{s[k]}^{BV}$) for the *maximum* or *minimum signed value* of width k, e.g., $\max_{s[4]}^{BV} = 0111$ and $\min_{s[4]}^{BV} = 1000$.

The theory $T_{IA} = (\Sigma_{IA}, I_{IA})$ of integer arithmetic is also defined as in the SMT-LIB 2 standard. The signature Σ_{IA} includes a single sort Int, function and predicate symbols $\{+, -, \cdot, \mathrm{div}, \mathrm{mod}, |...|, <, \leq, >, \geq\}$, and a constant symbol for every integer value. We further extend Σ_{IA} to include exponentiation, denoted in the usual way as a^b. All interpretations $\mathcal{I} \in I_{IA}$ are identical except for the values they assign to variables. We write T_{UFIA} to denote the (combined) theory of uninterpreted functions with integer arithmetic. Its signature is the union of the signature of T_{IA} with a signature containing a set of (freely interpreted) function symbols, called *uninterpreted functions*.

2.1 Parametric Bit-Vector Formulas

We are interested in reasoning about (classes of) Σ_{BV}-formulas that hold independently of the sorts assigned to their variables or terms. We formalize the notion of parametric Σ_{BV}-formulas in the following.

We fix two sets X^* and Z^* of variable and constant symbols, respectively, of bit-vector sort of undetermined bit-width. The bit-width is provided by the first component of a separate function pair $\omega = (\omega^b, \omega^N)$ which maps symbols $x \in X^* \cup Z^*$ to Σ_{IA}-terms. We refer to $\omega^b(x)$ as the *symbolic bit-width* assigned by ω to x. The second component of ω is a map ω^N from symbols $z \in Z^*$ to Σ_{IA}-terms. We call $\omega^N(z)$ the *symbolic value* assigned by ω to z. Let $v = FV(\omega)$ be the set of (integer) free variables occurring in the range of either ω^b or ω^N. We say that ω is *admissible* if for every interpretation $\mathcal{I} \in I_{IA}$ that interprets each variable in v as a positive integer, and for every $x \in X^* \cup Z^*$, $\mathcal{I}$ also interprets $\omega^b(x)$ as a positive integer.

Let φ be a formula built from the function symbols of Σ_{BV} and $X^* \cup Z^*$, ignoring their sorts. We refer to φ as a *parametric Σ_{BV}-formula*. One can interpret φ as a class of fixed-size bit-vector formulas as follows. For each symbol $x \in X^*$ and integer $n > 0$, we associate a unique variable x_n of (fixed) bit-vector sort $\sigma_{[n]}$. Given an admissible ω with $v = FV(\omega)$ and an interpretation $\mathcal{I}$ that maps each variable in v to a positive integer, let $\varphi|_{\omega[\mathcal{I}]}$ be the result of replacing all symbols $x \in X^*$ in φ by the corresponding bit-vector variable x_k and all symbols $x \in Z^*$ in φ by the bit-vector constant of sort $\sigma_{[k]}$ corresponding to $\omega^N(x)^{\mathcal{I}} \mod 2^k$, where in both cases k is the value of $\omega^b(x)^{\mathcal{I}}$. We say a formula φ is *well sorted under* ω if ω is admissible and $\varphi|_{\omega[\mathcal{I}]}$ is a well-sorted Σ_{BV}-formula for all $\mathcal{I}$ that map variables in v to positive integers.

Example 1. Let X^* be the set $\{x\}$ and Z^* be the set $\{z_0, z_1\}$, where $\omega^N(z_0) = 0$ and $\omega^N(z_1) = 1$. Let φ be the formula $(x +^{BV} x) +^{BV} z_1 \not\approx z_0$. We have that φ is well sorted under (ω^b, ω^N) with $\omega^b = \{x \mapsto a, z_0 \mapsto a, z_1 \mapsto a\}$ or $\omega^b = \{x \mapsto 3, z_0 \mapsto 3, z_1 \mapsto 3\}$. It is not well sorted when $\omega^b = \{x \mapsto a_1, z_0 \mapsto a_1, z_1 \mapsto a_2\}$ since $\varphi|_{\omega[\mathcal{I}]}$ is not a well sorted Σ_{BV}-formula whenever $a_1^{\mathcal{I}} \neq a_2^{\mathcal{I}}$. Note that an

ω where $\omega^b(\mathsf{x}) = a_1 - a_2$ is not admissible, since $(a_1 - a_2)^{\mathcal{I}} \leq 0$ is possible even when $a_1^{\mathcal{I}} > 0$ and $a_2^{\mathcal{I}} > 0$.

Notice that symbolic constants such as the maximum unsigned constant of a symbolic length w can be represented by introducing $\mathsf{z} \in Z^*$ with $\omega^b(\mathsf{z}) = w$ and $\omega^N(\mathsf{z}) = 2^w - 1$. Furthermore, recall that signature Σ_{BV} includes the bit-vector extract operator, which is parameterized by two natural numbers u and l. We do not lift the above definitions to handle extract operations having symbolic ranges, e.g., where u and l are Σ_{IA}-terms. This is for simplicity and comes at no loss of expressive power, since constraints involving extract can be equivalently expressed using constraints involving concatenation. For example, showing that every instance of a constraint $s \approx t[u : l]^{\mathrm{BV}}$ holds, where $0 < l \leq u < n - 1$, is equivalent to showing that $t \approx y_1 \circ^{\mathrm{BV}}(y_2 \circ^{\mathrm{BV}} y_3) \Rightarrow s \approx y_2$ holds for all y_1, y_2, y_3, where y_1, y_2, y_3 have sorts $\sigma_{[n-1-u]}$, $\sigma_{[u-l+1]}$, $\sigma_{[l]}$, respectively. We may reason about a formula involving a symbolic range $\{l, \ldots, u\}$ of t by considering a parametric bit-vector formula that encodes a formula of the latter form, where the appropriate symbolic bit-widths are assigned to symbols introduced for y_1, y_2, y_3.

We assume the above definitions for parametric Σ_{BV}-formulas are applied to parametric Σ_{BV}-terms as well. Furthermore, for any admissible ω, we assume ω can be extended to terms t of bit-vector sort that are well sorted under ω such that $t|_{\omega[\mathcal{I}]}$ has sort $\sigma_{[\omega^b(t)^{\mathcal{I}}]}$ for all $\mathcal{I}$ that map variables in $\mathrm{FV}(\omega)$ to positive integers. Such an extension of ω to terms can be easily computed in a bottom-up fashion by computing ω for each child and then applying the typing rules of the operators in Σ_{BV}. For example, we may assume $\omega^b(t) = \omega^b(t_2)$ if t is of the form $t_1 +^{\mathrm{BV}} t_2$ and is well sorted under ω, and $\omega^b(t) = \omega^b(t_1) + \omega^b(t_2)$ if t is of the form $t_1 \circ^{\mathrm{BV}} t_2$.

Finally, we extend the notion of validity to parametric bit-vector formulas. Given a formula φ that is well sorted under ω, we say φ is T_{BV}-valid under ω if $\varphi|_{\omega[\mathcal{I}]}$ is T_{BV}-valid for all $\mathcal{I}$ that that map variables in $\mathrm{FV}(\omega)$ to positive integers.

3   Encoding Parametric Bit-Vector Formulas in SMT

Current SMT solvers do not support reasoning about parametric bit-vector formulas. In this section, we present a technique for encoding such formulas as formulas involving non-linear integer arithmetic, uninterpreted functions, and universal quantifiers. In SMT parlance, these are formulas in the UFNIA logic. Given a formula φ that is well sorted under some mapping ω, we describe this encoding in terms of a translation $\mathcal{T}$, which returns a formula ψ that is valid in the theory of uninterpreted functions with integer arithmetic only if φ is T_{BV}-valid under ω. We describe several variations on this translation and discuss their relative strengths and weaknesses.

Overall Approach. At a high level, our translation produces an implication whose antecedent requires the integer variables to be in the correct ranges (e.g., $k > 0$ for every bit-width variable k), and whose conclusion is the result of converting each (parametric) bit-vector term of bit-width k to an integer term.

Operations on parametric bit-vector terms are converted to operations on the integers modulo 2^k, where k can be a symbolic constant. We first introduce uninterpreted functions that will be used in our translation. Note that SMT solvers may not support the full set of functions in our extended signature Σ_{IA}, since they typically do not support exponentiation. Since translation requires a limited form of exponentiation we introduce an uninterpreted function symbol pow2 of sort $Int \to Int$, whose intended semantics is the function $\lambda x.2^x$ when the argument x is non-negative. Second, for each (non-predicate) n-ary (with $n > 0$) function f^{BV} of sort $\sigma_1 \times \ldots \times \sigma_n \to \sigma$ in the signature of fixed-size bit-vectors Σ_{BV} (excluding bit-vector extraction), we introduce an uninterpreted function f^{N} of arity $n + 1$ and sort $Int \times Int \times \ldots \times Int \to Int$, where the extra argument is used to specify the bit-width. For example, for $+^{BV}$ with sort $\sigma_{[n]} \times \sigma_{[n]} \to \sigma_{[n]}$, we introduce $+^{N}$ of sort $Int \times Int \times Int \to Int$. In its intended semantics, this function adds the second and third arguments, both integers, and returns the result modulo 2^k, where k is the first argument. The signature Σ_{BV} contains one function, bit-vector concatenation $\circ^{BV}$, whose two arguments may have different sorts. For this case, the first argument of $\circ^{N}$ indicates the bit-width of the third argument, i.e., $\circ^{N}(k, x, y)$ is interpreted as the concatenation of x and y, where y is an integer that encodes a bit-vector of bit-width k; the bit-width for x is not specified by an argument, as it is not needed for the elimination of this operator we perform later. We introduce uninterpreted functions for each bit-vector predicate in a similar fashion. For instance, $\geq_u^{N}$ has sort $Int \times Int \times Int \to Bool$ and encodes whether its second argument is greater than or equal to its third argument, when these two arguments are interpreted as unsigned bit-vector values whose bit-width is given by its first argument. Depending on the variation of the encoding, our translation will either introduce quantified formulas that fully axiomatize the behavior of these uninterpreted functions or add (quantified) lemmas that state key properties about them, or both.

Translation Function. Figure 1 defines our translation function T_A, which is parameterized by an axiomatization mode A. Given an input formula φ that is well sorted under ω, it returns the implication whose antecedant is an *axiomatization* formula $AX_A(\varphi, \sigma)$ and whose conclusion is the result of converting φ to its encoded version via the conversion function CONV. The former is dependent upon the axiomatization mode A which we discuss later. We assume without loss of generality that φ contains no applications of bit-vector extract, which can be eliminated as described in the previous section, nor does it contain concrete bit-vector constants, since these can be equivalently represented by introducing a symbol in Z^* with the appropriate concrete mappings in ω^b and ω^N.

In the translation, we use an auxiliary function CONV which converts parametric bit-vector expressions into integer expressions with uninterpreted functions. Parametric bit-vector variables x (that is, symbols from X^*) are replaced by unique integer variables of type Int, where we assume a mapping χ maintains this correspondence, such that range of χ does not include any variable that occurs in $FV(\omega)$. Parametric bit-vector constants z (that is, symbols from set Z^*) are replaced by the term $\omega^N(z) \bmod pow2(\omega^b(z))$. The ranges of the maps

$\mathcal{T}_A(\varphi, \omega)$:

    Return $\mathrm{AX}_A(\varphi, \omega) \Rightarrow \mathrm{CONV}(\varphi, \omega)$.

$\mathrm{CONV}\,(e, \omega)$:

    Match e:

x	$\rightarrow \chi(\mathsf{x})$	if $\mathsf{x} \in X^*$
z	$\rightarrow \omega^N(\mathsf{z}) \bmod \mathsf{pow2}(\omega^b(\mathsf{z}))$	if $\mathsf{z} \in Z^*$
$t_1 \approx t_2$	$\rightarrow \mathrm{CONV}(t_1, \omega) \approx \mathrm{CONV}(t_2, \omega)$	
$f^{BV}(t_1, \ldots, t_n)$	$\rightarrow \mathrm{ELIM}(f^N(\omega^b(t_n), \mathrm{CONV}(t_1, \omega), \ldots, \mathrm{CONV}(t_n, \omega)))$	
$\bowtie(\varphi_1, \ldots, \varphi_n)$	$\rightarrow \bowtie(\mathrm{CONV}(\varphi_1, \omega), \ldots, \mathrm{CONV}(\varphi_n, \omega))$	$\bowtie \in \{\wedge, \vee, \Rightarrow, \neg, \Leftrightarrow\}$

$\mathrm{ELIM}\,(e)$:

    Match e:

$+^N(k, x, y)$	$\rightarrow (x + y) \bmod \mathsf{pow2}(k)$
$-^N(k, x, y)$	$\rightarrow (x - y) \bmod \mathsf{pow2}(k)$
$\cdot^N(k, x, y)$	$\rightarrow (x \cdot y) \bmod \mathsf{pow2}(k)$
$\mathrm{div}^N(k, x, y)$	$\rightarrow \mathrm{ite}(y \approx 0, \mathsf{pow2}(k) - 1, x \,\mathrm{div}\, y)$
$\mathrm{mod}^N(k, x, y)$	$\rightarrow \mathrm{ite}(y \approx 0, \mathsf{pow2}(k) - 1, x \bmod y)$
$\sim^N(k, x)$	$\rightarrow \mathsf{pow2}(k) - (x + 1)$
$-^N(k, x)$	$\rightarrow (\mathsf{pow2}(k) - x) \bmod \mathsf{pow2}(k)$
$\ll^N(k, x, y)$	$\rightarrow (x \cdot \mathsf{pow2}(y)) \bmod \mathsf{pow2}(k)$
$\gg^N(k, x, y)$	$\rightarrow (x \,\mathrm{div}\, \mathsf{pow2}(y)) \bmod \mathsf{pow2}(k)$
$\circ^N(k, x, y)$	$\rightarrow x \cdot \mathsf{pow2}(k) + y$
$\bowtie_u^N(k, x, y)$	$\rightarrow x \bowtie y$ $\bowtie \in \{<, \leq, >, \geq\}$
$\bowtie_s^N(k, x, y)$	$\rightarrow \mathsf{uts}_k(x) \bowtie \mathsf{uts}_k(y)$ $\bowtie \in \{<, \leq, >, \geq\}$
e	$\rightarrow e$ otherwise

Fig. 1. Translation $\mathcal{T}_A$ for parametric bit-vector formulas, parametrized by axiomatization mode A. We use $\mathsf{uts}_k(x)$ as shorthand for $2 \cdot (x \bmod \mathsf{pow2}(k - 1)) - x$.

in ω may contain arbitrary Σ_{IA}-terms. In practice, our translation handles only cases where these terms contain symbols supported by the SMT solver, as well as terms of the form 2^t, which we assume are replaced by $\mathsf{pow2}(t)$ during this translation. For instance, if $\omega^b(\mathsf{z}) = w + v$ and $\omega^N(\mathsf{z}) = 2^w - 1$, then $\mathrm{CONV}(\mathsf{z})$ returns $(\mathsf{pow2}(w) - 1) \bmod \mathsf{pow2}(w + v)$. Equalities are processed by recursively running the translation on both sides. The next case handles symbols from the signature Σ_{BV}, where symbols f^{BV} are replaced with the corresponding uninterpreted function f^N. We take as the first argument $\omega^b(t_n)$, indicating the symbolic bit-width of the last argument of e, and recursively call CONV on $t_1, \ldots, t_n$. In all cases, $\omega^b(t_n)$ corresponds to the bit-width that the uninterpreted function f^N expects based on its intended semantics (the bit-width of the second argument for bit-vector concatenation, or of an arbitrary argument for all other functions and predicates). Finally, if the top symbol of e is a Boolean connective we apply the conversion function recursively to all its children.

We run ELIM for all applications of uninterpreted functions f^N introduced during the conversion, which eliminates functions that correspond to a majority of the bit-vector operators. These functions can be equivalently expressed using integer arithmetic and $\mathsf{pow2}$. The ternary addition operation $+^N$, that represents addition of two bit-vectors with their width k specified as the first argument, is translated to integer addition modulo $\mathsf{pow2}(k)$. Similar considerations are applied for $-^{N}$ and $\cdot^{N}$. For div^{N} and mod^{N}, our translation handles the special case where the second argument is zero, where the return value in this case is the maximum value for the given bit-width, i.e. $\mathsf{pow2}(k) - 1$. The integer operators corresponding to unary (arithmetic) negation and bit-wise negation can be eliminated in a straightforward way. The semantics of various bitwise shift operators can be defined arithmetically using division and multiplication with $\mathsf{pow2}(k)$. Concatenation can be eliminated by multiplying its first argument x by $\mathsf{pow2}(k)$, where recall k is the bit-width of the second arugment y. In other words, it has the effect of shifting x left by k bits, as expected. The unsigned relation symbols can be directly converted to the corresponding integer relation. For the elimination of signed relation symbols we use an auxiliary helper uts (unsigned to signed), defined in Fig. 1, which returns the interpretation of its argument when seen as a signed value. The definition of uts can be derived based on the semantics for signed and unsigned bit-vector values in the SMT LIB standard. Based on this definition, we have that integers v and u that encode bit-vectors of bit-width k satisfy $<_{s}^{N}(k, u, v)$ if and only if $\mathsf{uts}_k(u) < \mathsf{uts}_k(v)$.

As an example of our translation, let $\varphi = (\mathsf{x} +^{BV} \mathsf{x}) +^{BV} \mathsf{z}_1 \not\approx \mathsf{z}_0$, $\omega^{N}(\mathsf{z}_0) = 0$, $\omega^{N}(\mathsf{z}_1) = 1$, and $\omega^{b}(\mathsf{x}) = \omega^{b}(\mathsf{z}_0) = \omega^{b}(\mathsf{z}_1) = a$ from Example 1. $\mathrm{CONV}(\varphi, (\omega^{b}, \omega^{N}))$ is $\mathrm{ELIM}(+^{N}(a, \mathrm{ELIM}(+^{N}(a, \chi(\mathsf{x}), \chi(\mathsf{x}))), 1 \bmod \mathsf{pow2}(a))) \not\approx 0 \bmod \mathsf{pow2}(a)$. After applying ELIM and simplifying, we get $(\chi(\mathsf{x}) + \chi(\mathsf{x}) + 1) \bmod \mathsf{pow2}(a) \not\approx 0$.

Thanks to ELIM, we can assume that all formulas generated by CONV contain only uninterpreted function symbols in the set $\{\mathsf{pow2}, \&^{N}, |^{N}, \oplus^{N}\}$. Thus, we restrict our attention to these symbols only in our axiomatization AX_A, described next.

Table 2. Full axiomatization of $\mathsf{pow2}$, $\&^{N}$, and $\oplus^{N}$. The axiomatization of $|^{N}$ is omitted, and is dual to that of $\&^{N}$. We use $\mathsf{ex}_i(x)$ for $(x \text{ div } \mathsf{pow2}(i)) \bmod 2$.

$\diamond$	$\mathrm{AX}_{\mathrm{full}}^{\diamond}$
$\mathsf{pow2}$	$\mathsf{pow2}(0) \approx 1 \land \forall k.\, k > 0 \Rightarrow \mathsf{pow2}(k) \approx 2 \cdot \mathsf{pow2}(k-1)$
$\&^{N}$	$\forall k, x, y.\ \&^{N}(k, x, y) \approx$ $\quad \mathsf{ite}(k > 1, \&^{N}(k-1, x \bmod \mathsf{pow2}(k-1), y \bmod \mathsf{pow2}(k-1)), 0) +$ $\quad \mathsf{pow2}(k-1) \cdot \min(\mathsf{ex}_{k-1}(x), \mathsf{ex}_{k-1}(y))$
$\oplus^{N}$	$\forall k, x, y.\ \oplus^{N}(k, x, y) \approx$ $\quad \mathsf{ite}(k > 1, \oplus^{N}(k-1, x \bmod \mathsf{pow2}(k-1), y \bmod \mathsf{pow2}(k-1)), 0) +$ $\quad \mathsf{pow2}(k-1) \cdot |\mathsf{ex}_{k-1}(x) - \mathsf{ex}_{k-1}(y)|$

Axiomatization Modes. We consider four different axiomatization modes A, which we call full, partial, combined, and qf (quantifier-free). For each of these axiomatizations, we define $\mathrm{AX}_A(\varphi, \omega)$ as the conjunction:

Table 3. Partial axiomatization of pow2, $\&^{\mathbb{N}}$, and $\oplus^{\mathbb{N}}$. The axioms for $|^{\mathbb{N}}$ are omitted, and are dual to those for $\&^{\mathbb{N}}$. We use $\max_k^{\mathbb{N}}$ for $\text{pow2}(k) - 1$.

$\diamond$	axiom	$\text{AX}_{\text{partial}}^{\diamond}$
pow2	base cases	$\text{pow2}(0) \approx 1 \wedge \text{pow2}(1) \approx 2 \wedge \text{pow2}(2) \approx 4 \wedge \text{pow2}(3) \approx 8$
	weak monotonicity	$\forall i \forall j.\, i \leq j \Rightarrow \text{pow2}(i) \leq \text{pow2}(j)$
	strong monotonicity	$\forall i \forall j.\, i < j \Rightarrow \text{pow2}(i) < \text{pow2}(j)$
	modularity	$\forall i \forall j \forall x.\, (x \cdot \text{pow2}(i)) \bmod \text{pow2}(j) \not\approx 0 \Rightarrow i < j$
	never even	$\forall i \forall x.\, \text{pow2}(i) - 1 \not\approx 2 \cdot x$
	always positive	$\forall i.\, \text{pow2}(i) \geq 1$
	div 0	$\forall i.\, i \text{ div } \text{pow2}(i) \approx 0$
$\&^{\mathbb{N}}$	base case	$\forall x \forall y.\, \&^{\mathbb{N}}(1, x, y) \approx \min(\text{ex}_0(x), \text{ex}_0(y))$
	max	$\forall k \forall x.\, \&^{\mathbb{N}}(k, x, \max_k^{\mathbb{N}}) \approx x$
	min	$\forall k \forall x.\, \&^{\mathbb{N}}(k, x, 0) \approx 0$
	idempotence	$\forall k \forall x.\, \&^{\mathbb{N}}(k, x, x) \approx x$
	contradiction	$\forall k \forall x.\, \&^{\mathbb{N}}(k, x, \sim^{\mathbb{N}}(k, x)) \approx 0$
	symmetry	$\forall k \forall x \forall y.\, \&^{\mathbb{N}}(k, x, y) \approx \&^{\mathbb{N}}(k, y, x)$
	difference	$\forall k \forall x \forall y \forall z.\, x \not\approx y \Rightarrow \&^{\mathbb{N}}(k, x, z) \not\approx y \vee \&^{\mathbb{N}}(k, y, z) \not\approx x$
	range	$\forall k \forall x \forall y.\, 0 \leq \&^{\mathbb{N}}(k, x, y) \leq \min(x, y)$
$\oplus^{\mathbb{N}}$	base case	$\forall x \forall y.\, \oplus^{\mathbb{N}}(1, x, y) \approx \text{ite}(\text{ex}_0(x) \approx \text{ex}_0(y), 0, 1)$
	zero	$\forall k \forall x.\, \oplus^{\mathbb{N}}(k, x, x) \approx 0$
	one	$\forall k \forall x.\, \oplus^{\mathbb{N}}(k, x, \sim^{\mathbb{N}}(k, x)) \approx \max_k^{\mathbb{N}}$
	symmetry	$\forall k \forall x \forall y.\, \oplus^{\mathbb{N}}(k, x, y) \approx \oplus^{\mathbb{N}}(k, y, x)$
	range	$\forall k \forall x \forall y.\, 0 \leq \oplus^{\mathbb{N}}(k, x, y) \leq \max_k^{\mathbb{N}}$

$$\bigwedge_{x \in \text{FV}(\varphi)} 0 \leq \chi(x) < \text{pow2}(\omega^b(x)) \wedge \left(\bigwedge_{w \in \text{FV}(\omega)} w > 0 \right) \wedge \text{AX}_A^{\text{pow2}} \wedge \text{AX}_A^{\&^{\mathbb{N}}} \wedge \text{AX}_A^{|^{\mathbb{N}}} \wedge \text{AX}_A^{\oplus^{\mathbb{N}}}$$

The first conjunction states that all integer variables introduced for parametric bit-vector variables x reside in the range specified by their bit-width. The second conjunction states that all free variables in ω (denoting bit-widths) are positive. The remaining four conjuncts denote the axiomatizations for the four uninterpreted functions that may occur in the output of the conversion function. The definitions of these formulas are given in Tables 2 and 3 for full and partial respectively. For each axiom, i, j, k denote bit-widths and x, y denote integers that encode bit-vectors of size k. We assume guards on all quantified formulas (omitted for brevity) that constrain i, j, k to be positive and x, y to be in the range $\{0, \ldots, \text{pow2}(k) - 1\}$. Each table entry lists a set of formulas (interpreted conjunctively) that state properties about the intended semantics of these operators. The formulas for axiomatization mode full assert the intended semantics of these operators, whereas those for partial assert several properties of them. Mode combined asserts both, and mode qf takes only the formulas in partial that are quantifier-free. In particular, $\text{AX}_{\text{qf}}^{\text{pow2}}$ corresponds to the base cases listed in partial, and $\text{AX}_{\text{qf}}^{\diamond}$ for the other operators is simply $\top$. The partial axiomatization of these operations mainly includes natural properties of them. For example, we include some base cases for each operation, and also the ranges of its inputs and output. For some proofs, these are sufficient. For $\&^{\mathbb{N}}$, $|^{\mathbb{N}}$ and $\oplus^{\mathbb{N}}$, we also included their behavior for specific cases, e.g., $\&^{\mathbb{N}}(k, a, 0) = 0$ and its variants. Other axioms (e.g., "never even") were added after analyzing specific benchmarks to identify sufficient axioms for their proofs.

Our translation satisfies the following key properties.

Theorem 2. *Let φ be a parameteric bit-vector formula that is well sorted under ω and has no occurrences of bit-vector extract or concrete bit-vector constants. Then:*

1. φ *is T_{BV}-valid under ω if and only if $T_{\mathrm{full}}(\varphi, \omega)$ is T_{UFIA}-valid.*
2. φ *is T_{BV}-valid under ω if and only if $T_{\mathrm{combined}}(\varphi, \omega)$ is T_{UFIA}-valid.*
3. φ *is T_{BV}-valid under ω if $T_{\mathrm{partial}}(\varphi, \omega)$ is T_{UFIA}-valid.*
4. φ *is T_{BV}-valid under ω if $T_{\mathrm{qf}}(\varphi, \omega)$ is T_{UFIA}-valid.*[1]

The proof of Property 1 is carried out by translating every interpretation $\mathcal{I}_{BV}$ of T_{BV} into a corresponding interpretation $\mathcal{I}_{N}$ of T_{UFIA} such that $\mathcal{I}_{BV}$ satisfies φ iff $\mathcal{I}_{N}$ satisfies $T_{\mathrm{full}}(\varphi)$. The converse translation can be achieved similarly, where appropriate bit-widths are determined by the range axioms $0 \leq \chi(x) < \mathrm{pow2}(\omega^b(x))$ that occur in $T_{\mathrm{full}}(\varphi, \omega)$. The rest of the properties follow from Property 1, by showing that the axioms in Table 3 are valid in every interpretation of T_{UFIA} that satisfies $\mathrm{AX}_{\mathrm{full}}(\varphi, \omega)$.

4   Case Studies

We apply the techniques from Sect. 3 to three case studies: (i) verification of invertibility conditions from Niemetz et al. [19]; (ii) verification of compiler optimizations as generated by Alive [17]; and (iii) verification of rewrite rules that are used in SMT solvers. For these case studies, we consider a set of verification conditions that originally use fixed-size bit-vectors, and exclude formulas involving multiple bit-widths.

For each formula ϕ, we first extract a parametric version φ by replacing each variable in ϕ by a fresh $x \in X^*$ and each (concrete) bit-vector constant by a fresh $z \in Z^*$. We define $\omega^b(x) = \omega^b(z) = k$ for a fresh integer variable k, and let $\omega^N(z)$ be the integer value corresponding to the bit-vector constant it replaced. Notice that, although omitted from the presentation, our translation can be easily extended to handle quantified bit-vector formulas, which appear in some of the case studies. We then define $\omega = (\omega^b, \omega^N)$ and invoke our translation from Sect. 3 on the parametric bit-vector formula φ. If the resulting formula is valid, the original verification condition holds independent of the original bit-width. In each case study, we report on the success rates of determining the validity of these formulas for axiomatization modes full, partial, combined, and qf. Overall, axiomatization mode combined yields the best results.

All experiments described below require tools with support for the SMT logic UFNIA. We used all three participants in the UFNIA division of the 2018 SMT

---

[1] A detailed proof, along with further details that were omitted from this paper can be found in its extended version at https://arxiv.org/abs/1905.10434.

competition: CVC4 [2] (GitHub master 6eb492f6), Z3 [8] (version 4.8.4), and Vampire [13] (GitHub master d0ea236). Z3 and CVC4 use various strategies and techniques for quantifier instantiation including E-matching [18], and enumerative [24] and conflict-based [27] instantiation. For non-linear integer arithmetic, CVC4 uses an approach based on incremental linearization [6,7,26]. Vampire is a superposition-based theorem prover for first-order logic based on the AVATAR framework [31], which has been extended also to support some theories including integer arithmetic [23]. We performed all experiments on a cluster with Intel Xeon E5-2637 CPUs with 3.5 GHz and 32 GB of memory and used a time limit of 300 s (wallclock) and a memory limit of 4 GB for each solver/benchmark pair. We consider a bit-width independent property to be proved if at least one solver proved it for at least one of the axiomatization modes.[2]

4.1   Verifying Invertibility Conditions

Niemetz et al. [19] present a technique for solving quantified bit-vector formulas that utilizes *invertibility conditions* to generate symbolic instantiations. Intuitively, an invertibility condition ϕ_c for a literal $\ell[x]$ is the exact condition under which $\ell[x]$ has a solution for x, i.e., $\phi_c \Leftrightarrow \exists x.\ell[x]$. For example, consider bit-vector literal $x \,\&^{\mathrm{BV}} s \approx t$ with $x \notin \mathrm{FV}(s) \cup \mathrm{FV}(t)$; then, the invertibility condition for x is $t \,\&^{\mathrm{BV}} s \approx t$.

The authors define invertibility conditions for a representative set of literals having a single occurrence of x, that involve the bit-vector operators listed in Table 1, excluding extraction, as the invertibility condition for the latter is trivially $\top$. A considerable number of these conditions were determined by leveraging syntax-guided synthesis (SyGuS) techniques [1]. The authors further verified the correctness of all conditions for bit-widths 1 to 65. However, a bit-width-independent formal proof of correctness of these conditions was left to future work. In the following, we apply the techniques of Sect. 3 to tackle this problem. Note that for this case study, we exclude operators involving multiple bit-widths, namely bit-vector extraction and concatenation. For the former, all invertibility conditions are $\top$, and for the latter a hand-written proof of the correctness of its invertibility conditions can be achieved easily.

Proving Invertibility Conditions. Let $\ell[x]$ be a bit-vector literal of the form $\diamond x \bowtie t$ or $x \diamond s \bowtie t$ (dually, $s \diamond x \bowtie t$) with operators $\diamond$ and relations $\bowtie$ as defined in Table 1. To prove the correctness of an invertibility condition ϕ_c for x independent of the bit-width, we have to prove the validity of the formula:

$$\phi_c \Leftrightarrow \exists x.\ell[x] \tag{1}$$

where occurrences of s and t are implicitly universally quantified. We then want to prove that Eq. 1 is T_{BV}-valid under ω. Considering the two directions of (1) separately, we get:

---

[2] All benchmarks, results, log files, and solver configurations are available at http://cvc4.cs.stanford.edu/papers/CADE2019-BVPROOF/.

$$\exists x.\ell[x, s, t] \Rightarrow \phi_{\mathrm{c}}[s, t] \tag{rtl}$$

$$\phi_{\mathrm{c}}[s, t] \Rightarrow \exists x.\ell[x, s, t] \tag{ltr}$$

The validity of (rtl) is equivalent to the unsatisfiability of the quantifier-free formula:

$$\ell[x, s, t] \wedge \neg \phi_{\mathrm{c}}[s, t] \tag{rtl'}$$

Eliminating the quantifier in (ltr) is much trickier. It typically amounts to finding a symbolic value for x such that $\ell[x, s, t]$ holds provided that $\phi_{\mathrm{c}}[s, t]$ holds. We refer to such a symbolic value as a *conditional inverse*.

Conditional Inverses. Given an invertibility condition ϕ_{c} for x in bit-vector literal $\ell[x]$, we say that a term α_{c} is a *conditional inverse* for x if $\phi_{\mathrm{c}} \Rightarrow \ell[\alpha_{\mathrm{c}}]$ is T_{BV}-valid. For example, the term s itself is a conditional inverse for x in the literal $(x \mid^{\mathrm{BV}} s) \leq_{\mathrm{u}}^{\mathrm{BV}} t$: given that there exists some x such that $(x \mid^{\mathrm{BV}} s) \leq_{\mathrm{u}}^{\mathrm{BV}} t$, we have that $(s \mid^{\mathrm{BV}} s) \leq_{\mathrm{u}}^{\mathrm{BV}} t$. When a conditional inverse α_{c} for x is found, we may replace (ltr) by:

$$\phi_{\mathrm{c}} \Rightarrow \ell[\alpha_{\mathrm{c}}] \tag{ltr'}$$

Clearly, (ltr') implies (ltr). However, the converse may not hold, i.e., if (ltr') is refuted, (ltr) is not necessarily refuted. Notice that if the invertibility condition for x is $\top$, the conditional inverse is in fact unconditional. The problem of finding a conditional inverse for a bit-vector literal $x \diamond s \bowtie t$ (dually, $s \diamond x \bowtie t$) can be defined as a SyGuS problem by asking whether there exists a binary bit-vector function C such that the (second-order) formula $\exists C \forall s \forall t. \phi_{\mathrm{c}} \Rightarrow C(s, t) \diamond s \bowtie t$ is satisfiable. If such a function C is found, then it is in fact a conditional inverse for x in $\ell[x]$. We synthesized conditional inverses for x in $\ell[x]$ for bit-width 4 with variants of the grammars used in [19] to synthesize invertibility conditions. For each grammar we generated 160 SyGuS problems, one for each combination of bit-vector operator and relation from Table 1 (excluding extraction and concatenation), counting commutative cases only once. We used the SyGuS feature of the SMT solver CVC4 [25] to solve these problems, and out of 160, we were able to synthesize candidate conditional inverses for 143 invertibility conditions. For 12 out of these 143, we found that the synthesized terms were not conditional inverses for every bit-width, by checking (ltr') for bit-widths up to 64.

Results. Table 4 provides detailed information on the results for the axiomatization modes full, partial, and qf discussed in Sect. 3. We use $\rightarrow$ and $\leftarrow$ to indicate that only direction left-to-right ((ltr) or (ltr')) or right-to-left (rtl'), respectively, were proved, and $\checkmark$ and $\times$ to indicate that both or none, respectively, of the directions were proved. Additionally, we use $\rightarrow_{\alpha_{\mathrm{c}}}$ (resp. $\rightarrow_{\mathrm{no}\,\alpha_{\mathrm{c}}}$) to indicate that for direction left-to-right, formula (ltr') (resp. (ltr)) was proved with (resp. without) plugging in a conditional inverse.

Overall, out of 160 invertibility conditions, we were able to fully prove 110, and for 19 (17) conditions we were able to prove only direction (rtl') (ltr'). For direction right-to-left, 129 formulas (rtl') overall were successfully proved to be unsatisfiable. Out of these 129, 32 formulas were actually trivial since the invertibility condition ϕ_c was $\top$. For direction left-to-right, overall, 127 formulas were proved successfully, and out of these, 102 (94) were proved using (resp. not using) a conditional inverse. Furthermore, 33 formulas could only be proved when using a conditional inverse. Thus, using conditional inverses was helpful for proving the correctness of invertibility conditions.

Considering the different axiomatization modes, overall, with 104 fully proved and only 17 unproved instances, combined performed best. Interestingly, even though axiomatization qf only includes some of the base cases of axiomatization partial, it still performs well. This may be due to the fact that in many cases, the correctness of the invertibility condition does not rely on any particular property of the operators involved. For example, the invertibility condition ϕ_c for literal $x \,\&^{\mathrm{BV}} s \approx t$ is $t \,\&^{\mathrm{BV}} s \approx t$. Proving the correctness of ϕ_c amounts to coming up with the right substitution for x, without relying on any particular axiomatization of $\&^{\mathrm{N}}$. In contrast, the invertibility condition ϕ_c for literal $x \,\&^{\mathrm{BV}} s \not\approx t$ is $t \not\approx 0 \vee s \not\approx 0$. Proving the correctness of ϕ_c relies on axioms regarding $\&^{\mathrm{BV}}$ and $\sim^{\mathrm{BV}}$. Specifically, we have found that from partial, it suffices to keep "min" and "idempotence" to prove ϕ_c. Overall, from the 2696 problems that this case study included, CVC4 proved 50.3%, Vampire proved 31.4%, and Z3 proved 33.8%, while 23.5% of the problems were proved by all solvers.

Table 4. Invertibility condition verification using axiomatization modes combined, full, partial, and qf. Column $\rightarrow_{\alpha_c}(\rightarrow_{\mathrm{no}\,\alpha_c})$ counts left-to-right proved with (without) conditional inverse.

Axiomatization	✓	←	→	×	$\rightarrow_{\alpha_c}$	$\rightarrow_{\mathrm{no}\,\alpha_c}$
full	64	18	22	56	72	51
partial	76	14	26	44	78	81
qf	40	22	22	76	50	51
combined	104	21	18	17	99	79
Total (160)	110	19	17	14	102	94

4.2 Verifying Alive Optimizations

Lopes et al. [17] introduces Alive, a tool for proving the correctness of compiler peephole optimizations. Alive has a high-level language for specifying optimizations. The tool takes as input a description of an optimization in this high-level language and then automatically verifies that applying the optimization to an arbitrary piece of source code produces optimized target code that is equivalent under a given precondition. It can also automatically translate verified optimizations into C++ code that can be linked into LLVM [16]. For each optimization, Alive generates four constraints that encode the following properties, assuming that the precondition of the optimization holds:

1. *Memory* Source and Target yield the same state of memory after execution.
2. *Definedness* The target is well-defined whenever the source is.
3. *Poison* The target produces so-called poison values (caused by LLVM's *nsw*, *nuw*, and *exact* attributes) only when the source does.
4. *Equivalence* Source and target yield the same result after execution.

From these verification tasks, Alive can generate benchmarks in SMT-LIB 2 format in the theory of fixed-size bit-vectors, with and without quantifiers. For each task, types are instantiated with all possible valid type assignments (for integer types up to a default bound of 64 bits). In the following, we apply our techniques from Sect. 3 to prove Alive verification tasks independently from the bit-width. For this, as in the Alive paper, we consider the set of optimizations from the *instcombine* optimization pass of LLVM, provided as Alive translations (433 total).[3] Of these 433 optimizations, 113 are dependent on a specific bit-width; thus we focus on the remaining 320. We further exclude optimizations that do not comply with the following criteria:

- In each generated SMT-LIB 2 file, only a single bit-width is used.
- All SMT-LIB 2 files generated for a property (instantiated for all possible valid type assignments) must be identical modulo the bit-width (excluding, e.g., bit-width dependent constants other than 0, 1, (un)signed min/max, and the bit-width).

As a useful exception to the first criterion, we included instances where all terms of bit-width 1 can be interpreted as Boolean terms. Overall, we consider bit-width independent verification conditions 1–4 for 180 out of 320 optimizations. None of these include memory operations or poison values, and only some have definedness constraints (and those are simple). Hence, the generated verification conditions 1–3 are trivial. We thus only consider the equivalence verification conditions for these 180 optimizations.

Results. Table 5 summarizes the results of verifying the equivalence constraints for the selected 180 optimizations from the *instcombine* LLVM optimization pass. It first lists all families, showing the number of bit-width independent optimizations per family (320 total). The next column indicates how many in each family were in the set of 180 considered optimizations, and the remaining columns show how many of those considered were proved with each axiomatization mode.

---

[3] At https://github.com/nunoplopes/alive/tree/master/tests/instcombine.

Table 5. Alive optimizations verification using axiomatizations combined, full, partial and qf.

Family	Considered	Proved				
		full	partial	qf	combined	Total
AddSub (52)	16	7	7	7	9	9
MulDivRem (29)	5	1	2	1	3	3
AndOrXor (162)	124	57	55	53	60	60
Select (51)	26	15	11	11	16	16
Shifts (17)	9	0	0	0	0	0
LoadStoreAlloca (9)	0	0	0	0	0	0
Total (320)	180	80	75	72	88	88

Overall, out of 180 equivalence verification conditions, we were able to prove 88. Our techniques were most successful for the AndOrXor family. This is not too surprising, since many verification conditions of this family require only Boolean reasoning and basic properties of ordering relations that are already included in the theory T_{IA}. For example, given bit-vector term a and bit-vector constants C_1 and C_2, optimization AndOrXor:979 essentially rewrites $(a <_s^{\mathrm{BV}} C_1 \land a <_s^{\mathrm{BV}} C_2)$ to $a <_s^{\mathrm{BV}} C_1$, provided that precondition $C_1 <_s^{\mathrm{BV}} C_2$ holds. To prove its correctness, it suffices to apply the transitivity of $<_s^{\mathrm{BV}}$ with Boolean reasoning. The same holds when lifting this equivalence to the integers, deducing the transitivity of $<_s^{\mathrm{N}}$ from that of the builtin $<$ relation of T_{IA}.

None of the 9 benchmarks from the Shifts family were proven. These benchmarks are more complicated than others. They combine bit-wise and arithmetical operations and thus rely on their axiomatization. Solving these benchmarks is an interesting challenge for future work. Adding specialized axioms to partial is one promising approach.

Interestingly, for this case study, the results from the different axiomatization modes are very similar. This can again be explained by the fact that many optimizations rely on properties of the integers that are already included in T_{IA}, without requiring any particular property of functions pow2, $\&^{\mathrm{N}}$, $|^{\mathrm{N}}$ and $\oplus^{\mathrm{N}}$ (as in the above example).

Note that we have also tried using our approach for proving the equivalence verification conditions for up to a bit-width of 64. However, all optimizations that were proven correct this way were already proven correct for arbitrary bit-widths, which suggests that this restriction did not make the benchmarks easier. Overall, from the 720 problems in this case study, CVC4 proved 42.6%, Vampire proved 36.2%, and Z3 proved 37.9%, while 32.5% of the problems were proved by all solvers.

4.3   BV Rewriting

SMT solvers for the theory of fixed-size bit-vectors heavily rely on rewriting to reduce the size of the input formula prior to solving the problem. Since these rewrite rules are usually implemented independently of the bit-width, verifying that they hold for any bit-width is crucial for the soundness of the solver. For this case study, we used a feature of the SyGuS solver in CVC4 that allows us to enumerate equivalent bit-vector terms/formulas (rewrite candidates) for a certain bit-width up to a certain term depth (nesting level of operators) [21]. We generated 1575 pairs of equivalent bit-vector terms of depth three and 431 equivalent pairs of formulas of depth two for bit-width 4 and translated them to integer problems with axiomatization modes full, partial, qf, and combined, resulting in $6300 + 1724 = 8024$ benchmarks in total. Since rewrites that have been proved can be used to further axiomatize the integer translation, we collected all proven rewrites after each run, added them as axioms to the initial problems and reran the experiments. This was repeated until we reached a fixpoint, i.e., no further rewrites were proved. With this approach, we were able to prove 409 out of the 435 formula equivalences (94%), reaching a fixpoint at the first iteration. For the equivalent terms, we initially proved 878 out of the 1575 equivalences, which increased to 935 (59%) after adding all axioms from the first run, reaching a fixpoint after two iterations. Overall, from the 8024 problems, CVC4 proved 64.2%, Vampire proved 66.5%, and Z3 proved 64.2%, while 63.8% of the problems were proved by all solvers.

5   Conclusion and Further Research

We have studied several translations from bit-vector formulas with parametric bit-width to the theories of integer arithmetic and uninterpreted functions. The translations differ in the way that the operator $2^{(\cdot)}$ and bitwise logical operators are axiomatized, namely, fully (using induction) or partially (using some of their key properties). Our empirical results show that state-of-the-art SMT solvers are capable of solving the translated formulas for various benchmarks that originate from the verification of invertibility conditions, LLVM optimizations, and rewriting rules for fixed-size bit-vectors.

In future research, we plan to investigate a translation of our results to a proof assistant such as Coq, for which a bit-vector library was recently developed [9]. This will involve supporting proofs in the SMT solver for non-linear arithmetic and quantifiers. We believe that our promising experimental results with an integer encoding indicate that this is a viable approach for automating bit-width independent proofs. We also plan to explore satisfiable benchmarks, and to extend our approach for translating models.

References

1. Alur, R., et al.: Syntax-guided synthesis. In: Formal Methods in Computer-Aided Design, FMCAD 2013, Portland, OR, USA, 20–23 October 2013, pp. 1–8 (2013)
2. Barrett, C., et al.: CVC4. In: Gopalakrishnan, G., Qadeer, S. (eds.) CAV 2011. LNCS, vol. 6806, pp. 171–177. Springer, Heidelberg (2011). https://doi.org/10. 1007/978-3-642-22110-1_14
3. Barrett, C., Stump, A., Tinelli, C.: The SMT-LIB standard: version 2.0. In: Gupta, A., Kroening, D. (eds.) Proceedings of the 8th International Workshop on Satisfiability Modulo Theories, Edinburgh, UK (2010)
4. BjØrner, N.S., Pichora, M.C.: Deciding fixed and non-fixed size bit-vectors. In: Steffen, B. (ed.) Tools and Algorithms for the Construction and Analysis of Systems, pp. 376–392. Springer, Berlin (1998). https://doi.org/10.1007/BFb0054184
5. Blanchette, J.C., Böhme, S., Paulson, L.C.: Extending sledgehammer with SMT solvers. J. Autom. Reasoning **51**(1), 109–128 (2013). https://doi.org/10.1007/ s10817-013-9278-5
6. Cimatti, A., Griggio, A., Irfan, A., Roveri, M., Sebastiani, R.: Experimenting on solving nonlinear integer arithmetic with incremental linearization. In: Beyersdorff, O., Wintersteiger, C.M. (eds.) SAT 2018. LNCS, vol. 10929, pp. 383–398. Springer, Cham (2018). https://doi.org/10.1007/978-3-319-94144-8_23
7. Cimatti, A., Griggio, A., Irfan, A., Roveri, M., Sebastiani, R.: Incremental linearization for satisfiability and verification modulo nonlinear arithmetic and transcendental functions. ACM Trans. Comput. Log. **19**(3), 19:1–19:52 (2018)
8. de Moura, L., Bjørner, N.: Z3: an efficient SMT solver. In: Ramakrishnan, C.R., Rehof, J. (eds.) TACAS 2008. LNCS, vol. 4963, pp. 337–340. Springer, Heidelberg (2008). https://doi.org/10.1007/978-3-540-78800-3_24. http://dl.acm.org/citation.cfm?id=1792734.1792766
9. Ekici, B., et al.: SMTCoq: a plug-in for integrating smt solvers into Coq. In: Majumdar, R., Kuncak, V. (eds.) CAV 2017. LNCS, vol. 10427, pp. 126–133. Springer, Cham (2017). https://doi.org/10.1007/978-3-319-63390-9_7
10. Enderton, H., Enderton, H.B.: A Mathematical Introduction to logic. Elsevier, Amsterdam (2001)
11. Gupta, A., Fisher, A.L.: Parametric circuit representation using inductive boolean functions. In: Courcoubetis, C. (ed.) CAV 1993. LNCS, vol. 697, pp. 15–28. Springer, Heidelberg (1993). https://doi.org/10.1007/3-540-56922-7_3
12. Gupta, A., Fisher, A.L.: Representation and symbolic manipulation of linearly inductive boolean functions. In: Proceedings of the 1993 IEEE/ACM International Conference on Computer-aided Design, pp. 192–199, ICCAD 1993. IEEE Computer Society Press, Los Alamitos (1993). http://dl.acm.org.stanford.idm.oclc.org/citation.cfm?id=259794.259827
13. Kovács, L., Voronkov, A.: First-order theorem proving and VAMPIRE. In: Sharygina, N., Veith, H. (eds.) CAV 2013. LNCS, vol. 8044, pp. 1–35. Springer, Heidelberg (2013). https://doi.org/10.1007/978-3-642-39799-8_1
14. Kovásznai, G., Fröhlich, A., Biere, A.: Complexity of fixed-size bit-vector logics. Theory Comput. Syst. **59**(2), 323–376 (2016). https://doi.org/10.1007/s00224-015-9653-1
15. Kroening, D., Strichman, O.: Decision Procedures - An Algorithmic Point of View. Texts in Theoretical Computer Science. An EATCS Series, 2nd edn. Springer, Berlin (2016)

16. Lattner, C., Adve, V.S.: LLVM: a compilation framework for lifelong program analysis & transformation. In: 2nd IEEE/ACM International Symposium on Code Generation and Optimization (CGO 2004), 20–24 March 2004, San Jose, CA, USA, pp. 75–88. IEEE Computer Society (2004). https://doi.org/10.1109/CGO.2004. 1281665

17. Lopes, N.P., Menendez, D., Nagarakatte, S., Regehr, J.: Provably correct peephole optimizations with alive. In: Proceedings of the 36th ACM SIGPLAN Conference on Programming Language Design and Implementation, pp. 22–32, PLDI 2015. ACM, New York (2015). https://doi.org/10.1145/2737924.2737965

18. de Moura, L., Bjørner, N.: Efficient E-matching for SMT solvers. In: Pfenning, F. (ed.) CADE 2007. LNCS (LNAI), vol. 4603, pp. 183–198. Springer, Heidelberg (2007). https://doi.org/10.1007/978-3-540-73595-3_13

19. Niemetz, A., Preiner, M., Reynolds, A., Barrett, C., Tinelli, C.: Solving Quantified Bit-Vectors Using Invertibility Conditions. In: Chockler, H., Weissenbacher, G. (eds.) CAV 2018. LNCS, vol. 10982, pp. 236–255. Springer, Cham (2018). https:// doi.org/10.1007/978-3-319-96142-2_16

20. Nipkow, T., Wenzel, M., Paulson, L.C. (eds.): Isabelle/HOL. LNCS, vol. 2283. Springer, Heidelberg (2002). https://doi.org/10.1007/3-540-45949-9

21. Nötzli, A., et al.: Syntax-guided rewrite rule enumeration for SMT solvers. In: Janota, M., Lynce, I. (eds.) SAT 2019. LNCS, vol. 11628. Springer, Cham (2019). https://doi.org/10.1007/978-3-030-24258-9_20

22. Pichora, M.C.: Automated reasoning about hardware data types using bit-vectors of symbolic lengths. Ph.D. thesis, Toronto, ON, Canada (2003). aAINQ84686

23. Reger, G., Suda, M., Voronkov, A.: Unification with abstraction and theory instantiation in saturation-based reasoning. In: Beyer, D., Huisman, M. (eds.) TACAS 2018. LNCS, vol. 10805, pp. 3–22. Springer, Cham (2018). https://doi.org/10.1007/ 978-3-319-89960-2_1

24. Reynolds, A., Barbosa, H., Fontaine, P.: Revisiting enumerative instantiation. In: Beyer, D., Huisman, M. (eds.) TACAS 2018. LNCS, vol. 10806, pp. 112–131. Springer, Cham (2018). https://doi.org/10.1007/978-3-319-89963-3_7

25. Reynolds, A., Deters, M., Kuncak, V., Tinelli, C., Barrett, C.: Counterexample-guided quantifier instantiation for synthesis in SMT. In: Kroening, D., Păsăreanu, C.S. (eds.) CAV 2015. LNCS, vol. 9207, pp. 198–216. Springer, Cham (2015). https://doi.org/10.1007/978-3-319-21668-3_12

26. Reynolds, A., Tinelli, C., Jovanović, D., Barrett, C.: Designing theory solvers with extensions. In: Dixon, C., Finger, M. (eds.) FroCoS 2017. LNCS (LNAI), vol. 10483, pp. 22–40. Springer, Cham (2017). https://doi.org/10.1007/978-3-319-66167-4_2

27. Reynolds, A., Tinelli, C., de Moura, L.M.: Finding conflicting instances of quantified formulas in SMT. In: Formal Methods in Computer-Aided Design, FMCAD 2014, Lausanne, Switzerland, 21–24 October 2014, pp. 195–202 (2014). https:// doi.org/10.1109/FMCAD.2014.6987613

28. Solidity Language Developers: Solidity (2018). https://solidity.readthedocs.io/en/ v0.4.25/

29. TC Development team: The Coq proof assistant reference manual version 8.9 (2019). https://coq.inria.fr/distrib/current/refman/

30. Tinelli, C., Zarba, C.G.: Combining decision procedures for sorted theories. In: Alferes, J.J., Leite, J. (eds.) JELIA 2004. LNCS (LNAI), vol. 3229, pp. 641–653. Springer, Heidelberg (2004). https://doi.org/10.1007/978-3-540-30227-8_53

31. Voronkov, A.: AVATAR: the architecture for first-order theorem provers. In: Biere, A., Bloem, R. (eds.) CAV 2014. LNCS, vol. 8559, pp. 696–710. Springer, Cham (2014). https://doi.org/10.1007/978-3-319-08867-9_46

On Invariant Synthesis
for Parametric Systems

Dennis Peuter and Viorica Sofronie-Stokkermans[✉]

Universität Koblenz-Landau, Koblenz, Germany
dpeuter@uni-koblenz.de, sofronie@uni-koblenz.de

Abstract. We study possibilities for automated invariant generation in parametric systems. We use (a refinement of) an algorithm for symbol elimination in theory extensions to devise a method for iteratively strengthening certain classes of safety properties to obtain invariants of the system. We identify conditions under which the method is correct and complete, and situations in which the method is guaranteed to terminate. We illustrate the ideas on various examples.

1 Introduction

In the verification of parametric systems it is important to show that a certain property holds for all states reachable from the initial state. One way to solve such problems is to identify an inductive invariant entailing the property to be proved. Finding suitable inductive invariants is non-trivial – the problem is undecidable in general; solutions have been proposed for specific cases: In [26], Kapur proposes methods for invariant generation in theories such as Presburger arithmetic, real closed fields, and for polynomial equations and inequations with solutions in an algebraic closed field. The main idea is to use templates for the invariant (polynomials with undetermined coefficients), and solve constraints for all paths and initial values to determine the coefficients. A similar idea was used by Beyer et al. [3] for constraints in linear real or rational arithmetic; it is shown that if an invariant is expressible with a given template, then it will be computed. Symbol elimination has been used for interpolation and invariant generation in many papers. The methods proposed in [26], where quantifier elimination or Gröbner bases computation are used for symbol elimination, are one class of examples. Quantifier elimination is also used by Dillig et al. in [9]. However, in some cases the investigated theories are complex (can be extensions or combinations of theories) and do not allow quantifier elimination. Methods for "symbol elimination" for such complex theories have been proposed, in many cases in relationship with interpolant computation. In [40] Yorsh et al. studied interpolation in combinations of theories; in [7], Brutomesso et al. extended these results to non-convex theories. Interpolation in data structures by reduction was analyzed by Kapur, Majumdar and Zarba in [27]. Independently, in [34,35] Sofronie-Stokkermans analyzed possibilities of computing interpolants

© Springer Nature Switzerland AG 2019
P. Fontaine (Ed.): CADE 2019, LNAI 11716, pp. 385–405, 2019.
https://doi.org/10.1007/978-3-030-29436-6_23

hierarchically, and in [38,39] proposed a method of hierarchical symbol elimination which was used for interpolant computation; already [37] mentions the possibility to infer constraints on parameters by hierarchical reasoning followed by quantifier elimination.

Symbol elimination can also be achieved using refinements of superposition. In [2], Bachmair et al. mention the applicability of a form of hierarchical superposition to second-order quantifier elimination (i.e. to symbol elimination). This idea and possible links to interpolation are also mentioned in Ganzinger et al. [13,14]. In [30], Kovács and Voronkov study inference systems and local derivations – in the context of interpolant generation – and symbol elimination in proofs in such systems. The ideas are concretized using the superposition calculus and its extension LASCA (ground linear rational arithmetic and uninterpreted functions). Applications to invariant generation (briefly mentioned in [30]) are explored in detail in, among others, [18,29] – there Vampire is used to generate a large set of invariants using symbol elimination; only invariants not implied by the theory axioms or by other invariants are kept (some of these tasks are undecidable). In [16], Gleiss et al. analyze functional and temporal properties of loops. For this, extended expressions (introduced in [29]) are used; symbol elimination à la [30] is used to synthesize invariants using quantification over iterations.

Various papers address the problem of strengthening a given formula to obtain an inductive invariant. In [5], Bradley proposes a goal-oriented invariant generation method for boolean/numeric transition systems, relying on finding counterexamples. Such methods were implemented in IC3 [4]. For programs using only integers, Dillig et al. [9] use quantifier elimination to obtain increasingly more precise approximations of inductive invariants (termination is not guaranteed). In [12], Falke and Kapur analyze various ways of strengthening the formulae; depending upon how strengthening is attempted, their procedure may also determine whether the original formula is not an invariant. Situations in which termination is guaranteed are identified. In [28], Karbyshev et al. propose a method to generate universal invariants in theories with the *finite model property* using diagram-based abstraction for invariant strengthening; Padon et al. [31] identify sufficient conditions for the decidability of inferring inductive invariants in a given language $\mathscr{L}$ and also present undecidability results. Invariant synthesis for array-based systems is studied by Ghilardi et al. in [15]; under local finiteness assumptions on the theory of elements and existence of well-quasi-orderings on configurations termination is guaranteed. In [1], Alberti et al. use lazy abstraction with interpolation-based refinement and discuss the applicability to invariant synthesis. A system for verifying safety properties that are "cubes" and invariant generation in array-based systems is described in [8]. In [17], Gurfinkel et al. propose an algorithm extending IC3 to support quantifiers for inferring universal invariants in theories of arrays, combining quantified generalizations (to construct invariants) with quantifier instantiation (to detect convergence).

Our Contribution. In this paper we continue our work on automated verification and synthesis in parametric systems [22,36,37] by investigating possibilities for automated goal-oriented generation of inductive invariants. Our method starts with a universally quantified formula Ψ and successively strengthens it, using a certain form of abductive reasoning based on symbol elimination. In case of termination we prove that we obtain a universal inductive invariant that entails Ψ, or the answer "no such invariant exists". We identify situations in which the method terminates. Our main results are:

- We refine the symbol elimination method in theory extensions described in [38,39] (Sect. 2.3). This helps us obtain shorter formulae during invariant synthesis.
- We propose a method for goal-oriented synthesis of universally quantified invariants which uses symbol elimination in theory extensions (Sect. 3).
- We identify conditions under which our invariant generation method is partially correct (Sect. 3) and situations in which the method terminates (Sect. 4.2).
- We further refine the method (Sect. 4) and provide examples in which the condition we impose on the class of transition systems can be relaxed (Sect. 4.1).

Illustration. Consider for instance the program in Fig. 1, using the subprograms $\text{copy}(a, b)$, which copies the array b into array a, and $\text{add1}(a)$, which adds 1 to every element of array a. The task is to prove that if b is an array with its elements sorted in increasing order then the formula $\Psi := d_2 \geq d_1$ is an invariant of the program. Ψ holds in the initial state; it is an inductive invariant of the while loop iff the formula

$$d_1 \leq d_2 \wedge \forall j(a'[j] = a[j] + 1) \wedge d'_1 = a'[i] \wedge$$
$$d'_2 = a'[i + 1] \wedge i' = i + 1 \wedge \ d'_1 > d'_2$$

```
d1 = 1; d2 = 1;
copy(a, b); i:= 0;
while (nondet()) {
    a = add1(a);
    d1 = a[i]; d2 = a[i+1];
    i:= i + 1}
```

is unsatisfiable. As this formula is satisfiable, Ψ is not an inductive invariant.

Fig. 1. Program using subprograms and global function updates

We will show how to obtain the condition $\forall i(a[i] \leq a[i + 1])$ which can be used to strengthen $\Psi := d_2 \geq d_1$ to the inductive invariant $(d_2 \geq d_1) \wedge \forall i(a[i] \leq a[i + 1])$.

While we rely on methods similar to the ones used in [5,9,12,15,17,28,31], there are several differences between our work and previous work. The methods proposed in [5,9,12,26] cannot be used to tackle examples like the one in Fig. 1: It is difficult to use templates in connection with additional function symbols; in addition, the methods of [5,9,12] can only handle numeric domains. The theories we analyze are typically extensions or combinations of theories and not required to have the finite model property – which is required e.g. in [28,31]. The method proposed in [17] does not come with soundness, completeness and termination guarantees. We here use possibilities of complete instantiation in local theory extensions and exploit (and refine) the methods for symbol elimination in theory extensions proposed in [38,39]. The algorithm proposed in [15] for theories of arrays uses a non-deterministic function ChooseCover that returns a cover of a formula (as an approximation of the reachable states). If the theory of elements is locally finite it is proved that a universal formula Ψ can be strengthened to a universal inductive invariant I iff there exists a suitable ChooseCover function for which the algorithm returns an inductive invariant strengthening Ψ. In contrast, our algorithm is deterministic; we prove completeness under locality assumptions (holding if updates and properties are in the array property fragment); our termination results are established for classes of formulae for which only finitely many atomic formulae formed with a fixed number of variables can be generated using quantifier elimination. In addition our method allows us to choose the language for the candidate invariants (we can search for invariants not containing certain constants or function symbols).

[18,29,30] use an approach different from ours: A large set of invariants are generated by symbol elimination using versions of superposition combined with symbolic solving of recurrences. Completeness/termination are not guaranteed, although the method works well in practice. In this paper we do not use quantification over the iterations.

Structure of the Paper. In Sect. 2 we present the verification problems we consider and the related reasoning problems; present some results on local theory extensions; present a method for symbol elimination in theory extensions introduced in [38,39] and propose an improvement of the method. In Sect. 3 we present an approach to invariant synthesis, and identify conditions under which it is partially correct. Section 4 presents refinements and a termination result. Section 5 contains conclusions and plans for future work. Full proofs and additional examples are included in the extended version of this paper [32].

2   Preliminaries

We consider signatures $\Pi = (\Sigma, \mathsf{Pred})$, where Σ is a family of function symbols and Pred a family of predicate symbols. We assume known standard definitions from first-order logic (e.g. Π-structures, satisfiability, unsatisfiability, logical theories). We denote "falsum" with $\bot$. If F and G are formulae we write $F \models G$ (resp. $F \models_{\mathscr{T}} G$ – also written as $\mathscr{T} \cup F \models G$) to express the fact that every model of F (resp. every model of F which is also a model of $\mathscr{T}$) is a model of G. $F \models \bot$ means that F is unsatisfiable; $F \models_{\mathscr{T}} \bot$ means that there is no model of $\mathscr{T}$ in which F is true.

2.1   Verification Problems for Parametric Systems

One of the application domains we consider is the verification of parametric systems. For modeling such systems we use transition constraint systems $T = (\Sigma, \mathsf{Init}, \mathsf{Update})$ which specify: the function symbols Σ (including a set V of functions with arity 0 – the "variables" of the systems) whose values change over time; a formula Init specifying the properties of initial states; a formula Update with function symbols in $\Sigma \cup \Sigma'$ (where Σ' consists of copies of symbols in Σ, such that if $f \in \Sigma$ then $f' \in \Sigma'$ is the updated function after the transition). Such descriptions can be obtained from system specifications (for an example cf. [11]). With every specification of a system S, a *background theory* $\mathcal{T}_S$ – describing the data types used in the specification and their properties – is associated. We can check in two steps whether a formula Ψ is an inductive invariant of a transition constraint system $T=(\Sigma, \mathsf{Init}, \mathsf{Update})$ by checking whether:

(1) $\mathsf{Init} \models_{\mathcal{T}_S} \Psi$; and
(2) $\Psi, \mathsf{Update} \models_{\mathcal{T}_S} \Psi'$, where Ψ' results from Ψ by replacing each $f \in \Sigma$ by f'.

Checking whether a formula Ψ is an invariant can thus be reduced to checking whether $\neg\Psi'$ is satisfiable or not w.r.t. a theory $\mathcal{T}$. Even if Ψ is a universally quantified formula (and thus $\neg\Psi'$ is a ground formula) the theory $\mathcal{T}$ can be quite complex: it contains the axiomatization $\mathcal{T}_S$ of the datatypes used in the specification of the system, the formalization of the update rules, as well as the formula Ψ itself. In [22,36,37] we show that the theory $\mathcal{T}$ can often be expressed using a chain of extensions, typically including:

$$\mathcal{T}_0 \subseteq \mathcal{T}_1 = \mathcal{T}_0 \cup \Psi \subseteq \mathcal{T} = \mathcal{T}_0 \cup \Psi \cup \mathsf{Update}$$

with the property that checking satisfiability of ground formulae w.r.t. $\mathcal{T}$ can be reduced to checking satisfiability w.r.t. $\mathcal{T}_1$ and ultimately to checking satisfiability w.r.t. $\mathcal{T}_0$. This is the case for instance when the theory extensions in the chain above are *local* (for definitions and further properties cf. Sect. 2.2).

Failure to prove (2) means that Ψ is not an invariant or Ψ is not inductive w.r.t. T. If Ψ is not an inductive invariant, we can consider two orthogonal problems:

(a) Determine constraints on parameters which guarantee that Ψ is an invariant.
(b) Determine a formula I such that $\mathcal{T}_S \models I \rightarrow \Psi$ and I is an inductive invariant.

Problem (a) was studied in [36,37]. In [38,39] we proposed a method for hierarchical symbol elimination in theory extensions which allowed us to show that for local theory extensions the formulae obtained using this symbol elimination method are *weakest* constraints on parameters which guarantee that Ψ is invariant. We present and improve this symbol elimination method in Sect. 2.3.

In this paper we address problem (b): in Sect. 3 we use symbol elimination for giving a complete method for goal-oriented invariant generation, for invariants containing symbols in a specified signature; we also identify some situations when termination is guaranteed. The safety property and invariants we consider are conjunctions of ground formulae and sets of (implicitly universally quantified) flat clauses of the form $\forall \overline{x}(C_i(\overline{x}) \vee C_v(\overline{x}, \overline{f}(\overline{x})))$, where $\overline{f}$ are functional parameters, C_i is a clause containing constants and universally quantified variables, and C_v a flat clause containing parameters, constants and universally quantified variables.[1]

---

[1] We use the following abbreviations: $\overline{x}$ for $x_1, \ldots, x_n$; $\overline{f}(\overline{x})$ for $f_1(\overline{x}), \ldots, f_n(\overline{x})$.

2.2   Local Theory Extensions

Let $\Pi_0 = (\Sigma_0, \mathsf{Pred})$ be a signature, and $\mathcal{T}_0$ be a "base" theory with signature Π_0. We consider extensions $\mathcal{T} := \mathcal{T}_0 \cup \mathcal{K}$ of $\mathcal{T}_0$ with new function symbols Σ (*extension functions*) whose properties are axiomatized using a set $\mathcal{K}$ of clauses in the extended signature $\Pi = (\Sigma_0 \cup \Sigma, \mathsf{Pred})$, which contain function symbols in Σ. If G is a finite set of ground Π^C-clauses[2] and $\mathcal{K}$ a set of Π-clauses, we will denote by $\mathsf{st}(\mathcal{K}, G)$ (resp. $\mathsf{est}(\mathcal{K}, G)$) the set of all ground terms (resp. extension ground terms, i.e. terms starting with a function in Σ) which occur in G or $\mathcal{K}$.[3] If T is a set of ground terms in the signature Π^C, we denote by $\mathcal{K}[T]$ the set of all instances of $\mathcal{K}$ in which the terms starting with a function symbol in Σ are in T. Let Ψ be a map associating with every finite set T of ground terms a finite set $\Psi(T)$ of ground terms. For any set G of ground Π^C-clauses we write $\mathcal{K}[\Psi_{\mathcal{K}}(G)]$ for $\mathcal{K}[\Psi(\mathsf{est}(\mathcal{K}, G))]$. We define:

(Loc_f^{Ψ}) For every finite set G of ground clauses in Π^C it holds that
$$\mathcal{T}_0 \cup \mathcal{K} \cup G \models \bot \text{ if and only if } \mathcal{T}_0 \cup \mathcal{K}[\Psi_{\mathcal{K}}(G)] \cup G \text{ is unsatisfiable.}$$

Extensions satisfying condition (Loc_f^{Ψ}) are called Ψ-*local* [22,24]. If Ψ is the identity, i.e. $\mathcal{K}[\Psi_{\mathcal{K}}(G)] = \mathcal{K}[G]$, we have a *local theory extension* [33].

Remark: In [22,24] we introduced and studied a notion of *extended locality*, in which the axioms in $\mathcal{K}$ are of the form $\forall \overline{x}(\phi(\overline{x}) \vee C)$, where ϕ is an arbitrary Σ_0-formula and C a clause containing extension symbols and the set G contains ground formulae of the form $\Psi \vee G_e$, where Ψ is a Σ_0-sentence and G_e a ground clause containing extension symbols. While most of the results in this paper can be lifted by replacing "locality" with "extended locality", in this paper we only refer to locality for the sake of simplicity.

For (Ψ)-local theory extensions hierarchical reasoning is possible. Below, we discuss the case of local theory extensions; similar results hold also for Ψ-local extensions. If $\mathcal{T}_0 \cup \mathcal{K}$ is a local extension of $\mathcal{T}_0$ and G is a set of ground Π^C-clauses, then $\mathcal{T}_0 \cup \mathcal{K} \cup G$ is unsatisfiable iff $\mathcal{T}_0 \cup \mathcal{K}[G] \cup G$ is unsatisfiable. We can reduce this last satisfiability test to a satisfiability test w.r.t. $\mathcal{T}_0$. The idea is to purify $\mathcal{K}[G] \cup G$ by (i) introducing (bottom-up) new constants c_t for subterms $t = f(g_1, \ldots, g_n)$ with $f \in \Sigma$, g_i ground $\Sigma_0 \cup \Sigma_c$-terms, (ii) replacing the terms t with the constants c_t, and (iii) adding the definitions $c_t \approx t$ to a set D. We denote by $\mathcal{K}_0 \cup G_0 \cup D$ the set of formulae obtained this way. Then G is satisfiable w.r.t. $\mathcal{T}_0 \cup \mathcal{K}$ iff $\mathcal{K}_0 \cup G_0 \cup \mathsf{Con}_0$ is satisfiable w.r.t. $\mathcal{T}_0$, where
$$\mathsf{Con}_0 = \{(\textstyle\bigwedge_{i=1}^n c_i \approx d_i) \rightarrow c \approx d \mid c \approx f(c_1, \ldots, c_n), d \approx f(d_1, \ldots, d_n) \in D\}.$$

Theorem 1 ([33]). *If $\mathcal{T}_0 \subseteq \mathcal{T}_0 \cup \mathcal{K}$ is a local extension and G is a finite set of ground clauses, then we can reduce the problem of checking whether G is satisfiable w.r.t. $\mathcal{T}_0 \cup \mathcal{K}$ to checking the satisfiability w.r.t. $\mathcal{T}_0$ of the formula $\mathcal{K}_0 \cup G_0 \cup \mathsf{Con}_0$ constructed as explained above. If $\mathcal{K}_0 \cup G_0 \cup \mathsf{Con}_0$ belongs to a*

---

[2] Π^C is the extension of Π with constants in a countable set C of fresh constants.

[3] We here regard every finite set G of ground clauses as the ground formula $\bigwedge_{K \in G} K$.

decidable fragment of $\mathcal{T}_0$, we can use the decision procedure for this fragment to decide the (un)satisfiability of $\mathcal{T}_0 \cup \mathcal{K} \cup G$.

As the size of $\mathcal{K}_0 \cup G_0 \cup \mathrm{Con}_0$ is polynomial in the size of G (for a given $\mathcal{K}$), locality allows us to express the complexity of the ground satisfiability problem w.r.t. $\mathcal{T}_1$ as a function of the complexity of the satisfiability of formulae w.r.t. $\mathcal{T}_0$.

(Ψ-)Local extensions can be recognized by showing that certain partial models embed into total ones [24]. Especially well-behaved are the theory extensions with property (Comp_f), stating that partial models can be made total without changing the universe of the model.[4] The link between embeddability and locality allowed us to identify many classes of local theory extensions:

Example 1 (Extensions with free/monotone functions [22,33]). *The following types of extensions of a theory $\mathcal{T}_0$ are local:*

(1) Any extension of $\mathcal{T}_0$ with uninterpreted function symbols ((Comp_f) holds).
(2) Any extension of a theory $\mathcal{T}_0$ for which $\leq$ is a partial order with functions monotone w.r.t. $\leq$ (condition (Comp_f) holds if all models of $\mathcal{T}_0$ are complete lattices w.r.t. $\leq$).

Example 2 (Extensions with definitions [22,25]). *Consider an extension of a theory $\mathcal{T}_0$ with a new function symbol f defined by axioms of the form:*

$$\mathsf{Def}_f := \{\forall \overline{x}(\phi_i(\overline{x}) \rightarrow F_i(f(\overline{x}),\overline{x})) \mid i = 1,\ldots,m\}$$

(definition by "case distinction") where ϕ_i and F_i, $i = 1,\ldots,m$, are formulae over the signature of $\mathcal{T}_0$ such that the following hold:

(a) $\phi_i(\overline{x}) \wedge \phi_j(\overline{x}) \models_{\mathcal{T}_0} \bot$ for $i \neq j$ and
(b) $\mathcal{T}_0 \models \forall \overline{x}(\phi_i(\overline{x}) \rightarrow \exists y(F_i(y,\overline{x})))$ for all $i \in \{1,\ldots,m\}$.

Then the extension is local (and satisfies (Comp_f)). Examples:

(1) Any extension with a function f defined by axioms of the form:

$$\mathsf{D}_f := \{\forall \overline{x}(\phi_i(\overline{x}) \rightarrow f(\overline{x}) \approx t_i) \mid i = 1,\ldots,n\}$$

where ϕ_i are formulae over the signature of $\mathcal{T}_0$ such that (a) holds.
(2) Any extension of $\mathcal{T}_0 \in \{\mathsf{LI}(\mathbb{Q}), \mathsf{LI}(\mathbb{R})\}$ with functions satisfying axioms:

$$\mathsf{Bound}_f := \{\forall \overline{x}(\phi_i(\overline{x}) \rightarrow s_i \leq f(\overline{x}) \leq t_i) \mid i = 1,\ldots,n\}$$

where ϕ_i are formulae over the signature of $\mathcal{T}_0$, s_i, t_i are $\mathcal{T}_0$-terms, condition (a) holds and $\models_{\mathcal{T}_0} \forall \overline{x}(\phi_i(\overline{x}) \rightarrow s_i \leq t_i)$ [22].

---

[4] We use the index f in (Comp_f) in order to emphasize that the property refers to completability of partial functions with a finite domain of definition.

Example 3 (The array property fragment [6,22]**).** *In [6] a decidable fragment of the theory of arrays is studied, namely the* array property fragment. *Arrays are regarded as functions with arguments of index sort and values of element sort. The index theory $\mathcal{T}_i$ is Presburger arithmetic; the element theory is parametric. The* array property fragment *consists of all existentially-closed Boolean combinations of quantifier-free formulae and array property formulae. Array property formulae are formulae of the form $(\forall i)(\varphi_I(i) \to \varphi_V(i))$, where*

- *φ_I is a positive Boolean combination of atoms of the form $t \leq u$ or $t = u$ where t, u are either variables or ground terms of index sort;*
- *φ_V has the property that any universally quantified variable of index sort i only occurs in a direct array read $a(x)$ in φ_V and array reads may not be nested.*

In [6] it is shown that formulae in the array property fragment have complete instantiation. In [22] we showed that this fragment satisfies a Ψ-locality condition.

2.3   Quantifier Elimination and Symbol Elimination

We now present possibilities of symbol elimination in complex theories.

A theory $\mathcal{T}$ over signature Π *allows quantifier elimination* if for every formula ϕ over Π there exists a quantifier-free formula ϕ^* over Π which is equivalent to ϕ modulo $\mathcal{T}$. Examples of theories which allow quantifier elimination are rational and real linear arithmetic ($\mathsf{LI}(\mathbb{Q})$, $\mathsf{LI}(\mathbb{R})$), the theory of real closed fields, and the theory of absolutely-free data structures.

Note first that if the theories $\mathcal{T}_1$ and $\mathcal{T}_2$ over disjoint signatures Π_1 resp. Π_2 allow elimination of existential quantifiers, then the two-sorted combination $\mathcal{T}$ of the theories $\mathcal{T}_1$ and $\mathcal{T}_2$, with signature $\Pi = (\{s_1, s_2\}, \Sigma_1 \cup \Sigma_2, \mathsf{Pred}_1 \cup \mathsf{Pred}_2)$ – where every n-ary operation $f \in \Sigma_i$ has sort $s_i^n \to s_i$, and every m-ary predicate symbol $p \in \mathsf{Pred}_i$ has arity s_i^m – allows elimination of existential quantifiers.

Symbol Elimination in Theory Extensions. Let $\Pi_0 = (\Sigma_0, \mathsf{Pred})$. Let $\mathcal{T}_0$ be a Π_0-theory and Σ_P be a set of parameters (function and constant symbols). Let Σ be a signature such that $\Sigma \cap (\Sigma_0 \cup \Sigma_P) = \emptyset$. We consider the theory extension $\mathcal{T}_0 \subseteq \mathcal{T}_0 \cup \mathcal{K}$, where $\mathcal{K}$ is a set of clauses in the signature $\Pi = \Pi_0 \cup \Sigma_P \cup \Sigma$ in which all variables occur also below functions in $\Sigma_1 = \Sigma_P \cup \Sigma$. Consider the symbol elimination method in Algorithm 1 [38,39].

Theorem 2 ([38,39])**.** *Assume that $\mathcal{T}_0$ allows quantifier elimination. For every finite set of ground Π^C-clauses G, and every finite set T of ground terms over the signature Π^C with $\mathsf{est}(G) \subseteq T$, Steps 1–5 yield a universally quantified $\Pi_0 \cup \Sigma_P$-formula $\forall \overline{x} \Gamma_T(\overline{x})$ such that $\mathcal{T}_0 \cup \forall \overline{y} \Gamma_T(\overline{y}) \cup \mathcal{K} \cup G$ is unsatisfiable.*

Theorem 3 ([38,39])**.** *Assume that the theory extension $\mathcal{T}_0 \subseteq \mathcal{T}_0 \cup \mathcal{K}$ satisfies condition (Comp_f) and $\mathcal{K}$ is flat and linear. Let G be a set of ground Π^C-clauses, and $\forall \overline{y} \Gamma_G(\overline{y})$ be the formula obtained with Algorithm 1 for $T = \mathsf{est}(\mathcal{K}, G)$. Then $\forall y \Gamma_G(y)$ is entailed by every universal formula Γ with $\mathcal{T}_0 \cup \Gamma \cup \mathcal{K} \cup G \models \bot$.*

Algorithm 1. Symbol elimination in theory extensions [38,39]

Step 1 Let $\mathscr{K}_0 \cup G_0 \cup \mathrm{Con}_0$ be the set of Π_0^C-clauses obtained from $\mathscr{K}[T] \cup G$ after the purification step described in Theorem 1 (with set of extension symbols Σ_1).

Step 2 Let $G_1 = \mathscr{K}_0 \cup G_0 \cup \mathrm{Con}_0$. Among the constants in G_1, we identify
  (i) the constants c_f, $f \in \Sigma_P$, where c_f is a constant parameter or c_f is introduced by a definition $c_f \approx f(c_1, \ldots, c_k)$ in the hierarchical reasoning method,
  (ii) all constants $\overline{c}_p$ occurring as arguments of functions in Σ_P in such definitions. Let $\overline{c}$ be the remaining constants. We replace the constants in $\overline{c}$ with existentially quantified variables $\overline{x}$, i.e. instead of $G_1(\overline{c}_p, \overline{c}_f, \overline{c})$ we consider the formula $\exists \overline{x} G_1(\overline{c}_p, \overline{c}_f, \overline{x})$.

Step 3 Using a method for quantifier elimination in $\mathscr{T}_0$ we can construct a formula $\Gamma_1(\overline{c}_p, \overline{c}_f)$ equivalent to $\exists \overline{x} G_1(\overline{c}_p, \overline{c}_f, \overline{x})$ w.r.t. $\mathscr{T}_0$.

Step 4 Let $\Gamma_2(\overline{c}_p)$ be the formula obtained by replacing back in $\Gamma_1(\overline{c}_p, \overline{c}_f)$ the constants c_f introduced by definitions $c_f := f(c_1, \ldots, c_k)$ with the terms $f(c_1, \ldots, c_k)$. We replace $\overline{c}_p$ with existentially quantified variables $\overline{y}$.

Step 5 Let $\forall \overline{y} \Gamma_T(\overline{y})$ be $\forall \overline{y} \neg \Gamma_2(\overline{y})$.

A similar result holds if T is the set of instances obtained from the instantiation of a chain of theory extensions $\mathscr{T}_0 \subseteq \mathscr{T}_0 \cup \mathscr{K}_1 \subseteq \cdots \subseteq \mathscr{T}_0 \cup \mathscr{K}_1 \cup \cdots \cup \mathscr{K}_n$, all satisfying condition (Comp_f), where $\mathscr{K}_1, \ldots, \mathscr{K}_n$ are all flat and linear and every variable is guarded by an extension symbol [39].

Remark. Algorithm 1 can be tuned to eliminate constants c in a set C_e which might occur as arguments to parameters: All these constants, together with all constants c_f introduced by definitions $c_f = f(c_1, \ldots, c_n)$ with some $c_i \in C_e$, are replaced with variables at the end of Step 2 and are eliminated in Step 3.

Quantifier elimination usually has high complexity and leads to large formulae. Often, Algorithm 1 can be improved such that QE is applied to smaller formulae:

Theorem 4. *Assume that* $\mathscr{K} = \mathscr{K}_P \cup \mathscr{K}_1$ *such that* $\mathscr{K}_P$ *contains only symbols in* $\Sigma_0 \cup \Sigma_P$ *and* $\mathscr{K}_1$ *is a set of* Π-*clauses such that*

$$\mathscr{T}_0 \subseteq \mathscr{T}_0 \cup \mathscr{K}_P \subseteq \mathscr{T}_0 \cup \mathscr{K}_P \cup \mathscr{K}_1$$

is a chain of theory extensions both satisfying condition (Comp_f) *and having the property that all variables occur below an extension function, and such that* $\mathscr{K}$ *is flat and linear. Let* G *be a set of ground* Π^C-*clauses. Then the formula* $\mathscr{K}_P \wedge \forall \overline{y} \Gamma_1(\overline{y})$, *where* $\forall \overline{y} \Gamma_1(\overline{y})$ *is obtained by applying Algorithm 1 to* $\mathscr{T}_0 \cup \mathscr{K}_1 \cup G$, *has the property that for every universal formula* Γ *containing only parameters with* $\mathscr{T}_0 \cup (\mathscr{K}_P \cup \Gamma) \cup G \models \bot$, *we have* $\mathscr{K}_P \wedge \Gamma \models \mathscr{K}_P \wedge \forall \overline{y} \Gamma_1(\overline{y})$.

Proof (Idea): Since $\mathscr{K}_P$ contains only functions in $\Sigma_0 \cup \Sigma_P$, its set of instances does not contain functions which we want to eliminate, so can be brought outside of the scope of the existential quantifiers after Step 2. Thus, quantifier elimination can be applied only to the sets of instances corresponding to

$\mathscr{K}_1 \cup G$ and yields a formula D. Step 5 yields a universally quantified disjunction between a formula corresponding to the negation of the instances of $\mathscr{K}_P$ and $\Gamma_1(\overline{y}) = \neg D(\overline{y})$, the negation of the formula obtained from D by replacing constants with variables. Thus, we only need $\forall \overline{y} \Gamma_1(\overline{y})$ to strengthen $\mathscr{K}_P$.   □

This improvement will be important for the method for invariant generation we discuss in what follows. Further improvements are discussed in Sect. 4.

3   Goal-Oriented Invariant Synthesis

Let S be a system, $\mathscr{T}_S$ be the theory and $T=(\Sigma_S, \mathsf{Init}, \mathsf{Update})$ the transition constraint system associated with S. We assume that $\Sigma_S = \Sigma_0 \cup \Sigma_P \cup \Sigma$, where Σ_0 is the signature of a "base" theory $\mathscr{T}_0$, Σ_P is a set of function symbols assumed to be parametric, and Σ is a set of functions (non-parametric) disjoint from $\Sigma_0 \cup \Sigma_P$. We assume that Init is a universal formula describing the initial states and Update is a universal formula describing (possibly global) updates of functions in a set $F \subseteq \Sigma$, and also variable updates.[5]

We assume given a universal formula Ψ (a conjunction of clauses $\forall \overline{x}(C_i(\overline{x}) \vee C_v(\overline{x}, \overline{f}(\overline{x}))$, where C_i is a $\mathscr{T}_0$-clause and C_v a flat clause over $\Sigma_0 \cup \Sigma_P$). Both Init and Ψ describe "global" properties of the function symbols in Σ_P at a given moment in time (for instance equality of two functions – or equality of arrays, monotonicity of a function – or sortedness of an array). Our goal is to obtain an inductive invariant I with $I \models_{\mathscr{T}_S} \Psi$.

We make the following assumptions: Let $\mathsf{LocSafe}$ be a class of universal Σ_S-formulae.

(A1) There exists a chain of local theory extensions $\mathscr{T}_0 \subseteq \cdots \subseteq \mathscr{T}_S \cup \mathsf{Init}$ such that in each extension all variables occur below an extension function.
(A2) For every $\Psi \in \mathsf{LocSafe}$ there exists a chain of local theory extensions $\mathscr{T}_0 \subseteq \cdots \subseteq \mathscr{T}_S \cup \Psi$ such that in each extension all variables occur below an extension function.
(A3) $\mathsf{Update} = \{\mathsf{Update}_f \mid f \in F\}$ consists of update axioms for functions in a set F, where, for every $f \in F$, Update_f has the form $\mathsf{Def}_f := \{\forall \overline{x}(\phi_i^f(\overline{x}) \rightarrow C_i^f(\overline{x}, f'(\overline{x}))) \mid i \in I\}$, such that (i) $\phi_i(\overline{x}) \wedge \phi_j(\overline{x}) \models_{\mathscr{T}_S} \bot$ for $i \neq j$, (ii) $\mathscr{T}_S \models \bigvee_{i=1}^{n} \phi_i$, and (iii) C_i^f are conjunctions of literals and $\mathscr{T}_S \models \forall \overline{x}(\phi_i(\overline{x}) \rightarrow \exists y(C_i^f(\overline{x}, y)))$ for all $i \in I$.[6]

In what follows, if ϕ is a formula containing function symbols in Σ we denote by ϕ' the formula obtained from ϕ by replacing every function symbol $f \in \Sigma$ with $f' \in \Sigma'$.

---

[5] Variables are 0-ary functions. Ground formulae are, in particular, also universal formulae.
[6] In particular we can consider definition updates of the form $\mathsf{D}_{f'}$ or updates of the form $\mathsf{Bound}_{f'}$ as discussed in Example 2.

Algorithm 2. Successively strengthening a formula to an inductive invariant

---

Input: $T = (\Sigma_S, \mathsf{Init}, \mathsf{Update})$ transition system; $\Sigma_P \subseteq \Sigma_S$; $\Psi \in \mathsf{LocSafe}$, formula over Σ_P
Output: Inductive invariant I of T that entails Ψ and contains only function symbols in Σ_P
          (if such an invariant exists).

1: $I := \Psi$
2: **while** I is not an inductive invariant for T **do:**
    if $\mathsf{Init} \not\models I$ **then return** "no universal inductive invariant over Σ_P entails Ψ"
    if I is not preserved under Update **then** Let Γ be obtained by eliminating
    all primed variables and symbols not in Σ_P from $I \wedge \mathsf{Update} \wedge \neg I'$;
    $I := I \wedge \Gamma$
3: **return** I is an inductive invariant

Theorem 5 ([22,36]). *The following hold under assumptions* **(A1)**–**(A3)***: (1) If ground satisfiability w.r.t. $\mathcal{T}_0$ is decidable, then the problem of checking whether a formula $\Psi \in \mathsf{LocSafe}$ is an inductive invariant of S is decidable. (2) If $\mathcal{T}_0$ allows quantifier elimination and the initial states or the updates contain parameters, Algorithm 1 yields constraints on these parameters that guarantee that Ψ is an inductive invariant.*

We now study the problem of inferring – in a goal-oriented way – universally quantified inductive invariants. The method we propose is described in Algorithm 2.

In addition to assumptions **(A1)**, **(A2)**, **(A3)** we now consider the following assumptions (where $\mathcal{T}_0$ is the base theory in assumptions **(A1)**–**(A3)**):

(A4) Ground satisfiability in $\mathcal{T}_0$ is decidable; $\mathcal{T}_0$ allows quantifier elimination.
(A5) All candidate invariants I computed in the while loop in Algorithm 2 are in $\mathsf{LocSafe}$, and all local extensions in $\mathsf{LocSafe}$ satisfy condition (Comp_f).

We prove that under assumptions **(A1)**–**(A5)** the algorithm is partially correct (Theorem 8). Then we identify conditions under which **(A5)** holds, so does not have to be stated explicitly (Sect. 4.1), and conditions under which the algorithm terminates (Sect. 4.2).

Lemma 6. *If Algorithm 2 terminates and returns a formula I, then I is an invariant of T containing only function symbols in Σ_P that entails Ψ.*

Proof: Follows from the loop condition.   □

Lemma 7. *Under assumptions* **(A1)**–**(A5)***, if there exists a universal inductive invariant J containing only function symbols in Σ_P that entails Ψ, then J entails every candidate invariant I generated in the while loop of Algorithm 2.*

Proof: Proof by induction on the number of iterations in which the candidate invariant I is obtained. If $i = 1$, then $I_1 = \Psi$, hence $J \models \Psi = I_1$.

Assume that the property holds for the candidate invariant generated in n steps. Let I_{n+1} be generated in step $n + 1$. In this case there exist candidate invariants $I_1, \ldots, I_n$ containing only function symbols in Σ_P s.t.: (i) $I_1 = \Psi$;

(ii) for all $1 \leq i \leq n$, $\mathsf{Init} \models I_i$; (iii) for all $1 \leq i \leq n$, I_i is not an inductive invariant, i.e. $I_i \wedge \mathsf{Update} \wedge \neg I_i'$ is satisfiable and Γ_i is obtained by eliminating the primed function symbols and all function symbols not in Σ_P; (iv) for all $1 \leq i \leq n$, $I_{i+1} = I_i \wedge \Gamma_i$.

We prove that $J \models_{\mathcal{T}_S} I_{n+1}$, i.e. that $J \models_{\mathcal{T}_S} I_n \wedge \Gamma_n$. By the induction hypothesis, $J \models_{\mathcal{T}_S} I_n$, hence $J \equiv_{\mathcal{T}_S} J \wedge I_n$. We know that J is an inductive invariant, i.e. $J \wedge \mathsf{Update} \wedge \neg J'$ is unsatisfiable. Therefore $(J \wedge I_n) \wedge \mathsf{Update} \wedge (\neg J' \vee \neg I_n')$ is unsatisfiable, hence, in particular, $J \wedge I_n \wedge \mathsf{Update} \wedge \neg I_n'$ is unsatisfiable. By Theorem 3, the way Γ_n is constructed, and the fact that J is a universal formula containing only function symbols in Σ_P, we know that $J \models_{\mathcal{T}_S} \Gamma_n$. Thus, $J \models_{\mathcal{T}_S} I_n \wedge \Gamma_n$, so $J \models_{\mathcal{T}_S} I_{n+1}$. This completes the proof.   □

Theorem 8 (Partial Correctness). *Under assumptions* **(A1)**–**(A5)**, *if Algorithm 2 terminates, then its output is correct.*

Proof (Sketch): If Algorithm 2 terminates with output I, then the condition of the while loop must be false for I, so I is an invariant. Assume that Algorithm 2 terminates because $\mathsf{Init} \not\models_{\mathcal{T}_S} I$ returning "no universal inductive invariant over Σ_P entails Ψ". Then there exists a model $\mathcal{A}$ of Init and $\mathcal{T}_S$ which is not a model of I. Assume that there exists a universal inductive invariant J over Σ_P that entails Ψ. By Lemma 7, J entails the candidate invariants generated at each iteration, thus entails I. But every model of Init (in particular $\mathcal{A}$) is a model of J, hence also of I. Contradiction. Therefore, the assumption that there exists a universal inductive invariant J that entails Ψ was false, i.e. the answer is correct.   □

4   Refinements

Assume that $\mathsf{Update} = \bigvee_{f \in F} \mathsf{Update}_f$, where $F \subseteq \Sigma$ (no f' with $f \in F$ is a parameter) such that Update_f satisfies the conditions in assumption **(A3)**.

Lemma 9. *We consider the computations described in Algorithm 2, iteration n, in Step 2, the case in which $\mathsf{Init} \models I_n$, but I_n is not invariant under updates. Let $\mathcal{K}$ be a set of constraints on parameters.*

(1) If $I_n = I_{n-1} \wedge \Gamma_{n-1}$ is not invariant under updates, then Algorithm 2 computes a formula $\Gamma_n = \bigwedge_{f \in F} \Gamma_n^f$, where Γ_n^f is obtained by symbol elimination applied to $\mathcal{K} \wedge I_n \wedge \mathsf{Update}_f \wedge G$, where G is obtained by Skolemization from $\neg \Gamma_{n-1}'$.

(2) If the only non-parametric functions are $\{f' \mid f \in F\}$, then with the improvement of Algorithm 1 in Theorem 4 we need to apply symbol elimination only to $\mathsf{Update}_f \wedge \neg \Gamma_{n-1}'$ to compute Γ_n^f.

Proof: (1) $I_n \wedge \mathsf{Update} \wedge \neg I_n' \equiv \bigvee_{f \in F} (I_n \wedge \mathsf{Update}_f \wedge \neg I_n')$, so it is satisfiable iff for some $f \in F$, the formula $\mathcal{K} \wedge I_n \wedge \mathsf{Update}_f \wedge \neg I_n'$ is satisfiable. We have:

$$\mathcal{K} \wedge I_n \wedge \mathsf{Update}_f \wedge \neg I'_n = \mathcal{K} \wedge (I_{n-1} \wedge \Gamma_{n-1}) \wedge \mathsf{Update}_f \wedge (\neg I'_{n-1} \vee \neg \Gamma'_{n-1})$$
$$\equiv \mathcal{K} \wedge (I_{n-1} \wedge \Gamma_{n-1}) \wedge \mathsf{Update}_f \wedge \neg \Gamma'_{n-1},$$

since Γ_{n-1} was introduced such that $\mathcal{K} \wedge (I_{n-1} \wedge \Gamma_{n-1}) \wedge \mathsf{Update}_f \wedge \neg I'_{n-1}$ is unsatisfiable. Then in Algorithm 2, $\Gamma_n = \bigwedge_{f \in F} \Gamma_n^f$, where Γ_n^f are the (weakest) formulae obtained with Algorithm 1, such that $\mathcal{K} \wedge I_n \wedge \Gamma_n^f \wedge \mathsf{Update}_f \wedge \neg \Gamma'_{n-1}$ is unsatisfiable.

(2) follows from Theorem 4. $\qquad \square$

Lemma 10. *If* $\phi_i \wedge \phi_j \models_{\mathscr{T}} \bot$ *for all* $i \neq j, 1 \leq i, j \leq n$ *and* $\models_{\mathscr{T}} \bigvee_{i=1}^n \phi_i$ *then* $\bigwedge_{i=1}^n (\phi_i \to C_i) \equiv \bigvee_{i=1}^n (\phi_i \wedge C_i)$.

We now analyze the formulae Γ_n^f generated at iteration n. For simplicity we assume that f is unary; the extension to higher arities is immediate.

Theorem 11. *Let* $\Psi \in \mathsf{LocSafe}$ *and* $\mathsf{Update} = \bigvee_{f \in F} \mathsf{Update}_f$ *of the form discussed above. Assume that the clauses in* Ψ *and* Update_f *are flat and linear for all* $f \in F$. *Let* m *be the maximal number of variables in a clause in* Ψ. *Assume that the only non-parametric functions which need to be eliminated are the primed symbols* $\{f' \mid f \in F\}$ *and that conditions (A1)–(A5) hold. Consider a variant of Algorithm 2, which uses for symbol elimination Algorithm 1 with the improvement in Theorem 4. Then for every step* n, *(i) the clauses in the candidate invariant* I_n *obtained at step* n *of Algorithm 2 are flat, and (ii) the number of universally quantified variables in every clause in* I_n *is* $\leq m$.

Proof: Proof by induction on n. For $n = 1$, $I_1 = \Psi$ and (i) and (ii) clearly hold. Assume that they hold for iteration n. We prove that they hold for iteration $n + 1$. By Lemma 9, we need to apply Algorithm 1 to $\mathsf{Update}_f \wedge G$, where G is obtained from $\neg \Gamma'_n$ after Skolemization. If Γ'_n is a conjunction of clauses, then G is a disjunction of conjunctions of literals; each disjunct can be processed separately, and we take the conjunction of the obtained constraints. Thus, we assume w.l.o.g. that G is a conjunction of literals. By the induction hypothesis the number k of universally quantified variables in Γ_n is $\leq m$, so G contains Skolem constants $\{d_1, \ldots, d_k, c_1, \ldots, c_r\}$ with $k + r \leq m$, where $d_1, \ldots, d_k$ occur below f'. For symbol elimination we first compute $G_1 = \mathsf{Update}_f[G] \wedge G$ (with $\mathsf{est}(G) = \{f'(d_1), \ldots, f'(d_k)\}$ where $k \leq m$) and purify it; in a second step we instantiate the terms starting with function symbols $g \in \Sigma_P \cup \Sigma$. By Lemma 10:

$$\mathsf{Update}_f[G] := \bigwedge_{j=1}^k \left(\bigwedge_{i=1}^{n_f} (\phi_i(d_j) \to C_i(d_j, f'(d_j))) \right) \equiv \bigwedge_{j=1}^k \bigvee_{i=1}^{n_f} (\phi_i(d_j) \wedge C_i(d_j, f'(d_j)))$$
$$\equiv \bigvee_{i_1, \ldots, i_k \in \{1, \ldots, n_f\}} \left(\bigwedge_{p=1}^k \phi_{i_p}(d_p) \wedge \bigwedge_{p=1}^k C_{i_p}(d_p, f'(d_p)) \right).$$

We thus obtained a DNF with $(n_f)^k \leq (n_f)^m$ disjuncts, where n_f (number of cases in the definition of f) and m (the maximal number of variables in $\mathcal{K} \cup I_n$) are constants depending on the description of the transition system. Both n_f and m are typically small, in most cases $n_f \leq 3$. Algorithm 1 is applied as follows:

In **Step 1** we introduce a constant $c_{f'd}$ for every term $f'(d) \in \text{est}(G)$, replace $f'(d)$ with $c_{f'd}$, and add the corresponding instances Con_0 of the congruence axioms. We may compute a disjunctive normal form $DNF(\text{Con}_0)$ for the instances of congruence axioms or not (Con_0 contains $k^2 \leq m^2$ conjunctions; $DNF(\text{Con}_0)$ contains $2^{k^2} \leq 2^{m^2}$ disjuncts, each of length k). In a second reduction we replace every term of the form $g(c) \in \text{est}(G_1)$, $g \in \Sigma_P$, with a new constant c_{gc}.

Steps 2 and 3: To eliminate f' we replace the constants $c_{f'd}$ with variables $x_{f'd}$ and obtain a formula $G_1^0(x_{f'd_1}, \ldots, x_{f'd_n})$. In $\exists x_{f'd_1}, \ldots x_{f'd_n}$ $G_1^0(x_{f'd_1}, \ldots, x_{f'd_n})$ the existential quantifiers can be brought inside the conjunctions and quantifier elimination can be used only on the part of the disjuncts that contain the variables $x_{f'd}$ (i.e. on relatively simple and short formulae). After quantifier elimination we obtain a formula Γ_2.

Steps 4 and 5: We replace back in the formula obtained this way all constants c_{gc}, $g \in \Sigma_P, g(c) \in \text{est}(G_1)$ with the terms $g(c)$. The constants $d_1, \ldots, d_k, c_1, \ldots, c_r$ are replaced with new variables $y_1, \ldots, y_k, y_{k+1}, \ldots, y_{k+r}$ respectively. We negate $\exists \overline{y}\Gamma_2(\overline{y})$ and obtain a conjunction $\Gamma_{n+1}^f(G)$ of universally quantified clauses.
All clauses in $\Gamma_{n+1}^f(G)$ are flat. By construction, the number of universally quantified variables in $\Gamma_{n+1}^f(G)$ is $k + r \leq m$.   □

Theorem 12. *Under the assumptions in Theorem 11, the number of clauses in Γ_n is at most $O(k_1^n)$; each clause in Γ_n contains at most $k_2 \cdot n + |\Psi|$ literals if the constraints C_i are all equalities, and can contain $O(|\Psi|^{k_3^n})$ literals if C_i are constraints in $\text{LI}(\mathbb{Q})$, where k_1, k_2, k_3 are constants of the system.*

If there are non-parametric functions that are being updated the number of variables in the clauses Γ_n might grow: Any constant $c \in F$ which is not a parameter, but occurs below a parameter in Update or G, is then being converted into a universally quantified variable by Algorithm 1 as the following example shows.

Example 4. *Consider the program in the introduction (Fig. 1). The task is to prove that if the parameter b is an increasingly sorted array then $\Psi := d_2 \geq d_1$ is an invariant of the program. $\mathcal{K}_P$ contains the sortedness axiom for b. Assume first that $\Sigma_P = \{b, d_1, d_2, a\}$. Ψ clearly holds in the initial state. To show that Ψ is an inductive invariant of the while loop, we would need to prove that the following formula is unsatisfiable:*

$$d_1 \leq d_2 \wedge \forall j(a'[j] \approx a[j]+1) \wedge d_1' \approx a'[i] \wedge d_2' \approx a'[i+1] \wedge i' \approx i+1 \wedge d_1' > d_2'.$$

We have the chain of local theory extensions

$$\mathbb{Z} \subseteq \mathbb{Z} \cup \text{UIF}_a \subseteq \mathbb{Z} \cup \text{UIF}_a \cup \text{Update}_a = \mathcal{T},$$

where $\text{Update}_a = \forall j(a'[j] \approx a[j]+1)$. $\text{Update}_{d_1} = d_1' \approx a'[i]$, $\text{Update}_{d_2} = d_2' \approx a'[i+1]$ and $\text{Update}_i = i' \approx i+1$ are ground formulae. Let $G = d_1' \approx a'[i] \wedge d_2' \approx$

$a'[i+1] \wedge i' \approx i+1 \wedge d'_1 > d'_2$. *Using the hierarchical reduction method for local theory extensions we can see that the formula above is satisfiable, so Ψ is not an invariant. To strengthen Ψ we use Algorithm 1; by Theorem 4 we can ignore $\mathcal{K}_P$ and $I_1 = d_1 \leq d_2$. In a first step, we compute $\mathsf{Update}_a[G]$ and obtain the set of instances $a'[i] \approx a[i]+1 \wedge a'[i+1] \approx a[i+1]+1$. After purification we obtain (with $\mathsf{Def} = a'_1 \approx a'[i] \wedge a'_2 \approx a'[i+1]$):*

$$G_0 \wedge (\mathsf{Update}_a)_0: a'_1 \approx a[i]+1 \wedge a'_2 \approx a[i+1]+1 \wedge$$
$$d'_1 \approx a'_1 \wedge d'_2 \approx a'_2 \wedge i' \approx i+1 \wedge d'_1 > d'_2.$$

In a second step we can use a similar hierarchical reduction for the extension with UIF_a; we obtain (with $\mathsf{Def} = a'_1 \approx a'[i] \wedge a'_2 \approx a'[i+1] \wedge a_1 \approx a[i] \wedge a_2 \approx a[i+1]$):

$$a'_1 \approx a_1 + 1 \wedge a'_2 \approx a_2 + 1 \wedge d'_1 \approx a'_1 \wedge d'_2 \approx a'_2 \wedge i' \approx i+1 \wedge d'_1 > d'_2.$$

We use quantifier elimination for eliminating $a'_1, a'_2, d'_1, d'_2, i'$ and obtain the constraint $a_1 > a_2$. After replacing the constants with the terms they denote we obtain $\exists i(a[i] > a[i+1])$; its negation, $\Gamma_1 = \forall i(a[i] \leq a[i+1])$, can be used to strengthen Ψ to the inductive invariant $I_2 = d_1 \leq d_2 \wedge \forall i(a[i] \leq a[i+1])$.

Assume now that $\Sigma_P = \{b, d_1, d_2, a, i\}$. All primed variables are eliminated as above, but in Step 2 of Algorithm 1 i is not existentially quantified. Ψ is strengthened to $I_2 := d_1 \leq d_2 \wedge a[i] \leq a[i+1]$ (no universally quantified variables, the same as in Ψ). However, I_2 is not an inductive invariant. It can be strengthened to $I_3 := d_1 \leq d_2 \wedge a[i] \leq a[i+1] \wedge a[i+1] \leq a[i+2]$ and so on. Ideas similar to those used in the melting calculus [21] (used e.g. in [19, 20]) could be used to obtain $d_1 \leq d_2 \wedge \forall i(a[i] \leq a[i+1])$. (This example indicates that it could be a good strategy to not include the variables controlling loops among the parameters.)

While testing our method, we noticed that in some cases in which Algorithm 2 does not terminate, if we eliminate more symbols (thus restricting the language of the formula that strengthens the property to be proved) we can obtain termination. Details are given in the extended version of this paper [32], Sect. 5.3.

Corollary 13. *The symbol elimination method in Algorithm 1 can be adapted to eliminate all constants not guarded by a function in Σ_P. With this change we can guarantee that in all clauses in I_n all variables occur below a function in Σ_P.*

Example 5. *Let $\mathcal{T}_0 = LI(\mathbb{Q})$. Let $m, M, g, L \in \Sigma_P$ satisfying $\mathcal{K} = \{m \leq M\}$. $\mathsf{Update}_f := \{\forall x(x \leq c_1 \rightarrow m \leq f'(x) \wedge f'(x) \leq M), \forall x(x > c_1 \rightarrow f'(x) \approx a)\}$. Assume that $\Psi = \forall x, y(g(y) \leq x \rightarrow f(x) \leq L(y))$. By the results in Examples 1 and 2 we have the following chain of local theory extensions:*

$$\mathcal{T}_0 \subseteq \mathcal{T}_0 \cup \mathsf{UIF}_{\{g,L\}} \subseteq \mathcal{T}_0 \cup \Psi \subseteq \mathcal{T}_0 \cup \Psi \cup \mathsf{Update}_f.$$

Ψ is invariant under the update of f iff $\mathcal{K} \wedge \Psi \wedge \mathsf{Update}_f \wedge G$ is unsatisfiable, where $G = g(c) \leq d \wedge f'(d) > L(c)$ is obtained from $\neg \Psi'$ after Skolemization. Since the formula is satisfiable, Ψ is not invariant. We can strengthen Ψ by computing the DNF of $\mathsf{Update}_f[G] = \{(d \leq c_1 \rightarrow m \leq f'(d) \wedge f'(d) \leq M), (d >$

$c_1 \to f'(d) \approx a)\}$, *as explained in Lemma 10, replacing $f'(d)$ with an existentially quantified variable $x_{f'd}$. As the constant d does not occur below a parameter, it is replaced in Step 2 of Algorithm 1 with a variable x_d. The terms $g(c)$, $L(c)$ are replaced with constants c_{gc} resp. c_{Lc}. We obtain:*

$$\exists x_d \exists x_{f'd} \, (x_d \leq c_1 \wedge m \leq x_{f'd} \wedge x_{f'd} \leq M \wedge c_{gc} \leq x_d \wedge x_{f'd} > c_{Lc}) \vee$$
$$(x_d > c_1 \wedge x_{f'd} \approx a \wedge c_{gc} \leq x_d \wedge x_{f'd} > c_{Lc})$$

After eliminating $x_{f'd}$ we obtain:

$$\exists x_d(x_d \leq c_1 \wedge c_{gc} \leq x_d \wedge m \leq M \wedge c_{Lc} < M) \vee (x_d > c_1 \wedge c_{gc} \leq x_d \wedge c_{Lc} < a).$$

The variable x_d does not occur below any function symbol and it can be eliminated; we obtain the equivalent formula $(c_{gc} \leq c_1 \wedge m \leq M \wedge c_{Lc} < M) \vee (c_{Lc} < a)$; after replacing back the constants c_{gc} and c_{Lc} with the terms they denote, replacing c with a new existentially quantified variable y (Step 4 of Algorithm 1) and negating the formula obtained this way (Step 5 of Algorithm 1) we obtain the constraint $\forall y(g(y) \leq c_1 \to M \leq L(y)) \wedge \forall y(a \leq L(y))$.

4.1   Avoiding Some of the Conditions (A1)–(A5)

Assumption (**A4**) ($\mathscr{T}_0$ allows quantifier elimination) is not needed if in all update axioms f' is defined using equality; then f' can easily be eliminated.

Assumption (**A5**) is very strong. Even if we cannot guarantee that assumption (**A5**) holds, it could theoretically be possible to identify situations in which we can transform candidate invariants which do not define local extensions into equivalent formulae which define local extensions – e.g. using the results in [19].

If all candidate invariants I generated in Algorithm 2 are ground, assumption (**A5**) is not needed. We now describe a situation in which assumption (**A5**) is fulfilled, so Lemma 7 and Theorem 8 hold under assumptions (**A1**)–(**A4**).

We consider transition systems $T = (\Sigma_S, \mathsf{Init}, \mathsf{Update})$ and properties Ψ, where $\mathscr{T}_S = \mathscr{T}_0 \cup \mathscr{K}$ and $\mathsf{Init}, \Psi, \mathscr{K}$ and Update_f, $f \in F$, are all in the *array property fragment*. Then assumptions (**A1**) and (**A2**) hold. We identify conditions under which we can guarantee that at every iteration of Algorithm 2, the candidate invariant I is in the array property fragment, so assumption (**A5**) holds and does not need to be mentioned explicitly.

Many types of systems have descriptions in this fragment; an example follows.

Example 6. *Consider a controller of a water tank in which the inflow and outflow in a time unit can be chosen freely between minimum and maximum values that depend on the moment in time. Assume that $0 \leq L_{\mathsf{alarm}} < L_{\mathsf{overflow}}$. At the beginning minimal and maximal values for the inflow and outflow are initialized as described by the formula $\mathsf{Init} = \mathsf{In}_1 \wedge \mathsf{In}_2 \wedge \mathsf{Out}_1 \wedge \mathsf{Out}_2 \wedge (t \approx 0) \wedge (L \approx L_0)$, where for $i = 1, 2$:*

$$\mathsf{In}_i = \forall t(0 \leq in_m^i(t) \leq in_M^i(t) \leq L_{\mathsf{overflow}} - L_{\mathsf{alarm}} - \epsilon_i) \; and$$
$$\mathsf{Out}_i = \forall t(in_M^i(t) \leq out_m^i(t) \leq out_M^i(t))$$

The updates are described by $\mathsf{Update}_{\mathsf{in}} \wedge L' \approx L + \mathsf{in}'(t) \wedge t' \approx t + 1$, *where:*

$$\mathsf{Update}_{\mathsf{in}} = \forall t(L \leq L_{\mathsf{alarm}} \wedge t \leq t_0 \rightarrow \mathsf{in}^1_m(t) \leq \mathsf{in}'(t) \leq \mathsf{in}^1_M(t))$$
$$\forall t(L \leq L_{\mathsf{alarm}} \wedge t > t_0 \rightarrow \mathsf{in}^2_m(t) \leq \mathsf{in}'(t) \leq \mathsf{in}^2_M(t))$$
$$\forall t(L > L_{\mathsf{alarm}} \wedge t \leq t_0 \rightarrow \mathsf{in}^1_m(t) - \mathsf{out}^1_M(t) \leq \mathsf{in}'(t) \leq \mathsf{in}^1_M(t) - \mathsf{out}^1_m(t))$$
$$\forall t(L > L_{\mathsf{alarm}} \wedge t > t_0 \rightarrow \mathsf{in}^2_m(t) - \mathsf{out}^2_M(t) \leq \mathsf{in}'(t) \leq \mathsf{in}^2_M(t) - \mathsf{out}^2_m(t))$$

All these formulae are in the array property fragment.

The following results follow from the definition of the array property fragment.

Lemma 14. *Under assumption* **(A3)**, Update_f *is in the array property fragment iff* $\phi_1, \ldots \phi_{n_f}$ *are conjunctions of constraints of the form* $x \leq g$ *or* $x \geq g$, *where* x *is a variable and* g *is a ground term of sort* index, *all* $\Sigma \cup \Sigma_P$ *terms are flat and all universally quantified variables occur below a function in* $\Sigma \cup \Sigma_P$.

Lemma 15. *Let* G *be the negation of a formula in the array property fragment (APF). Then the following are equivalent:*

(1) The formula obtained by applying Algorithm 1 to $\mathsf{Update}_f \wedge G$ *is in the APF.*
(2) No instances of the congruence axioms need to be used for $\mathsf{est}(G)$.
(3) Either $\mathsf{est}(G)$ *contains only one element, or whenever* $f'(\overline{d}), f'(\overline{d'}) \in \mathsf{est}(G)$, *where* $\overline{d} = d_1, \ldots, d_n, \overline{d'} = d'_1, \ldots, d'_n$, *we have* $\mathscr{T}_0 \cup \mathscr{K} \cup G \models \bigvee_{i=1}^n d_i \not\approx d'_i$.

Proof (Idea): The formula $\bigwedge_{p=1}^k \phi_{i_p}(y_p) \wedge \bigwedge_{(d_1,d_2) \in D} y_1 \not\approx y_2 \wedge G_0^g(\overline{y}, \overline{g}(y))$ obtained after applying Algorithm 1, can be an index guard only if it does not contain the disequalities $y_1 \not\approx y_2$. This is the case when $|\mathsf{est}(G)| = 1$ or else if for all $f(d_1), f(d_2) \in \mathsf{est}(G)$, $\mathscr{T}_0 \cup G_0 \models d_1 \not\approx d_2$.   □

Theorem 16 *Let* $T = (\Sigma_S, \mathsf{Init}, \mathsf{Update})$ *be a transition system with theory* $\mathscr{T}_S = \mathscr{T}_0 \cup \mathscr{K}$. *Assume that* $\mathscr{T}_0$ *is the disjoint combination of Presburger arithmetic (sort* index*) and a theory of elements (e.g. linear arithmetic over* $\mathbb{Q}$*). Assume that all functions in* Σ *are unary. If* $\mathscr{K}, \mathsf{Init}, \mathsf{Update}$ *and* Ψ *are in the array property fragment and all clauses in* Ψ *have only one universally quantified variable, then the formulae* Γ_n *obtained by symbol elimination in Step 2 at every iteration of Algorithm 2 are again in the array property fragment and are conjunctions of clauses having only one quantified variable.*

4.2 Termination

Algorithms of the form of Algorithm 2 do not terminate in general even for simple programs, handling only integer or rational variables (cf. e.g. [9]). We identify situations in which the invariant synthesis procedure terminates. (For proofs cf. the extended version [32].)

Lemma 17 (A termination condition). *Assume that conditions* **(A1)**–**(A5)** *hold and the candidate invariants* I *generated at each iteration are conjunctions of clauses which contain, up to renaming of the variables, terms in a given finite family* Ter *of terms. Then the algorithm must terminate with an invariant* I *or after detecting that* $\mathsf{Init} \not\models I$.

A situation in which this condition holds is described below.[7]

Theorem 18. *Let* $\Sigma = \{f_1, \ldots, f_n\} = \Sigma_P$. *Assume that conditions* (**A1**)–(**A5**) *hold,* $\mathcal{T}_0 = \mathsf{LI}(\mathbb{Q})$ *and that:*

- *All clauses used for defining $\mathcal{T}_S$ and the property Ψ contain only literals of the form: $x \triangleright t$, $u \triangleright v$, $f_i(x) \triangleright s$, $f_i(x) \triangleright y$, where x, y are (universally quantified) variables, $f_i \in \Sigma$, s, t, u, v are constants, and $\triangleright \in \{\leq, <, \geq, >, \approx\}$.*
- *All axioms in* Update *are of the form $\forall \overline{x} \left(\phi_i^k(\overline{x}) \to C_i(\overline{x}, f'_k(\overline{x})) \right)$ as in Assumption (**A2**), where $C_i(\overline{x}, y)$ and $\phi_i^k(\overline{x})$ are conjunctions of literals of the form above.*

Then all the candidate invariants I generated during the execution of Algorithm 2 are equivalent to sets of clauses, all containing a finite set Ter *of terms formed with variables in a finite set* Var. *Since only finitely many clauses (up to renaming of variables) can be formed this way, after a finite number of steps no new formulae can be generated, thus the algorithm terminates.*

5   Conclusion

We proposed a method for property-directed invariant generation and analyzed its properties. Our results extend the results in [4] and [9], as we consider more complex theories. There are similarities to the method in [31], but our approach is different: The theories we analyze do not typically have the finite model property (required in [28,31] where, if a counterexample A to the inductiveness of a candidate invariant I is found, a formula is added to I to avoid finding the same counterexample again in the next iteration; to construct this formula the finite model property assumption is used). In our work we use the symbol elimination method in Algorithm 1 to strengthen I; this should help to accelerate the procedure compared to the diagram-based approach. The decidability results in [31] are presented in a general framework and rely on the well-foundedness of certain relations. In this paper we consider extensions of arithmetic (or other theories allowing quantifier elimination) with additional function symbols; the theories we consider are not guaranteed to have the finite model property. For the situations in which we guarantee termination the abstract decidability or termination arguments in [31] might be difficult to check or might not hold (the arguments used for the case of pointers are not applicable). In contrast to the algorithm proposed in [15], our algorithm is deterministic. To prove termination we show that the length of the quantifier prefix in the candidate invariants generated in every iteration does not grow; termination is then guaranteed if only finitely many atomic formulae formed with a fixed number of variables can be generated using quantifier elimination when applying the algorithm.

We analyzed the applicability of our methods on several examples. In our tests, we used H-PILoT [23] for the hierarchical reduction (Step 1 in Algorithm 1)

---

[7] To simplify the notation, we assume that the functions in Σ have arity ≤ 1. Similar arguments can be used for n-ary functions.

and Redlog [10] for quantifier elimination (Step 3 in Algorithm 1); implementing Step 2 is ongoing work.

Future work. We here restricted to universally quantified invariants and theories related to the array property fragment, but an extension to a framework using the notion of "extended locality" (cf. [22,24]) seems unproblematic. We plan to identify additional situations in which our invariant generation method is correct, terminates resp. has low complexity – either by considering other theories or more general first-order properties.

Acknowledgments. We thank the reviewers for their helpful comments.

References

1. Alberti, F., Bruttomesso, R., Ghilardi, S., Ranise, S., Sharygina, N.: An extension of lazy abstraction with interpolation for programs with arrays. Formal Methods Syst. Des. **45**(1), 63–109 (2014)
2. Bachmair, L., Ganzinger, H., Waldmann, U.: Refutational theorem proving for hierarchic first-order theories. Appl. Algebra Eng. Commun. Comput. **5**, 193–212 (1994)
3. Beyer, D., Henzinger, T.A., Majumdar, R., Rybalchenko, A.: Invariant synthesis for combined theories. In: Cook, B., Podelski, A. (eds.) VMCAI 2007. LNCS, vol. 4349, pp. 378–394. Springer, Heidelberg (2007). https://doi.org/10.1007/978-3-540-69738-1_27
4. Bradley, A.R.: IC3 and beyond: incremental, inductive verification. In: Madhusudan, P., Seshia, S.A. (eds.) CAV 2012. LNCS, vol. 7358, pp. 4–4. Springer, Heidelberg (2012). https://doi.org/10.1007/978-3-642-31424-7_4
5. Bradley, A.R., Manna, Z.: Property-directed incremental invariant generation. Formal Asp. Comput. **20**(4–5), 379–405 (2008)
6. Bradley, A.R., Manna, Z., Sipma, H.B.: What's decidable about arrays? In: Emerson, E.A., Namjoshi, K.S. (eds.) VMCAI 2006. LNCS, vol. 3855, pp. 427–442. Springer, Heidelberg (2005). https://doi.org/10.1007/11609773_28
7. Bruttomesso, R., Ghilardi, S., Ranise, S.: Quantifier-free interpolation in combinations of equality interpolating theories. ACM Trans. Comput. Log. **15**(1), 5:1–5:34 (2014)
8. Conchon, S., Goel, A., Krstić, S., Mebsout, A., Zaïdi, F.: Cubicle: a parallel SMT-based model checker for parameterized systems. In: Madhusudan, P., Seshia, S.A. (eds.) CAV 2012. LNCS, vol. 7358, pp. 718–724. Springer, Heidelberg (2012). https://doi.org/10.1007/978-3-642-31424-7_55
9. Dillig, I., Dillig, T., Li, B., McMillan, K.L.: Inductive invariant generation via abductive inference. In: Hosking, A.L., Eugster, P.T., Lopes, C.V., (eds.) Proceedings of the 2013 ACM SIGPLAN International Conference on Object Oriented Programming Systems Languages & Applications, OOPSLA 2013, part of SPLASH 2013, pp. 443–456. ACM (2013)
10. Dolzmann, A., Sturm, T.: REDLOG: computer algebra meets computer logic. ACM SIGSAM Bull. **31**(2), 2–9 (1997)
11. Faber, J., Jacobs, S., Sofronie-Stokkermans, V.: Verifying CSP-OZ-DC specifications with complex data types and timing parameters. In: Davies, J., Gibbons, J. (eds.) IFM 2007. LNCS, vol. 4591, pp. 233–252. Springer, Heidelberg (2007). https://doi.org/10.1007/978-3-540-73210-5_13

12. Falke, S., Kapur, D.: When is a formula a loop invariant? In: Martí-Oliet, N., Ölveczky, P.C., Talcott, C. (eds.) Logic, Rewriting, and Concurrency. LNCS, vol. 9200, pp. 264–286. Springer, Cham (2015). https://doi.org/10.1007/978-3-319-23165-5_13

13. Ganzinger, H., Sofronie-Stokkermans, V., Waldmann, U.: Modular proof systems for partial functions with weak equality. In: Basin, D., Rusinowitch, M. (eds.) IJCAR 2004. LNCS (LNAI), vol. 3097, pp. 168–182. Springer, Heidelberg (2004). https://doi.org/10.1007/978-3-540-25984-8_10

14. Ganzinger, H., Sofronie-Stokkermans, V., Waldmann, U.: Modular proof systems for partial functions with Evans equality. Inf. Comput. **204**(10), 1453–1492 (2006)

15. Ghilardi, S., Ranise, S.: Backward reachability of array-based systems by SMT solving: Termination and invariant synthesis. Logical Methods Comput. Sci. **6**(4), 1–48 (2010)

16. Gleiss, B., Kovács, L., Robillard, S.: Loop analysis by quantification over iterations. In: Barthe, G., Sutcliffe, G., Veanes, M., (eds.) 22nd International Conference on Logic for Programming, Artificial Intelligence and Reasoning, volume 57 of EPiC Series in Computing, LPAR-22, pp. 381–399 (2018). EasyChair

17. Gurfinkel, A., Shoham, S., Vizel, Y.: Quantifiers on demand. In: Lahiri, S.K., Wang, C. (eds.) ATVA 2018. LNCS, vol. 11138, pp. 248–266. Springer, Cham (2018). https://doi.org/10.1007/978-3-030-01090-4_15

18. Hoder, K., Kovács, L., Voronkov, A.: Interpolation and symbol elimination in Vampire. In: Giesl, J., Hähnle, R. (eds.) IJCAR 2010. LNCS (LNAI), vol. 6173, pp. 188–195. Springer, Heidelberg (2010). https://doi.org/10.1007/978-3-642-14203-1_16

19. Horbach, M., Sofronie-Stokkermans, V.: Obtaining finite local theory axiomatizations via saturation. In: Fontaine, P., Ringeissen, C., Schmidt, R.A. (eds.) FroCoS 2013. LNCS (LNAI), vol. 8152, pp. 198–213. Springer, Heidelberg (2013). https://doi.org/10.1007/978-3-642-40885-4_14

20. Horbach, M., Sofronie-Stokkermans, V.: Locality transfer: From constrained axiomatizations to reachability predicates. In: Demri, S., Kapur, D., Weidenbach, C. (eds.) IJCAR 2014. LNCS (LNAI), vol. 8562, pp. 192–207. Springer, Cham (2014). https://doi.org/10.1007/978-3-319-08587-6_14

21. Horbach, M., Weidenbach, C.: Deciding the inductive validity of $\forall \exists^*$ queries. In: Grädel, E., Kahle, R. (eds.) CSL 2009. LNCS, vol. 5771, pp. 332–347. Springer, Heidelberg (2009). https://doi.org/10.1007/978-3-642-04027-6_25

22. Ihlemann, C., Jacobs, S., Sofronie-Stokkermans, V.: On local reasoning in verification. In: Ramakrishnan, C.R., Rehof, J. (eds.) TACAS 2008. LNCS, vol. 4963, pp. 265–281. Springer, Heidelberg (2008). https://doi.org/10.1007/978-3-540-78800-3_19

23. Ihlemann, C., Sofronie-Stokkermans, V.: System description: H-PILoT. In: Schmidt, R.A. (ed.) CADE 2009. LNCS (LNAI), vol. 5663, pp. 131–139. Springer, Heidelberg (2009). https://doi.org/10.1007/978-3-642-02959-2_9

24. Ihlemann, C., Sofronie-Stokkermans, V.: On hierarchical reasoning in combinations of theories. In: Giesl, J., Hähnle, R. (eds.) IJCAR 2010. LNCS (LNAI), vol. 6173, pp. 30–45. Springer, Heidelberg (2010). https://doi.org/10.1007/978-3-642-14203-1_4

25. Jacobs, S., Kuncak, V.: Towards complete reasoning about axiomatic specifications. In: Jhala, R., Schmidt, D. (eds.) VMCAI 2011. LNCS, vol. 6538, pp. 278–293. Springer, Heidelberg (2011). https://doi.org/10.1007/978-3-642-18275-4_20

26. Kapur, D.: A quantifier-elimination based heuristic for automatically generating inductive assertions for programs. J. Syst. Sci. Complexity **19**(3), 307–330 (2006)

27. Kapur, D., Majumdar, R., Zarba, C.G.: Interpolation for data structures. In: Young, M., Devanbu, P.T., (eds.) Proceedings of the 14th ACM SIGSOFT International Symposium on Foundations of Software Engineering, FSE 2006, pp. 105–116. ACM (2006)

28. Karbyshev, A., Bjørner, N., Itzhaky, S., Rinetzky, N., Shoham, S.: Property-directed inference of universal invariants or proving their absence. J. ACM **64**(1), 7:1–7:33 (2017)

29. Kovács, L., Voronkov, A.: Finding loop invariants for programs over arrays using a theorem prover. In: Chechik, M., Wirsing, M. (eds.) FASE 2009. LNCS, vol. 5503, pp. 470–485. Springer, Heidelberg (2009). https://doi.org/10.1007/978-3-642-00593-0_33

30. Kovács, L., Voronkov, A.: Interpolation and symbol elimination. In: Schmidt, R.A. (ed.) CADE 2009. LNCS (LNAI), vol. 5663, pp. 199–213. Springer, Heidelberg (2009). https://doi.org/10.1007/978-3-642-02959-2_17

31. Padon, O., Immerman, N., Shoham, S., Karbyshev, A., Sagiv, M.: Decidability of inferring inductive invariants. In: Bodík, R., Majumdar, R., (eds.) Proceedings of the 43rd Annual ACM SIGPLAN-SIGACT Symposium on Principles of Programming Languages, POPL 2016, pp. 217–231. ACM (2016)

32. Peuter, D., Sofronie-Stokkermans, V.: On invariant synthesis for parametric systems. CoRR http://arxiv.org/abs/1905.12524 (2019)

33. Sofronie-Stokkermans, V.: Hierarchic reasoning in local theory extensions. In: Nieuwenhuis, R. (ed.) CADE 2005. LNCS (LNAI), vol. 3632, pp. 219–234. Springer, Heidelberg (2005). https://doi.org/10.1007/11532231_16

34. Sofronie-Stokkermans, V.: Interpolation in local theory extensions. In: Furbach, U., Shankar, N. (eds.) IJCAR 2006. LNCS (LNAI), vol. 4130, pp. 235–250. Springer, Heidelberg (2006). https://doi.org/10.1007/11814771_21

35. Sofronie-Stokkermans, V.: Interpolation in local theory extensions. Logical Methods Comput. Sci. **4**(4), 1–31 (2008)

36. Sofronie-Stokkermans, V.: Hierarchical reasoning for the verification of parametric systems. In: Giesl, J., Hähnle, R. (eds.) IJCAR 2010. LNCS, vol. 6173, pp. 171–187. Springer, Berlin (2010). https://doi.org/10.1007/978-3-642-14203-1_15

37. Sofronie-Stokkermans, V.: Hierarchical reasoning and model generation for the verification of parametric hybrid systems. In: Bonacina, M.P. (ed.) CADE 2013. LNCS (LNAI), vol. 7898, pp. 360–376. Springer, Heidelberg (2013). https://doi.org/10.1007/978-3-642-38574-2_25

38. Sofronie-Stokkermans, V.: On interpolation and symbol elimination in theory extensions. In: Olivetti, N., Tiwari, A. (eds.) IJCAR 2016. LNCS (LNAI), vol. 9706, pp. 273–289. Springer, Cham (2016). https://doi.org/10.1007/978-3-319-40229-1_19

39. Sofronie-Stokkermans, V.: On interpolation and symbol elimination in theory extensions. Logical Methods Comput. Sci. **14**(3), 1–41 (2018)

40. Yorsh, G., Musuvathi, M.: A combination method for generating interpolants. In: Nieuwenhuis, R. (ed.) CADE 2005. LNCS (LNAI), vol. 3632, pp. 353–368. Springer, Heidelberg (2005). https://doi.org/10.1007/11532231_26

The Aspect Calculus

David A. Plaisted$^{(\boxtimes)}$

UNC Chapel Hill, Chapel Hill, NC 27599-3175, USA
plaisted@cs.unc.edu

Abstract. For theorem proving applications, the aspect calculus for reasoning about states and actions has some advantages over existing situation calculus formalisms, and also provides an application domain and a source of problems for first-order theorem provers. The aspect calculus provides a representation for reasoning about states and actions that is suited to modular domains. An aspect names a portion of a state, that is, a substate, such as a room in a building or a city in a country. Aspects may have aspects of their own. A state is assumed to be either a *leaf state* that cannot be further decomposed, or to be composed of substates, and actions associated with one substate do not influence other, disjoint substates. This feature can reduce the number of frame axioms that are needed if the domain has a modular structure. It can also permit planning problems on independent substates to be solved independently to some degree. However, interactions between independent substates are also permitted.

Keywords: Situation calculus · Frame problem · Aspects ·
Equational reasoning

1 Introduction

The situation calculus permits reasoning about properties of situations that result from a given situation by sequences of actions [MH69]. In the situation calculus, situations (states) are represented explicitly by variables, and actions a map states s to states $do(a, s)$. Predicates and functions on a situation or state are called *fluents*. In some formalisms, a situation denotes a state of the world, specifying the values of fluents, so that two situations are equal if the values of all their fluents are the same. Other formalisms reserve the term situation for a sequence of states. A problem with the situation calculus or any formalism for reasoning about actions is the necessity to include a large number of *frame axioms* that express the fact that actions do not influence many properties (fluents) of a state. Since the early days of artificial intelligence research the frame problem has been studied, beginning with McCarthy and Hayes [MH69]. Lin [Lin08] has written a recent survey of the situation calculus.

Reiter [Rei91] proposed an approach to the frame problem in first-order logic that avoids the need to specify all of the frame axioms. The method of Reiter,

© Springer Nature Switzerland AG 2019
P. Fontaine (Ed.): CADE 2019, LNAI 11716, pp. 406–424, 2019.
https://doi.org/10.1007/978-3-030-29436-6_24

foreshadowed by Haas [Haa87], Pednault [Ped89], Schubert [Sch90] and Davis [Dav90], essentially solves the frame problem by specifying that a change in the truth value of a fluent, caused by an action, is equivalent to a certain condition on the action. In this formalism, it is only necessary to list the actions that change each fluent, and it is not necessary to specify the frame axioms directly. If an action does not satisfy the condition, the fluent is not affected. In the following discussion the term "Reiter's formalism" will be used for simplicity even though others have also contributed to its development. The *fluent calculus* [Thi98] is another interesting approach to the frame problem. In this approach, a state is a conjunction of known facts.

In the present paper, yet another approach to the frame problem using *aspects* is presented. This approach is based on the idea that the world is hierarchical or modular to a large extent. Aspects permit one to structure fluents and actions in a modular way.

The aspect formalism considers a situation, or state, to be composed of substates, These substates are named by aspects. Substates may have substates of their own. The aspect calculus constructs a tree of aspects. For example, the top node could be "earth", its children could be various countries, each country could have its states as children, and each state could have its cities as children. An aspect is a sequence of identifiers such as (earth, USA, North Carolina, Chapel Hill). The aspect calculus is suitable if actions in a substate do not have much influence on fluents from a disjoint substate, roughly speaking. Thus the action of teaching a class in Chapel Hill would have aspect (earth, USA, North Carolina, Chapel Hill) and would only influence fluents that also had the same aspect, or an aspect referring to a part of Chapel Hill. This action would not have any effect on fluents with aspects of a different city, state, or country. However, calling someone in Washington DC from Chapel Hill would influence fluents in both cities and would have to be given an aspect of (earth, USA). Instead of sequences of names, the formal theory of aspects uses sequences of numbers.

Hayes actually mentioned "frames" which are very similar to aspects as a possible solution to the frame problem. He did not reject frames, but felt that they would not solve the frame problem in all cases. He wrote [Hay73], "In the long run I believe that a mixture of frame rules and consistency-based methods will be required for non-trivial problems ..." (page 56).

Petrick [Pet08] has adapted Reiter's formalism to knowledge and belief and has also introduced the notion of a Cartesian situation that can decompose a situation into parts, in a way that appears to be similar to the aspect calculus. However, his formalism also considers a situation to include a sequence of states.

The aspect calculus has some advantages over Reiter's formalism, especially in its suitability for first-order theorem provers. In Reiter's formalism, the successor state axiom for a fluent essentially says that the fluent is true on a situation $do(a, s)$ for fluent a and situation s if a is an action that makes the fluent true, or if the fluent was already true and a is not one of the actions that makes the fluent false. This requires one to know under what conditions an action changes the value of the fluent to "true" or "false." If for example the action is nondeterministic this may be difficult to know. Also, to formulate the successor state axiom, one needs a theory of equality between actions. If there are only a small number of actions that can make a fluent false, then Reiter's formalism is concise because one need not list all of the actions that do not influence the fluent (the frame axioms for the fluent). However, if there are many actions (possibly thousands or millions) that influence the fluent, then this successor state axiom can become very long. Further, when converting Reiter's approach to clause form, one needs an axiom of the form "For all actions a, $a = a_1 \vee a = a_2 \vee \cdots \vee a = a_n$" where a_i are all the possible actions, as well as the axioms $a_i \neq a_j$ for all $i \neq j$. If there are many actions, the first axiom will be huge. It is also difficult for many theorem provers to handle axioms of this form.

Even the successor state axiom itself, when translated into clause form, produces clauses having a disjunction of an equation and another literal. Using $\Phi(p, s)$ to denote the value of fluent p on situation s, a simple form of the successor state axiom would be

$$\Phi(p, do(x, s)) \equiv [(\Phi(p, s) \wedge (x \neq a_1) \wedge (x \neq a_2)) \vee (x = b_1 \vee x = b_2)]$$

where a_1 and a_2 are the only actions that can make p false and b_1 and b_2 are the only actions that make p true. Consider an even simpler form:

$$\Phi(p, do(x, s)) \equiv [(\Phi(p, s) \wedge (x \neq a_1)) \vee (x = b_1)]$$

The clause form of the latter is $\neg\Phi(p, do(x, s)) \vee \Phi(p, s) \vee x = b_1, \neg\Phi(p, do(x, s)) \vee x \neq a_1 \vee x = b_1, x \neq b_1 \vee \Phi(p, do(x, s)), \neg\Phi(p, s) \vee x = a_1 \vee \Phi(p, do(x, s))$. Such conjunctions of equations and inequations can be difficult for theorem provers to handle, especially if there are more actions in which case there would be more equations and inequations in the clauses.

The aspect calculus by contrast introduces many axioms that are unit equations, which are particularly easy for many theorem provers to handle. If the underlying domain is first-order then the aspect calculus is entirely expressed in first-order logic, so powerful first-order theorem provers can be applied to planning problems by framing a query of the form "There exists a situation having certain properties" and attempting to prove it. For this, a reflexive and transitive predicate *reachable* can be defined, the axioms $reachable(s, do(a, s))$ can be added for all actions a, and theorems of the form $(\exists s)(reachable(s_0, s) \wedge A[s])$ can be proved where s_0 is some starting state and A is a first-order formula. However, Reiter's formalism can handle domains without a clear hierarchical structure, especially if there are only a small number of actions that influence each fluent. Also, the aspect calculus does not handle knowledge and belief. Reiter's formalism attempts to make it easy to decide if a fluent is true on a situation obtained from a starting situation by a sequence of actions. The aspect calculus by contrast only attempts to preserve provability in the underlying theory while reducing the number of frame axioms.

The aspect calculus has other advantages independent of its suitability for theorem provers. Locality can be incorporated into the planning process. For example, if one wants to obtain a state t from s and the only difference is that a room in a building has changed, then one can first look for a plan that does not change anything outside the room. If that does not work, one can look for a plan that only changes rooms on that floor, changes to the other rooms being only temporary. If that does not work, one can look for a plan that only changes properties of the building, and nothing outside of it, and so on. Also, if the state space is finite, then the search space for planning problems in the aspect calculus is also finite. With Reiter's approach [Rei91], situations contain sequences of states, so the search space can be infinite. Planning in disjoint sub-states (aspects) of a state can be done independently to some extent. This reduces redundancies due to the order of actions involving independent modules not affecting the result.

Further, a possible problem with Reiter's approach, noted in Scherl and Levesque [SL93], is the *ramification problem*, namely, it can be difficult to incorporate *constraints* between fluents, such as when one fluent implies another. The successor state axiom essentially implies that the only way a fluent can become true is for an action to make it true. A great deal of work [Sha99, LR94, DT07, McI00, Ter00, MM97] has been done to handle the ramification problem in Reiter's system. No special treatment for the ramification problem is needed in the aspect calculus, but the theory needs to be hierarchical, that is, it should be possible to assign aspects so that disjoint aspects are largely independent.

2   Underlying Theory

We assume that there is some underlying set T of axioms in first-order logic concerning states, fluents, and actions. The semantics of this axiomatization will have domains for states and actions, with fluents mapping from states to various domains. We do not necessarily assume that T is encoded in any particular situation calculus, such as Reiter's [Rei91]. We will modify such a state theory T to obtain an axiomatization T^{aspect} that in some cases can more economically encode frame axioms than T does. In some cases T^{aspect} can be custom designed without transformation from a theory T.

Actions in T are typically indicated by the letter a, possibly with subscripts, and fluents are typically indicated by the letters p and q, possibly with subscripts. $\mathcal{F}$ is the set of all fluents and $\mathcal{A}$ is the set of actions. States are denoted by s, t, and u, possibly with subscripts. The set of states is $\mathcal{S}$.

If a is an action and s is a state then $do(a, s)$ is the result of applying action a in state s. For nondeterminism, instead of $do(a, s) = t$ one would write $do(a, s, t)$ indicating that t is a possible result of applying action a in state s. It appears that the aspect formalism can handle this without a problem, but this has not been formally investigated. If p is a fluent then $\Phi(p, s)$ is the value of p on state s. Thus fluents are essentially functions from states to various domains. If the value of a fluent is *true* or *false*, and it is not parameterized, then $\Phi(p, s)$ may be written as $p(s)$ instead. The semantics (interpretation) of the underlying theory T is assumed to have sorts for fluents, states, and actions, in addition to possibly others.

The semantics of operations is defined by assertions of the following form:

$$\lambda x_1 x_2 \ldots x_n . E[x_1, \ldots, x_n] : \psi_i \cdots \psi_n \to \psi_0$$

indicating that in the expression E, x_i are assumed to have sort ψ_i and E returns a value of sort ψ_0. One can then define the semantics of do and Φ as follows:

$\lambda as.do(a, s) : \mathcal{A} \times \mathcal{S} \to \mathcal{S}$

$\lambda ps.\Phi(p, s) : \mathcal{F} \times \mathcal{S} \to \mathcal{D}$ for some domain $\mathcal{D}$

We assume that $\mathcal{T}$ satisfies the action dependency condition if the fluents of $do(a, s)$ only depend on the fluents of s. This is formally defined as follows:

Definition 1. *The theory $\mathcal{T}$ satisfies the* action dependency condition *if $\mathcal{T} \models$ $(\forall s, t \in \mathcal{S})(\forall a \in \mathcal{A}), ((\forall p \in \mathcal{F})\Phi(p, s) = \Phi(p, t)) \to ((\forall p \in \mathcal{F})\Phi(p, do(a, s)) = \Phi(p, do(a, t)))$.*

This constraint must be satisfied in order to use the aspect representation.

Example 1. We give an example state theory $\mathcal{L}_n$ in the "classical representation." For simplicity, fluents are written as $ron(i, s)$, $lon(i, s)$, $lonall(s)$, $ronall(s)$, and $onall(s)$ instead of $\Phi(ron(i), s)$, $\Phi(lon(i), s)$, $\Phi(lonall, s)$, $\Phi(ronall, s)$, and $\Phi(onall, s)$, respectively. In general, fluents are functions, but because these are all Booleans, we write $ron(i, s)$ instead of $ron(i, s) = true$, et cetera.

Suppose there are two banks of n switches that can be turned on and off and each switch controls a light. So there are actions $lton(i)$ (turn i on in the left bank) and $ltof(i)$ (turn i off in the left bank) for $1 \le i \le n$, also $rton(i)$ and $rtof(i)$ for the right bank. There are also fluents $lon(i, s)$ and $ron(i, s)$ telling whether the i-th light is on in the left and right banks. There is also a fluent $lonall(s)$ telling whether all the lights are on in the left bank, and similarly $ronall$ for the right bank, and $onall(s)$ for both banks being all on. A state is defined by whether the switches are on or off; all fluents other than $lon(i)$ and $ron(i)$ are functions of these. Thus there are 4^n states in all, one for each combined setting of the $2n$ switches. We can indicate a state in which $lon(i) = b_i$ and $ron(i) = c_i$ for Booleans b_i, c_i by $[b_1, \ldots, b_n, c_1, \ldots, c_n]_S$ where the subscript S may be omitted. The fluents $lonall, ronall$, and $onall$ can be determined from b_i and c_i and are not explicitly shown in this notation.

In the following equations for $\mathcal{L}_n$, the free variables s are states and are universally quantified. $(A5)^c$ through $(A8)^c$ are the frame axioms, and they make this representation quadratic in n.

$$lon(i, do(lton(i), s)) \wedge ron(i, do(rton(i), s)), 1 \le i \le n(\text{A1})^c$$
$$\neg lon(i, do(ltof(i), s)) \wedge \neg ron(i, do(rtof(i), s)), 1 \le i \le n(\text{A2})^c$$
$$lonall(s) \equiv lon(1, s) \wedge \cdots \wedge lon(n, s)(\text{A3})_l^c$$
$$ronall(s) \equiv ron(1, s) \wedge \cdots \wedge ron(n, s)(\text{A3})_r^c$$
$$onall(s) \equiv lonall(s) \wedge ronall(s) \ (\text{A4})^c$$
$$lon(i, do(lton(j), s)) \equiv lon(i, s), 1 \le i, j \le n, i \ne j(\text{A5})_l^c$$
$$ron(i, do(rton(j), s)) \equiv ron(i, s), 1 \le i, j \le n, i \ne j(\text{A5})_r^c$$
$$lon(i, do(rton(j), s)) \equiv lon(i, s), 1 \le i, j \le n(\text{A6})_l^c$$
$$ron(i, do(lton(j), s)) \equiv ron(i, s), 1 \le i, j \le n(\text{A6})_r^c$$
$$lon(i, do(ltof(j), s)) \equiv lon(i, s), 1 \le i, j \le n, i \ne j(\text{A7})_l^c$$
$$ron(i, do(rtof(j), s)) \equiv ron(i, s), 1 \le i, j \le n, i \ne j(\text{A7})_r^c$$
$$lon(i, do(rtof(j), s)) \equiv lon(i, s), 1 \le i, j \le n(\text{A8})_l^c$$
$$ron(i, do(ltof(j), s)) \equiv ron(i, s), 1 \le i, j \le n(\text{A8})_r^c$$
$$\exists s(s \in S)(\text{A9})^c$$

3   Aspects

The theory T will be extended to a theory T^{aspect} that may permit many of the frame axioms of T to be omitted but will still permit the same plans to be derived. T^{aspect} is constructed so that any model M of the underlying theory T can be extended to a model M^{aspect} of T^{aspect}. This implies the relative consistency of T^{aspect} with respect to T, which essentially means that incorrect plans cannot be derived in T^{aspect}. With notation as in the introduction, this means that $(\exists s)(reachable(s_0, s) \wedge A[s])$ is derivable in T^{aspect} iff it is derivable in T, but T^{aspect} may have many fewer frame axioms. When presenting aspects the model M^{aspect} is essentially being described.

In T^{aspect} there are *aspects* and *statelets* in addition to the states, actions, and fluents of T. Also, Ψ is the set of aspects and $\hat{S}$ is the set of statelets.

The aspects are organized in T^{aspect} in an *aspect tree*. This can be regarded as part of the model M^{aspect}.

Definition 2. *The* aspect tree Υ *is a finite tree with a root node. Every other node in the tree is either a leaf with no children or else has finitely many children ordered from left to right. The nodes in the tree are labeled with sequences or strings of integers. The root is labeled with ϵ, the empty string. If a node N is labeled with α and has n children then its n children left to right are labeled $\alpha 1$ through αn. These sequences or strings of integers are called* aspects. *Aspects are indicated by Greek letters α, β, γ, possibly with subscripts. If node N with n children has aspect α then the aspects $\alpha 1 \cdots \alpha n$ are called the* children *of aspect α, and α is called the* parent *of αi for all i. Sometimes aspects can be written with commas between the numbers, as, $1, 2, 1$ or $(1, 2, 1)$. If node L has aspect α and node N has aspect β and L is an ancestor of N in the aspect tree, then we* *say that α is an* ancestor *of β and β is a* descendant *of α. Thus if α is a prefix of β then α is an* ancestor *of β and β is a* descendent *of α. If α is $(3, 2, 4)$ then αi is $(3, 2, 4, i)$.*

Definition 3. *There is an ordering relation $<$ on aspects with $\alpha < \beta$ if α is an ancestor (proper prefix) of β, $\alpha < \beta$ iff $\beta > \alpha$ and $\geq$, $\leq$ are defined as usual. Thus for example $1, 2 > 1$.*

Also, if two aspects α and β are neither ancestors or descendants of one another, so that neither one is a prefix of the other, they are said to be incomparable, independent, *or* disjoint, *written $\alpha \# \beta$.*

Actions and fluents have unique aspects assigned to them in $\mathcal{T}^{aspect}$. This assignment has to be done manually. If the theory has a natural hierarchical structure then this should be easier.

We write $a : \alpha$ to indicate that action a has aspect α, and $p : \alpha$ to indicate that a fluent p has aspect α; one can also write $aspect(p) = \alpha$ and $aspect(a) = \alpha$.

Example 2. Continuing with the example from Example 1, for $\mathcal{L}_3$ (three switches in the left and right banks) in $\mathcal{L}_3^{aspect}$ there would be aspects ϵ, (1), (2) and (i, j) for $i = 1, 2$ and $j = 1, 2, 3$. The aspect ϵ refers to the whole problem, (1) to the left bank of switches, (2) to the right bank, and (i, j) to switch j in the left or right bank.

4   Statelets

In addition to states, there is a set $\hat{S}$ of *statelets* or *modules* in $\mathcal{T}^{aspect}$. Statelets can be indicated by the letters s, t, and u, possibly with subscripts. In $\mathcal{T}^{aspect}$, actions and fluents are extended from states to statelets. Thus

$\lambda as.do(a, s) : \mathcal{A} \times \hat{S} \to \hat{S} \cup \{\bot\}$ where $\bot$ is "don't care."

$\lambda ps.\Phi(p, s) : \mathcal{F} \times \hat{S} \to \mathcal{D} \cup \{\bot\}$ for some domain $\mathcal{D}$ where $\bot$ is "don't care."

An assignment of aspects will be called *unconstraining* if it does not impose additional restrictions on $\mathcal{T}$, in a way that will be made precise later (Definition 16).

In general, statelets have unique aspects; writing $s : \alpha$ indicates that the aspect of statelet s is α. Equality for statelets $s : \alpha$ and $t : \beta$ is defined by their fluents and their aspect, as follows:

$$\text{If for all } p \text{ in } \mathcal{F}, \Phi(p, s) = \Phi(p, t) \text{ and } \alpha = \beta, \text{ then } s = t. \tag{1}$$

Thus statelets are entirely determined by how fluents map them, and by their aspect. This differs from states, which may have additional properties not used by our formalism. Also, there is a new value $\bot$ such that for all fluents p and all states s, $\Phi(p, s) \neq \bot$. Further, $\bot$ is not equal to any state or statelet. If s is a statelet and p is a fluent then $\Phi(p, s)$ can be $\bot$ (don't care).

Example 3. For $\mathcal{L}_3^{aspect}$, there would be 64 statelets at aspect ϵ, indicating the combined setting of all six switches. Therefore if statelet s has aspect ϵ then $lon(i, s)$ and $ron(i, s)$ would be *true* or *false* for all i. There would be eight statelets at aspect (1), specifying the combined setting of the three left switches, and similarly eight statelets at aspect (2). Also, there would be two statelets at aspects (i, j) for $i = 1, 2$ and $j = 1, 2, 3$, specifying the two possible settings of the corresponding switch.

Definition 4. *The $\perp$ values of a statelet are specified as follows: If a statelet s has aspect α then $(\forall p \in \mathcal{F})(\forall \beta \in \Psi)[(p : \beta) \to (\beta \geq \alpha \equiv (\Phi(p, s) \neq \perp))]$.*

Letting the aspect be part of the statelet eliminates some complexities from the system; one can then speak unambiguously about the parent and children of a statelet.

Statelets in $\mathcal{L}_n^{aspect}$ can be indicated by $[b_1, \ldots, b_n, c_1, \ldots, c_n]_{\hat{S}}$ where the b_i and c_i can be Booleans or $\perp$ and the subscript $\hat{S}$ may be omitted. Technically one should also indicate the aspect as well as the values of the fluents, but in this example the values of the fluents are enough to determine the aspect.

For $\mathcal{L}_3^{aspect}$, if $s : (1)$ (statelet s has aspect (1)) then $lon(i, s) = true$ or *false* and $ron(i, s) = \perp$ for $i = 1, 2, 3$. Thus statelets at aspect (1) are of the form $[b_1, b_2, b_3, \perp, \perp, \perp]$ where the b_i are Booleans. If $s : (2)$ (statelet s has aspect (2)) then $ron(i, s) = true$ or *false* and $lon(i, s) = \perp$ for $i = 1, 2, 3$. Thus statelets at aspect (2) are of the form $[\perp, \perp, \perp, c_1, c_2, c_3]$ where the c_i are Booleans. If $s : (1, i)$ then $lon(j) = \perp$ for $j \neq i$ and $ron(j) = \perp$ for $j = 1, 2, 3$ but $lon(i, s) = true$ or *false*. If $s : (2, i)$ then $ron(j) = \perp$ for $j \neq i$ and $lon(j) = \perp$ for $j = 1, 2, 3$ but $ron(i, s) = true$ or *false*. So a statelet at aspect $(1, 2)$ is of the form $[\perp, b_2, \perp, \perp, \perp, \perp]$ and a statelet at aspect $(2, 3)$ is of the form $[\perp, \perp, \perp, \perp, \perp, c_3]$.

Definition 5. *For states or statelets s and t, one writes $s \equiv_\alpha t$ if for all fluents p with $p : \beta$ and $\beta \geq \alpha$, $\Phi(p, s) = \Phi(p, t)$. Corresponding to this there is the assertion $s \equiv_{[\alpha]} t$ in $\mathcal{T}$ that does not mention aspects. This is defined as $\Phi(p_1, s) = \Phi(p_1, t) \wedge \Phi(p_2, s) = \Phi(p_2, t) \wedge \cdots \wedge \Phi(p_n, s) = \Phi(p_n, t)$ where $\{p_1, p_2, \cdots, p_n\}$ is the set of all fluents having aspects β in M^{aspect} with $\beta \geq \alpha$.*

Thus $s \equiv_\epsilon t$ if s, t agree on all fluents in $\mathcal{F}$. In $\mathcal{L}_3^{aspect}$, $[b_1, b_2, b_3, c_1, c_2, c_3] \equiv_{(1)} [b_1, b_2, b_3, c_1', c_2', c_3']$.

In M^{aspect}, states are related to statelets as follows:

Definition 6. *The bridging axioms are the following: If s is a state then s^ϵ is a statelet and $\Phi(p, s^\epsilon) = \Phi(p, s)$ for all $p \in \mathcal{F}$. Also, if a is an action and s, t are states and $do(a, s) = t$ then $do(a, s^\epsilon) = t^\epsilon$. Furthermore, for all statelets s at aspect α there is a state t such that $s \equiv_\alpha t$.*

In $\mathcal{L}_3^{aspect}$, $[b_1, b_2, b_3, c_1, c_2, c_3]_{\hat{S}}^\epsilon = [b_1, b_2, b_3, c_1, c_2, c_3]_{\hat{S}}$.

There is also a function that restricts statelets at an aspect to statelets at another aspect. The function s^β with semantics $\lambda s \beta. s^\beta : \hat{S} \times \Psi \to \hat{S}$ defined as follows:

Definition 7. *If s is a statelet, $s : \alpha$, and $\beta \geq \alpha$ then s^β is defined as the statelet at aspect β such that $\Phi(p, s^\beta) = \Phi(p, s)$ if $aspect(p) \geq \beta$, else $\Phi(p, s^\beta) = \bot$. Thus $s^\beta : \beta$ and $s^\beta \equiv_\beta s$. If $\beta \leq \alpha$ or $\alpha \# \beta$ then s^β is not defined. If s is a state then $s^\alpha = (s^\epsilon)^\alpha$.*

Thus in $\mathcal{L}_3^{aspect}$, $[b_1, b_2, b_3, c_1, c_2, c_3]^{(1)} = [b_1, b_2, b_3, \bot, \bot, \bot]$ and $[b_1, b_2, b_3, c_1, c_2, c_3]^{(1,2)} = [\bot, b_2, \bot, \bot, \bot, \bot]$. Also $[b_1, b_2, b_3, \bot, \bot, \bot]^{(1,3)} = [\bot, \bot, b_3, \bot, \bot, \bot]$. In general, $\hat{\mathcal{S}}$ is $\{s^\alpha : s \in \mathcal{S}, \alpha \in \Psi\}$.

There is also a function f^α, the composition function, that combines statelets (sub-modules) at aspects $\alpha 1 \cdots \alpha n$ to produce a statelet (module) at aspect α. It has the semantics $\lambda \alpha s_1 s_2 \ldots s_n . f^\alpha(s_1, \ldots, s_n) : \Psi \times \hat{\mathcal{S}}^n \to \hat{\mathcal{S}}$ where n is the number of children of α.

Recall that αi is the sequence α with i added to the end.

Definition 8. *Suppose α is an aspect with n children (which are $\alpha 1, \ldots, \alpha n$). Suppose $s_1 : \alpha 1, \cdots, s_n : \alpha n$ for statelets s_i. Then $f^\alpha(s_1, s_2, \cdots, s_n) = s$ where s is a statelet at aspect α, and where for fluent p, if $p : \beta$ with $\beta \geq \alpha i$ then $\Phi(p, s) = \Phi(p, s_i)$. For fluents p with $p : \alpha$, $\Phi(p, s)$ is defined by the leaf dependency constraint, Definition 9, below. For other fluents p with $p : \beta$ for $\beta \not\geq \alpha$, $\Phi(p, s) = \bot$.*

In $\mathcal{L}_3^{aspect}$, $f^\epsilon([b_1, b_2, b_3, \bot, \bot, \bot], [\bot, \bot, \bot, c_1, c_2, c_3]) = [b_1, b_2, b_3, c_1, c_2, c_3]$. The first argument of f^ϵ is a statelet at aspect (1) and the second argument is a statelet at aspect (2). The value of f^ϵ is a statelet at aspect ϵ. Also, $f^{(1)}([b_1, \bot, \bot, \bot, \bot, \bot], [\bot, b_2, \bot, \bot, \bot, \bot], [\bot, \bot, b_3, \bot, \bot, \bot]) = [b_1, b_2, b_3, \bot, \bot, \bot]$. $f^{(1)}$ can also be written f^1.

From this definition it follows that $s \equiv_{\alpha i} s_i$ for all i and $s^{\alpha i} = s_i$. Definition 8 also implies the following *aspect composition equation* for non-leaf aspects α and statelets s at aspect α:

$$f^\alpha(s^{\alpha 1}, s^{\alpha 2}, \cdots, s^{\alpha n}) = s \tag{2}$$

In addition, there is a dependency constraint on fluents. That is, non-leaf fluents have to depend on fluents at the leaves of the aspect tree.

Definition 9. *The* leaf dependency constraint *on fluents is the following: If p is a fluent at non-leaf aspect α, s and t are statelets at aspect α, and $\Phi(q, s) = \Phi(q, t)$ for all fluents q at leaf aspects γ with $\gamma > \alpha$, then $\Phi(p, s) = \Phi(p, t)$.*

In terms of $\mathcal{T}$, this is expressed as a collection of assertions

$$\{A(p, q_1, \cdots, q_n) : (p : \alpha), \alpha \text{ is a non-leaf aspect, and } \{q_1, \cdots, q_n\} \text{ is the set of } fluents \text{ at leaf aspects } \gamma \text{ with } \gamma > \alpha\}$$

where $A(p, q_1, \cdots, q_n)$ is the following assertion:

$$For \text{ all states } s \text{ and } t,$$
$$\Phi(q_1, s) = \Phi(q_1, t) \wedge \cdots \wedge \Phi(q_n, s) = \Phi(q_n, t) \to \Phi(p, s) = \Phi(p, t)$$

The leaf dependency constraint on fluents is necessary for f^α to be a mathematical function. This is the first constraint that must be satisfied when assigning aspects to actions and fluents. If one wants a statelet s to have properties that do not depend on the children aspects, then one can add a "virtual" child of the aspect of s that includes the extra information about s.

For $\mathcal{L}_3^{aspect}$, the leaf aspects are $(1, i)$ and $(2, i)$ for $i = 1, 2, 3$. The fluents at these aspects are $lon(i)$ and $ron(i)$, respectively. Thus the values of all other fluents have to be determined by these. For statelet s at aspect ϵ or (1), $\Phi(lonall, s)$ is determined by $\Phi(lon(i), s)$ for $i = 1, 2, 3$. Also, for $\mathcal{L}_3^{aspect}$ and statelet s at aspect ϵ or (2), $\Phi(ronall, s)$ is determined by $\Phi(ron(i), s)$ for $i = 1, 2, 3$ so this constraint is satisfied. Similarly, for statelet s at aspect ϵ, $\Phi(onall, s)$ is determined by the values $\Phi(lon(i), s)$ and $\Phi(ron(i), s)$ for $i = 1, 2, 3$.

Definition 10. *The* combining axiom *is the following: For all aspects α with n children and for all states $s_1, \cdots, s_n$ there is a state s such that*

$$s \equiv_{[\alpha 1]} s_1 \wedge \cdots \wedge s \equiv_{[\alpha n]} s_n.$$

The combining axiom is the second constraint that must be satisfied when assigning aspects to fluents and actions. This is satisfied for $\mathcal{L}_3^{aspect}$ because all combinations of all switch settings are permitted. This follows from $(A9)^c$ and the effects of the actions.

5 Actions

For action a at aspect α, $do(a, s)$ is defined for statelets s at aspect β iff $\beta \leq \alpha$. Otherwise, $do(a, s) = \perp$. Thus $do(a, s)$ is not always a statelet or a state, because it can be $\perp$. If $do(a, s) \neq \perp$ then $aspect(do(a, s)) = aspect(s)$.

There are some locality constraints on actions that need to be respected for $\mathcal{T}^{aspect}$ to be unconstraining. Taken collectively, these are the third constraint that must be satisfied by the assignment of aspects to fluents and actions.

Definition 11. *The* locality constraints *on actions are as follows: Suppose $a : \alpha$ and $p : \beta$. If $\alpha \# \beta$ then $\Phi(p, do(a, s)) = \Phi(p, s)$ for all states s. (Formally, this has to be a theorem of $\mathcal{T}$ for all such α and β). Also, if $s \equiv_\alpha t$ for states s and t (expressed in $\mathcal{T}$ by $s \equiv_{[\alpha]} t$) and $\beta \geq \alpha$ then $\Phi(p, do(a, s)) = \Phi(p, do(a, t))$.*

These constraints are satisfied for $\mathcal{L}_3^{aspect}$ because the action $lton(i)$ does not change the values of any fluents except $lon(i)$ at aspect $(1, i)$ and possibly $lonall$ and $onall$, but these are at aspects (1) and ϵ which are smaller than the aspect $(1, i)$ of $lton(i)$. Similar comments apply to $rton(i)$ and the fluents $ron(i)$, $ronall$, and $onall$.

5.1 Frame Axioms

Definition 12. *If for fluent p and action a and for some state s, $\Phi(p, s) \neq \Phi(p, do(a, s))$ then we say that action a influences fluent p. If for all states s and t, $\Phi(p, s) = \Phi(p, do(a, s))$ (if this is a theorem of $\mathcal{T}$) then a does not influence p.*

Frame axioms are encoded in the aspect system by the following *action locality* equation:

$$do(a, f^\alpha(s_1 \cdots s_n)) = f^\alpha(s_1 \cdots do(a, s_i) \cdots s_n) \qquad (3)$$

for all a, α such that $aspect(a) \geq \alpha i$. Also, there is the *fluent locality* equation:

$$\Phi(p, f^\alpha(s_1 \cdots s_n)) = \Phi(p, s_i) \qquad (4)$$

for all p, α such that $aspect(p) \geq \alpha i$.

These equations imply that if one has $p : \alpha$ and $a : \beta$ and α, β are incomparable then a does not influence p. This is how frame axioms are encoded in the aspect system. For $\mathcal{L}_3^{aspect}$, $do(lton(2), f^{(1)}(s_1, s_2, s_3)) = f^{(1)}(s_1, do(lton(2), s_2), s_3)$ because turning on left switch 2 does not influence left switches 1 or 3. Also, $\Phi(lon(2), f^{(1)}(s_1, s_2, s_3)) = \Phi(lon(2), s_2)$ because the fluent $lon(2)$ only depends on the setting of switch 2.

Definition 13. *Given T, an aspect tree Υ, and an assignment Π of aspects to fluents and actions, $\mathcal{M}_{\Upsilon,\Pi}$ (or just $\mathcal{M}$) is the conjunction of Eq. 1 for statelet equality, the bridging axioms, Definition 6, the aspect composition equation, Eq. 2, and the locality axioms, Eqs. 3 and 4.*

Theorem 1. *From $\mathcal{M}$ it follows that if one has $p : \alpha$ and $a : \beta$ and α, β are incomparable then $\Phi(p, do(a, s)) = \Phi(p, s)$ for statelets s such that $s : \gamma$ where γ is the greatest lower bound of α and β, that is, γ is the largest aspect such that $\gamma < \alpha$ and $\gamma < \beta$.*

Proof. Since γ is the greatest lower bound of α and β, $\alpha > \gamma i$ for some i and $\beta > \gamma j$ for some $j \neq i$. Suppose γ has n children. Then $s = f^\gamma(s^{\gamma 1} \cdots s^{\gamma n})$ by Eq. 2. Thus $\Phi(p, do(a, s)) = \Phi(p, s)$ is equivalent to $\Phi(p, do(a, f^\gamma(s^{\gamma 1} \cdots s^{\gamma n}))) = \Phi(p, f^\gamma(s^{\gamma 1} \cdots s^{\gamma n}))$. However, by Eq. 4, $\Phi(p, f^\gamma(s^{\gamma 1} \cdots s^{\gamma n})) = \Phi(p, s^{\gamma i})$. Also, by Eq. 3, $do(a, f^\gamma(s^{\gamma 1} \cdots s^{\gamma n})) = f^\gamma(s^{\gamma 1}, \cdots, do(a, f^{\gamma j}), \cdots, s^{\gamma n})$. Thus $\Phi(p, do(a, f^\gamma(s^{\gamma 1} \cdots s^{\gamma n}))) = \Phi(p, f^\gamma(s^{\gamma 1}, \cdots, do(a, f^{\gamma j}), \cdots, s^{\gamma n})) = \Phi(p, s^{\gamma i})$, again by Eq. 4, so the equation $\Phi(p, do(a, s)) = \Phi(p, s)$ holds with both sides equal to $\Phi(p, s^{\gamma i})$. $\square$

Lemma 1. *Suppose ξ is an aspect and for some i, $aspect(p) \geq \xi i$ and $aspect(a) \geq \xi i$. Suppose $s : \xi$ and let s be $f^\xi(s_1 \cdots s_n)$. Then from $\mathcal{M}$ it follows that $\Phi(p, do(a, s)) = \Phi(p, s)$ implies $\Phi(p, do(a, s_i)) = \Phi(p, s_i)$, and the reverse implication also holds.*

Proof. Suppose $\Phi(p, do(a, s)) = \Phi(p, s)$. Then by Eq. 3, $do(a, s) = f^\alpha(s_1 \cdots, do(a, s_i) \cdots s_n)$, so by Eq. 4, $\Phi(p, do(a, s)) = \Phi(p, do(a, s_i))$, and by Eq. 4 again, $\Phi(p, s) = \Phi(p, s_i)$. Therefore $\Phi(p, do(a, s_i)) = \Phi(p, do(a, s)) = \Phi(p, s) = \Phi(p, s_i)$ so $\Phi(p, do(a, s_i)) = \Phi(p, s_i)$. The reverse implication is shown in a similar way. $\square$

Theorem 2. *From $\mathcal{M}$ it follows that if one has $p : \alpha$ and $a : \beta$ and α, β are incomparable then $\Phi(p, do(a, s)) = \Phi(p, s)$ for statelets s with $s : \xi$ where $\xi \leq \alpha$ and $\xi \leq \beta$. Also, it follows that $\Phi(p, do(a, s)) = \Phi(p, s)$ for all states s.*

Proof. The first part follows by repeated application of Lemma 1. For the rest, letting ξ be ϵ, $\Phi(p, do(a, s)) = \Phi(p, s)$ for statelets s with $s : \epsilon$ and therefore by the bridging axioms, $\Phi(p, do(a, s)) = \Phi(p, s)$ for all states s. $\qquad\square$

This result shows that in $\mathcal{T}^{aspect}$ one can omit any frame axioms involving fluents and actions at incomparable aspects.

6   Encoding a Domain in the Aspect Formalism

A domain in the aspect calculus can be obtained in two ways: 1. By systematic translation from an existing domain. 2. By custom design. We first discuss the first possibility.

Definition 14. *Suppose one has an underlying state theory $\mathcal{T}$ with states, actions, and fluents and some axioms relating them. We want to encode $\mathcal{T}$ in the aspect formalism to obtain $\mathcal{T}^{aspect}$ that encodes as many of the frame axioms of $\mathcal{T}$ as possible in a more efficient manner, but does not imply frame axioms that are not theorems of $\mathcal{T}$. Suppose that an aspect tree Υ has been defined and aspects have been assigned for fluents and actions. Let $\mathcal{T}'$ be some theory such that $\mathcal{T}' \cup \mathcal{M}_{\Upsilon,\Pi}$ is equivalent to $\mathcal{T} \cup \mathcal{M}_{\Upsilon,\Pi}$. Typically $\mathcal{T}'$ can be $\mathcal{T}$ with frame axioms implied by $\mathcal{M}_{\Upsilon,\Pi}$ deleted. Then $\mathcal{T}^{aspect}_{\Upsilon,\Pi}$ is $\mathcal{T}' \cup \mathcal{M}_{\Upsilon,\Pi}$ for some such $\mathcal{T}'$.*

Thus there is some flexibility in defining $\mathcal{T}^{aspect}_{\Upsilon,\Pi}$. For concreteness, here is a more specific definition:

Definition 15. *Suppose one has an underlying theory $\mathcal{T}$ that can be expressed as $d_1 \wedge d_2 \wedge \cdots \wedge d_n$. Let $\mathcal{T}'$ be $e_1 \wedge e_2 \wedge \cdots \wedge e_m$ where $\{e_1, e_2, \cdots, e_m\} = \{d_i : 1 \leq i \leq n, \mathcal{M} \not\models d_i\}$. Then $\mathcal{T}^{aspect}_{\Upsilon,\Pi}$ is $\mathcal{T}' \cup \mathcal{M}$.*

Here is an example of such an underlying theory, in this case in first-order logic:

7   Switches Example

Let $\mathcal{T}$, that is, $\mathcal{L}_n$, be the theory from Example 1. We construct the theory $\mathcal{L}_n^{aspect}$ in the aspect representation.

7.1   Aspect Representation

The aspect tree Υ has a root node with two children, child 1 for the left bank and child 2 for the right bank. Each child has in turn n children numbered 1 through n, one for each switch. So the aspects are $\epsilon, (1), (2), (1, 1), (1, 2), \cdots, (1, n)$, $(2, 1), (2, 2), \cdots, (2, n)$. The actions $lton(i)$ and $ltof(i)$ have aspects $(1, i)$, and $rton(i)$ and $rtof(i)$ have aspects $(2, i)$. Also, $lon(i)$ has aspect $(1, i)$ and $ron(i)$ has aspect $(2, i)$. The fluent $lonall$ has aspect 1, $ronall$ has aspect 2, and $onall$ has aspect ϵ.

This is $\mathcal{T}'$, that is, $\mathcal{L}_n^{aspect}$; frame axioms are not needed and are omitted. Also, free occurrences of s refer to universally quantified states as before.

$$lon(i, do(lton(i), s)) \wedge ron(i, do(rton(i), s)), 1 \le i \le n(A1)^c$$
$$\neg lon(i, do(ltof(i), s)) \wedge \neg ron(i, do(rtof(i), s)), 1 \le i \le n(A2)^c$$
$$lonall(s) \equiv lon(1, s) \wedge \cdots \wedge lon(n, s)(A3)_l^c$$
$$ronall(s) \equiv ron(1, s) \wedge \cdots \wedge ron(n, s)(A3)_r^c$$
$$(onall(s) \equiv lonall(s) \wedge ronall(s))(A4)^c$$
$$(\exists s)(s \in S)(A9)^c$$

Here is $\mathcal{M}_\mathcal{T}$, consisting of the necessary portion (fluents at leaf aspects) of the bridging axioms, Definition 6, the locality axioms, Eqs. 3 and 4, and the aspect composition equation, Eq. 2.

$$(lon(i, s) = lon(i, s^\epsilon)) \wedge (ron(i, s) = ron(i, s^\epsilon)), 1 \le i \le n$$
$$do(lton(i), s)^\epsilon = do(lton(i), s^\epsilon), 1 \le i \le n$$
$$do(rton(i), s)^\epsilon = do(rton(i), s^\epsilon), 1 \le i \le n$$
$$do(ltof(i), s)^\epsilon = do(ltof(i), s^\epsilon), 1 \le i \le n$$
$$do(rtof(i), s)^\epsilon = do(rtof(i), s^\epsilon), 1 \le i \le n$$
$$\forall t \in \hat{\mathcal{S}}(t : \alpha \to \exists s \in \mathcal{S}(s^\alpha = t))$$

In the following lines, the t_i refer to statelets.

$$do(lton(i), f^\epsilon(t_1, t_2)) = f^\epsilon(do(lton(i), t_1), t_2)$$
$$do(rton(i), f^\epsilon(t_1, t_2)) = f^\epsilon(t_1, do(rton(i), t_2))$$
$$do(ltof(i), f^\epsilon(t_1, t_2)) = f^\epsilon(do(ltof(i), t_1), t_2)$$
$$do(rtof(i), f^\epsilon(t_1, t_2)) = f^\epsilon(t_1, do(rtof(i), t_2))$$
$$do(lton(i), f^1(t_1, \ldots, t_n)) = f^1(t_1, \ldots, do(lton(i), t_i), \ldots, t_n)$$
$$do(rton(i), f^2(t_1, \ldots, t_n)) = f^2(t_1, \ldots, do(rton(i), t_i), \ldots, t_n)$$
$$do(ltof(i), f^1(t_1, \ldots, t_n)) = f^1(t_1, \ldots, do(ltof(i), t_i), \ldots, t_n)$$
$$do(rtof(i), f^2(t_1, \ldots, t_n)) = f^2(t_1, \ldots, do(rtof(i), t_i), \ldots, t_n)$$

$$lon(i, f^\epsilon(t_1, t_2)) = lon(i, t_1)$$
$$ron(i, f^\epsilon(t_1, t_2)) = ron(i, t_2)$$
$$lonall(f^\epsilon(t_1, t_2)) = lonall(t_1)$$
$$ronall(f^\epsilon(t_1, t_2)) = ronall(t_2)$$
$$lon(i, f^1(t_1, \ldots, t_n)) = lon(i, t_i), 1 \le i \le n$$
$$ron(i, f^2(t_1, \ldots, t_n)) = ron(i, t_i), 1 \le i \le n$$

In the following lines, t refers to a statelet and superscripts refer to the composition function of Definition 8.

$$t : \epsilon \rightarrow f^\epsilon(t^1, t^2) = t$$
$$t : 1 \rightarrow f^1(t^{1,1}, \ldots, t^{1,n}) = t$$
$$t : 2 \rightarrow f^2(t^{2,1}, \ldots, t^{2,n}) = t$$

Equation 1 for statelet equality also is included in $\mathcal{M}$. The *onall*, *lonall*, and *ronall* predicates are allowed in the aspect representation because they are determined by fluents at their descendant leaves in the aspect tree according to the leaf dependency constraint of Definition 9.

A close examination shows that most of $\mathcal{L}_n^{aspect}$ is of complexity (size) linear in n. However, the number of axioms involving f^α for various aspects α is bounded by the depth of the aspect tree times the number of fluents and actions. Assuming the depth of the aspect tree is small compared to n, the complexity of $\mathcal{L}_n^{aspect}$ will be small relative to the classical version. Many of the lines in $\mathcal{L}_n^{aspect}$ mention the n variables t_i and this gives another quadratic factor, but the constant factor is at least smaller than the quadratic factor for the classical theory. However, even this factor can be reduced; the idea is to make the aspect tree a binary tree. This increases the number of equations while keeping the total number linear, but each equation will have a constant size. Also, the depth of the aspect tree will be at most logarithmic in n assuming the aspect tree is an approximately balanced binary tree. Many of the axioms are equations, which tend to be easy for first-order provers to handle, so the new equations should not make planning harder than for the classical representation.

7.2 Transmitting Switch Settings

Without going into detail, the switches example can be modified by also having an action $ltr(i)$ that transmits the state of left switch i to left switch $i + 1$, $1 \le i < n$ and similarly rtr for right switches. Then $ltr(i)$ could have aspect 1 but not $(1, i)$ or $(1, i+1)$ and $rtr(i)$ could have aspect 2 but not $(2, i)$ or $(2, i+1)$, even though the switches they modify have aspects that are children of 1 and 2, respectively. The axiom for $ltr(2)$ in $\mathcal{T}$, for example, could be

$$lon(3, do(ltr(2), s)) \equiv lon(2, s).$$

This example shows how sub-modules (incomparable aspects) are not completely independent but can influence one another. Now, the aspect representation would automatically give frame axioms implying that ltr does not modify right switches and rtr does not modify left switches. However, it would not, for example, give the frame axiom that $ltr(2)$ does not modify left switch 1, because the aspects of left switch 1 and the action are not incomparable. Such frame axioms would be included in $\mathcal{T}'$. On this example, a custom translation can give a more succinct representation of these frame axioms. In particular, one can axiomatize ltr and rtr in $\mathcal{T}$ as follows, where $1 \le i < n$, the statelets s_j with $s_j : (1, j)$ are universally quantified in the first two equations, and $s_j : (2, j)$ in the second two equations. Also, $ltr'(i, s_i)$ returns a statelet at aspect $(1, i + 1)$ and $rtr'(i, s_i)$ returns a statelet at aspect $(2, i + 1)$.

$$lon(i + 1, ltr'(i, s_i)) = lon(i, s_i)$$
$$do(ltr(i), f^1(s_1, \cdots, s_n)) = f^1(s_1, \cdots, s_i, ltr'(i, s_i), s_{i+2}, \cdots, s_n)$$
$$ron(i + 1, rtr'(i, s_i)) = ron(i, s_i)$$
$$do(rtr(i), f^2(s_1, \cdots, s_n)) = f^2(s_1, \cdots, s_i, rtr'(i, s_i), s_{i+2}, \cdots, s_n)$$

The binary tree idea can further reduce the complexity, as before.

This example and many similar examples involving transmitting information between disjoint aspects can be handled in a more systematic way by allowing some actions to have a set of aspects instead of just a single aspect. The $ltr(i)$ action would have aspects $(1, i)$ and $(1, i+1)$. Without a fully rigorous treatment, the idea is to modify Eq. 3 as follows for actions a with more than one aspect and more than one i such that αi is a prefix of at least one of the aspects of action a:

$$do(a, f^\alpha(s_1, \ldots, s_n)) = f^\alpha(s'_1, \ldots, s'_n)$$

where $s'_i = s_i$ if the aspect αi is disjoint from all the aspects of action a. Otherwise, s'_i is a statelet defined by axioms such as the first and third equations above. However, if there is only one i such that αi is a prefix of at least one of the aspects of a, then the original form of Eq. 3 can be used. Thus for example $do(ltr(i), f^\epsilon(s_1, s_2)) = f^\epsilon(do(ltr(i), s_1), s_2)$.

8   The Unconstraining Property

Definition 16. *An assignment of aspects to actions and fluents in a state theory T that satisfies the action dependency condition, Definition 1, is* unconstraining *if it satisfies the locality constraints on actions of Definition 11, the leaf dependency constraint on fluents of Definition 9, and the combining axiom of Definition 10; that is, these must be theorems of T.*

Theorem 3. *For any state theory T satisfying the action dependency condition and any aspect tree Υ, it is possible to find an assignment of aspects to fluents and actions that is unconstraining.*

Proof. The leaf dependency constraint on fluents can be satisfied by putting all fluents at the same leaf of Υ if necessary and the locality constraints on actions can be satisfied by assigning all actions the aspect of ϵ at the root of the tree. However, such an assignment of aspects would not encode any frame axioms, so it would not serve any purpose.   □

8.1   Relative Consistency

We now show that if $\mathcal{M}_{\Upsilon.\,\Pi}$ is unconstraining and $\mathcal{T}$ satisfies the action dependency condition then $\mathcal{T}^{aspect}$ is relatively consistent with $\mathcal{T}$. This implies that $\mathcal{T}^{aspect}$ does not imply any new theorems on the assertions over the symbols in $\mathcal{T}$.

Theorem 4. *Suppose $\mathcal{T}$ is a theory of states, actions, and fluents that satisfies the action dependency condition, Definition 1. Suppose that an aspect tree Υ is chosen and aspects are assigned to fluents and actions of $\mathcal{T}$ in an unconstraining manner (Definition 16). Then $\mathcal{T}^{aspect}$ is relatively consistent with $\mathcal{T}$.*

Proof. We show that any model M of $\mathcal{T}$ can be extended to a model M^{aspect} of $\mathcal{T}^{aspect}$. M^{aspect} interprets the symbols of $\mathcal{T}$ on the domains of $\mathcal{T}$ the same way that M does. M^{aspect} has additional domains, the set of statelets and the set of aspects, and an additional element $\perp$ that can be the value of fluents and of $do(a,s)$ in M^{aspect}. Also, M^{aspect} has the functions f^α for aspects α in Υ mapping from tuples of statelets to statelets, and the function mapping states and statelets s to statelet s^α, for aspects α.

For every state s of M, there is a statelet s^ϵ of M^{aspect} such that for all fluents $p \in \mathcal{F}$, $\Phi(p, s^\epsilon) = \Phi(p, s)$. Two statelets that have the same aspect and the same value on all fluents in $\mathcal{F}$ are equal in M^{aspect}; other statelets are not equal in M^{aspect}.

The functions s^α from states or statelets s to statelets are defined as in Definition 7. The functions f^α are defined by $f^\alpha(s^{\alpha 1} \cdots s^{\alpha n}) = s^\alpha$ where the aspect α has n children. In M^{aspect}, the set $\hat{\mathcal{S}}$ of statelets is $\{s^\alpha : s \in \mathcal{S}, \alpha \in \Psi\}$.

Fluents of M are extended from states of M to statelets in M^{aspect}. The value $\perp$ is allowed as a value of $\Phi(p, s)$ for fluents p and statelets s, where $\perp$ is not equal to any state or statelet and $\Phi(p, s) \neq \perp$ for fluents p and states s. A fluent p of M that is assigned an aspect of α in M^{aspect} is defined on all statelets s^β for $\beta \leq \alpha$ and $\Phi(p, s^\beta) = \Phi(p, s^\epsilon)$ for all such β. If a statelet s has aspect γ and $\gamma \not\leq \alpha$ then $\Phi(p, s^\gamma) = \perp$.

Actions a of M are extended from states to statelets in M^{aspect}. Actions a of M with aspect α satisfy $do(a, s^\beta) = \perp$ for statelets s^β with $\beta \not\leq \alpha$. Actions a of M with aspect α are defined on all statelets s^β for $\beta \leq \alpha$. The value of $do(a, s^\beta)$ in this case is a statelet t with $t : \beta$ such that $t \equiv_\alpha do(a, s^\epsilon)$. This completely defines t because fluents q with aspects γ with $\alpha \# \gamma$ satisfy $\Phi(q, t) = \perp$ in M^{aspect}, and fluents with aspects γ with $\gamma \leq \alpha$ are specified by the leaf dependency constraint on fluents. This completely defines M^{aspect}.

It remains to show that M^{aspect} is a model of $\mathcal{T}^{aspect}$. Now, M^{aspect} is a model of $\mathcal{T}$ because it agrees with M there. So it remains to show that M^{aspect} is a model of $\mathcal{M}_\Upsilon$. Recall from Definition 13 that $\mathcal{M}_\Upsilon$ is the conjunction of Eq. 1 for statelet equality, the bridging axioms, Definition 6, the aspect composition equation, Eq. 2, and the action and fluent locality axioms, Eqs. 3 and 4.

The issue is that one can have $s^\alpha = t^\alpha$ even for unequal states s and t, so one has to show that all the functions and properties depend only on the fluents of s^α and not directly on s.

The proof is routine, so the details are omitted.   □

9   Solving Planning Problems Bottom up

For a binary relation R, $R(x, y)$ indicates that $(x, y) \in R$. If A is a logical assertion then $\{x : A\}$ is the set of x having property A. If α is an aspect then $x : \alpha$ indicates that x has aspect α. Let M be a model of $\mathcal{T}^{aspect}$ and let the relations R^α, R_1^α, and R_2^α be defined as follows, where a superscript of $*$ indicates transitive closure and I^α is the identity relation on statelets at aspect α:

$$R^\alpha = (R_1^\alpha \cup R_2^\alpha)^* \cup I^\alpha \tag{5}$$

$$R_1^\alpha = \{(f^\alpha(s_1 \cdots s_n), f^\alpha(t_1 \cdots t_n)) : R^{\alpha i}(s_i, t_i), 1 \le i \le n\} \tag{6}$$

$$R_2^\alpha = \{(s, t) : M \models do(a, s) = t, a \in \mathcal{A}, s : \alpha, aspect(a) \ge \alpha\} \tag{7}$$

R^α gives the set of pairs (s, t) of statelets at aspect α such that t is reachable in M from s by a finite sequence of actions at aspect α or larger aspects. Computing R^α can be helpful for solving planning problems by exhaustive search, and it avoids repetitive search due to actions on independent (incomparable) aspects commuting. Of course, if the number of states is finite, R^α will always be finite. This differs from Reiter's formalism [Rei91], in which the number of situations can be infinite even if the number of states is finite because situations are defined by sequences of states.

Theorem 5. *With R^α defined as in Eqs. 5, 6, and 7, $R^\alpha(s, t)$ for statelets s and t with $s : \alpha$ and $t : \alpha$ iff there is a sequence $s_1 : \alpha, s_2 : \alpha, \ldots, s_n : \alpha$ of statelets where $s = s_1$, $t = s_n$, and for all i, $1 \le i < n$, there is an action a_i with $a_i : \beta_i$ such that $\beta_i \ge \alpha$ and $M \models s_{i+1} = do(a_i, s_i)$.*

The proof is omitted for lack of space. Of course, this implies that $R^\epsilon(s^\epsilon, t^\epsilon)$ for states s and t iff t can be obtained in M from s by a finite sequence of actions.

10   Conclusion

The aspect calculus expresses frame axioms involving incomparable aspects of a state efficiently for modular theories. Aspects are sequences of integers that correspond to substates of a state; for example, in the sequence (i, j, k), i may indicate the earth, j a country, and k a state in a country. These sequences are ordered so that sequences are larger than (greater than) their proper prefixes. Fluents are assigned aspects based on which portion of the state they describe, so a fluent may have an aspect corresponding to North Carolina if it describes something about North Carolina. Then actions can be assigned aspects that are the greatest lower bound (longest common prefix) of the aspects of all fluents that they influence or depend on. This implies for example that actions in North Carolina do not influence fluents from outside North Carolina, thereby encoding many frame axioms.

This formalism is entirely in first-order logic, and powerful first-order theorem provers can be applied to it if the underlying theory T is first-order. When converted to clause form, the resulting clauses appear to be easier for first-order theorem provers to handle than clauses from Reiter's formalism. Also, for some theories, clauses from Reiter's formalism can become very long. Two examples are given and relative consistency is shown assuming that the unconstraining property holds. This formalism also permits an exhaustive method of solving planning problems that has some advantages for modular domains. The ramification problem does not require any special methods in the aspect calculus. However, this formalism does not handle knowledge and belief, but is only concerned with logical correctness. It is also only suitable for modular theories.

References

[Dav90] Davis, E.: Representations of Commonsense Knowledge. Morgan Kaufmann, Burlington (1990)

[DT07] Denecker, M., Ternovska, E.: Inductive situation calculus. Artif. Intell. **171**(5–6), 332–360 (2007)

[Haa87] Haas, A.R.: The case for domain-specic frame axioms. In: Brown, F.M. (ed.) The Frame Problem in Artificial Intelligence, Proceedings of the 1987 Workshop, pp. 343–348. Morgan Kaufmann (1987)

[Hay73] Hayes, P.: The frame problem and related problems in artificial intelligence. In: Elithorn, A., Jones, D. (eds.) Artificial and Human Thinking, pp. 45–59. Jossey-Bass Inc., Elsevier Scientific Publishing Company, San Francisco, Amsterdam (1973)

[Lin08] Lin, F.: Situation calculus. In: van Harmelen, F., Lifschitz, V., Porter, B. (eds.) Handbook of Knowledge Representation, pp. 649–669. Elsevier, Amsterdam (2008)

[LR94] Lin, F., Reiter, R.: State constraints revisited. J. Logic Comput. **4**(5), 655–678 (1994)

[McI00] McIlraith, S.A.: Integrating actions and state constraints: a closed-form solution to the ramification problem (sometimes). Artif. Intell. **116**(1), 87–121 (2000)

[MH69] McCarthy, J., Hayes, P.: Some philosophical problems from the standpoint of artificial intelligence. In: Meltzer, B., Michie, D. (eds.) Machine Intelligence 4, pp. 463–502. Edinburgh University Press, Edinburgh (1969)

[MM97] Matos, P.A., Martins, J.P.: Contextual logic of change and the ramification problem. In: Coasta, E., Cardoso, A. (eds.) EPIA 1997. LNCS, vol. 1323, pp. 267–278. Springer, Heidelberg (1997). https://doi.org/10.1007/BFb0023928

[Ped89] Pednault, E.P.D.: ADL: exploring the middle ground between STRIPS and the situation calculus. In: Proceedings of the International Conference on Principles of Knowledge Representation (KR-1998), pp. 324–332. Morgan Kaufmann Inc. (1989)

[Pet08] Petrick, R.P.A.: Cartesian situations and knowledge decomposition in the situation calculus. In: Principles of Knowledge Representation and Reasoning: Proceedings of the Eleventh International Conference, KR 2008, Sydney, Australia, 16–19 September 2008, pp. 629–639 (2008)

[Rei91] Reiter, R.: The frame problem in the situation calculus: a simple solution (sometimes) and a completeness result for goal regression. In: Lifschitz, V. (ed.) Artificial Intelligence and Mathematical Theory of Computation: Papers in Honor of John McCarthy, pp. 359–380. Academic Press, Cambridge (1991)

[Sch90] Schubert, L.: Monotonic solution of the frame problem in the situation calculus: an efficient method for worlds with fully specified actions. In: Kyburg, H.E., Loui, R.P., Carlson, G.N. (eds.) Knowledge Representation and Defeasible Reasoning, vol. 5, pp. 23–67. Kluwer Academic Publishers, Dordrecht (1990)

[Sha99] Shanahan, M.: The ramification problem in the event calculus. In: Proceedings of the 16th International Joint Conference on Artifical Intelligence - Volume 1, IJCAI 1999, pp. 140–146. Morgan Kaufmann Publishers Inc., San Francisco (1999)

[SL93] Scherl, R.B., Levesque, H.J.: The frame problem and knowledge-producing actions. In: Proceedings of the Eleventh National Conference on Artificial Intelligence (AAAI-1993), Washington, D.C., USA, pp. 689–697. AAAI Press/MIT Press (1993)

[Ter00] Ternovska, E.: Id-logic and the ramification problem for the situation calculus. In: ECAI (2000)

[Thi98] Thielscher, M.: Introduction to the fluent calculus. Electron. Trans. Artif. Intell. **2**, 179–192 (1998)

Uniform Substitution at One Fell Swoop

André Platzer[1,2]($\boxtimes$) (iD)

[1] Computer Science Department, Carnegie Mellon University, Pittsburgh, USA
aplatzer@cs.cmu.edu
[2] Fakultät für Informatik, Technische Universität München, Munich, Germany

Abstract. Uniform substitution of function, predicate, program or game symbols is the core operation in parsimonious provers for hybrid systems and hybrid games. By postponing soundness-critical admissibility checks, this paper introduces a uniform substitution mechanism that proceeds in a linear pass homomorphically along the formula. Soundness is recovered using a simple variable condition at the replacements performed by the substitution. The setting in this paper is that of differential hybrid games, in which discrete, continuous, and adversarial dynamics interact in differential game logic dGL. This paper proves soundness and completeness of one-pass uniform substitutions for dGL.

1 Introduction

After a number of false starts on substitution [11,12,22], even by prominent logicians, did Church's *uniform substitution* [5] [§35,40] provide a mechanism for substituting function and predicate symbols with terms and formulas in first-order logic. Given a mechanism for applying a uniform substitution σ to formulas ϕ with result denoted $\sigma\phi$ uniform substitutions are used with Church's proof rule:

$$\text{(US)} \quad \frac{\phi}{\sigma\phi}$$

Contrary to casual belief, quite some care is needed in the substitution process, even of only function symbols [23], in order to prevent replacing functions with terms that denote incompatible values in different places depending on which variables are being used in the replacements and in which formula contexts. Due to their subtleties, there have even been passionate calls for banishing substitutions [10] and using more schemata. This paper moves in the opposite direction, making substitutions even more subtle, but also faster and, nevertheless, sound.

In Shakespeare's Macbeth, "at one fell swoop" was likened to the suddenness with which a bird of prey fiercely attacks a whole nest at once. The idiom has since retained only its meaning of suddenly doing all at once, although the connotation of fierceness is also befitting of the ignorance with which one-pass uniform substitution trespasses operator scopes. This research is supported by the Alexander von Humboldt Foundation and by the AFOSR under grant number FA9550-16-1-0288.

P. Fontaine (Ed.): CADE 2019, LNAI 11716, pp. 425–441, 2019.
https://doi.org/10.1007/978-3-030-29436-6_25

The biggest theoretical advantage of uniform substitutions is that they make instantiation explicit, so that proof calculi can use axioms (concrete object-level formulas) instead of axiom schemata (meta-level concepts standing for infinitely many formulas). Their biggest practical advantage is that this avoidance of schemata enables parsimonious theorem prover implementations that only consist of copies of concrete formulas as axioms together with *one* algorithm implementing the application of uniform substitutions (plus renaming). Similar advantages exist for concrete axiomatic proof rules instead of rule schemata [16]. This design obviates the need for algorithms that recognize all of the infinitely many instances of schemata and check all of their (sometimes pretty subtle) side conditions to soundly reject improper reasoning. These practical advantages have first been demonstrated for hybrid systems [8] and for hybrid games [18] proving, where uniform substitution led to significant reductions in soundness-critical size (down from 66000 to 1700 lines of code) or implementation time (down from months to minutes) compared to conventional prover implementations.

These uses of the uniform substitution principle required generalizations from first-order logic [5] to differential dynamic logic dL for hybrid systems [16] and differential game logic dGL for hybrid games [18], including substitutions of programs or games, respectively. The presence of variables whose values change imperatively over time, and of differential equations $x' = \theta$ that cause intrinsic links of variables x and their time-derivatives x', significantly complicate affairs compared to the simplicity of first-order logic [5,23] and λ-calculus [4]. Pure λ-calculus has a single binder and rests on the three pillars of α-conversions (for bound variables), β-reductions (by capture-avoiding substitutions), and η-conversions (versus free variables), which provide an elegant, deep, but solid foundation for functional programs (with similar observations for first-order logic). Despite significant additional challenges,[1] just two elementary operations, nevertheless, suffice as a foundation for imperative programs and even hybrid games: bound renaming and uniform substitution (based on suitably generalized notions of free and bound variables). Uniform substitutions generalize elegantly and in highly modular ways [16,18]. Much of the conceptual simplicity in the correctness arguments in these cases, however, came from the fact that Church-style uniform substitutions are applied by checking *at each operator* admissibility, i.e., that no free variable be introduced into a context in which it is bound. Such checks simplify correctness proofs, because they check each admissibility condition at every operator where they are necessary for soundness. The resulting substitution mechanism is elegant but computationally suboptimal, because it repeatedly checks admissibility recursively again and again at every operator. For example, applying a uniform substitution σ checks at every sequential composition $\alpha; \beta$ again that the entire substitution σ is admissible for the remainder β compared to the bound variables of the result of having applied σ to α:

---

[1] The area of effect that an assignment to a variable has is non-computable and even a single occurrence of a variable may have to be both free and bound to ensure correctness. Such overlap is an inherent consequence of change, which is an intrinsic feature of dynamical systems theory (the mathematics of change) and game theory (the mathematics of effects resulting from strategic interaction by player decisions).

$$\sigma(\alpha;\beta) = (\sigma(\alpha);\sigma(\beta)) \quad \text{if } \sigma \text{ is } \mathsf{BV}(\sigma(\alpha))\text{-admissible for } \beta \qquad (1)$$

where σ is U-admissible for β iff the free variables of the replacements for the part of σ having function/predicate symbols that occur in β do not intersect U, which, here, are the bound variables $\mathsf{BV}(\sigma(\alpha))$ computed from the result of applying the substitution σ to α [18]. This mechanism is sound [16,18], even verified sound for hybrid systems in Isabelle/HOL and Coq [2], but computationally redundant due to its repeated substitution application and admissibility computations.

The point of this paper is to introduce a more liberal form of uniform substitution that *substitutes at one fell swoop*, forgoing admissibility checks during the operators where they would be needed with a monadic computation of taboo sets to make up for that negligence by checking cumulative admissibility conditions locally only *once* at each replacement that the uniform substitution application performs. This *one-pass uniform substitution* is computationally attractive, because it operates linearly in the output, which matters because uniform substitution is the dominant logical inference in uniform substitution provers [8]. The biggest challenge is, precisely, that correctness of substitution can no longer be justified for all operators where it is needed (because admissibility is no longer recursively checked at every operator). The most important technical insight of this paper is that modularity of correctness arguments can be recovered, regardless, using a neighborhood semantics for taboos. Another value of this paper is its straightforward completeness proof based on [15,16]. Overall, the findings of this paper make it possible to verify hybrid games (and systems) with faster small soundness-critical prover cores than before [18,21], which, owing to their challenges, are the only two verification tools for hybrid games. Uniform substitutions extend to differential games [6,7], where soundness is challenging [13], leading to the first basis for a small prover core for differential hybrid games [17]. The accelerated proving primitives are of interest for other dynamic logics [1,9]. All proofs are in [20] and those till Theorem 19 were then formalized [19].

2 Preliminaries: Differential Game Logic

This section recalls the basics of differential game logic [15,18], the logic for specifying and verifying hybrid games of two players with differential equations.

2.1 Syntax

The set of all variables is $\mathbf{V}$, including for each variable x a differential variable x' (e.g., for an ODE for x). Higher-order differential variables x'' etc. are not used in this paper, so a finite set $\mathbf{V}$ suffices. The terms θ of (differential-form) dGL are polynomial terms with real-valued function symbols and *differential terms* $(\theta)'$ that are used to reduce reasoning about differential equations to reasoning about equations of differentials [16]. Hybrid games α describe the permitted discrete and continuous actions by player Angel and player Demon. Besides the operators of first-order logic of real arithmetic, dGL formulas ϕ can be built using $\langle\alpha\rangle\phi$, which expresses that Angel has a winning strategy in the hybrid game α to reach the region satisfying dGL formula ϕ. Likewise, $[\alpha]\phi$ expresses that Demon has a winning strategy in the hybrid game α to reach the region satisfying ϕ.

Definition 1 (Terms). Terms *are defined by the following grammar (with θ, η, $\theta_1, \ldots, \theta_k$ as terms, $x \in \mathbf{V}$ as variable, and f as function symbol of arity k):*

$$\theta, \eta ::= x \mid f(\theta_1, \ldots, \theta_k) \mid \theta + \eta \mid \theta \cdot \eta \mid (\theta)'$$

Definition 2 (dGL formulas). *The* formulas of differential game logic dGL *are defined by the following grammar (with ϕ, ψ as dGL formulas, p as predicate symbol of arity k, θ, η, θ_i as terms, x as variable, and α as hybrid game):*

$$\phi, \psi ::= \theta \geq \eta \mid p(\theta_1, \ldots, \theta_k) \mid \neg\phi \mid \phi \wedge \psi \mid \exists x\, \phi \mid \langle \alpha \rangle \phi$$

The usual operators can be derived, e.g., $\forall x\, \phi$ is $\neg \exists x\, \neg\phi$ and similarly for $\rightarrow, \leftrightarrow$ and truth $\top$. Existence of Demon's winning strategy in hybrid game α to achieve ϕ is expressed by the dGL formula $[\alpha]\phi$, which can be expressed indirectly as $\neg\langle\alpha\rangle\neg\phi$, thanks to the hybrid game determinacy theorem [15, Thm. 3.1].

Definition 3 (Hybrid games). *The* hybrid games of differential game logic dGL *are defined by the following grammar (with α, β as hybrid games, a as game symbol, x as variable, θ as term, and ψ as dGL formula):*

$$\alpha, \beta ::= a \mid x := \theta \mid x' = \theta \,\&\, \psi \mid ?\psi \mid \alpha \cup \beta \mid \alpha; \beta \mid \alpha^* \mid \alpha^d$$

The operator precedences make all unary operators, including modalities and quantifiers, bind stronger. Just like the meaning of function and predicate symbols is subject to interpretation, the effect of game symbol a is up to interpretation. In contrast, the assignment game $x := \theta$ has the specific effect of changing the value of variable x to that of term θ. The differential equation game $x' = \theta \,\&\, \psi$ allows Angel to choose how long she wants to follow the (vectorial) differential equation $x' = \theta$ for any real duration within the set of states where evolution domain constraint ψ is true. Differential equation games with trivial $\psi = \top$ are just written $x' = \theta$. The test game $?\psi$ challenges Angel to satisfy formula ψ, for if ψ is not true in the present state she loses the game prematurely. The choice game $\alpha \cup \beta$ allows Angel to choose if she wants to play game α or game β. The sequential game $\alpha; \beta$ will play game β after game α terminates (unless a player prematurely lost the game while playing α). The repetition game α^* allows Angel to decide, after having played any number of α repetitions, whether she wants to play another round (but she cannot play forever). Finally, the dual game α^d will have both players switch sides: every choice that Angel had in α will go to Demon in α^d, and vice versa, while every condition that Angel needs to meet in α will be Demon's responsibility in α^d, and vice versa.

Substitutions are fundamental but subtle. For example, a substitution σ that has the effect of replacing $f(x)$ with x^2 and $a(x)$ with zy is unsound for the following formula while a substitution that replaces $a(x)$ with zx^2 would be fine:

$$\text{clash} \notin \frac{\langle x' = f(x), y' = a(x)y \rangle \, x \geq 1 \leftrightarrow \langle x' = f(x) \rangle \, x \geq 1}{\langle x' = x^2, y' = zyy \rangle \, x \geq 1 \leftrightarrow \langle x' = x^2 \rangle \, x \geq 1}$$

The introduction of a new variable z by the substitution σ is acceptable, but, even if y was already present previously, its introduction by σ makes the inference unsound (e.g., when $x = y = 1/z = 1/2$), because this equates a system with a solution that is exponential in y with a hyperbolic solution of more limited duration, even if both solutions are already hyperbolic of limited time from x. By contrast, the use of the previously present variable x to form $x' = x^2$ is fine. The difference is that, unlike z, variable y has a differential equation that changes the value of y and, while x also does, $f(x)$ and $a(x)$ may explicitly depend on x. It is crucial to distinguish correct and incorrect substitutions in all cases.

2.2 Semantics

A *state* ω is a mapping from the set of all variables $\mathbf{V}$ to the reals $\mathbb{R}$. The state ω_x^r agrees with state ω except for variable x whose value is $r \in \mathbb{R}$ in ω_x^r. The set of all states is denoted $\mathcal{S}$ and the set of all its subsets is denoted $\wp(\mathcal{S})$.

The semantics of function, predicate, and game symbols is independent from the state. They are interpreted by an *interpretation* I that maps each arity k function symbol f to a k-ary smooth function $I(f) : \mathbb{R}^k \to \mathbb{R}$, each arity k predicate symbol p to a k-ary relation $I(p) \subseteq \mathbb{R}^k$, and each game symbol a to a monotone $I(a) : \wp(\mathcal{S}) \to \wp(\mathcal{S})$ where $I(a)(X) \subseteq \mathcal{S}$ are the states from which Angel has a winning strategy to achieve $X \subseteq \mathcal{S}$ in game a. Differentials $(\theta)'$ have a differential-form semantics [16]: the sum of partial derivatives by all variables $x \in \mathbf{V}$ multiplied by the values of their associated differential variable x'.

Definition 4 (Semantics of terms). *The semantics of a term θ in interpretation I and state $\omega \in \mathcal{S}$ is its value $I\omega[\![\theta]\!]$ in $\mathbb{R}$. It is defined inductively as*

1. *$I\omega[\![x]\!] = \omega(x)$ for variable $x \in \mathbf{V}$*
2. *$I\omega[\![f(\theta_1, \ldots, \theta_k)]\!] = I(f)\big(I\omega[\![\theta_1]\!], \ldots, I\omega[\![\theta_k]\!]\big)$ for function symbol f*
3. *$I\omega[\![\theta + \eta]\!] = I\omega[\![\theta]\!] + I\omega[\![\eta]\!]$*
4. *$I\omega[\![\theta \cdot \eta]\!] = I\omega[\![\theta]\!] \cdot I\omega[\![\eta]\!]$*
5. *$I\omega[\![(\theta)']\!] = \sum_{x \in \mathbf{V}} \omega(x') \frac{\partial I\omega[\![\theta]\!]}{\partial x}$ for the differential $(\theta)'$ of θ*

The semantics of differential game logic in interpretation I defines, for each formula ϕ, the set of all states $I[\![\phi]\!]$, in which ϕ is true. Since hybrid games appear in dGL formulas and vice versa, the semantics $I[\![\alpha]\!](X)$ of hybrid game α in interpretation I is defined by simultaneous induction as the set of all states from which Angel has a winning strategy in hybrid game α to achieve $X \subseteq \mathcal{S}$.

Definition 5 (dGL semantics). *The semantics of a dGL formula ϕ for each interpretation I with a corresponding set of states $\mathcal{S}$ is the subset $I[\![\phi]\!] \subseteq \mathcal{S}$ of states in which ϕ is true. It is defined inductively as follows*

1. $I[\![\theta \geq \eta]\!] = \{\omega \in \mathcal{S} : I\omega[\![\theta]\!] \geq I\omega[\![\eta]\!]\}$
2. $I[\![p(\theta_1, \ldots, \theta_k)]\!] = \{\omega \in \mathcal{S} : (I\omega[\![\theta_1]\!], \ldots, I\omega[\![\theta_k]\!]) \in I(p)\}$
3. $I[\![\neg\phi]\!] = (I[\![\phi]\!])^{\complement} = \mathcal{S} \setminus I[\![\phi]\!]$ *is the complement of* $I[\![\phi]\!]$
4. $I[\![\phi \wedge \psi]\!] = I[\![\phi]\!] \cap I[\![\psi]\!]$
5. $I[\![\exists x\,\phi]\!] = \{\omega \in \mathcal{S} : \omega_x^r \in I[\![\phi]\!]$ *for some* $r \in \mathbb{R}\}$
6. $I[\![\langle\alpha\rangle\phi]\!] = I[\![\alpha]\!](I[\![\phi]\!])$

A dGL *formula* ϕ *is* valid *in* I, *written* $I \models \phi$, *iff it is true in all states, i.e.,* $I[\![\phi]\!] = \mathcal{S}$. *Formula* ϕ *is* valid, *written* $\models \phi$, *iff* $I \models \phi$ *for all interpretations* I.

Definition 6 (Semantics of hybrid games). *The* semantics of a hybrid game α *for each interpretation* I *is a function* $I[\![\alpha]\!](\cdot)$ *that, for each set of states* $X \subseteq \mathcal{S}$ *as Angel's winning condition, gives the* winning region, *i.e., the set of states* $I[\![\alpha]\!](X) \subseteq \mathcal{S}$ *from which Angel has a winning strategy to achieve* X *in* α *(whatever strategy Demon chooses). It is defined inductively as follows*

1. $I[\![a]\!](X) = I(a)(X)$
2. $I[\![x := \theta]\!](X) = \{\omega \in \mathcal{S} : \omega_x^{I\omega[\![\theta]\!]} \in X\}$
3. $I[\![x' = \theta \,\&\, \psi]\!](X) = \{\omega \in \mathcal{S} : \omega = \varphi(0)$ *on* $\{x'\}^{\complement}$ *and* $\varphi(r) \in X$ *for some function* $\varphi : [0, r] \to \mathcal{S}$ *of some duration* $r \in \mathbb{R}$ *satisfying* $I, \varphi \models x' = \theta \wedge \psi\}$ *where* $I, \varphi \models x' = \theta \wedge \psi$ *iff* $\varphi(\zeta) \in I[\![x' = \theta \wedge \psi]\!]$ *and* $\varphi(0) = \varphi(\zeta)$ *on* $\{x, x'\}^{\complement}$ *for all* $0 \leq \zeta \leq r$ *and* $\frac{\mathrm{d}\varphi(t)(x)}{\mathrm{d}t}(\zeta)$ *exists and equals* $\varphi(\zeta)(x')$ *for all* $0 \leq \zeta \leq r$ *if* $r > 0$.
4. $I[\![?\psi]\!](X) = I[\![\psi]\!] \cap X$
5. $I[\![\alpha \cup \beta]\!](X) = I[\![\alpha]\!](X) \cup I[\![\beta]\!](X)$
6. $I[\![\alpha; \beta]\!](X) = I[\![\alpha]\!](I[\![\beta]\!](X))$
7. $I[\![\alpha^*]\!](X) = \bigcap\{Z \subseteq \mathcal{S} : X \cup I[\![\alpha]\!](Z) \subseteq Z\}$ *which is a least fixpoint* [15]
8. $I[\![\alpha^d]\!](X) = (I[\![\alpha]\!](X^{\complement}))^{\complement}$

Along $x' = \theta \,\&\, \psi$, variables x and x' enjoy an intrinsic link since they co-evolve.

2.3   Static Semantics

Sound uniform substitutions check free and bound occurrences of variables to prevent unsound replacements of expressions that might have incorrect values in the respective replacement contexts. The whole point of this paper is to skip admissibility checks such as that in (1). Free (and, indirectly, bound) variables will still have to be consulted to tell apart acceptable from unsound occurrences.

Hybrid games even make it challenging to characterize free and bound variables. Both are definable based on whether or not their values affect the existence of winning strategies under variations of the winning conditions [18]. The *upward projection* $X{\uparrow}V$ increases the winning condition $X \subseteq \mathcal{S}$ from variables $V \subseteq \mathbf{V}$ to all states that are "on V like X", i.e., similar on V to states in X. The *downward projection* $X{\downarrow}\omega(V)$ shrinks the winning condition X, fixing the values of state ω on variables $V \subseteq \mathbf{V}$ to keep just those states of X that agree with ω on V.

Definition 7. *The set* $X{\uparrow}V = \{\nu \in \mathcal{S} : \exists \omega \in X \, \omega = \nu \text{ on } V\} \supseteq X$ *extends* $X \subseteq \mathcal{S}$ *to the states that agree on* $V \subseteq \mathbf{V}$ *with some state in* X *(written* $\exists$ *). The set* $X{\downarrow}\omega(V) = \{\nu \in X : \omega = \nu \text{ on } V\} \subseteq X$ *selects state* ω *on* $V \subseteq \mathbf{V}$ *in* $X \subseteq \mathcal{S}$.

Projections make it possible to (*semantically!*) define free and bound variables of hybrid games by expressing variable dependence and ignorance. Such semantic characterizations increase modularity and are used for the correctness of syntactic analyzes that compute supersets [16, Sect. 2.4]. Variable x is free in hybrid game α iff two states that only differ in the value of x differ in membership in the winning region of α for some winning condition $X{\uparrow}\{x\}^{\complement}$ that does not distinguish values of x. Variable x is bound in hybrid game α iff it is in the winning region of α for some winning condition X but not for the winning condition $X{\downarrow}\omega(\{x\})$ that limits the new value of x to stay at its initial value $\omega(x)$.

Definition 8 (Static semantics). *The* static semantics *defines the* free *variables, which are all variables that the value of an expression depends on, as well as* bound *variables,* $\mathsf{BV}(\alpha)$*, which can change their value during game* α*, as:*

$$\mathsf{FV}(\theta) = \{x \in \mathbf{V} : \exists I, \omega, \tilde{\omega} \text{ such that } \omega = \tilde{\omega} \text{ on } \{x\}^{\complement} \text{ and } I\omega[\![\theta]\!] \neq I\tilde{\omega}[\![\theta]\!]\}$$

$$\mathsf{FV}(\phi) = \{x \in \mathbf{V} : \exists I, \omega, \tilde{\omega} \text{ such that } \omega = \tilde{\omega} \text{ on } \{x\}^{\complement} \text{ and } \omega \in I[\![\phi]\!] \not\ni \tilde{\omega}\}$$

$$\mathsf{FV}(\alpha) = \{x \in \mathbf{V} : \exists I, \omega, \tilde{\omega}, X \text{ with } \omega = \tilde{\omega} \text{ on } \{x\}^{\complement} \text{ and } \omega \in I[\![\alpha]\!](X{\uparrow}\{x\}^{\complement}) \not\ni \tilde{\omega}\}$$

$$\mathsf{BV}(\alpha) = \{x \in \mathbf{V} : \exists I, \omega, X \text{ such that } I[\![\alpha]\!](X) \ni \omega \notin I[\![\alpha]\!](X{\downarrow}\omega(\{x\}))\}$$

Beyond assignments, note complications with ODEs such as (2), where, due to their nature as the solution of a fixpoint condition, the *same* occurrences of variables are free, because they depend on their initial values, but they are also bound, because their values change along the ODE. All occurrences of x and y but not z on the right-hand side of $x' = x^2, y' = zx^2y$ and occurrences of x, y, x', y' also after this ODE are bound, since they are affected by this change. Variables x, y, z but not x', y' are free in this ODE. The crucial need for overlap of free and bound variables is most obvious for ODEs, but also arises for loops, e.g., $(x := x + 1; x' = -x)^*$. If x were not classified as free, its initial value could be overwritten incorrectly. If x were not classified as bound, its initial value could be incorrectly copy-propagated across the loop. This also applies to the *same* occurrence of x in $x + 1$ and $-x$, respectively. If it were not classified as a bound but a free occurrence, it could be incorrectly replaced by a term of the same initial value. If it were not classified as a free but a bound occurrence, it could, e.g., be boundly renamed, incorrectly losing its initial link. [2]

Coincidence lemmas [18] show truth-values of dGL formulas only depend on their free variables (likewise for terms and hybrid games). The bound effect lemma [18] shows only bound variables change their value when playing games.

---

[2] These intricate variable relationships in games and the intrinsic link of x and x' from ODEs significantly complicate substitutions beyond what is supported for first-order logic [5,23], λ-calculi [4], de Bruijn indices [3], or higher-order abstract syntax [14].

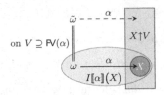 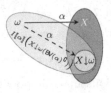

Fig. 1. Illustration of coincidence and bound effect properties of hybrid games

Supersets satisfy the same lemmas, so corresponding *syntactic* free and bound variable computations can be used correctly and are defined accordingly [16,18]. Since FV() and BV() are the smallest such sets, no smaller sets can be correct, including, e.g., the usual definitions that classify occurrences mutually exclusively.

Lemma 9 (Coincidence for terms [18]**).** FV(θ) *is the smallest set with the coincidence property for* θ: *If* $\omega = \tilde{\omega}$ *on* FV(θ), *then* $I\omega[\![\theta]\!] = I\tilde{\omega}[\![\theta]\!]$.

Lemma 10 (Coincidence for formulas [18]**).** FV(ϕ) *is the smallest set with the coincidence property for* ϕ: *If* $\omega = \tilde{\omega}$ *on* FV(ϕ), *then* $\omega \in I[\![\phi]\!]$ *iff* $\tilde{\omega} \in I[\![\phi]\!]$.

Lemma 11 (Coincidence for games [18]**).** FV(α) *is the smallest set with the coincidence property for* α: *If* $\omega = \tilde{\omega}$ *on* $V \supseteq$ FV(α), *then* $\omega \in I[\![\alpha]\!](X{\uparrow}V)$ *iff* $\tilde{\omega} \in I[\![\alpha]\!](X{\uparrow}V)$; *see Fig. 1(left).*

Lemma 12 (Bound effect [18]**).** BV(α) *is the smallest set with the bound effect property for* α: $\omega \in I[\![\alpha]\!](X)$ *iff* $\omega \in I[\![\alpha]\!](X{\downarrow}\omega(\text{BV}(\alpha)^\complement))$; *see Fig. 1(right).*

The correctness of one-pass uniform substitution will become more transparent after defining when one state is a variation of another on a set of variables. For a set $U \subseteq \mathbf{V}$, state $\tilde{\omega}$ is called a *U-variation* of state ω iff $\tilde{\omega} = \omega$ on complement $U^\complement$. Variations satisfy properties of monotonicity and transitivity. If $\tilde{\omega}$ is a U-variation of ω, then $\tilde{\omega}$ is a V-variation of ω for all $V \supseteq U$. If $\tilde{\omega}$ is a U-variation of ω and ω is a V-variation of μ, then $\tilde{\omega}$ is a $(U \cup V)$-variation of μ. Coincidence lemmas say that the semantics is insensitive to variations of nonfree variables. If $\tilde{\omega}$ is a U-variation of ω and FV(ϕ) $\cap U = \emptyset$, then $\omega \in I[\![\phi]\!]$ iff $\tilde{\omega} \in I[\![\phi]\!]$.

3   Uniform Substitution

Uniform substitutions for dGL affect terms, formulas, and games [18]. A *uniform substitution* σ is a mapping from expressions of the form $f(\cdot)$ to terms $\sigma f(\cdot)$, from $p(\cdot)$ to formulas $\sigma p(\cdot)$, and from game symbols a to hybrid games σa. Here $\cdot$ is a reserved function symbol of arity 0 marking the position where the argument, e.g., argument θ to $p(\cdot)$ in formula $p(\theta)$, will end up in the replacement $\sigma p(\cdot)$ used for $p(\theta)$. Vectorial extensions would be accordingly for other arities $k \geq 0$.

The key idea behind the new recursive one-pass application of uniform substitutions is that it simply applies σ by naïve homomorphic recursion without checking any admissibility conditions along the way. But the mechanism makes up for that soundness-defying negligence by passing a cumulative set U of taboo variables along the recursion that are then forbidden from being introduced free by σ *at the respective replacement* of function $f(\cdot)$ and predicate symbols $p(\cdot)$, respectively. No corresponding condition is required at substitutions of game symbols a, since games already have unlimited access to and effect on the state.

$$\sigma^U(x) = x \qquad\qquad \text{for variable } x \in \mathbf{V}$$
$$\sigma^U(f(\theta)) = (\sigma^U f)(\sigma^U \theta) \overset{\text{def}}{=} \{\cdot \mapsto \sigma^U \theta\}^\emptyset \sigma f(\cdot) \text{ if } \mathsf{FV}(\sigma f(\cdot)) \cap U = \emptyset$$
$$\sigma^U(\theta + \eta) = \sigma^U \theta + \sigma^U \eta$$
$$\sigma^U(\theta \cdot \eta) = \sigma^U \theta \cdot \sigma^U \eta$$
$$\sigma^U((\theta)') = (\sigma^{\mathbf{V}} \theta)'$$

$$\sigma^U(\theta \geq \eta) = \sigma^U \theta \geq \sigma^U \eta$$
$$\sigma^U(p(\theta)) = (\sigma^U p)(\sigma^U \theta) \overset{\text{def}}{=} \{\cdot \mapsto \sigma^U \theta\}^\emptyset \sigma p(\cdot) \text{ if } \mathsf{FV}(\sigma p(\cdot)) \cap U = \emptyset$$
$$\sigma^U(\neg \phi) = \neg \sigma^U \phi$$
$$\sigma^U(\phi \wedge \psi) = \sigma^U \phi \wedge \sigma^U \psi$$
$$\sigma^U(\exists x\, \phi) = \exists x\, \sigma^{U \cup \{x\}} \phi$$
$$\sigma^U(\langle \alpha \rangle \phi) = \langle \sigma_V^U \alpha \rangle \sigma^V \phi$$

$$\sigma_{U \cup \mathsf{BV}(\sigma a)}^U(a) = \sigma a \qquad\qquad \text{for game symbol } a$$
$$\sigma_{U \cup \{x\}}^U(x := \theta) = x := \sigma^U \theta$$
$$\sigma_{U \cup \{x,x'\}}^U(x' = \theta \,\&\, \psi) = (x' = \sigma^{U \cup \{x,x'\}} \theta \,\&\, \sigma^{U \cup \{x,x'\}} \psi)$$
$$\sigma_U^U(?\psi) = ?\sigma^U \psi$$
$$\sigma_{V \cup W}^U(\alpha \cup \beta) = \sigma_V^U \alpha \cup \sigma_W^U \beta$$
$$\sigma_W^U(\alpha; \beta) = \sigma_V^U \alpha ; \sigma_W^V \beta$$
$$\sigma_V^U(\alpha^*) = (\sigma_V^V \alpha)^* \qquad\qquad \text{where } \sigma_V^U \alpha \text{ is defined}$$
$$\sigma_V^U(\alpha^d) = (\sigma_V^U \alpha)^d$$

Fig. 2. Recursive application of one-pass uniform substitution σ for taboo $U \subseteq \mathbf{V}$

The result $\sigma^U \phi$ of *applying uniform substitution σ for taboo set* $U \subseteq \mathbf{V}$ to a dGL *formula* ϕ (or term θ or hybrid game α, respectively) is defined in Fig. 2. For proof rule US, the expression $\sigma\phi$ is, then, defined to be $\sigma^\emptyset \phi$ without taboos.

The case for $\exists x\, \phi$ in Fig. 2 conjoins the variable x to the taboo set in the homomorphic application of σ to ϕ, because any *newly introduced* free uses of x within that scope would refer to a different semantic value than outside that scope. In addition to computing the substituted hybrid game $\sigma_V^U \alpha$, the recursive application of one-pass uniform substitution σ to hybrid game α under taboo set U also performs an analysis that results in a new output taboo set V, written in subscript notation, that will be tabooed after this hybrid game. Superscripts as inputs and subscripts as outputs follows static analysis notation and makes the $\alpha; \beta$ case reminiscent of Einstein's summation: the output taboos V of $\sigma_V^U \alpha$ become the input taboos V for $\sigma_W^V \beta$, whose output W is that of $\sigma_W^U(\alpha; \beta)$. Similarly, the output taboos V resulting from the uniform substitute $\sigma_V^U \alpha$ of a hybrid game α become taboo during the uniform substitution application forming $\sigma^V \phi$ in the postcondition of a modality to build $\sigma^U(\langle\alpha\rangle\phi)$.

Repetitions $\sigma_V^U(\alpha^*)$ are the only complication in Fig. 2, where taboo U would be too lax during the recursion, because earlier repetitions of α bind variables of α itself, so only the taboos V obtained after one round $\sigma_V^U \alpha$ are correct input taboos for the loop body. These two passes per loop are linear in the output when considering repetitions α^* as their equivalent $?\top \cup \alpha; \alpha^*$ of double size.

Unlike in Church-style uniform substitution [5,16,18], attention is needed at the replacement sites of function and predicate symbols in order to make up for the neglected admissibility checks during all other operators. The result $\sigma^U(p(\theta))$ of applying uniform substitution σ with taboo U to a predicate application $p(\theta)$ is *only* defined if the replacement $\sigma p(\cdot)$ for p does not introduce free any tabooed variable, i.e., $\mathsf{FV}(\sigma p(\cdot)) \cap U = \emptyset$. Arguments are put in for placeholder $\cdot$ recursively by the taboo-free use of uniform substitution $\{\cdot \mapsto \sigma^U \theta\}$, which replaces arity 0 function symbol $\cdot$ by $\sigma^U \theta$. Taboos U are respected when forming (*once!*) the uniform substitution to be used for argument $\cdot$, but empty taboos $\emptyset$ suffice when substituting the resulting $\sigma^U \theta$ for $\cdot$ in the replacement $\sigma p(\cdot)$ for p.

All variables $\mathbf{V}$ become taboos during uniform substitutions into differentials $(\theta)'$, because any newly introduced occurrence of a variable x would cause additional dependencies on its respective associated differential variable x'.

If the conditions in Fig. 2 are not met, the substitution σ is said to *clash* for taboo U and its result $\sigma^U \phi$ is not defined and cannot be used. *All subsequent applications of uniform substitutions are required to be defined* (no clash).

Whether a substitution clashes is only checked once at each replacement, instead of also once per operator around it as in Church style from Eq. (1). The free variables $\mathsf{FV}(\sigma p(\cdot))$ of each (function and) predicate symbol replacement are best stored with σ to avoid repeated computation of free variables.

This inference would unsoundly equate linear solutions with exponential ones:

$$\text{clash}_{\not z}\frac{\langle v := f\rangle p(v) \leftrightarrow p(f)}{\langle v := -x\rangle[x' = v]\, x \geq 0 \leftrightarrow [x' = -x]\, x \geq 0}$$

Indeed, $\sigma = \{p(\cdot) \mapsto [x' = \cdot]\, x \geq 0, f \mapsto -x\}$ clashes so rejects the above inference since the substitute $-x$ for f has free variable x that is taboo in the context $[x' = \cdot]\, x \geq 0$. By contrast, a sound use of rule US, despite its change in multiple binding contexts with $\sigma = \{p(\cdot) \mapsto [(x := x + \cdot; x' = \cdot)^*]\, x + \cdot \geq 0, f \mapsto -v\}$, is:

$$\text{US}\frac{\langle v := f\rangle p(v) \leftrightarrow p(f)}{\langle v := -v\rangle[(x := x + v; x' = v)^*]\, x + v \geq 0 \leftrightarrow [(x := x - v; x' = -v)^*]\, x - v \geq 0}$$

Uniform substitution accurately distinguishes such sound inferences from unsound ones even if the substitutions take effect deep down within a dGL formula. Uniform substitutions enable other syntactic transformations that require a solid understanding of variable occurrence patterns such as common subexpression elimination, for example, by using the above inference from right to left.

3.1 Taboo Lemmas

The only soundness-critical property of output taboos is that they correctly add bound variables and never forget variables that were already input taboos.

Lemma 13 (Taboo set computation). *One-pass uniform substitution application monotonously computes taboos with correct bound variables for games:*

$$\text{if } \sigma_V^U \alpha \text{ is defined, then } V \supseteq U \cup \mathsf{BV}(\sigma_V^U \alpha)$$

Any superset of such taboo computations (or the free variable sets used in Fig. 2) remains correct, just more conservative. The change from input taboo U to output taboo V is a function of the hybrid game α, justifying the construction of $\sigma_V^U(\alpha^*)$: if $\sigma_V^U \alpha$ and $\sigma_W^V \alpha$ are defined, then $\sigma_V^V \alpha$ is defined and equal to $\sigma_W^V \alpha$. By Lemma 13, no implementation of bound variables is needed when defining game symbols via $\sigma_{U \cup V}^U (a) = \sigma a$ where $\{\}_V^\emptyset (\sigma a)$ with identity substitution $\{\}$. But bound variable computations speed up loops via $\sigma_V^U(\alpha^*) = (\sigma_V^{U \cup B} \alpha)^*$ since $B = \mathsf{BV}(\sigma_M^\emptyset \alpha)$ can be computed and used correctly in one pass when $U \cup B = V$.

3.2 Uniform Substitution Lemmas

Uniform substitutions are syntactic transformations on syntactic expressions. Their semantic counterpart is the semantic transformation that maps an interpretation I and a state ω to the adjoint interpretation $\sigma_\omega^* I$ that changes the meaning of all symbols according to the syntactic substitution σ. The interpretation $I_\cdot^d$ agrees with I except that function symbol $\cdot$ is interpreted as $d \in \mathbb{R}$.

Definition 14 (Substitution adjoints). *The* adjoint *to substitution σ is the operation that maps I, ω to the* adjoint interpretation *$\sigma_\omega^* I$ in which the interpretation of each function symbol f, predicate symbol p, and game symbol a are modified according to σ (it is enough to consider those that σ changes):*

$$\sigma_\omega^* I(f) : \mathbb{R} \to \mathbb{R}; \; d \mapsto I_\cdot^d \omega [\![\sigma f(\cdot)]\!]$$
$$\sigma_\omega^* I(p) = \{d \in \mathbb{R} : \omega \in I_\cdot^d [\![\sigma p(\cdot)]\!]\}$$
$$\sigma_\omega^* I(a) : \wp(\mathcal{S}) \to \wp(\mathcal{S}); \; X \mapsto I [\![\sigma a]\!](X)$$

The uniform substitution lemmas below are key to the soundness and equate the syntactic effect that a uniform substitution σ has on a syntactic expression in I, ω with the semantic effect that the switch to the adjoint interpretation $\sigma_\omega^* I$ has on the original expression. The technical challenge compared to Church-style uniform substitution [16, 18] is that no admissibility conditions are checked at the game operators that need them, because the whole point of one-pass uniform substitution is that it homomorphically recurses in a linear complexity sweep by postponing admissibility checks. All that happens during the substitution is that different taboo sets are passed along. Yet, still, there is a crucial interplay of the particular taboos imposed henceforth at binding operators and the retroactive checking at function and predicate symbol replacement sites.

In order to soundly deal with the negligence in admissibility checking of one-pass uniform substitutions in a modular way, the main insight is that it is imperative to generalize the range of applicability of uniform substitution lemmas beyond the state ω of original interest where the adjoint $\sigma_\omega^* I$ was formed, and make them cover *all* variations of states that are so similar that they might arise during soundness justifications. By demanding more comprehensive care at replacement sites, soundness arguments make up for the temporary lapses in attention during all other operators. This gives the uniform substitution algorithm broader liberties at binding operators, while simultaneously demanding broader compatibility in semantic neighborhoods on its parts. Due to the recursive nature of function substitutions, the proof [20] of the following result is by structural induction lexicographically on the structure of σ and θ, for all U, ν, ω.

Lemma 15 (Uniform substitution for terms). *The uniform substitution σ for taboo $U \subseteq \mathbf{V}$ and its adjoint interpretation $\sigma_\omega^* I$ for I, ω have the same semantics on U-variations for all terms θ:*

$$\text{for all } U\text{-variations } \nu \text{ of } \omega\text{:} \quad I\nu[\![\sigma^U \theta]\!] = \sigma_\omega^* I\nu[\![\theta]\!]$$

Recall that all uniform substitutions are only defined when they meet the side conditions from Fig. 2. A mention such as $\sigma^U \theta$ in Lemma 15 implies that its side conditions during the application of σ to θ with taboos U are met. Substitutions are antimonotone in taboos: If $\sigma^U \theta$ is defined, then $\sigma^V \theta$ is defined and equal to $\sigma^U \theta$ for all $V \subseteq U$ (accordingly for ϕ, α). The more taboos a use of a substitution tolerates, the more broadly its adjoint generalizes to state variations.

The corresponding results for formulas and games are proved by simultaneous induction since formulas and games are defined by simultaneous induction, as games may occur in formulas and, vice versa. The inductive proof [20] is lexicographic over the structure of σ and ϕ or α, with a nested induction over the closure ordinals of the loop fixpoints, simultaneously for all ν, ω, U, X.

Lemma 16 (Uniform substitution for formulas). *The uniform substitution σ for taboo $U \subseteq \mathbf{V}$ and its adjoint interpretation $\sigma_\omega^* I$ for I, ω have the same semantics on U-variations for all formulas ϕ:*

$$\text{for all } U\text{-variations } \nu \text{ of } \omega\text{:} \quad \nu \in I[\![\sigma^U \phi]\!] \text{ iff } \nu \in \sigma_\omega^* I[\![\phi]\!]$$

Lemma 17 (Uniform substitution for games). *The uniform substitution σ for taboo $U \subseteq \mathbf{V}$ and its adjoint interpretation $\sigma_\omega^* I$ for I, ω have the same semantics on U-variations for all games α:*

$$\text{for all } U\text{-variations } \nu \text{ of } \omega\text{:} \quad \nu \in I[\![\sigma_V^U \alpha]\!](X) \text{ iff } \nu \in \sigma_\omega^* I[\![\alpha]\!](X)$$

3.3   Soundness

With the uniform substitution lemmas having established the crucial equivalence of syntactic substitution and adjoint interpretation, the soundness of uniform substitution uses in proofs is now immediate. The notation $\sigma\phi$ in proof rule US is short for $\sigma^\emptyset\phi$, so the result of applying σ to ϕ without taboos (more taboos may still arise during the substitution application), and only defined if $\sigma^\emptyset\phi$ is. A proof rule is *sound* when its conclusion is valid if all its premises are valid.

Theorem 18 (Soundness of uniform substitution). *Proof rule US is sound.*

$$(\text{US})\ \ \frac{\phi}{\sigma\phi}$$

Theorem 18 is all it takes to soundly instantiate concrete axioms. Uniform substitutions can instantiate whole inferences [16], which makes it possible to avoid proof rule schemata by instantiating axiomatic proof rules consisting of pairs of concrete formulas. This enables uniformly substituting premises and conclusions of entire proofs of *locally sound* inferences, i.e., those whose conclusion is valid in any interpretation that all their premises are valid in.

Theorem 19 (Soundness of uniform substitution of rules). *All uniform substitution instances for taboo* $\mathbf{V}$ *of locally sound inferences are locally sound:*

$$\frac{\phi_1\ \ \cdots\ \ \phi_n}{\psi}\ \textit{locally sound}\ \ \textit{implies}\ \ \frac{\sigma^{\mathbf{V}}\phi_1\ \ \cdots\ \ \sigma^{\mathbf{V}}\phi_n}{\sigma^{\mathbf{V}}\psi}\ \textit{locally sound}$$

USR marks the use of Theorem 19 in proofs. If $n = 0$ (so ψ has a proof), USR preserves local soundness for taboo-free $\sigma^\emptyset\psi$ instead of $\sigma^{\mathbf{V}}\psi$, as US proves $\sigma^\emptyset\psi$ from the provable ψ and soundness is equivalent to local soundness for $n = 0$.

3.4   Completeness

Soundness is the property that every formula with a proof is valid. This is the most important consideration for something as fundamental as a uniform substitution mechanism. But the converse question of completeness, i.e., that every valid formula has a proof, is of interest as well, especially given the fact that one-pass uniform substitutions check differently for soundness during the substitution application, which had better not lose otherwise perfectly valid proofs.

Completeness is proved in an easy modular style based on all the nontrivial findings summarized in schematic relative completeness results, first for schematic dGL [15, Thm. 4.5], and then for a uniform substitution formulation of dL [16, Thm. 40]. The combination of both schematic completeness results makes it fairly easy to lift completeness to the setting in this paper. The challenge is to show that all instances of axiom schemata that are used for dGL's schematic relative completeness result are provable by one-pass uniform substitution.

A dGL formula ϕ is called *surjective* iff rule US can instantiate ϕ to any of its axiom schema instances, i.e., those formulas that are obtained by just

$$[\cdot] \quad [a]\langle c\rangle\top \leftrightarrow \neg\langle a\rangle\neg\langle c\rangle\top$$

$$\langle:=\rangle_= \quad \langle x:=f\rangle\langle c\rangle\top \leftrightarrow \exists x\,(x=f \wedge \langle c\rangle\top)$$

$$\text{DS} \quad \langle x'=f\rangle\langle c\rangle\top \leftrightarrow \exists t{\geq}0\,\langle x:=x{+}ft\rangle\langle x':=f\rangle\langle c\rangle\top$$

$$\langle?\rangle \quad \langle?q\rangle p \leftrightarrow q \wedge p$$

$$\langle\cup\rangle \quad \langle a\cup b\rangle\langle c\rangle\top \leftrightarrow \langle a\rangle\langle c\rangle\top \vee \langle b\rangle\langle c\rangle\top$$

$$\langle;\rangle \quad \langle a;b\rangle\langle c\rangle\top \leftrightarrow \langle a\rangle\langle b\rangle\langle c\rangle\top$$

$$\langle^*\rangle \quad \langle a^*\rangle\langle c\rangle\top \leftrightarrow \langle c\rangle\top \vee \langle a\rangle\langle a^*\rangle\langle c\rangle\top$$

$$\langle^d\rangle \quad \langle a^d\rangle\langle c\rangle\top \leftrightarrow \neg\langle a\rangle\neg\langle c\rangle\top$$

$$\text{M} \quad \frac{\langle c\rangle\top \to \langle d\rangle\top}{\langle a\rangle\langle c\rangle\top \to \langle a\rangle\langle d\rangle\top}$$

$$\text{FP} \quad \frac{\langle c\rangle\top \vee \langle a\rangle\langle d\rangle\top \to \langle d\rangle\top}{\langle a^*\rangle\langle c\rangle\top \to \langle d\rangle\top}$$

$$\text{MP} \quad \frac{p \quad p\to q}{q}$$

$$\forall \quad \frac{\langle c\rangle\top}{\forall x\,\langle c\rangle\top}$$

Fig. 3. Differential game logic axioms and axiomatic proof rules

replacing game symbols a uniformly by any game, etc. An axiomatic rule is called *surjective* iff USR of Theorem 19 can instantiate it to any of its proof rule schema instances.

Lemma 20 (Surjective axioms). *If ϕ is a dGL formula that is built only from game symbols but no function or predicate symbols, then ϕ is surjective. Axiomatic rules consisting of surjective dGL formulas are surjective.*

Instead of following previous completeness arguments for uniform substitution [18], this paper presents a pure game-style uniform substitution formulation in Fig. 3 of a dGL axiomatization that makes the overall completeness proof most straightforward. For that purpose, the dGL axiomatization in Fig. 3 uses properties $\langle c\rangle\top$ of a game symbol c, which, as a game, can impose arbitrary conditions on the state even for a trivial postcondition (the formula $\top$ is always true).

All axioms of Fig. 3, except test $\langle?\rangle$, equational assignment $\langle:=\rangle_=$, and constant solution DS, are surjective by Lemma 20. The US requirement that no substitute of f may depend on x is important for the soundness of DS and $\langle:=\rangle_=$. Axiom $\langle?\rangle$ is surjective, as it has no bound variables, so generates no taboos and none of its instances clash: $\sigma^{\emptyset}(\langle?q\rangle p \leftrightarrow q \wedge p) = (\langle\sigma_{\emptyset}^{\emptyset}q\rangle\sigma^{\emptyset}p \leftrightarrow \sigma^{\emptyset}q \wedge \sigma^{\emptyset}p)$. Similarly, rule MP is surjective [16], and the other rules are surjective by Lemma 20. Other differential equation axioms are elided but work as previously [16].

Besides rule US, *bound variable renaming* (rule BR) is the only schematic principle, mostly for generalizing assignment axiom $\langle:=\rangle_=$ to other variables.

Lemma 21 (Bound renaming). *Rule BR is locally sound, where ψ_x^y is the result of uniformly renaming x to y in ψ (also x' to y' but no x'', x''' etc. or game symbols occur in ψ, where the rule BR for $[x:=\theta]\psi$ is accordingly):*

$$(\text{BR}) \quad \frac{\phi \to \langle y:=\theta\rangle\langle y':=x'\rangle\psi_x^y}{\phi \to \langle x:=\theta\rangle\psi} \quad (y,y' \notin \psi)$$

Theorem 22 (Relative completeness). *The dGL calculus is a sound and complete axiomatization of hybrid games relative to any differentially expressive logic L, i.e., every valid dGL formula is provable in dGL from L tautologies.*

This completeness result assumes that no game symbols occur, because uniform renaming otherwise needs to become a syntactic operator. A logic L closed under first-order connectives is *differentially expressive* (for dGL) if every dGL formula ϕ has an equivalent $\phi^\flat$ in L and all differential equation equivalences of the form $\langle x' = \theta \rangle G \leftrightarrow (\langle x' = \theta \rangle G)^\flat$ for G in L are provable in its calculus.

4 Differential Hybrid Games

Uniform substitution generalizes from dGL for hybrid games [15] to dGL for *differential* hybrid games [17], which add differential games as a new atomic game. A *differential game* $x' = \theta \,\&^d\, y \in Y \,\&\, z \in Z$ allows Angel to control how long to follow the differential equation $x' = \theta$ (in which variables x, y, z may occur) while Demon provides a measurable input for y over time satisfying the formula $y \in Y$ always and Angel, knowing Demon's current input, provides a measurable input for z satisfying the formula $z \in Z$. All occurrences of y, z in $x' = \theta \,\&^d\, y \in Y \,\&\, z \in Z$ are bound, and $y \in Y$ and $z \in Z$ are formulas in the free variables y or z, respectively. It has been a long-standing challenge to give mathematical meaning [6,7] and sound reasoning principles [17] for differential games. Both outcomes can simply be adopted here under the usual well-definedness assumptions [17].

Uniform substitution application in Fig. 2 lifts to differential games by adding:

$$\sigma_U^U(x' = \theta \,\&^d\, y \in Y \,\&\, z \in Z) = (x' = \sigma^{\bar{U}} \theta \,\&^d\, y \in \sigma^{\bar{U}} Y \,\&\, z \in \sigma^{\bar{U}} Z)$$

where $\bar{U}$ is $U \cup \{x, x', y, y', z, z'\}$. Well-definedness assumptions on differential games [17] need to hold, e.g., only first-order logic formulas denoting compact sets are allowed for controls and the differential equations need to be bounded.

As terms are unaffected by adding differential games to the syntax, Lemma 9 and 15 do not change. The proofs of the coincidence Lemmas 10 and 11 and bound effect Lemma 12 [18] transfer to dGL with differential hybrid games in verbatim thanks to their use of *semantically defined* free and bound variables, which carry over to differential hybrid games. The proof of Lemma 13 generalizes easily by adding a case for differential games with the above $\bar{U}$. The uniform substitution Lemmas 16 and 17 inductively generalize to differential hybrid games because of:

Lemma 23 (Uniform substitution for differential games). *Let* $U \subseteq \mathbf{V}$. *For all U-variations ν of ω:*

$$\nu \in I[\![\sigma_U^U(x' = \theta \,\&^d\, y \in Y \,\&\, z \in Z)]\!](X) \;\; \textit{iff} \;\; \nu \in \sigma_\omega^* I[\![x' = \theta \,\&^d\, y \in Y \,\&\, z \in Z]\!](X)$$

The proof [20] makes clever use of differential game refinements [17] to avoid the significant complexities and semantic subtleties of differential games.

5   Conclusion

This paper introduced significantly faster uniform substitution mechanisms, the dominant logical inference in axiomatic small core hybrid systems/games provers. It is also first in proving soundness of uniform substitution for differential games.

Implementations exhibit a linear runtime complexity compared to the exponential complexity that direct implementations [8] of prior Church-style uniform substitutions exhibit, except when applying aggressive space/time optimization tradeoffs where that drops down to a quadratic runtime in practice.

Acknowledgment. I thank Frank Pfenning for useful discussions and the anonymous reviewers for their helpful feedback. I appreciate the kind advice of the Isabelle group at TU Munich for the subsequent formalization [19] of the proofs.

References

1. Ahrendt, W., Beckert, B., Bubel, R., Hähnle, R., Schmitt, P.H., Ulbrich, M. (eds.): Deductive Software Verification - The KeY Book, LNCS, vol. 10001. Springer, Cham (2016). https://doi.org/10.1007/978-3-319-49812-6
2. Bohrer, R., Rahli, V., Vukotic, I., Völp, M., Platzer, A.: Formally verified differential dynamic logic. In: Bertot, Y., Vafeiadis, V. (eds.) Certified Programs and Proofs - 6th ACM SIGPLAN Conference, CPP 2017, Paris, France, pp. 208–221. ACM, New York, 16–17 January 2017. https://doi.org/10.1145/3018610.3018616
3. de Bruijn, N.: Lambda calculus notation with nameless dummies, a tool for automatic formula manipulation, with application to the Church-Rosser theorem. Indagationes Math. **75**(5), 381–392 (1972). https://doi.org/10.1016/1385-7258(72)90034-0
4. Church, A.: A formulation of the simple theory of types. J. Symb. Log. **5**(2), 56–68 (1940). https://doi.org/10.2307/2266170
5. Church, A.: Introduction to Mathematical Logic. Princeton University Press, Princeton (1956)
6. Elliott, R.J., Kalton, N.J.: Cauchy problems for certain Isaacs-Bellman equations and games of survival. Trans. Amer. Math. Soc. **198**, 45–72 (1974). https://doi.org/10.1090/S0002-9947-1974-0347383-8
7. Evans, L.C., Souganidis, P.E.: Differential games and representation formulas for solutions of Hamilton-Jacobi-Isaacs equations. Indiana Univ. Math. J. **33**(5), 773–797 (1984). https://doi.org/10.1512/iumj.1984.33.33040
8. Fulton, N., Mitsch, S., Quesel, J.-D., Völp, M., Platzer, A.: KeYmaera X: an axiomatic tactical theorem prover for hybrid systems. In: Felty, A.P., Middeldorp, A. (eds.) CADE 2015. LNCS (LNAI), vol. 9195, pp. 527–538. Springer, Cham (2015). https://doi.org/10.1007/978-3-319-21401-6_36
9. Harel, D., Kozen, D., Tiuryn, J.: Dynamic Logic. MIT Press, Cambridge (2000). https://doi.org/10.7551/mitpress/2516.001.0001
10. Henkin, L.: Banishing the rule of substitution for functional variables. J. Symb. Log. **18**(3), 201–208 (1953). https://doi.org/10.2307/2267403
11. Hilbert, D., Ackermann, W.: Grundzüge der theoretischen Logik. Springer, Berlin (1928)

12. Hilbert, D., Bernays, P.: Grundlagen der Mathematik, vol. I, 2nd edn. Springer, Heidelberg (1934). https://doi.org/10.1007/978-3-642-86894-8
13. Mitchell, I., Bayen, A.M., Tomlin, C.: A time-dependent Hamilton-Jacobi formulation of reachable sets for continuous dynamic games. IEEE Trans. Autom. Control **50**(7), 947–957 (2005). https://doi.org/10.1109/TAC.2005.851439
14. Pfenning, F., Elliott, C.: Higher-order abstract syntax. In: Wexelblat, R.L. (ed.) PLDI, pp. 199–208. ACM (1988). https://doi.org/10.1145/53990.54010
15. Platzer, A.: Differential game logic. ACM Trans. Comput. Logic **17**(1), 1:1–1:51 (2015). https://doi.org/10.1145/2817824
16. Platzer, A.: A complete uniform substitution calculus for differential dynamic logic. J. Autom. Res. **59**(2), 219–265 (2017). https://doi.org/10.1007/s10817-016-9385-1
17. Platzer, A.: Differential hybrid games. ACM Trans. Comput. Logic **18**(3), 19:1–19:44 (2017). https://doi.org/10.1145/3091123
18. Platzer, A.: Uniform substitution for differential game logic. In: Galmiche, D., Schulz, S., Sebastiani, R. (eds.) IJCAR 2018. LNCS (LNAI), vol. 10900, pp. 211–227. Springer, Cham (2018). https://doi.org/10.1007/978-3-319-94205-6_15
19. Platzer, A.: Differential game logic. Archive of Formal Proofs 2019 (2019). http://isa-afp.org/entries/Differential_Game_Logic.html. formal proof development
20. Platzer, A.: Uniform substitution at one fell swoop. CoRR abs/1902.07230 (2019). http://arxiv.org/abs/1902.07230
21. Quesel, J.-D., Platzer, A.: Playing hybrid games with keymaera. In: Gramlich, B., Miller, D., Sattler, U. (eds.) IJCAR 2012. LNCS (LNAI), vol. 7364, pp. 439–453. Springer, Heidelberg (2012). https://doi.org/10.1007/978-3-642-31365-3_34
22. Quine, W.V.O.: A System of Logistic. Harvard University Press, Cambridge (1934)
23. Schneider, H.II.: Substitutions for predicate variables and functional variables. Notre Dame J. Formal Logic **21**(1), 33–44 (1980). https://doi.org/10.1305/ndjfl/1093882937

A Formally Verified Abstract Account of Gödel's Incompleteness Theorems

Andrei Popescu[1(✉)] and Dmitriy Traytel[2(✉)]

[1] Department of Computer Science, Middlesex University, London, UK
a.popescu@mdx.ac.uk
[2] Institute of Information Security, Department of Computer Science, ETH Zürich,
Zurich, Switzerland
traytel@inf.ethz.ch

Abstract. We present an abstract development of Gödel's incompleteness theorems, performed with the help of the Isabelle/HOL theorem prover. We analyze sufficient conditions for the theorems' applicability to a partially specified logic. In addition to the usual benefits of generality, our abstract perspective enables a comparison between alternative approaches from the literature. These include Rosser's variation of the first theorem, Jeroslow's variation of the second theorem, and the Świerczkowski–Paulson semantics-based approach. As part of our framework's validation, we upgrade Paulson's Isabelle proof to produce a mechanization of the second theorem that does not assume soundness in the standard model, and in fact does not rely on any notion of model or semantic interpretation.

1 Introduction

Gödel's incompleteness theorems [10,13] are landmark results in mathematical logic. Both theorems refer to consistent logical theories that satisfy some assumptions, notably that of "containing enough arithmetic." The first incompleteness theorem ($\mathcal{IT}_1$) says that there are sentences that the theory cannot decide (i.e., neither prove nor disprove); the second theorem ($\mathcal{IT}_2$) says that the theory cannot prove (an internal formulation of) its own consistency. It is generally accepted that $\mathcal{IT}_1$ and $\mathcal{IT}_2$ have a wide scope, covering many logics and logical theories. However, when it comes to rigorous presentation, typically these results are only proved for particular, albeit paradigmatic cases, such as theories of arithmetic or hereditarily finite (HF) sets, within classical first-order logic (FOL); and even in these cases the constructions and proofs tend to be "incomplete and (apparently) irremediably messy" [4, p. 16]. Hence, the theorems' scope remains largely unexplored on a rigorous/formal basis.

The emergence of powerful theorem provers has changed the rules of the game and, we argue, the expectation. Using interactive theorems provers, we can reliably keep track of all the constructions and their properties. Proof automation (often powered by fully automatic provers [18,28]), makes complete, fully rigorous proofs feasible. And indeed, researchers have successfully met the challenge

© Springer Nature Switzerland AG 2019
P. Fontaine (Ed.): CADE 2019, LNAI 11716, pp. 442–461, 2019.
https://doi.org/10.1007/978-3-030-29436-6_26

of mechanizing $\mathcal{IT}_1$ [15,25,27,35] and recently $\mathcal{IT}_2$ [27]. Besides reassurance, these verification *tours de force* have brought superior technical insight into the theorems. But they have taken place within the same solitary confinement of scope as the informal proofs.

This paper takes steps towards a more comprehensive prover-backed exploration of the incompleteness theorems, by a detailed analysis of their assumptions. We use Isabelle/HOL [24] to establish general conditions under which the theorems apply to a partially specified logic. Our formalization is publicly available [31]. An extended technical report gives more details [30].

We start with a notion of logic (Sect. 2) whose terms, formulas and provability relation are kept abstract (Sect. 2.1). In particular, substitution and free variables are not defined, but axiomatized by some general properties. On top of this logic substratum, we consider an arithmetic substratum, consisting of a set of closed terms called *numerals* and an order-like relation (Sect. 2.2). Also factored in our abstract framework are encodings of formulas and proofs into numerals, the representability of various functions and relations as terms or formulas (Sect. 2.3), variations of the Hilbert-Bernays-Löb derivability conditions [16,23] (Sect. 2.4), and standard models (Sect. 2.5).

Overall, our assumptions capture the notion of "containing enough arithmetics" in a general and flexible way. It is general because only few assumptions are made about the exact nature of formulas and numerals. It is flexible because different versions of the incompleteness theorems consider their own "amount of arithmetics" that makes it "enough," as proper subsets of these assumptions. Indeed, our formalization of the theorems (Sect. 3) proceeds in an austere-buffet style: Every result picks just enough infrastructure needed for it to hold—ranging from diagonalization which requires very little (Sect. 3.1) to Rosser's version of $\mathcal{IT}_1$ which is quite demanding. This approach caters for a sharp comparison between different formulations of the theorems, highlighting their trade-offs: Gödel's original formulation of $\mathcal{IT}_1$ versus Rosser's improvement (Sect. 3.2), proof-theoretic versus semantic versions of $\mathcal{IT}_1$ (Sect. 3.2), and Gödel's original formulation of the $\mathcal{IT}_2$ versus Jeroslow's improvement (Sect. 3.3).

Abstractness is our development's main strength, but also a potential weakness: Are our hypotheses reasonable? Are they consistent? These questions particularly concern our axiomatization of free variables and substitution—a notoriously error-prone area. As a remedy, we instantiate our framework to Paulson's semantics-based $\mathcal{IT}_1$ and $\mathcal{IT}_2$ for HF set theory [27], also performing an upgrade of Paulson's $\mathcal{IT}_2$ to a more general and standard formulation: for consistent (not necessarily sound) theories (Sect. 4). In the rest of this section, we discuss some formalization principles and related work.

Formal Design Principles. Our long-term goal is a framework that makes it easy to instantiate the incompleteness theorems and related results to different logics. This is a daunting task, especially for $\mathcal{IT}_2$, where a lot of seemingly logic-specific technicalities are required to even formulate the theorem. The challenge is to push as much as possible of the technical constructions and lemmas to a largely logic-independent layer.

To this end, we strive to make minimal assumptions in terms of structure and properties when inferring the results—we will call this the *Economy* principle. For example, we do not define, but axiomatize syntax in terms of a minimalistic infrastructure. We assume a generic single-point substitution, then define simultaneous substitution and infer its properties. This is laborious, but worthwhile: Any logic that provides a single-point substitution satisfying our assumptions gets the simultaneous substitution for free.

As another instance of Economy, when faced with two different ways of formulating a theorem's conclusion we prefer the one that is *stronger under fewer assumptions*. (And dually, we prefer weakness for a theorem's assumptions.) For example, we discuss two variants of consistency: (1) "does not prove false" or (2) "there exists no formula such that itself and its negation are provable" (Sect. 3.3). While the statements are equivalent at the meta-level, their representations as object-logic formulas are not necessarily equivalent; in fact, (1) implies (2) under mild assumptions but not *vice versa*. So in our abstract theorems we prefer (1). Indeed, even if (2) implies (1) in all reasonable instances, why postpone for the instantiation time any fact that we can show abstractly?

Applying the Economy principle not only stocks up generality for instantiations, but also accurately outlines trade-offs: How much does it cost (in terms of other added assumptions) to improve the conclusion, or to weaken an assumption of a theorem? For example, an Economy-based proof of Rosser's variant of $\mathcal{IT}_1$ reveals how much arithmetic we must factor in for weakening the ω-consistency assumption into consistency.

Related Work. Gödel initially gave a proof of $\mathcal{IT}_1$ and the rough proof idea of $\mathcal{IT}_2$ [13]. Hilbert and Bernays gave a first detailed proof of $\mathcal{IT}_2$ [16]. A vast literature was dedicated to the (re)formulation, proof, and analysis of these results [4,33,38,39]. The now canonical line of reasoning goes through the derivability conditions devised by Bernays and Hilbert [16] and simplified by Löb [23]. These conditions have inspired a new branch of modal logic called provability logic [4]. Jeroslow has argued that, unlike previously believed, one condition is redundant when proving $\mathcal{IT}_2$ [17].

Kreisel [20] and Jeroslow [17] were the first to study abstract conditions on logics under which the incompleteness theorems apply. Buldt [5] surveys the state of the art focusing on $\mathcal{IT}_1$. Our abstract approach, based on generic syntax and provability and truth predicates, resembles the style of institution-independent model theory [9,14] and our previous work on abstract completeness [3] and completeness of ordered resolution [34]. Dimensions of generality that our formalized work does not (yet) explore include quantifier-free logics [17] and arithmetical hierarchy refinements [19]. Our syntax axiomatization is inspired by algebraic theories of the λ-calculi syntax [11,12,29].

In the realm of mechanical proofs, the earliest substantial development was due to Sieg [36], who used a prover based on TEM (Theory of Elementary Meta-Mathematics) to formalize parts of the proofs of both $\mathcal{IT}_1$ and $\mathcal{IT}_2$. But the first full proof of $\mathcal{IT}_1$ was achieved by Shankar [35] in the Boyer-Moore prover, followed by Harrison in HOL Light [15] and O'Connor in Coq [25]. $\mathcal{IT}_2$ has only been fully proved recently—by Paulson in Isabelle/HOL [26, 27] (who also proved $\mathcal{IT}_1$). All these mechanizations target theories over a fixed language in classical FOL: that of arithmetic (Harrison and O'Connor) and that of HF sets or a variation of it (Sieg, Shankar and Paulson). These mechanizations are mostly focused on "getting all the work done" in a particular setting (although Harrison targets a more abstract class of theories in the given language). On their way to $\mathcal{IT}_1$, Shankar and O'Connor also prove representability of all-partial, respectively primitive recursive functions—important standalone results. Also, there has been work on fully automating parts of the proofs of these theorems [1, 6, 32, 37].

By contrast, we explore conditions that enable different formulations for an abstract logic, where aspects such as recursiveness are below our abstraction level. The two approaches are complementary, and they both contribute to formally taming the complex ramifications of the incompleteness theorems. When instantiating our abstract assumptions to recover and upgrade Paulson's results, we took advantage of Paulson's substantial work on proving the many low-level lemmas towards the derivability conditions. More should be done at an abstract level to avoid duplicating some of these laborious lemmas when instantiating the theorems to different logics. This will be future work.

2   Abstract Assumptions

Roughly, the incompleteness theorems are considered to hold for logical theories that (1) contain enough arithmetic and (2) are "effective" in that they themselves can be arithmetized. Our goal is to give a general expression of these favorable conditions. To this end, we identify some logic and arithmetic substrata consisting of structure and axioms that express the containment of (various degrees of) arithmetic more abstractly and flexibly than relative interpretations [41]. We also identify abstract notions of encodings and representability that have just what it takes for a working arithmetization.

2.1   The Logical Substratum

We start with some unspecified sets of variables (Var, ranged over by x, y, z), terms (Term, ranged over by s, t) and formulas (Fmla, ranged over by φ, ψ, χ). We assume that variables are particular terms, Var $\subseteq$ Term, and that Var is infinite. Free-variables and substitution operators, FVars and $\_[\_/\_]$, are assumed for both terms and formulas. We think of FVars(t) as the (finite) set of free variables of the term t, and similarly for formulas. We call *sentence* any formula with no free variable, and let Sen denote the set of sentences. We think of $s[t/x]$ as the term obtained from s by the (capture-avoiding) substitution of t for the free occurrences of variable x; we think of $\varphi[t/x]$ as the formula obtained from φ by the substitution of t for the free occurrences of variable x.

In FOL, terms introduce no bindings, so any occurring variable is free. FOL terms fall under our framework, and so do terms with bindings as in λ-calculi and higher-order logic (HOL). To achieve this degree of inclusiveness while also being able to prove interesting results, we work under some well-behavedness assumptions about the free-variables and substitution operators. For example, free-variables distribute over substitution, $\mathsf{FVars}(\varphi\,[s/x]) = \mathsf{FVars}(\varphi) - \{x\} \cup \mathsf{FVars}(s)$ if $x \in \mathsf{FVars}(\varphi)$, and substitution is compositional, $\varphi\,[s_1/x_1]\,[s_2/x_2] = \varphi\,[s_2/x_2]\,[(s_1\,[s_2/x_2])\,/\,x_1]$ if $x_1 \neq x_2$ and $x_1 \notin \mathsf{FVars}(s_2)$. Our extended report [30] contains the full list of our generic syntax axioms.

The incompleteness theorems rely heavily on simultaneous substitution, written $\varphi\,[t_1/x_1,\ldots,t_n/x_n]$, whose properties are tricky to formalize—for example, Paulson's formalization paper dedicates them ample space [27, 6.2]. To address this problem once and for all generically, we define simultaneous substitution from the single-point substitution, $\varphi\,[t/x]$, and infer its properties from the single-point substitution axioms. For example, we prove that $\mathsf{FVars}(\varphi\,[s_1/x_1,\ldots,s_n/x_n]) = \mathsf{FVars}(\varphi) \cup \bigcup\{\mathsf{FVars}(s_i) - \{x_i\} \mid i \in \{1,\ldots,n\}$ and $x_i \in \mathsf{FVars}(\varphi)\}$. The technicalities are delicate: To avoid undesired variable replacements, $\varphi\,[s_1/x_1,\ldots,s_n/x_n]$ must be defined as $\varphi\,[y_1/x_1]\ldots[y_n/x_n]$ $[s_1/y_1]\ldots[s_n/y_n]$ for some fresh $y_1,\ldots,y_n$, the choice of which we must show to be immaterial. This definition's complexity is reflected in the properties' proofs. But again, this one-time effort benefits any "customer" logic: In exchange for a well-behaved single-point substitution, it gets back a well-behaved simultaneous substitution.

We let $v_1,v_2,\ldots$ be fixed mutually distinct variables. We write Fmla_k for the set of formulas whose free variables are precisely $\{v_1,\ldots,v_k\}$, and $\mathsf{Fmla}_k^{\subseteq}$ for the set of formulas whose variables are among $\{v_1,\ldots,v_k\}$. Note that $\mathsf{Fmla}_k \subseteq \mathsf{Fmla}_k^{\subseteq}$ and $\mathsf{Fmla}_0 = \mathsf{Fmla}_0^{\subseteq} = \mathsf{Sen}$. Given $\varphi \in \mathsf{Fmla}_k^{\subseteq}$, we write $\varphi\,(t_1,\ldots,t_n)$ instead of $\varphi\,[t_1/v_1,\ldots,t_n/v_n]$.

In addition to free variables and substitution, our theorems will require formulas to be equipped with term equality ($\equiv$), Boolean connectives ($\bot$, $\top$, $\rightarrow$, $\neg$, $\wedge$, $\vee$), universal and existential quantifiers ($\forall$, $\exists$). In our formalization, we assume a minimal list of the above with respect to intuitionistic logic, and define the rest from this minimal list. They are not assumed to be constructors (syntax builders), but operators on terms and formulas, e.g., $\equiv\,:\mathsf{Term} \rightarrow \mathsf{Term} \rightarrow \mathsf{Fmla}$, $\bot \in \mathsf{Fmla}$, $\forall\,:\mathsf{Var} \times \mathsf{Fmla} \rightarrow \mathsf{Fmla}$. This caters for logics that do not have them as primitives. For example, HOL defines all connectives and quantifiers from λ-abstraction and either equality or implication.

We fix a unary relation $\vdash\,\subseteq \mathsf{Fmla}$ on formulas, called *provability*. We write $\vdash \varphi$ instead of $\varphi \in \vdash$, and say the formula φ is *provable*. Whenever certain formula connectives or quantifiers are assumed present, we will assume that $\vdash$ behaves intuitionistically w.r.t. them—namely, we assume the usual (Hilbert-style) intuitionistic FOL axioms with respect to the abstract connectives and quantifiers. Stronger systems, such as those of classical logic, also satisfy these assumptions.

Consistency, denoted Con, is defined as the impossibility to prove false, namely $\nvdash \bot$. Another central concept is ω-consistency—we carefully choose a formulation that works intuitionistically, with conclusion reminiscent of Gödel's negative translation [8]:

OCon: For all $\varphi \in \mathsf{Fmla}_1^{\subseteq}$, if $\vdash \neg \varphi(n)$ for all $n \in \mathsf{Num}$ then $\nvdash \neg\neg(\exists x.\, \varphi(x))$.

Assuming classic deduction in $\vdash$, this is equivalent to the standard formulation: For all $\varphi \in \mathsf{Fmla}_1^{\subseteq}$, it is not the case that $\vdash \varphi(n)$ for all $n \in \mathsf{Num}$ and $\vdash \neg(\forall x.\, \varphi(x))$.

Occasionally, we will consider not only provability but also explicit proofs. We fix a set Proof of (entities we call) *proofs*, ranged over by p, q, and a binary relation between proofs p and sentences φ, written $p \Vdash \varphi$ and read "p is a proof of φ." We assume $\vdash$ and $\Vdash$ to be related as expected, in that provability is the same as the existence of a proof:

Rel$_{\vdash}^{\Vdash}$: For all $\varphi \in \mathsf{Sen}$, $\vdash \varphi$ iff there exists $p \in \mathsf{Proof}$ such that $p \Vdash \varphi$.

2.2   The Arithmetic Substratum

We extend the generic syntax assumptions with a subset $\mathsf{Num} \subseteq \mathsf{Term}$, of *numerals*, ranged over by m, n, which are assumed to be closed, i.e., have no free variables.

Convention 1. In all the shown results we implicitly assume: (1) the generic syntax (free variable and substitution) axioms, (2) at least $\rightarrow$ and $\perp$ plus whatever connectives and quantifiers appear in the statement, (3) closedness of $\vdash$ under intuitionistic deduction rules, and (4) the existence of numerals. Other assumptions (e.g., order-like relation axioms, consistency, standard models, etc.) will be indicated explicitly.

On one occasion, we will assume an order-like binary relation modeled by a formula $\prec \in \mathsf{Fmla}_2$. We write $t_1 \prec t_2$ instead of $\prec (t_1, t_2)$ and $\forall x \prec n.\, \varphi$ instead of $\forall x.\, x \prec n \rightarrow \varphi$. It turns out that at our level of abstraction it does not matter whether $\prec$ is a strict or a non-strict order. Indeed, we only require the following two properties, where $x \in M$ denotes $\bigvee_{m \in M} x \equiv m$ and $\bigvee$ expresses the disjunction of a finite set of formulas:

Ord$_1$: For all $\varphi \in \mathsf{Fmla}_1$ and $n \in \mathsf{Num}$, if $\vdash \varphi(m)$ for all $m \in \mathsf{Num}$, then $\vdash \forall x \prec n.\, \varphi(x)$.

Ord$_2$: For all $n \in \mathsf{Num}$, there exists a finite set $M \subseteq \mathsf{Num}$ such that $\vdash \forall x.\, x \in M \vee n \prec x$.

Ord$_1$ states that if a property φ is provable for all numerals, then its universal quantification bounded by any given numeral n is also provable. Having in mind the arithmetic interpretation of numerals, it would also make sense to assume a stronger version of Ord$_1$, replacing "if $\vdash \varphi(m)$ for all $m \in \mathsf{Num}$" by the weaker hypothesis "if $\vdash \varphi(m)$ for all $m \in \mathsf{Num}$ such that $\vdash m \prec n$". But this stronger version will not be needed.

Ord$_2$ states that, for any numeral n, any element x in the domain of discourse is either greater than n or equal to one of a finite set M of numerals. If we instantiate our syntax to that of first-order arithmetic, then the natural number model satisfies Ord$_1$ and Ord$_2$ when interpreting $\prec$ as either $<$ or $\leq$. Moreover, these properties are provable in intuitionistic Robinson arithmetic, again for both $<$ and $\leq$.

2.3   Encodings and Representability

Central in the incompleteness theorems are functions that encode formulas and proofs as numerals, $\langle \_ \rangle : \mathsf{Fmla} \to \mathsf{Num}$ and $\langle \_ \rangle : \mathsf{Proof} \to \mathsf{Num}$. For our abstract results, the encodings are not required to be injective or surjective.

Let $A_1, \ldots, A_m$ be sets, and let, for each of them, $\langle \_ \rangle : A_i \to \mathsf{Num}$ be an "encoding" function to numerals. Then, an m-ary relation $R \subseteq A_1 \times \ldots \times A_m$ is said to be *represented* by a formula $\textcircled{R} \in \mathsf{Fmla}_m$ if the following hold for all $(a_1, \ldots, a_m) \in A_1 \times \ldots \times A_m$:

- $(a_1, \ldots, a_m) \in R$ implies $\vdash \textcircled{R}(\langle a_1 \rangle, \ldots, \langle a_m \rangle)$
- $(a_1, \ldots, a_m) \notin R$ implies $\vdash \neg\textcircled{R}(\langle a_1 \rangle, \ldots, \langle a_m \rangle)$

Let A be another set with $\langle \_ \rangle : A \to \mathsf{Num}$. An m-ary function $f : A_1 \times \ldots A_m \to A$ is said to be *represented* by a formula $\textcircled{f} \in \mathsf{Fmla}_{m+1}$ if for all $(a_1, \ldots, a_m) \in A_1 \times \ldots \times A_m$:

- $\vdash \textcircled{f}(\langle a_1 \rangle, \ldots, \langle a_m \rangle, \langle f(a_1, \ldots, a_m) \rangle)$
- $\vdash \forall x, y. \ \textcircled{f}(\langle a_1 \rangle, \ldots, \langle a_m \rangle, x) \wedge \textcircled{f}(\langle a_1 \rangle, \ldots, \langle a_m \rangle, y) \to x \equiv y$

The notion of a function being represented is stronger than that of its graph being represented (as a relation)—but with enough deductive power they are equivalent [38, §16]. We will need an even stronger notion: A function f as above is *term-represented* by an operator $\textcircled{f} : \mathsf{Term}^m \to \mathsf{Term}$ if $\vdash \textcircled{f}(\langle a_1 \rangle, \ldots, \langle a_m \rangle) \equiv \langle f(a_1, \ldots, a_m) \rangle$ for all $(a_1, \ldots, a_m) \in A_1 \times \ldots \times A_m$. When the formula by which a relation/function P is represented or term-represented is irrelevant, we call P *representable* or *term-representable*.

We will also need an enhancement of relation representability: Given $i < m$, we call the representation of an m-ary relation R by $\textcircled{R}$ i-*clean* if $\vdash \neg \textcircled{R}(n_1, \ldots, n_m)$ for all numbers $n_1, \ldots, n_m$ such that n_i (the i'th number among them) is outside the image of $\langle \_ \rangle$ (i.e., there is no $a \in A_i$ with $n_i = \langle a \rangle$). Cleanness would be trivially satisfied if the encodings were surjective. However, surjectivity is not a reasonable assumption. For example, most of the numeric encodings used in the literature are injective but not surjective.

We let $\mathsf{S} : \mathsf{Fmla}_1 \to \mathsf{Sen}$ be the *self-substitution* function, which sends any $\varphi \in \mathsf{Fmla}_1$ to $\varphi(\langle \varphi \rangle)$, i.e., to the sentence obtained from φ by substituting the encoding of φ for the unique variable of φ. An alternative is the following "soft" version of S, which sends any $\varphi \in \mathsf{Fmla}_1$ to $\exists v_1. \ v_1 \equiv \langle \varphi \rangle \wedge \varphi$, where v_1 is the single free variable of φ. The soft version yields provably equivalent formulas and has the advantage that it is easier to represent inside the logic, since it does not require formalizing the complexities of capture-avoiding substitution. All our results involving S have been proved for both versions.

We will consider the properties $\mathsf{Repr}_\neg$, Repr_S, and $\mathsf{Repr}_\Vdash$, stating the representability of the functions $\neg$ and S, and of the relation $\Vdash$. In addition, $\mathsf{Clean}_\Vdash$ will state that the considered representation of $\Vdash$ is 1-clean, i.e., it is clean on the proof component. For the representing formulas for the above relations and functions we will use their circled names, $\ominus$, $\oplus$, etc.; for example, $\mathsf{Repr}_\Vdash$ means that (1) $p \Vdash \varphi$ implies $\vdash \oplus(\langle p \rangle, \langle \varphi \rangle)$ and (2) $p \nVdash \varphi$ implies $\vdash \neg\oplus(\langle p \rangle, \langle \varphi \rangle)$ for all $p \in \mathsf{Proof}$ and $\varphi \in \mathsf{Sen}$.

2.4   Derivability Conditions

Most of our assumptions refer to representability. An important exception is the provability relation $\vdash$, for which only a weakening of representability is reasonable. Let $\ominus \in \mathsf{Fmla}_1$ be the formula for this task. We consider the following assumptions about $\ominus$, known as the Hilbert-Bernays-Löb derivability conditions:

$\mathsf{HBL_1}$: $\vdash \varphi$ implies $\vdash \ominus\langle\varphi\rangle$ for all $\varphi \in \mathsf{Sen}$.
$\mathsf{HBL_2}$: $\vdash \ominus\langle\varphi\rangle \wedge \ominus\langle\varphi \to \psi\rangle \to \ominus\langle\psi\rangle$ for all $\varphi, \psi \in \mathsf{Sen}$.
$\mathsf{HBL_3}$: $\vdash \ominus\langle\varphi\rangle \to \ominus\langle\ominus\langle\varphi\rangle\rangle$ for all $\varphi \in \mathsf{Sen}$.

Above and elsewhere, to lighten notation we omit parentheses when instantiating one-variable formulas with encodings of formulas—e.g., writing $\ominus\langle\varphi\rangle$ instead of $\ominus(\langle\varphi\rangle)$.

$\mathsf{HBL_1}$ states that, if a sentence is provable, then its encoding is also provable inside the representation. $\mathsf{HBL_3}$ is roughly a formulation of $\mathsf{HBL_1}$ "one level up," inside the proof system $\vdash$. Finally, note that the provability relation is closed under *modus ponens*, in that $\vdash \varphi$ and $\vdash \varphi \to \psi$ implies $\vdash \psi$ for all $\varphi, \psi \in \mathsf{Sen}$. Thus, $\mathsf{HBL_2}$ roughly states the same property inside the proof system. In short, the derivability conditions state that the representation of provability acts partly similarly to the provability relation. Note that the representability of "proof of" implies $\mathsf{HBL_1}$, taking $\ominus(x)$ to be $\exists y. \circleddash(y, x)$.

Convention 2. We focus on the standard provability representation in this paper: Whenever we assume explicit proofs and representability of "proof of," the formula $\ominus$ will be defined from $\circleddash$ as shown above.

We will also be interested in the following variations of the derivability conditions:

$\mathsf{HBL_4}$: $\vdash \ominus\langle\varphi\rangle \wedge \ominus\langle\psi\rangle \to \ominus\langle\varphi \wedge \psi\rangle$ for all $\varphi, \psi \in \mathsf{Sen}$.
$\mathsf{HBL_1^\Leftarrow}$: $\vdash \ominus\langle\varphi\rangle$ implies $\vdash \varphi$ for all $\varphi \in \mathsf{Sen}$.
$\mathsf{SHBL_3}$: $\vdash \ominus(t) \to \ominus\langle\ominus(t)\rangle$ for all closed terms t.
$\mathsf{WHBL_2}$: $\vdash \varphi \to \psi$ implies $\vdash \ominus\langle\varphi\rangle \to \ominus\langle\psi\rangle$ for all $\varphi, \psi \in \mathsf{Sen}$.

$\mathsf{HBL_4}$ has a similar flavor as $\mathsf{HBL_2}$, but refers to conjunction: It states that the conjunction introduction rule holds inside the proof system. $\mathsf{HBL_1^\Leftarrow}$ is the converse of $\mathsf{HBL_1}$. Finally, $\mathsf{SHBL_3}$ is a strengthening of $\mathsf{HBL_3}$ holding for all closed terms and not only those that encode sentences, and (if we assume $\mathsf{HBL_1}$) $\mathsf{WHBL_2}$ is a weakening of $\mathsf{HBL_2}$.

2.5   Standard Models

We fix a unary relation $\models \subseteq \mathsf{Sen}$, representing *truth of a sentence in the standard model*. We write $\models \varphi$ instead of $\varphi \in \models$, and read it as "φ is true." We consider the assumptions:

$\mathsf{Syn}_\models$: Syntactic entities (logical connectives and quantifiers) handle truth as expected:

(1) $\not\models \perp$; (2) for all $\varphi, \psi \in \mathsf{Sen}$, $\models \varphi$ and $\models \varphi \to \psi$ imply $\models \psi$;

(3) for all $\varphi \in \mathsf{Fmla}_1$, if $\models \varphi(n)$ for all $n \in \mathsf{Num}$ then $\models \forall x. \varphi(x)$;

(4) for all $\varphi \in \mathsf{Fmla}_1$, if $\models \exists x. \varphi(x)$ then $\models \varphi(n)$ for some $n \in \mathsf{Num}$;

(5) for all $\varphi \in \mathsf{Sen}$, $\models \varphi$ or $\models \neg \varphi$.

Soundness (of provability with respect to truth): $\vdash \varphi$ implies $\models \varphi$ for all $\varphi \in \mathsf{Sen}$.

$\mathsf{Syn}_\models(1\text{--}4)$ only contains a partial description of the syntactic entities' behavior—corresponding to elimination rules for $\perp$, $\to$ and $\exists$ and introduction rule for $\forall$. For our results this suffices. $\mathsf{Syn}_\models(5)$ states that standard models decide every sentence.

On his way to formalizing $\mathcal{IT}_2$ for extensions of the HF set theory, after proving HBL_1 Paulson notes [27, p. 21]: "The reverse implication [namely $\mathsf{HBL}_1^{\Leftarrow}$], despite its usefulness, is not always proved." In his abstract account, Buldt also assumes $\mathsf{HBL}_1^{\Leftarrow}$ in his most general formulation of $\mathcal{IT}_1$ [5, Theorem 3.1]; that formulation has in mind not necessarily the standard provability representation (our Convention 2), but any formula that weakly represents $\vdash$, which is acceptable for $\mathcal{IT}_1$ but not for $\mathcal{IT}_2$ [2].

We avoid such an $\mathcal{IT}_1$ versus $\mathcal{IT}_2$ divergence by remaining focused on the standard provability representation. In this case, for arithmetics and related theories, $\mathsf{HBL}_1^{\Leftarrow}$ cannot be inferred without assuming soundness in the standard model (which Paulson does), or at least ω-consistency. We can depict the situation abstractly, without knowing what standard models look like:

Lemma 3. (1) Assume $\mathsf{Rel}_{\vdash}^{\Vdash}$, $\mathsf{Repr}_{\Vdash}$, $\mathsf{Clean}_{\Vdash}$ and OCon. Then $\mathsf{HBL}_1^{\Leftarrow}$ holds.

(2) Assume Soundness and $\mathsf{Syn}_\models(1, 2, 3)$. Then OCon holds.

(3) Assume $\mathsf{Rel}_{\vdash}^{\Vdash}$, $\mathsf{Repr}_{\Vdash}$, $\mathsf{Clean}_{\Vdash}$, Soundness and $\mathsf{Syn}_\models(1, 2, 4)$. Then $\models \ominus\langle\varphi\rangle$ implies $\vdash \varphi$ for all $\varphi \in \mathsf{Sen}$. In particular, $\mathsf{HBL}_1^{\Leftarrow}$ holds.

Thus, staying in a proof-theoretic world, ω-consistency ensures $\mathsf{HBL}_1^{\Leftarrow}$ if the "proof of" relation is cleanly represented (1). In turn, ω-consistency is ensured by minimal semantic requirements, including the soundness of provability (2). Finally, putting together representability and semantics, we can infer something stronger than $\mathsf{HBL}_1^{\Leftarrow}$: That the mere truth (and not just the provability) of a sentence's provability representation implies the provability of the sentence itself (3).

It follows from either points (1, 2) or point (3) of the lemma that, in the presence of standard models and soundness, clean representability of the "proof of" relation implies $\mathsf{HBL}_1^{\Leftarrow}$; and recall that it also implies HBL_1. So it implies an "iff" version of HBL_1: $\vdash \varphi$ if an only if $\vdash \ominus\langle\varphi\rangle$. Interestingly, a converse of this implication also holds. To state it, we initially assume there is no "outer" notion of proof (i.e., no set Proof and no relation $\Vdash$), but only an "inner" one, given by a formula $\mathsf{P} \in \mathsf{Fmla}_2$ such that:

$\mathsf{Rel}_{\ominus}^{\mathsf{P}}$: $\vdash \ominus\langle\varphi\rangle \longleftrightarrow \exists x. \mathsf{P}(x, \langle\varphi\rangle)$.

$\mathsf{Compl}_{\mathsf{P}}$: $\models \mathsf{P}(n, \langle\varphi\rangle)$ implies $\vdash \mathsf{P}(n, \langle\varphi\rangle)$ for all $n \in \mathsf{Num}$ and $\varphi \in \mathsf{Sen}$.

$\mathsf{Compl}_{\neg\mathsf{P}}$: $\models \neg \mathsf{P}(n, \langle\varphi\rangle)$ implies $\vdash \neg \mathsf{P}(n, \langle\varphi\rangle)$ for all $n \in \mathsf{Num}$ and $\varphi \in \mathsf{Sen}$.

$\mathsf{Rel}^{\mathsf{P}}_{\oplus}$ is the inner version of $\mathsf{Rel}^{\Vdash}_{\vdash}$: It expresses that, *inside the representation*, proofs and provability are connected as expected. $\mathsf{Compl_P}$ and $\mathsf{Compl_{\neg P}}$ state that provability is complete on P statements about formula encodings, as well as their negations; in traditional settings, this is true thanks to P being a bounded arithmetical formula ($\varDelta_0$). Now the converse result states that, thanks to (standard models and) the "iff" version of HBL_1, we can define an outer notion of proof that is represented by the inner notion P:

Lemma 4. Assume $\mathsf{Rel}^{\mathsf{P}}_{\oplus}$, $\mathsf{Compl_P}$, $\mathsf{Compl_{\neg P}}$, Soundness, $\mathsf{Syn}_{\models}(4,5)$, HBL_1 and $\mathsf{HBL}^{\Leftarrow}_1$. Take Proof = Num and define $\Vdash$ by $n \Vdash \varphi$ iff $\vdash \mathsf{P}(n, \langle\varphi\rangle)$. Then $\mathsf{Rel}^{\Vdash}_{\vdash}$, $\mathsf{Repr}_{\Vdash}$ and $\mathsf{Clean}_{\Vdash}$ hold, with $\Vdash$ being represented by P.

3 Abstract Incompleteness Theorems

After last section's preparations, we are now ready to discuss different versions of the incompleteness theorems and their major lemmas, based on alternative assumptions.

3.1 Diagonalization

The formula diagonalization technique (due to Gödel and Carnap [7]) yields "self-referential" sentences. All we need for it to work is the representability of substitution.

Proposition 5. Assuming $\mathsf{Repr_S}$, for all $\psi \in \mathsf{Fmla}_1$ there exists $\varphi \in \mathsf{Fmla}_1$ with $\vdash \varphi \longleftrightarrow \psi\langle\varphi\rangle$.

A sentence $\varphi \in \mathsf{Sen}$ is called a *Gödel sentence* if $\vdash \varphi \longleftrightarrow \neg \oplus\langle\varphi\rangle$; it is called a *Rosser sentence* if $\vdash \varphi \longleftrightarrow \neg(\exists x. \oplus(x, \langle\varphi\rangle) \wedge \mathsf{RosserTwist}(x, \langle\varphi\rangle))$, where we define $\mathsf{RosserTwist}(x, y) = \forall x'. x' \prec x \to \forall y'. \ominus(y, y') \to \neg \oplus(x', y')$. The existence of Gödel and Rosser sentences follows immediately from diagonalization.

Proposition 6. Assuming $\mathsf{Repr_S}$, there exist Gödel and Rosser sentences.

Thus, any Gödel sentence is provably equivalent to the negation of its own provability; in Gödel's words [13], it "says about itself that it is not provable." A Rosser sentence φ asserts its own unprovabilty in a weaker fashion: Rather than saying "Myself, φ, am not provable" (i.e., "it is not the case that there exists a proof p of φ"), it says "it is not the case that there exists a proof p of φ such that, for all smaller proofs q, q is not a proof of $\neg \varphi$." Here, "smaller" refers to the order the encoding of proofs as numerals imposes.

3.2   The Incompleteness Theorems

$\mathcal{IT}_1$ identifies sentences that are neither provable nor disprovable—which often holds for Gödel and Rosser sentences with the help of a provability relation satisfying HBL_1.

Proposition 7. Assume Con and HBL_1. Then $\nvdash$ G for all Gödel sentences G.

For showing that the Gödel sentences are not disprovable, a standard route is to assume explicit proofs, strengthen the consistency assumption to ω-consistency, and strengthen HBL_1 to representability of the "proof of" relation.

Proposition 8. Assume OCon, $\mathsf{Rel}_{\vdash}^{\Vdash}$, $\mathsf{Repr}_{\Vdash}$, $\mathsf{Clean}_{\Vdash}$. Then $\nvdash \neg$ G for all Gödel sentences G.

Proof. Let G be a Gödel sentence. We prove $\nvdash \neg$ G by contradiction. Assume (1) $\vdash \neg$ G.

- By consistency (which is implied by OCon), we obtain $\nvdash$ G.
- From this and $\mathsf{Rel}_{\vdash}^{\Vdash}$, we obtain $p \nVdash$ G for all $p \in$ Proof.
- From this, $\mathsf{Repr}_{\Vdash}$ and $\mathsf{Clean}_{\Vdash}$, we obtain $\vdash \neg \oplus(n, \langle G \rangle)$ for all $n \in$ Num.
- From this and OCon, we obtain $\nvdash \neg\neg \exists x.\ \oplus(x, \langle G \rangle)$, i.e., $\nvdash \neg\neg \ominus \langle G \rangle$.
- Hence, since G is a Gödel sentence, we obtain $\nvdash \neg$ G, which contradicts (1).

$\square$

While the line of reasoning in the above proof is mostly well-known, it contains two subtle points about which the literature is not explicit (due to the usual focus on classical first-order arithmetic and particular choices of encodings).

First, we must assume the representation of the "proof of" relation to be 1-*clean*, i.e., clean with respect to the proof component. Indeed, the argument crucially relies on converting the statement "$p \nVdash$ G for all $p \in$ Proof" into "$\vdash \neg \oplus(n, \langle G \rangle)$ for all $n \in$ Num," which is only possible for 1-clean encodings. This assumption will be repeatedly needed in later results. By contrast, cleanness is never required with respect to the sentence component of "proof of" or for the provability relation (which only involves sentence encodings). In short, cleanness is only needed for proofs, not for sentences.

Second, to reach the desired contradiction for our intuitionistic proof system $\vdash$, from "$\vdash \neg \oplus(n, \langle G \rangle)$ for all $n \in$ Num" it is not sufficient to employ standard ω-consistency, which would only give us $\nvdash \exists x.\ \oplus(x, \langle G \rangle)$, i.e., $\nvdash \ominus \langle G \rangle$; the last together with $\vdash$ G $\longleftrightarrow \neg \ominus \langle G \rangle$ would be insufficient for obtaining $\nvdash \neg$ G. However, our stronger version of ω-consistency, OCon, does the trick. $\mathcal{IT}_1$ now follows by putting together Propositions 6–8:

Theorem 9. ($\mathcal{IT}_1$) Assume OCon, $\mathsf{Rel}_{\vdash}^{\Vdash}$, $\mathsf{Repr}_{\Vdash}$, $\mathsf{Clean}_{\Vdash}$, and $\mathsf{Repr}_{\mathsf{S}}$. Then:

(1) There exists a Gödel sentence.   (2) $\nvdash$ G and $\nvdash \neg$ G for all Gödel sentences G.

Rosser's contribution to $\mathcal{IT}_1$ was an ingenious trick for weakening the ω-consistency assumption into plain consistency—as such, it is usually seen as a *strict improvement* over Gödel's version. While this is true for the concrete case of FOL theories extending arithmetic, from an abstract perspective the situation is more nuanced: The improvement is achieved at the cost of asking more from the logic. Our framework makes this trade-off clearly visible. The idea is to use Rosser sentences instead of Gödel sentences to "repair" the ω-consistency assumption of Theorem 9 (inherited from Proposition 8):

Theorem 10. ($\mathcal{IT}_1$ *à la* Rosser)   Assume Con, Ord$_1$, Ord$_2$, Repr$_\neg$, Rel$_\vdash^{\Vdash}$, Repr$_{\Vdash}$, Clean$_{\Vdash}$, and Repr$_S$. Then:

(1) There exists a Rosser sentence.
(2) $\nvdash$ R and $\nvdash \neg$ R for all Rosser sentences R.

Highlighted is the assumption trade-off between the two versions: Rosser's weakening of ω-consistency into consistency is paid by additionally assuming representability of negation and an order-like relation satisfying Ord$_1$ and Ord$_2$. Certainly, negation representability is not a big price, since for concrete logics this tends to be a lemma that is anyway needed when proving HBL$_1$. On the other hand, the ordering assumptions seem to be a significant generality gap in favor of Gödel's version. A clear manifestation of this gap is in our inference of a semantic version of $\mathcal{IT}_1$—which we obtain from Theorem 9 with the help of Lemmas 3(2) and 4:

Theorem 11. (Semantic $\mathcal{IT}_1$)   Assume Rel$_{(\models)}^{\mathsf{P}}$, Compl$_{\mathsf{P}}$, Compl$_{\neg\mathsf{P}}$, Soundness, Syn$_{\models}$, HBL$_1$, HBL$_1^{\Leftarrow}$, and Repr$_S$. Then:

(1) There exists a Gödel sentence.
(2) $\models$ G, $\nvdash$ G, and $\nvdash \neg$ G for all Gödel sentences G.

We have highlighted the assumptions specific to the semantic treatment. They replace OCon, Rel$_\vdash^{\Vdash}$, Repr$_{\Vdash}$ and Clean$_{\Vdash}$ from the proof-theoretic Theorem 9. Also highlighted is the additional fact concluded: that the Gödel sentences are true.

We have inferred the semantic version from Gödel's proof-theoretic version (Theorem 9), and not from Rosser's variation (Theorem 10). This is because in the semantic version ω-consistency comes for free (from Lemma 3(2)). By contrast, for deploying Rosser's version we would need to explicitly consider the order-like relation with its own hypotheses. This would have led to a *strictly less general* abstract result (if we ignore the difference in the way Gödel and Rosser sentences are actually defined).

The semantic $\mathcal{IT}_1$ relies on HBL$_1^{\Leftarrow}$. If we commit to classical logic (i.e., assume $\vdash \neg\neg\varphi \to \varphi$), we can more directly show, taking advantage of HBL$_1^{\Leftarrow}$, that the Gödel sentences are not disprovable, which immediately proves $\mathcal{IT}_1$:

Theorem 12. (Classical $\mathcal{IT}_1$) Assume classical logic, Con, HBL$_1$, HBL$_1^{\Leftarrow}$, Repr$_S$. Then:

(1) There exists a Gödel sentence.
(2) $\nvdash$ G and $\nvdash \neg$ G for all Gödel sentences G.

Classical logic also offers two alternatives to our semantic Theorem 11 (where the second is strictly more general than the first):

Theorem 13. (Classical Semantic $\mathcal{IT}_1$) The conclusions of Theorem 11 still hold if we assume classical logic and perform either of the following changes in its assumptions: (1) remove Compl$_{\neg P}$, or (2) replace Rel$_{\ominus}^P$, Compl$_P$ and Compl$_{\neg P}$ with "$\models \ominus\langle\varphi\rangle$ implies $\vdash \varphi$ for all $\varphi \in$ Sen."

Even though $\mathcal{IT}_1$ needs a predicate $\ominus$ that satisfies HBL$_1$ (and sometimes also HBL$_1^{\Leftarrow}$, meaning that it weakly represents provability), its conclusion, the existence of undecided sentences, is meaningful regardless of whether $\ominus$ *adequately expresses provability*. By contrast, the meaning of $\mathcal{IT}_2$'s conclusion, the theory cannot prove its own consistency, relies on this (non-mathematical) "intensional" assumption [2]. In this case, consistency is adequately expressed by the sentence $\neg \ominus\langle\bot\rangle$. The standard formulation (and proof) of $\mathcal{IT}_2$ uses all three derivability conditions:

Theorem 14. ($\mathcal{IT}_2$) Assume Con, HBL$_1$, HBL$_2$, HBL$_3$ and Repr$_S$. Then $\nvdash$ $\neg\ominus\langle\bot\rangle$.

3.3 Jeroslow's Approach

Next we study an alternative line of reasoning due to Jeroslow [17], often cited as a simplification of the canonical route to prove $\mathcal{IT}_2$ [33,38,39]. To study its features and pitfalls, we need some standard notation used by Jeroslow. A *pseudo-term* is a formula $\varphi \in$ Fmla$_{m+1}$ expressing a provably functional relation via "exists unique": $\vdash \forall x_1, \ldots, x_m. \exists! y. \varphi(x_1, \ldots, x_m, y)$. We only discuss the case $m = 2$; the general case is similar.

Notation 15. Given a pseudo-term $\varphi \in$ Fmla$_2$, we treat it as if it is a one-variable term:

– for any terms s and t, we write $t \equiv \varphi(s)$ instead of $\varphi(s, t)$;
– for any term s and formula $\psi \in$ Fmla$_1$, we write $\psi(\varphi(s))$ instead of $\exists y. \varphi(s, y) \wedge \psi(y)$.

This notation smoothly integrates pseudo-terms with terms: If $\vdash t \equiv \varphi(s)$ and $\vdash \psi(\varphi(s))$ then $\vdash \psi(t)$, where $\psi(t)$ denotes actual substitution of terms in formulas.

Jeroslow relies on an abstract class of m-ary functions, $\mathcal{F}_m \subseteq$ Num$^m \to$ Num, for all arities $m \in \mathbb{N}$, on which he considers the following assumptions:

$\mathsf{Repr}_{\mathcal{F}}$: Every $f \in \mathcal{F}_m$ is represented by some pseudo-term $⟨f⟩ \in \mathsf{Fmla}_{m+1}$ under the identity encoding $\mathsf{Num} \to \mathsf{Num}$.

CapN: Some $\mathsf{N} \in \mathcal{F}_1$ correctly captures negation: $\mathsf{N}⟨\varphi⟩ = ⟨\neg\varphi⟩$ for all $\varphi \in \mathsf{Sen}$.

CapSS: Some $\mathsf{ssap} : \mathsf{Fmla}_1 \to \mathcal{F}_1$ correctly captures substituted self-application: $\mathsf{ssap}\,\psi\,⟨f⟩ = ⟨\psi(f⟨f⟩)⟩$ for all $\psi \in \mathsf{Fmla}_1$ and $f \in \mathcal{F}_1$.

In CapSS, following Jeroslow we employed Notation 15 taking advantage of the fact that $⟨f⟩$ are pseudo-terms: The highlighted text denotes $\exists y.\ ⟨f⟩(⟨⟨f⟩⟩, y) \wedge \psi(y)$. Moreover, using the same notation, the statement of $\mathsf{Repr}_{\mathcal{F}}$ for some $f \in \mathcal{F}_1$ and $n \in \mathsf{Num}$ would be written as $\vdash f(n) \equiv ⟨f⟩(n)$. Similarly, combining CapN with the instance of $\mathsf{Repr}_{\mathcal{F}}$, we obtain a fact that can be written as $\vdash ⟨\neg\varphi⟩ \equiv \mathsf{N}⟨\varphi⟩$.

When our logical theory is a recursive extension of Robinson arithmetic and $\mathsf{Num} = \mathbb{N}$, $\mathcal{F}_m$ could be the set of m-ary computable functions. Then every $f \in \mathcal{F}_m$ would indeed be represented by a formula $⟨f⟩$. Moreover, assuming a computable and injective encoding of formulas, $⟨\_⟩ : \mathsf{Fmla}_1 \to \mathbb{N}$, we can take $\mathsf{N} : \mathbb{N} \to \mathbb{N}$ to be the following computable function: Given input n, it checks if n has the form $⟨\varphi⟩$; if so, it returns $⟨\neg\varphi⟩$; if not, it returns any value (e.g., 0). And $\mathsf{ssap}\,\psi$ can be defined similarly, obtaining the desired property for every $\varphi \in \mathsf{Fmla}_2$, not necessarily of the form $⟨f⟩$. In short, Jeroslow's assumptions cover arithmetic (but also potentially many other systems).

At the heart of Jeroslow's approach lies an alternative diagonalization technique, producing *term* fixpoints, not just formula fixpoints:

Lemma 16. Assume CapSS and $\mathsf{Repr}_{\mathcal{F}}$ and let $\psi \in \mathsf{Fmla}_1$. Then there exists a closed pseudo-term t such that $\vdash t \equiv ⟨\psi(t)⟩$. Moreover, taking $\varphi = \psi(t)$, we have $\vdash \varphi \longleftrightarrow \psi⟨\varphi⟩$.

Proof. Let $f = \mathsf{ssap}\,\psi$ and $t = ⟨f⟩⟨⟨f⟩⟩$. From CapSS, we obtain $f⟨f⟩ = ⟨\psi(f⟨f⟩)⟩$. From this and $\mathsf{Repr}_{\mathcal{F}}$, we obtain $\vdash ⟨f⟩⟨f⟩ \equiv ⟨\psi(f⟨f⟩)⟩$, i.e., $\vdash t \equiv ⟨\psi(t)⟩$. With the equality rules, we obtain $\vdash \psi(t) \longleftrightarrow \psi(⟨\psi(t)⟩)$, i.e., $\vdash \varphi \longleftrightarrow \psi⟨\varphi⟩$. $\square$

This lemma offers us Gödel and Rosser sentences, which can be used like in Sects. 3.1 and 3.2, leading to corresponding variants of $\mathcal{IT}_1$. But Jeroslow's main innovation affects $\mathcal{IT}_2$: While traditionally $\mathcal{IT}_2$ requires all three derivability conditions, Jeroslow's version does not make use of the second, HBL_2:

Theorem 17. ($\mathcal{IT}_2$ *à la* Jeroslow) Assume Con, HBL_1, $\boxed{\mathsf{SHBL}_3}$, $\mathsf{Repr}_{\mathcal{F}}$, CapN, CapSS. Then $\boxed{\nvdash \mathsf{jcon}}$, where jcon denotes $\forall x.\ \neg(⊕(x) \wedge ⊕(\mathsf{N}(x)))$.

Like with Rosser's trick, we analyze this innovation's trade-offs from an abstract perspective. A first trade-off is in the employment of a stronger version of the third condition, SHBL_3 (extended to affect all closed pseudo-terms via Notation 15). Another is in the way consistency is expressed in the logic. Jeroslow does not conclude $\nvdash \neg⊕⟨\bot⟩$, but something more elaborate, namely

$\nvdash$ jcon. While the formula $\neg \ominus \langle \perp \rangle$ internalizes the statement $\nvdash \perp$, jcon internalizes the equivalent statement "for all φ, it is not the case that $\vdash \varphi$ and $\vdash \neg \varphi$." But are the internalizations themselves equivalent, i.e., is it the case that $\vdash \neg \ominus \langle \perp \rangle$ iff $\vdash$ jcon? This surely holds for many concrete logics, but it is one direction that we can infer logic-independently: Assuming HBL_1, $\mathsf{Repr}_{\mathcal{F}}$ and CapN, $\vdash$ jcon implies $\vdash \neg \ominus \langle \perp \rangle$. And it seems we cannot infer the other direction without knowing what $\ominus$ looks like more concretely. Therefore, $\nvdash \neg \ominus \langle \perp \rangle$, the conclusion of the original $\mathcal{IT}_2$, is *abstractly stronger than*, hence *preferable to* $\nvdash$ jcon. In short, Jeroslow somewhat weakens the theorem's conclusion.

Let us now look at (a slight rephrasing of) Jeroslow's proof:

Proof of Theorem 17. We assume (1) $\vdash$ jcon and aim to reach a contradiction.

- Applying Lemma 16 to $\ominus(\mathbb{N}(x))$, obtain a closed term t where (2) $\vdash t \equiv \langle \ominus(\mathbb{N}(t)) \rangle$.
- By SHBL_3 applied to $\mathbb{N}(t)$, we obtain $\vdash \ominus(\mathbb{N}(t)) \to \ominus\langle \ominus(\mathbb{N}(t)) \rangle$.
- From (2) and the equality rules, we obtain $\vdash \ominus(\mathbb{N}(t)) \to \ominus(\mathbb{N}\langle \ominus(\mathbb{N}(t)) \rangle)$.
- The last two facts give us $\vdash \varphi \to \ominus\langle \varphi \rangle \wedge \ominus(\mathbb{N}\langle \varphi \rangle)$, where φ denotes $\ominus(\mathbb{N}(t))$.
- On the other hand, (1) instantiated with $\langle \varphi \rangle$ gives us $\vdash \neg(\ominus\langle \varphi \rangle \wedge \ominus(\mathbb{N}\langle \varphi \rangle))$.
- From the last two facts, we obtain (3) $\vdash \neg \varphi$.
- With HBL_1, we obtain $\vdash \ominus\langle \neg \varphi \rangle$ and with CapN and $\mathsf{Repr}_{\mathcal{F}}$, we obtain $\vdash \ominus(\mathbb{N}\langle \varphi \rangle)$.
- From (2) and the equality rules, we obtain $\vdash \ominus(\mathbb{N}\langle \ominus(\mathbb{N}(t)) \rangle) \to \ominus(\mathbb{N}(t))$, i.e., $\vdash \ominus(\mathbb{N}\langle \varphi \rangle) \to \varphi$
- From the last two facts, we obtain $\vdash \varphi$. With (3) this contradicts (1). $\square$

A first major observation is that, under the stated assumptions, the above proof is *incorrect*. It uses an implicit assumption, hidden under Notation 15: When we disambiguate the notation, we see that Lemma 16 gives us a pseudo-term t that does not exactly satisfy (1) $\vdash t \equiv \langle \psi(t) \rangle$ (which is what the theorem's proof needs), but something weaker, namely (2) $\vdash t \equiv \langle \chi \rangle$, where χ is $\vdash \exists x.\ \mathcal{J}(\langle \langle \mathcal{J} \rangle, x) \wedge \psi(x)$. And although $\vdash \chi \longleftrightarrow \psi(t)$, we still cannot infer (1) from (2), unless *the encodings of provably equivalent formulas are assumed provably equal.* But this assumption is unreasonable: Usually formula equivalence is undecidable, so no computable encoding can achieve that. (Incidentally, this problem is also the reason why we need SHBL_3 instead of HBL_3: In the proof's application of SHBL_3 to obtain $\vdash \ominus(\mathbb{N}(t)) \to \ominus\langle \ominus(\mathbb{N}(t)) \rangle$, we cannot work with $\langle \neg \varphi \rangle$ instead of $\mathbb{N}(t)$, even though $\vdash \langle \neg \varphi \rangle \equiv \mathbb{N}(t)$.)

To repair that, we can replace representation by pseudo-terms with actual term-representation. More precisely (also factoring in the observation that Jeroslow's proof does not need $\mathcal{F}_n$ for all n, but $\mathcal{F}_1$ suffices), we change $\mathsf{Repr}_{\mathcal{F}}$ into:

$\mathsf{Repr}_{\mathcal{F}}$: Every $f \in \mathcal{F}_1$ is term-represented, under the identity encoding $\mathsf{Num} \to \mathsf{Num}$, by some $\widehat{f}$ taken from a set $\mathsf{Ops} \subseteq (\mathsf{Term} \to \mathsf{Term})$ for which an encoding as numerals $\langle \_ \rangle : \mathsf{Ops} \to \mathsf{Num}$ is given, and such that $\mathsf{FVars}(g(t)) = \mathsf{FVars}(t)$ and $(g(t))[s/x] = g(t[s/x])$ for all $g \in \mathsf{Ops}$, $s, t \in \mathsf{Term}$ and $x \in \mathsf{Var}$.

(In concrete logics, the elements of Ops can be constructors or derived operators on terms.) Then CapSS, Lemma 16, and all proofs work with terms rather than pseudo-terms and everything becomes formally correct. In summary, Jeroslow's approach to $\mathcal{IT}_2$ seems to fail for pseudo-terms representing computable functions, but to require actual terms. This usually means that the logic has built-in Skolem symbols and axioms.

Finally, let us see what it takes to alleviate the second trade-off: from $\nvdash$ jcon to the more desirable $\nvdash \neg \ominus \langle \bot \rangle$. We see that Theorem 17's proof uses $\vdash$ jcon not at jcon's full generality but only instantiated with formula encodings, which thanks to Repr$_\mathcal{F}$ and CapN would follow from (*) $\vdash \neg (\ominus \langle \varphi \rangle \wedge \ominus \langle \neg \varphi \rangle)$. And it only takes WHBL$_2$ (a weaker version of HBL$_2$) and HBL$_4$ to prove $\vdash (\ominus \langle \varphi \rangle \wedge \ominus \langle \neg \varphi \rangle) \rightarrow \ominus \langle \bot \rangle$, allowing us to infer (*) from $\vdash \neg \ominus \langle \bot \rangle$; meaning that the latter could have been used. We obtain:

Theorem 18. If in the (corrected) Theorem 17 we additionally assume WHBL$_2$ and HBL$_4$, its conclusion can be upgraded to $\nvdash \neg \ominus \langle \bot \rangle$.

Whether WHBL$_2$ and HBL$_4$ are a good trade-off for HBL$_2$ will of course depend on the logic's specificity, in particular, on its primitive rules of inference.

Jeroslow presented his approach for an abstract logical theory over a FOL language, which is not necessarily a FOL theory—so it found a natural fit in our generic framework. To our knowledge, very few subsequent authors present Jeroslow's approach rigorously, and none at its original level of generality. Smith's monograph gives a rigorous account for arithmetic [38, §33], silently performing the correction we have shown here, but failing to detect the need for SHBL$_3$ instead of HBL$_3$ (which Jeroslow had noticed). A mechanical prover is of invaluable help with detecting such nuances and pitfalls.

Summary. Using our generic infrastructure (Sect. 2), we have formally proved several abstract incompleteness results. They include four versions of $\mathcal{IT}_1$:

- Gödel's original $\mathcal{IT}_1$ (Theorem 9) and an $\mathcal{IT}_1$ based on classical logic (Theorem 12) required the formalization of some well-known arguments without change.
- Rosser's $\mathcal{IT}_1$ (Theorem 10) involved the generalization of a well-known argument: distilling two abstract conditions, Ord$_1$ and Ord$_2$.
- Novel semantic variants of $\mathcal{IT}_1$ (Theorems 11 and 13) were born from abstractly connecting standard models, the "iff" version of HBL$_1$ and proof representability.

They also include two versions of $\mathcal{IT}_2$:

- The standard $\mathcal{IT}_2$ based on the three derivability conditions (Theorem 14) again only required formalizing a well-known argument.
- The alternative, Jeroslow-style $\mathcal{IT}_2$ (Theorems 17 and 18) involved a detailed analysis and correction of an existing abstract result.

4 Instances of the Abstract Results

We first validate the assumptions about our abstract logic and arithmetic:

Proposition 19. (1) Any FOL theory that extends Robinson arithmetic or the
HF set theory satisfies all the axioms in our logical and arithmetical substrata
(in Sects. 2.1 and 2.2).

(2) If, in addition, the theory is sound, then, together with its corresponding
standard model, it also satisfies all our model-theoretic axioms (in Sect. 2.5).

In particular, point (2) shows that our discussion of standard models applies
equally well to $\mathbb{N}$ and the datatype of HF sets. (In the latter case, Num becomes
the entire set of closed terms, so that numerals can denote arbitrary HF sets. This
shows the versatility of our abstract concept of numeral.) Then we instantiate
three of our main theorems:

Theorem 20. (1) Any FOL theory that extends the HF set theory with a finite
set of axioms and is sound in the standard HF set model satisfies the hypothe-
ses of Theorems 13 and 14. Hence $\mathcal{IT}_1$ (semantic version) and $\mathcal{IT}_2$ hold for it.

(2) Any FOL theory that extends the HF set theory with a finite set of axioms
and is consistent satisfies Theorem 14's hypotheses. Hence $\mathcal{IT}_2$ holds for it.

These instances are heavily based on the lemmas proved by Paulson in his
formalization of $\mathcal{IT}_1$ and $\mathcal{IT}_2$ [26,27], who follows and corrects Świerczkowski's
detailed informal account [40]. Point (1) is a restatement of Paulson's formalized
results: theorems *Goedel_I* and *Goedel_II* in [27]. (His theorems also assume consistency, but that is redundant: Consistency follows from his underlying soundness assumption.)

By contrast, point (2) is an upgrade of Paulson's *Goedel_II*, applicable to
any consistent, though possibly unsound theory. This stronger version is in fact
$\mathcal{IT}_2$'s standard form, free from any model-theoretic considerations. Paulson had
proved both HBL_1 and $\mathsf{HBL}_1^{\Leftarrow}$ taking advantage of soundness, so we needed to
discard $\mathsf{HBL}_1^{\Leftarrow}$ and re-prove HBL_1 by replacing any semantic arguments with
proofs within the HF calculus. We also removed all invocations of a convenient
"truth implies provability for Σ-sentences" lemma, which depended on soundness
due to Paulson's choice of Σ-sentence definition.

This instantiation process has offered important feedback into the abstract
results. A formal development such as ours is (largely) immune to reasoning
errors, but not to missing out on useful pieces of generality. We experienced this
firsthand with our assumptions about substitution. An *a priori* natural choice
was to assume representability of the numeral substitution $\mathsf{Sb} : \mathsf{Fmla}_1 \times \mathsf{Num} \to$
Sen (defined as $\mathsf{Sb}(\varphi, n) = \varphi(n)$), part of which means $(1) \vdash \circledS\mathsf{b}(\langle\varphi\rangle, n, \mathsf{Sb}(\varphi, n))$.
But Paulson had instead proved $(2) \vdash \circledS\mathsf{b}(\langle\varphi\rangle, \langle n \rangle, \mathsf{Sb}(\varphi, n))$. The key difference
from (1) is that (2) applies the term encoding function $\langle\_\rangle : \mathsf{Term} \to \mathsf{Num}$ to
numerals as well (as particular terms); and since his $\langle\_\rangle$ function is injective, it is
far from the case that $\langle n \rangle = n$ for all numerals n. Paulson's version makes more
sense than ours when building the results bottom-up: Representability should not

discriminate numerals, but filter them through the encodings like other terms. However, top-down our version also made sense: It yielded the incompleteness theorems under reasonable assumptions, which do hold, by the way, for the HF set theory—even though in a bottom-up development one is unlikely to prove them. We resolved this discrepancy through a common denominator: the representability of self-substitution $S : \mathsf{Fmla}_1 \to \mathsf{Sen}$ (Sect. 2.3), which made our results more general.

Paulson's formalization has also inspired our abstract treatment of standard models (Sect. 2.5). Since Paulson proves $\mathsf{HBL}_1^{\Leftarrow}$ and uses classical logic, an obvious "port of entry" of his $\mathcal{IT}_2$ into our framework is Theorem 12. But this theorem tells us nothing about the Gödel sentences' truth. Delving deeper into Paulson's proof, we noted that he (unconventionally) completely avoids $\mathsf{Repr}_{\Vdash}$, and does not even define $\Vdash$. This raised the question of whether $\mathsf{HBL}_1^{\Leftarrow}$ and $\mathsf{Repr}_{\Vdash}$ are somehow interchangeable in the presence of standard models—and we found that they indeed are, under mild assumptions about truth. Incidentally, these assumptions were also sufficient for establishing the Gödel sentences' truth, leading to our semantic $\mathcal{IT}_1$ (Theorem 11). However, Theorem 11 was not easy to instantiate to Paulson's $\mathcal{IT}_1$. All its assumptions were easy to prove, except for $\mathsf{Compl}_{\neg P}$. Whereas Paulson proved that his proof-of predicate is a Σ-formula (which implies Compl_P by Σ-completeness), he did not prove the same for its negation (which would imply $\mathsf{Compl}_{\neg P}$). We are confident that this is true (any reasonable proof-of predicate is a Δ-formula), but we leave the laborious formal proof of this fact as future work. Instead, we recovered Paulson's result as an instance of our Theorem 13.

As future work, we will consider even more general variants of our semantic Theorems 11 and 13, as in Smorynski's account [39]: by distinguishing between a sound "base" provability relation $\vdash_0$ and an extension $\vdash$ only required to be consistent or ω-consistent. For example, $\vdash_0$ could be deduction in HF set theory or a weaker theory and $\vdash$ deduction in a consistent (not necessarily sound) extension of the HF set theory. This two-layered approach would have also benefited Paulson's original formalization.

Many other logics and logical theories satisfy our theorems' assumptions. We do *not* require the logic to be reducible to a single syntactic category of formulas, Fmla, a single syntactic judgment, $\vdash$, etc.; but only that such (well-behaved) formulas, provability relation, etc. are identifiable as part of that logic, e.g., localized to a given type and/or relativised by a given predicate. This allows our framework to capture most variants of higher-order logic and type theory (including the variant underlying Isabelle/HOL itself [21, 22]), and also, we believe, many of the logics surveyed by Buldt [5], including non-classical and fuzzy. But enabling "mass instantiation" that is both formal and painless requires more progress on the agenda we started here: recognizing reusable construction and proof patterns and formalizing them as abstract results.

Acknowledgments. We thank Bernd Buldt for his patient explanations on material in his monograph, and the reviewers for insightful comments and suggestions.

References

1. Ammon, K.: An automatic proof of Gödel's incompleteness theorem. Artif. Intell. **61**(2), 291–306 (1993)
2. Auerbach, D.: Intensionality and the Gödel theorems. Philos. Stud. Int. J. Philos. Anal. Tradit. **48**(3), 337–351 (1985)
3. Blanchette, J.C., Popescu, A., Traytel, D.: Unified classical logic completeness. In: Demri, S., Kapur, D., Weidenbach, C. (eds.) IJCAR 2014. LNCS (LNAI), vol. 8562, pp. 46–60. Springer, Cham (2014). https://doi.org/10.1007/978-3-319-08587-6_4
4. Boolos, G.: The Logic of Provability. Cambridge University Press, Cambridge (1993)
5. Buldt, B.: The scope of Gödel's first incompleteness theorem. Log. Univers. **8**(3), 499–552 (2014)
6. Bundy, A., Giunchiglia, F., Villafiorita, A., Walsh, T.: An incompleteness theorem via abstraction. Technical report, Istituto per la Ricerca Scientifica e Tecnologica, Trento (1996)
7. Carnap, R.: Logische syntax der sprache. Philos. Rev. **44**(4), 394–397 (1935)
8. Davis, M.: The Undecidable: Basic Papers on Undecidable Propositions, Unsolvable Problems, and Computable Functions. Dover Publication, Mineola (1965)
9. Diaconescu, R.: Institution-Independent Model Theory, 1st edn. Birkhäuser, Basel (2008)
10. Feferman, S., Dawson Jr., J.W., Kleene, S.C., Moore, G.H., Solovay, R.M., van Heijenoort, J. (eds.): Kurt Gödel: Collected Works. Vol. 1: Publications 1929–1936. Oxford University Press, Oxford (1986)
11. Fiore, M.P., Plotkin, G.D., Turi, D.: Abstract syntax and variable binding. In: Logic in Computer Science (LICS) 1999, pp. 193–202. IEEE Computer Society (1999)
12. Gabbay, M.J., Mathijssen, A.: Nominal (universal) algebra: equational logic with names and binding. J. Log. Comput. **19**(6), 1455–1508 (2009)
13. Gödel, K.: Über formal unentscheidbare Sätze der Principia Mathematica und verwandter Systeme I. Monatshefte für Mathematik und Physik **38**(1), 173–198 (1931)
14. Goguen, J.A., Burstall, R.M.: Institutions: abstract model theory for specification and programming. J. ACM **39**(1), 95–146 (1992)
15. Harrison, J.: HOL light proof of Gödel's first incompleteness theorem. http://code.google.com/p/hol-light/, directory Arithmetic
16. Hilbert, D., Bernays, P.: Grundlagen der Mathematik, vol. II. Springer, Heidelberg (1939)
17. Jeroslow, R.G.: Redundancies in the Hilbert-Bernays derivability conditions for Gödel's second incompleteness theorem. J. Symb. Log. **38**(3), 359–367 (1973)
18. Kaliszyk, C., Urban, J.: HOL(y)Hammer: online ATP service for HOL light. Math. Comput. Sci. **9**(1), 5–22 (2015)
19. Kikuchi, M., Kurahashi, T.: Generalizations of Gödel's incompleteness theorems for $\sum$ n-definable theories of arithmetic. Rew. Symb. Logic **10**(4), 603–616 (2017)
20. Kossak, R.: Mathematical Logic. SGTP, vol. 3. Springer, Cham (2018). https://doi.org/10.1007/978-3-319-97298-5
21. Kunčar, O., Popescu, A.: A consistent foundation for Isabelle/HOL. In: Urban, C., Zhang, X. (eds.) ITP 2015. LNCS, vol. 9236, pp. 234–252. Springer, Cham (2015). https://doi.org/10.1007/978-3-319-22102-1_16

22. Kunčar, O., Popescu, A.: Comprehending Isabelle/HOL's consistency. In: Yang, H. (ed.) ESOP 2017. LNCS, vol. 10201, pp. 724–749. Springer, Heidelberg (2017). https://doi.org/10.1007/978-3-662-54434-1_27
23. Löb, M.: Solution of a problem of Leon Henkin. J. Symb. Log. **20**(2), 115–118 (1955)
24. Nipkow, T., Wenzel, M., Paulson, L.C. (eds.): Isabelle/HOL. LNCS, vol. 2283. Springer, Heidelberg (2002). https://doi.org/10.1007/3-540-45949-9
25. O'Connor, R.: Essential incompleteness of arithmetic verified by Coq. In: Hurd, J., Melham, T. (eds.) TPHOLs 2005. LNCS, vol. 3603, pp. 245–260. Springer, Heidelberg (2005). https://doi.org/10.1007/11541868_16
26. Paulson, L.C.: A machine-assisted proof of Gödel's incompleteness theorems for the theory of hereditarily finite sets. Rew. Symb. Logic **7**(3), 484–498 (2014)
27. Paulson, L.C.: A mechanised proof of Gödel's incompleteness theorems using Nominal Isabelle. J. Autom. Reason. **55**(1), 1–37 (2015)
28. Paulson, L.C., Blanchette, J.C.: Three years of experience with Sledgehammer, a practical link between automatic and interactive theorem provers. In: The 8th International Workshop on the Implementation of Logics, IWIL 2010, Yogyakarta, Indonesia, 9 October 2011, pp. 1–11 (2010)
29. Popescu, A., Roşu, G.: Term-generic logic. Theor. Comput. Sci. **577**, 1–24 (2015)
30. Popescu, A., Traytel, D.: A formally verified abstract account of Gödel's incompleteness theorems (extended report) (2019). https://bitbucket.org/traytel/abstract_incompleteness/downloads/report.pdf
31. Popescu, A., Traytel, D.: Formalization associated with this paper (2019). https://bitbucket.org/traytel/abstract_incompleteness/
32. Quaife, A.: Automated proofs of Löb's theorem and Gödel's two incompleteness theorems. J. Autom. Reason. **4**(2), 219–231 (1988)
33. Raatikainen, P.: Gödel's incompleteness theorems. In: The Stanford Encyclopedia of Philosophy. Metaphysics Research Lab, Stanford University (2018)
34. Schlichtkrull, A., Blanchette, J.C., Traytel, D., Waldmann, U.: Formalizing Bachmair and Ganzinger's ordered resolution prover. In: Galmiche, D., Schulz, S., Sebastiani, R. (eds.) IJCAR 2018. LNCS (LNAI), vol. 10900, pp. 89–107. Springer, Cham (2018). https://doi.org/10.1007/978-3-319-94205-6_7
35. Shankar, N.: Metamathematics, Machines, and Gödel Proof. Cambridge University Press, Cambridge (1994)
36. Sieg, W.: Elementary proof theory. Technical report, Institute for Mathematical Studies in the Social Sciences, Stanford (1978)
37. Sieg, W., Field, C.: Automated search for Gödel's proofs. Ann. Pure Appl. Logic **133**(1–3), 319–338 (2005)
38. Smith, P.: An Introduction to Gödel's Incompleteness Theorems. Cambridge University Press, Cambridge (2007)
39. Smorynski, C.: The incompleteness theorems. In: Barwise, J. (ed.) Handbook of Mathematical Logic, pp. 821–865. North-Holland, Amsterdam (1977)
40. Świerczkowski, S.: Finite sets and Gödel incompleteness theorems. Diss. Math. **422**, 1–58 (2003)
41. Tarski, A., Mostowski, A., Robinson, R.: Undecidable Theories. Studies in Logic and the Foundations of Mathematics. North-Holland, Amsterdam (1953). 3rd edn. 1971

Old or Heavy? Decaying Gracefully
with Age/Weight Shapes

Michael Rawson$^{(\boxtimes)}$ and Giles Reger

University of Manchester, Manchester, UK
`michael@rawsons.uk`

Abstract. Modern saturation theorem provers are based on the given-clause algorithm, which iteratively selects new clauses to process. This clause selection has a large impact on the performance of proof search and has been the subject of much folklore. The standard approach is to alternate between selecting the *oldest* clause and the *lightest* clause with a fixed, but configurable *age/weight ratio* (AWR). An optimal fixed value of this ratio is shown to produce proofs significantly more quickly on a given problem, and further that varying AWR during proof search can improve upon a fixed ratio. Several new modes for the Vampire prover which vary AWR according to a "shape" during proof search are developed based on these observations. The modes solve a number of new problems in the TPTP benchmark set.

1 Introduction

Currently, the most successful theorem provers (such as Vampire [4], E [12], and SPASS [17]) for first-order logic are saturation-based, utilising the well-known *given-clause algorithm*. Simply, this algorithm *saturates* a set of clauses by iteratively selecting a clause and performing all non-redundant inferences with it until all clauses have been selected or the empty clause (witnessing inconsistency) has been found. Clearly, the order in which clauses are selected is key to the performance of the algorithm. Over the past few decades a certain amount of folklore has built up around the best methods for clause selection and recent work by Schulz and Möhrmann [13] systematically studied these. Our work extends this study with new results and also introduces the concept of a *variable* clause selection strategy (one that changes over time), instantiated with two simple patterns (or *shapes*) that prove to be pragmatically useful.

Clause selection strategies that alternate between selecting clauses based on age (i.e. in a first-in-first-out manner) and weight (i.e. those with the fewest symbols first) are the subject of this work. It was confirmed by Schulz and Möhrmann that alternating these two heuristics outperforms either by itself. The ratio of these selections is the *age/weight ratio* (AWR), as this is the terminology employed by the Vampire theorem prover, the vehicle for our study.

After covering relevant background material in Sect. 2 the remainder of the paper makes two main contributions. Firstly, Sect. 3 experimentally confirms the

© Springer Nature Switzerland AG 2019
P. Fontaine (Ed.): CADE 2019, LNAI 11716, pp. 462–476, 2019.
https://doi.org/10.1007/978-3-030-29436-6_27

folklore that (i) the choice of age/weight ratio often has a significant effect on the performance of proof search, and (ii) there is no "best" age/weight ratio: indeed, a large range of pragmatically useful ratios exist. Section 4.1 demonstrates that varying the age-weight ratio over time can achieve better performance than a fixed ratio, and therefore motivates the addition of so-called *age/weight shapes* for varying the ratio over time. Experiments (Sect. 5) with these new options implemented in the Vampire theorem prover show a significant improvement in coverage, proving many new problems unsolvable by any previous configuration of Vampire.

2 Background

This section introduces the relevant background for the rest of the paper.

First-Order Logic and Weight. Our setting is the standard first-order predicate logic with equality. A formal definition of this logic is not required for this paper but an important notion is that of the *weight* of a clause. In first-order logic, terms are built from function symbols and variables, literals are built from terms, and clauses are disjunctions of literals. The weight of a term/literal is the number of symbols (function, variable, or predicate) occurring in it. The weight of a clause is the sum of the weights of its literals.

Saturation-Based Proof Search. Saturation-based theorem provers *saturate* a set of clauses S with respect to an inference system $\mathbb{I}$: that is, computing a set of clauses S' by applying rules in $\mathbb{I}$ to clauses in S until no new clauses are generated. If the empty clause is generated then S is unsatisfiable. Calculi such as resolution and superposition have conditions that ensure *completeness*, which means that a saturated set S is satisfiable if it does not contain the empty clause as an element. As first-order logic is only semi-decidable, it is not necessarily the case that S has a finite saturation, and even if it does it may be unachievable in practice using the available resources. Therefore, much effort in saturation-based first-order theorem proving involves controlling proof search to make finding the empty clause more likely (within reasonable resource bounds). One important notion is that of *redundancy*, being able to remove clauses from the search space that are not required. Another important notion are literal selections that place restrictions on the inferences that can be performed. Both notions come with additional requirements for completeness. Vampire often gives up these requirements for pragmatic reasons (incomplete strategies have been found to be more efficient than complete ones in certain cases) and in such cases the satisfiability of S upon saturation is *unknown*.

The Given Clause Algorithm and AWR Clause Selection. To achieve saturation, the *given clause algorithm* organises the set of clauses into two sets: the *active* clauses are those that have been active in inferences, and the *passive* clauses are those that have not. Typically, a further *unprocessed* set is required in order to manage the clauses produced during a single iteration of the loop. Realisations of the given clause algorithm generally differ in how they organise simplifications. There are two main approaches (both implemented by Vampire, originally found in the eponymous theorem provers Otter [5] and DISCOUNT [1]): the Otter loop uses both *active* and *passive* for simplifications, whereas the Discount loop uses only *active*.

The algorithm is centred around the *clause selection* process. As previously mentioned, there are two main heuristics for this:

- *By Age (or First-in/First-out)* clause selection prefers the oldest clause (produced earlier in proof search), simulating a *breadth-first* search of the clause space. In Vampire the age of a clause is the number of inferences performed to produce it (input clauses have age 0).
- *By Weight (or symbol-counting)* clause selection prefers the lightest clause. The intuition behind this approach is that the sought empty clause has zero symbols and lighter clauses are in some sense closer to this. Furthermore, lighter clauses are more general in terms of subsumption and tend to have fewer children, making them less explosive in terms of proof search.

Schulz and Möhrmann show that alternating these heuristics is beneficial. In Vampire this alternation is achieved by an age/weight ratio (AWR) implemented by a simple *balancing* algorithm. The balance is initialised to 0 and used as follows: a negative balance means that a clause should be selected by age, whereas a positive balance means that a clause should be selected by weight; given a ratio of $a : w$ the balance is incremented by a when selecting by age and decremented by w when selecting by weight. Figure 1 gives the Discount algorithm along with balance-based AWR clause selection. The lines relevant to clause selection are marked with ✓.

Portfolio Solvers. Vampire is a portfolio solver and is typically run in a mode that attempts multiple different *strategies* in quick succession, e.g. in a 30 s run it may attempt 10 or more different strategies, and may run these in parallel with different priorities [8]. These strategies employ many different options including different saturation algorithms (including Otter and Discount), preprocessing options, literal selection strategies, inference rules, and clause selection heuristics. The portfolio mode is a significant improvement on any single strategy.

Vampire's portfolio mode also includes an additional option relevant to clause selection: the `--nongoal_weight_coefficient` option specifies a multiplier to apply to the weight of non-goal clauses, thus preferring clauses in or derived from the problem conjecture in clause selection. Use of this heuristic is orthogonal to the age/weight ratio and is not investigated further here.

Related Work. Many clause selection approaches are taken by other solvers. Otter 3.3 [6] selects *either* by age, by weight or manually. Prover9 [7] allows a configurable age/weight ratio. E [12] allows the user to specify an arbitrary number of priority queues and a weighted round-robin scheme that determines how many clauses are picked from each queue. The default is to use a combination

```
      input: init: set of clauses;, a : w age-weight ratio
      var active, passive, unprocessed: set of clauses;
      var given, new: clause;
      active := ∅;
      unprocessed := init;
✓     balance := 0;
      loop
          while unprocessed ≠ ∅
              new :=pop(unprocessed);
              if new = □ then return unsatisfiable;
              if retained(new) then                          (* retention test *)
                  simplify new by clauses in active;         (* forward simplification *)
                  if new = □ then return unsatisfiable;
                  if retained(new) then                      (* another retention test *)
                      simplify active using new ;            (* backward simplification *)
                      move the simplified clauses to unprocessed;
                      add new to passive
          if passive = ∅ then return satisfiable or unknown
✓         if balance > 0 then
✓             given := lightest clause in passive;
✓             balance:= balance − w;
✓         else
✓             given := oldest clause in passive;
✓             balance:= balance + a;
          move given from passive to active;
          unprocessed:=infer(given, active);                 (* generating inferences *)
```

Fig. 1. The discount saturation algorithm with AWR clause selection

of age and weight selection, although there is also a complex strategy developed by a genetic algorithm [11]. SPASS [17] uses symbol-counting based clause selection. iProver [3] follows E in having a number of configurable queues but relies mainly on age and weight heuristics in those queues. The general idea in this paper of a *varying age/weight ratio over time* is applicable to any ratio-based clause selection strategy, and our specific results apply to those that take a ratio between age and weight.

3   Optimising Age/Weight Ratios

Two assumptions from folklore are confirmed experimentally:

1. The choice of age/weight ratio often has a significant effect on the performance of proof search.
2. There is in general no single best age/weight ratio for a given set of problems.

These are supported by the work of Schulz and Möhrmann but are explored in more depth here.

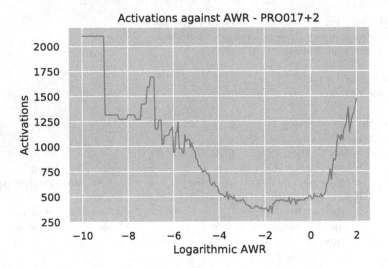

Fig. 2. The number of given-clause loops reported by Vampire after finding a proof with 1-s runs on a TPTP problem, PRO017+2. In between the peaks on either side, the function of L is discontinuous with large peaks and troughs, but follows an approximate trend and settles toward the global optimum. PRO017+2 exhibits typifying behaviour for TPTP, based on manual inspection of several hundred such plots.

3.1   Logarithmic AWR

Visualising AWR values is more easily achieved if they have a continuous scale. AWR values are mathematically $\mathbb{Q}^+$, the positive rational numbers, but in practice are more easily visualised logarithmically. Therefore, the *logarithmic* AWR L is defined in terms of age A and weight W as

$$L = \log_2\left(\frac{A}{W}\right)$$

As L tends to positive infinity, Vampire selects only by weight, whereas if L tends to negative infinity Vampire selects only by age. $L = 0$ represents the middle ground of a 1:1 age/weight ratio. Note that the balancing algorithm used by Vampire does not make use of this value (it still requires two numbers) but the quantity is used in this work to show continuous AWR values.

3.2   Experiments

As an initial illustrative example of how varying the AWR effects the number of clauses required to be processed before a proof is found consider Fig. 2. This demonstrates the effect that varying AWR can have: a smaller number of activations means that fewer clauses were processed, which in general means that a proof was found faster[1]. On the problem shown, a good AWR value is over 400% better by this metric than the worst AWR value.

Table 1. Relative performance gain, showing the ratio in activations between the best AWR setting for a given problem and another base setting. A comparison is drawn between 1:1 (Vampire's default), 1:5 (the best-behaved from Schulz and Möhrmann), and the worst setting for the problem. Where the problem is not solved at all by the base setting, it is ignored.

Base setting	% Maximum gain	% Mean gain	(Standard deviation)
1:1	13,356	126	163
1:5	13,367	144	170
(worst)	22,201	395	760

This experiment was repeated on the whole TPTP problem set, excluding problems Vampire does not currently support (e.g. higher-order problems). Vampire ran for 1 s in default mode with the `discount` saturation algorithm[2] using a sensible set of AWR values (see Table 2)—these are the values used in Vampire's portfolio mode. These tend to favour weight-first over age-first as this has been experimentally shown to be preferable. Problems not solved by any of these, or those solved trivially (e.g in preprocessing) are removed. The whole set yielded data for 7,947 problems.

The first result is that choosing a good AWR value for a problem is well-rewarded. Table 1 summarises the impact that choosing the best AWR can have. Compared to the default, Vampire can perform, on average, 1.26 times fewer activations, which is modest but (as Table 2 shows) just under 10% of problems are no longer proven by choosing the default. It is more relevant to note that there are cases where Vampire can do *much* better by selecting a different AWR value. Therefore, choosing a better AWR value *can* go from no solution to a solution and *can* do so faster, but not necessarily. In the worst case (choosing the pessimal AWR value) Vampire performs almost 4 times as many activations.

The second result is that there is no "best" AWR across this full set of problems. *Drop in performance* is defined to be how many times more activations were required for a proof under a given AWR, compared to the best AWR. Table 2 shows, for each AWR value, the % of problems solved, the number solved uniquely, and the maximum and mean drop in performance. No AWR value solves all problems, with the best being 1:5. A ratio of 1:4 produces an unusually small maximum performance drop. Schulz and Möhrmann found that 1:5 had a similar property, but this might be explained by differences in prover and test

---

[1] It should be noted that if a small number of clauses are extremely expensive to process it may be slower than a larger number of less-expensive clauses, but in general this is a good heuristic measure for prover performance. It also avoids reproducibility issues involved with using system timing approaches.

[2] The default LRS [10] saturation algorithm can be non-deterministic.

environment. It is interesting to note that the extreme AWR values solve fewer problems overall but solve the most uniquely. This is typical in saturation-based proof search: approaches that do not perform well in general may perform well in specific cases where the general approach does not.

In summary, these results confirm the previous assumptions often made in folklore. It should be noted that this is a small experiment (1 s runs in default mode) and the relative performance of different AWR values cannot be generalised, but the general result that they are complementary can.

Table 2. Per-AWR value results on 1 s runs over 7,947 TPTP problems.

AWR	% Solved	Uniques	% Maximum drop	% Mean drop	(Standard deviation)
8:1	85.25	16	15,067	137	198
5:1	86.10	1	12,222	133	164
4:1	86.93	1	10,144	132	142
3:1	87.63	2	10,500	129	141
2:1	88.62	3	11,267	127	145
3:2	89.83	2	11,989	127	151
5:4	89.98	4	12,500	126	155
1:1	90.56	4	13,356	126	163
2:3	91.20	9	14,767	128	179
1:2	91.68	0	16,267	131	197
1:3	91.81	5	19,056	137	230
1:4	91.85	3	**1,741**	138	67
1:5	92.00	2	13,367	144	170
1:6	91.57	1	10,644	147	146
1:7	91.49	1	10,489	149	144
1:8	91.09	2	10,133	153	145
1:10	90.52	1	10,178	160	153
1:12	90.00	0	10,167	165	162
1:14	89.29	4	10,300	170	175
1:16	89.42	5	10,133	174	176
1:20	88.61	3	10,089	182	194
1:24	88.26	2	10,133	189	208
1:28	87.57	2	9,922	196	224
1:32	87.01	1	10,000	199	236
1:40	86.23	4	9,878	209	264
1:50	84.93	1	9,878	217	288
1:64	84.17	2	10,122	228	319
1:128	81.34	3	10,744	257	416
1:1024	73.11	23	22,201	283	755

4   Variable AWR for Vampire

This section motivates and defines a clause selection approach which varies the AWR value over time.

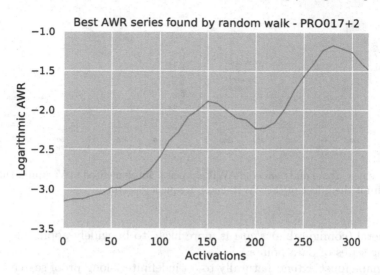

Fig. 3. The AWR series that produced the lowest number of activations on a particular problem, smoothed in order to show the actual effect on proof search. This is a search strategy that a single fixed AWR cannot reproduce.

4.1   The Optimal AWR over Time

Although choosing a good AWR value is important, this is covered in part by the use of strategy scheduling in which many AWR values are tried in sequence (along with other prover options). Additionally, given that varying the AWR can have such a large impact, it seems likely that a constant AWR fixed for the entire proof search is unlikely to be optimal for any given problem. This can be shown by running Vampire with a randomised sequence of age/weight ratios given by a random walk repeatedly, then finding the best after a large number of repetitions. Applying this method with 10,000 repetitions to the problem seen earlier (PRO017+2) yields the example AWR trend shown in Fig. 3, which reduces the best number of activations from 330 with a fixed AWR, to 287 with a varying AWR. Unsurprisingly, in ad-hoc experiments on other problems, the best shape is rarely constant. This suggests that implementing other shapes, such as an increasing or decreasing trend, might lead to quicker proofs in the Vampire theorem prover.

4.2   Varying AWR (in Vampire)

An implementation of dynamically-varying AWR values in Vampire is described below. In general any possible sequence that the AWR could follow during proof search can be used. However, some details constrain the design space:

1. Changing the AWR too frequently or sharply has little effect, due to the "balancing" algorithm—see Sect. 1.

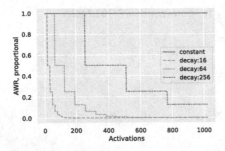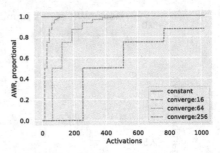

Fig. 4. The new *decay* and *converge* AWR shapes as implemented in Vampire. Different curves exhibit the effect of the AWR shape frequency setting.

2. A general (configurable) *shape* is more likely to be widely applicable than a specific series of data points.
3. The shape must extend naturally to an indefinitely-long proof search.

In this work two general trends are explored: a trend away from a given *start* AWR toward 1:1 ("decay"), and a trend from 1:1 toward a given *end* AWR ("converge"). Investigation showed that even fluctuating sequences had a general trend, and further that these two fixed trends are reasonable approximations of these trends. The start/end AWR values are taken from the portfolio mode: these values are known to be useful in a fixed-AWR context, and while this may not generalise to a dynamic-AWR context, it is a useful starting point pending integration of AWR shape parameters into strategy scheduling.

Since a simple linear shape does not extend well to indefinite proof search (it is unclear what should happen after either 1:1 or the target AWR is reached), an exponential decay function is used instead. These exponential shapes are further parameterised by an integral *shape frequency* setting, which controls the rate of decay or convergence: every n steps, the difference between the current and the target AWR is halved, rounding where necessary. In future, this might allow the use of repeating patterns such as a sinusoid, hence *frequency*. Figure 4 illustrates rates at which the new configurations converge or decay from the fixed AWR setting for some indicative frequency settings.

Our approach here was restricted by the balancing algorithm used internally, as AWR steps must be discrete and do not take effect immediately. An alternative approach might be to use an age/weight probability, rather than a ratio, from which age or weight decisions would be pseudo-randomly (but reproducibly) taken with the use of a seeded pseudo-random number generator, permitting use of continuous age/weight functions.

Two new options are implemented: `--age_weight_ratio_shape` can take the values *constant*, *decay*, or *converge* and selects one of the above shapes; and `--age_weight_ratio_shape_frequency` specifies the frequency (rate) or convergence/decay (default is 100). These are used with the existing `--age_weight_ratio` option (default 1:1) to give a number of new option combinations, which can be used in conjunction with Vampire's portfolio mode pending integration into the strategy schedules. This version of the prover is currently in a separate branch in the main Vampire source repository[3]. Another option, `--age_weight_ratio_b` is implemented (default 1:1), controlling the initial AWR value of *converge* or the final AWR value of *decay*.

Table 3. Results for the tested configurations. *Proved* refers to the total number of problems a configuration solved. *Fresh* is the number of problems a configuration solved which were not solved by the baseline. *Uniques* is the number of problems a configuration solved which were not solved by any other configuration. *u-score* is a refined unique score which correlates to a configuration's utility in solving new problems, as used in Hoder *et al.* [2].

Configuration	Frequency	Proved	Fresh	Uniques	u-score
Baseline	–	**13,057**	0	1	714.2
Converge	1	13,039	24	3	714.3
Converge	5	13,029	27	1	709.5
Converge	10	13,028	35	5	714.3
Converge	50	13,015	45	5	712.8
Converge	100	12,976	51	1	705.9
Converge	500	12,895	63	4	698.3
Converge	1000	12,837	52	0	688.6
Converge	5000	12,775	53	1	682.4
Converge	10000	12,751	53	0	678.7
Decay	1	12,698	48	1	673.6
Decay	5	12,702	51	1	674.9
Decay	10	12,698	48	1	674.2
Decay	50	12,712	49	2	679.1
Decay	100	12,726	46	1	678.8
Decay	500	12,795	29	1	685.5
Decay	1000	12,860	29	2	692.6
Decay	5000	12,982	16	2	707.1
Decay	10000	13,002	7	0	706.3
Converge	(Combined)	13,167	117	41	–
Decay	(Combined)	13,106	93	17	–

5   Experimental Evaluation

Two experiments evaluate the new techniques. The first compares the various options attempting to draw some conclusions about which option values work

---

[3] https://github.com/vprover/vampire/tree/awr-shapes.

well together. The second looks at how useful the new options are in the context of portfolio solving. Both experiments use the TPTP (version 7.1.0) benchmark [16] and were run on StarExec [14].

5.1   Comparing New Options

Vampire ran in default mode (with the `discount` saturation algorithm) for 10 s whilst varying `age_weight_ratio` and `age_weight_ratio_shape_frequency` for several AWR shapes: constant, converging from 1:1, decaying to 1:1, converging from 1:4 and decaying from 1:4.

Results are given in Table 4. The results for the different shapes are grouped into columns and then by frequency with rows giving results per AWR value. The total number of problems solved and those solved uniquely are also reported. The best combination of options overall was decaying from an initial age/weight of 1:100 with frequency 1000. Longer frequencies tended to do better, suggesting that more time at the intermediate AWR values is preferable. Unique solutions are distributed well in general, showing that the new options are complementary.

5.2   Contribution to Portfolio

Our next experiment aims to answer the question "How much can the portfolio mode of Vampire be improved using these new options?". To address this the new options ran on top of the portfolio mode used in the most recent CASC competition CASC-J9 [15]. Note that the CASC-J9 portfolio mode contains techniques completely unrelated to the age/weight ratio, e.g. finite model building [9], as well as other options related to clause selection, e.g. non-goal weight coefficient and set-of-support.

Vampire first ran to establish baseline performance in the given portfolio mode on all problems in TPTP, with a wallclock time limit of 300 s. New options were applied on top of the portfolio mode options, using the existing AWR values in the various strategies as the starting point. Three shapes are employed: constant (baseline), converging from 1:1 and decaying to 1:1. The purpose is to gauge what impact adding such options to a new portfolio mode could have. In this experiment the aim was to find new solved problems and identify new strategies that could be added to a portfolio mode. Therefore, it makes sense to consider the union of all experiments.

Overall, the baseline solved the most problems (13,057). No experimental configuration improved on this figure, but some problems not solved by baseline were solved by the new configurations, and some entirely new problems were solved. The union of all *converge* and *decay* configurations improved on the baseline, with 13,167 and 13,106 solved problems respectively.

Figure 3 shows the performance in terms of solved problems of all the configurations tested. These data show that configurations which select clauses in a similar way to the baseline (i.e. slow decay or fast convergence) achieve similar performance, as expected. In total, 134 (117 + 17, 93 + 41) problems were solved by the new configurations that were not solved by the baseline. This is an

Table 4. Number of problems solved (top) and unique problems solved (bottom) by various configurations varying start/end AWR values, AWR shape, and AWR frequency. Bold numbers indicate the best result within a given shape.

AWR	constant	converge from 1:1 — Freq 1	10	100	1000	Union	decay to 1:1 — Freq 1	10	100	1000	Union	converge from 1:4 — Freq 1	10	100	1000	Union	decay to 1:4 — Freq 1	10	100	1000	Union
									Problems Solved												
10:1	7967	7972	7976	8050	8245	8972	8448	8441	8380	8169	8614	7983	7990	8094	8323	8485	8579	8574	8493	8272	8797
1:10	8575	8565	**8578**	8550	8489	8778	8458	8456	8484	8268	8787	8575	**8584**	8582	8535	8729	8584	8574	8590	8608	8764
1:100	8079	8084	8079	8039	8279	8560	8454	8484	8537	**8636**	8907	8088	8084	8071	8216	8399	8572	8584	**8615**	8592	8855
1:1000	7276	7279	7297	7418	8133	8379	8470	8492	8492	8473	8873	7283	7300	7364	7927	8076	8567	8567	8566	8446	8830
Union	9019	9028	9016	8981	8871	9194	8572	8674	8725	8978	9048	9038	9038	9016	8967	9180	8697	8759	8800	8927	9026
									Uniquely Solved												
10:1	2	2	1	1	6	10	0	0	0	2	2	1	0	0	0	2	0	0	0	4	6
1:10	1	1	0	0	4	2	0	0	0	6	6	0	1	0	0	1	0	0	0	0	0
1:100	0	0	0	5	4	9	2	3	3	3	8	0	0	0	2	2	0	1	1	0	2
1:1000	0	0	0	0	1	1	2	0	0	2	4	0	1	**3**	**3**	7	0	0	0	0	0
Union	3	3	1	6	12	22	4	3	3	13	20	1	2	3	6	12	0	1	3	4	8

Table 5. Total number of problems solved compared to other solvers.

Solver	Total solved	Uniquely solved	
		All	Excluding Vampire (old)
Vampire (old)	13,057	0	-
Vampire (new)	13,191	54	1030
E	10,845	190	190
iProver	8,143	215	215
CVC4	9,354	501	502

impressive result—it is rare to be able to improve portfolio mode by this many new problems with a single new proof search option.

The *u-score* is computed by giving $1/n$ points per problem solved where n is the number of strategies solving a problem [2]. This gives a measure of contribution per strategy. Options with the largest u-score will be prioritised for extending the existing portfolio mode, but only those with unique solutions overall.

Finally, two problems were solved which were marked with an "Unknown" status (with rating 1.00) in the TPTP headers. Only converging with frequency 50 solved SET345-6 and only decaying with frequency 1 solved LAT320+3.

5.3   Comparison with Other Solvers

To place these results in context, the overall number of problems solved by our new strategies are compared with the results of other solvers, using their CASC-J9 These results are from 300-s runs in identical conditions and are given in Table 5. In this table *Vampire (old)* stands for the CASC-J9 competition version whilst *Vampire (new)* stands for the union of all problems solved by new options in the previous section. Between them, the two versions of Vampire solve 1,030 problems uniquely. 54 unique problems found in the previous section remain unique when compared to other competitive solvers.

6   Conclusions and Future Work

Clause selection is a key part of any saturation-based theorem prover and age/weight ratios have a significant effect on the performance of proof search in the Vampire theorem prover. Known folklore that there is no clear optimal age/weight ratio is supported. Further, varying the age/weight ratio over time *during* proof search can improve further on an optimal, but fixed age/weight ratio in terms of the number of activations. Experiments within Vampire on the TPTP benchmark set suggest that these *age/weight shapes* show promise for future developments in this novel approach to proof search. Indeed, including our relatively simple shapes already leads to significant performance gains.

Future directions for research include trying a greater number of "shapes" (such as repeating patterns), other approaches for parameterising these shapes, a pseudo-random approach to age/weight instead of the balancing algorithm, and integration of the new approaches into existing strategy schedules.

References

1. Denzinger, J., Kronenburg, M., Schulz, S.: Discount-a distributed and learning equational prover. J. Autom. Reason. **18**(2), 189–198 (1997)
2. Hoder, K., Reger, G., Suda, M., Voronkov, A.: Selecting the selection. In: Olivetti, N., Tiwari, A. (eds.) IJCAR 2016. LNCS (LNAI), vol. 9706, pp. 313–329. Springer, Cham (2016). https://doi.org/10.1007/978-3-319-40229-1_22
3. Korovin, K.: iProver – an instantiation-based theorem prover for first-order logic (system description). In: Armando, A., Baumgartner, P., Dowek, G. (eds.) IJCAR 2008. LNCS (LNAI), vol. 5195, pp. 292–298. Springer, Heidelberg (2008). https://doi.org/10.1007/978-3-540-71070-7_24
4. Kovács, L., Voronkov, A.: First-order theorem proving and VAMPIRE. In: Sharygina, N., Veith, H. (eds.) CAV 2013. LNCS, vol. 8044, pp. 1–35. Springer, Heidelberg (2013). https://doi.org/10.1007/978-3-642-39799-8_1
5. McCune, W.: Otter 2.0. In: Stickel, M.E. (ed.) CADE 1990. LNCS, vol. 449, pp. 663–664. Springer, Heidelberg (1990). https://doi.org/10.1007/3-540-52885-7_131
6. McCune, W.: Otter 3.3 reference manual. arXiv preprint, arXiv:cs/0310056 (2003)
7. McCune, W.: Release of prover9. In: Mile High Conference on Quasigroups, Loops and Nonassociative Systems, Denver, Colorado (2005)
8. Rawson, M., Reger, G.: Dynamic strategy priority: empower the strong and abandon the weak. In: Proceedings of the 6th Workshop on Practical Aspects of Automated Reasoning co-located with Federated Logic Conference 2018 (FLoC 2018), Oxford, UK, 19 July 2018, pp. 58–71 (2018)
9. Reger, G., Suda, M., Voronkov, A.: Finding finite models in multi-sorted first-order logic. In: Creignou, N., Le Berre, D. (eds.) SAT 2016. LNCS, vol. 9710, pp. 323–341. Springer, Cham (2016). https://doi.org/10.1007/978-3-319-40970-2_20
10. Riazanov, R., Voronkov, A.: Limited resource strategy in resolution theorem proving. J. Symb. Comput. **36**(1–2), 101–115 (2003)
11. Schäfer, S., Schulz, S.: Breeding theorem proving heuristics with genetic algorithms. In: Global Conference on Artificial Intelligence, GCAI 2015, Tbilisi, Georgia, 16–19 October 2015, pp. 263–274 (2015)
12. Schulz, S.: E - a brainiac theorem prover. Ai Commun. **15**(2–3), 111–126 (2002)
13. Schulz, S., Möhrmann, M.: Performance of clause selection heuristics for saturation-based theorem proving. In: Olivetti, N., Tiwari, A. (eds.) IJCAR 2016. LNCS (LNAI), vol. 9706, pp. 330–345. Springer, Cham (2016). https://doi.org/10.1007/978-3-319-40229-1_23
14. Stump, A., Sutcliffe, G., Tinelli, C.: StarExec: a cross-community infrastructure for logic solving. In: Demri, S., Kapur, D., Weidenbach, C. (eds.) IJCAR 2014. LNCS (LNAI), vol. 8562, pp. 367–373. Springer, Cham (2014). https://doi.org/10.1007/978-3-319-08587-6_28

15. Sutcliffe, G.: The 9th IJCAR automated theorem proving system competition-CASC-J9. AI Commun. **31**(1), 1–13 (2015)
16. Sutcliffe, G.: The TPTP problem library and associated infrastructure, from CNF to TH0, TPTP v6.4.0. J. Autom. Reason. **59**(4), 483–502 (2017)
17. Weidenbach, C.: Combining superposition, sorts and splitting. In: Robinson, A., Voronkov, A. (eds.) Handbook of Automated Reasoning, vol. II, chap. 27, pp. 1965–2013. Elsevier Science (2001)

Induction in Saturation-Based Proof Search

Giles Reger[1][(✉)] and Andrei Voronkov[1,2]

[1] University of Manchester, Manchester, UK
giles.reger@manchester.ac.uk
[2] EasyChair, Manchester, UK

Abstract. Many applications of theorem proving, for example program verification and analysis, require first-order reasoning with both quantifiers and theories such as arithmetic and datatypes. There is no complete procedure for reasoning in such theories but the state-of-the-art in automated theorem proving is still able to reason effectively with real-world problems from this rich domain. In this paper we contribute to a missing part of the puzzle: automated induction inside a saturation-based theorem prover. Our goal is to incorporate lightweight automated induction in a way that complements the saturation-based approach, allowing us to solve problems requiring a combination of first-order reasoning, theory reasoning, and inductive reasoning. We implement a number of techniques and heuristics and evaluate them within the Vampire theorem prover. Our results show that these new techniques enjoy practical success on real-world problems.

1 Introduction

Saturation-based proof search has been the leading technology in automated theorem proving for first-order logic for some time. The core idea of this approach is to saturate a set of clauses (including the negated goal) with respect to some inference system with the aim of deriving a contradiction and concluding that the goal holds. Over the last few years this technology has been extended to reason with both quantifiers, and theories such as arithmetic and term algebras (also known as algebraic, recursive or inductive datatypes), making it highly applicable in areas such as program analysis and verification, which were previously the sole domain of SMT solvers. However, so far little has been done to extend saturation-based proof search with *automated induction*. Most attempts to date have focussed on using saturation-based methods to discharge subgoals once an induction axiom has been selected.

The aim of this work is to extend saturation-based proof search with *lightweight* methods for automated induction where those techniques are integrated directly into proof search i.e. they do not rely on some external procedure

This work was supported by EPSRC Grant EP/P03408X/1. Andrei Voronkov was also partially supported by ERC Starting Grant 2014 SYMCAR 639270 and the Wallenberg Academy Fellowship 2014 – TheProSE.

P. Fontaine (Ed.): CADE 2019, LNAI 11716, pp. 477–494, 2019.
https://doi.org/10.1007/978-3-030-29436-6_28

to produce subgoals. We achieve this by the introduction of new inference rules capturing inductive steps and new proof search heuristics to guide their application. Our approach is based on the research hypothesis that many problems requiring induction only require relatively simple applications of induction.

Example 1. As an introductory example, consider the problem of proving the commutativity of $(\forall x \forall y)\mathsf{plus}(x, y) \approx \mathsf{plus}(y, x)$, where x and y range over natural numbers. We now briefly described how this approach will handle this problem.

When we Skolemise its negation, we obtain the clause $\mathsf{plus}(\sigma_0, \sigma_1) \not\approx \mathsf{plus}(\sigma_1, \sigma_0)$. In this paper, we will denote by σ_i fresh Skolem constants introduced by converting formulas to clausal form.

Our approach will immediately apply induction to σ_0 in the negated conjecture by resolving this clause with the (clausal form of the) induction axiom

$$\left((\forall z) \left(\begin{array}{l} \mathsf{plus}(\mathsf{zero}, \sigma_1) \approx \mathsf{plus}(\sigma_1, \mathsf{zero}) \wedge \\ \left(\begin{array}{l} \mathsf{plus}(z, \sigma_1) \approx \mathsf{plus}(\sigma_1, z) \to \\ \mathsf{plus}(\mathsf{succ}(z), \sigma_1) \approx \mathsf{plus}(\sigma_1, \mathsf{succ}(z)) \end{array} \right) \end{array} \right) \right) \to (\forall x)\mathsf{plus}(x, \sigma_1) \approx \mathsf{plus}(\sigma_1, x)$$

to produce the following subgoals:

$$\begin{array}{l} \mathsf{plus}(\mathsf{zero}, \sigma_1) \not\approx \mathsf{plus}(\sigma_1, \mathsf{zero}) \vee \mathsf{plus}(\mathsf{succ}(\sigma_2), \sigma_1) \not\approx \mathsf{plus}(\sigma_1, \mathsf{succ}(\sigma_2)) \\ \mathsf{plus}(\mathsf{zero}, \sigma_1) \not\approx \mathsf{plus}(\sigma_1, \mathsf{zero}) \vee \mathsf{plus}(\sigma_1, \sigma_2) \approx \mathsf{plus}(\sigma_2, \sigma_1) \end{array} \quad (1)$$

Clause splitting is then used to split the search space into two parts to be considered separately. This splitting is important to our approach and can be used in any saturation theorem prover implementing some version of it, for example using splitting with backtracking as in SPASS [24] or the AVATAR architecture as in Vampire [22]. The first part contains $\mathsf{plus}(\mathsf{zero}, \sigma_1) \not\approx \mathsf{plus}(\sigma_1, \mathsf{zero})$ and is refuted by deriving $\mathsf{plus}(\sigma_1, \mathsf{zero}) \not\approx \sigma_1$ using the definition of plus and applying a second induction step to σ_1 in this clause. By resolving with a similar induction axiom to before, the following clauses are produced and are refuted via the definition of plus and the injectivity of datatype constructors.

$$\begin{array}{l} \mathsf{zero} \not\approx \mathsf{plus}(\mathsf{zero}, \mathsf{zero}) \vee \mathsf{succ}(\sigma_3) \not\approx \mathsf{plus}(\mathsf{succ}(\sigma_3), \mathsf{zero}) \\ \mathsf{zero} \not\approx \mathsf{plus}(\mathsf{zero}, \mathsf{zero}) \vee \mathsf{plus}(\sigma_3, \mathsf{zero}) \approx \sigma_3 \end{array}$$

The second part of the clause splitting then contains the other half of the clauses given above. Superposition is then applied to these clauses and the axioms of plus to derive

$$\mathsf{succ}(\mathsf{plus}(\sigma_1, \sigma_2)) \not\approx \mathsf{plus}(\sigma_1, \mathsf{succ}(\sigma_2))$$

and a third induction step is applied to this clause on σ_1. The resulting subgoals can again be refuted via the definition of plus and the injectivity of datatype constructors.

While inductive reasoning in this example may seem to be the same as in almost any other inductive theorem prover, there is an essential difference: instead of reducing goals to subgoals using induction and trying to prove these subgoals using theory reasoning or again induction, we simply consider induction as an additional inference rule adding new formulas to the search space. In a way, every clause generated during the proof search becomes a potential target for applying induction and induction becomes integrated in the saturation process.

In this example there were three applications of induction to ground unit clauses in the search space, however our implementation performs 5 induction steps with 2 being unnecessary for the proof. This is typical in saturation-based proof search where many irrelevant consequences are often derived. This is an important observation; our general approach is to derive consequences (inductive or otherwise) in a semi-guided fashion, meaning that we may make many unnecessary induction steps. However, this is the philosophy behind saturation-based approaches.

During proof search for this example it was necessary to (i) decide which clauses to apply induction to, (ii) decide which term within that clause to apply induction to, and (iii) decide how to apply induction. We address issues (ii) and (iii) in this paper, whilst relying on the clause selection techniques of saturation-based theorem provers for (i). We begin in Sect. 2 by introducing the necessary preliminary definitions for the work. In Sect. 3 we address (iii), how we apply induction, through the introduction of a set of new inference rules. In Sect. 4 we consider (ii) through a number of heuristics for selecting goals for induction. Then in Sect. 5 we show how standard clause splitting techniques can be used in our induction proofs (without any additional work) for case splitting. Section 6 describes implementation and experimental evaluation. We then consider related work in Sect. 7 before concluding in Sect. 8.

2   Preliminaries

Multi-sorted First-Order Logic. We consider standard multi-sorted first-order predicate logic with equality. We allow all standard boolean connectives and quantifiers in the language. We denote terms by s, t, variables by x, y, z, constants by a, and function symbols by f. We consider equality $\approx$ as part of the language, that is, equality is not a symbol. An *atom* is an equality or a predicate applied to a list of terms. A *literal* is an atom A or its negation $\neg A$. Literals that are atoms are called *positive*, while literals of the form $\neg A$ are *negative*. If $L = \neg A$ is a literal we write $\neg L$ for the literal A. A *clause* is a disjunction of literals $L_1 \vee \ldots \vee L_n$, where $n \geq 0$. When $n = 0$, we will speak of the empty clause, denoted by $\square$. We denote atoms by A, literals by L, clauses by C, and formulas by F, all possibly with indices. Formulas can be *clausified* (transformed into a set of clauses) via standard techniques (e.g. [13] and our recent work in [15]). We write clausify(F) for the set of clauses obtained from F by clausification.

By an *expression* E we mean a term, atom, literal, or clause. We write $E[t]$ to mean an expression E with a particular occurrence of a term t and then $E[s]$ for that expression with the particular occurrence of t replaced by term s.

A *multi-sorted signature* is a finite set of symbols and a finite set of sorts with the accompanying function *srt* providing sorts for the symbols.

The Theory of Finite Term Algebras. In this paper we consider induction for finite term algebras, also known as algebraic, inductive, or recursive datatypes. A definition of the first-order theory of term algebras over a finite signature can be found in e.g. [17] and a description of how saturation-based proof search may be extended to reason with such structures is given in [9]. Let Σ be a finite set of function symbols containing at least one constant. Denote by $\mathcal{T}(\Sigma)$ the set of all ground terms built from the symbols in Σ. The Σ-*term algebra* is the algebraic structure whose carrier set is $\mathcal{T}(\Sigma)$ and defined in such a way that every ground term is interpreted by itself (we leave details to the reader).

We will often consider extensions of term algebras by additional symbols. Elements of Σ will be called *term constructors* (or simply just *constructors*), to distinguish them from other function symbols. We will differentiate between *recursive* constructors that are recursive in their arguments and *base* constructors that are not. Where we wish to differentiate we may write $\mathcal{T}(\Sigma_B, \Sigma_R)$ for base constructors Σ_B and recursive constructors Σ_R.

In practice, it can be useful to consider multiple sorts, especially for problems taken from functional programming. In this setting, each term algebra constructor has a type $\tau_1 \times \cdots \times \tau_n \to \tau$. The requirement for at least one constant is replaced by the requirement that for every sort, there exists a ground term of this sort. We also consider theories, which mix constructor and non-constructor sorts. That is, some sorts contain constructors and some do not (e.g. arithmetic).

Finally, we associate n *destructor* (or projection) functions with every constructor c of arity n such that each destructor returns one of the arguments of c. Note, that the behavior of destructors is unspecified on some terms.

Example 2. We introduce two term algebras. Firstly, that of natural numbers

$$nat := \mathsf{zero} \mid \mathsf{succ}(\mathsf{dec}(nat))$$

and secondly that of integer lists

$$list := \mathsf{nil} \mid \mathsf{cons}(\mathsf{hd}(Int), \mathsf{tail}(list)).$$

Note that this second term algebra relies on a built-in integer sort.

Saturation-Based Proof Search. An important concept in this work is that of saturation with respect to an inference system. Inference systems are used in the theory of superposition [12] implemented by several leading automated first-order theorem provers, including Vampire [10] and E [18]. Superposition theorem provers implement proof-search algorithms in $\mathcal{S}$ using so-called *saturation algorithms*, as follows. Given a set S of formulas, superposition-based theorem provers try to saturate S with respect to $\mathcal{S}$, that is build a set of formulas that contains S and is closed under inferences in $\mathcal{S}$. At every step, a saturation algorithm selects an inference of $\mathcal{S}$, applies this inference to S, and adds conclusions of the inferences to the set S. If at some moment the empty clause $\square$ is obtained, by soundness of $\mathcal{S}$, we can conclude that the input set of clauses is unsatisfiable. Figure 1 gives a simple saturation algorithm. This is missing an important notion

input: *Init*: set of clauses;
var *active, passive, unprocessed*: set of clauses; **var** *given, new*: clause;
active := ∅; *unprocessed* := *Init*;
loop
  while *unprocessed* ≠ ∅
    new :=*pop*(*unprocessed*);
    if *new* = □ **then** **return** *unsatisfiable*;
    add *new* to *passive*
  if *passive* = ∅ **then** **return** *satisfiable* or *unknown*
  given := *select*(*passive*);   (* *clause selection* *)
  move *given* from *passive* to *active*;
  unprocessed :=*infer*(*given, active*);   (* *generating inferences* *)

Fig. 1. Simple saturation algorithm.

of *redundancy*. We have omitted this as it does not interact with the elements of proof search we consider here. However, it is core to the implementation in the Vampire theorem prover. It is important to note that the only way to guide proof search is via how we select clauses and how we perform inferences on them.

3   Performing Induction

This section introduces inference rules for induction on term algebras.

3.1   General Approach

We begin by describing our general approach. The idea is to add inference rules that capture the application of induction to the selected clause in proof search. These inference rules will be applied during proof search to selected clauses in the same way as other inference rules such as resolution. We define an *induction axiom* to be any valid (in the underlying theory) formula of the form

$$formula \rightarrow (\forall x)(L[x]).$$

For simplicity we assume that this formula is closed, leaving out the general case due to the lack of space. The idea is to *resolve* this with a clause $\neg L[t] \vee C$ obtaining *formula* → C. Again, for simplicity we assume that t is a ground term. As long as the induction axiom is valid, this approach is always *sound*. If the resulting formula is not a clause, it should then be converted to its CNF.

The idea is that $L[t]$ is a *(sub)goal* we are trying to prove (by induction). This is an interesting point. Typically, saturation-based proof search is not goal-oriented (although one can introduce heuristics that support this) but this app-roach to induction is goal-oriented in nature as the conclusion of an induction inference is a subgoal that, if refuted, proves the goal represented by the premise. Also, similar to [6] by resolving the induction axiom to reduce the goal to sub-goals we bypass the literal selection used in saturation algorithms. This means that, if we would just add the (clausal form of) the induction axiom to the search space, we would most likely never use it to resolve against the goal in the same way as above since the literal $L[x]$ would not necessarily be selected.

Below we consider two different kinds of induction axioms, introducing three inference rules, parametrised by some (general) term algebra. To formalise the selection of goals that can be proved by induction we introduce a predicate $sel(C, L, t)$ that is true if C is clause, L a literal in C and t a term in L. We will call this predicate the *induction heuristic* since it will be used to decide when induction should be applied. In this case we will informally say that t is the induction term and L the induction literal in C.

Here we concentrate on how induction should be performed once an induction term and literal have been selected. Section 4 discusses choices for selection.

3.2   Structural Induction

We begin by motivating the inference rule by the simple example of inductively proving that the length of a list is non-negative.

Example 3 (Structural Induction on Lists). Consider the following conjecture $(\forall x : list)(\mathsf{len}(x) \geq 0)$ for integer lists (defined in Example 2) given the axioms $\mathsf{len}(\mathsf{nil}) \approx 0$ and $(\forall x : Int, y : list)(\mathsf{len}(\mathsf{cons}(x, y)) \approx 1 + \mathsf{len}(y))$ for the len function. To prove this conjecture we must first negate it to get $\neg(\mathsf{len}(\sigma) \geq 0)$ and then introduce the induction axiom

$$\mathsf{len}(\mathsf{nil}) \geq 0 \land (\forall x, y)(\mathsf{len}(x) \geq 0 \to \mathsf{len}(\mathsf{cons}(y, x)) \geq 0) \to (\forall x)(\mathsf{len}(x) \geq 0)$$

which is then resolved against $\neg(\mathsf{len}(\sigma) \geq 0)$ to give, after conversion to CNF, two clauses
$$\neg(\mathsf{len}(\mathsf{nil}) \geq 0) \lor \mathsf{len}(\sigma_1) \geq 0$$
$$\neg(\mathsf{len}(\mathsf{nil}) \geq 0) \lor \neg(\mathsf{len}(\mathsf{cons}(\sigma_2, \sigma_1)) \geq 0),$$

which can be refuted using the axioms for len. The question now is what inference rule is needed for performing the above induction step. To do so, we define the induction heuristics $sel(C, L, t)$ to hold when L is the only literal in C and t is a constant of the sort *list*. This rule effectively results in the following inferences performed by a saturation theorem prover:

$$\frac{\neg A[a]}{\neg A[\mathsf{nil}] \lor A[\sigma_1] \\ \neg A[\mathsf{nil}] \lor \neg A[\mathsf{cons}(\sigma_2, \sigma_1)]}$$

where a is a constant, $A[a]$ is ground, $srt(a) = \mathsf{list}$ and σ_1, σ_2 are fresh constants.

3.3   Well-Founded Induction

Suppose that $x \succ y$ is any binary predicate that is interpreted as a well-founded relation (which is not necessarily an ordering). We require both arguments of $\succ$

to be of the same sort. Then the following is a valid formula, which represents well-founded induction on this relation:

$$\forall x(\neg L[x] \rightarrow \exists y(x \succ y \wedge \neg L[y])) \rightarrow \forall x L[x].$$

When we skolemize this formula, we obtain two clauses

$$\neg L[\sigma_1] \vee L[x] \qquad \neg \sigma_1 \succ y \vee L[y] \vee L[x]$$

We can use the following two equivalent clauses instead:

$$\neg L[\sigma_1] \vee L[x] \qquad \neg \sigma_1 \succ y \vee L[y] \qquad (2)$$

Well-founded induction is the most general form of induction (though in practice it can only be used when the relation $\succ$ can be expressed in the first-order language we are using). We are interested in finding special cases of well-founded induction for term algebras. There are two obvious candidates for it: the immediate subterm relation $\succ_1$ and the subterm relation discussed in the sequel.

Let us begin with the immediate subterm relation. Note that the relation $\succ$ must have both arguments of the same sort, so the corresponding induction rule will only be useful for term algebras where at least one argument of a constructor has the same sort as the constructor itself. Fortunately, this is the case for the three most commonly used inductive data types: natural numbers, lists and trees.

Let us provide a complete axiomatisation of the immediate subterm relation $\succ_1$ first for natural numbers and lists:

$$\neg(\text{zero} \succ_1 x) \qquad\qquad\qquad \neg(\text{nil} \succ_1 x)$$
$$\text{succ}(x) \succ_1 y \leftrightarrow x \approx y \qquad\qquad \text{cons}(x, y) \succ_1 z \leftrightarrow y \approx z$$

The subterm relation is generally not axiomatisable. However, this is not a problem in general, since we can use as an incomplete axiomatisation of the subterm relation any set of formulas which are true on this relation (though this restricts what can be proved about the relation). If we then prove anything using this set of formulas, then our proof will be correct for the subterm relation too, which makes the corresponding induction rule valid too.

We can generalise the immediate subterm and subterm relation also to trees and some other (but not all!) inductively defined types. We do not include general definitions here as they become very involved with multiple sorts and mutually recursive type definitions.

3.4   Inductive Strengthening

We now consider a different form of induction axiom (inspired by [16]).

Example 4. Given the negated conjecture $\neg(\text{len}(\sigma_1) \geq 0)$ given in Example 3 we consider a different way in which to inductively demonstrate $L[x]$ and thus refute this claim. The idea here is to argue that if there does not exist a *smallest* list of non-negative length then the length of all lists is non-negative. This can be captured in the induction axiom

$$\neg(\exists x)\left(\begin{array}{l}\neg(\text{len}(x) \geq 0)\wedge \\ (\forall y)(\text{subterm}_{list}(x,y) \rightarrow \text{len}(\text{tail}(y)) \geq 0)\end{array}\right) \rightarrow (\forall z)(\text{len}(z) \geq 0)$$

where $\text{subterm}_{list}(x,y)$ is true if y is a subterm of x of $list$ sort. However, as argued in [9], the subterm relation needs to be axiomatised and these axioms (which include transitivity) can have a large negative impact on the search space. Therefore, we can consider two alternative inductive axioms. The first is the *weak* form where we consider only *direct* subterms of x as follows.

$$\neg(\exists x)\left(\begin{array}{l}\neg(\text{len}(x) \geq 0)\wedge \\ (x \approx \text{cons}(\text{hd}(x),\text{tail}(x)) \rightarrow \text{len}(\text{tail}(x)) \geq 0)\end{array}\right) \rightarrow (\forall y)(\text{len}(y) \geq 0)$$

This is clausified as

$$\text{len}(x) \geq 0 \vee \neg(\text{len}(\sigma_2) \geq 0)$$
$$\text{len}(x) \geq 0 \vee \sigma_2 \not\approx \text{cons}(\text{hd}(\sigma_2),\text{tail}(\sigma_2)) \vee \text{len}(\text{tail}(\sigma_2)) \geq 0$$

which can be resolved against the conjecture $\neg(\text{len}(\sigma_1) \geq 0)$ as before.

The second (taken from [9]) is where we represent the subterm relation in a way that is more friendly to saturation-based theorem provers i.e. we introduce a fresh predicate less_x and then add axioms such that it holds for exactly those terms smaller than the existential witness x. This can be written as follows.

$$\neg(\exists x)\left(\begin{array}{l}\neg(\text{len}(x) \geq 0) \wedge (\forall z)(\text{less}_x(z) \rightarrow \text{len}(z) \geq 0) \\ \wedge \; (x \approx \text{cons}(\text{hd}(x),\text{tail}(x)) \rightarrow \text{less}_x(\text{tail}(x))) \wedge \\ (\forall y)(\text{less}_x(\text{cons}(\text{hd}(y),\text{tail}(y))) \rightarrow \text{less}_x(\text{tail}(y)))\end{array}\right) \rightarrow (\forall y)(\text{len}(y) \geq 0)$$

Again, the specific approach taken in this example can be generalised to the arbitrary term algebra $ta = \mathcal{T}(\Sigma_B \cup \Sigma_R)$. The existential part $exists_{ta}(L)$ of the general induction axiom can be given as

$$(\exists x)\left(\neg L[x] \bigwedge_{\text{con}(\ldots,d_i,\ldots)\in\Sigma_R} \bigwedge_{j\in rec(\text{con})} (x \approx \text{con}(\ldots,d_i(x),\ldots) \rightarrow L[d_j(x)])\right)$$

for the first approach and as

$$(\exists x)\left(\begin{array}{l}\neg L[x] \wedge (\forall z)(\text{less}(z) \rightarrow L[z]) \wedge \\ \bigwedge_{\text{con}(\ldots,d_i,\ldots)\in\Sigma_R} \bigwedge_{j\in rec(\text{con})} x \approx \text{con}(\ldots,d_i(x),\ldots) \rightarrow \text{less}_x(d_j(x)) \wedge \\ (\forall y)(\bigwedge_{\text{con}(\ldots,d_i,\ldots)\in\Sigma_R} \bigwedge_{j\in rec(\text{con})} \text{less}_x z(\text{con}(\ldots,d_i(y),\ldots)) \rightarrow \text{less}_x(d_j(y)))\end{array}\right)$$

for the second approach. The general induction rule then becomes

$$\frac{L[t] \vee C}{\text{clausify}(exists_{ta}(\neg L) \vee C)}$$

for ground literal $L[t]$, clause C and term t, where $srt(t) = ta$ and $sel(L[t] \vee C, L[t], t)$.

One could consider an optimisation where this approach is applied directly to the input (as is done in [16]). However, this would introduce induction axioms too early in proof search i.e. it goes against the saturation-based philosophy. One could also consider reusing Skolem constants instead of introducing new ones where t in the above rule is already a Skolem constant. However, this could only be done for each Skolem constant at most once.

Table 1. Illustrating the induction inference schemas for the *rbtree* term algebra.

Approach One

$$\frac{L[t] \vee C}{}$$

$C \vee L[\mathsf{empty}] \vee L[\mathsf{leaf}(\sigma_1)] \vee \neg L[\sigma_4] \vee \neg L[\sigma_2]$
$C \vee L[\mathsf{empty}] \vee L[\mathsf{leaf}(\sigma_1)] \vee \neg L[\sigma_4] \vee \neg L[\sigma_6]$
$C \vee L[\mathsf{empty}] \vee L[\mathsf{leaf}(\sigma_1)] \vee \neg L[\sigma_7] \vee \neg L[\sigma_2]$
$C \vee L[\mathsf{empty}] \vee L[\mathsf{leaf}(\sigma_1)] \vee \neg L[\sigma_7] \vee \neg L[\sigma_6]$
$C \vee L[\mathsf{empty}] \vee L[\mathsf{leaf}(\sigma_1)] \vee L[\mathsf{black}(\sigma_3, \sigma_7, \sigma_4)] \vee \neg L[\sigma_2]$
$C \vee L[\mathsf{empty}] \vee L[\mathsf{leaf}(\sigma_1)] \vee L[\mathsf{black}(\sigma_3, \sigma_7, \sigma_4)] \vee \neg L[\sigma_6]$
$C \vee L[\mathsf{empty}] \vee L[\mathsf{leaf}(\sigma_1)] \vee L[\mathsf{red}(\sigma_5, \sigma_2, \sigma_6)]] \vee \neg L[\sigma_7]$
$C \vee L[\mathsf{empty}] \vee L[\mathsf{leaf}(\sigma_1)] \vee L[\mathsf{red}(\sigma_5, \sigma_2, \sigma_6)] \vee \neg L[\sigma_4]$
$C \vee L[\mathsf{empty}] \vee L[\mathsf{leaf}(\sigma_1)] \vee L[\mathsf{black}(\sigma_3, \sigma_7, \sigma_4)] \vee L[\mathsf{red}(\sigma_5, \sigma_2, \sigma_6)]$

Approach Two

$$\frac{L[t] \vee C}{}$$

$C \vee \mathsf{red}(\mathsf{rval}(\sigma_1), \mathsf{rleft}(\sigma_1), \mathsf{rright}(\sigma_1)) \not\approx \sigma_1 \vee \neg L[\mathsf{rleft}(\sigma_1)]$
$C \vee \mathsf{red}(\mathsf{rval}(\sigma_1), \mathsf{rleft}(\sigma_1), \mathsf{rright}(\sigma_1)) \not\approx \sigma_1 \vee \neg L[\mathsf{rright}(\sigma_1)]$
$C \vee \mathsf{black}(\mathsf{bval}(\sigma_1), \mathsf{bleft}(\sigma_1), \mathsf{bright}(\sigma_1)) \not\approx \sigma_1 \vee \neg L[\mathsf{bleft}(\sigma_1)]$
$C \vee \mathsf{black}(\mathsf{bval}(\sigma_1), \mathsf{bleft}(\sigma_1), \mathsf{bright}(\sigma_1)) \not\approx \sigma_1 \vee \neg L[\mathsf{bright}(\sigma_1)]$
$C \vee L[\sigma_1]$

Approach Three

$$\frac{L[t] \vee C}{}$$

$C \vee L[\sigma_1]$
$C \vee \neg \mathsf{less}_x(x) \vee \neg L[x]$
$C \vee \mathsf{red}(\mathsf{rval}(\sigma_1), \mathsf{rleft}(\sigma_1), \mathsf{rright}(\sigma_1) \not\approx \sigma_1 \vee \mathsf{less}_x(\mathsf{rleft}(\sigma_1))$
$C \vee \mathsf{red}(\mathsf{rval}(\sigma_1), \mathsf{rleft}(\sigma_1), \mathsf{rright}(\sigma_1) \not\approx \sigma_1 \vee \mathsf{less}_x(\mathsf{rright}(\sigma_1))$
$C \vee \mathsf{black}(\mathsf{bval}(\sigma_1), \mathsf{bleft}(\sigma_1), \mathsf{bright}(\sigma_1) \not\approx \sigma_1 \vee \mathsf{less}_x(\mathsf{bleft}(\sigma_1))$
$C \vee \mathsf{black}(\mathsf{bval}(\sigma_1), \mathsf{bleft}(\sigma_1), \mathsf{bright}(\sigma_1) \not\approx \sigma_1 \vee \mathsf{less}_x(\mathsf{bright}(\sigma_1))$
$C \vee \neg \mathsf{less}_x(\mathsf{red}(\mathsf{rval}(x), \mathsf{rleft}(x), \mathsf{rright}(x))) \vee \mathsf{less}_x(\mathsf{rleft}(x))$
$C \vee \neg \mathsf{less}_x(\mathsf{red}(\mathsf{rval}(x), \mathsf{rleft}(x), \mathsf{rright}(x))) \vee \mathsf{less}_x(\mathsf{rright}(x))$
$C \vee \neg \mathsf{less}_x(\mathsf{black}(\mathsf{bval}(x), \mathsf{bleft}(x), \mathsf{bright}(x))) \vee \mathsf{less}_x(\mathsf{bleft}(x))$
$C \vee \neg \mathsf{less}_x(\mathsf{black}(\mathsf{bval}(x), \mathsf{bleft}(x), \mathsf{bright}(x))) \vee \mathsf{less}_x(\mathsf{bright}(x))$

3.5   Comparing the Approaches with an Example

To illustrate the differences in the clauses produced by the above three approaches we give, in Table 1, the introduced inference rules instantiated with $ta = rbtree$ defined as

$rbtree :=$ empty $\ |\ $ leaf(lval(Int)) $\ |\ $ red(rval(Int), rleft($rbtree$), rright($rbtree$))
$\qquad\qquad\qquad\qquad\ |\ $ black(bval(Int), bleft($rbtree$), bright($rbtree$))

This covers all the important cases from above (i) non-zero arity base constructors, and (ii) multiple base and multiple recursive constructors. Notice how the structural induction rule, in this case introduces 7 new Skolem constants and 9 clauses (although this could be slightly optimised here) whilst the inductive strengthening approaches introduce one Skolem constant.

4   Selecting Where to Apply Induction

We now consider how to define various induction heuristics.

4.1   Goal-Directed Search

In our introductory example (Example 1, proving commutativity of addition) we (usefully) applied induction three times. The first time was directly to the goal and the second two times were to unit clauses derived directly from the result of this first induction. We hypothesise that this is a typical scenario and introduce heuristics for this common case. An important observation is that an implicative universal goal becomes a set of unit ground clauses once negated.

Unit Clauses. A unit clause represents a single goal or subgoal that, if refuted, will lead to a final proof. Conversely, applying the above induction inference rules to non-unit clauses will lead to applications of induction that may not be as general as needed. This selection can be defined as follows for some literal $L[t]$ and term t.

$$sel_U(L[t], L[t], t)$$

Negative Literals. Typically, goal statements are positive and therefore proof search is attempting to derive a contradiction from a negative statement. Applying induction to a negative statement leads to a mixture of positive and negative conclusions. As we saw in the introductory example, it is common to apply further induction to the negative conclusions. This selection can be defined as follows for clause C, atom A and term t.

$$sel_N(C \vee \neg A[t], \neg A[t], t)$$

However, it is easy to see cases where this is too restrictive. For example, the goal from Example 3 could have been rewritten as $(\forall x)(\neg(\mathsf{len}(x) < 0))$ and the negated goal on which induction should be performed would have been positive.

Constants. Given a purely universal goal, the terms of interest will be Skolem constants (whether this Skolemisation occurred within the solver or not) and terms introduced by induction for repeated induction are also typically Skolem constants. Therefore, to restrict application of induction to this special case, we can restrict it to constants only. This selection can be defined as follows for clause C, literal L and constant a.

$$sel_C(C \vee L[a], L[a], a)$$

Special Symbols. The goal will typically contain the symbols on which induction should be performed. Additionally, further induction steps are often performed on the Skolem constants introduced by a previous induction. We define a selection predicate parameterised by a set of symbols α as follows for clause C, literal L and term t.

$$sel_\alpha(C \vee L[t], L[t], t) \Leftrightarrow (t = f(t_1, \ldots, t_n) \to f \in \alpha) \wedge (t = a \to a \in \alpha)$$

and define the functions sel_G and sel_I for sets of goal symbols G and induction Skolem constants I.

The *sel* function is defined as any *conjunction* of zero or more of the above with the trivial selection function that is true on all inputs of term algebra sort.

4.2   Inferring Goal Clause(s)

One issue with the above heuristics is that we may not have an explicit goal in our input problem. Indeed, SMT-LIB [1] has no syntax for indicating the goal (unlike TPTP [21]). To address this we define a notion of *goal symbol* that is independent of the notion of an explicit goal being given.

Given a set of input formulas $F_1, \ldots, F_n$ and a set $\mathcal{G}$ containing zero or more formulas F_i marked as goal formulas, a *goal symbol* is a symbol such that

- It appears in a formula $F \in \mathcal{G}$, or
- It is a Skolem constant introduced in the clausification of some $F \in \mathcal{G}$, or
- It appears in at most *limit* formulas, or
- It is a Skolem constant introduced by the Skolemisation of some formula F_i of the form $\exists x. F$

where *limit* is a parameter to the process. In the case where this is a single goal formula we would expect *limit* to be 1. However, the input may have been subject to some additional preprocessing meaning that the goal is represented by a few clauses in the input. The last point is because many goals will take the form of negated universal statements; this is also how formulas for induction are identified in [16] (our approach is more general).

Once all such goal symbols have been identified, the set $\mathcal{G}$ is extended to include all formulas containing a goal symbol. This is done as $\mathcal{G}$ typically plays another role in proof search as clauses derived from formulas in $\mathcal{G}$ may be prioritised in clause selection, providing some heuristic goal-directionality.

5   Case Splitting for Free

An important part of inductive proofs is typically the case splitting between the base case and the inductive step. In this section we describe a clause splitting approach (implemented in Vampire as AVATAR [14,22]) that achieves this.

We briefly describe the ground part of the AVATAR framework for clause splitting as case splitting for induction only requires the ground part. The general idea is that given a set of clauses S and a ground clause $L_1 \lor L_2$ we can consider the two sub-problems $S \cup \{L_1\}$ and $S \cup \{L_2\}$ independently.

Let name be a function from ground literals to labels that is injective up to symmetry of equality. Let $C \leftarrow A$ be a *labelled clause* where A is a set of labels. We can lift an inference system on clauses to one on labelled clauses where all conclusions take the union of the labels in premises. The previous rules for induction can be extended such that the consequent clauses take the labels of the premise clause. Figure 2 shows how the simple saturation algorithm from Sect. 2 can be extended to perform ground clause splitting. It uses a SAT procedure that we add clauses of labels to and then request the *difference* between a new model and the previous model in terms of added/removed labels.

---

input: *Init*: set of clauses;
var *active, passive, unprocessed*: set of clauses; **var** *given, new*: clause;
active := ∅;   *passive* := ∅;   *unprocessed* := *Init*;
loop
  while *unprocessed* ≠ ∅
    new := pop(*unprocessed*);
    if *new* = □ **then return** *unsatisfiable*;
    if *new* = □ ← A **then** add ¬A to SAT;
    if *new* is ground **then** add label(*new*) to SAT;
    else add *new* to *passive*;
  if *passive* = ∅ **then return** *satisfiable* or *unknown*
  (*add_labels, remove_labels*) = *new_model*(SAT);   (* *compute new model* *)
  active := {$C \leftarrow L \in active \mid L \cap remove\_labels = \emptyset$};
  passive := {$C \leftarrow L \in passive \mid L \cap remove\_labels = \emptyset$};
  passive := *passive* ∪ {retrieve(l) ← $l \mid l \in add\_labels$};
  given := *select*(*passive*);   (* *clause selection* *)
  move *given* from *passive* to *active*;
  unprocessed := *infer*(*given, active*);   (* *generating inferences* *)

Fig. 2. Simple saturation algorithm with ground clause splitting.

To understand why this is useful consider the conclusions of the inference rules given in Table 1. These clauses are all ground and multi-literal i.e. they capture multiple *cases*. As an example, when proving the conjecture height(t) ≥ 0 our implementation considers and refutes between 6 and 8 different cases depending on which form of induction rule is used.

6   Experimental Evaluation

In this section we describe the implementation and evaluation of the techniques described in this paper.

Implementation. We extended the Vampire [10] theorem prover with additional options to capture the techniques described in the previous sections. Table 2 gives an overview of these new options. The `sik` option captures the different approaches introduced in Sect. 3. The `indm` option limits the *depth* of induction. The remaining options capture the choices made in Sect. 4. Our implementation of the induction inference rules ensures that we never instantiate the same induction axiom more than once and that proof search when there are no term algebra sorts in the problem is unaffected. Furthermore, this implementation is fully compatible with all other proof search options and heuristics in Vampire. Our implementation is available online[1].

Table 2. New options and their values.

Name	Values	Description
ind	<u>none</u>, struct	Whether structural induction should be applied or not
sik	<u>1</u>, 2, 3, all	The kind of structural induction to apply. The numbers 1,2, 3 refer to the three kinds introduced in Sect. 3 and `all` applies them all
indmd	$n \geq 0$ (<u>0</u>)	The maximum *depth* to which induction is applied where 0 indicates it is unlimited
indc	goal, goal_plus, <u>all</u>	Choices for the sel_α predicate (see Sect. 4) where `goal` uses goal symbols only, `goal_plus` uses goal and induction symbols, and `all` is unrestricted
indu	<u>on</u>, off	Whether to include the sel_U predicate
indn	<u>on</u>, off	Whether to include the sel_N predicate
gtg	on, <u>off</u>	Whether goal clauses in the input should be inferred
gtgl	$n \geq 1$ (<u>1</u>)	The *limit* of times a symbol should appear in input formulae to be identified as a goal symbol

Experimental Setup. We use two sets of benchmarks from SMT-LIB from the UFDT and UFDTLIA logics where UF stands for Uninterpreted Functions, DT stands for DataTypes and LIA stands for Linear Integer Arithmetic; we do not consider AUFDTLIA as it does not contain problems interesting for induction. UFDT consists of 4376 problems *known not to be satisfiable* (we excluded problems either marked as, or found to be, satisfiable during experiments) and UFDTLIA consists of 303 problems that formed the TIP benchmark set in 2015 as used in [16]. Experiments are run on StarExec [20].

---

[1] See https://github.com/vprover/vampire.

6.1   Research Questions

In this section we look at two research questions that naturally arise in our work.

Which Options are Useful? Given the set of introduced options, we would like to know which will be useful in general. Vampire is a portfolio solver and would normally run a series of strategies combining different options. Therefore, any options able to solve problems uniquely may be useful for a portfolio mode. Table 3 compares the option values across the SMT-LIB problems. All option values with the exception of `--sik three` and non-zero values for `indmd` solve some problems uniquely. For each option there is a clear choice for default value. The fact that non-zero values for `indmd` were not useful in general suggests that there was not a problem with an explosion of iterative induction steps. This is most likely due to the fact that clause selection will favour a breadth-first exploration of the space. The solved problems did not rely heavily on inferring goal symbols or selection via special symbols. This suggests that the problems of interest either had shallow proofs that followed quickly from the input, or contained few relevant symbols for induction.

Table 3. Comparing option values.

Value	Count	Unique	Value	Count	Unique	Value	Count	Unique
`sik`			`indmd`			`indc`		
`one`	3088	20	0	3096	37	`all`	3069	104
`two`	3028	3	1	3044	0	`goal`	2989	7
`three`	3019	0	2	3051	0	`goal_plus`	2985	1
`all`	3043	2	3	3048	0			
`indu`			`indn`			`gtg`		
`on`	3095	43	`on`	3088	50	`on`	2992	27
`off`	3053	1	`off`	3046	8	`off`	3069	104

What Do the Proofs Look Like? We ran Vampire in a portfolio mode using the additional options `-sik one -indm 0 -indc all` on the SMT-LIB UFDTLIA problem set and recorded (i) the number of induction inferences appearing in proofs, and (ii) the maximum depth of these inductions. The results are in Table 4. In the majority of cases only a few induction steps are used but there are 11 problems where more than 10 inductions are required and the proof of `induction-vmcai2015/leon/heap-goal3.smt2` uses 145 induction steps. As suggested above, induction is relatively shallow with the maximum depth in proofs being 6 and most necessary inductions not being nested.

Table 4. Statistics from 165 successful problems in UFDTLIA.

Number of induction inferences	Count
0	44
1	82
2	16
3	6
5	2
10-50	7
50-145	4

Max induction depth	Count
1	84
2	25
3	4
4	3
6	1

6.2 Comparative Evaluation

We compare the new techniques to CVC4 on the SMT-LIB benchmarks in Table 5 running both solvers with and without induction. We currently restrict our attention to CVC4 as this is the only solver available that runs on these problems and supports induction (Z3 does not support induction). It is worth noting that CVC4 was reported comparable to Zipperposition in [4] but has improved considerably in the meantime.

Table 5. Comparative results with CVC4 on SMT-LIB benchmarks.

Logic	Size	No induction		With induction	
		CVC4	Vampire	CVC4	Vampire
UFDT	4376	2270	2226 (2)	2275 (5)	2294 (37)
UFDTLIA	303	69	76	224 (69)	165 (9)

Overall CVC4 solves more problems but Vampire solves 48 problems that CVC4 (or any other solver) does not. We consider it an impressive result for a first implementation and believe that Vampire will solve many more previously unsolved problems when more heuristics, options and induction axioms are implemented.

It is interesting to note that the majority of problems are solvable without induction, suggesting the need for better benchmarks. However, we also observe that Vampire will commonly use induction to solve a problem more quickly even when induction is not required. This is also a very interesting observation since normally the addition of new rules other than simplification slows down saturation theorem provers.

The fact that the UFDTLIA benchmarks are a version of TIP allows us to indirectly compare to other inductive theorem provers. Table 6 uses historical data from the literature to show that Vampire is competitive with these solvers but does not perform as well in general. This can be explained by missing features specialised for induction that have not yet been implemented in Vampire.

Table 6. Using published data to compare to induction provers. Data for CVC4 and Vampire taken from our experiments, other data taken from [23].

	CLAM	HipSpec	Zeno	Pirate	ACL2s	IsaPlanner	Dafny	CVC4	Vampire
isaplanner	-	80	82	87	74	47	45	71	58
clam	41	47	21	47	-	-	-	41	29

7 Related Work

We focus on *explicit* induction approaches, rather than *implicit* induction, e.g. the inductionless induction [3] approach. Within this we identify two areas of relevant work - the specialised area of *inductive theorem proving* and the general approach of extending first-order theorem provers with induction.

Tools that use theorem provers as backends often include induction hypotheses in the input. For example, Dafny was extended to wrap SMT solvers with an induction layer inserting useful induction hypotheses [11] within Dafny.

There are a number of *inductive theorem provers* such as ACL2 [7], IsaPlanner [5], Zeno [19], and Hipspec [2] that differ in architecture fro our approach. ACL2 relies on a special procedure for deciding when to apply induction, HipSpec is based on a technique called *theory exploration* and IsaPlanner and Zeno follow a top-down approach. Therefore, in these other techniques most of the proof search effort is dedicated to deciding where to apply induction (as it is quite costly) whereas our approach is less guided in this sense but induction is, in some sense, cheap. In general, inductive solvers are well suited to problems that require complex induction but only require relatively simple reasoning otherwise. Our focus is the converse case.

The main previous attempt to extend a saturation-based superposition theorem prover with induction is in Zipperposition by Cruanes [4]. This approach is formulated for (generally defined) structural induction over inductive datatypes. The main difference between this previous work and ours is the way in which [4] puts together datatype reasoning, inductive reasoning, and reasoning by cases using AVATAR, whereas our work keeps all three parts separate. As a result, our approach is more general; our definition of induction does not depend on inductive datatypes and works without AVATAR, so it can be with little effort added to existing saturation theorem provers. For example, our generality results in the ability to implement well-founded induction.

Although we do note that Cruanes explores heuristics for *where to apply induction* from the broader inductive theorem proving literature that we have not yet explored.

Finally, we note that the experimental results of [4] have a different focus from our own as they focus on problems suited for inductive theorem provers whereas our research (and our experiments) focus on problems requiring a little bit of induction and a lot of complex first-order reasoning.

Another approach [23] wraps superposition-based proof search in an extra process that iteratively explores the space of possible inductions. There has also been work on incorporating induction for natural numbers into the superposition calculus [8]. CVC4 has been extended with a set of techniques for induction [16]. There rules are similar to ours but the setting is different as CVC4 is a DPLL(T)-based SMT solver using quantifier instantiation to handle quantifiers.

8 Conclusion

In this paper we introduce a new method for integrating induction into a saturation-based theorem prover using superposition. Our approach utilises the clause-splitting framework for case splitting. Experimental results show that the new options allow us to solve many problems requiring complex (e.g. nested) inductions.

Acknowledgements. We thank Andrew Reynolds for helping with obtaining CVC4 results.

References

1. Barrett, C., Fontaine, P., Tinelli, C.: The Satisfiability Modulo Theories Library (SMT-LIB) (2016). www.SMT-LIB.org
2. Claessen, K., Johansson, M., Rosén, D., Smallbone, N.: Automating inductive proofs using theory exploration. In: Bonacina, M.P. (ed.) CADE 2013. LNCS (LNAI), vol. 7898, pp. 392–406. Springer, Heidelberg (2013). https://doi.org/10.1007/978-3-642-38574-2_27
3. Comon, H.: Inductionless induction. In: Handbook of Automated Reasoning (in 2 vols.), pp. 913–962 (2001)
4. Cruanes, S.: Superposition with structural induction. In: Dixon, C., Finger, M. (eds.) FroCoS 2017. LNCS (LNAI), vol. 10483, pp. 172–188. Springer, Cham (2017). https://doi.org/10.1007/978-3-319-66167-4_10
5. Dixon, L., Fleuriot, J.: Higher order rippling in IsaPLANNER. In: Slind, K., Bunker, A., Gopalakrishnan, G. (eds.) TPHOLs 2004. LNCS, vol. 3223, pp. 83–98. Springer, Heidelberg (2004). https://doi.org/10.1007/978-3-540-30142-4_7
6. Gupta, A., Kovács, L., Kragl, B., Voronkov, A.: Extensional crisis and proving identity. In: Cassez, F., Raskin, J.-F. (eds.) ATVA 2014. LNCS, vol. 8837, pp. 185–200. Springer, Cham (2014). https://doi.org/10.1007/978-3-319-11936-6_14
7. Kaufmann, M., Strother Moore, J., Manolios, P.: Computer-Aided Reasoning: An Approach. Kluwer Academic Publishers, Norwell (2000)
8. Kersani, A., Peltier, N.: Combining superposition and induction: a practical realization. In: Fontaine, P., Ringeissen, C., Schmidt, R.A. (eds.) FroCoS 2013. LNCS (LNAI), vol. 8152, pp. 7–22. Springer, Heidelberg (2013). https://doi.org/10.1007/978-3-642-40885-4_2
9. Kovács, L., Robillard, S., Voronkov, A.: Coming to terms with quantified reasoning. SIGPLAN Not. **52**(1), 260–270 (2017)
10. Kovács, L., Voronkov, A.: First-order theorem proving and VAMPIRE. In: Sharygina, N., Veith, H. (eds.) CAV 2013. LNCS, vol. 8044, pp. 1–35. Springer, Heidelberg (2013). https://doi.org/10.1007/978-3-642-39799-8_1

11. Leino, K.R.M.: Automating induction with an SMT solver. In: Kuncak, V., Rybalchenko, A. (eds.) VMCAI 2012. LNCS, vol. 7148, pp. 315–331. Springer, Heidelberg (2012). https://doi.org/10.1007/978-3-642-27940-9_21

12. Nieuwenhuis, R., Rubio, A.: Paramodulation-based theorem proving. In: Robinson, A., Voronkov, A. (eds.) Handbook of Automated Reasoning, vol. I, chap. 7, pp. 371–443. Elsevier Science (2001)

13. Nonnengart, A., Weidenbach, C.: Computing small clause normal forms. In: Handbook of Automated Reasoning (in 2 vols.), pp. 335–367 (2001)

14. Reger, G., Bjørner, N., Suda, M., Voronkov, A.: AVATAR modulo theories. In: 2nd Global Conference on Artificial Intelligence, GCAI 2016. EPiC Series in Computing, vol. 41, pp. 39–52. EasyChair (2016)

15. Reger, G., Suda, M., Voronkov, A.: New techniques in clausal form generation. In: 2nd Global Conference on Artificial Intelligence, GCAI 2016. EPiC Series in Computing, vol. 41, pp. 11–23. EasyChair (2016)

16. Reynolds, A., Kuncak, V.: Induction for SMT solvers. In: D'Souza, D., Lal, A., Larsen, K.G. (eds.) VMCAI 2015. LNCS, vol. 8931, pp. 80–98. Springer, Heidelberg (2015). https://doi.org/10.1007/978-3-662-46081-8_5

17. Rybina, T., Voronkov, A.: A decision procedure for term algebras with queues. ACM Trans. Comput. Logic 2(2), 155–181 (2001)

18. Schulz, S.: E - a brainiac theorem prover. AI Commun. 15(2–3), 111–126 (2002)

19. Sonnex, W., Drossopoulou, S., Eisenbach, S.: Zeno: an automated prover for properties of recursive data structures. In: Flanagan, C., König, B. (eds.) TACAS 2012. LNCS, vol. 7214, pp. 407–421. Springer, Heidelberg (2012). https://doi.org/10.1007/978-3-642-28756-5_28

20. Stump, A., Sutcliffe, G., Tinelli, C.: StarExec, a cross community logic solving service (2012). https://www.starexec.org

21. Sutcliffe, G.: The TPTP problem library and associated infrastructure. J. Autom. Reason. 43(4), 337–362 (2009)

22. Voronkov, A.: AVATAR: the architecture for first-order theorem provers. In: Biere, A., Bloem, R. (eds.) CAV 2014. LNCS, vol. 8559, pp. 696–710. Springer, Cham (2014). https://doi.org/10.1007/978-3-319-08867-9_46

23. Wand, D.: Superposition: types and induction. (Superposition: types et induction). Ph.D. thesis, Saarland University, Saarbrücken, Germany (2017)

24. Weidenbach, C.: Combining superposition, sorts and splitting. In: Robinson, A., Voronkov, A. (eds.) Handbook of Automated Reasoning, vol. II, chap. 27, pp. 1965–2013. Elsevier Science (2001)

Faster, Higher, Stronger: E 2.3

Stephan Schulz[1]([⊠]), Simon Cruanes[2], and Petar Vukmirović[3]

[1] DHBW Stuttgart, Stuttgart, Germany
schulz@eprover.org
[2] Aesthetic Integration, Austin, TX, USA
simon.cruanes.2007@m4x.org
[3] Vrije Universiteit Amsterdam, Amsterdam, The Netherlands
p.vukmirovic@vu.nl

Abstract. E 2.3 is a theorem prover for many-sorted first-order logic with equality. We describe the basic logical and software architecture of the system, as well as core features of the implementation. We particularly discuss recently added features and extensions, including the extension to many-sorted logic, optional limited support for higher-order logic, and the integration of SAT techniques via PicoSAT. Minor additions include improved support for TPTP standard features, *always-on* internal proof objects, and lazy orphan removal. The paper also gives an overview of the performance of the system, and describes ongoing and future work.

1 Introduction

E is a fully automated theorem prover for first-order logic with equality. It has been under development for about 20 years, adding support for full first-order logic with E 0.82 in 2004, many-sorted first-order logic with E 2.0 in 2017, and both optional support for λ-free higher-order logic (LFHOL) and improved handling of propositional logic with the current release, E 2.3.

The basic architecture of the clausal inference core has previously been described in [15] (covering E 0.62), and the last updated description of E 1.8 was published in 2013 [18]. The recent support for λ-free higher-order logic is covered in detail in [30,31]. In this paper, we describe the current state of the prover, with a particular focus on recent developments.

E is available as free software under the GNU General Public License. Official point releases are available as source distributions from https://www.eprover. org. Development versions and the full history of changes can be found at https://github.com/eprover.

2 System Design and Architecture

The system is designed around a pipeline of largely distinct processing steps (compare Fig. 1): *Parsing, preliminary analysis, axiom selection, clausification,*

© Springer Nature Switzerland AG 2019
P. Fontaine (Ed.): CADE 2019, LNAI 11716, pp. 495–507, 2019.
https://doi.org/10.1007/978-3-030-29436-6_29

clausal preprocessing, auto-mode CNF analysis, saturation and *proof object extraction.* Parsing, clausification and saturation are necessary for actual theorem proving, the other steps are optional and enabled by command line options.

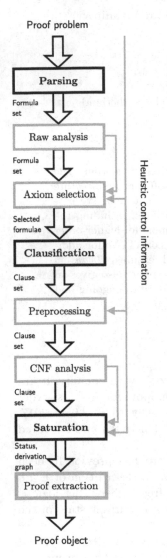

Fig. 1. Logical pipeline

In the first step, the input problem is parsed as a set of annotated formulas, where each logical formula is represented as a shared term over a signature including the usual logical operators, and wrapped in a data structure that allows annotations to capture additional extra-logical properties such as the formula role (in particular *axiom* and *conjecture*), the name of the formula, and its provenience.

The next step is an optional analysis of the parsed problem, primarily to automatically determine if and how an axiom selection scheme should be applied in the third step to reduce the number of axioms. Axiom selection is based on a variant of the SInE algorithm [8]. This step is optional. Axiom selection can be manually triggered or blocked by the user or triggered automatically based on the results of the preceding analysis step.

At the core of the prover is a refutational proof procedure for first-order clausal logic with equality. It is based on the superposition calculus (with some extensions and modifications), and works on a clausal representation of the problem. The *clausification* step converts the full first-order problem into a set of clauses. It is based on the ideas presented by Nonnengart and Weidenbach [13]. As usual with refutational theorem provers, if an explicit conjecture is given, it is negated before clausification, so that the resulting clause set is unsatisfiable if the conjecture logically follows from the axioms.

The prover optionally performs preprocessing of the clause set. Preprocessing removes redundant literals and tautologies, optionally unfolds some or all equational definitions, and orders literals and clauses in a canonical ordering so that the prover behaves in a more deterministic way.

The resulting clause set can be extracted after this stage. Indeed, several other clausal provers use E as an external clausifier. If E continues, the clause set is then analyzed to determine the search control strategy to be used by the inference core. The superposition calculus is parameterized by a term ordering and (optionally) a literal selection function. The implementation uses a variant of the *given-clause algorithm* (Fig. 2). The main additional search parameter for this algorithm is the scheme for the selection of the *given clause* for each iteration of the main loop. However, there are a large number of additional flags controlling e.g. different options for simplification. All aspects of the search strategy can again be explicitly set by the user, or automatically determined by the automatic mode of the prover.

The inference core performs a classical saturation of the clause set, optionally interspersed with calls to the CDCL-based SAT-solver *PicoSAT* [3] to detect conflicts hidden in (so far) unprocessed clauses. The procedure terminates successfully when either the empty clause has been derived directly, when the SAT-solver detects unsatisfiability of the proof state, or when the clause set is saturated. It terminates unsuccessfully, if it cannot reach success within user-defined limits (e.g. CPU time, memory, iterations, elementary term operations).

In the case of success, an optional final step can extract a proof object from the search state and present the proof to the user.

3   Calculus and Implementation

3.1   Superposition for Many-Sorted Logic

E was originally built around untyped first-order logic, distinguishing only predicate symbols (returning a Boolean value) and function symbols (returning an individual, represented as a term). Variables would implicitly range over all terms, and hence could be bound to any term. As of version 2.0, the prover has been extended to support many-sorted first order logic in the style described by Sutcliffe, Schulz, Claessen and Baumgartner [27].

In this logic, every plain function symbol has an associated function type, accepting a fixed number of arguments of defined sorts, and constructing a term of a defined return sort. Predicate symbols also accept terms of the correct sorts only. An exception is the equality-predicate, which is ad-hoc polymorphic, but requires terms of the same sort for both arguments.

Supporting many-sorted logic unlocks access to many useful features:

- expressing some size constraints over models, using axioms such as $\exists a, b : \tau, \forall x : \tau, x \simeq a \lor x \simeq b$;
- enabling more efficient encodings from systems with richer logics, such as proof assistants [4] or program verification tools [5]. While types can be encoded within plain first-order logic, these encodings tend to bloat formulas, adding sort predicates to every axiom, and to bloat terms, which reduces the effectiveness of many simplification rules;
- supporting some built-in theories, as SMT solvers typically do; indeed, the SMT-LIB language [2] is typed;
- supporting the FOOL extension [10] of first-order logic and its realization in the TFX format [26], allowing Boolean sub-terms as well as `let` and `if-then-else` constructs.

Basic support for interpreted numbers is planned for the near future, full support for TFX is already in progress and will most likely be included in the next release.

The superposition calculus readily generalizes to this logic. E implements the standard inference rules from [1]: Superposition, equality resolution, and equality factoring. In addition, it implements a large array of simplification rules, the most important of which are unconditional rewriting, subsumption, equational literal cutting and contextual literal cutting. A more detailed description of the calculus (and its realization in the proof procedure) is provided in the manual [19].

In practice, supporting simple types requires every variable and term to be annotated with its sort. Unification and retrieval of terms from indices (e.g. for demodulation) check that types are compatible before binding a variable to any given term. This is what prevents an axiom such as $\forall x : \text{side}, x \simeq \text{left} \vee x \simeq \text{right}$ to rewrite another clause's subterm of an incompatible type. This change had negligible impact on performance, but significantly improves the expressiveness of the logic.

E can currently parse the TFF0 sub-grammar of the TPTP TFF format [27], and prints typed terms and formulas using the same syntax.

Sorts were originally represented as indices into a sort table. The LFHOL extension of E 2.3 [31] further generalizes this representation to support higher-order simple types and partially applied terms. The implementation of types now uses a lightweight term-like structure, in which complex types are build from basic sorts and the arrow operator. Like terms, types are perfectly shared for efficient type equality comparisons.

3.2   Implementation

The system is being developed in C, providing good performance and maximal portability. The code of the prover proper largely restricts itself to features from C99, with some POSIX extensions. It has been successfully built on a large range of different UNIX-style operating systems, in particular OS-X/macOS (with both LLVM and GCC as compilers) and Linux, the two main development and testing platforms. It has also been compiled and run under versions of Windows, using the CygWin libraries for POSIX/UNIX compatibility.

In the past, supporting software for testing and optimizing the system has been built in a number of scripting languages, but more recently has been largely moved to Python.

While C is an excellent language for performance and portability, it offers a relatively small number of built-in data structures and programming constructs. As a consequence, E has been built on a layer of libraries providing generic data types such as unlimited size stacks, splay trees, dynamic arrays, as well as convenient abstractions for a number of operating system services.

On top of these generic libraries, the prover implements logical data types and operations. At the heart of the system is the term bank data type, an efficient and garbage-collected data structure originally for aggressively shared first-order terms. All persistent terms are inserted in a bottom-up manner into this term bank. Thus, identical terms are represented by identical pointers. This results in a saving in the number of cells needed to represent the proof state of several orders of magnitude [11]. It also enables us to precompute a number of properties and store them in the term cells. Examples include the number of function symbols in the term and the number of variable occurrences. Thus, we can e.g. decide if a shared term is ground in constant time. More importantly, we can cache the result of rewrite attempts at the term level—in the case of success with a link to the result (and, for proof reconstruction, with the clause used as a side premise), in the case of failure with the age of the youngest clause tried, so that future attempts can be restricted to newer clauses.

The term bank data structure and its API has proven to be efficient and convenient. In particular, the mark-and-sweep garbage collector makes the creation and destruction of terms very convenient and reduces programmer effort and errors. As a result, shared terms are now also used to represent formulas and in some roles even clauses (which, as of E 2.2, are parsed as a special case of formulas).

Literals and clauses for the inference core are implemented as dedicated data structures. Internally, all literals are equational. In addition to the two terms making up the equation, literals include polarity (positive or negative), a number of Boolean flags, and a pointer for creating linked lists. Clauses consist of such a linked list of literals, wrapped in a container for meta-data, heuristic evaluations, and information about the derivation of the clause.

Proof Procedure. Figure 2 depicts the main saturation procedure. It is a modified version of the DISCOUNT loop [6], one of the variants of the *given-clause algorithm*. The proof state is represented by two disjoint subsets of clauses, the *processed* clauses P and the *unprocessed* clauses U. Initially, all clauses are unprocessed. At each iteration of the main loop, the prover heuristically selects a *given clause* from U, adds it to P, and performs all generating inferences between this clause and all clauses in P. The resulting new clauses are added to U. This maintains the invariant that all direct consequences between clauses in P have been performed. Forward simplification is performed on the given clause (using clauses in P as side premises) before it is used for generation, and on new clauses before they are added to U. In addition, clauses in P are back-simplified with the given clause, and simplified clauses are moved to U. This maintains the additional invariant that the clauses in P are interreduced, or maximally simplified with respect to other clauses in P.

In addition to saturation, the current version may trigger a propositional check for unsatisfiability of a grounded version of the proof state, as described below.

Internal Proof Objects. Originally, E only offered the option to log all inferences to an external medium and then generate a proof object in a post-mortem analysis. Since these logs often reached extreme sizes, this was costly and not even practically possible for long runs.

Search state: (U, P)
U contains *unprocessed* clauses, P contains *processed* clauses.
Initially, P is empty and all clauses are in U.
The *given clause* is denoted by g.

---

while $U \neq \{\}$
    if prop_trigger(U,P)
        if prop_unsat_check(U,P)
            SUCCESS, Proof found
    $g = \text{extract\_best}(U)$
    $g = \text{simplify}(g, P)$
    if $g == \square$
        SUCCESS, Proof found
    if g is not subsumed by any clause in P (or otherwise redundant w.r.t. P)
        $P = P \backslash \{c \in P \mid c \text{ subsumed by (or otherwise redundant w.r.t.) } g\}$
        $T = \{c \in P \mid c \text{ can be simplified with } g\}$
        $P = (P \backslash T) \cup \{g\}$
        $T = T \cup \text{generate}(g, P)$
        $T' = \{\}$
        foreach $c \in T$
            $c = \text{cheap\_simplify}(c, P)$
            if c is not trivial
                $T' = T' \cup \{c\}$
        $U = U \cup T'$
SUCCESS, original U is satisfiable

Fig. 2. The modified *given-clause* algorithm as implemented in E

With E 1.8, we finally found a way to use the invariants of the given-clause algorithm to very compactly represent the derivation graph internally [22]. Since the overhead in time and memory turned out to be negligible, we have simplified the code and now always build an internal proof object. In addition to efficiently providing a checkable proof object in TPTP syntax [28], the presence of the derivation information enables the detection of vacuous proofs (based on an inconsistent axiomatization). It also enables an elegant lazy implementation of *orphan killing*. An orphan is a generated clause which has lost at least one of its parents to interreduction before being selected for processing, and which hence can be deleted as well. Older versions of E maintained an explicit list of direct descendants for processed clauses, and actively removed such descendents if the parent clause became redundant. As of E 2.2, we instead check the status of the parent clauses (which are either active or archived) only when the clause is selected for processing. This removes the bookkeeping overhead and simplifies both code and data structures.

In addition to the generation of proof objects, the system supports the proposed TPTP standard for answers [29]. An *answer* is an instantiation for an existential conjecture (or *query*) that makes the conjecture true. E can supply bindings for the outermost existentially quantified variables in a TPTP formula with type `question`.

Indexing. Most of the generating and simplifying inference rules require two premises - the main premise and a side premise. For generating inferences, one of the inference partners is the given clause, the other one is a clause in P. E uses a *fingerprint index* [16] to efficiently find clauses with (sub-)terms that are unifiable with the maximal terms of inference literals of the given clause.

For simplification, the DISCOUNT loop distinguishes two situations. In *forward simplification*, all clauses in P are used as side premises to simplify a given clause - either *the* given clause, or a newly generated clause. E uses *perfect discrimination trees* [12] with size- and age-constraints for forward rewriting. Backward simplification uses a single clause to simplify all clauses from P. E uses fingerprint indexing for backwards rewriting. Subsumption and contextual literal cutting use *feature vector indexing* [17], a clause indexing technique that supports the finding of both generalizations and instances.

SAT Integration. SAT solvers have greatly improved performance in the last decades, and can handle propositional problems that are far beyond the practical scope of classical first-order provers with ease. Following other attempts [9, 14], we want to utilize this power to improve the performance of the prover both for problems with a significant propositional component as well as for first-order problems where contradictory instances are generated early, but are not detected until all involved clauses have been selected for processing.

We have thus integrated the CDCL solver PicoSAT [3] with E. The saturation loop is periodically interrupted, and all clauses in the current proof state are grounded, i.e. all variables are bound to a constant of the proper sort. The instantiated clauses are efficiently translated into propositional clauses and handed to PicoSAT. Our original implementation used PicoSAT as an external tool via files and UNIX pipes [20], but as of E 2.2 we link PicoSAT as a library and use its documented C API. If PicoSAT refutes the given propositional problem, E extracts the unsatisfiable core and relates it back to the original first-order clauses to construct a proof object. If PicoSAT fails to find unsatisfiability, the saturation is resumed.

E users can control this process by choosing the following options:

- the point when PicoSAT is called – currently it is after N generated or processed clauses or after N new subterms created, where N is a user-chosen constant
- the way variables are instantiated with constants – some of the options are to use the most or the least frequent constant, a fresh constant (for each type), or a frequent or infrequent constant appearing in the conjecture.

We have only started to explore the parameter space. With current configurations, E finds about 1% more proofs on TPTP when PicoSAT is enabled. While this number seems low, it is significant among hard problems - 90% of solutions are found before the first run of the SAT solver.

3.3   Higher-Order Logic Support

One of the most recent updates for E adds support for λ-free higher-order logic (LFHOL). Supporting richer logics in a highly optimized theorem prover without compromising performance required some changes to fundamental data structures and algorithms. Here we will only briefly describe the changes. We refer the reader to [31] for details.

LFHOL is a fragment of simply-typed higher-order logic, with no λ-abstraction, but supporting functional variables and partial application of terms. It is expressive enough to axiomatize, for example, frequently used functional programming combinators such as map. We have generalized E's term representation to allow applied variables, as well as the type system to support partially applied terms. The most laborious change was the extension of all three indexing data structures to support more complex terms. Our experimental results show that E extended to support LFHOL natively outperforms the traditional encoding-based approaches. E 2.3 users can specify LFHOL problems in TPTP THF syntax. Support for LFHOL can be specified as an option at compile time.

3.4   Search Control

All provers for first-order logic search for proofs in an infinite search space. While *fairness* is a minimal requirement for completeness, practical performance depends critically on making the right choices. The prover supports a large number of options for controlling preprocessing and actual search control.

The most important parameters for the saturation are the *term ordering*, the *literal selection strategy*, and *clause evaluation heuristics*. Term orderings primarily determine in which direction equations can be applied (and as a consequence, which terms are overlapped for superposition inferences), and which literals are maximal and hence available for inferences. Literal selection can be used to overwrite the default inference literals and restrict inferences to particular (negative) literals. Finally, clause evaluations determine the order in which the given-clause algorithm processes clauses. In the simplest case, this is a single value, representing the number of symbols in the clause (known as a *symbol-counting* heuristic—smaller is better). E generalizes this concept and allows the user to specify an arbitrary number of priority queues and a weighted round-robin scheme that determines how many clauses are picked from each queue. Each queue is ordered by a particular evaluation function. A major feature is the use of goal-directed evaluation functions. These give a lower weight to symbols that occur in the goal, and a higher weight to other symbols, thus preferring clauses likely connected to the conjecture. We have so far only evaluated a small part of the possibility space opened by this design [21].

More complex clause evaluation functions allow the system to evaluate clauses based on a user-provided *watch list*. Clauses that match clauses on the watch list are preferred over other clauses. Watch lists can either be created based on human intuition, by manual analysis of similar proofs, or by automated mining of related proofs. The watch list mechanism in E has been improved several times, with the current incarnation [7] being successfully used for challenging mathematical problems.

Automatic Prover Configuration. Finding good heuristics for a given problem is challenging even for an experienced user. E supports a number of *automatic modes* that analyze the problem and apply either a single strategy or a schedule of several strategies. The selection of strategies and generation of schedules for each class of problems is determined automatically by analyzing previous performance of the prover on similar problems.

3.5 Usage and Formats

Recent versions of E have made minor changes to the usage and options, as well as to I/O formats. These are mostly conservative, i.e. they should not significantly impact integration of the prover into larger systems.

The first such change is automatic detection of the input format. E supports three different formats: The original LOP format inherited from SETHEO, the old TPTP format (TPTP format version 1/2) and the current TPTP format version 3. The prover has originally used command line options to select the desired format. However, with E 1.9.1, we introduced automatic detection of the input format (and automatic setting of the corresponding output format). This feature is implemented by checking the first proper input token, and selecting TPTP-3 format if it is one of the TPTP-3 language identifiers (`cnf`, `fof`, ...), or `include`, TPTP-2 format if it is one of `input_clause` or `input_formula`, and LOP otherwise. It is not completely foolproof (it can e.g. misidentify LOP input that uses TPTP-3 language identifiers as normal function symbols), but it works very well in practice. If it misidentifies the format, it fails towards the more modern TPTP-3 format. We have not yet encountered that situation. If TPTP-3 syntax is identified, the output syntax is also set to TPTP-3, otherwise it is set to PCL2 (E's original, more limited format). These choices can be independently overwritten via explicit use of the existing command line options.

The second change is more strict checking of TPTP language constraints. In particular, E now requires FOF, TFF and TCF style formulas to be fully quantified. CNF formulas are implicitly considered universally quantified. This change was prompted by frequent user errors dur to misjudging quantifier scopes and hence inadvertently creating free variables. Such cases will now be flagged as errors.

Similarly, E will now automatically type numerical constants as `$int`/`$rat` or `$real` (which will result in errors if they are used in untyped formulas) unless they are explicitly marked as free constants by a command line switch.

Finally, the prover now can detect proofs resulting from an inconsistent axiom set, and explicitly report the problem status as `ContradictoryAxioms`.

4   Experimental Evaluation

We have performed an evaluation of E 2.3 on the 16094 CNF and FOF problems of the TPTP problem library [25], release 7.2.0. Experiments were run on the StarExec cluster [23], i.e. on machines with an Intel Xeon E5/2.40 GHz processor and at least 128 GB of main memory. We used a CPU time limit of 300 s per problem and the prover was configured to optimize memory usage to at most 2 GB.

Table 1. Proofs and (counter-)saturations found within 300 s

Strategy Class size	UEQ (1193)	CNE (2383)	CEQ (4442)	FNE (1771)	FEQ (6305)	All (16094)
Auto (proofs)	814	1603	2360	1156	3704	9637
Auto (sat)	16	280	220	304	203	1023
Auto (all)	830	1883	2580	1460	3907	10660
E 1.8 Auto (all)	*812*	*1851*	*2561*	*1456*	*3909*	*10589*
Schedule (proofs)	829	1625	2470	1165	3961	10050
Schedule (sat)	16	286	219	307	206	1034
Schedule (all)	845	1911	2689	1472	4167	11084
E 1.8 Schedule (all)	*828*	*1889*	*2655*	*1463*	*4113*	*10948*

Table 1 summarizes the results of the experiment. We list the performance for unit-equational problems, clausal and non-clausal problems with and without equality. The two tested strategies are the automatic mode and the automatic strategy scheduler. For each strategy, we list the number of proofs found, the number of counter-saturations (i.e. saturations not including the empty clause), and the total number of successes. For comparison, we have also included data for E 1.8, the last version with a formally published description. The full data, including the exact command line options, is available at http://www.eprover.eu/E-eu/E_2.3.html.

5   Future Work

While E is quite mature and widely used, there is a number of projects for further improvement - in data structures, search control, and supported language. In particular, terms can be more compactly represented with variable length arrays (a feature not yet available in standard C when the data type was first designed), and priority queues can be more efficiently realized with heaps. Feature vector indexing works very well for classical theorem proving problems, but is less than optimal for problems with very large and sparsely used signatures. We plan to develop it into a more adaptive and efficient variant.

On the language side, we plan to support the full TFX language [26] and hence the FOOL logic. We also plan to add at least basic support for interpreted arithmetic sorts.

A lot of recent improvements have only been evaluated in isolation, not in concert. A major project is such a large-scale evaluation and a regeneration of the automatic modes to make better use of the new features.

Finally, E has grown over more than 20 years now. While we have tried to integrate new techniques in as modular and elegant a way as possible, some of the higher level-code can profit from significant refactoring and streamlining.

6 Conclusion

E is a mature and yet still developing fully automated theorem prover for first-order logics and some extensions. It has good performance, as demonstrated in the yearly CASC competitions [24].

The prover is available as free and open source software, and has been used and extended by a large number of parties. We hope and expect that this success will continue throughout the third decade of its lifetime.

References

1. Bachmair, L., Ganzinger, H.: Rewrite-based equational theorem proving with selection and simplification. J. Logic Comput. **3**(4), 217–247 (1994)
2. Barrett, C., Stump, A., Tinelli, C.: The SMT-lib standard: version 2.0. In: Proceedings of the 8th International Workshop on Satisfiability Modulo Theories (Edinburgh, UK) (2010). http://homepage.cs.uiowa.edu/~tinelli/papers/BarST-SMT-10.pdf
3. Biere, A.: PicoSAT essentials. J. Satisfiability Boolean Model. Comput. **4**, 75–97 (2008)
4. Blanchette, J.C., Kaliszyk, C., Paulson, L.C., Urban, J.: Hammering towards QED. J. Formal Reason. **9**(1), 101–148 (2016). https://doi.org/10.6092/issn.1972-5787/4593
5. Bobot, F., Filliâtre, J.C., Marché, C., Paskevich, A.: Why3: shepherd your herd of provers. In: First International Workshop on Intermediate Verification Languages, Boogie 2011, Wrocław, Poland, pp. 53–64, August 2011. http://proval.lri.fr/publications/boogie11final.pdf
6. Denzinger, J., Kronenburg, M., Schulz, S.: DISCOUNT: a distributed and learning equational prover. J. Autom. Reason. **18**(2), 189–198 (1997). Special Issue on the CADE 13 ATP System Competition
7. Goertzel, Z., Jakubův, J., Schulz, S., Urban, J.: ProofWatch: watchlist guidance for large theories in E. In: Avigad, J., Mahboubi, A. (eds.) ITP 2018. LNCS, vol. 10895, pp. 270–288. Springer, Cham (2018). https://doi.org/10.1007/978-3-319-94821-8_16
8. Hoder, K., Voronkov, A.: Sine Qua Non for large theory reasoning. In: Bjørner, N., Sofronie-Stokkermans, V. (eds.) CADE 2011. LNCS (LNAI), vol. 6803, pp. 299–314. Springer, Heidelberg (2011). https://doi.org/10.1007/978-3-642-22438-6_23

9. Korovin, K.: Inst-Gen – a modular approach to instantiation-based automated reasoning. In: Voronkov, A., Weidenbach, C. (eds.) Programming Logics. LNCS, vol. 7797, pp. 239–270. Springer, Heidelberg (2013). https://doi.org/10.1007/978-3-642-37651-1_10

10. Kotelnikov, E., Kovács, L., Reger, G., Voronkov, A.: The Vampire and the FOOL. In: Avigad, J., Chlipala, A. (eds.) Proceedings of the 5th ACM SIGPLAN Conference on Certified Programs and Proofs, Saint Petersburg, USA, pp. 37–48. ACM (2016)

11. Löchner, B., Schulz, S.: An evaluation of shared rewriting. In: de Nivelle, H., Schulz, S. (eds.) Proceedings of the 2nd International Workshop on the Implementation of Logics, pp. 33–48. MPI Preprint, Max-Planck-Institut für Informatik, Saarbrücken (2001)

12. McCune, W.: Experiments with discrimination-tree indexing and path indexing for term retrieval. J. Autom. Reason. **9**(2), 147–167 (1992)

13. Nonnengart, A., Weidenbach, C.: Computing small clause normal forms. In: Robinson, A., Voronkov, A. (eds.) Handbook of Automated Reasoning, vol. I, chap. 5, pp. 335–367. Elsevier Science and MIT Press (2001)

14. Reger, G., Suda, M., Voronkov, A.: Playing with AVATAR. In: Felty, A.P., Middeldorp, A. (eds.) CADE 2015. LNCS (LNAI), vol. 9195, pp. 399–415. Springer, Cham (2015). https://doi.org/10.1007/978-3-319-21401-6_28

15. Schulz, S.: E – a brainiac theorem prover. J. AI Commun. **15**(2/3), 111–126 (2002)

16. Schulz, S.: Fingerprint indexing for paramodulation and rewriting. In: Gramlich, B., Miller, D., Sattler, U. (eds.) IJCAR 2012. LNCS (LNAI), vol. 7364, pp. 477–483. Springer, Heidelberg (2012). https://doi.org/10.1007/978-3-642-31365-3_37

17. Schulz, S.: Simple and efficient clause subsumption with feature vector indexing. In: Bonacina, M.P., Stickel, M.E. (eds.) Automated Reasoning and Mathematics. LNCS (LNAI), vol. 7788, pp. 45–67. Springer, Heidelberg (2013). https://doi.org/10.1007/978-3-642-36675-8_3

18. Schulz, S.: System description: E 1.8. In: McMillan, K., Middeldorp, A., Voronkov, A. (eds.) LPAR 2013. LNCS, vol. 8312, pp. 735–743. Springer, Heidelberg (2013). https://doi.org/10.1007/978-3-642-45221-5_49

19. Schulz, S.: E 2.0 User Manual. EasyChair preprint no. 8 (2018). https://doi.org/10.29007/m4jw

20. Schulz, S.: Light-weight integration of SAT solving into first-order reasoners - first experiments. In: Kovács, L., Voronkov, A. (eds.) Vampire 2017, Proceedings of the 4th Vampire Workshop. EPiC Series in Computing, vol. 53, pp. 9–19. EasyChair (2018). https://doi.org/10.29007/89kc. https://easychair.org/publications/paper/94vW

21. Schulz, S., Möhrmann, M.: Performance of clause selection heuristics for saturation-based theorem proving. In: Olivetti, N., Tiwari, A. (eds.) IJCAR 2016. LNCS (LNAI), vol. 9706, pp. 330–345. Springer, Cham (2016). https://doi.org/10.1007/978-3-319-40229-1_23

22. Schulz, S., Sutcliffe, G.: Proof generation for saturating first-order theorem provers. In: Delahaye, D., Woltzenlogel Paleo, B. (eds.) All About Proofs, Proofs for All, Mathematical Logic and Foundations, vol. 55, pp. 45–61. College Publications, London, January 2015

23. Stump, A., Sutcliffe, G., Tinelli, C.: StarExec: a cross-community infrastructure for logic solving. In: Demri, S., Kapur, D., Weidenbach, C. (eds.) IJCAR 2014. LNCS (LNAI), vol. 8562, pp. 367–373. Springer, Cham (2014). https://doi.org/10.1007/978-3-319-08587-6_28

24. Sutcliffe, G.: The 8th IJCAR automated theorem proving system competition-CASC-J8. AI Commun. **29**(5), 607–619 (2016)
25. Sutcliffe, G.: The TPTP problem library and associated infrastructure - from CNF to TH0, TPTP v6.4.0. J. Autom. Reason. **59**(4), 483–502 (2017)
26. Sutcliffe, G., Kotelnikov, E.: TFX: the TPTP extended typed first-order form. In: Konev, B., Urban, J., Rümmer, P. (eds.) Proceedings of the 6th Workshop on Practical Aspects of Automated Reasoning (PAAR), Oxford, UK. CEUR Workshop Proceedings, vol. 2162, pp. 72–87 (2018). http://ceur-ws.org/Vol-2162/#paper-07
27. Sutcliffe, G., Schulz, S., Claessen, K., Baumgartner, P.: The TPTP typed first-order form with arithmetic. In: Bjørner, N., Voronkov, A. (eds.) LPAR 2012. LNCS, vol. 7180, pp. 406–419. Springer, Heidelberg (2012). https://doi.org/10.1007/978-3-642-28717-6_32
28. Sutcliffe, G., Schulz, S., Claessen, K., Van Gelder, A.: Using the TPTP language for writing derivations and finite interpretations. In: Furbach, U., Shankar, N. (eds.) IJCAR 2006. LNCS (LNAI), vol. 4130, pp. 67–81. Springer, Heidelberg (2006). https://doi.org/10.1007/11814771_7
29. Sutcliffe, G., Stickel, M., Schulz, S., Urban, J.: Answer extraction for TPTP. http://www.cs.miami.edu/~tptp/TPTP/Proposals/AnswerExtraction.html. Accessed 08 July 2013
30. Vukmirović, P., Blanchette, J.C., Cruanes, S., Schulz, S.: Extending a brainiac prover to lambda-free higher-order logic - report version. Technical report, Matryoshka Project (2018). http://matryoshka.gforge.inria.fr/pubs/ehoh_report.pdf
31. Vukmirović, P., Blanchette, J.C., Cruanes, S., Schulz, S.: Extending a brainiac prover to lambda-free higher-order logic. In: Vojnar, T., Zhang, L. (eds.) TACAS 2019. LNCS, vol. 11427, pp. 192–210. Springer, Cham (2019). https://doi.org/10.1007/978-3-030-17462-0_11

Certified Equational Reasoning
via Ordered Completion

Christian Sternagel$^{(\boxtimes)}$ and Sarah Winkler$^{(\boxtimes)}$

Department of Computer Science, University of Innsbruck, Innsbruck, Austria
{christian.sternagel,sarah.winkler}@uibk.ac.at

Abstract. On the one hand, equational reasoning is a fundamental part of automated theorem proving with ordered completion as a key technique. On the other hand, the complexity of corresponding, often highly optimized, automated reasoning tools makes implementations inherently error-prone. As a remedy, we provide a formally verified certifier for ordered completion based techniques. This certifier is code generated from an accompanying Isabelle/HOL formalization of ordered rewriting and ordered completion incorporating an advanced ground joinability criterion. It allows us to rigorously validate generated proof certificates from several domains: ordered completion, satisfiability in equational logic, and confluence of conditional term rewriting.

Keywords: Equational reasoning · Ordered completion ·
Ground joinability · Certification

1 Introduction

Equational reasoning constitutes a main area of automated theorem proving in which completion has evolved as a fundamental technique [8]. Completion aims to transform a given set of equations into a terminating and confluent rewrite system that induces the same equational theory. Thus, on success, such a rewrite system can be used to decide equivalence of terms with respect to the initial set of equations. The original completion procedure may fail due to unorientable equations. As a remedy to this problem, ordered completion—also known as unfailing completion—was developed [3]. As the name suggests, unfailing completion always yields a result (which may however be infinite and thus take infinitely many inference steps to compute). This time, the result is an ordered rewrite system (given by a ground total reduction order, a set of rules which are oriented with respect to this order, and a set of equations) that is still terminating, but in general only ground confluent (that is, confluent on ground terms). Thus, the resulting system can be used to decide equivalence of *ground* terms with respect to the initial set of equations. This suffices for

This work is supported by Austrian Science Fund (FWF) projects T789 and P27502.

P. Fontaine (Ed.): CADE 2019, LNAI 11716, pp. 508–525, 2019.
https://doi.org/10.1007/978-3-030-29436-6_30

many practical purposes: A well-known success story of ordered completion is the solution of the long-standing Robbins conjecture [10], followed by applications to other problems from (Boolean) algebra [11]. More recent applications include the use of ordered completion in algebraic data integration [14] and in confluence proofs of conditional term rewrite systems [20].

As an introductory example, let us illustrate ordered completion on the following set of equations describing a group where all elements are self-inverse:

$$f(x,y) \approx f(y,x) \quad f(x,f(y,z)) \approx f(f(x,y),z) \quad f(x,x) \approx 0 \quad f(x,0) \approx x$$

Using ordered completion, the tool MædMax [24] transforms it into the following rules ($\rightarrow$) and equations ($\approx$), together with a suitable ground total reduction order $>$ that orients all rules from left to right.

$$f(x,f(x,y)) \rightarrow f(0,y) \qquad f(x,f(y,x)) \rightarrow f(0,y) \quad f(x,x) \rightarrow 0 \quad f(x,0) \rightarrow x$$
$$f(f(x,y),z) \rightarrow f(x,f(y,z)) \qquad \quad f(0,x) \rightarrow x$$
$$f(x,f(y,z)) \approx f(y,f(x,z)) \qquad \quad f(x,y) \approx f(y,x)$$

This ordered rewrite system can be used to decide a given equation between ground terms, by checking whether the unique normal forms (with respect to ordered rewriting using $>$) of both terms coincide.

Automated reasoning tools are highly sophisticated pieces of software, not only because they implement complex calculi, but also due to their high degree of optimization. Consequently, their implementation is inherently error-prone.

To improve their trustability we follow a two-staged certification approach and (1) add the relevant concepts and results regarding ordered completion to a formal library using the proof assistant Isabelle/HOL [12] (version Isabelle2019), and from there (2) code generate [5] a trusted certifier that is correct by construction. Our formalization strengthens the originally proposed procedure [3] by using a relaxed version of the inference system, while incorporating a stronger ground joinability criterion [9]. Our certifier allows us to rigorously validate generated proof certificates from several domains: ordered completion, satisfiability in equational logic, and confluence of conditional term rewriting.

More specifically, our contributions are as follows:

- We extend the existing **Isabelle Formalization of Rewriting**[1] (IsaFoR for short) by ordered rewriting and a generalization of the ordered completion calculus oKB [3], and prove the latter correct for finite completion runs with respect to ground total reduction orders (Sect. 3).
- We establish ground totality of the Knuth-Bendix order and the lexicographic path order in IsaFoR (Sect. 3).
- We formalize two criteria for ground joinability [3,9] known from the literature, that allow us to apply our previous results to concrete completion runs (Sect. 4). In fact, we present a slightly more powerful version of the latter, and fix an error in its proof, as described below.

---

[1] http://cl-informatik.uibk.ac.at/isafor

- We apply ordered completion to satisfiability in equational logic and infeasibility of conditions in conditional rewriting (Sect. 5).
- We extend the XML-based *certification problem format* (CPF for short) [18] by certificates for ordered completion and formalize corresponding executable check functions that verify the supplied derivations (Sect. 6).
- Finally, we extend the completion tool MædMax [24], as well as the confluence tool ConCon [20] by certificate generation and evaluate our approach on existing benchmarks (Sect. 7).

As a result, CeTA (the certifier accompanying IsaFoR) can now certify (a) ordered completion proofs and (b) satisfiability proofs of equational logic produced by the tool MædMax, as well as (c) conditional confluence proofs by ConCon where infeasibility of critical pairs is established via equational logic. To the best of our knowledge, CeTA constitutes the first proof checker in all of these domains.

In the remainder we provide hyperlinks (marked by ☑) to an HTML rendering of our formalization.

This work is an extension of an earlier workshop paper [19]. Further note that the IsaFoR formalization of the results in this paper is, apart from very basic results on (ordered) rewriting, entirely disjoint from our previous formalization together with Hirokawa and Middeldorp [6]. On the one hand, we consider a relaxed completion inference system where more inferences are allowed. This is possible since we are only interested in finite completion runs. On the other hand, we employ a stronger ground joinability criterion. Another major difference is that our new formalization enables actual certification of ordered completion based techniques, which is not the case for our work with Hirokawa and Middeldorp.

2   Preliminaries

In the sequel, we use standard notation from term rewriting [2]. Let $\mathcal{T}(\mathcal{F}, \mathcal{V})$ denote the *set of all terms* over a signature $\mathcal{F}$ and an infinite set of variables $\mathcal{V}$, and $\mathcal{T}(\mathcal{F})$ the *set of all ground terms* over $\mathcal{F}$ (that is, terms without variables). A *substitution* σ is a mapping from variables to terms. As usual, we write $t\sigma$ for the *application* of σ to the term t. A *variable permutation* (or *renaming*) π is a bijective substitution such that $\pi(x) \in \mathcal{V}$ for all $x \in \mathcal{V}$. Given an equational system (ES) $\mathcal{E}$, we write $\mathcal{E}^{\leftrightarrow}$ to denote its *symmetric closure* $\mathcal{E} \cup \{t \approx s \mid s \approx t \in \mathcal{E}\}$. A *reduction order* is a proper and well-founded order on terms which is closed under contexts and substitutions. It is $\mathcal{F}$-*ground total* if it is total on $\mathcal{T}(\mathcal{F})$. In the remainder we often focus on the Knuth-Bendix order (KBO), written $>_{\mathsf{kbo}}$, and the lexicographic path order (LPO), written $>_{\mathsf{lpo}}$. Given a reduction order $>$ and an ES $\mathcal{E}$, the term rewrite system (TRS) $\mathcal{E}_>$ consists of all rules $s\sigma \to t\sigma$ such that $s \approx t \in \mathcal{E}^{\leftrightarrow}$ and $s\sigma > t\sigma$.

Given a reduction order $>$, an *extended overlap* consists of two variable-disjoint variants $\ell_1 \approx r_1$ and $\ell_2 \approx r_2$ of equations in $\mathcal{E}^{\leftrightarrow}$ such that $p \in \mathcal{P}os_{\mathcal{F}}(\ell_2)$ and ℓ_1 and $\ell_2|_p$ are unifiable with most general unifier μ. An extended overlap which in addition satisfies $r_1\mu \not> \ell_1\mu$ and $r_2\mu \not> \ell_2\mu$ gives rise to the *extended critical pair* $\ell_2[r_1]_p\mu \approx r_2\mu$. The set $\text{CP}_>(\mathcal{E})$ consists of all extended critical pairs between equations in $\mathcal{E}$. A relation on terms is *(ground) complete*, if it is terminating and confluent (on ground terms). A TRS $\mathcal{R}$ is (ground) complete whenever the induced rewrite relation $\to_{\mathcal{R}}$ is. Finally, we say that a TRS $\mathcal{R}$ is a *presentation* of an ES $\mathcal{E}$, whenever $\leftrightarrow^*_{\mathcal{E}} = \leftrightarrow^*_{\mathcal{R}}$ (that is, their equational theories coincide).

A substitution σ is *grounding* for a term t if $\sigma(x) \in \mathcal{T}(\mathcal{F})$ for all $x \in \mathcal{V}ar(t)$. Two terms s and t are called *ground joinable* over a rewrite system $\mathcal{R}$, denoted $s \downarrow^g_{\mathcal{R}} t$ if $s\sigma \downarrow_{\mathcal{R}} t\sigma$ for all substitutions σ that are grounding for s and t.

For any complete rewrite relation $\to$, we denote the (necessarily unique) *normal form* of a term t (that is, the term u such that we have $t \to^* u$ but $u \not\to v$ for all terms v) by $t\downarrow$. By an *ordered rewrite system* we mean a pair $(\mathcal{E}, \mathcal{R})$, consisting of an ES $\mathcal{E}$ and a TRS $\mathcal{R}$, together with a reduction order $>$. Then, *ordered rewriting* is rewriting with respect to the TRS $\mathcal{R} \cup \mathcal{E}_>$. Note that ordered rewriting is always terminating if $\mathcal{R} \subseteq >$. Take commutativity $x * y \approx y * x$ for example, which causes nontermination when used as a rule in a TRS. Nevertheless, the ordered rewrite system $(\{x * y \approx y * x\}, \varnothing)$ together with KBO, say with precedence $* > \mathsf{a} > \mathsf{b}$, *is* terminating and we can for example rewrite $\mathsf{a} * \mathsf{b}$ to $\mathsf{b} * \mathsf{a}$ since applying the substitution $\{x \mapsto \mathsf{a}, y \mapsto \mathsf{b}\}$ to the commutativity equation results in a KBO-oriented instance.

3   Formalized Ordered Completion

Ordered completion is commonly presented as a set of inference rules, parameterized by a fixed reduction order $>$. This way of presentation conveniently leaves a lot of freedom to implementations. We use the following inference system, with some differences to the original formulation [3] that we discuss below.

Definition 1 (Ordered Completion ☑). *The inference system* oKB *of ordered completion operates on pairs* $(\mathcal{E}, \mathcal{R})$ *of equations* $\mathcal{E}$ *and rules* $\mathcal{R}$ *over a common signature* $\mathcal{F}$. *It consists of the following inference rules, where* $\mathcal{S}$ *abbreviates* $\mathcal{R} \cup \mathcal{E}_>$ *and* π *is a renaming.*

$$\text{deduce } \frac{\mathcal{E}, \mathcal{R}}{\mathcal{E} \cup \{s\pi \approx t\pi\}, \mathcal{R}} \text{ if } s \underset{\mathcal{R}\cup\mathcal{E}\hookleftarrow}{\leftarrow \cdot \to} t \qquad \text{compose } \frac{\mathcal{E}, \mathcal{R} \uplus \{s \to t\}}{\mathcal{E}, \mathcal{R} \cup \{s\pi \to u\pi\}} \text{ if } t \to_{\mathcal{S}} u$$

$$\text{orient } \begin{array}{c} \dfrac{\mathcal{E} \uplus \{s \approx t\}, \mathcal{R}}{\mathcal{E}, \mathcal{R} \cup \{s\pi \to t\pi\}} \text{ if } s > t \\[2em] \dfrac{\mathcal{E} \uplus \{s \approx t\}, \mathcal{R}}{\mathcal{E}, \mathcal{R} \cup \{t\pi \to s\pi\}} \text{ if } t > s \end{array} \qquad \text{simplify } \begin{array}{c} \dfrac{\mathcal{E} \uplus \{s \approx t\}, \mathcal{R}}{\mathcal{E} \cup \{u\pi \approx t\pi\}, \mathcal{R}} \text{ if } s \to_{\mathcal{S}} u \\[2em] \dfrac{\mathcal{E} \uplus \{s \approx t\}, \mathcal{R}}{\mathcal{E} \cup \{s\pi \approx u\pi\}, \mathcal{R}} \text{ if } t \to_{\mathcal{S}} u \end{array}$$

$$\text{delete } \frac{\mathcal{E} \uplus \{s \approx s\}, \mathcal{R}}{\mathcal{E}, \mathcal{R}} \qquad \text{collapse } \frac{\mathcal{E}, \mathcal{R} \uplus \{t \to s\}}{\mathcal{E} \cup \{u\pi \approx s\pi\}, \mathcal{R}} \text{ if } t \to_{\mathcal{S}} u$$

We write $(\mathcal{E}, \mathcal{R}) \vdash (\mathcal{E}', \mathcal{R}')$ if $(\mathcal{E}', \mathcal{R}')$ is obtained from $(\mathcal{E}, \mathcal{R})$ by employing one of the above inference rules. A finite sequence of inference steps

$$(\mathcal{E}_0, \varnothing) \vdash (\mathcal{E}_1, \mathcal{R}_1) \vdash \cdots \vdash (\mathcal{E}_n, \mathcal{R}_n)$$

is called a *run*. Definition 1 differs from the original formulation of ordered completion [3] (as well as the formulation in our previous work together with Hirokawa and Middeldorp [6]) in two ways. First, collapse and simplify do not have an encompassment condition.[2] This omission is possible since we only consider *finite* runs. Second, we allow variants of rules and equations to be added. This relaxation tremendously simplifies certificate generation in tools, where facts are renamed upon generation to avoid the maintenance and processing of many renamed versions of the same equation or rule. Also note that the deduce rule admits the addition of equations that originate from arbitrary peaks. In practice, tools usually limit its application to extended critical pairs.

The following two results establish that the rules resulting from a finite oKB run are oriented by the reduction order $>$ and that the induced equational theories before and after completion coincide.

Lemma 1 (☑).   *If $(\mathcal{E}, \mathcal{R}) \vdash^* (\mathcal{E}', \mathcal{R}')$ then $\mathcal{R} \subseteq \; >$ implies $\mathcal{R}' \subseteq \; >$.*   □

Lemma 2 (☑).   *If $(\mathcal{E}, \mathcal{R}) \vdash^* (\mathcal{E}', \mathcal{R}')$ then $\leftrightarrow^*_{\mathcal{E} \cup \mathcal{R}} = \leftrightarrow^*_{\mathcal{E}' \cup \mathcal{R}'}$.*   □

If the employed reduction order is $\mathcal{F}$-ground total then the above two results imply the following conversion equivalence involving *ordered rewriting* with respect to the final system.

Lemma 3 (☑).   *Suppose $>$ is $\mathcal{F}$-ground total and $\mathcal{R} \subseteq \; >$. If $(\mathcal{E}, \mathcal{R}) \vdash^* (\mathcal{E}', \mathcal{R}')$ such that $\mathcal{E}'$, $\mathcal{R}'$, and $>$ are over the signature $\mathcal{F}$, then $\leftrightarrow^*_{\mathcal{E} \cup \mathcal{R}} = \leftrightarrow^*_{\mathcal{E}'_{\geq} \cup \mathcal{R}'}$ holds for conversions between terms in $\mathcal{T}(\mathcal{F})$.*   □

This result is a key ingredient to our correctness results in Sect. 4. In order to apply it, however, we need ground total reduction orders. To this end, we formalized the following two results in IsaFoR.

Lemma 4 (☑).   *If $>$ is a total precedence on $\mathcal{F}$ then $>_{\mathsf{kbo}}$ is $\mathcal{F}$-ground total.*   □

Lemma 5 (☑).   *If $>$ is a total precedence on $\mathcal{F}$ then $>_{\mathsf{lpo}}$ is $\mathcal{F}$-ground total.*   □

In addition, we proved that for any given KBO $>_{\mathsf{kbo}}$ (LPO $>_{\mathsf{lpo}}$) defined over a total precedence $>$ there exists a minimal constant, that is, a constant c such that $t \geqslant_{\mathsf{kbo}} c$ ($t \geqslant_{\mathsf{lpo}} c$) holds for all $t \in \mathcal{T}(\mathcal{F})$ (which will be needed in Sect. 4). In earlier work by Becker et al. [4] ground totality of a lambda-free higher-order variant of KBO is formalized in Isabelle/HOL. However, for our purposes it makes sense to work with the definition of KBO that is already widely used in IsaFoR.

By Lemma 3, any two ground terms convertible in the initial equational theory are convertible with respect to ordered rewriting in the system obtained from an oKB run. The remaining key issue is to decide when the current ordered rewrite system is ground confluent, such that a tool implementing oKB can stop. Instead of defining a fairness criterion as done by Bachmair et al. [3], we use the following criterion for correctness involving ground joinability.

---

[2]   The encompassment condition demands that if a rule or equation $\ell \approx r$ is used to rewrite a term $t = C[\ell\sigma]$ then C is non-empty or σ is not a renaming.

Lemma 6 (☑).   *If for all equations $s \approx t$ in $\mathcal{E}$ we have $s > t$ or $t \approx s$ in $\mathcal{E}$ and $\mathrm{CP}_>(\mathcal{E}) \subseteq \downarrow^g_{\mathcal{E}_>}$ then $\mathcal{E}$ is ground confluent with respect to $>$.*   □

Note that the symmetry condition on $\mathcal{E}$ above is just a convenient way to express the split of $\mathcal{E}$ into rewrite rules with fixed orientation, and equations applicable in both directions, which allows us to treat an ordered rewrite system as a single set of equations. Lemmas 3 and 6 combine to the following correctness result.

Corollary 1 (☑).   *If $>$ is $\mathcal{F}$-ground total and $(\mathcal{E}_0, \varnothing) \vdash^* (\mathcal{E}, \mathcal{R})$ such that $\mathcal{E}'$, $\mathcal{R}'$, and $>$ are over the signature $\mathcal{F}$ and $\mathrm{CP}_>(\mathcal{R} \cup \mathcal{E}^\leftrightarrow) \subseteq \downarrow^g_{\mathcal{R} \cup \mathcal{E}^\leftrightarrow_>}$, then $\mathcal{S} = \mathcal{R} \cup \mathcal{E}^\leftrightarrow_>$ is ground complete and $\leftrightarrow^*_{\mathcal{E}_0} = \leftrightarrow^*_{\mathcal{S}}$ holds for conversions between terms in $\mathcal{T}(\mathcal{F})$.*

Before we can apply this result in order to obtain ground completeness we need to be able to discharge its ground joinability assumption on extended critical pairs. This is the topic of the next section.

4   Formalized Ground Joinability Criteria

In general, ground joinability is undecidable even for terminating rewrite systems [7]. Below, we formalize two sufficient criteria.

4.1   A Simple Criterion

We start with the criterion that Bachmair et al. [3] proposed when they introduced ordered completion.

Lemma 7 (☑).   *Suppose $>$ is a ground total reduction order over $\mathcal{F}$ with a minimal constant. Then, $\mathcal{E}_>$ is $\mathcal{F}$-ground complete whenever for all $s \approx t \in \mathrm{CP}_>(\mathcal{E}^\leftrightarrow)$ it holds that $s \downarrow_{\mathcal{E}_>} t$, or $s \approx t = (s' \approx t')\sigma$ for some $s' \approx t' \in \mathcal{E}^\leftrightarrow$.*   □

A minimal constant c is needed to turn arbitrary ordered rewrite steps into ordered rewrite steps over $\mathcal{T}(\mathcal{F})$: when performing an ordered rewrite step using an equation $u \approx v$ with $V = \mathcal{V}ar(v) \setminus \mathcal{V}ar(u) \neq \varnothing$, a step over $\mathcal{T}(\mathcal{F})$ is obtained by instantiating all variables in V to c. We illustrate the criterion on an example.

Example 1. The following equational system $\mathcal{E}_0$ is derived by ConCon while checking infeasibility of a critical pair of the conditional rewrite system Cops #361:

$$x \div y \approx \langle 0, y \rangle \qquad\qquad x \div y \approx \langle \mathsf{s}(q), r \rangle \qquad\qquad x - 0 \approx x$$
$$0 - y \approx 0 \qquad\qquad \mathsf{s}(x) - \mathsf{s}(y) \approx x - y \qquad\qquad \mathsf{s}(x) > \mathsf{s}(y) \approx x > y$$
$$\mathsf{s}(x) > 0 \approx \mathsf{true} \qquad\qquad \mathsf{s}(x) \leqslant \mathsf{s}(y) \approx x \leqslant y \qquad\qquad 0 \leqslant x \approx \mathsf{true}$$

In an ordered completion run, MædMax transforms $\mathcal{E}_0$ into the following rules $\mathcal{R}$ and equations $\mathcal{E}$:

$$x - 0 \to x \qquad\qquad 0 - x \to 0 \qquad\qquad \mathsf{s}(x) - \mathsf{s}(y) \to x - y$$
$$0 \leqslant x \to \mathsf{true} \qquad \mathsf{s}(x) \leqslant \mathsf{s}(y) \to x \leqslant y \qquad\quad x \div y \to \langle 0, y \rangle$$
$$\mathsf{s}(x) > 0 \to \mathsf{true} \qquad \mathsf{s}(x) > \mathsf{s}(y) \to x > y$$
$$\langle \mathsf{s}(x), y \rangle \approx \langle \mathsf{s}(q), r \rangle \qquad \langle 0, y \rangle \approx \langle \mathsf{s}(q), r \rangle \qquad \langle 0, x \rangle \approx \langle 0, y \rangle$$

Ground confluence of this system can be established by means of Lemma 7. For example, the extended overlap between the first two equations gives rise to the extended critical pair $\langle 0, y \rangle \approx \langle \mathsf{s}(x), y \rangle$, which is just an instance of the second equation (and similarly for the other extended critical pairs).

4.2   Ground Joinability via Order Closures

The criterion discussed in Subsect. 4.1 is rather weak. For instance, it cannot handle associativity and commutativity, as illustrated next [9, Example 1.1].

Example 2. Consider the system $\mathcal{E}$ consisting of the three equations

$$(1) \quad (x * y) * z \approx x * (y * z) \quad (2) \quad x * y \approx y * x \quad (3) \quad x * (y * z) \approx y * (x * z)$$

and the reduction order $>_{\mathsf{kbo}}$ with $w_0 = 1$ and $w(*) = 0$. The first equation can be oriented from left to right, whereas the other ones are unorientable.

We obtain the following extended critical peak from equations (2) and (1):

$$z * (x * y) \leftarrow (x * y) * z \to x * (y * z)$$

The resulting extended critical pair is neither an instance of an equation in $\mathcal{E}$ nor joinable. Thus the criterion of Lemma 7 does not apply.

However, this extended critical pair is ground joinable, which we show in the following. The reduction order $>_{\mathsf{kbo}}$ is contained in an $\mathcal{F}'$-ground total one on any extension of the signature $\mathcal{F}' \supseteq \mathcal{F}$ (using the well-order theorem and incrementality of KBO). Thus, for any grounding substitution σ the terms $x\sigma$, $y\sigma$, and $z\sigma$ are totally ordered. Suppose for instance that $x\sigma > z\sigma > y\sigma$. Then there is an ordered rewrite sequence witnessing joinability:

$$z\sigma * (x\sigma * y\sigma) \qquad\qquad\qquad\qquad\qquad\qquad\qquad x\sigma * (y\sigma * z\sigma)$$
$$\xrightarrow{\;(2)\;} z\sigma * (y\sigma * x\sigma) \qquad\qquad\qquad y\sigma * (x\sigma * z\sigma) \xleftarrow{\;(2)\;}$$
$$\xrightarrow{\;(3)\;} y\sigma * (z\sigma * x\sigma) \xleftarrow{\;(3)\;}$$

If, on the other hand, $x\sigma = y\sigma > z\sigma$ holds, there is a joining sequence as well:

$$x\sigma * (x\sigma * z\sigma) = x\sigma * (y\sigma * z\sigma)$$
$$x\sigma * (z\sigma * x\sigma) \xleftarrow{\;(2)\;}$$
$$z\sigma * (x\sigma * y\sigma) = z\sigma * (x\sigma * x\sigma) \xleftarrow{\;(3)\;}$$

By ensuring the existence of a joining sequence for all possible relationships between $x\sigma$, $y\sigma$, and $z\sigma$, ground joinability can be established. Using this approach to show that all extended critical pairs are ground joinable, it can be verified that $\mathcal{E}$ is in fact ground complete.

The ground joinability test by Martin and Nipkow [9] is based on the idea illustrated in Example 2 above: perform a case analysis by considering ordered rewriting using all extensions of $>$ to instantiations of variables. Below, we give the corresponding formal definitions used in IsaFoR. For any relation R on terms, let $\sigma(R)$ denote the relation such that $s\sigma\ \sigma(R)\ t\sigma$ holds if and only if $s\ R\ t$.

Definition 2 (☑). *A closure $\mathcal{C}$ is a mapping between relations on terms that satisfies the following properties:*

(1) If $s\ \mathcal{C}(R)\ t$ then $s\sigma\ \mathcal{C}(\sigma(R))\ t\sigma$, for all relations R, substitutions σ, and terms s and t.
(2) If $R \subseteq R'$ then $\mathcal{C}(R) \subseteq \mathcal{C}(R')$, for all relations on terms R and R'.

The closure $\mathcal{C}$ is compatible *with a relation on terms R if $\mathcal{C}(R) \subseteq R$ holds.*

In the remainder of this section we assume $\mathcal{F}$ to be the signature of the input problem, we consider an $\mathcal{F}$-ground total reduction order $>$ as well as a closure $\mathcal{C}$ that is compatible with $>$. Furthermore, we assume for every finite set of variables $V \subseteq \mathcal{V}$ and every equivalence relation $\equiv$ on V a representation function $\mathsf{rep}_\equiv$ such that for any $x \in V$ we have $x \equiv \mathsf{rep}_\equiv(x)$, $\mathsf{rep}_\equiv(x) \in V$ and $x \equiv y$ implies $\mathsf{rep}_\equiv(x) = \mathsf{rep}_\equiv(y)$. Given an equivalence relation $\equiv$ on V, let $\hat{\equiv}$ denote the substitution such that $\hat{\equiv}(x) = \mathsf{rep}_\equiv(x)$ for all $x \in V$.

Definition 3 (☑). *Given an ES $\mathcal{E}$ and a reduction order $>$, terms s and t are $\mathcal{C}$-joinable, written $s \downarrow^{\mathcal{C}}_{\mathcal{E}} t$, if for all equivalence relations $\equiv$ on $\mathsf{Var}(s,t)$ and every order $\succ$ on the equivalence classes of $\equiv$ it holds that*

$$s\hat{\equiv} \xrightarrow[\mathcal{E}_{\mathcal{C}(\succ)}]{*} \cdot \xleftrightarrow[\mathcal{E}]{=} \cdot \xleftarrow[\mathcal{E}_{\mathcal{C}(\succ)}]{*} t\hat{\equiv} \tag{1}$$

Example 3. For instance, consider the terms $s = z*(x*y)$ and $t = x*(y*z)$ from Example 2. One possible equivalence relation $\equiv$ on $\mathsf{Var}(s,t) = \{x,y,z\}$ is given by the equivalence classes $\{x,y\}$ and $\{z\}$; one possible order on these is $\hat{\equiv}(x) \succ \hat{\equiv}(z)$ (corresponding to the second example for an order on the instantiations $x\sigma$ and $z\sigma$ in Example 2). By taking $\mathcal{C}$ to be the KBO closure (see Definition 5 below), we have $x*z\ \mathcal{C}(\succ)\ z*x$ and $x*(z*x)\ \mathcal{C}(\succ)\ z*(x*x)$. Using the ES $\mathcal{E}$ from Example 2 we thus obtain the ordered rewrite sequence

$$t\hat{\equiv} = x*(x*z) \xrightarrow[\mathcal{E}_{\mathcal{C}(\succ)}]{} x*(z*x) \xrightarrow[\mathcal{E}_{\mathcal{C}(\succ)}]{} z*(x*x) = s\hat{\equiv}$$

Ground joinability follows from $\mathcal{C}$-joinability. Since this is the key result for the ground joinability criterion of this subsection, we also sketch its proof.

Lemma 8 (☑). *If $s \downarrow^{\mathcal{C}}_{\mathcal{E}} t$ then $s \downarrow^{g}_{\mathcal{E}_>} t$.*

Proof. We assume $s \downarrow_{\mathcal{E}}^{\mathcal{C}} t$ and consider a grounding substitution σ to show $s\sigma \downarrow_{\mathcal{E}_>} t\sigma$. There is some equivalence relation $\equiv$ on $\mathcal{V}ar(s,t)$ such that $x \equiv y$ holds if and only if $\sigma(x) = \sigma(y)$ for all $x, y \in \mathcal{V}ar(s,t)$. Note that this implies $s\sigma = s\hat{\equiv}\sigma$ and $t\sigma = t\hat{\equiv}\sigma$.

We can define an order $\succ$ on the equivalence classes of $\equiv$ such that $[x]_\equiv \succ [y]_\equiv$ if and only if $\sigma(x) > \sigma(y)$. Hence $\sigma(\succ) \subseteq >$ holds, and by Definition 2(2) we have $\mathcal{C}(\sigma(\succ)) \subseteq \mathcal{C}(>)$. Compatibility implies $\mathcal{C}(>) \subseteq >$, and thus $\mathcal{C}(\sigma(\succ)) \subseteq >$.

From Definition 2(1) we can show that $u \to_{\mathcal{E}_{\mathcal{C}(\succ)}} v$ implies $u\sigma \to_{\mathcal{E}_{\mathcal{C}(\sigma(\succ))}} v\sigma$ for all terms u and v. So using the assumption $s \downarrow_{\mathcal{E}}^{\mathcal{C}} t$ we can apply σ to a conversion of the form (1) to obtain

$$s\sigma = s\hat{\equiv}\sigma \xrightarrow[\mathcal{E}_{\mathcal{C}(\sigma(\succ))}]{*} \cdot \xleftrightarrow[\mathcal{E}]{=} \cdot \xleftarrow[\mathcal{E}_{\mathcal{C}(\sigma(\succ))}]{*} t\hat{\equiv}\sigma = t\sigma \tag{2}$$

Ordered rewriting is monotone with respect to the order, and hence $\mathcal{C}(\sigma(\succ)) \subseteq >$ implies $\to_{\mathcal{E}_{\mathcal{C}(\sigma(\succ))}} \subseteq \to_{\mathcal{E}_>}$. Thus (2) implies the existence of a conversion

$$s\sigma \xrightarrow[\mathcal{E}_>]{*} \cdot \xleftrightarrow[\mathcal{E}_>]{=} \cdot \xleftarrow[\mathcal{E}_>]{*} t\sigma$$

where the $\leftrightarrow_{\mathcal{E}_>}$ step exists as any two $\mathcal{F}$-ground terms are comparable in $>$. $\square$

Note that the proof above uses the monotonicity assumption for closures (Definition 2(2)), which is not present in [9]. The following counterexample illustrates that monotonicity is indeed necessary.

Example 4. Consider the ES $\mathcal{E} = \{f(x) \approx a\}$ and suppose that $> = \mathcal{C}(>)$ is an LPO with precedence $a > b > c > f$. Moreover, take $s = f(b)$ and $t = f(c)$. Any order $\succ$ as in Definition 3 is empty since $\mathcal{V}ar(s,t) = \varnothing$. As $\mathcal{C}$ is not required to be monotone, the relation $\mathcal{C}(\succ)$ may contain $(f(b), a)$ and $(f(c), a)$. Then $s \to_{\mathcal{E}_{\mathcal{C}(\succ)}} a$ and $t \to_{\mathcal{E}_{\mathcal{C}(\succ)}} a$ imply $s \downarrow_{\mathcal{E}}^{\mathcal{C}} t$ even though $s \downarrow_{\mathcal{E}_>}^{g} t$ does not hold.

Below, we define an inductive predicate gj which is used to conclude ground joinability of a given equation.

Definition 4 (☑).   *Given an ES $\mathcal{E}$ and a reduction order $>$, gj is defined inductively by the following rules:*

delete	$\mathsf{gj}(t, t)$
closure	$s \downarrow_{\mathcal{E}}^{\mathcal{C}} t \implies \mathsf{gj}(s, t)$
step	$s \leftrightarrow_{\mathcal{E}} t \implies \mathsf{gj}(s, t)$
rewrite left	$s \xrightarrow{\mathcal{E}_>} u$ and $\mathsf{gj}(u, t) \implies \mathsf{gj}(s, t)$
rewrite right	$t \xrightarrow{\mathcal{E}_>} u$ and $\mathsf{gj}(s, u) \implies \mathsf{gj}(s, t)$
congruence	$\mathsf{gj}(s_i, t_i)$ for all $1 \leqslant i \leqslant n \implies \mathsf{gj}(f(s_1, \ldots, s_n), f(t_1, \ldots, t_n))$

This test differs from the one due to Martin and Nipkow [9] by the two rewrite rules, which were added to allow for more efficient checks, as illustrated next.

Example 5. Consider the ES $\mathcal{E}$

$$f(x) \approx f(y) \qquad\qquad g(x, y) \approx f(x)$$

together with a KBO that can orient the second equation (for instance, one can take as precedence $g > f > c$ and let all function symbol weights as well as w_0 be 1). Then $gj(f(x), f(z))$ holds by the step rule, $gj(g(x, y), f(z))$ follows by an application of rewrite left, and $gj(g(x, y), g(z, w)))$ by rewrite right. By Lemma 9 below it thus follows that the equation $g(x, y) \approx g(z, w)$ is ground joinable.

However, the criterion by Martin and Nipkow [9] lacks the rewrite steps. Hence ground joinability of $g(x, y) \approx g(z, w)$ can only be established by applying the closure rule. This amounts to checking ground joinability with respect to 81 relations between the four variables. Since the number of variable relations is in general exponential, the criterion stated in Definition 4 can in practice be exponentially more efficient than the test by Martin and Nipkow [9].

Using Lemma 8 it is not hard to show the following correctness results.

Lemma 9 (☑). *Suppose for all $s \approx t$ in $\mathcal{E}$ we have $s > t$ or $t \approx s$ in $\mathcal{E}$. Then $gj(s, t)$ implies $s \downarrow^{g}_{\mathcal{E}_>} t$.* □

Lemma 10 (☑). *If for all $s \approx t$ in $\mathcal{E}$ we have $s > t$ or $t \approx s$ in $\mathcal{E}$ and $CP_>(\mathcal{E}) \subseteq \downarrow^{g}_{\mathcal{E}_>}$ then $\mathcal{E}$ is ground confluent with respect to $>$.* □

This test can not only handle Example 2 but also the group theoretic problem from the introduction. Moreover, it subsumes Lemma 7 since whenever for some equation $s \approx t$ we have $s \downarrow^{g}_{\mathcal{E}_>} t$ by Lemma 7 then $gj(s, t)$ holds.

Closures for Knuth-Bendix Orders. Definition 2 requires abstract properties on closures. In the following we define closures for KBO as used in IsaFoR/CeTA.

Similar to the already existing definition of KBO in IsaFoR [17] we define the closure $>^{R}_{kbo}$ as follows.

Definition 5 (☑). *Let R be a relation on terms, $>$ a precedence on $\mathcal{F}$, and (w, w_0) a weight function. The KBO closure $>^{R}_{kbo}$ is a relation on terms inductively defined as follows: $s >^{R}_{kbo} t$ if $s\ R\ t$, or $|s|_x \geqslant |t|_x$ for all $x \in \mathcal{V}$ and either*

(a) $w(s) > w(t)$, or
(b) $w(s) = w(t)$ and one of
    (1) $s \notin \mathcal{V}$ and $t \in \mathcal{V}$, or
    (2) $s = f(s_1, \ldots, s_n)$, $t = g(t_1, \ldots, t_m)$ and $f > g$, or
    (3) $s = f(s_1, \ldots, s_n)$, $t = f(t_1, \ldots, t_n)$ and there is some $i \leqslant n$ such that $s_j = t_j$ for all $1 \leqslant j < i$ and $s_i >^{R}_{kbo} t_i$

Note that even though Definition 5 resembles the usual definition of KBO, it defines a *closure* of a relation R in a KBO-like way rather than a reduction order. For instance, if $x \succ z$, as in Example 3, then $x * z >^{\succ}_{kbo} z * x$ holds.

We prove that $>^{R}_{kbo}$ is indeed a closure that is compatible with $>_{kbo}$ based on the same weight function and precedence.

Lemma 11. *Let R be a relation on terms, $>$ a precedence on $\mathcal{F}$, and (w, w_0) a weight function. Then all of the following hold:*

(a) *If $s >_{\mathsf{kbo}} t$ then $s >_{\mathsf{kbo}}^{R} t$ for all terms s and t.*   ☑

(b) *If $R \subseteq R'$ then $>_{\mathsf{kbo}}^{R} \subseteq >_{\mathsf{kbo}}^{R'}$.*   ☑

(c) *If $s >_{\mathsf{kbo}}^{R} t$ then $s\sigma >_{\mathsf{kbo}}^{\sigma(R)} t\sigma$, for all substitutions σ, and terms s and t.*   ☑

(d) *The closure $>_{\mathsf{kbo}}^{R}$ is compatible with $>_{\mathsf{kbo}}$.*   ☑

5 Applications

Ground complete rewrite systems can be used to decide equivalence of ground terms with respect to their induced equational theory. Here we highlight applications of this decision problem.

Deciding Ground Equations. Suppose we obtain the ordered rewrite system $(\mathcal{E}, \mathcal{R})$ and the reduction order $>$ by applying ordered completion to an initial set of equations $\mathcal{E}_0$. Then it is easy to decide whether two ground terms s and t are equivalent with respect to $\mathcal{E}_0$ (that is, whether $s \leftrightarrow_{\mathcal{E}_0}^{*} t$): it suffices to check if the (necessarily unique) normal forms of s and t with respect to $\mathcal{R} \cup \mathcal{E}_>$ coincide. Also if all variables of a non-ground goal equation are universally quantified, the goal can be decided by substituting fresh constants for its variables.

Equations with Existential Variables. The following trick by Bachmair et al. [3] allows us to reduce equations with existentially quantified variables to the ground case: Let $\mathcal{E}$ be a set of equations and $s \approx t$ a goal equation where all variables are existentially quantified. This corresponds to the question whether there is a substitution σ such that $s\sigma \leftrightarrow_{\mathcal{E}}^{*} t\sigma$ holds. We employ three fresh function symbols eq, true, and false, and define $\mathcal{E}_{s,t}^{\mathsf{eq}}$ to denote $\mathcal{E}$ extended by the two equations $\mathsf{eq}(x, x) \approx \mathsf{true}$ and $\mathsf{eq}(s, t) \approx \mathsf{false}$.

If a ground complete system equivalent to $\mathcal{E}_{s,t}^{\mathsf{eq}}$ is found—for instance discovered by ordered completion—then it can be used to decide the goal, as stated next.

Lemma 12 (☑).   *Let s, t, and $\mathcal{E}$ all be over signature $\mathcal{F}$ and let S be a ground complete TRS such that $\leftrightarrow_{\mathcal{E}_{s,t}^{\mathsf{eq}}}^{*} \subseteq \leftrightarrow_{S}^{*}$ on $\mathcal{T}(\mathcal{F})$. If $s\sigma \leftrightarrow_{\mathcal{E}}^{*} t\sigma$ then $\mathsf{true}{\downarrow}_S = \mathsf{false}{\downarrow}_S$.*

Proof. Since $s\sigma \leftrightarrow_{\mathcal{E}}^{*} t\sigma$, there is a conversion $s\sigma \leftrightarrow_{\mathcal{E}_{s,t}^{\mathsf{eq}}}^{*} t\sigma$ by construction of $\mathcal{E}_{s,t}^{\mathsf{eq}}$. Moreover, (appealing to an earlier formalization about signature extensions [16]) there exists an $\mathcal{F}$-grounding substitution τ such that $s\tau \leftrightarrow_{\mathcal{E}_{s,t}^{\mathsf{eq}}}^{*} t\tau$. So we have

$$\mathsf{true} \xleftarrow{}_{\mathcal{E}_{s,t}^{\mathsf{eq}}} \mathsf{eq}(s\tau, s\tau) \xleftrightarrow[\mathcal{E}_{s,t}^{\mathsf{eq}}]{*} \mathsf{eq}(s\tau, t\tau) \xrightarrow[\mathcal{E}_{s,t}^{\mathsf{eq}}]{} \mathsf{false}$$

and by the assumed conversion inclusion an S-conversion between true and false. Several applications of ground confluence of S yield joinability of $\mathsf{true}{\downarrow}_S$ and $\mathsf{false}{\downarrow}_S$. Since both of these terms are normal forms they coincide.   □

Infeasibility of Conditions. A decision procedure for ground equations can also be harnessed to prove infeasibility of conditions in conditional term rewriting. Here a condition c is a sequence of pairs of terms $s_1 \approx t_1, \ldots, s_k \approx t_k$ and we say that c is infeasible whenever there is no substitution such that $s_i\sigma \rightarrow^*_{\mathcal{R}} t_i\sigma$ holds for all $1 \leqslant i \leqslant k$. Now, it is obviously a sound overapproximation to ensure that there is no σ such that $s_i\sigma \leftrightarrow^*_{\mathcal{R}} t_i\sigma$ for all $1 \leqslant i \leqslant k$. This suggests that completion methods might be applicable.

But there are still two complications before we are able to achieve an infeasibility check: (1) the rules of a conditional term rewrite system (CTRS for short) $\mathcal{R}$ may be guarded by conditions, making $\mathcal{R}$ an unsuitable input for ordered completion, and (2) the conditions c are most of the time not ground. As is conventional when adopting TRS methods to conditional rewriting, we solve (1) by dropping all conditions from the rules of $\mathcal{R}$, resulting in the unconditional TRS $\mathcal{R}_u$ whose rewrite relation overapproximates the one of $\mathcal{R}$. Of course if we can establish that there is no σ such that $s_i\sigma \rightarrow^*_{\mathcal{R}_u} t_i\sigma$ for all $1 \leqslant i \leqslant k$, then we also obtain infeasibility of c with respect to the CTRS $\mathcal{R}$. In order to solve (2) we use a fresh function symbol c and apply Lemma 12 to decide the equation $s = \mathsf{c}(s_1, \ldots, s_k) \approx \mathsf{c}(t_1, \ldots, t_k) = t$ by applying ordered completion to $\mathcal{R}_{u\,s,t}^{\mathsf{eq}}$. If $s \not\leftrightarrow^*_{\mathcal{R}_{u\,s,t}^{\mathsf{eq}}} t$ we can conclude infeasibility of c.

Checking for infeasibility is for example useful when analyzing the confluence of a conditional rewrite system, since whenever we encounter a conditional critical pair whose conditions are infeasible, we can ignore it entirely. Since 2019 the Confluence Competition (CoCo)[3] also features a dedicated infeasibility category.

6   Certification

In this section we describe the proof certificates for the different certifiable properties and summarize the corresponding Isabelle/HOL check functions.

Here, *check functions* are the formal connection between general, abstract results and concrete certificates. For example, a check function for a KBO termination proof takes a certificate, containing a concrete TRS, a specific precedence, and fixed weight functions, as input. It checks that the KBO instance is admissible and orients all rules of the TRS from left to right. By appealing to the abstract result that compatibility of a TRS with an admissible KBO implies termination, it then concludes termination of the concrete instance.

Only check functions that are both executable and proven sound are allowed in the certifier. The latter means that success of the check function implies a concrete instance of the corresponding general result (in our example success proves termination of the given TRS). In case of failure it is customary for CeTA check functions to give a human readable reason for why a certificate is rejected.

---

[3] http://project-coco.uibk.ac.at/2019/

Ordered Completion Certificates. Here, the certificate consists of

- a set of initial equations $\mathcal{E}_0$,
- an ordered completion result $(\mathcal{E}, \mathcal{R})$ together with a reduction order $>$, and
- a sequence of inference steps according to Definition 1.

The corresponding check function verifies that (1) the inference steps form a valid run $(\mathcal{E}_0 \pi, \varnothing) \vdash^* (\mathcal{E}, \mathcal{R})$ for some renaming π, (2) all extended critical pairs are joinable, by default according to Lemma 10, and (3) the reduction order is admissible, in case of KBO.

Next, we illustrate such an ordered completion proof by an example.

Example 6. The certificate corresponding to Example 1 contains the equations $\mathcal{E}_0$, the resulting system $(\mathcal{E}, \mathcal{R})$, and the reduction order $>_{\mathsf{kbo}}$ with precedence $> \,>\, \mathsf{s} \,>\, \leqslant \,>\, \mathsf{true} \,>\, - \,>\, \div \,>\, \langle \cdot, \cdot \rangle \,>\, 0$, $w_0 = 1$, and $w(0) = 2$, $w(\div) = w(\mathsf{true}) = w(\mathsf{s}) = 1$, and all other symbols having weight 0. In addition, a sequence of inference steps explains how $(\mathcal{E}, \mathcal{R})$ is obtained from $\mathcal{E}_0$:

simplify$_{\mathsf{left}}$	$x \div y \approx \langle \mathsf{s}(q), r \rangle$ to $\langle 0, y \rangle \approx \langle \mathsf{s}(q), r \rangle$	
deduce	$\langle 0, x \rangle \leftarrow \langle \mathsf{s}(u), v \rangle \rightarrow \langle 0, y \rangle$	
deduce	$\langle \mathsf{s}(x), y \rangle \leftarrow \langle 0, u \rangle \rightarrow \langle \mathsf{s}(q), r \rangle$	
deduce	$x > y \leftarrow \mathsf{s}(x) > \mathsf{s}(y) \rightarrow \mathsf{s}(\mathsf{s}(x)) > \mathsf{s}(\mathsf{s}(y))$	
orient$_{\mathsf{lr}}$	$0 \leqslant x \rightarrow \mathsf{true}$	
orient$_{\mathsf{rl}}$	$\mathsf{s}(\mathsf{s}(x)) > \mathsf{s}(\mathsf{s}(y)) \rightarrow x > y$	$(\star)$

. . .

orient$_{\mathsf{lr}}$	$\mathsf{s}(x) - \mathsf{s}(y) \rightarrow x - y$
orient$_{\mathsf{lr}}$	$0 - x \rightarrow 0$
orient$_{\mathsf{lr}}$	$\mathsf{s}(x) \leqslant \mathsf{s}(y) \rightarrow x \leqslant y$
collapse	$\mathsf{s}(\mathsf{s}(x)) > \mathsf{s}(\mathsf{s}(y)) \rightarrow x > y$ to $x > y \approx x > y$
collapse	$\mathsf{s}(\mathsf{s}(x)) > \mathsf{s}(0) \rightarrow \mathsf{true}$ to $\mathsf{s}(x) > 0 \approx \mathsf{true}$
simplify$_{\mathsf{left}}$	$\mathsf{s}(x) > 0 \approx \mathsf{true}$ to $\mathsf{true} \approx \mathsf{true}$
delete	$x > y \approx x > y$
delete	$\mathsf{true} \approx \mathsf{true}$

The first collapse step using rule $(\star)$ above illustrates our relaxed inference rule, it would not have been possible according to the original inference system [3] due to the encompassment condition since $\mathsf{s}(\mathsf{s}(x)) > \mathsf{s}(\mathsf{s}(y)) \not\vartriangleright \mathsf{s}(\mathsf{s}(x)) > \mathsf{s}(\mathsf{s}(y))$.

We briefly comment on the differences to the certification of standard Knuth-Bendix completion as already present in CeTA [17]. For standard completion, the certificate contains the initial set of equations $\mathcal{E}_0$, the resulting TRS $\mathcal{R}$ together with a termination proof, and stepwise $\mathcal{E}_0$-conversions from ℓ to r for each rule $\ell \rightarrow r \in \mathcal{R}$. The certifier first checks the termination proof to guarantee termination of $\mathcal{R}$. Then, confluence of $\mathcal{R}$ can be guaranteed by ensuring that all critical pairs are joinable. At this point it is easy to verify the inclusion $\leftrightarrow^*_{\mathcal{E}_0} \subseteq \leftrightarrow^*_{\mathcal{R}}$: for each equation $s \approx t \in \mathcal{E}_0$ the $\mathcal{R}$-normal forms of s and t are computed and checked for syntactic equality. The converse inclusion $\leftrightarrow^*_{\mathcal{R}} \subseteq \leftrightarrow^*_{\mathcal{E}_0}$ is taken care of by the provided $\mathcal{E}_0$-conversions. Overall, we obtain that $\mathcal{R}$ is a complete presentation of $\mathcal{E}_0$ without mentioning a specific inference system.

Unfortunately, the same approach does not work for ordered completion: The inclusion $\leftrightarrow^*_{\mathcal{E}_0} \subseteq \leftrightarrow^*_{\mathcal{R} \cup \mathcal{E}_>}$ cannot be established by rewriting equations in $\mathcal{E}_0$ to normal form, since they may contain variables but $\mathcal{R} \cup \mathcal{E}_>$ is only ground confluent. Moreover, since ground joinability is undecidable no complete check can be performed. Therefore, we instead ask for certificates that contain explicit inference steps, as described above.

Equational Satisfiability Certificates. We use the term "satisfiability" of unit equality problems in line with the terminology of TPTP [22]: given a set of equations $\mathcal{E}_0$ and a ground goal *in*equality $s \not\approx t$, show that this axiomatization is satisfiable. To this end, completion-based tools try to find a ground complete presentation $\mathcal{S}$ of $\mathcal{E}_0$ and verify that $s{\downarrow}_\mathcal{S} \neq t{\downarrow}_\mathcal{S}$.

A certificate for this application extends an ordered completion certificate by the goal terms. The corresponding check function verifies that

- the presented ordered completion proof is valid as described above,
- the goal inequality is ground,
- the signature of $\mathcal{E}_0$, $\mathcal{E}$, and $\mathcal{R}$ is included in the signature of $>$, and
- the terms in the goal have different normal forms.

We chose the symbols mentioned by the reduction order to be the considered signature $\mathcal{F}$. In comparison to picking the signature of $\mathcal{E}_0$, this has the advantage that it is easy to add additional function symbols. Moreover, since KBO precedences in the CPF input are lists of function symbols, no additional checks are required to ensure $\mathcal{F}$-ground totality of the constructed reduction order.

As a side note, unsatisfiability proofs are much easier to certify: a tool only needs to output a conversion between the two goal terms. Support for the corresponding certificates has already been added to CeTA earlier [21].

Infeasibility Certificates. Actually we check (generalized) nonreachability [15] of a target t from a source s with respect to a TRS $\mathcal{R}$, that is, the property that, given a TRS $\mathcal{R}$ and two terms s and t, there is no substitution σ with $s\sigma \rightarrow^*_\mathcal{R} t\sigma$.

The corresponding certificates list function symbols eq, true, and false, together with an equational satisfiability certificate. The check function first constructs, using eq, true, and false from the certificate the TRS $\mathcal{R}^{\text{eq}}_{s,t}$ and then verifies that the equation true $\approx$ false is not satisfiable according to the supplied equational satisfiability certificate with $\mathcal{R}^{\text{eq}}_{s,t}$ as initial set of equations.

7 Experiments

Below we summarize experiments with our certifier on different problem sets. More details are available from the accompanying website.[4]

---

[4] http://cl-informatik.uibk.ac.at/experiments/okb/

Ordered Completion. Martin and Nipkow [9] give 10 examples. The criterion of Lemma 10 with KBO applies to 7 of those and MædMax produces corresponding proofs. Six of these proofs are certified by CeTA. The missing example uses a trick also used by Waldmeister [1]: certain *redundant* equations need not be considered for critical pair computation. This simplification is not yet supported by CeTA.

We also ran MædMax on the 138 problems [13] for standard completion collected from the literature. Using KBO, MædMax can complete 55 of them, and 52 of those are certified. (Using LPO and KBO, 91 are completed.) For the three remaining (AC) group examples, MædMax uses a stronger criterion [23] which is currently not supported by CeTA. Overall, this amounts to 58% certification coverage of all ordered completion proofs by MædMax.

Satisfiable Unit Equality Problems. There are 144 unit equality problems (UEQ) in the TPTP 7.2.0 [22] benchmark that are classified as satisfiable, of which MædMax using KBO only can prove 11. All these proofs are certified by CeTA. With its general strategy MædMax can handle 14 problems, but two of those require duplicating rules, such that KBO is not applicable, and one has multiple goals, which is currently not supported by CeTA.

Infeasibility Problems. There are 148 oriented CTRSs in version 807 of the Cops[5] benchmark (that is, the version of Cops where the highest problem number is 807) of CoCo. Here *oriented* means that a condition $s \approx t$ is satisfied by a substitution σ, whenever $s\sigma \to_{\mathcal{R}}^* t\sigma$. (This is the class of systems ConCon is specialized to, hence we restrict our experiments to the above 148 systems.)

Out of those 148 CTRSs, the previous version of ConCon (1.7) can prove (non)confluence of 109 with and of 112 without certification. The new version of ConCon (1.8), extended by infeasibility checks via ordered completion with MædMax, can handle 111 CTRSs with and 114 without certification. We thus obtain two new certified proofs, namely for Cops #340 and #361.

8   Conclusion

We presented our Isabelle/HOL formalization of ordered completion and two accompanying ground joinability criteria—now part of IsaFoR 2.37. It comes with check functions for ordered completion proofs, equational satisfiability proofs, and infeasibility proofs for conditional term rewriting. Formalizing soundness of these check functions allowed us to add support for corresponding certificates to the certifier CeTA that is code generated from IsaFoR. To the best of our knowledge, CeTA constitutes the first proof checker for ordered completion proofs. Indeed, it already helped us to detect a soundness error in MædMax, where in certain corner cases some extended critical pairs were ignored. Our experiments show that we can certify 58% of ordered completion proofs (corresponding to 94%

---

[5] http://cops.uibk.ac.at?q=1..807

of the KBO proofs) and 85% of the satisfiability proofs produced by MædMax (100% for KBO). The number of certified proofs of ConCon increased by two.

Moreover, CeTA is the only certifier used in the Confluence Competition; by certifying infeasibility proofs our work thus helps to validate more tool output. Regarding the recent CoCo 2019, certification currently covers roughly 83% of the benchmarks in the two categories (CTRS and TRS) that have certified counterparts (CPF-CTRS and CPF-TRS).

In the future, we plan to add support for closures of LPO and extend our certifier to verify proofs of pure, not necessarily unit, equality formulas, as well as ground confluence proofs by tools participating in the confluence competition.

Acknowledgments. We thank the anonymous referees for their constructive comments and various suggestions for improvements.

References

1. Avenhaus, J., Hillenbrand, T., Löchner, B.: On using ground joinable equations in equational theorem proving. J. Symb. Comput. **36**(1–2), 217–233 (2003). https://doi.org/10.1016/S0747-7171(03)00024-5
2. Baader, F., Nipkow, T.: Term Rewriting and All That. Cambridge University Press (1998). https://doi.org/10.1017/CBO9781139172752
3. Bachmair, L., Dershowitz, N., Plaisted, D.A.: Completion without failure. In: Aït-Kaci, H., Nivat, M. (eds.) Resolution of Equations in Algebraic Structures, Rewriting Techniques, vol. 2, pp. 1–30. Academic Press (1989). https://doi.org/10.1016/B978-0-12-046371-8.50007-9
4. Becker, H., Blanchette, J.C., Waldmann, U., Wand, D.: A transfinite Knuth–Bendix order for lambda-free higher-order terms. In: de Moura, L. (ed.) CADE 2017. LNCS (LNAI), vol. 10395, pp. 432–453. Springer, Cham (2017). https://doi.org/10.1007/978-3-319-63046-5_27
5. Haftmann, F., Nipkow, T.: Code generation via higher-order rewrite systems. In: Blume, M., Kobayashi, N., Vidal, G. (eds.) FLOPS 2010. LNCS, vol. 6009, pp. 103–117. Springer, Heidelberg (2010). https://doi.org/10.1007/978-3-642-12251-4_9
6. Hirokawa, N., Middeldorp, A., Sternagel, C., Winkler, S.: Infinite runs in abstract completion. In: Proceedings of the 2nd FSCD. LIPIcs, vol. 84, pp. 19:1–19:16 (2017). https://doi.org/10.4230/LIPIcs.FSCD.2017.19
7. Kapur, D., Narendran, P., Otto, F.: On ground-confluence of term rewriting systems. Inform. Comput. **86**(1), 14–31 (1990). https://doi.org/10.1016/0890-5401(90)90023-B
8. Knuth, D.E., Bendix, P.: Simple word problems in universal algebras. In: Leech, J. (ed.) Computational Problems in Abstract Algebra, pp. 263–297. Pergamon Press (1970). https://doi.org/10.1016/B978-0-08-012975-4
9. Martin, U., Nipkow, T.: Ordered rewriting and confluence. In: Stickel, M.E. (ed.) CADE 1990. LNCS, vol. 449, pp. 366–380. Springer, Heidelberg (1990). https://doi.org/10.1007/3-540-52885-7_100
10. McCune, W.: Solution of the Robbins problem. J. Autom. Reasoning **19**(3), 263–276 (1997). https://doi.org/10.1023/A:1005843212881
11. McCune, W., Veroff, R., Fitelson, B., Harris, K., Feist, A., Wos, L.: Short single axioms for Boolean algebra. J. Autom. Reasoning **29**(1), 1–16 (2002). https://doi.org/10.1023/A:1020542009983

12. Nipkow, T., Paulson, L.C., Wenzel, M.: Isabelle/HOL – A Proof Assistant for Higher-Order Logic, LNCS, vol. 2283. Springer (2002). https://doi.org/10.1007/3-540-45949-9

13. Sato, H., Winkler, S.: Encoding dependency pair techniques and control strategies for maximal completion. In: Felty, A.P., Middeldorp, A. (eds.) CADE 2015. LNCS (LNAI), vol. 9195, pp. 152–162. Springer, Cham (2015). https://doi.org/10.1007/978-3-319-21401-6_10

14. Schultz, P., Wisnesky, R.: Algebraic data integration. J. Funct. Program. **27**(e24), 51 (2017). https://doi.org/10.1017/S0956796817000168

15. Sternagel, C., Sternagel, T.: Certifying confluence of almost orthogonal CTRSs via exact tree automata completion. In: Proceedings of the 1st FSCD. LIPIcs, vol. 52, pp. 29:1–29:16. Schloss Dagstuhl (2016). https://doi.org/10.4230/LIPIcs.FSCD.2016.29

16. Sternagel, C., Thiemann, R.: Signature extensions preserve termination. In: Dawar, A., Veith, H. (eds.) CSL 2010. LNCS, vol. 6247, pp. 514–528. Springer, Heidelberg (2010). https://doi.org/10.1007/978-3-642-15205-4_39

17. Sternagel, C., Thiemann, R.: Formalizing Knuth-Bendix orders and Knuth-Bendix completion. In: Proceedings of the 24th RTA. LIPIcs, vol. 21, pp. 287–302. Schloss Dagstuhl (2013). https://doi.org/10.4230/LIPIcs.RTA.2013.287

18. Sternagel, C., Thiemann, R.: The certification problem format. In: Proceedings of the 11th UITP. EPTCS, vol. 167, pp. 61–72 (2014). https://doi.org/10.4204/EPTCS.167.8

19. Sternagel, C., Winkler, S.: Certified ordered completion. In: Proceedings of the 7th IWC (2018), arXiv:1805.10090

20. Sternagel, T., Middeldorp, A.: Conditional confluence (system description). In: Dowek, G. (ed.) RTA 2014. LNCS, vol. 8560, pp. 456–465. Springer, Cham (2014). https://doi.org/10.1007/978-3-319-08918-8_31

21. Sternagel, T., Winkler, S., Zankl, H.: Recording completion for certificates in equational reasoning. In: Proceedings of the 4th CPP, pp. 41–47 (2015). https://doi.org/10.1145/2676724.2693171

22. Sutcliffe, G.: The TPTP problem library and associated infrastructure: the FOF and CNF Parts. J. Autom. Reasoning **43**(4), 337–362 (2009). https://doi.org/10.1007/s10817-009-9143-8

23. Winkler, S.: A ground joinability criterion for ordered completion. In: Proceedings of the 6th IWC, pp. 45–49 (2017)

24. Winkler, S., Moser, G.: MædMax: a maximal ordered completion tool. In: Galmiche, D., Schulz, S., Sebastiani, R. (eds.) IJCAR 2018. LNCS (LNAI), vol. 10900, pp. 472–480. Springer, Cham (2018). https://doi.org/10.1007/978-3-319-94205-6_31

JGXYZ:
An ATP System for Gap and Glut Logics

Geoff Sutcliffe[1]([⊠]) [iD] and Francis Jeffry Pelletier[2] [iD]

[1] University of Miami, Miami, USA
geoff@cs.miami.edu
[2] University of Alberta, Edmonton, Canada
http://www.cs.miami.edu/~geoff
https://sites.ualberta.ca/~francisp

Abstract. This paper describes an ATP system, named JGXYZ, for some gap and glut logics. JGXYZ is based on an equi-provable translation to FOL, followed by use of an existing ATP system for FOL. A key feature of JGXYZ is that the translation to FOL is data-driven, in the sense that it requires only the addition of a new logic's truth tables for the unary and binary connectives in order to produce an ATP system for the logic. Experimental results from JGXYZ illustrate the differences between the logics and translated problems, both technically and in terms of a quasi-real-world use case.

Keywords: Multi-valued logic · Gap logic · Glut logic · ATP system

1 Gap and Glut Logics

Logic "is a subject concerned with the most general laws of truth, and is now generally held to consist of the systematic study of the form of valid inference", and "A valid inference is one where there is a specific relation of logical support between the assumptions of the inference and its conclusion." [21]. Classical first-order logic (FOL), with its truth values **True** and **False** has "been the logic suggested as the ideal for guiding reasoning" and "For this reason, classical logic has often been called the one right logic." [18]. Despite this view, in 1920 Łukasiewicz noted that future contingent statements like "There will be a sea-battle tomorrow" are not true (now), nor are they false (now). To reason about such statements Łukasiewicz invented a new truth-value, **Neither**[1], to form the logic Ł3 [12]. Łukasiewicz basically wanted to use classical logic, except to allow **N** to be "in the *gap* between" **T** and **F**. He kept the usual connectives of ¬, ∨, ∧, and →, but found it necessary to change the definition of the conditional connective.

In contrast to statements that appear to have no truth value, paradoxical statements such as the Liar Paradox "This sentence is false." provide motivation for dialetheic logics [17] that allow statements to be one of **True**, **False**, or "have the *glut* of" **Both** true and false. Dialetheic logics are paraconsistent, so that a contradiction in the input

---

[1] Actually, Łukasiewicz called it (the Polish equivalent for) **Indeterminate**, but to keep things consistent with other works, we use **Neither**.

© Springer Nature Switzerland AG 2019
P. Fontaine (Ed.): CADE 2019, LNAI 11716, pp. 526–537, 2019.
https://doi.org/10.1007/978-3-030-29436-6_31

does not lead to logical omniscience. The most famous – and persistent – advocate of dialetheism is Graham Priest, who developed the Logic of Paradox [16], which provides a foundation for the dialetheic logics RM3 [19] and a logic that we call A3, after [1]. As with the gap logic Ł3, these *glut* logics require particular conditional connectives in order to retain useful reasoning properties.

In 1977 Nuel Belnap published two articles, "How a Computer Should Think" and "A Useful Four-Valued Logic" [5]. One of the leading ideas was of a then-futuristic knowledge based system that would not only retrieve explicitly stored data, but would also reason and deduce consequences of the stored data. A further idea was that such a knowledge base might be given contradictory data to store, and that there might be topics for which no data is stored. This led to the development of the FDE logic

Fig. 1. The truth diamond

[4,6], which merges the ideas of gap and glut logics by including all four truth values: **T**, **B**, **N**, and **F**. Belnap envisaged the four truth values of FDE in a lattice, the "Truth Diamond" shown in Fig. 1. The Truth Diamond represents the amount of truth in the four truth values, with **T** having the most (only truth) and **F** the least (no truth). **B** and **N** are between the two extremes of **T** and **F**, with different ways of balancing their true and false parts, and therefore have incomparable amounts of truth. Again, the choice of conditional connective for FDE is important, with different choices leading to different theories [9,20].

This work deals with the development of an ATP system called JGXYZ[2] for these and other first-order logics. The system is "data-driven", in the sense that it requires only the addition of a new logic's truth tables for the unary and binary connectives in order to produce an ATP system for the logic. The data-driven approach is also taken in MUltlog [2], leading to the specification of a logic and deduction systems, but no actual running ATP system like JGXYZ. An implemented ATP system for multi-valued logics was ₃TAP [3], but it is no longer supported. A survey of work done around the end of the last century is provided by [8]. Note that the input language for gap/glut logics is the same as for FOL – it is the semantics and reasoning that changes when a gap/glut logic is adopted (and consequently it does not make sense to compare an ATP system's reasoning in gap/glut logics with the reasoning of a FOL ATP system).

2   A Motivating Example

As a quasi-real-world use case, consider the situation faced by script writers for a TV series that features "undead" characters [11]. In such shows there are characters who are alive, characters who are not alive, and undead characters who are both alive and not alive. Additionally, there will be (in future episodes) new characters whose liveliness is yet unknown. All characters that have ever appeared in an episode are either alive or have been buried. Each week the script writer must provide the necessary dialogue

---

[2] Named after the authors Jeff and Geoff, for any logic **XYZ**.

and placement of the characters who appear in the episode.[3] Characters who are alive need words and placement. Characters who are not alive need no words but still need placement. For now, let there be four characters: Alan, who is alive; Désirée, who is not alive and has been buried; Umberto, who is undead (i.e., both alive and not alive); and Nigel, who has not yet appeared in the script. The kinds of questions the script write might ask include:

- Does Désirée need words?
- Does Nigel need placement?
- Is Umberto both alive and not alive?
- Is Nigel alive or (inclusively) not alive?
- Has Umberto been buried?
- Was Désirée buried because she is not alive?

If such a scenario is to be formalized so that the questions can be correctly (logically!) answered, the possibility of characters being both alive and not alive requires a glut logic that supports the truth value **Both**, and the possibility of new characters whose liveliness is unknown requires a gap logic that supports the truth value **Neither**. The gap and glut logics discussed in Sect. 1 are appropriate, and the JGXYZ ATP system can provide the necessary reasoning.

The formalization in TPTP syntax is as follows:

```
%----Axioms of the undead
fof(alive_or_buried,axiom,! [X] : ( alive(X) | buried(X) )).
fof(alive_scripting,axiom,
    ! [X] : ( alive(X) => ( script(X,words) & script(X,placement) ))).
fof(not_alive_scripting,axiom,
    ! [X] : ( ~alive(X) => ( ~script(X,words) & script(X,placement) ))).

%----Current characters
fof(alan_alive,axiom,     alive(alan) ).
fof(desiree_dead,axiom,   ~alive(desiree) ).
fof(desiree_buried,axiom, buried(desiree)).
fof(umberto_alive,axiom,  alive(umberto) ).
fof(umberto_dead,axiom,   ~alive(umberto) ).

%----Queries
fof(desiree_needs_words,conjecture,    script(desiree,words) ).
fof(nigel_needs_placement,conjecture, script(nigel,placement)).
fof(umberto_alive_and_not,conjecture, alive(umberto) & ~alive(umberto)).
fof(nigel_alive_or_not,conjecture,     alive(nigel) | ~alive(nigel)).
fof(umberto_buried,conjecture,         buried(umberto)).
fof(not_alive_buried,conjecture,       ~alive(desiree) => buried(desiree)).
```

The answers to these queries, for each of the logics that are presented in Sect. 3, are presented in Sect. 5.

---

[3] Computer geeks ... think of the characters as UNIX processes, which can be alive, not alive, or zombies. Burial corresponds to reaping the process from the process table. FDE can thus be used to reason about UNIX processes. (Thanks to Josef Urban for this interpretation.)

3   Truth Values and Conditional Connectives

Section 1 briefly introduced four gap/glut logics: Ł3, RM3, A3, and FDE. These differ in terms of the truth values they support, and the conditional connective that they use. This section provides further details of these logics, and examines their conditional connectives.

Section 1 provided motivation for having the four truth values used by gap and glut logics: **T**, **B**, **N**, and **F**. As usual, the truth values are divided into those that are *designated* – the values that "true" statements should have (like being **T** in classical logic), and those that are *undesignated*. Logical truths are formulae that are always designated regardless of the truth values of their atomic components, and are the formulae that a reasoning tool should be able to prove. The truth tables for negation, disjunction, and conjunction over the four truth values are given in Table 1. The truth value of a conjunction (disjunction) is the meet (join) of its conjuncts (disjuncts) in the truth diamond, and negation inverts the order in the diamond.

Table 1. Truth tables for negation, disjunction, and conjunction

¬		∨	T	B	N	F	∧	T	B	N	F
T	F	**T**	T	T	T	T	**T**	T	B	N	F
B	B	**B**	T	B	T	B	**B**	B	B	F	F
N	N	**N**	T	T	N	N	**N**	N	F	N	F
F	T	**F**	T	B	N	F	**F**	F	F	F	F

In this work, two conditional connectives are used:

- Classical Material Implication $\rightarrow_{cmi}$ [1,9,20]. This conditional was proposed in response to the observation that modus ponens (MP) fails in FDE if the classical FOL conditional $\rightarrow_{cls}$ defined in terms of ∨ and ¬, $(\varphi \rightarrow_{cls} \psi) =_{df} (\neg\varphi \vee \psi)$, is used [20]. $\rightarrow_{cmi}$ does however emphasize the classical aspects of a conditional. In the cases when the antecedent is designated, the value of the consequent is assigned to the conditional. In the cases when the antecedent is undesignated, **T** is assigned to the conditional.
- The "Łukasiewicz" conditional $\rightarrow_{Luk}$ [13]. One of the features missing from $\rightarrow_{cmi}$ is contraposition with respect to negation, i.e., $(\varphi \rightarrow_{cmi} \psi) \neq (\neg\psi \rightarrow_{cmi} \neg\varphi)$. Contraposition can be added by taking a conjunction of $\rightarrow_{cmi}$ and its contraposed form, $(\varphi \rightarrow_{Luk} \psi) =_{df} ((\varphi \rightarrow_{cmi} \psi) \wedge (\neg\psi \rightarrow_{cmi} \neg\varphi))$. This can be seen as a generalization of Łukasiewicz' implication from Ł3, hence the name "Łukasiewicz".

Table 2 shows the definitions of $\rightarrow_{Luk}$ and $\rightarrow_{cmi}$. It is clear that they are very similar, differing only in the values of $\mathbf{T} \rightarrow \mathbf{B}$, $\mathbf{N} \rightarrow \mathbf{B}$, and $\mathbf{N} \rightarrow \mathbf{F}$. The biconditional connective is understood to be the conjunction of the conditional and its converse, hence the differences between the two conditionals are propagated to the bi-conditionals. These differences are enough to produce some quite different theorems between the logics that use them, as can be seen in the experimental results presented in Sect. 5.

Table 2. Truth tables for $\rightarrow_{Luk}$ and $\rightarrow_{cmi}$

$\rightarrow_{Luk}$	T	B	N	F		$\rightarrow_{cmi}$	T	B	N	F
T	T	F	N	F		T	T	B	N	F
B	T	B	N	F		B	T	B	N	F
N	T	N	T	N		N	T	T	T	T
F	T	T	T	T		F	T	T	T	T

Given the choices of truth values and conditional connectives, five logics are considered:

- Ł3: The truth values are **T**, **N**, and **F**, with **T** designated. The conditional is $\rightarrow_{Luk}$, restricted to the three truth values.
- RM3: The truth values are **T**, **B**, and **F**, with **T** and **B** designated. The conditional is $\rightarrow_{Luk}$, restricted to the three truth values.
- A3: The truth values are **T**, **B**, and **F**, with **T** and **B** designated. The conditional is $\rightarrow_{cmi}$, restricted to the three truth values.
- FDE$^{\rightarrow Luk}$: The truth values are **T**, **B**, **N**, and **F**, with **T** and **B** designated. The conditional is $\rightarrow_{Luk}$.
- FDE$^{\rightarrow cmi}$: The truth values are **T**, **B**, **N**, and **F**, with **T** and **B** designated. The conditional is $\rightarrow_{cmi}$.

The relationship between FOL and these logics is shown in Fig. 2.

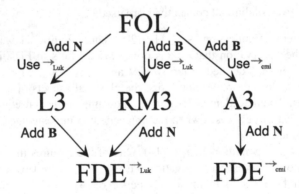

Fig. 2. The relationships between the logics

4   System Architecture and Implementation

JGXYZ proves theorems in the gap/glut (and other) logics by translating the problem to an equi-provable FOL problem, then using a FOL ATP system to find a proof (or countermodel) for the FOL problem. In [15] two translations from RM3 to FOL were presented, and in [20] the "truth evaluation" translation was extended to FDE$^{\rightarrow cmi}$. The truth evaluation translation function *trs* takes a target formula (e.g., in $FDE^{\rightarrow cmi}$) and a target truth value (e.g., one of **T**, **B**, **N**, or **F**) as arguments, and translates the target formula, either directly for atoms, or recursively on the subformulae for non-atoms, to produce a FOL formula. Intuitively, *trs* captures the necessary and sufficient conditions for the target formula to have the target truth value. Prior implementations of JGXYZ (called JGRM3 in [15], and later JGXYZ 0.1 in [20]) encoded *trs* directly. This meant that extending the translation to a new logic required significant effort. The new implementation of JGXYZ (version 0.2) is the same as for version 0.1 for quantified and atomic formulae, but makes the translation data-driven for formulae under a unary or binary connective. For each logic, its truth values and the designated subset of them are specified, and the truth tables for the logic's negation, disjunction, conjunction, and conditional connectives are provided.

Universally qualified formulae are treated as a conjunction of their ground instances, requiring that there exists an instance that has the target truth value, and that there do not exist any instances that have a truth value lower in the truth diamond. For example, for a universally quantified formula in $FDE^{\rightarrow cmi}$ and the target truth value **B**, the translation requires that there exists an instance of the formula whose translation is **B**, and that there do not exist any instances whose translation is **F**, i.e., $trs(\forall x\ \varphi, \mathbf{B}) \Rightarrow \exists x\ trs(\varphi, \mathbf{B}) \wedge \neg \exists x\ trs(\varphi, \mathbf{F})$. Existentially quantified formulae are treated as a disjunction of their ground instances, requiring that there exists an instance that has the target truth value, and that there do not exist any instances that have a truth value higher in the truth diamond. For example, for an existentially quantified formula in $FDE^{\rightarrow cmi}$ and the target truth value **B**, the translation requires that there exists an instance of the formula whose translation is **B**, and that there do not exist any instances whose translation is **T**, i.e., $trs(\exists x\ \varphi, \mathbf{B}) \Rightarrow \exists x\ trs(\varphi, \mathbf{B}) \wedge \neg \exists x\ trs(\varphi, \mathbf{T})$.

For formulae under a unary or binary connective, the appropriate truth table is consulted to find tuples of truth values such that the value of the connective for those inputs is the target truth value. The tuple elements are then the target truth values for the arguments of the connective in the formula. The translation is the disjunction (one disjunct for each tuple) of conjunctions (one conjunct for element of the tuple), applied to the translations of the arguments of the connective. For the *n*-ary connective $\oplus$ and the target truth value TTV:

$$trs(\oplus \varphi, TTV) \Rightarrow \bigvee_{i=1}^{k} \bigwedge_{j=1}^{n} trs(\varphi_j, inputs_{i,j}(\oplus, TTV))$$

where $inputs_{i,j}(\oplus, TTV)$ is the jth element of the ith tuple of the k tuples from the truth table for $\oplus$ such that the value of $\oplus$ for those inputs is TTV, and φ_j is the jth argument of φ (*n* is 1 for a unary connective and 2 for a binary connective, etc.). For example, for the $FDE^{\rightarrow cmi}$ conditional formula $\varphi \rightarrow_{cmi} \psi$ and the target truth value **B**, k is 2 and the input tuples are [**T**, **B**] and [**B**, **B**]. Then:

$$trs(\varphi \rightarrow_{cmi} \psi, \mathbf{B}) \Rightarrow ((trs(\varphi, \mathbf{T}) \wedge trs(\psi, \mathbf{B})) \vee (trs(\varphi, \mathbf{B}) \wedge trs(\psi, \mathbf{B}))).$$

Atoms are translated to FOL atoms that capture what it means for the atom to have the target truth value. Equality atoms are treated classically[4], so that for a target truth value of **T** an equality atom is unchanged, for a target truth value of **F** an equality atom is negated, and for a target truth value of **B** or **N** an equality atom is translated to the FOL truth value **F**. A non-equality atom Φ that has predicate symbol $\mathcal{P}$ and arity n is translated to a FOL atom with predicate symbol $\mathcal{P}^{TTV}$ and arity n, where TTV is the target truth value. The FOL atom has the same term arguments as $\mathcal{P}$ in Φ. *Definition axioms* are added to relate each predicate symbol $\mathcal{P}^{LTV}$ to atoms that correspond to the two FOL truth values **T** and **F**, where LTV is each of the truth values used by the logic. The axioms introduce two new predicate symbols, $\mathcal{P}^{cT}$ and $\mathcal{P}^{cF}$ (for classical True and False) for each predicate symbol $\mathcal{P}$ in the input problem. The axioms are:

$$\forall \overline{x}\,(\mathcal{P}^{T}(\overline{x}) \leftrightarrow (\mathcal{P}^{cT}(\overline{x}) \wedge \neg\mathcal{P}^{cF}(\overline{x}))) \qquad \forall \overline{x}\,(\mathcal{P}^{B}(\overline{x}) \leftrightarrow (\mathcal{P}^{cT}(\overline{x}) \wedge \mathcal{P}^{cF}(\overline{x})))$$
$$\forall \overline{x}\,(\mathcal{P}^{N}(\overline{x}) \leftrightarrow (\neg\mathcal{P}^{cT}(\overline{x}) \wedge \neg\mathcal{P}^{cF}(\overline{x}))) \qquad \forall \overline{x}\,(\mathcal{P}^{F}(\overline{x}) \leftrightarrow (\neg\mathcal{P}^{cT}(\overline{x}) \wedge \mathcal{P}^{cF}(\overline{x})))$$

Finally, *exhaustion axioms* are added to enforce that each of the FOL atoms takes on exactly one of the truth values of the logic. By example, the axioms for FDE$^{\rightarrow cmi}$ are:

$$\forall \overline{x}\,(\mathcal{P}^{T}(\overline{x}) \vee \mathcal{P}^{B}(\overline{x}) \vee \mathcal{P}^{N}(\overline{x}) \vee \mathcal{P}^{F}(\overline{x}))$$

(The exclusive disjunction of the disjuncts, so that each of the FOL atoms takes on only one of the truth values, is a logical consequence of the exhaustion and definition axioms.)

For a set of formulae ϕ, let $def(\phi)$ be the set of definition axioms and $exh(\phi)$ the set of exhaustion axioms, for the predicate symbols that occur in ϕ. Define

$$des(\phi) =_{df} \bigvee_{i=1}^{n} trs(\phi, DTV_i)$$

where DTV is the set of designated truth values of the logic. For a problem $\phi \vDash \psi$ define

$$trans(\phi) = des(\phi) \cup exh(\phi \cup \{\psi\}) \cup def(\phi \cup \{\psi\})$$

Then $\phi \vDash_{logic} \psi$ iff $trans(\phi) \vDash_{FOL} des(\psi)$. A theorem prover for the logic is simply implemented by submitting $trans(\phi) \vDash_{FOL} des(\psi)$ to a FOL ATP system.

The JGXYZ translation is implemented in Prolog, and the full ATP system uses some scriptin' magic to connect the translation to a FOL ATP system. By default, 80% of the CPU time is allocated to searching for a proof, and if no proof is found the remaining 20% is used to search for a countermodel. Currently Vampire 4.2.2 [10] is used for the FOL reasoning, in CASC mode for proving, and in finite model finding mode for finding countermodels. JGXYZ for FOL,[5] Ł3, A3, RM3, FDE$^{\rightarrow Łuk}$, and

---

[4] The classical interpretation of equality is due to the classical interpretation of terms. Since a term is interpreted as an element of the domain, if two terms are interpreted as the same element then their equality is **True**, and if they are interpreted as different elements then their equality is **False**. There is no middle ground (**Both** or **Neither**). [7,14].

[5] This can be used to empirically check that the translation does produce equi-provable problems. For more fun, it is possible to repeatedly apply the translation to a FOL problem to produce a new FOL problem, to produce a sequence of ever more difficult FOL problems.

FDE$^{\rightarrow cmi}$ are available through the SystemOnTPTP interface at http://www.tptp.org/cgi-bin/SystemOnTPTP.

5   Experimental Results

The implementation has been tested for all the logics encoded, on a set of problems, taken from [20]. All the problems are valid in FOL. Testing was done on an Intel(R) Xeon(R) CPU E5-2609 v2 @ 2.50 GHz, with a CPU time limit of 600 s per problem. Note that the time taken to translate a problem is negligible, so that almost all of the time is available to the FOL ATP system. The test problems in TPTP format are available at http://www.tptp.org/JGXYZ, and they can be run through SystemOnTPTP.

Table 3 gives the results of the testing, using the default JGXYZ settings described in Sect. 4. The results with a CPU time were proved, countermodels were found for those marked CSA, and no result was obtained within the CPU time limit for those marked GUP. The results marked GUP$^+$ are known (from previous experiments [15,20]) to be theorems for that logic, and the results marked GUP$^-$ are known to have countermodels for that logic.

As is expected, there are differences in the results between the various logics because of their different truth values and also their different conditional connectives. Problem 1 shows how purely glut logics such as RM3 and A3 can prove FOL tautologies, while logics that include the gap truth value **N** cannot. In contrast, Problems 8 and 14 show that there are some theorems of purely gap logics that are not theorems of glut logics. Problem 8 in particular shows that Ł3 is not paraconsistent. Problems 2 and 12 illustrate a difference between $\rightarrow_{Łuk}$ and $\rightarrow_{cmi}$: e.g., for Problem 2, in RM3 and FDE$^{\rightarrow Łuk}$ with q set to **B** and p set to **T**, the conjecture is **F** and hence not a theorem, while in A3 and FDE$^{\rightarrow cmi}$ the conjecture is **B**. In contrast, Problem 11 shows how this difference can work the other way. Problem 7 shows the difference between FOL and the gap/glut logics with their extra truth values and extended conditional connectives. In Ł3 and FDE$^{\rightarrow Łuk}$ with p to **N** and q to **F** the conjecture is **N**; in A3 and FDE$^{\rightarrow cmi}$ with p to **B** and q to **F** the conjecture is **F**; and in RM3 with p to **B** and q to **F** the conjecture is **N**. In contrast, Problem 6 is a theorem for all the logics, despite the extra truth values and extended conditional connectives.

Problems 16–20 are interesting both from a historical and also a contemporary point of view of the foundations of mathematics. They represent some of the motivating claims that drove the modern development of axiomatic set theory and mathematics. Read the relation $E(x, y)$ as saying that x *is an element of the set* y. Then each formula represents a crucial part of the various paradoxes of set theory. For example, Russell's paradox is in part captured by Problem 16, which says that there cannot be a set (y) all of whose members (x) are not members of themselves. See [20] for a more detailed discussion of these problems.

Problem 20, which is a theorem for Ł3, RM3, A3, and FDE$^{\rightarrow Łuk}$, is quite hard for JGXYZ. An examination of syntactic characteristics of the translated problems illustrates how the translation blows up the problem. Table 4 provides some measures of the

Table 3. Example axiom-conjecture pairs and their provability

#	Axioms ⊨ Conjecture		Ł3	RM3	A3	FDE→	
						Łuk	cmi
1		⊨ $p \lor \neg p$	CSA	0.1	0.1	CSA	CSA
2	q	⊨ $p \to q$	0.1	CSA	0.1	CSA	0.1
3	$\neg p$	⊨ $p \to q$	0.1	CSA	CSA	CSA	CSA
4	$\neg(p \to q)$	⊨ p	0.1	0.1	0.1	0.1	0.1
5		⊨ $p \to (q \lor \neg q)$	CSA	CSA	0.1	CSA	CSA
6		⊨ $p \to (p \lor \neg p)$	0.1	0.1	0.1	0.1	0.1
7		⊨ $(p \land \neg p) \to q$	CSA	CSA	CSA	CSA	CSA
8	$p, \neg p$	⊨ q	0.1	CSA	CSA	CSA	CSA
9	$p \lor q, \neg p$	⊨ q	0.1	CSA	CSA	CSA	CSA
10		⊨ $(\neg p \lor q) \leftrightarrow (p \to q)$	CSA	CSA	CSA	CSA	CSA
11		⊨ $((p \to q) \land (q \to p)) \to$ $(p \lor q \lor \neg(p \to q) \lor \neg(q \to p) \lor$ $((\neg p \to \neg q) \land (\neg q \to \neg p)))$	3.7	3.8	4.4	39.9	CSA
12	$H(a)$	⊨ $\exists x\, G(x) \to H(a)$	0.1	CSA	0.1	CSA	0.1
13		⊨ $\exists x\, (G(x) \land \neg G(x)) \to H(b)$	CSA	CSA	CSA	CSA	CSA
14	$\exists x\, (G(x) \lor H(x)), \neg \exists y\, G(y)$	⊨ $\exists z\, H(z)$	0.1	CSA	CSA	CSA	CSA
15	$H(a)$	⊨ $\forall x\, (H(x) \to G(x)) \leftrightarrow$ $\forall x\, ((H(x) \land G(x)) \lor (\neg H(x) \land G(a)))$	CSA	CSA	CSA	CSA	CSA
16		⊨ $\neg \exists y \forall x\, (E(x,y) \leftrightarrow \neg E(x,x))$	CSA	0.1	0.1	CSA	CSA
17		⊨ $\forall z \exists y \forall x\, (E(x,y) \leftrightarrow (E(x,z) \land \neg E(x,x)))$ $\to \neg \exists w \forall u\, E(u,w)$	CSA	GUP⁻	GUP⁻	GUP	CSA
18		⊨ $\neg \exists y \forall x\, (E(x,y) \leftrightarrow$ $\neg \exists z\, (E(x,z) \land E(z,x))$	CSA	162.1	37.6	GUP	CSA
19		⊨ $\exists y \forall x\, (E(x,y) \leftrightarrow E(x,x)) \to$ $\neg \forall x \exists y \forall z\, (E(z,y) \leftrightarrow \neg E(z,x))$	CSA	430.8	GUP⁺	GUP	CSA
20	$\forall y \exists z \forall x\, (E(x,z) \leftrightarrow x = y)$	⊨ $\neg \exists w \forall x\, (E(x,w) \leftrightarrow \forall u\, (E(x,u) \to$ $\exists y\, (E(y,u) \land \neg \exists z\, (E(z,u) \land E(z,y)))))$	73.3	263.1	GUP⁺	412.3	CSA

original and translated problems.[6] The translation blows up the problem significantly, with the effect being least for the purely gap logic Ł3, greater for the purely glut logics RM3 and A3, and most for the gap/glut logics FDE→Łuk and FDE→cmi. The use of →Łuk by RM3 and FDE→Łuk apparently has a greater effect than the use of →cmi by A3 and FDE→cmi. As RM3 and A3 are both purely glut logics, this difference is attributed to the different values for **T → B**. The different values for **N → B** and **N → F** further contribute to the differences between the translations for FDE→Łuk and FDE→cmi. The different blow ups naturally contribute correspondingly to the difficulty of the translated problems for the FOL ATP system.

For the motivating example of Sect. 2, the different logics again produce interestingly different results, as shown in Table 5. A proof is a positive answer to the query,

---

[6] Thanks to Giles Reger for providing a special version of Vampire that normalises the formulae into comparable forms.

Table 4. Syntactic measures for problem 20

Measure	FOL	Ł3	RM3	A3	FDE$^\rightarrow$	
					Łuk	cmi
Number of formulae	2	6	6	6	7	7
Number of atoms	7	2080	9912	8356	45496	41130
Maximal formula depth	12	29	33	31	43	45
Number of connectives	7	2182	10418	8780	47920	43364
Number of predicates	2	6	6	6	7	7
Number of variables	8	460	2173	1847	7835	7211

Table 5. Provability of queries about the undead

#	Query	FOL′	Ł3′	RM3	A3	FDE$^\rightarrow$	
						Łuk	cmi
1	Does Désirée need words?	CSA	CSA	CSA	CSA	CSA	CSA
2	Is Nigel alive or not alive?	0.1	CSA	0.2	0.2	CSA	CSA
3	Does Nigel need placement?	0.1	CSA	0.1	0.2	CSA	CSA
4	Is Umberto both alive and not alive?	CSA	CSA	0.3	0.2	0.2	0.2
5	Has Umberto been buried?	0.1	0.1	CSA	CSA	CSA	CSA
6	Was Désirée buried because she is not alive?	0.1	0.2	CSA	0.1	CSA	0.1

while a CSA result is a negative answer. For FOL and Ł3, the axioms are contradictory (Umberto is alive and not alive), thus all the conjectures are theorems. For interest, the axiom stating that Umberto is alive was removed to make the axioms consistent in FOL and Ł3, then Vampire and JGXYZ were run on the resulting problems - these results are shown in the columns marked FOL′ and Ł3′. Problem 1 shows that all the logics understand that Désirée does not need words, because she is not known to be alive. Problem 2 should have a negative answer, because Nigel is not known to be alive nor is he known to be not alive. However, FOL′ assumes that he is either alive or not alive. RM3 and A3 do not escape from this conclusion because the only other possibility they offer is that he is both alive and not alive. In contrast, Ł3′, FDE$^{\rightarrow Łuk}$, and FDE$^{\rightarrow cmi}$ allow Nigel to be neither alive nor not alive. Problem 3 extends Problem 2, so that FOL′, RM3, and A3 conclude that Nigel needs placement, while Ł3′, FDE$^{\rightarrow Łuk}$, and FDE$^{\rightarrow cmi}$ do not. Problem 4 should have a positive answer, which all the logics (taking the original FOL and Ł3) support. However, for FOL and Ł3 with the contradictory axioms the positive answer might be for the wrong reason, depending on how the ATP system uses the axioms. Problem 5 is answered positively by FOL′ and Ł3′ as it is known that Umberto is not alive (recall, the axiom stating that Umberto is alive is removed). In contrast, for the other logics it is known that Umberto is alive and hence has not necessarily been buried. Problem 6 illustrates the difference between $\rightarrow_{Łuk}$ and $\rightarrow_{cmi}$. For RM3 and FDE$^{\rightarrow Łuk}$, which both use $\rightarrow_{Łuk}$, it is possible that Désirée is definitely (**T**) not alive, but has been both (**B**) buried and not buried. Under $\rightarrow_{Łuk}$ the implication is false

(F) and hence a negative answer is returned. For A3 and $FDE^{\rightarrow cmi}$, which both use $\rightarrow_{cmi}$, the conditional would be both (B) true and false, and thus a positive answer is returned. The only way for the implication to not be a theorem in A3 and $FDE^{\rightarrow cmi}$ would be for Désirée to have been neither (N) buried nor not buried, or definitely not buried, which is not the case because it's an axiom that she has been buried.

6 Conclusion

This paper has described an ATP system, named JGXYZ, for some gap and glut logics. JGXYZ is based on an equi-provable translation to FOL, followed by use of an existing ATP system for FOL. A key feature of JGXYZ is that the translation to FOL is data-driven, in the sense that it requires only the addition of a new logic's truth tables for the unary and binary connectives in order to produce an ATP system for the logic. Experimental results from JGXYZ have illustrated the differences between the logics and translated problems, both technically and in terms of a quasi-real-world use case.

Future work includes a more comprehensive investigation of gap and glut logics, their implementation in JGXYZ, and full experimental evaluation.

References

1. Avron, A.: Natural 3-valued logics: characterization and proof theory. J. Symb. Log. **56**(1), 276–294 (1991)
2. Baaz, M., Fermüller, C.G., Salzer, G., Zach, R.: MUltlog 1.0: towards an expert system for many-valued logics. In: McRobbie, M.A., Slaney, J.K. (eds.) CADE 1996. LNCS, vol. 1104, pp. 226–230. Springer, Heidelberg (1996). https://doi.org/10.1007/3-540-61511-3_84
3. Beckert, B., Hähnle, R., Oel, P., Sulzmann, M.: The tableau-based theorem prover $3^{T\!A\!P}$ version 4.0. In: McRobbie, M.A., Slaney, J.K. (eds.) CADE 1996. LNCS, vol. 1104, pp. 303–307. Springer, Heidelberg (1996). https://doi.org/10.1007/3-540-61511-3_95
4. Belnap, N.D.: A Useful Four-Valued Logic. In: Dunn, J.M., Epstein, G. (eds.) Modern Uses of Multiple-Valued Logic. EPIS, vol. 2, pp. 5–37. Springer, Dordrecht (1977). https://doi.org/10.1007/978-94-010-1161-7_2
5. Belnap, N.: A useful four-valued logic: how a computer should think. In: Anderson, A., Belnap, N., Dunn, J. (eds.) Entailment: The Logic of Relevance and Necessity, vol. 2, pp. 506–541. Princeton University Press (1992)
6. Dunn, J.: Intuitive semantics for first degree entailment and coupled trees. Philos. Stud. **29**, 149–168 (1976)
7. Evans, G.: Can there be vague objects? Analysis **38**, 208 (1978)
8. Hähnle, R.: Advanced Many-Valued Logics. In: Gabbay, D.M., Guenthner, F. (eds.) Handbook of Philosophical Logic. HALO, vol. 2, pp. 297–395. Springer, Dordrecht (2001). https://doi.org/10.1007/978-94-017-0452-6_5
9. Hazen, A., Pelletier, F.: K3, Ł3, LP, RM3, A3, FDE, M: How to Make Many-Valued Logics Work for You. In: Omori, H., Wansing, H. (eds.) New Essays on Belnap-Dunn Logic. Springer, Berlin (1980). To appear. Synthese Library
10. Kovács, L., Voronkov, A.: First-order theorem proving and VAMPIRE. In: Sharygina, N., Veith, H. (eds.) CAV 2013. LNCS, vol. 8044, pp. 1–35. Springer, Heidelberg (2013). https://doi.org/10.1007/978-3-642-39799-8_1

11. Levine, E., Parks, L.: Undead TV. Duke University Press, Durham (2007)
12. Łukasiewicz, J.: On three-valued logic. Ruch Filozoficny **5**, 170–171 (1920)
13. Omori, H., Wansing, H.: 40 years of FDE: an introductory overview. Stud. Log. **105**(6), 1021–1049 (2017)
14. Pelletier, F.: Another argument against vague identity. J. Philos. **86**, 481–492 (1989)
15. Pelletier, F., Sutcliffe, G., Hazen, A.: Automated reasoning for the dialetheic logic RM3. In: Rus, V., Markov, Z. (eds.) Proceedings of the 30th International FLAIRS Conference, pp. 110–115 (2017)
16. Priest, G.: The logic of paradox. J. Philos. Log. **8**, 219–241 (1979)
17. Priest, G., Routley, R., Norman, J.: Paraconsistent Logic: Essays on the Inconsistent. Philosophia Verlag (1989)
18. Shapiro, S., Kouri Kissel, T.: Classical logic. In: Zalta, E. (ed.) The Stanford Encyclopedia of Philosophy. Metaphysics Research Lab, Stanford University (2018). https://plato.stanford.edu/archives/spr2018/entries/logic-classical/
19. Sobociński, B.: Axiomatization of a partial system of three-valued calculus of propositions'. J. Comput. Syst. **1**, 23–55 (1952)
20. Sutcliffe, G., Pelletier, F., Hazen, A.: Making Belnap's "useful four-valued logic" useful. In: Brawner, K., Rus, V. (eds.) Proceedings of the 31st International FLAIRS Conference, pp. 116–121 (2018)
21. Wikipedia contributors: logic - Wikipedia, the free encyclopedia (2018). https://en.wikipedia.org/w/index.php?title=Logic&oldid=875884116

GKC: A Reasoning System for Large Knowledge Bases

Tanel Tammet(✉)

Tallinn University of Technology, Tallinn, Estonia
`tanel.tammet@taltech.ee`

Abstract. This paper introduces GKC, a resolution prover optimized for search in large knowledge bases. The system is built upon a shared memory graph database Whitedb, enabling it to solve multiple different queries without a need to repeatedly parse or load the large parsed knowledge base from the disk. Due to the relatively shallow and simple structure of most of the literals in the knowledge base, the indexing methods used are mostly hash-based. While GKC performs well on large problems from the TPTP set, the system is built for use as a core system for developing a toolset of commonsense reasoning functionalities.

Keywords: Automated reasoning · Knowledge base

1 Introduction

We present the first release of GKC (acronym for "Graph Knowledge Core"), version 0.1: an automated theorem prover for first order logic, optimized for handling large knowledge bases. GKC is intended to become a building block for developing specialized methods and strategies for commonsense reasoning, including nonmonotonic reasoning, probabilistic reasoning and machine learning methods. We envision natural language question answering systems as the main potential application of rule-applying commonsense reasoning methods.

The immediate focus of GKC is implementing core technologies for efficient handling of large knowledge bases like DBpedia, YAGO, NELL and OpenCyc. The reason for this focus is the recognition that any useful commonsense reasoning system would necessarily contain a very large set of facts and rules, most of which have a relatively simple structure.

Due to the complexities of handling large knowledge bases, the most common current approach is to rely on specialized query tools like SPARQL or reasoning systems built for RDFs or some restricted subset of OWL, focusing mostly on taxonomies, while complex relations between different objects are rarely handled. On the other hand, the natural language question answering systems currently rely mainly on so-called shallow reasoning using methods based on word vectors.

Our hypothesis is that enabling efficient "deep" reasoning with more complex rules would complement and significantly enhance the capabilities of commonsense reasoning systems. This approach has been pursued in several papers and implementations. In particular, we note the papers [4,6,8,15,17].

© Springer Nature Switzerland AG 2019
P. Fontaine (Ed.): CADE 2019, LNAI 11716, pp. 538–549, 2019.
https://doi.org/10.1007/978-3-030-29436-6_32

GKC is undergoing active development and the current version 0.1 of GKC is the first public release of the system [18]. Hence the set of implemented search strategies and indexing technologies is limited, with heavy stress on implementing efficient core algorithms. The main algorithmic and technical features of GKC are:

1. The use of a shared memory database to enable fast startup of proof search and independent parallel searches on the same knowledge base.
2. Using hash indexes instead of tree indexes.
3. Efficient clause-to-clause subsumption algorithm using hashes of ground literal structure.
4. Simplification of derived clauses by hash-based search of contradicting units from all derived clauses.
5. Using several separate queues for picking clauses for the set of support strategy.

We expect GKC to become significantly stronger in near future. We have already started experiments with building nonmonotonic and probabilistic reasoning on a separate layer on top of GKC. However, the GKC system itself will be developed as a conventional first order reasoner without including the experimental features.

2   Architecture

GKC is a conventional first order theorem prover with the architecture and algorithms tuned for large problems. It is implemented in C on top of the data structures and functionality of the shared memory database WhiteDB [14]. GKC is available for both Linux and Windows under GNU AGPLv3 and is expected to be highly portable, see [18].

The prover is run from the command line, indicating the command, the input file, the strategy selection file using JSON syntax and optionally the parsed and prepared knowledge base as a shared memory handle number. Both a detailed configurable running log and a detailed proof is printed for each solution found.

The shared memory database makes it possible to start solving a new problem in the context of a given knowledge base very quickly: parsing and preprocessing the large knowledge base can be performed before the GKC is called to do proof search: the preprocessed database can be assumed to be already present in the memory. Since GKC does not write into the shared database during search, several GKC-calling processes can run simultaneously without locking while using the single copy of a knowledge base in memory. The memory database can be dumped and read from the disk and there could be multiple memory databases present in shared memory simultaneously.

WhiteDB is a lightweight NoSQL database library written jointly by the author of this paper and Priit Järv as a separate project. It is available under the GPL licence and can be compiled from C source or installed as a Debian package. All the data is kept in main memory and can be dumped and read back to and from the disk as a whole. There is no server process, data is read and written directly from/to shared memory, no sockets are used between WhiteDB and the application program. Since data is kept in shared memory, it is accessible to separate processes.

GKC implements a parser for the [1] first order formula syntax. The parser is implemented using GNU tools Flex and Bison. There is also a parser for the Otter clause normal form syntax and a simplified Prolog syntax. The parsed formula is converted to a clause normal form (CNF) using both ordinary CNF conversion rules and replacement of subformulas with introduced predicates in cases there is a danger of the CNF size exploding, using a simple top-down procedure: any time we see that the distribution should be applied to $(a\&b) \vee (c\&d)$, renaming is performed.

3   Algorithms, Strategies and Optimizations

The derivation rules currently implemented in GKC are very basic. The preference stems from our focus of optimizing for the set of support strategy (see [9] for core terminology).

1. Binary resolution with optionally the set of support strategy, negative or positive ordered resolution or unit restriction.
2. Factorization.
3. Paramodulation with the Knuth-Bendix ordering.

In particular, we note that neither the demodulation, hyperresolution, unit--resulting resolution nor purely propositional methods like AVATAR have been implemented so far. We plan to add these rules, but they have not been a priority for GKC development.

The overall iteration algorithm of GKC is based on the common *given-clause algorithm* where newly derived clauses are pushed into the *passive list* and then selected (based on the combination of creation order and clause weight) as a *given clause* into an *active list*. The derivation rules are applied only to the given clause and active clauses. In the following we explain how we perform clause simplification with all the derived clauses present in the active list. We will also explain the use of different clause selection queues used by GKC.

The *set of support strategy* we rely upon for large problems basically means that the large knowledge base is immediately put into the active list and no direct derivations between the clauses in the knowledge base are performed. As an additional limitation we do not perform subsumption of given clauses with non-unit clauses in the knowledge base: during our experiments the time spent for this did not give sufficient gains for the efficiency of proof search.

3.1   Hash Indexes and Their Use

Perhaps the most interesting innovation in GKC is the pervasive use of hash indexes instead of tree indexes. In contrast, all state-of-the-art provers implementing resolution rely on tree indexes of various kinds. Research into suitable tree indexes has been an important subfield of automated reasoning: see [12] for an early overview of common indexing techniques.

Our experiments demonstrate that hash indexes are a viable alternative and possibly a superior choice in the context of large knowledge bases. The latter are expected to consist mostly of ground clauses representing known "facts" and a significant percentage of derived literals are ground as well.

Hash indexes are particularly well suited for ground literals. The motivation for using hash indexes can be summed up as:

1. Hash indexes take up much less space than tree indexes.
2. Hash indexes are possibly faster for our primary scenario of large knowledge bases with a shallow term structure, although confirming this hypothesis would need further research.
3. Hash indexes are simpler to implement than tree indexes.

A hash index of a term or an atom is an integer. We compute the hash of a term by sequentially adding the hashes of constants and variables (hash in the formula) to the previous value with a popular addition function *sdbm* developed for strings: value + (hash << 6) + (hash << 16) - hash. The same iterative function is used for calculating hashes of constants interpreted as strings, to be used in the hash calculation of the term. These hashes are cached in the data structure of the constant to avoid regular recomputation. A hash of a variable is based on the order of a first variable occurrence in the clause: i.e. if hashes of two literals in two separate clauses are equal, then the literals are equal modulo renaming the variables in the whole clause.

As a hash index we use a simple integer array, elements of which point to hash chains. We currently use the arrays with a length of one million. A minor drawback of this approach is the fact that the hash arrays have to be zeroed during the initialization phase of proof search, which takes time proportional to the array size.

The first important use of hash indexes in GKC is simplifying the newly derived clauses. Each derived clause immediately undergoes simplification and subsumption attempts by looking for existing unit clauses in the passive or active clause list, either deleting some of its literals or subsuming the clause. For this we search for exactly equal literals with the same or negative polarity by looking up the atoms in the hash index. Each match is followed by an actual equality check with atoms in the hash chain. Every unit clause derived is pushed to this hash index. We note that the simplification algorithm can also cut off literals containing variables.

GKC uses an analogous hash index for forward subsumption of newly selected given clauses with unit clauses from the list of active clauses.

Finally, we use hashes of head predicate and function symbols while processing a given clause for the purpose of looking for literals to resolve and paramodulate upon and terms to paramodulate into.

3.2   Hash Features for Clause-to-clause Subsumption

Efficient clause-to-clause subsumption is important for forward subsumption of long clauses. Deriving and using long clauses is very common for the set of support strategy crucial for large knowledge bases. In our experiments the forward subsumption of newly given clause by a given-clause algorithm dominated the time spent on search until we implemented hash features. We note that GKC performs full subsumption only for given clauses, and not for newly derived clauses: for the latter we only perform fast hash-based subsumption with units for memory conservation. Also, we do not perform full self-subsumption of the axiom set for the set-of-support strategy.

It is well known that the tree indexing methods do not perform well for subsumption of long clauses. Earlier work has presented algorithms for efficiently filtering out impossible subsumption cases by feature vectors, see [3] and [13].

The well-known core idea for checking whether a clause A could subsume a clause B is to look at a short vector of meta-information – *features* – stored along with the clause A and compare it to the corresponding meta-information of B. For example, a longer clause cannot subsume a shorter clause, a deeper clause cannot subsume a shallower clause, etc.

The basic features GKC uses for comparison are ground/non-ground, clause length, size, depth, length of a negative subset, length of a ground subset.

Additionally – what turned out to have a significant effect – we compute and compare *hash features* as the hashes of ground prefixes. A *ground prefix* denotes the part of the sequential atom representation until the first occurrence of a variable. As one of the non-hash features we use the longest ground prefix.

We look at ground hashes of several short lengths (currently 1, 2 and 3) of ground prefixes: length 1 corresponds to (signed) predicate symbols, length 2 to a predicate symbol plus the first the argument, assuming it is ground, etc. Each integer hash of the ground prefix is again hashed to a small integer $0 \ldots 29$ corresponding to a single set bit position in an integer.

Hence, for 30-bit integers as used in the WhiteDb encoding we essentially have 30 different representations for ground prefixes. Finally, the one-bit representations of ground prefix hashes of all literals in a clause are put together by using the bit-wise logical *or*. As a consequence we can use the following observation during clause-to-clause subsumption: a clause A cannot subsume a clause B if the bit-wise representation of ground prefixes of the same length of A are not a bit-wise subset of the same bit-wise representation for B.

We will bring examples of the performance of hash features in the later section.

3.3   Clause Selection Queues

Clause selection is, in our understanding, the most crucial choice point of resolution provers, see [11]. Hence we plan to carry out more research and experimentation with GKC for this direction.

Currently we perform the selection of a given clause by using several queues in order to spread the selection relatively uniformly over different important categories of derived clauses. The queues are organized in two layers.

As a first layer we use the common ratio-based algorithm [11] of alternating between selecting N clauses from a weight-ordered queue and one clause from the FIFO queue with the derivation order. This *pick-given ratio* N is set to 4 by default.

As a second layer we use four separate queues based on the derivation history of a clause. Each queue in the second layer contains the two sub-queues of the first layer.

We note that formulas in TPTP are normally annotated as either being axioms or conjectures/goals to be proved or assumptions/hypothesis posed and relevant for the goal. This annotation can be seen to arise naturally in question answering tasks from a large knowledge base: the latter consists of axioms and the question can be often split into the goal and the assumptions part.

We split all the input and derived clauses into four classes based on their history according to the annotations:

1. Clauses having both the goal and assumption in the derivation history.
2. Clauses having some goal clauses in the derivation history.
3. Clauses having some assumption clauses in the derivation history.
4. Clauses having only axioms in the derivation history.

These four queues are disjoint and if conditions are not mutually exclusive, the higher (earlier) one has priority.

Our initial experiments with different ratios for these queues indicate that giving more preference to the first two seems to be a better strategy for large problems than a uniform approach. Obviously, an optimal ratio is highly dependent on the type of the problem.

All in all, the use of these four queue classes has been highly beneficial for the performance of GKC, both for the set of support strategy and all the other resolution strategies.

4   Term Representation

GKC uses WhiteDB data structures for term representation: each term or clause is represented as a WhiteDB database record containing meta-information followed by term elements encoded as integers. Meta-information for literals in the clause is kept on the clause level to avoid the need to follow a pointer to access the literal meta-information.

WhiteDB database records – and hence also the main data structures in GKC – are tuples of N elements, each element encoded as an integer in the WhiteDB-s data encoding scheme. Since the WhiteDB data structures can be kept in the shared memory where absolute pointers do not work (processes map memory areas to different address spaces), conventional pointers are not used in the main data structures: this role is given to integers indicating offset to the current memory area, thus enabling the data in memory to be independent of its exact location.

Low bits of an integer in a record indicate the type of data stored in high bits. Pointers (offsets) have always zeros in low bits. Predicate and function symbols are represented as URI-s. Small integers, floats, boolean constants and variables fit into one integer directly, while large integers, doubles, strings and URI-s are represented as an offset to a separate data structure. In particular, URI-s are stored uniquely and contain various statistical and cached information in addition to the namespace and main strings.

WhiteDB uses our own implementation of a malloc-like allocator for shared memory and simple continuous allocation from memory pools for terms, literals and clauses. In particular, memory space for subterms and literals in a clause is continuous, which improves cache locality, important for walking through an atom or a term.

5   Performance

We describe the performance of GKC by comparing it to the results from the first order proof search category FOF of the latest CASC competition CASC-J9 held in 2018, see [16]. The detailed logs of all proof attempts as well as a working system for experimentation can be found in the GKC repository release v0.1–alpha [18].

The long-term winner of CASC – since 2002 – is the prover Vampire [10] with a clearly superior performance to all the other competitors. Incidentally, an early prover Gandalf [2] of the current author won an analogous division of CASC in 1997 and 1998. GKC has no direct relations to Gandalf nor shares any code.

The FOF division presents 500 randomly chosen problems from TPTP (see [1] and [7]) to the competitors with the goal to solve as many as possible under the given time limit. The competition was run on a quad-core Intel(R) Xeon(R) E5-2609 chip, with each problem solution attempt having access to all the cores for a maximum of 300 s.

We note that the problems were selected from a wide variety of different problem classes and for the most part are not very large. GKC is not designed for the majority of these classes.

For comparison purposes we ran GKC on a laptop with Ubuntu Linux 16.04 and the Intel(R) Core(TM) i7-5500U chip, using just one core. Shared memory was not used, i.e. each proof attempt started from scratch and included parsing and problem preparation.

A fixed sequence of simple strategies was run inside the limit of 200 s. The core strategies were binary ordered resolution, unit resolution and the set of support resolution. These were combined with none or small static limits (1, 2, and 4) for term depth and either using four beforementioned clause selection queue classes for giving preference to goal- and assumption-derived clauses or only one, common queue class, giving preference to smaller and older clauses regardless of history. For the set of support strategy stronger preference was given to the clauses containing goals and assumptions in their history. For unit and ordered binary resolution we used either no history-based preference at all or equal preference to the queues of clauses derived from goals, assumptions, combination of these or axioms only.

It is worth noting that on average the binary ordered resolution with several equally preferred history-based queues performed better than having no history-based preference. On the other hand, strong preference to queues formed from goal- and assumption-derived clauses performed on average worse than equal preference among the queues. The same cannot be said of the set of support strategy, where stronger goal- and assumption preference of said queues was better on average.

Equality was always handled by paramodulation with the Knuth-Bendix ordering. No demodulation was used. In short, the strategies selected were basic, not specially tuned or dependent upon a problem given.

In this setting GKC showed satisfactory performance, landing in the first half of the result list.

The following table inserts the GKC result into the official list of CASC-J9 results for comparison purposes. GKC did not take part of this competition (Table 1).

Table 1. CASC-J9 FOF results with GKC inserted.

System	Proofs
Vampire 4.3	461
Vampire 4.2	454
CSE_E 1.0	363
E 2.2pre	350
CVC4 1.6pre	298
GKC 0.1	**260**
Leo-III 1.3	256
iProver 2.8	248
leanCoP 2.2	143
nanoCoP 1.1	126
CSE 1.1	123
CSE 1.0	122
Prover9 1109a	122
Twee 2.2	74
Geo-III 2018c	50

Next we will have a look at the performance of hash features for clause-to-clause subsumption described earlier. We will consider all clause-to-clause subsumption attempts of non-ground-unit clauses for the two hardest problems for GKC from the seven largest problems from CASC-J9.

The subsumption pre-filter runs in stages, each stage detecting that subsumption of A by B is impossible due to some features stored as meta-information. As described earlier, the first, top features stage, considers ordinary features like clause length, depth etc. The hash prefix stages introduced in GKC check the bit-wise inclusion of encoded hashes of ground prefixes of length 1, 2 and 3. Only the subsumption attempts passing all these filters will continue to the stage where the subsumption of literals in respective clauses is considered (Table 2).

Table 2. Subsumption prefilter performance example.

Filter stage	CSR056+6	CSR033+6
All subsumptions attempted	360280255	669782763
Passed top features stage	13818803	6288334
Passed hash prefix length 1	772059	437145
Passed hash prefix length 2	448353	78176
Passed hash prefix length 3	435218	54881

5.1   Performance on the Largest Problems in TPTP

The experiments in this section are conducted using a newer release 0.1-epsilon of GKC, having better command-line support for using shared memory databases and being roughly twice faster for large problems than the release 0.1-alpha used in the previously described experiments.

The largest problems in TPTP, CSR025 ... CSR074, ask questions from the axioms built from the OpenCyc database: 50 problems for the axiom set CSR002+5.ax with over three million formulae and 50 problems for the subset of the latter, the axiom set CSR002+4.ax with over half a million formulae. Importantly, the larger set CSR002+5.ax is itself unsatisfiable, while the smaller CSR002+4.ax is satisfiable. We note that CASC-J9 contained seven problems based on the set CSR002+5.ax and only Vampire and iProver could solve any of these problems.

The default strategy of GKC for large formulas is binary resolution with the set-of-support strategy and earliest-derived vs. lightest-clause picking ratio four, with no special limits or preferences.

GKC parses and indexes the CSR002+5.ax set into shared memory in ca 23 s. After that the proof searches are run as new independent command-line commands which do not need to parse or do initial indexing and could be run in parallel. In this setting GKC proves 44 of the problems with the default strategy, most of them under 1 s and the longest time being 31 s. The remaining six of the problems are proved with a few variations of the clause picking ratio and set of support preferences, with the longest time being 3 min.

Since CSR002+5.ax is itself unsatisfiable, the problems based upon it are not well suited for comparison with other provers. Although the GKC strategy appears to use the given question in the derivation, there is no strict obligation to do so.

Next we look at the same 50 problems asked about the smaller, satisfiable axiom set CSR002+4.ax. GKC parses and indexes the CSR002+4.ax set into shared memory in ca 3.7 s. Again, using the shared memory database, GKC proves 45 of the problems with the default strategy and the remaining five hard problems either with a unit strategy limit (one of the clauses resolved upon must be a unit clause) or a derived clause size limit of 2. 36 of the problems are solved under 0.1 s, 12 between 0.1 and 1 s and the slowest two under 3 s.

We have compared GKC performance on the same problems with Vampire 4.2.2 in the "casc" mode. Most of the problems are solved in ca 10 s and most of this time is spent on parsing and initial indexing. The default initial strategy of Vampire solves 41 problems, while the remaining nine hard problems are solved after sequentially trying several strategies. These sequential attempts take ca one minute and in one case two minutes until the proof is found. The five hard problems for GKC are a subset of the nine hard problems for Vampire.

6   Summary and Further Work

We have presented a new automated theorem prover GKC optimized for search in large knowledge bases. While the development of GKC is ongoing, it is already a usable and performant generic theorem prover. The main outstanding practical capabilities of GKC as it stands now are its ability to use prepared knowledge bases in shared memory and top of the line performance for handling large knowledge bases.

From a research perspective we note that our experiments with GKC indicate that it is feasible for a theorem prover to rely purely on the hash indexes and avoid tree indexes altogether. We have introduced hash prefix filters for clause-to-clause subsumption and demonstrated their good performance. This said, we acknowledge that tree indexes do have superior performance in scenarios with deep term structures.

We plan to pursue the following directions for future work:

1. Improving the general-purpose performance of GKC by implementing additional derivation rules, algorithms and strategies. We do plan to participate in the next CASC competition.
2. Implementing specialized methods for large knowledge bases, like precomputation and built-in handling of transitive properties.
3. Improving the functionality of knowledge base preparation and precomputation with methods like vector-based statistical analysis for likely interdependencies.
4. Measuring the performance of hash indexes when compared to tree indexes for different problem classes.

5. Developing an experimental toolset of commonsense reasoning functionalities on top of GKC, with the principal aim to make GKC usable as a component in natural language understanding systems.

References

1. TPTP homepage. http://tptp.cs.miami.edu/~tptp/
2. Tammet, T.: Gandalf. J. Autom. Reason. **18**(2), 199–204 (1997)
3. Tammet, T.: Towards efficient subsumption. In: Kirchner, C., Kirchner, H. (eds.) CADE 1998. LNCS, vol. 1421, pp. 427–441. Springer, Heidelberg (1998). https://doi.org/10.1007/BFb0054276
4. Pease, A., Sutcliffe, G.: First order reasoning on a large ontology. In: Proceedings of the CADE-21 Workshop on Empirically Successful Automated Reasoning in Large Theories, vol. 257, pp. 61–70. CEUR Workshop Proceedings (2007)
5. Reagan, S.P., Sutcliffe, G., Goolsbey, K., Kahlert, R.C.: The Cyc TPTP Challenge Problem Set. Unpublished manuscript. http://www.opencyc.org/doc/tptp_challenge_problem_set
6. Suchanek, F., Kasneci, G.m Weikum, G.: YAGO: a core of semantic knowledge. In: Proceedings of the 16th International World Wide Web Conference, Banff, Canada, pp. 697–706
7. Sutcliffe, G.: The TPTP world – infrastructure for automated reasoning. In: Clarke, E.M., Voronkov, A. (eds.) LPAR 2010. LNCS (LNAI), vol. 6355, pp. 1–12. Springer, Heidelberg (2010). https://doi.org/10.1007/978-3-642-17511-4_1
8. Suda, M., Weidenbach, C., Wischnewski, P.: On the saturation of YAGO. In: Giesl, J., Hähnle, R. (eds.) IJCAR 2010. LNCS (LNAI), vol. 6173, pp. 441–456. Springer, Heidelberg (2010). https://doi.org/10.1007/978-3-642-14203-1_38
9. Bachmair, L., Ganzinger, H.: Resolution theorem proving. In: Handbook of Automated Reasoning, pp. 19–99. Elsevier (2001)
10. Kovács, L., Voronkov, A.: First-order theorem proving and VAMPIRE. In: Sharygina, N., Veith, H. (eds.) CAV 2013. LNCS, vol. 8044, pp. 1–35. Springer, Heidelberg (2013). https://doi.org/10.1007/978-3-642-39799-8_1
11. Schulz, S., Möhrmann, M.: Performance of clause selection heuristics for saturation-based theorem proving. In: Olivetti, N., Tiwari, A. (eds.) IJCAR 2016. LNCS (LNAI), vol. 9706, pp. 330–345. Springer, Cham (2016). https://doi.org/10.1007/978-3-319-40229-1_23
12. Sekar, R., Ramakrishnan, I., Voronkov, A.: Term indexing. In: Handbook of Automated Reasoning, vol. II, chap. 26, pp. 1853–1964. Elsevier Science (2001)
13. Schulz, S.: Simple and efficient clause subsumption with feature vector indexing. In: Bonacina, M.P., Stickel, M.E. (eds.) Automated Reasoning and Mathematics. LNCS (LNAI), vol. 7788, pp. 45–67. Springer, Heidelberg (2013). https://doi.org/10.1007/978-3-642-36675-8_3
14. Tammet, T., Järv, P.: WhiteDB homepage. https://whitedb.org
15. Furbach, U., Schon, C.: Commonsense reasoning meets theorem proving. In: Proceedings of the Workshop on Bridging the Gap between Human and Automated Reasoning co-located with 25th International Joint Conference on Artificial Intelligence IJCAI 2016, pp. 74–85. CEUR (2016)
16. Sutcliffe, G.: The 9th IJCAR automated theorem proving system competition - CASC-J9. AI Commun. **31**(1), 1–13 (2018)

17. Lopez Hernandez, J.C., Korovin, K.: An abstraction-refinement framework for reasoning with large theories. In: Galmiche, D., Schulz, S., Sebastiani, R. (eds.) IJCAR 2018. LNCS (LNAI), vol. 10900, pp. 663–679. Springer, Cham (2018). https://doi. org/10.1007/978-3-319-94205-6_43
18. Tammet, T.: Repository of the GKC system and experiment logs (2019). https:// github.com/tammet/gkc

Optimization Modulo the Theory of Floating-Point Numbers

Patrick Trentin[✉] and Roberto Sebastiani

DISI, University of Trento, Trento, Italy
patrick.trentin@unitn.it

Abstract. Optimization Modulo Theories (OMT) is an important extension of SMT which allows for finding models that optimize given objective functions, typically consisting in linear-arithmetic or pseudo-Boolean terms. However, many SMT and OMT applications, in particular from SW and HW verification, require handling *bit-precise* representations of numbers, which in SMT are handled by means of the theory of Bit-Vectors ($\mathcal{BV}$) for the integers and that of Floating-Point Numbers ($\mathcal{FP}$) for the reals respectively. Whereas an approach for OMT with (unsigned) $\mathcal{BV}$ has been proposed by Nadel & Ryvchin, unfortunately we are not aware of any existing approach for OMT with $\mathcal{FP}$.

In this paper we fill this gap. We present a novel OMT approach, based on the novel concept of *attractor* and *dynamic attractor*, which extends the work of Nadel & Ryvchin to signed $\mathcal{BV}$ and, most importantly, to $\mathcal{FP}$. We have implemented some OMT($\mathcal{BV}$) and OMT($\mathcal{FP}$) procedures on top of OptiMathSAT and tested the latter ones on modified problems from the SMT-LIB repository. The empirical results support the validity and feasibility of the novel approach.

1 Introduction

Optimization Modulo Theories (OMT) [5, 15, 16, 19–21, 23, 25–27] is an important extension to Satisfiability Modulo Theories which allows for finding models that optimize one or more objectives, which typically consist in some linear-arithmetic or Pseudo-Boolean function application.

However, many SMT and OMT applications, in particular from SW and HW verification, require handling *bit-precise* representations of numbers, which in SMT are handled by means of the theory of Bit-Vectors ($\mathcal{BV}$) for the integers and that of Floating-Point Numbers ($\mathcal{FP}$) for the reals respectively. (For instance, during the verification process of a piece of software, one may look for the minimum/maximum value of some int [resp. float] parameter causing an SMT($\mathcal{BV}$) [resp. SMT($\mathcal{FP}$)] call to return SAT—which typically corresponds to the presence of some bug—so that to guarantee a safe range for such parameter.)

We would like to thank the anonymous reviewers for their insightful comments and suggestions, and we thank Alberto Griggio for support with MathSAT5 code.

P. Fontaine (Ed.): CADE 2019, LNAI 11716, pp. 550–567, 2019.
https://doi.org/10.1007/978-3-030-29436-6_33

OMT for the theory of (unsigned) bit-vectors (OMT($\mathcal{BV}$)) was proposed by Nadel and Ryvchin [21], although a reduction to the problem to MaxSAT was already implemented in the SMT/OMT solver Z3 [6]. The work in [21] was based on the observation that OMT on unsigned $\mathcal{BV}$ can be seen as lexicographic optimization over the bits in the bitwise representation of the objective, ordered from the most-significant bit (MSB) to the least-significant bit (LSB).

In this paper we address—for the first time to the best of our knowledge—OMT for the theory of signed Bit-Vectors and, most importantly, for the theory of Floating-Point Arithmetic (OMT($\mathcal{FP}$)), by exploiting some properties of the two's complement encoding for signed $\mathcal{BV}$ and of the IEEE 754-2008 encoding for $\mathcal{FP}$ respectively.

We start from introducing the notion of *attractor*, which represent (the bitwise encoding of) the target value for the objective which the optimization process aims at. This allows us for easily leverage the procedure of [21] to work with both *signed* and *unsigned* Bit-Vectors, by minimizing lexicographically the bitwise distance between the objective and the attractor, that is, by minimizing lexicographically the bitwise-xor between the objective and the attractor.

Unfortunately there is no such notion of (fixed) attractor for $\mathcal{FP}$ numbers, because the target value moves as long as the bits of the objective are updated from the MSB to the LSB, and the optimization process may have to change dynamically its aim, even at the opposite direction. (For instance, as soon as the minimization process realizes there is no solution with a negative value for the objective and thus sets its MSB to 0, the target value is switched from $-\infty$ to $0+$, and the search switches direction, from the maximization of the exponent and the significand to their minimization.)

To cope with this fact, we introduce the notions of *dynamic attractor* and *attractor trajectory*, representing the dynamics of the moving target value, which are progressively updated as soon as the bits of the objective are updated from the MSB to the LSB. Based on these ideas, we present novel OMT($\mathcal{FP}$) procedures, which require at most $n + 2$, incremental calls to an SMT($\mathcal{FP}$) solver, n being the number of bits in the representation of the objective. Notice that these procedures do not depend on the underlying SMT($\mathcal{FP}$) procedure used, provided the latter allows for accessing and setting the single bits of the objective.

We have implemented these OMT($\mathcal{BV}$) and OMT($\mathcal{FP}$) procedures on top of the OPTIMATHSAT OMT solver [27]. We have run an experimental evaluation of the OMT($\mathcal{FP}$) procedures on modified SMT($\mathcal{FP}$) problems from the SMT-LIB library. The empirical results support the validity and feasibility of the novel approach.

The rest of the paper is organized as follows. In Sect. 2 we provide the necessary background on $\mathcal{BV}$ and $\mathcal{FP}$ theories and reasoning. In Sect. 3 we provide the novel theoretical definitions and results. In Sect. 4 we describe our novel OMT($\mathcal{FP}$) procedures. In Sect. 5 we present the empirical evaluation. In Sect. 6 we conclude, hinting some future directions. The proofs of the theoretical results from Sect. 3 are in the extended version of this paper [28].

2   Background

We assume some basic knowledge on SAT and SMT and briefly introduce the reader to the Bit-Vector and Floating-Point theories.

Bit-Vectors. A *bit* is a Boolean variable that can be interpreted as 0 or 1. A Bit-Vector ($\mathcal{BV}$) variable $\mathbf{v}^{[n]}$ is a vector of n bits, where $v[0]$ is the Most Significant Bit (MSB) and $v[n-1]$ is the Least Significant Bit (LSB).[1] A $\mathcal{BV}$ constant of width n is an interpreted vector of n values in $\{0,1\}$. We $\overline{overline}$ a bit value or a $\mathcal{BV}$ value to denote its complement (e.g., $\overline{[11010010]}$ is $[00101101]$). A $\mathcal{BV}$ variable/constant of width n can be *unsigned*, in which case its domain is $[0, 2^n - 1]$, or *signed*, which we assume to comply with the *Two's complement* representation, so that its domain is $[-2^{(n-1)}, 2^{(n-1)} - 1]$. Therefore, the vector $[11111111]$ can be interpreted either as the unsigned $\mathcal{BV}$ constant $\mathbf{255}^{[8]}$ or as the signed $\mathcal{BV}$ constant $-\mathbf{1}^{[8]}$. Following the SMT-LIBv2 standard [3], we may also represent a $\mathcal{BV}$ constant in *binary* (e.g. $\mathbf{28}^{[8]}$ is written $\#b00011100$) or in *hexadecimal* (e.g. $\mathbf{28}^{[8]}$ is written $\#x1C$) form. A $\mathcal{BV}$ term is built from $\mathcal{BV}$ constants, variables and interpreted $\mathcal{BV}$ functions which represent standard RTL operators: word concatenation (e.g. $\mathbf{3}^{[8]} \circ \mathbf{x}^{[8]}$), sub-word selection (e.g. $(\mathbf{3}^{[8]}[6:3])^{[4]}$), modulo-n sum and multiplication (e.g. $\mathbf{x}^{[8]} +_8 \mathbf{y}^{[8]}$ and $\mathbf{x}^{[8]} \cdot_8 \mathbf{y}^{[8]}$), bit-wise operators (like, e.g., $\mathbf{and}_n$, $\mathbf{or}_n$, $\mathbf{xor}_n$, $\mathbf{nxor}_n$, $\mathbf{not}_n$), left and right shift $<<_n$, $>>_n$. A $\mathcal{BV}$ atom can be built by combining $\mathcal{BV}$ terms with interpreted predicates like $\geq_n$, $<_n$ (e.g. $\mathbf{0}^{[8]} \geq_8 \mathbf{x}^{[8]}$) and equality. We refer the reader to [3] for further details on the syntax and semantics of Bit-Vector theory.

There are two main techniques for $\mathcal{BV}$ satisfiability, the "*eager*" and the "*lazy*" approach, which are substantially complementary to one another [18]. In the *eager* approach, $\mathcal{BV}$ terms and constraints are encoded into SAT via bit-blasting [13,17,22]. In the *lazy* approach, $\mathcal{BV}$ terms are not immediately expanded –so to avoid any scalability issue– and the $\mathcal{BV}$ solver is comprised by a layered set of techniques, each of which deals with a sub-portion of the $\mathcal{BV}$ theory [7,12,14].

Floating-Point. The theory of *Floating-Point Numbers* ($\mathcal{FP}$), [3,10,24], is based on the IEEE standard 754-2008 [4] for floating-point arithmetic, restricted to the binary case. A $\mathcal{FP}$ sort is an indexed nullary sort identifier of the form (_ FP <ebits> <sbits>) s.t. both *ebits* and *sbits* are positive integers greater than one, *ebits* defines the number of bits in the exponent and *sbits* defines the number of bits in the significand, including the hidden bit. A $\mathcal{FP}$ variable $\mathbf{v}^{[n]}$ with sort (_ FP <ebits> <sbits>) can be indifferently viewed as a vector of $n \overset{\text{def}}{=} ebits + sbits$ bits, where $v[0]$ is the Most Significant Bit (MSB) and $v[n-1]$ is the Least Significant Bit (LSB), or as a triplet of Bit-Vectors $\langle \mathbf{sign}, \mathbf{exp}, \mathbf{sig} \rangle$ s.t. $\mathbf{sign}$ is

---

[1] Although most often in the literature the indexes $i \in [0, \ldots, n-1]$ use to grow from the LSB to the MSB, in this paper we use the opposite notation because we always reason from the MSB down to the LSB, so that to much simplify the explanation.

a $\mathcal{BV}$ of size 1, **exp** is a $\mathcal{BV}$ of size *ebits* and **sig** is a $\mathcal{BV}$ of size *sbits* $-$ 1. A $\mathcal{FP}$ constant is a triplet of $\mathcal{BV}$ constants. Given a fixed floating-point sort, i.e. a pair $\langle ebits, sbits \rangle$, the following $\mathcal{FP}$ constants are implicitly defined:

value	Symbol	$\mathcal{BV}$ Repr.
plus infinity	(_ +oo <*ebits*> <*sbits*>)	(fp #b0 #b1...1 #b0...0)
minus infinity	(_ -oo <*ebits*> <*sbits*>)	(fp #b1 #b1...1 #b0...0)
plus zero	(_ +zero <*ebits*> <*sbits*>)	(fp #b0 #b0...0 #b0...0)
minus zero	(_ -zero <*ebits*> <*sbits*>)	(fp #b1 #b0...0 #b0...0)
not-a-number	(_ NaN <*ebits*> <*sbits*>)	(fp t #b1...1 s)

where t is either 0 or 1 and s is a $\mathcal{BV}$ which contains at least a 1.

Setting aside special $\mathcal{FP}$ constants, the remaining $\mathcal{FP}$ values can be classified to be either normal or subnormal (a.k.a. denormal) [4]. A $\mathcal{FP}$ number is said to be *subnormal* when every bit in its exponent is equal to zero, and *normal* otherwise. The significand of a normal $\mathcal{FP}$ number is always interpreted as if the leading binary digit is equal 1, while for denormalized $\mathcal{FP}$ values the leading binary digit is always 0. This allows for the representation of numbers that are closer to zero, although with reduced precision.

Example 1. Let x be the normal $\mathcal{FP}$ constant (_ FP #b0 #b1100 #b0101000), and y be the subnormal $\mathcal{FP}$ constant (_ FP #b0 #b0000 #b0101000), so that their corresponding sort is (_ FP <4> <8>). Then, according to the semantics defined in the IEEE standard 754-2008 [4], the floating-point value of x and y in decimal notation is given by:

$$x = (-1)^0 \cdot 2^{(12-7)} \cdot \left(1 + \sum_{i=1}^{7} \left(x[4+i] \cdot 2^{-i}\right)\right) = 1 \cdot 2^5 \cdot \left(1 + \frac{1}{2^2} + \frac{1}{2^4}\right) = 42$$

$$y = (-1)^0 \cdot 2^{(0-7+1)} \cdot \left(0 + \sum_{i=1}^{7} \left(y[4+i] \cdot 2^{-i}\right)\right) = 1 \cdot 2^{-6} \cdot \left(\frac{1}{2^2} + \frac{1}{2^4}\right) = \frac{5}{2^{10}}.$$

$\diamond$

The theory of $\mathcal{FP}$ provides a variety of built-in floating-point operations as defined in the IEEE standard 754-2008. This includes binary arithmetic operations (e.g. $+, -, \star, \div$), basic unary operations (e.g. $abs, -$), binary comparison operations (e.g. $\leq, <, \neq, =, >, \geq$), the remainder operation, the square root operation and more. Importantly, arithmetic operations are performed *as if with infinite precision*, but the result is then *rounded* to the "nearest" representable $\mathcal{FP}$ number according to the specified *rounding mode*. Five *rounding modes* are made available, as in [4].

The most common approach for $\mathcal{FP}$-satisfiability is to encode $\mathcal{FP}$ expressions into $\mathcal{BV}$ formulas based on the circuits used to implement floating-point operations, using appropriate under- and over-approximation schemes –or a mixture of both– to improve performance [11,29,30]. Then, the $\mathcal{BV}$-Solver is used to deal with the $\mathcal{FP}$ formula, using either the *eager* or the *lazy* $\mathcal{BV}$ approach. An alternative approach, based on *abstract interpretation*, is presented in [8,9].

With this technique, called *Abstract CDCL* (ACDCL), the set of feasible solutions is over-approximated with floating-point intervals, so that intervals-based conflict analysis is performed to decide $\mathcal{FP}$-satisfiability.

3   Theoretical Framework

We present our generalization of [21] to the case of signed/unsigned Bit-Vector Optimization, and then move on to deal with Floating-Point Optimization.

3.1   Bit-Vector Optimization

Without any loss of generality, we assume that every objective function $f(...)$ is replaced by a variable obj of the same type by conjoining "obj $= f(...)$" to the input formula. We use the symbol n to denote the bit-width of obj, and obj$[i]$ to denote the i-th bit of obj, where obj$[0]$ and obj$[n-1]$ are the Most Significant Bit (MSB) and the Least Significant Bit (LSB) of obj respectively. (See footnote 1)

Definition 1 *(OMT($\mathcal{BV}$)). Let φ be a SMT($\mathcal{BV}$) formula and obj be a –signed or unsigned– $\mathcal{BV}$ variable occurring in φ. We call an* **Optimization Modulo $\mathcal{BV}$ problem, OMT($\mathcal{BV}$),** *the problem of finding a model $\mathcal{M}$ for φ (if any) whose value of obj, denoted with $\min_{obj}(\varphi)$, is minimum w.r.t. the total order relation $\leq_n$ for signed $\mathcal{BV}$s if obj is signed, and the one for unsigned $\mathcal{BV}$s otherwise. (The dual definition where we look for the maximum follows straightforwardly)*

Hereafter, we generalize the unsigned $\mathcal{BV}$ maximization procedures described in [21] to the case of signed and unsigned $\mathcal{BV}$ optimization. To this extent, we introduce the novel notion of $\mathcal{BV}$ *attractor*.

Definition 2 *(Attractor, attractor equalities). When minimizing [resp. maximizing], we call* **attractor** *for obj the smallest [resp. greatest] $\mathcal{BV}$-value attr of the sort of obj. We call* **vector of attractor equalities** *the vector A s.t. $A[k] \stackrel{def}{=} (obj[k] = attr[k])$, $k \in [0..n-1]$.*

Example 2. If obj$^{[8]}$ is an *unsigned* $\mathcal{BV}$ objective of width 8, then its corresponding attractor *attr* is $\mathbf{0}^{[8]}$, i.e. [00000000], when obj$^{[8]}$ is minimized and it is $\mathbf{255}^{[8]}$, i.e. [11111111], when obj$^{[8]}$ is maximized. When obj$^{[8]}$ is instead a *signed* $\mathcal{BV}$ objective, following the two's complement encoding, the corresponding *attr* is $-\mathbf{128}^{[8]}$, i.e. [10000000], for minimization and $\mathbf{127}^{[8]}$, i.e. [01111111], for maximization.   ◇

In essence, the *attractor* can be seen as the target value of the optimization search and therefore it can be used to determine the desired improvement direction and to guide the decisions taken by the optimization search. By construction, if a model $\mathcal{M}$ satisfies all equalities $A[i]$, then $\mathcal{M}(obj) = attr$.

We use the symbol μ_k to denote a generic (possibly partial) assignment which assigns at least the k most-significant bits of obj. We use the symbol τ_k to denote an assignment to all and only the k most-significant bits of obj. Given $i < k$, we denote by $\mu_k[i]$ [resp. $\tau_k[i]$] the value in $\{0,1\}$ assigned to obj$[i]$ by μ_k [resp. τ_k]. Moreover, we use the expression $\llbracket\mu_k\rrbracket_i$ where $i \leq k$ to denote the restriction of μ_k to all and only the i most-significant bits of obj, obj$[0], \ldots,$ obj$[i-1]$. Given a model $\mathcal{M}$ of φ and a variable v, we denote by $\mathcal{M}(v)$ the evaluation of v in $\mathcal{M}$. With a little abuse of notation, and when this does not cause ambiguities, we sometimes use an attractor equality $A[i] \stackrel{\text{def}}{=} (\text{obj}[i] = attr[i])$ to denote the single-bit assignment obj$[i] := attr[i]$ and its negation $\neg A[i]$ to denote the assignment to the complement value obj$[i] := \overline{attr[i]}$.

Definition 3 *(lexicographic maximization).   Consider an OMT instance $\langle\varphi, \text{obj}\rangle$ and the vector of attractor equalities A. We say that an assignment τ_n to* obj **lexicographically maximizes** *A **w.r.t.** φ iff, for every $k \in [0..n-1]$,*

- *$\tau_n[k] = \overline{attr[k]}$ if $\varphi \wedge \llbracket\tau_n\rrbracket_k \wedge A[k]$ is unsatisfiable,*
- *$\tau_n[k] = attr[k]$ otherwise.*

where $A[k]$ is the attractor equality (obj$[k] = attr[k]$). Given a model $\mathcal{M}$ for φ, we say that $\mathcal{M}$ lexicographically maximizes A w.r.t. φ iff its restriction to obj *lexicographically maximizes A w.r.t. φ.*

Starting from the MSB to the LSB, τ_n [resp. $\mathcal{M}$] in Definition 3 assigns to each obj$[k]$ the value $attr[k]$ unless it is inconsistent w.r.t. φ and the assignments to the previous obj$[i]$s, $i \in [0..k-1]$. Notice that this corresponds to minimize [resp. maximize] the value $\sum_{k=0}^{n-1} 2^{n-1-k} \cdot (\text{obj}[k]\,\mathbf{xor}_1\,attr[k])$ [resp. $\sum_{k=0}^{n-1} 2^{n-1-k} \cdot (\text{obj}[k]\,\mathbf{nxor}_1\,attr[k])$],—where $\mathbf{xor}_n$ is the bitwise-xor operator and $\mathbf{nxor}_n$ is its complement—because $2^{n-1-i} > \sum_{k=i+1}^{n-1} 2^{n-1-k}$.

The following fact derives from the above definitions and the properties of two's complement representation adopted by the SMT-LIBv2 standard for signed $\mathcal{BV}$.

Theorem 1. *An optimal solution of an OMT($\mathcal{BV}$) problem $\langle\varphi, \text{obj}\rangle$ is any model $\mathcal{M}$ of φ which lexicographically maximizes the vector of attractor equalities A.*

Definitions 2 and 3 with Theorem 1 suggest thus a direct extension to the minimization/maximization of *signed $\mathcal{BV}$* of the algorithm for unsigned $\mathcal{BV}$ in [21]: *apply the unsigned-$\mathcal{BV}$ maximization* [resp. *minimization*] *algorithm of* [21] *to the objective* obj$' \stackrel{\text{def}}{=} (\text{obj}\,\mathbf{nxor}_n\,attr)$ [resp. obj$' \stackrel{\text{def}}{=} (\text{obj}\,\mathbf{xor}_n\,attr)$]*instead than simply to* obj [resp. $\overline{\text{obj}}$].

Example 3. Let obj$^{[3]}$ be a signed $\mathcal{BV}$ goal of 3 bits to be minimized and $attr \stackrel{\text{def}}{=}$ [100] be its attractor, so that the corresponding vector of attractor equalities A is equal to [obj$[0] = 1$, obj$[1] = 0$, obj$[2] = 0$].

An assignment $\tau_3 \stackrel{\text{def}}{=} \{A[0], \neg A[1], \neg A[2]\}$ (for which obj$^{[3]} = -1^{[3]}$) is lexicographically better than $\tau_3' \stackrel{\text{def}}{=} \{\neg A[0], A[1], A[2]\}$ (for which obj$^{[3]} = 0^{[3]}$), because the former satisfies the *attractor equality* corresponding to the MSB while the latter does not. Moreover, the assignment τ_3 is lexicographically worse than the assignment $\tau_3'' \stackrel{\text{def}}{=} \{A[0], \neg A[1], A[2]\}$ (for which $\text{obj}^{[3]} = -2^{[3]}$), because –all the rest being equal– the latter assignment makes the *attractor equality* ($\text{obj}[2] = 0$) true.   ◇

3.2   Floating-Point Optimization

We define the *Floating-Point Optimization problem* as follows.

Definition 4 *(OMT($\mathcal{FP}$)).* *Let φ be a SMT($\mathcal{FP}$) formula and* obj *be a $\mathcal{FP}$ variable occurring in φ. We call an* **Optimization Modulo $\mathcal{FP}$ problem***, the problem of finding a model $\mathcal{M}$ for φ (if any) whose value of* obj*, denoted with* $\min_{\text{obj}}(\varphi)$*, is either*

- *minimum w.r.t. the usual total order relation $\leq$ for $\mathcal{FP}$ numbers, if φ is satisfied by at least one model $\mathcal{M}'$ s.t. $\mathcal{M}'(\text{obj})$ is not* NaN,
- *some binary representation of* NaN*, otherwise.*

(The dual definition where we look for the maximum follows straightforwardly.)

Definition 4 is made necessarily convoluted by the fact that obj can be NaN. In fact, in the SMT-LIBv2 standard the comparisons $\{\leq, <, \geq, >\}$ between NaN and any other $\mathcal{FP}$ value are always evaluated false because NaN has multiple representations at the binary level. Also, requiring the optimal solution to be always different from NaN makes the resulting OMT($\mathcal{FP}$) problem $\langle \varphi \wedge \neg\mathsf{IsNaN}(\text{obj}), \text{obj} \rangle$ unsatisfiable when φ is satisfied only by models $\mathcal{M}$ s.t. $\mathcal{M}(\text{obj})$ is NaN. For these reasons, we admit NaN as the optimal solution value for obj if and only if φ is satisfied only by models $\mathcal{M}$ s.t. $\mathcal{M}(\text{obj})$ is NaN.

In the rest of this section we assume that we have already checked, in sequence, that

(i) the input formula φ is satisfiable—by invoking an SMT($\mathcal{FP}$) solver on φ. If the solver returns UNSAT, then there is no need to proceed;
(ii) φ is satisfied by at least one model $\mathcal{M}'$ s.t. $\mathcal{M}'(\text{obj})$ is not NaN—by invoking an SMT($\mathcal{FP}$) solver on $\varphi \wedge \neg\mathsf{IsNaN}(\text{obj})$ if the model $\mathcal{M}$ returned by the previous SMT call is s.t. $\mathcal{M}(\text{obj})$ is NaN. If the solver returns UNSAT, then we conclude that the minimum is NaN.

After that, we can safely focus our investigation on the restricted OMT($\mathcal{FP}$) problem $\langle \varphi_{\text{noNaN}}, \text{obj} \rangle$, where $\varphi_{\text{noNaN}} \stackrel{\text{def}}{=} \varphi \wedge \neg\mathsf{IsNaN}(\text{obj})$, knowing it is satisfiable.

Definition 5 *(Dynamic Attractor).* *Let $\langle \varphi_{\text{noNaN}}, \text{obj} \rangle$ be a restricted OMT($\mathcal{FP}$) problem, where $\varphi_{\text{noNaN}} \stackrel{\text{def}}{=} \varphi \wedge \neg\mathsf{IsNaN}(\text{obj})$ is a satisfiable SMT($\mathcal{FP}$) formula and* obj *is a $\mathcal{FP}$ objective to be minimized [resp. maximized]. Let $k \in [0..n]$ and τ_k be an assignment to the k most-significant bits of* obj.

Then, we say that an $\mathcal{FP}$-value $attr_{\tau_k}$ for obj *is a* **dynamic attractor for** obj**w.r.t.** τ_k *iff it is the smallest [resp. largest] $\mathcal{FP}$ value different from* NaN *s.t. the k most-significant bits of $attr_{\tau_k}$ have the same value of the k most-significant bits of* obj *in τ_k. We call* **vector of attractor equalities** *the vector A_{τ_k} s.t. $A_{\tau_k}[i] \stackrel{\text{def}}{=} (\text{obj}[i] = attr_{\tau_k}[i])$, $i \in [0..n-1]$.*

The following fact derives from the above definitions and the properties of IEEE 754-2008 standard representation adopted by SMT-LIBv2 standard for $\mathcal{FP}$.

Lemma 1. *Let* $\langle \varphi_{\mathsf{noNaN}}, \mathsf{obj} \rangle$ *be a restricted minimization [resp. maximization] OMT($\mathcal{FP}$) problem, let* τ_k *be an assignment to* $\mathsf{obj}[0]...\mathsf{obj}[k-1]$ *and* $attr_{\tau_k}$ *be its corresponding dynamic attractor, for some* $k \in [0..n-1]$. *Let* $\tau_{k+1} \stackrel{def}{=} \tau_k \cup \{\mathsf{obj}[k] := attr_{\tau_k}[k]\}$ *and* $\tau'_{k+1} \stackrel{def}{=} \tau_k \cup \{\mathsf{obj}[k] := \overline{attr_{\tau_k}[k]}\}$, *and let* $\mathcal{M}$, $\mathcal{M}'$ *two models for* φ_{noNaN} *which extend* τ_{k+1} *and* τ'_{k+1} *respectively.*
Then $\mathcal{M}(\mathsf{obj}) \leq \mathcal{M}'(\mathsf{obj})$ *[resp.* $\mathcal{M}(\mathsf{obj}) \geq \mathcal{M}'(\mathsf{obj})$].

Lemma 1 states that, given the current assignment τ_k to the k most-significant-bits of obj, $\mathsf{obj}[k] = attr_{\tau_k}[k]$ is always the best extension of τ_k to the next bit (when consistent). A dynamic attractor $attr_{\tau_k}$ can thus be used by the optimization search to guide the assignment of the $k+1$-th bit of obj towards the direction of maximum gain which is allowed by τ_k, so that to obtain the "best" extension τ_{k+1} of τ_k. Once the (new) assignment τ_{k+1} is found, the OMT solver can compute the dynamic attractor $attr_{\tau_{k+1}}$ for obj w.r.t. τ_{k+1} and then use it to assign the $k+2$-th bit of obj, and so on.

Let $\langle \varphi_{\mathsf{noNaN}}, \mathsf{obj} \rangle$ be an OMT($\mathcal{FP}$) instance, s.t. obj is a $\mathcal{FP}$ variable of n bits, and τ_0 be an initially empty assignment. If at each step of the optimization search the assignment of the k-th bit of obj is guided by the dynamic attractor for obj w.r.t. τ_k, then the corresponding sequence of n dynamic attractors (of increasing order k) is unique and depends exclusively on φ_{noNaN}. Intuitively, this is the case because the (current) dynamic attractor always points in the direction of maximum gain. We illustrate this in the following example.

Example 4. Let $\langle \varphi_{\mathsf{noNaN}}, \mathsf{obj} \rangle$ be an OMT($\mathcal{FP}$) problem where obj is a $\mathcal{FP}$ objective, of sort (_ FP 3 5), to be minimized. At the beginning of the search, nothing is known about the structure of the solution. Therefore, $\tau_0 = \emptyset$ and, since obj is being minimized, the *dynamic attractor* for obj w.r.t. τ_0 (i.e. $attr_{\tau_0}$) is equal to (fp #b1 #b111 #b0000) (i.e. $-\infty$), which gives a preference to any feasible value of obj in the negative domain.

If at some point of the optimization search we discover that the domain of the objective function can only be positive, so that the first bit of obj is permanently set to 0 in τ_1, then the new dynamic attractor for obj w.r.t. τ_1 (i.e. $attr_{\tau_1}$) is equal to (fp #b0 #b000 #b0000) (i.e. $+0$).

Furthermore, if later on we also find out that at least one bit in the exponent of obj can be assigned to 0 in a feasible solution of the problem that extends τ_i, for some i, then we can remove $+\infty$ from the optimization search interval.   ◇

Definition 6 *(Attractor Trajectory $\mathcal{A}_\varphi$).* *Consider the restricted OMT($\mathcal{FP}$) problem* $\langle \varphi_{\mathsf{noNaN}}, \mathsf{obj} \rangle$ *s.t.* $\varphi_{\mathsf{noNaN}} \stackrel{def}{=} \varphi \wedge \neg\mathsf{IsNaN}(\mathsf{obj})$ *as in Definition 5, a triplet of inductively-defined sequences* $\langle \{\tau_0, \tau_1, \ldots, \tau_n\}, \{attr_{\tau_0}, attr_{\tau_1}, \ldots, attr_{\tau_n}\},$ $\{A_{\tau_0}, A_{\tau_1}, \ldots, A_{\tau_n}\} \rangle$ *—where each* τ_k *is an assignment to the first* k *most-significant bits of* obj *s.t.* $\tau_k \subset \tau_{k+1}$, $attr_{\tau_k}$ *is its corresponding dynamic attractor* and A_{τ_k} is its corresponding vector of attractor equalities—so that, for every $k \in [0..n-1]$:

(i) $\tau_{k+1}[k] = \overline{attr_{\tau_k}[k]}$ if $\varphi_{\mathsf{noNaN}} \wedge \tau_k \wedge A_{\tau_k}[k]$ is unsatisfiable,
(ii) $\tau_{k+1}[k] = attr_{\tau_k}[k]$ otherwise.

Then we define the **attractor trajectory** $\mathcal{A}_\varphi$ as the vector $[A_{\tau_0}[0], \ldots, A_{\tau_{n-1}}[n-1]]$.

The attractor trajectory $\mathcal{A}_\varphi$ contains those attractor equalities ($\mathsf{obj}[k] = attr_{\tau_k}[k]$) which are of critical importance for the decisions taken by the optimization search. Intuitively, this is the case because the value of the k-th bit of obj (i.e. $\mathsf{obj}[k]$) is still undecided in τ_k.

$$\tau_0 = \emptyset \qquad attr_{\tau_0} = (\texttt{fp \#b1 \#b111 \#b0000}) = [\underline{1}.111.1111] \quad [\text{i.e.} -\infty] \Rightarrow \text{UNSAT}$$
$$\tau_1 = \tau_0 \cup \{\mathsf{obj}[0] = 0\} \qquad attr_{\tau_1} = (\texttt{fp \#b0 \#b000 \#b0000}) = [0.\underline{0}00.0000] \quad [\text{i.e.} +0] \Rightarrow \text{UNSAT}$$
$$\tau_2 = \tau_1 \cup \{\mathsf{obj}[1] = 1\} \qquad attr_{\tau_2} = (\texttt{fp \#b0 \#b100 \#b0000}) = [0.1\underline{0}0.0000] \quad [\text{i.e.} +2] \Rightarrow \text{UNSAT}$$
$$\tau_3 = \tau_2 \cup \{\mathsf{obj}[2] = 1\} \qquad attr_{\tau_3} = (\texttt{fp \#b0 \#b110 \#b0000}) = [0.11\underline{0}.0000] \quad [\text{i.e.} +8] \Rightarrow \text{SAT}$$
$$\tau_4 = \tau_3 \cup \{\mathsf{obj}[3] = 0\} \qquad attr_{\tau_4} = (\texttt{fp \#b0 \#b110 \#b0000}) = [0.110.\underline{0}000] \quad [''\ ''] \Rightarrow \text{UNSAT}$$
$$\tau_5 = \tau_4 \cup \{\mathsf{obj}[4] = 1\} \qquad attr_{\tau_5} = (\texttt{fp \#b0 \#b110 \#b1000}) = [0.110.1\underline{0}00] \quad [\text{i.e.} +12] \Rightarrow \text{UNSAT}$$
$$\tau_6 = \tau_5 \cup \{\mathsf{obj}[5] = 1\} \qquad attr_{\tau_6} = (\texttt{fp \#b0 \#b110 \#b1100}) = [0.110.11\underline{0}0] \quad [\text{i.e.} +14] \Rightarrow \text{SAT}$$
$$\tau_7 = \tau_6 \cup \{\mathsf{obj}[6] = 0\} \qquad attr_{\tau_7} = (\texttt{fp \#b0 \#b110 \#b1100}) = [0.110.110\underline{0}] \quad [''\ ''] \Rightarrow \text{UNSAT}$$
$$\tau_8 = \tau_7 \cup \{\mathsf{obj}[7] = 1\} \qquad attr_{\tau_8} = (\texttt{fp \#b0 \#b110 \#b1101}) = [0.110.1101] \quad [\text{i.e. } 29/2]$$

$$A_{\tau_0} = [\underline{\mathsf{obj}[0] = 1}, \mathsf{obj}[1] = 1, \mathsf{obj}[2] = 1, \mathsf{obj}[3] = 1, \mathsf{obj}[4] = 0, \mathsf{obj}[5] = 0, \mathsf{obj}[6] = 0, \mathsf{obj}[7] = 0]$$
$$A_{\tau_1} = [\mathsf{obj}[0] = 0, \underline{\mathsf{obj}[1] = 0}, \mathsf{obj}[2] = 0, \mathsf{obj}[3] = 0, \mathsf{obj}[4] = 0, \mathsf{obj}[5] = 0, \mathsf{obj}[6] = 0, \mathsf{obj}[7] = 0]$$
$$A_{\tau_2} = [\mathsf{obj}[0] = 0, \mathsf{obj}[1] = 1, \underline{\mathsf{obj}[2] = 0}, \mathsf{obj}[3] = 0, \mathsf{obj}[4] = 0, \mathsf{obj}[5] = 0, \mathsf{obj}[6] = 0, \mathsf{obj}[7] = 0]$$
$$A_{\tau_3} = [\mathsf{obj}[0] = 0, \mathsf{obj}[1] = 1, \mathsf{obj}[2] = 1, \underline{\mathsf{obj}[3] = 0}, \mathsf{obj}[4] = 0, \mathsf{obj}[5] = 0, \mathsf{obj}[6] = 0, \mathsf{obj}[7] = 0]$$
$$A_{\tau_4} = [\mathsf{obj}[0] = 0, \mathsf{obj}[1] = 1, \mathsf{obj}[2] = 1, \mathsf{obj}[3] = 0, \underline{\mathsf{obj}[4] = 0}, \mathsf{obj}[5] = 0, \mathsf{obj}[6] = 0, \mathsf{obj}[7] = 0]$$
$$A_{\tau_5} = [\mathsf{obj}[0] = 0, \mathsf{obj}[1] = 1, \mathsf{obj}[2] = 1, \mathsf{obj}[3] = 0, \mathsf{obj}[4] = 1, \underline{\mathsf{obj}[5] = 0}, \mathsf{obj}[6] = 0, \mathsf{obj}[7] = 0]$$
$$A_{\tau_6} = [\mathsf{obj}[0] = 0, \mathsf{obj}[1] = 1, \mathsf{obj}[2] = 1, \mathsf{obj}[3] = 0, \mathsf{obj}[4] = 1, \mathsf{obj}[5] = 1, \underline{\mathsf{obj}[6] = 0}, \mathsf{obj}[7] = 0]$$
$$A_{\tau_7} = [\mathsf{obj}[0] = 0, \mathsf{obj}[1] = 1, \mathsf{obj}[2] = 1, \mathsf{obj}[3] = 0, \mathsf{obj}[4] = 1, \mathsf{obj}[5] = 1, \mathsf{obj}[6] = 0, \underline{\mathsf{obj}[7] = 0}]$$
$$A_{\tau_8} = [\mathsf{obj}[0] = 0, \mathsf{obj}[1] = 1, \mathsf{obj}[2] = 1, \mathsf{obj}[3] = 0, \mathsf{obj}[4] = 1, \mathsf{obj}[5] = 1, \mathsf{obj}[6] = 0, \mathsf{obj}[7] = 1]$$

Fig. 1. An example of $\mathcal{FP}$ optimization using the dynamic attractor. ("$\Rightarrow$ SAT/UNSAT" denotes the satisfiability of $\varphi_{\mathsf{noNaN}} \wedge \tau_k \wedge A_{\tau_k}[k]$, the symbols "$''$ $''$" stand for "the same as above". For ease of illustration, we have underlined the critical bit $attr_{\tau_k}[k]$ in the attractors and each attractor equality of the attractor trajectory $\mathcal{A}_\varphi$ inside the vectors of attractor equalities.)

Example 5. Let $\langle \varphi_{\mathsf{noNaN}}, \mathsf{obj} \rangle$ be a restricted OMT($\mathcal{FP}$) problem where obj is a $\mathcal{FP}$ objective, of sort (_ FP 3 5), to be minimized. We consider the case in which the input formula φ_{noNaN} requires obj to be larger or equal $29/2$ and it does not impose any other constraint on the value of obj. Given the sequence of (partial) assignments $\tau_0, \ldots, \tau_8$ in Fig. 1, the corresponding list of dynamic attractors and the corresponding vectors of attractor equalities, then the attractor trajectory $\mathcal{A}_\varphi$ is equal to the vector $[\mathsf{obj}[0] = 1, \mathsf{obj}[1] = 0, \mathsf{obj}[2] = 0, \mathsf{obj}[3] = 0, \mathsf{obj}[4] = 0, \mathsf{obj}[5] = 0, \mathsf{obj}[6] = 0, \mathsf{obj}[7] = 0]$. ◇

Lemma 2.
Consider $\langle \varphi_{\mathsf{noNaN}}, \mathsf{obj} \rangle, \tau_0, \ldots, \tau_n, attr_{\tau_0}, \ldots, attr_{\tau_n}, A_{\tau_0}, \ldots, A_{\tau_n},$ *and* $\mathcal{A}_\varphi$ *as in Definition 6. Then* τ_n *lexicographically maximizes* $\mathcal{A}_\varphi$ *w.r.t.* φ_{noNaN}.

Theorem 2. *Let* $\langle \varphi_{\mathsf{noNaN}}, \mathsf{obj} \rangle, \tau_0, \ldots, \tau_n, attr_{\tau_0}, \ldots, attr_{\tau_n}, A_{\tau_0}, \ldots, A_{\tau_n},$ *and* $\mathcal{A}_\varphi$ *be as in Definition 6. Then, any model* $\mathcal{M}$ *of* φ_{noNaN} *which lexicographically maximizes the attractor trajectory* $\mathcal{A}_\varphi$ *is an optimal solution for the* OMT($\mathcal{FP}$) *problem* $\langle \varphi_{\mathsf{noNaN}}, \mathsf{obj} \rangle$.

4   OMT($\mathcal{FP}$) Procedures

In this paper, we consider two approaches for dealing with OMT($\mathcal{FP}$): a basic linear/binary search, based on the inline OMT schema for OMT($\mathcal{LRA} \cup \mathcal{T}$) presented in [25], and *Floating-Point Optimization with Binary Search* (OFP-BS), a brand-new engine inspired by the OBV-BS algorithm for unsigned Bit-Vectors in [21] and by Theorem 2 and relative definitions in Sect. 3.2.

4.1   OMT-Based Approach

The OMT-based approach for OMT($\mathcal{FP}$) adapts the linear- and binary-search schemata for OMT($\mathcal{LRA} \cup \mathcal{T}$) presented in [25] to deal with $\mathcal{FP}$ objectives.

In the basic linear-search schema, the optimization search is advanced by means of a sequence of linear cuts, each of which forces the OMT solver to look for a new model $\mathcal{M}'$ which improves the value of obj w.r.t. the most recent model $\mathcal{M}$. In the binary-search schema, instead, the OMT solver learns an incremental sequence of cuts which bisect the current domain of the objective function.

In general, it is reasonable to expect the binary-search schema to converge towards the optimal solution faster than the linear-search schema, because the feasible domain of a $\mathcal{FP}$ goal can be comprised by an exponentially large number of values (w.r.t. the bit-width of the cost function).

In either schema, whenever the optimization engine encounters for the first time a solution s.t. $\mathsf{obj} = \mathrm{NAN}$, the OMT solver learns a unit-clause of the form $\neg(\mathrm{ISNAN}(\mathsf{obj}))$ so as to look for an optimal solution different from NAN (if any).

When dealing with $\mathcal{FP}$ objectives, differently from the case of $\mathcal{LRA}$ in [25], it is not necessary to implement a specialized optimization procedure within the $\mathcal{FP}$-Solver in order to guarantee the termination of the optimization search.

4.2   Floating-Point Optimization with Binary Search

The *Floating-Point Optimization with Binary Search* algorithm is a new engine for OMT($\mathcal{FP}$) which is inspired by the OBV-BS algorithm for OMT($\mathcal{BV}$) [21] and is a direct implementation of Definition 6 and Theorem 2.

The optimization search tries to lexicographically maximize an implicit *attractor trajectory* vector $\mathcal{A}_\varphi$, which is incrementally derived from the current value of the dynamic attractor. The raw value of the dynamic attractor's bits drive the optimization search towards the direction of maximum gain at any given point in time, without disrupting any decision that has been already made. The dynamic attractor is incrementally updated along the search, based on the outcome of the previous rounds of the optimization search. At each round, one bit of the objective function is assigned its final value. The first round decides the sign, the next batch of rounds decides the exponent and the remaining rounds decide the fine-grained details of the significand.

function OFP-BS (φ, obj)
1: $\langle res, \mathcal{M} \rangle := $ SMT.CHECK_UNDER_ASSUMPTIONS($\varphi, \emptyset$)
2: **if** ($res ==$ UNSAT) **then**
3:     **return** $\langle res, \emptyset \rangle$ // φ is unsatisfiable
4: **if** ($\mathcal{M}(\text{obj}) ==$ NaN) **then**
5:     $\langle res, \mathcal{M}' \rangle := $ SMT.CHECK_UNDER_ASSUMPTIONS($\varphi \wedge \neg\mathsf{IsNaN}(\text{obj}), \emptyset$)
6:     **if** ($res ==$ UNSAT) **then**
7:         **return** $\langle$SAT$, \mathcal{M} \rangle$ // obj can only be NaN
8:     **else**
9:         $\mathcal{M} := \mathcal{M}'$
10:         $\varphi := \varphi \wedge \neg\mathsf{IsNaN}(\text{obj})$
11: $\tau := \emptyset$ // from now on, obj cannot be equal NaN
12: $attr_\tau := $ UPDATE_DYNAMIC_ATTRACTOR(τ)
13: SMT.SET_BRANCHING_PREFERENCE(obj)
14: SMT.UPDATE_BITS_POLARITY_TO(obj, $attr_\tau$)
15: **for** $i := 0$ **up to** $n - 1$ **do**
16:     $eq := (\text{obj}[i] = attr_\tau[i])$ // attractor equality $A_\tau[i]$
17:     **if** ($\mathcal{M} \models eq$) **then**
18:         $\tau := \tau \cup \{eq\}$
19:     **else**
20:         SMT.SET_BRANCHING_PREFERENCE(obj)
21:         SMT.UPDATE_BITS_POLARITY_TO(obj, $attr_\tau$)
22:         $\langle res, \mathcal{M}' \rangle := $ SMT.CHECK_UNDER_ASSUMPTIONS($\varphi, \tau \cup \{eq\}$)
23:         **if** ($res ==$ SAT) **then**
24:             $\tau := \tau \cup \{eq\}$
25:             $\mathcal{M} := \mathcal{M}'$
26:         **else**
27:             $\tau := \tau \cup \{\neg eq\}$
28:             $attr_\tau := $ UPDATE_DYNAMIC_ATTRACTOR(τ)
29: **return** $\langle$SAT$, \mathcal{M} \rangle$

Fig. 2. OFP-BS Algorithm for Floating-Point optimization.

The pseudo-code of OFP-BS is shown in Fig. 2. The arguments of the algorithm are the input formula φ and the $\mathcal{FP}$ objective obj, where obj is a

$\mathcal{FP}$ variable with *ebits* bits in the exponent, *sbits* $-$ 1 in the significand and $n \stackrel{\text{def}}{=} ebits + sbits$ bits overall.

The procedure starts by checking whether the input formula φ is satisfiable and immediately terminates if that is not the case (lines 1–3). If obj $=$ NaN in $\mathcal{M}$ then the procedure checks whether there exists a model $\mathcal{M}'$ for $\varphi \wedge \neg\mathsf{IsNaN}(\mathsf{obj})$ (lines 4–5). If this is not the case, the procedure terminates immediately and returns the pair $\langle \text{SAT}, \mathcal{M} \rangle$ (line 7). Otherwise, the model $\mathcal{M}$ is updated with the new model $\mathcal{M}'$, and φ is permanently extended with the constraint $\neg\mathsf{IsNaN}(\mathsf{obj})$ (lines 9–10).

At this point, the procedure initializes the value of the dynamic attractor by invoking an external function UPDATE_DYNAMIC_ATTRACTOR() with the empty assignment τ as parameter, so that the returned value is equal to $-\infty$ when minimizing and $+\infty$ when maximizing (lines 11–12). Then, the execution moves to the section of code implementing the core part of the OFP-BS algorithm (lines 15–28), which consists of a loop over the bits of obj, starting from the MSB obj[0] down to the LSB obj[$n-1$].

Inside this loop, OFP-BS first checks whether the value of obj[i] in $\mathcal{M}$ matches the i-th bit of the (current) dynamic attractor $attr_\tau$. If this is the case, then the i-th bit is already set to its "best" value in $\mathcal{M}$. Thus, the assignment τ is extended so as to permanently set obj[i] $= attr_\tau[i]$ (line 16), and the optimization search moves to the next iteration of the loop. If instead obj[i] $\neq attr_\tau[i]$ in $\mathcal{M}$, we need to verify whether the value of the objective function in $\mathcal{M}$ can be improved by forcing the i-th bit of obj equal to the i-th bit of the dynamic attractor. To do so, we incrementally invoke the underlying SMT solver, this time checking the satisfiability of φ under the list of assumptions $\tau \cup \{\mathsf{obj}[i] = attr_\tau[i]\}$ (line 22). If the SMT solver returns SAT, then the value of the objective function has been successfully improved. Hence, τ is extended with an assignment setting obj[i] equal to $attr_\tau[i]$, and $\mathcal{M}$ is replaced with the new model $\mathcal{M}'$ (lines 23–25). Otherwise, it is not possible to improve the objective function by toggling the value of obj[i], and τ is extended so as to permanently set obj[i] $\neq attr_\tau[i]$ (line 27). At this point, there is a mismatch between the value of the first $i+1$ bits of obj in $\mathcal{M}$, corresponding to the assignment τ, and those of the current dynamic attractor. This mismatch is resolved by calling the function UPDATE_DYNAMIC_ATTRACTOR() with the updated assignment τ as parameter (line 28). In either case, the execution moves to the next iteration of loop.

After exactly n iterations of the loop, the optimization search terminates with the pair $\langle \text{SAT}, \mathcal{M} \rangle$, where $\mathcal{M}$ is the optimum model of the given OMT($\mathcal{FP} \cup \mathcal{T}$) instance. The OFP-BS algorithm requires at most $n + 2$ incremental calls to an underlying SMT($\mathcal{FP}$) solver. The test in rows 17–18 allows for saving lots of such SMT calls when the current model already assigns obj[i] to its corresponding value in the attractor.

The function UPDATE_DYNAMIC_ATTRACTOR() takes as input τ, a (partial) assignment over the k most-significant bits of obj and, when obj is minimized[2],

---

[2] The implementation of UPDATE_DYNAMIC_ATTRACTOR() is dual when obj is maximized.

and it essentially works as follows. If $\tau = \emptyset$, then nothing is known about the solution of the problem, so $-\infty$ is returned. Otherwise, the procedure must compute the smallest $\mathcal{FP}$ value different from NaN (if any) which extends τ. Since $\tau \neq \emptyset$ then we know that the sign of the objective function has been permanently decided in τ. If $\mathsf{obj}[0] = 0$ in τ, i.e. obj must be positive, the procedure must return the smallest positive $\mathcal{FP}$ value admitted by τ. Hence, we extend τ with $\bigcup_{i=|\tau|}^{i=n-1} \mathsf{obj}[i] = 0$ and return the corresponding $\mathcal{FP}$ value. If $\mathsf{obj}[0] = 1$ in τ, i.e. obj can be negative values, the procedure must return the largest negative $\mathcal{FP}$ value admitted by τ. We first check whether there exists a bit in the exponent of obj which is assigned to 0 in τ. If that is the case, we extend τ with $\bigcup_{i=|\tau|}^{i=n-1} \mathsf{obj}[i] = 1$ and return the corresponding $\mathcal{FP}$ value. Otherwise, the procedure returns the value $-\infty$, which is still a viable extension of τ.

4.3   Search Enhancements

Given a $\mathcal{FP}$ value *attr* and a $\mathcal{FP}$ goal obj, (a combination of) the following techniques can be used to adjust the behavior of the optimization search, similarly what has been proposed for the case of OMT($\mathcal{BV}$) by Nadel et al. in [21].

- **branching preference:** the bits of the $\mathcal{FP}$ objective obj are marked, inside the OMT solver, as preferred variables for branching starting from the MSB down to the LSB. This ensures that conflicts involving the value of the objective function are handled as early as possible, possibly reducing the amount of work that needs to be redone after each back-jump.
- **polarity initialization:** the phase-saving value of each $\mathsf{obj}[i]$ is initialized with the value of $attr[i]$. This encourages the OMT solver to assign the bits of obj so as to reassemble the bits of *attr*, thus possibly speeding-up the convergence towards the optimal value.

In the case of the basic OMT schema described in Sect. 4.1, the effectiveness of either technique depends on the initial choice for *attr*. In the lucky case, the value of *attr* pulls the optimization search in the right direction and speeds up the search. In the unlucky case, when *attr* pulls in the wrong direction, there is no visible effect or an overall slow down. For instance, in the case of the *linear-search* optimization schema, enabling both options with an unlucky choice of *attr* can cause the OMT solver to start the search from the furthest possible point from the optional solution, and thus enumerate an exponential number of intermediate solutions.

In the case of the OFP-BS algorithm described in Sect. 4.2, we use the latest value of the dynamic attractor $attr_\tau$ for both the *branching preference* (lines 11 and 18 of Fig. 2) and the *polarity initialization* (rows 12 and 19 of Fig. 2) techniques. We observe that the value of every bit in the dynamic attractor can change after the sign of the objective function has been decided. Furthermore, the value of all the significand's bits in the dynamic attractor can also change during the process of determining the optimal exponent value of the objective function. As a consequence, if the OMT solver applies either enhancement before the correct improving direction is known, this may cause the underlying OMT engine to advance the search starting from a sub-optimal set of initial decisions. Enabling both enhancements at the same time could make things even worse. In order to mitigate this issue, we have designed a variant of our optimization-search approach which does not apply either enhancement on those bits of the objective function for which the best improving direction is not yet known. We have called this variant **safe bits restriction**.

5   Experimental Evaluation

We assess the performance of OptiMathSAT (v. 1.6.2) on a set of OMT($\mathcal{FP}$) formulas that have been automatically generated using the SMT($\mathcal{FP}$) benchmark-set of [3]. The formulas, the results and the scripts necessary to reproduce these results are made publicly available and can be downloaded from [1].

Experiment Setup. This experiment has been performed on an *i7-6500U 2.50*GHz *Intel Quad-Core* machine with 16 GB of ram and running *Ubuntu Linux* 17.10. For each formula being tested we used a timeout of 600 s. The OMT($\mathcal{FP}$) instances used in this experiment have been automatically generated starting from the satisfiable formulas included in the SMT($\mathcal{FP}$) benchmark-set of [3]. We did not consider any of the unsatisfiable instances that are present in the remote repository.

We consider two OMT-based baseline configurations, OptiMath-SAT(omt+lin) and OptiMathSAT(omt+bin), that run the linear- and the binary-search respectively. These configurations have been tested using both the *eager* and the *lazy* $\mathcal{FP}$ approaches. The third baseline approach, named Opti-MathSAT(eager+obv-bs), is based on a reduction of the OMT($\mathcal{FP}$) problem to OMT($\mathcal{BV}$) and it uses OptiMathSAT's implementation of the obv-bs engine[3] presented by Nadel et al. in [21]. For this test, we have generated an OMT($\mathcal{BV}$) benchmark-set using a $\mathcal{BV}$ encoding that mimics the essential aspects of the ofp-bs algorithm described Sect. 4.2.

We compared these baseline approaches with a configuration using the ofp-bs algorithm and the *eager* $\mathcal{FP}$ approach, namely OptiMath-SAT(eager+ofp-bs).

We have separately tested the effect of enabling the *branching preference* (bp), the *polarity initialization* (pi) and the *safe bits restriction* (so) enhancements described in Sect. 3.2, whenever these options were supported by the given configuration.

We have not included other tools in our experiment because we are not aware of any other OMT($\mathcal{FP}$) solver. For all problem instances, we verified the correctness of the optimal solution found by each configuration with an SMT

---

[3] The binaries of the original OMT($\mathcal{BV}$) tools presented in [21] are not publicly available.

solver (MATHSAT5). When terminating, all tools returned the same optimum value.

Table 1. Comparison among various OPTIMATHSAT configurations on the OMT($\mathcal{FP}$) benchmark-set. The columns list the total number of instances (inst.), the number of instances solved (term.), the number of timeouts (t.o.), the number of instances uniquely solved by the given configuration (u), the number of instances solved faster than any other configuration (bt), the total number of instances solved in the shortest amount of time (st) and the total solving time for all solved instances (time).

Tool, configuration & encoding	inst.	term.	t.o.	u	bt	st	time (s.)
OPTIMATHSAT(EAGER+OMT+LIN)	1120	1003	117	0	5	73	76375
OPTIMATHSAT(EAGER+OMT+LIN+PI)	1120	1003	117	0	5	71	76785
OPTIMATHSAT(EAGER+OMT+LIN+BP)	1120	956	164	0	6	105	77480
OPTIMATHSAT(EAGER+OMT+LIN+BP+PI)	1120	873	247	0	77	217	54859
OPTIMATHSAT(EAGER+OMT+BIN)	1120	1014	106	0	11	281	67834
OPTIMATHSAT(EAGER+OMT+BIN+PI)	1120	970	150	0	8	285	69765
OPTIMATHSAT(EAGER+OMT+BIN+BP)	1120	1016	104	0	14	205	68255
OPTIMATHSAT(EAGER+OMT+BIN+BP+PI)	1120	991	129	0	65	**321**	56941
OPTIMATHSAT(LAZY+OMT+LIN)	1120	868	252	0	93	203	29832
OPTIMATHSAT(LAZY+OMT+BIN)	1120	900	220	0	90	243	33260
OPTIMATHSAT(EAGER+OBVBS) [REDUCTION]	1120	1013	107	0	14	141	65954
OPTIMATHSAT(EAGER+OFPBS)	1120	1017	103	0	9	171	70732
OPTIMATHSAT(EAGER+OFPBS+PI)	1120	**1019**	101	0	34	280	64896
OPTIMATHSAT(EAGER+OFPBS+PI+SO)	1120	1018	102	0	7	179	71430
OPTIMATHSAT(EAGER+OFPBS+BP)	1120	975	145	0	2	145	65543
OPTIMATHSAT(EAGER+OFPBS+BP+SO)	1120	1000	120	0	3	124	68390
OPTIMATHSAT(EAGER+OFPBS+BP+PI)	1120	1001	119	0	77	273	60365
OPTIMATHSAT(EAGER+OFPBS+BP+PI+SO)	1120	1006	114	**19**	32	245	59463
VIRTUAL BEST	1120	**1074**	46	-	559	1074	27788

Experiment Results. The results of this experiment are listed in Table 1.

For what concerns OMT-based *linear-search* optimization, we observe that OPTIMATHSAT performs the best when no enhancement is enabled. In particular, the empirical evidence suggests that enabling *branching preference* significantly increases the number of timeouts, generally deteriorating the performance. Enabling only *polarity initialization* does not result in an appreciable change on the running time of the solver. In contrast, enabling both enhancements at the same time generally worsens the performance and results in a drastic increase in the number of timeouts (Table 1). We justify these results as follows. First, when only *polarity initialization* is used, the phase-saving value that is being set by OPTIMATHSAT does not really matter because the optimization search is dominated by the structure of the formula itself rather than by the bits of the $\mathcal{FP}$ objective. Second, when *polarity initialization* is used on top of *branching preference*, there is an even more drastic decrease in performance due to the fact that the initial phase-saving value that is statically assigned by the OMT solver to the bits of the $\mathcal{FP}$ objective cannot be expected to be "good enough" for any situation.

In the case of the OMT-based *binary-search* optimization approach, we observe that it solves more formulas than linear-search and it generally appears to be faster. Overall, *polarity initialization* does not seem to be beneficial, whereas enabling *branching preference* increases the number of formulas solved within the timeout. This behavior is different from the linear-search approach, and we conjecture that it is due to the fact that, with the OMT-based binary-search approach, branching over the bits of the objective function can reveal in advance any (partial) assignment to the bits of the objective function that it is inconsistent w.r.t. the pivoting cuts learned by the optimization engine.

Using the *lazy* $\mathcal{FP}$ engine results in fewer formulas being solved, although a significant number of these benchmarks is solved faster than with any other configuration.

The OPTIMATHSAT(EAGER+OBV-BS) configuration is able to solve 1013 formulas within the timeout, showing that OMT($\mathcal{FP}$) can be reduced to OMT($\mathcal{BV}$) effectively, and that –on the given benchmark-set– the performance of this approach are comparable with the best OMT($\mathcal{FP}$) configurations being tested.

Overall, the best performance is obtained by using the OFP-BS engine, with up to 1019 benchmark-set instances being solved in correspondence to the OPTIMATHSAT(EAGER+OFP-BS+PI) configuration. Similarly to the case of OMT-based optimization with linear-search, we observe that enabling *branching preference* generally makes the performance worse. Instead, when *polarity initialization* is used we observe a general performance improvement that does not only result in an increase in the number of formulas being solved within the timeout, but also a noticeable reduction of the solving time as a whole. This is in contrast with the case of OMT-based optimization, and it can be explained by the fact that OFP-BS uses an internal heuristic function to dynamically determine and update the most appropriate phase-saving value for the bits of the objective function. An equally important role is played by the *safe bits restriction*, that limits the effects of *branching preference* and *polarity initialization* to only certain bits of the *dynamic attractor*. This feature is particularly effective when used in combination with *branching preference*.

6 Conclusions and Future Work

We have presented for the first time OMT procedures (for signed Bit-Vectors and) Floating-Point numbers, based on the novel notions of attractor, dynamic attractor and attractor trajectory, which we have implemented in OPTIMATHSAT and tested on modified problems from SMT-LIB.

Ongoing research involves implementing our OFP-BS procedure on top of the ACDCL SMT($\mathcal{FP}$) procedure—which is not immediate to do efficiently because the latter approach does not allow directly accessing and setting the single bits of the objective (since $\mathcal{BV}$ and $\mathcal{FP}$ are not signature-disjoint). Future research involves experimenting the new OMT procedure directly on problems coming from bit-precise SW and HW verification, produced, e.g., by the NuXmv model checker [2].

References

1. http://disi.unitn.it/trentin/resources/floatingpoint_test.tar.gz
2. NUXMV. https://nuxmv.fbk.eu
3. SmtLibv2. www.smtlib.cs.uiowa.edu/
4. IEEE standard 754 (2008). http://grouper.ieee.org/groups/754/
5. Bjorner, N., Phan, A.-D.: νZ - maximal satisfaction with Z3. In: Proceedings of the International Symposium on Symbolic Computation in Software Science, Gammarth, Tunisia, December 2014. EasyChair Proceedings in Computing (EPiC) (2014)
6. Bjørner, N., Phan, A.-D., Fleckenstein, L.: νZ - an optimizing SMT solver. In: Baier, C., Tinelli, C. (eds.) TACAS 2015. LNCS, vol. 9035, pp. 194–199. Springer, Heidelberg (2015). https://doi.org/10.1007/978-3-662-46681-0_14
7. Bozzano, M., et al.: Encoding RTL constructs for MathSAT: a preliminary report. In: Proceedings of the 3rd Workshop of Pragmatics on Decision Procedure in Automated Reasoning, PDPAR 2005, ENTCS. Elsevier (2005)
8. Brain, M., D'Silva, V., Griggio, A., Haller, L., Kroening, D.: Interpolation-based verification of floating-point programs with abstract CDCL. In: Logozzo, F., Fähndrich, M. (eds.) SAS 2013. LNCS, vol. 7935, pp. 412–432. Springer, Heidelberg (2013). https://doi.org/10.1007/978-3-642-38856-9_22
9. Brain, M., D'Silva, V., Griggio, A., Haller, L., Kroening, D.: Deciding floating-point logic with abstract conflict driven clause learning. Formal Methods Syst. Des. **45**(2), 213–245 (2014)
10. Brain, M., Tinelli, C., Rümmer, P., Wahl, T.: An automatable formal semantics for IEEE-754 floating-point arithmetic. In: ARITH, pp. 160–167. IEEE (2015)
11. Brillout, A., Kroening, D., Wahl, T.: Mixed abstractions for floating-point arithmetic. In: 2009 Formal Methods in Computer-Aided Design, pp. 69–76, November 2009
12. Brinkmann, R., Drechsler, R.: RTL-datapath verification using integer linear programming. In: Proceedings of the ASP-DAC 2002, pp. 741–746. IEEE (2002)
13. Brummayer, R., Biere, A.: Boolector: an efficient SMT solver for bit-vectors and arrays. In: Kowalewski, S., Philippou, A. (eds.) TACAS 2009. LNCS, vol. 5505, pp. 174–177. Springer, Heidelberg (2009). https://doi.org/10.1007/978-3-642-00768-2_16
14. Bruttomesso, R., et al.: A lazy and layered SMT($\mathcal{BV}$) solver for hard industrial verification problems. In: Damm, W., Hermanns, H. (eds.) CAV 2007. LNCS, vol. 4590, pp. 547–560. Springer, Heidelberg (2007). https://doi.org/10.1007/978-3-540-73368-3_54
15. Cimatti, A., Franzén, A., Griggio, A., Sebastiani, R., Stenico, C.: Satisfiability modulo the theory of costs: foundations and applications. In: Esparza, J., Majumdar, R. (eds.) TACAS 2010. LNCS, vol. 6015, pp. 99–113. Springer, Heidelberg (2010). https://doi.org/10.1007/978-3-642-12002-2_8

16. Fazekas, K., Bacchus, F., Biere, A.: Implicit hitting set algorithms for maximum satisfiability modulo theories. In: Galmiche, D., Schulz, S., Sebastiani, R. (eds.) IJCAR 2018. LNCS, vol. 10900, pp. 134–151. Springer, Cham (2018). https://doi.org/10.1007/978-3-319-94205-6_10

17. Ganesh, V., Dill, D.L.: A decision procedure for bit-vectors and arrays. In: Damm, W., Hermanns, H. (eds.) CAV 2007. LNCS, vol. 4590, pp. 519–531. Springer, Heidelberg (2007). https://doi.org/10.1007/978-3-540-73368-3_52

18. Hadarean, L., Bansal, K., Jovanović, D., Barrett, C., Tinelli, C.: A tale of two solvers: eager and lazy approaches to bit-vectors. In: Biere, A., Bloem, R. (eds.) CAV 2014. LNCS, vol. 8559, pp. 680–695. Springer, Cham (2014). https://doi.org/10.1007/978-3-319-08867-9_45

19. Larraz, D., Oliveras, A., Rodríguez-Carbonell, E., Rubio, A.: Minimal-model-guided approaches to solving polynomial constraints and extensions. In: Sinz, C., Egly, U. (eds.) SAT 2014. LNCS, vol. 8561, pp. 333–350. Springer, Cham (2014). https://doi.org/10.1007/978-3-319-09284-3_25

20. Li, Y., Albarghouthi, A., Kincad, Z., Gurfinkel, A., Chechik, M.: Symbolic optimization with SMT solvers. In: POPL (2014)

21. Nadel, A., Ryvchin, V.: Bit-vector optimization. In: Chechik, M., Raskin, J.-F. (eds.) TACAS 2016. LNCS, vol. 9636, pp. 851–867. Springer, Heidelberg (2016). https://doi.org/10.1007/978-3-662-49674-9_53

22. Niemetz, A., Preiner, M., Fröhlich, A., Biere, A.: Improving local search for bit-vector logics in SMT with path propagation. In: Proceedings of the 4th International Workshop on Design and Implementation of Formal Tools and Systems (DIFTS 2015), p. 10 (2015)

23. Nieuwenhuis, R., Oliveras, A.: On SAT modulo theories and optimization problems. In: Biere, A., Gomes, C.P. (eds.) SAT 2006. LNCS, vol. 4121, pp. 156–169. Springer, Heidelberg (2006). https://doi.org/10.1007/11814948_18

24. Ruemmer, P., Wahl, T.: An SMT-LIB theory of binary floating-point arithmetic. In: SMT 2010 Workshop, July 2010. http://www.philipp.ruemmer.org/publications/smt-fpa.pdf

25. Sebastiani, R., Tomasi, S.: Optimization modulo theories with linear rational costs. ACM Trans. Comput. Log. **16**(2), 12 (2015)

26. Sebastiani, R., Trentin, P.: Pushing the envelope of optimization modulo theories with linear-arithmetic cost functions. In: Baier, C., Tinelli, C. (eds.) TACAS 2015. LNCS, vol. 9035, pp. 335–349. Springer, Heidelberg (2015). https://doi.org/10.1007/978-3-662-46681-0_27

27. Sebastiani, R., Trentin, P.: OptiMathSAT: a tool for optimization modulo theories. J. Autom. Reason. (2018)

28. Trentin, P., Sebastiani, R.: Optimization modulo the theories of signed bit-vectors and floating-point numbers. arXiv e-prints arXiv:1905.02838, May 2019

29. Zeljić, A., Backeman, P., Wintersteiger, C.M., Rümmer, P.: Exploring approximations for floating-point arithmetic using UppSAT. In: Galmiche, D., Schulz, S., Sebastiani, R. (eds.) IJCAR 2018. LNCS, vol. 10900, pp. 246–262. Springer, Cham (2018). https://doi.org/10.1007/978-3-319-94205-6_17

30. Zeljić, A., Wintersteiger, C.M., Rümmer, P.: Approximations for model construction. In: Demri, S., Kapur, D., Weidenbach, C. (eds.) IJCAR 2014. LNCS, vol. 8562, pp. 344–359. Springer, Cham (2014). https://doi.org/10.1007/978-3-319-08587-6_26

FAME(Q): An Automated Tool for Forgetting in Description Logics with Qualified Number Restrictions

Yizheng Zhao[1,2,3](✉) and Renate A. Schmidt[3]

[1] National Key Laboratory for Novel Software Technology, Nanjing University, Nanjing, China
yizheng.zhao1@gmail.com
[2] School of Artificial Intelligence, Nanjing University, Nanjing, China
[3] School of Computer Science, The University of Manchester, Manchester, UK

Abstract. In this paper, we describe FAME(Q), a Java-based implementation of a forgetting method developed for eliminating concept and role names from $\mathcal{ALCOQH}$-ontologies. FAME(Q) is presently the only tool for concept forgetting in description logics with qualified number restrictions and nominals, and the only tool for role forgetting in description logics with qualified number restrictions. FAME(Q) can be used as a stand-alone tool or a Java library for forgetting, or related tasks. An evaluation of FAME(Q) on a large corpus of biomedical ontologies shows that the tool is able to compute forgetting solutions in 90% of the test cases; in most cases, the solutions are computed within a few seconds.

1 Introduction

Forgetting is an ontology re-engineering technique that seeks to produce new ontologies from existing ones using only a subset of their signature while preserving all logical consequences up to the names in the subset. This is done by eliminating from an ontology a set of concept and role names (the *forgetting signature*) in such a way that all logical consequences are preserved up to the names in the remaining signature. The ontology produced by forgetting (the *forgetting solution*), can be seen as a *view* of the original ontology. In traditional databases, a view is a subset of a database, whereas in ontologies, a view is more than a subset; it may contain not only axioms contained in the original ontology, but also contains those entailed by the ontology (implicitly contained in the ontology). Forgetting is potentially useful for many ontology processing tasks such as ontology reuse, alignment, versioning, merging, debugging, repair, and logical difference computation [1,3,5,6,10,12–15]. Forgetting is also useful for other tasks such as information hiding and explanation generation [2,5].

At present, practical methods for forgetting in description logics with qualified number restrictions are the resolution-based approach of the LETHE system [7–9] and the one developed by [17,19]. FAME(Q) is a Java implementation of the latter, which computes uniform interpolants for $\mathcal{ALCOQH}$-ontologies. The

© Springer Nature Switzerland AG 2019
P. Fontaine (Ed.): CADE 2019, LNAI 11716, pp. 568–579, 2019.
https://doi.org/10.1007/978-3-030-29436-6_34

method is a hybrid approach that makes use of both resolution and Ackermann's Lemma. It is so far the only approach able to forget concept and role names in description logics with qualified number restrictions.

In this paper, we describe the forgetting method used by FAME(Q), the implementation of FAME(Q), and details of an evaluation of FAME(Q) on a large corpus of publicly accessible biomedical ontologies. The current version of FAME(Q) can be downloaded via http://www.cs.man.ac.uk/~schmidt/sf-fame/.

2 Forgetting for $\mathcal{ALCOQH}$-Ontologies

Let N_C, N_R and N_I be (countably infinite and pairwise disjoint) sets of *concept names*, *role names* and *individual names* (*nominals*), respectively. *Concepts* in $\mathcal{ALCOQH}$ have one of the following forms:

$$\top \mid \bot \mid a \mid A \mid \neg C \mid C \sqcap D \mid C \sqcup D \mid {\geq}mr.C \mid {\leq}nr.C,$$

where $a \in N_I$, $A \in N_C$, $r \in N_R$, C and D denote arbitrary concepts, and $m \geq 1$ and $n \geq 0$ are natural numbers. Further concepts are defined as abbreviations: $\exists r.C = {\geq}1r.C$, $\forall r.C = {\leq}0r.\neg C$, $\neg{\geq}mr.C = {\leq}nr.C$ and $\neg{\leq}nr.C = {\geq}mr.C$, where $n = m - 1$. Concepts of the form ${\geq}mr.C$ and ${\leq}nr.C$ are referred to as *(qualified) number restrictions*.

An $\mathcal{ALCOQH}$-ontology is comprised of a TBox, an RBox and an ABox. A TBox is a finite set of axioms of the form $C \sqsubseteq D$ (*concept inclusions*), where C and D are concepts. An RBox is a finite set of axioms of the form $r \sqsubseteq s$ (*role inclusions*), where $r, s \in N_R$. An ABox is a finite set of axioms of the form $C(a)$ (*concept assertions*) and $r(a, b)$ (*role assertions*), where $a, b \in N_I$, $r \in N_R$, and C is a concept.

Forgetting can be defined in two closely related ways. In particular, it can be defined as the dual of *uniform interpolation* or model-theoretically as *semantic forgetting* [4,6,17]. The two notions differ in the sense that uniform interpolation preserves all *logical consequences* whereas semantic forgetting preserves *semantic equivalence* up to certain names. The results of semantic forgetting (the *semantic solutions*), are in general stronger than those of uniform interpolation (the *uniform interpolants*). This means that semantic solutions always entail uniform interpolants, but the converse does not hold. Uniform interpolants are always expressible in the source logic, while semantic solutions are often not, and may require an extended target language to express them.

By $\mathsf{sig}_C(X)$ and $\mathsf{sig}_R(X)$ we denote respectively the sets of the concept names and role names that occur in X, where X ranges over concepts, roles, clauses, axioms, sets of clauses and sets of axioms (ontologies). By $\mathsf{sig}(X)$ we denote the union of $\mathsf{sig}_C(X)$ and $\mathsf{sig}_R(X)$.

Definition 1 (Uniform Interpolation for $\mathcal{ALCOQH}$). *Let $\mathcal{O}$ be an $\mathcal{ALCOQH}$-ontology and let $\mathcal{F} \subseteq \mathsf{sig}_C(\mathcal{O})$ be a set of concept and role names. An ontology $\mathcal{V}$ is an $\mathcal{ALCOQH}$-uniform interpolant of $\mathcal{O}$ for $\mathsf{sig}(\mathcal{O}) \backslash \mathcal{F}$ iff the following conditions hold: (i) $\mathsf{sig}(\mathcal{V}) \subseteq \mathsf{sig}(\mathcal{O}) \backslash \mathcal{F}$, and (ii) for any axiom α with*

$sig(\alpha) \subseteq sig(\mathcal{O})\backslash\mathcal{F}$, $\mathcal{V} \models \alpha$ iff $\mathcal{O} \models \alpha$. In this case, $sig(\mathcal{O})\backslash\mathcal{F}$ is called the interpolation signature, i.e., the set of concept and role names to be preserved.

Definition 1 says that uniform interpolants have the same logical consequences with the original ontologies up to the interpolation signature.

Definition 2 below says that semantic solutions preserve equivalence up to the interpretations of the names in the forgetting signature $\mathcal{F}$. We say that $\mathcal{I}$ and $\mathcal{I}'$ are *equivalent up to a set $\mathcal{F}$ of concept and role names*, or *$\mathcal{F}$-equivalent*, if $\mathcal{I}$ and $\mathcal{I}'$ coincide but differ possibly in the interpretations of the names in $\mathcal{F}$.

Definition 2 (Semantic Forgetting for $\mathcal{ALCOQH}$). *Let $\mathcal{O}$ be an $\mathcal{ALCOQH}$-ontology and let $\mathcal{F} \subseteq sig(\mathcal{O})$ be a set of concept and role names. An ontology $\mathcal{V}$ is a semantic solution of forgetting $\mathcal{F}$ from $\mathcal{O}$ iff the following conditions hold: (i) $sig(\mathcal{V}) \subseteq sig(\mathcal{O})\backslash\mathcal{F}$ and (ii) for any interpretation $\mathcal{I}$: $\mathcal{I} \models \mathcal{V}$ iff $\mathcal{I}' \models \mathcal{O}$, for some interpretation $\mathcal{I}'$ $\mathcal{F}$-equivalent to $\mathcal{I}$. $\mathcal{F}$ is called the* forgetting signature, *i.e., the set of concept and role names to be forgotten.*

3   The Forgetting Method

Next, we briefly describe the forgetting method implemented in FAME(Q). The method is mainly based on two calculi: a calculus for concept name elimination and a calculus for role name elimination. The former was presented in our recent work [19] and the latter in [17]. The method is terminating and sound.

Both calculi operate on $\mathcal{ALCOQH}$-ontologies in *clausal normal form*, which are obtained from axioms using the standard transformations based on logical equivalence such as $\neg\neg \geq mr.C = \geq mr.C$. In the following, we always use the notation $\mathcal{N}$ to denote a set of clauses (clausified from an $\mathcal{ALCOQH}$-ontology).

Definition 3 (Clausal Normal Form). *A TBox literal in $\mathcal{ALCOQH}$ is a concept of the form a, $\neg a$, A, $\neg A$, $\geq mr.C$ or $\leq nr.C$, where $a \in N_I$, $r \in N_R$, C is a concept, and $m > 1$ and $n > 0$ are natural numbers. A TBox clause in $\mathcal{ALCOQH}$ is a disjunction of a finite number of TBox literals. An RBox clause in $\mathcal{ALCOQH}$ is a disjunction of a role name and a negated role name. A clause is called an S-clause if it contains S, for any concept/role name S in $N_C \cup N_R$.*

Our method is a rounds-based method, where forgetting solutions (uniform interpolants and semantic solutions) are computed by iteratively eliminating the (concept and role) names in $\mathcal{F}$. We call the name under consideration for forgetting in the current round the *pivot*.

The calculus for eliminating a concept name from a set $\mathcal{N}$ of clauses includes two purify rules and one combination rule.[1] The purify rules are applied when the pivot occurs only positively or only negatively in $\mathcal{N}$, i.e., the pivot is *pure* in $\mathcal{N}$. The purify rules say that if the pivot occurs only positively (negatively) in $\mathcal{N}$, it is eliminated by substitution with the top (bottom) concept. The combination rule is applied when the pivot occurs both positively and negatively in $\mathcal{N}$, i.e.,

---

[1] In [19], the combination rule is named the Ackermann rule.

the pivot is *impure* in $\mathcal{N}$. It is applicable iff $\mathcal{N}$ is in a specialized normal form called *A-reduced form*, if A is the concept pivot.

Definition 4 (A-Reduced Form). *Let $\mathcal{N}$ be a set of clauses. Let $A \in sig_C(\mathcal{N})$. A clause is in A-reduced form if it has the form $C \sqcup A$, $C \sqcup \neg A$, $C \sqcup \geq mr.A$, $C \sqcup \geq mr.\neg A$, $C \sqcup \leq nr.A$ or $C \sqcup \leq nr.\neg A$, where $r \in N_R$, C is a clause that does not contain A, and $m \geq 1$ and $n \geq 0$ are natural numbers. A set $\mathcal{N}$ of clauses is in A-reduced form if all A-clauses in $\mathcal{N}$ are in A-reduced form.*

A-clauses not in A-reduced form can be transformed into A-reduced form by introducing *definer names* (or *definers* for short). Once $\mathcal{N}$ is in A-reduced form, one can immediately apply the combination rule to $\mathcal{N}$ to eliminate A. For space reasons we do not present and describe the combination rule in this paper, but refer the reader to [19] for a comprehensive description of the rule.

The calculus for eliminating a role name from $\mathcal{N}$ includes two purify rules and five combination rules.[2] The purify rules are applied when the pivot is *pure* in $\mathcal{N}$. The combination rules are applied when the pivot is *impure* in $\mathcal{N}$. They are applicable iff $\mathcal{N}$ is in *r-reduced form*, where r is the pivot.

Definition 5 (r-Reduced Form). *Let $\mathcal{N}$ be a set of clauses. Let $r \in sig_R(\mathcal{N})$. A TBox clause is in r-reduced form if it has the form $C \sqcup \geq mr.D$ or $C \sqcup \leq nr.D$, where C and D are concepts that do not contain r, and $m \geq 1$ and $n \geq 0$ are natural numbers. An RBox clause is in r-reduced form if it has the form $\neg s \sqcup r$ or $s \sqcup \neg r$, where $s \in N_R$ and $s \neq r$. A set $\mathcal{N}$ of clauses is in r-reduced form if all r-clauses in $\mathcal{N}$ are in r-reduced form.*

r-clauses not in r-reduced form can be transformed into r-reduced form by introducing *definers* as in concept forgetting. Once $\mathcal{N}$ is in r-reduced form, we apply an appropriate combination rule to $\mathcal{N}$ to eliminate r. We refer the reader to [19] for presentation and a comprehensive description of the rules.

In order to be able to express more semantic solutions of concept forgetting, the target language is $\mathcal{ALCOQH}$ extended with the top role, role negation, role conjunction and role disjunction.

4   The Implementation

FAME(Q) is a Java-based implementation of the forgetting method described in the previous section. In this section we describe the implementation in detail, and discuss some of its notable features. For users' convenience, FAME(Q) provides a graphic user interface, shown in Fig. 1. FAME 1.0 [18] is a preceding system for forgetting in description logics without number restrictions, but since the inference rules used by FAME(Q) are different from those in FAME 1.0, FAME(Q) is not simply an improvement of FAME 1.0, but is a novel system.

---

[2] In [17], the purify rules are named Ackermann rules I and II, and the combination rules are named the Ackermann rules III, IV and V.

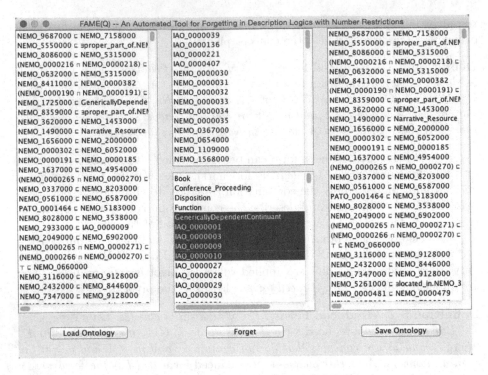

Fig. 1. Graphic user interface of FAME(Q)

FAME(Q) has a modular design consisting of six main modules: Load Ontology, Parse into Own Data Structure, Role Forgetting, Concept Forgetting, Unparse into OWL Data Structure, and Save Ontology, which are linked as depicted in Fig. 2. Each successively undertakes a particular task. FAME(Q) uses the OWL API Version 3.5.6[3] for the tasks of loading, parsing, unparsing and saving ontologies. The ontology to be loaded must be an OWL/XML file, or a URL pointing to an OWL/XML file. Internally (during the forgetting process), FAME(Q) uses own data structures to store and manipulate data so it can be processed efficiently.

4.1 Forgetting Process

Central to FAME(Q) are the Role Forgetting process and Concept Forgetting process, in which the role names and concept names in $\mathcal{F}$ are eliminated. FAME(Q) eliminates role names and concept names in a focused manner, that is, it performs role forgetting and concept forgetting separately. Although FAME(Q) can eliminate role and concept names in any specified order, it defaults to eliminating role names first. This is because during the concept forgetting process, role negation and role disjunction may be introduced, and the calculus for role name elimination does not support these two role constructs.

---

[3] http://owlcs.github.io/owlapi/.

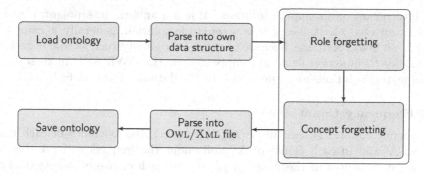

Fig. 2. Top-level design of FAME(Q)

The role forgetting process is an iteration of several rounds in each of which a role name in the forgetting signature $\mathcal{F}$ is eliminated using the calculus for role name elimination. The concept forgetting process has two phases executed in sequence. In the first phase concept names in $\mathcal{F}$ are eliminated using only the purify rules. These iterations are intended to eliminate those concept names that are pure in $\mathcal{N}$. This is because purification does not require the ontology to be normalized or in reduced form, and thus is relatively cheap. Another reason is that purification introduces the top concept into clauses which are immediately simplified or eliminated; this makes subsequent forgetting less challenging. The second phase contains several rounds in each of which a concept name in the forgetting signature $\mathcal{F}$ is eliminated using not only the combination rule, but also the purify rules. This guarantees that all concept names in $\mathcal{F}$ are considered for elimination from $\mathcal{F}$.

Once a name has been eliminated from the clause set $\mathcal{N}$, it is removed from the forgetting signature $\mathcal{F}$. A name that cannot be eliminated in the current round may become eliminable after the elimination of another name [16]. The elimination rounds are therefore implemented in a do-while loop. The break condition checks if there were names eliminated in the previous rounds. If so, FAME(Q) repeats the iterations, attempting to eliminate the remaining names. The loop terminates when $\mathcal{F}$ becomes empty or no names were eliminated in the previous rounds.

Introduced definers are eliminated as part of the concept forgetting process using the calculus for concept name elimination. Unlike regular concept names, there is no guarantee that all definers can be eliminated. If the original ontology contains cyclic dependencies over the names in the forgetting signature $\mathcal{F}$, it may not be possible to eliminate all definers, see [17,19] for examples. This means the forgetting method is incomplete.

Our method can eliminate any concept and role names, though this is at the cost that the definers introduced may not be all eliminated. If the ontology computed by FAME(Q) does not contain any definers, we say that FAME(Q)/the forgetting is successful. In the successful cases, the forgetting solution is a uniform interpolant or a semantic solution.[4] If it is a uniform interpolant, it can be saved as an OWL/XML file. If it is a semantic solution, generally it cannot be saved as an OWL/XML file, because of extra expressivity such as role negation/-conjunction/disjunction being not supported by the OWL API. In these cases, the forgetting solutions are represented in the data structure of FAME(Q).

4.2 Frequency Count

A frequency counter is used in FAME(Q) to check the existence of each name of $\mathcal{F}$ in $\mathcal{N}$ and in each clause of $\mathcal{N}$, and count the frequency of positive and negative occurrences of the name in $\mathcal{N}$ and in each clause of $\mathcal{N}$. Algorithm 1 below computes the frequency counts of positive occurrences of a concept name, where AtomicConcept denotes a concept name, GreaterThan and LessThan denote the ternary number restriction operators $\geq$ and $\leq$, respectively, and Conjunction and Disjunction denote the n-nary operators of $\sqcap$ and $\sqcup$, respectively. The first operand of GreaterThan and LessThan is a positive integer and a non-negative integer, respectively, the second operand is a role name, and the third operand is a concept. The operands of Conjunction and Disjunction are concepts. Operands are stored in a list, an ordered collection of objects allowing duplicate values. We used a list, not a set, because the insertion order is preserved in a list, and allows positional access and insertion of elements. The algorithms (for counting negative frequency of a concept name and for counting positive frequency and negative frequency of a role name) were implemented similarly.

4.3 Definer Reuse

FAME(Q) reuses definers whenever possible. For example, consider the case of forgetting $A \in \mathsf{sig}_C(\mathcal{N})$ from $\mathcal{N}$, when a concept has been replaced by a specific definer in an A-clause, it is replaced uniformly by the definer in all A-clauses. We do not introduce new definer names for the same concept in other A-clauses. On the other hand, if a concept C has been replaced by a definer D, the concept of $\neg C$ is replaced (if necessary) by $\neg$D, rather than a fresh definer, that is, FAME(Q) introduces definers in a conservative manner (as few as possible). This significantly improves the efficiency of FAME(Q). Definers and the concepts replaced by them (the corresponding concepts) are stored as keys and values respectively in a Java HashMap, which allows for easy insertion and retrieval of paired elements.

5   The Evaluation

In order to understand the practicality and usefulness of FAME(Q), we evaluated the current version on a corpus of ontologies taken from the NCBO BioPortal repository,[5] a resource currently including more than 600 ontologies originally

---

[4] Because in some cases a uniform interpolant and a semantic solution coincide, when we say a forgetting solution is a semantic solution, we means it is only a semantic solution but not a uniform interpolant.

[5] https://bioportal.bioontology.org/.

Algorithm 1. POSITIVE(A, cls)

    Input   : a concept name A
                a clause cls
    Output: an integer i

```
1  if cls instance of AtomicConcept then
2  |   if cls equals to A then
3  |   |   return 1;
4  |   else
5  |   |   return 0;
6  else if cls instance of Negation then
7  |   Clause operand = cls.getOperands().get(0);
8  |   return NEGATIVE(A, operand);
9  else if cls instance of GreaterThan or LessThan then
10 |   Clause operand = cls.getOperands().get(1);
11 |   return POSITIVE(A, operand);
12 else if cls instance of Conjunction or Disjunction then
13 |   initialize Integer sum to 0;
14 |   List<Clause> operand_list = cls.getOperands();
15 |   foreach clause operand in operand_list do
16 |   |   sum = sum + POSITIVE(A, operand);
17 |   end
18 |   return sum;
19 else
20 |   return 0;
```

---

developed for clinical research. The corpus was based on a snapshot of the repository taken in March 2017 [11], containing 396 OWL API compatible ontologies. Statistical information about these ontologies can be found in [18].

Table 1 lists the types of axioms handled by FAME(Q). All these can be encoded as SubClassOf axioms. Axioms not expressible in $\mathcal{ALCOQH}$ were removed from each ontology as FAME(Q) only accommodated $\mathcal{ALCOQH}$-ontologies.

To reflect real-world application scenarios, we evaluated the performance of FAME(Q) for forgetting different numbers of concept names and role names from each ontology. We considered the cases of forgetting 10%, 30% and 50% of concept and role names from the signature of each ontology. LETHE was the only existing tool for forgetting in description logics with number restrictions; it handled $\mathcal{ALCQH}$ but only for concept forgetting. We compared the results of concept forgetting computed by FAME(Q) with those by LETHE on the $\mathcal{ALCQH}$-fragments. The fragments were obtained similarly as for the $\mathcal{ALCOQH}$-fragments. In order to allow a fair comparison with LETHE which was evaluated on randomly chosen forgetting signatures we did the same. The experiments were run on a desktop with an Intel® Core™ i7-4790 processor, four cores running at up to 3.60 GHz, and 8 GB of DDR3-1600 MHz RAM. The experiments were

Table 1. Types of axioms that can be handled by FAME(Q)

	Type of axiom	Representation
TBox	SubClassOf(C1 C2)	SubClassOf(C1 C2)
	EquivalentClasses(C1 C2)	SubClassOf(C1 C2), SubClassOf(C2 C1)
	DisjointClasses(C1 C2)	SubClassOf(C1 ObjectComplementOf(C2))
	DisjointUnion(C C1...Cn)	EquivalentClasses(C ObjectUnionOf(C1...Cn)) DisjointClasses(C1...Cn)
	SubObjectPropertyOf(R1 R2)	SubObjectPropertyOf(R1 R2)
	EquivalentObjectProperties(R1 R2)	SubObjectPropertyOf(R1 R2) SubObjectPropertyOf(R2 R1)
	ObjectPropertyDomain(R C)	SubClassOf(ObjectSomeValuesFrom(R owl:Thing), C)
	ObjectPropertyRange(R C)	SubClassOf(owl:Thing ObjectAllValuesFrom(R C))
ABox	ClassAssertion(C a)	SubClassOf(a C)
	ObjectPropertyAssertion(R a1 a2)	SubClassOf(a1 ObjectSomeValuesFrom(R a2))

Table 2. Results of concept and role forgetting computed by FAME(Q)

Settings		Results					
Forgetting	Forget %	Time	Timeout	Success rate	N_D left	$\nabla, \neg, \sqcap, \sqcup$
Concept Forgetting	10%	3.1 s	1.3%	96.2%	2.5%	10.6%
	30%	9.0 s	4.0%	89.7%	6.3%	31.6%
	50%	14.2 s	7.5%	83.7%	8.8%	53.3%
	Avg.	8.8 s	4.3%	89.8%	5.9%	31.8%
Role Forgetting	10%	4.0 s	1.5%	96.7%	1.8%	18.3%
	30%	9.1 s	4.6%	90.1%	5.3%	25.3%
	50%	15.2 s	7.8%	82.7%	9.5%	41.9%
	Avg.	9.5 s	4.7%	89.8%	5.5%	25.4%

run 100 times on each ontology and we averaged the results in order to verify the accuracy of our findings. A timeout of 1000 s was imposed on each run.

The results obtained from forgetting 10%, 30% and 50% of concept names and role names from the $\mathcal{ALCOQH}$-ontologies are shown in Table 2, where one can observe that, on average, FAME(Q) was successful in nearly 90% of the test cases (89.8% for both concept forgetting and role forgetting). In most successful cases, the forgetting solutions were computed within 10 s (8.8 s for concept forgetting and 9.5 s for role forgetting). The column headed N_D Left shows the percentages of the test cases where the definers were present in the resulting ontologies. The column headed $\nabla, \neg, \sqcap, \sqcup$ shows the percentages of the test cases where the forgetting solutions involved role constructs.

According to the results given in Table 3 FAME(Q) was considerably faster than LETHE on the $\mathcal{ALCQH}$-fragments; on average, it was 8 times faster. An important reason is that LETHE introduces definers in a systematic and exhaus-

Table 3. Results of concept forgetting computed by FAME(Q) and LETHE

Settings		Results						
Tool	Forget%	Time	Timeout	Success rate	N_D intro	$\nabla, \neg, \sqcap, \sqcup$	Fixpoints
FAME(Q) $\mathcal{ALCQH}$	10%	2.9 s	1.0%	96.2%	16.3%	10.6%	0.0%
	30%	7.5 s	3.5%	89.7%	27.2%	31.6%	0.0%
	50%	7.4 s	6.7%	83.7%	35.8%	53.3%	0.0%
	Avg.	8.1 s	3.4%	89.8%	5.9%	31.8%	0.0%
LETHE $\mathcal{ALCQH}$	10%	25.2 s	7.4%	92.6%	97.2%	0.0%	11.4%
	30%	59.5 s	20.5%	79.5%	100.0%	0.0%	14.9%
	50%	91.7 s	35.1%	64.9%	100.0%	0.0%	18.2%
	Avg.	58.8 s	21.0%	79.0%	99.1%	0.0%	14.8%

tive manner. The column headed N_D Intro shows the percentages of the test cases where definers were introduced during the forgetting process. It can be seen that LETHE introduced definers in nearly 100% of the test cases. In addition, FAME(Q) attained notably better success rates over LETHE (90.5% over 79.0%). Most failures of LETHE were due to the timeout.

Another advantage is that solutions computed by FAME(Q) are in general stronger than those by LETHE. Often, a stronger solution means a better one. For example, the solution of forgetting the concept name {Male} from the ontology

$$\{A \sqsubseteq \geq 2\text{hasSon.Male}, \ A \sqsubseteq \geq 3\text{hasDaughter.}\neg\text{Male},$$
$$\text{hasSon} \sqsubseteq \text{hasChild}, \text{hasDaughter} \sqsubseteq \text{hasChild}\}$$

computed by LETHE is

$$\{A \sqsubseteq \geq 2\text{hasSon.}\top, \ A \sqsubseteq \geq 3\text{hasDaughter.}\top,$$
$$\text{hasSon} \sqsubseteq \text{hasChild}, \text{hasDaughter} \sqsubseteq \text{hasChild}\},$$

while the solution of FAME(Q) includes an additional axiom

$$A \sqsubseteq \geq 5(\text{hasSon} \sqcup \text{hasDaughter}).\top,$$

where role disjunction is used. Upon the solution of LETHE, if we further forget the role names hasSon and hasDaughter, the uniform interpolant is {A $\sqsubseteq$ ≥ 3hasChild.$\top$}, while on the intermediary solution of FAME(Q), the solution is {A $\sqsubseteq$ ≥ 5hasChild.$\top$}, which is stronger and closer to the fact: A has at least 5 children. This shows an advantage of semantic forgetting where extra expressivity allows intermediary information (A $\sqsubseteq$ ≥ 5(hasSon $\sqcup$ hasDaughter).$\top$) to be captured which produces a better solution.

For users such as SNOMED CT and NCIT who do not have the flexibility to easily switch to a more expressive language, or are bound by the application, the available support and tooling, to a specific language, FAME(Q) is not satisfactory. Tracking the logical difference between different versions of ontologies is an application where the target language should coincide with the source language. In these cases, LETHE would be more suited.

6   Conclusions

This paper describes the tool of FAME(Q) for forgetting in $\mathcal{ALCOQH}$-ontologies. FAME(Q) is at present the only tool able to forget concept and role names in description logics with number restrictions. Compared to LETHE, a tool that can perform concept forgetting in $\mathcal{ALCQH}$, FAME(Q) fared better with respect to success rates and time efficiency on $\mathcal{ALCQH}$-fragments of realistic ontologies.

References

1. Bicarregui, J., Dimitrakos, T., Gabbay, D.M., Maibaum, T.S.E.: Interpolation in practical formal development. Log. J. IGPL 9(2), 231–244 (2001)
2. Del-Pinto, W.M., Schmidt, R.A.: ABox abduction via forgetting in $\mathcal{ALC}$. In: Proceedings of AAAI 2019. AAAI Press (2019, to appear)
3. Eiter, T., Ianni, G., Schindlauer, R., Tompits, H., Wang, K.: Forgetting in managing rules and ontologies. In: Web Intelligence, pp. 411–419. IEEE Computer Society (2006)
4. Gabbay, D.M., Schmidt, R.A., Szałas, A.: Second Order Quantifier Elimination: Foundations, Computational Aspects and Applications. College Publications, London (2008)
5. Grau, B.C., Motik, B.: Reasoning over ontologies with hidden content: the import-by-query approach. J. Artif. Intell. Res. 45, 197–255 (2012)
6. Konev, B., Walther, D., Wolter, F.: Forgetting and uniform interpolation in large-scale description logic terminologies. In Proceedings of IJCAI 2009, pp. 830–835. IJCAI/AAAI Press (2009)
7. Koopmann, P.: Practical uniform interpolation for expressive description logics. Ph.D. thesis, University of Manchester, UK (2015)
8. Koopmann, P., Schmidt, R.A.: Count and forget: uniform interpolation of $\mathcal{SHQ}$-ontologies. In: Demri, S., Kapur, D., Weidenbach, C. (eds.) IJCAR 2014. LNCS (LNAI), vol. 8562, pp. 434–448. Springer, Cham (2014). https://doi.org/10.1007/978-3-319-08587-6_34
9. Koopmann, P., Schmidt, R.A.: LETHE: saturation-based reasoning for non-standard reasoning tasks. In: Proceedings of DL 2015. CEUR Workshop Proceedings, vol. 1387, pp. 23–30. CEUR-WS.org (2015)
10. Lang, J., Liberatore, P., Marquis, P.: Propositional independence: formula-variable independence and forgetting. J. Artif. Intell. Res. 18, 391–443 (2003)
11. Matentzoglu, N., Parsia, B.: BioPortal Snapshot 30.03.2017, March 2017
12. Qi, G., Wang, Y., Haase, Y., Hitzler, P.: A forgetting-based approach for reasoning with inconsistent distributed ontologies. In: Proceedings of WoMO 2008. CEUR Workshop Proceedings, vol. 348. CEUR-WS.org (2008)
13. Wang, K., Antoniou, G., Topor, R., Sattar, A.: Merging and aligning ontologies in dl-programs. In: Adi, A., Stoutenburg, S., Tabet, S. (eds.) RuleML 2005. LNCS, vol. 3791, pp. 160–171. Springer, Heidelberg (2005). https://doi.org/10.1007/11580072_13

14. Wang, K., Wang, Z., Topor, R.W., Pan, J.Z., Antoniou, G.: Eliminating concepts and roles from ontologies in expressive descriptive logics. Comput. Intell. **30**(2), 205–232 (2014)
15. Zhao, Y., Alghamdi, G., Schmidt, R.A., Feng, H., Stoilos, G., Juric, D., Khodadadi, M.: Tracking logical difference in large-scale ontologies: a forgetting-based approach. In: Proceedings of AAAI 2019. AAAI Press (2019)
16. Zhao, Y., Schmidt, R.A.: Forgetting concept and role symbols in $\mathcal{ALCOIH}\mu^{+}(\nabla, \sqcap)$-ontologies. In: Proceedings of IJCAI 2016, pp. 1345–1352. IJCAI/AAAI Press (2016)
17. Zhao, Y., Schmidt, R.A.: Role forgetting for $\mathcal{ALCOQH}(\nabla)$-ontologies using an Ackermann-based approach. In: Proceedings of IJCAI 2017, pp. 1354–1361. IJCAI/AAAI Press (2017)
18. Zhao, Y., Schmidt, R.A.: FAME: an automated tool for semantic forgetting in expressive description logics. In: Galmiche, D., Schulz, S., Sebastiani, R. (eds.) IJCAR 2018. LNCS (LNAI), vol. 10900, pp. 19–27. Springer, Cham (2018). https://doi.org/10.1007/978-3-319-94205-6_2
19. Zhao, Y., Schmidt, R.A.: On concept forgetting in description logics with qualified number restrictions. In: Proceedings of IJCAI 2018, pp. 1984–1990. IJCAI/AAAI Press (2018)

Author Index

Printed in the United States
by Baker & Taylor Publisher Services